# GATEWAY TO JAPAN

*June Kinoshita and
Nicholas Palevsky*

KODANSHA INTERNATIONAL
Tokyo • New York • London

**Book design** by Ed Marquand Book Design, Seattle, Wa.

**Illustration credits.** Base art for the local maps are from the Blue Guide Pack series published by Jitsugyō no Nihonsha in Tokyo; mechanicals by Terri Axe and June Kinoshita. Regional maps and transit diagrams by Terri Axe and June Kinoshita. Family crests and figures 1, 3, 5, 9, 14–22, 24, 25, 27, 33, and 34 courtesy of Yamakawa Shuppansha. Figures 4, 6–8, 10, 11 and 13 courtesy of the Japan Architecture Institute. Figures 3 and 12 courtesy of Kodansha International. Figure 28 by Diana Stiles. Figure 29 by Kawabata Naoshi, courtesy of Jitsugyō no Nihonsha. Figures 30–32, 35, and 36 courtesy of the Japan Information Center in New York. Figures 37–44 and 46–47 from Sekai Bunka Photo in New York. Figure 45 courtesy of Geoffrey Oliver (Max Palevsky collection).

ii

Distributed in the United States by Kodansha America, Inc., 114 Fifth Avenue, New York, New York 10011, and in the United Kingdom and continental Europe by Kodansha Europe Ltd., Gillingham House, 38-44 Gillingham Street, London SW1V 1HU. Published by Kodansha International Ltd. 17-14, Otowa 1-chome, Bunkyo-ku, Tokyo 112 and Kodansha America, Inc. Copyright © 1990, 1992 by June Kinoshita and Nicholas G. Palevsky. All rights reserved. Printed in Japan.
First edition, 1990
Second edition, updated, 1992
92 93 94 10 9 8 7 6 5 4 3 2 1

**Library of Congress Cataloging-in-Publication Data**
Kinoshita, June.
    Gateway to Japan/by June Kinoshita & Nicholas G. Palevsky, — Rev. ed.
      p. cm
    Includes bibliographical references.
    1. Japan — Description and travel — Guidebooks.
1. Palevsky, Nicholas G.        II. Title.
DS805.2.K56    1992          92- 7290
915.204′49—dc20               CIP

ISBN 4-7700-1631-X

*To our parents,*
*and to the Tsutsumi family*
*and Kiyoshi, who sustained us*
*through the difficult years*

# Contents

# MAP OF JAPAN

0   100   200   300km

HOKKAIDŌ

SAPPORO

AOMORI

TŌHOKU          Hiraizumi 卍

SENDAI

Sado Is.

KANTŌ          Nikkō 卍

Sea of Japan

KANAZAWA                          Narita Airport

CHŪBU       Gokayama          TOKYO
Shirakawa-gō   ●TAKAYAMA      YOKOHAMA
                              Fuji-san ▲
            ●Tsumago          KAMAKURA

KINKI                NAGOYA

L. Biwa

KYOTO        Uji
         ŌSAKA 卍  NARA
CHŪGOKU      卍 Hōryū-ji

HIMEJI

KURASHIKI        Kōya-san        Pacific Ocean

HIROSHIMA
Miyajima 卍   Inland Sea

SHIKOKU

HAKATA
        ▲Aso

KYŪSHŪ

NAGASAKI

KAGOSHIMA

NAHA

OKINAWA

vi

# Introduction

A friend from Seattle once showed us a nifty pocket compass, a compact device about the size of a bottle cap, which he always carried with him in Japan. He said it was particularly useful when he took the subway: the instrument would enable him to find his bearings when he emerged above ground. I later thought that this book should be to the traveler what that compass is to our friend. No guidebook, no matter how thorough, can anticipate the uncharted territory into which travelers will stumble. In any case, it is the little accidents — the impromptu village festival, the nameless temple, the hospitable stranger — that are the finest rewards of travel. So, although this book supplies an abundance of detail, its real aim is to encourage you, the traveler, to learn to find your bearings for yourself — to recognize the cultural and historical signposts by which you can orient yourself no matter where you wind up. This book may not fit into your pocket, but we hope it will be the only book you will need.

When Nick and I headed for Japan to write this book, our goal was to produce the kind of guide we wished we had had when we visited Japan two years earlier. (Why else does anyone write guidebooks?) At the time, Japan's image abroad was undergoing a dramatic shift, from quaint land of cherry blossoms and Madame Butterfly to economic superpower and international trend setter in technology and fashion. The bizarreness of the contrasts delighted us, and we wanted to serve them up — Noh theater, love hotels, Comme des Garçons, and thatched farmhouses — like assorted hors d'oeuvres on a tray. But as we began to travel around the country and to delve into its past, our thinking changed. We realized that anyone can see the signs of Japan's economic achievement. What is harder to discern is the foundation on which it stands.

Japan in the past century has undergone a series of wrenching transformations, having changed from an insular, agrarian state into a modern industrial nation, won military victories over China and Russia, boogied through the roaring Twenties, aspired to engulf Asia, suffered utter defeat at the end of World War II, and risen again, in four decades, to economic superstardom. Yet rather than tear apart the fabric of Japanese culture, these stresses have only exposed the strength of the threads that hold it together. Two themes in particular stand out in my mind: the love of novelty and a fierce conservatism. From the earliest recorded history, the Japanese have been eager for novelty. When novelty was in the form of swords, written language and laws, or useful industries, it bestowed power. Like the esoteric mantras and rituals handed down by Shingon Buddhist priests to their chosen disciples, trade secrets and scholarly treatises were transmitted by masters to their most accomplished apprentices. For every person who eagerly pursues the latest gadget, there is another who cleaves even more fanatically to tradition. In the land of Sony Walkmans and capsule hotels, one also finds actors who devote their lives to perfecting medieval techniques, and tea masters who prepare their brew in a manner that originated in Sung dynasty China.

This is not to say that the Japanese are adept only at mimicry and conservation. Everything that is adopted from abroad is also transformed, reinvented — and recodified. This is the singular charm of the culture, and it is also perhaps why Japanese people often believe that their art, literature, language, cuisine, and mannerisms cannot be understood by neophytes and outsiders. A painting is unfinished until a knowledgeable viewer has written down an erudite comment in a corner of the painting. A Noh play is incomplete without the presence of a responsive audience. A tea ceremony can be shared only among the cognoscenti. The belief runs deep that words are not capable of conferring understanding.

What we have set out to do, then, is somewhat iconoclastic; we think that much can, and should, be explained. That is the underlying concern of this book, particularly of the History and Culture section, where we have endeavored in broad brushstrokes to capture the essential features of religion, architecture, and the various arts. Our task would have been impossible were it not for the Japanese propensity to codify. Why does a particular temple face south? More often than not, there is a reason. Sometimes the reasons given are not supported by fact, but that in itself is interesting; myths can sometimes be more revealing than reality. All of this seems abstract, however, if it is divorced from physical reality. History and culture are not merely self-contained entities but are also part of the geographic landscape. That is why we have planted a series of historical essays throughout the regional chapters, wherever major events occurred. We have also devised an extensive cross-referencing system between the cultural chapters and the regional chapters.

In the regional section, we provide the practical information that can remove some of the aggravation of traveling in Japan. You can rest assured that, in spite of our efforts, plenty of challenges will remain. Foremost is the absence of a common language and writing system with the West. You should always carry the name of your destination written in Japanese, as well as the business card of your hotel. You can also point to the Japanese characters in this book. Pencil and paper are helpful for writing out questions in simple English; many Japanese can cope with written English far, far better than with the spoken version. Thanks to the byzantine address system, almost everybody is, of necessity, skilled at drawing maps.

Cost is also a cause for anxiety, although not to the extent that it has been made out to be in the press. First-class travel is as expensive in Japan as it is in Manhattan. But if you choose modest inns, eat in ordinary restaurants, and ride the superb public transportation system, you can get excellent value—and learn a great deal more about Japan. For example, a minshuku, a type of accommodation offered in people's homes, includes dinner and breakfast and will run about forty dollars. Any minshuku will give you a dose of Japanese daily life, and the exceptional ones, such as the massive farmhouses of Shirakawa-gō or the Edo-period post-town inns of the Kiso Valley, will provide an extraordinary cultural experience.

The timing of your trip is an important consideration. Festivals are integral to Japanese life. If you want to schedule your trip around a major festival, refer to the directory at the end of the Matsuri chapter and to the calendar at the beginning of each regional chapter. The peak tourist season is in October and November, when the weather is relatively dry and maples blaze on the mountainsides. The cuisine is enriched by wild mushrooms, chestnuts, and fattened fish. Rarely seen art masterpieces, including the eighth-century treasures of the Shōsō-in, are aired in public. April and May also bring out huge numbers of tourists. During the spring and fall, be prepared to share your travels with millions of uniformed school children from all over Japan. This semiannual ritual originated from a Meiji-era edict aimed at fostering a sense of nationhood among the people (who had not been allowed to travel freely by the Tokugawa shogunate). The middle of June to the middle of July is a period of constant drizzle. The summer is stiflingly humid, but it is a colorful time of year marked by boisterous festivals. December and January are an underrated and excellent time to travel. Days are brisk and clear, and except in northern or mountainous regions, the temperature is tolerably mild. You will be comfortable as long as you stay in well-heated hotels.

The goodwill and honesty of the people will go a long way toward making Japan a less daunting place. You will have many other things on your side as well. Trains and buses are punctual, and there are usually romanized signs indicating the name of each station and of the stations that precede and follow it. Station employees will write out the schedule for the train to your next destination. In major cities, the hotels, department stores, and train stations often have information booths, where the staff will patiently try to help you as best it can. Theft and violent crime are exceedingly rare, and hygiene standards are among the highest in the world. These factors give independent travelers the latitude to explore—and take risks in—a completely alien universe, a luxury that few other exotic destinations in the world can offer.

# GUIDE TO THE GUIDE

When friends want to know where to go in Japan, I always ask, "What are you interested in?" One friend spent every day at the Kabuki theater in Tokyo. Another ventured north to savor the culinary traditions of Tōhoku. We know people who adore Tokyo, exulting in the energy of the world's most futuristic megapolis. Others loath it and flee to tranquil Kyoto, the former imperial city that epitomizes the refinement of traditional culture. Still others visit both cities and wonder at the extremes represented by these opposing poles of the Japanese experience. The diversity of cultural and geographic offerings can be intimidating. The two sections of this book, History and Culture and Japan by Region, are designed to make them more manageable. History and Culture focuses on specific topics and recommends where to go. Japan by Region gives the practical information you need to make the trip.

### History and Culture
"A Brief History" introduces the major historical periods and includes a list of the most important figures in Japanese history and culture; their names appear in uppercase letters throughout the book. The chapters that follow provide both an overview and a practical reference on various subjects. For example, "Cuisine" contains bilingual "menus" from which you can order food in restaurants. Most of the chapters conclude with a list of recommendations. Any place that is mentioned in both the main text and the list appears in uppercase.

### Japan by Region
The ten regional chapters appear in geographic order, from north to south (see map on p. vi). The largest of Japan's four main islands, Honshū, and the smallest, Shikoku, together make up seven chapters. The remaining three chapters are devoted to Hokkaidō, Kyūshū, and the Okinawan archipelago. Each chapter begins with a brief introduction and lists the best attractions, special interests, and seasonal events.

**Transit Diagrams.** The transit diagram at the beginning of each regional chapter shows the main trunk line (usually the bullet train) traversing the region, together with other train and bus lines that branch off. The main junctions on the trunk line are assigned roman numerals and treated as jumping-off points from which to explore side routes; the stations along the side routes are assigned arabic numerals. The text describes in numerical order each main junction, followed by the side routes; their direction is denoted by the letters "N" for north, "E" for east, and so forth. For example, suppose you want to visit Dewa Sanzan (transit key number IV:W3) in Tōhoku. To see how to get there, turn to the Tōhoku transit diagram (p. 152); go down the trunk line to the fourth city, Sendai (IV), then go west three notches. The text follows the same organization and is, in effect, a series of mini-itineraries.

**Dining, Lodgings, and Local Maps.** Dining and lodging facilities are listed at the end of each town or locale. Telephone area codes are usually listed beside the Lodgings heading. Shops, restaurants, and hotels will appear on local maps according to a number-key system. (See inside front cover for a key to symbols.) Ratings are awarded on a scale of from one to three stars based on quality, service, and atmosphere. Credit-card information is supplied for every establishment for which the information was available.

# ACKNOWLEDGEMENTS

We take pleasure in thanking the many people who have given practical and moral support over the years, in particular Albert Goldman, Hatashin Moriya, Kasai Masaaki, Ray Kinoshita, Kojiro Yuichiro, Kokubu Ayako, Joy Morrell, and Howard Smith. Special thanks are due to Yoshio Morita, editor of Blue Guide Pack, who was instrumental in supplying the maps for this book. Tak Nagaoka, Etsuko Penner, Mary Testa, Grace Herget, Seiko Taniguchi and other past and present employees of the Japan National Tourist Organisation provided invaluable assistance in a diversity of matters. Suggestions and comments were offered by: Ando Tadao and Yumiko, Tim Appenzeller, David Aronson, Marie-Christine Aquarone, Ed Bell, Monica Bethe, Dorothy Britton, Alice and Otis Cary, Rand Castile, William Coaldrake, Ellen and Ted Conant, Judith Conner, Helene Cornevin, Peter Davison, Enbutsu Sumiko, Barbara Ford, Dana Friis-Hansen, Janet Goldenberg, Richard Greer, Peter Grilli, Roy Gyongy, Clyde Haberman, Jere Herzenberg, Thomas Imoos, Christi Keller, David Kidd, J. Edward Kidder, Kinoshita Yoko, Isozaki Arata, Dana Levy, Masuda Hajime, David MacEachron, Nishimura Minoru, Miya Nobuho, Munakata Naoko, Alexandra Munroe, Morimoto Takeshi, Murata Norio, Taggert Murphy, Leticia O'Conner, Andrew Pekarik, Donald Richie, Marian and Howard Rogers, Henry Scott-Stokes, Edward Seidensticker, Alistair Seton, Marc Treib, Kazuko Saito, the Sasaki family in Morioka, Frederick Schultz, Kazuko and Robert Smith, Suzuki Shiroyasu and Mari, Takeda Shiro and Yuriko, Watanabe Hiroshi, Watanabe Makoto, Andrew Watsky, Yamada Hisashi, and Ann Yonemura. Our research assistants Ikeda Shigeru and Kurimoto Noriko chased down thousands of details with boundless energy and resourcefulness. Tanaka Noriko, Yagi Seiya, Nishiue Itsuko, Nosé Mai and Iwata Yoshiko also rendered valuable assistance. We of course accept credit for any errors that have made it past the fact-checkers. Finally, we are grateful to our editors at Kodansha International, Les Pockell, Prue Moodie, Mia Nielsen and Meagan Calogeras, for helping to bring this book to publication.

ix

---

**Please Write!**

Your comments, complaints and suggestions will help us serve our readers better. Send correspondence to June Kinoshita, c/o Kodansha America, Inc., 114 Fifth Avenue, New York, NY 10011.

"Times go by turns, and chances change by course,
From foul to fair, from better hap to worse."
— Robert Southwell (ca. 1595)

Change may be eternal, but it is the bane of the guidebook writer. Establishments go out of business, change ownership, slouch into bad habits. All prices were updated in the summer of 1991. Even with Japan's low rate of inflation, they will no doubt creep upward over time. If you find gross disparities between the quoted prices, ratings, or descriptions in this book, please sound off. Write to June Kinoshita c/o Kodansha America, Inc., 114 Fifth Avenue, New York, NY 10011.

**Romanization and Japanese terms.** We generally stick to the Hepburn system of romanization. Differences in the length of vowel sounds change the meaning of words, and so long vowels are indicated by macrons (bars) above the letter; exceptions are words such as sumo, shogun, and Shinto, and the names of such cities as Tokyo and Kyoto, which by now are so familiar to Westerners that it seemed anachronistic to employ macrons.

The most common Japanese terms that appear in this book, such as -ji (temple) and jinja (shrine), appear without translation; see inside front cover for a glossary of terms that are usually not translated in the text. Singular and plural forms are the same in Japanese. Hence we write, "jinja are shrines."

Names of Japanese people are always given with the family name first, followed by the given name. We also follow the Japanese convention of calling historical figures by their given names, rather than by their family names; there are many eminent members of the Tokugawa family, but only one of them is called Ieyasu. (The system can be arbitrary at times; the author Natsume Sōseki is popularly called Sōseki, but Mishima Yukio is always referred to as Mishima.)

# Preliminaries

# Practical Advice

3

# BEFORE YOU GO

There's no better way to get to know a country than to make your own travel arrangements. Japan, with perhaps the most varied culture in the world today, presents astounding and delightful choices: whether to stay in a temple or a computer-controlled hotel room, to see Noh or Butō, to dine on *nouvelle Japonaise* or slurp noodles in a 500-year-old shop.

**Expenses.** With the rise of the mighty yen, Japan has undoubtedly become an expensive travel destination. It is not necessary to impoverish yourself, however. If you are willing to rely on the superb public transportation system and to try the accommodations and restaurants that the average Japanese themselves use, you will be able to stretch your budget considerably further than if you were to stick to international hotels and fancy French restaurants. What's more, you will have a much more interesting experience. Minshuku, which are Japanese-style "bed-and-breakfasts" (they include dinner), cost about $35 to $50 and will give you an opportunity to see how ordinary people live. Food can be shockingly expensive, but it is possible to dine cheaply. Commuter railway stations and shopping districts abound with inexpensive restaurants where you can get a nourishing meal for about $10. The huge food marts in department store basements sell beautiful and inexpensive *bentō* (lunch boxes), perfect for picnics or for taking back to your room. Restaurant lunch specials are often a bargain. Railway travel in Japan operates with clockwork efficiency, but it is expensive. Sometimes it is cheaper to fly—especially if you count in the time savings. Note that during peak vacation periods (Mar. 21–Apr. 15, Apr. 28–May 6, July 21–Aug. 31, Dec. 25–Jan. 10) JR and many hotels charge higher rates. The Japan Rail Pass can be a money saver depending on your itinerary. A one-week pass costs about the same as the round-trip bullet-train fare from Tokyo to Kyoto. Here are two entirely realistic possibilities for daily expenses:

| Item | First-class | Budget |
|---|---|---|
| Lodgings | Y11,000/person (twin room in first-class hotel) | Y6000 (minshuku) |
| Breakfast | Y1800 (hotel coffee shop) | (incl. in lodging) |
| Lunch | Y4000 | Y650 (set menu lunch) |
| Dinner | Y8000 | (incl. in lodging) |
| Transport* | Y3000 (taxi) | Y1000 (public) |
| Entertainment | Y9000 (Kabuki, best seats) | Y2000 (Kabuki, one act) |
| Total | Y36,800 ($263) | Y9650 ($69) |

* Japan Rail Pass additional. $1.00 = Y130 (Y1000 = $7.70)

**JNTO Offices Abroad.** For information on travel in Japan and locations of travel agents selling Rail Pass vouchers:

| | |
|---|---|
| USA | 630 Fifth Ave., NY, NY 10111 (212-757-5640, fax 212-307-6754) |
| | 401 N. Michigan Ave., Chicago, IL 60611 (312-222-0874, fax 312-222-0876) |
| | 2121 San Jacinto St., Dallas, TX 75201 (214-754-1820, fax 214-754-1822) |
| | 360 Post St., San Francisco, CA 94108 (415-989-7140, fax 415-398-5461) |
| | 624 S. Grand Ave., Los Angeles, CA 90017 (213-623-1952, fax 213-623-6301) |
| Brazil | Av. Paulista, 509-S/405, 01311 São Paulo (011-289-2931, fax 011-285-0595) |
| Mexico | Temístocles 246 — P.B., Col. Reforma Polanco, Deleg. Miguel Hídalgo, 11550-Mexico, D.F. (05-254-6666, fax 05-254-6666) |
| Korea | 10 Da-Dong, Chung-Ku, Seoul (752-7968, fax 755-5149) |
| Canada | 165 University Ave., Toronto, Ont. M5H 3B8 (416-366-7140, fax 416-366-4530) |
| England | 167 Regent St., London W.1 (071-737-9638, fax 071-734-4290) |
| Australia | 115 Pitt St., Sydney, N.S.W. 2000 (232-4522, fax 232-1494) |
| Hong Kong | Suite 3606, 8 Connaught Pl., Central (5255295, fax 8684930) |
| Thailand | 33/61 Suriwong Rd., Bangkok (233-5108, fax 236-8356) |
| France | 4-8 Rue Sainte-Anne, 75001 Paris (4296-2029, fax 4020-9279) |
| Switzerland | Rue de Berne 13, Geneva (7318140, fax 7381314) |
| Germany | Kaiserstrasse 11, 6000 Frankfurt a/M (20353, fax 284281) |

4

**Reservations.** Train and hotel reservations are essential if you want everything to go smoothly. Reservations should be made as far in advance as possible during peak vacation periods: Mar. 21–Apr. 15, Apr. 28–May 6, July 21–Aug. 31, Dec. 25–Jan. 10. But if you want a flexible schedule and don't mind being inconvenienced at times, you needn't reserve too early, because Japan has a huge number of inns, and it's always possible to find lodgings of *some* kind. Seats on the *Hikari* bullet train can be sold out at peak times, but may be available on the slightly slower *Kodama* express. In Kyoto, reservations are needed to see the imperial villas and the Saihō-ji moss garden. See pp. 330 and 363 for details. JTB and Kintetsu are major Japanese travel agencies operating in the United States that can reserve affiliated hotels in Japan:

**JTB:** 11th Floor, Equitable Tower, 787 Seventh Ave., NY, NY 10019 (212-489-1919, fax 212-246-5607). Suite 190, 5600 North River Rd., Rosemont, IL 60018 (708-698-9090, fax 708-698-1232). Suite 300, 360 Post St., San Francisco, CA 94108 (415-986-4764, fax 415-986-3989). Suite 3800, 707 Wilshire Blvd., Los Angeles, CA 90017 (213-687-9881, fax 213-621-2318).

**Kintetsu:** 1270 Avenue of the Americas, Suite 1813, New York, NY 10020 (212-632-3725, fax 212-489-8642). Japan Center, 1737 Post St., San Francisco, CA 94115 (415-922-7171). 10900 E. 183rd St., Suite 320, Cerritos, CA 90701 (213-924-4600).

**Japan Rail Pass.** A great convenience as well as a money saver if you plan to travel widely, the Rail Pass is good for unlimited travel on all JR (Japan Railways) trains, buses, and ferries, including the Shinkansen ("bullet train"). All express and reservation charges (except sleeper charges) are included. It is available to people whose legal residence is not in Japan who are visiting the country as a tourist (business-visa holders are ineligible). Rail Pass vouchers are sold only outside Japan, at JAL, JAL-appointed travel agents, JTB, Kintetsu, and Nippon Travel. To receive the Rail Pass, you must present the voucher, together with your passport, at one of thirteen JR Travel Service Centers in Japan within three months of purchase. The centers are located at Narita Airport and the main JR stations in Sapporo, Sendai, Niigata, Tokyo, Yokohama, Nagoya, Kyoto, Ōsaka, Hiroshima, Hakata, Kumamoto, and Nishi-Kagoshima. A ticket for a Green Car (first class) is approximately 45 percent more. Tall travelers may find it worthwhile to pay for the roomier cars. Note that on the Shinkansen, only half of the Green Car is reserved for nonsmokers.

**Tours.** In addition to the numerous overseas tour operators, there are many companies in Japan that offer regular package tours to major cities and regions. They range in duration from one to thirteen days. JNTO can supply you with details on these as well as on overseas tour operators. Cruise ships sailing the Japan coast are the latest rage. *M.S. Oceanic Grace* offers interesting itineraries, including many remote and scenic ports of call. For information, contact Bill Balfour of Tourism Marketing Specialists, 5757 W. Century Blvd., Suite 390, Los Angeles, CA 90045 (213-215-0191, fax 213-215-0346).

**Required documents.** A valid passport is required of U.S. citizens. No visa is required for tourists who intend to stay in Japan for less than ninety days.

**Language.** English speakers will get by, but even a few lessons in Japanese yields abundant returns. For starters, become familiar with the Hepburn system for romanization so that you can pronounce words and place names properly. If you learn the *katakana* syllabary, you'll be able to read coffee shop menus. A knowledge of the numeric characters will enable you to read prices. A few quick lessons before you go should give you enough not only to survive, but also to have fun with it. See "One-hour Japanese" for basic phrases.

**When to Go.** Spring and fall, the best seasons, offer comfortable temperatures and relatively dry weather. Summers are hot and very humid, winters are cold and damp. From mid-June to mid-July is a season of constant drizzle and mold. Temperatures vary considerably from north to south; see regional introductions for average temperatures and precipitation. See the Matsuri chapter for a description of seasonal rites and outstanding festivals. Millions of Japanese visit family at New Years and Bon (August 14–16) and go on holiday during "Golden Week" (April 29–May 5); it is almost impossible to secure train and hotel reservations at these times.

**What to Wear.** Bring clothes that are comfortable for sitting on tatami floors and (not to be indelicate) for squatting over a Japanese toilet. For women, loose, medium-length skirts have decided advantages. A critical item is a pair of very good walking shoes that can be slipped on and off easily and are sturdy enough to take you over stone pavements and gravel walks. In cold months, carry warm socks to shield your feet from icy floors in temples. Long underwear is more useful than a heavy coat at underheated inns. One lifesaver is the cheap and terrific heat-generating pocket warmer (*kairo*), which lasts twenty-four hours; *kairo* are sold in supermarkets. For raingear, a folding umbrella is best; excellent lightweight models are sold in Japan. The Japanese will judge you by your outward appearance, so make sure your dress will send the right message. Discreet, respectable clothes are best, no matter what your mode of travel. Torn or soiled garments and too-revealing clothes (short shorts, halter tops) are out. On the other hand, apart from business, the Japanese are not formal dressers; few restaurants require jackets and ties, for example.

**Exercises.** Limber legs will get you through Japan with less anguish. Easy yoga stretches are perfect. Make sure you can squat for a minute and then stand up again without the aid of your hands.

**Packing.** Imagine yourself running up and down stairs to catch a train, and then struggling to a seat. (There are almost no porters in railway stations.) Pack accordingly. Luggage with a shoulder strap is most practical; the convertible, backpack/soft luggage type is ideal. If you plan to make excursions out of a base city, bring a soft overnight bag or daypack. Take only essentials — extra eyeglasses, prescription drugs. Anything else (except large-size clothes and shoes) can be bought in Japan.

**Money.** Airport money changers offer the standard exchange rates.

# GETTING INTO AND OUT OF JAPAN

U.S. citizens must carry a valid passport. Tourists don't need a visa, but students, business travelers and workers must have proper visas. Japan forbids entry of narcotics, firearms and pornography.

**By Air**
Most travelers arrive and depart by New Tokyo International (Narita) Airport. Some carriers also serve Ōsaka, which offers fewer hassles than Narita and quick access to Kyoto. A few airlines land at Nagoya, and Fukuoka has direct service to and from Hawaii.

**New Tokyo International (Narita) Airport.** Served by nonstop flights from Atlanta (JAL), Chicago (JAL, Northwest, United), Dallas (American), Detroit (Northwest), Honolulu (Continental, JAL, JAS, Northwest), Los Angeles (ANA, Delta, JAL, Northwest, United), Minneapolis (Northwest), New York/Newark (ANA, JAL, Northwest, United), Portland, OR (Delta), San Francisco (JAL, Northwest, United), San Jose (American), Seattle (American, JAL, Northwest), Washington, D.C. (ANA, JAL). Major carriers from other nations also land at Narita. JAL has the most frequent flights. It's strongly geared to business travelers, and can provide bilingual business cards (order two weeks in advance) and make JR train reservations. Its planes consist mainly of roomier, "executive class" seats. Of the U.S. carriers, United and Northwest have the most flights from each city, and are the only airlines permitted to continue to other Asian countries.

    **Airport to Town.** Airport limousine bus (Y2500, 1:10h) offers frequent service to the Tokyo City Air Terminal (TCAT), a 0:10h cab ride from Tokyo Station. Other buses (Y2600-2700, 1:20h) go to Tokyo Station and major hotels. A cheap, fast service is the Keisei Skyliner express (Y1,630, 1:00h) or limited express (Y840, 1:15h) from Keisei Narita Station (lower level of Narita air terminal) to Keisei Ueno Station in Tokyo.

    The JR Narita Express Train, or JR NEX (Y2,890, coach), is 0:53h nonstop from Narita air terminal to Tokyo Station. Trains continue onward to Shinjuku, Ikebukuro, or Yokohama. The JR Rail Pass applies. Amenities include dressing rooms, telephones and wheelchair access. A big drawback: all seats are reserved. Those coming from abroad can book through JAL or on arrival, but this consumes so much time that limousine buses may prove faster in the end. A maze of stairs and escalators makes for less-than-ideal access to the train platforms.

    **Layover tours.** JTB offers tours to the National Museum of Japanese History, Narita-san temple, and other nearby attractions (see p. 256), as well as a six-hour trip into Tokyo, and tours of Tokyo Disneyland. Reserve through JTB in New York (212-698-4919 or 800-223-6104).

**Haneda Airport.** Tokyo's domestic airport. Served internationally by China Air Lines. Haneda is 0:15h by monorail (Y300) from Hamamatsuchō station in Tokyo, or about 0:20h (Y2000) by taxi from downtown Tokyo.

**Nagoya International Airport.** Served by nonstop flights from Guam and Saipan (Air Micronesia, Northwest), Honolulu (ANA, JAL) and Portland, OR (Delta).

**Ōsaka International Airport.** Served by nonstop flights from Honolulu (JAL, Northwest, United), Los Angeles (Northwest), San Francisco (United), and Seattle (Northwest). Non-U.S. carriers include JAL, ANA, JAS, Korean Airlines, Singapore Airlines, Cathay Pacific, British Airways, Air France, Air India, China Air Lines and Royal Thai.

    **Airport to Ōsaka.** About 0:25h (Y380) by limousine bus to Shin-Ōsaka Station. Taxis take 0:15-0:20h (about Y4500) to central Ōsaka.

    **Airport to Kyoto.** About 1:00h (Y830) by limousine bus to Kyoto Station. 1:00h (about Y14,000) to central Kyoto.

**Arrival tips.** Banks at the airports offer the standard foreign currency exchange rates. Package delivery services in the airport terminals will deliver excess baggage to any destination in Japan for a reasonable charge.

**Departure tips.** Lines at check-in counters and immigration at Narita can be monstrous. Smart travelers take the limousine bus (departs every 0:15h) from Tokyo City Air Terminal, where they can check bags to final destinations and pass through immigration. Travelers leaving from Narita must pay an exit fee of Y2000 (Y1000 for children age 2-11 years). Change unused yen before going through customs, as there are no money changers in the international departure lounge. Travelers can take up to five million yen out of the country. Certain restrictions apply to old art objects. Call 03-3581-3632 (Tokyo) or 075-541-1151 (Kyoto) for information.

### By Sea
Passenger ships ply the following routes: Between Vladivostok, CIS, and Yokohama, June–Sept., 3–7 times per month by Tōyō Kyōdo Kaiun (Tokyo, 03-3475-2841; in the U.S. contact International Cruise Center, Inc., 185 Willis Ave., Minneola, NY 11501). Between Shanghai, China, and Yokohama and Ōsaka by Nichū Kokusai Ferry (Tokyo, 03-3294-3351). Between Shanghai and Kōbe twice a month by China-Japan International Ferry Co. (Kōbe, 078-392-1021). Between Tianjin, China, and Kōbe once a week by China Express Line (Tokyo, 03-3278-6703; Kōbe, 078-321-5791). Between Pusan, Korea, and Ōsaka, twice a week by Ōsaka Kokusai Ferry (Ōsaka, 06-263-0200). Between Pusan and Shimonoseki daily by Kampū Ferry, Inc. (Ōsaka, 06-345-2245; Shimonoseki, 0832-24-3000). Between Pusan and Hakata daily by JR Kyūshū Senpaku Jigyōbu (Hakata, 092-281-2315). Between Keelung, Taiwan and Naha once a week by Arimura Sangyō Co. (Tokyo, 03-3562-2091).

# MONEY

The exchange rate as we write is about Y130 to the dollar, or roughly Y1000 to $7.70. Japanese denominations are indicated in Arabic numerals (except 5 yen, a brass coin with a hole). *Coins*: Y1, Y5, Y10, Y50, Y100, Y500. *Bills*: Y500, Y1000, Y5000, Y10,000.

**Changing money.** Major tourist hotels offer the same exchange rates as banks, and have English-speaking clerks, less bureaucracy, and longer "banking hours."

**Carry plenty of cash.** The Japanese still rely heavily on hard cash, a habit made practical by the low crime rate. Even houses and cars are paid for in briefcase-loads of cash, as much to demonstrate the buyer's sincerity as to prove ability to pay. Don't assume that you can walk into a store or inn and pay with a credit card or travelers' check.

**Credit cards.** These are increasingly accepted at tourist hotels, restaurants, shops, and travel agencies, but it is rare to find a country inn that will take them. Visa and Diners Club are the most widely accepted. American Express is accepted in many beaten-track locations. Offices:

    **Visa.** In Tokyo, Sumitomo Credit Card, 5-2-10 Shibashi, Minato-ku (03-3459-4800; in emergencies, 3459-4700). In Ōsaka, Teisan Nakanoshima Bldg., 2-2-8 Nakanoshima, Kita-ku (06-228-1221; in emergencies, 228-1200).

    **Japan Diners Club.** In Tokyo, Senshu Bldg., 1-13-7 Shibuya, Shibuya-ku (03-3499-1311; 24 hours, 3499-1181). In Ōsaka, 3-3-7 Kawaramachi, Chūō-ku (06-202-4616; 24 hours, 201-0921).

    **American Express.** In Tokyo, 4-30-16 Ogikubo, Suginami-ku (03-3220-6000). In Ōsaka, Ushu Honmachi Bldg., 3-1-6 Honmachi, Chūō-ku (06-264-5400). 24-hour toll-free number, 0120-376-100.

**Travelers' checks.** In general, only major banks and tourist hotels will accept them.

**JTB coupons** for transportation and lodgings, which can be purchased with cash or credit card when you make reservations through major JTB offices, are a good way to reduce your hard cash needs. Coupons are fully refundable up to 5 days before the date of the reservation.

# INFORMATION IN JAPAN

**Tourist Information Centers (TIC).** Free information centers operated by the JNTO for the benefit of foreign visitors. Pick up English maps for major tourist destinations, up-to-date matsuri lists, and information on lodgings and places to visit. Office locations are:

    **Narita:** Airport Terminal Bldg. (0476-32-8711)
    Hrs: M–F 9:00–20:00; Sa 9:00–12:00; clsd Su, NH.
    **Tokyo:** Kotani Bldg. 1-6-6 Yūrakuchō (03-3502-1461)
    Hrs: M–F 9:00–17:00; Sa 9:00–12:00; clsd Su, NH.
    **Kyoto:** Kyoto Tower Bldg. (075-371-5649 or 371-0486)
    Hrs: M–F 9:00–17:00; Sa 9:00–12:00; clsd Su, NH.

JNTO provides toll-free numbers that will connect you to a bilingual operator who can offer assistance 9:00–17:00 daily. In eastern Japan, dial 0120-222-800; in western Japan, dial 0120-444-800. JNTO's "i" offices (look for a question-mark logo) help English-speaking travelers. They're located in or near 75 train stations around Japan.

**English-language newspapers and magazines.** These are available in major hotels and at Kinokuniya and Maruzen bookstores (see Tokyo, Kyoto, and Ōsaka entries for locations). The four daily newspapers and monthly *Tokyo Journal* and *Kansai Time Out* (Kyoto area) are the best sources for current events.

**Prefectural information offices.** Prefectural tourism offices in Tokyo provide brochures, maps, lists of accommodations, and bus schedules in Japanese and often in English. Most of the offices are located in two buildings flanking the Yaesu exit of Tokyo station: the Kokusai Kankō Kaikan is on the left side of the exit, and the Tetsudō Kaikan is to the right side, on the upper floors of Daimaru Department Store.

### Kokusai Kankō Kaikan:

| Prefecture or City | Region | TEL (03) |
|---|---|---|
| Aomori | Tōhoku | 3216-6010 |
| Chiba | Kantō | 3216-6017 |
| Fukui | Chūbu | 3211-8054 |
| Fukuoka | Kyūshū | 3231-1750 |
| Gumma | Kantō | 3231-4836 |
| Hiroshima | Chūgoku | 3215-5010 |
| Hokkaidō | Hokkaidō | 3214-2481 |
| Ibaraki | Kantō | 3231-2642 |
| Ishikawa | Chūbu | 3231-4030 |
| Kagawa | Shikoku | 3231-4840 |
| Kanagawa | Kantō | 3231-3901 |
| Kyoto (city) | Kinki | 3201-2147 |
| Miyazaki | Kyūshū | 3216-9587 |
| Nagano | Chūbu | 3214-5651 |
| Nagasaki | Kyūshū | 3216-2047 |
| Nagoya | Chūbu | 3212-0761 |
| Nara | Kinki | 3216-5955 |
| Niigata | Kantō | 3215-4618 |
| Ōita | Kyūshū | 3231-5096 |
| Okayama | Chūgoku | 3211-5767 |
| Okinawa | Okinawa | 3287-1661 |
| Saga | Kyūshū | 3216-6596 |
| Saitama | Kantō | 3215-2031 |
| Shiga | Kinki | 3231-6131 |
| Shizuoka | Kantō | 3213-4831 |
| Tochigi | Kantō | 3215-4050 |
| Toyama | Chūbu | 3231-5032 |
| Wakayama | Kinki | 3231-2041 |
| Yamaguchi | Chūgoku | 3231-4980 |
| Yamanashi | Kantō | 3231-0760 |

### Tetsudō Kaikan (Daimaru Department Store):

| | | |
|---|---|---|
| Aichi | Chūbu | 3212-0761 |
| Akita | Tōhoku | 3211-1775 |
| Ehime | Shikoku | 3231-1804 |
| Gifu | Chūbu | 3231-1775 |
| Iwate | Tōhoku | 3231-2613 |
| Kōchi | Shikoku | 3231-1833 |
| Mie | Chūbu | 3211-2737 |
| Miyagi | Tōhoku | 3231-0944 |
| Shimane | Chūgoku | 3212-1091 |
| Tokushima | Shikoku | 3216-2081 |
| Tottori | Chūgoku | 3211-8286 |
| Yamagata | Tōhoku | 3215-2222 |

**Kankō annaijo.** These are tourist information booths in or near the rail stations of virtually every tourist destination throughout Japan. Though most handle only Japanese, they can supply maps and information on museum hours, bicycle rental, places to eat, lodgings, time and cost of getting to various sites, and so on.

# LODGINGS

### Japanese-style
Though the finest ryokan (traditional Japanese inns) are quite expensive, but if you're traveling alone or with one other person, a medium-priced inn may offer a better value than a Western-style hotel (see the Ryokan chapter for a description). Similar features will be found in minshuku (lodgings in private homes), pensions, and *kokuminshukusha* (government-run "peoples' lodges"). The quoted rate is a per-person charge; it includes dinner, breakfast, tax, and service. Infants and children stay for free or at a reduced rate. For room only, ask for

7

*sudomari ryōkin* (charge for room only). Reserve in advance so the inn can make provisions for your meals. If you must cancel, inform the inn without fail; otherwise the staff will fix dinner and wait for you.

**Ryokan.** A traditional inn. Older inns often have separate bath and toilet facilities, but newer and renovated inns offer rooms with bath and toilet. All provide a clean *yukata* that doubles as bathrobe and pajamas, as well as a tiny bath-towel and toothbrush. Depending on the size and nature of the ryokan, meal and bath hours are set within certain limits. (Dinner is not served much later than 7:30 or 8:00 p.m.; there tends to be no hot water in the morning, etc.) All these matters are settled with your maid. The best inns serve superb cuisine. Average inns feature ambitious spreads that are fun once every few days, but may prove a bit much for daily fare. Price: from Y6000. Y10–25,000 for a quality inn.

**Minshuku.** These are "bed-and-breakfast-and-dinner" lodgings in private homes, although often they are separate from the owner's house. Think of them as no-frills ryokan. You eat in a common room, meals are home-cooked fare, and you lay out your own *futon*. *Yukata* robes are provided, but not towels. The best minshuku rival a good ryokan in the beauty of their buildings and quality of service. Price: Y5–7000.

**Pensions.** These are small inns, usually run by couples. Many of them are near tourist attractions, often in beautiful, isolated spots. The pension idea came from Europe, but the decor is often aimed at the young Japanese female's fantasies about the U.S. It is, if nothing else, another kind of cultural experience. Pensions often have excellent home-cooked Western-style food, served in a dining room. Toilets are often Western style. *Yukata* and towel are not provided. Some pensions will send a van to pick you up at the station. Price: Y5500–8000.

**Kokuminshukusha.** These government-sponsored lodges are institutional and economical. They are often located near travel attractions. Meals are served in a dining hall. Shared toilets and a large, common bath are usual. *Yukata* and towel provided. Price: approximately Y2800 for the room and Y2200 for the meals.

8

### Western-style

Usually tax and service charges are added to the quoted room rate (which does not include meals). *Yukata*, towels, and disposable toothbrush are provided.

**Full-service hotels.** Mostly found in major cities and famous tourist resorts. Price: Twin room rates are about Y14,000.

**Business hotels.** Economical, no-frills hotels oriented to business travelers. Rooms are small and usually come with a Western-style bathroom. They are efficient, usually have some English-speaking staff, and tend to be in good locations, although they often lack atmosphere. Many of the newer ones offer brighter decor and a little more comfort. Price: Single Y5–7000, Twin Y8–10,000.

**Kaikan (conference halls).** Hotel-style lodgings subsidized by various public or government organizations, which sometimes offer rooms to non-members at very reasonable rates. Usually business-hotel class or better. Yūbin Chokin Kaikan (Postal Savings) and Yayoi Kaikan run a dozen *kaikan* each, in various cities.

**Chain hotels.** These are useful to know about if you require a predictable Western-style hotel room with toilet, reservation services, and usually some English-speaking staff. Two chains, ANA and Washington, have been consistently good.

**ANA Hotels.** An excellent group of city hotels affiliated with All-Nippon Airways. Spacious, pleasant rooms and good service, English-speaking staff. Average price: Single from Y7000, Twin from Y12,000. ANA Hotel Tokyo is deluxe class. Reservations: U.S., 800-235-9262; Tokyo, 03-3505-1181.

**Washington Hotels.** A chain of cozy, well-run business hotels. In some cities, they've expanded to include a second Washington, which is newer and better. Price: Single from Y5000, Twin from about Y11,000. Reservations: 03-3434-5211.

**Prince Hotels.** A large chain of luxury resort hotels. Maintenance is substandard, and in terms of taste, they're aimed at hedonistic honeymooners. English-speaking staff, large rooms, and full service; located in prime areas. Price varies from hotel to hotel, with higher rates during tourist seasons. Reservations: U.S., 800-542-8686; Tokyo, 03-3209-8686.

**Tōkyū Hotels.** First-class city hotels, led by the Capitol Tōkyū in Tokyo. The standard in other hotels, however, is uneven. Price: Single from about Y7200, Twin from Y13,800 (Capitol Tōkyū is more expensive). Reservations: New York, 212-764-4750 and 800-822-0016; Los Angeles, 213-622-0354 and 800-624-5068; Tokyo, 03-3462-0109; Ōsaka, 06-314-1090.

**Tōkyū Inn.** Rather ascetic business hotels, with erratic maintenance quality. Price: Single from Y6300, Twin Y12,600. Reservations: Tokyo, 03-3406-0109; Ōsaka, 06-314-1090; Sapporo, 011-521-1090.

### Youth hostels, temples, and cycling terminals

**Youth hostels.** (*"Yūsu"* in Japanese-English.) Japan has more than 520 youth hostels in cities, nature spots, and many tourist attractions. These are usually institutional, but there are also many lovely private homes, temples, inns, and farms. A few have private rooms for couples and families. There's no age limit, and often a membership can be purchased at one of them. Check in from 15:00, check out by 10:00. Arrive no later than 18:30 (with dinner), 20:00 (no dinner). Very crowded from July 20–Aug. 31. Reserve by mail or phone. Some hostels are on a computerized reservation network, but there are only a few booking centers: Tokyo (Keiō, Seibu-Ikebukuro, and Sogō department stores); Ōsaka (Sogō department store,

Namba City YH center). Price: about Y2300 (bed), Y1300 (meals), additional charges for sheets, heating, kitchen use. The *Youth Hostel Handbook*, which includes some English, is invaluable. You can buy it at a hostel or by writing Japan Youth Hostels, Inc., Hoken Kaikan, 1-2 Sadohara-chō, Ichigaya, Shinjuku-ku, Tokyo 162, tel: 03-3269-5831.

**Shukubō (temple and shrine lodgings).** Not long ago, most temples provided free lodgings to all, but no longer. Today, it is primarily the important pilgrimage temples and shrines that still offer accommodations, and most charge a set fee. Rules about vegetarian meals and attendance at morning services have become lax. Most *shukubō* offer very modest accommodations, but the best provide surroundings of great beauty, exquisite gardens, and art treasures; an overnight stay is a unique, highly recommended experience. Sacred Mt. Kōya (three hours from Kyoto) is the best place to experience *shukubō*. Price: from Y5000 with meals.

**Cycling terminals.** About forty cycling terminals all over Japan rent bicycles and offer simple, modern lodgings, generally tatami rooms or bunks. Price: Y5000 with two meals.

### Reservations and Information

It's best to reserve by the morning of the day you want to stay at a ryokan, minshuku, pension, or youth hostel, so that there is time to get meals ready. If language is a problem, ask your present inn or hotel to call for you. Doing it through JTB saves hassles, but it means you have to pre-pay in exchange for a coupon. JTB handles reservations only for inns with which it has a commission contract. To make your own reservations, write or fax the hotels. Most, if not all, hotels should respond.

**Welcome Inns System.** This free reservation service books rooms at inexpensive (under Y8000) hotels, ryokan, minshuku, pensions, and kokuminshukusha. No fees or deposits required. Write or phone JNTO for a free directory and mail/fax reservation forms. Six hundred establishments should be registered with the service by 1992.

**Pacific Select** can make reservations at a group rate in first-class ryokan from the U.S. Send away for their brochure at 1500 Broadway, New York, NY 10036 (tel: 800-722-4349 and 212-575-2460).

**Economical Japanese Inn Group.** An association of budget ryokan in tourist areas, geared to foreigners. Room charges are given Western-style, with meal charges extra. Write for their handy English pamphlet: c/o Hiraiwa Ryokan, 314 Hayao-chō, Kaminoguchi-agaru, Ninomiyachō-dori, Shimogyō-ku, Kyoto 600.

**In a Pinch.** In a town where you don't know of an inn, visit the *ryokan annaijo*, a lodgings information window found in many train stations. The first thing the clerk always wants to know is how much you want to spend. Someone will call every place in town and nearby to find you appropriate lodgings. When a reservation is confirmed, the clerk will give you a voucher, for which you pay all or part of the room charge on the spot.

One alternative the *annaijo* is unlikely to explore is **love hotels**, which are discreet little inns that rent rooms to couples—often married—for a few hours or overnight. Even on the day of a major festival, you can usually get a clean, pleasant room with bath and toilet for less than the price of a business hotel. Check-in is usually after 22:00. Ask your taxi driver.

# TRANSPORTATION INSIDE JAPAN

### JR (Japan Railways)

In 1987, the national railway system was formally broken up into a half-dozen regional corporations, which are now collectively called JR. The Japan Rail Pass can be used on all JR lines. The trains and buses are extraordinary—punctual and with service to virtually anywhere in Japan. Shinkansen (bullet train) lines and major trunk lines are expected to remain intact, but unprofitable minor local lines may be replaced by buses. Phone 03-3423-0111 for schedules in English. Hrs: M–F 10:00–18:00.

**Travel Service Centers.** Hrs: 5:45–24:00 (9:00–18:00 at Tokyo Station). Here you can exchange Rail Pass vouchers, figure out train schedules, and make reservations for trains, hotels, and car rentals. Locations: Narita, and at the main stations in Sapporo, Sendai, Niigata, Tokyo, Yokohama, Nagoya, Kyoto, Ōsaka, Hiroshima, Shimonoseki, Hakata, Kumamoto, Nishi-Kagoshima. Large stations without Travel Service Centers have **Green Windows**, which handle reservations, train passes, big fares, and other complicated tasks. Many trains now have nonsmoking cars, called *kin'en-sha*. Rail-pass holders can reserve train seats at no charge. It's worth doing so to secure seats in nonsmoking sections or in center cars, which are closest to platform escalators. **Fare types.** There are *futsū* (milk-run), *kyūkō* (express), and *tokkyū* (limited express) trains, and the high-speed Shinkansen (bullet train). Except for the Shinkansen, express surcharges can be paid to the conductor. *Kyūkō* and *tokkyū* fares end up being about twice the *futsū* fare, but are often worth the time saved. Moreover, the express trains are newer, more comfortable, and offer food service, toilets, and a nonsmoking car.

**Shinkansen (bullet train).** Cars # 1, 2, and 10 are usually nonsmoking cars. **Tokyo to Shin-Ōsaka:** Departures from 6:00 to 20:30. About eight per hour. *Hikari* trains stop in Nagoya and Kyoto. *Kodama* trains stop at nine other stops, taking 0:30h longer to get to Ōsaka. It's usually not necessary to reserve seats except on weekends and holidays in peak tourist seasons. If you board at Tokyo you can always get an unreserved seat. **Shin-Ōsaka to Hakata:** Departures from 6:00 to 20:00. Most Hikari trains continue west of Shin-Ōsaka to Hakata, but not all stop at the same stations; always ask the platform conductor for the train that will stop at your destination. **Tokyo/Ueno to Morioka:** Departures from 6:00 to 20:00. *Yamabiko* trains are more frequent and stop only at Utsunomiya, Kōriyama, Fukushima,

9

and Sendai. Hourly, one continues to Morioka. The *Aoba* terminates at Sendai, making every stop on the way, taking 0:30h longer to arrive in Sendai. **Tokyo/Ueno to Niigata:** Departures 6:20 to 21:00. The *Asahi* express is faster and more frequent. The *Toki* express makes every stop on the way, and takes 0:15h longer to reach Niigata.

**Money-saving passes.** If you don't have a Japan Rail Pass, you can save money by planning a round trip (say from Kyoto) to a region (such as Tōhoku), and buying a *shūyū-ken* or *free-kippu*, which can be purchased at JR stations and JTB. You must obtain the pass outside the designated region. The pass gives you unlimited use of all JR transport within the region, including limited expresses, plus round-trip travel from the point of origin. Good only for unreserved, ordinary seats. Shinkansen express and sleeper charges are generally extra.

## Buses and scheduled tour buses

Most buses operate on the following system: Take a numbered ticket from the dispenser upon boarding. When getting off, pay the fare indicated under the corresponding number displayed on a chart at the front of the bus. Keep change handy; drivers can change up to a Y1000 bill only. If boarding at a bus station, it's convenient to buy the ticket there.

**Teiki Kankō bus.** These regularly scheduled local tour buses are popular with Japanese tourists. The tours often include many places that would be considered way off the beaten track for foreigners. The guides usually speak only Japanese, but you do get to see the main sights quickly without getting lost, and at reasonable cost. Inquire at the station *annaijo*.

## Jikokuhyō timetables

A must for independent travelers, the *JTB Speed Jikokuhyō* is a bilingual, pocket-sized book that lists limited express train schedules throughout Japan. It is sold in large bookstores (though many shops do not realize the *JTB Speed Jikokuhyō* is in English). The *Jikokuhyō* has a series of maps in front (starting with Kyūshū, ending in Hokkaidō), with page cross-references beside every transport line. There is also an exhaustive version that includes every bus, boat, plane and train; it is in Japanese only.

## Domestic airlines

With rail travel becoming increasingly expensive, it often costs almost the same and may save a day or more of travel time to fly between distant cities. See the regional introductions for recommended air routes. Flights to medium and small towns radiate out of the following hub airports: Sapporo, Tokyo (Haneda), Ōsaka, Fukuoka, Nagoya, and Naha (Okinawa). The hub airports are connected by frequent flights. The major domestic carriers are ANA, JAS, and JAL. ANA has more flights to the big cities, while JAS routes include smaller cities and towns, often of touristic interest. Bilingual schedules and prices are available at all travel agencies. Round-trip fares are ten percent cheaper if the return trip is made within seven to ten days of the departure date. Main reservation numbers (most can handle English):

| | | |
|---|---|---|
| ANA | Tokyo: 03-5489-8800 (daily, 6:30–21:00) | |
| | Ōsaka: 06-534-8000 (daily, 6:30–21:00) | |
| | Kyoto: 075-211-5471 (daily, 6:30–21:00) | |
| JAS | Tokyo: 03-3432-6111 (daily, 6:30–21:00) | |
| | Ōsaka: 06-345-8111 (daily, 8:00–20:00) | |
| JAL | Tokyo: 03-3457-1121 (daily, 9:00–18:00); 03-5489-2111 (daily, 6:30–21:00) | |
| | Ōsaka: 06-201-1231 (daily, 7:00–21:00) | |
| | Kyoto: 075-231-2311 (daily, 7:00–21:00) | |

## Taxis

With few exceptions, fares are by the meter. A tip is not expected, but if you have a large quantity of luggage, you should offer to add Y200 per piece to the fare. That's if you can get it to fit; the trunk is often full of the driver's personal property, leaving no room for large bags. You may need an *ōgata* (large) taxi, which is slightly more expensive than *kogata* (small).

## Driving, car rental, and hitchhiking

Not recommended for novices. To drive in Japan, you'll need an International Driver's License as well as your real driver's license. Drive on the left side of the road. Nearly all road signs are in Japanese only. Gasoline and expressway tolls are very expensive.

**Car rentals** range from Y6500–18,000 for twenty-four hours with unlimited mileage, for S-class cars (subcompacts). You should have an International Driver's License, but a credit card is not necessary. **Nippon Rent-a-Car** (Tokyo: 03-3468-7126) is affiliated with Hertz. It has a widespread dropoff network and reasonable rates. Reservations can be made through National in the U.S. **Avis** (03-3583-0911), **Orix** (03-3779-0543), **Dollar** (03-3567-2818), and **Aloha** (03-3415-4691). The Japanese rental company **Japaren** (Tokyo: 03-3354-5531) has branches in various cities, but no dropoff; however, it offers the cheapest rates and is recommended for local touring.

**Hitchhiking** is relatively safe. Carry cardboard and black magic marker: drivers will be much more willing to pick you up if they see you holding up a sign with your destination written *in Japanese*.

# PRACTICAL INFORMATION A TO Z

**Addresses.** The Japanese system is to list addresses from greater to lesser: prefecture, city, ward, block or street, number, and finally addressee's name. When written in roman letters, however, the order is reversed, gratuitously conforming to Western convention. We follow this rule so as not to confound the postal authorities. Locating a place by its address is another problem. Upon arriving in the right general area, one usually must make local inquiries. Rice dealers, saké shops, and local police boxes are the best informed. Whenever you set out for a possibly obscure spot, have someone call ahead for exact directions, which should be *written down in Japanese*. Useful terms:

| | | | | | |
|---|---|---|---|---|---|
| -ken | prefecture | -ku | ward | -chōme | block |
| -gun | ward | -mura | village | -ban | number |
| -shi | city | -dōri | avenue | -biru | building |
| -machi | town or quarter | -chō | street | | |

**Banks.** Bank hours: M–F 9:00–15:00; clsd Sa, Su, NH. Large banks can exchange currency and cash traveler's checks, but hotels offer the same rates of exchange, without the red tape.

**Baths.** (Also see Ryokan chapter.) The Japanese bath (*o-furo*) is for everyone to use, so don't soap in the tub and don't pull the plug. Scrub and rinse outside. In ryokan and min-shuku, guests typically take turns rather than plunging in with strangers. Bathing before dinner is customary. Bathing in the morning is unheard of, except at onsen (hot springs), which often have baths that are open around the clock. *Sentō* (public baths) charge about Y250–300, and towels can be rented or purchased, along with soap. Almost every hot-spring town has one or more public onsen baths.

**Business hours.** Government offices: M–F 9:00–17:00; Sa (two per month only) 9:00–12:00; clsd Su. Private companies: M–F 9:30–17:00; Sa 9:30–12:00; clsd Su (many are also closed Sa). Department stores: 10:00–19:00; clsd one day a week.

11

**Business travel.** Without a *meishi*, or business card, you are a nonperson in Japan. Bilingual cards can be printed overnight at major hotels; JAL has an in-flight service. Train ticket stubs are collected when you disembark, so make sure to ask for a separate receipt when you buy the ticket. Useful phrase: *Reshiito kudasai*, "Receipt, please."

**Children.** Trains, subways and buses are free for children under 6, half-fare up to age 12 (except for reserved seats). Hotels and inns accommodate infants for free and young children at a reduced rate. Baby-sitting services are rare, but you can always ask. Try taking fussy eaters to a kissaten (p. 119), for almost-familiar sandwiches, spaghetti, and ice cream. Department-store eateries offer *okosama ranchi* ("honorable child lunch") — kid foods like macaroni, fried chicken, and mixed rice, arranged in animal shapes, etc.

**Crime.** Dial 110 for police. The neighborhood police box is called a *kōban*. Though Japan's low crime rate is the envy of the Western world, obviously one should take normal precautions. Professional pickpockets prey on train passengers and festival throngs. Few foreigners, including women alone, ever find themselves in actual physical danger. Troubles begin only when foreigners try to work as English teachers, hostesses, and so on without proper visas, which is illegal and exposes one to exploitation and blackmail.

**Embassies and consulates**

| | |
|---|---|
| Canadian Embassy | 7-3-38 Akasaka, Minato-ku, Tokyo (03-3408-2101) |
| UK Embassy | 1 Ichiban-chō, Chiyoda-ku, Tokyo, (03-3265-5511) |
| Consulates | Hong Kong-Shanghai Bank Bldg. 4F, 3-6-1 Awaji-chō, Chūō-ku, Ōsaka (06-231-3355) |
| US Embassy | 1-10-5 Akasaka Minato-ku, Tokyo (03-3224-5000) |
| Consulates | 2-11-5 Nishi-tenma, Kita-ku, Ōsaka (06-315-5900) |
| | 2-5-26 Ōhori, Chūō-ku, Fukuoka (092-751-9331) |
| | 1 Kita, 28 Nishi, Chūō-ku, Sapporo (011-641-1115) |
| | 254 Nishihara, Urasoe-shi, Naha, Okinawa (0988-76-4211) |

**Emergencies.** Most public phones have a red button. Lift the receiver, push it, and dial.

| Police | 110 (Can set up conference call with translator.) |
|---|---|
| Fire, Ambulance | 119 (Calls must be in Japanese.) |

**English.** Japan's "second language," English, only works in major hotels, tourist restaurants, and other places specifically designated for foreigners. Out in the real Japan, one must remember a few facts. All Japanese high-school graduates have had English for six years, but very few have ever heard a native speaker. Even fewer have tried to speak it. The brave ones who try it on a foreigner are amazed to see that it works. When asking directions, pick a likely target — a student or a businessman — and speak slowly, evenly, with precise diction. If speech fails, write it down. The Japanese do infinitely better with written English. Also, bear in mind that not every foreigner is a tourist; there are many resident *gaijin*, especially in Tokyo and Kyoto, who can assist you.

**English-language Assistance.** The following phone services provide aid to English-speaking travelers and residents. Toll free (dial from anywhere in Japan):

**Japan Travel Phone** (0120-222-800 in east Japan, 0120-444-800 in west Japan) Hrs: 9:00–17:00, daily.

**Japan Helpline** (0120-461-997) 24-hours, daily. Staffed by volunteers.

Other numbers (when phoning from outside Tokyo, first dial 03):

**Directory Information** (3277-1010) Hrs: M–F 9:00–17:00.
**Japan Railways** (3423-0111) Hrs: M–F 10:00–18:00.
**Japan Hotline** (3586-0110) Hrs: M–F 10:00–16:00. General information service.
**Foreign Residents' Advisory Corner** (3211-4433) Hrs: M–F 9:30–16:00. Questions answered by the Tokyo Metropolitan Government.
**Immigration Office** (3213-8523) M–F 9:00–16:00, 1st and 3rd Sa 9:00–12:00. Information in English, Chinese, Korean, Spanish and Portuguese.

**Etiquette.** Fastidiousness rules. It is considered rude to sneeze or to blow your nose in public. Eating while walking along the street is also not done, except at festivals. Speaking loudly in public places is considered uncouth. You can shake hands with Japanese people—they accept it as Western custom—but never give a lady a friendly peck on the cheek; kissing is regarded as a sexual act. Feet are "unclean," so be careful not to bump your feet into other people. When trying to sit comfortably on the floor, it is acceptable for men to sit crosslegged, but not for women. Women should sit with legs tucked to the side, like the Little Mermaid.

**Footwear.** Most tourists have heard about the Japanese custom of removing one's shoes before entering a house, but can't quite figure out the details of its application. The principle is to keep street dirt from defiling the living space. Just inside the doorway, there's a street-level area where shoes are okay, and a raised level—the floor of the house—which is off-limits to shoes. Position yourself by the raised floor, step out of street shoes, and set your foot down on the raised floor; if you just step back onto the lower level, all that street dirt will get on the bottoms of your feet, defeating the purpose of the exercise. Walking barefoot outside, and then tromping into the house, is also not done. Inside the house, shared slippers are provided. Remember, remove slippers before stepping on tatami. This is because tatami is fragile, and also because one eats and sleeps on it, and so it has to be kept extra clean. The **toilet slippers** are for use in the obviously "dirty place." Don't forget to change out of them when leaving the toilet.

**Gift-giving.** If you have a Japanese host, by all means bring a gift from home. You may also want to come prepared with a few small items to give to friends and kindly people you meet on your travels. Handcrafts (Navaho jewelry), food products (Vermont maple sugar candy, Macadamia nuts), baseball pennants, and the like are good bets. If you're invited to someone's home, you won't go wrong with liquor (imported whiskey) or fruit.

**Handicapped Travelers.** Few public or private facilities accommodate wheelchairs.

**Health.** Food hygiene in Japan is the best in the world, but sometimes things appear on the table that should be declined. Don't eat raw freshwater fish, raw bear meat (*kuma-sashi*) or raw wild boar meat (*botan niku*). Don't drink from mountain streams. If you are allergic to mold, avoid the humid months of June to September. Don't wade barefoot in rice paddies and other bodies of standing water; the schistosomiasis parasite, which can permanently damage vital organs, still exists in Japan. *Urushi* (lacquer) and *haze* (wax) trees, and raw lacquer produce an allergic rash like poison ivy.

**Hospitals.** The following have English-speaking doctors:

| | |
|---|---|
| Tokyo | Hibiya Clinic, Hibiya Mitsui Bldg., B1, 1-1-2 Yūrakuchō, Chiyoda-ku (03-3502-2681) |
| | International Catholic Hospital, 2-5-1 Nakaochiai, Shinjuku-ku (3951-1111) |
| | St. Luke's Hospital & Clinic, 10-1, Akashichō, Chūō-ku (3541-5151) |
| | Tokyo Medical and Surgical Clinic, No. 32 Mori Bldg., 3-4-30 Shiba-kōen, Minato-ku (3436-3028) |
| Kyoto | Japan Baptist Hospital, 47 Yamanomotochō, Kitashirakawa, Sakyō-ku (075-781-5191) |
| Ōsaka | Yodogawa Christian Hospital, 2-9-26 Awaji, Higashi-Yodogawa-ku (06-322-2250) |

**Immigration.** (See "Before You Go" for visa requirements.) Visitors who wish to stay beyond ninety days should know the following:

**Alien registration.** Foreigners staying for more than ninety days must apply at a ward office (*kuyakushō*) for a Certificate of Alien Registration within ninety days of landing.
**Extension of length of stay.** Apply at an immigration office (*hōmugōdō chōsha*) at least ten days prior to expiration date. One must explain the reason for the extension, prove financial support during the extension period, supply a letter from a guarantor (form provided by immigration offices), and pay a fee.
**Location of immigration offices:**

| | |
|---|---|
| Sapporo | Kita-sanjō Nishi 4-chōme, Chūō-ku (011-261-9211) |
| Sendai | 3-20 Gorin 1-chōme, Miyagino-ku (022-256-6076) |
| Tokyo | 1-3-1 Ōtemachi, Chiyoda-ku (03-3213-8111) |
| Narita | Narita Airport (0476-32-6771) |
| Yokohama | 37-9 Yamashita-chō, Naka-ku (045-681-6801) |
| Nagoya | 4-3-1 Sannomaru, Naka-ku (052-951-2391) |
| Kyoto | 72-2 Nambu-machi, Fushimi-ku (075-612-0660) |
| Ōsaka | 2-1-17 Tanimachi, Chūō-ku (06-941-0771) |
| Kōbe | Kaigan-dōri, Chūō-ku (078-391-6377) |
| Hiroshima | 6-30 Kamihatchōbori, Naka-ku (082-221-4412) |

12

| Fukuoka | 1-22 Okihama-chō, Hakata-ku (092-281-7431) |
| Kagoshima | 18-2-40 Izumi-chō (0992-22-5658) |
| Naha (Okinawa) | 1-15-15 Hikawa (098-832-4185) |

**Lost-and-found.** People are pretty scrupulous about turning in lost articles. In Tokyo, check with the appropriate office. JR trains lost-and-found: Tokyo station (03-231-1880), Ueno station (03-841-8069). Subways (Teitō RTA): Ueno subway station (03-834-5577). Tokyo metropolitan buses and subways (03-216-2953). Taxis (Tokyo Taxi Kindaika Center), Shinjuku (03-648-0300). After three to five days, all lost items go to the central lost-and-found office of the Central Metropolitan Police Board (03-814-4151).

**National holidays.** Banks and public offices close on national holidays. Museums generally stay open. If the national holiday falls on a Sunday, the following Monday becomes a holiday. The period from April 29 to May 5, with its three national holidays, is known as Golden Week; millions of Japanese take the whole week off to travel, so be prepared for extreme crowding on trains and in hotels. Two other extremely crowded periods are August 13–16 and New Year.

| | | | |
|---|---|---|---|
| Jan. 1 | New Year's Day | Sept. 15 | Respect for the Aged Day |
| Jan. 15 | Coming of Age Day | Sept. 23 | Autumnal Equinox |
| Feb. 11 | National Foundation Day | Oct. 10 | Health-Sports Day |
| Mar. 21 | Vernal Equinox | Nov. 3 | Culture Day |
| Apr. 29 | Greenery Day | Nov. 23 | Labor Thanksgiving Day |
| May 3 | Constitution Memorial Day | Dec. 23 | Emperor's Birthday |
| May 5 | Children's Day | | |

**Parcel delivery.** To ship purchases and excess baggage back to your base camp, use one of the *takkyū-bin* (home delivery) services. They are cheap, fast, and reliable. Ask your hotel to arrange it, or stop by one of the numerous outlets, which is often the neighborhood rice shop. Two large companies are easily identifiable by their signs: a pelican (Perikan-bin) and black cat (Kuroneko). Simple packaging is provided for a small fee. Suitcases, boxes, and sealed bags are okay. Prices shown are for 2 kg and 20 kg packages.

| | Sapporo | Tokyo | Kyoto | Fukuoka |
|---|---|---|---|---|
| Sapporo | — | | | |
| Tokyo | Y1300/1400 | — | | |
| Kyoto | 1340/1650 | 1000/1100 | — | |
| Fukuoka | 1960/2270 | 1200/1300 | 720/1340 | — |

**Postal system.** The post office (*yūbin kyoku*) is marked by a scarlet . Central post offices handle overseas parcels. Hrs: 9:00–19:00; Sa 9:00–17:00; Su and NH 9:00–12:30. Small post offices: 9:00–17:00; Sa 9:00–12:30; clsd. Su, 2nd Sa. Smaller branch post offices cannot handle overseas parcels; take them to a main office. Central post offices in the major cities are located by the central train stations:

| Tokyo: | 2-7-2 Marunouchi, Chiyoda-ku (03-3284-9539) |
| Kyoto: | 843 Higashi-Shiokōji, Shimogyō-ku (075-365-2555) |
| Ōsaka: | 3-2-4 Umeda-chō, Kita-ku (06-347-8060) |

**Postage Rates**

| Zone | Postcard | Letter (10 gm) |
|---|---|---|
| Within Japan | Y 41 | Y 62 |
| N. and C. America | 80 | 100 |
| E. Asia | 80 | 80 |
| Europe, Africa, S. America | 80 | 120 |
| Oceania | 80 | 100 |

**Shopping.** Though prices are not cheap, there are good buys for the discerning shopper in every budget class. Crafts can be unique and reasonably priced (see Crafts chapter). Old silk kimono, a mainstay at flea markets, are remarkably cheap, an infinitely better deal than the acetate imitations aimed at the tourist trade. Cameras and electronic goods are now cheaper in Hong Kong and Singapore, but the big discount shops in Tokyo's Akihabara and Shinjuku districts offer selections second to none. Bargaining is not done, except at flea markets, antique shops, and discount electronics shops. Even here, there's no drawn-out haggling; the price is set after one or two exchanges. Major discount outlets and department stores have tax-free shopping; you must pay the tax at the time of purchase and then visit a special desk and present your passport to get an immediate tax refund. Duty-free items: articles made of, or incorporating, precious metals and stones, pearls, coral, cloisonné, furs, sporting guns, electronic products, cameras, projectors, binoculars, watches, tobacco pipes.

**Taxes.** There is a value-added tax of three percent on all expenditures. A six-percent tax is charged on hotel bills exceeding Y10,000 and restaurant bills exceeding Y5,000.

**Telephone and telegraph.** A three-minute local phone call is Y10. Local numbers are from five to eight digits long. Area codes are from two to five digits long (always beginning with zero) and change from town to town. A typical phone number might look like this:

```
area code  local number
 012  - 345-6789
 0123 - 45-6789
```

Long-distance calls of between 60 and 320 km are discounted 40 percent between 19:00 and 8:00 a.m. Calls of greater than 320 km are discounted 50 percent from 21:00 to 6:00 a.m. Calls of more than 60 km are reduced 40 percent Sa, Su, and NH. International direct-dial calls are 40 percent cheaper between 23:00 and 5:00 a.m.

13

**Useful numbers:**

| | |
|---|---|
| 100 | to place a domestic call and find out the charge |
| 104 | directory assistance for all parts of Japan (Y30 per inquiry) |
| 106 | collect calls (to the TIC, for example) |
| 0041 | Direct-dial international call |
| 0051 | international operator |
| 0039111 | Direct to AT&T operator, for charge calls only |

**Public phones (kōshū denwa).** Public phones used to come in a rainbow of color-coded types, but they have now been replaced almost completely by one shade: lime green. These phones often take Y10 and Y100 coins (no change on Y100), and most accept magnetic cards, which can be purchased in Y500, Y1000 and Y3000 denominations from vending machines and magazine kiosks. International calls can be made from green phones that are labeled as such, often located near major JR stations.

**Private phones.** Sometimes a shop will let you use the phone if no public phone is available. Be sure to pay Y10 for each local call. Place long-distance domestic calls through the 100 operator. Afterward the operator will call to tell you how much it cost.

**International calls and telegrams.** To place an overseas phone call you must use a private phone, hotel phone, an international public green phone or visit a KDD office. To send an overseas telegram, phone or visit KDD. Office locations:

| | |
|---|---|
| Sapporo | Chūō-ku, Kitashijō-nishi, 5-chōme, 1-3. Nihon Seimei Kitamonkan Biru 1F (011-241-6802). Hrs: M–F 9:00–17:00, clsd Sa, Su, NH. |
| Narita | Airport Terminal (0476-32-8730). Hrs: M–F 9:00–20:00, Sa, Su, NH 9:00–18:00. |
| Tokyo | Chiyoda-ku, Ōtemachi, 1-chōme, 8-1 (03-3275-4343). Hrs: M–F 9:00–18:00; Sa, Su, NH 9:00–17:00. |
| | Nishi-Shinjuku, 2-chōme, 3-2, KDD Biru 1F (03-3347-5000). Hrs: M–F 9:00–18:00, clsd Sa, Su, NH. (There are many others; call JNTO for the one nearest you.) |
| Kyoto | Shimogyō-ku, Kawaramachi-dōri Shijō-sagaru, Sumitomo Biru 1F (075-341-2733). Hrs: M–F 9:00–17:00, clsd Sa, Su, NH. |
| Ōsaka | Chūō-ku, Bingo-chō, 1-chōme, 5-2 (06-228-2151). Hrs: 9:00–18:00, clsd Sa, Sun, NH. |
| | Umeda Station Area: Kita-ku, Umeda, 2-chōme, 2-25, Shin-Hanshin Biru 1F (06-343-2571). Hrs: M–F 9:00–18:00; Sa, Su, NH 9:00–17:00. |
| | Ōsaka International Airport: Terminal Bldg. 3F (06-856-7387). Hrs: 9:00–17:00, daily. |
| Hiroshima | Naka-ku, Ōtemachi, 1-chōme 1-23 Okajū Biru, 1F (082-241-2411). Hrs: M–F 9:00–17:00, clsd Sa, Su, NH. |
| Fukuoka | Hakata-ku, Nakatsu 5-chōme, 5-13, KDD Biru (092-281-9111). Hrs: M–F 9:00–17:00, clsd Sa, Su, NH. |
| Okinawa | Naha-shi, Higashi-machi, 4-1 (098-865-3374). Hrs: M–F 9:00–18:00, Sa 9:00–17:00, clsd Su, NH. |

14

**Time zone.** Japan Standard Time is nine hours ahead of Greenwich Mean Time, or fourteen hours ahead of New York (EST). Japan has no daylight savings time, so subtract one hour from the time difference in summer.

**Tipping.** Don't. A ten-percent service charge is included in most restaurant and hotel bills. In a ryokan, if a maid is especially attentive (launders your clothes, arranges a tour of the city), you may give her a *chadai* (tea money) of Y2–3000, although it is not expected. (Be discreet; put the money in an envelope or folded paper and slip it to her when she comes to serve tea.)

**Toilet (W.C.).** *Toilet?* will be understood. The Japanese toilet is flush to the floor; squat over it, facing the hood. Before using one for the first time, make certain you are able to complete a deep knee bend without using your hands. Be careful not to spill the contents of your pants pockets. Public facilities are numerous and reasonably clean in stations, public parks, department stores, and buildings. For Western-style facilities, try first-class hotels or new department stores. Away from major cities, one can still find pre-modern plumbing. Just think of it as another aspect of Japan's incredible variety. Carry pocket tissues and handkerchiefs, since toilet paper and towels are usually not provided.

**Travel agents.** Most visitors use the vast JTB (Japan Travel Bureau). The main offices in Tokyo and Kyoto have English-speaking personnel. JTB can only book at lodgings with which it has a commission agreement; though these include some minshuku and youth hostels, the choices dwindle as you move down the price scale. On the other hand, some of the most exclusive inns cannot be booked through JTB.

**Weights and measures.** Japan is on the metric system.

**Women travelers.** It is generally safe for women to walk alone at night. A woman traveling alone may be harassed by men, but this is more annoying than threatening. A firm "no!" should do the trick. Women pinned inside a sardine-packed rush-hour train sometimes are subject to groping by unseen hands; Japanese women are usually too chagrined to make a fuss, unlike one American lady who seized the offending hand, held it aloft, and demanded, "whose hand is this?" The owner of the hand disembarked at the next stop.

**Voltage.** 100 volts, AC, but cycles are different. Eastern Japan, including Tokyo, is on fifty cycles; western Japan, including Nagoya, Kyoto, and Ōsaka, is on sixty cycles.

# History and Culture

**EARLY JAPAN**
Asuka period (538–645)
Hakuhō period (645–710)

16

**CLASSICAL JAPAN**
Nara period (710–794)
Early Heian period (794–894)
Late Heian (Fujiwara) period (894–1185)

**THE MIDDLE AGES**
Kamakura period (1185–1333)
Muromachi (Ashikaga) period (1334–1573)

**PREMODERN JAPAN**
Momoyama (Azuchi-Momoyama) period (1573–1615)
Edo (Tokugawa) period (1615–1868)

**MODERN JAPAN**
Meiji period (1868–1912)
Taishō period (1912–1926)
Shōwa period (1926–1988)
Heisei period (1989–)

# A Brief History of Japan

Japan underwent three distinct cultural transformations during its prehistoric era (ca. 100,000 B.C.–A.D. 538). With the introduction of writing and Buddhism in the sixth century, Japan entered its historical phase. During the classical period (710–1185), a permanent capital was established at Nara and later at Kyoto. At first, Japan was an earnest and agile student of China, but by the tenth century, it had developed a distinct and sophisticated culture of its own. During the turbulent middle ages (1185–1573), when various warrior clans battled to rule the country, Zen Buddhism worked profound changes on Japanese civilization. In premodern times (1573–1868), power was consolidated under three successive military leaders, the last of whom, Tokugawa Ieyasu, founded a dynasty of shoguns who would rule oppressively but peacefully for 250 years. During this period, an urban middle class emerged. After the Meiji Restoration (1868), in which the Emperor was "restored to power," Japan started down the road to becoming a modern nation.

17

## EARLY JAPAN (ca. 100,000 B.C.–A.D. 710)

369    Japanese colony of Mimana established in Korea
538    Buddhism introduced into Japan
607    Shōtoku Taishi builds Hōryū-ji
645    Nakatomi no Kamatari helps overthrow the Soga clan; Taika Reform the following year

### Jōmon, Yayoi, and Kofun Periods (ca. 10,000 B.C.–A.D. 538)

Japan was inhabited perhaps as early as 100,000 years ago, but it is not clear whether these people were ancestors of the present-day Japanese. Eventually, two distinct pottery-making cultures emerged. The **Jōmon** (ca. 10,000–300 B.C.) is known for pots with rope impressions. It bears some relation to present **Ainu** culture and probably to mainstream Japanese culture as well (see Hokkaidō, p. 146). The rice-cultivating **Yayoi** (ca. 300 B.C.–ca. A.D. 300) are clearly identified with the modern Japanese. They produced plainer but technically more advanced pots and used metal tools, probably imported (see Art, p. 100).

During the **Kofun period** (A.D. 300–ca. 700), large earthen tombs (*kofun*) were built throughout Japan. These were often encircled with *haniwa*, clay figures of warriors and servants. Inside the mounds were placed bronze mirrors, glass beads, and other objects indicating both sophisticated production at home and extensive trade with the Asian continent. From the fourth century, in fact, Japan seems to have had a colony in Korea called Mimana (see Kyūshū History, p. 469). This colony was administered by the **Yamato** state, whose leaders—progenitors of the imperial house—extended their control over most of Japan during this time and also built the large *kofun* in the Kinki area. The history of these putative ancestors of the present emperor is shrouded in myth (see Shinto, p. 24–26).

### Asuka (538–645) and Hakuhō Periods (645–710)

While large *kofun* were still being built by local rulers in eastern Japan and elsewhere, Buddhism was introduced from Korea and made its way into the Yamato court under the aegis of the **Soga clan** (see Asuka History, p. 407). SHŌTOKU TAISHI built Hōryū-ji, which now has the world's oldest wooden buildings and famous masterpieces of early Buddhist sculpture.

In 645, Nakatomi no Kamatari, the founder of the FUJIWARA clan, helped overthrow the tyrannical Soga and participated in the **Taika Reform**, an ambitious plan to set up a centralized, Chinese-style court bureaucracy (see Hōryū-ji History, p. 400). During the **Hakuhō period**, Chinese cultural influence gained ascendancy over the Korean. The Buddhist art of this era exhibits great fluidity and grace.

# CLASSICAL JAPAN (710–1185)

| | |
|---|---|
| 710 | First permanent capital at Nara |
| 752 | Great Buddha completed at Nara |
| 794 | Capital moves to Kyoto; the Heian period begins |
| 805 | Voyages of the monks Saichō and Kūkai |
| 894 | Imperial court terminates official missions to China |
| 966 | Fujiwara no Michinaga becomes regent |
| 1000 | Lady Murasaki writes *The Tale of Genji* |
| 1053 | Fujiwara no Yorimichi builds the Byōdō-in at Uji |
| 1156–1160 | Hōgen and Heiji rebellions; Taira no Kiyomori defeats the Minamoto |
| 1185 | The Minamoto defeat the Taira at Dan no Ura |
| 1220–1240 | *Tales of the Heike* takes form |

### Nara Period (710–794)
In 710, Japan's first successful permanent capital, Nara, was built on the pattern of Ch'ang-an, the Tang Chinese capital; the FUJIWARA established Kōfuku-ji and Kasuga Shrine there. Emperor Shōmu built Tōdai-ji to serve as the head of a national system of temples. Delegations from all over Asia attended the "eye-opening" ceremony for Tōdai-ji's Great Buddha, housed in the largest wooden building in the world. The exotic gifts received on the occasion—beautiful lutes, Persian cut-glass bowls, and brocades—are preserved in the Shōsō-in imperial repository (see Nara History, p. 392).

### Early Heian Period (794–894)
In 794, the emperor moved to an even grander capital at Heian-kyō, present-day Kyoto, also laid out on a grid like China's Ch'ang-an. In 805, the monks Saichō and KŪKAI went to study in China. Saichō returned to establish the Tendai sect. He built his headquarters at Enryaku-ji, on Kyoto's Mt. Hiei. Kūkai founded Shingon, a form of Esoteric Buddhism (see Buddhism, p. 36); he built a seminary at Kyoto's Tō-ji and another on Mt. Kōya. The elaborate rituals and fashions of the imperial court took form at this time (see Kyoto History, p. 319).

### Late Heian (Fujiwara) Period (894–1195)
The FUJIWARA family, which had long held power, gradually monopolized it, ruling as regents for the emperor and exiling political rivals. In 894, the imperial court ended all official communication with the faltering Tang Chinese empire. Cut off from China, court culture became inward-looking. Court life was documented by the women in diaries and novels such as *Genji Monogatari* (The Tale of Genji), written by LADY MURASAKI around the year 1000. This was during the rule of the regent MICHINAGA, when Fujiwara power was at its height. His son, the regent Yorimichi, built the famous Phoenix Hall at Byōdō-in (see Uji History, p. 387).

Gradually Fujiwara power waned as retired emperors, the MINAMOTO and TAIRA warrior clans, and the monks of Enryaku-ji became increasingly independent and restive. TAIRA NO KIYOMORI defeated the Minamoto and became all-powerful, marrying off his daughter to an emperor, as the Soga and Fujiwara had done before him. The Taira in turn were defeated and destroyed by MINAMOTO NO YORITOMO and YOSHITSUNE. The war between these two clans forms the basis for *Tales of the Heike*, the Japanese Iliad (see Drama, p. 81).

# THE MIDDLE AGES (1185–1573)

| | |
|---|---|
| 1180 | Yoritomo establishes the military capital at Kamakura |
| 1195 | Tōdai-ji rebuilt at Nara; the Kei School of sculptors flourishes |
| 1199 | Yoritomo dies; the Hōjō family takes control |
| 1274–1281 | First and second Mongol attacks |
| 1331–1333 | Emperor Go-Daigo's second and third rebellions; the fall of Kamakura |
| 1338 | Ashikaga Takauji becomes shogun and makes Kyoto his capital |
| 1397 | Ashikaga Yoshimitsu "retires" to the Golden Pavilion |
| 1467–1477 | The Ōnin Wars devastate Kyoto, ushering in a century of anarchy |
| 1482 | Ashikaga Yoshimasa completes the Silver Pavilion |
| 1543 | Portuguese shipwreck at Tanegashima; firearms enter Japan |
| 1549 | Francis Xavier arrives in Japan |
| 1573 | Oda Nobunaga deposes the last Ashikaga shogun |

### Kamakura Period (1185–1333)
The victorious Minamoto no Yoritomo moved the de facto capital to Kamakura, where he became the first governing shogun, marking the arrival of the samurai as the true ruling class of Japan. The emperors, now mere figureheads, remained in Kyoto. Yoritomo rebuilt the temples of Nara and Kyoto that had been destroyed in the war with the Taira; many statues were carved for these temples by UNKEI, KAIKEI, and other members of the KEI SCHOOL. After Yoritomo's death, his wife Masako and her family, the Hōjō, seized control (see Kamakura History, p. 261–262). When Mongol armies overran China, Chinese Zen priests escaped to Japan and helped the Japanese repel two Mongol attacks. Zen gained powerful patrons in Kamakura and Kyoto (see Kamakura History, p. 258–259). Several emperors attempted to wrest power back from the samurai. Emperor Go-Daigo eventually succeeded in overthrowing the Kamakura shogunate.

## Muromachi (Ashikaga) Period (1333–1573)

After his victory over Kamakura, Emperor Go-Daigo had a falling out with his principal military supporter, ASHIKAGA TAKAUJI. The emperor was forced to flee to the mountains of Yoshino, where he and his descendants resisted Ashikaga rule during the **period of the Southern and Northern Courts** (1334–1393; see Yoshino History, p. 411).

Takauji meanwhile established the Ashikaga shogunate in Kyoto. His religious and esthetic advisor, the Zen priest MUSŌ SOSEKI, is credited with inventing the meditation garden. Takauji's grandson YOSHIMITSU built the Golden Pavilion, patronized KAN'AMI and ZEAMI, inventors of the Noh drama, and founded the painting academy where SESSHŪ and KANŌ MOTONOBU, founder of the KANŌ SCHOOL, studied. Yoshimitsu's grandson, YOSHIMASA, built the famous Silver Pavilion and through misgovernment allowed most of Kyoto to burn during the **Ōnin Wars** (1467–1477; see Kyoto History, p. 321).

During the following century of anarchy, known as the **Sengoku (Country at War) period** (1467–1573), much of the cultural and political focus shifted to Sakai, Yamaguchi, and Nagasaki, the last of which developed as a port for the newly arrived Portuguese traders. Nagasaki became a center of Christianity, which had been introduced by the Jesuit Francis Xavier (see Nagasaki History, p. 483). With the Portuguese came guns, which ODA NOBUNAGA skillfully exploited in his bid to reunite central Japan. He marched into Kyoto in 1568. Five years later, the last Ashikaga shogun fled Kyoto, ending the Muromachi period.

# PREMODERN JAPAN (1573–1868)

| | |
|---|---|
| 1576 | Oda Nobunaga builds Azuchi Castle |
| 1582 | Nobunaga assassinated. Toyotomi Hideyoshi rises to power |
| 1588 | Hideyoshi initiates sword hunt and declares fixed social classes |
| 1592 | Hideyoshi begins his disastrous Korean campaign |
| 1598 | Hideyoshi dies |
| 1600 | Tokugawa Ieyasu defeats his rivals in the Battle of Sekigahara, becomes shogun soon after |
| 1615 | Defeat of Hideyoshi's son at Ōsaka; the Edo period begins |
| 1636 | Tokugawa Iemitsu completes Ieyasu's mausoleum at Nikkō |
| 1637–1638 | Shimabara Rebellion and subsequent closing of Japan |
| 1688–1703 | Genroku era—the rise of urban popular culture |
| 1853 | Commodore Perry arrives in Japan |
| 1858 | Townsend Harris signs trade treaty with Japanese |
| 1868 | Meiji Restoration |

19

## Momoyama (Azuchi-Momoyama) Period (1573–1615)

Oda Nobunaga built Japan's first important feudal castle, Azuchi-jō, in 1575; other warlords soon followed suit and erected hundreds more by the end of the century (see Castles, p. 46). After Nobunaga was assassinated in 1582, Toyotomi Hideyoshi, one of the most fascinating figures in Japanese history, completed the reunification of Japan (see Kyoto History, p. 323). He built several palatial fortresses, including Fushimi-jō (south of Kyoto). Thanks to Hideyoshi's love of extravagance, the period is known for its gilded screens, ornate buildings, and general lavishness in the arts. Hideyoshi was also a patron of SEN NO RIKYŪ's restrained *wabi* tea ceremony. Hideyoshi's disastrous invasions of Korea (1592, 1597) are called the Pottery Wars because of the numerous captured Korean potters who introduced the production of porcelain and other types of pottery favored by tea masters. In the following decades, KOBORI ENSHŪ and HON'AMI KŌETSU elaborated on the arts associated with the tea ceremony, such as garden design and calligraphy.

Hideyoshi, before he died in 1598, entrusted his young heir, HIDEYORI, to a council of warlords that included TOKUGAWA IEYASU. In the ensuing power struggle Ieyasu emerged the victor at the **Battle of Sekigahara** in 1600. Edo (now Tokyo), Ieyasu's castle town, became the military capital. In 1615, a year before Ieyasu's death, Tokugawa forces destroyed Ōsaka Castle and killed Hideyori, leaving the Tokugawa claim to power undisputed (see Nikkō History, p. 242).

## Edo (Tokugawa) Period (1615–1868)

The early Tokugawa shoguns, especially IEMITSU, devised draconian measures to ensure their dominance over the provincial daimyo, such as forcing them to spend half their time in Edo. A strict social code defined the status and duties of the samurai, the peasants, and the merchants, who were theoretically at the bottom of the social scale. After mercilessly crushing a massive Japanese Christian uprising at **Shimabara**, the shogunate, which had already banned Christianity, closed Japan to the outside world. Only the Dutch and Chinese were allowed to continue a carefully monitored trade in Nagasaki.

Although of low social status, merchants and craftsmen prospered during the long Tokugawa peace. They were the principal patrons of an urban culture, which first flourished in the **Genroku era** (1688–1703) in Kyoto and Ōsaka. At this time the playwright CHIKAMATSU began to write for the puppet theater of Ōsaka, and the poet BASHŌ made his literary pilgrimage to Tōhoku. Eventually, the center of urban culture shifted to the expanding city of Edo, especially to the famed Yoshiwara pleasure quarter (see Tokyo History, p. 195–197). The Edo Kabuki (see Drama, p. 86), the courtesans of the Yoshiwara, and the scenic wonders of Japan were portrayed by the woodblock-print artists of the era (see Art, p. 99).

In spite of the closed-door policy, foreign influences — mainly Chinese and Dutch — trickled into Japan through Nagasaki, greatly influencing medicine, painting, and military science. The floodgates opened wide when **Commodore Perry** concluded a friendship treaty and the first American Consul, **Townsend Harris**, backed by the threat of force, negotiated the opening of treaty ports (see Izu History, p. 269). Internal problems and external pressures were pushing the shogunate to the brink of collapse. Political factions were temporarily united by the rallying cry, "Revere the emperor, expel the barbarians" (see Hagi History, p. 460). In 1867, the shogunate was overthrown, and in 1868, the newly enthroned EMPEROR MEIJI was "restored," although not to any real power. The nation's capital was moved from Kyoto to Edo, which was renamed Tokyo (Eastern Capital).

# MODERN JAPAN (1868–present)

| | |
|---|---|
| 1889 | The Meiji Constitution is adopted |
| 1894 | Japan wins Sino-Japanese War; China cedes Taiwan |
| 1905 | Japan wins Russo-Japanese War |
| 1910 | Official annexation of Korea |
| 1912 | Death of Emperor Meiji; the Taishō period begins |
| 1923 | Great Kantō Earthquake |
| 1931 | Manchurian Incident |
| 1937 | Japan invades China |
| 1941 | Pearl Harbor |
| 1945 | Atom bombs at Hiroshima and Nagasaki; World War II ends |
| 1952 | American Occupation ends |
| 1964 | Tokyo Olympics |
| 1972 | Okinawa reverts to Japan |
| 1988 | Emperor Hirohito dies. Akihito ascends throne in 1989. |

20

In the decades after the Meiji Restoration, the Japanese carried out sweeping reforms. Daimyo were deprived of their fiefs, and samurai of their swords. Children of all classes received compulsory education, and the government adopted European parliamentary and legal forms. Japan's rapid modernization made it possible for it to pursue imperialist ambitions in Asia, annexing Taiwan, Korea, and Manchuria. Japan's incursions into Asia led to war with the United States and its allies, and just seven decades after opening its doors to Western technology, Japan was able to mount one of the greatest war efforts in modern history. World War II ended shortly after atom bombs were dropped on Hiroshima and Nagasaki. The ensuing American Occupation carried out sweeping political and social reforms. The 1964 Tokyo Olympics, symbolized by the soaring profile of architect Tange Kenzō's Olympic Stadium, announced the reemergence of Japan on the world stage, where it gains in prominence every day.

# HISTORICAL SETTINGS

In Japan, every hero and villain has his place. History, much of it legend, has a pleasant tendency to focus upon events that occurred at a small number of locations, like stage settings in a play. This is good for the traveler, who can become acquainted with specific historical figures while looking at the tangible evidence of their times and their deeds. The preceding introductory history is only a skeleton, a kind of monochromatic timeline and map populated by stick figures; the flesh of personality is left to the appropriate locales as follows:

After Japan was opened to the West, Japanese history became infinitely more complicated. Not only did Japan's history become part of world history, but with the spread of universal education, its main actors were no longer limited to a tiny elite. Richard Storry's *A History of Modern Japan* offers an excellent account of post-Meiji history.

# TEN GREAT NAMES IN JAPANESE HISTORY

These names appear in uppercase letters throughout the book. Since the middle ages, the military clans used family crests to identify their troops on the battlefield and to emblazon buildings. The crests associated with the great historical figures are displayed next to their names. Often clans had several crests—we are showing the most prominent one.

**SHŌTOKU TAISHI (572–621).** As the imperial regent, he promoted Buddhism and Chinese culture; he is the first great culture hero of Japan. He is revered as a saint, and is also the object of an agricultural fertility cult. As a cult image, he is often portrayed as a two-year-old child. He is credited with founding many temples, the most important of which, Hōryū-ji, was built near his retirement villa (see Hōryū-ji History, p. 400).

**The FUJIWARA.** This family dominated the imperial court during the classical period. The Fujiwara name was given to its founder, **Nakatomi no Kamatari** (614–669), who restructured the central government according to the Chinese model. His son **Fuhito** dominated court politics at Nara (see Nara History, p. 392). The regency of **Michinaga** (966–1028) marked the height of Fujiwara power; his son built the famous Byōdō-in, a temple that has become the symbol of the era (see Uji History, p. 387). The family power declined at the end of the Heian period, although its members remained prominent aristocrats.

**KŪKAI (774–835).** Known posthumously as **Kōbō Daishi**, Kūkai is Japan's most venerated saint. After studying in China, he returned to Japan in 807 and founded the Shingon sect. He is buried on Mt. Kōya (Kinki, p. 419). He is credited with numerous miracles and is associated with Japan's most famous pilgrimage, the Shikoku eighty-eight-temple circuit (see Buddhism, p. 36; Kyoto History, p. 319).

**The TAIRA.** Also known as the **Heike** (the "Chinese" reading of "house of Taira"). The clan patriarch, **Kiyomori** (1118–1181), defeated the Minamoto and became all-powerful. His daughter became Empress **Kenreimon-in** (1155–1213). Shortly after Kiyomori's death, the Minamoto rose in revolt and exterminated the Taira in an epic naval battle at Dan no Ura, bringing the Heian period to an end (see Miyajima History, p. 449). Most of the great warrior families of the middle ages are descended from the Taira and Minamoto.

21

**The MINAMOTO.** Also known as **Genji** (the "Chinese" reading of "Minamoto clan"). In 1160, Taira no Kiyomori exiled three small sons of his dead enemy, Minamoto no Yoshitomo. Led by the eldest, **Yoritomo** (1147–1199), the brothers grew up to vanquish the Taira and found the Kamakura shogunate, with Yoritomo as shogun (see Kamakura History, p. 261). This was Japan's first military government. The Minamoto victory was led by Yoritomo's charismatic younger half-brother, **Yoshitsune** (1159–1189). Persecuted by the jealous Yoritomo, Yoshitsune fled to Hiraizumi, where he met his death. He is the foremost tragic hero of Japan (see Drama, p. 81; Hiraizumi History, p. 169).

**The ASHIKAGA.** This family governed as shoguns in the Muromachi period. **Takauji** (1305–1358) established the Ashikaga shogunate in Kyoto. The third shogun, **Yoshimitsu** (1358–1408), an able leader, patronized the new Noh theater and built the Golden Pavilion. The dissolute eighth shogun, **Yoshimasa** (1436–1490), built the Silver Pavilion (see Kyoto History, p. 320).

**ODA NOBUNAGA (1534–1582).** Nobunaga began the reunification of Japan after a century of anarchy. He was the first warlord to use Western firearms. He built the first great castle, and he entertained Jesuit missionaries. He is remembered for his cruelty and ruthlessness, particularly the slaughter of the warrior monks on Mt. Hiei (see Kyoto History, p. 322).

**TOYOTOMI HIDEYOSHI (1536–1598).** Hideyoshi completed Nobunaga's task of reunifying Japan. He is the only premodern Japanese ruler of common descent and is arguably the most fascinating character in Japanese history. Small of stature and monkey-faced, he was known for his generosity and extravagance. Only fragments remain of the lavish temples, shrines, and palaces he built. His heir, **Hideyori**, perished in the 1615 siege of Ōsaka Castle by Tokugawa Ieyasu (see Kyoto History, p. 322).

**The TOKUGAWA.** They were the shoguns of Edo (Tokyo) for over 250 years. The first shogun, **Ieyasu** (1543–1616), a man of monumental patience, carefully laid the foundation for his descendants' long rule. His grandson and great admirer **Iemitsu** (1604–1651) completed his nation-building and two important edifices: Nijō Castle in Kyoto and Ieyasu's mausoleum at Nikkō (see Nikkō History, p. 242). The last shogun, Yoshinobu, returned the mandate to rule "to the Emperor" in 1867.

**EMPEROR MEIJI (1852–1912).** Figurehead ruler for a group of young samurai who transformed Japan into a modern nation (see Hagi History, p. 460). After the Meiji Restoration in 1868, much was done in this man's name, including shifting the imperial capital to Tokyo and building numerous State Shinto shrines. The Meiji Shrine in Tokyo was built in his memory. A son reigned during the Taishō period (1912–1926), and his grandson Hirohito (Emperor Shōwa) reigned from 1926–1988. Strictly speaking, Meiji, Taishō, and Shōwa are the names not of the monarchs themselves, but of their reign periods. The reign of the current emperor, Akihito, will be called Heisei.

# TWELVE GREAT NAMES IN THE ARTS

**TORI BUSSHI (early 7th C).** A *busshi* (Buddhist sculptor) of Korean or Chinese descent, he is Japan's first artist to be known by name. He or his school cast the bronze Shaka trinity and Yakushi Nyorai of Hōryū-ji (see Art, p. 91).

**LADY MURASAKI (ca. 1000).** Member of an obscure branch of the FUJIWARA family, she is the author of *The Tale of Genji*, possibly the world's first novel. It deals with the life and amorous adventures of "the Shining Genji," an emperor's son who is made a commoner and assigned to the MINAMOTO clan. Paintings, plays, incense games, and even the garden at Katsura Imperial Villa were inspired by the novel (see Uji History, p. 387).

**The KEI SCHOOL.** The most illustrious Kamakura-period school of sculptors, descended from **Jōchō** (11th C), who perfected the multiblock (*yosegi*) method and carved the Amida Buddha at Uji's Byōdō-in. He and his numerous artistic descendants, especially **Unkei**, **Kaikei** and **Tankei**, were connected with the FUJIWARA temple of Kōfuku-ji at Nara. The pair of Niō at Nara's Tōdai-ji, the "portraits" of Muchaku at Kōfuku-ji and of Kūya Shōnin and Taira no Kiyomori at Rokuharamitsu-ji are among the school's finest works (see Art, p. 94).

**MUSŌ SOSEKI (1275–1351).** Zen priest, also known as **Musō Kokushi** (Musō, the National Teacher). He became ASHIKAGA TAKAUJI's spiritual advisor. He is said to have invented the meditation garden, and is credited with designing the gardens of Zuisen-ji in Kamakura and of Tenryū-ji and Saihō-ji in Kyoto (see Villas, p. 62).

**SESSHŪ (1420–1506).** Japan's greatest medieval painter, Sesshū journeyed to Ming China, where he was acclaimed a master. He spent much of his life around Yamaguchi (Chūgoku, p. 457). His famous paintings include *Haboku Landscape*, *Four Seasons Landscape Scroll*, *Ama no Hashidate* and *Hui-k'o Presenting His Arm to Daruma* (see Art, p. 95).

**KAN'AMI (1333–1384) and ZEAMI (1363–1443).** Kan'ami was a minor priest at Kasuga Shrine in Nara, who refined old folk plays to create a new theatrical art form called Noh. His son Zeami received ASHIKAGA YOSHIMITSU's patronage (he is thought to have been the shogun's lover), and adapted Noh to Zen esthetics. Zeami wrote many plays, and his essays remain the essential texts on the theory of Noh (see Drama, p. 82).

**The KANŌ SCHOOL.** This was the official painters' academy for four hundred years, from the late Muromachi through the Edo period. It was founded by **Masanobu** (1434–1530) and systemized by his son, **Motonobu** (1476–1559). The school is famous for the lavishly gilded screens of the Momoyama period, especially those painted by **Eitoku** (1543–1590) and **Sanraku** (1559–1635). Eitoku's masterpieces include a screen known as *Cypress Trees*, currently housed at the Tokyo National Museum. The most skilled of the Edo-period painters was **Tan'yū** (1602–1674; see Art, p. 96).

**SEN NO RIKYŪ (1522–1591).** Japan's most famous tea master, credited with perfecting the restrained *wabi* tea ceremony, he had enormous influence on the design of tea utensils, tea gardens, and tea architecture (see Villas, p. 65–67). He was tea master to ODA NOBUNAGA and TOYOTOMI HIDEYOSHI; Hideyoshi eventually ordered him to commit suicide. His grandson **Sōtan** founded the **Senke** (House of Sen) tea school, which now has three branches: Ura Senke, Omote Senke, and Mushanokōji Senke.

**KOBORI ENSHŪ (1579–1647).** A daimyo and leading tea master who is credited with inventing the Edo-period stroll garden (see Villas, p. 67). He advised on the design of the gardens of Nijō-jō, the Konchi-in subtemple of Nanzen-ji, and the Sentō Palace. His name is indirectly linked to the garden of the Katsura Imperial Villa. Enshū's influence dominates Edo-period gardens.

**The RIMPA SCHOOL.** The artists of this school, based in the Kyoto area, developed a bold decorative style, a blend of courtly tastes and tea ceremony esthetics, that make Rimpa paintings, pottery, and other works among the most appealing in Japanese art. Its foremost exponents include **Hon'ami Kōetsu** (1557–1637), **Tawaraya Sōtatsu** (d. 1643?), **Ogata Kōrin** (1658–1716), and **Ogata Kenzan** (1663–1743; see Art, p. 97).

**BASHŌ (1644–1694).** This poet elevated the seventeen-syllable haiku to a high literary art. His *nom de plume* comes from his fondness for the flowerless, droopy-leafed *bashō*, or plantain. Bashō often traveled in the guise of a pilgrim, and his most famous work is a travel sketch, *Oku no Hosomichi* (The Narrow Road to the Deep North), which contains descriptions of the famous ancient places of Tōhoku interspersed with evocative poems. There are Bashō memorabilia at his birthplace of Iga-Ueno (Kinki, p. 405).

**CHIKAMATSU (1653–1724).** Japan's foremost playwright, who wrote mainly for the Bunraku puppet theater. His masterpieces include *Sonezaki Shinjū*, the tale of the love-suicide of a shop clerk and a prostitute, and *Koxinga*, the tale of the half-Japanese pirate general who ruled Taiwan briefly in the seventeenth century (see Drama, p. 86, 89).

# Shinto
# and Shrines

Shinto, a term that embraces a diverse body of beliefs and practices making up Japan's indigenous faith, is an anachronism among the religions of modern societies, one that would seem to have little relevance to Japan today. Unlike more organized religions, Shinto is characterized not by scriptures and churches but by archaic myths, a concern for purity and defilement, and a chaotic amalgamation of shrines and rituals centered on the most primitive terms of survival—the need for food and for protection from draughts, plagues, and enemies. It revolves around the rites and festivals of the community, not of the individual, in a way that can only be described as tribal. In other words, Shinto is not so much a matter of personal belief as it is of being Japanese.

To most Japanese, Shinto is part of the backdrop of daily life, a set of customs that are to be followed more or less, but not to be pondered deeply. As such, it coexists easily with other aspects of life, including other religions. For all its unprepossessing character, however, Shinto is fascinating because it embodies two millennia of historical memory—ancient conquests, disasters, changes in political structure, and changes in livelihood. It is a kind of Rosetta stone that encodes the mysteries of origins, community rites and beliefs, local differences, and other features that have exerted, and continue to exert, a subtle yet pervasive influence over Japanese culture.

## ORIGINAL SHINTO

Visitors to Japan who hear the imperial ISE SHRINES described as "the most sacred place of the Shinto religion" may imagine Ise to be a kind of mecca where the faithful gather. But this is an incomplete, if not altogether misleading, impression. What is remarkable about Shinto is not its nationally organized form, but the persistence of its local character. Long before the Yamato clan set up the imperial line as descendants of the Sun Goddess enshrined at Ise, each village and clan had its own **kami** (deities). Even today, it is the local kami that are celebrated in a community's most serious rituals.

The kami are numinous entities that govern natural forces or occupy natural places. Most important are those connected with food production: water, fertility, the cycle of seasons, the movement of fish and game. Others are associated with special natural features, such as islands, caves, natural springs, waterfalls, and great trees. The kami come from the sky or from beyond the horizon, and they land at a sacred place during designated times of the year.

Mountain peaks, being closest to the sky, and being also the source of life-giving water, are especially favored; Fuji is but the most famous of Japan's innumerable sacred peaks. The kami of the mountain, usually a female, like the goddess of Fuji, is the most typical of the Shinto deities. Originally, a sacred place was marked simply, with a rope or some other delimiter. Nowadays there is usually a small shrine at the summit of the mountain, while the main shrine—the one at which people normally pray—is at the base, near the community, preferably in a place of great natural beauty. Cryptomeria groves are a favorite site.

The mountain goddess ages according to the cycle of the seasons, much like the universal archetypes Fraser describes in *The Golden Bough*; she is in particular credited with sending fresh, pure water from her lofty domain down to the paddy fields. In spring, when she is a young virgin, she must be enticed down to the fields. By harvest, she is a spent old hag, and must be properly thanked if the villagers wish to avoid her jealous wrath. Any woman who ventured into the mountains was said to court disaster; until the Meiji period, most sacred mountains, including Mt. Fuji, were generally forbidden to women. Men too had to be careful; in a recent movie, men engaged in mountain work—lumbering and hunting—placate the goddess by exposing their private parts.

The act of approaching the kami, then, entails some danger. Whether one could safely be in the kami's presence depends on one's state of purity—the overriding concern in Shinto. Priests and others who participate in rites undergo days of purification, avoiding contact with sex, birth, menstruation, and death. (Blood and death are especially polluting.) White robes, water, saké and salt symbolize ritual purity. The sacred ground of a shrine precinct is delimited by gates (*torii*, fig. 1), rope (*shimenawa*, fig. 2), fences, and expanses of white gravel (*yuniwa*). Most Japanese who are in mourning or otherwise ritually polluted will not cross these boundaries.

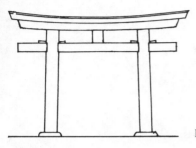

Figure 1. Torii

# MATSURI

Matsuri (festivals) are held by the thousands throughout the year. The processions, dances, plays, and other spectacles draw many onlookers, but in fact the ritual function of a matsuri is to delight and entertain noncorporeal guests, the kami, so that they will continue to bestow blessings—or abstain from causing misfortune. Indeed, the slow, stately Kagura (sacred dances) offered at matsuri, while fascinating to watch, seem intended for the enjoyment of beings for whom a century passes like an instant.

Primal Shinto beliefs are reflected in matsuri. The archetypal spring matsuri is a ritual to coax the mountain or fertility kami into the village and, more important, to the rice paddies, where it transmits its powers to the seedlings. In autumn festivals, the kami is given thanks for the harvest. A temporary shrine, the *otabisho* ("traveling place"), is set up in the village or fields, and the kami is transported there from the main shrine for the duration of the matsuri. This is accomplished by means of *gohei* (fig. 2), zigzags of paper, usually white, which are a kind of antenna to attract the kami. The *mikoshi* (portable shrine) developed relatively late, but is a central feature in today's matsuri. With *gohei* fixed atop, it is paraded around on the shoulders of villagers; if the *mikoshi* shakes violently, that is considered a sign of the kami's favor.

Figure 2. Shimenawa with gohei

Before the matsuri can begin, priests and other direct participants spend several days purifying themselves and the ritual sites. The *otabisho* is prepared, along with offerings of food and saké. The matsuri begins with the head priest invoking the kami's name. The kami is greeted, escorted through the villages and fields to the *otabisho*, and offered saké, a sticky rice cake called *mochi*, and other kinds of food. The purified participants also partake of these offerings, in an important act of communion with the kami. Then the kami is entertained. There are offerings of Kagura dances, and perhaps *yabusame* (archery), sumo wrestling, or plays. Youths full of life and intoxicated with saké are especially pleasing to the kami. The kami is then taken once more through fields and villages before being escorted back to the main shrine, from which it returns to the spirit world (see Matsuri chapter).

# MYTHOLOGY

In the eighth century (by tradition), the scribes of the Yamato state wrote down the official, glorified history of their nation. What resulted were two of the earliest written records in Japan, *Kojiki* and *Nihon Shoki*, which painstakingly "document" the origins of the Japanese nation from "the age of the gods" through the establishment of the imperial line and the succeeding generations of emperors and empresses. These naturally were the versions of the myths most acceptable to the Yamato court. According to them Japan was originally a land of gods:

> In the dawn of time, two gods appeared, the female **Izanami** and the male **Izanagi**. They were given a long spear with which they stirred the primordial muck, causing the islands of Japan to form. Then they descended. Izanami complained that her body was deficient in one place, and Izanagi observed that he had an excess in the same place. So they joined these parts together and begat various other islands and kami to populate Japan. All went well until Izanami gave birth to Fire. She was burned terribly and went into the Land of Death. The grief-stricken Izanagi insisted on following her there, only to see her maggot-covered corpse. Horrified, he fled from the scene. Finally, he came to a river where he washed, and from his purification were born the three mightiest kami, **Amaterasu** (goddess of the heavens and giver of light), **Susano'o** (god of the oceans), and Tsukuyomi (goddess of darkness and the moon).

But there was trouble brewing in paradise. Japan has few wide, flat plains on which to grow rice. Since antiquity, clans vied for control over such areas, which then became centers of early civilization. Great earthen mound tombs called *kofun* dot the centers of early political power such as Yamato (near Nara), Kumamoto (central Kyūshū), Saitobaru (southern Kyūshū), Kibi (facing the Inland Sea), and Izumo (on the Japan Sea). By the time the Yamato had pacified or conquered rival clans in western Japan, it had to justify its hegemony and find appropriate new roles for the other clans. The continuation of the genesis myth contains clues to how the Yamato achieved this goal:

> It was decided that Amaterasu should rule the High Plain of Heaven and Susano'o should rule the ocean. But Susano'o was a wild, unruly kami who angered his father by storming and wailing that he missed his mother. Exiled by his father, he visited his sister, but she was suspicious of him. Susano'o proposed a test to prove his sincerity, and when the results favored him, he went on a joyous, drunken rampage, trampling Amaterasu's rice fields and smearing excrement over her palace. But then he threw a skinned pony into her weaving room, killing one of the sacred weavers. This was too much for Amaterasu. She hid in a cave and vowed never to come out again. With the Sun Goddess shut away in a cave, the world was plunged in darkness. The millions of kami hastily gathered and tried various ploys to coax Amaterasu to reappear, but in vain. Finally, a female kami performed a ribald dance, causing the assembled kami to roar with laughter. Amaterasu inquired after the cause of their merriment and was told that a kami superior to her had appeared. Amaterasu peered out and saw her reflection in a mirror that the kami had set up. As she stepped closer to investigate, two kami seized her hands and drew her out of the cave. Light was restored to the world.
>
> Susano'o, banished from heaven for his misdeeds, wandered despondently around Japan. One day, in the land of Izumo, he met an old couple and their daughter, who were weeping. Inquiring, he learned there had once been eight daughters but every year an eight-headed dragon had devoured a daughter, and this very night the monster was coming for the last one. Susano'o offered to slay the dragon in return for the maiden's hand in marriage. Who were they to refuse? That night, he set out eight barrels of saké (knowing how divine beings love saké) and sure enough, the dragon *gabu gabu* guzzled it all down. Soon, the eight heads started nodding. When Susano'o saw that the monster was fast asleep, he leapt up and smote off all eight heads. Susano'o found a fine sword in the dragon's tail, which he gave to Amaterasu. As promised, the rescued daughter became his bride. Among their descendants was the kindly **Ōkuninushi no Mikoto**, who became the kami of Izumo and protector of Japan. Later, when **Ninigi no Mikoto**, grandson of Amaterasu, descended to earth, Ōkuninushi turned over the land to him. This greatly pleased Amaterasu, who ordered the Izumo Shrine built for Ōkuninushi—the very first shrine in Japan.

The usual interpretation of this tale is that the Izumo clan had been especially difficult to subdue, and that their pacification had been achieved only by giving their local tutelary kami an important—if clearly subordinate—place in the mythological pantheon. Significantly, the sword Susano'o found in the dragon's tail became one of the three imperial regalia. (The sword is now enshrined at Atsuta Shrine in Nagoya.) As a reward for submitting, Izumo was declared one of the country's most important shrines, second only to the imperial shrine of Amaterasu at Ise. But all of this is pure conjecture; archeologists have yet to find evidence that the prehistoric Izumo tribe was as powerful as the myths imply it to have been.

# IZUMO AND EARLY SHRINE ARCHITECTURE

IZUMO TAISHA is said to have been modeled on an early emperor's dwelling. Its great size indicated that a divine being resides there. It is the largest shrine hall in Japan. In early times it was said to have been truly immense; ancient legends claim that it stood on tall posts and was nearly a hundred meters tall, although this seems technically impossible.

## The Architecture of Izumo

*Taisha-zukuri*, the Izumo Taisha style, is considered the oldest and most basic style of shrine architecture (fig. 3). On a much reduced scale, it can be seen all over the Izumo region. Izumo Taisha has been rebuilt many times (most recently in 1744) with uncertain fidelity to the original. It cannot accurately reflect ancient shrine forms, but nevertheless it does represent an archetype. Here are particular features to look for:

**Demarcation of sacred space.** Several large torii mark the approach. The shrine is enclosed by a fence, which ordinary people cannot enter. The courtyard is covered with pebbles, giving it a clean, bare appearance.

**Natural wood construction, on posts.** The beautiful, utterly unadorned wood construction is considered a native feature, as is the practice of setting buildings on posts. In this respect, the Shimmei style of Ise (see next page) is "purer," because the pillars are embedded directly in the earth; Izumo's pillars rest on foundation stones, a building technique that came later from the Asian continent.

**Simple gabled (kirizuma) roof.** "Native" style indicates a simple gabled roof. Buddhist temples, and other buildings influenced by Chinese architecture, have a hipped or hip-and-gable roof.

**Entrance under the gable.** Early native dwellings had their entrance on the narrow side, under the gable. Shrines that have their main entrance in the side parallel to the roof ridge have either been influenced by Chinese temple architecture or are based not on dwellings, but on storehouses (as at Ise).

**Chigi and katsuogi.** The *chigi*, hornlike protrusions above the roof ridge, evolved from the crossed bargeboards that support and decorate the gable. *Katsuogi* were loglike elements perched along the roof ridge to hold the roof and ridge-cover down. As these features became emblematic of power, their use in humbler dwellings was sometimes restricted.

26

Figure 3. Izumo Taisha

# THE IMPERIAL CULT AND THE ISE SHRINES

Mythology assigns the earthly beginnings of the Yamato clan, which united Japan and founded the imperial line, to TAKACHIHO, in Kyūshū.

> Amaterasu decided to send her grandson, **Ninigi no Mikoto**, down to Earth to rule it. She gave him the mirror that lured her out of her cave, the sword Susano'o found in the dragon's tail, and a curved jewel. Ninigi landed on Mt. Takachiho. He took a beautiful goddess as consort, but when her father also offered her ugly older sister, Ninigi refused. This shamed the father and he put a curse on Ninigi's offspring so that their lives would be short. Thus the race of humans was born. **Jimmu**, Ninigi's grandson, established himself as the first emperor, and the mirror, sword, and jewel became the Three Imperial Regalia. Other descendants formed the aristocratic clans, such as the Imbe and Nakatomi (progenitor of the FUJIWARA).

Gradually the Yamato made their way up the Japanese archipelago to the area south of Nara, the Yamato plain. To the east, near the sea, they established the ISE SHRINES, consecrated to Amaterasu, the imperial ancestor, and thus the most important in Japan. There are two shrines at Ise, the Nai-kū (Inner Shrine) of Amaterasu and the Ge-kū (Outer Shrine) of the grain deity, who was perhaps enlisted to bolster the new imperial cult. Even today the emperor conducts rites to ensure a rich harvest, including secret rituals in which he symbolically mates with the earth. The high priestess of Ise was traditionally an imperial princess, reflecting Japan's early history of shamanesses, priestesses, and ruling empresses.

The Nai-kū at Ise houses the sacred mirror, which forms a part of the imperial regalia, along with the sword and jewel (the comma-shaped *magatama*). These are symbols of divine authority, supposedly received from Amaterasu herself. The same types of objects were buried in the tombs of important early personages as evidence of their wealth and power. The first emperors built the huge *kofun* tomb mounds to symbolize their authority over lesser chieftains. The largest, constructed for **Nintoku** (by tradition the sixteenth emperor), is an immense, keyhole-shaped mound surrounded by a triple ring of moats; it exceeds the Great Pyramid of Cheops in volume.

As the Yamato emperors asserted their divinity, a theological problem arose. If the emperor lived in a palace, shouldn't the kami also have a dwelling? Early shrines, such as Izumo Taisha, are thought to have been modeled after the early imperial dwellings. Shrines and imperial palaces still share such features as a fenced white gravel enclosure. In early recorded history, each new emperor had to build a new palace—even a new capital—to avoid pollution from the death of his predecessor. When the first permanent capital was established near Nara in the seventh century, the palace could no longer be moved so readily. Instead, it was rebuilt on an adjoining plot whenever a new emperor was installed. This practice had a parallel in shrines, which were periodically torn down and completely rebuilt on adjoining plots. Today, Ise is the only shrine to continue this practice. It is rebuilt every twenty-one years, a tradition that has continued almost uninterrupted for 1,300 years.

### The Architecture of Ise

Ise's architecture, the **Shimmei style** (fig. 4), is thought to be based not on an emperor's palace but on his storehouse, because of its function as the repository for the sacred mirror of the imperial regalia. Here are features to look for:

**Entrance parallel to the roof ridge.** Storehouses were built this way to provide a wider and more convenient opening for stowing and removing their contents.

**Straight roof lines.** This is considered a native feature. Shrines affected by Buddhist styles, including the current Izumo Shrine, have roof lines that sweep upward at the eaves.

**Posts embedded in the soil.** This is also a native feature. Though it speeds rot, this does not matter at Ise because the shrines are rebuilt so often. The rebuilding of Ise is a long, complicated ritual involving the preparation of special timber, building a new shrine, transporting the kami, and dismantling the old shrine. The next rebuilding will be in 1993.

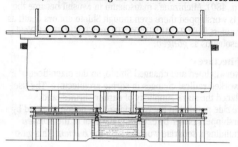

27

Figure 4. Ise Jingū

# SHINTO AND BUDDHISM

So far we have been describing Shinto in an era when, in fact, the word "Shinto" did not even exist. Around the seventh century, when Buddhism, introduced via China and Korea, was declared Japan's national faith, it became necessary to distinguish native beliefs as Shinto, or "way of the kami." This was not done with great precision, however, because Buddhism, with its articulated cosmic view, ethics, impressive cultural baggage, and long tradition of tolerance, simply absorbed the native beliefs. Buddhist theologians did not dismiss Shinto as "pagan," but viewed it as a lesser truth. Thus, when Emperor Shōmu consulted the Ise Shrines on his proposed project to build a Great Buddha, Amaterasu declared her approval by revealing herself to be a manifestation of the cosmic Buddha. Shinto shrines came to be established as guardians of Buddhist temples. One famous example is KASUGA TAISHA, the FUJIWARA family's tutelary shrine that is paired with Kōfuku-ji in Nara.

### Esoteric Buddhism and the Yamabushi

After the ninth century, Esoteric Buddhism made great headway in absorbing Shinto (see Buddhism, p. 36). These sects stressed that the Buddhist deities—indeed all beings—were ultimately emanations of the cosmic Buddha. Just as Amaterasu was identified with the cosmic Buddha, so all kami could be identified with appropriate Buddhist deities, forming a native "mirror" of the Esoteric universe. Mandalas, geometric diagrams representing the Buddhist cosmos, inspired shrine mandalas that explained the Buddhist nature of various kami (see Art, p. 93).

Esoteric Buddhism included belief in the holiness of mountains, much like native mountain worship. The headquarters of the two Esoteric sects, Enryaku-ji (on Mt. Hiei) and Kongōbu-ji (on Mt. Kōya), were among the first mountain-top monasteries in Japan. These sects absorbed a more ancient syncretic practice, **Shugendō**, whose practitioners are called **yamabushi** (those who prostrate themselves toward the mountain). The *yamabushi* wore a distinctive costume: a tiny black hat held on the head with a band, and deer-skin leggings. An exaggerated version is worn by the warrior-monk Benkei (YOSHITSUNE's sidekick) in Noh and Kabuki plays (see Drama, p. 86). **En no Gyōja**, the legendary seventh-century founder of Shugendō, was a shadowy figure who cast spells on demons and was eventually exiled by the Yamato court. His skills as an exorcist enabled him to "enlighten" the kami of various mountains and show them that they were really avatars of the Buddha. Shugendō is thought to have evolved from an ancient tradition of female shamans, which also existed (and still exists) in Okinawa and Korea. The *yamabushi*'s pilgrimage up the mountain is said to represent a return to the womb, and his backpack, besides its obvious practical use, is said to symbolize the uterus. Significantly, ŌMINE-SAN, the most important mountain "opened" by En no Gyōja, remains forbidden to women to this day.

During the classical period, the *yamabushi* occupied mountains all over Japan, including DEWA SANZAN, Haku-san, Togakushi, Daigo-yama, Daisen, and Mitoku-san. Because of their exorcism skills, *yamabushi* were popular with the peasants—although they were sometimes viewed as sorcerers—and they played a major role in spreading their brand of Buddhism among the common people. Rural Kagura dances, heavily imbued with Esoteric concepts, were introduced largely by the *yamabushi* (see Matsuri, p. 74).

The Esoteric sects tried to control the *yamabushi*; the *yamabushi* mountains near Kyoto tended to be under Shingon influence, and those in Kyūshū or Tōhoku tended to belong to the Tendai sect. Tendai *yamabushi* approached En no Gyōja's holy mountain of Ōmine from KUMANO, and Shingon adherents approached from YOSHINO. The deity of Ōmine-san, **Zaō Gongen**, is a fierce avatar of the evil-quelling Myō-ō, Buddhist patron deities of ascetics. From 1873 to 1945, under State Shinto ideology, Shugendō was regarded as "impure" and was outlawed. Nearly all Shugendō temples were destroyed or "purged" and turned into shrines. The subversive notion of a *gongen*, a kami avatar of the Buddha, had become so deeply embedded in Shinto, however, that even a strong nationalist movement could not root it out entirely.

A curious and celebrated event illustrates how strongly intertwined Buddhist and Shinto beliefs had become. In the early tenth century, Sugawara no Michizane, an ordinary mortal, was deified as the *gongen* **Tenjin**, reflecting Buddhist teachings that human beings were capable of achieving buddhahood. Moreover, Michizane's deification came about through the Buddhist belief that angry souls cling to their earthly abodes (his soul was angry because he had been unjustly exiled; see Kyūshū, p. 480). Michizane's mausoleum in Kyūshū became the shrine DAZAIFU TENMAN-GŪ, and he is worshipped there even though Shinto abhors death as a "pollution." Much later, the military rulers TOYOTOMI HIDEYOSHI and TOKUGAWA IEYASU had themselves enshrined at their mausoleums as *gongen*.

28

### Buddhist Influence on Shrine Architecture

Just as powerful Buddhist doctrines overwhelmed and changed Shinto, so the magnificent Chinese-style architecture of temples worked radical changes in shrine architecture. The use of color and metal ornamentation replaced the stark simplicity of earlier shrines, and entrances were regularly placed on the side parallel to the roof ridge. One notion inspired by temples was to provide a space for worshippers either by extending the roof of the *honden* (where the kami is enshrined) or by building a separate worship hall, the *haiden*. This gave rise to a number of new styles:

**Kasuga style.** Named for KASUGA TAISHA in Nara. The entrance is under the gable, and a deep eave extension is built over the steps. It is the second most common style (fig. 5).

**Nagare style.** The most common shrine style. The entrance is on the long side (like the Shimmei style), but the front eave sweeps out over the front steps, providing a shelter for worshippers (fig. 6). The best examples are the Kamo Shrines in Kyoto.

**Hachiman style.** Used for shrines to Hachiman, the kami of war, identified with Emperor Ōjin and appointed protector of Nara's Great Buddha temple, Tōdai-ji. *Honden* and *haiden* are built so close together that their roofs are linked by a rain gutter (fig. 7).

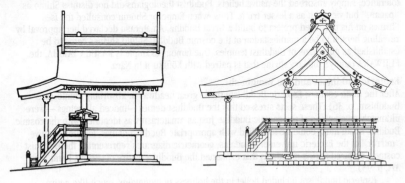

Figure 5. Kasuga style          Figure 6. Nagare style

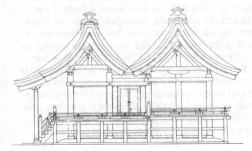

Figure 7. Hachiman style

**Gongen style.** This beautiful style was used for the shrines of deified humans. It resembles the Hachiman style, but *haiden* and *honden* are linked by a kind of hallway (*ishi no ma*) with a roof that slices perpendicularly through the *haiden* and *honden* roofs, creating a complex roof that appears to have five gables. The *ishi no ma* signifies the *gongen*'s existence in both this world and the divine realm. Famous examples include the KITANO TENMAN-GŪ in Kyoto and Tokugawa Ieyasu's mausoleum, NIKKŌ TŌSHŌ-GŪ, which is the penultimate example of the ornate Momoyama style—elaborate carvings and brilliant colors.

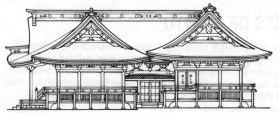

Figure 8. Gongen style

# STATE SHINTO

Though Buddhism exerted a profound influence over Shinto, various people over time attempted to reformulate Shinto as a separate, native tradition, and to place it above the foreign Buddhism. In the Edo period, the National Learning movement rejected Buddhism altogether and sought to go back to Japan's "pure" pre-Buddhist roots. It centered Shinto on the person of the emperor, who was considered divine, and was one of the intellectual currents leading to the Meiji Restoration of 1868.

After 1868, all shrines were required to join a national organization, with Ise reigning supreme; some small shrines were eliminated. More drastically, shrines and temples had to separate, and this led to an unofficial campaign in which many valuable Buddhist buildings and art treasures were destroyed. Syncretisms such as Shugendō all but disappeared. Still, shrine precincts often betray a syncretic past by the presence of Buddhist edifices, such as pagodas or Niō Gates (with the Buddhist Niō guardians replaced by a pair of courtierlike archers), or a nearby temple that was once related to the shrine.

Meanwhile, the newly established State Shinto organization constructed beautiful, monumental shrines of unfinished wood and vast spaces, dedicated to a variety of figures, mythical and historical, who had contributed to the greater glory of the imperial institution. These shrines are built in the Shimmei style, supposedly untainted by Buddhist influence, and bear the imperial chrysanthemum crest. They are usually called *jingū* (imperial shrines), rather than *jinja*. Famous State Shinto shrines built before the war include MEIJI JINGŪ, dedicated to EMPEROR MEIJI; Yasukuni Jinja, dedicated to all soldiers who have died for imperial cause since 1853; and Kashihara Jingū, dedicated to the mythic first emperor, Jimmu. Because of its close ties to the militarism that led to World War II, State Shinto as a national organization was disestablished in 1945 by the Allied Occupation.

# POPULAR SHRINES AND THEIR DEITIES

Thousands of small shrines are scattered throughout the towns and countryside. They are dedicated to various popular kami connected to the livelihood and well-being of the people. Most of these kami have an emblematic animal servant, such as the fox of Inari and the ox of Tenjin, which is represented by a statue on the shrine grounds.

**Inari.** Bright vermilion torii gates and fox guardians are the trademark of Inari shrines, which are dedicated to the kami of rice and, by extension, commercial prosperity. There are some forty thousand throughout Japan. Many are tiny, found on streets or tucked away on the grounds of other shrines and temples. Fried bean curd, the fox's favorite food, is offered at Inari shrines (fried bean curd sushi is called Inari-zushi). FUSHIMI INARI TAISHA in Kyoto, with its thousands of red torii, is the most prominent.

**Sumiyoshi.** The legendary, warlike Empress Jingū founded this shrine, dedicating it to the deities who protected her when she crossed the sea to invade Korea. A guardian of seafarers, Sumiyoshi's two thousand branches are commonly found in seaports. The most famous is the Sumiyoshi Jinja south of Ōsaka.

**Hachiman.** This shrine worships a combination of Emperor Ōjin, his "mother" Jingū, and his "wife," who in turn were identified with three Korean war gods enlisted in the seventh century to protect Japan against a feared invasion from Korea. This confusing hybrid became Japan's god of war (see Kyūshū History, p. 469). Kyūshū's Usa Jingū is the founding shrine. Iwashimizu Hachiman, south of Kyoto, became the patron shrine of the MINAMOTO, one of whom, Yoriyoshi, founded the famous TSURUGAOKA HACHIMAN-GŪ at Kamakura. There are some twenty-five thousand Hachiman shrines throughout Japan.

**Tenjin.** This is the shrine of the deified Heian-period scholar Sugawara no Michizane, patron of poetry and scholarship. He remains very popular in this education-minded country, especially among youths cramming for exams. Tenjin shrines are associated with plum trees, the "gentleman" flower favored by Chinese scholars, and thus of course by Michizane. The

29

grounds often contain a statue of an ox, Tenjin's messenger, which you can rub to cure an ailment. The most famous Tenjin shrines are KITANO TENMAN-GŪ in Kyoto and DAZAIFU TENMAN-GŪ in Kyūshū.

**Tōshō-gū.** Though there are only about one hundred Tōshō-gū shrines, they are architecturally and historically prominent, being branches of the celebrated NIKKŌ TŌSHŌ-GŪ, dedicated to TOKUGAWA IEYASU (see Nikkō History, p. 242). Other Tōshō-gū tend to be in castle towns.

# OTHER ASPECTS OF SHINTO

**Fertility cults.** Shinto once had an overtly sexual aspect that was connected to widespread fertility rituals. Stone or wood phalli were enshrined, and matsuri rites included symbolically enacted sexual intercourse. However, the spread of Victorian prudishness led to a successful campaign to remove such embarrassments from public view. Today, fertility cult relics remain visible only in a few remote shrines and matsuri, such as the Tagata Jinja near Nagoya, dedicated to the creative couple, Izanagi and Izanami.

**Gods of the hearth.** In a traditional home or shop, you will see a small *kamidana*, a miniature shrine dedicated to a local kami or one from a famous shrine, and containing an appropriate shrine amulet. Other types of gods have small shrines in various parts of the house; the all-important god of the hearth has his shrine in the kitchen. A special shrine is erected to welcome the kami of the New Year.

**Manufactures.** Creative processes, such as house building, pottery, metalworking, and saké brewing, are governed by kami. Today one still sees a sacred rope over the kiln door, or a swordsmith wearing the robes and ceremonial hat of a Shinto priest. When people build a new house, a party is held when the frame has been completed. A Shinto priest comes to purify it and seek the goodwill of the kami who may have been disturbed. Priests also bless modern factories.

**Seven Lucky Gods.** These gods of Chinese and Indian, Buddhist, Taoist, and Hindu origin came to be worshipped as a group during the Edo period. The five gods (Ebisu, Daikoku-ten, Bishamon-ten, Jurōjin, and Hōtei) and two goddesses (Kisshō-ten and Benten), are often depicted riding a treasure ship. They are particularly popular as New Year's good luck symbols.

30

# VISITING A SHRINE

**Torii.** These "gates" mark the entrance to a shrine. Each major shrine style has a corresponding torii style. A series of torii may span the approach to a shrine, and the path may be lined with lanterns, cryptomeria trees, or, if it's popular with pilgrims, souvenir shops.

**Pairs of koma-inu** ("Korean dogs"), or **Yatori** (archers). These often flank the main entrance to the grounds. Fox guardians indicate an Inari shrine.

**Ablutions.** These are performed by rinsing hands and mouth from a stone basin of pure water before praying at the shrine. Rinse both hands with the scoop and then transfer water to a cupped hand to rinse the mouth.

**Shimenawa.** These are straw ropes often festooned with white paper strips, called *gohei*. They appear on torii, around sacred rocks and trees, and above the entry to a shrine structure itself. They are symbols marking the boundary between sacred and profane spaces.

**To pay respects.** Stand in front of the cashbox and the long ropes dangling from a gong. The shrine may contain offerings of food and saké placed before a symbol of the kami, typically white paper *gohei* or a mirror. Most people toss a coin in the box, sound the gong a couple of times, bow deeply twice, clap hands firmly twice, bow once deeply, once lightly and then back away politely to avoid turning their backs on the shrine.

**Amulets.** These are sold at the shrine office. Especially popular are *ema* ("picture horses"), small, wooden votive plaques with a picture or inscription on one side, and a blank surface on the other to write one's wish. Most are pleas to pass an exam, get into Tokyo University, win someone's love, or have healthy babies.

**Priests and shrine maidens.** Only large shrines have official priests. Priesthood is generally hereditary; eldest sons are sent to Kokugakuin, the Shinto University. Shrine vestments are white and are worn with loose, pleated trousers of aqua or vermilion (for the maidens). For ceremonies, the head priest dons more colorful overgarments and an *eboshi*, a black cap of stiff gauze with an "antenna," a long, stiff band of material protruding vertically from the back of the cap, and doubled over in the middle. (Only the emperor wears a fully erect "antenna," to indicate his supreme position in the Shinto priesthood.) The shrine maidens are thought to originate from shamanesses of antiquity. Along with their other duties, they perform Kagura dances, a vestige of ancient trances in which shamanesses served as the kami's mouthpiece.

**Common rites.** The most common is *oharai*, a purification by waving what looks like a featherduster of shredded paper. This "dusts" away defilements. People will have *oharai* done over a new car to ensure against traffic accidents. Individuals can also pay to have a performance of Kagura dances offered to the kami.

# FAMOUS SHRINES AND SACRED MOUNTAINS

## TŌHOKU

** **Osore-zan.** This desolate volcanic plateau is regarded as a gateway to hell. It retains a last vestige of shamanist-Buddhist syncretism, with shamanesses, known as *itako*, who "communicate" with the dead (p. 159).

** **DEWA SANZAN.** "The Three Mountains of Dewa" were an ancient *yamabushi* center. Haguro Jinja retains a pagoda (NT); the mountain cryptomeria forest setting is breathtaking. Long ago, holy men underwent severe austerities to prepare their bodies for natural mummification. These mummies are revered as Buddhas (p. 175).

## TOKYO (***)

*** **MEIJI JINGŪ.** State Shinto shrine to EMPEROR MEIJI, it stands in a vast parkland. The most popular shrine in Tokyo, and thronged at New Year (p. 219).

## KANTŌ

*** **NIKKŌ TŌSHŌ-GŪ.** Fabulously ornate shrine to TOKUGAWA IEYASU — "Gongen-sama" in his Shinto-Buddhist incarnation (p. 239).

*** **TSURUGAOKA HACHIMAN-GŪ.** Guardian shrine of Kamakura, the medieval military capital. Famous for *yabusame* (horseback archery) during its spring and fall festivals (in *** Kamakura, p. 263).

## CHŪBU

*** **ISE JINGŪ.** Shrine in two parts, the outer, to the grain goddess, and the inner, to Amaterasu, mythic ancestor of the imperial house. Celebrated for the simplicity and beauty of its buildings and setting (p. 307).

## KYOTO (***)

** **FUSHIMI INARI TAISHA.** The most famous — and perhaps oldest — Inari shrine. The grounds contain thousands of vermilion torii (p. 333).

** **Heian Jingū.** Though founded only in 1895, this shrine, modeled on the Heian-period imperial palace, is impressive to behold (p. 340).

* **KITANO TENMAN-GŪ.** The main hall (NT) is a stunning example of the Gongen style. The shrine owns a famous scroll (NT) depicting the legend of Sugawara no Michizane (p. 352).

## KINKI

*** **KASUGA TAISHA.** Tutelary shrine of the FUJIWARA, and guardian of Nara. Origin of the Kasuga style of shrine architecture. Closely associated with the Fujiwara temple, Kōfuku-ji, Kasuga was an early syncretic center (in *** Nara, p. 395).

** **YOSHINO, KUMANO, AND ŌMINE-SAN.** The most famous center of Shugendō is at Mt. Yoshino's Kimpusen-ji. Kumano-Nachi Taisha is near the sacred Nachi waterfall. Every summer, *yamabushi* and pilgrims — men only — climb Ōmine-san (p. 414).

## CHŪGOKU AND SHIKOKU

*** **Kibitsu Jinja.** A beautiful and unique shrine hall (NT) dedicated to Momotarō, a mythical hero. The tumulus-dotted Kibi plain was the ancient stronghold of the Kibi clan, early rivals to the imperial house (in * Kibi Plain, p. 430).

** **Kotohira-gū.** A highly popular pilgrimage shrine to the guardian of seafarers (p. 435).

** **IZUMO TAISHA.** The largest and, by tradition, oldest shrine hall in Japan. The Susano'o legend is enacted in Izumo Kagura (p. 443).

*** **Ōyamazumi Jinja.** On an island in the Inland Sea, this shrine is renowned for its vast collection of arms and armor, placed there as offerings by great historical figures (on ** STS Inland Sea Route, p. 446).

*** **Miyajima.** Itsukushima Jinja, the tutelary shrine of the TAIRA clan, is on this sacred island. One of the most famous buildings in Japan, it was inspired by paintings of the Buddhist Paradise. The various halls are linked by covered galleries and are built on piles in a tidal cove. The shrine was meant to be approached by sea, and at high tide seems to float on the water (p. 449).

## KYŪSHŪ

*** **DAZAIFU TENMAN-GŪ.** Founded at the tomb of Sugawara no Michizane in Dazaifu, a military outpost to which he was exiled by the Heian court (at ** Dazaifu, p. 480).

** **TAKACHIHO.** This mountain village is claimed to be the place where Ninigi no Mikoto landed in Japan. Ama no Iwato Jinja enshrines a cave, said to be the very one in which Amaterasu hid herself. Iwato Kagura are sacred dances that reenact the creation myths (p. 497).

# Buddhism and Temples

32

Buddhist temples in Japan are rich in history and romance. They contain many of the most exalted masterpieces of Japanese art and architecture. Temples dominate the average sight-seer's itinerary, and rightly so. Yet without an understanding of basic Buddhist beliefs or the development of sects, they can seem to be a dreary repetition of dark halls filled with inscrutable icons. It is well worth the effort, therefore, to learn to "read" temples and Buddhist images. Often, a temple's sect, history, location, buildings, and sacred images fit together in a coherent pattern. In this chapter, we explain how the structure of temples reflects the basic tenets of each major sect. Buddhist art is discussed more fully in the Art chapter. The deities are introduced with the sects and periods in which they are particularly prominent, but in reality one will see most of these deities in all types of temples, and from all periods.

| Period | Deities | Architecture |
|---|---|---|
| | Nyorai, Bosatsu | Pagodas |
| Asuka-Hakuhō | Shaka, Yakushi, Miroku | Seven-hall garan |
| Nara | Niō, Shi-Tennō, | Chinese style |
| Early Heian | Dainichi, Myō-ō | Mountain temples |
| Late Heian | Amida, Kannon | Paradise halls |
| Kamakura | Jizō, Emma-ō | Daibutsu style |
| Kamakura-Muromachi | Rakan | Zen garan, Zen style |

## AN INDIAN PRINCE AND HIS ENLIGHTENMENT

Buddhism was a thousand years old by the time it reached Japan. It was founded in the fifth century B.C. by an Indian prince who at the age of twenty-nine renounced a life of sheltered luxury to seek the meaning of life. In his struggle to learn the cause of misery in the world, he became a wanderer. At one point, he underwent harsh ascetic discipline, nearly starving to death, but found that this brought him no clarity. He determined that a "middle way," in which there is neither pain nor pleasure, was better. One day, as he was meditating under a great pipal tree, he suddenly understood everything:

> That the world is an illusion, forever in a state of flux.
> That living beings are filled with worldly desire.
> That desire is never fulfilled because the world and the self are an illusion.
> That suffering is caused by unfulfilled desire.

This suggested a solution:

> That desire can end by realizing that the world is illusion.
> With the end of desire comes the end of suffering.
> By ending attachment to this world, one escapes the endless cycle of being;
> one attains nirvana, or nothingness.

And to achieve enlightenment, one must follow the Eightfold Way:

> Right outlook, resolve, speech, conduct, livelihood, effort, mindfulness, and
> concentration. By diligently pursuing these eight principles during every
> moment, one will pierce through illusion, and so end desire.

The enlightened prince was Sakyamuni, known in Japan as **Shaka**. He was given the honorary title of Buddha, or "enlightened one," which the Japanese call nyorai.

### Deities: Nyorai and Bosatsu

Early Buddhism centered on monastic life, in which Shaka's teaching was followed strictly in the quest for personal enlightenment. The Buddhism that entered Japan, however, was mainly the more complex **Mahayana**, or "Greater Vehicle," Buddhism, which stressed compassion for others and introduced the notion of the bosatsu (bodhisattva), who put off his own salvation in order to bring enlightenment to others. During Buddhism's long journey to Japan—through India, Central Asia, China, and Korea—local gods and goddesses were also adopted into the Mahayana pantheon as protectors of the faith. The end result was that, although early Indian Buddhism seems to have been egalitarian, the Mahayana Buddhism that arrived in Japan in the sixth century A.D. consisted of an intricately ranked pantheon of deities, which conveniently mirrored the stratification of Japanese society. At the top were the nyorai and the bosatsu.

**Nyorai (Buddha).** Fully enlightened beings. Mahayana Buddhism worships several nyorai besides the historical Buddha, Shaka. Each nyorai is a different aspect of the same ultimate truth, and the relationships between them are adduced according to complicated theories about reincarnations, different "worlds," and different eras. In sculpture, their identifying marks include simple monk's robes devoid of ornamentation, hair composed of snail curls, and a lump on the top of the head, signifying superior wisdom. They are often seated on a lotus, a flower that symbolizes the capacity of every living being to rise out of the slime of existence and achieve nirvana.

**Bosatsu (Bodhisattva).** These compassionate beings postpone their own nirvana in order to save all sentient beings. At the same time, they are manifestations of a nyorai, and do his work in the world at large. In sculpture, two bosatsu often flank an image of this nyorai, forming a trinity. They are princely figures, with long tresses and jeweled ornaments, because they need to impress ordinary people with Buddha's wisdom. Because bosatsu do the "legwork," they are commonly portrayed in active or standing poses.

### Architecture: The Pagoda

The pagoda was the most important building in early temples, because it contained a relic of Shaka—perhaps a tooth or chip of bone. This practice originated in India, where early believers entombed the Buddha's remains in large, hemispherical mounds called *stupa* (fig. 9). As Buddhism spread through Asia, there evolved an amazing number of local variations on the *stupa's* shape. Under the influence of Chinese wooden, post-and-lintel architecture, stupas evolved into lovely, multistoried pagodas. The relic container is buried under the heart pillar, and the pagoda is crowned by a spire, often having nine tiers to represent the nine spheres of heaven (fig. 10). The important point about pagodas is that they are a symbol of Shaka.

33

Figure 9. Stupa at Sanchi, India

Figure 10. Hōryū-ji pagoda

# A JAPANESE PRINCE AND HIS TEMPLE

### Asuka and Hakuhō Periods (538–710)

The arrival of Buddhism in the mid-sixth century precipitated a profound cultural transformation in Japan. It began innocuously enough in 538, when a Korean king sent the Yamato court a small image of Shaka. The Soga clan seized on the foreign faith as a means for overturning the entrenched political order. Several bloody battles later (during which the historic statue was dumped into a canal), the Soga crushed their foes and established Buddhism under their protection (see Asuka History, p. 407).

SHŌTOKU TAISHI, crown prince and regent during this seminal period, sent Japan's first official embassy to China, introduced Chinese culture on a sweeping scale, and built the first true Buddhist temples in Japan. Shōtoku intended to replace the clan-based hierarchy with a Chinese-style system of court ranks, and was not loath to use the temples he built to bolster his political influence. Temples also served as powerful "magic" to cure ailments more physical than spiritual. One such temple was HŌRYŪ-JI, south of Nara.

Hōryū-ji, the most celebrated temple in Japan, was dedicated to **Yakushi**, the Nyorai of

Healing, to fulfill a vow made by Shōtoku when his imperial sire became gravely ill. Because of its immense fame—it includes the oldest surviving wooden structures in the world—and its intimate association with Shōtoku, Hōryū-ji is regarded as the birthplace of Buddhism in Japan. There are other temples older and more important than Hōryū-ji, such as Gangō-ji in Asuka and Shitennō-ji in Ōsaka, but none of their original buildings have survived. These early temples, concentrated around the Yamato plain south of Nara, shared similar features, adapted from continental temples.

### Deities: Shaka, Yakushi, Miroku

Nyorai such as Shaka and Yakushi can be distinguished by their characteristic *mudra*, or hand gestures, and by the attendants who accompany them.

**Shaka.** Shaka commonly has his right hand raised in a "do not fear" *mudra*, with his left palm extended downward to the worshipper in the attitude of giving a sermon; for this reason, he is often shown standing. His two bosatsu attendants are usually **Monju**, who rides a lion, and **Fugen**, who rides an elephant (neither animal existed in pre-Tokugawa Japan). Hōryū-ji has a famous Shaka trinity ascribed to TORI BUSSHI (fig. 17). Hōryū-ji's pagoda houses a famous sculpted scene showing a prostrate, dying Shaka surrounded by grieving disciples.

**Yakushi.** Yakushi also holds his right hand in a gesture of "do not fear." His left hand usually holds a medicine jar; sometimes, instead, he is seated on a rectangular dais, which represents a medicine chest. He often has seven little nyorai in his halo (for his seven manifestations) and is generally flanked by the two bosatsu, **Nikkō** and **Gakkō** (Sunlight and Moonlight). He is also often surrounded by the Twelve Divine Generals, who are associated with the animals of the Chinese zodiac. Hōryū-ji's main image is a TORI-school Yakushi. The Yakushi trinity at Yakushi-ji is one of the great landmarks of Japanese art (fig. 18).

**Miroku Bosatsu.** A follower of Shaka, Miroku is promised to appear as a nyorai billions of years in the future to save all beings; he is therefore also called the Nyorai of the Future. Miroku Bosatsu is portrayed as a youth sitting with one leg crossed over the other, a hand resting lightly on his cheek, deep in thought (fig. 21). This iconography was introduced in the Asuka period from Korea, where there flourished a cult of Miroku. Offerings of thousands of small Miroku statues are preserved at Hōryū-ji. Japan's most beautiful statue of Miroku Bosatsu is at Kōryū-ji (Kyoto, p.5:1). Miroku is also portrayed as a nyorai.

### Architecture: The Garan (Temple Court)

The ancient Yamato temples, such as Hōryū-ji, are strikingly different from temples elsewhere in Japan. These early temples convey openness, grandeur, and clarity of plan. They are also rather stark, without that organic luxuriance that makes later temples, such as those in Kyoto, so pleasant to roam. Their builders thought of these early temples as divine worlds, where neither man nor nature impinges upon an ideal of perfection. Though it is often said the Japanese have an innate preference for asymmetry, these temples are symmetrical, in strict accordance with the Chinese pattern. The temple layout is called the *shichi-dō garan*, or temple court with seven halls. The seven prescribed halls are: pagoda (*tō*), main hall (*kondō* or *hondō*), lecture hall (*kōdō*), drum and bell tower (*korō* and *shōrō*), sutra repository (*kyōzō*), dormitories (*sōbō*), and dining hall (*jikidō*).

By the time Buddhism reached Japan, the importance of Shaka was rivaled by other nyorai. In Japan, the status and significance of the pagoda as a symbol of Shaka diminished, whereas the Main Hall, which could enshrine other nyorai, gained in stature. A fascinating example is Hōryū-ji itself, which when first built featured the pagoda in the preeminent position, with the other halls lined behind it. However, when the temple was rebuilt after a fire, the rising status of the images in the *kondō* caused the hall to be built alongside the pagoda, on an equal footing.

YAKUSHI-JI, in Nara, was built around 690 for much the same reason as Hōryū-ji—an empress was sick—and, as the name suggests, it was also dedicated to the Nyorai of Healing, who is enshrined in a great central hall. But the pagoda has lost all its original significance; Yakushi-ji, in fact, has two pagodas, decoratively flanking the main approach. (The surviving East Pagoda is an unusual masterpiece.) Later, when symmetry became less important in temple architecture, the pagoda was often placed in a corner of the temple and sometimes was omitted altogether.

# STATE MAGNIFICENCE

### Nara Period (710–794)

By the time the capital at Nara was completed in 710, Buddhism and Chinese culture were firmly entrenched in Japan. The old clans had been replaced with an elaborate system of court ranks suitable to an aristocratic society. In 742, **Emperor Shōmu** established a system of national temples, called Kokubun-ji, in every province, thereby linking the propagation of the faith with the consolidation of state power. One can still see Kokubun-ji ruins or even a functioning temple in the countryside. Standing at the head of all the provincial Kokubun-ji was the greatest temple of all, the TŌDAI-JI of Nara.

In 752, a great crowd of envoys and priests from as far away as Persia gathered in Nara for the eye-opening ceremony of the Tōdai-ji Great Buddha. An eminent Indian priest was invited to paint in the statue's eyes. Even today, the colossal bronze image, housed in the world's largest wooden building, is astonishing. The image represents a newly introduced

Buddhist deity, **Rushana** (largely equivalent to the deity Dainichi, discussed below under Esoteric Buddhism). This nyorai was a cosmic, or solar, Buddha, who sits at the center of the universe. Shaka appeared in India as a manifestation and envoy of Rushana; similarly, other Shakas appear in other worlds throughout the universe. The Great Buddha's lotus pedestal is etched with representations of the infinite Shakas of the infinite worlds in the universe. The message being impressed upon the assembled nobles was of centralized religious authority and, by implication, centralized state power.

### Deities: Defenders of the Faith
Many Indian deities were absorbed into Mahayana Buddhism, and an extended family of Central Asian and Chinese deities was adopted during the journey across Asia. These deities were ranked in the *ten* (*deva*) category, and were appointed "defenders of the faith." From the very beginning of Japanese Buddhism, *ten* were placed as guardians around a temple's principal image. During the aristocratic, status-conscious Nara period, many of these heavenly vassals acquired greater prominence.

**Niō.** Two important Hindu deities, Brahma and Indra, are known in Japan as **Bon-ten** and **Taishaku-ten**. Tōdai-ji's Hokke-dō hall has a famous pair of statues of these two deities. Taishaku-ten more commonly manifests himself as two half-naked musclemen, the Niō (two deva kings), who stand guard in the temple gate (fig. 26). One of the Niō has his mouth open, *ah*, the other's lips are pursed, *un*. The two sounds are the alpha and omega of the Sanskrit alphabet, and thus represent eternity and completeness.

**Shi-Tennō.** These four "heavenly kings" stand at the four corners around the main image, guarding the cardinal directions. The most important is **Bishamon-ten**, guardian of the north (the "dangerous" direction, by Chinese geomantic convention); he holds a pagoda in his palm (fig. 25). The Shi-tennō usually stomp demons underfoot, but in rare instances, Bishamon-ten stands on the shoulders of an "earth goddess" that belongs to Central Asian iconography.

**Indian Goddesses.** Heavenly beings are sexless, but just as the guardian kings are shown as masculine, so several deities are clearly feminine. The matronly **Kisshō-ten** brings riches, and **Benzai-ten** (or **Benten**) is associated with music, love, jealousy, and white snakes. There is a famous painting of Kisshō-ten at Yakushi-ji. Both goddesses are worshipped in popular Shinto shrines. They are included among the Seven Lucky Gods of folk religion.

35

### Architecture: Monumental Chinese Style
As we noted in the Shinto chapter, the native style of housing had a simple roof, with an entrance under the projecting gables. In contrast, Chinese-style temple and palace halls were entered from the "long" side, parallel to the roof ridge. A heavy tile roof held everything underneath in place, and it became the showiest part of the building, supported by complicated bracketing that was partly decorative and partly dictated by structural requirements. The most formal Chinese style is the simple hipped roof; less formal buildings adopted a hip-and-gabled roof (fig. 11). The Nara-period temples are characterized by their huge formal hipped roofs, which are not seen in most later Japanese temples. The Daibutsu-den at Tōdai-ji has an impressive hipped roof, decorated with two large golden *shibi*, stylized birds atop the roof ridge. The most graceful examples of this style are the Main Hall and Lecture Hall of TŌSHŌDAI-JI; the latter, donated by a prince, is the only surviving Nara-period palace hall.

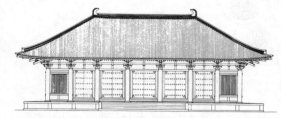

Figure 11. Tōshōdai-ji

The Nara temples copied the key features of Chinese architecture, such as the symmetrical layout, tile floor, and hipped roof covered with tile. Symmetry extended to forms like the octagonal **Yumedono** at Hōryū-ji, which is the only surviving such hall from the Nara period. As Chinese influence waned in the Heian period, a native preference for wood floors, shingled hip-and-gable roofs, and asymmetrical plans asserted itself. Symmetry, tile floors, and hipped roofs would enjoy a brief revival under the Zen sect, which was a vehicle for the resurgence of Chinese influence in Japan starting in the late twelfth century.

# ESOTERIC BUDDHISM: THE SEARCH FOR ENLIGHTENMENT
### Early Heian Period (794–894)

Japan's early Buddhist period coincided with the religion's zenith in Korea and China. Temples, images, and all the panoply of continental culture were imported wholesale into Japan. But whether the Japanese possessed a profound understanding of Buddhist teachings, especially of enlightenment, remains in doubt. Temples were built for the good of the state, and common people were drafted by the thousands to become monks and nuns, whether they had any interest in doing so or not. Japanese Buddhism came of age in the early ninth century with the arrival of *mikkyō*, or Esoteric Buddhism, which was brought back from China by two priests, **Saichō** and KŪKAI (see Kyoto History, p. 319). Saichō studied at Tien T'ai in southern China and returned to Japan first; he founded the **Tendai sect** at ENRYAKU-JI on Mt. Hiei, near Kyoto. The teachings of the sect were based on the Lotus Sutra, which subscribes to different levels of truth, and thus the sect absorbed most other contemporaneous teachings as valid. Enlightenment is sought through a combination of meditation, study, chants, and *mikkyō*, or secret practices. The eclectic nature of Tendai led to numerous spinoffs, giving rise to most of the later Japanese sects.

The only major sect not to have Tendai roots was the one founded by Saichō's fellow seeker, Kūkai, who brought back a purer form of *mikkyō*, which he established as the **Shingon (mantra) sect**. *Mikkyō* adopted the magical rituals and meditation practices of Indian Tantrism; Tantric influence can be seen in the fierce faces and multiple arms and heads of *mikkyō* iconography. It is called an esoteric or secret teaching because its closely guarded secrets are handed down from priest to priest, master to chosen disciple. Two different versions of *mikkyō*—one traveling via Southeast Asia, the other through Central Asia— eventually arrived at the Chinese capital of Ch'ang-an. There, the two versions were "reunited" in the person of a great priest, who became convinced that the teachings were fated to reach Japan, through Kūkai, where they would attain their fullest development. In Shingon, magical chants, secret rituals, and other methods are practiced so that one may become a Buddha in one's own body. Kūkai, known posthumously as KŌBŌ DAISHI, was entombed in the Okuno-in, a hall on KŌYA-SAN. The faithful believe he has become a Buddha and is sitting there in meditation to this day, awaiting the coming of Miroku.

The two teachings that Kūkai received were conveyed in the **Two Worlds Mandala**, a pair of huge, kaleidoscopic paintings of Dainichi Nyorai surrounded by his other nyorai manifestations and their manifestations in turn, as bosatsu and *ten*. One is called the Womb Mandala and the other the Diamond (or Vajra) Mandala. The two traditions relate to each other in a "secret" dialectic that is explained—rather vaguely—to outsiders as the dichotomy between the outer (womb) universe, or realm of action, and the inner (diamond) universe, or realm of wisdom and compassion. They are the two aspects of the one reality, and both are needed for enlightenment. The easiest way to tell the difference between the two mandalas is by the halos. A figure sitting against a full, round halo (like the man in the moon), is pure spirit and belongs to the diamond world. A figure with a head halo and a body halo represents the active body and mind, and belongs to the womb world (fig. 12). A simplified, sculpted version of the center of the Womb Mandala can be seen at TŌ-JI.

Figure 12. Womb mandala

### Deities: The Womb World

**Dainichi ("Great Sun") Nyorai.** This is the unified cosmic Buddha; all other beings are aspects of Dainichi. He sits at the center of the Womb Mandala and wears a crown. Dainichi's right hand is clasped around the index finger of the left; this *mudra* signifies the unity of the Two Worlds (fig. 20). He is surrounded by four directional nyorai and four bosatsu (originally female deities called *dakini*), who are his direct manifestations.

**Kokuzō Bosatsu.** These five bosatsu are manifestations of Dainichi and the four nyorai of the cardinal points. They are gentle bosatsu who confer wisdom.

**The Five Myō-ō.** These are fierce manifestations of Dainichi; their job is to conquer evil and illusion (the same thing). The Myō-ō were Hindu gods drafted into the Buddhist pantheon; their black, red, or otherwise strangely colored faces, fangs, dreadlocks, and rocky perches make them memorable. **Fudō**, the chief Myō-ō, holds a sword upright in one hand, and dangles a snare from the other. He has a tightly coiled lock of hair hanging down one cheek, and is often enveloped in flames. He is especially popular and is often singled out for worship (fig. 24). The five Myō-ō are often enshrined in a hall called a Godai-dō.

## Architecture: Mountain Temples

Since prehistoric times, the holiness of mountains has been an integral part of native belief (see Shinto, p. 23). As *mikkyō* became the dominant form of Buddhism during the Heian period, enlightenment became a personal quest, achieved through an intense spiritual "climb." Mountains, physically elevated and sacred, were the obvious place to build the monasteries where aspiring monks would practice rituals and undergo austerities—much like followers of the syncretic *yamabushi* cult (see Shinto, p. 27). Mountain sites made the ordered, symmetric *garan* impossible. Instead, temples were built to fit the natural terrain, with halls scattered on different levels and joined by mountain paths. Sometimes halls were perched on precipices atop stilts in gravity-defying feats of engineering. This can be seen especially in temples associated with the *yamabushi*.

The *mikkyō* sects stressed gradual initiation into secret rites, and, for this reason, the main halls of Mikkyō temples have a central barrier dividing the interior into an outer part for the uninitiated, and an inner sanctum where there is an altar and, behind it, space for additional images. A raised wooden floor replaced the tile floor of earlier times, and the eave protruded over wooden front steps (fig. 13). Elegant cypress shingles began to be favored instead of tile for the roof. This style, though derived from Tang Chinese architecture, came to be known in the Kamakura period as **Wayō**, or "Japanese" style, to distinguish it from the Zen style, which was imported later from Sung China. A variant of Wayō, known as Setchūyō (mixed style), preserved the Wayō style's basic plan but incorporated features of the Zen style.

The *mikkyō* sects also introduced a new kind of pagoda, the **tahō-tō**, which retains something of the shape of the original Indian stupa, although it picked up a pair of square canopy eaves during its migration to Japan (fig. 14). This form of pagoda alludes to the Lotus Sutra and is therefore favored by both the Tendai and Nichiren sects, although it is also found in Shingon temples. Ishiyama-dera, for example, has both a lovely Wayō main hall and Japan's oldest extant *tahō-tō*. It is only one of many Wayō temple halls hidden in the hills encircling Lake Biwa, near Kyoto.

37

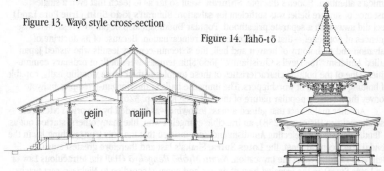

Figure 13. Wayō style cross-section

gejin  naijin

Figure 14. Tahō-tō

# AMIDISM: AN EASY WAY TO PARADISE

### Late Heian Period (894-1185)

During the Fujiwara period, a *fin de siècle* mood pervaded the Heian court. This subtle pessimism was partly motivated by the belief that the world was entering **Mappō**, a degenerate, dark epoch in which the Buddhist law would be in eclipse (see Uji History, p. 387). During Mappō, even monastic austerities will not save a person who does not place his faith in **Amida**, the nyorai of **Jōdo**, the Pure Land across the Western Ocean. A number of Tendai priests, such as Kūya and Genshin, elaborated the portions of Tendai teachings involving Amida (see Kyoto, p. 349). These early Amidists taught that Amida was a compassionate being who would save earnest believers. Just as Amida will descend from the Pure Land to welcome souls, so the temples began to come down from their mountaintops.

### Deities: Amida, Kannon

**Amida Nyorai.** This deity is usually represented in one of two poses: Amida presiding over Jōdo, seated, with hands resting in the lap forming the meditating *mudra* (fig. 19); and Amida in *raigō*, descending to welcome souls, with one hand raised in the "do not fear" *mudra*, and one hand extended downward in the giving *mudra*. Amida mandalas depict Amida in Jōdo, seated in a palace surrounded by rejoicing attendants, dancers, and musicians. Before them is a pond representing the Western Ocean. Amida often forms a trinity with the bosatsu **Seishi** and **Kannon**.

**Kannon Bosatsu.** This is the "goddess of mercy," a manifestation of Amida and highly venerated in her own right, with temples and pilgrimages dedicated to her. Kannon has promised to appear in thirty-three forms to save humankind. The most popular are **Shō Kannon**, a graceful, human-shaped being usually standing and holding a lotus and vial (fig. 22), **Jūichi-men Kannon**, with eleven faces, and **Senju Kannon**, whose thousand arms are cast wide to save all beings. The **Batō Kannon** has a fierce face with a horse's head in the crown. Whatever the form, a tiny image of Amida is embedded in Kannon's crown as a reminder that Kannon is Amida's manifestation.

## Architecture: Heaven on Earth

The Amida-dō, or Amida Hall, became the main structure in Amidist temples. These halls are three-dimensional Amida mandalas, depicting Amida in Paradise. Sanzen-in, in the north of Kyoto, has one of the earliest styles of Amida-dō, built in 1086. The small, square hall houses a large, gilded Amida surrounded by attendants painted on the walls and ceilings. The hall sits in a serene grove, lush with moss. Heian nobles built even more elaborate halls modeled on Amida's palace. The area around Uji, a favorite retreat, had several such Gokuraku Jōdo (Paradise Pure Land) Amida halls. The best surviving example is the BYŌDŌ-IN, an ethereal Tang-style pavilion set in a garden. The Amida in the hall faces east across a large pond representing the Western Ocean, as though beckoning to us from his Paradise. Other outstanding examples are Hōkai-ji, near Uji (Kinki, p. 386), the Golden Hall of CHŪSON-JI at Hiraizumi, in northern Japan, and Jōruri-ji (outside Nara), which is set in a paradise garden and houses nine Amida images (based on the nine ranks of heaven).

# SAVIORS FOR THE COMMON PEOPLE

## Kamakura Period (1185–1333)

The dream world of the Heian aristocrats was shattered at the end of the twelfth century when two warrior clans fought a devastating war for supremacy. The victorious MINAMOTO moved their capital to Kamakura, severing links with the classical age. The savage war led many people to conclude that the world had indeed entered Mappō, and out of this conviction arose new sects that promised salvation to all, even the common people, who had hitherto been neglected.

The priest **Hōnen** founded the **Jōdo**, or Pure Land sect, which taught that salvation through Amida's mercy could be achieved by endlessly reciting *Namu Amida Butsu* (Hail Amida Buddha), the more times the better, for countless others were also clamoring for Amida's attention. Hōnen's disciple, **Shinran**, went so far as to teach that even a single instance of sincere belief was sufficient for salvation. Shinran's **Jōdo Shin** (True Pure Land) sect did away with a separate priesthood. Popular Buddhism also began to stress the consequences of nonbelief—that is, hell, or endless reincarnation. Because of its doctrine of salvation and dichotomy of heaven and hell, the sixteenth-century Jesuits who visited Japan called Amidism "the Devil's Christianity." Jōdo Shin temples were built in ordinary communities. One of the notable characteristics of these temples is their large worship halls, capable of holding hundreds of worshippers. The immense halls of the Hongan-ji temples in Kyoto convey the intensely popular nature of the sect (see Kyoto, p. 326).

Another major sect that gained a mass following was founded by the priest **Nichiren** (see Kamakura History, p. 258), an irascible evangelist who, like many others, started out as a Tendai acolyte but, rejecting Amidism and Zen, insisted that the only true teaching lay in the Tendai sect's central tenet, the **Lotus Sutra**, Shaka's last and therefore greatest sutra. Believers rapidly repeat the invocation, *Namu Myōhō Rengekyō* (Hail the Miraculous Law of the Lotus Sutra) to the frenzied beat of drums and gongs. According to Nichiren-sect teachings, the Lotus Sutra's highest meaning would become manifest only during Mappō, in Japan, through Nichiren, who was claimed to be a reincarnation of the bosatsu Jōgyō. The sect is virtually a cult of Nichiren's personality. One of its sacred icons is a "mandala" of the invocation *Namu Myōhō Rengekyō* written in the saint's bristling script—called the "mustache style." The *tahō-tō*, as a symbol of the Lotus Sutra, is also common in Nichiren temples. Temples in working-class neighborhoods tend to belong to either the Nichiren or Jōdo sects.

## Deities: Jizō Bosatsu and Emma-ō

**Jizō Bosatsu.** Like Kannon, this deity became the object of a widespread Amidist cult from the late Heian period onward. Jizō is the bosatsu assigned by Amida to save souls during Mappō. He is depicted as a mendicant monk, with shaved head, dressed in simple robes, and carrying a pilgrim's staff (fig. 23). Jizō is especially beloved because of his power to save children and sinners from purgatory and hell. He is also a road guardian and often stands by the roadside in groups of six, one for each of the six realms of reincarnation.

**Emma-ō.** The King of Hell; he became popular in the Kamakura period. He is dressed as a Chinese bureaucrat and presides with nine other judges, who record each soul's past deeds of good and evil. According to Emma's judgment, all beings are reborn into one of the six realms of reincarnation: *ten*, human, ashura, animals, hungry ghosts, and hell.

## Architecture: The Daibutsu (Great Buddha) Style

The rebuilding of Tōdai-ji in Nara, which was destroyed in the war between the Minamoto and Taira, was entrusted to the Amidist priest **Chōgen**. He decided to rebuild it in a style rarely seen in Japan; sometimes called the Indian style, it in fact came from southern China. It is characterized by multitiered brackets that lie in vertical planes. The roof is supported by tall columns hewn from enormous trees, which had to be brought from distant forests. Bold and unsubtle, the style suited the newly dominant warrior class. The best example is the **Nandai-mon** (Great South Gate) of Tōdai-ji (fig. 15).

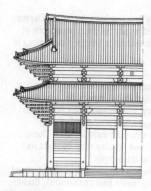

Figure 15. Nandai-mon at Tōdai-ji

# ZEN

## Kamakura and Muromachi Periods (1185-1568)

Zen was the last major Buddhist sect to be introduced from China. Zen was already an integral part of Tendai practice when, in the late twelfth century, it was reintroduced from Sung China as an independent sect, bringing a new wave of Chinese culture into Japan. The medieval samurai were attracted to the new sect and helped Zen to become established in Japan.

Zen was founded by the Indian priest **Daruma** (Bodhidharma), who is caricatured by the bright red Daruma dolls sold at New Year markets in Japan. The roly-poly dolls, with their amusingly angry faces, have no legs because, according to the legend, Daruma sat in meditation for so many years that his legs withered away. Daruma attained enlightenment and introduced his way of Buddhism to China in the fifth century. He is often depicted in Zen paintings with a heavy beard and fierce, large eyes. Daruma taught that "You are the Buddha": by dint of hard meditation, one can become enlightened.

As Daruma's experience shows, the basic practice of Zen revolves around long bouts of *zazen* (seated Zen), which are supposed to help one to empty one's mind of illusion and thereby attain *satori*, or enlightenment. Rationalism, which assumes that the world can be understood through observation and thought, produces nothing but illusion, according to Zen, because the world and self are illusions. All sorts of methods were devised to jolt the disciple out of his rational wits: shouts, loud noises, and bizarre exchanges called *mondō* between master and pupil. Particularly memorable to those who have "sat" is the large stick, called a *kyōsaku*, used to strike anyone who dozes off.

Even facing this arsenal of weapons, disciples found themselves persisting in rational thought, so *kōan* were invented. These are mind-twisters with no rational answers: "Two hands clapped together make a sound. What is the sound of one hand clapping?" A disciple is obliged to keep this puzzle in mind day and night until through utter exhaustion he or she eschews rational thought and returns to the roots of consciousness. Two schools of Zen took hold in Japan. The **Sōtō** school emphasized *zazen* and gradual enlightenment. The **Rinzai** school put more stress on *kōan* and a sudden, sometimes violent, enlightenment.

For the visitor to Japan, the most significant difference between the Sōtō and Rinzai schools has less to do with their teachings than with the worldliness of their practitioners. Sōtō was introduced to Japan by **Dōgen**, who established a small Zen hall in Kyoto in 1223. He soon grew tired of Kyoto and set out north, to the mountains on the Japan Sea, where he founded the monastery of EIHEI-JI. Eihei-ji is an orderly complex of buildings on a thickly wooded mountainside where, to this day, many monks lead an austere life, waking at three in the morning, meditating for hours, eating sparse, vegetarian meals, and doing manual work around the grounds. Sōtō has enjoyed some popularity in the United States recently.

The Rinzai school is larger, more worldly, and because of its eclecticism, has left a deeper imprint on Japanese culture. Rinzai was brought back by **Eisai**, who established Japan's first Zen temple, Shōfuku-ji, in Fukuoka in 1191. Tradition has it that Eisai brought tea plants back to Japan and promoted tea-drinking as an effective remedy for drowsiness, hangovers, and other ailments. Rinzai monasteries were established in Kyoto and Kamakura and deeply influenced Japan's medieval arts, including the tea ceremony (see Villas, p. 65).

### Deities: Rakan

**Rakan.** In contrast to the many exotic deities of the Mahayana pantheon, the rakan are humans who have reached a state of enlightenment equal to that of Shaka. Rakan statues are often seen in Zen temples, which prefer these human examples to those of idealized divinity. They typically form numbered groups such as the Jūroku (Sixteen) Rakan, the Jū Daideshi (Ten Great Disciples), and the Gohyaku (Five Hundred) Rakan. They are certainly down to earth; one can have no illusions about fellows who pick at their gums and nostrils, scratch their scruffy heads, and wear such dumbly blissful grins.

**Priest Portraits.** The portraits of famous priests, especially Zen teachers, including Daruma and various historical founders of temples, should be counted as part of the iconography of Zen temples. Like Rakan images, priest portraits are realistic and often inspired depictions of the human form.

### Architecture: The Zen Garan and Zen Style

Zen stresses monastic life, but unlike the Esoteric sects, it does not reject ordinary humanity. Monks in training try to forswear the five desires (property, sex, food, reputation, and sleep) and live strictly regulated by a series of bells and gongs. Every activity, no matter how mundane, must be done with utmost awareness. Waking, walking, eating, washing, bathing, excreting, if done with total concentration, aid the acolyte in stripping away illusion. These practices affected temple architecture: kitchens, bathhouses, and latrines were brought into the *garan* and were considered intrinsic to the organization of the temple.

**The Zen Garan.** Temple plans are arranged according to the formal, rectilinear plan favored in China. Important halls are aligned along a north-south axis: main gate (*san-mon*), Buddha hall (*butsu-den*), lecture hall (*hattō*), monk's dormitory (*sōdō*), kitchen (*kuin*), lavatory (*tōsu*), and bath hall (*yokushitsu*).

In many Zen temples, the symmetrical *garan* is usually overwhelmed by an organic chaos of subtemples that have grown up around it. It became customary for important priests to establish small residential subtemples, called *tatchū*, within the monastery grounds. The most independant of the great Rinzai monasteries, such as Kyoto's DAITOKU-JI, encouraged the residents of these subtemples to pursue various arts—calligraphy, gardening, tea ceremony—and thereby became rich repositories of culture.

**The Zen Style.** With Zen came Sung Chinese temple halls built in a distinctive style, called **Kara-yō**, or Chinese style (fig. 16). Zen-style halls stand on stone podiums and have tile floors. The main columns rest on two-layered, carved stone plinths. Roof bracketing became more elaborate, with intercolumnar brackets and greater use of cantilevers. Decorative features include the bell-shaped window (*katō-mado*). Because of the cold tile floors, Chinese-style chairs are often found inside such halls. The octagonal pagoda of Anraku-ji, a Kamakura-period Zen temple near Nagano, harkens to the same Chinese esthetic as found in the Nara-period Yumedono, an octagonal chapel at Hōryū-ji.

Figure 16. Shari-den at Engaku-ji

# BUDDHISM AFTER THE AGE OF FAITH

### The Ōbaku Zen Sect

The last Buddhist sect to arrive from China was Ōbaku Zen, introduced around 1600, some four hundred years after the Rinzai and Sōtō sects. The Ōbaku sect established temples in Nagasaki (Shōfuku-ji and Kōfuku-ji) and a headquarters at MAMPUKU-JI, south of Kyoto. Ōbaku temples preserved the Ming Chinese temple styles, such as plaster "dragon gates," sharply uptilted eaves, and Chinese sculpture. Also associated with the Ōbaku school is a unique Chinese-influenced vegetarian cuisine called *fucha-ryōri* (see Cuisine, p. 117).

### Buddhism and New Religions in Modern Japan

During the Edo period, religion took a back seat to popular culture. Because the authoritarian Tokugawa government required all Japanese to register their families at a temple, formal membership exceeded, and still exceeds, the number of actual believers. After the Meiji Restoration (1868), these unfortunate ties to the hated shogunate made many people indifferent or even hostile to temples. When the Meiji government decreed that Shinto shrines and Buddhist temples must be separated, many temples and treasures of Buddhist art were neglected or destroyed (see Shinto, p. 29). The Japanese today protect historic temples as part of their cultural heritage. With the exception of the Nara sects, all the Japanese Buddhist sects thrive in the modern world.

Presently, the biggest temple builders are the popular sects, such as Jōdo Shin and Nichiren, or various "new religions," such as **Sōka Gakkai**, a Nichiren-based sect dedicated to the pursuit of worldly success. Perhaps the most salient characteristic of these temple halls is their ability to hold huge congregations. In this respect, the headquarters of the Jōdo Shin sects, Kyoto's Hongan-ji temples, built in the early seventeenth century, are not so different from the recently built Sōka Gakkai world headquarters near Mt. Fuji.

# VISITING A TEMPLE

**Main Gate.** This is often a large, free-standing structure that symbolically marks the entrance to the precincts. It may contain a pair of Niō.

**Main Hall.** In Nara, Tendai, and Shingon temples, this hall is called the *kondō* and faces south. In Zen temples, the main hall is called *hattō*. In most other temples, the main hall is called *hondō*. In Jōdo and Jōdo Shin temples, this hall usually faces east (Amida faces east from his Western Paradise) and is flanked by a huge congregational hall.

**Main Image (Honzon).** The main image occupies the central altar of the main hall. Offerings of food, flowers, and incense are placed in front of it. In Tendai and Shingon temples, the main image is behind a central partition and is usually hidden from view. In Jōdo and Jōdo Shin temples, the venerated image is Amida Nyorai. Zen temples often enshrine Shaka and Rakan images in the main hall, and place portraits of important Zen teachers in a *kaisan-dō* (founder's hall).

**Cemetery.** Most people still have a Buddhist funeral. In historic temples, one often finds the tombs of important figures of the past; a *gorin-tō*, a five-level (or five-element) stupa, indicates a person of high status. A tombstone shaped like the tip of a huge baseball bat marks the grave of an important priest.

**Nearby Shrine or Okuno-in (Inner Sanctum).** Many temples are historically associated with a nearby shrine. Temples such as DAIGO-JI, which have an Okuno-in up on a mountain, belong to either the Tendai or Shingon sects, which had strong syncretic elements in pre-Meiji times (see Shinto, p. 27).

# Mountains and Enlightenment

From the earliest times, mountains were sacred (Shinto, p. 23). Each sect tended to build its temples to reflect its philosophy of the relation between the world of humans and the world of the divine, symbolically represented by mountains.

**The early Nara sects (6th–8th C).** Major temples were laid out in flat, open areas, but were no more accessible for it; surrounded by cloisters, they were off limits to ordinary people, who at the time knew little of Buddhism anyway.

**Esoteric sects, Tendai and Shingon (8th C–).** With the introduction of Esoteric Buddhism, the search for enlightenment became an active quest. All beings contain within themselves a mirror of Buddhahood, but it takes strenuous austerities and knowledge of secret rituals to polish it. Tendai and Shingon temples were built on mountaintops, in close proximity to the sacred.

**Amidist sects, Jōdo (10th C–).** There is a barrier between the ordinary, impure world and the Pure Land, but Amida will descend to the barrier to welcome those who sincerely invoke his name. Early Jōdo temples are built at the foot of mountains, the symbolic border between the profane and the sacred.

**Jōdo Shin (True Pure Land) sects.** Belief in Amida is carried further. Amida will descend all the way into the world of mortals to save all believers, regardless of their state of degradation. Jōdo Shin temples are built in town centers and have immense halls to hold the masses of believers.

**Zen sects (12th C–).** Buddha nature lives in everyone, but can be realized only by piercing through illusion. Unlike the Esoteric sects, which try to elevate humans to a pure state through austerities, secret chants, and rituals, Zen seeks enlightenment in the everyday "profane" world; "the world of the divine" is a delusion. Reflecting Zen's stress on everyday life, the formal temple *garan* includes kitchens, bath halls, and lavatories. Every human function becomes part of the Way. Rinzai Zen temples, more worldly and eclectic than Sōtō Zen temples, are often located close to towns.

**Buddhist sects and social class.** The Tendai and Shingon sects, in which enlightenment depends on an elite body of knowledge, were favored by emperors and nobles. Zen, in which enlightenment is achieved by an effort of will (or non-will) attracted the warriors. In the Jōdo Shin and Nichiren sects, salvation is obtained by single-minded devotion. These sects were favored by the common people.

B
U
D
D
H
I
S
M

# Summary of the Buddhist Deities

**Nyorai**

These are fully enlightened beings, or Buddhas, at the top of the pantheon. Their identifying marks include simple robes devoid of ornamentation, hair composed of snail curls, a lump on the top of the head, signifying superior wisdom, long earlobes, a radiant curl of hair on the forehead, and webbed fingers for scooping up souls. The four important nyorai can often be distinguished by their hand gestures, or *mudra*.

**Fig. 17. Shaka Nyorai.** The historical Buddha; holds the right hand up and extends the left palm downward, toward the worshipper, in a preaching pose. Often shown standing. May be flanked by Monju (the Bosatsu of Wisdom) astride a lion and Fugen Bosatsu astride an elephant. (Here Shaka is portrayed in the company of two unidentified bosatsu.)

**Fig. 18. Yakushi Nyorai.** The Buddha of Healing; holds the right hand up and extends the left palm, holding a medicine jar, toward the worshipper. Because he appears in seven manifestations, he often has seven small nyorai in his halo. Often accompanied by the sun and moon bosatsu, Nikkō and Gakkō, and the Twelve Directional Generals, or Jūnishinshō.

**Fig. 19. Amida Nyorai.** The Buddha of the Western Paradise; usually depicted in meditation, with hands resting in his lap, knuckles pressed together; or in *raigō*, descending to welcome souls into his paradise, with one hand held up in the "do not fear" *mudra* and the other extended downward in welcome. Often attended by Kannon Bosatsu and Seishi Bosatsu.

**Fig. 20. Dainichi Nyorai.** The cosmic or solar Buddha of Esoteric Buddhism; often shown wearing a crown, in a characteristic *mudra* with one hand clasped around the index finger of the other hand. This sexual gesture symbolizes the unification of action and wisdom and has origins in Tantrism. Sits at the center of the Womb Mandala surrounded by eight directional nyorai and bosatsu and hundreds of other deities, including five Myō-ō.

42

Figure 17. Shaka Nyorai (Hōryū-ji)

Figure 18. Yakushi Nyorai (Yakushi-ji)

Figure 19. Amida Nyorai (Byōdō-in)

Figure 20. Dainichi Nyorai (Enjō-ji)

## Bosatsu

These compassionate beings postpone their own nirvana in order to help save all sentient beings. Here are some important bosatsu:

**Fig. 21. Miroku.** The Bosatsu of the Future; usually shown as a youth sitting cross-legged, meditating on ways to save all beings.

**Fig. 22. Kannon.** The Goddess of Mercy; a compassionate bosatsu who appears to people in need. Kannon has many manifestations, including this Shō-Kannon (Sainted Kannon), a graceful, human-shaped being who is usually shown standing, holding a lotus and vial. Other forms include Jūichimen Kannon, with eleven faces, and Senju Kannon, who has a thousand arms to save all beings.

**Fig. 23. Jizō.** The bosatsu assigned to save souls during the dark age of Mappō; commonly depicted as a mendicant monk, with simple robes, shaved head, and pilgrim's staff. Jizō saves children and sinners from purgatory and hell; he is also a road guardian and is often found in groups of six by the roadside.

**Fig. 24. Myō-ō.** Wisdom Kings; fiery, ogrelike beings of equal rank as bosatsu, they fight evil and illusion. When people became lazy and began to rely on the kindness of the bosatsu, the Myō-ō frightened them back onto the right path. The most popular is the one shown here, Fudō, the "immovable."

## Ten (Heavenly Beings)

These guardians of Buddhism, mostly adopted from the Hindu pantheon, include Bon-ten (Brahma), Taishaku-ten (Indra), the female Kisshō-ten and Benzai-ten, as well as the Central Asian Daikoku-ten. They are usually depicted standing.

**Fig. 25. Shi-Tennō.** The Four Heavenly Kings; they stand at the four corners around the main image to guard the cardinal directions. They often stomp demons underfoot. Shown here is Bishamon-ten, guardian of the "dangerous" north, who holds a pagoda in his palm.

**Fig. 26. Niō.** Deva Kings; huge, half-naked musclemen who stand guard in temple gates. They are two aspects of Taishaku-ten. One has his mouth open, pronouncing the first letter of the Sanskrit alphabet, *ah*; the other has his mouth closed, pronouncing the last letter, *un*.

43

Figure 21. Miroku Bosatsu    Figure 22. Shō Kannon    Figure 23. Jizō Bosatsu

Figure 24. Fudō Myō-ō    Figure 25. Bishamonten    Figure 26. Niō

# BEST TEMPLES

### KYOTO (∗∗∗)
∗∗∗ **TŌ-JI.** Shingon seminary founded by KŪKAI. Fabulous sculpture mandala (p. 325).
∗∗∗ **Sanjūsangen-dō.** Rebuilt at the beginning of the 13th century; its famous long hall is filled with a thousand and one gilded images of Kannon (p. 334).
∗∗∗ **Kiyomizu-dera.** One of the most ancient and enduring temples in Kyoto. The great wooden hall, balanced on stilts on a steep slope, is an architectural marvel (p. 336).
∗∗∗ **DAITOKU-JI.** The finest Rinzai Zen sect monastery, with numerous subtemples containing noted gardens and works of art (p. 352).

### KINKI
∗∗∗ **BYŌDŌ-IN.** Temple of the celebrated Phoenix Hall, the most lavish of the Fujiwara-period Paradise Halls (in ∗∗∗ Uji, p. 386).
∗∗∗ **TŌDAI-JI.** The temple of the Great Buddha, housed in the largest wooden building in the world. In a sense, this is still Japan's national temple (in ∗∗∗ Nara, p. 394).
∗∗∗ **TŌSHŌDAI-JI.** A beautifully preserved Nara monastery, rich in fine halls and statuary (in ∗∗∗ Nara, p. 387).
∗∗∗ **HŌRYŪ-JI.** Priceless repository of early Buddhist architecture and art. Hōryū-ji has the oldest wooden structures in the world. Built by SHŌTOKU TAISHI (p. 399).
∗∗∗ **KŌYA-SAN.** Mountaintop city of temples, founded by KŪKAI. The holiest place in Japanese Buddhism (p. 419).

# OTHER IMPORTANT TEMPLES

### TŌHOKU
∗∗∗ **CHŪSON-JI.** The 12th-century Konjiki-dō (Golden Hall) lavishly depicts Amida's Paradise in gilded lacquer, mother-of-pearl, and gilt bronze. (in ∗∗ Hiraizumi, p. 168).

### KANTŌ
∗∗∗ **Zenkō-ji.** One of the most popular pilgrimage temples (in ∗∗ Nagano, p. 350).
∗∗∗ **Kenchō-ji.** Head of the Kamakura Zen monasteries. Preserves the austere plan of the Zen *garan* (in ∗∗∗ Kamakura, p. 261).
∗∗∗ **Kōtoku-in.** Temple of the Great Buddha, a giant bronze image of Amida built with popular donations in the Kamakura period (in ∗∗∗ Kamakura, p. 264).

### CHŪBU
∗∗ **EIHEI-JI.** The leading Sōtō Zen sect monastery, founded by Dōgen in 1244. The *garan*, a series of great halls, galleries, and courtyards, ranges up a forested mountainside (p. 306).

### KYOTO(∗∗∗)
∗∗ **ENRYAKU-JI.** Founding temple of the Tendai sect, located on Mt. Hiei, overlooking Kyoto. Though much reduced in scale, it remains of great historical importance (p. 347).

### KINKI
∗∗ **DAIGO-JI.** Famous Shingon temple; its upper region is an ancient preserve of mountain ascetics. Its subtemple Sambō-in is famous for fine buildings and gardens (p. 382).
∗∗ **MAMPUKU-JI.** Ming Chinese-style temple, headquarters of the Ōbaku Zen sect (in ∗∗∗ Uji, p. 389).
∗∗∗ **YAKUSHI-JI.** The east pagoda, Yakushi trinity, and Shō Kannon bronzes are the supreme masterpieces of the early eighth century (in ∗∗∗ Nara, p. 397).
∗∗ **Murō-ji.** Shingon mountain temple, known as the women's Mt. Kōya. Exquisite halls in a beautiful setting, with an important group of early Heian sculpture (p. 404).

## Sanskrit and Japanese Equivalents

| Sanskrit | Japanese | Sanskrit | Japanese |
|---|---|---|---|
| Buddha | Nyorai | Vidyaraja | Myō-ō |
| Sakyamuni | Shaka | Acalanatha | Fudō |
| Bhaisajyaguru | Yakushi | Deva | Ten |
| Amitabha | Amida | Brahma | Bon-ten |
| Mahavairocana | Dainichi | Indra | Taishaku-ten |
| Vairocana | Rushana | Mahasri | Kisshō-ten |
| Bodhisattva | Bosatsu | Sarasvati | Benzai-ten |
| Maitreya | Miroku | Vaisrovana | Bishamon-ten |
| Avalokitesvara | Shō Kannon | Vajradara | Niō |
| Ksitigarbha | Jizō | Arhat | Rakan |
| Manjusri | Monju | Yama | Emma-ō |

# Castles and Castle Towns

One of the most brutal and romantic eras of Japan's history was the Sengoku Jidai, the Period of the Country at War, a century of turmoil and warfare throughout the Japanese archipelago. It was an age of legendary feats, when small lords rose to overthrow great medieval houses, and the political geography of the land was plunged into chaos. Faced with the constant danger of war, petty lords everywhere built *yamashiro*, mountaintop fortresses, where they could retreat when attacked. But even down in the lowlands, where they resided in peacetime, it was necessary to always be on the alert, and watchtowers were built atop the lord's manor. MARUOKA-JŌ, built in 1576, the oldest extant keep in Japan, is of this early type.

A year before Maruoka-jō was built, however, an event occurred that would make this simple watchtower style, innovative as it was, obsolete. In one of the decisive battles of his career, ODA NOBUNAGA (1534–1582) armed his soldiers with guns, stationed them behind wooden palisades, and proceeded to demolish the cavalry of his great enemy, Takeda Matsu-yori. This was the first really effective use in battle of Western firearms, which had arrived in Japan around 1543. During the brief span of the Azuchi-Momoyama period (1573–1615), firearms and new battle tactics forced a change from the crude keeps and mountain fortresses to the edifices of beauty and grandeur we see today. At the same time, they enabled a few foresighted leaders to pacify and reunify Japan.

Nobunaga, the first to understand the new nature of warfare, was also the first to build a fortress of the new type, Azuchi-jō, in 1579. Although he needed a well-defended place in case an enemy attacked, he could not retreat to an isolated fort as earlier warlords had done, because he had to administer his growing army and preside over a spreading web of alliances. Instead of building his castle in an inaccessible place, Nobunaga chose a low hill on the shores of Lake Biwa, with a sweeping view of the surrounding plains; this setup is called *hirayamajiro* or "flatland-mountain castle." The *tenshu*, or keep, was made especially tall and impressive. From then on the trend was toward the *hirayamajiro*, such as Azuchi-jō, and even *hirajiro*, "flatland castles." In the space of a few decades, hundreds of *tenshu* were built.

Japanese architecture was so strongly biased toward building in wood that stone castle keeps like those in Europe never developed. The *tenshu* was therefore much more vulnerable than a European keep. For protection, it was built atop a high stone palisade, and its wooden walls, exposed in earlier castles, were armored with thick layers of clay and plaster against fire and artillery. A series of overhanging eaves and gables sheltered the walls from rain, their graceful curves arranged into the lively, rhythmic compositions that make Japanese keeps so beautiful. The alternating layers of *kara hafu* (rounded gables) and *chidori hafu* (pointed gables), the cusped windows of the upper floors, the pendants hanging from the eaves, and the *shachi*, dolphins mounted on top of the roof as a charm against fire, all originated in temple and palace architecture and were intended to lend beauty and dignity to the *tenshu*.

Nobunaga's Azuchi-jō set an extravagant, *arriviste* tone for the entire Azuchi-Momoyama

45

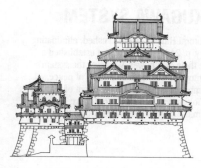

Figure 27. Himeji-jō

period. Its keep was a fantastical layer cake built up of rectangular, square, and octagonal floor plans. The foremost painter in the land, KANŌ EITOKU, was commanded to illuminate the interior with brilliantly gilded screens. Nobunaga's successor HIDEYOSHI built Ōsaka-jō, considered an invincible stronghold, as well as two fortified palaces, Juraku-tei in Kyoto proper and Fushimi-jō to the city's south, on a hill called Momoyama. Unlike Nobunaga, Hideyoshi felt secure enough to live in airier quarters outside the *tenshu*; the keep was reserved for emergencies. Gorgeous gilded screens of the time depict the pavilions and colorful Chinese gates of Fushimi-jō and Juraku-tei. The Tokugawa-period lords followed Hideyoshi's precedent and continued to live outside the gloomy keep, in magnificent quarters such as NIJŌ-JŌ. Lavish as these were, however, they never equaled the exuberant decor of Hideyoshi's palaces. Both Fushimi-jō and Juraku-tei were destroyed or dismantled by 1615, when the Tokugawa, using trickery, sacked Ōsaka-jō and forced the suicide of its lord, Hideyoshi's son HIDEYORI.

# HIMEJI-JŌ: THE ULTIMATE JAPANESE CASTLE

HIMEJI-JŌ, located a hundred and thirty kilometers west of Kyoto, was built by TOKUGAWA IEYASU's son-in-law in 1609. It is the most beautiful and militarily formidable Japanese castle in existence. Himeji-jō is a "flatland-mountain castle" with an elaborate central citadel consisting of a principal tower connected to three subsidiary ones (fig. 27). These white towers, floating like birds over the plain, have earned Himeji-jō the nickname "White Egret Castle." The *tenshu* housed the lord in times of war, and had well water, ample space to store arms and provisions, and a vantage point from which to watch the enemy's movements. Though heavily armored with plaster, it was still vulnerable to bombardment and fire. The task of defending this structure fell to the moats, walls, outer guardtowers, and elevated passageways that surround it. Radiating out from the *tenshu* is a maze of fortified corridors and parapets, where soldiers could position themselves to fire on the enemy. The citadel stands atop huge stone palisades which, although built steeply, are slanted slightly to protect against erosion. The corners and other more vulnerable places along the palisade are protected by *ishi-otoshi* (rock chutes), designed to send an avalanche of stones — and sometimes boiling oil — down on any invaders attempting to scale them.

46

The entrance to the keep is a classic ambush. The approach, a long series of stairs, doubles back on itself as it zigzags up the palisade. In the walls above each switchback are loopholes — tall, narrow openings for arrows and round or triangular ones for firearms — from which defending soldiers could fire on the pursuing enemy. If, under this barrage of arrows and bullets, the enemy nevertheless advanced, the defenders needed only to retreat to the next higher switchback and continue firing.

Himeji-jō's labyrinthine approach, through a series of twisting passages, narrow gates, and ambushes, provided an exceptionally formidable defense. Most castles made do with somewhat simpler devices, such as the *masugata* gate (fig. 28). This gate consisted of two portals placed at right angles to each other in the walls of a box-shaped courtyard. The first portal was narrow, sometimes incorporating a dip, to block the view of the interior. If an enemy charged this gate, he would have to turn ninety degrees and try to breach the heavily fortified second gate while trapped in the cramped courtyard, with defenders shooting at him from all directions; especially lethal was the squad of sharpshooters firing down from the upper story of the second portal. The Sakurada gate of the TOKYO IMPERIAL PALACE (formerly Edo-jō) is a fine example of this style. Ironically, because of the 250-year peace imposed by the Tokugawa, neither this gate nor the elaborate defenses of Himeji-jō was ever put to the test of battle.

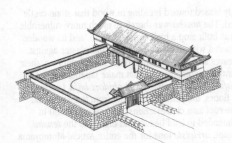

Figure 28. Masugata gate

# THE CASTLE AND THE TOKUGAWA SYSTEM

With the fall of Ōsaka-jō in 1615, the forces of Toyotomi Hideyori were crushed, eliminating the last threat to Tokugawa rule (see Nikkō History, p. 242). The Tokugawa established a vigilant feudal police state, designed to perpetuate their own power. Whatever the system's drawbacks, it blessed Japan, after more than a century of war, with 250 years of peace.

Under Tokugawa rule, the castle remained important not as an instrument of war but as a symbol of authority. In a famous proclamation, Tokugawa Ieyasu declared there be one and only one castle in each province. This meant that many daimyo had to tear down the castles they had erected on their borders. Others, who neither had a castle nor felt they needed one, were nevertheless obliged to build one. During the course of the Edo period several castles had to be rebuilt, usually because of fire. Many were rebuilt without the defensive features employed in a working castle, and became mere symbols of the lord's authority. KŌCHI-JŌ, for example, rebuilt in 1747, has first-floor living quarters built in the residential style and opening onto a garden, an impossibly vulnerable arrangement if it were ever to be attacked.

## Inner and Outer Lords

The lord of a castle was called a daimyo (literally "big name"), and under the Tokugawa system there were three kinds: relatives of the shogun, "inner" daimyo, and "outer" daimyo. The most important relatives were the three collateral Tokugawa branches at **Mito**, **Nagoya** (Owari), and **Wakayama** (Kii), which were established by three of Ieyasu's sons; if the main Tokugawa line failed to produce an heir, one was adopted from one of these families. Other sons of Ieyasu and lesser relatives were awarded the name **Matsudaira**, Ieyasu's original family name, and were given smaller fiefs.

Ieyasu and his successors also raised several vassals to daimyo rank. These **fudai daimyō**, or "inner lords," received small fiefs, with revenues averaging fifty thousand *koku* (one *koku*, about five bushels of rice, was designated as the amount needed to feed one retainer for a year). Other vassals, who received smaller estates or salaries, were not allowed to build castles, but often held important posts in the shogun's government.

The **tozama daimyō**, or "outer lords," were originally Ieyasu's peers who had pledged fealty to him. The *tozama daimyō* were wealthier and considered themselves socially superior to the *fudai daimyō*. Among the most important were the Maeda, Date, Mōri, Hosokawa, and Shimazu; the Maeda were the wealthiest, with 1,300,000 *koku*.

## Sankin Kōtai: Alternate Attendance

Even *tozama daimyō* who had long been allies of Ieyasu, such as the Hosokawa, were viewed with suspicion; despite protestations of fealty, they owed neither their rank nor their fiefs to the Tokugawa. Ieyasu and his successors settled on the strategy of surrounding these potential enemies with the reliable *fudai daimyō*, many of whom had to change fiefs several times during the early days of the shogunate's musical-chairs style of power politics.

Ieyasu's main strategy, however, was to keep all the daimyo so busy and their lives so minutely regulated that they would have no extra time or resources with which to plot rebellion. Marriages between daimyo families had to be approved by the shogun. To keep an eye on the more powerful lords, Ieyasu often invited them to attend him in Edo. IEMITSU, the third Tokugawa shogun, made these visits regular and compulsory under a system called **sankin kōtai**, or "alternate attendance," whereby the *fudai daimyō* had to stay in Edo six months out of the year, and the *tozama daimyō* were required to stay one year out of every two. Each daimyo had to keep an estate in Edo, with lodgings for himself, his Edo staff, and his family, who had to live permanently in Edo.

Particularly bothersome were the processions the daimyo had to mount on their way to and from Edo. The wealthier were attended by thousands of bannermen, halberd bearers, soldiers, ladies, and servants, forming a procession many kilometers long. Even lesser daimyo had to have a few hundred in their entourages (see Villages, p. 53). It is estimated that a daimyo spent about half his time and three-quarters of his income on *sankin kōtai*. Another drain was the numerous construction projects for which the daimyo were forced to pay, the most famous being the extravagant mausoleums of Ieyasu and Iemitsu at Nikkō.

# THE CASTLE TOWN (JŌKAMACHI)

There were more than two hundred castle towns in Edo-period Japan, and each was the urban center of its region. Many still are. The town was basically designed as an extension of the castle's defenses. The houses of low-ranking samurai were placed at the outer fringes of town, to give early warning of an enemy attack. A *teramachi*, or temple quarter, surrounded by a maze of walls, would also be located on the periphery. The temples served as a moral and physical barrier to an attacking army, and also provided barracks for the defenders. A pleasure district was often found nearby; this arrangement kept both religion and vice at a comfortably safe distance from the castle.

If enemy forces should breach the outer defenses of the town, they would be confronted (as is the traveler today) by a maze of dead ends, T junctions, and narrow, twisting lanes. The defenders, familiar with the idiosyncrasies of the town plan, would be at a decided advantage. Sometimes, a straight street leading to the *ōte-mon* (the main gate of the castle) served as a device to draw the enemy to the most heavily fortified part of town. On either side of this approach were the homes of higher-ranking retainers, who would be waiting in ambush with a contingent of followers.

The very highest ranks of samurai were housed inside the castle walls. Since every daimyo had to spend extended periods of time in Edo, the day-to-day administration of the fief was left to the *karō* (the house elder) and his assistants. Also stationed at each castle were the *metsuke*, officials sent by the shogunate to monitor the rulers of each province. Like many types of shogunate officials, they were appointed in pairs—to keep an eye on each other as well. The castle grounds also housed low-ranking samurai guards, who lived in long barracks called *nagaya*.

47

### Samurai and Townsman

The Tokugawa shogunate ranked the four classes—samurai, farmer, craftsman, and merchant—in order of "importance" to society. The samurai endowed the nation with peace—or so Tokugawa theory went—whereas the merchant was an unproductive social parasite; farmers and craftsmen were of intermediate status. The emblem of the samurai's rank was his pair of swords. During the Sengoku period, most warriors also worked as farmers, rallying to the castle only when a battle was in the offing. In order to pacify the countryside, TOYOTOMI HIDEYOSHI forced these "land samurai" to choose between the occupations of warrior and farmer. In 1588, he launched his famous sword hunt, forcing all but the samurai to give up their swords. The samurai thus gained an exclusive badge of authority, but having lost his means of support, was forced to move into the castle town. There, many low-ranking samurai, dependent on their lord for a small stipend of rice, barely eked out a living. Some lords bent the rules about the separation of the four classes and introduced an industry, such as the cherry-bark crafts of KAKUNODATE, in which only samurai could engage. Pasting paper onto umbrella frames was considered a suitable trade, because umbrellas were placed above the user's head. (Footwear, on the other hand, was made by an untouchable caste called the *eta*.)

A recurrent theme in Edo-period literature is that of the poor samurai trying to keep up appearances. According to an old saying, "A samurai uses a toothpick, even on an empty stomach." A samurai house, even if very plain, is nearly always surrounded by a walled garden and boasts a formal gate. The size and appearance of this gate was strictly determined by the samurai's status within the clan hierarchy. Today many samurai houses have been replaced by modern dwellings, but the residents are often loath to do away with their fine samurai gates. The least fortunate samurai were the *rōnin*, "masterless samurai," many of whom wandered from town to town, often getting into brawls. But most samurai in castle towns engaged in peaceful pursuits, becoming teachers, policemen, and tax collectors. They also had to fulfill ceremonial duties, such as accompanying their lord to and from Edo on his *sankin kōtai* processions.

Merchants and craftsmen were required to live in designated quarters, separate from the samurai. Different crafts and specialities—dyers, saké merchants, swordsmiths, and the like—were grouped into different quarters, called *machi* or *chō*. In practice not much distinction was made between merchants and craftsmen, but merchants generally were located on the larger thoroughfares, whereas craftsmen lived and worked in the alleys behind. This separation of trades into neighborhoods, reminiscent of European trade guilds, can be seen today in modern cities. Names such as Konya-chō (dyer town), Kōji-machi (yeast town) and Zaimoku-chō (lumber town) are found in provincial castle towns as well as in Tokyo, particularly in the Shitamachi district.

In contrast to the samurai house, the homes of even wealthy merchants rarely had gates, and had only small courtyard gardens. Merchants had to deal with innumerable restrictions on the size, materials, and shapes of their houses. A tax on the street frontage of merchant houses ensured that the facades would be narrow and modest (see Villages, p. 54). All these efforts to keep merchants in their place notwithstanding, in practice many samurai, and also their overlords the daimyo, were deeply in debt to wealthy merchants.

The elite of the townsmen were the merchants and craftsmen who supplied the daimyo's household. Many lords patronized the fine crafts, sometimes even inviting artisans from Kyoto. KANAZAWA is renowned for crafts introduced from Kyoto, such as *yūzen* silk, *maki-e* lacquer, and Raku-style tea bowls, as well as Kanazawa's own Kutani porcelain. The local souvenirs of former castle towns include numerous crafts first promoted by Edo-period daimyo.

# VISITING A CASTLE TOWN TODAY

Of the more than one hundred Edo-period castle keeps, only about forty survived the Meiji Restoration. In the years after 1868, many of these were pulled down by the fledgling Meiji government or dismantled by local patriots as undesirable relics of feudalism. Castles were so unvalued during the Meiji period that one, in western Japan, was sold for the equivalent of fifteen dollars. Castle sites, however, remained important municipal centers; the grounds of many old castles contain schools, athletic fields, parks, museums, and other public institutions. Because of World War II and other disasters, only twelve genuine castle keeps survive: Maruoka-jō (1576), MATSUMOTO-JŌ (ca. 1596), Inuyama-jō (ca. 1601), HIKONE-JŌ (1606), HIMEJI-JŌ (1609), MATSUE-JŌ (1611), Marugame-jō (1660), Uwajima-jō (1665), BITCHŪ-MATSUYAMA-JŌ (ca. 1684), KŌCHI-JŌ (1747), HIROSAKI-JŌ (1810), and MATSUYAMA-JŌ (1854).

Many of the best preserved, most atmospheric castle towns never had impressive castles. These are often smaller towns in remote areas that have lagged in development and so have retained more of the old atmosphere.

### The Castle Museum

As a matter of civic pride, many castle keeps have been reconstructed in impressive, but not always accurate or esthetic, ferro-concrete reproductions. Inside (or near) the castle there is often a local history museum; these are of varying quality and selectivity. Typical displays

48

# Five Famous Daimyo

Nearly as famous as Japan's military hegemons (see "Ten Great Names in Japanese History," p. 21) are the following five families, the most powerful among the *tozama daimyō*. Other important families include the **Ii** of Hikone, hereditary ministers to the TOKUGAWA, and the **Uesugi** of Yonezawa, who are well known as descendants of one of the greatest warlords of Japanese history, Uesugi Kenshin. Many of Japan's important daimyo families trace their ancestry to the MINAMOTO or the TAIRA; the Hosokawa and the Shimazu, for example, are of Minamoto descent.

 **Date of Sendai** (Tōhoku, p. 172). Date Masamune founded Sendai as his castle town and also built Zuigan-ji in Matsushima; he was an important ally of Tokugawa Ieyasu at Sekigahara. When he was a boy he lost the sight in one eye and came to be known as the "One-eyed Dragon." In the hope of engaging in trade with the West, he sent his vassal Hasekura Tsunenaga on a mission to the Vatican in 1613. In the mid-seventeenth century, the Date were divided by a bloody succession struggle that formed the basis for the Kabuki play *Sendai Meiboku Hagi*. Old province name: Rikuzen.

 **Maeda of Kanazawa** (Chūbu, p. 298). Maeda Toshiie, born to a minor daimyo family in the region of Nagoya, rose in the service of Nobunaga and Hideyoshi and eventually established the wealthiest daimyo family of the Edo period, worth more than one million *koku*. Although Toshiie was the principal guardian of Toyotomi Hideyori, his heirs ended up siding with the Tokugawa in the Battle of Sekigahara. During the Edo period, the Maeda castle town of Kanazawa flourished as an elegant, Kyoto-influenced cultural center. Old province name: Kaga.

 **Mōri of Hagi** (Chūgoku, p. 459). Mōri Motonari, originally lord of the area around Hiroshima, became a vassal of the Ōuchi of Yamaguchi. When the Ōuchi lord was murdered, Motonari killed the assassin and took over the Ōuchi domain, holding most of western Japan and part of Kyūshū. In the movie *Ran*, Kurosawa Akira based an early scene on Motonari's advice to his three sons to remain allied; he demonstrated that a single arrow could be broken, but three together could not. A Mōri crest shows three circles united under a single bar. Unlike the sons in *Ran*, the Mōri took their father's advice and thus remained powerful, even after they had lost more than half of their domain by fighting against Tokugawa Ieyasu at Sekigahara. They were avenged two-and-a-half centuries later, when the Mōri clan played a leading role in the Meiji Restoration (see Hagi History, p. 460). Chōshū samurai dominated the pre-World War II army. Old province name: Chōshū.

 **Hosokawa of Kumamoto** (Kyūshū, p. 493). The Hosokawa became governors of Shikoku and shogunal deputies with the rise of their relatives, the ASHIKAGA (1334–1573). Under Hosokawa Katsumoto, the family fought the Yamana for control of Kyoto during the Ōnin Wars (1467–1477) and also built Ryōan-ji, famed for its rock garden. Later, Hosokawa Yūsai (1534–1610), a famous literary figure, broke with the last Ashikaga shogun and followed Nobunaga, Hideyoshi, and Tokugawa Ieyasu in succession. His son Tadaoki built Daitoku-ji's Kōtō-in subtemple and was a disciple of SEN NO RIKYŪ. Tadaoki ordered his wife, the famous Christian Hosokawa Gracia (1563–1600), killed to prevent her capture by anti-Tokugawa forces. After the Battle of Sekigahara, Tadaoki and his son were awarded a large domain at Kumamoto. Old province name: Higo.

 **Shimazu of Kagoshima** (Kyūshū, p. 498). This is one of Japan's oldest daimyo families, founded in 1197 by Shimazu Tadahisa, a relative and retainer of MINAMOTO NO YORITOMO. In the late sixteenth century the Shimazu controlled nearly all of Kyūshū. After their defeat by Tokugawa Ieyasu at Sekigahara, they were allowed to keep only the core of their fief, still very large, around Kagoshima. In 1865, they struck an alliance with the Mōri (see above) to overthrow the Tokugawa shogunate, which they did in late 1867, precipitating the Meiji Restoration. In 1873, Saigō Takamori led the abortive Satsuma Rebellion against the new Meiji government. Satsuma samurai dominated the pre-World War II navy. Old province name: Satsuma.

include treasured objects, such as a fine sword or tea utensils, and a woodblock print or old photograph of the castle and of notable figures from the era of the Meiji Restoration.

An inevitable part of the display is some relic of the pomp and splendor of a *sankin kōtai* procession, often a palanquin used by the lord or his ladies, decorated with his family crests. These beautiful designs functioned much like European coats of arms and are often emblazoned on the roof tiles of castle buildings, as well as on the clothing, banners, armor, and weapons shown in the museum. An elaborate lacquerware bridal set, brought with a bride when she entered her husband's castle, will bear her own family crest. Gifts from the Tokugawa bear the triple hollyhock crest; those from the imperial family bear the sixteen-petalled chrysanthemum.

## Formal Daimyo Palaces

During the Tokugawa peace, the daimyo lived outside the *tenshu* in palaces that resembled, on a more modest scale, the ornate *shoin* of NIJŌ-JŌ (see Villas, p. 64). Because the shogunate sent spies and assassins into the realms of suspect daimyo—IGA-UENO has a small museum devoted to the most famous of these spies, the *ninja*—these villas also had defensive devices similar to those at Nijō-jō. Hallways were equipped with *uguisu bari*, "nightingale flooring," designed to squeak when stepped on and warn of intruders. In the early years of the Edo period, when a samurai visited the daimyo's palace, he was required to wear the formal *nagabakama*, or "long pants," which were so long that they trailed on the floor and effectively hobbled the samurai, making him harmless; he had to learn a special technique just to walk in them. As additional protection, there were hidden compartments for guards, who were ready to leap out and defend their lord at the slightest sign of trouble. Only a few towns, such as Kawagoe and Kōchi, preserve parts of these palaces.

## Informal Villas and Gardens

50

Many daimyo built themselves pleasure villas with large gardens, lavish parks for the lord and his retinue to stroll around in. Often a daimyo would go to great pains to secure a famous tea master and fine tea utensils from Kyoto and build an exquisite tea hut in the garden. Unlike the formal style required for the official palace, the more informal Sukiya style of tea huts was also favored for the villa (see Villas, p. 67). Many of Japan's famous provincial stroll gardens, such as Kanazawa's Kenroku-en and Kumamoto's Suizen-ji, were once part of a daimyo's pleasure estate.

## "High Collar" Mansions

After the Meiji Restoration, many daimyo became noblemen in the new order. To fit their new titles—marquis, count, baron—the more extravagant daimyo built mock châteaux, while the more conservative incorporated Western flourishes and conveniences into a traditional-style residence. Good examples of these "high collar" (semi-Westernized) villas can be seen in YONEZAWA, MATSUYAMA, Hōfu, Fukue, YANAGAWA, and OBI.

## Samurai Houses

Along with the local civic museum, a castle town often has a *buke-yashiki*, or samurai house, which can be viewed for a small admission fee. If the old quarter's earthen walls, gates, gardens, and houses are well preserved, the atmosphere can be strikingly reminiscent of another time. House and garden are apt to be plain, although the house may display heirlooms such as screens or calligraphy. Edo-period samurai are best thought of as civil servants, generally underpaid. The samurai class accounted for five to ten percent of the population; it was not the select elite the European aristocracy was. Even well-to-do samurai lived simply, according to the spartan dictates of their class. Often, the rank of the occupant can be gauged by the distance from the castle; the greater the distance, the lower the rank. Since the houses of the highest-ranking samurai were inside the castle compound itself, few of these survived the turmoil of the Meiji Restoration.

The status symbols of a samurai house were its wide frontage, walled enclosure, gate, and garden. Generally a samurai house had two entrances, one for receiving those higher in station, the other for ordinary folk. There was sometimes a *jōdan no ma*, a special room where the master entertained honored guests. During most of the Edo period, only samurai houses were legally entitled to have a second story or a coffered ceiling (*gō-tenjō*). Samurai houses generally had a wide veranda facing out onto the garden. Many features, such as floor space and the thickness of the beams, were fixed according to the samurai's rank.

Even in times of peace, certain defensive features were incorporated into the construction of the samurai house. Slatted Judas windows enabled guards to spy on people entering or passing the gate. Trapdoors, hidden rooms, and escape routes were sometimes built into the house. Often exhibited in the *buke-yashiki* are a set or two of the paired swords the samurai was privileged to wear. Relating to the samurai's later role as administrator and man of letters, several documents of a literary or official nature may also be on display. In many castle towns, in particular HAGI, low-ranking samurai houses were preserved because a son of the house became an important figure in the Meiji Restoration. Despite Japan's rapid modernization, feudal consciousness remained so strong that until World War II, all citizens were officially classified as being of noble, samurai, or common descent.

## Merchant Quarter

Old merchant townhouses are packed together in rows (now often hidden behind modern facades). Look for famous old shops selling pickles, sweets, or regional crafts.

**Temples and Shrines**

The lord of a province usually patronized at least two temples, one for prayers concerning this world, called a *kigan-ji*, the other for his burial and prayers for his salvation, called a *bodai-ji*. The *bodai-ji* is generally the more interesting, with its often elaborate tombstones or mausoleums. The more extravagant daimyo, such as Date Masamune in Sendai and Katō Kiyomasa in Kumamoto, built ornate mausoleums resembling that of Ieyasu, the Nikkō Tōshō-gū. A castle town often had two "temple towns," or *teramachi*, one spacious temple district for the samurai, who favored the Zen sect, and one amid the cramped clutter of the townsmen, who leaned toward the Nichiren, Jōdo, or Jōdo-Shin sects. Usually there is a noted garden, often in a Zen temple. Castle-town Zen temples, however, often look forlorn, since their patrons, the samurai, have lost their social position.

If the lord wanted a domain that was strong in the arts of war, prosperous, and boasted a high level of scholarship, he would support, respectively, the town's Hachiman, Inari, and Tenjin shrines (see Shinto, p. 29). There would generally be a guardian shrine for the castle, often in the "dangerous" northeast direction. As a gesture of fealty to the shogunate, a lord might build a Tōshō-gū, a shrine consecrated to the apotheosis of Tokugawa Ieyasu. Shrines were often dedicated to the founding daimyo of the domain.

# USEFUL TERMS

**Castles**

| | |
|---|---|
| shiro | Castle |
| -jō | Castle |
| hori | Moat (*sotobori* is the outer moat, *uchibori* is the inner moat) |
| ishi-otoshi | A chute from which rocks were dropped on attackers |
| maru | Major enclosures of defensive walls around the castle's main towers |
| ōte-mon | Main gate, often built in *masugata* style |
| tenshu | Donjon, castle keep |
| uguisu-bari | "Nightingale flooring" that squeaks when trod upon, to warn of intruders |
| yagura | Guard tower and armory |

**Castle Towns**

| | |
|---|---|
| bodai-ji | A daimyo family's funerary temple |
| buke-yashiki | A samurai house |
| fudai daimyō | An "inside lord," a hereditary vassal of the Tokugawa shogunate |
| goyō shōnin | Merchant patronized by the daimyo |
| Judas window | Boxlike windows covered with wooden slats from which guards can spy |
| kigan-ji | A temple where the daimyo prayed for well-being in this world |
| sankin kōtai | Compulsory attendance in Edo, required of all daimyo |
| teramachi | Temple quarter |
| tozama daimyō | An "outside lord," regarded by the shogunate with suspicion |

# BEST CASTLES AND CASTLE TOWNS

## TŌHOKU

**\*\* Hirosaki.** Honshū's northernmost castle town has an original castle keep, a preserved samurai quarter, two impressive temple towns, and mazelike streets filled with artisans' workshops. This proudly provincial cultural center is nationally famous for its Neputa festival, lacquerware, and *Tsugaru-jamisen* music (p. 157).

**\*\* Kakunodate.** This small, northern castle town has an avenue lined with well-preserved samurai houses. Kakunodate's poorer samurai once made the cherry-bark crafts that are the town's most famous product today (p. 164).

## CHŪBU

**\*\*\* MATSUMOTO-JŌ** (1596). This national treasure is one of the oldest extant castles, designed to withstand a real battle. The majestic donjon is covered with black planks, which contrast strikingly with the white mortar. Situated on a plateau surrounded by snowcapped peaks (in \* Matsumoto, p. 283).

**\*\*\* KANAZAWA.** Castle town of the Maeda, the wealthiest Edo-period daimyo, Kanazawa is famous for its elegant culture. Although now a bustling modern city, it has a splendid stroll garden and villa, samurai houses, sprawling temple towns, old pleasure quarters, fine crafts, a Noh theater, and what many consider to be the best cuisine in Japan (p. 298).

## KYOTO (\*\*\*)

**\*\*\* NIJŌ-JŌ** (1602–03, Ninomaru Palace added 1624–26). The Tokugawa castle in Kyoto. Although the donjon burned in 1750, the audience halls and living quarters, sumptuously decorated with KANŌ SCHOOL paintings, give a picture of the life of the shoguns. Nearby Nijō Jinya, a lodging for high officials, is equipped with defensive devices (p. 329).

**KINKI**

**✳ IGA-UENO.** This small, poor castle town was a stronghold of the *ninja*, mercenary spies trained in the deadly arts of assassination. Their legacy is preserved in a "*ninja* mansion." Iga-Ueno was also the birthplace of the poet BASHŌ. The town's distinctive culture can be seen in its curious festivals, old neighborhoods, and crafts (p. 405).

**✳✳✳ HIMEJI-JŌ** (1609). The celebrated "White Egret," Japan's most complete and beautiful extant feudal castle. Famous for its mazelike plan and elaborate defenses (p. 424).

**CHŪGOKU AND SHIKOKU**

**✳✳✳ MATSUYAMA-JŌ** (1854). An impressive array of turrets and donjons, second only to Himeji-jō in preserving the effect of a complete fortress (in ✳ Matsuyama, p. 452).

**✳✳ HAGI.** The seat of the powerful Mōri lords, Hagi is renowned for its well-preserved samurai quarter, a labyrinth of earthen walls shaded by citrus groves. Hagi-yaki, patronized by the Mōri, is one of Japan's finest tea ceremony wares. Hagi samurai led the move to overthrow the shogunate, (p. 460).

**KYŪSHŪ**

**✳✳✳ Kumamoto-jō.** Reconstruction. This castle, with its superb masonry, was originally built by Katō Kiyomasa, a powerful Sengoku daimyo who was also a renowned castle architect. Intended as a refuge for Hideyori, it was virtually invincible (in ✳ Kumamoto, p. 494).

# OTHER INTERESTING CASTLES AND CASTLE TOWNS

52 **HOKKAIDŌ**

**✳✳✳ Goryōkaku.** Star-shaped, Western-style fort, built in 1864. After the Meiji Restoration, the shogun's navy founded the short-lived Republic of Hokkaidō here (in ✳ Hokadate, p. 149).

**TŌHOKU**

**✳✳ Morioka.** Castle town with excellent crafts and museums (p. 161).

**Taga-jō.** Ruins of a Chinese-style quadrangular fortress, built in the Nara period during campaigns to subdue northern tribes (p. 179).

**✳ YONEZAWA.** Unusual country castle town known for safflower-dyed silks and "poor daimyo's cuisine" (p. 181).

**✳ Aizu-Wakamatsu.** Celebrated throughout Japan for samurai youths who committed suicide in the early Meiji period (p. 183).

**TOKYO (✳✳✳)**

**✳✳✳ TOKYO IMPERIAL PALACE** (formerly Edo-jō). Once the largest castle in the world, it still preserves vestiges of its former immensity in the massive walls and moat (p. 208).

**KYOTO**

**✳ Ōmi-Hachiman.** Charming castle town laced with canals (p. 378).

**✳✳✳ HIKONE-JŌ** (1606). This graceful castle on the shores of Lake Biwa was the seat of the Ii family, important ministers to the Tokugawa (in ✳ Hikone, p. 379).

**KINKI**

**✳ ŌSAKA-JŌ.** Now an ugly concrete reconstruction, this is historically one of the most famous castles in Japan. Built by Hideyoshi as a refuge for his young son, Hideyori, it was the site of a great siege by Tokugawa forces in 1615 (in ✳ Osaka, p. 416).

**✳ Tamba-Sasayama.** Country castle town in famed pottery area (p. 418).

**CHŪGOKU AND SHIKOKU**

**✳✳ KŌCHI-JŌ** (1747). This castle preserves the lord's living quarters (in ✳ Kōchi, p. 436).

**✳✳ BITCHŪ-MATSUYAMA-JŌ** (ca. 1684). Built on a high, steep hill, this is the only mountaintop castle to preserve a keep. Hideyoshi was laying siege to its predecessor when ODA NOBUNAGA was assassinated. Pleasant castle town (in ✳ Bitchū-Takahashi, p. 440).

**✳✳ MATSUE-JŌ** (1611). This castle's dark-walled keep presides over the city much beloved by Lafcadio Hearn (p. 441).

**✳ Iwakuni.** The Brocade Sash Bridge is a marvel of engineering (p. 454).

**✳ Tsuwano.** Small castle town in beautiful narrow valley (p. 458).

**KYŪSHŪ**

**✳✳ YANAGAWA.** Boats glide through lovely canals that were once castle moats (p. 491).

**✳ Bungo-Takeda.** Magnificent ruined castle in the highlands (p. 498).

**✳ OBI.** Remote castle town on the Nichinan Coast (p. 504).

**OKINAWA**

**✳✳✳ Nakagusuku.** Fifteenth-century Okinawan fortress (in ✳ Central Okinawa, p. 516).

# Villages, Roads, and Merchant Towns

*Tabi no haji wa kakisute.*
"While traveling, shame doesn't stick." — An old adage; or loosely translated, "A traveler's deeds can be completely rotten, because he knows they'll soon be forgotten."

Although castle towns were the dominant urban unit in old Japan, it was the towns of trade and travel that inspired poets and artists. The castle town was the home of Confucian correctness and duty. The road offered the romance and terror of freedom. It may seem surprising that a country as small as Japan can generate so much wanderlust. In modern times this passion has been focused on the train, which is the setting of many popular novels. In earlier times the traveler, depending on social class, either trudged in straw sandals or was borne by horse or palanquin. Whether one walked or rode, travel was an opportunity to cast aside everyday inhibitions, forget duties and responsibilities, and, for a brief while, pursue dreams.

Little wonder that Japan's artists have been great wanderers; dreams, rather than duties, are the stuff of art. The poet BASHŌ's masterpiece *Oku no Hosomichi* (The Narrow Road to the Deep North) is a haiku-filled diary of his journeys around the Tōhoku region. An Edo-period comic novel, Ikku Jippensha's *Shank's Mare*, chronicles the adventures of two ne'er-do-wells who flee their debts in Edo and set out on Japan's most celebrated road, the **Tōkaidō**, outfoxing and being outfoxed by a succession of dishonest officials, priests, pilgrims, thieves, "teahouse girls," and "begging nuns," who offer their favors in return for a "donation." The Tōkaidō was also the subject of the most famous series of ukiyo-e prints, *The Fifty-three Stations of the Tōkaidō*, by Andō Hiroshige. Hiroshige and other artists of the mid-nineteenth century depicted the great and humble sights of Japan in intimate — if not always accurate — detail, portraying post towns, market towns, quaint farming and fishing villages, famous shrines and temples, and the interesting goings-on around them. Most of Hiroshige's world has disappeared without a trace, but the special kind of traveler who is willing to get off the main train lines and tourist routes can still find hints of this romantic world, if he knows where to look for them.

## ROADS, BARRIERS, AND POST TOWNS

The Tōkaidō was one of five roads maintained by the shogunate for official purposes, including the *sankin kōtai* (attendance at Edo) required of the daimyo of every province (see Castles, p. 47). It ran from Edo to Kyoto along, near, and, at one point, through, the Pacific Ocean, and was Japan's most famous road. It remains the most heavily trafficked part of the country today, and so only a few old post towns, such as AKASAKA and GOYU, retain a hint of the Tōkaidō's original atmosphere.

At HAKONE, a famous onsen (hot spring) area near Mt. Fuji, the long and narrow barrier gatehouse has been reconstructed as a small museum. The shogunate erected barriers to check travelers' documents; farmers, for example, had to prove they had permission to travel before they could set out on a pilgrimage. To mutilate this document even slightly was a crime; to try to circumvent a barrier was a grave offense.

The shogunate was most concerned to learn whether the *tozama daimyō* to the west might be preparing a rebellion. Since the rules of *sankin kōtai* required the daimyo's wives and children to reside in Edo, the officials who manned the barrier were on the lookout for women heading west (home) and rifles heading east toward Edo, where the daimyo's retainers might mount a surprise attack on the shogun. Inside the Hakone barrier gatehouse, mannequins portray a woman of high rank being searched by a female official, stationed by the shogunate at the barrier just for this purpose.

Most of Hiroshige's Tōkaidō has given way to the Tōkaidō industrial belt. Fortunately, parts of the other four official roads—the Nikkō Kaidō, Kōshū Kaidō, Ōshū Kaidō, and Nakasendō—are at a safer distance from economic progress. Particularly beautiful is a section of the Nakasendō called the Kiso Kaidō, with the well-preserved post towns of MAGOME, TSUMAGO, and NARAI, and the barrier station at KISO-FUKUSHIMA. The three post towns, especially Tsumago, still look much as they were portrayed in the Kiso Kaidō print series by Hiroshige and Eisen.

The long, narrow post towns hugged the road they served, and so each shop and tavern had a shot at the passing traveler. Many post towns became known for a local specialty. The Kiso Valley's Hirosawa lacquerware and Hakone's *yosegi zaiku* boxes still make popular souvenirs. Yodo, south of Kyoto, was famous for *Fushimi ningyō*, festive clay dolls. Like many another post town, Yoshida, on the Tōkaidō, was known for its girls; in 1843, the town had 2,772 women, while men numbered only 1,505.

Official requirements and restrictions on facilities and buildings gave post towns a pleasing uniformity. Stations were set up to provide travelers with fresh horses, runners, and palanquin bearers. (Wheeled vehicles, which caused ruts, were prohibited.) A shogunate official received these services free, as a form of tax payment, while daimyo on *sankin kōtai* journeys paid a set fee. Both lodged at the town's **honjin**, or "main encampment," an appellation that betrays its military origins. In peacetime the *honjin* became luxurious inns, with exquisite gardens and interior ornamentation. Overflow guests from the *honjin* lodged at the auxiliary *waki-honjin*, which could accept paying guests if there was room. For commoners, there were numerous inns. One that survives today is the Echigoya in Narai. At the edge of town were wooden signboards, with tiny eaves to keep off the rain, bearing official notices such as offers of a reward for information on the whereabouts of any Christians, Christianity being outlawed.

The five official roads connected the various holdings and territories of the Tokugawa families and thereby served as the main arteries of travel for central Japan. Farther afield, in the west and in the north, were other ancient roads, post towns, and *honjin* maintained by individual daimyo. The Yakumo Honjin near Izumo was used by the daimyo of Matsue during his annual pilgrimage to Izumo Shrine, and is now a wonderfully atmospheric inn.

# TOWNS OF TRADE

One type of shogunate official traveling the post roads was a *daikan*, an administrator of one of the more remote parts of the shogun's lands. *Daikan* were appointed in pairs, each alternating between Edo and his jurisdiction. *Daikan* towns became busy marketplaces, because goods could be shipped from one to any other, as well as to Edo, without incurring the tariffs that local daimyo charged. TAKAYAMA, deep in the mountains of the Chūbu region, preserves Japan's only remaining *daikan*'s office, which includes large storehouses for tax rice as well as the *shirasu* pit, where confessions were extracted from suspected criminals. Nearby, the morning market still draws farm women from the surrounding villages. During the Edo period, Takayama's merchants habitually bribed the shogunate officials to overlook violations of sumptuary laws, so today, there still stand rows of beautiful merchant houses. They survived because they were very well built to start with, and because the town has not grown explosively the way most Japanese cities have.

It is the towns that were once prosperous and later on left by the economic wayside that retain their old flavor. FUKIYA, in the mountains of western Honshū, produced copper and a red ochre called *bengara*, a prized pigment used for porcelain, lacquer, and to stain the walls and woodwork of elegant Kyoto teahouses; it was also widely used in Fukiya itself. TAKEHARA, which prospered from salt, has several salt-mechants' houses. UCHIKO, in Shikoku, got rich in the Meiji era on vegetable wax; the wealthy wax-merchant's houses survive because the town center shifted elsewhere. IMAI-CHŌ, an unusual self-governing merchant town in the Yamato plain, was a center of the lumber trade. The layout of this town is preserved from the fifteenth century; in the space of a square kilometer are several hundred old merchant houses, protected against fire by thick walls of brilliant white plaster and black tile, a luxury only the most prosperous communities could afford.

## A Typical Machiya (Merchant House)

In a well-preserved town of trade, one can see classic Edo-period townhouses, or *machiya*, standing in neat rows, wall-to-wall. Unlike the samurai house, which had a long outer wall fronting onto the street and a fairly spacious yard, the *machiya* began with the narrow facade of the merchant's store—narrow because it was taxed by its street frontage—and continued a surprisingly long way back from the street. Until the end of the Edo period, *machiya* were generally forbidden to have a full second story, although often they got around the law by building a kind of attic or "half-second story." The prohibition was intended to prevent any merchants, who according to Confucian theory were parasites at the bottom of the social ladder, from "looking down" on a samurai.

One mild form of public display was an *udatsu*, a plaster wall extension covered by its own little eaves and placed between a house and its neighbors. They jut out like a pair of blinders, ostensibly to protect against fire in the house next door. In fact, they were built as impressively as possible to advertise their owner's wealth; an unsuccessful man was said to have "failed to build an *udatsu*." The Tōkaidō post town of ARIMATSU, famous for luxurious tie-dyed silks, has particularly prominent examples.

Other forms of display include doors and windows decorated with fine slats called *kōshi*. Kyoto's GION district is known for facades ornamented with *bengara-gōshi*, slats stained with red ochre, and convex bamboo-lath fences along the lower wall, called *inuyarai*, "dog repellers," which have the putative function of keeping the walls clean. These were particularly favored by houses in the entertainment trades, such as restaurants and brothels, which were also among the only *machiya* allowed to have full two-story facades, a second floor being almost essential for privacy.

In a regular merchant house, however, the customer entered only as far as the shop at the front of the house. It usually consisted of a *doma*, or earthen floor, and beside it, a raised area called a *chōba*, where customers sat while carrying out transactions. Honored guests and high-ranking customers were ushered down the earthen corridor at one side of the house to an inner area, where there would be an elegant little courtyard garden and next to it a formal room for entertaining guests. A wealthy merchant might, in defiance of regulations, embellish this room with the finest woods and a coffered ceiling, as well as many other appurtenances of the luxurious aristocratic styles.

Behind this reception room were the living quarters and the kitchen. The latter consisted of a large earthen-floored space and a raised floor, usually next to the living quarters. The large clay stoves on the earthen floor boasted of the number of servants and other house dependents to be fed. A small shrine to the hearth god was placed nearby. The earthen-floored corridor in fact extended from the entrance of the house all the way to the back, where there was a *kura* (storehouse) for valuables. Here, at the very rear of the house, was another garden, as well as the toilet and bath.

There were at least as many variations on this plan as there were trades. All *machiya*, however, were constructed on a scale of increasing privacy away from the street. Even today, in traditional towns such as Kyoto, outsiders rarely penetrate beyond the rooms reserved for entertaining clients or guests. Luckily, many famous merchant towns have a fine old *machiya* open to the public as a museum. The finest examples include the Kusakabe and Yoshijima houses in Takayama. These magnificent edifices were erected by rich merchants in the Meiji period, when, free of the old sumptuary laws, they could rebuild their traditional homes on a luxurious scale. Particularly striking is the intricate scaffolding of the ceiling rafters; although also found in the humble farmhouse, here the use of fine timbers and exquisite carpentry serves to emphasize its elegance of form.

## Kura (Storehouses)

Fires were the plague of merchant towns, which were densely packed with wooden houses. Disastrous conflagrations were so common in the shogun's city that they were called "flowers of Edo." To protect tax-rice and valuables, merchants and tax collectors built *kura*, storehouses with thick walls of earth and plaster, often made sparkling white by mixing in ground oyster shells. The river at Edo's Nihonbashi, "the bridge of Japan" where all roads terminated, was lined with *kura*. The most famous place to see *kura* today is KURASHIKI, an old rice-trading town, which later became the site of a large textile mill. Kurashiki's museums, shops, and even inns are housed in sturdy old *kura* that face a willow-lined canal—a scene right out of an ukiyo-e print.

Although somewhat dark and dank, *kura* were adapted for residences in many merchant towns such as KAWAGOE—a "little Edo"—and KITAKATA, after fires leveled the towns in the late nineteenth century. The doors and window of *kura* shops and dwellings are in a style called *Kannon-biraki*, "altar doors," and have a "male" side and a "female" side that interlock and can be sealed with clay in the event of fire. Thanks to the durability of *kura*, these towns preserve a pleasing appearance today. On the Izu Peninsula, houses have *kura*-style walls armored with tiles set in a gay diamond pattern to withstand ocean gales. These *namako-kabe*, or "sea cucumber walls," so-called for the cylindrical plaster moldings that hold the tiles in place, can be seen in Matsuzaki, on the Izu Peninsula.

Figure 29. Townhouse

# VILLAGES AND FARMHOUSES

Farming villages were part of the landscape appreciated by poets and artists. The romance of the road, however, was not for the hapless farmers, who were not normally allowed to leave their farms and villages. This oppressive law helped preserve Japan's many distinct provincial subcultures. One of the special pleasures of traveling in the remoter parts of Japan is that each few hours of travel will reveal new crafts, a different, delicious regional cuisine and, among the elderly, a yet more incomprehensible dialect. Among the most charming regional deviations is in the style of the **minka**, or farmhouse. (The term *minka*, "houses of the people," includes merchant houses, but is typically used to refer to farmhouses.)

The simplest style of farmhouse was separated into the dirt-floor *doma* area and a raised area, much as in a merchant's shop, except that the raised area normally contained an *irori*, a square, open hearth. Farm families spent most daylight hours working outdoors, so there was less need in their homes for the many rooms and partitions of samurai and merchant houses. The raised area served for eating, sleeping, and "night work," such as fashioning sacks and rope out of rice straw. The *irori* provided heat, light, and a place to cook. Suspended above it might be a wooden fish, which served not only as part of the pot-suspension system, but also as a charm against fire (the fish being associated with water). Seating around the *irori* was strictly fixed according to family hierarchy. The master of the house sat on the side farthest from the *doma*. His wife sat to his left, while guests sat to his right. Farmhands, children, and daughters-in-law sat nearest the *doma*.

Because of differences in climate and occupation, an amazing number of regional styles developed from this basic model. In the TŌNO area of Tōhoku, raising horses was such an important income supplement for farming families that the beasts were treated and cared for almost as if they were members of the family. These farmers built L-shaped *minka*, called *magariya*, or "bent houses," which housed horses in one wing and humans in the other; this way, the farmers could keep an eye on the animals and also have added protection from cold winds.

Many *minka* types developed in response to the increase in silk raising that occurred when silk became a major export item during the Meiji period. Because worms and cocoons require warmth and varying amounts of light, multistoried *minka* were built with spacious, windowed upper floors. The *kabuto-zukuri*, or "helmet-style," *minka* has a voluminous roof that allows light and air into the upper floors. The *minka* of TAMUGIMATA, in the Dewa Sanzan area, were a variant of this style that included an extra gable. In winter, when the snow was piled deep, these *minka* could be entered through the second-floor gable; the multiple-floor arrangement also conserved heat. The huge *gasshō*-style houses of SHIRAKAWA-GŌ and GOKAYAMA were originally reserved for the families of priests and village headmen, but other households built them when they started to raise silkworms. The devout villagers, members of the Jōdo Shin sect, named these three- to four-story A-frame houses "hands clasped in prayer."

Other distinctive styles include the *honmune* style around Matsumoto, the Yamato style around Nara, and the *kudo* style, a complex form said to resemble an oven, found in Saga prefecture. The NIHON MINKA-EN (Japan Farmhouse Museum) outside Tokyo, and many other fine *minka* museums, enable the visitor to compare regional styles.

CHIRAN, south of Kagoshima, was a particularly unusual farming village because its inhabitants were samurai. Surrounding the village are the tea fields these gentlemen farmers tended. Although the Tokugawa forbade samurai from farming, Kagoshima's Satsuma clan was distant and powerful enough to flaunt Edo's strictures. The fine, clipped-hedge gardens of Chiran's samurai houses offer the sightseer a charming juxtaposition of the rustic and the refined. The stone walls of Chiran are thought to show the influence of the expert masons of Okinawa, which Satsuma held as a quasi-colony. In Okinawa, the island of TAKETOMI, on roughly the same latitude as Taipei, is the best place to see the distinctive coral walls enclosing the pretty courtyards and houses with red-tile roofs surmounted by guardian lions.

# PILGRIMAGES AND MONZENMACHI

In the Edo period, the religious pilgrimage provided the one chance for farmers and many townsmen to put their responsibilities aside and travel. In Japan, this form of travel is as old as history. Many ancient pilgrimages were associated with a mystical cult, called **Shugendō**, which incorporates Buddhist and Shinto elements (see Shinto, p. 28). Shugendō is tied to Japan's primordial mountain worship. From the sixth century on, its practitioners, the *yama-bushi*, wandered around Japan proselytizing among the common people and "converting" mountains, the domain of Shinto *kami*, to its syncretic brand of Buddhism. The *yamabushi* practiced austerities on these mountains, as would lay pilgrims. *Monzenmachi*, literally "towns below the gate," with inns and shops catering to pilgrims, sprang up in places such as YOSHINO, MT. TOGAKUSHI, and in the Dewa Sanzan region at the villages of TŌGE and TAMUGIMATA.

During the Edo period, Mt. Fuji, Japan's highest mountain, became the object of a similar climbing cult, especially among Edo townsmen. Miniatures of the famous cone—including one near Asakusa Kannon Temple—were built within Edo itself so that worshippers unable to afford the trip could gain the same merit climbing up and down the model. Today

Fuji is a quick trip; during the summer white-clad pilgrims, as well as ordinary hikers, crowd the trails to the summit. Fuji Yoshida, at the base of one of the trails up Fuji, is the site of a Sengen Jinja (a shrine to the goddess of Fuji). The approach is lined with pilgrims' inns once owned by *oshi*, the proselytizers who guided pilgrims from Edo.

Villages and towns throughout Japan in the Edo period formed associations to finance pilgrimages to various destinations. These associations held lotteries every year, and the pot went to defray the winner's expenses. The imperial shrines of Ise were the most popular destination. At times Ise became the focus for hysterical mass pilgrimages. In the fifty days between April 9 and May 29, 1705, more than three million people, a tenth of Japan's population, flocked to Ise. As in the children's crusade in Europe, bands of unescorted children vanished from their villages and joined the pilgrimage; shrine officials were at a loss as to how to feed and shelter them all.

Ise's *monzenmachi* featured a perpetual carnival of food, souvenir stands, teahouses, inns, "teahouse girls," and "archery girls." Some vestiges of this atmosphere—now minus the archery girls—can be savored in Tokyo along Nakamise-dōri in front of the Asakusa Kannon temple. SANNENZAKA and NINENZAKA, shop-lined streets that lead up to Kyoto's Kiyomizu Temple, are architecturally the best-preserved *monzenmachi*.

Japan's most impressive *monzenmachi* is at KOTOHIRA, which lies near the end of Japan's most famous pilgrimage, the Shikoku eighty-eight-temple circuit. Before the era of buses and trains, it took staff-carrying, white-robed pilgrims, called *henro*, six weeks to complete the circuit around Japan's fourth largest island of eighty-eight temples dedicated to Japan's most revered saint, KŌBŌ DAISHI. Kōbō Daishi's Shingon sect, along with the Tendai sect, incorporated the *yamabushi* cult; this pilgrimage, as well as another famous one, the thirty-three Kannon temple pilgrimage in Kansai, each have some connection with the *yamabushi*. The high point of the Shikoku pilgrimage is a visit to Zentsū-ji, Kōbō Daishi's birthplace. Nearby is Kotohira Shrine, more familiarly called "Kompira-san," whose *monzen-machi* includes the only Edo-period Kabuki playhouse remaining in Japan, as well as many inns and shops. The *kami* of Kompira is thought to have originated with the crocodile god of the Ganges of India. He is the *kami* of the sea, guardian of sailors and fishermen, many of whom skipped the temple pilgrimage and headed directly to Kompira-san.

57

# FISHING VILLAGES AND PORTS

Fishing villages often have a torii and a small shrine, usually a branch of the Kompira or Sumiyoshi shrines, the latter dedicated to four deities, one of whom is Susano'o, the god of storms. A festive procession of boats, rather than a procession on dry land, honors these protectors of the sea. INE, on the Tango Peninsula, not only features such a matsuri, but its houses, built on stilts with "boat garages" underneath, are practically out in the water as well. Such houses, while common in Southeast Asia, are seen in Japan only here. Fishing villages such as IWAIJIMA, an islet in the Inland Sea, and SOTODOMARI and OKINOSHIMA, in southwest Shikoku, feature houses wrapped in mazes of stone walls, protection against typhoons; this use of stone walls might have been introduced from Okinawa.

Houses in most fishing villages, however, tend to be less distinctive; it is the setting of the villages that makes them spectacular. HEDA, situated on a stunning cove on the west coast of the Izu Peninsula, is hemmed in by steep mountains and is almost inaccessible by land. TOMO NO URA, in the Inland Sea, was a way station for Korean embassies to the Tokugawa shogunate. The temple where they lodged looks out onto a vista of jewellike islands, which recede into the haze of the Inland Sea. On the nearest islands is a small pagoda, rather overwhelmed by the surrounding scenery, which is reminiscent of the Chinese ink-painting tradition common to both the Koreans and the Japanese. SAKITSU, in a remote corner of the Amakusa Islands, was a refuge of crypto-Christians; it was nearly inaccessible by land and, even today, an old house or two fronts onto the sea. BŌNOTSU, another hidden port, offered Satsuma the perfect place to carry on its secret trade with China, via Okinawa. This trade, begun in the early seventeenth century, continued until the 1850s, when contacts with the outside world were reestablished.

Much of the charm of Hiroshige's world was that it was a world unto itself, without the disturbing influences of the West. Aside from minor exceptions such as Bōnotsu, the primary door open to the West was NAGASAKI (see Nagasaki History, p. 483). After the conclusion of Townsend Harris's Open Port Treaty (see Izu History, p. 269), other cities took on a "foreign" atmosphere, especially KŌBE, Yokohama, and HAKODATE. Although such pockets of "Victorian" houses may not seem particularly exotic to the foreign tourist, they have a particular fascination for the Japanese. The architect Taniguchi Yoshio has amassed a truly outstanding collection of incongruous and beautiful architectural half-breeds at MEIJI MURA, near Nagoya. Among the exhibits, all dating from the Meiji and Taishō periods, are part of Frank Lloyd Wright's Imperial Hotel and novelist Natsume Sōseki's "Cat House."

# BEST TOWNS AND VILLAGES

## HOKKAIDŌ

✽ **HAKODATE.** This city was one of Japan's first open ports. It preserves many early Western buildings, including an onion-domed Russian Orthodox church (p. 149).

## TŌHOKU

✽ **TŌNO.** This scattered rural area features L-shaped *minka*, called *magariya*. The region is famed for legends concerning *kappa*, changelings, and other supernatural creatures (p. 166).
✽✽ **DEWA SANZAN.** Three sacred mountains, forming one of the holiest *yamabushi* centers. TŌGE and TAMUGIMATA are *monzenmachi* with a strongly rural flavor. They preserve a number of thatched-roof pilgrim's lodges (p. 175).
✽ **Ōuchijuku.** This remote post town preserves rows of thatched farmhouse-inns (p. 185).
✽ **KITAKATA.** This town preserves two thousand *kura*, now put to all kinds of uses (p. 186).

## KANTŌ

✽✽ **Nagano.** The magnificent Zenkō-ji temple is the object of one of Japan's most popular pilgrimages. The faithful believe it enshrines the first Buddhist statue brought to Japan. The approach is flanked by shops and rows of temple-inns (p. 250).
✽ **TOGAKUSHI.** A former Shugendō center, Togakushi now consists of a series of three shrines straggling up the mountainside. At the base of the middle shrine there remains a considerable number of thatched-roof inns for pilgrims and, in winter, skiers (p. 252).
✽ **NIHON MINKA-EN.** Farmhouses from various parts of Japan (p. 255).
✽ **HAKONE.** Historically, the most famous post town in Japan. It preserves a tree-lined stretch of the Tōkaidō and has a reconstructed barrier gate, now a museum (p. 265).
✽✽ **HEDA.** A beautifully situated fishing village (on ✽✽ Izu Peninsula, p. 271).

## CHŪBU

**AKASAKA and GOYU.** Two tiny but rather well-preserved Tōkaidō post towns, once noted for numerous and aggressive teahouse girls. One former Akasaka brothel is now an inn (p. 277).
**ARIMATSU.** A well-preserved Tōkaidō post town famous for tie-dyed silk and old merchant houses, which boast particularly fine examples of *udatsu* (p. 278).
✽✽ **MAGOME.** A sprawling, bucolic Nakasendō post town preserving many atmospheric inns. The hike over the Magome Pass to Tsumago follows the old Nakasendō through mountain forests (p. 279).
✽✽✽ **TSUMAGO.** A picture-perfect post town, revived from near-abandonment by local residents. Many Edo-period inns have now been turned into minshuku (p. 280).
✽ **KISO-FUKUSHIMA.** The main town of the Kiso-Kaidō. The Kiso-Fukushima barrier gate has been reconstructed and is now a museum. The governor's mansion survives and is open to the public (p. 281).
✽✽ **NARAI.** This Nakasendō post town, less of a "museum town" than Tsumago or Magome, preserves rows of Edo-period lodgings, exchange stations for porters and horses, and the Echigoya, a famous inn (p. 282).
✽✽ **MEIJI MURA.** Absolutely not to be missed by anybody interested in Meiji and Taishō architecture or history (p. 287).
✽✽✽ **TAKAYAMA.** A former *daikan* town, famous for fine merchant houses, crafts, and its spring and fall matsuri, which feature ornate floats. The Hida Minzoku Mura is a collection of farmhouses of the Takayama and Shōkawa Valley regions (p. 289).
✽✽✽ **SHIRAKAWA-GŌ.** Isolated farm hamlet famous for its multi-storied *gasshō* houses, many of which are now minshuku (p. 296).
✽✽✽ **GOKAYAMA.** Downriver from Shirakawa-gō, Gokayama also has many *gasshō* houses (p. 297).
✽✽ **Edo Mura.** Museum of traditional Kaga architecture (in ✽✽✽ Kanazawa, p. 302).

## KYOTO (✽✽✽)

✽✽✽ **SANNENZAKA, NINENZAKA.** These secondary pilgrim's approaches to the popular Kiyomizu temple are beautifully preserved, their stone-paved streets lined with small inns and old Kyoto-style shops (p. 336).
**INE.** A fishing village on the Sea of Japan. The houses are built on stilts over water (p. 378).

## KINKI

✽ **IMAI.** An autonomous, walled merchant town during the Muromachi period, Imai is remarkably well preserved. Many houses date from the Edo period (p. 403).
✽✽ **YOSHINO.** This *monzenmachi* snakes along a narrow mountain ridge from the Shugendō headquarters of Kimpusen-ji toward sacred Mt. Ōmine. The houses are perched atop a steep ridge (p. 411).
**KŌBE.** Several restored Western houses are the city's main tourist attraction. The excellent City Museum has an impressive collection of Western-influenced art from the 16th and 17th centuries (p. 422).

## CHŪGOKU AND SHIKOKU

**\*\*\* Shikoku Mura.** Farmhouses of Shikoku (\* Takamatsu, p. 434).

**\*\* KOTOHIRA.** The long climb to the popular Kompira-san shrine is lined with inns and teahouses. If the climb proves daunting, there are palanquins to take you to the top (p. 435).

**# OKINOSHIMA.** A tiny island off southwest Shikoku. The houses are sheltered against typhoons by high stone walls (p. 437).

**\*\*\* KURASHIKI.** A popular town with many museums and which is itself a museum; white-washed rice storehouses line a scenic former transport canal (p. 438).

**\*\* FUKIYA.** Isolated mountain village that prospered from its copper mine and *bengara* (red ochre) factory—until the mines ran out. Fukiya became a ghost town, but now the fine ochre-stained houses are being restored. The countryside is beautiful (p. 440).

**\*\* TOMO NO URA.** A picturesque fishing village where Korean envoys in the Edo period enjoyed its "Chinese" landscape (p. 445).

**TAKEHARA.** A salt-producing town. Its old merchant houses and salt *kura* are now a pre-served zone (p. 447).

**\* UCHIKO.** Preserves a street of magnificent wax-merchants' homes from the early Meiji period (p. 453).

**# SOTODOMARI.** A remote fishing hamlet in southwest Shikoku (p. 454).

**# IWAIJIMA.** A tiny Inland Sea island with fine stone walls (p. 456).

## KYŪSHŪ

**\*\* NAGASAKI.** Japan's only open port for over two centuries, Nagasaki offers a charming blend of Western, Chinese, and Japanese cultures (p. 482).

**SAKITSU.** Crypto-Christians during the Edo period sought refuge in this isolated village (# Amakusa Islands, p. 489).

**\*\* CHIRAN.** A tea-growing village of samurai-farmers. Many of their houses have fine gardens. Chiran was a base for kamikaze pilots during World War II (p. 500).

**BŌNOTSU.** Secret port for the Satsuma fief's illegal trade with China (p. 502).

## OKINAWA

**\*\* Kumejima.** This Okinawa island was the center of the Ryūkyū Kingdom's silk trade. Kumejima's exquisite silk pongee is still woven at the village of Nakazato, where one can also see rows of Okinawan houses enclosed by hedges and stone walls (p. 520).

**\*\* TAKETOMI.** The best-preserved Okinawan village is situated on a tiny blossoming island in the midst of the Yaeyama islands. Local women weave *minsā* belts beneath the red-tile roofs (p. 523).

59

# Pilgrimage Bus Tours

The Iyo Rail Company in Matsuyama runs bus tours of the famous pilgrimage circuits in Japan. The most impressive tour is the **Saikoku Sanjūsankasho Junrei** (Western Japan Thirty-three Kannon temple circuit), which includes Himeji, Kyoto, Nara, Hikone, Daigo-ji, Uji, Nara, Asuka, Kumano, Ise, and Mt. Kōya on a whirlwind thirteen-day tour. Lodgings are at temples and ryokan. Some Japanese language abil-ity is essential, and you will spend twenty-four hours a day with a busload of jolly retirees. Cost is Y213,000. It includes transportation, lodgings, meals, and temple fees. The tour can be joined in Matsuyama, Takamatsu, Okayama, or Himeji, and ended in Ōsaka or Matsuyama. Departures Mar. 28, Apr. 7, May 27, Sept. 16, Oct. 16. Main office: 0899-48-3114. Tokyo: 03-3274-3681. Ōsaka: 06-344-2101.

# Villas and Gardens

> A house should be built with summer in mind. In winter it is possible to live any-
> where, but a badly made house is unbearable when it gets hot.
> —Yoshida Kenko, *Tsurezuregusa*
> (trans. Donald Keene)

The sophisticated Japanese house has always been open to the elements — frigid in winter,
pleasantly breezy in summer. Building materials are light to the point of flimsiness, and the
integration of house and garden has been a primary concern from classical times to the
present day. The European formal garden stretched expansively away from the residence;
the Japanese garden brought nature into the living space.

This interplay of garden and architecture owes much to the Shinto shrine. Early shrines
were not sacred halls but sacred spaces, marked off from the impure world only by
*shimenawa* ropes, torii gates, simple fences, or an expanse of white gravel. Only priests, who
had specially purified themselves, could cross these sacred delimiters and tread the hallowed
ground of the kami. Shrines began to change when the kami took on human characteristics.
This occurred in the early centuries A.D., when the emperors were apotheosized. Echoing this
change, Shinto shrines incorporated buildings, while imperial palaces, as abodes of a kami,
adopted the delimiters of the shrine. From the word *yuniwa*, meaning the sacred quadrangle
of white sand in a shrine or palace compound, comes the word *niwa*, or garden.

## PALACES AND GARDENS OF THE HEIAN NOBLES

### Heian Period (894–1185)

Under the influence of mainland culture, palace and shrine architecture diverged; by the
Nara and Heian periods, palaces were being built in formal Chinese style. The ornate HEIAN
SHRINE, a two-thirds scale replica of the Great Hall of State of the Heian Palace, conveys
something of the stiff formality of these ceremonial halls. The Japanese apparently found
such cavernous halls uncongenial; they have not been rebuilt for a thousand years. The
present formal halls of the KYOTO IMPERIAL PALACE (last rebuilt in 1855) evolved from
the emperor's everyday quarters. These were built in the **Shinden style** which, although it
owes much to continental architecture, was infused with the naturalness and simplicity of the
native esthetic. The Kyoto Imperial Palace, DAIKAKU-JI, and NINNA-JI all contain buildings
in a modified Shinden style.

### The Aristocratic Shinden Villa

No pure Shinden-style buildings remain, but scholars have reconstructed the general
appearance of ancient mansions from early picture scrolls and from excavations.
*Shinden* means "sleeping hall," and originally referred only to the central hall of the compound, where the master slept and entertained visitors. Extending out from the main *shinden*
hall were long, graceful, covered wooden corridors that connected to subsidiary wings where
wives and other dependents lived. Around each subsidiary pavilion, in the enclosed spaces
between buildings, were little gardens, called *tsubo* (pots or planters). Many of the women
in *The Tale of Genji*, the eleventh-century classic, are named after their place of residence:
Fujitsubo (Wisteria Pot), whose apartment looks out on a garden of wisteria vines; and
Akikonomu (Prefers Autumn), who has maples and other autumn trees in her garden.

That the amorous Genji was so easily able to gain access to the apartments of so many ladies was due not only to his irresistible charm, but also to the flimsiness of Shinden fixtures. Each hall had on all sides either hinged doors or reticulated shutters (*shitomido*), which during the summer were raised, leaving the interior open to the breezes. Bamboo blinds (*sudare*) were hung to give minimal privacy. Since it was considered indelicate for aristocratic ladies to be seen, they surrounded themselves with curtains and free-standing screens. Partitions, as well as tatami mats, which today help to define rooms in a Japanese house, were freely moved about in the *shinden* mansion. Two or three mats—either rectangular or round—were placed where people sat or slept. The rest of the floor was of bare polished wood. *The Tale of Genji* vividly describes the chilling drafts to which such structures were subject in winter.

### The Shinden Garden

According to Chinese geomantic rules, the main garden lay to the south of the master's hall. In the foreground was a courtyard, used for entertainments such as Gagaku and Bugaku (see Drama, p. 88). Beyond the courtyard was a garden consisting of a lake, islands, and bridges. From both ends of the hall, long covered corridors stretched down to the lake, terminating in the "fishing pavilion" on one side and the "spring pavilion" on the other. These open pavilions, built on stilts over the lake, offered relief from the summer heat. From them the master and his guests could watch Chinese-style dragon-boat races, drink saké, exchange poems, and enjoy the view.

A stream, coming from the northeast, meandered elegantly under the connecting corridors of the compound before it fed the lake, bringing the sound of rushing water to the various apartments, further uniting house and garden. The overall effect was of a lush, languid natural paradise. Yet it was anything but natural, since raw nature was abhorred. In these gardens every pebble and tuft of moss was arranged by a human hand. Considerable thought and effort went into achieving an idealized version of nature, as the *Sakuteiki*, an eleventh-century compilation of gardening rules reveals:

> The "large river style" (of stone arrangement) should have an appearance resembling the track left by a crawling dragon or serpent. Running water will damage what stands in its way, and banks and elevations would not keep their forms without stones ... [Water flowing downhill slowly modifies the character of the stream], so it is better to put stones in a manner so that the feeling gradually changes ... White sand should be placed where [the stream] is ... wide and the water flows gently. (Excerpted in *A Guide to the Gardens of Kyoto*, by Marc Treib and Ron Herman.)

61

### Amida Halls and Paradise Gardens

In the late Heian period, when the Jōdo, or Pure Land, Buddhist sect became influential among the aristocracy, wealthy believers incorporated Pure Land pavilions and paradise gardens into their estates. They created three-dimensional renderings of Amida mandalas showing Amida Buddha in his Pure Land across the mythical Western Ocean. BYŌDŌ-IN, located south of Kyoto, was built on the estate of an eleventh-century FUJIWARA regent. It remains the oldest and best surviving example of an Amida hall (see Buddhism, p. 37).

Facing east, Byōdō-in's Phoenix Hall and the Amida statue inside it are mirrored in a pond that represents the Western Ocean (fig. 30). Beyond the ocean lies the profane world of humankind. This eastern orientation distinguishes the Amida Halls from most temples, which, like the *shinden*, face south. The Phoenix Hall is like a stage set, a full-scale mockup of the palaces pictured in the Amida mandala, which is itself inspired by a Tang Chinese palace. Both the Amidist temple and its Chinese prototype have a principal hall flanked by ornate wings. In the Japanese version, however, the wings have no function; they exist solely to represent accurately the image of the mandala. The wisteria bowers and willows around the pond add a gentle sensuality to the scene. Hōkai-ji, also near Uji, and the ruins of MŌTSŪ-JI in Tōhoku are other examples of Paradise pavilions that were originally private chapels. JŌRURI-JI, near Nara, is a more complex paradise garden, enshrining several different Buddhas around a central pond.

Figure 30. Byōdō-in

# SUNG PAVILIONS AND ROCK LANDSCAPES
## Muromachi Period (1334–1573)

Starting in the Kamakura period, Zen Buddhism and Chinese Sung culture exerted a profound influence on Japan. Sung landscape paintings portrayed China's remote and craggy mountains, and the lesson they taught was of human insignificance and vulnerability in the face of nature; dizzying cliffs jut up to the sky, dwarfing tiny pavilions and antlike humans. Not surprisingly, this imagery was taken up by garden designers. During the Muromachi period, pictorial art and gardening became as closely tied as they were ever to become. SESSHŪ, Japan's most famous ink painter, designed several gardens for his patrons, the Ōuchi lords of Yamaguchi, during the late fifteenth century.

The influential Zen priest MUSŌ SOSEKI was among the first to carry Sung painting into garden design; his broad interpretation of Zen principles led him to promote the idea that gardens could be an aid to meditation. His earliest garden, ZUISEN-JI in Kamakura, consists of a simple pond, devoid of greenery, next to a rocky cliff in which there is a cave for meditation. When Musō came to Kyoto, he converted two older gardens. One, a paradise garden, became SAIHŌ-JI; the other, an old *shinden* garden, became TENRYŪ-JI. The major innovation in Tenryū-ji's garden is the painterly composition of upward-jutting rocks at the rear of the pond. There is also a Dragon's Gate, named after the cascade on China's Yellow River where a legendary carp swam up the fall and was transformed into a dragon, the symbol of the emperor. Saihō-ji, in contrast, with its lush trees, murky pond, and emerald-green moss, seems to bear no relation to later Zen gardens. Yet the essence is there. In a corner of the garden Musō arranged boulders as though to receive a nonexistent waterfall and placed a boulder nearby where he could sit in meditation.

62

At Saihō-ji, Musō built the Ruriden, or Lapis-lazuli Hall, a two-storied pavilion modeled on those depicted in Sung paintings. The Ruriden did not survive the vicissitudes of later eras, but it left its mark on the design of the famed Golden Pavilion of KINKAKU-JI (fig. 31), built by the third ASHIKAGA shogun YOSHIMITSU, and on the Silver Pavilion of GINKAKU-JI, built by the eighth Ashikaga shogun YOSHIMASA. The Golden Pavilion is noted for the delicacy of its proportions and is an innovative fusion of the older idioms of *shinden* and paradise hall with features from the new Zen style, such as the cusped window (see Buddhism, p. 39). It was dedicated to Amida, but also served, much like the ancient "fishing pavilion" of the *shinden* palace, as a place for the entertainment of guests. A small dock extends from the ground floor so that guests could board boats and make expeditions around the pond. In the 1480s, Yoshimasa, imitating his grandfather Yoshimitsu, built the Silver Pavilion to provide a setting for his own esthetic pursuits. Yoshimasa's Higashiyama (Eastern Mountain) culture saw the emergence of the tea ceremony and flower arrangement as independent arts. The Silver Pavilion is a more modest private hall dedicated to Kannon; its garden, a fascinating juxtaposition of pure sand and lush plantings, seems to have come from a later period. Both the Golden and Silver Pavilions stood amid larger villa complexes that have all but disappeared.

Figure 31. Kinkaku-ji

Figure 32. Daisen-in

Around 1480, **Sōami**, one of Yoshimasa's official painters and connoisseurs, is said to have cooperated with his friend, the priest Kogaku, to build one of Japan's earliest and most famous "dry landscape" gardens (*karesansui*) at the abbot's residence of DAISEN-IN, a subtemple of Daitoku-ji. This garden is a Sung painting executed in rock and sand (fig. 32). It portrays Mt. Hōrai, home of the Taoist immortals, a river, and a "treasure boat," represented by an unusually shaped rock. Like a painting, this garden is an object of meditation; it cannot be entered, but instead is viewed from the veranda. Another famous *karesansui* garden, attributed to the painter KANŌ MOTONOBU, is at TAIZŌ-IN, a subtemple of Myōshin-ji.

Roughly contemporaneous with Daisen-in is another precedent-breaking dry garden, the abbot's garden at RYŌAN-JI. Unlike Daisen-in, which literally represents a landscape, Ryōan-ji is almost abstract. It is a quietly authoritative composition of five groupings of small dark rocks embedded in raked white gravel and framed by a rectangular earthen wall. Each group alternates between an upward and a horizontal thrust; complex linear relations exist between stones in each grouping. Because the garden was built during the chaotic period after the Ōnin Wars (1467–1477), its exact age and creator are unknown. The nature of those troubled times may have influenced the garden's designer, whoever he was, to eschew facile representations and aim for something deeper, closer to the essence of the Zen spirit.

# THE WORLD INSIDE THE ZEN SUBTEMPLE
## Muromachi to Early Edo Periods (1333–1615)

Under the influence of Musō Soseki and later priests, followers of the Rinzai sect of Zen ventured more deeply into the arts — ink painting, calligraphy, gardening, and the tea ceremony. Just as religious teachings were handed down from teacher to pupil, so the same was done with artistic traditions. For this reason, artistic achievements often occurred inside the *tatchū*, subtemples where individual abbots lived independently. These *tatchū*, particularly at temples such as DAITOKU-JI, MYŌSHIN-JI, and NANZEN-JI, have become great repositories of ink paintings, tea arbors, and gardens. The abbots' residences are called *hōjō*, literally "ten-foot-square huts," a name that often belies their luxurious appointments.

Each *hōjō* had to have its garden, usually a dry landscape like those at Daisen-in and Ryōan-ji. Eventually the gardens became conventionalized, the work of professional gardeners rather than the esthetic expression of priests and painters. Although these later gardens were often superb examples of decorative technique, they had less of the artistic power of the earlier ones. The best of the later gardens remained the work of artists; the garden at KONCHI-IN (in Nanzen-ji), designed by tea master and garden designer KOBORI ENSHŪ in the early Edo period, combines a "sea" of sand with a "mountain" of Enshū's characteristic clipped hedges. The nearby HŌJŌ of Nanzen-ji has a good example of a more conventional dry garden of the same period.

### Shoin Architecture

The Shoin (writing hall) style developed in the *hōjō* (which are among the oldest surviving residences in Japan). The *shoin* was originally a small, private study for the abbot that looked out on a garden. The finest room of the abbot's residence, it evolved into an audience chamber for important guests. It was in the *shoin* that many of the familiar features of Japanese interiors developed: floors completely covered by tatami mats placed in fixed arrangements; the *tokonoma* alcove; sliding screens (*fusuma*) to divide rooms; wood-latticed paper windows (*shōji*); and wooden outer shutters (*amado*) to protect the paper from the elements. The *shoin* had a raised area, called *jōdan no ma*, which was reserved for people of high status. The dimensions of tatami mats, columns, bays, and windows were all set according to fixed proportions, presaging Japan's famed modular system of architecture.

The earliest surviving *shoin* is also Japan's oldest tea arbor, the DŌJIN-SAI (shown by application) at Ginkaku-ji, the temple of the Silver Pavilion. The Dōjin-sai, a room in the Tōgu-dō hall, was built for Japan's first famous tea master, Murata Shukō (see p. 65). It included *chigaidana* (staggered shelves) and a built-in desk, called a *tsuke-shoin*, that resembles a wide windowsill or bench. The *tsuke-shoin* is set against a large window overlooking a garden, so that the abbot could reflect on the beauties of nature as he studied or wrote.

The mature *shoin* interior included not only the desk and shelves, but also the *tokonoma* alcove and the *chōdaigamae* decorative doors. The *chōdaigamae* originated as armored doors to a protected bedchamber, but by the time they had been incorporated into *shoin* architecture, they had become decorative elements. The *tokonoma* evolved from a small altar used in temples. Like the desk and shelves, it was originally movable but gradually came to be built into a wall. The position of the four *shoin* elements came to be rigidly fixed at the back of the room, around the *jōdan no ma*. The *tokonoma* and the *chigaidana* occupy the back wall of the room, the *chōdaigamae* are on the right-hand wall, and, opposite, on the left-hand wall, is the *tsuke-shoin* (see fig. 33).

The most elaborate temple *shoin* are found not in Zen subtemples, but in Esoteric Buddhist temples. These, with their aristocratic associations, often played host to high court nobles and other important guests. The most famous is at KANGAKU-IN, a subtemple of

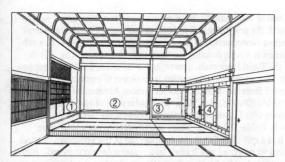

Figure 33. Shoin interior

① tsukeshoin
② tokonoma
③ chigaidana
④ chōdaigamae

Miidera (ca. 1601), a portion of which has been replicated at New York's Metropolitan Museum of Art. Unfortunately, Kangaku-in can be seen only by appointment. One fine example that is open to the public is at KANCHI-IN, a subtemple of Kyoto's Tō-ji.

# THE WARRIOR MANSION—THE GRAND SHOIN AND ITS GARDEN

## Momoyama and Edo Periods (1573–1868)

From the end of the Muromachi period, the grand reception rooms of warrior mansions began to incorporate the Shoin style. Meetings and alliances became increasingly important during this and the following Momoyama periods, and the Shoin style maintained the fiction of intimacy—even though such meetings were often strained—while clearly separating ranks. The lord sat on the *jōdan no ma*, which provided a properly impressive frame, with its coffered ceiling and lavishly constructed *tokonoma* and *chigaidana*; retainers and other inferiors sat before him on a lower level. The function of a *shoin* as a place for contemplation disappeared. The four *shoin* elements were now built to impress, rather than to be used. The intimate alcove for the *tsuke-shoin* disappeared, and the desk became a mere decoration; its window faced a dark hallway instead of the garden. Conversely, the *chōdaigamae* doors found a new purpose—behind them, in dark, windowless rooms, bodyguards were poised to rescue their lord in case of trouble.

The layout of the warrior mansion as a whole was likewise built with defense in mind. In the violence and insecurity of the Kamakura and Muromachi periods, the expansive Shinden-style mansion became impractical. Warrior mansions became more compact; separate wings were linked either by short hallways or directly at the corners, rather than by long, exposed corridors. In place of several entrances at the side of the compound, as in the *shinden*, the warrior mansion had a single ostentatious entrance; in front of it was a large gate and an enclosed courtyard that could be defended easily.

The final development of the Shoin style in the Momoyama and early Edo periods integrated the layout of the samurai mansion and the *shoin* interior. The classic example is the NINOMARU PALACE of Nijō-jō, which acquired its present form under TOKUGAWA IEMITSU in the 1620s. One of the innovations of this palace was a covered carriage approach to shelter visitors from the elements while they removed their footwear; this is the ancestor of the *genkan*, the entrance hall of the modern Japanese house. The zigzag arrangement of halls contains four *shoin* lavishly decorated with coffered ceilings, elaborate bronze nail covers, and *fusuma* (sliding doors) painted by the finest painters of the age. The other outstanding example of the grand Shoin style is the SHIRO SHOIN at Nishi Hongan-ji in Kyoto.

The warriors also appropriated the rock garden as a form of display. Fine garden rocks were difficult to find and a lot of trouble to transport. In the Muromachi period, they became objects of great value, traded among warlords as gifts, wrapped in silk and accompanied by processions. The antithesis of the austere Zen rock garden was reached at SAMBŌ-IN, a subtemple at Daigo-ji that was refurbished by TOYOTOMI HIDEYOSHI in 1598. This garden contains nearly eight hundred valuable rocks; but although they are cleverly placed, the arrangement is restless and obtrusive, rather than calm and focused. At Nijō-jō too, the Ninomaru Palace opens onto a garden, supposedly supervised by Kobori Enshū, which features massive groupings of upright rocks.

The Ninomaru Palace set the standard for formal palaces and mansions throughout the Edo period. Today, few traces of these mansions survive. Instead, it is the more informal *sukiya shoin*, influenced by the tea ceremony, that has endured and has continuing relevance in private Japanese houses today.

# THE TEA HUT AND ITS GARDEN

## Late Muromachi and Momoyama Periods (1422–1615)

It is because tea served as an aid in staying awake during long meditations that the histories of tea and Zen are so closely intertwined. According to legend, when Daruma (Bodhidharma) brought Zen from India to China, he carried tea plants with him. An early form of the tea ceremony is still carried out in Zen monasteries of Japan in honor of Daruma. The Sung Chinese method of powdering tea, and the strain of tea plant needed for it, are thought to have been introduced by Eisai, founder of Japan's Rinzai sect of Zen, when he returned from China in 1191. *Matcha*—leaf-green tea, thick like Turkish coffee and whipped to a froth—is still used in the Japanese tea ceremony. This method of preparing tea, long extinct in China, survives in Japan, like so many other arts, as a kind of living cultural fossil.

In the middle of the fifteenth century lived the eccentric priest **Ikkyū**, the unrecognized son of an emperor. Although he was abbot of Daitoku-ji, he spent most of his time at the wine-shops, brothels, and rollicking "tea parties" of the prosperous merchant town of Sakai, south of present-day Ōsaka. At these tea parties, which Ikkyū's disciple **Murata Shukō** (1422–1502) also attended, merchants who were engaged in the China trade showed off their precious celadons and other imported treasures. Ikkyū, who in typical Zen fashion always railed against the hypocritical "wooden Zen" of the Kyoto monasteries, told Shukō to forget about Zen and just make tea. Then he presented Shukō with a valuable Chinese scroll, a customary parting gift given by a Zen master to his disciple, and admonished Shukō to give the tea ceremony the same intense, focused attention Zen monks had earlier given to painting, gardening, and calligraphy. Ikkyū's gift supposedly set a precedent for using calligraphy, rather than landscapes, to decorate the *tokonoma* of the tea arbor.

From Daitoku-ji, to this day a mecca of tea culture, "Shukō's way" spread to the **Higashiyama circle** at Ginkaku-ji. The shogun Yoshimasa is said to have built the Dōjin-sai, mentioned previously as an early example of the Shoin style, especially for Shukō to use in the tea ceremony. The Dōjin-sai is the first known tea arbor, and it embodies the now-canonical arrangement of four-and-a-half tatami mats. This arrangement is supposed to be the same size as the home of the Indian merchant Yuima (Vimalarkti), who appears in a sutra of the same name. Wealthy though he was, he lived as an ideal lay Buddhist in a "ten-foot-square hut."

## Wabi Tea and the Tea Arbor

Although—or more likely because—the tea ceremony attracted such powerful patrons, tea masters stressed the humble and plain: the rustic hermitage and the imperfectly formed bowl. A Sakai merchant named **Takeno Jō-ō** (1504–1555) and his famous pupil, SEN NO RIKYŪ (1522–1591), are credited with perfecting **wabi tea**, which stressed extreme simplicity. Central to *wabi* is the idea of *mitate*, or "reseeing," an awareness of beauty in unexpected forms. Crude Korean peasant rice bowls were admired for their uncontrived beauty and became the standard for the *wabi* tea bowl. The only tea arbor attributed with certainty to Rikyū is TAI-AN, a tiny hut only two tatami mats in size, built in the *sōan*, or "grass hut" style. The *sōan* is a *mitate* of the rustic farmhouse. Through subtle artifice, it is made to transcend its humble origins and become something infinitely more sophisticated.

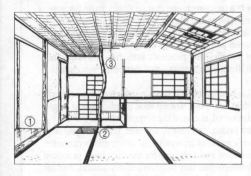

Figure 34. Tea arbor interior

① tokonoma
② fire pit
③ nakabashira

When visiting a tea hut, you should note some typical features (see fig. 34). The *nijiriguchi* is a square aperture barely two feet high through which guests crawl on hands and knees, equally humble regardless of rank, and which reminds all who enter to leave behind excess baggage—in former times, swords, and today, briefcases, jewelry, and especially wristwatches—that might disrupt the spirit of harmony within. Certain tea masters have considered some guests "more equal than others," however, and have installed a taller entrance for persons of high rank. A square is cut in the tatami for the fire pit; in summer, a brazier is substituted. The *tokonoma* alcove, like that in the *shoin*, evolved from a type of small Buddhist altar; the hanging scroll in the alcove is, like a Buddhist image, complemented by flowers. According to one tale, TOYOTOMI HIDEYOSHI invited himself to Rikyū's tea arbor to see the master's much-talked-about garden of morning glories. When he arrived, however, the vines had been stripped of their flowers; he stormed into the tea hut, and was stopped short by the sight of a single perfect blossom, floating in a bowl of water. Unlike the monumental arrangements found on Buddhist altars, tea flowers are arranged as modestly and naturally as possible.

There is a separate room for the host's preparations; it contains the *mizuya*, a corner equipped with shelves and a bamboo drainboard. The host's entrance is separated from the tea room by a "sleeve wall" stretching across the upper space between two posts. The free end of this sleeve wall is called the *nakabashira*, or central pillar. It serves little structural purpose, but is considered the spiritual and esthetic focus of the tea hut. It is often left in its natural state—barks, kinks, and all.

The construction of a tea arbor poses intricate problems in both design and execution. The humble and ordinary materials of rustic huts—mud and wattle, bamboo, unvarnished woods, paper, and thatch—are finished with exquisite care to bring alive the innate beauty of natural grains and textures. The vine frame for the tea hut's mud walls is often left exposed in windows, forming a pleasing, yet seemingly accidental, decorative lattice. The limited space of the tea arbor calls for subtle ingenuity. Windows, for example, of which there are several types, with no set rules on number or combination, are placed with painstaking consideration for the lighting conditions that prevail at the site during certain seasons or hours of the day. Considerations of overall esthetic balance became so complex that paper models, called *okoshiezu*, were invented to ensure that the tea hut really achieved the effects its designer intended before the expense of building was undertaken.

The tea hut, small as it is, brought a revolution in architecture. Previously, buildings had consisted of a conventional shell, suitably divided into rooms. Tea architecture grew from the inside out, redefining a building as an ensemble of rooms suited to personal taste. The *sukiya shoin* continued this revolution on a larger scale.

# The Tea Ceremony

Make a delicious bowl of tea; lay the charcoal so that it heats the water; arrange the flowers as they are in the field; in summer suggest coolness, in winter, warmth; do everything ahead of time; prepare for rain; and give those with whom you find yourself every consideration.
— *The Seven Rules of Sen no Rikyū*

At the 1872 Kyoto International Exposition, the URA SENKE school of tea, or *chanoyu*, offered a new tea ceremony using stools and benches. The objective was to give Westerners participating in the tea ceremony "every consideration." And since the publication in 1906 of *The Book of Tea*, Okakura Kakuzō's apologia for Eastern culture written for a Western audience, the tea ceremony has been offered as a microcosm of Japanese culture, a paradigm of a certain ethic of harmony and tranquility.

To call *chanoyu* a ceremony is a misnomer, one that no doubt arose because of the ritualistic way in which every movement and phrase is rigidly prescribed. The guests move from garden to tea hut, admire the scroll, with its suitably seasonal aphorism, and receive their dry sweets and tea. A series of signals is exchanged between guests and host to ensure that the event proceeds smoothly. Everything follows a prescribed sequence, much like the conventions that dictate the movements in Noh drama and the martial arts.

What, one might ask, does this have to do with serenity, tranquility, or "international understanding"? Since the Meiji era, when women took up *chanoyu* in large numbers, it has sometimes been dismissed as one of the genteel arts, part of the mandatory trousseau of prospective brides. At its ideal, however, this elaborate step-by-step ritual is supposed to induce a mood of tranquility, in which minds can meet. Although the set movements are awkward and confining for the untrained, practiced hands can execute them with such finesse that they become entirely natural. And for the Japanese, who loath social awkwardness, the prescribed formality ensures that there will be no misunderstanding or hesitation before serenity descends on the small group of friends enjoying the tea together. The ritual is a preliminary designed to achieve a creative unfolding of the moment, what tea men refer to as *sabi*, or patina (literally "rust"). The gathering moves toward a certain informality, as guests converse, unburdened of their everyday cares. Some compare *chanoyu* to Zen meditation. At the very least, in a society where the individual is hemmed in by duties and obligations, *chanoyu* provided—and in traditional circles, still provides—a sophisticated escape from these strictures.

For the tourist, opportunities to partake of *chanoyu* are understandably limited. The Ura Senke headquarters in Kyoto offers weekly lecture-demonstrations. Some luxury tourist hotels in Tokyo and Kyoto offer regular demonstrations. As a foreigner, you are not expected to know the procedure; just relax and copy the guest who preceded you. (Guests are served one by one, from the person closest to the host.) Some pointers: Eat your sweet while the host is preparing your tea. When the tea is placed before you, take up the bowl and turn it ninety degrees clockwise before sipping. (This is called "declining to drink from the front of the bowl"—a gesture of humility and respect.) After draining the bowl, cradle it in both hands and silently admire its beauty before returning the bowl.

### The Roji, or "Dewy Path"

The tea ceremony brought motion back into the garden. In the tea ceremony, the mood progresses from formal to informal, from *shin* to *gyō* to *sō* (formal, semiformal, and informal), terms borrowed from calligraphy. A similar progression from formal to informal can be seen in the *roji*, or "dewy path," the small tea garden so economical in its use of space that most people think of it as little more than a path of steppingstones, as its name implies. As in the case of the tea arbor, appearances are deceptive; the tiny *roji* transformed the Japanese garden. The Zen dry garden evolved to the point where it could be viewed only from fixed vantage points. The *roji* preserves tight control over a succession of small views, experienced by those who walk through it. Each effect is carefully designed to transport the viewer from the cares of everyday life into the world of tea.

One should imagine the steppingstones of the *roji* shining darkly with water, sprinkled by the host as a silent message of welcome. Among them might be a millstone or foundation stone, humble, functional stones that were a *mitate* of the host. Steppingstones placed at irregular intervals, called *tobi-ishi*, force the viewer to look down and watch his step, and then look up and view this millstone — or perhaps a stone lantern taken from an old temple — in a new light. An "informal" steppingstone might be balanced by a more "formal" stone bridge; lanterns, as well, come in *shin*, *gyō*, and *sō* varieties. The hard-packed earth is swept clean, but always retains a few fallen leaves or other suggestions of the season, of life and decay. The few other components include a bench for waiting guests, a stone basin of water with a stone to crouch on while rinsing one's hands and mouth, and a stone on which to rest a candle for evening tea.

The transition achieved by the *roji* is subtle. It dispenses with sweeping views, stone arrangements, and exotic plants in favor of that which is modest, natural, and in keeping with present time and place — by the tenets of tea, the most true and beautiful. Sweeping, dramatic transitions would develop with the *sukiya* and the Edo-period stroll garden.

67

# VILLAS AND GARDENS OF EDO-PERIOD LORDS
### Edo Period (1615–1868)

After Sen no Rikyū's death — he was ordered to commit *seppuku* by Hideyoshi — widely varied tea styles developed according to the tastes and predilections of various masters. Among them were HON'AMI KŌETSU, Rikyū's grandson **Sen no Sōtan**, who founded the three Senke schools of tea ceremony, and **Furuta Oribe**. Oribe created a fanciful tea ceremony that incorporated such quirks as crooked *tokobashira* (the column in the *tokonoma*) and an appealing and colorful tea pottery that bears his name. He and his pupil KOBORI ENSHŪ developed a dazzling tea for the upper classes (they were themselves daimyo), incorporating elements from the extravagant *shoin* and gardens of formal warrior mansions. Emperors, shogun, daimyo, and court aristocrats adopted Enshū's style as a standard for their own private villas. These villas, called *sukiya*, combined the principles and tastes of the tea ceremony with luxury, and were designed from the inside out, like tea arbors. Each was one-of-a-kind, an often whimsical expression of the owner-designer's personal taste.

### The Sukiya Shoin

The two characters that form the word *suki* are said to have been inscribed by Murata Shukō on the plaque of an early tea arbor. Together, they constitute a pun meaning both "asymmetry" and "personal taste." Although *sukiya* was originally used to refer to a building in which the tea ceremony takes place, the *sukiya shoin* specifically denotes the early Edo-period application of tea taste to the Shoin style: light openwork replaces ornate carving on the transoms, poetic ink landscapes replace gilded bird-and-flower screens, and light, unbevelled posts — often unfinished — replace sturdy square pillars. Great sums were lavished on rare, top-quality materials, laboriously finished to bring out their innate perfection. The rigid, symmetrical arrangement of the four *shoin* features — decorative alcove and shelves at the back, desk and *chōdaigamae* doors balancing each other on the right and left, goes pleasingly awry in this house of asymmetry. The *chōdaigamae* disappear, while the three other elements are arranged freely, often ingeniously. The shelves were redesigned with particular cleverness, and become a real delight to the eye.

The classic *sukiya* mansion is the KATSURA IMPERIAL VILLA, built by a noble family during the first half of the seventeenth century. The leisure of the owner-designers, who were barred from politics, is apparent in the villa's exquisite details. Not only each room, but each nail cover, transom, and door pull is an individualized work of art. Katsura became famous in the 1930s because it conformed to modern European architectural theories; it created sophisticated interior spaces, used natural materials, was deceptively simple in form, and, most important, skillfully blended house and garden (fig. 35). With the exception of its interior spaces, however, Katsura is merely the culmination of themes that have been present in Japanese architecture since the *shinden* mansion; as Fosco Maraini put it, "the Japanese have always been modern."

Whereas the formal *shoin*, with their opulent audience rooms, were built exclusively by the elite, the Sukiya style crossed class barriers. Although it took considerable wealth to afford a *sukiya* mansion, such mansions were built by prosperous townsmen as well as by emperors, court nobles, and samurai. A modified, gaudier version of the Sukiya style became the rule for the *chaya* (teahouses), which were *maisons de rendezvous* for geisha and other

Figure 35. Katsura Rikyū

68

Figure 36. Shūgaku-in Rikyū

female entertainers; the Sukiya-style rooms of the SUMIYA in Kyoto's Shimabara quarter are famous for the delicate patterning on window screens and transoms. Although nobody builds formal *shoin* any more, the *sukiya* continues to exert its influence on the humblest abodes as well as on the most elegant traditional houses and inns.

### The Stroll Garden

The stroll garden, which complemented the *sukiya* villa, combined the showy magnificence of warrior gardens such as Sambō-in and Nijō-jō with the principles of movement and *mitate* found in the *roji* tea garden. Instead of directing the viewer's attention to a humble object such as a millstone, the garden path takes the stroller through a succession of scenes and panoramas. Kobori Enshū, the putative inventor of this style, designed the stroll garden at Kyoto's SENTŌ GOSHO (Retired Emperor's Palace) in collaboration with Emperor Go-Mizuno'o. Go-Mizuno'o went on to design the breathtaking grounds of SHŪGAKU-IN IMPERIAL VILLA (fig. 36). Enshū may have given advice on the garden at Katsura, although he probably did not actually design it. Katsura's aristocratic founder, Prince Toshihito, was one of the most cultured men in Japan, deeply versed in the literature of the Heian period, when the nobility still ruled as well as reigned; subtle allusions to classical poetry and *The Tale of Genji* are scattered throughout the garden.

The provincial daimyo also built stroll gardens for their private *sukiya* retreats. Whereas Katsura alludes to Heian-period literature, the daimyo gardens seem to favor the Chinese classics. The Mito Tokugawa, who were interested in combining Chinese Confucianism with native Shinto traditions, filled Tokyo's Kōraku-en with miniature versions of famous scenes of China and Japan and loaded the garden with allusions to Confucian aphorisms. Daimyo stroll gardens were built for display and pleasure, on huge plots of land. Their artificial hills, lakes, huge stone bridges, and many lanterns tend to produce an impression of sumptuousness and cleverness of design, rather than of artistic depth. The best, such as Kanazawa's KENROKU-EN, Takamatsu's RITSURIN KŌEN, Okayama's KŌRAKU-EN, and Kumamoto's SUIZEN-JI, are wonderful exercises in pure landscaping.

# SOME DESIGN PRINCIPLES

**Mt. Hōrai.** A focal element, usually a rock, symbolizing the legendary island peak of the Taoist immortals (or Mt. Sumeru, the central mountain of the Buddhist cosmos). Often combined with a rock symbolizing a bridge, over which only the worthy ones can cross.

**Tortoise and crane.** A pair of rocks, islets, or trees—one low, one high—corresponding to these Chinese symbols of longevity.

**Shin-gyō-sō.** The trichotomy of formal, semiformal, and informal, which originated in the various styles of calligraphy and was borrowed by the tea ceremony. In the tea garden, this concept is applied to achieve a transition from the formal exterior to the informal interior. Katsura Villa is famous for the *shin-gyō-sō* progression of its garden path. The beginning consists of a regular pavement (*shin*), then changes to irregular (*gyō*), and ends in mere steppingstones (*sō*).

**Hide-and-reveal.** The careful placement of hedges, buildings, and other obstructions to control the way in which garden elements are revealed. The entrance to Kyoto's Ginkaku-ji, for example, passes through a corridor of stone walls and towering hedges. Bends in the path prevent views into the garden, and when the path finally opens onto the garden area, the view is again partially obstructed by a white wall with a bell-shaped window, giving a glimpse of the garden beyond. This sophisticated combination of elements successfully bridges the space, mental and physical, between the busy shop-lined street outside and the cloistered serenity of the garden. The path to the upper garden at Shūgaku-in, where spaces suddenly open up to reveal a spectacular view, is another superb example.

**Shakkei (borrowed scenery).** The use of distant scenery which is not physically a part of the garden but becomes a part of the total effect. The dry gardens of Zen *hōjō* often employ a high wall to block out undesirable elements in the middle distance, such as neighboring buildings, thereby juxtaposing the garden with a distant view. ENTSŪ-JI and SHŌDEN-JI both use this technique to incorporate Kyoto's Mt. Hiei, which looms in the background. In the famous view from Shūgaku-in's Upper Villa, the embankment of an artificial lake blocks out undesirable elements; the lake blends with Kyoto's northern mountains across the valley. This carefully orchestrated view is especially spectacular during the autumn, when it becomes a blaze of color.

**Seasons.** In the tea ceremony, only fresh flowers and calligraphy scrolls that pertain to the season are appropriate. Although certain gardens are deemed to be at their best in a particular season—Shūgaku-in in autumn, for example—in principle a garden should adapt to the beauties of every season, even those known for inclement weather. Ryōan-ji's garden is considered at its best when its rocks are darkened by rain. Kinkaku-ji is considered at its most beautiful after a snowfall.

69

# VILLA AND GARDEN STYLES: A SUMMARY

### Buildings

**Tang Chinese palace style.** A symmetrical, monumental style, used for the formal halls of the Heian-period imperial palace. Heian Shrine and, indirectly, Byōdō-in, are replicas.

**Shinden style.** The open, flowing style of Heian-period aristocratic mansions. No authentic examples remain today. (The term *shinden* literally means "sleeping hall," and sometimes refers to any sleeping quarter.)

**Shoin style.** Originally developed as the study for a temple abbott, the Shoin style became the preferred formal style in the Edo period. A formal *shoin* consists of a rigid arrangement of *tokonoma*, *chōdaigamae*, *chigaidana*, and *tsuke-shoin*. The style was adopted for warrior palaces such as Nijō-jō.

**Sukiya Shoin, or Sukiya style.** A freer, lighter version of the formal Shoin style favored for informal retreats. (Confusingly, the term *sukiya* can also refer to any kind of tea arbor, while individual rooms in the Sukiya style are often called *shoin* or even *shinden*.)

**Tea huts.** The Sōan style was invented for *wabi* tea arbors, which are based on the farmhouse and rustic retreat, and are usually four-and-a-half mats in size. Tea arbors are also built in the Shoin and Sukiya styles.

### Gardens

**Shinden garden.** A courtyard-and-pond garden, with "spring pavilions" and "fishing pavilions" at the water's edge, all devised for aristocratic entertainments. Only ruins and reconstructions of such gardens remain.

**Paradise garden.** The dominant style in the late Heian and Kamakura periods, this kind of garden has a pavilion that represents the palace of Amida, and a pond that represents the Western Ocean.

**Zen garden.** Gardens designed for Zen meditation. Early Zen gardens were adaptations of the previous styles, but placed greater emphasis on rock and terrain than on vegetation. Dry landscape gardens (*karesansui*) include rock-and-sand renderings of Sung-style ink paintings, as well as more abstract compositions, such as the celebrated garden at Ryōan-ji. These gardens are usually confined to a sharply delimited rectangle, surrounded by a wall on three sides and a veranda on the fourth.

**Tea garden (roji).** The small garden and path of steppingstones that constitute the approach to the tea hut.

**Stroll garden.** A large garden, built by Edo-period daimyo and aristocrats, which consists of a succession of carefully orchestrated views.

# BEST VILLAS AND GARDENS

Unless otherwise indicated, all of the following gardens are in Kyoto. Note: † means permission is required from the Imperial Household Agency (see p. 330).

## HEIAN SHINDEN PALACES (RECONSTRUCTIONS)
† ✳✳ **KYOTO IMPERIAL PALACE.** Rebuilt in the late Edo period (p. 331).
✳✳ **HEIAN JINGŪ.** This shrine is a two-thirds scale reconstruction of the Great Hall of State of the Heian-period imperial palace, set in a reconstructed garden (p. 340).
✳✳ **NINNA-JI.** Meiji-era reconstruction (p. 356).
✳✳ **DAIKAKU-JI.** *Shinden* halls were formerly at the Kyoto Imperial palace (p. 360).

## PARADISE GARDENS
✳✳ **MŌTSŪ-JI.** Ruins of a 12th-century garden (in ✳✳ Hiraizumi, Tōhoku, p. 171).
✳✳✳ **BYŌDŌ-IN.** Phoenix Hall modeled on Tang palaces (in ✳✳✳ Uji, Kinki, p. 386).
✳✳ **JŌRURI-JI.** Unusual paradise hall housing nine Amidas (in ✳✳✳ Nara, Kinki, p. 398).

## SUNG-STYLE PAVILIONS AND LANDSCAPES
✳ **ZUISEN-JI.** An early garden by Musō Soseki (in ✳✳✳ Kamakura, Kantō, p. 263).
✳✳ **TENRYŪ-JI.** Large pond garden restored by Musō Soseki (p. 358).
✳✳✳ **SAIHŌ-JI.** Famous "Moss Garden"; contains an early dry landscape (p. 363).
✳✳✳ **KINKAKU-JI.** The Golden Pavilion (rebuilt), famous for its perfect form (p. 354).
✳✳✳ **GINKAKU-JI.** The Silver Pavilion; unique garden (p. 343).
✳✳✳ **RYŌAN-JI.** The quintessential abstract rock garden (p. 355).
✳✳✳ **DAITOKU-JI, DAISEN-IN.** Celebrated dry landscape (p. 352).
✳✳ **MYŌSHIN-JI, TAIZŌ-IN.** Dry garden ascribed to the painter Kanō Motonobu (p. 356).

## TEMPLE SHOIN AND HŌJŌ GARDENS
✳✳✳ **TŌ-JI, KANCHI-IN.** A fine example of a Momoyama-period temple *shoin* (p. 325).
✳✳ **NANZEN-JI, KONCHI-IN.** Garden likely to have been designed by Kobori Enshū (p. 341).
✳✳ **NANZEN-JI HŌJŌ.** A conventional late Zen garden (p. 341).
✳✳✳ **DAITOKU-JI.** Numerous examples of Zen *shoin* architecture and gardens (p. 352).
✳✳ **MYŌSHIN-JI.** Major Zen monastery with excellent architecture and gardens (p. 356).
✳✳✳ **MII-DERA, KANGAKU-IN and Kōjō-in.** These subtemples have two of the finest examples of temple *shoin*. By appointment only (in ✳ Ōtsu, p. 377).

## THE GRAND SHOIN AND GARDEN
✳✳✳ **Zuigan-ji.** Opulent Momoyama-period *shoin* halls (in ✳ Matsushima, Tōhoku, p. 179).
✳✳✳ **NIJŌ-JŌ, NINOMARU PALACE.** The Tokugawa palace in Kyoto (p. 329).
✳✳ **NISHI HONGAN-JI, SHIRO SHOIN.** Sumptuous audience rooms (p. 326).
✳✳✳ **SAMBŌ-IN.** Exquisite halls and flamboyant garden (in ✳✳ Daigo-ji, Kinki, p. 383).

## TEA ARBORS AND ROJI
✳✳✳ **Jo-an.** Of the three tea arbors that are national treasures, this fine *wabi* hut by Oda Urakusai is the easiest to see (in ✳ Inuyama, Chūbu, p. 288).
✳ **URA SENKE.** Weekly tea-ceremony demonstrations. Its famous tea arbors can be seen by appointment (p. 351).
✳✳✳ **DAITOKU-JI.** Kōtō-in and Shinji-an have fine tea rooms (p. 352).
✳ **Kōetsu-ji.** Tea arbors and bamboo fence designed by Hon'ami Kōetsu (p. 354).
✳✳ **MYŌSHIN-JI, Kihaku-ken.** Keishun-in subtemple's Sōan-style arbor (p. 356).
**TAI-AN.** Only documented arbor by Sen no Rikyū. Request appointment in writing (p. 365).
**Hassō-an.** The Nara National Museum's Oribe-style tea arbor (in ✳✳✳ Nara, Kinki, p. 393).
✳✳ **Meimei-an.** By Matsudaira Fumai, lord of Matsue and leading master of daimyo tea (in ✳ Matsue, Chūgoku, p. 442).

## SUKIYA VILLAS, STROLL GARDENS, AND BORROWED SCENERY
✳✳✳ **Sankei-en.** A collection of fine *sukiya* buildings (in Yokohama, Kantō, p. 257).
**SUMIYA.** Japan's oldest standing house of assignation; interior not shown (p. 326).
† ✳✳✳ **KATSURA RIKYŪ.** The ultimate Sukiya-style villa and stroll garden (p. 364).
† ✳ **SENTŌ GOSHO (Retired Emperor's Palace).** Large stroll garden, said to be a collaboration between Emperor Go-Mizuno'o and Kobori Enshū (p. 331).
† ✳✳✳ **SHŪGAKU-IN RIKYŪ.** Vast stroll garden dotted with *sukiya* arbors (p. 345).
✳✳✳ **KENROKU-EN.** Fine daimyo stroll garden. The adjacent Seisonkaku is a Sukiya-Shoin villa (in ✳✳✳ Kanazawa, Chūbu, p. 299).
✳✳✳ **RITSURIN KŌEN.** Daimyo garden and Sukiya villa (in ✳ Takamatsu, Chūgoku, p. 434).
✳✳✳ **KŌRAKU-EN.** A large, well-composed daimyo garden (in ✳ Okayama, Chūgoku, p. 429).
✳✳✳ **SUIZEN-JI.** Garden on the theme of the Tōkaidō highway, including a miniature of Mt. Fuji. Kokin Denju no Ma tea arbor from Katsura Villa (in ✳ Kumamoto, Kyūshū, p. 494).
✳ **SHŌDEN-JI.** A classic example of borrowed scenery, using a white wall to blend its dry garden with Mt. Hiei in the background (p. 354).
✳ **ENTSŪ-JI.** "Borrows" Mt. Hiei in a more sophisticated way, with hedges and trees to blend the foreground with the distant peak (p. 346).

# Matsuri

No one can claim to have seen Japan who has not experienced the primal, stirring rhythms of a matsuri, the Japanese festival. Every community has its annual cycle of matsuri—a living link to the land and its burden of history. Villages celebrate the gods that make the land fertile. Cities placate the gods of pestilence that run wild in summer. A Tōhoku town drives away midsummer spirits of lethargy with a deafening bacchanal that lasts for a week. A mountain village in Kyūshū, early home of the gods, celebrates its mythic past with ancient dances in the stillness of the winter night. Inevitably, many matsuri have vanished or changed with the times, but others have endured for a millennium.

## WHAT HAPPENS IN A MATSURI

The matsuri is a communion between the divine and the human. Farmers, fishermen, merchants, and artisans all depend on the good will of the deities: the kami of grain and fertility, the kami of the sea, the kami of commerce and craft. In Japan, where rice is the staff of life, it is naturally the kami of rice and the matsuri revolving around rice-growing that set the pattern. The rice deity (*ta no kami*) doesn't dwell in the paddies, but on the mountains—the source of snow melt that flows down to irrigate the fields in spring. The kami is fertility itself, so at planting time it must be invited down to the village and field, feted, and prayed to, to ensure a fruitful harvest. In the autumn, it must be thanked and escorted back to the mountain (see Shinto, p. 23). All but the most nontraditional matsuri observe this basic form.

**Purification.** The kami must be approached with care. All matsuri participants are thoroughly purified and isolated from defilements such as death and blood. Often, the ablutions—a plunge into a chilly sea, a shower of sparks—become part of the spectacle.

**A tree is erected.** The kami are attracted to trees, often represented by branches of glossy-leaved *sakaki* or a tall pole.

**The kami is invoked by the priest.** Prayers are offered along with sacred music and Kagura dances, and participants partake of special food and saké in the kami's presence.

**The kami is escorted to a temporary dwelling (otabisho).** The kami picks an *otabisho*, perhaps a farmer's house or a hillock, in which to spend the festival. Commonly, the kami is transported in an ornate portable shrine borne on the shoulders of village men and escorted by a gay procession, which winds along the pathways, spreading the kami's power over the fields and tying the community with an invisible but binding knot.

**Entertainments are offered at the otabisho.** Today, it may seem that the dances and spectacles are put on solely for the benefit of the tourists. But the original intent was religious, both to receive an oracle from the kami and to make an offering to it. Kagura, sacred dances, were performed by dancers who fell into trances and uttered messages from the kami. Contests—naked men struggling for an amulet, sumo wrestling, horseback archery, races—also foretold the coming year.

**The kami is escorted back to its shrine.** Further prayers and Kagura may be offered as the kami is sent back to its home.

## TYPICAL MATSURI

With every locale celebrating its own deities in its own distinctive way, the sheer number and variety of matsuri is enormous. Many matsuri, however, share common elements, such as the basic form described above, and the use of fire and water for purification. Often the festivals fit into an annual cycle, as outlined in the following section. By becoming familiar with these patterns, a visitor can venture an intelligent guess as to a matsuri's significance.

**Water.** Purification by water is universal. Participants and objects used in a matsuri are often sprinkled or dipped in water, or even plunged into the sea. Kyoto's GION MATSURI, Japan's greatest festival, originated in the ninth century to subdue a plague. Floats with halberds thrusting above were dipped in the Shinsen-en pond at the south end of the Imperial Palace. Contests in the sea—a tug of war or a struggle for possession of a ball—purify combatants and at the same time produce an oracle. The famous Doll Festival (March 3) was originally a rite to exorcise bad luck by setting simple dolls adrift on a river.

**Fire.** The spectacularly pyromaniacal fire festivals, or *hi-matsuri*, are also purification rites. All over Japan, New Year decorations are burned in great bonfires. In Nara's OMIZUTORI, fire purifies water drawn from a sacred well, and torches are shaken over the crowds, showering them with sparks to ward off sickness. Like water matsuri, fire matsuri are common in summer, the season of plague and insect pests. In autumn, there's the spectacular KURAMA HI-MATSURI near Kyoto, which reenacts a torch-purified procession that brought the shrine deity to Kurama; village youths groaning under the weight of huge, fiercely burning torches demonstrate their virility to the kami. Not only are fires purifying, but the fire itself must be pure. On New Year's Eve, tens of thousands of people visit Kyoto's Yasaka Jinja to receive a purified flame with which to light their hearths in the New Year.

**Processions.** Matsuri processions are often colorful, showy affairs, with flying banners, drums, gorgeous floats, and costumed paraders. The procession may head to the shrine to invoke the kami, then accompany the kami around the community, and finally send it off. One of the most primordial is held at the ancient Izumo Shrine in the tenth lunar month, when the so-called "eight million kami" of Japan assemble there. The kami arrive from across the sea, so a delegation of priests and pilgrims gather at the beach at dusk to light bonfires and await their coming. The kami are then escorted in a lantern procession to temporary abodes on the grounds of Izumo Shrine. More typically, the kami rides in a *mikoshi*, an ornate portable shrine crowned by a glittering phoenix or flower and borne by dozens of men. The *mikoshi* heaves about because the god inside goes on a joyful rampage—the more violent the better, according to diviners.

Costume parades often re-create a historical episode connected to a matsuri. Kyoto's Aoi Matsuri reenacts the colorful journey of an imperial messenger to the Kamo Shrines. At Nikkō, the Thousand-Man Parade reenacts the samurai procession that escorted TOKUGAWA IEYASU's spirit to its final resting place. Kyoto's Jidai Matsuri, or Festival of the Ages, a costume parade that depicts the history of the city, was invented in 1895 to salve the injured pride of the former imperial capital.

**Dashimono (Floats).** Kyoto's Gion Matsuri is renowned for its fabulous floats, great wheeled structures encrusted in ornaments and draped with rich cloths. Each carries a life-sized doll in which various deities reside; only the lead float still has a living child-god. The floats belong to merchant neighborhoods that have vied with one another for centuries to provide the most magnificent vehicles. Some are decorated with Nishijin brocades and finery from the Nagasaki trade, such as Gobelin tapestries, and carry musicians who play gongs and flutes. The Gion floats were depicted in Momoyama-period genre screens of famous scenes in the imperial capital and were widely copied in provincial towns. The HIE JINJA SANNŌ MATSURI and HACHIMAN MATSURI in Takayama and the CHICHIBU YO-MATSURI are famous in their own right for the splendor of their floats.

**Contests.** These served as oracles and are often mingled with purification rites. In the famous Naked Festival of Saidai-ji (Okayama), hundreds of men, clad only in loincloths, purify themselves by water, crowd into a temple, and struggle for a lucky amulet. In many locales, loinclothed braves struggle over possession of a ball or have a tug-of-war in the sea, sometimes in the dead of winter. At Hachiman shrines, feats of military skill, such as *yabusame* (equestrian archery), are offered to the god of war. The *yabusame* on September 16 at Kamakura's Tsurugaoka Hachiman Shrine is especially famous.

**Entertainments.** Sacred dances, called Kagura, and many other forms of folk performing arts, ranging from rain dances and exorcisms to Buddhist miracle plays and antique forms of Noh, may be offered at matsuri. Remote villages often preserve sacred plays and dances in forms that are not only archaic, but may no longer exist anywhere else. These are a fascinating topic in themselves, of great importance to historians of theater and folklore; they are described briefly under "Folk Performing Arts."

**Buddhist Matsuri.** Although the matsuri's basic form is Shinto in character, there are many festivals connected with Buddhist observances. Foremost is **Bon**, the festival of the dead, observed nationwide in summer. Higan, the spring and autumn equinoxes, are believed to be days on which souls can enter Paradise, and many families visit cemeteries to clean the ancestors' graves and offer food. Typical Buddhist observances include the revelation of a secret image; a religious service such as *hari-kuyō*, a mass to console the spirits of broken needles; or an anniversary, such as Shaka's birth or death. They include folk dramas, such as Kyoto's Mibu Kyōgen, medieval miracle plays that illustrated Buddhist teachings to the illiterate masses.

# THE MATSURI CYCLE

The basic pattern is the rice-growing year, the cycle of planting, driving away pests, harvest, thanksgiving, and prayers for a bountiful new year. In the Heian period, the imperial court added many ceremonies, largely Chinese in origin, and created its calendar of Nenjū Gyōji, or seasonal observances. Kyoto is still famed for its numerous Nenjū Gyōji; the most important, such as Hina Matsuri (March 3), Tango no Sekku (May 5), and Tanabata (July 7), are observed throughout Japan. Together with Buddhist rituals and the local festivals peculiar to each community, they make up Japan's annual cycle of matsuri. The following are just a few examples of typical rites performed at different times of the year. (*Note:* See Matsuri Directory, p. 76, for locations of the matsuri described below. L 7/15 = 7th lunar month, 15th day. An explanation and chart of the traditional lunar calendar is given on p. 75.)

72

## New Year
Purifying fire and water festivals are common from New Year's Eve through the month of January. Auspicious symbols such as *kadomatsu*, the pine and bamboo ornaments placed by gates, ensure that the New Year will be lucky. *Otoso*, sweet saké steeped in fragrant herbs, is drunk to ensure health. *Mochi*, sticky pounded rice cake, represents the bounty of the past year and a prayer for continued prosperity. Renewal of time is a basic feature of Shinto belief; hence the importance of "firsts" of the year.

**Jan. 1–3: Hatsumōde.** First visit to a shrine or temple.

**Jan. 2: Kakizome.** First writing (calligraphy) of the year.

**Jan. 4: Goyō Hajime.** First business. Many traditional shops open for business on this day.

**Jan. 15: Koshōgatsu (Little New Year).** Willow branches are decorated with "flowers" of pink and white *mochi*, symbolizing the human toil of growing food. New Year *kadomatsu* are burned in bonfires.

## Early Spring
Planting dances on snow-covered ground and fertility festivals are held for the coming planting season. Exorcisms, to start the year on a clean note, were part of the old court calendar.

**Feb. 2–3: Setsubun.** On the first day of New Year by the ancient solar calendar. An ancient Chinese custom of exorcism is carried out by throwing soybeans around and shouting *Oni wa soto! Fuku wa uchi!* (Demons out! Fortune in!).

**Early Feb.: Onta Matsuri.** Asuka. A very explicit sexual dance performed by a pair of masked dancers.

**Mar. 3: Hina Matsura (Doll Festival).** A ceremony of the Heian court, this was an exorcism in which bad luck is transferred to dolls which are then set adrift on water; still performed in Tottori by the lunar calendar (L 3/3). In most of Japan, it has simply become an occasion for families to display lavish sets of dolls representing the imperial court, a prayer for the future domestic bliss of the little girls of the household.

**Mar. 15: Hōnen-sai.** Tagata Jinja. The *mikoshi* for this festival is a three-meter-long wooden phallus.

**May 5: Tango no Sekku (Children's Day).** Originally a Heian court rite to distribute medicinal irises as a protection against illness, over time it became a day to pray for healthy boys. The custom of displaying miniature suits of armor is recent. Families fly carp banners (the carp being a hardy, and therefore auspicious, fish), one for each son.

## Rice Planting (Taue)
With the advent of modern agriculture, these once all-important rites are in decline. A common feature of rice-planting rites is that women do the planting, ostensibly to impart their fertility to the seedlings.

**June (1st Su): Hana Taue.** Chiyoda. A colorful spectacle in which costumed young women sing and plant while village men beat drums to set the pace.

**June 24: Izōnomiya Otaue Shinji.** Fifteen-hundred-year-old rite to plant sacred rice for the Ise Shrines. Half-naked men trample through a sacred paddy. Young girls then plant rice seedlings to the beat of drums.

## Summer
This was a dangerous season, when crops might be destroyed by pests or drought, and cities were threatened with epidemics. City matsuri are most numerous in summer.

**July 1–30: Gion Matsuri.** Kyoto. Begun in the ninth century to end a plague.

**July 7: Tanabata (Weaver Festival).** A Heian court rite in which the weaver and the herdsman (the stars Vega and Altair) are reunited by a bridge of magpies over the Milky Way, according to a Chinese legend. Wishes are written on paper streamers hanging from bamboo branches. These are set adrift on rivers or rice paddies to ward off pests and ill fortune.

**Aug. 1–7: Nebuta.** Aomori. A rousing festival with thousands of frenzied dancers and spectacular, illuminated floats, held at the peak of summer to drive off lethargy.

## Bon (The Feast of the Dead)
In the middle of the seventh lunar month, which most areas today approximate by August 14–16, the spirits of the dead return to their earthly homes. Lanterns and prayer fill the cemeteries, and in some places people still leave their doors open and prepare a special feast of vegetables for the returning souls. Bon Odori, hypnotic outdoor dancing, is held everywhere. Local versions of ancient Bon dances are of special interest. On the last night, lanterns are set adrift on a body of water to guide the spirits back across the sea.

**Aug. 12–15: Awa-Odori.** Tokushima. The streets are packed with tens of thousands of dancers performing a peculiar "crazy dance" to the sound of *shamisen* and clanging gongs.

**Aug. 16: Daimonji Okuribi.** Kyoto. The dead are sent off with fires burning on the hills surrounding the city.

## Harvest
The rice-field kami is feted in thanksgiving rites and ushered back to the mountains.

**L 8/15: Jūgoya (Harvest Moon).** Rice dumplings and pampas-grass decorations are offered to the harvest moon, said to be the most beautiful of the year. The pampas grass, resembling ripe rice stalks, represents a prayer for a good harvest. Some temples and shrines hold a moon-viewing festival.

73

**Sept. 1–3: Owara Kaze no Bon.** Etchū Yatsuo. As harvest nears, the villagers dance for three days and nights as a prayer to prevent typhoons from destroying their crops.
**Sept. 14–16: Hachiman Festival.** Tōno. Harvest festival dedicated to the war deity; famous for its deer dances. Similar festivals are held throughout Japan. The most famous, in Kamakura, features equestrian archery.
**Oct. 14–19: Doburoku Matsuri.** Shirakawa-gō. Rustic harvest festival with gay processions through the fields, lion dances, and communal drinking of a special home-brewed saké, called *doburoku*.

**End of Year**
This is the time of year-end fairs and of house-cleaning. In the **Iwato Kagura** in Takachiho and **Hanamatsuri** in the mountains of southern Chūbu, sacred dances are performed through the night to offer thanks and prayers for a good harvest in the New Year.
**Nov. 15: Shichigosan (7-5-3 Festival).** Girls aged three and seven and boys aged five are taken to a shrine to receive divine protection. This custom is thought to have originated as a rite of passage.
**Dec. 16–18: On-Matsuri.** Nara. This festival preserves the archaic matsuri form combined with grand outdoor offerings of Noh and Bugaku. The festival traditionally marked the end of the harvest in the Yamato region.
**Dec. 31: New Year's Eve.** In Kyoto, people visit Yasaka Jinja to receive a purified fire. At Dewa Sanzan Jinja in Tōhoku, a fire festival burns away pestilence and gives an oracle for the coming year. On the Oga Peninsula, **Namahage** demons frighten small children in the middle of the night. At midnight all over Japan, temple bells toll **Joya no Kane**, 108 strokes for the 108 delusions of humankind.

# FOLK PERFORMING ARTS

Japan's formal dramatic traditions (Noh, Kyōgen, Bunraku puppet drama, and Kabuki) are but a small part of a gigantic and diverse body of performing arts offered at matsuri. They are classified as:

    **Kagura.** Sacred dances for the celebration and renewal of life
    **Furyū.** Performances to exorcise harmful spirits
    **Dengaku.** Performances connected with rice growing

In addition, there are Chinese- or Buddhist-inspired performances and early forms of Noh, Kyōgen, puppet plays, and Kabuki, introduced at different stages in their history to various areas, often by the *yamabushi* (see Shinto, p. 27). No other modern nation preserves such a diverse and historically complex legacy of folk performing arts.

It all began in the age of the gods, when a goddess performed a striptease to lure Amaterasu Ōmikami out of her cave (see Shinto, p. 25). This is, by tradition, the origin of Kagura. Shrine visitors today are most likely to see Miko Kagura (Vestal Kagura), a demure dance by shrine maidens, hardly reminiscent of its mythic antecedent. The Iwato Kagura, by contrast, is an earthy, thirty-three-dance cycle based on the creation myths. It is performed at Kyūshū's Takachiho, claimed to be the very site of Amaterasu's cave. Izumo is the setting for myths about Amaterasu's unruly brother, Susano'o. Traveling troupes perform Izumo Kagura, famous for a spectacular dance depicting Susano'o's rescue of a beautiful maiden from a lustful, eight-headed dragon; it is thought to have been inspired by Noh drama. Yudate Kagura, which originated at Ise, evokes shamanistic roots. It centers on a boiling cauldron that delivers an oracle, and a masked dancer through whom the kami converses with spectators. No longer performed at Ise, it survives in the interior of the Chūbu region.

Shishi Kagura, or lion dances, are a type of Furyū. Farmers venerated the lion's fabled power to drive away the wild animals that marauded in their fields. Furyū performances typically center on a flamboyant prop, such as the Gion Matsuri floats, colorful parasols (Kyoto's Yasurai Matsuri), or enormous, flaring sprays of artificial flowers (Kyūshū's Usudaiko), accompanied by vigorous music and dances. The spectacle attracts harmful spirits, which are then exorcised by rites, burning, or other such measures.

Dengaku includes the songs and dances offered in prayer for bountiful harvests, the colorful rice-planting rites, and dances—in the dead of winter—enacting the whole cycle of planting and harvest. This quasi-theatrical tradition is one of the antecedents of Noh. Nishiure Dengaku (L 1/18) is a famous example.

The other precursor of Noh is **Sarugaku**, an acrobatic entertainment of Chinese origin that included pantomime and conjuring tricks, which gradually turned into spoken plays that were performed at temples and shrines for the edification of the illiterate masses. At Kyoto's Mibu Temple, Sarugaku evolved into Mibu Kyōgen, mimed Buddhist miracle plays concerning the Buddhist hell and salvation. These plays are believed to have been performed continuously for seven hundred years.

Of equal antiquity is **Ennen no Mai**, an ancient repertory of song, dance, and plays performed in Buddhist temples, preserved at Nikkō's Rinnō-ji and Hiraizumi's Mōtsu-ji. In one form, Bugaku dances are offered to a figure representing the emperor of Japan or China—in effect, it is a play within a play. Later forms of dance and drama also entered the repertory of folk performing arts. The most famous may be Kurokawa Noh, a sacred Noh offered to a shrine deity by farmers in Kurokawa village (Tōhoku, p. 177). It is thought to have been transmitted to the region five hundred years ago. Sado Island (Kantō, p. 246) has a legacy of Noh established by Noh's founder, ZEAMI, when he was exiled to the island. Sado is also noted for its Bun'ya Ningyō, a rustic puppet drama. On Awajishima, birthplace of Bunraku, puppet plays remain very much part of the local culture. Kabuki and Bunraku were widely admired and incorporated into many regional matsuri, where they are often performed upon lavishly decorated floats.

# Lunar Calendar

Borrowed from the Chinese in 604, the lunar calendar remained Japan's official calendar until the 1870s, when the Gregorian system was adopted. Generally, a lunar month falls 20 to 50 days behind the corresponding month in the Gregorian calendar. The resulting chaos can be illustrated with the example of the Bon festival. Originally, Bon was observed in the middle of the 7th lunar month, so some locales hold it in mid-July. But most set it on August 14–16, closer to its original season. And a few die-hards have it on the proper lunar date. In our listings, a lunar calendar date is designated as follows: L 7/15 = 7th lunar month, 15th day.

The lunar calendar starts with the first new moon between January 21 and February 19, and has twelve months of 29 or 30 days (the lunar cycle). Important lunar dates are the 1st (new moon) and the 15th (full moon). A thirteenth month, called *urūzuki*, is occasionally added to bring the lunar calendar in line with the solar year. The *urūzuki* occurs about once every 30 months, although exactly when is up to calendrical authorities (a role fulfilled before World War II by the Ise Imperial Shrines).

**Projected Lunar Calendar 1992–1994**
This chart gives the first of each lunar month in the left column, and its corresponding date (new moon) by the Western calendar in the right column.

|      | Lunar Date       | Western Date   |
|------|------------------|----------------|
| 1992 | 1/1              | Feb. 4         |
|      | 2/1              | Mar. 4         |
|      | 3/1              | Apr. 3         |
|      | 4/1              | May 3          |
|      | 5/1              | June 1         |
|      | 6/1              | June 30        |
|      | 7/1              | July 30        |
|      | 8/1              | Aug. 28        |
|      | 9/1              | Sept. 26       |
|      | 10/1             | Oct. 25        |
|      | 11/1             | Nov. 24        |
|      | 12/1             | Dec. 24        |
| 1993 | 1/1              | Jan. 22        |
|      | 2/1              | Feb. 21        |
|      | 3/1              | Mar. 23        |
|      | 3/1 (*urūzuki*)  | Apr. 21        |
|      | 4/1              | May 21         |
|      | 5/1              | June 20        |
|      | 6/1              | July 19        |
|      | 7/1              | Aug. 17        |
|      | 8/1              | Sept. 16       |
|      | 9/1              | Oct. 15        |
|      | 10/1             | Nov. 13        |
|      | 11/1             | Dec. 13        |
|      | 12/1             | Jan. 11        |
| 1994 | 1/1              | Feb. 10        |
|      | 2/1              | Mar. 12        |
|      | 3/1              | Apr. 11        |
|      | 4/1              | May 10         |
|      | 5/1              | June 9         |
|      | 6/1              | July 8         |
|      | 7/1              | Aug. 7         |
|      | 8/1              | Sept. 5        |
|      | 9/1              | Oct. 5         |
|      | 10/1             | Nov. 3         |
|      | 11/1             | Dec. 2         |
|      | 12/1             | Jan. 1, 1995   |

75

# BEST MATSURI (THREE-STAR EVENTS)

**Mar. 12: O-Mizutori.** Tōdai-ji, Nara (Kinki, p. 390). Buddhist rite performed continuously for over 1,200 years. Based on an ancient dream, this festival centers on the drawing of water from a sacred well. Great torches rain sparks down on spectators, and in the early hours water is drawn from the well and purified with fire. An ancient Tartar dance is performed.

**Apr. 14–15: HIE JINJA SANNŌ MATSURI.** Takayama (Chūbu, p. 289). Large, ornate wheeled floats are pulled through the town. The floats are famous for their clever mechanical puppets, which perform tricks to the delight of the crowd.

**July 14: Nachi no Hi-Matsuri.** Kumano Nachi Taisha (Kinki, p. 415). Spectacular fire festival commemorating Jimmu, Japan's mythical first emperor, who prayed at the sacred Nachi falls when he arrived from Kyūshū. Twelve portable "shrines"—tall edifices festooned with gilt fans—are taken to sacred Nachi falls. Twelve large torches are set ablaze and rice-planting dances are offered.

**July 14–17: GION MATSURI.** Kyoto (p. 311). The festival of Yasaka Jinja, famous for its thirty-one lavishly decorated floats. On the evenings of the 14th–16th, the streets of central Kyoto are jammed with spectators who come to see the lantern-festooned floats and hear the music of gongs, drums, and flutes. On the morning of the 17th, the floats are pulled through the streets of the city.

**July 23–25: Sōma Nomaoi.** Sōma (Tōhoku, p. 172). Spectacular samurai equestrian feats. On the 24th, hundreds of horsemen vie with one another to retrieve flags shot up by a small rocket out onto a plain.

**Aug. 2–7: NEBUTA.** Aomori (Tōhoku, p. 155). Huge, illuminated paper floats, shaped like Kabuki warriors battling mythical monsters, are pulled through the city as tens of thousands of young people go beserk with dance and saké. The festival, coming at the height of the Tōhoku summer, is said to have originated to drive away lethargy. The spirits of sleep are set adrift on the river in a rite called *neburi-nagashi*.

**Oct. 7–9: Okunchi.** Nagasaki (Kyūshū, p. 482). The annual matsuri of Suwa Jinja envelops the whole city in festivities. Antique floats are presented at various shrines. The famous dragon dance, accompanied by the crash of Chinese gongs, evokes Nagasaki's exotic history.

**Oct. 9–10: HACHIMAN MATSURI.** Takayama (Chūbu, p. 289). Similar to the April matsuri (see above).

**Oct. 21: KURAMA NO HI-MATSURI.** Kurama-dera (Kyoto, p. 311). Large, furiously burning torches are borne through the single narrow street of this tiny mountain village by sweating, near-naked men, who strain under the weight as the embers shower down on them. Magnetic, exciting, and dangerous.

**Dec. 2–3: CHICHIBU NO YO-MATSURI.** Chichibu (Kantō, p. 254). The male and female deities of two shrines meet on this occasion. Gorgeous lantern-festooned floats and electrifying drumming attract large crowds. During the day, Kabuki and dance are performed on the floats. Main night is Dec. 3, when fireworks illuminate the winter night.

# MATSURI DIRECTORY

**Rating Key:**

*** Best in Japan. Worth timing your trip to Japan.

** Best in region. Worth planning a regional itinerary around. (See beginning of each regional section.)

\* Special interest/local bests. Includes many purely religious rites, good but not especially important spectacles, and folk performing arts that are sometimes difficult to see and require somewhat specialized knowledge or interest.

**Principal Features:**

Ⓟ Performing arts          Ⓔ Energetic          Ⓢ Shinto rite

Ⓕ Fire festival           Ⓥ Visual beauty       Ⓑ Buddhist rite

| Location | Date | Name | Features |
|---|---|---|---|
| Kinki, p. 423 | Daily | \* Puppet plays. Awajishima. | Ⓟ |
| **January** | | | |
| Chūbu, p. 310 | Jan. 1 | \* Okina Matsuri. Ago-chō. | Ⓟ |
| Kinki, p. 403 | Jan. 1 | \* Miwa Nyōdō-sai. Sakurai. | Ⓕ |
| Chūgoku, p. 449 | Jan. 2, 3, 5 | \* Bugaku. Miyajima. | Ⓟ |
| Kyūshū, p. 474 | Jan. 3 | \* Tamaseseri. Hakata. | Ⓔ |
| Chūbu, p. 277 | Jan. 4–5 | \*# Sakabe no Fuyu Matsuri. | Ⓟ |
| Tōhoku, p. 183 | Jan. 7 | \* Hadaka Mairi. Yanaizu. | Ⓔ |
| Kyūshū, p. 480 | Jan. 7 | \* Usokae, Onisube. Dazaifu. | Ⓕ Ⓔ |
| Kyūshū, p. 490 | Jan. 7 | \* Oniyo. Kurume. | Ⓕ |
| Tokyo, p. 192 | Jan. 8 | \* Dondo-yaki. Torigoe Jinja. | Ⓕ |
| Kyoto, p. 378 | Jan. 8 | \* Hadaka Matsuri. Yōkaichi. | Ⓔ |
| Kyoto, p. 378 | Jan. 8 | \* Moriyama no Himatsuri. Moriyama. | Ⓕ |
| Tōhoku, p. 172 | Jan. 14–15 | \* Donto-sai. Sendai. | Ⓕ |

| | | | | |
|---|---|---|---|---|
| Kantō, p. 245 | Jan. 14 | ** Nakanojō no Tori-oi. Nakanojō. | E | |
| Chūbu, p. 277 | Jan. 14 | *# Niino Yuki Matsuri. Niino. | P | |
| Kinki, p. 386 | Jan. 14 | * Hadaka-odori. Hōkai-ji. | E | |
| Kinki, p. 416 | Jan. 14 | * Doya-doya. Ōsaka, Shitennō-ji. | E | |
| Kantō, p. 252 | Jan. 15 | * Nozawa Onsen Hi-matsuri. Nozawa Onsen. | F E | |
| Kyoto, p. 316 | Jan. 15 | * Tōshi-ya (archery). Sanjūsangen-dō. | | |
| Kyoto, p. 378 | Jan. 15 | * Suichū Tsunahiki. Mihama. | E | |
| Kinki, p. 391 | Jan. 15 | ** Yamayaki. Nara. | F | |
| Tōhoku, p. 168 | Jan. 20 | * Hatsuka Yasai. Hiraizumi. | P B | |

**Lunar 12/10 to 1/9**

| | | | | |
|---|---|---|---|---|
| Kyūshū, p. 472 | L 1/7 | *# Ten'nen-ji Shujō Onie. Takada. | F E B | |

**February**

| | | | | |
|---|---|---|---|---|
| Kinki, p. 406 | Feb. (1st Su) | ** Onta Matsuri. Asuka. | P S | |
| Tōhoku, p. 178 | Feb. 1–2 | * # Kurokawa Noh. Kurokawa. | P S | |
| Kyoto, p. 316 | Feb. 3 | * Setsubun. | P | |
| Kinki, p. 391 | Feb. 3 | * Setsubun. Nara. | P | |
| Kinki, p. 399 | Feb. 3 | * Setsubun. Hōryū-ji. | P | |
| Hokkaidō, p. 140 | Feb. 9–11 | ** Sapporo Yuki Matsuri. Sapporo. | V | |
| Tokyo, p. 192 | Feb. 11 | * Ta Asobi. Kitano Jinja. | P S | |
| Tōhoku, p. 165 | Feb. (3rd Sa–Su) | * Kamakura. Yokote. | V | |
| Tōhoku, p. 177 | Feb. 15–17 | * Kuromori Kabuki. Kuromori. | P | |
| Chūbu, p. 277 | Feb. 15 | * # Suikai Dengaku. Ikeda-chō. | P | |
| Tōhoku, p. 166 | Feb. 16–17 | * Bonten. Yokote and Ōmagari. | V S | |
| Tōhoku, p. 155 | Feb. 17–20 | * # Emburi. Hachinohe. | P S | |
| Chūgoku, p. 429 | Feb. (3rd Sa) | ** Saidai-ji Eyō. Okayama. | E | |
| Kinki, p. 382 | Feb. 23 | * Godairikison Jinnō-e. Daigo-ji. | F E | |

**Lunar 1/10 to 2/9**

| | | | | |
|---|---|---|---|---|
| Chūbu, p. 277 | L 1/18 | * # Nishiure Dengaku. Misakubo. | P S | |
| Okinawa, p. 511 | L 1/20 | ** Juriuma. Naha. | P | |

**March**

| | | | | |
|---|---|---|---|---|
| Kantō, p. 256 | Mar. 9 | * Kashima Saitōsai. Kashima. | V | |
| Kinki, p. 391 | Mar. 12 | *** Omizutori. Nara. | F E B | |
| Chūbu, p. 287 | Mid-Mar. | * Ōagata Jinja Matsuri (Su before 15th). Ōagata Jinja. | V S | |
| Kyoto, p. 378 | Mid-Mar. | * Sagichō-sai. Ōmi-Hachiman. | F V | |
| Chūbu, p. 287 | Mar. 15 | ** Tagata Hōnen-sai. Tagata Jinja. | V S | |
| Kyoto, p. 316 | Mar. 15 | * Sagano Taimatsu. | P F | |
| Kantō, p. 265 | Mar. 27 | * Yudate Shishi-mai. Hakone. | P | |

**Lunar 2/10 to 3/9**

| | | | | |
|---|---|---|---|---|
| Chūgoku, p. 432 | L 3/3 | * Hina-nagashi. Tottori. | V | |

**April**

| | | | | |
|---|---|---|---|---|
| Chūbu, p. 283 | Apr., May | * Onbashira-sai. Suwa (every 6 yr). | E S | |
| Kantō, p. 239 | Apr. 2 | * Gōhan-shiki. Nikkō. | E | |
| Chūbu, p. 294 | Apr. 5 | * Tejikara no Himatsuri. Tejikara. | F E | |
| Chūbu, p. 307 | Apr. 5–7 | * Kagura-sai. Ise Jingū. | P | |
| Chūgoku, p. 441 | Apr. 7 | * Aofushigaki no Shinji. Miho. | E S | |
| Kantō, p. 250 | Apr. 7–May 26 | * Gokaichō. Nagano (every 7 yr). | E B | |
| Kinki, p. 391 | Apr. 8 | * Otaimatsu. Nara. | F | |
| Kantō, p. 255 | Apr. (Su nearest 10th) | * Tenzushimai. Kōfu. | P V | |
| Kantō, p. 244 | Apr. (1st or 2nd Sa–Su) | * Furyūmono. Hitachi. | V P | |
| Kyoto, p. 316 | Apr. (2nd Su) | * Yasurai Matsuri. | P | |
| Kyoto, p. 376 | Apr. 12–14 | * Sannō Matsuri. Hiyoshi Taisha. | E V | |
| Chūbu, p. 289 | Apr. 14–15 | *** Sannō Matsuri. Takayama. | P V | |
| Kyoto, p. 380 | Apr. 14–16 | ** Hikiyama Matsuri. Nagahama. | P V | |
| Kyoto, p. 378 | Apr. 14–15 | * Taimatsu Matsuri. Ōmi- Hachiman. | F E | |
| Chūgoku, p. 449 | Apr. 15 | * Hiwatari. Miyajima. | F E | |
| Chūgoku, p. 449 | Apr. 16–18 | * Jin-Noh. Miyajima. | P | |
| Chūbu, p. 293 | Apr. 19–20 | * Furukawa Matsuri. Furukawa. | E V | |
| Kyoto, p. 316 | Apr. 21–29 | ** Mibu Kyōgen. | P V B | |

**May**

| | | | | |
|---|---|---|---|---|
| Tōhoku, p. 168 | May 1–5 | * Fujiwara Spring Festival. Hiraizumi. | P | |
| Chūbu, p. 298 | May 1 | * Takaoka Mikurumayama. Takaoka. | V | |
| Kyoto, p. 316 | May 1–3 | * Senbon Emma-dō Kyōgen. | P B | |
| Chūbu, p. 289 | May 3–4 | * Kabuki. Gero Onsen. | P | |
| Chūbu, p. 277 | May 3–5 | ** Tako-Gassen. Hamamatsu. | E V | |
| Chūgoku, p. 433 | May 3 | * Farmer's Kabuku. Shōdoshima. | P | |
| Kyūshū, p. 497 | May 2–3 | * Nishi Hongū-taisai. Takachiho. | P S | |
| Okinawa, p. 511 | May 3–4 | ** Hārī. Naha. | E | |
| Tokyo, p. 192 | May 5 | * Kitano Jinja Shishi-mai. | P | |

| | | | |
|---|---|---|---|
| Tokyo, p. 192 | May 5–6 | ** Kurayami Matsuri. | E |
| Chūbu, p. 293 | May 5 | * Hikiyama. Etchū-Yatsuo. | V |
| Kinki, p. 391 | May 11–12 | * Takigi-Noh. Kōfuku-ji, Nara. | P V |
| Tōhoku, p. 186 | May 12–18 | * # Atago Jinja Sairei. Hinoemata. | P |
| Chūbu, p. 304 | May 13–15 | ** Seihaku-sai. Nanao. | E V |
| Chūgoku, p. 443 | May 14–16 | Izumo Taisha Daisairei. Izumo. | P S |
| Tokyo, p. 192 | May (Sa–Su before 15th) | ** Kanda Matsuri. | E |
| Kinki, p. 410 | May 14 | * Nerikuyō-shiki. Taima-dera. | P V B |
| Chūbu, p. 298 | May 15 | * Jōhana Hikiyama. Jōhana. | V |
| Kyoto, p. 316 | May 15 | ** Aoi Matsuri. | P V |
| Tokyo, p. 194 | May (3rd F–Su) | ** Sanja Matsuri. | E |
| Kantō, p. 239 | May 17 | * Ennen no Mai. Nikkō. | P B |
| Kantō, p. 239 | May 17–18 | ** Grand Festival of Tōshō-gū. Nikkō. | V |
| Kyoto, p. 317 | May 18 | * Kamigoryō-sai. | V |
| Chūbu, p. 306 | May 24 | * Baka-bayashi. Fukui. | P |

**Lunar 4/10 to 5/9**

| | | | |
|---|---|---|---|
| Okinawa, p. 515 | L 5/4 | ** Hārī. Itoman and Ishigaki. | E |
| Chūgoku, p. 446 | L 5/5 | * Rice Planting. Ōmishima. | P S |

**June**

| | | | |
|---|---|---|---|
| Kyoto, p. 317 | June 1–2 | * Takigi Noh. Heian Jingū. | P V |
| Chūgoku, p. 447 | June (1st Su) | ** Hana-taue. Chiyoda. | P V S |
| Tokyo, p. 194 | June (Su nearest the 9th) | ** Yomatsuri. Torigoe Jinja. | E V |
| Kantō, p. 246 | June (2nd wknd) | * Takigi Noh. Sado Island. | P |
| Tokyo, p. 194 | June 10–16 | ** Sannō Matsuri. Hie Jinja. | V |
| Tōhoku, p. 161 | June 15 | ** Chagu-chagu Umakko. Morioka. | V |
| Kantō, p. 246 | June 15 | * Tsuburosashi. Sado Island. | P |
| Chūbu, p. 310 | June 24 | * Izōnomiya Otaue Shinji. Shima. | P |

**July**

| | | | |
|---|---|---|---|
| Kyoto, p. 317 | July 1 | * Mitoshiro Noh. Kamigamo Jinja. | P |
| Kyūshū, p. 474 | July 1–15 | ** Gion Yamagasa. Hakata. | E V |
| Chūbu, p. 294 | July 7–8 | * Abare Matsuri. Ushitsu. | F E |
| Kinki, p. 410 | July 7 | * Kaeru-tobi. Yoshino. | P B |
| Kyūshū, p. 471 | July 10–12 | ** Kokura Gion-daiko. Kokura. | E |
| Kyūshū, p. 471 | July 13–15 | * Tabata Gion Yamagasa. Kokura. | E V |
| Kyoto, p. 317 | July 14–17 | *** Gion Matsuri. | E V |
| Kinki, p. 415 | July 14 | *** Nachi no Hi-matsuri. Kumano Nachi Taisha. | P F |
| Kantō, p. 249 | July (Su nearest 15th) | * Nobori-no-Bessho-no-take. Bessho Onsen. | P V B |
| Kantō, p. 265 | July 15 | * Yudate Shishi-mai. Hakone. | P |
| Kyūshū, p. 498 | July (3rd wk) | * Soga-don no Kasayaki. Kagoshima. | F |
| Tōhoku, p. 159 | July 20–24 | ** Osore-zan Taisai. Osore-zan. | S B |
| Kyūshū, p. 483 | July (3rd Su) | * Pēron. Togitsu. | E |
| Hokkaidō, p. 144 | July (4th Sa) | ** Orochon no Hi-matsuri. Abashiri. | P F |
| Kyūshū, p. 483 | July (4th Su) | * Pēron. Nagasaki. | E |
| Tokyo, p. 194 | July (last Sa) | * Sumidagawa Fireworks. | V |
| Tōhoku, p. 172 | July 24–25 | *** Sōma Nomaoi. Sōma. | E V |
| Chūgoku, p. 453 | July 24–24 | ** Warei Jinja Matsuri. Uwajima. | E V |
| Kinki, p. 415 | July 24–25 | ** Mifune Matsuri. Kozagawa-chō | P V |
| Kinki, p. 416 | July 24–25 | * Tenjin Matsuri. Ōsaka. | V |
| Kantō, p. 245 | July 25–27 | ** Yama'age Matsuri. Karasuyama. | P V |
| Kantō, p. 246 | July 27–28 | * Noh. Sado Island. | P |
| Kyūshū, p. 495 | July 28 | ** Onda Matsuri. Aso. | P B |
| Tōhoku, p. 166 | July 31–Aug. 1 | * # Hayachine Jinja Matsuri. Tōno. | P |
| Chūbu, p. 304 | July 31 | * Gonjinjo Daiko. Nabune. | P E |

**Lunar 6/10 to 7/9**

| | | | |
|---|---|---|---|
| Okinawa, p. 522 | L 6 | ** Yaeyama Hōnen-sai. Ishigaki. | P E |
| Chūbu, p. 304 | L 6/15 | ** Ishizaki Hōtō-sai. Nanao. | P E V |
| Chūgoku, p. 449 | L 6/17 | ** Kangen-sai. Miyajima. | P E |

**August**

| | | | |
|---|---|---|---|
| Tōhoku, p. 157 | Aug. 1–7 | ** Neputa. Hirosaki. | V |
| Tōhoku, p. 155 | Aug. 2–7 | *** Nebuta. Aomori. | E V |
| Tōhoku, p. 166 | Aug. 4–7 | ** Kantō Matsuri. Akita. | V |
| Tōhoku, p. 172 | Aug. 6–8 | * Tanabata. Sendai. | V |
| Kyoto, p. 317 | Aug. 7–10 | * Pottery Fair, Rokudō-mairi. | V |
| Kyoto, p. 317 | Mid-Aug. | * Rokusai Nembutsu. | P B |
| Chūgoku, p. 434 | Aug. 12–15 | ** Awa Odori. Tokushima. | E |
| Chūbu, p. 295 | Aug. 13–16 | * Gujō Odori. Gujō-Hachiman. | E |
| Kyūshū, p. 480 | Aug. 13–15 | * Chankoko Odori. Gotō Islands. | P |

| Region, page | Date | Festival | Symbols |
|---|---|---|---|
| Tōhoku, p. 168 | Aug. 14 | * Noh. Hiraizumi. | P |
| Chūbu, p. 277 | Aug. 14–15 | * Ōmi Hōka. Shinshiro. | P B |
| Kyoto, p. 317 | Aug. 14–16 | * Mantō-e. | V B |
| Chūgoku, p. 439 | Aug. 14–16 | * Shiraishi Odori. Shiraishi. | P |
| Kyūshū, p. 472 | Aug. 14–17 | * # Himejima Bon Odori. | P |
| Kantō, p. 254 | Aug. 15 | * Funatama-sai. Nagatori. | V |
| Chūbu, p. 277 | Aug. 15 | * Tokuyama Shikan-mai. Nakakawane. | P |
| Chūbu, p. 307 | Aug. 15 | ** Kanko Odori. Ise-shi. | P |
| Kyoto, p. 317 | Aug. 15 | * # Hanase Hi-matsuri. | F V |
| Kyūshū, p. 482 | Aug. 15 | * Urabon-e. Nagasaki. | V |
| Tōhoku, p. 166 | Aug. 16–18 | * # Nishimonai Bon Odori. | P |
| Kantō, p. 256 | Aug. 16 | * Kiraigō. Hikari-machi. | P B |
| Kyoto, p. 318 | Aug. 16 | ** Daimonji. | F V |
| Kyoto, p. 377 | Aug. 16 | * Miyazu Tōrō-nagashi. | V |
| Kinki, p. 422 | Aug. 16 | * Hi-odori. Awajishima. | P |
| Chūgoku, p. 443 | Aug. 16 | * # Sha'ara-bune. Oki Islands | V |
| Tōhoku, p. 186 | Aug. 18 | * # Kabuki. Hinoemata. | P |
| Hokkaidō, p. 148 | Aug. 20 | * Funamatsuri. Niputani. | P |
| Kyoto, p. 318 | Aug. 23–24 | * Jizō-bon. | B |
| Kyoto, p. 318 | Aug. 23 | * # Hirogawara Hi-matsuri. | F V |
| Kantō, p. 244 | Aug. 23–24 | * Tsunabi Ningyō. Ina-mura. | P V |
| Kantō, p. 254 | Aug. 26–27 | ** Yoshida no Hi-matsuri. Fuji Yoshida. | F E |
| Tōhoku, p. 177 | Aug. 31–Sept. 1 | * Hassaku Matsuri. Haguro Jinja. | F |
| Chūgoku, p. 460 | Aug. 31 | * Itsukushima Jinja Jūshichiya Matsuri. Abu-machi. | P V |

**Lunar 7/10 to 8/9**

| Region, page | Date | Festival | Symbols |
|---|---|---|---|
| Okinawa, p. 516 | L 7/13–15 | ** Eisā Bon Odori. Koza. | P E |
| Okinawa, p. 516 | L 7 | ** Unjami Matsuri. Shioya. (First day of the boar after L 7/15). | V S |
| Okinawa, p. 521 | L 7/15 | * Kuichā Yuichā. Miyako Island. | P |
| Okinawa, p. 523 | L 7/16 | * Angamā. Taketomi Island. | P B |
| Kyūshū, p. 482 | L 7/26–28 | * Chinese Ura Bon. Nagasaki. | V |
| Okinawa, p. 521 | L 8 | * # Hōnen Matsuri. Taramajima. (Sa-M between lunar 1st–15th). | P |
| Tōhoku, p. 157 | L 8/1 | ** Oyama-sankei. Hirosaki. | V S |
| Kyūshū, p. 482 | L 8/1 | ** Usudaiko Odori. Saito. | P V |

**September**

| Region, page | Date | Festival | Symbols |
|---|---|---|---|
| Chūbu, p. 293 | Sept. 1–3 | ** Owara Kaze-no-bon. Etchū-Yatsuo. | P V |
| Chūbu, p. 293 | Sept. 5 | * Sugō Matsuri. Furukawa. | P |
| Tōhoku, p. 164 | Sept. 7–9 | * Oyama-bayashi. Kakunodate. | E V |
| Tōhoku, p. 166 | Sept. 14–15 | ** Hachiman Jinja Saiten. Tōno. | P V |
| Kantō, p. 257 | Sept. 14–16 | * Tsurugaoka Hachiman-gū Matsuri. Kamakura. | P V |
| Kinki, p. 416 | Sept. 14–15 | * Kishiwada-shi Danjiri Matsuri. Ōsaka. | E |
| Kantō, p. 257 | Sept. 18 | * Menkake Gyōretsu. Kamakura. | P |
| Chūgoku, p. 447 | Sept. (around 3rd wknd) | * Nishi-Chūgoku Senbatsu Kagura. Kyō-en Taikai. Kakei. | P |
| Kantō, p. 257 | Sept. 21–22 | * Takigi-Noh. Kamakura. | P |
| Kyūshū, p. 497 | Sept. 22–23 | * Higashi Hongū-taisai. Takachiho. | P S |
| Hokkaidō, p. 148 | Sept. 23 | * Shakushain Matsuri. Shizunai. | P |
| Chūgoku, p. 441 | Sept. 24–25 | * Sada Goza-kae Shinji. Kajima. | P S |
| Kyūshū, p. 490 | Sept. (late) | * Yame Tōrō Ningyō. Yame. | P |
| Chūbu, p. 297 | Sept. 26–27 | * Kokiriko Matsuri. Gokayama. | P |
| Chūgoku, p. 443 | Sept. 28 | * Izumo Kagura. Daitō. | P |

**Lunar 8/10 to 9/9**

| Region, page | Date | Festival | Symbols |
|---|---|---|---|
| Kyoto, p. 318 | L 8/15 | * Kangetsu no Yūbe. Daikaku-ji. | V |
| Kyūshū, p. 500 | L 8/15 | * Jūgoya Sorayoi. Chiran. | P F |
| Okinawa, p. 515 | L 8/15 | ** Itoman no Tsunahiki. Itoman. | P E |
| Okinawa, p. 524 | L 8 or L 9 | * Setsu Matsuri. Iriomote (at tsuchi no toi day of the Chinese lunar calendar). | P E |
| Chūgoku, p. 446 | L 9/9 | * Oyamazumi Jinja Nukihosai. Ōmishima. | P S |

**October**

| Region, page | Date | Festival | Symbols |
|---|---|---|---|
| Kyoto, p. 318 | Early Oct. | ** Mibu Kyōgen. | P B |
| Kinki, p. 422 | Oct. 1 | * Hachiman Jinja Fall Festival. Hirokawa. | P |
| Kyoto, p. 318 | Oct. 1–5 | * Zuiki Matsuri. | V |

| Region, page | Date | Festival | Symbols |
|---|---|---|---|
| Kyūshū, p. 471 | Oct. 1 | * Kaijō Jinkō-sai. Munakata Taisha. | P V |
| Chūbu, p. 283 | Oct. 3–4 | * Torch Festival. Asama Onsen. | F |
| Kantō, p. 254 | Oct. 5 | * Muku Jinja Ryūsei Matsuri. Yoshida-mura. | E V |
| Kyūshū, p. 482 | Oct. 7–9 | *** Okunchi. Nagasaki. | P E V |
| Chūbu, p. 289 | Oct. 9–10 | *** Hachiman Matsuri. Takayama. | P V |
| Kyoto, p. 318 | Oct. 9–10 | * Ōtsu Matsuri. Ōtsu. | P V |
| Kyūshū, p. 472 | Oct. 9–11 | * Usa Jingū Hōjōe. Usa. | V |
| Hokkaidō, p. 142 | Oct. 10 | ** Ainu Kotan Matsuri. Asahikawa. | P |
| Tokyo, p. 194 | Oct. 10 | * Kusajishi. Yasukuni Junja. | P |
| Kyoto, p. 318 | Oct. 10 | * Ushi Matsuri. Kōryū-ji. | P B |
| Chūgoku, p. 433 | Oct. 10 | * Farmer's Kabuki. Shōdoshima. | P |
| Okinawa, p. 511 | Oct. 10 | ** Naha Ōtsunahiki. Naha. | E |
| Kyoto, p. 318 | Oct. (2nd Su) | * Nijū-go Bosatsu Oneri Kuyō. | P B |
| Chūgoku, p. 433 | Oct. 11–18 | * Aki Matsuri. Shōdoshima. | P E |
| Kantō, p. 253 | Oct. 14–15 | * Kawagoe Matsuri. Kawagoe. | V |
| Chūbu, p. 296 | Oct. 14–19 | ** Doburoku Matsuri. Shirakawa-gō. | P V |
| Kinki, p. 424 | Oct. 14–15 | ** Mega Kenka Matsuri. Himeji. | E |
| Kyūshū, p. 472 | Oct. 14 | * # Kebesu Matsuri. Kunisaki. | F E |
| Kantō, p. 246 | Oct. 15 | * Bun'ya Puppets. Sado Island. | P |
| Kantō, p. 246 | Oct. 16 | * Chitochin-ton. Sado Island. | P |
| Kantō, p. 239 | Oct. 17 | * Autumn Festival. Nikkō. | V |
| Kyoto, p. 318 | Oct. 22 | * Jidai Matsuri. | V |
| Kyoto, p. 318 | Oct. 22 | *** Kurama Hi-matsuri. | F E |
| Kinki, p. 405 | Oct. 23–25 | * Ueno Tenjin Matsuri. Iga-Ueno. | V |
| Chūgoku, p. 453 | Oct. 28–29 | ** Uwatsuhiko Jinja Matsuri. Uwajima. | P |

**Lunar 9–10 to 10/9**

| Region, page | Date | Festival | Symbols |
|---|---|---|---|
| Okinawa, p. 521 | | * Yūkui. Miyako, Ikemajima (on lucky day at end of L 9). | P S |

**November**

| Region, page | Date | Festival | Symbols |
|---|---|---|---|
| Tokyo, p. 194 | Nov. | ** Tori no Ichi. Ōtori Jinja (on days of the cock). | V |
| Tōhoku, p. 168 | Nov. 1–3 | * Fujiwara Fall Festival. Hiraizumi. | P |
| Chūbu, p. 289 | Nov. 2–3 | * Kabuki. Gero Onsen. | P |
| Kyūshū, p. 475 | Nov. 2–4 | ** Karatsu Kunchi. Karatsu. | E V |
| Chūgoku, p. 453 | Nov. 3 | * Mishō Hachiman-sai. Mishō. | P |
| Kyūshū, p. 497 | Nov. 3 | * Yo-Kagura Kōkai Matsuri. Takachiho. | P S |
| Chūgoku, p. 449 | Nov. 15 | * Hi-watari. Miyajima. | F E |
| Kyūshū, p. 495 | Nov. 18 | ** Myōken-sai. Yatsushiro. | E V |
| Chūbu, p. 277 | Late Nov.–Jan. | * # Hana Matsuri. | P S |
| Kyūshū, p. 497 | Late Nov.–Feb. | ** Takachiho no Yo-Kagura. | P S |

**Lunar 10/10 to 11/9**

| Region, page | Date | Festival | Symbols |
|---|---|---|---|
| Okinawa, p. 523 | L 10 | ** Tantoi. Taketomi (for 10 days from ki no esaru day) | P |
| Chūgoku, p. 443 | L 10/11–17 | * Kamiari-sai. Izumo Taisha. | S |

**December**

| Region, page | Date | Festival | Symbols |
|---|---|---|---|
| Kyoto, p. 318 | Dec. 1–26 | * Kaomise (Kabuki). | P |
| Kantō, p. 254 | Dec. 2–3 | *** Yo-Matsuri. Chichibu. | P E V |
| Chūgoku, p. 441 | Dec. 3 | * Morotabune Shinji. Miho. | S |
| Tokyo, p. 194 | Mid to end Dec. | * Gasa-ichi. Asakusa Kannon. | V |
| Kantō, p. 254 | Dec. 15 | * Teppō Matsuri. Ogano. | P E |
| Kinki, p. 390 | Dec. 16–18 | ** On-Matsuri. Nara. | P V S |
| Chūbu, p. 307 | Dec. 24 | ** Ise Ō-kagura. Kuwana. | P |
| Tōhoku, p. 177 | Dec. 31–Jan. 1 | * Shōrei-sai. Haguro Jinja. | F |
| Tōhoku, p. 166 | Dec. 31 | ** # Namahage. Oga Peninsula. | P |
| Kyoto, p. 318 | Dec. 31 | ** Okera Mairi. | E |
| Chūgoku, p. 449 | Dec. 31 | * Chinkasai. Miyajima. | E V |

**Lunar 11/10 to 12/9**

| Region, page | Date | Festival | Symbols |
|---|---|---|---|
| Okinawa, p. 515 | L 11/15–19 | * Izaihō. Kudakajima (once every 13 yr in yr of the horse). | P S |

# Drama

Every visitor should attend a performance of at least one of Japan's traditional dramatic arts, if for no other reason than that they are visual spectacles of unparalleled beauty. But there are other compelling reasons. These theatrical arts are among the oldest still performed in the world, and though language is a formidable barrier, it is possible for visitors to appreciate Japanese theater as a dramatic experience. With some background on history, basic literary themes, and theatrical conventions, and with the aid of English-language play guides, translations, and the earphone services available in major theaters, it is possible to enjoy the great dramas of Japan to the fullest. The effort is richly rewarding.

There are four major types of traditional drama: Noh, Kyōgen, Bunraku, and Kabuki. These sophisticated arts have roots in shrine dances and popular entertainments. Remarkably, many of these earlier forms are still performed today.

**Noh.** This is a medieval theater that strives to create sheer artistic beauty through poetry, song, and dance. It is a drama of fate and anguished souls, gods and joy, deeply felt, so deeply, perhaps, that too overt an expression of it would render it shallow or false. Passion is expressed with the utmost restraint, played upon the barest of stages, with a minimum of actors and props. It demands more of the audience than perhaps any other theatrical art in the world.

**Kyōgen.** These comic vignettes interspersed in Noh programs are the most accessible form of Japanese drama. Kyōgen is often regarded as subsidiary to Noh — a kind of palate refresher between main courses. This is a shame, because Kyōgen is good theater in its own right, with traditions and acting quality as exceptional as those in Noh. Kyōgen is rarely bawdy or side-splittingly funny; its droll, gentle humor keeps its own standards of refinement. (ZEAMI insisted: "On no account must vulgar words and gestures be introduced, however funny they may be.") Programs consisting entirely of Kyōgen have become popular.

**Bunraku.** It was in Bunraku puppet dramas that popular theater reached its highest artistic development. Lacking star actors to attract fans, playwrights found it necessary to write plays that by their merit would win an audience. The large, beautiful puppets, nearly two-thirds life size, are manipulated by up to three black-robed puppeteers who work in plain view of the audience. Narration, also performed in view of the audience, is a paragon of dramatic recitation. To shift between consciousness of the human artistry and total absorption in the world of the puppets is a unique and startling experience.

**Kabuki.** Kabuki is gorgeous, energetic, gimmicky, and incredibly varied; the only demands it makes on its dedicated, enthusiastic fans is that they watch and enjoy. Staging is elaborate, and the plots are laden with improbable twists. To satisfy its fun-loving audiences, Kabuki borrowed liberally from Noh, Kyōgen, Bunraku, historical epics, current events, scandals, and the latest novelties. It enjoys the largest following today and offers the most frequent and varied programming.

## JAPAN'S GREAT EPIC AND THE THEATER

In the late twelfth century, fighting broke out between two powerful military clans, the Genji (MINAMOTO) and the Heike (TAIRA). The war ended in 1185 with the annihilation of the Heike in the great sea battle at Dan no Ura, a cataclysmic event that brought Japan's classical age, the Heian period, to a close. The war, with its cast of thousands, heroes and villains, and acts of bravery and betrayal, inspired medieval minstrels to compose an epic ballad known as the *Heike Monogatari* (Tales of the Heike).

The minstrels who recited the *Heike Monogatari* were the *biwa bōshi*, blind mendicant monks who sang to the plaintive twangs of a lute called the *biwa*. This music evolved from Buddhist liturgical music. The opening lines of the *Heike Monogatari* resound with Buddhist themes of impermanence and the passing of glory:

> The sound of the bell of Jetavana echoes the impermanence of all things. The hue of the flowers of the teak tree declares that they who flourish must be brought low. Yea, the proud ones are but for a moment, like an evening dream in springtime. The mighty are destroyed at the last, they are but as the dust before the wind.

> (Trans. A. L. Sadler)

81

If the Genji had crushed the Heike from the start, there would be no epic. But in the first round it was the Heike who won, and their patriarch, KIYOMORI, arranged for his daughter to marry the emperor. She bore a son, who became the child-emperor Antoku. By maneuvering this grandson onto the throne, Kiyomori succeeded in becoming the de facto ruler of Japan. Kiyomori was not noted for his magnanimity, yet for some reason, he spared three sons of his vanquished rival. The eldest, YORITOMO, then thirteen, was exiled to the eastern provinces, while his half-brother YOSHITSUNE, then an infant, was put in the care of Kurama Temple, north of Kyoto. Yoritomo and Yoshitsune grew up to avenge their clan and utterly annihilate the Heike.

In history books, Yoritomo ranks among Japan's towering figures. But in literature and drama, it is Yoshitsune who achieves immortality; no other figure appears in as many legends, ballads, poems, and scenarios as he does. The Yoshitsune of legend is a rather exotic hero. In appearance he is an effete aristocrat, with white skin, blackened teeth, and a frail physique. He plays the flute. He is also a consummate military genius.

## The Yoshitsune Legend

Many Noh plays are based on the *Heike Monogatari*, just as early Greek drama borrows heavily from the *Iliad* and the *Odyssey*. The following Noh plays, adapted from the *Heike Monogatari* and a later work called the *Gikeiki* (The Record of Yoshitsune), form an outline of the Yoshitsune legend.

**Kurama Tengu.** Ushiwaka, as the child Yoshitsune was called, slips away from sutra studies to learn martial skills from a mysterious supernatural being called a *tengu*.

**Benkei on the Bridge.** In Kyoto, at Gojō Bridge, a huge *yamabushi* monk named Benkei is forcibly "collecting" swords from passersby to finance the rebuilding of a temple. Ushiwaka saunters across and vanquishes him with his fan. Benkei, upon learning Ushiwaka's identity, swears eternal devotion.

**Atsumori.** Yoshitsune won fame as a Genji general, leading a series of brilliant attacks that forced the Heike to flee westward. His most memorable display of tactics was at Ichinotani, where he led his troops down the face of an impossibly steep incline, taking the Heike completely by surprise. This play is about one of Yoshitsune's lieutenants, Kumagai, and the sixteen-year-old courtier Atsumori.

As the Heike flee, Kumagai captures Atsumori, but moved by his youth and beauty, decides to let him escape. Just then, members of Kumagai's party appear on the scene: "'Alas! look there,' he exclaims, with tears running down his face. 'Though I would spare your life, the whole countryside swarms with our men, and you cannot escape them. If you must die, let it be by my hand, and I will see that prayers are said for your rebirth in bliss.'" Later, Kumagai becomes a priest to atone for the death and to pray for Atsumori's soul. (Source of quote: *The Ten Foot Square Hut and the Tales of the Heike* translated by A. L. Sadler.)

**Ōhara Gokō.** Finally, at Dan no Ura, the Heike fleet found itself outmaneuvered, and defeat was imminent. The widow of Kiyomori, taking her grandson, the child-emperor Antoku, into her arms and consoling him, "In the depths of the Ocean we have a Capital," leaped into the waves and so drowned. Others followed, but the former empress, Antoku's mother KEN-REIMON-IN, was rescued against her will and taken to Kyoto. In this play, she has retired to a convent at Ōhara, a village north of Kyoto, to pray for the salvation of her son and slaughtered kin. Her father-in-law, the retired emperor Go-Shirakawa, who has also fallen from glory, comes to visit her, and she describes the death of Antoku to him as she witnessed it.

**Funa Benkei.** Ironically, after the Genji victory, Yoshitsune becomes a tragic figure. He is forced to part with the beautiful dancer, Shizuka Gozen, and become a fugitive because of the envy of his older brother, the shogun Yoritomo.

**Ataka.** Yoshitsune, Benkei, and their loyal followers evade Yoritomo's manhunt and pose as *yamabushi* traveling to collect funds to rebuild Tōdai-ji in Nara. Barrier guards are on the alert for suspicious-looking monks, and Benkei decides to lessen the danger to Yoshitsune by disguising him as a lowly porter. At Ataka barrier gate they are almost discovered, but at the critical instant, Benkei strikes Yoshitsune to convince suspicious guards that he is in fact a mere servant. The barrier chief sees through the ploy, but is so moved by Benkei's desperate act that he lets them through.

The Yoshitsune epic ends in Hiraizumi, where Yoshitsune and Benkei perish in a final battle against impossible odds (see Hiraizumi History, p. 169). This is anything but an exhaustive list of the Noh plays treating Yoshitsune and his world; others include *Eboshi-ori*, *Kumasaka*, and *Futari Shizuka*.

# NOH

In Noh plays, stories are often interpreted within a Buddhist framework: *karma* (destiny) and salvation—escape from attachment to the earthly world—are basic themes. Those familiar with *The Tale of Genji* know that the Japanese believed the souls of people who died while holding some deep, earthly attachment—whether love or hatred—became ghosts, unable to achieve salvation. This is true of the ghosts in Noh plays. But as Zeami commented: "[even if] the outward form is a ghost, the inward form is a human being."

## Features

**Stage.** Noh and Kyōgen are played on a bare cypress wood stage, six meters square, with a bridge on the left where the actor makes his entrance; the bridge symbolically connects "this world" with "the other world." A shrine roof is built over the stage, supported by a pillar at each corner. The back wall is painted with a gnarled pine tree—a symbol of the kami for whom Noh was originally performed. Huge pottery crocks are placed beneath the stage floor as acoustic devices to enhance the sound of stamping feet.

**Actors.** Performers are all male. Women are represented by masked actors. The **Waki**, or assistant, appears first to explain the circumstances surrounding the main actor, or **Shite**. The Waki might be a wandering priest, and the Shite a ghost who cannot sever his bonds with this world. The Shite might wear a mask, but the Waki never does. Children and roles that call for a certain delicacy, such as that of Yoshitsune, are called *kogata*, and are played by young boys. Finally, there is a Noh role called Kyōgen, played by a Kyōgen actor, identifiable by his plainer dress and yellow *tabi* socks, who takes the part of the commoner, and who recapitulates the story in easy-to-understand colloquial language during the interlude between the two parts of some Noh plays.

**Music and chorus.** A chorus of six to eight men in formal dress is seated in two rows on the right side of the stage. Their function is similar to that of a Greek chorus; they explain and comment on the action and also serve as the voice of the Shite during dance climaxes, when due to physical exertion it would be impossible for the actor himself to declaim. Music consists of three types of drums and a flute. The drum players punctuate their playing with sharp cries—like the call of a strange bird. The flute playing is not so much melodic, in the Western sense, as it is atmospheric, rising in intensity to mark climaxes.

**Masks and costumes.** The Noh mask is a masterpiece of the sculptor's art, in which the movement of inner emotions is subtly expressed by the play of light and shadow on the mask. Tilted slightly up, the face smiles faintly; tilted down, it seems profoundly sad. Masks are used for women, old people, aristocratic youths, demons, gods, and ghosts. Masks possess a character of their own; a weak actor is said to be "upstaged by his own mask" (*omote ni makeru*). Costumes are of the most sumptuous brocades, threaded with gold. They are not strictly representational, but are intended to create an illusion of volume and unearthly beauty. Even a beggar's costume is elegant. Gods' and demons' robes are especially resplendent.

**The action.** No matter how emotionally charged, the drama is performed with a maximum of restraint. In the highly symbolic world of Noh, a few steps across the bare stage can represent a journey of hundreds of miles. Zeami, in his remarkable fourteenth-century essays on the theory of Noh, refers repreatedly to the term **yūgen**, which means "what lies beneath the surface." It carries connotations of mystery, elegance, and naturalness: "To watch the sun sink behind a flower-clad hill, to wander on and on in a huge forest with no thought of return...." Zeami also wrote:

> In representing anger the actor should retain some gentleness in his mood, else he will portray not anger but violence. In representing the mysterious (yūgen) he must not forget the principle of energy. When the body is in violent action, the hands and feet must be quiet. When the feet are in lively motion, the body must be held in quietness.

### The Construction of a "Dream World Play"

In this most typical type of Noh play, the Waki is an observer and the Shite appears in the first act in the guise of an ordinary mortal. In the second act, it becomes clear that the Shite is a ghost; the story he recounts has occurred long before the action of the play.

*Atsumori* (see above), written by Zeami, is a good example. The action begins *after* Atsumori has been slain. Kumagai (the Waki), has become Rensei, a wandering priest, in order to pray for Atsumori's soul. Rensei, charmed by the beauty of their song, converses with a group of reapers. As he speaks to one young reaper, the others vanish. This reaper says he is of Lord Atsumori's family and asks Rensei to pray for him.

In the second act, it is evening and Rensei begins rites for Atsumori's soul. The young reaper appears in his true guise, as the ghost of Atsumori. He wears the mask of a beautiful young man. Rensei wonders if he must be dreaming, but the ghost replies that whether he is dreaming or not, the karma that binds Atsumori's soul to the world and its torments is quite real. Rensei says he has been praying constantly for Atsumori's salvation, and the ghost retorts: "As the sea by the rocky shore/Yet should I be saved by prayer." Atsumori and the chorus reenact the death scene, which comes to a head when Atsumori advances towards Rensei with uplifted sword:

> "There is my enemy," he cries, and would strike
> But the other is grown gentle
> And calling on Buddha's name
> Has obtained salvation for his foe;
> So that they shall be re-born together
> On one lotus-seat
> "No, Rensei is not my enemy.
> Pray for me again, oh pray for me again."

(trans. Arthur Waley)

Atsumori's ghost has broken his bonds of hate and escaped the suffering that comes of being tied to the mortal world.

### Other Kinds of Noh Plays

In the Edo period, a typical Noh performance took all day. Plays were divided into five types, and one of each was given in the following sequence: god play, warrior play, woman play, madman play, and devil play. The god and devil plays are based on myths and legends, and correspond to the greeting and sending-off of the god in the Kagura performed at Shinto shrines. These plays center on a gorgeous costumed dance rather than a dramatic story. Warrior plays (such as *Atsumori*) tend to be in the "dream time" described above. Madman plays are more aptly called "real time" plays, and resemble Western dramas in their sense of time. *Hagoromo* (Feathered Robe), perhaps the most frequently staged Noh play, demonstrates the arbitrariness of these categories. Although *Hagoromo* resembles a god play in form, it is classified as a woman play. A fisherman steals the feathered robe of an angel, without which she cannot fly back to heaven. He agrees to return it to her only if she will dance for him; her dance forms the conclusion of the play.

# KYŌGEN

An all-day Noh performance was an exhausting event, in need of some relief. This was provided by Kyōgen ("crazy words"), comic vignettes given between Noh plays. Kyōgen is the world of Noh turned topsy-turvy; the protagonists are not anguished ghosts, but bumbling humans. In Noh, warriors are brave, and priests pray in earnest. In Kyōgen, warriors are craven and stupid, and priests can barely recite their sutras, for their time is taken up in lechery and the pursuit of worldly gain. Kyōgen takes the point of view of the common man, who likes to see the high and mighty of the world taken down a notch or two. It is hardly subversive, however; Kyōgen's favorite victim is a shiftless servant named Tarō Kaja (Number One Boy). Other figures of ridicule include daimyo, sons-in-law, blind men, *oni* (demons), and *yamabushi* priests. Like Noh, Kyōgen also includes plays that are basically dances in praise or celebration.

### Features

**Stage.** Same as for Noh.

84

**Actors.** There are two central characters, the Shite (protagonist) and Ado (antagonist). For example, in a play where Tarō Kaja is the Shite, his enraged master would be the Ado. The Ado never wears a mask. Kyōgen actors belong to their own traditional schools, separate from Noh schools.

**Costumes.** Although Kyōgen actors wear masks for comic effect, generally they rely on their own mobile faces. A woman is represented by a prim-faced actor wearing a white headband with long, dangling ends. Costumes tend toward the plain indigo, olive, brown, and yellow cotton prints worn by commoners. Tarō Kaja often wears a yellow plaid cotton kimono, a stiff vestlike garment, and wide trousers. The trademark of all Kyōgen actors is yellow *tabi* socks.

### Types of Plays

**Daimyo plays.** A large number of Kyōgen plays are about country daimyo—conniving, petty, and ineffectual—who are made out to be fools. In *Futari Daimyo*, two daimyo journey to Kyoto, but soon find their swords growing heavy. A commoner comes along, and they draft him, over his protests, to carry their swords. When the commoner has the swords firmly in his possession, he threatens to kill the two daimyo. When they have been reduced to utter terror, he decides to have a little fun by ordering them to strip down to their underwear and imitate animals and toys. At an opportune moment, he makes his escape.

**Tarō Kaja plays.** These are the most satisfying Kyōgen, because, like *Futari Daimyo* above, they treat underlying class frictions. Tarō Kaja's enduring appeal is described insightfully by Donald Richie:

> A lord has a stupid servant, always called Tarō Kaja ... who cannot tell a fan from an umbrella, or who inadvertently gives away to his mistress his master's philanderings, or who drinks up all the saké and fills up the bottles with hot water and then tries to talk the master into thinking he is getting drunk. Tarō is joined by a large cast of comic characters, each as distinctive as himself, just as sublimely stupid, as gloriously sly, as eternally innocent.
>
> (Introduction to *A Guide to Kyōgen*)

In *Kane no Ne*, the master wishes to make a ceremonial sword for his son's coming of age and orders Tarō to find the best price for iron (*kane no ne*). Tarō sets off, but he's a bit puzzled as to why the master wants the best sound of a bell (also *kane no ne*). In any case, he does his best, going from temple to temple until at last he finds one that has a worthy boom. He eagerly sets out for home to report his findings, only to be rewarded with a pummeling.

### The Fan as a Universal Prop

The large fan, or *ōgi*, is the most important prop in Noh and Kyōgen. In the imperial court, an *ōgi*-like staff was a mark of authority. In Noh, a god spreads a fan to indicate bestowing of fortune, a woman uses it to perform a dance, and a warrior uses a closed fan as a sword. In a Kyōgen play, the irate master might use his fan to beat Tarō Kaja.

# BUNRAKU (NINGYŌ JŌRURI)

In Kyōgen, Tarō Kaja is the object of humor, rather than pity. Roughly three centuries later, Bunraku puppet plays were portraying the sufferings of commoners in deadly earnest. The protagonists were ordinary townspeople and denizens of the pleasure quarters. These plays, called *sewamono*, were perfected by CHIKAMATSU (1653–1724), to whom Bunraku owes much of its literary excellence. Edo-period society was one of strictly delineated duties—between retainer and lord, wife and husband, child and parent—in which human feelings accounted for little. Chikamatsu made special use of the tension between duty (*giri*) and human feelings (*ninjō*)—a conflict that in the Japanese scheme of things inevitably leads to tragedy.

## Features

**Stage.** The stage, measuring nearly eleven meters in width, is large compared to stages used for Western puppet theaters. The puppet manipulators operate in full view, so that the "floor" is at waist level. Narrator and shamisen player sit to the right, on a raised dais. Because these performers—considered more important than the puppeteers themselves—have such demanding jobs, the dais is designed to revolve so that a performer can relieve his exhausted confrère without disrupting the action of the play.

**Puppets and puppeteers.** Bunraku puppets are about four feet tall. Heads are individually carved from wood, painted, given eyes, eyebrows, and mouths that sometimes move, and have real human hair. Hands are mobile and expressive. Male dolls have feet. Costumes are as elaborate as for any Kabuki actor, and employ the same conventions. Some dolls are capable of spectacular, crowd-pleasing effects; one puppet, a *hannya* (derived from Noh), has the face of a beautiful young woman, which becomes transformed into that of a frightful horned demon. The chief manipulators wear formal clothes, but assistants wear a black gauze mask and black clothes.

**Narrator (Gidayū).** The Bunraku narrator's art is one of the most demanding in all Japanese theater. He not only narrates the action, but also speaks all of the parts, while maintaining the rhythm and dramatic tension of the moment. A dialogue between a cruel, chortling villain and a weeping young geisha might provoke laughter in a vaudeville show, but in Bunraku it raises real lumps in the throat. The job is so exhausting that by the end of an act, the narrator is usually drenched in sweat and tears. Narration is carried out by three or four pairs of narrator and shamisen-player. These teams rotate throughout the play.

**Shamisen Player.** The shamisen accompanist's art often goes unnoticed, but it is he who "directs" the Bunraku play. Through his music, he controls the tension and speed of the play. The twanging shamisen not only expresses the emotions of the characters, but also provides sound effects—for example, a loud clap of the plectrum when the heroine is beheaded.

## Sewamono (Plays about Ordinary People)

Most typical of the *sewamono* are the "love-suicide plays," the oldest and most famous of which is CHIKAMATSU's *Sonezaki Shinjū*. The plot is archetypal. O-Hatsu, a famous courtesan, and Tokubei, a clerk, are in love. When Tokubei refuses a prearranged marriage, his angry uncle demands that Tokubei return the dowry. Tokubei, a simple soul, foolishly lends the money to an unscrupulous friend, Kuheiji, who then refuses to acknowledge the loan and accuses Tokubei of lying. Worse, Kuheiji announces his intention to ransom O-Hatsu with the money. O-Hatsu, in despair, pretends to agree. She announces that she is willing to run away with her lover that very night and put an end to their unhappiness. Unbeknown to Kuheiji, Tokubei is hiding under the veranda, and as O-Hatsu speaks to Kuheiji, she stretches her bare foot out to Tokubei to make it clear she is really addressing him, not Kuheiji. Tokubei, to let her know he understands, gently draws her foot across his throat (the audience can see all this going on). Late that night, the two lovers flee to a lonely wood. Back at the teahouse, Tokubei's uncle discovers the truth and sets off to find them, but it is too late. The lyrical scene in which the lovers flee is called a *michi-yuki* (travel scene). *Sonezaki Shinjū* owes its enduring place in the Bunraku and Kabuki repertories to the intricate stylization and interplay of music and movement, and to the beauty of its poetry, especially in the *michi-yuki* scene:

> Farewell to this world
> And to the night, farewell
> We who walk the way to death
> To what should we be likened?
> To the frost on the road
> To the graveyard
> Vanishing with each
> Step ahead:
> This dream of a dream
> Is sorrowful.
> (trans. Donald Keene)

## Historical Plays

Although Chikamatsu perfected the *sewamono*, he wrote primarily in Bunraku's other great genre, the historical play. Into this he injected *sewamono* elements, such as the conflict between duty and human feelings. Moreover, many "historical" plays are so in name only; Edo-period audiences were avidly interested in current events, but because of official censorship, it was necessary to disguise them (very thinly) by changing names and dates. Once the events became old news, and the danger of censorship receded, the casting of plays into different "worlds" (as the practice was called) became a kind of game. Some works go to the extreme of shifting time and place in mid-play, relying on analogies between Chinese and Japanese history and other elaborate parallels.

*Chūshingura*, Japan's most celebrated play, has both current and "historical" versions. Known in English as *The Tale of the Forty-seven Rōnin* (*rōnin* are masterless samurai),

*Chūshingura* is based on events that took place in 1703. The playwrights changed the names of the characters and set the events in the fourteenth century, during the early days of the ASHI-KAGA shogunate. Most people know the characters by their real names, however, and one later Kabuki version, *Genroku Chūshingura*, uses real names and sets the action in real time.

   *Chūshingura* centers on a vendetta carried out by the loyal retainers of Lord Asano, who was condemned to commit *seppuku* after he drew his sword and injured Lord Kira, an odious official. Asano's retainers then become *rōnin*. Over a two-year period, they scatter to make it appear they are not planning their revenge. The leader of the band holes up in the Ichiriki-tei (a famous Gion teahouse, see Kyoto, p. 337) and pretends to abandon himself entirely to a life of pleasure and debauchery. Finally, one snowy night the rōnin, reunited, steal through the silent streets and attack Kira's mansion. They slay the villain and lay his head on their master's grave (see Tokyo History, p. 195). The Kabuki adaptation of a 1748 puppet play is the most popular version today, with *Genroku Chūshingura* running second; the play is always performed around December 14, the anniversary of the vendetta.

# KABUKI

Kabuki is actor-centered theater, and borrows anything and everything—*Chūshingura* is only one example—to create a vehicle for its star. Among Kabuki's innovations are magnificent acting displays, such as those of *onnagata* (female impersonator) and *aragoto* (rough stuff) roles. Another example of acting virtuosity in Kabuki is found in plays adapted from Bunraku. In these there is always a scene in which actors mimic the movements of puppets, and a Bunraku-style narrator and shamisen player tell the story.

### Features
**Stage.** Modern Kabuki stages are large and, unlike Noh stages, do not protrude into the audience. For the stars' spectacular entrances and exits, a long raised ramp, the *hanamichi*, cuts through the audience to the stage. Kabuki stages are famous for their flashy effects—revolving scenes, moving backdrops, and trapdoors. A pine tree backdrop signifies that the play was appropriated from Noh.

**Actors.** All actors are male. Audiences come as much to see a favorite star as to enjoy the play. With practiced timing, genuine fans will call out an actor's *ya-gō* (a sort of trade name for each acting family, ending in *ya*, or "shop") as he makes his entrance or strikes a climactic pose; there are also professionals in the audience who perform this excitement-heightening service. Leading actors usually specialize in certain types of roles. The *onnagata* devotes his acting skills to creating an illusion of idealized femininity, an art that has to do with style rather than looks (some of the greatest *onnagata* are quite ugly). During the Edo period, *onnagata* set many of the fashions for women in clothing and behavior.
   The counterpart to *onnagata* acting is the *aragoto* style used to portray superhero-like characters. *Aragoto* actors wear fantastic cosmetic "masks" and perform bombastic dances. At climactic moments, they strike a powerful pose and grimace, crossing their eyes, to express wrath or intense emotion. *Aragoto* was invented by **Ichikawa Danjūrō**, the seventeenth-century actor and playwright. The Danjūrō name has been handed down from generation to generation to the chosen successor of the Ichikawa family. Fans will pay a small fortune for a piece of cloth imprinted with the makeup worn by star actors such as the current Ichikawa Danjūrō XII. Famous actors often indulge in ad-libs, cracking jokes about baseball or a current scandal, to the delight of their following.
**Musicians.** The most distinctive sound associated with Kabuki is a loud, ringing percussion produced by a pair of wooden clappers. It serves to announce and accentuate the beginning and end of acts and the climax of a scene. Musicians and singers usually perform from behind slatted wooden screens in a separate "house" near the *hanamichi*; if they are in full view, they are imitating Bunraku or Noh. Kabuki employs a great variety of instruments, including a violinlike string instrument (for heartbreak music), the *koto*, and bells and gongs.
**Costumes.** Every character has prescribed costumes and makeup, codified since at least the nineteenth century. Some of the basic conventions: Princesses wear elaborate crowns of twinkling, silver-foil flowers. Courtesans have headdresses bristling with long, tortoiseshell pins, wear their huge *obi* (sashes) tied in front, and walk atop clogs a foot high. Indoors, samurai wear formal trousers with exceedingly long hems that trail behind them as they walk; this style was developed to prevent fighting at the shogun's court. Dandies dress in feminine, colorful silk kimono (purple is a favorite color). Townspeople dress in plain plaid or striped hempen cloth. White faces denote nobility, whereas red faces generally belong to villains; an exception is the masklike *kumadori* makeup used in historical plays, where red streaks signify passion and virtue, whereas blue signifies fear and jealousy. Ichikawa Danjūrō is said to have been inspired by Chinese opera when he created this style of makeup.

### Jidaimono (Historical Plays)
As in Bunraku, this is a major Kabuki genre. The protagonists are great lords, warriors, and princesses. These plays are the great spectacles of Kabuki, with sets depicting sumptuous mansions and heroes and heroines dressed in colorful—often utterly fanciful—costumes. As in Noh, many plays are based on the *Heike Monogatari*.
**Kumagai Jinya.** Adapted from a Bunraku play, in turn adapted from the death-of-Atsumori episode of the *Heike Monogatari*, it differs markedly from the Noh version. In order to

introduce a clear conflict between duty and human feelings, *Kumagai Jinya* employs an improbable but dramatically effective twist: Kumagai's wife and son owe a debt of honor to Atsumori's mother. Through a complicated plot, Kumagai's son poses as Atsumori, while Atsumori himself is captured alive and safely hidden. On the day of the battle, Kumagai fights and finally kills "Atsumori" — actually his own son. The climactic scene involves a head inspection at which Kumagai's wife, who does not realize what has happened, is inadvertently present. Confronted with her son's head, she must struggle to retain her composure in order not to give the ruse away. Kumagai, overcome by what circumstances have forced him to do, becomes a priest.

**Kanjinchō (The Subscription List).** This play is based on the Noh play *Ataka*, about Benkei's effort to smuggle his fugitive master, Yoshitsune, past the checkpoint at the Ataka barrier. The role of Benkei, who performs a grand dance finale, is played by an *aragoto* actor. Because *Kanjinchō* is one of the Kabuki Eighteen of the Ichikawa family (see below), this most beloved of parts is traditionally played by the current Ichikawa Danjūrō. (Kurosawa Akira has in turn made a movie adaptation, *The Men Who Tread on the Tiger's Tail*.)

### The "Kabuki Eighteen" and the Ichikawa Family

A group of eighteen plays "owned" by the Ichikawa family forms a classification unto itself because of the prevalence of *aragoto* roles and the related *otokodate* (chivalrous commoner) parts. The Ichikawa family has become almost synonymous with Edo Kabuki (the tradition in Kyoto and Ōsaka stressed the *sewamono*). The *otokodate* parts were inspired by gangsters who fought against equally rowdy groups of samurai during the early days of Edo. In the Kabuki, however, the *otokodate* become sensitive, gallant men who defend the rights of the common people against arrogant and corrupt samurai. *Sukeroku* is about an *otokodate* of the same name and is described in the Tokyo history (p. 195).

Tied with *Sukeroku* as the most popular of the eighteen plays is *Shibaraku*, the most famous *aragoto* play. The *aragoto* hero, Kamakura no Gongorō Kagemasa, transplants the *otokodate*'s righteousness and energy into a historical pageant. Just as a valorous MINAMOTO warrior is about to be executed by a wicked courtier, Gongorō makes his first entrance shouting *Shibaraku!!* (Wait a moment!!). This superhuman figure, who easily saves the day, is usually played by Ichikawa Danjūrō. *Shibaraku* is perhaps the ultimate in "actor-centered" Kabuki; Gongorō is so closely identified with Ichikawa Danjūrō that he is addressed by other characters in the play as "Narita-ya," the *ya-gō* name of the Ichikawa family (taken from the Narita temple near Narita International Airport).

87

### Onnagata (Female) Roles

Certain Kabuki plays are especially famous for their demanding *onnagata* roles, such as the heroine of *Meiboku Sendai Hagi*, the faithful nursemaid Masaoka. The play is based on an eighteenth-century succession dispute in the house of Date, although, like *Chūshingura*, it is set in an earlier period. Masaoka is trying to keep the young heir from being murdered by conspirators, but her own son is killed in front of her when he, in accordance with her training, gobbles up some poisoned cakes intended for the heir. She retains her composure, convincing the conspirators that she is in on the plot and has actually posed the heir as her son. Masaoka is congratulated, and the conspirators leave. Later, Masaoka expresses her pride and anguish for her dead son in a virtuoso scene, done in Bunraku mode: The male *onnagata* must play a puppet portraying a woman.

### Sewamono and Later Sewamono

As in Bunraku, this is an important genre; most *sewamono* plays in Kabuki, such as *Sonezaki Shinjū*, or plays with *sewamono* elements, such as *Meiboku Sendai Hagi*, originated as Bunraku plays. An exception are the *kizewamono* (later sewamono) written exclusively for the Kabuki during the late eighteenth and nineteenth centuries, which emphasize the sleaziness of all classes — especially the lower ones. They often portrayed real criminals. The latest gory murder would be reenacted on stage almost before the corpse had been buried. These plays are especially realistic, with people and houses accurately depicted in the costumes and sets; in this respect, the plays function as a record of everyday life — at least lowlife — in the Edo period. Like later ukiyo-e prints, these plays were exaggerated to cater to a jaded public. Among the most famous is *Benten Kozō*, about a colorful thief and rogue. Ghost stories, such as *Yotsuya Kaidan*, were also favored by this audience.

### Shosagoto

These plays, consisting mainly of dance or mime, correspond to dance pieces in Noh and Kyōgen. Musicians and singers appear on stage, together with the actors. One of the most famous *shosagoto* plays is *Musume Dōjō-ji*, adapted from the Noh play *Dōjō-ji*. Priests gather to dedicate a new bell at Dōjō-ji. The temple had a bell long ago, but a girl, Kiyohime, fell in love with one of the monks and pursued him so avidly that the abbot hid him by lowering the bell over him. In her jealousy, Kiyohime turned into a giant serpent, coiled herself around the bell, and breathed fire until both bell and hapless monk were burned to cinders. Because of this old story, women are barred from the precincts during the dedication of the new bell. But Hanako, a dancer, arrives and pleads to be allowed to dance in honor of the new bell. Finally, the priests relent. Of course, the girl turns into a serpent during the dance. The fame of the play lies in the extravagant way in which this transformation is accomplished. Related to *shosagoto* are the *michi-yuki* scenes, originated by Chikamatsu, which became gorgeous dance pieces in Kabuki.

# HISTORY OF THE JAPANESE THEATER

## Dances for the Gods

The roots of Japanese theater are found in Shinto sacred dances, called Kagura, which are performed at shrines and festivals. Youths or shrine maidens become "possessed" by the kami and dance for it. Though intended as a religious rite and offering, human spectators naturally found such performances diverting and developed them into secular entertainments. Many dance pieces in Japanese theater are derived from shrine dances. Some Kagura are a form of mime theater based on Japanese mythology. The music of Kagura—drums, flutes, and chanting—produces a primal and mysterious effect (see Matsuri, p. 71).

## Dances for the Court

In the Nara period, Japanese music and dance were vastly enriched by an influx of continental culture. The exquisite lutes in the Shōsō-in imperial storehouse, with their inlaid designs of parrots, camels, palm trees, and arabesques, point to Central Asian origins. Along with music, dance dramas came from the continent. **Gigaku**, or "skill music," introduced in the early seventh century, is no longer performed. It seems to have been a bawdy mime-dance procession and Buddhist mystery play. Gigaku dancers wore wooden or dry-lacquer masks which covered the head. Often works of great sculptural skill, these masks depict characters from continental Buddhist and Hindu lore, such as Baramon (Brahma) and Karura (Garuda), as well as earthier fellows like Sanron, whose nature is indicated by his phallic nose. Sanron seems to have been a stock character whose main activity was making amorous advances. The Nara National Museum and the Tokyo National Museum have wonderfully expressive Gigaku masks. Gigaku entertainments were often led off by a *shishi-mai*, or lion dance, which has since become a mainstay of folk festivals throughout Japan.

Gigaku is not to be confused with **Gagaku**, "elegant music," which entered Japan during the Nara period and attained its final form in the early Heian period. Gagaku is still performed today. It is easier to appreciate when it is accompanied by dancing, in which case it is called **Bugaku** (dance music). The imperial court had a special Gagaku/Bugaku bureau, and even today Bugaku is performed publicly on the Imperial Palace grounds by direct descendants of the Nara court musicians' guild. It is also performed at a number of important shrines, notably Kasuga in Nara and Itsukushima at Miyajima, near Hiroshima.

Gagaku orchestras are large ensembles consisting of several types of drums, flutes, and stringed instruments. The *hichiriki*, a reed instrument of Central Asian origin, emits an eerie, multitonal blare that sets a mystical, stately mood. Climaxes are punctuated by the boom of a pair of huge drums spectacularly decorated with the thunder symbol and flaming halos. Bugaku is performed by costumed dancers, some of whom wear masks depicting fantastical figures with colorful faces and fierce, bulging eyes. Unlike Gigaku masks, Bugaku masks cover only the face; masks in the formal dramatic arts shrank steadily until they reached elegant compactness in Noh.

The silk costumes of Bugaku represent robes of civic and military officials of the Heian court whose ranks, in imitation of the Chinese and Korean courts, were divided into "right" and "left" sides. The Bugaku repertory is similarly divided, based on the putative origins of the pieces. "Tang-style" pieces, attributed to the Chinese court, are "left music," played on the great drum on the left, and dancers typically wear red costumes. "Korean-style" pieces are "right music," played on the right drum, and dancers wear blue or green. "Native" performances, which stem from shrine Kagura, are performed without the great drums, by unmasked dancers in white. Each of the three categories uses a different kind of flute.

## From Sacred Dance to Theater

The sole ornament of a Noh stage is the lone pine tree painted on the back wall. It is said to represent a sacred pine at Kasuga Shrine in Nara, where Sarugaku no Noh was performed at the shrine, as a type of shrine Kagura. KAN'AMI (1333–1384), a priest at the shrine, as a type of shrine Kagura. Sarugaku, which originally consisted of acrobatics and broad farce, together with Dengaku, form the basis of Noh theater. The farces became Kyōgen. The serious plays became Noh which, though deeply imbued with religious elements, was pursued as an artistic end in itself, resulting in works of poetry, song, and visual beauty.

Kan'ami and his son Zeami (1363–1443) are credited with the invention of Noh. The -ami suffix of their name stands for Amida and was often found among lower-class artisans belonging to an Amidist sect. Certain aspects of Noh—transience, purgatory, paradise, and a melancholy sense of loss—derive from Amidism. Esoteric Buddhism influenced Noh as well. It was, however, under the influence of Zen, the Buddhist sect favored by the shogunate, that Noh became high art. The two performers, father and son, attracted the attention of the third ASHIKAGA shogun, YOSHIMITSU, when they performed in Kyoto, and soon after came under his patronage. Zeami became a particular favorite of Yoshimitsu. Zeami wrote his own plays and modified the existing repertory according to the principles of restraint, suggestion, and mystery, or *yūgen*. His essays remain the essential teachings of Noh.

Noh experienced a rebirth in the Momoyama period, when HIDEYOSHI became an enthusiastic practitioner. In the Edo period it continued to enjoy the patronage of the daimyo, but as a result, it became highly formalized—almost ceremonial—until it took three times longer to perform a play than in Zeami's day. After the Meiji Restoration, Noh almost vanished; it was kept alive by a tiny handful of performers. Today, it is experiencing a small but solid revival. Twentieth-century writers, from Ezra Pound and William Butler Yeats to Mishima Yukio, have found inspiration in Noh, the world's oldest continually performed drama.

## Bunraku (Ningyō Jōruri)

The *Biwa hōshi* (blind minstrels) continued to chant the *Heike Monogatari* and its variants throughout Japan's Middle Ages. In the late fifteenth century, a new, more colorful style of recitation evolved. It was called *jōruri*, after an early work about a romance between Yoshitsune and a certain Lady Jōruri. Gradually, the lute was replaced by the exotic three-stringed *shamisen*, introduced from Okinawa (where it is called a *jabisen* and is still very popular). In the early seventeenth century, *jōruri* chanting was combined with the folk puppet theater of the island of Awaji, between Ōsaka and Shikoku. This amalgamation came to be known as *ningyō* (doll) *jōruri* and can still be seen, in a relatively well-preserved state, on Awaji and at Tokushima on Shikoku. An entrepreneur named Bunzaemon took a troupe of performers from Awaji to Ōsaka; lending the first syllable of his name, he called it the Bunraku troupe. Bunraku became the generic name for *ningyō jōruri*.

Bunraku's heyday was from about 1690 to 1750. An Ōsaka chanter, Takemoto Gidayū (1651–1714), won acclaim for a new, powerful, and beautiful style of recitation, a style that came to be called *Gidayū-bushi*. Gidayū made Bunraku so popular that the budding playwright CHIKAMATSU MONZAEMON, who was writing for Kabuki, defected to Bunraku, for which he wrote his greatest plays. During the first performance of *Sonezaki Shinjū* in 1703 (see p. 85), several innovations took place. A famous (and good-looking) puppet master came out on stage and manipulated the puppets in full view of the audience. Two masked assistants appeared some time later. Soon Gidayū, the famous chanter, also appeared in view of the audience. At the same time, there was growing realism in the puppets. In 1727, puppet makers developed movable eyelids and gripping hands. By 1736, a puppet could roll its eyes and wiggle its eyebrows. The faces were modeled on famous Kabuki actors. By 1750, Bunraku had taken the form it has today. Japan scholar Donald Keene suggests that realism was always balanced by a show of artifice; as Chikamatsu wrote: "The theater is unreal, and yet not unreal, real and yet not real. Entertainment lies between the two."

## Kabuki

Shijō-Kawaramachi is the heart of Kyoto's shopping and entertainment district, where department stores, boutiques, bars, restaurants, and movie houses are clustered. There was a time, however, when this area lay on the outskirts of the city and was inhabited only by outcasts, called *kawaramono*, or riverbed people. The *kawaramono* were restricted to the most menial work, and so many preferred to become artisans or entertainers. So it was that, in 1603, one Okuni, a shrine dancer of Izumo, "frolicked" (*kabuku*) on the bank of the Kamo River. Okuni and her all-woman troupe performed a lively mix of dances and comic skits, which proved a great success. However, the shogunate shut down her show and banned female performers after several skirmishes by patrons over the women's sexual favors. Kabuki became, and has remained, the province of male actors. For a time, handsome youths and boys played female roles, but they too engaged in prostitution, and once more the authorities clamped down. Kabuku was obliged to use only adult males, who were required to perform Kyōgen and Noh pieces in an effort to turn it into legitimate theater. One result was that, for the first time, some of the treasures of the Noh drama became widely available to the common people.

At first Kabuki was performed on a Noh stage, but this was abandoned in the 1660s in favor of a broader stage. Around the same time, the addition of a draw curtain made it possible to change sets and develop longer plays with many acts. The *hanamichi* was invented to give the actors a prominent place to grandstand. In 1673, Ichikawa Danjūrō (1660-1704) created the show-stopping *aragoto* style. The world's first revolving stage was invented in the mid-eighteenth century by the famous Kyoto *sewamono* playwright Namiki Shōzō.

Though Noh and Kyōgen were important to early Kabuki, it is to Bunraku that Kabuki owes its greatest debt. Chikamatsu abandoned the Kabuki in order to write plays for Bunraku because he saw greater artistic possibilities in the latter: puppets don't have actors' egos. For a time, Bunraku was so popular that Kabuki actors had to imitate the puppets just to attract an audience. Toward the middle of the eighteenth century, however, about the time of the rise of the *nishiki-e*, or color print, Kabuki surpassed Bunraku in popularity.

What often goes unsaid is that, to the end of the Edo period, Kabuki actors remained outcasts. They have been allowed to live among "respectable" people only since the Meiji period, when even the emperor attended a Kabuki performance. Today, Kabuki enjoys a status similar to the national theaters of other countries.

## Theater in Modern Japan

Many Japanese film directors have made movies inspired by Noh and Kabuki classics, such as *The Men Who Tread on the Tiger's Tail*, Kurosawa's exquisite 1945 adaptation of *Kanjinchō*, and versions of *Chūshingura* too numerous to mention. Japanese of a new generation are developing a deeper interest in their theatrical inheritance. For Japan's avant garde, the traditional theater is a well of inspiration that is just beginning to be tapped by people like Suzuki Tadashi of Waseda University, founder of the Toga International Arts Festival (see Chūbu, p. 293).

# PRACTICAL TIPS

George Bernard Shaw quipped, "The Noh drama is no drama at all." Your experience will be considerably more rewarding than his was if you take care to choose the theater form that best suits your own tastes. The next step is to purchase an English-language play guide, sold at major bookstores and sometimes at theaters. We recommend: *The Kabuki Handbook*, by Aubrey & Giovanni Halford, *A Guide to Nō*, by P. G. O'Neill, and *A Guide to Kyōgen*, by Don Kenny. For Bunraku, the Kabuki guide will serve.

**Hints for Noh.** The Japanese bring scripts to help them follow the antiquated language. You can bring along *The Nō Plays of Japan*, Arthur Waley's lyrical translations, or *20 Plays of the Nō Theater*, edited by Donald Keene, both of which convey some of the poetic richness of the Noh theater. *On the Art of the Nō Drama*, a fine translation of Zeami's treatises, is compelling reading for anyone who wants to delve deeper into the esthetic theory behind Noh.

**Hints for Kyōgen.** There is one book of twenty-two translated Kyōgen plays, *Japanese Folk Plays: The Ink-Smeared Lady and Other Kyōgen* (trans. Shio Sakanishi, published by Tuttle); only the translated titles are listed, with no cross-index to the Japanese titles.

**Hints for Bunraku.** Try to sit in the first ten rows for good views of the puppets and of the fascinating technique of the manipulators, narrator, and shamisen player.

**Hints for Kabuki.** Kabuki programs at the commercial theaters favor unrelated vignettes from a variety of plays, chosen to showcase a star actor. By the time you've figured out the plot, the vignette is over. The national theaters tend to present longer acts and plays in full. Among the leading stars: the *onnagata* Utaemon (now over eighty years old) and the glamorous Tamasaburō, *aragato* Ichikawa Danjūrō XII, and Ichikawa Ennosuke.

Plays are known by both a popular name and a "formal" name, chosen for euphony and stylistic flourish rather than sense: For example, the full title of *Chūshingura* is *Kanadehon Chūshingura* (An Alphabetized Treasury of Loyal Retainers).

# MAJOR THEATERS AND SCHEDULES

**TOKYO** (Tel 03)
**National Theater** (3265-7411). Near Akasaka-Mitsuke and Nagata-chō subway stations. Kabuki every month except Feb., May, and Sept. Bunraku in small theater Feb., May, Sept., Dec. Closed at beginning and end of each month.
**National Noh Theater** (3423-1331). Near Sendagaya subway station. Beautiful theater. Regular program (1 Noh, 1 Kyōgen) first Wednesday (13:00) and third Friday (18:30) of each month. Lecture performance second Saturday (13:30). All-Kyōgen program, fourth Friday of odd-numbered months (18:30). Special (2 Noh, 1 Kyōgen), fifth Sunday (13:00).
**Kanze Nohgaku-dō** (3469-5241). 1-16-4 Shōtō, Shibuya. First Sunday (11:00), every Wednesday (17:30), and second Thursday of odd-numbered months (17:00).
**Tessenkai Nohgaku Kenshūjo** (3401-2285). Last Wednesday of each month at their beautiful Aoyama theater. Also on second Friday at the Suidōbashi Hōshō Nohgaku-dō.
**Kabuki-za** (3541-3131). Ginza. Landmark theater. Daily matinees and early evening shows of Kabuki every month.

**KYOTO** (TEL 075)
**Kanze Nohgaku-dō Kaikan** (771-6114). Kanze school regular performance, every Sa, Su, NH, 9:00-17:00.
**Kongō Nohgaku-dō** (221-3049). Fourth Sunday of each month except Aug. Lecture program roughly three times per month, 14:00-21:00.
**Minami-za** (561-1155). Kabuki all-star program daily from end of Nov. through Dec.

**ŌSAKA** (TEL 06)
**National Bunraku Theater** (212-2531). Bunraku in Jan., Apr., June, July, Sept., Nov.
**Shin Kabuki-za** (631-2121). One month of Kabuki every year, variable schedule.

**NAGOYA** (TEL 052)
**Misono-za** (211-1451). In Oct., a month of all-star Kabuki performances.

# Art

The Japanese skill at assimilating new influences and transforming them into uniquely Japanese styles is particularly apparent in art. Continental forms of Buddhist sculpture, ink painting, and ceramics were avidly collected, faithfully copied, and then redefined, often with breathtaking inventiveness, to express native concerns. We divide art history into two major phases. The first, dominated by religious art, began with the introduction of Buddhism in the sixth century and lasted through the Kamakura period. The second, from the Muromachi period onward, was increasingly secular, and the emphasis shifted to painting and decorative arts. The examples described here can be seen today; they are listed under "Selected Collections." The Japanese have been fanatic conservers of art objects throughout their history. Their continuing fascination with their own art ensures a steady supply of excellent exhibitions.

# THE GREAT AGE OF BUDDHIST ART (593-1333)

### The Naive and the Sublime
### Asuka and Hakuhō Periods (593–710)

In the Asuka period, Buddhism and mainland Asian culture began to enter Japan by conscious design. With it came a new and sophisticated art that was, for a while, almost purely continental. TORI BUSSHI, the grandson of a Korean immigrant, was the foremost sculptor of the period. To him and his school are attributed the celebrated bronze Shaka Trinity and the statue of Yakushi Nyorai (fig. 37) in the main hall of HŌRYŪ-JI. Although Tori worked in bronze, the modeling of these statues has a simple forcefulness and the faces a kind of "archaic smile" that shows the influence of the stone statuary of the Northern Wei dynasty in China. The ethereally gentle wooden images of Miroku Bosatsu at the CHŪGŪ-JI nunnery near Hōryū-ji and at KŌRYŪ-JI in Kyoto show much smoother modeling and tenderness. The statues are remarkably similar to two bronze statues in the Seoul National Museum (Korea). The paintings on the Tamamushi-zushi, a small lacquered shrine at Hōryū-ji, are the oldest from the historical period; the shrine was once inlaid with the iridescent wings of *tamamushi* (jewel beetles), a technique imported from Korea.

Figure 37. Yakushi Nyorai (Hōryū-ji)

In the sixth century, the Yamato state lost its territory on the Korean peninsula, and Japanese interest shifted to China, which had recently regained a central government that supported a strong Buddhist establishment. Tang China at the time was the most cosmopolitan country in the world, with a vast empire and trade routes extending to Rome. Traders and envoys from throughout the civilized world rubbed shoulders in Ch'ang-an, the magnificent Tang capital. As this vibrant culture spread eastward, exciting advances occurred in Japan, the effects of which are especially visible in art.

Across a dangerous sea, these influences were more easily transmitted by drawings than by statues. A voluptuous new esthetic of sinuous bodies, bejeweled and swathed in diaphanous drapery, probably inspired by Chinese sketches of Indian art, can be seen in the early eighth-century frescoes in Hōryū-ji's main hall (damaged in 1949), on Hōryū-ji's Tachibana Shrine, and in the magnificent bronze Shō Kannon and Yakushi Trinity at Nara's YAKUSHI-JI. The Shō Kannon's sensual physique contrasts with the archaism of its square, frontal stance and the flattened, stylized hems of its drapery. It is almost as though the statue were poised midway in the move from two dimensions to three. The Yakushi Trinity, although possibly a slightly earlier work, shows the full development of this trend: the celebrated bosatsu attendants, Nikkō and Gakkō, are fully three-dimensional, dynamic and delightful to view from all sides. The grapevine motif on the central image's pedestal betrays western Asian influences; grapes were not native to East Asia but were introduced by the trade in Roman wine on the Silk Road. Many musical instruments, such as the *biwa* (lute) and the *koto* (zithern) were also introduced. The bronze finial atop Yakushi-ji's East Pagoda depicts slender angels playing flutes and harps embedded in lyrical openwork; art historian Noma Seiroku suggests that the lightness of Hakuhō art echoes a "musical awakening."

## The Courtly Art of Nara
### Nara Period (710–794)
If the Asuka and Hakuhō periods were the dawn of Japan's Buddhist golden age, then the Nara period was its high noon. This was a period of monumental Buddhism on a scale never to be repeated. The Great Buddha Hall at TŌDAI-JI, dedicated in 752, was the biggest and grandest in a succession of splendid temple halls. The hall and the Great Buddha have been repaired and rebuilt so many times, however, that today neither accurately reflects Nara's art. Instead, the true greatness of the period can be seen in many smaller objects, such as the octagonal bronze lantern that stands in the courtyard before the Great Buddha Hall. The heavenly musicians in high relief decorating its sides are lyrical and gay, like those at Yakushi-ji, but their bodies are fleshier and more richly adorned.

As life at the Nara court became more elaborate, ethereality gave way to opulent realism. The small painting of Kisshō-ten at Yakushi-ji, probably painted in the 770s, portrays this Indian goddess as a voluptuous court matron. The tendency toward realism coincided with the Great Buddha project, which severely depleted Japan's supply of bronze. Sculptors were forced to turn to clay and dry lacquer, with the happy result that their work became more fluid and lifelike. Great examples include the remote and dignified Bon-ten and Taishaku-ten of Tōdai-ji's HOKKE-DŌ, the stern and wise Shi-Tennō (four kings) of the KAIDAN-IN, and the dry-lacquer Ashura (fig. 38) at KŌFUKU-JI, originally a wrathful demon, here rendered tender and boyish. The Nara period's mastery of sculpture also extended to the expressive Gigaku masks used in court dances.

Figure 38. Ashura (Kōfuku-ji)

Thousands of lesser masterpieces have been preserved in the famed SHŌSŌ-IN imperial repository, which some call the world's oldest museum. Besides objects used in temples and at court, the collection includes gifts presented to Emperor Shōmu by envoys from throughout Asia, perhaps as far away as Persia, on the occasion of the dedication of Tōdai-ji's Great Buddha in 752. It is often said that the Silk Road ends at the Shōsō-in. Many items are in a superb state of preservation; they include drawings, documents, textiles, cosmetics, ritual implements, cut glass from Persia, silver vessels, and musical instruments with exquisite mother-of-pearl decoration. Some objects, once assumed to have been foreign gifts, are now thought to be Japanese copies, evidence of a rapidly developing native skill.

Toward the close of the Nara period, Buddhist reformers reacted against opulent realism. Ganjin, the indomitable Chinese who was the most important priest in Japan, sought to reform Japanese Buddhism by establishing TŌSHŌDAI-JI as a seminary to train Nara priests, who had grown lax amid the luxury of the capital. Ganjin's Chinese artisans carved from single blocks of wood, producing weighty and remote images intended to induce deeper meditations on Buddhist mysteries, whereas earlier images had inspired only enchanted reveries upon physical beauty. Tōshōdai-ji's Senju Kannon, an awe-inspiring thousand-armed Goddess of Mercy, possesses none of the tenderness of middle Nara-period art. In contrast, the temple's venerated portrait statue of Ganjin depicts the blind, aged priest with unstinting realism.

Figure 39. Nyoirin Kannon (Murō-ji)

## Esoteric and Syncretic Mysteries
### Heian to Kamakura Periods (794–1333)

In 794, Emperor Kammu founded a new capital at Kyoto (Heian-kyō), partly to escape the politically ambitious temples of Nara. The art of the first century of the Heian period was formed by the demands of the new Esoteric Buddhist sects, Shingon and Tendai. These sects called for sculpture and painting to aid in ritual and meditation, instead of serving merely as objects for veneration. Single-block wood sculpture achieved a high degree of mastery; images became deliberately unrealistic, with heavy heads and limbs and "inscrutable" faces, all intended to convey divine mystery (fig. 39). The Hindu influence on Esoteric Buddhism can be seen in the grotesque faces and multiple limbs of the deities. At TŌ-JI, near the Kyoto station, one can see a three-dimensional mandala, an array of twenty-one statues said to have been carved and arranged by KŪKAI himself.

93

Although mandalas originated in India as sculptural arrangements like the group at Tō-ji, they became so complex that they were most often depicted in painting, long before they ever reached Japan. The two mandalas favored by Shingon, the Diamond and Womb Mandalas (see Buddhism, p. 36), are especially intricate; the Diamond Mandala calls for the minute depiction of 414 deities. Artistic expression was saddled by the fact that each deity had a prescribed color scheme and iconography. The average believer, for whom mandalas were too abstract, preferred larger, freer depictions of the wrathful Myō-ō, enemies of evil. Particularly popular was Fudō Myō-ō, who was believed to aid those undergoing religious austerities. There are many famous images of him, such as the *Red Fudō* painting at KŌYA-SAN.

Because Esoteric Buddhist deities have multiple manifestations, their introduction into Japan enhanced a trend, already present in the Nara period, toward combining Shinto and Buddhism (see Shinto, p. 27). Just as Buddhist and Shinto deities were identified with one another, so Buddhist images led to the depiction of the hitherto invisible Shinto kami. Beginning in the ninth century, kami were portrayed in wood statuary, compactly and realistically in the form of Heian nobles, in contrast to the often grotesque, fantastic forms of Buddhist deities. Tō-ji and Nara's Yakushi-ji own famous statues of Hachiman, the deified Emperor Ōjin, in the guise of a Buddhist priest.

Syncretic mandalas also appeared, although much later, because a great amount of metaphysical juggling was needed to pair the multitudes of Shinto kami with corresponding Buddhist deities. The Kamakura-period *Kasuga Shrine Mandala* (TOKYO NATIONAL MUSEUM) is characteristic in that it sidesteps the issue of the kami's appearance, portraying only the shrine precincts and using Sanskrit letters to show where the corresponding Buddhist deities are supposed to reside. The painting, *Nachi Waterfall* (NEZU ART MUSEUM), simply depicts the sacred waterfall, which was regarded as an avatar of Kannon Bosatsu.

## The Art of Paradise
### Late Heian Period (894–1185)

Toward the end of the ninth century, Heian courtiers became increasingly reluctant to undertake the dangerous voyages to China. Moreover, Buddhism, which had served to link the two cultures, had been subject to severe persecution in China during the previous fifty years. In any case, the Tang empire was beginning to crumble. In 894, Japan curtailed its relations with Tang China and entered a period of isolation during which native esthetic inclinations were allowed to develop. The Heian court culture that resulted was one of the most peculiar and refined in the history of civilizations (see Uji History, p. 387).

During the late Heian, or Fujiwara, period, sculpture took on a new aura of compassion and tranquility. A conviction arose that the Buddhist law was in decline, and that Esoteric Buddhist teachings, limited to a few, were no longer adequate. Many people turned to the belief that Amida, the Buddha of the Pure Land, would save all who sincerely invoked his name. Just as the Esoteric mandala expressed Esoteric Buddhist mysteries, so the Amida Mandala, a radiant picture of the Pure Land depicting Amida in his glittering palace, attended by heavenly dancers and musicians, became the icon of this new faith.

This vision is gloriously realized at the famous BYŌDŌ-IN at Uji, south of Kyoto, a

Fujiwara villa built, as was the fashion of the time, to resemble the jeweled palaces depicted in Amida mandalas. The large, gilded Amida Buddha inside the temple's main hall is the work of JŌCHŌ, the most gifted sculptor of the age. Jōchō set a new standard of physical proportions and facial expression to convey Amida's omniscience and compassion. High up on the surrounding walls are small wood carvings of Bosatsu riding on clouds, dancing and playing musical instruments. Jōchō revolutionized wood sculpture by perfecting the technique for multiblock construction, which permitted greater fluidity of expression—and mass production. His descendants, the KEI SCHOOL, would bring the method to its zenith.

In painting, there matured a native style called Yamato-e, which reached its most sophisticated form in *e-makimono*, or narrative picture scrolls, inspired by the literary outpouring that is the hallmark of this period. With the invention of *kana*, a script better suited for the expression of Japanese, native themes replaced Chinese ideas in the court literature; *waka* poetry, folk tales, and full-blown novels such as *The Tale of Genji* were read avidly. Such works were illustrated with pictures not of exotic China, but of native scenes, emotionally subtle yet powerful. The undisputed masterpiece of illustrated court literature is the *Tale of Genji Scrolls* (late 12th C), painted by Fujiwara no Takayoshi. The long, flowing hair of the ladies, the lavish costumes, and the backgrounds were carefully composed to convey both the melancholy mood of the novel and its sumptuous setting (fig. 40). Colors suggest the emotional undercurrents of a scene, while the pale, expressionless faces of the characters invite the reader to imagine their mood and appearance. Because much of the activity takes place indoors, the artist devised an ingenious technique of removing the roof and arranging the walls to reveal the persons within; he also used linear elements to heighten the sense of drama, with effects that verge on the abstract. The Genji scrolls are now in the TOKUGAWA ART MUSEUM in Nagoya and the GOTŌ ART MUSEUM in Tokyo.

94

Figure 40. *Genji Monogatari* scroll

One of the supreme Japanese achievements in the decorative arts, *maki-e* lacquer, developed in this environment. Lacquerware was introduced early—tradition has SHŌTOKU TAISHI ordering lac trees planted—but decoration had been limited to painting and inlaying. *Maki-e*, a Japanese invention, is created by sprinkling gold and silver dust on wet lacquer, a technique that permits shading, texture, and a subtlety of design unequaled elswhere. Motifs taken from daily life—waves, ox-cart wheels, birds, fans—were treated as pure patterns, a distinctively Japanese approach to design that has continued to the present.

The same refinement and elegance appears in religious art. Buddhist sculpture of the period was covered with hair-thin lines of gold leaf, called *kirikane*. The Byōdō-in was once richly decorated inside with gold leaf and shell-inlay, but these have been lost to the ravages of time. However, the Konjiki-dō of CHŪSON-JI, far to the north, preserves its splendid ornamentation. The *Heike Nōkyō*, Lotus Sutra scrolls donated by the TAIRA clan to ITSUKUSHIMA JINJA, also rank among the great masterpieces of the age. Each scroll has a lavish frontispiece drawn in gold, silver, and bright pigments, and the text itself is embellished with gold and silver flakes. The fittings of crystal and finely worked metal, the silken cords, and the bronze case decorated with dragons and clouds complete a picture of a culture that was moved as much by an exquisite sense of worldly beauty as by faith.

### The Kei School Sculptors
### Kamakura Period (1185–1333)

The Heian period, Japan's classical age, ended violently in a great war between two feuding clans, the MINAMOTO and the Taira. The victor, MINAMOTO NO YORITOMO, undertook to rebuild war-damaged temples around Kyoto and Nara; foremost was the rebuilding of Tōdai-ji and its Great Buddha Hall. Many of the hundreds of statues needed for this vast project were sculpted by the KEI SCHOOL, a family of gifted sculptors based in Nara; its leading exponents— UNKEI (1151–1223), KAIKEI, and TANKEI—were descendants of Jōchō, the genius of the Byōdō-in. Using the multiblock method perfected by Jōchō, they were able to work at a feverish pace, assigning rough shaping and assembly to apprentices and saving their own skills for the finishing touches. The multiblock method also allowed them to insert eerily lifelike crystal eyes.

In Kyoto, the Kei School worked on famous "portraits" of Kūya Shōnin (fig. 41) and Taira no Kiyomori at ROKUHARAMITSU-JI, as well as statues at SENBON SHAKADŌ and SANJŪSANGEN-DŌ. The most famous masterpieces, however, are in Nara. The Niō in Tōdai-ji's Great South Gate, a pair of Herculean Deva kings carved by Unkei and Kaikei, boast rippling muscles and popping veins that convey a tremendous impression of physical power. Spiritual power is just as strikingly captured in the imaginary portrait statues of the priests Muchaku and Seshin, owned by Nara's Kōfuku-ji, the temple most closely associated with the Kei

Figure 41. Kūya Shōnin (Rokuharamitsu-ji)

School. Tōdai-ji owns the equally remarkable Portrait of Chōgen, the priest who supervised the rebuilding of Tōdai-ji, a task that must have required a will of iron. The portrait's stubbornly set jaw captures the old man's grim resolve.

Chōgen was a follower of the Jōdo Sect, which along with the Jōdo Shin sect propagated a doctrine of faith and salvation among the common people. The supreme symbol of the devotional and artistic forces of this age is the Great Bronze Amida at Kamakura, which was built with donations from the faithful. These new sects precipitated a demand for a huge number of Amida, Kannon, and Jizō images, which were often gaudily gilded and had compassionate and lovely faces that appealed to everyone. With the proliferation of so much undistinguished statuary, the momentum that had carried the religious sculpture of the Kei School to great heights dissipated within a few decades. With a few exceptions, such as portraits of Zen priests, Japanese sculpture never again regained its vitality.

95

### Narrative Picture Scrolls
### Kamakura Period (1185–1333)

During the late Heian and Kamakura periods, there emerged a lively and realistic new style of scroll painting. Often humorous or grotesque, it offered startling contrasts to the exquisite, static beauty of the Genji scrolls. The *Shigisan Engi* (Legends of Mt. Shigi) scrolls, dated circa 1156–1180, depicted real faces and details of common life. The famous episode of the Flying Storehouse portrays the tale of a hermit who is fed by a magic alms bowl that flies daily between his retreat and a rich man's storehouse. One day, the bowl gets locked inside the storehouse; it flies back to the hermit carrying the entire storehouse with it, generating great excitement among onlookers. The scrolls are long, continuous pictures, drawn in a lively style, and feature "cinematic" storytelling conventions, such as having one scene fade into the next and reversing the action to provide a flashback.

The early Kamakura-period *Chōjū Giga* (Frolicking Animals Scrolls) of Kōzan-ji, now at the Tokyo National Museum, is a cartoonish satire of society; the best-known portion shows frogs, rabbits, and monkeys playing games and conducting Buddhist rites. Although Amida's Paradise had long been portrayed in painting, during the Kamakura period imaginatively gruesome Yamato-e picture scrolls depicted the Amidist hell, as well as the other five Realms of Reincarnation—hungry ghosts, animals, evil spirits, human beings, and divinities. Also portrayed were the lives of saints such as Hōnen Shōnin and Ippen Shōnin. The Yamato-e tradition continued in the Muromachi, Momoyama, and Edo periods under the aegis of the Tosa School; this tradition would form the artistic basis for Momoyama-period genre painting and the ukiyo-e school of the Edo period.

# SECULAR ART AND THE DECORATIVE TRADITION (1334–1912)

### Zen Painting
### Muromachi Period (1334–1573)

When the ASHIKAGA shoguns returned the seat of power to Kyoto, Zen influence merged with a revival of courtly life and art connoisseurship to produce a great cultural flowering. Much of what we think of today as forming the core of Japanese art—tea ceremony, rock gardens, Noh drama, and ink painting—emerged at this time, primarily at the shogun's court and the great Kyoto Zen temples.

Zen priests, well versed in the culture of Sung China, were the only Japanese who could write the missives and handle the diplomatic protocol required for the official trading missions to China. They also became skilled appraisers of the fine porcelains and *suibokuga* (ink paintings) that came back from China, destined for the shogun. The most admired ink paintings were not, however, of the contemporary Ming dynasty, but of the earlier Sung dynasty, where the roots of Japanese Zen lay. Especially revered was the Huangzhou priest-painter Much'i. When the shogun YOSHIMITSU founded the official painting academy at Shōkoku-ji at the end of the fourteenth century, it was the Sung style that was taught and that determined the course

Figure 42. *Winter*, by Sesshū

of Japanese painting for the next two centuries; the great Muromachi masters—Josetsu, Shūbun, SESSHŪ, KANŌ MASANOBU—were all students and teachers there.

In China, *suibokuga* developed primarily as a literary and esthetic, rather than religious, form of painting. In Japan also, *suibokuga* heralded a secularization of art, even though its first practitioners were Zen monks. Arcadian ink landscapes invited contemplation by depicting the grand solitude of Nature, rather than a religious icon. Buddhist and Taoist themes remained central, but were significantly altered; Shaka was depicted as a man, not a divinity, and the Immortals were shown as mountain hermits. In the hands of Zen monks, ink paintings became spare and impressionistic—produced by a flash of insight. By refraining from literal representations of color and form, the painters seem to suggest that appearances are illusory, that the essence of being can only be intuited.

Shōkoku-ji's first painter of note was **Josetsu**, an early fifteenth-century master who painted *Catching a Catfish with a Gourd*, a humorous sketch based on a Zen allegory about a hermit who attempts this impossible feat. **Shūbun**, who was placed in charge of the painter's academy, was a virtuoso of landscapes. The greatest *suibokuga* master was SESSHŪ (1420–1506), a student of Shūbun's. Sesshū left Kyoto and the academy shortly before the disastrous Ōnin Wars (1467–1477) and found a patron in Lord Ōuchi of Yamaguchi, whose trading mission to China he accompanied in 1467–69. To his disappointment, he found few living Chinese masters whose work he respected, but he was able to travel and sketch in the countryside, an experience of great importance, for almost no Japanese artists had actually seen the landscapes they so carefully copied from Chinese paintings. Returning to Japan, Sesshū continued to work from nature. He broke with the conventions of the Shōkoku-ji academy, adding hints of color wherever he pleased to enhance the mood of his compositions. He worked in a variety of styles, from bold, Chinese-influenced landscapes and impressionistic "splashed ink" compositions to warmly atmospheric Japanese landscapes (fig. 42). His most celebrated works—*Four Seasons Landscape Scroll, Haboku (Splashed Ink) Landscape, Hui'ko Presenting his Arm to Daruma, Ama no Hashidate*—are testaments to his versatility. Sesshū is a pivotal figure who stands at the point where religious art gave way to purely esthetic art. It seems no accident that he was the first Japanese painter to place a prominent signature—the mark of an individual artist—on his work.

**The early Kanō School.** Decorative paintings on *fusuma* (sliding screens) and *byōbu* (folding screens) had been used since the Heian period, but they became an important artistic medium in the later Muromachi period, with the advent of *shoin* architecture (see Villas, p. 63). KANŌ MASANOBU, another student of Shūbun's at Shōkoku-ji, succeeded him as head of the academy and founded the hereditary KANŌ SCHOOL, which was to dominate decorative screen painting for the next four hundred years. His son MOTONOBU skillfully married Chinese ink painting to Yamato-e techniques, such as the liberal use of color and picture elements that wander on and off the plane or into an abstract golden cloud. He developed the mature Kanō style, which can be seen in the superb screens at Daisen-in and the Myōshin-ji subtemple, REIUN-IN. (Taizō-in, another Myōshin-ji subtemple, has a garden ascribed to Motonobu.) Motonobu also established a studio system that enabled the Kanō line to perpetuate itself through generations of only moderate talents.

## Golden Screens and Peasant Pottery
## Momoyama Period (1573–1615)

The Momoyama period is distinguished by the contrast between gorgeous decoration and the restraint of the tea ceremony. During its brief forty years, hundreds of castles, palaces, temples, and shrines were built, and artistic production had to keep pace. *Arriviste* military rulers such as ODA NOBUNAGA and TOYOTOMI HIDEYOSHI used gold lavishly to display their new power and wealth; decorative arts reached an apex of sumptuousness. At Kyoto's Kōdai-ji, built by Hideyoshi's widow, the altar was covered with a beautiful lacquer, renowned as Kōdai-ji *maki-e*, that was decorated with flowering plants and musical instruments of gold. Newly acquired techniques for incorporating gold and silver thread into brocades, embroidery, and appliqués brought an unparalleled lavishness to the costumes of the ruling class.

The warlords also demanded golden screens to brighten their gloomy castles. The foremost master of the ornate Momoyama screen was KANŌ EITOKU (1543–1590), Motonobu's grandson. He was commissioned to paint Nobunaga's Azuchi-jō and Hideyoshi's Ōsaka-jō and Juraku-tei palace. These edifices, and the screens inside them, have been destroyed, but a few of his paintings survive, such as the *Chinese Lions Screen* (now owned by the Imperial Household Agency), *Cypress Trees* (Tokyo National Museum), and a set of screens at Jukō-in, a subtemple of Daitoku-ji in Kyoto. In Eitoku, the Kanō School reached its zenith.

Eitoku's main rival was the independent **Hasegawa Tōhaku** (1539–1610), who painted the exquisite *Maple and Cherry Tree Screens* at CHISHAKU-IN, a temple in Kyoto. His *Pine Trees Screen* (Tokyo National Museum), an ink painting of impressionistic brush strokes, shows the remarkable range of this artist. Eitoku's adopted heir, KANŌ SANRAKU, painted the *Peony Screens* at DAIKAKU-JI, *Birds in Plum Trees Screen* at TENKYŪ-IN, and *Landscape Screens* at SHŌDEN-JI. During the Edo period, the Kanō School remained the official academy under the TOKUGAWA shogunate, whose rigidity caused the school to lapse into stiff conventionality. The most famous painter of this period is KANŌ TAN'YŪ (1602–1674), who painted the *Pine Tree Screens* at NIJŌ-JŌ, as well as screens for Edo-jō and NAGOYA-JŌ. He also directed the artwork for the Nikkō Tōshō-gū.

**Tea Bowls.** Coexisting with the lavish Momoyama decor was the restrained esthetic of the tea ceremony. In the Muromachi period, tea ceremonies offered occasions to admire expensive imported Chinese wares. The Momoyama-period tea master SEN NO RIKYŪ, however, insisted that native crafts and humble objects, with their subtle, unpretentious beauty, were worthy of even greater admiration. He was especially taken with the ordinary Korean peasant rice-bowl, called Ido, which he used in the tea ceremony. Ido bowls became extravagantly prized; chips and cracks were mended with gold. Rikyū commissioned the potter Chōjirō to make a special type of tea bowl, now known as Raku ware. It is broad-bottomed, to accommodate the beating tea whisk, light and hand-formed to fit into the hand, and typically glazed black, salmon, or white. Raku, Hagi (an Ido type of ware made in western Honshū), and Karatsu (a Korean-influenced ware made in northern Kyūshū), with their refined rustic quality, are considered ideal for the tea ceremony. By the time of Hideyoshi's campaigns in Korea, Korean wares were so favored that Korean potters were captured and taken back to Japan. The craze for tea ware brought major developments in Japanese ceramic art (see Crafts, p. 103); many artists of the period dabbled in tea and tea utensils. Sen no Rikyū's disciple, Furuta Oribe, invented a style of pottery. In the mid-seventeenth century, the Kyoto potter **Nonomura Ninsei** developed an elegant enameled stoneware; his celebrated tea urns are decorated with designs inspired by Yamato-e.

### The Design Genius of the Rimpa School
### Edo Period (1615–1868)

**Kōetsu and Sōtatsu.** The remarkable RIMPA SCHOOL evolved as a reaction to Momoyama extravagance. Drawing on Heian courtly traditions and the nature esthetic of the tea ceremony, it formulated a new decorative esthetic that gives works of the school an enduring appeal. HON'AMI KŌETSU (1558–1637) received a gift of land from TOKUGAWA IEYASU in the Takagamine district in northern Kyoto (where there is now a temple in his memory, KŌETSU-JI). Kōetsu worked in a variety of media, including lacquer, pottery, metal, and bamboo, producing playfully innovative pieces that would have been impossible for professional artisans. His famous ink-stone box (Tokyo National Museum) bears the design of a boat passing under a bridge; the gold lacquer relief of boat and water plays against the dull, beaten-lead strip representing the bridge, over which some scrawling lines of poetry have been inlaid in silver. Like many of his designs, this scene serves as a background for Kōetsu's distinctive calligraphy, the art for which this multitalented man was most famous.

Figure 43. Folding screen by Tawaraya Sōtatsu

97

Kōetsu is perhaps most celebrated for his series of poems brushed against exquisite grounds, thought to be painted by his brother-in-law TAWARAYA SŌTATSU (d. 1643), a fanmaker and one of Japan's most original and versatile painters (fig. 43). Sōtatsu painted birds, flowers, and landscapes using a distinctive style called *tarashikomi*, a "puddling" technique that involves applying inks with a wet brush so that they bleed, as in watercolor. He also took an interest in the old Yamato-e tradition; he produced many works adapted from the Genji scrolls and the Heike Sutra Scrolls, which he helped to restore in 1602. Sōtatsu treated classical themes in a fresh and whimsical way; his famous *Wind and Thunder Gods Screen* (Kyoto National Museum) is an amusing caricature of its thirteenth-century sculptural prototype at the Kyoto temple Sanjūsangen-dō.

**Kōrin and Kenzan.** The term Rimpa comes from the last syllable in the name of OGATA KŌRIN (1658–1716), a great-grandnephew of Kōetsu. Kōrin, like Sōtatsu, painted from classical themes, such as the Yatsuhashi Bridge from *The Tale of Ise*; he combined decorativeness, simplicity, and naturalism with extraordinary skill, as exemplified in his famous *Iris Screen* (Nezu Art Museum). His careful drawing is often breathtakingly combined with purely decorative elements, borrowed and stylized from the classical repertoire. The *Red and White Plum Trees Screen* (MOA ART MUSEUM) is particularly pleasing, with its delicately painted plum blossoms standing out against a boldly abstract rivulet. Kōrin's younger brother KENZAN (1663–1743), although also a painter, is most famous as a ceramic artist. A student of the potter Nonomura Ninsei, Kenzan converted his brother Kōrin's designs into a unique style of pottery. Strongly influenced by the tea ceremony and Zen, Kenzan's work has an abstract, casual quality. His version of the Yatsuhashi Bridge, for example, is freely brushed and much less realistic than Kōrin's. The Ogata brothers were among the last great exponents of the courtly Kyoto tradition.

## Pictures from the Floating World
## Momoyama to Meiji Periods (1573–1912)

**Genre painting.** The Tosa School, official painters to the imperial court, continued to work in the classical Yamato-e style. They frequently painted the Nenjū Gyōji, or annual rites, of the imperial court and the various shrines, and depicted the seasons and famous places. In the early Momoyama period, as Kyoto regained its magnificence, gilded screens called *rakuchū rakugai-zu* (Scenes of the Capital and its Environs) became popular; they showed pavilions of Kyoto and the floats of the Gion Matsuri peeking out between golden clouds. They were painted in pairs, one screen showing central Kyoto and the other the temples of Higashiyama, east of the Kamo River. The painters exploited the folds of the screens to produce lively, three-dimensional effects. *Namban byōbu* (Screens of the Southern Barbarians) are another type of genre screen that comes in sets of two: one screen shows Portuguese sailors with their ships at Nagasaki and the other is a portrait of the exotic port town itself (fig. 44).

Figure 44. Namban screen by Kanō Naizen

Such genre paintings of popular scenes quickly spread among artists outside the Tosa School, who adopted the school's style and techniques. In fact, many of the most famous screens were painted by moonlighting Kanō artists. For example, Kanō Eitoku painted the famous *Uesugi Screens*, which ODA NOBUNAGA gave to the famous warlord, Uesugi Kenshin. (The screens are now in the KEISHŌDEN in Yonezawa.) Other famous Kanō School genre paintings are *Maple Viewing at Takao* by Kanō Hideyori and *Merrymaking under the Blossoms* by Kanō Naonobu (Tokyo National Museum).

By the early Edo period, wealthy townsmen were commissioning genre paintings on a smaller scale from minor artists. Their subjects were Kyoto's pleasure quarters, the women's Kabuki (see Drama, p. 89), and other scenes of daily life. *The Hanging Scroll of Yuna* (MOA Art Museum) is a cruelly humorous depiction of bathhouse prostitutes. Compositions began to focus on small groups of figures; the *Hikone Screen* (Hikone Art Museum) depicts men and women in an unspecified, dreamlike space. The *Matsu'ura Screen* (YAMATO BUNKAKAN) focuses on the gorgeous costumes of women, giving them very much the same sort of treatment as the ukiyo-e or "floating world" pictures did, especially of the Kaigetsu-dō School, which specialized in ukiyo-e portraits (called *nikuhitsu*) of beautiful courtesans. (See Ryokan, p. 125 for an explanation of *ukiyo*.)

**Ukiyo-e prints.** Aside from the Kaigetsu-dō School and a few other Kansai artists, the home of the ukiyo-e—especially the woodblock print—was Edo, where a burgeoning population of ordinary townsmen clamored for amusements and diversions. **Hishikawa Moronobu**, who painted the genre screens called *Nakamura-za Kabuki Theater* and *Flower-Viewing at Edo* (SUNTORY ART MUSEUM), was the first great name in black-and-white ukiyo-e prints; continuing the trend of genre screens, his prints focused on the related worlds of the actor and the prostitute. Among his successors was the Torii School, which specialized in actor prints; since costumes were at least as important as faces in these early "portraits," the black-and-white outlines were often filled in with color, especially with a luxurious red safflower dye called *beni*, which was worth more than its weight in gold.

The first full-color prints were made by **Suzuki Harunobu** (1724–1770) for a calendar in 1765. The yearly disposition of the lunar calendar (see Matsuri, p. 75), which was made public on the New Year, determined when debts could be collected; expensive limited editions were distributed in advance to merchants with this insider information cleverly hidden in the illustrations. The expense of using multiple blocks for the different colors was covered by the calendar's exorbitant price. Harunobu's dainty, neotenic women suited the new color technique (fig. 45). Both were widely imitated instant successes; the print, aside from illustrated books, was from then on in color.

99

Figure 45. Ukiyo-e print by Suzuki Harunobu

The golden age of the ukiyo-e print began around 1790. The ukiyo-e craftsman began to take on some of the idiosyncrasies of the independent artist. The portraits of handsome actors and the diminutive, Harunobu-style *bijin* (beautiful women) gave way to more grotesque actors and statuesque women. **Sharaku**, a mysterious genius who worked a mere ten months from 1794 to 1795, portrayed bony-faced *onnagata* (female impersonators) and comically fierce *aragoto* actors (see Drama, p. 87). **Torii Kiyonaga**, who began working in the 1780s, challenged Harunobu's feminine ideal with his images of statuesque beauties. **Utamaro**, who began to work in the 1790s, softened, individualized, and eroticized this taller ideal. Utamaro was a denizen of the pleasure quarter, and his understanding of feminine erotic psychology also made him a master of the pornographic *shunga*, or "spring pictures," which had been a major subgenre of the ukiyo-e print from its inception. Indeed, the *bijin* portrait itself had first developed as a guide to the courtesans of the Yoshiwara pleasure quarter (see Tokyo History, p. 195). *Shunga* were generally printed in books called *sharebon*, with comparatively innocent covers that belied the explicit contents.

**The Ukiyo-e landscape and after.** From this time on, ukiyo-e became extremely popular and were printed in great quantity; the quality of later impressions of a print was very poor, because blocks were used until they disintegrated. As the print-buying public became broader, the kimono of the *bijin* portraits became coarser and the poses more exaggerated. Moreover, people were beginning to tire of actors and prostitutes. Their interest was instead captured by landscape series, aimed at a public fascinated by, but rarely able to, travel (see Villages, p. 56). In essence, these were more artistically rendered versions of the "scenes of famous places," illustrated guidebooks to every province of Japan.

**Katsushika Hokusai** (1760–1849), "the old man mad with painting," had studied with the Tosa, Kanō, and Rimpa schools. In addition, he had learned about Western perspective drawing from Shiba Kōkan (see following page). Hokusai brought his learning and talent to bear on his *Thirty-six Views of Fuji*, which was an instant success when published in 1823. In addition to having a superb sense of composition, Hokusai was a supremely gifted draftsman, and even his countless sketches of animals and human physiognomies are imbued with startling vitality. Hokusai's younger rival in landscape prints, **Andō Hiroshige** (1797–1858), was a master at capturing the atmosphere of each locale. In his most famous work, *The Fifty-three Stations of the Tōkaidō*, the human figures blend harmoniously with the mood of the landscape. In collaboration with another artist, Eisen, he also created the Kiso Kaidō series.

**Utagawa Kuniyoshi** (1798–1861), a contemporary of Hiroshige's, began to paint ghosts and other vividly imaginative scenes as well as landscapes. Kuniyoshi was anticipating an increasingly jaded, sensation-loving public. Ghost stories such as *Yotsuya Kaiden* now dominated the Kabuki as well. Because gaudy aniline dyes, imported from the West, were cheap and consonant with the public mood, they were adopted overnight. (The older dyes, which had produced the subtle tints of Hiroshige and Hokusai prints, were so completely abandoned that their composition is now a subject of debate.) **Taiso Yoshitoshi** (1839–1892), who used aniline dyes to depict lurid goblins and battle scenes, showed great originality in composition as well as an understanding of Western painting techniques. **Kobayashi Kiyochika** (1847–1915), known for his landscape prints, served as a "correspondent" during the Sino-Japanese War (1894) and sent gory propaganda prints of battle scenes to the Japanese newspapers.

### Other Schools of the Edo Period

During the Edo period, the works of Chinese Ming and Ch'ing literati artists entered Japan through Nagasaki and the Ōbaku Zen sect, and influenced the formation of the Japanese literati, or *bunjin*, school. Its most famous exponents were **Ike no Taiga** and **Yosa Buson**. For this school, painting was only one aspect of a *bunjin's* achievements, which included knowledge of calligraphy and of the Chinese classics that provided the themes for their art. Paintings were constructed out of spontaneous, impressionistic brushstrokes, as suited amateurs.

The Realist School was founded by **Maruyama Ōkyo** (1733–1795), who studied Chinese and Western painting and depicted nature scenes in a realistic yet economical style. **Shiba Kōkan**, also known for his forgeries of the ukiyo-e artist Harunobu, is probably the best known of the early Western-style painters; his work foreshadowed the *yō-ga* (Western painting) movement in the early Meiji period.

# A Note on Prehistoric Art

**Jōmon Period (ca. 10,000–300 B.C.).** The Jōmon people were primarily hunters and gatherers who made the world's oldest known pottery—carbon dated to before 10,000 B.C.—for which they are named. Jōmon pottery was built up from coils of clay and the soft surface was boldly imprinted with rope (*jōmon* means "rope pattern") or other objects, and fired at a low temperature. Because the pots were porous, they were sometimes painted with ochre to help prevent leaks. Particularly beautiful is the flaming Jōmon pottery of the early Middle Jōmon Period (3500 B.C.–2000 B.C.). This pottery, made in north central Japan, as far north as Aizu-Wakamatsu, is decorated along the rim with flamboyant sculptural forms that resemble highly stylized roosters, dragonflies, and other motifs (fig. 46). In addition to making vessels for cooking and food storage, these ancient potters created female fertility figures, often in an abstract, geometrical style.

Figure 46.
Flaming Jōmon pot

**Yayoi Period (300 B.C.–A.D. 300).** By 300 B.C., when Yayoi culture emerged, wet rice agriculture had been introduced from Korea. Yayoi pottery seems to be a hybrid of the Jōmon tradition and techniques imported from the continent, and is much plainer in design. It was fired at higher temperatures, often to a pleasing orange-brown color, and was decorated (but not as yet thrown) on a potter's wheel. Most Yayoi pottery served the needs of an agricultural life. In addition, a type of stemmed tray on which other pots were placed seems to have been used for ritual offerings. In Kyūshū, cylindrical pottery coffins have been found. The Yayoi people not only had iron tools, such as shovels and plows, but also implements of bronze, including mirrors and the mysterious *dōtaku*, which were clearly modeled on Chinese bells, but did not have a musical tone. They were probably objects of religious veneration and must have been imported from the mainland; certainly the superior cultures of China and Korea must have filled the Japanese with awe.

**Kofun Period (A.D. 300–ca. 700).** During this last phase of Japanese prehistory, local kings and chieftains were entombed in huge burial mounds called *kofun*, which were round, square, or keyhole-shaped. Armor, horse-tack, weapons, bronze mirrors, and jewelry were buried with the body to serve the dead in the next world. Placed inside or on top of the *kofun* were *haniwa*, clay models of warriors, servants, animals, and objects (fig. 47). Most *haniwa* were made like Haji pottery, which developed from Yayoi ware but were plainer, more regular, and fired in a more advanced type of kiln. The *haniwa* often exhibit touching artistry, portraying mischievous monkeys, gentle deer, and loving couples. Huge *haniwa* cylinders were planted upright along the periphery of the *kofun*. Clay houses, servants attending to their duties, and warriors in armor, with shields and horses, give a picture of ancient life.

Real bridles, saddle fittings, stirrups, horse bells, plated armor, swords, shields, and helmets, all found in abundance, make it clear that the aristocrats were mounted warriors. Some scholars think these people originated among the continental nomads of North Asia (see Kyūshū History, p. 469). The tombs also contain numerous bronze mirrors bearing Chinese and North Asian patterns; others have a *chokko-mon* (straight-and-curved pattern) also found on some *haniwa*, and one famous mirror shows ancient thatched houses. Curved jewels, called *magatama*, are also found. Some are made of materials, such as glass, that may have come from distant parts of Asia. The *magatama*, as well as the golden crowns, belts, rings, and slippers excavated from *kofun*, closely resemble objects excavated from Korean tombs.

Figure 47. Haniwa depicting a shamaness

101

# SELECTED COLLECTIONS

## CHŪBU

**✶✶ NAGOYA-JŌ.** A large group of decorative screens (p. 278).
**✶✶ TOKUGAWA ART MUSEUM.** *Tale of Genji Scrolls*; shown rarely (Nagoya, p. 278).
**✶✶ Nihon Ukiyo-e Museum.** Respected collection of Ukiyo-e prints (✶ Matsumoto, p. 283).

## KYOTO (✶✶✶)

**✶✶✶ TŌ-JI.** Esoteric Buddhist art (p. 325).
**✶✶ Nishi Hongan-ji.** Hasegawa Tōhaku screens (p. 326).
**✶✶✶ NIJŌ-JŌ.** Kanō Tan'yū and other Kanō painters (p. 329).
**✶✶ Raku Museum.** Devoted to Raku tea bowls (p. 331).
**✶✶✶ SANJŪSANGEN-DŌ.** A thousand statues of Kannon carved by the Kei School (p. 334).
**✶✶ KYOTO NATIONAL MUSEUM.** Repository for the art of Kansai-area temples. A fine group of Heian statuary, numerous narrative scrolls, and other paintings of all periods (p. 334).
**✶ CHISHAKU-IN.** Gilded screens by Hasegawa Tōhaku (p. 334).
**✶ ROKUHARAMITSU-JI.** Kamakura-period portrait statues (p. 335).
**✶ SEMBON SHAKA-DŌ.** Six Kannon and ten disciples by Kei School sculptors (p. 351).
**✶ Kitano Tenman-gū.** *Tenjin Engi* scroll shown the 25th of each month (p. 352).
**✶✶✶ DAITOKU-JI, DAISEN-IN.** Sōami screens (p. 352).
**✶ KŌETSU-JI.** Small museum displays the versatile style of Hon'ami Kōetsu (p. 354).
**✶ SHŌDEN-JI.** Kanō Sanraku Chinese landscapes (p. 354).
**✶✶ MYŌSHIN-JI, TENKYŪ-IN.** Kanō Sanraku screens (p. 356).
**✶✶ MYŌSHIN-JI, REIUN-IN.** Kanō Motonobu screens (p. 356).
**✶✶ KŌRYŪ-JI.** Famed 8th-century Korean statue of Miroku Bosatsu (p. 357).
**✶✶ DAIKAKU-JI.** Kanō Sanraku peony screens (p. 360).
**Ike no Taiga Museum.** Large group of paintings by this prominent literati painter (p. 364).

## 102 KINKI

**✶✶✶ BYŌDŌ-IN.** Amida by Jōchō; Bosatsu Riding on the Clouds (✶✶✶ Uji, p. 386).
**✶✶✶ KŌFUKU-JI.** Dry-lacquer Ashura and other masterpieces of Nara Buddhist art. Muchaku and Seshin portrait statues and other works of the Kei School (✶✶✶ Nara, p. 393).
**✶✶✶ NARA NATIONAL MUSEUM.** Many objects belonging to Nara-area temples are kept here. A portion of the incredible Shōsō-in collection is usually displayed here from late Oct. to early Nov. (✶✶✶ Nara, p. 393).
**✶✶✶ TŌDAI-JI.** Statuary in Hokke-dō and Kaidan-in. Kamakura-period Niō and portrait of Chōgen (✶✶✶ Nara, p. 394).
**✶✶ Shin-Yakushi-ji.** Masterpieces of Nara-period clay sculpture (✶✶✶ Nara, p. 396).
**✶✶ YAMATO BUNKAKAN.** Superb general collection (✶✶✶ Nara, p. 397).
**✶✶✶ TŌSHŌDAI-JI.** Awesome array of late Nara statuary (✶✶✶ Nara, p. 397).
**✶✶✶ YAKUSHI-JI.** Bronze Yakushi Trinity and Shō-Kannon, finial of East Pagoda, Kisshō-ten painting, and Hachiman portrait statue (✶✶✶ Nara, p. 397).
**✶✶✶ HŌRYŪ-JI.** Yakushi and Shaka Trinity by Tori Busshi or his school; Tamamushi and Tachibana shrines. The Chūgū-ji nunnery is famous for its statue of Miroku Bosatsu (p. 399).
**✶✶ Murō-ji.** Rich in early Heian sculpture (p. 404).
**✶✶✶ Nara Prefectural Archeological Museum.** Lavish museum of Yamato *kofun* culture (✶ Kashiwara, p. 406).
**✶✶✶ National Research Center for Asuka Material.** Fine displays on Yamato *kofun* and early Buddhist culture in Japan (✶✶ Asuka, p. 409).
**✶✶✶ Museum of Oriental Ceramics.** Superb collection of Asian ceramics (✶ Ōsaka, p. 416).
**✶✶ Fujita Art Museum.** Noted for tea ware and Rimpa art (✶ Ōsaka, p. 416).
**Daijō-ji.** Called Ōkyo Temple for its screens painted by Maruyama Ōkyo (Kasumi, p. 419).
**✶✶✶ KŌYA-SAN TREASURE HOUSE.** Vast collection of Esoteric Buddhist art (✶✶✶ Kōya-san, p. 420).
**✶✶ Kōbe City Museum.** *Namban* paintings (Kōbe, p. 422).

## CHŪGOKU AND SHIKOKU

**✶✶✶ ITSUKUSHIMA JINJA.** *Heike Sutra Scrolls* (✶✶✶ Miyajima, p. 451).
**✶✶✶ Mōri Museum.** Sesshū's *Four Seasons Landscape Scroll* (Hōfu, p. 456).

## KYŪSHŪ

**✶✶✶ Kyūshū Historical Museum.** Fine museum on early culture in northern Kyūshū, especially late Yayoi (✶✶ Dazaifu, p. 481).

### Japanese Art in America

Boston's **Museum of Fine Art** has the finest collection outside Japan; includes *Ban Dainagon Ekotoba* (Kamakura-period scroll), Kōrin's *Matsushima*, and a gallery for Buddhist statuary. New York's **Metropolitan Museum of Art** has a *Tenjin Engi* scroll, a Kōrin *Iris* screen, and a reproduction of a Momoyama-style temple *shoin*. The **Freer Gallery** in Washington, D.C., has an outstanding Rimpa collection, including a Sōtatsu dragon and a screen of cranes by Kōrin. The **Los Angeles County Museum** has a large group of Edo-period paintings. Other noted collections: the **Brooklyn Museum** and **Asia Society Gallery**, New York, the **Seattle Art Museum**, the **Asian Art Museum** in San Francisco, and the **Cleveland Art Museum**.

# Crafts

The boundary between art and craft has never been sharply defined in Japan as it has been in the West and in China. Since ancient times, when bronze and iron working, silk cultivation, lacquer, and papermaking were introduced from the continent to the isolated islanders, cultured and powerful people have supported crafts equally with the fine arts. Potters, swordsmiths, and fanmakers have been honored alongside painters and sculptors, and their work was esteemed for seamlessly fusing practical function with spiritual and esthetic qualities. To this day, craft secrets are treated as sacred treasures, handed down through the same family over many generations.

The continuity of Japanese crafts was gravely threatened after the Meiji Restoration (1868), when customs and traditions were discarded in the feverish pursuit of westernization and modernity. Many artisans abandoned their trades. In the 1920s, **Yanagi Sōetsu** (1889–1961), who thought machine-made objects were esthetically and spiritually impoverished, led a revival of Japan's crafts with his folk-art movement. Sōetsu coined the term *mingei*, or "people's art," to describe the humble work of the "unknown craftsman," who made objects for daily use, objects with a spontaneous beauty that was "born, not made." He organized and supported craftsmen, and built the Nihon Mingeikan (Japan Folk Art Museum) in Tokyo. Sōetsu was particularly interested in Japan's minority and neighboring cultures—Korean, aboriginal Taiwanese, Okinawan, and Ainu—and spoke out against the forced assimilation of these peoples by Japanese colonial policies before World War II.

Today, thanks to renewed appreciation of traditional crafts, outstanding artisans (as well as performing artists) are honored by the Ministry of Education as holders of important Intangible Cultural Properties. Popularly known as Living National Treasures, these artisans receive a modest stipend to further their studies and train apprentices. (Having won fame, they can also charge a fortune for their work.) The designation applies only to crafts of a practical nature, such as swordmaking, stencil-cutting, papermaking, and pottery. It includes both the elegant products once made for the upper classes and *mingei*, though nowadays, the indiscriminate application of this term to any vaguely rustic souvenir discourages many people from using it. The preferred term, *kōgei*, covers nearly every preindustrial product that is still made in a traditional manner, ranging from luxurious *yūzen*-dyed silk and fine porcelain to roofing tiles and kitchen knives. To protect this heritage, the government has further designated about one hundred crafts with histories of more than a century as *dentō kōgeihin* (traditional craft products).

103

## STONEWARE AND PORCELAIN

Ceramics is the most vigorous of Japanese crafts. It has the greatest number of artisans—probably more per capita than in any other country—and a steady, discerning clientele among the average Japanese. This is due both to the tea ceremony, with its connoisseur's appreciation of folk-style pottery, and the artistry demanded by Japanese cuisine.

Stoneware is made from high-grade clay which is fired at 600 to 900°C, making it hard and nonporous. The variety and history of Japanese kilns almost defy description. Perhaps a hundred pottery villages still exist. Among the so-called Six Ancient Kilns, pottery communities dating to the thirteenth century, BIZEN and Shigaraki still produce rough-textured wares encrusted with molten ash, originally simple peasant wares that were praised and collected by sixteenth-century tea masters. TAMBA produces attractive, inexpensive dishes, crocks, and *bonsai* pots, glazed in rich black-browns, ambers and bluish whites little changed since the Momoyama period. The biggest, Seto, is a highly automated commercial center (famous abroad for Noritake china). It also has individual artisans working in such venerable traditions as *temmoku*, the Sung Chinese "oil drop" or "hare's fur" glazes, and Ki-Seto, a yellow-green imitation celadon, both originating in the Kamakura period; Oribe, a yellowish ware with brushed designs in iron underglaze covered by translucent splashes of blue-green, supposedly invented by the Momoyama-period tea master Furuta Oribe (see Villas, p. 67); and Shino, also prized by tea connoisseurs.

In Kyūshū and western Honshū, there are numerous kilns that show strong Korean influence; many were founded in the Momoyama period as a legacy of HIDEYOSHI's ill-fated Korean campaigns. Among Hideyoshi's generals were tea enthusiasts who, although they failed to conquer Korea, managed to capture hundreds of potters and bring them back to Japan, where they were made to produce the prized Korean-style bowls. This is why the Korean campaigns are often called "the pottery wars." HAGI, a lovely castle town in western Honshū, is famous for Hagi-yaki, a pinkish-beige ware that resembles the Ido rice bowls that first ignited the interest of Japan's tea masters. KARATSU, an ancient port on the northern Kyūshū coast, is typified by E-Garatsu (picture Karatsu), similar to Korean Yi dynasty wares, with handsome floral or geometric motifs freely brushed in deep-brown iron oxides and covered with translucent or whitish glazes. Other types of Karatsu ware employ Korean techniques such as *hakeme*, broad swatches of white slip applied with a wide brush over undecorated clay, and *mishima*, in which the clay surface is punched with small holes and filled with white slip.

Satsuma-yaki, made by Korean descendants in KAGOSHIMA, includes both the refined mock-porcelain called Shiro (White) Satsuma, a stoneware with colorful overglaze enamel decoration over a finely crazed ivory skin, and Kuro (Black) Satsuma, a folk pottery made for the potters' own use. ONTA and KOISHIWARA, two mountain villages in northeastern Kyūshū, produce genuine folk pottery derived from Korean wares, with decorative techniques such as *tobi-kanna*, a "flying blade" that is chattered across the leather-hard surface as the piece is turned on the wheel, creating a fine, spokelike pattern. These are among the most attractive and distinctive folk potteries made today.

Kyūshū was also the birthplace of Japanese porcelain. Production was established in the early seventeenth century after Ri Sanpei, a Korean potter, discovered kaolin near present-day ARITA. Porcelain is a medium quite unlike stoneware; made from the purest white clay (kaolin) and fired at much higher temperatures (1300–1400°C), it vitrifies into an impermeable, translucent material that rings like a bell when struck. The technical demands are much greater, and, whereas stoneware can be prized for an earthy naturalness and "kiln accidents" (cracks, streaks, and grains that form during firing), porcelain never is. It is judged by the technical perfection of its form and glaze. At a kiln such as Imaizumi Imaemon, heir to the exalted Iro-Nabeshima tradition, ninety percent of the output was judged below standard and destroyed. Iro-Nabeshima, considered one of the finest porcelains ever made, was for the exclusive use of the Nabeshima daimyo and until the Meiji period was unknown in the West. This was not the case with the celebrated kiln of Kakiemon, whose founder perfected the use of brilliant overglaze enamels thirteen generations ago.

Although the Nabeshima domain jealously guarded its porcelain industry, the secrets leaked out, and porcelain spread to a few other regions, notably KANAZAWA, KYOTO, and Seto. Kutani-yaki, patronized by the Maeda lords of Kanazawa, is distinctive, with a bold mix of pictorial and geometric motifs executed in a near-black underglaze and rich overglazes of blues, green, purple, and yellow. Kyoto's Kiyomizu-yaki, sold around the approach to Kiyomizu Temple, consists mainly of porcelain, which began to be produced on a large scale in the late Edo period. As one might expect, it is colorful and elegant, drawing upon an eclectic tradition — not only in ceramics, but in textiles, lacquer design, and painting — molded to Kyoto taste.

With such a burden of history, it is fortunate that Japanese potters continue to develop in exciting new ways, nourished rather than smothered by tradition. Leaders in the folk-art revival were **Hamada Shōji** (1894–1978), **Kawai Kanjirō** (1890–1966), and **Tomimoto Kenkichi** (1886–1963). (Tomimoto is often considered not to be a folk potter because he worked in elegant, enameled porcelain and signed his pieces.) Hamada's farmhouse studio in the now-famous pottery town of MASHIKO, Kawai's house in Kyoto, and Tomimoto's house near Nara's Hōryū-ji are now museums, worth a visit by anyone with an interest in modern Japanese ceramic art.

### Useful Terms

**Climbing kiln (Noborigama).** This type of kiln, introduced from Korea, consists of many linked chambers built on a slope. The chambers are fired from the bottom up, with heat from a lower chamber going to preheat the next chamber, which is fueled in turn through a small side portal when its temperature reaches the flashpoint. The *noborigama* is easier to control than earlier types of kilns, and reaches temperatures of 1300–1400°C, high enough to fire porcelain. Red pine is the favored fuel, but gas and oil are now more common. The enormous kilns typically take weeks to fill and ten days to fire. The Kawai Kanjirō House in Kyoto has an old *noborigama*. These brick and mud kilns, with their stacks of split red pine and sacred straw rope over the firebox, add greatly to the atmosphere of a pottery town. Tamba, Bizen, and Onta still have numerous *noborigama*.

**Ash glaze.** Molten wood ash, yellow to olive in color, was originally a natural by-product of firing. Ash glazes came to be applied deliberately to produce a more regular effect.

**Kiln accident.** In stoneware, uncontrollable factors in the firing, such as flying ash, oxidation and reduction, warping, and sand grains "blossoming" through the surface, can produce highly desirable features. Because a piece with an attractive kiln accident can fetch a high price, potters often induce the accidents by applying ash, wrapping pots in straw, or positioning them in a certain part of the kiln. Characteristic wares: Bizen, Shigaraki, and Iga.

**Overglaze enamels.** Colored, glassy substances applied over the glaze on a fired piece of porcelain or stoneware to complete the design. Most enameled porcelains are first given a cobalt underglaze design and fired at 1300–1400°C to vitrify the clay. The overglaze is then applied and the piece is refired at around 800°C to bond the enamel to the surface. Enameled stonewares include certain Kyoto wares and Satsuma-yaki.

**Folk pottery.** Wares made mostly by preindustrial methods for daily use, generally by a community of potters working in the same tradition. Best examples: Tamba, Onta, and Koishiwara. Others include: Tsuboya-yaki from NAHA in Okinawa; Shikoku's Tobe-yaki (blue-and-white heavy porcelain, some of which is quite handsome and utilitarian). The pottery of Mashiko, near Tokyo, is mainly of commercial quality.

# TEXTILES

Readers of *The Tale of Genji* are always struck by the characters' obsession with their dress — not so much with its cut as with its colors and textures — and with cloth in general as an expression of style and social position. These lords and ladies are forever giving out bolts of fine figured silk as rewards and gifts. Although styles changed, textiles have remained an obsession in Japan, providing a powerful stimulus for the evolution of dyeing and weaving. It almost seems that the kimono, sewn in straight lines from full widths of material, was designed to provide the ideal showcase for fine cloth.

Aristocrats in the Edo period wore silk robes lavishly embroidered with gold thread, but sumptuary laws forbade such luxuries to the merchants, who developed new decorative techniques to circumvent the laws. *Yūzen* dyeing, which originated in the Genroku period (1688–1704), is a way of creating colorful pictorial designs on silk by applying a rice-paste resist in very fine lines with a "pastry tube." Dyes can then be brushed onto the silk without bleeding from one area to an adjacent one. The process can be repeated to create a design of great complexity. When finished, the rice paste is rinsed out; one can sometimes see a demonstration in the rivers of Kyoto (on Aug. 15) and Kanazawa, the two cities famous for *yūzen*.

Another method of paste-resist dyeing is *katazome*, or stencil dyeing. A stencil of paper stiffened with persimmon tannin is cut with razor-sharp tools into intricate floral patterns, arabesques, minute dots, or — most cunning of all — pinstriping, which mimics a simple striped weave but is ineffably more subtle and elegant. The paste resist is applied through the stencil; matching the edges of the pattern is tricky. In Okinawa, the dye is applied by hand to individual areas, with the use of a distinctive shading technique. This type of textile, called Bingata, is still made in SHURI, the old royal capital. *Katazome* is widespread; one good place to see it is at Ono Sensaisho in MORIOKA.

*Shibori*, or tie-dyeing, is employed to create patterns of various sizes, ranging down to tiny dots, sometimes tens of thousands to a single kimono. The resulting finely puckered texture is prized (and being quite labor-intensive, very expensive). *Shibori* is often seen on an informal *obi*, fancy *yukata* (cotton summer kimono), and drawstring purses. ARIMATSU, an old Tōkaidō post town near Nagoya, is famous for its *shibori*.

*Kasuri* is woven from warp and weft threads that are tie-dyed before being woven, producing a pleasingly soft-edged yet lively pattern. Like *shibori* and resist-dyeing, this method originated in India and was transmitted to Japan via Southeast Asia, China, and Okinawa. The Indonesian *ikat* is similar. Okinawa produces the finest *kasuri* in Japan today, including such prized textiles as Miyako-jōfu, Ryūkyū-tsumugi, Kumejima-tsumugi, and Bashōfu. Only high-quality natural fiber — fine ramie, silk pongee, the plantain fiber of Bashōfu — and dyes derived from native plants and minerals are used. This tradition dates to the early 1600s, when the impoverished outer islands of Okinawa had to pay taxes in cloth (see Okinawa History, p. 509).

In other parts of Japan *kasuri* was widespread, but it is popularly associated with the town of KURUME, in northern Kyūshū, where it was supposedly reinvented by a farmgirl. Until fairly recently, the large, snowflakelike white spots on indigo of Kurume-gasuri *mompe* (baggy trousers) was a common sight in the countryside. Today, only a few workshops make it all by hand using real indigo. At a thousand dollars a bolt, it is hardly something one could wear to hoe the cabbage rows.

*Ai*, or indigo, is the quintessential Japanese color, as much a part of the landscape as blue denim is in America. Indigo-dyed work clothes were sturdy, with a sharp, not unpleasant smell that was said to repel biting insects. It is a color that acquires character with wear. Today, most indigo cloth is dyed with synthetic chemicals, perhaps with a final dip in real indigo to give it the distinctive smell. The reason is that *ai* is a living thing, requiring vigilant care that few are willing to give. Made from the fermented leaves of Japanese indigo plants, the deep blue dye is activated by a bacterium that requires oxygen and adequate warmth. A typical *aizome* workshop has a dozen huge crocks of *ai*, buried up to the rim; so many are needed because each time cloth is dipped into a vat, the vat must "rest" and recover its potency before it can be used again. The dyer judges when a vat is ready by the taste and color of the foam floating on top. In winter, coals are placed in a small sunken brazier to keep the vats warm. *Ai* "coats" the cloth, building up a deeper color with each dipping. To achieve a dark blue requires a dozen or more dippings.

In Aomori, farmers used to embroider their plain indigo hemp clothes with white cotton thread, so finely stitched in intricate diamonds and rectilinear patterns as to be mistaken for weaving. This method, called *kogin*, is now used to decorate purses and table runners from HIROSAKI. In TAKAYAMA one can find another type of quilting called *sashiko*, a running stitch executed in such geometric patterns as intersecting circles or squares. Other plant-dyeing methods are known collectively as *kusaki-zome* (grass-and-tree dyeing). A noted example is Yamagata's *benibana-zome* (safflower dyeing).

# WOOD CRAFTS

Japan has wood crafts to equal its exquisite wooden architecture. Japanese woodworkers avoid painting or heavily carving fine wood, preferring to let the natural grain show. Among the most beautiful woods commonly used in crafts are the straight-grained *hinoki* (cypress) and *sugi* (cryptomeria), the oaklike *tochi* (horse chestnut) and *keyaki* (zelkova), and light, silvery *kiri* (paulownia). Places such as the Kiso Valley, famed since early times for its timber forests, are noted for excellent wood crafts.

One of the Kiso Valley's famous products is a wooden comb known as *Oroku-gushi*, now carved by hand at only one shop in the old post town of Yabuhara (one station from NARAI). The combs were named for a local girl, Oroku, who was cured of a disfiguring disease by using a comb carved of *minebari* (a type of birch). Later these combs were sold as souvenirs to travelers on the Nakasendō, and still are. Other types of wooden combs are sold in Tokyo and Kyoto at famous comb shops and department stores. *Tsuge* (boxwood) is a favored wood because it polishes to a lustrous sheen. They come in many shapes — semicircular, rat-tailed — designed for the elaborate coiffures of the past.

*Magemono* are bentwood vessels and utensils made from thin planes of *sugi* or *hinoki*. Similar to Shaker boxes, they bring out the fragrant, satiny essence of *sugi*. In good-quality *magemono*, the seams are secured with strips of cherry bark. *Magemono* include such objects as *mempa* (covered lunchboxes), *seiro* (steamers), water scoops (often seen at shrines), and trays. In Akita's Ōdate, *magemono* boxes are coated inside with red lacquer to protect against food stains.

Lathe-carved objects such as bowls, toy tops, tea caddies, and coasters are found in many regions. Tōhoku is associated with *kokeshi*, simple wooden dolls with globular heads affixed to a cylindrical body and painted with a few quick strokes of ink, typically black and red. The Sendai area is noted for its thriving *kokeshi* towns, now catering to ordinary people, among whom collecting *kokeshi* is a popular pastime.

*Kabazaiku*, or "bark craft," makes use of the bark of a tree. KAKUNODATE's *kabazaiku*, made from the beautifully burnished bark of the wild cherry, is the most famous craft of this type. The bark is used to make or laminate a number of items, such as tea caddies, toothpick boxes, cigarette cases, trays, clogs, and small pieces of furniture. They are sold everywhere in Kakunodate and are available at fine craft shops throughout the country.

Fine wood *tansu* (chests) are prized by collectors around the world, but really good ones — solid hardwood or light *kiri*, fitted with hand-wrought metal ornaments — are rare these days, even in antique stores. *Funadansu*, or "ship chests," are heavily reinforced, waterproof strongboxes, featuring secret compartments. *Sashimono*, hand-crafted delicate household articles and furniture, with fitted joints, wood or ivory pegs instead of nails, and wood-inlay decorations, are expensive, but the workmanship is unexcelled. Edo (Tokyo) *sashimono* favors a clear lacquer coat, whereas Kyoto *sashimono* is usually unlacquered.

# BAMBOO AND BASKETS

Certain regions such as Beppu and Kagoshima still produce baskets from the abundant local bamboo, but in general the cheap bamboo baskets sold in souvenir shops are imported from China. Bamboo artisans mostly produce such items as flower containers and charcoal baskets for the tea ceremony. Among the most prized pieces are those woven from dark, polished bamboo — bamboo salvaged from old farmhouses, blackened and cured by smoke. Less costly yet wonderful and often overlooked examples of design and workmanship are the bamboo ladles (*hishaku*) and whisks (*chasen*) used in the tea ceremony. These wear out quickly with use, so they don't receive the reverence or the high price tags of tea bowls and other more durable artifacts. In this respect, they embody the true *mingei* spirit: made by unknown craftsmen, with an elegant economy of design and construction perfectly suited to their function. *Akebi* baskets are woven from the tough, glossy brown vine of the *akebi* plant. They are durable, lasting much longer than bamboo, and stand up well to everyday use. Handwoven *akebi* baskets are made and sold at Miyamoto Kōgei in Hirosaki.

# LACQUERWARE

Lacquerware, introduced from China in ancient times, attained an extraordinary level of technical perfection and artistic beauty in Japan, where it is called *shikki* or *nurimono*. Obtained from the sap of the lac tree, related to poison sumac (and capable of causing an itchy rash), lacquer hardens in warm, moist air to form an odorless, impermeable surface. Most of Japan's lacquer now comes from China. There are also many imitations, such as cashew lacquer and "plastic lacquer."

106

Shunkei-nuri, a famous product of Takayama, is a marmalade-colored translucent lacquer that allows the wood grain underneath to show through. It generally requires only a few layers. HIRASAWA, a town on the Kiso Kaidō, is known for another relatively simple lacquerware, made by applying clear lacquer over a base stained deep maroon or rust color with persimmon tannin or red ochre. More often, lacquer is opaque; it is usually colored black, red, brown, green, or yellow. A base of well-cured wood is primed and reinforced with layers of cloth soaked in clay and lacquer. The successive coats of lacquer are applied, layer by layer. Each time, the lacquer is left to harden in a moist, warm, dust-free place for about a week, then polished with a piece of charcoal before the next layer is applied. Depending on quality, a piece may require ten to fifteen coats of lacquer. Finally, it is carefully polished to a soft, deep sheen. To practiced hands, the luxurious feel of genuine lacquerware bears as much resemblance to plastic lacquer as silk does to acetate.

Lacquerware is often decorated by painting with colored lacquer, carving, and inlay. Most exquisite of all is the technique called *maki-e*: The design is painted in wet lacquer, then sprinkled with fine gold or silver dust, and finally sealed with a coat of clear lacquer. The subtle contours, shades, and delicate forms that can be attained by this method are remarkable. Another highly refined technique is *raden*, inlay of mother-of-pearl and also of egg shells. Kyoto, Kanazawa, and Wajima are all noted for refined lacquerware.

The Tōhoku region produces types of lacquerware that can be used for ordinary purposes. Hirosaki's Tsugaru-nuri, for example, is made by putting down dozens of different colored layers of lacquer over a bumpy base. The surface is then polished smooth to reveal multicolored bands and rings, resembling bird's-eye maple. Kurume's Rantai-shikki employs a similar technique, applied over a basketware base. When the lacquer is polished down, it brings out the basketweave texture in a most attractive way. Okinawa's Ryūkyū-shikki is an excellent lacquerware influenced by both Japanese and Chinese ware. It was traditionally primed with pig's blood, and the colors are unusually clear and bright, said to be due to the practice of warming the lacquer with direct sunlight.

107

# PAPER AND PAPER GOODS

Traditional paper is so esteemed that it is called *washi* (*wa* means "Japanese") to distinguish it from *yōshi* (Western paper). Durable, beautiful, and ranging from tough, parchmentlike stuff to gossamer tissue, it is used for the translucent *shōji* windows, *fusuma* sliding panels, garments, umbrellas and parasols, and lighting fixtures. In shrines, strips of white paper are symbols of the kami. *Washi* found its way to Europe, where it was prized by such artists as Rembrandt.

The technique used today, mainly in the fifty-odd locations that still make *washi* by hand, was first invented in China in the second century B.C. and was probably known in Japan by the fifth or sixth centuries. The inner bark of *kōzo* (paper mulberry) is the most common source of fiber; *mitsumata* and *gampi*, indigenous to most of Japan, are also used, by themselves or in blends, to make a variety of *washi*. The raw branches are steamed, the white inner bark scraped clean and bleached by exposure to snow, icy cold streams, or cold air. The fibers are then boiled with ash lye and rinsed again. The pulp is beaten, chopped to give the fibers the desired length, and, in a process unique to Japan, suspended in a solution thickened with a tarolike starch called *tororo aoi*. To produce colored or patterned *washi*, dyes, textured fibers, flakes of bark and other such materials are added to the mixture. The suspended fibers are scooped up in a large, rectangular mesh and jiggled to entangle the fibers. As the liquid drains, a sheet of wet *washi* forms on the mesh. The sheet holds together, and when flipped out onto a growing stack of newly made sheets, it won't stick to the damp sheet below it, not even after the stack has been pressed between weights to squeeze out excess water. Finally, the damp *washi* is spread out sheet by sheet to dry on pine planks in the sun or, more commonly, on stainless-steel steam-drying boards. The process is fascinating to see. Good places to visit include MINO, Etchū-Yatsuo (Chūbu, p. 293), GOKAYAMA, Kurodani (near Kyoto), and Yame (near Kurume).

There are a variety of paper products to choose from. *Washi* namecards, stationery, wallets, and notebooks are sold in craft shops and at *washi*-making locales. Inexpensive, light, and unusually attractive, they make ideal gifts. Gifu (Chūbu, p. 294) is famous for its delicate lanterns and paper umbrellas; *bangasa* are made of plain, oiled paper, and are meant to be marked with the name of the family or inn to which they belong. *Janome* (snake eye) are elegant parasols marked with a bull's eye. Marugame (Chūgoku, p. 435) produces eighty percent of Japan's *uchiwa*, the flat, round fans used in summer; its classic persimmon-red *uchiwa* has the character for *kin* (gold) emblazoned in black, from the name of the popular pilgrimage shrine nearby, Kompira-san (written Kinpira). Hirosaki and Nagasaki have distinctive kites. The ancient capital of Nara is noted for two crafts that entered Japan in conjunction with paper: *sumi* (ink sticks) and brushes.

# METALWORK

Nothing in Japan commands a greater mystique than the samurai sword, the finest cutting blade ever forged. The secret rests in a method of folding high-carbon steel to create microscopically thin layers, and in bonding this sharp, brittle cutting edge to a low-carbon steel, which has the resilience and strength needed for the sword's backbone. The technique for forging swords reached its zenith in the thirteenth century. Prized even by the Chinese, swords were a major export item for Japan; indeed, as the Kamakura shogunate battled the Mongol armadas in the bay of Hakata, Japanese profiteers were getting rich selling swords to the enemy. A handful of master swordsmiths still create fine swords—now appreciated mainly for their artistic beauty—but don't come to Japan expecting to pick one up as a souvenir. They are extremely expensive masterpieces, best left to connoisseurs. What one can avail oneself of, however, are the excellent cutlery and carpenter's tools. These enjoy a venerable tradition in their own right. In addition to cutlery shops in Tokyo and Kyoto, one might visit MINO-SEKI, an ancient sword-making town that is now Japan's leading producer of cutlery (and swords).

Iron tea kettles, or *tetsubin*, are another craft in which the Japanese have excelled. The finest kettles, for use in the tea ceremony, are works of art. Morioka is noted for Nambu-tetsubin, first made for its castle lords. One of the simplest designs, a small iron tea pot decorated with a design of small raised knobs, can be seen anywhere. These are mostly mass-produced in Morioka's factories. For excellently designed, hand-cast *tetsubin*, visit Kamasada Kōbō in Morioka.

# FIGURINES AND TOYS

*Kyō-ningyō* (Kyoto dolls) and Hakata clay dolls are well-known and expensive—and they are decorative objects, not toys. Many people find the folk toys (*kyōdo gangu*), of which there is a tremendous variety, more appealing. KURASHIKI and Takayama have toy museums where one can see and buy some of these. *Hariko* (papier-mâché) and *tsuchi-ningyō* (clay dolls) are figurines made in simple molds, with facial features and clothing provided by bright daubs of paint. Favorite figures include Yamauba (the mountain hag, nursing the lusty red infant Kintarō at her breast), and the lucky gods Ebisu and Daikoku. Papier-mâché yellow tigers and red oxen with swinging heads are also quite popular. Many toys are talismans associated with a local shrine. Lathe craftsmen have created a diversity of wooden toys, from simple *kokeshi* dolls to ingenious tops (*koma*) that whistle, fly apart, or flip upside down.

108

# BUYING CRAFTS

When shopping, don't confuse shoddy work with "rusticity." Look for excellent design and workmanship—it can be found even in inexpensive items, such as handmade *washi* post-cards and bamboo utensils. Train your eye by visiting places such as Tokyo's Dentō Kōgei Center, the Nippon Mingeikan, the craft floor at Maruzen, and leading craft shops. Avoid arcades and souvenir shops.

**Stoneware and Porcelain.** Some of the best buys in Japan are everyday dishes. A good, ordinary pottery shop should yield an attractive, handmade piece for a few hundred yen. Texture and feel are important; handle a cup for weight, balance, and ease of use to judge whether it is as well made as it is pleasing to the eye.

**Textiles.** Kimono fabric is usually sold in bolts called *tan*, which are about 12 meters long and 33 centimeters wide, enough to make one kimono (always custom-sewn). New kimono are extremely expensive; to find affordable good silk kimono, *obi*, and fragments, visit a flea market or used-kimono shop (the Japanese have an aversion to wearing used clothes, so these can be real bargains). A new blue-and-white cotton *yukata* can be quite reasonable, but the fabric is sold only in summer. Since few people can afford a hand-dyed, hand-woven kimono, some workshops also sell table runners, *noren* (curtains that hang in doorways), and other small items.

**Woodwork, Lacquerware, and Bamboo.** Beware of clever imitations! Many objects are often laminated with an expensive wood; check an object such as a small chest of drawers inside and out to see if its quality lives up to its price. Cheap bamboo baskets are now mostly imported from China. Lacquerware is prone to fading in sunlight and cracking in dry climates; it demands special care.

# BEST MUSEUMS, SHOPS, AND LOCALES

### TŌHOKU

**✶✶ HIROSAKI.** Handmade kites, fantastic wooden tops, clay figurines, vine baskets, *kogin* quilting, Tsugaru-nuri lacquer (p. 157).

**✶✶ MORIOKA.** Nambu *tetsubin* kettles are still made by hand in some shops, as are fine textiles of various types (p. 161).

**✶✶ KAKUNODATE.** Polished cherry-bark *kabazaiku* is fashioned into a variety of handsome objects. Also wooden folk toys (p. 164).

**✶ Yonezawa.** *Benibana* (safflower) dyeing, various plant-fiber weaves, Yonezawa silk, and traditional toys (p. 181).

**✶ Aizu-Wakamatsu.** Lacquerware, candles, papier-mâché toy oxen, cotton textiles, and pottery (p. 183).

## TOKYO (∗∗∗)

**Maruzen Bookstore.** Carries a tasteful selection of modern crafts (p. 211).
∗∗ **Nihon Mingeikan (Japan Folk Art Museum).** Famed collection begun by Yanagi Sōetsu (p. 223).
∗ **Nihon Zenkoku Dentō Kōgeihin Center (Traditional Craft Center).** Surveys crafts made throughout Japan (p. 218).
**Bingoya.** Well-known craft shop (p. 226).

## KANTŌ

**MASHIKO.** Commercial folk pottery. The **Sankō-kan** (Hamada Shōji Collection) should not be missed (p. 245).
∗∗∗ **Kamakura.** Medieval technique for carving and lacquering temple fixtures, called Kamakura-bori, has been turned to the creation of strikingly handsome everyday objects: trays, mirrors, coasters, and furniture (p. 265).

## CHŪBU

**ARIMATSU.** Old Tōkaidō post town famed for tie-dyed silk *shibori* fabric (p. 278).
∗ **NARAI.** Kiso Valley lacquerware (made in nearby HIRASAWA) and wood crafts (p. 282).
**MINO-SEKI.** Swords and cutlery. Occasional sword-forging demonstrations (p. 289).
**MINO.** The papermaking technique preserved here is designated an Important Intangible Cultural Asset (p. 289).
∗∗∗ **TAKAYAMA.** Shunkei-nuri lacquerware and *sashiko* quilting (p. 289).
∗∗∗ **GOKAYAMA.** Remote papermaking region famous for its farmhouses (p. 297).
∗∗∗ **KANAZAWA.** Numerous elegant craft traditions. The Ishikawa Prefectural Museum is noted for old Kutani porcelain; the Ishikawa Prefectural Handcraft Museum surveys Kanazawa's refined crafts (p. 298).

109

## KYOTO (∗∗∗)

**Yamato Mingei-ten.** Folk-craft shop specializing in rustic designs (p. 366).
**Maruzen Bookstore.** Excellent modern crafts on sale (p. 366).
∗∗ **Kawai Kanjirō House.** Home of famous folk-art potter (p. 335).
**Kyoto Craft Center.** Excellent selection of contemporary crafts (p. 337).
∗ **Museum of Traditional Crafts and Industry.** Exhibits, demonstrations, and sales of the traditional crafts of Kyoto (p. 341).

## KINKI

∗ **TAMBA-SASAYAMA.** Has an excellent museum of old Tamba pottery. Kilns are located nearby at Tachikui village (p. 418).

## CHŪGOKU

∗ **IMBE (BIZEN).** Excellent museums and kilns for Bizen pottery (p. 430).
∗∗∗ **KURASHIKI.** Folk Art Museum and shop-museum of Japanese folk toys (p. 438).
∗∗ **HAGI.** Beautiful castle town famed for Hagi-yaki tea pottery (p. 459).

## KYŪSHŪ

**KOISHIWARA.** Korean-style folk pottery (p. 481).
∗ **KARATSU.** Home of Karatsu pottery. Visit the Nakazato kilns (p. 475).
∗ **IMARI and ARITA.** Huge porcelain center with numerous excellent museums; visit charming Ōkawachiyama pottery village and Imaemon and Kakiemon kilns (p. 476–477).
**KURUME.** Kurume-gasuri textiles, Rantai-shikki lacquerware, handmade paper (p. 490).
∗ **ONTA.** Folk pottery in a lovely mountain village (p. 492).
**KAGOSHIMA.** Naeshirokawa, a half-hour from the city, is the original community of Satsuma-yaki potters. Visit the lovely gallery of Chin Ju-kan (p. 499).

## OKINAWA

∗∗ **NAHA.** Tsuboya pottery, Bingata and Ryūkyū-tsumugi textiles, and lacquerware (p. 511). In Kijoka, a village in the north, women weave Bashōfu plantain textiles (p. 519).
∗∗ **Kumejima.** Silk pongee dyed with clay and plants (p. 521).
∗ **Miyakojima.** Miyako-jōfu ramie textiles (p. 521).
∗∗ **Taketomi.** *Minsā* weaving (p. 523).

## Annual Exhibitions

**Dentō Kōgeihin Annual Fair.** Held at Seibu Department Store in Tokyo in January; demonstrations of traditional craft skills.
**Dentō Kōgei-ten.** National exhibition and sales of recent work by major artisans, held in major cities: Tokyo (Mitsukoshi Department store, mid-Sept.); Nagoya (mid-Oct.); Ōsaka (late Oct.); Kanazawa (early Nov.); Okayama (mid-Nov.); Takamatsu (early Jan.); Fukuoka (late Jan.); Hiroshima (early Feb.); Kyoto (variable; call 075-828-9789).

# Cuisine

110
The basement food market of a Japanese department store is a vast and minutely detailed map of Japan's gastronomic universe. Every visitor will want to investigate one, to watch and to taste, for a whirlwind tour of the world of Japanese food. But to go the next step, you will have to do more than brave a mob of shouting hawkers and housewives. You will have to locate, identify, and enter a restaurant, decipher its menu, make your desires known, and figure out how to eat what you have ordered. To help you, this chapter is divided into types of cuisines, because Japanese restaurants usually specialize. With each description, there's a simple guide to ordering and a typical menu, with Japanese characters supplied so that you can point to items if speech fails. Also, it's acceptable in most places to point at any dish that appeals (but be prepared for people to try to dissuade you from what they think you won't like). Two very useful words to memorize are **teishoku**, a set meal including rice and soup, and **moriawase**, which simply means "an assortment."

## PRACTICAL MATTERS

**Plastic Food Models.** Many restaurant windows display this form of nonverbal menu. Say *Mihon no shō-uindō e kite kudasai* (Please come to the show window) and point.
**Manners.** It's perfectly polite, when using *bashi* (chopsticks), to pick up the small dish you're eating from and hold it chest-high under your chin; the dish provides a safety net if the food slips from your grasp. Or use your rice bowl for this purpose. A bowl of soup or noodles is picked up and the broth sipped from it.
**Budget Dining.** The *shokudō* is a Japanese diner, where students and working people can get a cheap, filling meal from a diverse menu; in these places, you usually pay when you order. Noodles, rice dishes, *okonomiyaki*, *yakitori*, and *oden* are also budget dining. Such shops are found in abundance around commuter stations and inside department stores and basement arcades. The food section in department stores also sells boxed *bentō* and sushi, for cheap and good picnics. A lunchtime *bentō* at a *ryōtei* (a good traditional restaurant) is a comparatively economical way to enjoy an elegant meal. In fact, lunch specials anywhere are a good deal; one would do well to turn lunch into the main meal of the day and settle for something light at dinner.
**Condiments.** Japanese cuisine emphasizes fresh, natural flavors, and so the seasoning comes on the side:

| | |
|---|---|
| sushi | plain soy sauce (*shōyu*) |
| sashimi | plain soy sauce with green horseradish (*wasabi*) |
| tempura | light, clear brown sauce w/grated radish and ginger (*ten-tsuyu*) |
| tonkatasu | thick, Worcestershire-type sauce (*sōsu*) |
| oden | mustard (*karashi*) |
| nabemono | soy sauce with citrus juice (*ponzu*), grated radish, and scallions |
| tofu | soy sauce with grated ginger and bonito flakes |

**Paying.** Say *gochisō-sama* (that was a fine meal) or *okanjō kudasai* (the bill, please) and make motions of getting ready to leave; this should cause the bill to materialize. EXPECT TO PAY CASH. Virtually no restaurants accept traveler's checks, and relatively few accept credit cards.

## Useful Phrases and Terms

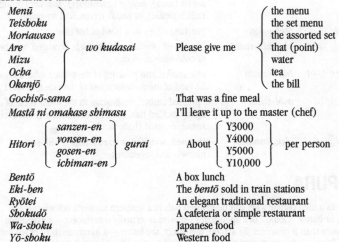

| Menū | | | the menu |
| Teishoku | | | the set menu |
| Moriawase | | | the assorted set |
| Are | *wo kudasai* | Please give me | that (point) |
| Mizu | | | water |
| Ocha | | | tea |
| Okanjō | | | the bill |

Gochisō-sama — That was a fine meal
Mastā ni omakase shimasu — I'll leave it up to the master (chef)

| Hitori | sanzen-en | | | Y3000 | |
| | yonsen-en | *gurai* | About | Y4000 | per person |
| | gosen-en | | | Y5000 | |
| | ichiman-en | | | Y10,000 | |

| Bentō | A box lunch |
| Eki-ben | The *bentō* sold in train stations |
| Ryōtei | An elegant traditional restaurant |
| Shokudō | A cafeteria or simple restaurant |
| Wa-shoku | Japanese food |
| Yō-shoku | Western food |

As a rule of thumb, if you add *-ya* (shop) to to the name of a dish, you get the name of the
type of restaurant that serves it:

| Fugu-ya | Sushi-ya |
| Nomi-ya (a "drinking shop," a pub) | Tempura-ya |
| Oden-ya | Tonkatsu-ya |
| Robata-ya | Unagi-ya |
| Soba-ya | Yakitori-ya |
| Sukiyaki-ya | |

111

# SUSHI AND SASHIMI

The sushi most familiar to Westerners is *nigiri-zushi*, assembled by deftly molding a small
fistful of cool, lightly vinegared rice into a bite-sized morsel, smearing it with green *wasabi*
"horseradish"—preferably freshly grated—and topping it with a slice of the freshest raw fish,
roe or shellfish. The connoisseur takes this up with fingers, lightly dips the *top* side in a small
dish of soy sauce—the secret to noncrumbling sushi is to avoid soaking the rice—and
dispatches it in two or three bites. Chopsticks are acceptable, but fingers add a touch of
bravado that suits the food. Between orders, refresh the palate with slices of vinegared ginger.
Sushi is consumed with saké, beer, or tea.

**Ordering.** The simplest way is to order *nigiri moriawase* (or *jō-nigiri*, superior), an
assortment of seven to nine pieces of *nigiri-zushi*. When ordering à la carte, one order
means two pieces. There are no rules, but many diners prefer to start with mild fish
(*maguro, toro, hirame, tai, ika*), and progress to stronger-flavored delicacies (*awabi,
ikura, uni*). One can also request especially choice cuts of the freshest seasonal fish to be
served plain, as sashimi (the best sashimi species are marked with an asterisk).

| 赤貝 | *akagai*∗ | ark shell |
| 甘海老 | *amaebi*∗ | sweet prawn (raw) |
| あなご | *anago* | sea eel (broiled) |
| あわび | *awabi*∗ | abalone |
| 海老 | *ebi* | prawn (boiled) |
| はまち | *hamachi*∗ | yellowtail |
| ひらめ | *hirame*∗ | sole |
| いか | *ika*∗ | squid |
| いくら | *ikura* | salmon roe |
| かずのこ | *kazunoko* | herring roe |
| まぐろ | *maguro*∗ | tuna |
| たい | *tai*∗ | sea bream |
| たこ | *tako* | octopus |
| たまご | *tamago* | sweet egg omelet |
| とり貝 | *torigai* | cockle |
| とろ | *toro*∗ | fatty tuna |
| うに | *uni*∗ | sea urchin roe |

The following are also standard items:

| | | |
|---|---|---|
| （手）巻きずし | *(te)maki-zushi* | (hand-)rolled tube or cone of crisp, purple-black *nori* (pressed seaweed) around rice and a choice of: *tekka* (tuna), *kappa* (cucumber), *takuan* (crunchy radish pickle), or *nattō* (fermented soybeans) |
| 鉄火丼 | *tekka-don* | raw tuna slices on a bowl of hot rice |
| ちらし寿司 | *chirashi-zushi* | "scattered" sushi—raw morsels arranged on a bed of cold, vinegared rice |
| いなり寿司 | *Inari-zushi* | rice stuffed into pouches of deep-fried tofu; a favorite food of foxes, messengers of the rice god Inari |
| おし寿司 | *oshi-zushi* | "pressed sushi," originating in the Kyoto area, of lightly pickled fish, such as *saba-zushi* (mackerel), *suzume-zushi* (baby sea bream) |
| 茶碗蒸 | *chawanmushi* | steamed, souplike custard studded with seafood morsels and vegetables |

# TEMPURA

Tempura as a high culinary art can be savored only at a tempura master's restaurant. The *koromo*, or batter "cloak," of a specialist's tempura is virtually translucent—a gauze that reveals more than it conceals. To achieve this effect, the batter—a lumpy mixture of ice water, egg, and flour—is barely stirred and never allowed to stand for long; it must be remade constantly lest it lose its airy lightness and turn tough and flat. Batter-covered morsels are dropped into a deep vat of oil, a few at a time, so as not to affect the crucial temperature. At the precise nanosecond when the tempura is perfect, it is plucked out and laid piping hot on a sheet of white paper before the customer. With tempura is served a dipping sauce called *ten-tsuyu*, made of *dashi* stock and sweet saké, to which one adds grated radish and ginger. The tempura should be dipped lightly in it, never left to soak. A true connoisseur, however, will savor the tempura with no embellishment other than a dab of salt or lemon juice.

**Ordering.** One economical lunch dish is *ten-don*, tempura prawns on a large bowl of rice, covered with a tasty sauce. For a full meal, order a *teishoku*. Typical items that can also be ordered à la carte are these:

Fish:

| | | |
|---|---|---|
| 鮎 | *ayu* | sweetfish (early summer) |
| あなご | *anago* | sea eel |
| はぜ | *haze* | goby |
| いか | *ika* | squid |
| 車海老 | *kuruma-ebi* | prawn |
| きす | *kisu* | smelt |
| めごち | *megochi* | flathead |
| 白魚 | *shirauo* | whitebait (early spring) |
| かきあげ | *kakiage* | mix of scallops, shrimp, and vegetables |

Vegetables:

| | | |
|---|---|---|
| 獅子唐 | *shishitō* | small green pepper |
| 銀杏 | *ginnan* | gingko nuts |
| かぼちゃ | *kabocha* | acorn squash |
| 茄子 | *nasu* | eggplant |
| 蓮根 | *renkon* | lotus root |
| 薩摩芋 | *satsumaimo* | sweet potato |
| しいたけ | *shiitake* | brown mushroom |
| しそ | *shiso* | beefsteak leaf |
| しょうが | *shōga* | ginger |
| 玉ねぎ | *tamanegi* | onion |

# GRILLS AND OTHER COUNTER CUISINES

Sushi and tempura are just two examples of the most popular style of casual dining—sitting at a counter, eating food prepared to order by a chef working behind that counter.

## Yakitori

Skewered pieces of chicken—almost no part gets wasted—are broiled over a sputtering charcoal fire and dipped into a dark glaze of soy sauce and sweet saké or sprinkled with salt. Yakitori, served in tiny, smoky, publike shops, is regarded as a snack to go with alcohol; many shops are clustered around commuter stations, such as Yūrakuchō and Shinjuku in Tokyo. But it's possible to turn yakitori into a filling and economical meal.

**Ordering.** Customers are served a complimentary cup of chicken broth. Some shops offer a "course" (a series of courses). Many shops also have *o-hitashi* (cooked spinach), *yasai sarada* (salad), and rice dishes (see the Rice section).

Chicken:

| ささみ | *sasami* | breast meat |
|---|---|---|
| もも焼 | *momoyaki* | thighs |
| 手羽さき | *tebasaki* | wings |
| つくね | *tsukune* | chicken meatballs |
| モツ | *motsu* | giblets |
| ハツ | *hatsu* | hearts |
| レバー | *rebā* | liver |
| うずら | *uzura* | hardboiled quail eggs |
| 鳥ねぎ | *tori-negi* | chicken and leeks |
| 鳥のベーコン巻 | *tori no beikonmaki* | chicken wrapped in bacon |
| 鳥のしそ巻 | *tori no shisomaki* | chicken wrapped in *shiso* leaf |
| つみれ | *tsumire* | shiitake stuffed with ground chicken |

Vegetables:

| アスパラ | *aspara* | asparagus |
|---|---|---|
| 銀杏 | *ginnan* | gingko nut |
| ねぎ | *negi* | leek |
| ピーマン | *piiman* | green pepper |
| しいたけ | *shiitake* | brown mushroom |
| 獅子唐 | *shishitō* | tiny green pepper |

113

## Robata-Yaki

"Hearthside grill" of seafood, vegetables, and hearty, home-style cooking, served, appropriately, in a smoky, "down home" farmhouse setting. The atmosphere is one of calculated rusticity. There's a great deal of shouting, and the salty fare encourages the free flow of saké and beer.

**Ordering.** Generally à la carte, and portions tend to be small; unless you're careful, the tab can really mount up. The fresh fish and vegetables are on view atop the counter, and the atmosphere is casual, so if words fail, simply point at whatever appeals to you. See the Sushi section for fish names; see the Rice section for rice dishes.

Popular Styles of Broiling:

| 田楽 | *dengaku* | broiled with sweet miso |
|---|---|---|
| ホイル焼き | *foiru-yaki* | broiled in tinfoil |
| ほうろく焼 | *hōroku-yaki* | baked on a bed of coarse salt |
| 味噌焼 | *miso-yaki* | broiled with salty miso (soy-bean paste) |
| 塩焼 | *shio-yaki* | fish sprinkled with salt and broiled |
| 照り焼 | *teri-yaki* | fish or meat broiled with teriyaki sauce |
| うに焼 | *uni-yaki* | broiled with sea-urchin paste |

Popular robata dishes:

| 揚げ出し豆腐 | *agedashi-dōfu* | deep-fried bean curd |
|---|---|---|
| あじのたたき | *aji no tataki* | a *ceviche* of minced raw pompano |
| あさりの酒蒸 | *asari no sakamushi* | small clams steamed with saké |
| かつおのたたき | *katsuo no tataki* | bonito, broiled on the outside, sliced and served with garlic, *shōyu*, and citrus |
| 肉じゃが | *nikujaga* | a meat and potato dish |
| にしん | *nishin* | broiled herring |
| さんま | *sanma* | broiled mackerel pike (autumn) |

Vegetables (see also Yakitori vegetables):

| えのき茸 | *enokidake* | straw mushrooms (baked in foil with butter) |
|---|---|---|
| 銀杏 | *ginnan* | gingko nuts (parched and salted) |
| じゃがバター | *jagabatā* | baked potato with butter |
| 茄子 | *nasu* | eggplant (*dengaku*) |
| とうもろこし | *tōmorokoshi* | corn on the cob (broiled, soy-brushed) |
| 焼きおにぎり | *yaki-onigiri* | broiled rice balls |

## Tonkatsu and Kushi-age

*Tonkatsu* is pork cutlet. The Japanese dislike greasy food, so very lean pork sirloin is used. The filet is dredged in flour, dipped in egg, rolled in breadcrumbs, and deep-fried. It is served piping hot with chopped fresh cabbage, mustard, and a Worcestershire-flavored sauce (each shop boasts a "secret formula"). *Kushi-age* is deep-fried skewers of meat, vegetables, prawns, and crab claws served with similar accompaniments.

**Ordering.** *Tonkatsu* is considered a meal in itself, so one orders a *teishoku*, which includes rice and *tonjiru*, a miso soup laced with minced pork and vegetables. There is a choice between two grades: *rōsu*, which has a bit of fat, and *hire* (filet), which is lean. *Kushi-age* shops offer a *moriawase* of a half-dozen skewers.

## Okonomiyaki

This is a kind of savory pancake, a mixture of chopped seafood or meat, vegetables, and batter that is cooked on a grill, usually by the customer. Cheap and filling, it's popular with young people and families. In a do-it-yourself place, you'll get a bowl of batter topped with minced cabbage, red ginger, a raw egg, and whatever ingredients you've ordered, such as beef, shrimp, or squid. These are mixed and poured onto the preheated griddle. A spatula is provided to flip it over when it's done on one side. When the okonomiyaki is golden-brown, the customer can brush the top with a sweet or spicy sauce, sprinklings of dried seaweed, ginger, and bonito shavings.

**Ordering.** These are some typical fillings:

| | | |
|---|---|---|
| ビーフ | *bīfu* | beef |
| エビ | *ebi* | shrimp |
| カキ | *kaki* | oyster |
| イカ | *ika* | squid |
| ミックス | *mikkusu* | mixed |
| ブタ | *buta* | pork |

## Oden

*Oden* is a mix of fishcakes, vegetables, and other savory morsels simmered together in a carefully tended tub of stock. It is served with a dab of mustard and chopped scallions. A popular and cheap cold-weather snack, it is available at *oden-ya*, street carts, and pubs.

**Ordering.** The vat of *oden* is in plain view, so simply point at what you like. Most shops price it by the *sara* (plate, usually with three pieces). To make a meal of it, ask for *oden teishoku*.

Fish:

| | | |
|---|---|---|
| ちくわ | *chikuwa* | hollow, cylindrical baked fish sausage |
| はんぺん | *hanpen* | fluffy white fishcake |
| 薩摩揚げ | *satsuma-age* | deep-fried fishcake |
| たこ | *tako* | octopus (cooked to tenderness) |

Tofu:

| | | |
|---|---|---|
| あつ揚げ | *atsu-age* | deep-fried tofu |
| ふくろ | *fukuro* | deep-fried tofu pouch filled with vegetables |
| がんもどき | *ganmodoki* | deep-fried tofu-and-vegetable dumpling |

Other:

| | | |
|---|---|---|
| 大根 | *daikon* | radish |
| こんにゃく | *konnyaku* | devil's tongue jelly (pure texture; spice it with plenty of mustard) |
| ロールキャベツ | *rōru kyabetsu* | stuffed cabbage |
| 里芋 | *sato-imo* | taro yam |
| 玉子 | *tamago* | hard-boiled egg |

# NABEMONO

One-pot "stews" cooked at the table in a large, earthenware casserole over a gas flame. Everyone eats out of the communal pot, plucking out morsels and dipping them in sauce. This is one of the most popular ways to dine in cold weather. The raw ingredients are beautifully arranged on large platters and presented to the diners before being put into the boiling stock. The waitress will start it off, but then it becomes "self-service," so it's worth knowing the basic rule. The first things to go in the pot are ingredients that give flavor to the stock: clams, chicken, fish, leeks, and shiitake mushrooms. Next comes everything else, except for delicate greens, usually *mitsuba* (trefoil) and *shungiku* (chrysanthemum leaves), which are thrown in at the last minute. Often added at the end are *udon* noodles or *mochi* (rice cakes), or cold rice and egg, to make *zōsui*. If the flame is too high, tell the waitress, *hi wo sagete kudasai*.

**Mizudaki.** This famous *nabemono* originated in Hakata, in northern Kyūshū, inspired, it is said, by the Chinese. *Mizudaki* is based on milky-white chicken stock. To it one adds chunks of chicken (on the bone), Chinese cabbage, carrot, tofu, leeks, and fine "glass noodles" of bean protein. It is served with a sauce of soy, citrus, grated radish, and hot pepper.

**Chanko-nabe.** This hearty *nabemono* of fish, meat, tofu, and vegetables in a tangy broth is a staple of the sumō wrestler's diet. Many *chanko-nabe* shops are opened by ex-wrestlers who proved to be more adept at cooking for their brethren than at winning in the ring.

**Ordering.** Some shops specialize in a certain type of *nabemono* such as *mizudaki* or *chanko-nabe*, but others serve many kinds, such as:

| | | |
|---|---|---|
| よせ鍋 | *yose-nabe* | seafood and chicken |
| たら鍋 | *tara-nabe* | codfish |
| どて鍋 | *dote-nabe* | oysters in a miso stock |
| 沖すき | *okisuki* | seafood |
| あんこう鍋 | *ankō-nabe* | angler fish (winter) |
| ぼたん鍋 | *botan-nabe* | wild boar in a miso stock (winter) |
| 湯豆腐 | *yudōfu* | tofu and vegetables |

# FUGU

The *fugu* is a plump fish with absurd little fins that is barely able to waddle its way through the ocean. Its main defenses are its ability to blow itself up into an imposing, spine-covered ball — hence its English names, puffer or globefish — and the presence of a deadly neurotoxin in its reproductive organs and liver. But this has not fazed the Japanese, who find its flesh delectable. Chefs are specially licensed to ensure perfectly safe dining. The *fugu*-eating season is winter, when the toxins from its reproductive cycle are at a minimum and the flesh "closes up," giving it the firmness that is one of its gustatory attractions.

115

A *fugu ryōtei* is very expensive, but many ordinary fish restaurants offer the fish at a reasonable price (about Y4000). A *fugu* dinner begins with *hirezaké*, an *aperitif* of saké scented with toasted fins, and *fugusashi*, sashimi sliced to a translucent thinness, spectacularly arranged like a chrysanthemum or crane on a porcelain platter and served with a sauce of soy, *sudachi* (bitter orange), minced scallions, and a dab of grated radish, scarlet with hot pepper. The taste is delicate and the texture is firm, almost crunchy. The skin is particularly good. It is followed by *fugunabe* (also called *tetchiri*), chunks of *fugu* cooked with vegetables. In this dish, the distinctive flavor of the fish asserts itself. Finally, cooked rice and egg are mixed into the delicious soup to make *zōsui*.

# BEEF

Japan's finest beef comes from Matsusaka, Yonezawa, Ōmi, and Tamba (source of "Kōbe beef"), where farmers hand-raise animals that are fattened on beer, massaged, and otherwise pampered to produce the buttery-rich marbled meat called *shimofuri* ("frosted").

**Sukiyaki.** Though beef-eating is barely a century old in Japan, sukiyaki is virtually the national dish. A lump of suet is melted in an iron pan, onions are sautéed in the fat, and very thin slices of beef are laid over the bottom of the pan and browned. They are then covered by the other ingredients — tofu, shiitake mushrooms, carrots, bamboo shoots, fluffy wheat gluten, *ito konnyaku* (noodles of devil's tongue jelly) — and doused in a piquant mixture of soy sauce, sweet saké, and sugar. The mixture is simmered briefly. At the last moment, *shungiku*, tender chrysanthemum leaves, are added. Each diner is provided with a raw egg, which is broken into a small bowl and beaten. Steaming morsels are dipped into the beaten egg, which forms a cool, silken cloak that perfectly complements the savory richness of the dish.

**Shabu-Shabu.** This typically Japanese dish, even less ancient than sukiyaki, was a postwar invention of a Kyoto chef who was inspired by the Mongolian "hot pot." Water with a piece of kelp in it is set to boil over a gas flame. Slices of extra thin beef are swished in it, *shabu-shabu*, for the few seconds it takes to cook, and dipped into a sauce, either a mild, peanut-colored concoction of sesame paste, or a tangy one of soy, citrus, and chopped scallions. As the water turns to broth, vegetables — Chinese cabbage, carrots, leeks — are added. Sometimes, flat *kishimen* noodles are heated in the broth.

**Teppan-yaki.** Japanese steakhouses, with their Western-style ambience, wine lists, and bilingual menus, offer an East-West mixture. On the countertop grill, a chef sautées steak, bean sprouts, mushrooms, and large cloves of garlic, followed by beef fried rice. *Teppan-yaki* shops also serve grilled seafood and chicken.

**Ordering.** Beef is most popularly served as sukiyaki, *shabu-shabu*, or *teppan-yaki*. *Amiyaki* is beef grilled over charcoal. *Gyū-sashi*, thin slices served raw with soy and ginger, is a classic appetizer. Since beef is a delicacy, price depends on the quantity (in grams — 250 grams is about half a pound) and grade, with the prized *shimofuri* being the most expensive.

# SPECIALTY CUISINES

## Unagi

The succulent eel, or *unagi*, is one of the great delicacies of Japan, where it has attained a kind of culinary apotheosis. Prepared in the classical *kabayaki* manner — creamy filets broiled and brushed with an aromatic brown glaze over a charcoal fire, spluttering and smoking from drips of eel fat — it is so delicious that it has become by custom a summer restorative; people eat it on days of the Ox to revive their appetite.

*Unagi* is not fast food; a properly cooked *kabayaki* is a time-consuming achievement. A live eel is rapidly dispatched, fileted, skewered, and carefully broiled with a mixture of soy sauce and sweet saké. In Kantō, the broiled filets are steamed to tenderize the meat and render out excess fat, and then returned to the broiler. In Kansai, the steaming process is left out, with richer, firmer results. *Unagi* is spiced with a dash of aromatic *sansho* pepper.

**Ordering.** Unagi dishes are served with rice, crunchy yellow radish pickles, and *kimosui*, a broth garnished with the delicate eel liver.

| 蒲焼 | *kabayaki* | broiled eel |
| 肝焼 | *kimoyaki* | an appetizer of eel liver, broiled on a skewer |
| うな丼 | *unadon* | *kabayaki* served on a bowl of rice, with sauce |
| うな重 | *unajū* | *kabayaki* on a bed of rice |
| うざく | *uzaku* | broiled eel and cucumber in vinegar |
| 八幡巻 | *yawatamaki* | eel wrapped around burdock root and broiled |

## Tofu

In the West, tofu (bean curd) is hailed as a cheap, cholesterol-free protein substitute. This is also essentially how it is viewed in the country of its origin, China, where it is said to have been invented by an honest and therefore poor official. In Japan, a land of scrupulous palates and semi-vegetarian history, tofu is appreciated for itself. The Japanese refined tofu to give it a more delicate flavor and texture. Kyoto tofu is claimed to be the finest. It is also in Kyoto that one finds the greatest variety of tofu-based foods.

Tofu is made by soaking soybeans overnight, grinding them, adding water, and boiling and straining the mixture to make soy milk. The wrinkled skin that forms on the surface of soy milk is *yuba*, itself a prized food. Bittern, salts of magnesium and calcium, is added to soy milk to coagulate it, like the use of rennet to make cheese. The mixture is poured into a cotton-lined mold and the "whey" is pressed out, leaving a block of firm, *momengoshi-dōfu* ("cotton" tofu). A stronger coagulant is used for *kinugoshi-dōfu* ("silk" tofu), which solidifies into a custardlike, delicate tofu. Tofu-based foods include *abura-age* (deep-fried), *ganmodoki* (deep-fried balls of tofu and vegetables), *Kōya-dōfu* (spongy, freeze-dried tofu, said to have been invented accidentally on Mt. Kōya), *goma-dōfu* (a rich, beige tofu of sesame).

Common tofu dishes:

| 冷奴 | *hiya-yakko* | chilled *momengoshi-dōfu*, served with soy sauce, chopped scallions, grated ginger, and bonito shavings; a refreshing summer dish |
| 湯豆腐 | *yudōfu* | tofu heated in hot, kelp-laced water, and served with *hiya-yakko* condiments |
| 豆腐田楽 | *tofu dengaku* | drained, pressed tofu broiled with a paste of sweet miso and garnished with peppertree buds, citrus peel, or poppy seeds |
| 揚げ出し豆腐 | *agedashi-dōfu* | tofu dredged in potato starch, deep-fried, and served with a light sauce and grated radish |

## Sansai (Mountain Greens) and River Fish

*Sansai-ryōri* is a kind of generic "local cuisine" that is in fact served in many mountainous regions. Wild, edible mountain plants — fiddlehead ferns, tender shoots, wild fungi — and river fish were part of the traditional diet of country people. Today, these are a delicacy for city people traveling in such regions as Tōhoku and Chūbu. In these areas, one can find *sansai-soba* (buckwheat noodles with wild greens), *sansai tempura*, and *sansai teishoku*, a simple set meal of wild greens, rice, soup, and perhaps a broiled river fish.

Among river fish, *ayu*, or sweetfish, is the undisputed gourmet's delight. This lithe little fish feeds only on river moss and disdains the fisherman's bait, so **ukai**, or cormorant fishing, was invented to catch it. *Ukai* is done on moonless nights, when the *ayu* are lured near the boat by the glow of a torch, there to be snapped up by trained cormorants. The birds wear rings around their gullets so they cannot swallow their catch. *Ukai* is a summer tourist spectacle in Gifu and Kyoto's Arashiyama. All this trouble is deemed worthwhile for the pleasure of tasting *ayu*, with its delicate layer of fat and sweet white flesh. Gourmets prize even more its bittersweet liver and entrails, so the fish is usually broiled whole and ungutted. It is served with *tadesu*, a green sauce of vinegar and nettles. *Ayu* deboning trick: gently but firmly massage the fish with chopsticks to loosen the flesh from the bones. Then break off the tail, separate the flesh of the body from the head, *leaving the spine intact*, and gently pull head and body apart. The spine and ribs should slip free of the body.

**Common sansai greens.** *Fuki* and *fuki-no-tō* (butterbur stalk and buds), *taranome* (angelica buds), *udo* (Japanese celery), *warabi* (fiddlehead fern), *yamabuki* (kerria rose), *zenmai* (fern).
**Common river fish.** *Ayu* (sweetfish), *masu* (trout), *iwana* (char).

### Shōjin-ryōri

This is a type of vegetarian cuisine that developed in the Zen monastery. Buddhism forbids the taking of life, so *shōjin-ryōri* includes no meat or fish, not even bonito stock, one of the pillars of Japanese cuisine. Also forbidden are the "five fragrant vegetables," including onions and garlic, that might arouse an unseemly desire for the food. Paradoxically, the result is one of Japan's most delicate and delicious cuisines. It features many forms of tofu and other soybean foods, and an astonishing variety of vegetables, prepared in intricate and ingenious ways, seasoned with soy sauce, miso, vinegar, sugar, and delicate herbs. *Shōjin-ryōri*, available at temples and special restaurants, is served as a set meal, in lacquered bowls arranged on trays, in monastic style. **Fucha-ryōri** is a "Chinese" *shōjin-ryōri* that was developed by the Ōbaku Zen sect in the early 1600s. It features elaborate and colorful Chinese-style hors d'oeuvres and dishes such as stir-fried vegetables. It is served banquet style, on communal platters, rather than on individual trays.

# HAUTE CUISINE

### Kaiseki

*Kaiseki* originated four centuries ago as a light repast served during the tea ceremony. Its name comes from the word for the warm stones placed over the stomach to quell the hunger pangs of Zen acolytes. In keeping with tea philosophy, this meal is a series of seasonal morsels, prepared simply, with careful distinctions between hot and cold dishes, appropriate vessels, and visual appeal. The aim is to showcase the natural essence of the food. This *chakaiseki* (tea *kaiseki*) introduced an esthetic code to the cuisine of Japan.

117

    *Kaiseki*, the beautiful, formal cuisine served at a traditional restaurant, or *ryōtei*, is deeply influenced by *chakaiseki*. But unlike its rarefied ancestor, it is not so codified or so frugal; to underscore this fact, it is sometimes written with different characters that mean "sitting together." *Kaiseki* is not simply food, but a total environment of elegant refinement. *Ryōtei* are typically located in a lovely house with gardens. Each party is given its own room, decorated with a seasonal scroll and flowers, and is assigned a bevy of kimonoed waitresses. It offers what for the Japanese is the ultimate luxury—privacy and a retreat from the world.

    A *kaiseki* meal is a sequence of small courses. Everything is seasonal, fresh, prepared with a light but often stunningly original touch. There is one soup and an odd number of dishes, accompanied by saké or beer. The dishes would certainly include sashimi and a variety of preparations of fish, vegetables, and perhaps chicken or beef. Rice, served only after the last of the alcohol has been drunk, marks the end of the meal. This might be followed by fresh fruit, tea, or perhaps a sweet and *matcha*, the frothy, thick, grass-green tea of the tea ceremony. All throughout, only the finest lacquerware and plates, often antiques, are used, and a quiet appreciation of them is also one of the pleasures of *kaiseki*.

**Ordering.** Order by set price. The menu is decided by the *ryōtei*, but when making a reservation, let the chef know if there is anything you cannot eat. Fine *ryōtei* require a reservation a day or more in advance, because they must procure fresh ingredients and plan each day's menus. Cancelling shortly before the reserved time is therefore just not done. *Kaiseki* is very expensive; expect it to *start* at around ¥8000. In Kyoto, the home of *kaiseki*, one economical and recommended way to dine in a *ryōtei* is to go at lunchtime and order a *bentō*, an elegant arrangement of tidbits and rice in a lacquered box. A cautionary note: the term *kaiseki* is often applied to any lavish meal (such as an average ryokan meal), good or otherwise.

# RICE AND NOODLES

### Rice and Pickles

Japanese rice is short-grained and more moist and glutinous than what Westerners are used to. It is also more fragrant and sweet, which is why the Japanese prefer it plain. It is usually served with tea and a dish of piquant, crisp pickles or perhaps *umeboshi*, a red, wrinkled, and mouth-puckeringly sour salted plum. One rule of thumb is that plain rice and alcohol are never consumed together. In addition to plain rice, there are many rice dishes:

| | | |
|---|---|---|
| 丼 | *domburi* | large bowl of rice with a topping, a meal in itself: *ten-don* is tempura domburi; *oyako-* (parent-child) *domburi* is chicken and egg |
| 釜めし | *kamameshi* | rice casserole cooked with vegetables, fish, chicken, or meat, arranged attractively on top |
| 餅 | *mochi* | cakes of pounded glutinous rice; *zōni*, toasted *mochi* in soup, is a New Year dish |

| おにぎり | onigiri | rice balls, the Japanese equivalent of a sandwich; the simplest has an *umeboshi* inside and is wrapped in dried seaweed or rolled in sesame seeds to provide a nonstick grip; other flavors: *shake* (salmon), *katsuo* (dried bonito), *shiokobu* (salt kelp) |
| ぞうすい | zōsui | rice mixed into soup with a beaten egg |

## Noodles

Like pasta in Italy, noodles in Japan came from China; but once entrenched, noodles acquired their own exalted place in their new home. There are many types. *Soba*, a buckwheat noodle, ranges from pale blond to a hearty dark gray; sometimes powdered green tea is mixed in, turning it into green *cha-soba*. *Udon* is a plump, white wheat noodle. Cheap, fast, and tasty, *soba* and *udon* are a popular lunch or snack. Most noodle shops serve both types. The Japanese practically inhale noodles, with a great slurping noise considered appropriate, indeed essential, for the act.

| ざるそば | zaru-soba | plain *soba* with dipping sauce (also called mori- or seiro-soba) |
| 天ざる | ten-zaru | zaru-soba with tempura on the side |
| 鍋焼うどん | nabe-yaki udon | tempura, vegetables, egg, and *udon*, cooked in an earthenware pot |
| うどんすき | udon-suki | a casserole of seafood, vegetables, with *udon* |
| きつね | kitsune soba/udon | with fried bean curd and leeks in broth |
| 天ぷら | tempura soba/udon | with tempura in broth |
| 鳥なんばん | tori-namban soba/udon | with chicken and leeks in broth |
| 月見 | tsukimi soba/udon | with raw egg on top |
| そうめん | sōmen | fine wheat noodle, served cold in summer |
| ラーメン | rāmen | Chinese-style noodles |

118

# BEVERAGES

Drinking is a major social activity and a private one as well, judging from the ubiquity of public vending machines that dispense beer, saké, and whiskey. In social situations, etiquette requires that drinking partners pour for one another. When your companion offers to pour, always lift up your glass or saké cup. Then return the gesture. Be ever ready to fill your companion's cup when it goes dry, and expect to be plied constantly and ruthlessly to drink more than you might ever want to. Alcohol is always consumed with food (except plain rice), particularly seafood, often of an unidentifiable type. Sushi, yakitori, and robata-yaki shops are also places where liquor flows freely. If you just want to drink, go to a *nomiya* or one of the trendy café-bars. Unless you're with a Japanese friend, avoid hostess bars and clubs, which are exclusive ripoff joints.

**Saké.** Japan's national brew is made from fermented rice. It is usually clear, with a yeasty fragrance and a taste that is a blend of sweet and acidic, astringent and mellow. Bottled saké is by law limited to 32 proof. There are no "vintages," as saké doesn't improve with age, and usually only the current year's saké is drunk. There are national brands, and there is *jizaké*, local saké, made by some three thousand breweries across the land. Though it isn't quite the national pastime that wine-tasting is in France, saké-tasting is a serious sport among connoisseurs. Saké is graded into *tokkyū* (premium), *ikkyū* (first class), and *nikyū* (second class); but any saké that hasn't been submitted for grading is *nikyū* by default, so some *nikyū* are really *ikkyū* or *tokkyū*, evading taxes under a cheap label. In addition to grade, saké-tasters distinguish between **amakuchi** (sweet) and **karakuchi** (dry). Saké is served in two ways, *atsukan* (heated) and *reishū* (chilled), the latter often favored in summer. One interesting way to drink saké is out of a *masu*, a cypress box used as a measure of rice, with a pinch of salt on the rim. For variety, one might try **nigori-zaké**, a milky, unfiltered brew often served in "country" restaurants, and **namazaké**, full-bodied raw saké (40 proof).

**Shōchū.** A potent, pungent-smelling distilled liquor of rice, barley, or sweet potatoes from Kyūshū, where the distillation process was introduced by the Dutch in the Edo period. Usually ordered *oyuwari* (with hot water). *Chūhai*, a "shōchū highball," is a modern concoction that has made *shōchū* more popular with young people.

**Beer.** Japanese beer is excellent and a tad richer than American beer. Popular brands are Kirin, Asahi, Sapporo, and Ebisu.

**Whiskey.** Domestic (Suntory, Nikka) or imported, it is typically drunk *mizu-wari* (with water) or *onzarokku* (with ice).

**Non-Alcoholic Drinks.** Typical soft drinks available in bars and restaurants include *kōra* (cola), *Kirin remon* (lemon-lime), and an orange liquid called, deceptively, *jūsu* (juice). If you want real juice, ask for *hyaku pāsento* (100 percent), but don't count on it being available. Plain soda water is *tanzan* (which is sometimes jazzed up with food coloring and a maraschino cherry). *Mizu* (water) and *cha* (tea) you can always count on.

# KISSATEN (CAFÉS)

The kissaten is a cultural institution of modern Japan not unlike the Parisian café, though in decor and food it may more closely resemble the American coffee shop. Perhaps because of the lack of privacy in most homes, dormitories, and workplaces, the kissaten is a favorite place to socialize. Many kissaten have distinctive decor to attract a particular type of customer—posters of Montmartre for artist types, floral prints for ladies, vinyl-upholstered barstools for salarymen. For the traveler, the kissaten offers a free cultural experience and cheap breakfast ("morning set"—coffee, inch-thick toast, and perhaps an egg or salad). It's a good place to rest. You can sit for as many hours as you like over just one cup of very good coffee. Japanese conglomerates have cornered the market for the world's best coffee beans, and even a working-class kissaten will brew it with ceremonial care. A more upscale place might have Burū Maunten (Blue Mountain) and other special varieties. The Japanese brew their coffee strong. If you prefer it weaker, ask for *Amerikan*.

Nearly all the items on a kissaten menu are "Japanese-English" terms, written in *katakana* syllabary, which is fairly easy to learn; if you have taken the trouble to learn *katakana*, you will be able to read any typical kissaten menu.

Beverage:

| | | |
|---|---|---|
| コーヒー | *kōhī* | coffee |
| ウインナコーヒー | *uinna kōhī* | Vienna coffee |
| カフェオーレ | *kafe ōre* | café au lait |
| 紅茶 | *kōcha* | black tea |
| ミルク | *miruku* | milk |
| オレンジジュース | *orenji jūsu* | orange juice |
| ヨーグルト | *yōguruto* | yoghurt |
| アイスクリーム | *aisu kurīmu* | ice cream |

Food:

| | | |
|---|---|---|
| モーニングセット | *mōningu setto* | morning set (toast, egg, coffee) |
| グラタン | *guratan* | potatoes à la gratin |
| カレーライス | *karē raisu* | curry rice |
| オムレツ | *omuretsu* | omelet |
| ピラフ | *pirafu* | pilaf |
| ピザ | *piza* | pizza: *sarami* (salami), *hamu* (ham), *mikkusu* (mix) |
| ポタージュ | *potāju* | potage (cream of corn soup) |
| サンドイッチ | *sandoitchi* | sandwich: *hamu-chīzu* (ham and cheese), *tsuna* (tuna), *mikkusu* (mix) |
| サラダ | *sarada* | salad |
| スパゲッティ | *supagettī* | spaghetti: *mīto* (meat), *tomato* (tomato), *bongore* (clam sauce), *bajiriko* (*shiso* "pesto") |

119

# TEA AND SWEETS

Japanese tea is green; the leaf is steamed, destroying an enzyme that would otherwise turn it black. The sweetest leaves are ground to a powder and whipped with hot water to make the frothy **matcha** of the tea ceremony. Normally, however, the Japanese drink steeped tea, such as **sencha** and humble **bancha**, a light brown tea made from the coarsest leaves and served free in any Japanese restaurant. In summer, one might be served cold **mugicha**, a refreshing infusion of roast barley. For the finest steeped tea, one should order **gyokuro**, "jewel dew," a fragrant, cloudy green brew with a sweet aftertaste, available in fine teashops.

Japanese sweets are designed to complement green tea. *Matcha* is typically served with *rakugan*, dry, sugary lozenges molded into beautiful shapes and eaten before sipping the strong, bitter tea. **Yōkan** is bean jelly, served in slices with *gyokuro* or *sencha*. **Mizuyōkan** is a light *yōkan* jelled with agar and served chilled in summer. **Mitsumame**, a colorful medley of agar cubes, fruit, and small brown beans, is another summer sweet. The ultimate hot-weather treat is **Uji-gōri**, a mountain of shaved ice flavored with sweetened *matcha*; Uji-Kintoki is a version embellished with a spoonful of bean jam. There are also numerous confections of *mochi*, sticky cakes of glutinous rice. **Zenzai** is toasted *mochi* in a hot sauce of sweet azuki beans. **Abekawa-mochi** is toasted *mochi* covered in sweetened soybean flour. **Sakura-mochi** is a delicate pink dumpling of glutinous rice, filled with bean jam and elegantly wrapped in preserved cherry leaves, which impart a sweet fragrance.

# FRUIT

The famous fruit boutiques of Tokyo's Ginza, with their tissue-wrapped fifty-dollar melons and five-dollar apples arranged like trophies on polished glass shelves, are something to see, but if you have a fruit craving, go to an ordinary market. Buy what's in season, for best prices and flavor:

| | |
|---|---|
| *ichigo* | strawberries |
| *momo* | peach; the expensive white ones are especially sweet and fragrant |
| *suika* | watermelon |
| *nashi* | Japanese pear; extremely crisp and juicy; *nijusseiki nashi* is juiciest |
| *kaki* | persimmon; the squarish variety are sweet and crisp; the ones with pointed bottoms are astringent and must be soft before they can be eaten |
| *budō* | grapes; the small seedless red grapes slip right out of their skins |
| *ringo* | apple; try the sweet Fuji or Mutsu varieties |
| *mikan* | mandarin orange |

# DINING ON TRAINS

The Shinkansen and limited express trains usually have a buffet or dining car, which serves food that is palatable if uninteresting. The true star of railroad meals is the **eki-ben** (from *eki bentō*, or station *bentō*), which is sold on the platform and from carts that move through the train. A typical *eki-ben* is a wooden box containing partitions, one for plain rice, the others for neatly arranged morsels of cooked fish, omelet, vegetables, and pickles. The box is smartly wrapped in paper and string and is sealed with a sticker showing the time and date of preparation (*eki-ben* must be sold within four hours of preparation). There are many varieties of *eki-ben*, including sushi and *unagi-bentō* (broiled eel on rice). Some stations are nationally famous for *eki-ben* featuring a regional specialty; the traveler can savor a local delicacy without ever getting off the train.

120

# Ryokan, Onsen, and Other Escapes

旅館

It may seem strange to include traditional inns, baths, and the sleazier entertainment trades in the same chapter. The three are connected, however, not only because they belong to the world of holidays and evenings, but also because all three correspond to deep national attitudes regarding self-indulgence and dependence on others. In Japan, self-indulgence, even childishness, is tolerated, even approved of, if it is practiced in moderation at the right place and time, with an appropriate attitude of gratitude and cooperation toward the person who is indulging you.

121

## RYOKAN 旅館          *straw bag* 俵屋 京都

The quiet world of the fine ryokan, or Japanese inn—so startlingly different from the noise and bustle of the cities—is one of Japan's great escapes. The ryokan is not simply a native-style alternative to a hotel, but a venerable cultural institution. At a ryokan like the three-hundred-year-old Tawaraya in Kyōto, history comes alive in the flickering shadows of its candle-lit halls. A fine ryokan, with water-splashed stone floors, gardens, and personalized service, is the easiest way for a foreigner to experience a gracious, timeless way of life—as close to entering an elegant traditional home as someone without a wealthy Japanese friend is likely to get. Such an inn is definitely worth a splurge (expect to pay Y10,000 to Y35,000 per person, with meals). The innumerable lesser ryokan are also well worth a stay and can be an excellent value. (Americans tend to pronounce ryokan as *ri-yo-kan*, but you must run the *r* and *y* together, without an intervening vowel, or you won't be understood.)

A reservation allows the staff to be prepared for your arrival. In Japan, being caught unprepared puts people in bad humor; a phone call from across the street is infinitely better than just showing up at the door. If language is a problem, ask a Japanese friend, the staff of your hotel, or a travel agent to handle it for you (see Practical Advice, p. 7). For communication with the inn staff, pencil and paper may prove invaluable, since written English and cartoons are more likely to be understood.

玄関

### From the Genkan to the Bath

After a tiring, perhaps even aggravating, day of travel, you arrive at your ryokan. The manager and maids greet you with a welcoming *Irasshaimase!* in the *genkan*, the vestibule of the inn where you take off your shoes and slide into slippers. During your stay you will be shod in various pairs of slippers and clogs, so it is advisable to familiarize yourself with the semiotics of Japanese footwear. The key is in the level of "cleanness" of the floor. Street shoes or clogs provided by the ryokan are for use outdoors—street, garden, and vestibule (an extension of the street). Slippers are used on public indoor areas such as the hallway and lobby. The slippers are removed for rooms where people sleep or sit on the floor, including your tatami-matted ryokan room. Toilets, being places of impurity, have their own set of slippers or clogs. Appropriate footgear is strategically placed throughout the ryokan both for the guests' convenience and to ensure that dirt and impurity stay where they belong.

As soon as the ryokan staff have identified you—generally a simple task if you are a foreigner with a reservation—the maid will take you to your room. The fine old inns that retain their wooden architecture often have several wings connected by long winding halls, occasionally punctuated by gardens and stairways. Rooms are typically named for the three auspicious trees: pine (*matsu*), bamboo (*take*), and plum (*ume*). Not only is each of these plants associated with long life, but also the name ranks the room; pine is considered more auspicious than bamboo, which is considered better than plum.

The interior of your room will be arranged in the tea-ceremony-influenced Sukiya

松 竹 梅          数寄屋

床の間　　　畳

style—in some measure, the finer its Sukiya style, the better the inn (see Villas, p. 67). There is a great deal of snobbery about giving only important or regular guests the rooms with the finest garden views and most impressive *tokonoma*, or decorative alcove. In a fine ryokan room, nature is all around you; the garden will be exquisitely conceived, the *tokonoma* will be decorated with fresh flowers, and even the walls are plastered with sand. (In cheaper inns, there is no garden, and the *tokonoma* becomes a receptacle for telephones, excess luggage, and coin-operated television sets). The room itself will be floored with *tatami*, although sometimes there will be a veranda with tables and chairs. A sink or toilet, if there is one, is likely to be to one side of this veranda, or else by the entrance to the room. The toilets in many inns are Japanese style, which means you squat over them; many of the better inns, however, have made a point of installing at least one Western-style fixture.

A large, low table occupies the center of your room. While the maid serves you green tea and sweets—often some local specialty—and once again welcomes you to the inn, you should fill out a registration form. The information required is simple: your name, occupation, address, and previous and next destinations. Write in English in what looks like the appropriate spaces. Nobody will care very much if the form is filled out incorrectly. The maid will want to know what time you want dinner and breakfast—neither of which can be had much past 7:30 or 8:00 (p.m. and a.m.). Your maid, usually a middle-aged woman, is your mother and protector in all matters. You may find it bizarre—or a pleasant surprise—to be coddled like a child by a total stranger; the pleasantness of your stay will depend on how well you get along with her.

Your room will have a closet or a traditional lacquered stand for your clothes and a square tray containing *yukata*—crisply starched cotton robes—and small towels for use in the bath. In winter, there may be woolen overgarments as well. Before heading for the bath, change into the *yukata*; your maid will try to find an extra-large one if necessary. Wear the left side over the right; only corpses are dressed right side over the left.

浴衣

## 122

## The Bath (O-furo)　お風呂

Towel in hand and attired in your *yukata*, you will be led by the maid to the spiritual center of the ryokan, and perhaps of all Japan: the bath. Early Shinto was above all a religion of cleanliness and purification; only after ritual bathing could worshippers take part in matsuri or enter holy places. Worshippers are often required to purify themselves in cold water, or *mizu* (水), under waterfalls or in freezing lakes. For pleasure, however, one bathes in *yu* (湯), scalding hot water in which the cares of the day melt away into stupor. By using two completely different words, the Japanese express the emotional gulf between cold water and hot water. Either as divine imperative or hedonistic luxury, in Japan bathing has always been regarded as more than a hygienic chore. In order to enjoy a relaxed evening meal, the Japanese bathe beforehand to soak away tension as well as wash away grime.

The door to the women's bath is marked (女), and the men's bath is marked (男). The changing room contains baskets for clothing; valuables, although best left in your room, are almost certainly safe. Along the walls of the bath hall are tiny benches and little tubs for washing. (Traditionally, toilets are not placed in the same room.) Unlike in the West, where one soaks in one's own sweat and grime, in Japan, one washes and rinses before entering the bath, using hot water scooped out of the bath with the small tubs or dispensed from the faucets placed along the wall. Some bathers give this preliminary rinse every effort, lathering and scrubbing every pore until their flesh is aglow. Others merely give themselves a token splash, comparable to the cursory ablutions worshippers make before entering a shrine. In any case, everybody makes sure that their bodies are free of obvious dirt—and *soap*, which is never used in the tub—thereby ensuring that the bath water remains pure.

Now you are ready to enjoy the **o-furo**, a large tub big enough to sit in with legs stretched out, immersed to the neck. Some baths are tiled. Others, called *iwa-buro*, are paved in stone. The most luxurious—and rare—are cypress baths, with their pleasant fragrance and smooth, velvety surface. *O-furo* often look out over beautiful views or gardens. The water is scalding hot, especially at the end of the tub where the *yu* is trickling in.

## Ryokan Evenings

By the time you have finished your bath, put on your *yukata*—which is, by the way, acceptable wear in any part of the ryokan—and returned to the room, your meal may already be laid out. There is likely to be an incredible array of dishes spread before each place setting; many of these dishes are for dips and sauces (see Cuisine, p. 110). Ryokan rates, calculated per person, include two meals. The rates sometimes vary according to the elaborateness of the meal; if given a choice, order lightly, as the food usually comes in large quantity. *Jūsu* (orange drink, not real juice) and alcohol can be ordered at extra charge from your maid. If there is a woman in your party, she will be entrusted (like it or not) with the tub of rice, that essential element that ends and completes the meal. Meals are usually a simplified form of *kaiseki*, but only in the very best inns are dishes brought out one at a time, in true *kaiseki* style.

岩風呂

After dinner, you may want to take a stroll in the garden or in the surrounding neighborhood. Except in large cities, most ryokan do not keep their doors open much past 10 p.m.

会席

祭り　敷蒲団　二枚下さい　掛け布団

(matsuri nights are an exception); consult with the innkeeper before planning a night on the town. During this time, the maid clears away the dinner table, and lays out the bedding. This consists of a mattress (*shiki-buton*) laid directly on the tatami, and quilt (*kake-buton*). A tall person should ask for two quilts (*kake-buton nimai kudasai*), which can be staggered to cover the full length of the body. Pillows are often bricklike devices filled with buckwheat chaff; a good substitute for this traveler's nightmare is a *zabuton*, the square cushion used for sitting on the *tatami*, covered with a shirt or a towel. Before saying goodnight, the maid asks if she can get you anything, such as a nightcap or a pitcher of water. 座蒲団

One particularly pleasant service provided by most ryokan and hotels is massage (*massāji*), which you can arrange with your maid even for a late hour. This occupation is traditionally plied by blind specialists called *anma*. (Lately, however, there has developed a new breed outfitted with an athletic suit and a walkie-talkie.) Massages are given on your futon (or bed), with you clad in *yukata*. You start on your side, then the *anma* tells you to 按摩 lie on your stomach (*utsubuse*) and finally on your back (*aomuki*). A masseuse may also walk on your back. Prices have been subject to inflation, but range from Y1500 to Y3500 for forty minutes. This is not cheap, but it is a reasonable price to pay to settle into the sleep of the dead. 俯伏せ　あおむ　仰むく　梅干し

In the morning, five or ten minutes before breakfast is due, the maid gives a cursory knock on the door, wishes you a good morning with a rousing *Ohayō-gozaimasu*, and without further ado barges in to put away the futon. She asks you if you slept well as she bustles about, restoring the table and bringing breakfast (some inns serve breakfast in a common dining hall). A Japanese breakfast typically consists of pickled plum (*umeboshi*), dried seaweed (*nori*), a raw egg, and broiled fish along with *miso* soup, white rice, and green tea. The 味噌 egg is to be mixed with soy sauce and poured over the rice, bite-size mouthfuls of which are then wrapped in the *nori* and eaten. You can ask for a "Western" breakfast (*Yō-shoku dekimasuka?*) the night before, but be warned that this usually consists of ham and *cold* fried eggs, salad, and thick toast. Try to make it clear beforehand what you want; some establishments, certain that you detest Japanese food, will go out of their way to prepare cutlets for dinner and cold eggs for breakfast. 海苔　洋食

123

Guests are expected to leave by around 10 a.m. The maid will do her best, given the language barrier, to arrange taxis or sightseeing tours and check train schedules. The bill, which you settle with the maid in your room, will include any extras you may have incurred. Generally, small parties need not tip the maid, but if she has been especially nice to you or done you some special service, you may want to give her a token of thanks. Inexpensive articles representative of your home country are useful in this and in other situations, where the currencies of exchange are small, often impractical gifts and gestures. When you leave, you will observe one such gesture; the inn staff will accompany you to the door, wish you a warm farewell, bid you come again, and bow. You can respond by saying *O-sewa ni narimashita* (Thanks for taking care of me). 五右衛門風呂　bath tub w. floating wooden lid　お世話になりました

# MINSHUKU AND SENTŌ 民宿　銭湯　妻籠

wife - ko, basket　wago, cage　kome (rice) filled w.

In old farmhouses, you may still occasionally see a bathtub that looks like a giant iron cauldron. This is called a *goemonburo* after a famous Japanese Robin Hood who was captured at Nanzen-ji in Kyoto and boiled to death. Voluntary bathers, wishing to avoid scorching their feet, would put their weight on a wooden disk that shielded them from the searing iron below. Only one person could bathe at a time, and somebody else had to tend the fire. Today's aluminum and plastic household wonders are more inviting, but they still accommodate only one person. In traditional homes, bathing follows a strict pecking order, starting with the father and finishing up with the daughter-in-law. The bath is made very hot to last through all these shifts; if you are a guest, be prepared to bathe first and scald!

Minshuku are cheap lodgings provided in private homes, something like a bed-and-breakfast (see Practical Advice, p. 7). Just as a stay at one of the finer ryokan is like a visit to an elegant Japanese home, so a stay at an exceptional minshuku is a quick entree into Japan's folk traditions. Among the best are the old post inns at Tsumago and the *gasshō* farmhouses of Shirakawa-gō. The household pecking order also applies at the minshuku. The mistress of the house will advise you when to bathe. In a minshuku, by the way, you are expected to bring your own towel and lay out your own futon. 白川郷　house w. a steep rafter roof

Although even the shabbiest farmhouse traditionally had a bath, city dwellers preferred communal bathing at the *sentō*, neighborhood baths that charge a fee—a few pennies not so long ago, these days about Y250. A *sentō* generally has two entrances, one for men on the left and one for women on the right. The character *yu* (湯) (hot water) or the onsen sign ♨ are often displayed on the *noren* shop-curtains that hang in the entrance. The very oldest *sentō* are built entirely of wood. Because homes in the city now have their own baths, many modern *sentō* feature all sorts of gimmicks to attract customers: cold pools, saunas, electrified baths, and Las Vegas decor. One of the earliest gimmicks were tile mosaics; typically, one wall portrays a Japanese landscape, such as Mt. Fuji surrounded by rustic *minka* farmhouses, while the opposite wall might portray the Swiss Alps, dotted with chalets. 暖簾

弘法大師 温泉
湯殿山 東北 隠し湯

# ONSEN

For Japanese bathing enthusiasts the search for the ultimate bath is something in the nature of a religious quest. That *yu*, hot water, is held to have divine powers is best demonstrated by remote shrines, such as Yudono-san (Bathtub Mountain), where a hot spring is regarded as the god incarnate (Tōhoku, p. 175). Volcanic activity gives rise to thousands of onsen (hot springs), but popular legends often ascribe hot springs to miracles worked by famous ascetics and priests. KŌBŌ DAISHI (774-835), in order to succor the sick, supposedly created many of Japan's most famous hot springs by striking the ground with his magic staff. During the war-torn Middle Ages, certain onsen called *kakushi-yu* (hidden hot water) were used by military generals as camp hospitals. An injured warrior was supposed to make his way secretly to the agreed-upon spring where, with the aid of the beneficial waters, he could recuperate to fight again. 湯治場 hot spring

Many rustic onsen, deep in the mountains, are set up purely for medicinal purposes. At these *tōjiba*, elderly people and convalescents can stay for a few dollars a night, living in simple lodgings and preparing their own food. Depending on the mineral content of the water—iron, sulfur, radium, and the like—the springs are thought to have a salutary effect on a wide range of conditions, including skin diseases, gout, and rheumatism. People stand under waterfalls of hot water or sit in wooden steam boxes with their heads sticking out. Patients with internal ailments drink large amounts of the health-giving water. Certain onsen are paired, and alternating between them is considered particularly effective for certain ailments.

山菜 露天風呂

Many *tōjiba* are located in beautiful, isolated areas. A few even lack electricity; they use the soft light of oil lamps. These lodges cater to hikers, skiers, and nature lovers, and may consist of a series of thatched huts and old wooden buildings. Meals consist of trout caught in nearby streams and *sansai* (mountain greens) gathered from the mountains (see Cuisine, p. 116). These inns generally boast a **rotemburo**, an outdoor bath, usually in some particularly idyllic spot. Here, in the midst of nature, is where the communal essence of the bath is most strongly felt. Young women may not bathe outside in broad daylight—grannies are out night and day—but late in the evening mixed groups bathe, sing, and drink saké, which is floated from person to person in little cypress tubs. In the summer, a broiled trout often flavors the saké tub. You may also encounter saké in which *mamushi*, a poisonous snake, is pickled; this elixir is said to increase sexual potency.

124

## Onsen Cities

熱海 open air 蝮 別府

This sense of communality—near-sacred in Japan—appeals to schools, company groups, sports clubs, and circles of friends who take an onsen vacation together not only for enjoyment, but also to enhance group solidarity. The usual choice is not an isolated spring, but a famous onsen mecca, such as Atami or Beppu. These groups can be seen strolling around the town, dressed in matching *yukata*. Onsen vacations are also great favorites of couples, especially those seeking anonymity. A typical hotel in a large onsen town, however, may not be the best place to find a quiet, undisturbed evening; large groups use the huge halls of these places for *enkai*, banquets, often attended by geisha or "companions," which start off quite formally but don't end that way. These too are considered exercises in group cohesion; any unpleasantness—and most of the later part of the evening—is usually forgotten by morning. Hangovers, and any other lingering sense of uncleanness, can be soaked away in the baths, which remain open around the clock. 宴会

The baths themselves are for the most part exuberant souvenirs of the Japanese Everyman's first encounters with affluence in the 1960's. There are sand baths, baths in cablecars, baths in caves, multi-story variety bathhouses, and vast "jungle baths" filled with water slides, tropical plants, pavilions, waterfalls, Buddhas, and white plaster Cupids. 伊勢

浮き世

# SEX, FANTASY, AND THE "WATER BUSINESS"

The term *ukiyo*, or "floating world," is derived from a Buddhist belief about the impermanence and futility of material existence. (In Japanese, the word "floating" can mean "fleeting.") In his *Tales of Ise*, the courtier Narihira finds in this pessimistic worldview a vivid sense of beauty:

| | |
|---|---|
| Most wonderful when | Chireba-koso |
| they scatter— still more | Itodo sakura wa |
| The cherry blossoms. | Medetakere happy occasion |
| In this floating world, | Ukiyo ni nani ka |
| does anything endure? | Hisashikarubeki |

散ればこそ
いとど桜は
めでたけれ
浮き世に何か
久しかるべき

By the early Edo period, the term *ukiyo* came to refer to the fashionable and hedonistic pleasure quarters. These "nightless cities" consisted of brothels, teahouses, and bathhouses, all engaged in prostitution. The ukiyo-e, or "pictures of the floating world," depicted actors and courtesans—demure, willow-waisted women, often in not-so-demure poses. The officially sanctioned districts, such as Yoshiwara in Edo, Shimabara in Kyoto, and Shinmachi in Ōsaka, were surrounded by a large wall and gate.

浮き世絵

吉原(江戸) 島原(京都) 新町(大阪)

## Soaplands

When the priest Nisei Shōnin revived Kōbe's Arima Onsen as a place of worship and healing in the twelfth century, he built twelve temple hostels, and within each temple he installed two women, called *yuna*, or "hot-water women," to wash pilgrims. These bathhouse girls soon drifted into prostitution. Later, the bathhouse girls of Edo achieved great notoriety when the authorities tried to outlaw them. What had happened was inevitable, since the bath is a primal physical experience that naturally leaves the bather in a hedonistic mood. Prostitutes and "onsen geisha" are still an integral, if partially hidden, part of the onsen scene. (For more on classical geisha—who are not prostitutes—see Kyoto, p. 338.)

The connection between bathing and sex is so strong that, although prostitution was outlawed in 1958, the institution persists quite openly in "soaplands," where the action centers around a bubble bath. These are tolerated partly because both the bath and what comes after are thought to have therapeutic value. Large "soapland cities" exist in Sapporo, Kawasaki, Gifu, and Shiga-ken, to name only the most famous. Soaplands used to be called *toruko*, or *toruko-buro* (Turkish baths), but were renamed soaplands, supposedly because of a misunderstanding involving a taxi-driver, the Turkish ambassador, and a *toruko* named Embassy. In response to protests by the Turkish government, these establishments across the nation agreed, on a set day, to change their names from *toruko* to the less offensive "soapland."

## Fantasy

Such names as Embassy, Palace, and Dreamland are often used not only for soaplands but also for *pachinko* (pinball) parlors, kissaten, and "love hotels," lodgings that offer bargain hourly rates because of the rapid turnover of their clients. All these establishments offer theme decor; love hotels offer fantasy beds and baths in addition to a fanciful exterior. The most famous, a Disneyland-type castle named Emperor that towers over the Meguro section of Tokyo, was a bit upstaged by the opening of a real Magic Kingdom outside Tokyo in 1984. Pension lodgings, often decorated to evoke rural American themes, have become popular (see Practical Advice, p. 7). Wholesome or sleazy, these various establishments offer an escape from the humdrum of everyday life, although perhaps less effectively than the primal succor of the bath or the elegant repose of a fine ryokan.

In modern Japanese society, nighttime entertainment has become big business. Such quaint terms as "hot-water girls" and "floating world" have given way to the cold, utilitarian *mizu-shōbai*, or "water business." Although soaplands are included in this term, by far the most common *mizu-shōbai* institutions are *sunakku* ("snacks"), hostess bars, and cabarets, which offer liquor and female companionship. These range in size from huge Tokyo cabarets, where hundreds of hostesses circulate among tables according to a computerized dispatching system, to tiny *sunakku* run by one woman behind a counter; dozens of the latter type of establishment can be fitted into a single building.

Added to the hostesses' flirting is some of the motherly understanding you may encounter in your ryokan maid; one of the hostess's objectives is to help the customer forget the aggravations and injured dignity of the day. If men come in a group, she will help them cement social or business relationships by keeping the party convivial. In a smaller club, there is no better way to emphasize shared sentiments than with *karaoke*: individuals stand up and sing a tune, accompanied by a recorded soundtrack. (The word literally means "empty orchestra.") "Yesterday" and "My Way" are often available for foreign guests. Video disks supply bouncing-ball lyrics and visual accompaniments, usually soft porn or soft-focus landscapes.

---

# A Note on Amae

Anthropologist Doi Takeo thinks the key to Japanese society lies in the verb *amaeru*, which means to "play baby," to expect indulgence the way a child might from its mother. The art of living, according to Doi's *Anatomy of Dependence*, lies in knowing the appropriate time to indulge others—and oneself—so that everyone can fulfill his or her need to *amaeru*, a need which is viewed as far from undesirable. Indulgence is not always the same as blind generosity, however; amid an atmosphere of seeming tolerance, the debit and credit of *who* is indulging *whom* is often carefully accounted.

125

## Sex Shops

Japan's sex-related businesses are subject to fads. The following list, courtesy of *Tokyo: A City Guide*, by Judith Conner and Mayumi Yoshida, describes the main ones, in increasing order of "difficulty":

1. **Nōpan Kissa** (No-panty Coffee Shop). Waitresses clad only in a skimpy apron serve coffee and tea. Mirrored floors are a common feature. Charge incl. coffee, Y2–3000. "Pleasure" course, Y3–8000.
2. **Nozoki Gekijō** (Peep Show). Watch a girl through the little hole of your tiny private room. Charge, Y2–3000. "Pleasure" course, Y3–8000.
3. **Sutorippu Gekijō** (Strip Show). Watch a live strip show. Sometimes volunteers from the audience take turns participating on stage. Charge, Y3–5000.
4. **Poruno Land** (Porn Land). Just like Disneyland—all the fun in one building. There's *nōpan kissa*, peep shows, massage, etc. Special "round trip" tickets available. Entrance fee and "pleasure" charge, Y9–15,000.
5. **Fasshion Massāji** (Fashion Massage). There is actually nothing fashionable about the massages given here. Entrance fee and "pleasure charge," Y9–15,000.
6. **Dēto Kissa** (Date Coffee Shop). Young women hang out in the coffee shop and wait for a "date" to take them to a hotel. Charge for one drink, hotel, and "super pleasure," Y25–40,000.
7. **Soapland**. A rather traditional form of naughty place. .... Part of what takes place goes on in a bath. Entrance fee, Y3–5000; "super pleasure," Y15–60,000.
8. **Hotetoru** (Turkish Bath in a Hotel). Set up through an agency, the "bath" takes place in a hotel. Japanese language ability required. Hotel and "super pleasure," Y25–40,000.
9. **Mantoru** (Turkish Bath in an Apartment). Same as above.
10. **Pink Kyabare** (Pink Cabaret). Cabaret where more happens off-stage than on. Drink and "pleasure," Y10–30,000.

126

Although most *mizu-shōbai* have connections with the *yakuza*, Japan's underworld, transactions are generally carried out with circumspection and decorum. The areas where these businesses cluster are surprisingly safe; teenage girls walk cheerfully past the worst-looking places. The best place for street voyeurism is Shinjuku's Kabuki-chō, a district of Tokyo densely packed with bars, *yakitori* stands, and thousands of the establishments mentioned above.

Women can safely stroll around the area but should use common sense in entering one of these shops. Places for gawkers—strip shows, *nōpan kissa*—might be okay, but places that rely on customers who do more than just gawk are best avoided. If you do go in, expect an enormous bar tab, not including the "extras." There are a few male strip shows and "host" bars that cater specifically to women. And there's a lively and innocuous gay nightclub scene (such as Shinjuku Ni-chōme in Tokyo) where both men and women are welcome.

# FAVORITE INNS AND ONSEN

### ELEGANT RYOKAN

These are a varied group, personal favorites offering a mixture of tradition, elegance, service, and history. By purely objective standards, some might rate higher than others (e.g., they have Western-style plumbing, TV and air conditioning, and accept credit cards). But subjectively, each is in its own way a quintessence of the Japanese inn.

** **Hōrai**. An elegant hot-spring inn, built in exquisite modern Sukiya style, overlooking the sea. Famous for its open-air cypress bath pavilion (Atami, Kantō, p. 268).

** **Ōsawa Onsen Hotel**. A hot-spring inn built on a samurai estate. Wonderful baths and atmosphere (** Izu Peninsula, Kantō, p. 272).

*** **Asadaya**. Modern ryokan, designed and serviced with exquisite taste. Prides itself on its extraordinary cuisine, served on the superb porcelain and lacquerware for which this region is famed (*** Kanazawa, Chūbu, p. 302).

*** **Tawaraya**. Lovely old buildings and gardens, flawless good taste, and elegant service have won it a place as one of the great small inns of the world (*** Kyoto, p. 373).

** **Sumiya**. Another venerable Kyoto inn, this one permeated in the tea ceremony. Sukiya architecture, *chakaiseki* cuisine (p. 373).

** **Kinmata**. A lovely two-hundred-year-old inn, modest but run by a warm, lovely family, who really look after you (*** Kyoto, p. 373).

*** **Miyama-sō**. A secluded inn in rustic mountains, an hour's drive north of Kyoto. Elegant amenities, lovely mountain cuisine, and beechwood baths overlooking a rushing stream (*** Kyoto, p. 375).

** **Ryokan Kurashiki**. An Edo-period merchant's house converted into a wonderful, antique-furnished inn. Fresh Inland Sea fish and *kaiseki* (*** Kurashiki, Chūgoku, p. 439).

** **Yakumo Honjin**. This marvelous inn near the ancient Izumo Shrine was originally built to lodge the local lord (Shinjō, Chūgoku, p. 443).

*** **Tamanoyu**. A refined country-style retreat, furnished in tasteful handcrafts. The hot-spring baths look out on Mt. Yufuin. The inn prides itself on its natural, home-grown food, prepared as an elegant, rusticized *kaiseki* (** Yufuin, Kyūshū, p. 473).

## SOME UNUSUAL INNS AND MINSHUKU

** **Minshuku Magariya.** Nambu *magariya* farmhouse (* Tōno, Tōhoku, p. 167).

** **Dōchū-an YH.** A refurbished farmhouse in a suburb just south of Sendai (* Sendai, Tōhoku, p. 174).

* **Haguro Sai-kan.** On Haguro-san, this is an atmospheric *shukubō* (temple inn) run by Haguro Jinja. **Daishin-bō**, in the village at the base, is a thatched-roof *shukubō*. The minshuku **Kayabukiya**, in nearby Tamugimata, is a magnificent farmhouse (** Dewa Sanzan, Tōhoku, p. 177).

** **Ryonin-kan.** Early Meiji-period fish wholesaler's fine shop and home have been converted into a charming inn (* Aizu-Wakamatsu, p. 185).

**Yamatoya.** One of many large, thatched-roof farmhouse inns that line the single street of a Tōhoku post town (* Ōuchijuku, Tōhoku, p. 185).

* **Kokuminshukusha and YH Yokokura.** A thatched pilgrim's inn (* Togakushi, Kantō, p. 252).

** **Minshuku Teppō.** An Izu headman's house. Guests dine on one-pot meals cooked at a hearth (** Izu Peninsula, Kantō, p. 272).

** **Echigoya.** A two-hundred-year-old post-town inn. Simple but atmospheric (** Narai, Chūbu, p. 283).

** **Adachi Minshuku.** A minshuku where one can stay in the lovely old house of a cormorant fisherman (Mino-Seki, Chūbu, p. 289).

* **Yosobei** in Ōgimachi and * **Yūsuke** in Ainokura are two among dozens of minshuku in an area famous for A-frame thatched-roof farmhouses (*** Shirakawa-gō and Gokayama, Chūbu, p. 298).

* **Asakichi.** An Edo-period bordello that catered to Ise pilgrims. Now a traditional and respectable inn (*** Ise, Chūbu, p. 310).

**Temple lodgings on *** Kōya-san.** Fifty-three temples on this holy mountain provide lodgings for pilgrims and tourists. The best offer gardens, lovely old rooms decorated with fine art, and exquisite vegetarian meals (Kinki, p. 421).

** **International Villas.** Okayama prefecture has created half a dozen excellent and inexpensive inns, many in beautiful, remote regions. Includes several refurbished old farmhouses (see p. 428).

** **Fukiya Sansō.** Handsomely renovated Meiji-period house in an idyllic mountain village (** Fukiya, Chūgoku, p. 441).

**Minshuku Izumiya.** A traditional Okinawan house with a beautiful garden (** Taketomi Island, Okinawa, p. 523).

127

## FAVORITE ROTEMBURO AND SPAS

** **Kamuiwakka Rotemburo.** A spectacular series of pools fed by a hot waterfall (* Shiretoko Peninsula, Hokkaidō, p. 145).

** # **Aoni Onsen.** An inn buried in a wild valley. Has a lovely *rotemburo* by a rushing river (* Towada Area, Tōhoku, p. 157).

** # **Tsurunoyu Onsen and Kuroyu Onsen.** Tsurunoyu is a quiet and rustic inn in a remote valley. Kuroyu's thatched bungalows are sprawled out along a slope streaming with hot water. Both inns offer a variety of baths in wooden halls (Tōhoku, p. 164).

# **Tamagawa.** A *tōjiba* buried in the Hachimantai mountains, where working people and hikers come to recuperate (Tōhoku, p. 164).

* **Shirabu Onsen.** Three wonderful inns in the center of this mountain hot-spring village preserve their thatched main buildings (Tōhoku, p. 182).

** **Hōshi Onsen.** A mountain inn with a spectacular wooden bath hall (Kantō, p. 245).

** **Takaragawa Onsen.** The one inn here boasts an enormous *rotemburo* in a stunning natural setting (Kantō, p. 246).

# **Takayama Onsen.** A large bath built against the living rock and canopied by trees, in the mountains of eastern Nagano (Kantō, p. 251).

* **Jigokudani Onsen.** This mountain spa attracts wild monkeys, which bathe in the pools in the winter. Lodgings at the rambling Gorakukan (Kantō, p. 251).

**Tokkonoyu.** At Shuzen-ji Onsen, this open-air bath, bubbling up in a boulder in the middle of the river, is said to have welled up when Kōbō Daishi struck the boulder with his staff (** Izu Peninsula, Kantō, p. 272).

**Ōdaru Onsen.** A group of baths by a thundering waterfall in central Izu (** Izu Peninsula, Kantō, p. 270).

* **Shirahone Onsen.** Near Matsumoto, in a prime hiking area. The rambling Saitō Ryokan offers a multitude of baths (Chūbu, p. 285).

** **Shirouma Yari Onsen.** Reached by a 3:00h climb from Hakuba station, it is the highest *rotemburo* in Japan, with a panoramic view of the Japan Alps (Chūbu, p. 287).

**Kanetsuri Onsen.** Inns and riverside baths in scenic Kurobe Gorge (Chūbu, p. 294).

** **Tarutama and Jigoku Onsen.** Two rustic spas (* Aso National Park, Kyūshū, p. 496).

**# Yakushima.** This island south of Kagoshima has open-air baths by the sea (Kyūshū, p. 502).

**✱✱ Ebino Kōgen Rotemburo.** A beautiful, boulder-lined *rotemburo* and simple cabins, surrounded by tall pampas grass, at the foot of Mt. Karakuni (**✱✱ Kirishima/Ebino Kōgen, Kyūshū, p. 503).

## ONSEN "LAS VEGAS" AND FAMOUS NIGHT TOWNS

**✱ Sapporo.** Susukino is this city's friendly nightlife district (Hokkaidō, p. 140).

**Noboribetsu.** The Dai-ichi Takimoto-kan's bath hall is one of the largest in Japan. Other attractions are Hell Valley and an Ainu Village (Hokkaidō, p. 148).

**✱✱✱ Tokyo.** Kabukichō, in Tokyo's booming Shinjuku, has become a byword for sex throughout Japan (p. 226).

**Atami.** High-rise hotels dominate this famous seaside spa. Considered to be rather sleazy, it is a favorite hideaway for illicit lovers (Kantō, p. 268).

**✱✱✱ Kyoto.** Geisha and bar hostesses work side by side in the elegant and tawdry Gion-Shinbashi quarter (p. 338).

**Katsu'ura.** The Hotel Urashima is famous for its sea-cavern bath. The Nakanoshima Hotel, on a small island of its own, has a *rotemburo* built on a scenic cove (Kinki, p. 415).

**✱ Ōsaka.** Shinchi in the north of Ōsaka and Soemon-chō in the south are the main nightlife districts. Namba is more of a dining-out area, but colorful nonetheless. Tsūtenkaku is a notorious low-life district, best avoided at night (Kinki, p. 417).

**Shirahama.** Famous seaside spa with white sand beaches, balmy weather, open-air baths, and fishing (Kinki, p. 422).

**Dōgo Onsen.** This ancient spa is famed for its classic bathhouse with three different grades of public baths and lounges, including an imperial suite. Nearby Oku-Dōgo has jungle baths (✱ Matsuyama, Chūgoku, p. 452).

**Beppu.** An onsen city, famous for huge volumes of hot water and sleazy atmosphere. Amusements include sand baths, a tour of the "hells," a sex museum, and the Suginoi Palace's jungle bath (Kyūshū, p. 473).

**Hakata (Fukuoka).** Nakasu is the heart of Hakata's nightlife district (Kyūshū, p. 474).

**✱✱ Ibusuki Onsen.** A spa on the scenic, balmy tip of the Satsuma Peninsula. One can be buried in steaming sand on the beach and cavort in the jungle bath at the Ibusuki Kankō Hotel (Kyūshū, p. 501).

# One-Hour Japanese

## BASIC QUESTION AND ANSWER

Japanese word order is roughly the reverse of that of English and the modern Romance languages. There are no plurals or articles (*a/the*). The vocabulary words chosen for the first part of this example are classic Japanese-English terms. The three forms of the verb *desu* (meaning "it is") exemplify the various levels of courtesy that are employed in Japanese.

**Basic questions**

| | | | |
|---|---|---|---|
| *Takushī* | | | taxi(s) |
| *Basu* | | | bus(es) |
| *Toire* | *wa doko desu-ka?* | Where is(are) the(a) | toilet(s) |
| *Hoteru* | | | hotel(s) |
| *Resutoran* | | | restaurant(s) |

**Possible answers**

| | | | |
|---|---|---|---|
| *Migi* | | | right |
| *Hidari* | *da* [abrupt] | | left |
| *Massugu* | *desu* [neutral] | It's | straight ahead |
| *Ue* | *degozaimasu* [polite] | | above |
| *Shita* | | | below |

## PRONUNCIATION: MASTERING JAPANESE-ENGLISH

A quick way to learn Japanese pronunciation is to pronounce English words as the Japanese do. Japanese is pronounced rather like Spanish or Italian, with similar vowel sounds and a pattern of consonant-vowel, consonant-vowel. According to the Hepburn system of romanizing Japanese, vowels are pronounced as follows:

*a, e* and *i* as in *spaghetti*
*u* and *o* as in *uno*

A long bar over the vowel means to stretch it while keeping the same sound: *takushī* is pronounced *takushee*. Final vowels are voiced: *toire* is pronounced *to-i-reh*.

Syllables are stressed evenly. English has a tendency to stress the second syllable, so "America" sounds to Japanese ears like "Merika." (Wheat flour is still called *meriken-ko*, American flour.) When Japanese words are pronounced this way, they become incomprehensible; the city of *Ōsaka*, pronounced American-style with the stress on the second syllable, sounds like *Saka* to Japanese ears.

English, especially as spoken in the American Midwest and South, tends to drawl, stretching the length of vowels; in Japanese, changes in vowel length change the meaning of a word. *Tori* means bird, while *torī* (or *torii*) means a Shinto shrine gate. *Tōri*, on the other hand, means a boulevard or street. Japanese with an American drawl sounds comical — which is no problem in itself — but it can also lead to serious misunderstandings.

There are many thousands of possible syllables in English, whereas Japanese has only a few hundred. For this reason, "Japanese English" sounds distorted to us. Moreover, a Japanese may not understand your English unless you similarly "Japanize" it. Don't, for example, ask for a *hotel*; ask for a *hoteru*.

**How to add extra vowels**

1. In Japanese, a consonant is usually followed by a vowel. Final consonants usually take an *i*, *u*, or *o*, as in *jūsu* (juice), *kēki* (cake), and *howaito hausu* (white house).
2. Consonant clusters are usually broken up with a *u* or *i* as in *tōsuto* for "toast."
3. Bothersome final consonants are dropped, as in *toire* (toilet) and *resutoran* (restaurant).

**How to Japanize your English consonants**

| English | Japanese | Examples |
|---------|----------|----------|
| *tu* | *tsu or chu* | *tsuna* (tuna) |
| *r* or *l* | *r* | *sarada* (salad), *sarami* (salami), *kōra* (cola) |
| *f* | *h* (except *f* before *u*) | *kōbī* (coffee), *fuddo* (hood), *pirafu* (pilaf) |
| *v* | *b* | *bideo* (video) |
| *si* | *shi* | *shisutemu* (system) |
| *di/zi* | *ji* | *rajio* (radio) |

# BASIC GRAMMAR

**Particles.** In *Hoteru wa doko desu-ka?* (Where is the hotel?), *wa* means that *hoteru* is the subject of the sentence, while *ka*, appended at the end, turns the entire sentence into a question. The basic particles include these:

| | |
|---|---|
| *wa* | indicates a grammatical subject |
| *wo* | indicates a grammatical object |
| *ni* | means "at" or "on"; *resutoran ni* means "at the restaurant" |
| *made* | means "until," "up to," or "to"; *hoteru made* means "(up) to the hotel" |
| *no* | means "of"; *hoteru no hidari* means "left of the hotel". It also creates the possessive; *hoteru no basu* means "bus of the hotel" (i.e., hotel's bus) |
| *ka* | placed at the end of a sentence, *ka* turns it into a question |

**"Pointing" pronouns.** These pronouns are highly patterned and easy to remember:

| Japanese | English | Japanese (adj./noun) | English |
|----------|---------|----------------------|---------|
| *doko* | where | *dono/dore* | which |
| *koko* | here | *kono/kore* | this |
| *soko* | there (by you) | *sono/sore* | that (by you) |
| *asoko* | over there | *ano/are* | that over there |

**More basic questions and answers**

*Basu wa* { *koko* / *soko* / *asoko* } *desu ka?*   Is the bus { here / there (by you)? / over there }

*Hai* / *Eh* / *Sō desu* } Yes.

*Ie* / *Chigaimasu* } No.

130

# NUMBERS, TIME, AND MONEY

**Numbers**

Japanese has several ways of counting, but the "Chinese" method given here is the simplest. The *kanji* character is included because prices are sometimes written this way:

| Number | Kanji | Japanese | Number | Kanji | Japanese |
|--------|-------|----------|--------|-------|----------|
| 0 | 0 * | *zero* | 10 | 十 | *jū* |
| 1 | 一 | *ichi* | 100 | 百 | *hyaku* |
| 2 | 二 | *ni* | 1,000 | 千 | *sen* |
| 3 | 三 | *san* | 10,000 | 万 | *man* |
| 4 | 四 | *shi (or yon)* | | | |
| 5 | 五 | *go* | | | |
| 6 | 六 | *roku* | | | |
| 7 | 七 | *shichi (or nana)* | | | |
| 8 | 八 | *hachi* | | | |
| 9 | 九 | *kyū* | | | |

*the Arabic numeral is used most often

Making compound numbers is straightforward. When written in kanji, numbers can take a traditional form or a "decimal form" corresponding to our use of Arabic numerals:

|  | | Traditional | "Decimal" |
|---|---|---|---|
| 2,500 | *ni-sen go-hyaku* | 二千五百 | 二五〇〇 |

Numbers are usually followed by a suffix indicating what type of object is being counted:

時 *-ji* (hour)
円 *-en* (yen)
枚 *-mai* (flat object, like a ticket)
人 *-nin* (persons)

Kippu { *ichi-mai* / *ni-mai* } *kudasai*   Please give me { one / two } ticket(s)

## Time

Add *-ji* to turn a number into the hour; add *-fun* to indicate the minute (after *jū*, the vowel gets shortened and *ppun* is added).

| *Basu wa nan-ji desu-ka?* | What time is the bus? |
|---|---|
| *Ichi-ji* | One o'clock |
| *Jū-ni-ji* | Twelve o'clock |
| *Roku-ji go-fun* | 6:05 |
| *Shichi-ji sanjuppun* | 7:30 |

## Duration

Add *-kan* to speak about duration.

| *Ōsaka made wa nan-ji-kan desu-ka?* | How many hours to Ōsaka? |
|---|---|
| *Go-ji-kan* | Five hours |
| *Roku-ji-kan* | Six hours |
| *Jū-ichi-ji-kan* | Eleven hours |
| *Hachi-ji-kan go-fun* | Eight hours and five minutes |

## Money

Append *-en* (yen) or *doru* (dollars) to the number.

| *Kore wa ikura desu-ka?* | How much is this? |
|---|---|
| *Hyaku-en* | One hundred yen |
| *San-byaku-en* | Three hundred yen |
| *Ni-sen-en* | Two thousand yen |
| *Ichi-man go-sen-en* | Fifteen thousand yen |
| *Go-man-en* | Fifty thousand yen |
| *Jū-go-man doru* | 150,000 dollars |

131

# TRAVELING

**Travel terms**

| *eki* | station |
|---|---|
| *chikatetsu* | subway |
| *jei-āru* | JR (Japan Railways) |
| *ressha* | long-distance train |
| *densha* | commuter train, streetcar |
| *-yuki* | -bound (direction) |
| *-ban sen* | track number |

{ *Jei-āru* / *Basu* / *Densha* / *Chikatetsu* } *no eki wa doko desu-ka?*   Where is the { JR / bus / train / subway } station?

Q. { *Kyoto* / *Nara* / *Tokyo* } *-yuki no* { *densha* / *ressha* / *basu* } *wa* { *nan-ban sen* / *doko* / *koko* / *nan-ji* } *desu-ka?*

The { *Kyoto* / *Nara* / *Tokyo* } -bound { train / train / bus } is { what track? / where? / here? / what time? }

A. { *Ichi* / *Ni* / *San* } *-ban sen desu*   It's track { one. / two. / three. }

{ *Ichi-ji san-juppun* / *San-ji yon-juppun* / *Jū-hachi-ji ni-juppun* } *desu*   It's at { 1:30 / 3:40 / 18:20 (6:20 p.m.) }

## Buying a ticket

| | |
|---|---|
| *kudasai* | please give me |
| *tokkyū* | limited express |
| *kyūkō* | express |
| *kippu* | ticket |
| *tokkyū-ken* | limited express ticket |
| *-mai* | a "counter" for flat objects like tickets. |
| *seki* | seat |
| *shitei-seki* | reserved seat |
| *shitei-ken* | reserved seat ticket |

| | |
|---|---|
| *Kippu ichi-mai kudasai.* | Please give me one ticket |

Ōsaka / Kyoto } *made no kippu kudasai*　　Please give me ticket(s) to { Ōsaka / Kyoto

Tokkyū-ken / Kyūkō-ken / Shitei-ken } *wa ikura desu-ka?*　　How much are { limited express tickets / express tickets / reserved seats?

# SHOPPING

| | |
|---|---|
| *Kore wo kudasai* | Please give me this |

Sore / Are } *wa ikura desu ka?*　　How much is { that (by you) / that (over there)

132

Atarashī / Furui / Ōkī / Chīsai } *hō wo kudasai*　　Please give me the { new(er) / old(er) / large(r) / small(er)

# LODGINGS

Making reservations in Japanese over the phone is really too complicated unless you are fluent. Convey your wishes to your hotel, JTB, and so on, and have them call for you. In a ryokan, it's useful to be able to assure the maids that you can eat Japanese food, know how to use a Japanese bath, and can sleep on the floor (see Ryokan chapter).

| | |
|---|---|
| *Shinguru arimasu ka?* | Do you have a　single? |

Tsuin / Heya / Ippaku ni-shoku / Zeikin sābisu-komi } *wa ikura desu ka?*　　How much is a { twin / room / room w/2 meals? / w/tax and service

Yonsen gohyaku-en / Hassen-en / Ichiman-en } *desu.*　　It's { Y4,500 / Y8,000 / Y10,000

Furonto / O-furo / Yukata } *wa doko desu-ka?*　　Where is the { front desk / bath / *yukata* (robe)

O-furo / Yū-shoku / Chō-shoku / Chekku-auto } *wa nan-ji desu-ka?*　　What time is { the bath / dinner / breakfast / check-out

Wa-shitsu / Wa-shoku / Nihon no o-furo } *de kekkō desu.*　　(A) Japanese { room / food　is fine / bath

*Wa-* and *yō-* are prefixes indicating "Japanese" and "Western," although they can't be applied universally:

Chō-shoku wa { yō-shoku / wa-shoku } desu-ka?　　Is breakfast { Western? / Japanese?

# POLITE PHRASES

The way you begin and end social interactions in Japan is as important as anything that goes on in the middle:

| | |
|---|---|
| *Ohayō gozaimasu.* | Good morning. |
| *Konnichiwa.* | Good day. |
| *Konbanwa.* | Good evening. |
| *Sayonara.* | Good-bye. |

| | |
|---|---|
| *Chotto o-tazune shimasu.* | I'd like to ask a question. |
| *Dōzo.* | Please go ahead. |
| *Sumimasen.* | Excuse me/ I'm sorry. |
| *Dōmo [arigatō (gozaimasu)].* | Thank you [polite (formal)]. |
| *O-sewa ni narimashita.* | Thanks for taking care of me. |
| *Gochisōsama deshita.* | Thank you for a fine meal. |
| *Chotto matte kudasai.* | Please wait a moment. |

# THE JAPANESE WRITING SYSTEM: KANA AND KANJI

Japanese is written with Chinese ideograms, called *kanji*, and two phonetic syllabaries, *hiragana* and *katakana*. *Hiragana* are rounded while *katakana* are angular; both systems represent the same set of forty-six syllables. *Hiragana* represent Japanese verb inflections and particles, which have no equivalent in Chinese, and are also used in place of Chinese characters in "easy" texts, such as children's books. *Katakana* express foreign — largely English — words that have been adopted into the Japanese vocabulary. Because there are many such words (e.g. *basu*, *hoteru*, and *takushi*), memorizing the *katakana* will open a small window in the daunting wall of cryptic symbols. For example, the menu of a *kissaten* or any restaurant that serves Western food consists largely of *katakana*, which can be deciphered into the "Japanese English" decribed above. (Also see Cuisine, p. 119). P.G. O'Neill's *A Japanese Kana Workbook* (see Recommended Reading) is a good programmed text for *kana*; a casual visitor to Japan should probably skip the section on *hiragana*.

Out of the thousands of *kanji*, or Chinese characters, here are a few simple and useful examples:

| Kanji | Meaning | Pronunciation |
|---|---|---|
| 口 | mouth | *kuchi* |
| 入 | enter/put in | *hai(ru), ire(ru)* |
| 出 | leave | *de(ru)* |
| 日 | sun | *hi* |
| 月 | moon | *tsuki* |
| 男 | man | *otoko* |
| 女 | woman | *onna* |

Two useful compounds:

| | | |
|---|---|---|
| 入口 | entrance | *iri-guchi* |
| 出口 | exit | *de-guchi* |

The character for *kuchi* obviously represents a mouth. *De(ru)* shows two mountains stacked one on top of the other, suggesting a departure on a long journey. *Otoko* shows the character for rice paddy over the character for strength, indicating that men were viewed as strength in the paddies. *Onna* is a rendition of a very pregnant woman. (These two characters are found on doors of toilets and bathrooms.) Dates are often given with the moon and sun symbols; December 14, for example, is written 12月14日 . Len Walsh's *Read Japanese Today* is a simple and excellent introduction to *kanji*.

# BRIEF HISTORY OF THE LANGUAGE

The Japanese language is totally unrelated to Chinese. It is clearly linked only with the languages of Japan's closest neighbors, Okinawa (now part of Japan) and Korea. These languages bear resemblances to the Altaic family, which includes Turkish and many Central Asian languages. Okinawan and Japanese also have some similarity to Malayo-Polynesian languages, particularly in the vocabulary relating to parts of the body, fishing, and the ocean.

Although Chinese and Japanese are grammatically as different as any two languages can be, the adoption of Chinese *kanji* (by the sixth century A.D.) had a tremendous impact on Japanese. Mastery of written Chinese was the mark of a gentleman, much as the mastery of Latin was in Europe. Chinese similarly served, over the centuries, to round out the limited vocabulary of the Japanese vernacular. Within the severe limits imposed by the small number of sounds in Japanese, these new words were pronounced as close to Chinese as possible, the distortion being comparable to that of "Japanese English." The Japanese also assigned *kanji* to native words that have the same meaning, so that most *kanji* can be pronounced in at least two ways, one Chinese and one Japanese. For example:

| Character | Meaning | Japanese Reading | Chinese Reading |
|---|---|---|---|
| 山 | mountain | *yama* | *san* |
| 寺 | temple | *tera* (or *dera*) | *-ji* |

There are striking parallels between the way the ancient Japanese responded to the onslaught of Chinese culture, which accompanied Chinese script, and the way modern Japanese have adapted to things Western. Today one usually eats Japanese food with chopsticks and Western food with silver. Similarly, one generally does not mix Chinese and Japanese readings. For example, the name of one famous temple, 山寺 (Yama-dera), means Mountain Temple, and uses Japanese readings for both characters, but the name of another famous temple, 高山寺 (Kōzan-ji), meaning High Mountain Temple, is pronounced purely by the "Chinese" readings. In traditional Japan, and to some extent today, the vocabulary of public life, particularly in government and academia, is heavy on "dry" Chinese compounds, whereas private life favors the more "emotional" Japanese of vernacular origin.

## The development of kana

According to legend, the priest KŪKAI invented the *kana* in the eighth century so that women and commoners could read about Buddhism. The *kana* originated as a small subset of the Chinese characters just for their sounds, something like a rebus. The two styles, *katakana* and *hiragana*, are simplified versions of the plain and cursive styles of those characters. In late Heian times, *kana* served as the script for novels composed by aristocratic women, such as *The Tale of Genji*. These women wrote in a poetic style that relied almost entirely on native Japanese words.

The modern language contains an abundance of homonyms, particularly compound words pronounced in the "Chinese" manner, and would be incomprehensible if written in *kana* alone. Newspapers use about two thousand *kanji*, partly in order to avoid this kind of ambiguity.

## Language and culture

Japanese verbs are inflected not only according to tense, but also according to many different levels of politeness that can be granted to the listener. These correspond to the listener's social status and also to whether he or she is considered "inside" or "outside" the speaker's group. In general, the greater the distance, the greater the politeness; in the absence of intimacy, familiar forms are felt to be disrespectful. Foreigners, or *gaijin* ("outside people"), being the very farthest "outside," are often regaled with particularly polite forms.

The psychological need to distinguish between "inside" and "outside" also extends to popular debate about the Japanese language itself. The theory that the brain processes Japanese differently from Western languages is extremely popular in Japan, even though there is no scientific evidence for it. And essayists and critics never lose an opportunity to point out how inalienably Japanese Japanese is. "Japanese English" is a case in point: most English speakers would not be able to understand it, and they certainly would not be able to read it — it has been made Japanese, albeit at the "outside" limit of the language. The notion of a cultural and linguistic inner core — which foreigners are supposed neither to understand nor to be able to penetrate — has enabled the Japanese to borrow extensively, in culture as well as in language, without losing their sense of inviolability.

134

# Japan
# by Region

# Hokkaidō

Japan's northernmost island is also its newest, having been fully settled by the Japanese only in the past century. Before that, it was a wild, inhospitable place inhabited mostly by the Ainu, a non-Yamato people who had been pushed out of Honshū by the Japanese. Today Hokkaidō, the most sparsely populated of Japan's main islands, offers wide-open landscapes for hikers, skiers, and bicyclists, as well as glimpses of vanishing Ainu culture and relics of Hokkaidō's frontier days. Though popular with Japanese vacationers, these attractions are of limited historical and cultural interest. Hokkaidō's principal attractions, its five national parks, take sizable amounts of time and money to visit because public transport is sparse and distances are great. Also, Japanese national parks often contain highly developed towns and populated areas; it takes some effort to find the unspoiled spots within them.

## BEST ATTRACTIONS

I.	\* **Sapporo.** Capital of Hokkaidō. A lively, entertaining city, and the logical base for your travels (p. 140).

I:NE3	\*# **Rishiri-Rebun-Sarobetsu National Park.** Remote, unspoiled islands (p. 142).

I:NE5	\*\* **Daisetsuzan National Park.** Volcanoes, alpine flowers, and some of the finest hiking in Japan (p. 143).

I:NE9	\*# **Shiretoko National Park.** Sea cliffs and a spectacular hot-spring waterfall (p. 145).

II	\* **Hakodate.** Early treaty port; star-shaped fort (p. 149).

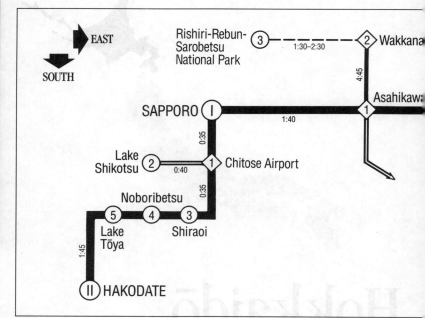

### Seasons

Hokkaidō's spring flowering is from May to June, summer is July and August, autumn foliage comes in September and October, and the long winter stretches from November to April. June is drier (no rainy season) and summer is cooler than in the rest of Japan. Midsummer is superb for colorful flowers, which bloom profusely on mountains and coasts. Hotel reservations must be made well in advance for the Sapporo Snow Festival, as well as for ski and summer resorts in season.

### Average Temperature °C (°F)/Days of Rain or Snow

|  | January | April | July | October |
|---|---|---|---|---|
| Sapporo | − 7.5 (18.5)/16 | 5.2 (41.4)/ 9 | 21.3 (70.3)/ 8 | 11.3 (52.3)/12 |
| Asahikawa | −12.2 (10.0)/18 | 3.2 (37.8)/10 | 21.8 (71.2)/10 | 8.7 (47.7)/13 |

### Traveling

Distances are long, so if time is short, consider flying to one end of the island and leaving by another (for example, travel overland from Sapporo to Kushiro and then fly out). Allow a week just to see a part of Hokkaidō; two to three weeks is adequate to make a circuit. For those who fly in, driving might be the best way to get around the island. Though there are few romanized signs, roads are wider, straighter, and simpler than in other parts of Japan. Train travelers in Hokkaidō should bear in mind that 20 percent of Hokkaidō's rail network is slated for liquidation over the next five years. Nevertheless, a Japan Rail Pass is a considerable cost-saver (see Practical Advice). Consult JNTO or a *Jikokuhyō* (rail schedule) for current schedules.

**By Train to Hokkaidō:** Hokkaidō is connected to Honshū by an undersea tunnel served by trains. The *Hokutōsei* limited express is a sleeper train that leaves Tokyo's Ueno station in the early evening and arrives in Sapporo in mid-morning; three departures a day.

**By Air to Hokkaidō: ANA:** to Sapporo from Tokyo, Sendai, Yamagata, Niigata, Komatsu (Kanazawa), and Hiroshima; to Hakodate from Tokyo and Nagoya; to Kushiro from Tokyo. **JAS:** to Sapporo from major cities, and from many Tōhoku and Kyūshū cities; from Tokyo to Asahikawa (Daisetsuzan), Kushiro and Obihiro (S. Daisetsuzan). **JAL:** to Sapporo from Tokyo, Narita, Ōsaka, Fukuoka, Okinawa.

**By Ferry to Hokkaidō: From Tōhoku:** Aomori-Muroran, Noheji-Hakodate, Ōma (tip of Shimokita Peninsula)-Hakodate, Hachinohe-Muroran, Hachinohe-Tomakomai, Sendai-Tomakomai, Tsuruga-Otaru. **From Tokyo:** Tokyo-Tomakomai, Tokyo-Kushiro.

**By Air within Hokkaidō:** There are *two* Sapporo airports, **Chitose** *(1:00h by express bus to Sapporo)*, and **Okadama** *(0:40h by bus to Sapporo)*. They are in opposite directions from the city; make sure connections are through the same airport. **ANK:** (reservations through ANA) from Sapporo to Nakashibetsu (Akan NP, Shiretoko NP), Wakkanai (Rishiri-Rebun NP), Monbetsu (Daisetsuzan, NE coast), and Kushiro (Akan NP, Shiretoko NP). **JAS:** from Sapporo to Memanbetsu, Kushiro, Obihiro, and Hakodate.

**Train Travel in Hokkaidō:** The *Hokkaidō Jikokuhyō*, a regional rail timetable, suitably lightweight for toting around, is sold at major bookstores.

**Car Rental:** 24-hour rates range from Y7000 to Y10,500 for a small car, Y14,000 to Y15,500 for a medium-size car. Nippon Rent-a-Car has offices in various cities in Hokkaidō, with drop-off options. Reservation, in Sapporo: 011-251-0909.

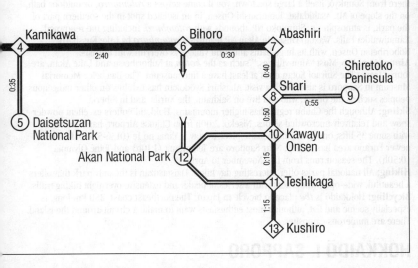

## HOKKAIDŌ TRANSIT DIAGRAM

Kamikawa — Bihoro — Abashiri

Shiretoko Peninsula

Shari

Daisetsuzan National Park

Kawayu Onsen

Akan National Park

Teshikaga

Kushiro

2:40  0:30  0:40  0:55  0:50  0:15  1:15  0:35

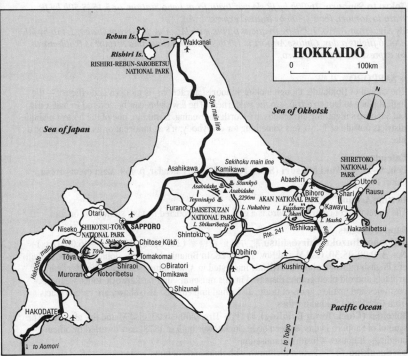

HOKKAIDŌ

0    100km

Rebun Is.
Rishiri Is.
RISHIRI-REBUN-SAROBETSU NATIONAL PARK
Wakkanai

Sea of Okhotsk
Sea of Japan

Sōya main line

SHIRETOKO NATIONAL PARK
Utoro
Rausu

Sekihoku main line

Asahikawa
Kamikawa
Sōunkyō
Asahidake
Asahidake 2290m
Tenninkyō
DAISETSUZAN NATIONAL PARK
L. Nukabira
Abashiri
Shari
AKAN NATIONAL PARK
L. Kussharo
L. Akan
Kawayu
Nakashibetsu
L. Mashū
Teshikaga

Furano

Otaru
SAPPORO
SHIKOTSU-TŌYA NATIONAL PARK
Niseko line
L. Shibetsu
Chitose Kūkō
Tōya
L. Tōya
Tomakomai
Shiraoi
Muroran
Noboribetsu
Shintoku
L. Shikaribetsu
Rte. 241
Obihiro
Sennmo line
Kushiro
Biratori
Tomikawa
Shizunai

Hakodate main line
HAKODATE
↓ to Aomori

to Tokyo

Pacific Ocean
N

# CALENDAR

**Feb. 5–11: ✳✳ Yuki Matsuri (Snow Festival).** Sapporo (I). Young and vigorous like the city, this festival arose spontaneously in 1950 after some high school students made six ice sculptures in Ōdori Park. Today, 200 elaborate edifices and figures of ice line the boulevard. Japanese pop stars are on hand to entertain the crowds. Smaller versions take place at around this time in Asahikawa, Shikotsu-ko, and Sōunkyō.

**July (4th Sa): ✳✳ Orochon no Himatsuri.** Abashiri (I:E7). Resurrected fire festival of the Gilyak people. Shamanistic rites, dances, and songs offered for good fishing and hunting.

**Aug. 20: ✳ Funamatsuri.** Biratori, Nibudani (I:S2). Ⓟ

**Sept. 23: ✳ Shakushain Matsuri.** Shizunai-chō (I:S2). Ⓟ

**Oct. 10: ✳✳ Ainu Kotan Matsuri.** Asahikawa (I:E1). One of the best Ainu festivals, offered as a prayer for safety when crossing the dangerous rapids on the Ishikari River. Followed by Ainu dances.

# SPECIAL INTERESTS

**Onsen:** Hokkaidō abounds with volcanoes; there are onsen virtually everywhere you might go. Asahidake Onsen, on the west side of Daisetsuzan NP, is very pleasant, and if you hike there from Sōunkyō, itself a large spa town, you'll come across a *rotemburo*, or outdoor bath, on the slope of Mt. Asahidake. Tomuraushi Onsen, in an isolated spot in the southern part of the park, is atmospheric. Shiretoko NP abounds with *rotemburo*, including the renowned Kamuiwakka Falls. Wakoto Onsen in Akan NP features a *rotemburo* by Lake Kussharo. Noboribetsu Onsen, with its huge baths and Ainu village, is overrun with tourists.
**Ainu:** See p. 146. Most "Ainu villages," such as the *kotan* at Noboribetsu and Lake Akan, are tourist traps. The Shiraoi Kotan does at least have a fine museum. The Batchelor Memorial Museum in Sapporo is also worth a visit. Abashiri Kyōdokan has exhibits on other indigenous peoples such as the Gilyak, who still live on Sakhalin, the Kurils, and in Siberia.
**Skiing:** Although the Chūbu region has higher mountains, Hokkaidō offers excellent powder snow and relatively uncrowded slopes. Niseko, 2:00h from Chitose Airport, has 5 ski areas with some 35 lifts; one good, inexpensive place to stay is Yama no Ie (0136-58-2611). The newer Furano area has 13 lifts. Near Sapporo are Teineyama (1:10h) and Teine Olympia (0:50h). The season runs from late November to April.
**Hiking:** All national parks offer interesting day hikes. Daisetsuzan is the only park that offers a beautiful, wide-open wilderness with a series of peaks and extensive overnight hiking trails.
**Bicycling:** Hokkaidō is *the* place to bicycle in Japan. The northeast coast, 250 km long, is especially scenic and flat, although most enthusiasts want to make a circuit around the island. There are numerous campsites.

# HOKKAIDŌ I. SAPPORO

140

**Tokyo to Sapporo:** *16:00h by JR sleeper train from Ueno Station, or 5:15–5:50h by JR train to Aomori, then 3:30h by limited express train.*
**By Air:** *From Tokyo, 1:25h by frequent flights with JAL, ANA, JAS. From Osaka, 1:45h by JAL, ANA, 6 flights a day. Chitose Airport is 1:00h south and Okadama Airport is 0:40h north by express bus from Sapporo.*

## ✳ SAPPORO　札幌
The capital of Hokkaidō, though lacking in tourist attractions, is modern and efficient—the logical place to launch a trip into the wilderness. The few sights can be covered in half a day, but Sapporo's nighttime attractions are worth an evening. Susukino, one of the hottest nightlife districts outside of Tokyo, has something for everybody; it's as innocent or as tawdry as you'd like.

### Calendar
**Feb. 5–11:** ✳✳ **Yuki Matsuri (Snow Festival).** See Calendar, p. 139. Main events are in Ōdōri Park.

### Getting Around
The street plan of central Sapporo is a grid, easily negotiated by taxi, subway, or on foot.

### Sapporo Sights
✳ **Hoppō Minzoku Shiryōshitsu** 北方民俗資料室 (221-0066). Hrs: 9:00–16:00; Oct. 1–Nov. 3, 9:00–15:30. Clsd M and Nov. 4–Apr. 28. In Botanical Gardens. John Batchelor, a Meiji-era English minister who was ardently interested in Ainu culture, collected the excellent artifacts and old photographs displayed in this museum: Ainu basketwork, tools, weapons, costumes and textiles, items of trade, and ritual implements. Also shown are rare artifacts from Gilyak and Sakhalin tribes.

**Tokeidai (Clock Tower Building)** 時計台　Hrs: 9:00–16:00; clsd M and day after NH. The symbol of Sapporo is this Western-style clock tower built in 1878, now dwarfed by office buildings. It houses a historical museum.

✳✳ **Susukino** 薄野　Famed nighttown with thousands of pubs, restaurants, coffee shops, massage parlors, and porn shows. Carnival atmosphere; patronized by throngs of business-men, students, middle-aged matrons, young couples, schoolgirls, and tourists. Theme "Soaplands" (schoolgirl, hospital, Hawaii, China) abound. One of the friendlier places to sample the seamier side of Japan.

✳ **Hokkaidō Kaitaku Kinenkan (Hokkaidō Development History Museum)** 北海道開拓記念館　Hrs: 9:30–16:30 (enter by 16:00); clsd M, NH, NY. *0:50h by bus east from Sapporo station.* A series of elaborately wrought displays on Hokkaidō history. Nearby is Hokkaidō Historical Village.

### Sapporo Dining
Hokkaidō specialties include fresh salmon, crab, corn, potatoes, and Sapporo *ramen* (noodles). Salmon dishes: *Ishikari-nabe* (a salmon stew), *ruibe* (sliced frozen salmon), *hizunamasu* (salmon head seasoned with daikon radish and vinegar). *Jingiskan* (Genghis Khan) is Mongolian lamb barbecue.

① **Sapporo Bīru-en (Bier Garten)** サッポロビール園　北 6 東 9 (742-1531). Hrs: 11:30–21:00, daily; clsd NY. Sapporo's first brewery, now done up like a German beer hall. Roaring fire in winter, outdoor garden in summer. *Jingiskan* (Y2800) and *Dosanko nabe*, a seafood stew, are served here with copious amounts of draft beer.

⑥ **Yakumo Soba** 八雲そば　北 4 西 4 (221-3640). Hrs: 11:00–20:20. In underground station arcade. Try the *goma* (sesame) *soba*, from Y360 per person.

⑦ **Ryūhō** 龍鳳　北 1 西 3 (222-3486). Tokyo Kaijō Bldg. Hrs: 11:00–21:00; NH 11:00–18:00; clsd Su, NY. Famous *ramen* shop. Varieties include stocks made of butter, cheese, milk, and toppings of roast pork, corn, asparagus, etc. From Y600.

⑨ **Matsuo Jingiskan** 松尾ジンギスカン　南 4 西 5 (511-0043). Hrs: 17:00–1:00; clsd Tu. Popular *jingiskan* shop. Try the tender lamb sashimi. About Y3000 per person.

⑩ **Matsukura** 松倉　南 4 西 3 (518-2103). Daiyan Green Bldg., 1F. Hrs: 17:00–23:30. Regional cuisine. Moderate to expensive.

Ramen Yokochō ラーメン横丁 This alley in Susukino is packed with cheap, popular *ramen* shops. Famous ones include Higuma and Karyu.

⑪ Hyōsetsu no Mon 氷雪の門 南5西2 (521-3046). Hrs: 11:00–23:00. The place for king crab. Course from Y5000.

⑫ Silo サイロ 南5西3 (531-5857). NC Hokusen Plaza Bldg., B1. Hrs: 17:00–23:00; clsd Su, NY. An old shop serving up Hokkaidō specialties such as *ruibe* and smoked Ezo deer. Y4000 per person.

## Sapporo Lodgings (TEL 011)

② ✳ Sapporo Washington Hotel II 第二札幌ワシントンホテル (222-3311). Kita 5-jō Nishi 6-chōme, Chūō-ku, Sapporo-shi, Hokkaidō. Newer hotel of this reliable chain. S Y9200+, Tw Y16,700+.

③ ✳ Sapporo Washington Hotel I 第一札幌ワシントンホテル (251-3211). Kita 4-jō Nishi 4-chōme, Chūō-ku, Sapporo-shi, Hokkaidō. S Y5900+, Tw Y15,600+.

④ Nakamuraya Ryokan 中村屋旅館 北3西7 (241-2111). Fax 241-2118. Kita 3-jō Nishi 7-chōme, Chūō-ku. 0:10h walk from station. S Y5500–8000, Tw Y10–16,000.

⑤ KKR Sapporo KKR札幌 (231-6711). Kita 4-jō Nishi 5-chōme, Chūō-ku. *0:04h walk from station.* Western and Japanese rooms. S from Y7,000 w/breakfast.

⑧ ✳✳ Hotel Alpha Sapporo ホテルアルファ札幌 (221-2333). Fax 221-0819. Minami 1-jō Nishi 5-chōme, Chūō-ku. Near Ōdori Kōen subway stop, not far from Susukino. Excellent city hotel. S Y17,000, Tw Y27,000.

# HOKKAIDŌ I:E. EAST HOKKAIDŌ

**Main Attraction:** Daisetsusan National Park (E5)

## E1 ASAHIKAWA 旭川

*1:40h by JR limited express from Sapporo. An important junction: express trains continue north to Wakkanai, and east to Kamikawa and Abashiri. Buses to Tennin-kyō and Asahidake Onsen, gateways to Daisetsuzan.* Asahikawa's **Kawamura Ainu Hakubutsukan** 川村アイヌ博物館 is a museum of Ainu culture; it is 0:15h by bus from Ichijō-hachi, a bus depot 0:03h on foot from Asahikawa station.

### Calendar

**Early Feb.: Winter Festival.** A smaller version of Sapporo's.
**Oct. 10: ✳✳ Ainu Kotan Matsuri.** See Calendar, p. 139. At Kamui Kotan, on the banks of the Ishikarigawa, 0:30h by bus from Ichijō-hachi bus depot.

### Asahikawa Lodgings (TEL 0166)

Asahikawa Tōkyū Inn 東急イン (26-0109). Hachijō-dōri 6-chōme, Asahikawa-shi, Hokkaidō. S Y7200, Tw Y12,300.

## E2 # WAKKANAI 稚内

*5:40h by JR Sōya main line express (Y8000) from Sapporo, or 1:00h by a morning NKK Airlines flight (Y14,400) from Sapporo Okadama Airport.* Ferry port to Rebun and Rishiri; travelers arriving by train from Sapporo should expect to spend one night here.

### Wakkanai Lodgings (TEL 0162)

Wakkanai Moshiripa YH 稚内モシリパYH (0162-24-0180). 2-9-5, Chūō, Wakkanai, Hokkaidō. 0:05h on foot from the station, has rent-a-cycles.

## E3 ✳ # RISHIRI-REBUN-SAROBETSU NATIONAL PARK 利尻礼文サロベツ国立公園

*Ferry service from Wakkanai at least once daily, most frequently July 20–Aug. 31. Flights daily except on the 14th of each month.* Rishiri and Rebun, two windswept islands off the northernmost tip of Hokkaidō, offer good hikes and dramatic, northern seacoast scenery. The entire park (including the Sarobetsu Coast on the Hokkaidō mainland) is a preserve for alpine wildflowers, which bloom profusely in July.

### Getting Around

Interisland ferries from Oshidomari to Kabuka and to Funadomari, and from Kutsugata to Kabuka. Check schedules in advance, as buses and ferries are slow, infrequent, and stop at sundown. Two days are required to see one island, three days for both. **Rent-a-cycle:** on Rishiri, at Higashi Rishiri-chō; on Rebun, at Kabuka.

### Park Sights

✳✳ **Rishiri** 利尻 *1:40h (Y1850) by ferry, or 0:20h (Y5880, one-way) by Air Nippon (ANK) flight from Wakkanai (connects with flight from Sapporo).* A graceful volcanic cone rising out of the sea. Main ports are Oshidomari and Kutsugata. The 6:00h round trip (18 km) ascent of **Rishiri-zan** (1781 m) is what people come for. Three trailheads, none more advantageous than the others, are located at the 2 ports and at Oniwaki. There's also a 40-km cycling circuit of the island that takes about 5:00h to complete.

** **Rebun** 礼文 *2:10h (Y2060) by ferry or 0:20h (Y6710) by ANK flight from Wakkanai.*
A long, low ridge of an island. Ferry terminals at **Kabuka** and **Funadomari**, near the S and N tips, respectively. The most famous activity is the 8:00h hike from **Sukoton Misaki** to **Momoiwa**. Go with one of the youth hostels, or come prepared to get lost a few times. Momoiwa, 0:15h by bus or 0:45h on foot from Kabuka, is near rocky beaches with cliffs, waterfalls, and **Jizō Iwa**, a tower of rock which split off from a cliff and now stands upright on the beach, like Jizō on the riverbank of hell. On the east coast, a scenic road (suitable for cycling) winds from Kabuka to Funadomari, passing weatherbeaten fishing shacks and tiny coves. Funadomari, the pleasanter port, has a small lake and campground. Sukoton Misaki (cape), the northern tip of Rebun, is 0:15h by bus or car or 2:00h on foot from Funadomari.

### Rishiri and Rebun Lodgings (TEL 01638)
Many minshuku are run by fishing families who can arrange to take you fishing. The three YHs on Rebun offer arrangements for the 8:00h hike. Hostelers get a lift to the trailhead at Sukoton Misaki and are guided safely to the beach near Jizō Iwa.
**Kitaguni Grand Hotel** 北国グランドホテル (2-1362). Oshidomari, Higashi Rishiri-chō, Rishiri-gun, Hokkaidō. *0:05h walk from Oshidomari.*
**YH Momoiwa-sō** YH桃岩荘 (6-1390). Motochi, Kabuka, Rebun-chō, Rebun-gun. Clsd Oct.-May.

## E4 KAMIKAWA 上川
*About 0:40h by JR Sekihoku Line from Asahikawa (E1).* Junction for buses to Sōunkyō Onsen, in Daisetsuzan National Park.

## E5 ** DAISETSUZAN NATIONAL PARK 大雪山国立公園
*Main gateways are as follows: (1) Sōunkyō: 16 km from Kamikawa station, 0:35h by bus. Last bus, 19:15. Or 1:55h by direct bus from Asahikawa (E1). (2) Tenninkyō: 1:20h by bus from Asahikawa; nice ride through farm country. Or 0:30h by bus or 2:00h hike from Asahidake Onsen. (3) Asahidake Onsen: 1:40h by bus from Asahikawa.* This beautiful national park, the largest in Japan, encompasses a massive cluster of volcanic peaks, rolling highlands, and scenic gorges. Unlike most Japanese national parks, Daisetsuzan is one unbroken mass, most of which is unspoiled. The park's outstanding feature is its network of hiking trails into the interior, where one can enjoy some of the loveliest natural scenery in Japan. Though the peaks that make up Daisetsuzan are not very high—Asahidake, the highest, is 2290 m—cold winds blowing down from Siberia create an alpine environment normally seen in Europe and America only at much higher elevations or more northern latitudes. In summer, alpine plants bloom spectacularly against a backdrop of dark, cinder-sloped volcanic cones and craters. For bath lovers, there are hot springs in abundance, including a *rotemburo* on the summit of Asahidake.

143

* **Sōunkyō Onsen** 層雲峡温泉 This busy hot-spring resort is situated in the middle of 20-km-long Sōunkyō Gorge. Recommended base for the spectacular, 5:30h hike across Mt. Asahidake to Asahidake Onsen; a ski lift takes you partway up the very steep beginning of the hike. Skiing in winter. East of the town on the main highway are two picturesque waterfalls, **Ryūsei no taki** and **Ginga no taki**, and near the end of the gorge are **Kobako** and **Ōbako**, ("small box" and "great box"), where the gorge narrows and the cliffs become quite perpendicular. The road winds in and out of tunnels, making it difficult to see the scenery from a car. Bicycles can be rented at the gorges for an exorbitant Y1000; they can be dropped off (downhill) in town at no extra charge.

*** **Asahidake Onsen** 旭岳温泉 Quiet and barely developed, with only a few lodge-style hotels and an outstanding youth hostel. This is the best base from which to enjoy the beauty of Daisetsuzan. There is a tramway to the foot of **Mt. Asahidake**, providing access to alpine fields dotted with small lakes and sulfur vents, all excellent for hiking. The ascent of Asahidake from this side takes 2:00h. There's a *rotemburo* near the summit.

* **Tenninkyō** 天人峡温泉 Modest development, with some half-dozen onsen hotels. Tenninkyō Gorge is smaller and less impressive than Sōunkyō, but has **Hagoromo no taki**, a diaphanous, seven-tiered waterfall named for its resemblance to a legendary robe of feathers belonging to a *tennin*, or angel. Trails lead to the interior of Daisetsuzan National Park.

### Hiking
From June to early September. The terrain is rocky, steep, and icy at higher elevations, so bring a good pair of hiking shoes and warm clothes. Carry food and water. Pick up a trail map at the mountaineering station near the top of the Sōunkyō tramway. Potable water at designated spots on trail. There are two cabins, one at Kurodake and the other near the top of the Asahidake Onsen tramway. To reserve the Kurodake cabin, call minshuku Yamagoya (01658-5-3325). **Sōunkyō to Kurodake:** About 3:00h, round trip. Take the two-stage lift from Sōunkyō up to the base of Kurodake (0:22h, Y860 one way, 15 percent discount to YH members). From there, it's a steep, 1:00h climb to the summit of Kurodake. Good alpine flora, views. **Sōunkyō to Asahidake Onsen:** About 7:00h total. From Kurodake, it is 3:00h to Asahidake. The terrain is rolling and skirts a series of craters. The ascent of Asahidake is very steep, and often covered with ice. Steep descent on the other side. Hike or take the tramway down to Asahidake Onsen (0:20h, Y1300 one way). It will take half a day to bus back to

Sōunkyō, so you may want to forward luggage to your next night's lodgings. **Asahidake Onsen to Asahidake:** 4:00h round trip. See above. **Asahidake Onsen to Tenninkyō:** 2:00h. A pretty hiking trail through lush, mosquito-infested forest.

## Daisetsuzan Lodgings (TEL 01658)

Sōunkyō has numerous hotels, plus two YHs (poor reports). For minshuku (summer only), call Sōunkyō Kankō Annaijo (5-3350).

**Sōunkyō Kan'i Hoken-hoyō Sentā** 層雲峡簡易保険保養センター （5-3331). Sōunkyō, Kamikawa-chō, Kamikawa-gun, Hokkaidō. In nice surroundings, 1.5 km from Sōunkyō Onsen (on the route from Kamikawa). Subsidized lodge and spa. Plain but economical. From Y5000 w/2 meals.

**Hotel Daisetsu** ホテル大雪 （5-3211). Address as above. Resort ryokan. From Y15,600–20,800 w/meals.

**Sōunkaku Grand Hotel** 層雲閣グランドホテル （5-3111). Address as above. Resort ryokan. From Y8200 w/meals.

**Mount View Hotel** マウントビューホテル （5-3011). Address as above. Seven-story A-frame in gleaming white, aimed at trendy skiers. From Y8000 w/meals.

**∗ Daisetsuzan Shirakaba-sō** 大雪山白樺荘 （0166-97-2246). 1418 Higashikawa-machi, Kamikawa-gun. Nice youth hostel at Asahidake Onsen. Lovely setting by onsen-fed brook. Good meals, onsen bath, including an open air bath.

**Hotel Shikishima-sō** ホテル敷島荘 （0166-97-2141). Tenninkyō, Biei-chō, Kamikawa-gun. Y5–12,000 w/meals.

## Exploring Daisetsuzan Interior

# The southern part of Daisetsuzan National Park is beautiful and unfrequented; some places cannot be reached by public transportation. From Sapporo, take the train or Rte. 38 junction at Takikawa toward Shintoku and Obihiro. On the way is **Furano**, a ski resort with the best powder snow in Japan. From **Shintoku**, in an area with many ski resorts, one can drive or hitchhike to **Tomuraushi Onsen**, a really rustic spa deep inside the national park. From here, with adequate backpacking preparations and food (available in Shintoku), it is a two-day hike to Tenninkyō, or three days to Sōunkyō, via Kurodake. Ask the Hokkaidō Tourism Office for details. From Shintoku, one can also drive to **Lake Shikaribetsu**, a pleasant wooded lake, and **Lake Nukabira**. From Lake Nukabira, Rte. 273 becomes a gravel road, running through a near-deserted valley and eventually joining Rte. 39, which heads back to Sōunkyō Onsen. **Lodgings:** At Furano: **Furano Prince Hotel** (0167-23-4111), Tw Y12–16,000. At Shintoku: **Lodge Sahoro** (01566-4-5353), Y12–28,000. 0:15h by bus from Shintoku station. At Tomuraushi: **Tomuraushi Higashi Daisetsusō Kokuminshukusha** (01566-5-3021), about Y5000.

## E6 BIHORO 美幌

*5:00h from Sapporo or 3:20h from Asahikawa* (E1) *by JR Sekihoku line limited express.* Buses to Akan National Park (E12) depart from this dingy little town.

### Bihoro Lodgings (TEL 01527)

**Bihoro YH** 美幌YH 字元町31 （3-2560). Motomachi, Bihoro-chō, Abashiri-gun, Hokkaidō. Clsd Nov. 1–4. In summer, there is a bus to the hostel. Good reputation.

## E7 ABASHIRI 網走

*Terminus of the JR Sekihoku line, 5:40h by limited express from Sapporo. Junction for the JR Senmō main line to Shari* (E8), *gateway to Shiretoko Peninsula* (E9). *From Sapporo Chitose Airport, 0:55h by JAS flight to Memambetsu, which is not far from Abashiri.* The sights of Abashiri, such as they are, center around **Tento-zan** 天都山, a hill about 3 km southwest on Rte. 39, and include an **∗∗ observation tower** with views of nearby peaks—O-Akan, Me-Akan, Rausudake—the Sea of Okhotsk; the **Ryuhyō-kan** 流氷館, a museum on the icebergs that drift past Abashiri in mid-Feb.; **Hakubutsukan Abashiri Kangoku** 博物館網走監獄, a museum on Abashiri's notorious penitentiary; and **Jakka Dofuni** ジャッカドフニ a museum on various peoples who lived in Hokkaidō before the Ainu (Hrs: 9:00–17:00. In winter 9:00–16:00; clsd Su). About 1 km east of the station is **Abashiri Kyōdo Hakubutsukan** 網走郷土博物館, with exhibits on local culture, archeology, and the Gilyak people (Hrs: 9:00–17:00. In winter 9:00–16:00; clsd M, NH, NY).

### Calendar

**Early Feb.: Iceberg Festival.** Ice sculpture, festivities.
**July (4th Sa): ∗∗ Orochon no Himatsuri.** See Calendar, p. 139. At Katsuragaoka Park.

### Abashiri Lodgings (TEL 0152)

**Minshuku Sakura-sō** 民宿さくら荘 大曲27-41 （44-2337). 27-41 Ōmagari, Abashiri-shi, Hokkaidō. Friendly. Near Tento-zan. Y5200 w/meals.

## E8 SHARI 斜里

*On the JR Senmō line between Abashiri and Kushiro* (E13). *0:40–0:50h by infrequent train from Abashiri. Buses to Shiretoko Peninsula* (E9) *depart about once in 2 hours.*

## E9 ✳ # SHIRETOKO NATIONAL PARK    知床国立公園

*Utoro and Rausu are the two main access towns; Utoro, 0:55h by bus from Shari, makes a better base.* Shiretoko, a wild peninsula jutting into the Sea of Okhotsk, is among the most dramatically beautiful areas in Hokkaidō, but you really need a car or a bicycle to get around. There's a nice hike up **Rausudake**, and excursion boats take tourists to see the sea cliffs. The peninsula is volcanic, so there are a few onsen to round out a visit. Kamuiwakka Falls has a truly memorable *rotemburo*, fed by a hot-spring waterfall.

### Getting Around

Buses are infrequent. A car is suggested for those who'd like to see the sights, take the boat excursion, and hike without spending more than a night in the park. Vehicles that can negotiate the gravel roads would be best. In Abashiri: Nissan Rent-a-Car 日産レンタカー 新町1-11-3 (0152-43-6191), Nippon Rent-a-Car ニッポンレンタカー 新町1-3-3 (45-0765). Dropoff option, Visa card accepted.

### Park Sights

**Utoro** ウトロ An eyesore of a spa town. Mildly interesting tourist boat rides along the north coast of Shiretoko depart from here. To get to the ticket office, go down the small incline from the main intersection (traffic signal), and turn left. Boat docks are through the tunnel. There are two trips, one to Kamuiwakka Falls, and one that continues out to the cape, Shiretoko Misaki. The latter offers similar scenery but is perhaps less crowded.

✳ **Shiretoko Go-ko (Five Lakes)** 知床五湖 *0:30h by bus east of Utoro*. A series of scenic ponds with boardwalks, views of the central mountains. Pretty at sundown or sunrise.

**Iwaobetsu Onsen** 岩尾別温泉 *0:45h by bus from Utoro*. The most pleasant spa on the peninsula, and a base for the popular ascent of Shiretoko's highest mountain, Rausudake.

✳✳ **Kamuiwakka no Taki (Falls)** カムイワッカの滝 *1:00h by bus from Utoro to Shiretoko Ōhashi, then 0:15h to this spectacular hot-spring falls.* A 0:30h climb up a wet, sulfurous stream bed leads to the ◆ **Kamuiwakka Rotemburo**, one of the most memorable open-air baths in Japan. At the uppermost *rotemburo*, fed by a hot cascade, bathers will be rewarded with a wonderful view—a wedge of ocean between the mountains. From here, one can hike up **Iōzan**, with its steaming fumeroles.

**Rausu** 羅臼 From Utoro, one can drive or bus across **Shiretoko Tōge** (pass) for a view of Rausudake, and continue down into Rausu, a dingy fishing village. **Takasuna** is a local restaurant that serves sea lion cuisine ("tough but tasty"); *teppanyaki* (grilled) from Y1000. The Rausu coast is less touristed and might appeal to explorers. Toward Aidomari are several *rotemburo*.

### Hiking

**Iwaobetsu Onsen to Rausudake:** 8–9:00h round trip. A favorite hike. You'll probably find someone to do it with at the YH. **Kamuiwakka Falls to Iōzan:** 7:00h round trip. This may be the more interesting hike. Iozan has steaming sulfur vents. On the way back down, you can take a dip in Kamuiwakka *rotemburo*.

### Shiretoko Lodgings (TEL 01522)

⬜1⬜ **Hotel Chinohate** ホテル地の涯 (4-2331). Iwaobetsu, Tō'onbetsu, Shari-chō, Shari-gun, Hokkaidō. Very friendly if slightly run down hotel at the end of a beautiful, tree-lined gravel road. Convenient to Rausudake hike. The inn's *rotemburo* is hidden among trees below the parking lot. Japanese rooms are much better maintained than Western-style rooms. Y8300–16,500 w/meals. Clsd in winter.

⬜2⬜ **Iwaobetsu YH** 岩尾別YH (4-2311). Address as above. Friendly and very knowledgeable about hiking. Clsd Nov.-May.

145

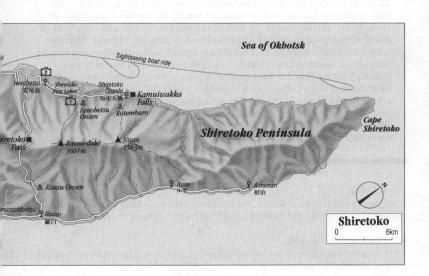

# The Ainu

The Ainu are thought to be descendants of a people who once occupied large parts of the Japanese islands and were pushed north by invaders from the south. Compared to the average Japanese, the Ainu have lighter skin, more body hair, a heavier brow-ridge, and deep-set eyes, which are occasionally gray or blue. Some anthropologists have called them proto-Caucasian because of their superficial resemblance to Caucasian people, but it is now believed that their unusual characteristics, such as "hairiness," are the result of long genetic isolation, and that they are related to Siberian groups such as the Gilyak. Until recently, there were Ainu in Sakhalin, the Kurils, and the lower Amur River, where the Gilyak also live.

In the Nara and Heian periods, the central Yamato government met with fierce resistance north of present-day Sendai from a people it called Emishi, Ezo, or "the hairy people," who were probably Ainu. Archeological remains suggest that the culture of these people was related to Jōmon culture, which in prehistoric times extended from Okinawa to Hokkaidō. Whether this similarity was a product of kinship, trade, or conquest is unknown. Place names throughout Japan—such as Mt. Fuji—are said to be originally Ainu words. Until the Edo period, the Ainu also lived in parts of Tōhoku, where they traded with the Japanese, exchanging salmon and bear skins for iron, swords, cotton, lacquerware, and saké, items important in Ainu ceremonies and daily life.

There are many intriguing resemblances between Ainu and Japanese religious customs. For example, the word kami (deity) in Japanese, is pronounced *kamui* among the Hokkaidō Ainu. Sticks adorned with long, curling ribbons of shaved wood, not unlike the *gohei* wands of Shinto ritual, are employed in Ainu rites. The spirit of the hearth is an important deity for both the Japanese and the Ainu, and like Japanese matsuri, Ainu ceremonies include much saké-drinking.

The most important Ainu *kamui* are spirits of animals, such as the bear, the owl, and the sea turtle. Among the most colorful of their festivals is **Iyomante**, dedicated to the bear spirit. In the original festival, a bear cub was breast-fed and raised by an Ainu woman. Today the bear is still ritually killed and its meat eaten. The head is then cleaned, adorned, and worshipped in a rite intended to return its spirit to the world of the *kamui*, with prayers of gratitude for the flesh and fur of the bear, and to ensure the continued bounty of nature.

Ainu ceremonial costumes are made of tan elm-fiber cloth or cotton, boldly decorated with appliquéd and embroidered whorls and bars. Similar patterns were tattooed on women's wrists and hands, along with a distinctive large tattoo around the lips, to signify a young woman's readiness for marriage. One can occasionally see tattoos on an older woman, although the Japanese government outlawed the practice in the Meiji period. Both the roofs and walls of Ainu dwellings were thatched. The hearth occupied the center, and there were several windows, including a "god window" on the east by which the deities entered the home.

The Ainu had no writing system, but instead recorded their histories and epics as *yukar*, oral recitations with prescribed flourishes to aid memory. These now remain only in transcriptions and wax-cylinder recordings made by ethnologists half a century ago. A recent television program showed some aged Ainu listening to one of these recordings; they are probably the last people who can still understand them. Thanks to past government policy to "assimilate" the Ainu by encouraging marriage with Japanese, forbidding many customs, and barring the language from schools or public media, virtually none of the 24,000 Hokkaidō Ainu descendants—nearly all of mixed parentage—can speak or understand the Ainu language. Although laws now grant special rights to the Ainu, discrimination keeps them among the poorest minorities in Japan, and most Ainu descendants see full assimilation as their only hope. Recently, however, there has been a revival of interest among younger Ainu in studying their ancestral tongue. About half of Hokkaidō's present-day Ainu live in the south-central Hidaka district. In daily life they are indistinguishable from the ethnic Japanese, but they have kept up or revived their traditional festivals, such as Iyomante. Few tourists venture to Hidaka, but one can get a superficial glimpse of vanished Ainu culture at a handful of exhibit villages and museums.

---

**E10 KAWAYU** 川湯
*0:50h from Shari* (E8) *by JR Senmō line express. A gateway to Akan National Park; convenient to Kussharo-ko and Mashū-ko; 0:10h bus ride to Kawayu Onsen.*

**E11 TESHIKAGA** 弟子屈
*0:15h south of Kawayu on JR Senmō line express. A gateway to Akan National Park. Convenient to Mashū-ko and Akan-ko.*

## E12 AKAN NATIONAL PARK 阿寒国立公園

*The main gateways are Bihoro (E6), Kawayu (E10), and Teshikaga (E11). From Bihoro, there is direct bus service via Bihoro Tōge (pass), which offers a fine panorama of the park. Kawayu is closest to Kussharo-ko and Mashū-ko (but depending on bus schedules, it might be faster to change at Teshikaga), while Akan-ko is most easily reached from Teshikaga.* This park is set up for tourists in tour buses, not for active outdoorsmen. There are few hiking trails. The park features crater lakes, volcanoes, steaming sulfur vents, and Akan Kotan, a depressing "Ainu village." Akan-ko (lake) is noted for the *marimo* weed, an odd little spherical algae.

### Getting Around

No regular public buses; only big, expensive, and infrequent tour buses with guides who chatter nonstop and sing "Ainu" songs. The buses circle the park, stopping for a few minutes at designated sights. You are not required to remain with one bus. Fares are by distance. Bihoro-Akan-ko circuit, 5:20h, Y5780. Alternatively, you can hitchhike, bicycle, or rent a car.

### Park Sights

**\*\* Kussharo-ko** 屈斜路湖 The less spoiled part of Akan National Park. 7 km from Kawayu is **Sunayu**, with geothermally heated sand along the beach, a crowded campsite, and fleets of swan-shaped pedal boats. It takes an hour of pedaling to reach the wooded islet in the middle (go at own risk). **Wakoto Onsen** has open-air hot-spring baths by the lakeshore. One km from Kawayu Onsen is **Iōzan**, Mt. Sulfur, which one can climb to inspect the steaming sulfur vents encrusted with canary-yellow crystals. Fumerole-steamed eggs are sold at exorbitant prices (but after all, they add years to your life).

**Mashū-ko** 摩周湖 A clear lake at the bottom of a steep-rimmed crater, beautiful on a sunny day, but usually fogged over. The vista point, Dai-ichi Tembōdai, is considered to have the better view.

**Akan-ko** 阿寒湖 Akan Kohan Onsen, the main town on the shores of this lake, is depressingly touristy and has no proper lakefront. There's no reason to visit it except to climb O-Akandake or Me-Akandake, two volcanoes overlooking the lake. On Oct. 8–10, the villagers hold the Marimo Matsuri, rowing out to collect *marimo*, feting it with Ainu song and dance, and ceremonially returning it to the lake.

### Hiking

**O-Akandake:** 10.7–km hike to summit from O-Akan Onsen, 4 km east of Akan Kohan.
**Me-Akandake:** 10.7 km from Akan Kohan, or 2.2 km from Me-Akan Onsen. No public buses. Me-Akandake has the more impressive view, with volcanic cones and fumeroles at the summit.

### Akan Lodgings

**\* Nibushi no Sato** にぶしの里 (01548-3-2294). Kussharo-kohan, Teshikaga-machi, Kawakami-gun, Hokkaidō. A charming hot-spring minshuku. Y5-7000 w/meals.
**Mashū-ko YH** 摩周湖YH (01548-2-3098). 883 Genya, Teshikaga-machi.
**Akan Engel YH** 阿寒エンジェルYH (0154-67-2309) 5-1 Shurikomanbetsu, Akan-kohan, Akan-machi, Akan-gun, Hokkaidō. Reputed to be good.

## E13 KUSHIRO 釧路

*1:15–1:25h by JR express from Teshikaga. Flights from Tokyo and Sapporo Chitose Airport. Direct buses to and from Akan NP and Rausu (Shiretoko NP).*

# HOKKAIDŌ I:S. SOUTH HOKKAIDŌ

## S1 CHITOSE KŪKŌ (AIRPORT) STATION 千歳空港

*0:35h by JR express from Sapporo, or 0:07h by bus from Chitose Airport, the main airport on Hokkaidō, served by JAL, ANA and JAS (see p. 138). Transport to nearby destinations: 0:50h by bus to Shikotsu-ko (S2); 1:15h by bus or 0:35h by express train to Shiraoi (S3); 1:50h by bus or 0:50h by limited express train to Noboribetsu (S4).*

## S2 SHIKOTSU-KO (LAKE) 支笏湖

*0:50h by bus from Sapporo. 0:40h by bus from Chitose. 0:45h by bus from Tomakomai. Buses run only 3–4 times a day.* This pretty caldera lake, the deepest in Hokkaidō, is the unspoiled part of **Shikotsu-Tōya National Park**. Facilities are at Shikotsu Kohan, a small village on the east shore. Sightseeing boats are launched from here. The lake is rimmed by several interesting and climbable volcanoes. Near the south shore is Koke no Dōmon, a volcanically formed canyon with steep rock walls, lushly carpeted with moss. The lake is popular for fishing, but the stony bottom, hazardous drops, and cold water make it unsuitable for swimming.

### Getting Around

There are no public buses circling the lake. The Shikotsu-ko YH rents bicycles and runs a van in the morning that shuttles hostelers to the Eniwadake trailhead or Koke no Dōmon, depending on the weather.

147

## Hiking

The flan-shaped cone of **Tarumaedake** is a popular climb. From May to October, a bus runs from Morrapu to the 7th station, 0:40h from the summit. The precipitous **Eniwadake** is more of a challenge, taking 4:30h round trip, but the view is spectacular. The trailhead is near Poropinai camp, reached from Shikotsu Kohan by ferry or car. A good rainy-day hike is **Koke no Dōmon**; the entrance is 10 km west of Morappu, along the road circling the lake. Hike in 1 km from the entrance sign.

### Shikotsu-ko Lodgings (TEL 0123)

There are 3 lakeside campgrounds at Morappu, Poropinai, and Bifue.

**Shikotsu-ko YH** 支笏湖 YH (25-2311/2312). Shikotsu Kohan, Chitose-shi, Hokkaidō. Members only. Pleasant A-frame lodge. *Jingiskan* dinner and folk dancing. Onsen. Bike rental. Organized hikes.

**Shikotsu Kohan Kokuminkyūkamura** 支笏湖畔国民休暇村 (25-2201). Bangai-ichi, Shikotsu-ko Onsen, Chitose-shi. Y6–10,000 w/meals. Open all year.

## TOMAKOMAI 苫小牧

*0:55h by JR express from Sapporo. Ferries from Hachinohe, Sendai, Tokyo, Nagoya. 3 buses a day to Shikotsu-ko. Junction to the Hidaka line, which heads SE along the coast.*

### Calendar

**Aug. 20:** \* # **Funamatsuri.** Biratori, Nibudani *(from Tomakomai, 1:35h by bus to Biratori, change buses and ride 0:10h to Nibudani, then walk 0:15h)*. Begun around 1970 to preserve Ainu boat culture. Prayers are offered to the gods of fire and rivers, and Ainu songs and dances are performed.

**Sept. 23:** \* **Shakushain Matsuri.** Shizunai-chō *(1:20h by local train from Tomakomai)*. Ainu dances and songs commemorate Shakushain, an Ainu hero who fought the Japanese in the 17th C.

## S3 SHIRAOI 白老

*1:10h by JR express from Sapporo or 1:15h by bus from Chitose Kūkō station* (S1). Main attraction is the **Ainu Minzoku Hakubutsukan** (Ainu Museum) アイヌ民族博物館 (Hrs: 8:00–17:00. Nov.–Mar. 8:30–16:30. Clsd NY, mid-Aug.) Nearby is the **Shiraoi Poroto Kotan** 白老ポロトコタン , a museum village with several Ainu houses. The museum publishes a nice pamphlet with photographs and English text.

## S4 NOBORIBETSU ONSEN 登別温泉

*1:30h from Sapporo or 0:50h from Chitose Kūkō station by JR express to Noboribetsu, then bus to Noboribetsu Onsen.* The most famous onsen town in Hokkaidō. Though located in a pretty gorge, huge hotels and "pink" entertainments give it a tawdry cast. Kumayama's Ainu museum village is of some interest.

\*\*\* **Dai-ichi Takimoto-kan.** Open 24:00h. The huge, famous bath halls of this hotel are a unique cultural experience in their own way. Anyone can partake of the baths by paying Y800. There are over 40 pools with different mineral contents, embellished with plastic plants and abstract sculptures. There is a walled-off women-only section, and a "mixed" section, about four times as spacious, with hot waterfalls, streams, and cool (chlorinated) pools. The few women in the mixed section wear bathing suits and stick with their kids in the cool pool. The scene is entertaining, but not relaxed.

\* **Jigokudani (Hell Gorge).** At the upper end of Noboribetsu Onsen village is this volcanic ravine from which gushes an enormous quantity of hot water to supply all the baths in Noboribetsu. Local vegetation includes lacquer trees that survive in the cold climate because of the heat from Jigokudani.

\*\* **Kumayama (Bear Mountain).** *0:10h by tramway from Noboribetsu Onsen (Y1900 round trip, incl. admission).* Open Apr. 29–Oct. 30, daily. A tiny Ainu "village" of about six thatched houses where some Ainu elders demonstrate traditional crafts such as basket weaving and wood carving. At 10:30, 15:30, 19:30, and 20:00 (the last two times only in summer), they demonstrate the important sacred rituals of the Ainu, including saké rites and the famous Iyomante rite (here, the clownish bear cub is harmlessly "shot" with an arrow). *No photographs.* The nearby bear museum and bear pits are a depressing spectacle, best avoided.

### Noboribetsu Lodgings (TEL 0143)

**Takinoya Ryokan** 滝乃家 (84-2222). 162 Noboribetsu Onsen-chō, Noboribetsu-shi, Hokkaidō. Has an open-air bath and garden. Y10,500–32,000 w/2 meals, tax, and service.

**Takimoto Inn** 滝本イン (84-2205). 76 Noboribetsu Onsen-chō. Small hotel annex of the Dai-ichi Takimoto-kan. Western-style rooms. Y11–13,000 w/meals.

**Dai-ichi Takimoto-kan** 第一滝本館 (84-2111). 55 Noboribetsu Onsen-chō. Glittering and impersonal. Famous for its bath. Deluxe ryokan style. Y12,500–22,000 w/meals.

**YH Noboribetsu Kannon-ji** YH登別観音寺 (84-2359/2970). 119 Noboribetsu Onsen-chō. Temple YH with reputation for good meals, friendliness. Onsen bath.

**Suzuki Ryokan** 鈴木旅館　カルルス町 (84-2285). Karurusu Onsen, Noboribetsu-shi. 0:25h by car from Noboribetsu, up in quieter mountains. Rambling old inn with a generous, multipool, wood-floored bath hall. Y8–10,000 w/meals.

## S5 TŌYA-KO (LAKE)  洞爺湖

*By bus to Tōya-ko Onsen: 2:45h from Sapporo, or 1:40h from Noboribetsu Onsen (June 1–Oct. 21). By train: 2:10h from Sapporo, or 1:45h from Hakodate* (HOKKAIDŌ II) *by JR express to Tōya, then 0:15–0:20h by bus. From Shikotsu-ko* (S2), *1:00h by car.* This is the developed area of Shikotsu-Tōya National Park. Its main attraction is **Shōwa Shinzan**, a smoldering pile of volcanic rubble that thrust up in the middle of a farmer's field in the winter of 1944. Towering over this new mountain is **Usu-zan**, a craggy cinder volcano that erupted spectacularly in August 1977, dumping 30 cm of ash on the town of Tōya-ko Onsen. Smashed cars, volcanic cinders, and a multimedia show of the disaster are on view at the **Abuta Kazan Kagakukan** (Volcano Science Museum), above the Tōya-ko Onsen bus terminal (clsd Dec.–Mar.). Neither mountain can be climbed to its summit, but there is a tramway part way up Usu-zan that affords the best view of Shōwa Shinzan. **Tōya-ko**, a caldera lake, has an island, Nakajima, in its center, and three islets. **Kannon-ji**, on Kannon islet, enshrines a rough-hewn image of Kannon attributed to the Edo-period mendicant monk-sculptor Enkū. Pleasure boats make trips to the islands.

### Getting Around
Bus service between Tōya-ko Onsen bus terminal, Tōya-ko Onsen, Kankō-kan YH, and Shōwa Shinzan. Rent-a-cycle near the bus terminal and at Kankō-kan YH.

### Tōya-ko Lodgings (TEL 01427)
**Shōwa Shinzan YH**  昭和新山YH (5-2283). 103 Sōbetsu Onsen, Sōbetsu-machi, Usu-gun, Hokkaidō. A run-down former ryokan. Large onsen baths.

# HOKKAIDŌ II. HAKODATE

149

*Tokyo to Hakodate: 1:35h by air, 6 flights a day with ANA and JAL.*
*Sapporo to Hakodate: 4:00h by JR limited express train.*
*Aomori to Hakodate: 3:50h by JR ferry, or 2:00h by limited express train.*

## * HAKODATE  函館
Hakodate's strategic location on a fine harbor with the promontory, Mt. Hakodate, overlooking the Tsugaru Straits, has made it an important city in Hokkaidō history. As far back as the 13th century, Hakodate was Japan's toe-hold on Hokkaidō. When Russian ships began prowling the Hokkaidō coast around 1740, they weighed anchor in Hakodate Bay. In 1854, Hakodate became one of Japan's first treaty ports, together with Nagasaki and Shimoda, and a small community of foreign traders settled in **Motomachi**. A decade later, Hakodate became the scene of a curious footnote to the Meiji Restoration when a band of shogunate loyalists re-treated here and declared an independent republic. The imperial army arrived less than a year later and crushed them in battle at the **Goryōkaku**, Hakodate's famous star-shaped fort. Some old foreign-settlement buildings have been converted to shops, hotels, and restaurants. The night view from Mt. Hakodate of the illuminated isthmus is rated among Japan's "Best Three," but the nightlife itself is rather quiet, even gloomy.

### Calendar
**Mid-May: Goryōkaku Matsuri.** On the weekend nearest May 18, the last battle between the imperial and shogunate armies is reenacted.

### Getting Around
The two main areas of interest are Motomachi and the Goryōkaku. To get to Motomachi, take a tram from the station 0:05h to **Jūjigai** 十字街 , or a taxi to Haristos-sei Kyōkai (Russian Orthodox Church). Goryōkaku is 0:10h by bus or tram in the opposite direction; the 4-km taxi ride is somewhat expensive but much simpler.

### Goryōkaku Area
**★★ Goryōkaku (Fortress)** 五稜郭 Japan's first Western-style fort was completed in 1864 by Takeda Ayasaburō, who had studied Western military techniques. The TOKUGAWA built it to defend northern Japan against the Russians. Ironically, it became the site of the shogunate's last gasp. In October 1868, eight warships and 2,000 shogunate loyalists fled to Hokkaidō and established a headquarters at this fortress. They declared an autonomous republic, and were even recognized by France and Britain. In May 1869, however, imperial troops attacked the fortress and soon after forced its surrender.
**Hakodate Hakubutsukan Bunkan.** Hrs: 10:00–16:30; Oct.–Mar. 9:00–16:00; clsd M, NH, last day of month, NY. Inside the fortress; museum on Hakodate history, including relics — swords, guns, blood-stained uniforms — from the battle.
**Goryōkaku Tower.** This tacky tower offers a worthwhile view of the fort's star shape. Small fee. The ground floor houses exhibits on Hakodate's history.

### Motomachi Area
A cluster of Western buildings remains from the old foreign community that grew up here during Hakodate's treaty-port era. The tourist information office is in Motomachi Park.
**Haristos-sei Kyōkai** ハリストス正教会 A Russian Orthodox Church with green onion domes, founded in 1861. It burned in 1907; the present structure was rebuilt in 1916.

✱ **Hakodate-yama** 函館山 0:10h on foot from Jūjigai is a tramway to the top of this mountain, where there is an excellent view, by day or night, of the town and the harbor. The foreigners' cemetery (*gaijin bochi*) is filled with graves of Russians, Chinese, English, French, and Americans.

**Hakodate Hakubutsukan Kyōdo Shiryōkan (Municipal Museum)** 函館博物館郷土資料館 (23-5480). Hrs: 9:00–16:30; Nov.–Mar. 9:00–16:00; clsd M, last F of month, NH. Near Suehiro-chō tram stop. Interesting collection of locally excavated objects, including Jōmon pots and a cache of Han-dynasty coins. Housed in the oldest Western-style brick building in Japan. The main branch of this museum is in Hakodate Kōen (park).

## Hakodate Dining

In Motomachi are numerous cafés and restaurants, some in renovated old buildings. Kissaten Goby and Hishii are in old *kura*. California Baby, on the wharf, was a post office.

② **Renga-tei** 煉瓦亭　東雲町13-11 (23-3091). Hrs: 18:00–24:00; clsd Su. Hokkaidō cuisine: broiled fish and *nabe* dishes from Y1100.

③ **Chat Noir** シャノワール　ユニオンスクエア1F (27-1200). Union Square Meijikan, 1F. Hrs: 11:00–24:00; clsd 1st and 3rd W. Chic design, inexpensive dishes. Pork curry set, Y700.

⑦ **Sei Sushi** 清寿し　末広町7-4 (22-0537). Hrs: 11:00–22:00, daily. Fresh, generous-sized sushi. *Teishoku* from Y1000.

⑧ **Marine House** マリンハウス　元町29-15 (27-0508). Hrs: 9:30–19:00; clsd Tu. Motomachi restaurant in a converted church. Coffee, and dairy and potato dishes. À la carte from Y300.

## Hakodate Lodgings (TEL 0138)

① **Hotel Hakodate Royal** ホテル函館ロイヤル (26-8181). Fax 27-4397. 16-9 Ōmori-chō, Hakodate-shi, Hokkaidō. One of the better hotels, but a little far from the sights. S Y9600＋, Tw Y19,200＋.

④ **Pension Kokian** ペンション古稀庵　末広町13-2 (26-5753). 13-2 Suehiro-chō. In old Motomachi building. Restaurant. Y7000 w/meals.

⑤ **Hotel New Hakodate** ホテルニュー函館 (22-8131). 23-9 Suehiro-chō. In a converted Meiji-period bank near Motomachi; a little gloomy. S from Y8000, Tw from Y18,000.

⑥ **Minshuku Muroya** 民宿室屋　大町9-17 (23-0033). 9-17 Ōmachi. Old Motomachi building. Y6000 w/meals.

⑨ **Hotel Hakodateyama** ホテル函館山 (23-7237). 19-1 Motomachi. Close to the Hakodate-yama tramway, convenient to the Motomachi area. S Y9000＋, Tw Y16,000＋.

150

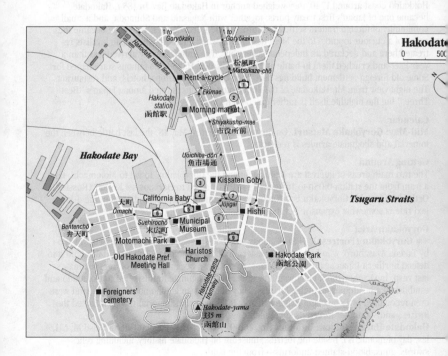

# Tōhoku

Tōhoku is where the traditional life of Japan is best pre-served today. Tōhoku's castle towns are among the most charming, its crafts are the earthiest, and its festivals are the lustiest. Still strongly rural, its people are plain-spoken and warm characters, who still retain vivid memories of the hardships that faced Tōhoku farmers until only a few dec-ades ago. To many, Tōhoku evokes scenes from Bashō's poetic pilgrimage, chronicled in *The Narrow Road to the Deep North*. The haiku in this travel diary are as famous as the places they immortalized.

## BEST ATTRACTIONS

I:W2   ✳✳ **Hirosaki.** An old castle town with a genuine castle keep, rustic handcrafts, and Tsugaru-jamisen music (p. 157).

I:E2   ✳✳ **Osore-zan and Shimokita Peninsula.** Where mediums mouth messages from dead souls. Spectacular sea cliffs and scenes of desolation (p. 159).

II   ✳✳ **Morioka.** A castle town with an artistic bent. Museums, *kura* coffee shops, good eating, and hand-cast iron kettles (p. 161).

II:W2   ✳✳ **Kakunodate.** Famous for its street of samurai houses (p. 164).

III:W1   ✳✳ **Hiraizumi.** One of the most fascinating historical places in Japan. Golden Hall of the ill-fated Northern Fujiwara (p. 168).

IV:W3   ✳✳ **Dewa Sanzan.** Three mountains that were a center of the ascetic *yamabushi* cult (p. 175).

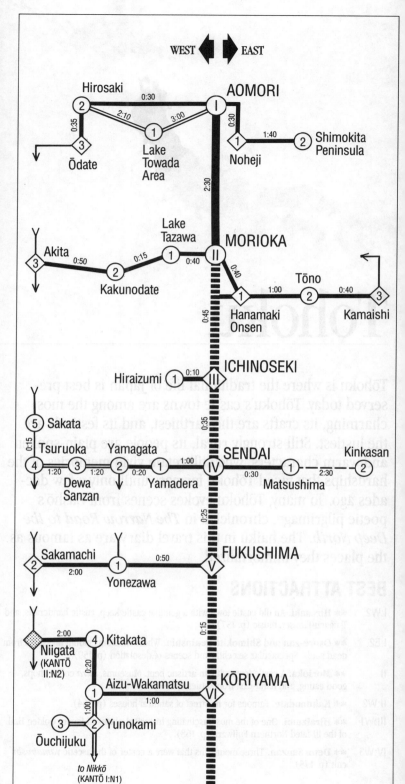

152

WEST ◀ ▶ EAST

Hirosaki
2 —— 0:30 —— AOMORI I
2:10   3:00
0:35         1
Lake
Towada
Area
3
Ōdate

0:30
1 —— 1:40 —— 2 Shimokita
Noheji          Peninsula

2:30

Lake
Tazawa
Akita   0:50   2   0:15   1   0:40   II  MORIOKA
3
Kakunodate

0:40
Tōno
1 —— 1:00 —— 2 —— 0:40 —— 3
Hanamaki          Kamaishi
Onsen

0:45

Hiraizumi 1 —— 0:10 —— III  ICHINOSEKI

0:35

Sakata 5
0:15
Tsuruoka 4   Yamagata
3   0:20   1 —— 1:00 —— IV  SENDAI   Kinkasan
1:20   Dewa   2                    0:30         2:30
Sanzan   Yamadera          1 ——— 2 ——
1:20                         Matsushima

0:25

Sakamachi
2   2:00   1   0:50   V  FUKUSHIMA
Yonezawa

0:15

Niigata   2:00   4   Kitakata
(KANTŌ
II:N2)
0:20

Aizu-Wakamatsu
1 —— 1:00 —— VI  KŌRIYAMA

Ōuchijuku
3 —— 2   Yunokami
1:00

to Nikkō
(KANTŌ I:N1)

1:20

to Tokyo

**TŌHOKU
TRANSIT DIAGRAM**

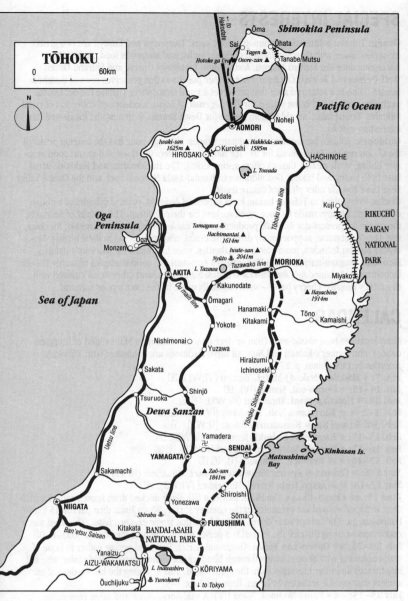

## Traveling

With the Tōhoku Shinkansen, it takes only 2:30h–3:30h to get to Morioka from Tokyo. What takes time is traveling on local lines that criss-cross the region.

## Seasons

Tōhoku's principal tourist season is during its comparatively drier and cooler summers. During the hottest time, in the first 10 days of August, the so-called "three big festivals" in Aomori, Akita, and Sendai draw millions of tourists, so reserve lodgings early. Mid-spring (cherry blossoms) comes in late April; full foliage starts around mid-October. Winters, especially on the Japan Sea coast, are very cold and snowy.

## Average Temperature °C (°F)/Days of Rain or Snow

|  | January | April | July | October |
|---|---|---|---|---|
| Aomori | −2.0 (28.4)/23 | 7.6 (45.7)/10 | 20.9 (69.6)/9 | 11.8 (53.2)/13 |
| Akita | −0.7 (30.7)/22 | 8.5 (47.3)/12 | 22.6 (72.7)/12 | 13.0 (55.4)/13 |
| Sendai | 0.6 (33.0)/6 | 9.6 (49.3)/8 | 22.1 (71.8)/13 | 14.0 (57.2)/9 |

# SPECIAL INTERESTS

**Onsen:** Tōhoku is littered with remote, rustic spas. Tsurunoyu and Kuroyu are two great mountain onsen with thatched lodges, open-air baths, and mountain food. Some other interesting ones are Tashiro Motoyu, Aoni Onsen, Tamagawa Onsen, and Shirabu Onsen.

**Well-Preserved Towns:** Ōuchijuku is a former post town that preserves rows of thatched houses. Tōno is a scattered area that preserves a rural atmosphere (ignore the occasional pachinko parlor) and is the setting for *The Legends of Tōno*, a celebrated collection of rural folktales. Tamugimata, an old pilgrim station for Dewa Sanzan, is in a mystic locale and has interesting *minka*.

**Outdoors:** Tōhoku has numerous mountain ranges, although none has the soaring peaks of the Chūbu region. Zaō, famous for its "ice monsters," offers the finest skiing and good summer hiking, while nearby Gassan offers spring skiing. The Hachimantai and Hakkōda areas have both skiing and hiking. Goshikinuma in Bandai-Asahi National Park and the Oirase Valley near Lake Towada offer pleasant nature trails.

**Crafts:** Every place in Tōhoku has its local version of *kokeshi*, painted cylindrical wooden dolls, originally toys made by poor woodworkers for their children. The vicinity of Sendai is the center for present-day *kokeshi* production. Old castle towns, such as Hirosaki, Morioka, and Aizu-Wakamatsu, support many distinctive crafts, often connected to their history. Morioka's Nambu *tetsubin*, hand-cast iron teakettles, were first made for Morioka's daimyo. Hirosaki's Tsugaru-nuri and Aizu-Wakamatsu's Aizu-nuri are good examples of sturdy Tōhoku lacquerware. Kakunodate's *kabazaiku*—boxes, tea caddies, and other items covered with beautifully finished cherry bark—were originally made by the town's poor samurai.

# CALENDAR

154

Many localities have *shishi-mai* (lion or deer dances), Ennen no Mai (a kind of liturgical dance), and farmer's Kabuki and Noh. All three traditions are connected with Tōhoku's *yamabushi* (see Shinto, p. 27).

**Jan. 7:** \* **Hadaka (Naked) Mairi.** Yanaizu (VI:W1). E

**Jan. 14–15:** \* **Donto-sai.** Sendai (IV). F

**Jan. 20:** \* **Hatsuka Yasai.** Hiraizumi (III:W1). P B

**Feb. 1–2:** \* # **Kurokawa Noh.** Kurokawa (IV:W4). P S

**Feb. 3rd Sa and Su:** \* **Kamakura.** Yokote (II:W2). V

**Feb. 15–17:** \* **Kuromori Kabuki.** Kuromori (IV:W5). P

**Feb. 16–17:** \* **Bonten.** Yokote and Ōmagari (II:W2). V S

**Feb. 17–20:** \* # **Emburi.** Hachinohe (I). P S

**May 1–5:** \* **Chūson-ji Spring Fujiwara Matsuri.** Hiraizumi (III:W1). P

**May 12–18:** \* # **Atago Jinja Sairei.** Hinoemata (VI:W3). P

**June 15:** \*\* **Chagu-Chagu Umakko.** Morioka (II). Gaily decked draft horses with tiny children strapped aboard are presented at the country shrine, Sōzen Jinja, then parade 15 km to Hachiman-gū. The horses wear donut-shaped bells that jangle *chagu-chagu*. This area was a major horse-raising district; the festival is a prayer for the safety of the horses. 9:00–14:00.

**July 20–24:** \*\* **Osore-zan Taisai.** Osore-zan (I:E2). Bereaved people gather in hope of communicating with dead relatives through blind female shamanesses called *itako*, who fall into trances and utter messages from the spirit world. This is among the last vestiges of an ancient shamanistic tradition in Japan. Repeated Sept. 1–5.

**July 23–25:** \*\*\* **Sōma Nomaoi.** Sōma (IV). A wild horse chase and other equestrian events were part of a festival begun by a 10th-C lord, TAIRA no Masakado (see Tokyo, p. 206, Kanda Myōjin). In the highlight (July 24) of today's festival, colored flags are shot into the air and 1,000 horses and riders decked out in feudal armor, saddles, and war banners skirmish to recover them; the victors present them at a hilltop shrine.

**July 31–Aug. 1:** \* # **Hayachine Jinja Matsuri.** Hayachine Jinja (II:E2). P

**Aug. 1–7:** \*\* **Neputa.** Hirosaki (I:W2). Beautiful, handpainted giant floats are paraded through the city to the mesmerizing sound of drums and gongs. Aomori's frenetic Nebuta is a participant's matsuri; Hirosaki's is visually entrancing, wonderful just to see.

**Aug. 2–7:** \*\*\* **Nebuta Matsuri.** Aomori (I). Giant lanternlike floats in the shapes of warriors and fantastic creatures are displayed, and on the 5th to the 7th, are dragged through the streets at night to the din of drums, flutes, and bells, while thousands of youths dance frenziedly to the chant of *rase-rase-rase-raa!* By tradition, Sakanoue Tamuramaro, the very first "barbarian-quelling shogun" in Japanese history, built the awesome floats in the 8th century to frighten away his northern (possibly Ainu) foes (see Hiraizumi History, p. 169). And indeed, the festival has the feel of a victory celebration. Others say that *nebuta* means to "drive away lethargy" during the peak of summer heat; the spirits of sleep are set adrift on the river in a rite called *neburi-nagashi*.

**Aug. 4–7:** \*\* **Kantō Matsuri.** Akita (II:W3). Legions of young men perform balancing feats with enormous, lantern-decked poles, or *kantō*, some of which weigh 60 kg. About 160 *kantō* appear on the street.

**Aug. 6–8:** \* **Tanabata.** Sendai (IV). V

**Aug. 14:** \* **Noh.** Hiraizumi (III:W1). P

**Aug. 16–18:** \* # **Nishimonai Bon Odori.** Nishimonai (II:W2). P
**Aug. 18:** \* # **Kabuki.** Hinoemata (VI:W3). P
**Aug. 31–Sept. 1: Hassaku Matsuri:** Haguro Jinja (IV:W3). F
**L 8/1:** \*\* **Oyama-Sankei.** Hirosaki (II:W2). One of the most colorful mountain pilgrimages. Local farmers climb Iwaki-san through the night to greet the sunrise and thank the kami for a bountiful harvest.
**Sept. 7–9:** \* **Oyama-bayashi.** Kakunodate (II:W2). F E
**Sept. 14–15:** \*\* **Hachiman Jinja Saiten.** Tōno (II:E2). Tōno's famous deer dances are performed. Lively country harvest matsuri.
**Nov. 1–3:** \* **Fujiwara Matsuri.** Hiraizumi (III:W1). P
**Dec. 31:** \*\* # **Namahage.** Oga (II:W3). Villagers disguised as fearsome *oni* (demons) go from house to house, brandishing butcher knives and roaring threats at terrified small children. The idea is to ensure that the children will grow up to be hard-working. A similar custom is practiced on the Noto Peninsula and in Kagoshima, the southernmost part of Kyūshū.
**Dec. 31–Jan. 1:** \* **Shōrei-sai.** Haguro Jinja (IV:W3). F

# TŌHOKU I. AOMORI

**Tokyo to Aomori:** *2:30–3:30h by Tōhoku Shinkansen to Morioka* (TŌHOKU II), *then 2:30h by JR Tōhoku main line limited express.*
**By Air:** *JAS flies from Tokyo's Haneda Airport to Aomori (1:45h), 3 times a day.*
**Prefectures:** Aomori

### AOMORI 青森
It was only in the Meiji period that Aomori, an important port town, usurped Hirosaki's place as the capital of the region. The city consequently has few cultural attractions (90 percent of the city was destroyed in World War II). But in early August, Aomori holds a not-to-be-missed event, the Nebuta Matsuri. Aomori has two good museums: **Aomori Kenritsu Kyōdokan** 青森県立郷土館 , a modern, well-arranged museum of local culture (Hrs: 9:30–16:30; clsd NY, NH, from Nov.–April; and **Munakata Kinenkan** 棟方志功記念館 , exhibiting the work of Japan's most famous modern print artist, the late Munakata Shikō, an Aomori native (Open Apr.–Sept. 9:30–16:30, Oct.–Mar. 9:30–16:30; clsd M, NH, end of month, NY).

155

### Calendar
**Feb. 17–20:** \* # **Emburi.** Hachinohe *(0:30h by Tōhoku main line express from Aomori).* 1,300-year-old dances by "ploughmen" wearing unusual tall hats, suggestive of a horse's head, who stamp the snow-covered ground to impart fertility to the rice paddies. In early morning (ends by 8:30), dances are offered at the Shinra shrine. Later, the dances are performed throughout the town.
**Aug. 2–7:** \*\*\* **Nebuta Matsuri.** See Calendar, p. 154. On the 5th–7th, the fabulous Nebuta floats are dragged through the streets at night. Most tourists just watch from the sidelines, but it's much, much better to join in the fray. The friendly dancers will sweep you right up. Hirosaki has a quieter version Aug. 1–7. Reserve hotels well in advance.

### Aomori's Minyō Sakaba (Folk-Music Pubs)
Tsugaru folk music has an enthusiastic following throughout Japan. The *shamisen* rhythms can be heard nightly at **Jintako** 甚太古  安方1丁目 6 (73-3522), five minutes from Aomori station. Clsd on 3rd Su.

### Aomori Lodgings (TEL 0177)
Reserve far in advance during Nebuta.
**Hotel Aomori** ホテル青森 (75-4141). Fax 73-5201. 1-1-23 Tsutsumi-machi, Aomori-shi, Aomori-ken. Central. S Y6–7000, Tw Y10–18,000.
**Aomori Green Hotel** 青森グリーンホテル 新町1-11-22 (23-2001). 1-11-22 Shin-machi. S Y6600, Tw Y10,000.

### Exploring Ura-Hakkōda
# The north side of Mt. Hakkōda can be reached by a bus that leaves in the morning from Aomori station, returning in late afternoon. Take it to **Tashiro Motoyu** (1:20h), a sublimely rustic hot spring in a forested river valley, with views of Mt. Hakkōda. From the bus stop, it's a 0:20h hike to the **Yamadakan**, a basic but clean inn, with several varieties of baths, indoors and outdoors (no electricity or plumbing). 0:10h on foot downstream, across a suspension bridge, is a splendid *rotemburo*. Reserve at 0177-66-0506 (no direct phone). Clsd Oct.–Mar. Y7000 w/meals.

# TŌHOKU I:W. SOUTHWEST FROM AOMORI

**Main Attractions:** Hirosaki (W2)

### W1 \* LAKE TOWADA AREA 十和田湖
*About 3:00h by JR and private buses from Aomori station, or 2:15h by bus from Morioka* (TŌHOKU II). This beautiful mountainous region offers rustic onsen, hiking, skiing, and the resort lake, Towada-ko. From mid-Apr. to Oct. 31, a bus departs about once an hour from Aomori station to Towada-ko. There are various attractions along the way. The "ropeway"

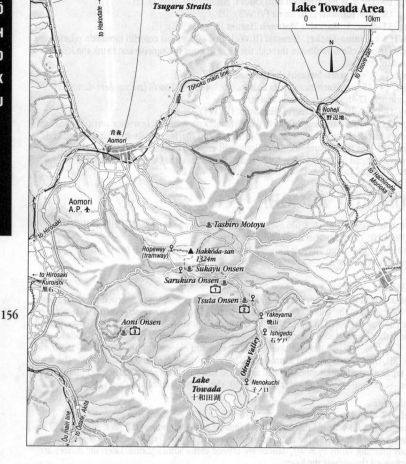

Lake Towada Area

Tsugaru Straits

to Hakodate

N

Tōhoku main line

to Osore-zan

Noheji
野辺地

青森
Aomori

to Hachinohe, Morioka

Aomori A.P.

to Hirosaki

Tashiro Motoyu

Ropeway (tramway)

Hakkōda-san 1324m

Sukayu Onsen

Sarukura Onsen

Tsuta Onsen

to Hirosaki
Kuroishi
黒石

Aoni Onsen

Yakeyama
焼山

Ishigedo
石ケ戸

Oirase Valley

Lake Towada
十和田湖

Nenokuchi
子ノ口

Ōu main line
to Ōdate, Akita

offers a nice vista. **Sukayu Onsen Hotel** 酸カ湯温泉 attracts busloads of tourists with its *senninburo* (1,000-person bath), a vast wooden bath hall. **Sarukura Onsen** is a simple but pleasant spa with a nice wood-and-rock bath hall. **Tsuta Onsen** is an atmospheric inn built in 1908, with a beautiful wooden bathhouse. There's a cluster of small lakes behind the inn, with a scenic loop trail (a bit muddy). The Towada-ko Onsen Hotel is a terminus of the Oirase Valley walking path and cycling trail.

## ** Oirase Valley 奥入瀬渓流

*In addition to the bus route described above, there are direct buses to and from Hirosaki (W2) (2:10b, 4 per day), Ōdate (W3) (2:15b, 4 per day), Misawa (2:15b, 3 per day), and Morioka (TŌHOKU II) (2:15b, 10 per day). Most buses run from Apr. through Oct. or early Nov.* The Oirase Valley offers a very popular **walking/cycling path** along a pretty, winding river with cascades gushing between moss-covered boulders. In autumn, it ranks foremost among Tōhoku's foliage-viewing spots and gets very crowded. At the Towada-ko Onsen Hotel, you can rent bicycles and arrange to have luggage delivered (Y400 per piece) to Nenokuchi, where you can drop off the bicycle and pick up waiting luggage. Walkers can also deposit luggage, but should be sure to hop right back on the bus and ride a little farther, to Ishigedo. The walking trail starts here. Walking is more pleasant than bicycling on the nearby highway, which is roaring with trucks. (This is the one blot on Oirase's beauty.) The hike is 9 km, about 2:30h. Cycling from Towada-ko Onsen Hotel is 15 km, about 1:30h. Be sure to take the JR buses; there are other buses, but they don't stop at the right places.

Nenokuchi, the boat landing for excursions on Towada-ko, is awful; both it and the boat ride can be skipped. You can do the Oirase course in the reverse direction from Nenokuchi—luggage delivery and all. From Nenokuchi, there are buses to Hirosaki (2:20h) via Kuroishi (1:45h).

## Lake Towada Area Lodgings (TEL 0176)

□1 **Ryokan Sarukura Onsen** 旅館猿倉温泉 (23-7500). Sarukura Onsen, Okuse, Towadako-machi, Kamikita-gun, Aomori-ken. Clsd Nov.–Apr. 15. Y10–14,000 w/meals.

□2 * **Tsuta Onsen Ryokan** 蔦温泉旅館 (74-2311). Tsutanoyu, Okuse. A classic Tōhoku mountain spa. Famous, so sometimes it fills up. Y13–25,000 w/meals.

## KUROISHI　黒石

*1:45h by bus from Nenokuchi, or 0:30h by bus or private Kōnan-tetsudō line from Hirosaki (W2).* Near Kuroishi is a wonderful hot-spring spa, Aoni Onsen (see below). Kuroishi has a small Neputa festival of its own (Aug. 1–7), and Edo-period *komise* (ICP), wooden eaves that shelter sidewalks from the winter snows. A convenient place for lunch is **Kurayoshi** 倉よし (01725-3-3396), 0:05h on foot from the station. At Tsugaru-Onoue station on the Kōnan-tetsudō line linking Hirosaki to Kuroishi is the Meiji-period **Seibi-en** 盛美園, a half-*sukiya*, half-Renaissance manor with a pleasant garden (Hrs: 8:00–sundown; clsd Nov. 15–Apr. 20). Its *kura* is extravagantly decorated inside with *maki-e* lacquer.

⟨3⟩ **\*\* # Aoni Onsen** 青荷温泉 (0172-and 52-3243). Takinoue, Aonisawa, Okiura, Kuroishi-shi, Aomori-ken. Clsd Nov.–Apr. Reserve several days ahead, and they'll send a van to pick you up twice a day at Kuroishi station (get there by 10:00 or 16:00). A wonderful place to rest from your travels. Aoni is a "lamp no yado," with oil lamps instead of electric lights in guest rooms and bath areas. The old thatched inn and bungalows have been replaced by trim new buildings, but it's still pretty nice. There are segregated baths and a nonsegregated *rotemburo* right beside a cold rushing stream where overheated bathers can cool off. Trout and mountain greens (*sansai*). Y6000+ w/meals.

## W2 \*\* HIROSAKI　弘前

*0:30h by JR limited express or 0:50h by local from Aomori, or 2:00h by limited express from Akita (TŌHOKU II:W3) on the Ōu line; or by bus via the Lake Towada area (W1). From Morioka (TŌHOKU II), 3:45–4:00h by direct JR train, several times a day.* As the castle town of the Tsugaru domain, which controlled the northwest tip of Honshū, Hirosaki was a cultural center of northern Tōhoku. The city, though spared during World War II, presents a modern, rather grimy face, yet it definitely has charm. Its twisting, alleys were designed to defend the fort. Hirosaki preserves many important cultural relics, including an original castle keep, samurai houses, a five-storied pagoda, and a large temple town. Hirosaki's Neputa Matsuri is more intimate and beautiful than the spectacularly rowdy Aomori Nebuta. Hirosaki's craft traditions thrive. Hirosaki also has a great *minyō sakaba*, Yamauta, where you can hear the live strains of Tsugaru-jamisen, a hot, foot-stomping Japanese "bluegrass" music.

157

### Calendar

Hirosaki castle is a famous cherry-viewing spot (Apr. 24–May 7). The apple orchards outside the town bloom in mid-May.

**Aug. 1–7: \*\* Neputa Matsuri.** See Calendar, p. 154. Aomori's frenetic Nebuta is a participant's matsuri; Hirosaki's is visually entrancing, wonderful just to watch.

**L 8/1: \*\* Oyama-Sankei.** See Calendar, p. 155.

### Getting Around

The Kankō Annaijo by the station provides a pamphlet in English. The sights can be seen in a day of vigorous walking. We suggest taking a bus or taxi to Kamenoko-chō kado bus stop and then walking from there.

### Hirosaki Sights

**Tōshō-gū (Shrine)** 東照宮 One of many shrines consecrated to TOKUGAWA IEYASU, usually indicative of a castle town's political status vis-à-vis the shogunate. In this case, the second Tsugaru lord had married one of Ieyasu's daughters.

**\*\* Tsugaru-han Neputa Mura** 津軽藩ねぷた村 (35-5755). Hrs: 9:00–17:00. Mid-Nov.–Mar. 9:00–16:00. *0:15h by bus from station.* Colorful Nebuta floats on display.

**\* Buke-Yashiki (Samurai Houses)** 武家屋敷 This area on the north side of the castle formed a major defense against attacks on its main gate. The streets retain their original rectilinear plan, devised to channel the enemy to the heavily fortified neighborhood (see Castles, p. 47). Supposedly the hedges were planted so that samurai hidden behind them could skewer enemy soldiers as they went charging past. A few old gates and houses are preserved. **Itō-ke** 伊藤家, a modest, 200-year-old samurai house, is open to the public. (Hrs: 10:00–16:00; clsd Tu, F.) Across the street from Kamenoko gate is **Ishiba-ke** 石場家 (ICP), a saké merchant's shop dating from the 1750s. Note the old *komise* eaves, designed to keep snow off the sidewalk.

**\*\*\* Hirosaki-jō (Castle)** 弘前城 (ICP). When Hirosaki-jō was built in 1611, peace was not yet firmly established, and so for defense purposes the castle had only one gate, the **Kamenoko-mon** on the north. It is still the most imposing and beautiful of the castle's gates. Most of the buildings were destroyed in an earthquake, but the **main keep**, several turrets, gates, and moats survive. The main keep houses a small museum on the castle's history (Hrs: 8:30–17:00; clsd Dec.–Mar.). The castle grounds are now a park, mobbed in spring by tourists coming to view its famous cherry blossoms.

**\* Shiritsu Hakubutsukan (Municipal Museum)** 市立博物館 (35-0700). Hrs: Apr.–Oct., Tu–Su 9:30–16:30; Nov.–Mar., Tu–Su 10:00–16:00; clsd M, NH, NY. A pleasant museum on local history, including interesting old photographs of the Neputa. One room is devoted to the history of the Tsugaru lords and their collateral branch in Kuroishi (W1). The Tsugaru lords used the *manji* (Buddhist swastika) as a family crest, a symbol since adopted by the city of Hirosaki. Look for it on manhole covers.

**∗∗ Chōshō-ji** 長勝寺 Hrs: 8:00–17:00. The temple-lined approach to this funerary temple of the Tsugaru lords is rich in history and atmosphere. Chōshō-ji was built on a strategically important bluff soon after Hirosaki-jō was completed. The daimyo gathered around it all the Zen temples in his domain, creating a fortified temple town. Morning is the best time to walk the approach; it takes 0:30h to walk from the **Kuromon Gate** (late 17th C) to Chōshō-ji proper. The temple's **main gate** (1692, ICP) has extra-deep eaves to handle Hirosaki's snows. The upper story (not open) houses images of Yakushi Nyorai and Rakan, typical of Zen temples. The belfry contains a bronze bell (ICP) cast in 1306. Directly behind the main hall is the **Miei-dō**, a polychrome, Momoyama-period hall containing a statue of Lord Tamenobu, the first Tsugaru daimyo. Nearby are the tombs of later Tsugaru lords. The main hall contains their mortuary tablets, flanked by those of their wives, and yet smaller ones for concubines. The tablet bearing the Tokugawa crest is for the wife of the second lord. The body of the eleventh lord, who died in 1855 at age 18, was excavated not long ago from the Hirosaki high school tennis court. It was in an excellent state of mummification. According to the priest, the reason he is so well preserved relates to the cause of his death: he was pathologically fond of sweets. The mummy, kept in a glass case in the main hall, is shown during cherry-blossom season.

**∗∗ Saishō-in** 最勝院 Not far from the Kuromon gate of Chōshō-ji is **Shin-Teramachi**, or "new temple town," another street lined with temples, mostly belonging to the Nichiren or Jōdo Shin sects. Few of the buildings are old, but Saishō-in, at the east end of the street, has a beautiful five-storied pagoda (1667, ICP). It was built to console the souls of warriors who had fallen in the various battles waged by the first lord of Tsugaru.

## Hirosaki Crafts and Shopping
Hirosaki's most famous craft is Tsugaru-nuri, also known as Baka-nuri (idiot lacquer) because of its durability. It was once the exclusive trade of poor samurai (see Crafts, p. 106).

4 **∗ Nakano Tako** 中野凧製作所　和徳町197　(32-7033). Ask locally to find this small shop, which sells Tsugaru kites handmade by a master who also creates Neputa floats. Designs are outlined in wax before being colored in. The translucent wax not only prevents the dyes from bleeding, but also gives kites and floats a vivid glow. Tsugaru kites have a paper strip across the back that buzzes when the kite is flown.

5 ＊**Miyamoto Kōgei** 宮本工芸店　南横町 7 (32-0796). Hrs: 9:00–17:00; clsd Su, Aug. 13–15, Dec. 12, NY. Handwoven *akebi* vine baskets are made and sold here. Visitors can see the baskets being woven.

7 ＊**Tanakaya** 田中屋　元寺町 7 (33-6666). Hrs: 10:00–19:00; clsd NY. This craft shop is a fine, one-stop introduction to Hirosaki crafts. AX, V, MC.

11 ＊＊**Tsugaru-han Neputa Mura** 津軽藩ねぷた村 (35-5755). Hrs: 9:00–17:00. Dec.– Mar. 9:00–16:00; clsd Dec. 31. Handmade *kokeshi*, tops, and other wooden lathe-turned objects. *Kijishi* (lathe craftsman) Mr. Honda designs some fabulous tops that fly apart, flip over, and do other amazing tricks. The tops are painted with gay vegetable dyes. "Only four *kijishi* in Japan can do this kind of work now," boasts his assistant.

14 **Takaya Jūji** 高谷充治　桔梗野1-20-8 (32-6888). Hrs: 9:00–12:30, 13:30–18:00; clsd irregularly. Simple, pigeon-shaped whistles (*hato-bue*) and dolls of clay, made by Mr. and Mrs. Takaya. The bright colors are a bit modern but still charming.

### Hirosaki Dining

1 ＊**Ishita** いした　弘前駅前3-3 (27-4905). Hrs: 8:30–19:00, clsd Su, NY. Local cuisine, light meals, in a folksy setting. Inexpensive to moderate.

2 ＊**Yamauta** 山唄　大町3-1-1 (36-1835). Hrs. 17:00–23:00, clsd NY. A wonderful bar-restaurant with nightly live performances of Tsugaru-jamisen by virtuoso Yamada Chisato. Food ranges from the familiar (*yakitori, soba*) to the gourmet (*warabi* ferns and *hoya*, a sea creature). Yamauta *teishoku* (set menus) are a good buy. Inexpensive to moderate.

6 **Kiku Fuji** 菊富士　坂本町 1 (36-3300). Hrs: 11:00–21:00. Pleasant interiors and varied menu. *Soba, teishoku* (set menus), sukiyaki. Moderate.

8 ＊**Kagi no Hana** かぎのはな　新鍛治町43-6　(36-1152). Hrs: 17:00–23:00; clsd Su. Friendly country-style pub. *Sansai-gozen* (several small dishes of mountain vegetables) served on lacquer trays, from Y1500.

### Hirosaki Lodgings (TEL 0172)

3 ＊**Hotel Hokke Club** ホテル法華クラブ　(34-3811). Fax 32-0589. 126-1 Dote-machi, Hirosaki-shi, Aomori-ken. Bright, modern hotel with efficient service and convenient location. S Y6800–8000, Tw Y13,000. AX, DC, V, MC.

9 **Ishiba Ryokan** 石場旅館　元寺町55 (32-9118). 55 Moto-Teramachi. A modest, old-fashioned ryokan. Y8–12,000. No CC.

10 ＊**Suimei-sō** 翠明荘　元寺町69 (32-8281). 69 Moto-Teramachi. Stunning old Japanese house and garden. Reservations necessary. Y8500–24,000 w/meals. No CC.

12 **Hirosaki YH** 弘前YH　森町11 (33-7066) 11 Mori-chō. Members, Y3500 w/meals.

13 **Henshō-ji** 遍照寺　新寺町 (32-8714). 107-3 Shin-Teramachi. A newish temple-minshuku. Y5000 w/meals.

### Exploring Iwaki-san Jinja

*1:20h by bus from Hirosaki station.* This scenic shrine is sacred to **Iwaki-san**, the majestic volcano dominating the Hirosaki plain. The shrine is said to have been founded 1,200 years ago as a guardian shrine against the Emishi, a northern people who fought against the Yamato state. The architecture of the shrine's 340-year-old gate and main hall reveals that it was originally a syncretic establishment (see Shinto, p. 27). Every fall, farmers from the surrounding area make a thanksgiving pilgrimage to the inner sanctum at the summit, to which they climb during the night (see Hirosaki Calendar).

## W3 ŌDATE 大館

*0:35h by JR limited express from Hirosaki. Important junction on the Ōu line.* This modest town is the foremost producer of **Akita dogs** (big show in May). While waiting for your train, you might visit the *wappa* factory, where handsome cryptomeria-wood trays and boxes are made by hand.

**Easy Access To:**
＊＊**Morioka** (TŌHOKU II): *2:55h by Hanawa line direct express from Ōdate, or 3:30h by direct express via Akita.*
**Lake Tazawa** (TŌHOKU II:W1): *From Ōdate, 1:10h by Hanawa line to Rikuchū-Hanawa or Hachimantai, transfer for 2:00–3:00h bus ride over the Hachimantai range to Lake Tazawa.*
**Akita** (TŌHOKU II:W3): *1:40h by Ōu line from Ōdate.*

# TŌHOKU I:E. EAST OF AOMORI

## E1 NOHEJI 野辺地

*0:30h by limited express or 0:45h by local from Aomori, or 2:00h by limited express from Morioka (TŌHOKU II) by JR Tōhoku main line. Gateway to Osore-zan and the Shimokita Peninsula; transfer to the Ōminato/Ōhata line to Tanabu/Mutsu Bus Terminal.*

## E2 ＊＊OSORE-ZAN AND THE SHIMOKITA PENINSULA 恐山・下北半島

*Main center of transportation is Tanabu station/Mutsu Bus Terminal: from Aomori, 2:10h by JR Tōhoku main line via Noheji, then change to the private Ōhata line; or 2:45h by direct bus from Aomori station.*

## Calendar

Buses run May–Oct. Osore-zan is closed in winter.

**July 20–24:** ✱✱ **Osore-zan Taisai.** See Calendar, p. 154.

**Oct. 9–11:** **Akimairi.** Repeat of Osore-zan Taisai.

## Getting Around

The Shimokita Peninsula is remote and unpretentious, but it is also time-consuming to get around; buses and trains are few and slow. Osore-zan alone can be visited in a half day, but to see any other place one must spend at least one night.

## Shimokita Peninsula Sights

✱✱✱ **Osore-zan.** *0:40h by bus from Mutsu Bus Terminal.* The Japanese believed this volcanic plateau, Mt. Terror, was a gathering place for dead souls. It is curiously beautiful in a desolate, creepy way. A pale green lake lies dead still against a dark, forested volcano, and nearby wastelands of steaming, sulfurous vents stretch starkly before the rhododendrons, the only plants able to survive here. To the Japanese, such places were gateways to hell, the banks of the river Sai, the Buddhist Styx; souls of dead children wander here, condemned to pursue salvation by building towers of stone, which are kicked down by sadistic demons. Jizō, the bosatsu who drives away the demons, is represented here by dozens of images, many wearing the bibs of dead infants. Scattered about are offerings of their toys—rattles, pacifiers, and red and pink pinwheels thrust in the ground, twirling noiselessly in the breeze. The tourist comes here, but so does the lone pilgrim who, kneeling, piles pebble towers to help his child to salvation. Osore-zan has a temple, **Entsū-ji,** said to have been founded by the priest Ennin (see Hiraizumi History, p. 169). Nearby are several free hot-spring baths and pilgrims' lodgings.

✱ **Yagen Onsen** 薬研温泉 *0:30h by bus from Ōhata (5 per day), or Y3000 by taxi from Osore-zan via a scenic, winding mountain road.* This spa, located in a picturesque river gorge at the north foot of Osore-zan, is the best choice for an overnight stay. The Yagen Kankō Hotel, 0:45h on foot from Yagen Onsen, has a very nice open-air bath.

✱✱✱ **Hotoke ga Ura** 仏ヶ浦 *From Ōhata, 1:40h by bus to Sai, then board the ferry to Aomori. A daily ferry arrives at 12:40 and leaves for Aomori at 13:20; the ride takes 4:40h one way (Y3090).* This ferry offers one of the best boat rides in Japan, with spectacular views of Hotoke ga Ura rock formations and sheer cliffs along the unspoiled "blade" of Shimokita's "axe." The few fishing villages huddled in the occasional coves are virtually locked in; the inhabitants claim descent from TOYOTOMI warriors who fled to this remote refuge after the fall of Ōsaka Castle in 1615. The ferry brings in supplies and carries out fish for the market in Aomori, making for amusing diversions during the long ride.

## Shimokita Peninsula Lodgings (TEL 0175)

**Hotel New Yagen** ホテルニュー薬研 (34-3311).
6-1 Yagen, Ōhata, Shimokita-gun, Aomori-ken.
A bit large and modern, but comfortable. Japanese and Western rooms. Wooded surroundings.
Y8–12,000 w/meals.

**Furuhata** 古畑旅館 (34-2763). 1 Yagen. An older, countrified place, with a wood-paneled bath.
Y11,000 w/meals.

**Yagen Kankō Hotel** 薬研観光ホテル (34-3411).
Oku Yagen. No bargain, but has a great *rotem-buro*, best enjoyed at night. Y11–12,000 w/meals.

## Easy Access To:

**Aomori (I):** *4:40h by scenic ferry ride from Sai (see above).*

✱ **Hakodate** (HOKKAIDŌ II): *Ferry twice a day from Ōma.*

# TŌHOKU II. MORIOKA

**Tokyo to Morioka:** *2:30–3:30h by Tōhoku Shinkansen from Tokyo station.*
**Prefectures:** *Iwate, Akita*

## ** MORIOKA 盛岡

Morioka is one of the most appealing old castle towns in Japan. Though few buildings actually
date to feudal times, Morioka's temples, old merchant quarter, crafts, and traditions convey a
powerful impression of the town's history. The people of Morioka have a flair for making the
most of their town's provincial charm, turning old storehouses into restaurants and art galleries, and building lively, handsome museums, all of which make Morioka a good place for
people who love old Japan.

### Calendar
**Jan. 14–15: Hadaka Mairi (Naked Pilgrimage).** Males undergo purification and parade
half-naked in subfreezing cold. At Kyōjō-ji on the 14th, Hachiman-gū on the 15th.
**June 15: ** Chagu-Chagu Umakko.** See Calendar, p. 154. The horses are presented
around 9:00 at Sōzen Jinja (*0:25h by taxi out in the countryside*), then form a procession
toward town. Around 13:00, horses and riders pause to rest and cool off in the river near
Nakanohashi before continuing to Hachiman-gū.
**Aug. 16: Funakko Nagashi.** A straw boat bearing the names of recently deceased people is
set afire on the river.
**Sept. 14–16: Hachiman-gū Festival.** Floats; *yabusame* (equestrian archery) on the 15th.

### Getting Around
City buses stop in front of Morioka station and the Bus Center Terminal, which is a 0:15h walk
or 0:05h bus ride from the railway station. **Teiki Kankō (scheduled) bus tours** are an easy
way to visit the outlying attractions (in Japanese only). Apr. 20–Nov. 10, except Mondays.
Inquire at the station Kankō Center.

161

### Central Morioka
**\* Kozukata-jō Ato (Castle Ruin)** 不来方城跡 *0:05h by bus from station to Uchimaru.*
Built in the early 17th C by the 27th Nambu lord, Toshinao, this castle was burned in the wars
that followed the Meiji Restoration. Only moats and walls remain. NW of the castle ruin is
Morioka's most famous tree, the **Ishiwari-zakura** (stone-splitting cherry); the roots of this
300-year-old cherry tree have split a large boulder in two.

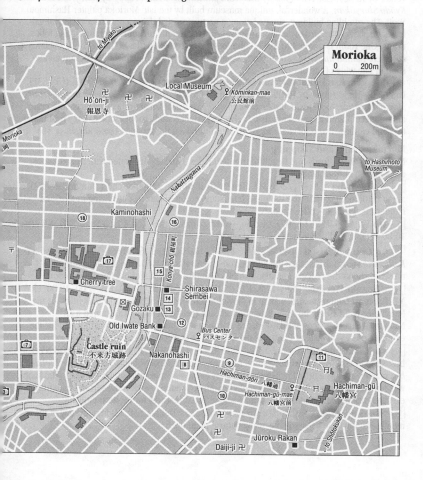

**\*\* Konya-chō** 紺屋町 *Cross the river at Nakanohashi (middle bridge), then turn left at the red-brick, Meiji-era Iwate Bank.* Konya-chō, or "dyers' town," stretches along the river because dyers used the clear, flowing water to rinse the paste-resist out of dyed cloth. There are still several dyeshops here, as well as many other interesting old-fashioned shops, like **Gozaku** (bamboo objects), **Kamasada Kōbō** (iron teakettles), and **Shirasawa Sembei** (handbaked crackers), easy to locate from the delicious aroma of roasting crackers wafting into the street. At the north end of the street are **Sasaki**, a *washi* (Japanese paper) store, and kissaten **Saiensu**, in an old storehouse. **Kaminohashi** (upper bridge), built by Lord Toshinao in 1609, has posts crowned with metal ornaments (ICP), now symbols of Morioka.

## Hachiman-gū Area

**\* Hachiman-gū** 八幡宮 Morioka's main shrine was founded by the 10th-C warrior MINAMOTO no Yoriyoshi (see Hiraizumi History, p. 169). Consecrated to the god of war, it remains the primary shrine for this former castle town.

**\* Jūroku Rakan** 十六羅漢 South of the shrine is a small park in which stand 16 large granite images of *rakan* carved by a priest around 1837–1849 to console victims of a famine. **Daiji-ji** 大慈寺 An Ōbaku Zen sect temple recognizable by its plaster, Chinese-style gate. It stands in a quiet area with many temples. Look for **Daiji-ji Shimizu**, a public spring, rare in Japanese towns today. There are three such wells in Morioka.

**\*\* Shōtokukan (Horse Museum)** 称徳館　茶畑2-15-10 (22-2022). By appointment, except on June 15, when it's open to the general public. The Nambu fief was famous in feudal Japan for breeding fine horses, a tradition celebrated in this outstanding private collection. Horses were not only valuable to warriors, but also sacred to the gods. Displays include horse images and amulets offered at shrines, ornate saddlery, horse toys, and Edo-period manuals on the care and training of horses.

## Northern Morioka

162　**\*\* Hō'on-ji** 報恩寺 (51-4415). Hrs: 9:00–16:00. This important Zen temple has a marvelous group of 500 *rakan* statues, carved between 1731 and 1735. The lacquered wooden images sit on shelves inside the main hall. Among them are Marco Polo and Kublai Khan, proving that anyone can be a disciple of the Buddha.

**\* Kyōdo Shiryō Tenjishitsu (Local Museum)** 郷土資料展示室　(54-5366). Hrs: 9:00–16:30; clsd M, NH, NY. Good exhibits on Morioka's castle town history, local festivals (on video). Adjacent is **Nakamura House** (1861, ICP), a fine merchant's house.

**\*\*\* Hashimoto Bijutsukan (Art Museum)** 橋本美術館　(52-5002). Hrs: 10:00–17:00 (enter by 16:30); clsd NY. *0:30h by bus from station, or 0:10h (Y600) by taxi from the Kyōdo Shiryōkan.* A wonderful, unique museum built by the late Morioka painter Hashimoto Yaoji. The rambling building, situated along a pretty, forested drive, contains a variety of galleries displaying Western-style oil paintings, bronzes, antique furniture, ceramics, and folk crafts. One room is devoted to fine Nambu *tetsubin* (iron teakettles). The top floor contains a complete Nambu *magariya* farmhouse, beautifully restored and furnished. Pleasant coffee shop in one wing of the museum.

**\* Iwate-kenritsu Hakubutsukan (Prefectural Museum)** 岩手県立博物館　(61-2831). Hrs: 9:30–16:30 (enter by 16:00); clsd M (Tu if M a NH), Sept. 1–10, NY. *0:40h by bus from Morioka station to Higashi Matsuzono, then 0:15h walk.* Local archeology, arts, folk crafts, and modern paintings and sculpture. In the "experience study room," one can try traditional toys and clothes. Two relocated *magariya* farmhouses on the grounds (see Villages, p. 56).

## Morioka Crafts and Shopping

Nambu *tetsubin*, sturdy and beautiful iron teakettles, typically decorated with raised knobs, are a classic craft of Japan.

4　**\* Kōgensha** 光原社 (22-2894). Hrs: 9:30–18:00. On Zaimoku-chō ("lumber street"), about 0:10h on foot from the station. A handsome group of shops specializing in Morioka handcrafts. Pleasant coffee shop.

5　**Ito Yū** 絲木綿 (51-5867). Clsd Su, 1st day of the month (2nd if 1st a Su or NH), NY. Hrs: 10:00–19:00. Traditional textiles.

6　**\*\* Ono Sensaisho** 小野染彩所　材木町10-16 (52-4116). Hrs: 8:30–18:00; clsd NY. *Katazome* stencil dyers since the Edo period (see Crafts, p. 105). The second-floor minimuseum shows the process and also exhibits beautiful examples of old Nambu *katazome*.

8　**\* Suzuki Morihisa** 鈴木盛久工房　南大通1-6-7 (22-3809). Hrs: 9:00–18:00; clsd NY. The most famous *tetsubin* shop in Morioka, founded in 1625 to make teakettles for the Nambu lords. In 1948, the 13th-generation master (now deceased) was named a Living National Treasure. Prices at this store are astronomical, but it's still well worth a visit for the exquisite pieces on display. Photos of the late master at work hang on the walls.

13　**\*\* Kamasada Kōbō** 釜定工房　紺屋町2-5 (22-3911). Hrs: 8:00–18:00; clsd NY. The best shop to visit to learn about Nambu *tetsubin*. Master Miya Nobuho, accomplished *tetsubin* master, speaks a little English and is happy to answer questions about his craft. The shop was founded a century ago by his grandfather. Miya Nobuho's work ranges from beautifully executed traditional designs to innovative and affordable wares for modern daily life.

14　**Sōshi-dō** 草紫堂　紺屋町2-15 (22-6668). Hrs: 9:00–17:30; clsd Su, 1st day of the month, NY. Intricate tie-dyed silks using natural plant dyes.

15 **Tomoe Some Kōjō** 巴染工場 (22-5334). Hrs: 9:00–17:00; clsd Su, NH, NY, mid-Aug., Sept. 14–16. Hand-dyed festival *happi* coats, kerchiefs, and other custom work.

\* **Iwachū Casting Works** 岩鋳鉄器館(35-2501). Hrs: 8:00–17:30, daily; restaurant, 11:00–21:00. *3.5km SE of station*. Handsome contemporary showroom for iron crafts. Watch artisans at work.

\* **Morioka Tezukuri Mura** 盛岡手作り村(89-2201). Hrs: 9:00–17:30; Dec.–Mar. 9:00–17:00; clsd NY. *0:30h from station by Tsunagi Onsen-yuki bus*. Lavish new center for promoting and selling regional crafts—cast iron, textiles, baskets, toys, ceramics. Lessons and demonstrations. Well designed as such places go, it's not a bad rainy-day option.

## Morioka Dining

The famous local "dish" is *wanko soba*: numerous small portions of buckwheat noodles served with a variety of accompaniments like raw tuna, salmon roe, wild ferns, and mushrooms, and a sweet sauce of walnuts and miso. Eating contests involve downing the little servings of *soba*, keeping count with a box of matches.

① **Faisan** フェザン  The basement of the station department store has dozens of restaurants for a wide range of cuisines, including several serving local dishes. Enter by 21:00.

⑨ \*\* **Nambu Robata** 南部炉ばた  八幡町番屋向 (22-5082). Hrs: 17:00–22:00. Fabulous farmhouse interior and seasonal country cuisine served on lacquered trays. Fixed course, Y2700. Wash it down with *nigori-zake*, a milky white country saké. The proprietor does each bill in vigorous calligraphy ("If you can read it, you don't have to pay—and if you can't it's twice as much!").

⑩ \*\* **Shiruichi** しる一 (22-7333). Hrs: 11:00–17:00; clsd Su, mid-Aug., NY. A plain shop with dark, country-style *soba*.

⑫ \* **Azumaya** 東家  中ノ橋通1丁目 (22-2252). Hrs: 11:00–20:00; clsd 1st and 3rd Tu, NY. An old *soba* shop with a cheery folkcraft interior. *Wanko Soba*, Y2000–3500, comes with an English guide. Other *soba* dishes, Y400–800. Station branch (22-2233), Hrs: 11:00–20:00, clsd 1st and 3rd Tu, NY.

⑯ \* **Saiensu** 彩園子  上ノ橋通1-48  (53-4646). Hrs: 10:00–19:00; clsd Su, NY, mid-Aug. Gallery and coffee shop in a renovated *kura*. Quiet, restful, spacious. Serves light meals.

⑱ \* **Bazoku** 馬賊  本町通2-9-28 (52-3105). Hrs: 12:00–15:00, 17:00–22:30 (last order 22:00); clsd Su, NY. Chinese-style natural foods in an antique-filled Japanese setting. Lunch Y1500; dinner Y3500–4000. By reservation.

## Morioka Lodgings (TEL 0196)

② \* **Metropolitan Morioka** メトロポリタン盛岡(25-1211). 1-44 Ekimae-dōri, Morioka-shi, Iwate-ken. Good city hotel adjoining Morioka station. S Y7000, Tw Y14,000.

③ **Taishōkan** 大正館(22-4436). Osawa Kawahara 2-5-30. *0:05h walk from station*. Old wooden ryokan/minshuku. Economical Inn Group member. Y5000 w/meals.

⑦ \* **Hotel Royal Morioka** ホテルロイヤル盛岡  (53-1331). Fax 53-3330. 1-11-11 Saien. An established city hotel. S Y6800–8400, Tw Y13,600.

⑪ **Sakura Kaikan** さくら会館  八幡町13-22 (51-8411). 13-12 Hachiman-chō. Wedding hall by Hachiman shrine, with inexpensive ryokan-style lodgings. Y6000 w/meals.

⑰ **Kita Hotel (Hotel du Nord)** 北ホテル  (25-2711). 17-45 Uchimaru. Business hotel, good location. S Y6000＋, Tw Y9000＋.

⑲ **Morioka YH** 盛岡YH  高松1-9-41 (62-2220). 1-9-41 Takamatsu.

163

# The Making of a Nambu Tetsubin

*Tetsubin* molds consist of two outer pieces that fit together around a single inner piece. An even space is left between the inner and outer molds; designs—raised knobs, a spray of pine branches—are carved by hand in the walls of the outer molds, which can be reused. The inner mold, broken after one casting, is of soft, porous clay, which absorbs and vents the hot gases escaping the molten iron.

Iron is melted at 1400°C and poured from long-handled ladles into the molds. The sheer physical violence of the encounter between molten iron, air, and the surface of the mold can shatter work that took weeks to create in a few seconds.

The successfully cast *tetsubin* is filed, tempered, and burnished with lacquer and tooth-black, a mixture of brown-rust, vinegar, and green tea, which in premodern times married women used to blacken their teeth. When water is boiled in a *tetsubin*, a white mineral fuzz builds up on the inner walls, which further protects the iron and, it is said, purifies and sweetens even the worst city tap water.

The most prized *tetsubin*, such as the stunning, silvery kettles at the Hashimoto Museum, were made of sand-iron panned from river beds. Also the raw material of the finest swords, sand-iron is a kind of "phantom metal" that is said to have extraordinary qualities. No one mines iron this way anymore, so sand-iron kettles, made from hoarded material, are extremely expensive.

# TŌHOKU II:W. WEST FROM MORIOKA

**Main Attraction:** Kakunodate(W2)

## W1 TAZAWA-KO (LAKE) 田沢湖

*0:40h by JR Tazawa line limited express from Morioka.* The shore of this pretty crater lake, the deepest in Japan, is being built up into a resort, but it still retains a rural flavor from the numerous surrounding farms (many are minshuku). The isolated inns around Nyūtō Onsen, deep in the mountains, are among the best rustic spas in Japan. Take the Nyūtō Onsen buses from Tazawa-ko. The inns will pick up guests who arrange for it in advance, though in fine weather the walks are pleasant. Long-term guests and budget travelers bring their own food and towels; the inns provide simpler rooms for under Y1500, with communal kitchens. Mixed and segregated baths.

** # **Tsurunoyu Onsen** 鶴ノ湯温泉 (0187-46-2814). Tazawako-machi, Senboku-gun, Akita-ken. *If you are being met, get off at Kōgen Onsen. If you prefer to walk, get off at Tsurunoyu-guchi (0:40h to the inn).* This intimate, rustic retreat began serving the daimyo of Kakunodate 350 years ago. A special pavilion for the lord once stood behind the present ryokan wing. The thatched long house is 100 years old and has an *irori* room where you can dine on a one-pot meal cooked over an open fire (arrange in advance). Wooden bathhouses and *rotemburo* offer milky white and "black" waters. Y2000 w/o meals, or Y6,500–12,000 in the ryokan part, with excellent meals.

** **Kuroyu Onsen** 黒湯温泉 (0187-46-2214). Address as above. The road to Kuroyu is paved and starts from Tazawa-ko Kōgen Kokumin Kyūkamura. With numerous thatched-roof lodgings and bathhouses sprawled out along a slope, Kuroyu is almost a village in itself. Hot springs bubble up at a nearby pool and run in streams and wooden gutters along the paths. There are indoor and outdoor baths and hot waterfalls to massage tired backs. The bungalow standing off by itself was built for the emperor's uncle and is now preserved as a memento. Y1500 w/o futon or meals, Y2100 w/futon only, from Y7500–8500 w/meals. Open June 1–Nov. 5.

164

### Exploring Hachimantai

# A mountainous region served by buses from Tazawa-ko. Long bus rides through mildly scenic areas. Onsen fans might enjoy the following: **Goshogake Onsen**, with an unusual steam bath heated by the earth (Y1000 for 6:00h, from Y10,000 for overnight stay w/meals). **Tamagawa Onsen**, a sprawling complex of homely buildings, is a classic Tōhoku rehabilitational onsen: Lots of people, young, old, male and female, seriously soak away ailments or fatigue. This is one of the few places left in Japan where even young women unabashedly take dips in the nonsegregated baths.

## W2 ** KAKUNODATE 角館

*0:55h by JR Tazawa line limited express from Morioka, or 0:50h by limited express from Akita (W3). Regular trains take slightly longer. The scenery through the mountains is pretty.* Kakunodate has one of the loveliest samurai neighborhoods left in Japan. The samurai quarter, Uchimachi (inner town) stands in a lush grove. Dark wood fences and samurai gates enclose a half-dozen original houses and their gardens. The idyllic atmosphere is a world apart from the cramped, bustling Tomachi (outer town), still very much a merchant quarter. For the poorer samurai, however, life was hard; many eked out a living by making objects of polished cherry bark. The unusually handsome craft is now famous throughout Japan. Kakunodate's **cherry trees** are renowned for their beauty as well as their bark, especially the weeping cherries brought from Kyoto by Kakunodate's lords, the **Ashina**, who were descended from Kyoto aristocrats; 153 of these ancient cherry trees, and thousands more along the river, enfold the town in clouds of pink from late April through early May.

### Calendar

**Sept. 7–9:** * **Oyama-bayashi.** A giant mountain-shaped float dominates activities. Smaller floats are rammed against each other in mock battles. Evening of the 8th and night of the 9th are said to be best for action.

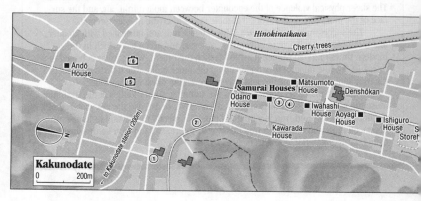

## Getting Around

Rent-a-cycles at the station, but Kakunodate is compact enough to see on foot. The sights can be seen in half a day, leaving time to browse or head for rustic spas at Tazawa-ko (W1).

## Kakunodate Sights

**\*\*\* Samurai Houses (Buke-Yashiki)** 武家屋敷 The Kakunodate samurai dwellings line the broad, central avenue leading to the hilltop castle of Lord Ashina. In the event of an attack, they provided a major line of defense. The street isn't perfect—many houses preserve only their outer walls and gates—but it remains highly evocative. Five original houses are open to the public, usually 9:00–17:00 (enter by 16:30), Apr.–Nov., and 9:00–16:30, Dec.–Mar. At the head of the avenue is the site of the lord's mansion, from which only a mud-walled storehouse remains. Beyond is **Furushiroyama Kōen**, the old castle park, which offers a view of Kakunodate.

> **Odano House** 小田野家 (18th–19th C). Only the quiet garden is open to visitors. This one is done in a natural style with dwarf bamboo, shrubs, and boulders amid a stand of ancient shade trees.
>
> **Kawarada House** 河原田家 (18th–19th C). This one has a handsome black *kura* in the rear, and interesting boulder arrangements in the front garden. Interiors can be viewed only from outside. Adjoins a *kura* displaying a hodgepodge of samurai gear.
>
> **Iwahashi House** 岩橋家 This house is usually open on all sides, so it's easy to appreciate the modest standard of living of its middle-ranking samurai residents.
>
> ◆ **Denshōkan** 伝承館 (54-1700). In winter clsd Th. A hard-to-miss structure of red brick with white neo-colonial trim and a metal roof shaped like a traditional thatched roof. Exhibits *kabazaiku* alongside the tools used to make them, as well as old folk crafts and a roomful of Ashina family belongings bearing their fan-shaped family crest, including silks, lacquerware, and art from Kakunodate's days as a "Little Kyoto."
>
> **Matsumoto House** 松本家 This house, off on a side street, is the much more modest home of a low-ranking samurai.
>
> ◆ **Aoyagi House** 青柳家 Built in 1860, this is the most extensive of the houses, with numerous outbuildings. The admission fee includes three mini-museums (finer things, folk items, and "high-collar" Western objects).
>
> **Ishiguro House** 石黒家 This high-ranking retainer's house has a magnificent thatched roof and lovely garden.

**\* Andō House** 安藤醸造元 (53-2008). Best to call in advance; this brewer of saké, miso, and soy sauce, located in Kakunodate's merchant quarter, has been doing a thriving business for a hundred years. Evidence of its prosperity shows in every gleaming wooden beam, the glossy black lacquer on the fermentation *kura*, the small courtyard, and the gilt *fusuma* inside a red-brick Meiji-period *kura*, shown on request.

## Kakunodate Crafts

*Kabazaiku* are items fashioned from the mottled bark of the wild cherry and painstakingly polished to a satiny finish. Once the exclusive trade of poor samurai, it is now made and sold all over town. A good-quality tea caddy is cherry bark inside and out. Cheaper, but still attractive, are those made of bark glued on a tin base. Another charming Kakunodate craft is *itayazaiku*, an example of a folk toy at its simple best; a cylinder of maple is split radially, and each wedge is carved to suggest a fox. Reassembled, they form a nose-to-nose congress of foxes.

## Kakunodate Dining and Lodgings (TEL 0187)

Try *iburi-zuke*, a crunchy, smoked radish pickle. *Sanazura* is wild-grape jelly, pressed between bamboo bark.

① **Kakunodate Club** 角館クラブ 竹原町 (54-3166). Hrs: 12:00–20:00. By reservation. Local cuisine in an old house with an open hearth. From Y1500.

② **Shōji** 東海林 岩瀬花場下 (54-2022). Hrs: 12:00–21:00; clsd 1st and 3rd Su, NY, mid-Aug. Local cuisine (river fish, *sansai*). Lunch from Y3000, dinner from Y5000. By reservation.

③ **Sakura no Sato** 桜の里 (54-2527). Hrs: 9:00–17:00, clsd Dec.–Mar. Pleasant teahouse inside a renovated *kura*. Light *bentō* lunches. Inexpensive.

④ **Kosen-dō** 古泉洞 (53-2902). Hrs: 8:30–17:00, clsd Dec.–Mar. *Soba*. Inexpensive.

⑤ **\* Ishikawa Ryokan** 石川旅館 (54-2030). 32 Iwase-chō, Kakunodate-machi, Senboku-gun, Akita-ken. The building is new but the family that runs this pleasant, unpretentious inn has been in business for ten generations. Warm service, wonderful food. Y8–17000.

⑥ **Minshuku Hyakusui-en** 民宿百穂苑 (55-5715). Shimonaka-machi. A minshuku with an atmospheric *irori* hearth, mini-museum, and local cuisine. Y5500+.

## ŌMAGARI 大曲

*1:10h from Morioka by JR Tazawa line express, or 0:40h from Akita. 0:20h to Yokote by JR Ōu line express; continues to Yamagata (TŌHOKU IV:W2).*

## Calendar

**Feb. 3rd Sa and Su: \* Kamakura.** Yokote. Famous but rather tame festival in which children build snow houses, called *kamakura*. They invite their friends and make offerings to the water kami to ensure the safety of crops.

**Feb. 16–17:** * **Bonten.** Yokote. Colorfully bedecked poles, called *bonten*, are twirled violently as people compete to make their offering to the shrine first; a prayer for a good harvest. At Ōmagari, *bonten* are ferried across a river.

**Aug. 16–18:** * # **Nishimonai Bon-Odori.** (*Ōu line to Yuzawa, then bus to Nishimonai*). Unusual Bon dances by dancers in black hoods. Hrs: 20:00–23:00.

## W3 AKITA 秋田

*1:50h by JR Tazawa line express from Morioka.* The castle town of the Satake, Akita is now a major city on the Japan Sea coast. The **Akita-kenritsu Hakubutsukan** 秋田県立博物館 (Prefectural Museum) is a 0:15h walk from Oiwake station. (Hrs: 9:30–16:30; clsd Th. Nov.– Mar. 9:30–16:00.) The grounds contain the **Nara House** (ICP), a magnificent farmhouse.

### Calendar
**Aug. 4–7:** ** **Kantō Matsuri.** See Calendar, p. 154.

### Akita Dining and Lodgings (TEL 0188)
Akita cuisine features two warming stockpot dishes for those cold winters: *Kiritampo* is made of chicken broth, vegetables, and chunks of rice that have been partially pounded and roasted on sticks over charcoal. *Shottsuru-nabe* is made from a stock of *hata-hata*, a small, flavorful Japan Sea fish.

* **Suginoya** 杉のや 中通2丁目 (35-5111). Hrs: 11:00–21:00, clsd Dec. 31, Jan. 1, Aug. 13. *0:05h walk from station. Wappa-meshi* (rice and fish or vegetables cooked in bentwood steamers), *kiritampo*, *shottsuru-nabe*. Moderate.

**Akita Castle Hotel** 秋田キャッスルホテル (34-1141). Fax 34-5588. 1-3-5 Naka-dōri, Akita-shi, Akita-ken. S Y8–10,000, Tw Y15–17,000.

**Akita New Grand Hotel** 秋田ニューグランド (34-5211). Fax 34-5365. 5-2-1. Naka-dōri. S Y6–8000 Tw Y11–20,000.

**Joshi-tei** 如斯亭 旭川南町2-73 (34-5641). 2-73 Asahikawa Minami-chō. A ryokan that was the villa of the Satake family. Has an Enshū-style garden. Y8500/person.

**Akita Park Hotel** 秋田パークホテル (62-1515). 4-5-10 Sannō. Business hotel. S Y5600, Tw Y9500.

## # OGA HANTŌ (PENINSULA) 男鹿半島
*Take the Oga line to Oga, from Akita (1:00h) or Oiwake (0:45h) both on the Ōu line. From Oga station, bus to Monzen (0:35h) or to Oga Onsen (0:55h).* Few people visit this hilly green peninsula, best known for its New Year's Eve rite, Namahage (see Calendar, below). Most of the time, Oga is quiet, mildly scenic, with some pleasant little fishing villages and eroded cliffs. The most developed part is around **Oga Onsen.** The bus continues to the Suizokukan (aquarium), from where sightseeing boats set out for a cruise along the scenic coast, arriving in **Monzen**, a rather pretty fishing village.

### Calendar
**Feb. 13–15: Namahage.** A version for tourists, at Shinzan Jinja in Oga-shi (town).
**Dec. 31:** ** # **Namahage.** See Calendar, p. 154. There is a tourist's version, but to see the real festival, you'll have to arrange to stay in someone's home, perhaps a minshuku.

### Oga Lodgings (TEL 0185)
**Oga Sakurajima-sō** 男鹿桜島荘 (37-2311). 1-466 Nakadai, Togakamo, Oga-shi. Hot-spring resort run by the prefecture; on a scenic outcropping. Y8600–13,000 w/meals.

### Easy Access To:
** **Hirosaki** (TŌHOKU I:W2): *2:10h by JR Ōu line limited express from Akita.*
* **Sakata** (TŌHOKU IV:W5): *1:30h by JR Uetsu line limited express.*

# TŌHOKU II:E. EAST FROM MORIOKA

## E1 HANAMAKI ONSEN 花巻温泉
*0:40h from Morioka by JR Tōhoku line, or by Shinkansen to Shin-Hanamaki station.* A famous spa, gateway to the Tōno basin.

### Hanamaki Lodgings (TEL 0198)
**Ryokan Kashō-en** 佳松園 (27-2111). Hanamaki Onsen, Hanamaki-shi, Iwate-ken. An expensive ryokan built in 1965; like a Sukiya-style country club. Y20–50,000 w/meals.
**Kikusui-kan** 菊水館 大沢温泉 (25-2233). At Ōsawa Onsen (*0:20h by bus or taxi from Hanamaki station*). A plain, old-fashioned ryokan known for its open-air riverside bath. Y4500–8500 w/ meals.

## E2 * TŌNO 遠野
*1:40h by direct express train from Morioka; or 0:50–1:00h by express or local train from Hanamaki or Shin-Hanamaki. From Kitakami, 1:10h by bus (2 per day).* The name Tōno is indelibly linked to the *Tōno Monogatari* (Legends of Tōno), a collection of tales that was recorded in writing in 1910 and became a classic work of folk literature—a *Grimm's Fairy Tales* of Japan. These strange legends, often fragmentary and frightening, laden with sexual or

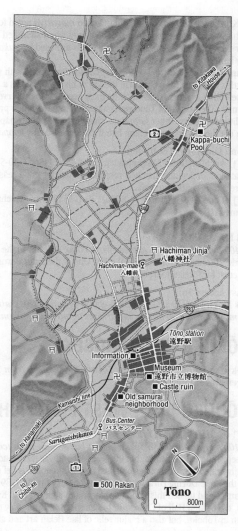

Kappa-buchi
Pool

Hachiman Jinja
八幡神社

Hachiman-mae
八幡前

Tōno station
遠野駅

Information

Museum
■ 遠野市立博物館

Castle ruin

Old samurai
neighborhood

Bus Center
バスセンター

Kamaishi line

Sarugaishikawa

to Hanamaki

to Kippkawa
House

to
Chiba-ke

■ 500 Rakan

**Tōno**

0 ———— 800m

occult themes, resurrect the spiritual life of old rural Japan. But the rustic charm one might expect to find in Tōno is rapidly vanishing. Visitors should read the excellent Ronald Morse translation, *The Legends of Tōno* (published by the Japan Foundation; sold in major Tokyo and Kyoto bookstores, and at the Tōno museum). In the Edo period, Tōno produced fine horses, one of the Nambu fief's most important commodities. The Nambu *magariya*, L-shaped farmhouses, were distinctive; the stables were attached at right angles to the family house. There are still a few scattered about Tōno (see Villages, p. 56).

**Calendar**
**July 31–Aug. 1: \* # Hayachine Jinja Matsuri.** Ōhazama-machi (*from Shin-Hanamaki, take Tozan express bus, 2 per day*). Performances of a simple, ancient style of Kagura and Yamabushi Kagura on the evening of the 31st and all day on the 1st.
**Sept. 14–15: \*\* Hachiman Jinja Saiten.** See Calendar, p. 155.

**Getting Around**
Unfortunately, it is difficult to see much or get very far on foot or public buses. Rent-a-cycles are available near the station; Y830 a day. A taxi is about Y3200 per hour.

**Tōno Sights**
**\*\*\* Tōno-shiritsu Hakubutsukan (Museum)** 遠野市立博物館 (2-2340). Hrs: 9:00–17:00 (enter by 16:30); clsd end of the month. Nov.–Mar. clsd M. *0:05h walk from station.* An excellent museum with displays of local folk objects, crafts, a video library on local customs and festivals, and slide presentations of two famous Tōno legends, "Oshirasama" and "Kappa no Okurimono."
**\*\* Gohyaku (500) Rakan** 五百羅漢 *0:15h on foot from Bus Center.* In 1782, a priest of Daiji-ji carved these *rakan* out of natural boulders in this peaceful ravine to console the victims of a great famine.
**\*\*\* Chiba-ke** 千葉家 Hrs: 8:00–17:00. *5 km from Tōno station.* A splendid, 200-year-old *magariya* that once belonged to a local strongman. Unlike ordinary farmhouses, it is built up on stone fortifications and commands a good view of the valley below.

**\* Kitakawa-ke** 北川家 An old thatched *magariya* noted for its altar to the folk deity, Oshirasama, represented by a rough stick of wood swaddled in bright cloths, with a simply carved head of a girl or a horse. The sticks are used by *itako* (blind shamanesses) to invoke the kami (see Osore-zan, p. 159).

**Kappa-buchi Pool** カッパ淵 A *kappa* is a river sprite with scaly skin, webbed feet, and a turtle's carapace for a back. On the top of his head, he has a saucer-shaped indentation resembling a friar's pate, which he must keep wet to preserve his supernatural strength. Occasionally, the women of Tōno were supposed to have gotten pregnant by *kappa* and given birth to little monsters. Other *kappa* mischief includes pulling hapless victims into rivers and tearing out their livers by reaching into their anuses. Many *kappa* are supposed to live in this pool.

### Tōno Lodgings (TEL 01986)

[1] **\*\* Minshuku Magariya** 民宿曲り家 (2-4564). 30-58-3 Niizato, Ayaori-chō, Tōno-shi, Iwate-ken. A genuine thatched-roof *magariya*; one good reason for visiting Tōno is to stay here. From Y6500 w/meals.

[2] **Tōno YH** 遠野YH (2-8736). 39-1, 13 Chiwari, Tsuchibuchi, Tsuchibuchi-chō. Small, homey YH.

### E3 KAMAISHI 釜石

*0:40h by Kamaishi line express from Tōno.* Gateway to the Rikuchū Kaigan (Coast) National Park, 200 km of eroded coastal cliffs. One of the natural wonders of Tōhoku, but of limited interest for foreign tourists.

**Easy Access To:**
**\*\* Morioka** (TŌHOKU II): *2:30–3:00h by infrequent train from Miyako, north of Kamaishi; or 2:10h by bus, departures about once an hour.*

# TŌHOKU III. ICHINOSEKI

**Tokyo to Ichinoseki:** *2:35h by Tōhoku Shinkansen from Tokyo.*
**Prefecture:** Iwate

# TŌHOKU III:W. WEST FROM ICHINOSEKI

## W1 \*\* HIRAIZUMI 平泉

*0:10h by train or 0:25h by a frequent bus service from Ichinoseki.* Hiraizumi today is a sleepy little country town, but 900 years ago it was the proud capital of the Northern Fujiwara, a clan that had established a semiautonomous fief and grown rich on the gold found in the area. During Hiraizumi's century of glory (1090–1189), the Fujiwara built palaces and temples and turned this Tōhoku outpost into a city to rival Kyoto itself. Today, only the Konjiki-dō, the Golden Hall of Chūson-ji, has survived. It is not only the pre-eminent cultural attraction in Tōhoku, but also a major relic of late Heian art and architecture.

### Calendar

**Jan. 20: \* Hatsuka Yasai.** Mōtsū-ji. Ancient Ennen no Mai, Dengaku, Noh-type performances (see Matsuri, p. 74; Kyoto, p. 357). Spectators hurl insults; the worse they are, the better the year's fortune. Also Noh at Chūson-ji.

**Apr. 22: Hitaka Hibuse Matsuri.** Mizusawa (*0:17h by local train from Hiraizumi*). Originated 300 years ago when the lord commanded a festival be held to ward off fires. Showy floats carry musical ensembles of prettily dressed little girls.

**May 1–5: \* Fujiwara Spring Festival.** Chūson-ji. May 2, folk performing arts; May 3, a parade reenacts Yoshitsune's escape to Hiraizumi; May 4, Noh and Kojitsu-shiki at Chūson-ji and Ennen no Mai at Mōtsū-ji; May 5, Noh at Chūson-ji.

**Aug. 14: \* Noh.** Chūson-ji.

**Nov. 1–3: \* Fujiwara Fall Festival.** Nov. 2, folk theater at Mōtsū-ji; Nov. 3, Noh and Shiki Sanban at Chūson-ji, and Ennen no Mai at Mōtsū-ji.

### Getting Around

Rent-a-cycle at Hiraizumi station. Bus tours cover Chūson-ji, Mōtsū-ji, Gembikei (a scenic gorge), and Takkoku no Iwaya (a cliffside temple); 3:20h, Y2400, departures daily at 10:00, 11:00, 12:00, and 13:00. Late Nov.–early Mar. at 11:00 only.

### Hiraizumi Sights

**\*\*\* Chūson-ji** 中尊寺 (46-2111). Hrs: 8:00–17:00. Nov.–Mar. 8:30–16:30. *0:20h on foot or 0:05h by bus from station.* Chūson-ji was founded around 850, and Fujiwara no Kiyohira restored it in the 12th C, turning it into the greatest monastery in Tōhoku. After the fall of the Fujiwara, a great fire in 1337 claimed all the remaining buildings except the Konjiki-dō and the Kyōzō (sutra library). From the road, a long approach climbs through a forest of ancient cryptomeria. Along the way is the **Benkei-dō** chapel and a thatched teahouse where BASHŌ is said to have rested, perhaps to compose his famous verse:

> The summer grass
> 'Tis all that's left
> Of ancient warriors' dreams.

# Hiraizumi History: Yoshitsune and the Northern Fujiwara

**Priest Ennin**    (794–864) Saichō's disciple and third abbot of the Tendai sect headquarters at Mt. Hiei, Ennin studied in Tang China from 838 to 847. He founded most of Tōhoku's famous temples, including Mōtsū-ji and Chūson-ji at Hiraizumi.

**The Minamoto**    Yoshiie (1039–1106), who crushed a rebellious Tōhoku lord, acquired a reputation as the most formidable warrior in the land. His descendant Yoritomo would found Japan's first military government at Kamakura, near the clan's traditional stronghold in eastern Japan.

**The Northern Fujiwara**    A warrior clan that ruled northern Tōhoku in the 11th and 12th C. Successive leaders of the clan were Kiyohira, Motohira, Hidehira, and Yasuhira. Hiraizumi was their capital.

**Yoshitsune**    (1159–1189) Japan's foremost tragic hero. Yoshitsune led the Minamoto to victory over the Taira clan, but was persecuted by his jealous brother, the shogun Yoritomo, and forced to flee to Hiraizumi, where he met his end.

To the courtiers of classical Kyoto, eastern Japan was a wilderness of uncivilized tribes, which, having been subdued by force of arms, was left in the charge of warrior clans. To this day, there is a clear division between the customs and even the speech of eastern and western Japan; in classical times, a court gentleman would do anything to avoid a career in the eastern provinces.

Kyoto's haughty nobles would have been surprised to learn that the disdained eastern warriors, not content to remain mere custodians of court lands, would come to rule Japan, first from Kamakura and later from Edo (Tokyo). Had the nobles been less complacent, they might have been alerted by events in their own time. The most startling, surely, was the rise in the eleventh century of a Tōhoku warrior clan that called itself the **Northern Fujiwara** and carved out a vast domain—virtually an autonomous kingdom—with its own splendid capital, Hiraizumi, a rival to Kyoto itself. Indeed, the **Konjiki-dō**, the golden mortuary chapel of Hiraizumi's lords, was without peer. It was only the ascendancy of another eastern clan, the Minamoto, that led to Hiraizumi's downfall. The Konjiki-dō, miraculously intact, remains as an eloquent testament to the impermanence of glory.

The first recorded incursion against the Emishi—"eastern barbarians" identified by some scholars with the Ainu (see Hokkaidō, p. 146)—is the stuff of legend. In the early centuries A.D., Emperor Keiko was alarmed to learn that his son, subsequently known as **Yamato Takeru** (The Yamato Brave), had savagely killed his twin brother in a privy. Setting an oft-repeated precedent, Keiko decided that his unruly offspring would better serve the state by killing Emishi instead. Yamato Takeru was sent east to wrestle with various "demons"—read "tribes"—before dying a lonely hero's death.

By the Nara period, better-organized expeditions were taking place. Large garrisons were stationed at fortresses such as Taga-jō (TŌHOKU IV:E) to defend the northern boundary of Yamato lands. This was no simple task; Taga-jō, although well staffed and equipped, was sacked by local tribes in 776 and had to be rebuilt. By the beginning of the ninth century after the campaigns of **Sakanoue no Tamuramaro**, tribal resistance was finally quelled. Tamuramaro became the first to receive the title *Sei-i Tai Shogun*, "barbarian-quelling generalissimo."

In the Heian period, excess imperial offspring were assigned to one of two large clans, the TAIRA or the MINAMOTO, and, following Yamato Takeru's example, sent off to the provinces. The Taira warriors sent to govern in the east eventually proved more troublesome than the barbarians; they quarreled with the government and each other, and did not pay their taxes. In the eleventh century, **Minamoto no Yoriyoshi** and his son **Yoshiie** were sent to chastise them. Yoshiie, who succeeded his father, proved so successful that landholders around the country begged to commit their lands to his protection, foremost among them the very Taira families he had been sent to punish. He was known as Hachiman Tarō (The War God's First Born), partly because his father had dedicated several shrines to the god Hachiman—including the famous Tsurugaoka Hachiman-gū at Kamakura—on his way to subdue Tōhoku in 1063. The descendants of Yoshiie would become the great eastern warrior families of the Middle Ages: the ASHIKAGA, Hosokawa, Satake, and TOKUGAWA. From Kamakura, Kyoto, and finally Edo, Yoshiie's heirs would rule under Tamuramaro's

169

title, *Sei-i Tai Shogun*, which by their time was just a name for the de facto ruler of the country: there were no barbarians left to quell. Court loyalists, who resented the loss of the court's political power, took to calling the shogun himself an "eastern barbarian"—but never to his face.

One eastern warrior at whom the courtiers would not have sneered was **Fujiwara no Kiyohira**. Though his father was killed by Yoriyoshi's forces, Kiyohira allied himself with Yoriyoshi's son, Yoshiie. After the Tōhoku campaigns were over, Yoshiie and his descendants concentrated their energies on the Kantō region and at the Kyoto court. Kiyohira was left to rule northern Tōhoku. He kept enlarging his territory until he was the greatest landholder in Japan. Kiyohira's Fujiwara name was probably an invention of one of his ancestors; nevertheless, the proud FUJIWARA aristocrats of the Kyoto court acknowledged Kiyohira's line as a branch of the family, mainly because of his considerable power but also because of his cultural accomplishments.

Hiraizumi, Kiyohira's new capital, began as a military outpost in the eighth century. In the ninth century, the priest **Ennin** came to Hiraizumi, where he founded **Mōtsū-ji** and **Chūson-ji** to assuage the souls of the warriors who died subduing the northern provinces. Ennin founded many other famous temples in northern Japan, including Rinnō-ji at Nikkō, Yamadera, Zuigan-ji at Matsushima, and the temple on Osore-zan. (At many of these, he introduced festivals in honor of the god Madarajin, and a ritual called Ennen no Mai; see Matsuri, p. 74.)

Hiraizumi's setting, similar to Kyoto's, led Kiyohira to build his capital there in 1094. Determined to make it worthy of his Fujiwara name, Kiyohira modeled the street plan on the imperial city and re-created the elegance of the capital in this remote outback. He rebuilt Chūson-ji, providing it with over forty halls and pagodas. The most exquisite was the Konjiki-dō, or Golden Hall. Heavily influenced by the Amidist beliefs then fashionable in the capital, Kiyohira sought, like the Kyoto aristocrats, to evoke Amida's Paradise in a personal worship hall (see Buddhism, p. 37). It is the only Amida Hall today that retains its lavish ornamentation. Because most of Japan's gold came from Kiyohira's province, he could well afford to gild the entire interior. Even the famous Byōdō-in, outside Kyoto, was no match for it. Kiyohira and his successors were buried in the Golden Hall, directly under the altar, as if to ensure that they would surpass the Kyoto Fujiwara in the next world as well.

Kiyohira's son **Motohira** (d. 1157) restored nearby Mōtsū-ji, building on its grounds a paradise garden with an Amida Hall modeled closely on the Byōdō-in; only the garden and foundation stones remain today. Motohira's son **Hidehira** (1096–1187) took his family's fascination for the capital too far, however; by sheltering a fugitive from Kyoto, he and his son **Yasuhira** (d. 1189) became enmeshed in a drama that proved the clan's undoing.

The young man who sought refuge in Hiraizumi was YOSHITSUNE, the great hero of the Genpei Wars. His father, Minamoto no Yoshitomo, had been killed by Taira forces, but young Yoshitsune's life was spared on condition that he become a priest at Kurama Temple. Legend has it that Yoshitsune learned the arts of military strategy from a *tengu*, a kind of superman, on Mt. Kurama. In his teens Yoshitsune, determined to avenge his father's death, fled to Hiraizumi and sought asylum from Hidehira, who took the youth in and became a father to him. In 1180, Yoshitsune heard that his half-brother YORITOMO had mustered an army against the Taira and went to join him. Yoshitsune proved a brilliant commander, driving the Taira across the Inland Sea, and finally defeating them at Dan no Ura in 1185. The victorious Yoshitsune returned to Kyoto, where he charmed the court; retired emperor Go-Shirakawa bestowed upon him the court rank of *hōgan* (Lieutenant of the Imperial Police), an exalted title for a mere warrior.

Yoritomo, however, accused Yoshitsune of defying orders forbidding retainers to accept court ranks without his approval. Yoritomo also seems to have been jealous of Yoshitsune (see Kamakura History, p. 261). Although born to a woman of much lower rank than Yoritomo's mother, Yoshitsune was successful both in battle and at court in a way the cold and calculating Yoritomo could never be. To posterity, the spartan and successful Yoritomo is a villain, whereas Yoshitsune is the ideal hero, a gallant warrior who is ultimately done in by his lack of guile (see Drama, p. 81).

Yoshitsune attempted to profess his loyalty at Kamakura, but was coldly rebuffed: he was not even allowed into the city. Desperate, he plotted a rebellion but could not gather a sufficient following. Finally, with the help of his faithful retainer, the giant **Benkei**, he fled, following the secret trails of the *yamabushi*, first to the hills of Yoshino (Kinki, p. 2S13), then to his childhood refuge of Hiraizumi, which alone lay outside Yoritomo's control. This afforded Yoritomo the perfect excuse to send an army against the Northern Fujiwara, who were the last obstacle to his hegemony.

In 1187, only a few months after Yoshitsune's arrival, Hidehira died. On his deathbed Hidehira made his heir Yasuhira vow to protect Yoshitsune, but in 1189, Yasuhira gave in to Yoritomo's threats and attacked Yoshitsune. Yoshitsune's nine followers put up a brave resistance against Yasuhira's army, allowing Yoshitsune time to make his farewells and end his life by his own hand. His wife and children were killed by a retainer, who then set fire to the house and immolated himself in the flames. Yoshitsune's head, rescued from the fire, was sent to Kamakura. Yoritomo was not yet satisfied, however. That same year, he sent a huge army against Hiraizumi. Yasuhira escaped to Hokkaidō, but was then betrayed and killed by a trusted retainer. His head arrived in Kamakura only a few months after Yoshitsune's. Afterward, it was returned to the ruins of Hiraizumi.

◆ **Konjiki-dō** 金色堂 (NT). The famed Golden Hall of Chūson-ji, now housed in a fireproof building. Three Amida trinities occupy the hall, flanked by groups of six Jizō and four guardian kings. The first three Fujiwara lords were mummified and interred beneath their respective Amida trinities. In 1962, when the hall was restored to its original splendor, the mummies were examined. A rich cache of artifacts was recovered from the tombs and put on display in the treasure house. A 15-minute film of this excavation is shown throughout the day in a nearby building.

◆ **Sankōzō (Treasure House)** 讃衡蔵 Fascinating temple treasures, including objects recovered from the Fujiwara coffins. National treasures include gilt-bronze *keman* (temple ornaments) of exquisite openwork; delicate furniture and daises with mother-of-pearl inlay; and a renowned set of sutras written in gold on indigo-blue paper. There's also a black-lacquer box that held the fourth Fujiwara lord's head.

**Kyōzō** 経蔵 (ICP). The library that held Chūson-ji's celebrated sutras. This hall (which lost its upper floor in the 1337 fire) houses an image of **Monju Bosatsu** riding a lion, which stands upon a wonderful **octagonal dais** (NT) decorated with nacre inlays of *vajra* and bronze reliefs of half-bird, half-human heavenly beings.

**Kyū Ōi-dō** 旧覆堂 (ICP). This wooden hall, built in 1288, sheltered the Konjiki-dō from the elements for 680 years. Nearby are the **Shiryōkan** 資料館 , a museum exhibiting documents and objects related to the festivals and Noh performances at Hakusan Jinja, Hiraizumi's guardian shrine, and the shrine's **Nohgaku-dō**, a lovely, thatched-roof outdoor Noh stage built in 1853.

** **Mōtsū-ji** 毛越寺 *0:10h on foot from the station or 0:20h from Chūson-ji.* Like Chūson-ji, this temple was founded by Ennin. It was restored by Fujiwara no Motohira. While the Konjiki-dō represents an early style of Amida Hall, Mōtsū-ji was built in the style of the celebrated Byōdō-in at Uji, south of Kyoto. Only foundations remain, but they clearly show the wings of the main pavilions. Over 40 buildings stood in a Jōdo-style paradise garden which, remarkably, survives. The garden's large, placid pond with islets, fringed by lawns and trees, is the best-preserved example of a Heian-period garden. The Hiraizumi nobles boated for pleasure on the pond and enjoyed dance and music performed on the central islet, which was once connected to the shore by bridges. The **treasure hall** exhibits objects belonging to the temple (Hrs: May–Aug. 8:00–18:00, Sept. 8:00–17:30, Oct.–Nov. and Mar.–Apr. 8:00–17:00, Dec.–Feb. 8:00–16:30).

**Gikei-dō** 義経堂 A small thatched hall purporting to mark the site of Yoshitsune's home in Hiraizumi.

171

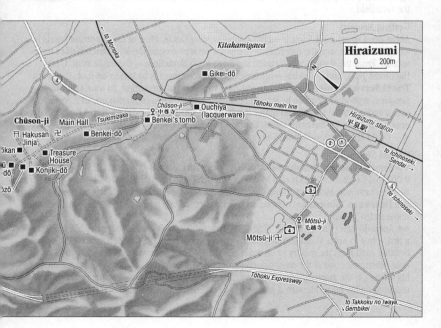

## Hiraizumi Crafts

Hidehira-nuri, red or black lacquerware decorated with floral motifs and diamond-shaped lozenges of goldleaf, has a charming blend of refinement and rusticity. Said to date from Hidehira's time.

## Hiraizumi Dining and Lodgings (TEL 0191)

① * **Izumiya** 泉屋　平泉駅前 (46-2038). Hrs: 8:00–19:00, daily. *Soba*. Inexpensive.

② **Bashō-kan** 芭蕉館　平泉駅前 (46-2524). Hrs: 8:00–20:00, daily. *Wanko soba*. Inexpensive.

③ * **Shirayama Ryokan** しら山　志羅山115–6 (46-2883). 115-6 Shirasan, Hiraizumi-chō, Nishiiwai-gun, Iwate-ken. Modest, well-appointed inn and restaurant run by a lovely couple. The superb meals feature local specialties such as *Hatto-jiru* (dumpling soup) and wild greens gathered by the innkeepers. Y6–8000 w/meals.

④ **Mōtsū-ji Temple Lodgings and YH** 毛越寺YH (46-2331). 58 Ōsawa, Hiraizumi-chō. Shared rooms: Y3000 for YH members, Y3700 for others. Y4500 w/meals and private room.

## Exploring

6 km SW of Hiraizumi is **Takkoku no Iwaya**, a temple built into the side of a cliff in which is carved a shallow relief of a Buddha (Dainichi Nyorai) said to date from the 11th C. 0:45h by bus from Ichinoseki is **Geibikei**, a scenic gorge with 100-m cliffs.

# TŌHOKU IV. SENDAI

**Tokyo to Sendai:** *2:00h by Tōhoku Shinkansen.*
**By Air:** *ANA flies from Nagoya, Ōsaka, and Okinawa. JAS flies from Nagoya and Fukuoka. Sendai's airport is 0:45h south of the city.*
**Prefectures:** Miyagi, Yamagata, Fukushima

## * SENDAI 仙台

Sendai, bombed flat during World War II, has few historic sights left. The handful that survive generally have to do with the Date family, Tōhoku's most powerful daimyo, who established their castle town here in 1600 (see Castles, p. 49). Starting with the remarkable Date Masamune, they turned Edo-period Sendai into the cultural center of Tōhoku. Postwar Sendai was rebuilt on a grid plan, with pleasant tree-lined streets; it is a good place to find a little breathing space and get oriented. Nearby Matsushima (E1) has more Date relics and, by tradition, is considered one of Japan's Three Famous Views. But the adventurous may prefer to plunge into the rustic, quintessential Tōhoku found in neighboring Yamagata prefecture.

## Calendar

**Jan. 14: * Donto-sai.** Sendai residents crowd the Ōsaki Hachiman shrine grounds to dance around a huge bonfire of New Year decorations.

**Aug. 6–8: * Tanabata.** The most famous of the "star" or "weaver" festivals (see Matsuri, p. 73), Sendai's Tanabata is counted among the "big three" Tōhoku summer festivals. Huge decorations festoon the shopping arcades and main streets. Colorful but tame.

**July 23–25: *** Sōma Nomaoi.** Sōma (*0:50h by express train south of Sendai, then 0:20h walk to festival site*). See Calendar, p. 154. Local inns are booked far in advance. Highlight on the 24th: parade at 9:30, races and rockets from around noon. Admission charged to the race field.

## Getting Around

**Aoba-dōri** spans the 1.5 km from the station to Aoba Castle. Most of the important hotels lie along this avenue, and the entertainment district centers around the **Ichibanchō-dōri** intersection. From the station, buses run to the three main attractions — the castle ruin, Ōsaki Hachiman Jinja, and Zuihōden — but transport between them is by taxi or on foot. There is a **Travel Service Center** (to exchange rail-pass vouchers) at the station. *In and Around Sendai* is a good local guide by foreign residents; sold at Maruzen bookstores in Tokyo and Kyoto, and at Sendai station and major hotels. **Teiki Kankō (Scheduled Tour) Bus:** In Japanese. Convenient for the main sights. Course C: Station (departs at 13:30) — Zuihōden — Aoba-jō — Ōsaki Hachiman — Station. The tour takes 3:00h and costs about Y2000.

## Sendai Sights

**** Sendai-shiritsu Hakubutsukan (City Museum)** 仙台市立博物館(225-2557). Hrs: 9:00–16:45 (enter by 16:15); clsd M unless M a NH, day after NH, NY. *0:10h by bus from Sendai station to Hakubutsukan-mae, at the foot of the castle hill.* Objects on the Date and **Hasekura Tsunenaga**, who led an official party of 180 Japanese to Mexico, Madrid, and Rome in 1613–1620.

**** Aoba-jō Ato (Castle Ruin)** 青葉城跡 Hrs: 9:00–17:00, clsd M, day after NH, NY. Take a taxi, a bus to Aoba-jō-ato Uzuminomon, or walk uphill from the City Museum (0:15h). The twisting road hugs the mighty stone walls of Aoba-jō. The castle was completed in 1602 by Date Masamune, one of the most colorful and powerful daimyo of his day. All that remains of his fortress is the *sumiyagura* (corner turret). Up on the hill, a bronze statue of Masamune mounted on his horse glowers at smog-bound Sendai. Close by is a statue of Hasekura

Tsunenaga, Masamune's emissary to Rome. The **Shiryō Tenjikan** (museum), above the souvenir shop, has handsome exhibits on the castle and the Date (Hrs: 9:00–17:00).

\* **Miyagi-ken Bijutsukan (Museum of Art)** 宮城県美術館 (221-2111). Hrs: 9:30–17:00 (enter by 16:30); clsd M (unless M a NH), day after NH, NY. Western art and post-Meiji works by Tōhoku artists, in a modern red-brick building.

\* **Zuihōden** 瑞鳳殿 Hrs: 9:00–16:00. *0:15h by bus from station to Otamayabashi.* The ornate mausoleum of Date Masamune, rebuilt after the war. Flanking it are stone tombs of retainers who committed suicide to follow him in death; nearby are the mausoleums of the second and third Date lords, and the Rinzai Zen temple, **Zuihō-ji**. Zuihō-ji's famous cherry trees, one pink and one white, were brought back by Masamune from HIDEYOSHI's Korean campaign.

\*\* □ **Ōsaki Hachiman Jinja** 大崎八幡神社 (NT). Hrs: 9:30–16:30. *0:15h by bus from station to Hachiman Jinja-mae.* This shrine to Hachiman, the god of war, is said to have been founded in 1100 by the great MINAMOTO warrior, Yoshiie (see Hiraizumi History, p. 169). The *shaden* (shrine hall), an ornate structure coated in lustrous black lacquer and decorated inside and out with colorful carvings of beasts and flowers, is among the oldest and finest examples of Momoyama-period Gongen-style architecture (see Shinto, p. 29). It was built by Date Masamune in 1607 and is one of the very few buildings to survive from Sendai's brilliant past.

## Sendai Crafts and Shopping

Sendai is Tōhoku's center for *kokeshi*, a simple wooden doll carved on a lathe, with a bulbous head attached to a cylindrical body. Faces and kimono patterns are painted on with quick brushstrokes in black and red ink. *Kokeshi* were once made by woodworkers as toys for their children. Some people think the dolls evolved from phallic emblems.

[5] **Ganguan Kokeshiya** 玩愚庵 国分町1丁目 (222-5889). Hrs: 8:00–18:00, daily; clsd NY. Shop overflowing with *kokeshi* from all over Japan.

[10] **Ishibashiya** 石橋屋 舟丁63 (222-5415). Hrs: 8:45–19:00, Su 9:00–18:00. Old shop famous for *dagashi*, old-fashioned sweets from a simpler age. Many Japanese wax nostalgic over the colorful lollipops and *karintō*, crisp lumps covered with black sugar.

## Sendai Dining

Sendai claims some of the best seafood in Japan. Local specialties include *hoya*, or "sea pineapple," a rust-orange, bumpy creature; the insides, which have a fresh, piney taste, are eaten raw, with a dash of vinegar.

② \*\* **Ambien-tei** あんびえん亭中央3-5-14ーセントラルパーク１階 (224-8255). Hrs: 11:30–14:00, 17:00–22:00; clsd Su, NH, NY. Superb Sendai seafood served in trendy surroundings—concrete walls played against the red-and-black lacquer counter, *hinoki* trays, beautiful ceramics. You can watch the chefs behind the counter and order what looks interesting, or try the *omakase* multicourse dinners, Y4500–Y8500.

⑦ **Matsuribayashi** 祭ばやし 大町2-7-7 (264-3205). Hrs: 17:00–22:00; clsd Su, NH. Hearty fare to go with saké. About Y4000.

173

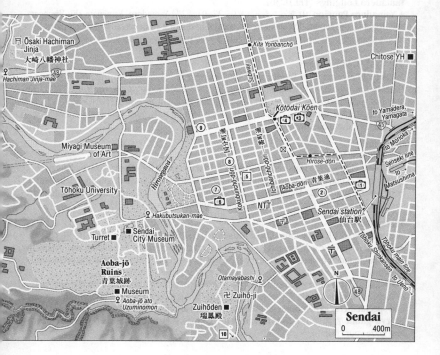

⑧ \* **Robata** 炉ばた 国分町2丁目 (266-0897). Hrs: 17:00–21:30 (last order); clsd Su, NH. A classic Tōhoku *robata* grill. Farmhouse atmosphere. Y1400 set comes with saké and three small dishes. Full course from Y3000.

⑨ **Baisaō** 売茶翁 春日町市民会館前 Hrs: 9:00–17:30; clsd 1st and 16th of each month. Famous old confectioner, with a teahouse where *matcha* and sweets are served.

## Sendai Lodgings (TEL 022)

① \* **Sendai Hotel** 仙台ホテル (225-5171). Fax 268-9325. Chūō 1-chōme, Sendai-shi, Miyagi-ken. Established city hotel across from the station. S Y11–13,000, Tw Y17–23,000.

③ \* **Hotel Sendai Plaza** ホテル仙台プラザ (262-7111). Fax 262-8169. Honchō 2-chōme. *0:05h taxi ride from the station.* S Y8800–15,500, Tw Y17–23,000.

④ \* **Sendai Mitsui Urban Hotel** 三井アーバンホテル (265-3131). Honchō 2-chōme. Trim, clean business hotel. S Y8000+, Tw Y15,000+.

⑥ \* **Washington Hotel II** 第二ワシントンホテル (222-2111). Ōmachi 2-chōme. *0:05h by taxi from station.* One of the best of this reliable chain. S Y7400, Tw Y14,000. The adjacent Washington Hotel I is older and cheaper.

\*\* **Dōchūan YH** 道中庵YH 大野田字北屋敷31 (247-0511). 31 Kitayashiki, Ōnoda, Taihaku-ku, Sendai-shi. *0:25h by bus from station.* There are three other YH closer to town center, but this one is worth going out of your way. The hostel is a renovated thatched-roof farmhouse set in a patch of country. There's a patio in summer and a hearth in winter.

# TŌHOKU IV:W. WEST FROM SENDAI

**Main Attraction:** Dewa Sanzan (W3)

## W1 \* YAMADERA 山寺

174 *1:00h by JR express from Sendai, or 0:15h from Yamagata (W2).* Hrs: 8:00–17:00, in winter 8:00–16:00. BASHŌ stopped at this mountaintop monastery on his Tōhoku journey and wrote one of his most famous haiku: "How still it is! / Piercing into the rocks / The cicada's shrill." Today, even with crowds, Yamadera preserves an air of stillness and mystery. The monastery was founded around 860 by the Tendai priest Ennin (see Hiraizumi History, p. 169). The precinct straggles up a steep, wooded mountainside, which served as a site for rigorous austerities by the monks. A number of the halls perch dramatically upon stilts on rock outcroppings; some can be reached only by clambering up chains (signs warn tourists away, but as they are written in Japanese, one might ignore them). From the station, cross the river, turn right, and walk to the large hall, **Konpon Chūdō**, named the same as its counterpart at the Tendai sect headquarters on Mt. Hiei, near Kyoto; a thousand-year-old sacred flame burns inside. To the left are a small **treasure house**, a bell tower, the **San-mon** (gate), and an admission booth. A stone-paved path ascends the mountain. Beyond the **Niō Gate** (0:25h), the path splits three ways. Straight ahead lies the incense-bathed **Okuno-in**, or inner sanctum. The left path leads to an observation platform, the right to the **Shaka-dō**; there are magnificent views from these side halls. It takes about two hours to circle the precincts. Festival on Jan. 17, Aug. 7.

## Yamadera Lodgings (TEL 0236)

\* **Yamadera Pension** 山寺ペンション (95-2240). 4274 Yamadera, Yamagata-shi, Yamagata-ken. Right by the station. Excellent meals, served in the first-floor restaurant. Each pair of rooms shares a bath. From Y7600 w/o bath, Y7600 w/bath. Meals included.

## W2 YAMAGATA 山形

*1:20h by JR express from Sendai, or 2:40h by direct JR "Type 400" express from Tokyo (part of the Tōhoku Shinkansen; splits off at Fukushima to go up the Ōu line).* This city is mainly a springboard for travelers to Dewa Sanzan, Zaō, and Yonezawa (TŌHOKU V:W1), but it does have a few attractions of its own. In its castle town days, Yamagata produced *beni*, a precious red dye made from safflowers.

## Calendar

**Jan. 10:** New Year's Fair.
**Aug. 6–8: Hanagasa.** Hundreds of *yukata*-clad dancers hit the streets wearing hats decorated with red pom-poms representing safflowers, which this festival originally celebrated.
**Sept.–Oct.: Imonikai.** An informal harvest celebration in which yams, beef, and onions are stewed in big pots on the riverbank. Reserve at Kuroki Shōten (22-7821).

## Yamagata Sights

\* **Yamagata-shi Kyōdo-kan (Local Museum)** 山形市郷土館 Hrs: 9:00–16:30; clsd M, 3rd Su, NH, NY. On castle grounds. The peculiar round, Western-style building was originally a hospital founded by an Austrian doctor. Nearby is the history museum and the prefectural museum.

\* **Hirashimizu Pottery Village** 平清水 *0:20h by bus from Yamagata, on the outskirts of town, at the foot of Mt. Chitose.* Hirashimizu-yaki is a pleasant folk pottery with caramel and speckled gray glazes. Some of the best examples are produced at Niwa Yoshitomo's kiln, **Seiryū-gama** 青龍窯 (31-2828). Farther up the road is **Nanaemon**, where you can throw and glaze your own.

## Yamagata Dining and Lodgings (TEL 0236)

**Mansei-an** 万盛庵 (22-2167). Hrs: 11:00–19:00; clsd M, 2nd Su, NY. Near Washington Hotel. Famous for *soba*. Inexpensive.

**Kappō Shōgetsu** 割烹松月 十日町2-2-5 (23-0415). Hrs: 12:00–21:00; clsd Su. Open Su by reservation. Near bus terminal. *Kaiseki* from Y10,000 by reservation.

* **Hotel Castle** ホテルキャッスル (31-3311). 4-2-7 Tōkamachi, Yamagata-shi, Yamagata-ken. Part of the reliable ANA group. S Y6600, Tw Y12,500. MC, AX, V, DC, CB.

**Washington Hotel** 山形ワシントンホテル (24-1515). 1-4-31 Nanokamachi. Reliable business hotel chain. S Y6000, Tw Y12,400. MC, AX, V, DC, CB.

**Ryokan Gotō Matabei** 旅館後藤又兵衛 (22-0357). 2-2-30 Hatagomachi. Atmospheric old inn. From Y8500 w/meals. V, MC, AX, DC, CB.

**Yamagata YH** 山形YH 黒沢293-3 (88-3201). 293-3 Kurosawa. At Kurosawa Onsen, near Zaō. Sounds like a homey, friendly place. Onsen bath. Y3200–3500 w/meals.

### Exploring Kahoku-chō Benihana Shiryōkan

# Tel: 0237-73-3500. This area north of Yamagata lies on a tributary of the Mogami River, at the terminus of one of Yamagata's *beni* routes, over which were transported dried *beni* (safflowers), source of a valuable crimson dye. This museum is on a large estate that belonged to a wealthy *beni* trader. Though not a samurai, he was allowed to keep weapons to protect the *beni*, which was worth more than its weight in gold. The place is fortified with moats, walls, and a strong gate, all impressive reminders of the wealth the *beni* trade brought to this impoverished area. The museum displays *beni*-dyed silks.

## ZAŌ 蔵王

*0:50h by bus from Yamagata station.* Zaō offers the best skiing in Tōhoku, livened with numerous spas and *juhyō*, or "snow monsters," ice-covered trees that give the scenery a little extra wintertime interest. The busy resort of **Zaō Onsen** is the main base; lifts to the best runs start from here. Summertime hiking is pretty good too.

175

### Zaō Lodgings (TEL 0236)

**Takamiya Ryokan** 高見屋旅館 (94-9333). 54 Zaō Onsen, Yamagata-ken. Onsen bath. Y8–15,000 w/meals. AX, V, MC.

**Ōhira Hotel** 大平ホテル (94-9422). Address as above. Ski-lodge style with Japanese and Western rooms. Open-air bath. From Y8000 w/meals.

**Pension Kiichigo** ペンション木いちご (79-2177) and **Pension Mominoki** ペンションもみのき (79-2330). *0:05h by pension vans from the Zaō Onsen bus terminal.* From about Y7500 w/o bath, Y7000 w/bath. At Zaō Yamabiko-mura, a "village" of chalet-style pensions.

## W3 ** DEWA SANZAN 出羽三山

The Three Mountains of Dewa were "opened" by Prince Hōshi, a disciple of the 7th-century holy man En no Gyōja, founder of the syncretic Shugendō sect (see Shinto, p. 27). Dewa was the old name for western Tōhoku, and the three peaks, Gassan, Yudono-san, and Haguro-san, were among the most sacred centers in Japan for the *yamabushi*, priests of the Shugendō sect. (The other sites were Ōmine-san near Yoshino, and Hakusan in Chūbu.) The *yamabushi* of Dewa Sanzan were a power to contend with; it is said that MINAMOTO NO YORITOMO was able to crush Hiraizumi only after making a pact with the Dewa *yamabushi* (see Hiraizumi History, p. 169). After the Meiji Restoration in 1868, Shugendō was "purged" and the temples of Dewa Sanzan were converted into pure Shinto shrines. Today, the few resurrected *yamabushi*, wearing their distinctive checked jerkin and small black cap, and toting *hora*-shell trumpets, pose for the benefit of tourists.

### Calendar

**July 15: Hanamatsuri.** Dewa Sanzan Jinja, on Haguro-san. *Bonden* staffs festooned with artificial flowers are paraded; the scattered flowers protect their keepers from harm.

**Aug. 31–Sept. 1: Hassaku Matsuri.** Dewa Sanzan Jinja. To mark the harvest, the *yamabushi* make a 5-day pilgrimage that ends with a fire festival on the night of the 31st.

**Dec. 31–Jan. 1:** * **Shōrei-sai.** Dewa Sanzan Jinja. One of Japan's famous fire festivals. *Yamabushi* who have undergone 100 days of austerities burn and scatter a pair of torches made from 1,333 bundles. Originally a harvest oracle, the flames also symbolize destruction of *tsutsugamushibyō*, a disease that once afflicted Japanese peasants.

### Getting Around

The leisurely route described below starts from Yamagata and covers all three mountains via Rte. 112 (8 express buses a day in winter, 10 a day in summer, departing from Yamagata station or bus terminal). Shōnai Kōtsū Co. buses also swing by Yamagata Airport. If time is limited, visit Haguro as a day trip out of Tsuruoka. From Tsuruoka, buses also depart for Tamugimata, Yudono-san, and Gassan. Bus routes off of Rte. 112 are closed in winter.

### Dewa Sanzan Sights

**Sagae** 寒河江 *0:35h from Yamagata by Rte. 112 express bus.* Hot spring. 0:05h farther by bus is **Jion-ji**, a pretty temple.

**Mazawa** 間沢 *1:05h from Yamagata by Rte. 112 express bus.* There is a famous restaurant here, ② ** **Dewaya** 出羽屋 (02377-4-2323). Hrs: 11:00–22:00 (last order 20:00); clsd NY, Aug. 13. It serves mountain greens: *Gassan sansai soba* Y1000, *teishoku* Y1000–4000, *sansai ryōri* Y5–8000.

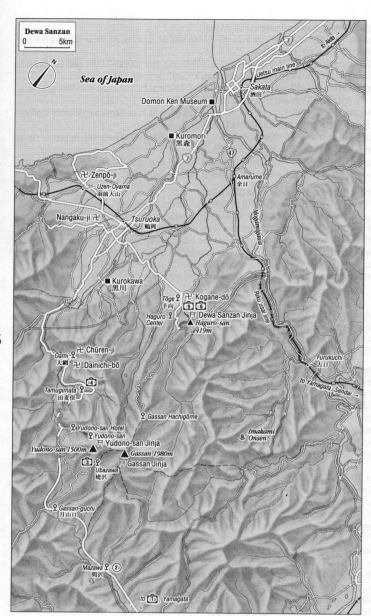

Dewa Sanzan
0       5km

Sea of Japan

Sakata
酒田

Domon Ken Museum ■

to Akita

Uetsu main line

7

Kuromori
黒森

47

卍 Zenpō-ji
Uzen-Oyama
羽前大山

Amarume
余目

7

Nangaku-ji 卍

Tsuruoka
鶴岡

Riku Usai line

Mogamigawa

■ Kurokawa
黒川

Tōge
手向
5  6

卍 Kogane-dō

Haguro
Center

Dewa Sanzan Jinja
▲ Haguro-san
419m

卍 Chūren-ji
Ōami
大網

Furukuchi
古口

to Yamagata, Sendai

卍 Dainichi-bō

4

Tamugimata
田麦俣

Gassan Hachigōme

Imakami
Onsen

Yudono-san Hotel
Yudono-san

Yudono-san Jinja

Yudono-san 1500m ▲

▲ Gassan 1980m
Gassan Jinja

3

Ubazawa
姥沢

Gassan-guchi
月山口

Mazawa
間沢     2

to 1 , Yamagata

176

**\* Gassan** 月山 *1:20h to Gassan-guchi/Kogetsu Sansō bus stop from Yamagata, or 1:10h from Tsuruoka. In summer, a bus runs from Yamagata to Ubazawa (2:00h).* Gassan (Moon Mountain), is one of the three sacred peaks. The **Gassan ski area** offers skiing from April 20 to early July. (Until buses to Ubazawa start running, you must arrange to have the ski hut send a van.) During the summer you can climb to **Gassan Jinja** at the summit in 3:30h starting from the ski area. The classic climb, however, is from Haguro-san: take the bus 1:30h from Tsuruoka via Haguro to Gassan Hachigōme (8th station), and then hike 2:00h (July 1–Oct. 10 only).

**\*\* Yudono-san (Bathtub Mountain)** 湯殿山 *Buses to shrine, June 1–mid-Nov. only. Otherwise, get off at Yudonosan Hotel, 1:40h from Yamagata or 1:00h from Tsuruoka by express bus.* Not far west of Gassan, this is the "innermost" of the three sacred peaks. From the bus stop, it is a 2.5 km walk up to **Yudono-san Jinja**. The *goshintai*, or object of worship, is a huge, rust-orange rock with bubbling, warm, sulfurous water flowing over it. On entering the precincts, pilgrims remove their shoes and await their turn to climb the rock and bathe their feet in the hot water. Below the rock, white-clad pilgrims stand under a cold waterfall.

**\*\* Tamugimata** 田麦俣 *0:20h from Yudono-san or 1:20h from Tsuruoka by local bus (no expresses).* This village offered lodgings to pilgrims on the Yudono-san pilgrimage in the Edo period. The houses were built to provide an entrance on the second floor when the winter snows piled deep, burying the ground floor. The magnificently sculpted end-gables protecting the second-floor entrance look like a samurai's helmet, and so this style is known as *kabuto-zukuri*, or helmet construction. 20 years ago there were perhaps 30 such houses; today, there are only 3 or 4. The **Endō house** is open to the public.

✳ **Dainichi-bō** 大日坊 **and Chūren-ji** 注蓮寺 *By Ōami bus stop, 0:10h from Tamugimata.* Two temples where one can view **mummified priests**, who are called "instant Buddhas." The reason for this practice turns on a point in Esoteric Buddhist theology about becoming a "Buddha in one's body." Holy men purified their bodies and spirits by reducing their food intake from vegetables to leaves and twigs, and finally to just water. Then they were entombed alive, seated in meditation. Because of what they had endured, after death their bodies did not decompose, but instead mummified naturally. Both temples stand along the old pilgrimage route that parallels Rte. 112. Chūren-ji is pretty, and its mummy has a personality; he was a murderer who repented, became a priest, and cured an epidemic of blindness by tearing out one of his own eyes.

✳✳✳ **Haguro-san (Dewa Sanzan Jinja)** 羽黒山 *0:35h by bus from Tsuruoka station to Haguro Center, at the top of Tōge village; the bus continues to the summit.* At Tōge, there are some thatched temple-inns along the street. As an ancient Shugendō center, Haguro is rooted in both Buddhist and Shinto tradition. After 1868, however, it became a Shinto shrine. The entrance gate, **Zuishin-mon,** was formerly a Buddhist Niō gate. A short distance beyond it, a bridge spans a mountain stream where pilgrims bathe. On the far side stands the beautiful 600-year-old ◆ **five-storied pagoda** (NT), the only Buddhist structure left undisturbed by the Shinto reformers. The pagoda marks the beginning of a steep, hour-long climb up a series of stone staircases leading through stands of immense cryptomeria. At the top of the second steep ascent is a teahouse that serves free tea, sells certificates proving you've made it that far, and has a fantastic view of the Mogami River Valley and the Japan Sea. A side path leads to the ruins of a temple where the poet BASHŌ stayed. The third and final steep ascent ends at ◆ **Gassai-den**, a shrine of distinctly Buddhist architecture, where the three kami of Dewa Sanzan are gathered. Before the hall is a pond into which believers once threw mirrors as offerings. Some of the mirrors were recovered from the pond and are on view in the nearby ◆ **Rekishi Hakubutsukan** (History Museum) 歴史博物館 , along with a group of Buddhist images saved from the Meiji purge and ritual objects of the *yamabushi*. The belfry contains a great bell (ICP), a gift of the Kamakura shogun. Nearby is the tomb of Prince Hōshi, the 7th-C founder of Dewa Sanzan. During the summer, white-robed pilgrims walk the 25 km to Gassan shrine (or take the bus to the eighth station; see Gassan, above). Back at Tōge, one can visit the **Kogane-dō** 黄金堂 (ca. 1189, ICP), which houses more Buddhist art that was formerly on Haguro-san.

177

## Dewa Sanzan Lodgings

①︎ **Yoshimoto** 吉本旅館 (0237-84-2138). 2-1-23 Honchō, Sagae-shi, Yamagata-ken. An onsen ryokan at Sagae. Y10–15,000.

③︎ **Ubazawa Koya** 姥沢小屋 (0237-75-2121). Shizu, Nishikawa-machi, Nishimurayama-gun. Clsd Oct. 21–Mar. 31. Gassan ski lodge with bunks, very friendly and right by the lifts. Call ahead and they'll pick you up at the Gassan-guchi bus stop (too far to walk).

④︎ **Minshuku Kayabukiya** かやぶき屋 (0235-54-6103). Tamugimata, Asahi-mura, Higashitagawa-gun. One of the remaining *kabuto-zukuri* houses. Y6000 w/meals.

⑤︎ **Daishin-bō** 大進坊 (0235-62-2372). Tōge, Haguro-machi, Higashitagawa-gun. Thatched-roof temple lodging. From Y6000 w/meals.

⑥︎ ✳ **Haguro Sai-kan** 羽黒山斎館 (0235-62-2355). Dewa Sanzan Jinja, Tōge, Haguromachi. Shrine lodgings, right on the mountain. One of the guest rooms is a very nice Sukiya-style tearoom. The inn serves *sansai ryōri* (Cuisine, p. 116), of which the *goma-dōfu* (sesame tofu) is their pride. Y6000 w/meals. You can also dine here at lunch time for Y1000–3500.

## Exploring Mogami River Boat Ride

# Apr. 1–Nov. 30, charters in winter. Departures from Furukuchi. The boats have motors, obnoxious public-address systems, and sing-alongs, but the scenery is quite beautiful (and the weather is chilly!) in autumn and winter. Deep in the mountains SW of Furukuchi is **Imakami Onsen**, also known as Nembutsu Onsen because Buddhist pilgrims bathe in it while reciting the *nembutsu*. Closed in winter.

## W4 ✳ TSURUOKA 鶴岡
*3:50h from Sendai by direct Riku'usai line Sakata-bound limited express (2 per day), changing to the Uetsu line at Amarume. 2:05h by Hokuriku main line limited express from Niigata (KANTŌ II:N2).* Tsuruoka is the main gateway to Dewa Sanzan, with buses departing regularly for all three mountains. As the castle town of the Sakai family, it has a few attractions of its own, mostly around the castle ruins, 2 km (0:10h by bus) from the station.

## Calendar
**Feb. 1–2:** ✳ # **Kurokawa Noh.** One of the most famous of Japan's sacred folk plays, performed at Kurokawa, a village 5 km SE of Tsuruoka. A huge sacred *ōgi* (folding fan), symbol of fertility, is brought to a farmhouse, and Noh plays are offered through the night. The Noh, performed by local farmers, is thought to have been introduced by the *yamabushi* of Haguro about 500 years ago. You must reserve a spot by Nov. 20 by sending a self-addressed postcard (give your name, address, occupation, and purpose of visit, in Japanese) to the Kurokawa Noh Hozon-kai, 100 Bunei, Kamiyamazoe, Higashitagawa-gun, Yamagata-ken 997-03 (tel: 0235-57-2111). Kurokawa Noh is also offered at matsuri on Mar. 23, May 3, and Nov. 23.

**May 25: Bakemono Matsuri.** Formerly, boys would *bakeru* (dress in their sisters' clothes and wear big hats) and offer saké to passersby. If a girl accepted saké from one boy for 3 years running, it was tantamount to exchanging nuptial vows. Today the *bakemono* consist mostly of members of local tourist associations.

**Aug. 15: Kurokawa Noh.** At Sōnai Jinja. Part of the shrine festival.

## Tsuruoka Sights

✱ **Chidō-kan** 致道館 Hrs: 9:00–16:30; clsd NY. *0:10h by bus from station to Shiyakusho-mae.* Just outside the SE corner of castle grounds. The clan school for sons of high-ranking families, built in 1806. Contains a small Confucian temple.

✱✱✱ **Chidō Hakubutsukan** 致道博物館 (22-1199). Hrs: 9:00–17:00 (enter by 16:30); clsd NY. On W side of the castle grounds. This museum is comprised of the old Sakai family villa and garden, two Meiji-period Western-style buildings, a *kabuto-zukuri* house (ICP) moved from Tamugimata village (see Dewa Sanzan), and several other structures. The museum collection includes a marvelous group of old *funadansu* (ship chests), fishing poles (Tsuruoka was the traditional center of fishing-pole production), and *iwai-bandori*, beautifully ornamented harnesses made as betrothal gifts by Tsuruoka men for their brides-to-be.

✱ **Nangaku-ji** 南岳寺 *0:15h by bus from station.* If you didn't get a chance to see a mummified priest on Yudono-san, you can see one here in Tsuruoka. This one "became a Buddha" in 1868.

## Tsuruoka Dining and Lodgings (TEL 0235)

From spring to fall there are vendors of roasted skewered meat along the riverbank.

**Sanmai-an** 三昧庵 (24-0736). Hrs: 10:00–17:00; clsd NY; on the 1st, 3rd, and 4th M (unless a NH); in winter every M. Delicious *soba* and *udon* noodles, on the grounds of the Chidō Hakubutsukan. Inexpensive.

**Tsuruoka Hotel** 鶴岡ホテル (22-1135). Baba-chō, Tsuruoka-shi, Yamagata-ken. Dark, tranquil old ryokan. Y7–10,000 w/meals. No CC.

178

## Exploring Zenpō-ji

*0:40h by bus from Tsuruoka station.* A large temple complex, now of the Sōtō Zen sect; founded a thousand years ago for a dragon god who dwells in a pond behind the temple.

## W5 ✱ SAKATA　酒田

*2:10h by direct JR limited express from Yamagata (only 2 per day at 7:34 and 19:19); 1:30h by limited express frm Akita); 2:20h by limited express from Niigata* (KANTŌ II:N2). Sakata was a flourishing port town from which the abundant rice of the neighboring Shōnai plain was shipped south. Although the Tsuruoka daimyo nominally ruled, it was the Homma family, rice merchants still wealthy today, who ran the city. The principal attractions of Sakata include two residences built by the Homma, the Homma warehouses, and—an unexpected contemporary addition—the Domon Ken Museum.

## Calendar

**Feb. 15–17: ✱ Kuromori Kabuki.** *In Morita, 0:50h by bus from Sakata.* Folk Kabuki performed on an open stage by farmers since 1735 as a shrine offering. Hrs: 10:00–16:00.

## Sakata Sights

✱✱ **Homma Bijutsukan (Art Museum)** 本間美術館 Hrs: 9:00–17:00, daily. Nov.–Mar. 9:00–16:30; Dec.–Mar. clsd M, NY. *0:05h walk from station.* The concrete museum is mildly interesting, but the real attraction is the garden and the old Homma villa. The villa was built about 200 years ago in Shoin style. The garden, Tsurumai-en, would be even more beautiful if the new museum building weren't there.

✱ **Homma-ke Kyū Hontei** 本間家旧本邸 (22-3562). Hrs: 9:30–16:00, clsd NY. *0:15h walk from station.* This mansion was built in 1768 by the Homma to provide lodgings for the Sakai lords and shogunate inspectors. The Homma sleeping quarters consist of just a few mats, but the quarters provided for their exalted guests were immense.

**Abumiya** 鐙屋 *200 m west of Homma-ke.* This is an old shipping-merchant's house. It is still lived in, but you can enter the front part and have a look.

✱✱ **Sankyo Sōko** 山居倉庫 *0:10h by bus from the station.* A row of eleven white *kura* storehouses for rice, belonging to the Homma. One houses a small history museum. The buildings date from 1893, but the site was also used for rice storage in the Edo period.

✱✱✱ **Domon Ken Kinenkan** 土門拳記念館 (31-0028). Hrs: 9:00–16:30; clsd M (unless a NH), NY. *2 km south of town center.* Domon Ken (1909– ) is famed for his photography of ancient temples and of postwar Japan: children playing on the street, Hiroshima victims, actors, and prostitutes. He donated most of his negatives to this museum in his home town. The work is riveting, as is the museum building itself, built on the bank of the Mogami River. It is designed to protect an Isamu Noguchi sculpture from winter winds.

## Sakata Dining and Lodgings (TEL 0234)

**Le Pot au Feu** ルポットフー　東急イン３階 (26-2218). Hrs: 11:30–14:00, 17:00–20:00; clsd W, NH, NY. Good French restaurant on the third floor of the Tōkyū Inn. Y2500–10,000 per person. DC, V, CB.

**Ryōtei Kamazaki** 料亭香梅咲　日吉町1-3-16 (23-3366). Hrs: 11:30–22:00; clsd 1st and 3rd Su. Elegant old inn specializing in fish cuisine. Y5000–15,000 for *omakase*.

**Wakaba Ryokan** 若葉旅館 本町2丁目 (24-8111). 2-3-9 Hon-chō, Sakata-shi, Yamagata-ken. A family hotel. Rooms w/bath, 2 meals, from Y8000. V, MC, AX, DC, CB.

**Tōkyū Inn** 東急イン (26-0109). 1-10-20 Saiwai-chō. Near station. S Y6000, Tw Y11,000. V, MC, DC, CB, AX.

**Easy Access To:**
**Akita** (TŌHOKU II:E3): *1:30h by JR Uetsu line limited express.*

# TŌHOKU IV:E. EAST FROM SENDAI

## # TAGA-JŌ 多賀城
*0:20h by Tōhoku main line local to Rikuzen-Sannō station, then 0:20h walk or taxi via the site to the museum. One can continue from here to Shiogama (4 km).* These are the ruins of a large, Chinese-style fortress built in 724 by the Nara government to fight the Emishi, a northern people who defied Yamato rule (see Hiraizumi History, p. 169). Taga-jō was used for 600 years before being abandoned.

∗ **Tōhoku Rekishi Shiryōkan (History Museum)** 東北歴史資料館 (022-368-0101). Hrs: 9:30–16:30; clsd M, NH. Handsome museum exhibiting excavated objects and other materials on Tōhoku history, including models of Taga-jō showing the fort's Chinese plan: a rectangular compound surrounded by an immense outer wall 3.5 km long.

∗ **Taga-jō Excavations** 多賀城跡 *0:15h walk from museum.* Near the site of Taga-jō's south gate is ∗ **Tsubo no Ishibumi** 壺の碑, a kind of milestone, now housed in a wooden cage. The inscription dates it to the year 762 and indicates distances to Nara (1500 *ri*), the Emishi (120 *ri*), and various boundaries of the Yamato kingdom. In *Narrow Road to the Deep North* (1694), the poet BASHŌ wrote: "This monument was made a thousand years ago and is a very real and vivid link with the past. Seeing it is one of the things that has made my trip worthwhile and one of the happiest moments of my life. ..." Some distance away (taxi advised) are the foundations of **Hai-ji**, a temple laid out like famed Hōryū-ji (see p. 33).

179

## E1 ∗ MATSUSHIMA 松島
*From Sendai, 0:15h to Hon-Shiogama, 0:30h to Matsushima-Kaigan, by Senseki line. A nice detour is to visit Shiogama Jinja near Hon-Shiogama station, then board the ferry to cross the bay to Matsushima.* The celebrated bay of Matsushima, studded with countless pine-covered islets, is by tradition one of Japan's Three Famous Views. The panorama was thought to be good for meditation, and the Kamakura shogunate directed Hoshin, who had recently studied Zen in China, to turn the ancient Zuigan-ji into a Zen temple. In 1606 Sendai's lord, **Date Masamune**, rebuilt Zuigan-ji in gorgeous Shoin style. When the poet BASHŌ saw Matsushima, he marveled, "O Great Creator of the Universe, what man could presume to describe this place in words?" The only people who would be rendered speechless by Matsushima today are those outraged by the rampant commercialism of the area and the ugly smokestacks in the distance. Oku-Matsushima is said to be less spoiled.

### Calendar
**Mar. 10: Shiogama Jinja Hote Matsuri.** Shiogama Jinja. Features a 250-year-old *mikoshi*, one of the "three largest" in Japan.
**Aug. 15: Lantern Floating.** Bon rite on Matsushima Bay. Services on the 16th at Zuigan-ji.

### Shiogama Sights
∗ **Shiogama Jinja** 塩釜神社 (1704, ICP). Situated on a beautiful, tree-covered hill. The treasure house features a motley assortment of floats and equipment for whaling and salt-making (the shrine's name means "Salt-Cauldron"). Nice view of Matsushima Bay.

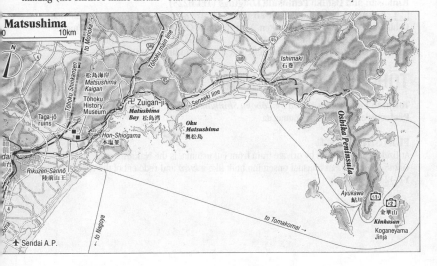

**\*\* Shiogama-Matsushima Ferry.** Hour-long cruises to Matsushima leave 17 times a day from Shiogama pier, nearest to Hon-Shiogama station. Base fare is Y1000; the more expensive upper deck has a better view. Most of the famous formations can be seen from the ferry. There are longer rides to more remote areas of the bay.

### Matsushima Along the Beach
A tourist information booth directly across from the wharf issues maps and a small pamphlet in English.

**\* Godai-dō** 五大堂 (ICP). This tiny temple hall, on an islet connected to the shore by a bridge of land, is the first thing you see upon arrival. It was built by Date Masamune in the early 1600s. Its images of the Godai Myō-ō are shown once every 33 years.

**\*\* Kanran-tei** 観瀾亭 Hrs: 8:30–17:00. Mid-Dec.–Mar. 8:30–16:30. S of tourist information. This tea arbor was originally in the Fushimi Castle in Kyoto and was given by TOYOTOMI HIDEYOSHI to Date Masamune after Masamune had sworn fealty to him. It contains door panels painted by KANŌ SANRAKU (ICP). The adjacent building is the Matsushima Museum, which displays Date family memorabilia, seashells, and archeological finds.

**\*\* Oshima** 雄島 *S of the railway station and aquarium.* This islet is linked to the land by a red "moon-crossing bridge." The island, an ancient site for monks' austerities, is riddled with meditation caves, whose wall are engraved with Buddhist images.

**\*\*\* Zuigan-ji** 瑞巌寺 Hrs: 7:30–17:00. Oct.–Mar. 8:30–16:30. *0:10h on foot from Matsushima Kaigan station.* This historically and artistically rich temple is the highlight of a visit to Matsushima. Zuigan-ji was founded by the indefatigable Tendai abbot **Ennin** (see Hiraizumi History, p. 169). Since the Kamakura period, it has been a Rinzai Zen monastery. In 1606, Date Masamune, lord of Sendai, rebuilt it in its present sumptuous Momoyama style and made it his funerary temple, though he isn't buried here. On the grounds are meditation caves and Buddhist images carved into the wall of a cliff. The ◆ **Hondō** (Main Hall), **Kairō** (gallery), **Onari-mon** (imperial gate), and **Kuri** (kitchen), are all NT. There are KANŌ SCHOOL paintings on the sliding panels of the Hondō. The **Seiryūden** houses the temple's sizable collection, including many gifts from the Date lords. Among the outstanding paintings are a Shaka ascribed to Shūbun and a Kannon by SESSHŪ. Sculptures include a Senju Kannon and a portrait of the one-eyed Date Masamune. Of special interest is a famous pair of cut-glass candlesticks given by Pope Paul V to Hasekura Tsunenaga, Masamune's envoy to Rome.

### Matsushima Dining
**Donjiki Teahouse** どんじき (354-5855). Hrs: 9:00–17:00, daily. Dec.–mid-Mar. open Sa, Su, NH only, 9:30–16:00. *Oden* under a thatched roof. Inexpensive.

**Taritsu-an** 田里津庵 (366-3328). Hrs: 11:00–21:00; clsd NY, Aug. 15–16. Fresh seafood.

## E2 \* # KINKASAN (ISLAND) 金華山
*Take the Senseki line to Ishimaki, 1:30h from Sendai. Switch to a bus to Ayukawa (7 per day, 1:45h). From Ayukawa, there are ferries to Kinkasan; departures are few—check schedules in advance. You may also charter a motorboat for Y10,000 (or Y1000 per person if shared).* Besides **Koganeyama Jinja** (dedicated to the deity of precious metals), one hotel, a lighthouse, and the dock, there is little else on Golden Mountain Island except for numerous deer, wild monkeys, and leeches (in summer). A steep hour's walk to the top of the mountain brings you to the tiny upper shrine, which stands next to a large stone phallus. From here, there is a beautiful view of the island and nearby Oshika Peninsula. On the east side of the island are tatami-like rock formations—supposedly 1,000 tatami mats in size. Ayukawa, the jumping-off point to Kinkazan, has a whaling museum (and whaling).

### Calendar
**1st and 2nd Su in Oct. and Oct. 10th:** Deer-horn-cutting ceremony.

### Kinkasan and Oshika Peninsula Lodgings (TEL 0225)
① **Kokuminshukusha Cobalt-sō** 国民宿舎コバルト荘 (45-2281). Ayukawahama, Oshika-chō, Oshika-gun, Miyagi-ken. Near the tip of Oshika Peninsula. Y4950 w/meals.
② **YH Kinkasan Jinja** YH金華山神社 (45-2264 or 45-2301). 5 Kinkasan, Ayukawahama. Nice, old-fashioned lodgings at Kinkasan Jinja. Y3000 w/meals.

# TŌHOKU V. FUKUSHIMA

**Tokyo to Fukushima:** *1:40h by Tōhoku Shinkansen from Ueno station.*
**Prefectures:** Fukushima, Yamagata

### FUKUSHIMA 福島
At Iizaka Onsen, 0:25h by private train from Fukushima, is the **Nakamuraya** 中村屋 (0245-42-4050), an unusual onsen inn built like a *kura* and redolent of the early Meiji era. Y7–12,000 w/meals.

# TŌHOKU V:W. WEST FROM FUKUSHIMA

## W1 ∗ YONEZAWA 米沢

*0:50h by JR express from Fukushima, or 0:40h by express from Yamagata (TŌHOKU IV:W2). 3:00h by bus from Aizu-Wakamatsu (TŌHOKU VI:W1) via Bandai-Asahi National Park (change at Bandai Kōgen).* Uesugi Kenshin, one of the most famous warriors of the Sengoku period, ruled an immense territory along the Japan Sea coast, worth some 2 million *koku*. His descendants, however, made the mistake of siding against TOKUGAWA IEYASU and found themselves removed to the poor, landlocked castle town of Yonezawa, a fief worth only 150,000 *koku*. The tenth daimyo, Yōzan, was a humanitarian and an innovator; he had his subjects keep carp ponds and plant hedges of *ukogi*, a thorny, edible plant that provided both a defensive barrier and food. "That's how poor Yonezawa was," locals recount. To further supplement income, Yonezawa produced *beni-bana* (safflower), source of a precious red dye, and handspun silk cloth, which was woven by low-ranking samurai households and is still one of the town's famous products. Yonezawa remains "backward": it is unpolluted; thatched roofs appear here and there in town; and streets are quiet and orderly.

## Calendar
**Apr. 29–May 3: Uesugi Matsuri.** Uesugi Kenshin's spirit is feted at various shrines around town. On the last day, townsmen, many wearing their ancestors' armor, form a colorful "samurai" procession and reenact Uesugi Kenshin's great battles with Takeda Shingen.

## Getting Around
Rent-a-cycle at Yonezawa station and Uesugi Kinenkan. The castle area, where many of the attractions are, is about 2 km from Yonezawa station. It might make sense to take a bus to the castle and walk from there or rent a bicycle at Uesugi Kinenkan.

## Yonezawa Sights

181

∗ **Jōshin-an** 常信庵 Near station. Noted for a mummy of one of the temple's nuns.
∗∗ **Keishō-den** 稽照殿 (22-3189). Hrs: 9:00–16:00; Dec.–Mar. open by reservation only. *0:05h by Shirabu Onsen bus to Uesugi Jinja-mae, on the ruined castle grounds.* The treasure house of **Uesugi Jinja** displays Uesugi family treasures, including one of Japan's finest
◆ *Rakuchū-Rakugai* (scenes of Kyoto) screens (ICP), painted by KANŌ EITOKU and given to Uesugi Kenshin by ODA NOBUNAGA. Other objects of note include Kenshin's gilded leather helmet, armor (ICP), late Heian-period paintings of Bishamon-ten and a Two Worlds Mandala (ICP). The collection is noted for old costumes (many are ICP).
∗∗ **Uesugi Kinenkan** 上杉記念館 (21-5121). Hrs: 9:00–17:00. Dec.–Mar. 10:00–16:00; clsd Tu (except if NH). The Meiji-period villa of the Uesugi family is a handsome Japanese-style house, roofed in copper, with a pleasant garden. Local crafts and family treasures are on display. The Kinenkan serves *kenzen-ryōri*, a cuisine based on Yōzan's writings in which he instructed people how to use available food resources. Dishes are prepared from wild plants, preserved fish, and fresh carp, and served in a room with a garden view.
∗ **Uesugi-ke Byōsho** 上杉家廟所 (23-3115). Hrs: 9:00–17:00, July–Aug. 8:30–17:30. *0:15h by bus from station, west of the castle.* Mausoleums of the first 12 Uesugi lords stand in somber rows beneath cryptomerias. The lone stone tomb is for the 14th descendant, Count Uesugi, who built the villa that is now the Uesugi Kinenkan.

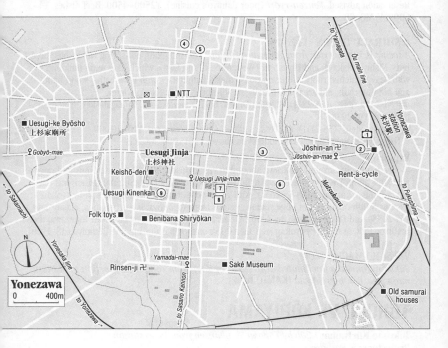

Yonezawa
0        400m

\* **Rinsen-ji** 林泉寺 The funerary temple of Uesugi Kenshin's original family, the Nagao. Beautiful garden.

\* **Sasano Kannon** 笹野観音 *0:25h by Shirabu Onsen bus.* A quiet country temple with a magnificent thatched roof. Said to have been founded in 807, the temple is dedicated to Senju Kannon.

## Yonezawa Crafts and Shopping

7 **Orimono Rekishi Shiryōkan (Weaving History Hall)** 織物歴史資料館 (23-3006). Hrs: 9:00–17:00, clsd. NY. Displays of Yonezawa silk weaving.

8 \*\* **Dewa no Oriza** 出羽の織座 (22-8141). By reservation. Hrs: 10:00–16:00; clsd mid-Dec.–Feb., mid-Aug. A handsome old house exhibiting textiles made from the inner bark of trees, wisteria vine fibers, and even used paper. Natural dyes only. Most of the weaving is done in winter by farm households.

10 \*\* **Ryōu Benibana Kōgeijo** 両羽紅花工芸所 (23-7717). Hrs: 10:00–12:00, 13:00–16:00; clsd Su, NH, 2nd Sa, NY, mid-Aug. The technique for *beni*, a bright red dye made from safflowers, had virtually disappeared by World War II, but the third-generation master of Nitta Textile Industries reinvented it, based on what may have been the only surviving use of *beni*, to dye vestments at the Ise Shrines. Nitta's exquisite colors have earned the company national fame; it supplies kimono to the Empress. Make an appointment to visit the lovely house and see the weavers at work.

11 \* **Sasano Ittō-bori** 笹野一刀彫 (38-4288). Hrs: 9:00–17:00; clsd Jan. 1. A classic Japanese wooden toy, these "one-blade carvings" of hawks and chickens have curling tails and wing feathers of shaved wood.

## Yonezawa Dining and Lodgings (TEL 0238)

Yonezawa's excellent cuisine developed out of the area's poverty. Carp, raised in garden ponds, are served blanched, or deep fried with a sweet-and-sour sauce. Yonezawa beef is among Japan's best; try it sashimi style (*gyū-sashi*). Even the *eki-ben* (station *bentō*) has beef in it. Yonezawa is a nice place to visit, but an even nicer place to stay is Shirabu Onsen (see below).

1 **Hotel Otowaya** ホテル音羽屋 (22-0124). 2-1-40 Ekimae, Yonezawa-shi, Yamagata-ken. An old, half-Western, half-Japanese hotel near the station. S Y5800–6500. Suite, Y16,000 w/meals.

2 **Ōgawara** 大河原 (23-4502). Hrs: 11:00–21:00; clsd 1st and 3rd Tu. Sukiyaki, steak, Shabu-shabu. Full course Y5300.

3 **Okiya** 黄木屋 (22-2240). Hrs: 11:00–21:00 (last order 20:00); clsd Tu (except if NH). Sukiyaki from Y2600.

4 **Tokiwa** 登起波 (23-5400). Hrs: 11:00–19:30 (last order 17:30); clsd NY, mid-Aug. Sukiyaki from Y2–5000. No CC.

5 **Chikusei-ken** 竹盛軒 (23-0040). Hrs: 11:00–14:00, 17:00–19:00. By reservation. Regional cuisine. Shiobiki-zushi (salmon sushi) set, Y1100. Full course, Y3000. Reservation required. No CC.

6 **Miyasaka** 宮坂鯉店 (22-7188). Hrs: 8:00–18:00; clsd NY. Carp cuisine. Take-out and delivery only. *Koi no Amani* (sweet-cooked carp) from Y450. No CC.

9 \*\* **Uesugi Kinenkan** (21-5121). Hrs: 11:00–16:00; Dec.–Mar. 11:00–15:00, clsd Tu. Reservation advised. *Kenzen-ryōri* (poor daimyo's cuisine), Y2500–4500. Beef dishes, Y4–6000. V, MC, CB.

\* **SHIRABU ONSEN** 白布温泉
*A scenic 0:50h bus ride from Yonezawa station.* This mountain hot-spring village has three inns, Nishiya, Nakaya, and Higashiya (West, Middle, and East), which have main buildings with heavy thatched roofs. All have wood-paneled bathhouses with rock baths, wood baths, and hot waterfalls. Ski areas are nearby, so Shirabu is accessible in winter.
\*\* **Nishiya** 西屋 (55-2211). Shirabu Onsen, Seki, Yonezawa-shi, Yamagata-ken. The most beautiful. Y9–20,000.
\* **Nakaya** 中屋 (55-2111). Address as above. Quaint courtyard. Y10–20,000.
\* **Higashiya** 東屋 (55-2011). Address as above. Y9–15,000. MC, CB.

## Exploring

# The mountains around Yonezawa abound in rustic onsen, all with wooden inns and open-air baths, about Y5000 w/meals. **Shin Takayu**, 0:30h on foot from Shirabu Onsen, has one old inn, the Azumaya (0238-55-2031), with great views. **Ubayu Onsen** is 0:45h by ryokan jeep, 0:40h on foot from Tōge station, 3 stops from Yonezawa; it has two inns, Masugataya (35-2633) and Fukushimaya (34-2250). **Ōdaira Onsen** is 0:50h by bus from Yonezawa, then 3:40h on foot, or 0:55h by ryokan jeep, then 0:15h on foot; has one inn, the Takimiya (38-3360).

## W2 SAKAMACHI 坂町
*2:00h by Yonesaka line limited express (2 per day) from Yonezawa. Junction to JR Uetsu main line, 0:40h to Niigata* (KANTŌ II:N2).

# TŌHOKU VI. KŌRIYAMA

**Tokyo to Kōriyama:** *1:20h by Tōhoku Shinkansen from Ueno station.*
**Prefecture:** Fukushima

# TŌHOKU VI:W. WEST FROM KŌRIYAMA

## INAWASHIRO-KO (LAKE)　猪苗代湖・磐梯朝日国立公園

*0:30h by train from Kōriyama. Or 0:30–0:40h by train or bus from Aizu-Wakamatsu.*
This developed lake and mountain resort is a gateway to Bandai-Asahi National Park. 0:15h by bus from the station is **Noguchi Hideyo Kinenkan** 野口英世記念館, the memorial museum and childhood home of the famous medical researcher (Hrs: 8:30–16:45, daily. Nov.–Mar. 9:00–16:00). Although one of his hands was crippled in infancy, Noguchi Hideyo (1876–1928) won world renown for isolating the syphilis spirochete and researching yellow fever, of which he died in Africa. Next door is the **Aizu Minzokukan** 会津民俗館, two thatched-roof farmhouses displaying farm tools and relics of fertility cults (Hrs: 8:00–17:00, daily. Nov. 15–Mar. 8:30–16:30).

The Bandai Plateau is dotted with ponds, formed when Mt. Bandai erupted in 1888, blasting off a third of the mountain and damming up streams. Best known are the **Goshi-kinuma**, "five-colored marshes," which can be seen along a 4-km nature trail between Goshikinuma Iriguchi (0:30h by bus from the Inawashiro-ko bus terminal) and Bandai Kōgen, a developed tourist center.

### Inawashiro-ko/National Park Lodgings

**Kokuminshukusha Okinajima-sō** 国民宿舎翁島荘 (0242-65-2811). 1048-6 Gotenzan, Okinasawa, Inawashiro-chō, Yama-gun, Fukushima-ken. A pleasant lodge on a wooded slope overlooking Inawashiro-ko. Y5450 w/meals. No CC.
**Ura-Bandai YH** 裏磐梯YH (0241-32-2811). Goshikinuma, Ura-bandai, Azuma-kyoku, Fukushima-ken. Near Goshikinuma Iriguchi bus stop.

## W1 ＊ AIZU-WAKAMATSU　会津若松

*1:00h by express from Kōriyama, or 2:00h by express from Niigata* (KANTŌ II:N2). *From Kinugawa Onsen, near Nikkō* (KANTŌ I:N1), *1:50h by bus to Aizu-Tajima, then 1:20h by train to Aizu-Wakamatsu. This back route is said to be scenic.* This small city is an unsightly sprawl, but its lack of pretension can be charming. The small city of Aizu-Wakamatsu was the castle town of the powerful Aizu fief, ruled by lords closely related to the TOKUGAWA shoguns and thus serving as a buffer between the *tozama* (outer) daimyo of northern Tōhoku and the capital at Edo. Aizu-Wakamatsu is famous for the Byakkotai, a legion of teenage samurai who committed suicide on Iimoriyama in 1868, during the brief Boshin War, in which their lord was defeated by the new imperial army. Other attractions include the castle, a reconstructed samurai house, and local crafts.

183

### Calendar

**Jan. 7: ＊ Hadaka Mairi (Naked Festival).** Yanaizu (*1:10h by Tadami line local from Aizu-Wakamatsu*). Mobs of youths in loincloths race up 113 icy steps to the main hall of Enzō-ji and climb a thick rope hanging from the ceiling. From 20:00.

### Getting Around

Nanukamachi-dōri, a street with many quaint shops, is a fine place to prowl on foot. The main sights are grouped around Iimoriyama, the Buke-Yashiki, and the castle. Taxi, bus, or bicycle advised for transport between these areas. Rent-a-cycles at **Urushiya Kōgei** (lacquer shop) by station. One- and two-day bus passes (Y770 and Y1380) permit unlimited rides on city buses. **Two handy bus routes:** From pier 6, Tsuruga-jō mawari route circles the town counterclockwise via the castle and Iimoriyama; the Iimoriyama mawari route goes in the reverse direction. From pier 4, Higashiyama Onsen route traverses the town via Onyaku-en and Bukeyashiki-mae. **Teiki Kankō (Scheduled Tour) Bus:** In Japanese. Apr. 6–Nov. 25. Tours leave from the station.

### Aizu-Wakamatsu Sights

**＊＊ Iimoriyama** 飯盛山 *0:10h by bus (Iimoriyama mawari) from station.* The graves of 19 teenage samurai of the Byakkotai (White Tiger Legion) are on this wooded bluff, where they committed suicide in 1868. Two nearby monuments call for explanation: The Pompeiian marble column topped by a bronze eagle was given by Rome in 1928, with the inscription, "...the city of the birthplace of civilization sends this Fascist Party symbol with a 1,000-year-old stone column, the symbol of eternal greatness, to the Flower of Bushido." The smaller black marble monument, given by a German military attaché to Japan, reads: "To Aizu's young samurai from one German man." During the Occupation these inscriptions were effaced. The German monument was restored in 1953. Today, souvenir stands crowd the grounds, and an escalator transports busloads of Japanese tourists up the hill to pose for photos in front of the Italian monument, which has become the symbol for Iimoriyama.
**＊＊ Sazae-dō (Conch Shell Hall)** さざえ堂 This hexagonal tower built in 1796 contains representations of each of the 33 temples in the Kansai region's Kannon Pilgrimage (see Villages, p. 56); its unique double-helix staircase enables worshippers to ascend and descend the tower without crossing the same "pilgrimage spot" twice.
**＊＊ Kyū Aizu-han Gohonjin** 会津藩御本陣 (ICP). Hrs: 8:30–17:00, daily. Built in 1679 as an inn for high officials. During the 1868 Boshin War, it served as the daimyo's military head-quarters; the pillars and doors are scarred with bullet holes and sword slashes from the battle.

\* **Onyaku-en** 御薬園 Hrs: Apr.–Oct. 8:30–17:00. Nov.–Mar. 8:30–16:30. Clsd 1st M, Th of July and 1st Tu, Th of Dec. The attractive stroll garden, tea arbors, and villa of the lord of Aizu. Adjacent is a garden of some 200 species of medicinal plants which gives this place its name, Medicine Garden. The souvenir shop displays intriguing photos of the last daimyo.

\*\*\* **Buke-Yashiki (Samurai Mansion)** 会津武家屋敷 (28-2525). Hrs: 8:30–17:00. Dec.–Mar. 9:00–16:30. This reconstruction of a grand samurai estate is superbly conceived. The sprawling complex includes the reconstructed estate of a senior Aizu vassal, a working water-powered rice mill, lacquer craft demonstrations, a wax museum depicting dramatic moments in Aizu's history, and a superb specimen of flaming Jōmon pottery.

**Matsudaira-ke Gobyō (Tombs)** 松平家御廟 *Walk 0:15h from In'nai, one bus stop past Buke-Yashiki.* The tombs of the Aizu lords lie in the shade of old cryptomeria trees, up a peaceful stone-paved walk.

**Tsuruga-jō** 鶴ガ城 *0:10h by Tsuruga-jō mawari bus from station.* A modern concrete keep built on the moat and fortifications of what was once the most ancient and powerful fortress in Tōhoku. The Edo-period lords, the Matsudaira, were a collateral branch of the TOKUGAWA and shared the same triple hollyhock crest. The last lord, Katamori, was the son of a shogun who was adopted into the Aizu lord's family. In 1863 he crushed an attempted coup d'état by the Chōshū clan, but lost to the "imperial" — read Chōshū — army in 1868 (see Hagi History, p. 460). The rebuilt citadel houses a local history museum.

\*\* **Aizu Shuzō Rekishikan (Saké History Museum)** 会津酒造歴史館 (26-0031). Hrs: Apr.–Nov. 8:30–17:00. Dec.–Mar. 9:00–16:30. This handsome old brewery is an interesting museum on saké brewing. The *sugidama*, a large ball of cryptomeria fronds hanging over the entrance, serves as a timer; the fronds are picked as brewing begins, and when they turn brown and dry, the saké is ready. The ground floor shows the brewing process; the second floor contains all kinds of serving vessels.

\* **Aizu Ichibankan** 会津一番館 (27-3750). Hrs: 8:00–20:00. Handsome black-walled *kura* with an antique-filled café on the ground floor and an upstairs gallery displaying memorabilia connected to local hero Noguchi Hideyo (see p. 183).

\* **Aizu Shuzō Hakubutsukan (Saké-Brewing Museum)** 会津酒造博物館 (28-0150). Hrs: 8:30–17:00; clsd NY. *Near Nishi-Wakamatsu station.* Where the Kono family has been brewing saké for 12 generations. Edo-period furnishings and art are on view.

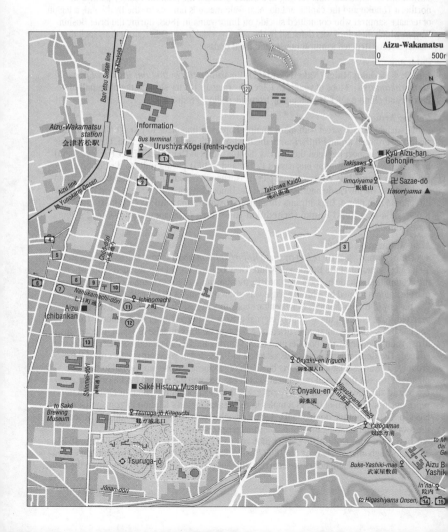

＊**Hongō** 本郷 *0:30h by bus.* This pottery village was founded in 1593 to make tiles for Tsuruga-jō. Later, the castle lord imported potters from Seto (near Nagoya) to teach Hongō potters to make functional, everyday wares. A few kilns, mostly mediocre, remain. Stop in first at the **Aizu Hongōyaki Shiryōkan** 会津本郷焼資料館 for a map. The exhibits of old Hongō pottery are worth a look. A short walk away is famed **Munakata-gama** 宗像窯 (56-2174), the only kiln that still makes the classic *nishin-bachi*, a rectangular crock for pickled herring, once a staple protein for the landlocked city. (Hrs: 8:30–17:00, clsd NY.)

## Aizu-Wakamatsu Crafts and Shopping

Aizu-shikki (lacquerware), Aizu *e-rōsoku* (candles hand-painted with flowers), *akabeko* (a red papier-mâché ox with a bobbing head), Aizu *momen* (indigo-dyed, striped cotton), and Hongō-yaki are nationally famous products of the town.

3 **Mingeidokoro Banshō** 会津若松民芸処番匠 (27-4358). Hrs: 8:30–17:00; clsd Su, NH, Aug. 12–18, NY. *Akabeko* made to order, Y720.

5 **Yamada Momen** 山田木綿　七日町 (22-1632). Hrs: 8:00–20:00; clsd NY. Indigo-dyed textiles.

8 ＊**Shirokiya** 白木屋漆器店 (22-0203). Hrs: 8:30–17:30; Nov.–Mar. 8:00–17:00; clsd NY. Behind the 1914 Western facade is the city's foremost lacquer store. Sample wares and lacquermaking process displayed in a free museum.

9 **Suzukiya Rihei Shōten** 鈴木屋利兵衛　大町1丁目 (22-0151). Hrs: 9:30–19:00; July–Oct. open daily, Nov.–June clsd 1st and 3rd Th. Aizu-shikki shop founded in the 1840s. Folkcrafts, souvenir on ground floor, antiques and better wares upstairs.

10 **Taketō** 竹藤　中央1丁目 (22-1068). Hrs: 9:30–20:00; Nov.–Apr. 9:30–19:00. Bambooware, in a fine old building. From souvenirs to fine craftwork.

13 ＊**Ozawa Rōsokuten** 小沢ローソク店 (27-0652). Hrs: 8:00–19:30; clsd NY. Candles.

## Aizu-Wakamatsu Dining

185

Around Ichinomachi bus stop and east on Nanukamachi-dōri are several old shops and restaurants.

7 ＊**Mitsutaya** 満田屋 (27-1345). Hrs 9:00–18:00; clsd 1st and 3rd W; Jan.–Mar. clsd every W. Atmospheric old shop famous for *dengaku* (tofu, yams, and fish, slathered with sweet miso and broiled over charcoal). *Dengaku* "A" set, Y1000. Vegetarian "B" set, Y600. No CC.

11 ＊**Ebiya** えびや　馬場町 (22-1288). Hrs: 11:00–14:30, 16:00–21:30. Grilled *unagi* (eel) in a rambling, old-style establishment. Informal and friendly. Courses Y1900＋. No CC.

12 ＊**Takino** 田季野 (25-0808). Hrs: 11:00–23:00, clsd NY. Famous for *wappa-meshi*, rice steamed in a bentwood steamer with a variety of toppings, such as salmon and roe, *ayu* (sweetfish), *sansai* (mountain greens), crabmeat, and wild fowl. Y1200–1800. No CC.

14 ＊**Tsuruizutsu** 鶴井筒 (26-5629). Hrs: 11:00–23:00; clsd Jan.–Mar. Higashiyama Onsen. Local country cuisine in a former headman's house. *Sansai soba* Y600. Courses from Y1500. No CC.

## Aizu-Wakamatsu Lodgings (TEL 0242)

1 **Aizu-Wakamatsu Washington Hotel** 会津若松ワシントン・ホテル (22-6111). S Y6500–7200, Tw Y12,500.

2 **Green Hotel Aizu** グリーンホテル会津 (24-5181). Ekimae, Aizu-Wakamatsu-shi, Fukushima-ken. Japanese-style rooms at same price as Western. Y5400 w/breakfast. V, AX, MC.

4 ＊**Ryokan Tagoto** 旅館田事 (24-7500). 5-15 Jōhoku-chō. This family inn prides itself on its cuisine. Meals are served around an *irori*. Y10–15,000. V.

6 ＊＊**Ryojin-kan** 旅人館 (28-4000). 3-28 Nanukamachi. A splendid early Meiji-period merchant's house. Rooms in the main house and, for ladies only, in a converted herring storehouse in back. Excellent local cuisine. Shared bathrooms. Y7000 w/meals, Y5500 w/o meals. No CC.

15 **Mukaidaki Ryokan** 向滝旅館 (27-7501). Higashiyama Onsen, Aizu-Wakamatsu-shi. One of the better inns at Higashiyama Onsen. Y18,000＋ w/meals. AX, DC.

**Aizu no Sato YH** 会津の里YH (0241-27-2054). 36 Hatakeda, Kofune, Aizu-Shiokawa-chō, Yama-gun. Toward Kitakata (see below). Clsd NY. Y1700, no meals. Nov.–Mar., Y1900.

## W2 YUNOKAMI ONSEN　湯野上温泉

*1:00h by train or bus from Aizu-Wakamatsu.* A small hot-spring resort. Turn off the main road to get to Ōuchijuku post town.

## W3 ＊ # ŌUCHIJUKU　大内宿

*From Yunokami Onsen, 0:20h by taxi or 1:30h on foot.* This charming, isolated hamlet preserves some 40 Edo-period houses, many with thatched roofs, from the days when it was a post town for the lords of Aizu. The village has been designated a traditional architecture preserve, which caused many residents to grumble because this meant they couldn't modernize their homes. The local shrine, in a pretty glade, has a festival on July 2. In autumn, bears come into the farmers' fields and sometimes end up supplementing minshuku dinners. Lodgings at one of the houses can be arranged through the Minshuku Kumiai (02416-8-2943). We liked **Yamatoya Minshuku** 大和屋 (8-2911). 46 Yamamoto, Ōuchi, Shimogō-chō, Minamiaizu-gun, Fukushima-ken. The granny is gruff but goodhearted, the house a little disheveled but atmospheric. Y6500 w/meals.

T
Ō
H
O
K
U

## Exploring

# Continue west along the Aizu line to Aizu-Tajima (1:20h from Aizu-Wakamatsu), a former post town with a folklore museum. From Tajima, there are buses to **Kinugawa Onsen**, **Hinoemata**, and **Ozenuma**, all near Nikkō National Park (Kantō, p. 246). Hinoemata is a rustic village famous for its * **Kabuki**, performed on a thatched outdoor stage on May 12–18 and Aug. 18. Local farmers learned it on their Ise pilgrimages and brought it home.

## W4 * KITAKATA 喜多方

*0:20–0:30h by Ban'etsu Saisen line from Aizu-Wakamatsu, or 2:00–3:00h from Niigata* (KANTŌ II:N2). In 1880, a major fire swept through this little town. In the aftermath, the townspeople were stunned to find their *kura*, mortar-and-tile storehouses, standing intact amid the ashes. This demonstration of the *kura*'s ability to withstand fire convinced them to rebuild their homes, shops, inns, and even temples in *kura* style (see Villages, p. 55). Kitakata was not the only town to perceive the advantages of fireproof buildings—Meiji-period Tokyo was a metropolis of *kura*—but it is rare today for having preserved so many, more than 2,500 by a recent count. They are vanishing from the main streets, but many survive in side lanes and backyards, giving Kitakata a visual appeal that has been lost in most modern Japanese towns. Visitors should also not miss Kumano Jinja.

## Getting Around

Areas noted for *kura* include Chūō-dōri, Hon-nakamachi, Nishimachi, and Higashimachi. Farther out in the countryside are Sugiyama and Mitsuya, the latter noted for its red-brick *kura* incorporating Western arches. A leisurely ramble on foot or bicycle is the best way to see them. Rent-a-cycle by the station. Leaving from near the station is a horse-drawn *kura*-shaped wagon that makes the rounds to the main attractions. 1:30h tours Apr.–Nov., three times a day, Y1300 (children Y800).

## 186 Kitakata Sights

**Yamatogawa Shuzō Kitakata Fūdokan (Saké-Brewing Museum)** 大和川酒造北方風土館 Hrs: 9:00–16:30. Housed in a *kura* built in 1790.

* **Anshō-ji** 安勝寺 A temple rebuilt in 1895 using *kura* architecture.

** **Kai Honke** 甲斐本家 Hrs: 9:00–17:00; clsd Dec.–mid-Mar. A prosperous saké merchant's black-mortar house, built in the 1920s. Has a pretty garden. Visitors can peek at the inner rooms.

* **Shimashin Shōten** 島新商店 A *kura* shop on Chūō-dōri. Open to public.

** **Urushigura Yamato** うるし倉やまと (24-2858). Hrs: 8:30–17:30. 130-year-old lacquer shop with a *kura* mini-museum on lacquerware production.

* **Aizu Urushi Bijutsu Hakubutsukan (Aizu Lacquer Art Museum)** 会津うるし美術博物館 (4-4111). Hrs: Apr.–Nov. 9:00–17:00. A lacquer shop exhibiting wares in a spacious Meiji-period residence.

*** **Kumano Jinja** 熊野神社 *From Kitakata station, 0:25h by infrequent bus to Shingū, or a 5-km taxi ride.* The torii is hung with a gargantuan *shimenawa* (twisted rope). The unusual and beautiful long hall, or ◆ Nagatoko (ICP), consists of a raised floor and 50 thick columns supporting an immense thatched roof. There are no walls, adornments, or implements save a few wisps of straw rope and a small offering stand on the bare floor. The shrine was founded by MINAMOTO no Yoriyoshi to enlist the aid of the Kumano Gongen (see Kinki, p. 415) in his fight against Tōhoku rebels (see Hiraizumi History, p. 169). His son, Yoshiie, built the Nagatoko on its present site in 1085. The hall was poorly repaired after a 16th-C earthquake, but in 1974 it was carefully restored, using many of the original columns. Nearby are a 14th-C bell and the **Monju-dō**, which houses some sculpture ascribed (dubiously) to the Kamakura period, including a Monju Bosatsu seated on a lion.

## Kitakata Dining and Lodgings (TEL 0241)

Kitakata's *ramen* noodles for some reason have a great reputation. For coffee, try **Renga**, a brick *kura* by the station, and **Ikoi**, which has a clock collection.

**Makoto Shokudō** まこと食堂　市役所東側 (22-0232). Hrs: 7:30–20:00, daily; clsd 1st and 3rd M (except if NH), Aug. 2–3, NY. Famed for *ramen*.

**Sasaya Ryokan** 笹屋旅館 (22-0008). 4844 3-chōme, Kitakata-shi, Fukushima-ken. A well-known *kura* ryokan. Y6500+.

**Green Hotel** グリーンホテル (22-0011). 4664 2-chōme. Business hotel. S Y4700, Tw Y10–12,000.

# Tokyo

Is there any city in the world today more intriguing than Tokyo? Other capitals may be more beautiful, more cultured, more sane — better, without question, at serving their function as preserves of art and history. But Tokyo is no museum. It is a laboratory. From a fecund brew of wealth, imagination and desire is emerging the city of the future. The air pulsates with a spirit of experimentation. The face of Tokyo is transmutating before our eyes, as whole expanses of drab, postwar structures give way to svelte architecture echoing the high-tech packaging of a Sony product. The streets swarm with invention. Fashions straddle science fiction and Kabuki. Vending machines speak politely in synthetic female voices. In Yoyogi Park, Elvis clones gyrate alongside performance artists of the apocalypse. These (to our eyes) weird juxtapositions of cultures, eras and technologies seem to spring from an intense collective hunger to redefine life. Like a galaxy condensing from a swirling molecular cloud, creating order out of chaos, Tokyo is spinning out an alternative universe of urban possibility.

# TOURING TOKYO

We have divided Tokyo into four areas. The development of these quarters has partly to do with the Edo-period distinction between High City and Low City (see Tokyo History). Naturally, our characterizations are only approximate; parts of Traditional Tokyo are avant-garde, just as parts of Contemporary Tokyo are quite staid.

(I) **Traditional Tokyo** (Northeast): Those brave enough to look for the flavor of old Japan in Tokyo are advised to look here; includes Asakusa and Ueno Park.

(II) **Establishment Tokyo** (East, Southeast): The center for banks, airlines, department stores, galleries, exclusive bars; includes the Imperial Palace and Ginza.

(III) **Contemporary Tokyo** (West, Southwest): This is the most internationalized, trendiest, and, to many, the most interesting part of town; includes Roppongi, Akasaka, Yoyogi/Harajuku and Shibuya.

(IV) **Commuter Tokyo** (West, Northwest): Those looking for an Orwellian future might come to these huge, furiously busy commuter centers; includes Shinjuku and Ikebukuro.

### Seasons

Summers are dreadful, winters are comparatively mild. September and June are damp. Best seasons are October–November and April–May.

### Average Temperature °C (°F)/Days of Rain or Snow

| January | April | July | October |
|---|---|---|---|
| 4.1 (39.4)/5 | 13.5 (56.3)/10 | 25.2 (77.4)/10 | 16.9 (62.4)/10 |

**Note: This transit diagram shows only selected train and subway lines.**

**TOKYO TRANSIT DIAGRAM**

WEST ◄► EAST

Ikebukuro ②

IV. COMMUTER TOKYO

Shinjuku ①

Marunouchi line

Harajuku ②

Chiyoda line

Aoyama-dōri

Akasaka-Mitsuke ②

Omotesandō

Shibuya ③

Roppongi ①

Gaien Higas

III. CONTEMPORARY TOKYO

Yamanote line

# BEST ATTRACTIONS

| I:1 | ★★★ Asakusa Kannon Temple |
| I:1 | ★★ Kappabashi |
| I:2 | ★★ Ueno Tōshō-gū (shrine) |
| I:2 | ★★★ Tokyo National Museum |
| I:2 | ★★★ Shitamachi Museum |
| II:1 | ★★★ Tokyo Imperial Palace |
| II:1 | ★★★ Idemitsu Art Museum |
| II:2 | ★★ Ginza Yon-chōme Crossing |
| II:2 | ★★ Riccar Art Museum |
| II:2 | ★★★ Kabuki-za (theater) |
| II:3 | ★★ Tsukiji Central Fish Market |
| III:1 | ★★ Roppongi Crossing |
| III:2 | ★★ Suntory Art Museum |
| III:2 | ★★ Sōgetsu Kaikan |
| III:2 | ★★ Aoyama Gochōme |
| III:2 | ★★ Nezu Art Museum |
| III:2 | ★★ Ōta Art Museum |
| III:2 | ★★ Takeshita-dōri |
| III:2 | ★★★ Yoyogi National Stadium |
| III:2 | ★★★ Meiji Shrine |
| III:3 | ★★ Japan Folk Art Museum |
| IV:1 | ★★ Kabukichō |
| IV:1 | ★★★ Tokyo Metropolitan Government Office Building |
| IV:2 | ★★ Seibu Department Store |
| IV:2 | ★★ Rikugi-en (garden) |

189

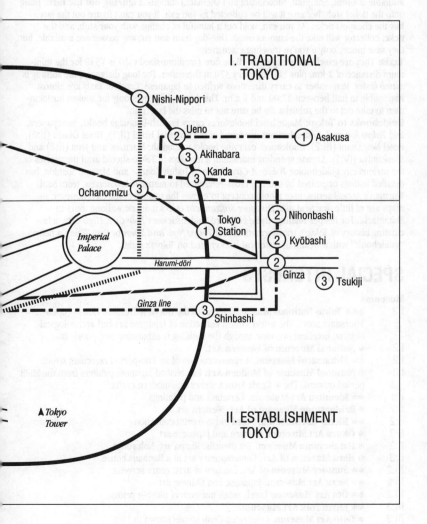

### Traveling and Navigating in Tokyo

**Getting There:** Downtown Tokyo is 1:00–2:00h from Narita International Airport (see Practical Advice, p. 5, for details on airlines and getting into town). For those coming from Kyoto or Ōsaka, Tokyo station is 3:00–3:30h by Shinkansen (bullet train).

**Getting Around:** Many districts of Tokyo were once outlying villages (Shinjuku was a post town, Ueno a temple town) that were absorbed into the expanding modern city without becoming integrated into a greater city plan. Each retains its own center and peculiar organization of streets, while the city's larger avenues and transport lines link the districts. The best way to get to know Tokyo is to plan your day within one or two of these districts; most can be seen on foot, and the trick is to orient yourself around the main subway or train station (a pocket compass comes in handy). **Maps:** Pick up a map at the Tourist Information Center (TIC) in Hibiya (p. 210). It includes maps of the subways and trains. **Addresses:** Carry a card from your hotel, with its address written in Japanese, and try to get written addresses or maps (with landmarks indicated) for your destinations. Even armed with an address, you will have problems: Tokyo is divided into areas, then blocks (*chōme*), subblocks, and finally buildings, numbered according to the order in which they were built. For example, to get to 6-3-15 Ginza, it's pretty easy to find 6-3 Ginza (it should be near 6-2 or 6-4); but once you've gotten this far, you may have to check every building on the block.

**Train Stations and Lines:** Trains and subways operate from 5:00 a.m.–midnight. See under listings for details of Ueno (I:2), Tokyo (II:1), Shibuya (III:3), and Shinjuku (IV:1) stations. **JR Yamanote line:** This line circles central Tokyo, hitting almost all the important stations. Though it may not be the most direct way to get around, it is easy. For the minimum fare of Y120, you can circle Tokyo in an hour. **JR Chūō line:** Cuts through the center of the Yamanote loop, providing the fastest link between Tokyo station and Shinjuku.

**Subways:** Ten lines crisscross the city. Except for the three Toei lines, which have a separate fare system, one can transfer freely between these lines. Subway entrances are indicated by blue circular signs inscribed with a white S. Subway lines are color-coded, with station names in roman letters. Buy tickets at vending machines or ticket windows. Assistance in English available at Ginza, Shinjuku, Nihonbashi and Ōtemachi stations. **Figuring out the fare:** Hang onto the ticket stub, because it will be collected as you exit. If you can't figure out the fare, buy the cheapest ticket. As you exit, hold out a handful of change with your stub, and the ticket collector will take the amount owed. One-day train and subway passes are available, but they save money only if you're traveling extensively.

**Taxis:** They are exorbitantly expensive. Base fare (medium-sized cab) is Y540 for the minimum distance of 2 km, plus Y80 for every 370 m thereafter. For long distances, the subway is *much* faster. Remember to carry directions written in Japanese. Caution: Taxis are almost impossible to hail between 22:00 and 2 a.m. The drivers have eyes only for soused businessmen to take out to the suburbs. So be sure not to miss the last train.

**Guidebooks to Tokyo:** Major hotel bookstores carry English-language books, newspapers, and *Tokyo Journal*. Best selections are found at the Imperial Hotel (II:1), Hotel Ōkura (II:3), Hotel New Ōtani (III:2). Bookstores carrying books in English: Maruzen and Jena (II:2) and Kinokuniya (IV:1). Anyone spending more than a few days in Tokyo should avail themselves of the various city guidebooks: *Tokyo: A City Guide* by Judith Connor and Mayumi Yoshida, has detailed listings organized by subject, cross-referenced to maps. *Tokyo Access*, from Saul Wurman's Access series, uses a bold concept to convey the texture of the city; however, its maps are of little practical use. *Discover Shitamachi* offers intimate walking tours in Shitamachi. For deeper reading, there's Edward Seidensticker's *Low City, High City*, a fascinating history of Tokyo's transformation, and *Tokyo Now and Then* by Paul Waley, a hefty "guidebook" with a wealth of historical background on Tokyo's sights.

# SPECIAL INTERESTS

### Museums

I:2    **✳✳✳ Tokyo National Museum.** Includes the Hōryū-ji Treasure House (open Thursdays only). The world's finest collection of Japanese art and archeological objects. Excellent overview, though the building is exhausting and poorly lit.

I:2    **✳ National Museum of Western Art.**

I:2    **✳✳ Shitamachi Museum.** A reconstruction of an Edo-period merchant street.

I:3    **✳ National Museum of Modern Art.** Established Japanese painters from the Meiji period onward. The ✳ **Craft Annex** shows fine modern crafts.

II:1    **✳✳ Idemitsu Art Museum.** Ceramics and paintings.

II:2    **✳ Bridgestone Museum of Art.** Western art.

II:2    **✳✳ Riccar Art Museum.** Noted ukiyo-e print collection.

II:3    **✳ Ōkura Art Museum.** Chinese and Japanese art.

II:3    **✳ Hatakeyama Museum.** Tea utensils, Rimpa art, Noh robes.

II:3    **✳ Hara Museum of Art.** Contemporary art in a Bauhaus house.

III:1    **✳✳ Suntory Museum of Art.** Decorative arts, genre screens.

III:2    **✳✳ Nezu Art Museum.** Japanese and Chinese art.

III:2    **✳✳ Ōta Art Museum.** Lovely small museum of ukiyo-e prints.

III:3    **✳✳ Japan Folk Art Museum.**

III:3    **✳ Gotō Art Museum.** Celebrated Genji scrolls shown in May.

## Contemporary Art Galleries

*Tokyo Journal* lists current shows. Most galleries are rented by the artist, so it's impossible to characterize them reliably. Here are some of the more interesting spaces:

**Gallery Ueda Ginza** (3574-7553). 6-6-7 Ginza, Asahi Bldg. Leading contemporary artists, mainly Japanese and Korean.

**Akira Ikeda** (3567-5090). 2-8-18 Kyōbashi. Established international artists.

**Kobayashi Gallery** (3561-0515). 3-8-12 Ginza, Yamato Bldg., B1. Hrs: 11:30–19:00; clsd Su.

**Gallery Yamaguchi** (3564-0633). 3-8-12 Ginza, Yamato Bldg., 3F. Hrs: 11:00–19:00; Sa 11:00–18:00; clsd Su, NH.

**Satani Gallery** (3564-6733). 4-2-6 Ginza, Daini Asahi Bldg., BF. Hrs: 11:00–18:00; clsd Su, NH.

**Sagachō Exhibit Space** (3630-3243). 1-8-13 Saga, Shokuryō Bldg., 3F. Hrs: 11:00–18:00; Th 11:00–20:00; clsd Su, NH. *Take Tozai line to Monzen-Nakamachi station, then walk 0:13h.* This beautiful large space run by Kazuko Koike is ranked among the most important galleries for contemporary art in Japan.

**Hosomi Contemporary Gallery** (3497-1328). Hrs: 11:00–19:00; clsd Su, NH. 6-5-17 Roppongi. Curated exhibits.

**Tepia** (5474-6111). 2-8-44 Kita Aoyama. Hrs: 10:00–18:00; Sa-Su, NH 10:00–17:00. Enter 1:00h before closing. Clsd M (except if NH, then clsd Tu). Interesting avant-garde exhibits in the large third-floor galleries. See p. 218.

**Spiral Building** (3498-1171). Hrs: 11:00–20:00. Western and Japanese avant-garde artists, performance art. Quality is generally high. See p. 219.

**Tokyo-to Shashin Bijutsukan (Museum of Photography)** (3280-0031). 4-19-24 Ebisu. Hrs: 10:00–18:00 (enter by 17:30); clsd 2nd and 4th W. Near Ebisu station. Japanese and international work, organized around varying themes.

**Sezon Bijutsukan (Museum of Art)** (5992-0155). Ikebukuro SMA-kan 1-2F. Hrs: 10:00–20:00 (enter by 19:30); clsd Tu. Attached to Ikebukuro's Seibu Department Store, long a mover and shaker in Tokyo's avant-garde scene.

## Tokyo Theaters

| | |
|---|---|
| I:2 | **Suzumoto Engeijō** (3834-5906). Hrs: 12:00–16:30, 17:00–20:40. *Rakugo* (traditional comedy). |
| II:1 | **∗∗ National Theater** (3265-7411). Kabuki every month except Feb., May, and Sept. Bunraku in Feb., May, Sept., Dec. Matinee and early evening programs. |
| II:2 | **∗∗∗ Kabuki-za** (3541-3131). Mainly Kabuki. Matinee and early evening performance almost daily. |
| III:1 | **Haiyū-za** (3470-2880). Tokyo's best contemporary theater. |
| III:2 | **∗ Tessenkai Noh Institute** (3401-2285). Performances usually the final Wednesday each month, and also on the 2nd Friday of each month at the Hōshō Nohgakudō near Suidōbashi station. |
| III:3 | **Kanze Nohgaku-dō** (3469-5241). Hrs: 11:00 on 1st Sunday of each month, 17:30 every Wednesday, and 17:00 on 2nd Thursday of odd-numbered months. |
| IV:1 | **∗ Suehirotei** (3351-2974). Hrs: 12:00–16:30, 17:00–21:30; Jan. 1-10, 11:00–16:00, 16:30–21:30. *Rakugo.* |
| IV:1 | **∗∗ National Noh Theater** (3423-1331). Program of one Noh and one Kyōgen play, 1st Wednesday (13:00) and 3rd Friday (18:30). Lecture performance 2nd Saturday (13:30). All-Kyōgen program 4th Friday of odd-numbered months (18:30). Special program 5th Sunday (13:00). |

## Shopping

Tokyo shops have a habit of clustering together in districts, as outlined below:

| | |
|---|---|
| I:1 | **Nakamise-dōri:** Traditional bazaar with Edo crafts. **Kappabashi:** Plastic food models. **Asakusabashi:** Toys. |
| I:2 | **Ameyoko-chō:** Cut-rate goods. **Yushima:** Traditional items. |
| I:3 | **Akihabara:** Discount electronic shops. **Jimbōchō:** Booksellers, antique books. |
| II:2 | **Nihonbashi** and **Ningyōchō:** Traditional goods—paper, Japanese cutlery, confections. **Ginza:** Expensive traditional and Western goods, and 7 department stores. |
| III:1 | **Roppongi:** Books, records, modern design. |
| III:2 | **Japan Traditional Craft Center. Killer-dōri** and **Omotesandō:** Avant-garde boutiques. **Kottohin-dōri:** Antiques. **Takeshita-dōri:** Imitation designer clothes. |
| III:3 | **Shibuya:** Tōkyū, Seibu, and Parco department stores. |
| IV:1 | **Shinjuku:** Discount cameras and electronics, major department stores. |
| IV:2 | **Ikebukuro:** Headquarters of Seibu Department Store (best in town). |

## Hot Night Spots

**Gold** ゴールド海岸3-1-6 (3453-3545). 3-1-6 Kaigan. Hrs: 18:00–wee hours. *0:15h walk from JR Tamachi Station.* Four-story disco in a former warehouse along the Tokyo bayfront. This club hit its peak in mid-1991, but it remains hot. All kinds of events and music. Decor can be described as apocalyptic. Cover: Y4000; F, Sa, day before NH Y5000.

**Juliana Tokyo** 芝浦1-13-10 (5484-4000). 1-13-10 Shibaura, Tokyo Port Bowl, 1F. Hrs: 18:00–wee hours. *0:15h walk from JR Tamachi station.* Millions of dollars were spent on this huge, 2,000-capacity dance club opened in May, 1991. Lavishly eclectic decor, varied music. Cover: Y5000 (men), Y4500 (women); Y500 more on F, Sa, day before NH.

**Ink Stick Suzue Factory** 海岸1-15-1 (3434-1677). 1-15-1 Kaigan. Hrs: 18:00–23:30, daily. *0:05h walk from south exit of JR Hamamatsuchō station.* Tokyo's best club for live, cutting-edge music.

**Tantra** タントラ 渋谷3-5-5 高橋ビル (5485-8414). 3-5-5 Shibuya, No. 5 Takahashi Bldg., B1F. Hrs: 22:00–8:00 a.m. *On Roppongi-dōri, near Shibuya Ni-chōme Kōsaten.* Incense-laden watering hole where eerily lit Thai buddhas and tree-sized floral sculptures loom over low tables. Attracts chic bohemians. Cover: Y1,000. Drinks from Y800. Light food served.

**Yakōchū** 夜光虫 恵比寿西1-34-17 (5489-5403). 1-34-17 Ebisu Nishi, The House Bldg., B3F. Hrs: 19:00–4:00 a.m. *0:05h walk from Daikanyama station.* Dark, gorgeous cavern lit by a bank of salt-water aquariums filled with luminous sea anemones. This pricey bar is hot with hip young Tokyoites. Cover: Y1000, drinks from Y1000.

**Contemporary Architecture in and near Tokyo**

| | |
|---|---|
| I:1 | **La Flamme d'Or.** Philippe Starck. |
| II:1 | **Supreme Court Building.** Okada Shin'ichi. |
| II:1 | **Wacoal Kōjimachi Building.** Kurokawa. |
| II:2 | **San'ai Dream Center.** Nikken Sekkei. |
| II:2 | **Sony Building.** Ashihara Yoshinobu. |
| II:2 | **Shizuoka Press and Broadcasting Building.** Tange. |
| II:2 | **Nakagin Capsule Building.** Kurokawa. |
| II:3 | **Keiō University New Library.** Maki. |
| III:1 | **Roppongi Prince Hotel.** Kurokawa. |
| III:2 | **Akasaka Prince Hotel.** Tange. |
| III:2 | **Sōgetsu Kaikan.** Tange. |
| III:2 | **Tepia.** Maki. |
| III:2 | **Spiral Building.** Maki. |
| III:2 | **Aoyama Gochōme.** Boutique buildings by Andō and others. |
| III:2 | **Hanae Mori Building.** Tange. |
| III:2 | **Yoyogi National Stadium.** Tange. |
| III:3 | **Hillside Terrace Apartments.** Maki. |
| IV:1 | **Ichibankan, Nibankan.** Takeyama Minoru. |
| IV:1 | **Tokyo Metropolitan Gymnasium.** Maki. |
| IV:1 | **Tokyo Metropolitan Government Office Building.** Tange. |
| IV:2 | **St. Mary's Cathedral.** Tange. |

# CALENDAR

**Jan. 1–3: Hatsumōde.** Year's first visit to shrines and temples. Asakusa Kannon (I:1) and Meiji Jingū (III:2) are especially popular. On the 2nd, the Imperial Palace grounds (II:1) are open to the public.

**Jan. 2–3: Daruma-ichi.** Haijima Daishi temple (*1:25h by Chūō and Itsukaichi lines from Shinjuku; get off at Haijima*). One of the biggest Daruma fairs in Tokyo; buyers of the furious, roly-poly dolls paint in one eye as a prayer, with a promise to paint in the other when the prayer is granted.

**Jan. 6: Dezome-shiki.** Parade of Tokyo's fire brigades, along Chūō-dōri in Harumi. Fire-fighters dressed as Edo-period firemen perform acrobatic stunts atop ladders.

**Jan. 8: ✳ Dondo-yaki.** Torigoe Jinja (I:1). Bonfire of New Year ornaments.

**Mid-Jan.: 15 days of sumo.** New Kokugikan (I:1).

**Jan. 18: Mōja-okuri.** Asakusa Kannon (I:1). Two priests in demon masks beat the floor of the temple with torches and run out, spraying sparks over onlookers. From 18:00.

**Feb. 3: Setsubun.** (See Matsuri, p. 73.) Bean-throwing at Asakusa Kannon and Torigoe Jinja (I:1), Kanda Myōjin (I:3), Hie Jinja (III:1).

**Feb. 8: Harikuyō.** Asakusa Kannon (I:1). Spirits of broken needles are consoled; the needles are stuck in tofu and other soft foods.

**Feb. 11: ✳ Ta Asobi.** Kitano Jinja (*Tōbu-Tōjō line to Tōbu-Nerima, then bus to Miyanoshita*). Millennium-old Field Play festival in which men and boys reenact a year's rice-growing cycle; performed annually since 1725. Get there by 17:00.

**Mid-Apr.: Gagaku.** Imperial Music Hall (II:1). Ancient court music. Call 3213-1111 up to two months in advance for exact date.

**Apr. 21–23: Spring Festival.** Yasukuni Jinja (I:3). Martial displays and folk performing arts are offered at the shrine.

**May 5–6: ✳✳ Kurayami Matsuri.** Fuchū, Okunitama Jinja (*take Keiō line from Shinjuku to Fuchū*). Rows of the largest drums in Japan are beaten. The 8 portable shrines head for the *otabisho* at 16:00.

**May 5: ✳ Shishi-mai.** *Take Tōbu-Tōjō line to Tōbu-Nerima, then bus to Kitano Jinja.* From 15:00, dancers disguised as female and male lions perform this spring planting rite. (May be canceled if dancers are unavailable.)

**May, Sa and Su before 14–15: ✳✳ Kanda Matsuri.** Kanda Myōjin (I:3). With the Sannō Matsuri, this festival was Edo's "Greatest Beneath Heaven." It was the sole occasion on which the townsmen could enter the castle and parade before the shogun. The full-scale matsuri is held only in odd-numbered years; the reason goes back to its rivalry with the Sannō Matsuri which often erupted into pitched battles. Eventually, the shogunate decreed that the festivals be held in alternate years. On the 9th, two ox-drawn *mikoshi* make the rounds. On the 15th, a procession of 70 *mikoshi* wends its drunken way through Kanda, Ōtemachi, and Nihonbashi,

# Tokyo, Architectural Dreamscape

The visitor to Tokyo may find it hard to believe this was once a supremely ordered city. Under the Tokugawa shoguns, every part of the city, then called Edo, had a designated role (see Tokyo history). Rational planning continued into the early modern era. Deciding that the city needed a Western facelift, the government invited architects such as Josiah Condor to build properly European structures in conspicuous places.

After World War II, which left Tokyo a charred flatland, Maekawa Kunio, the first Japanese architect to gain international stature, designed museums and halls in Ueno Park in, appropriately, the International Style of his mentor, Le Corbusier (who also built a hall in the park). Outside the orderly confines of the park, however, anarchy reigned. Cheap, practical concrete structures sprang up willy nilly, turning Tokyo into a vast sea of ugliness.

By the 1960s Japan's economy was running at full steam. Tange Kenzō, Maekawa's star disciple, worried that the city, in its rush to expand, would fail to provide adequate public spaces. His concern inspired the design of his famed Olympic Stadium (1964) in Yoyogi Park. The stadium's shiplike profile soars above an open site that draws weekend throngs directed there by a confluence of train lines, subways, and a trendy shopping boulevard. Three decades after it was created, this remains the most vibrant public space in the city.

Tokyo's explosive growth challenged Tange and his followers to propose a new kind of city, one flexible enough to accommodate both physical and economic expansion. Their idea, known as Metabolism, distinguished between stable infrastructure (expressways, public spaces) and unstable modules (housing, businesses) that would be replaced as people got richer and technology improved. Proposals such as Tange's Tokyo Plan and Isozaki Arata's Cities in the Sky were too ambitiously outrageous to be realized. One of the few metabolist designs actually built was Kurokawa Kishō's Nakagin Capsule Tower (1972), a modest structure consisting of replaceable, boxlike apartment units plugged into a central tower containing elevator shafts.

Still, Metabolism was a milestone. It created an avant-garde in architecture that saw Japan's urban, consumerist culture as its main concern. Architecture offered visions, some dreamlike, some nightmarish, of what the city was becoming. Takeyama Minoru, for example, covered two of his early buildings, Ichibankan (1969) and Nibankan (1970), with black-and-white traffic stripes and supergraphics as a sly comment on Tokyo's overbearing, ad-cluttered visual environment.

A shifting view of the city can be traced in Maki Fumihiko's work. In the 1970s Maki rejected the metabolist division between urban elements and infrastructure, and advocated a more ambiguous spatial interplay of buildings and their context. At Hillside Terrace (1976) he gracefully integrated a series of residences, offices and shops by using courtyards and passageways to link them to one another and to the street environment. By the 1980s Maki realized his concept of the relation between buildings and their context would have to change. Tokyo was moving too fast. His Spiral building (1985) integrates a cafe, art gallery, theater, shop, and offices within a lively structural collage of off-kilter geometries and diverse materials that echoes the restlessness of the street. Recently, Maki seems to have retreated from the city. At Tepia and Tokyo Municipal Gymnasium, he encloses the buildings within walls and fountains that divide rather than unify inner and outer spaces.

Isozaki Arata, famous abroad for such works as the Museum of Contemporary Art in Los Angeles and the Barcelona Olympic stadium, has also lost the pure vision of his youth. (Curiously, Isozaki has yet to design a major work in Tokyo, where he lives and works.) His early buildings were assertive compositions of large geometric forms — cubes, grids, tubes. The Tsukuba Center Building (1983), on the other hand, is fragmented and selfconscious. He calls it "a group portrait," an amalgam of borrowings from Western postmodern architects. The building's parts are arranged around a large, empty plaza. Could this be a metaphor for Japan's voracious consumerism, its plunder of other cultures for diversions to feed its empty soul?

Andō Tadao's work, in contrast, draws on Japanese tradition to create a subtle architectural language that is fresh and universal. Like Sukiya designers of the past, he coaxes forth the beauty of materials — steel, glass and concrete — and masterfully manipulates space to suggest an entire world within the confines of a townhouse plot. Andō's Corezone, one of several boutique buildings that adorn fashionable Aoyama Gochōme, creates a calm, shadowy refuge from the city.

Other architects of the rising generation continue to comment on the urban scene. Hara Hiroshi's Yamato International office complex on Tokyo Bay offers a shining vision of a city that is harmonious and yet individualized. Others, such as Shinohara Kazuo, Takamatsu Shin and Kitagawara Atsushi, explore the dynamic interplay of technology and urban culture. Each in his own way confronts the future, and offers an alternative to the nostalgic postmodernism of the West.

lasting into the night. A "shadow matsuri"—minus the parade—is held in even-numbered years.

**Mid-May: 15 days of sumo.** New Kokugikan (I:1).

**May (3rd F–Su): ✴✴ Sanja Matsuri.** Asakusa Jinja (I:1). A great Shitamachi festival, which draws huge crowds. The three main *mikoshi* exit the shrine at 7:00 on Sunday morning; for this and the return to the shrine in the evening, people come from miles away to join in carrying the *mikoshi*. There is also a parade of 100 smaller *mikoshi* accompanied by townsmen and geisha. One feature of the festival is *binzasara-mai*, a series of dances begun in 1312 that includes lion dances, seed-scattering dances, and others, accompanied by flutes, drums, and *sasara* (108 pieces of wood strung together and played with a snapping motion).

**May 31–June 1: Potted Plant Fair.** At Sengen Jinja, a shrine north of Asakusa Kannon temple that is famous for its miniature Mt. Fuji.

**June Su nearest the 9th: ✴✴ Yomatsuri.** Torigoe Jinja (I:1). A 4-ton *mikoshi* borne by 200 men is carried about the neighborhood during the day and welcomed home in the evening (20:00) in a magnificent, lantern-lit spectacle.

**June 10–16: ✴✴ Sannō Matsuri.** Hie Jinja (III:2). Main version held in even-numbered years, alternating with the Kanda Matsuri (see above); a "shadow matsuri" is held in odd-numbered years. This was a matsuri of the High City and, with the Kanda Matsuri, the only one allowed into the castle grounds. Unlike the hot-blooded Kanda Matsuri, the Sannō Matsuri culminates in a stately procession (in even-numbered years) on the 15th, led by an ox-drawn sacred carriage and accompanied by mounted samurai. The parade circles the palace and continues down to Ginza and Kyōbashi.

**Late June: Irises** in peak bloom at Meiji Jingū (III:2).

**July 1: Nagoshi Harae.** Torigoe Jinja (I:1). To ward off summer epidemics, people walk through a large straw ring and leave paper effigies, which are set adrift on Tokyo Bay the following day.

194 **July 9–10: Hozuki-ichi.** Japanese-lantern plants, believed to ward off insects, are sold at Asakusa Kannon (I:1).

**July 13–16: Mitama Matsuri.** Yasukuni Jinja (I:3). The approach is festooned with lanterns. Noh, traditional dance, and folk music are offered. Lasts until 22:00.

**July 15: Bon Odori** at Tsukudajima, since 1580.

**July–Aug.: Edo Engei Taikai.** Ueno Shinobazu Pond (I:2). Folk songs, *rakugo*, and other traditional Edo entertainments are performed at the music hall and Benten shrine. Mostly on weekends from mid-July to early August.

**July, last Sa: ✴ Sumidagawa Fireworks.** Revival of the Edo spectacle in which the river was officially opened for summer pleasure boats by a tremendous display of fireworks. Bridges around Asakusa are closed to traffic, but spectators are advised to avoid the crush and cross to Honjo, on the east side of the river. Kiyosumi street, on either side of Ryōgoku station (I:1), offers good views.

**Early Aug.: Takigi (Torchlight) Noh.** Hie Jinja (III:2). From 18:00. Tickets at shrine office (581-2471).

**Mid-Aug.: Fukagawa Hachiman Matsuri.** Tomioka Hachiman-gū. Once every three years (next in 1993). Great procession of *mikoshi*, which, along with participants, are doused with water.

**Mid-Sept.: 15 days of sumo.** New Kokugikan (I:1).

**Oct. (1st Sa): Exhibition of acrobatic skills by loggers** who once floated timber down the river in Fukagawa. On Sendaibori River, at Kurofunabashi (bridge) (*take Tōzai line to Monzen-nakamachi*). Hrs: 13:00–14:00.

**Early Oct.: Gagaku.** Imperial Music Hall. See early April.

**Oct. 10: ✴ Kusajishi.** Yasukuni Jinja (I:3). Archery in the old style and other martial displays. From 11:00 and 13:00.

**Oct. 17–19: Autumn Festival.** Yasukuni Jinja (I:3). See Apr. 21–23.

**Oct. 18: Asakusa Kannon Matsuri.** Asakusa Kannon (I:1). The festival officially extends from Oct. 11 to Nov. 15. On this day, there's a special offering of chrysanthemums and a golden dragon dance.

**Oct. 31–Nov. 3: Autumn Festival.** Meiji Jingū (III:2). Noh, Bugaku, martial arts, archery, horsemanship.

**Nov.: ✴✴ Tori no Ichi.** Ōtori Jinja (I:1). Held on Cock days of the zodiac calendar, when the birds were presented to the god of war. On these days, the girls of the Yoshiwara were allowed out of the gates. Today the festival remains popular with people in the entertainment trades, who crowd the grounds to buy *kumade* (bear claws), bamboo rakes spectacularly festooned with good-luck charms, effective for "raking in fortune."

**Nov. 3: Shirasagi-no-mai (White Egret Dance).** Asakusa Kannon (I:1).

**Dec. 14: Gishi-sai.** Sengaku-ji (II:3). Memorial rites for the 47 *rōnin* (see Drama, p. 86). There is also a rite to console the villain, Lord Kira, at the site of his mansion in Ryōgoku (I:1).

**Mid- to end Dec.: ✴ Gasa-ichi.** Asakusa Kannon (I:1). Lively year-end market for New Year's ornaments. From 17–19th, ornamental battledores are sold (wholesale only).

**Dec. 15–16: Setagaya Boro-ichi (Flea Market).** Daikan Yashiki in Setagaya-ku (*Tōkyū-Shintamagawa line from Shibuya to Sangenjaya, transfer to Tōkyū-Setagaya line, get off at Uemachi*). A market begun in 1578 by the lord of Odawara. Today, magazines, old kimono, "antiques," and plants are hawked from a thousand booths set up along the road.

**Dec. 23: Emperor's Birthday.** The emperor makes a public appearance at the Palace.

# Tokyo (Edo) History: The Rise of an Urban Culture

**Tokugawa Ieyasu**  (1543–1616) Shogun who built Edo and made it his capital (see Nikkō History, p. 239).

**Tsunayoshi**  (1646–1709) The eccentric "Dog Shogun," who presided over the flowering of urban culture called the Genroku period (1688–1704). His deeply religious mother, Keishō-in, was a compulsive rebuilder of temples.

**The Edokko**  (ca. 1700–present) The cockneylike resident of Shitamachi who knew, at least in fantasy, how to deflate a conceited samurai's ego.

In 1457, a local warrior, **Ōta Dōkan**, built a castle at the village of Edo ("rivergate"), near the mouths of three rivers, the Sumidagawa, the Arakawa, and the Edogawa. These rivers drained Japan's largest alluvial basin, the great **Kantō Plain**. The region would become the richest rice-producing area in Japan, but at the time, it was unimproved; Edo itself sat in a mosquito-ridden marsh. Dōkan seems to have tried to develop the land's potential, but in 1486 he was brutally murdered by his suspicious overlords, the Uesugi. The man fated to realize Edo's potential was TOKUGAWA IEYASU, who in 1590 led his bewildered retainers through the surrounding marshes into Edo. In little over a century, this tiny fishing village would become the most populous city in the world.

Ieyasu initiated a vast landfill and waterworks project, turning Edo's major drawback—its abundance of rivers and marshes—to his advantage. Spiraling out from Ieyasu's huge new castle was a network of canals and moats designed to provide an outer defense. The inner coil of the spiral, together with the bulwark of hills to the castle's west and north—what Edward Seidensticker has dubbed the **High City**— were the domain of the samurai. Ieyasu positioned his retainers and vassal lords in the inner part of the spiral. Farther out, at a safe distance among the hills of the High City, were the Edo residences of the powerful *tozama daimyō*. Continuing full circle to the outer ring of the spiral was the bayfront—a flat, damp landfill. While some daimyo had villas here, much of the land, considered unfit for samurai, was given over to merchants and craftsmen who poured into the booming city. This **Shitamachi**, or Low City, began east of Ōtemachi, at **Ginza** and **Nihonbashi**, and sprawled east to the river and north toward **Asakusa**.

The institution that shaped the High City—the reason why every lord had a residence there—was the infamous *sankin kōtai*, or "alternate attendance" (see Castles, p. 47). Under *sankin kōtai*, every daimyo had to live periodically in Edo, each time mounting an expensive parade, with legions of retainers, to mark his progress to and from Edo. He also had to maintain a mansion in Edo, where his wife and children were required to live permanently, as hostages. The mansions are gone, but two stroll gardens, Kōraku-en and Rikugi-en, remain to evoke the times. Every daimyo mansion had such gardens, a fact which the shogunate exploited by creating a gardeners' guild that was, in truth, a nest of spies. These measures were not limited to the daimyo. Official shogunate posts were always filled in duplicate—Edo, for instance, had two magistrates—so that each could keep tabs on the other, and there were official spies to watch both. In the later Edo period, elaborate precautions were taken to keep the shogun from becoming an embarrassment to the shogunate. A woman official was stationed by the shogun's bed so that no concubine could cajole a political promise out of him. The day-to-day affairs of state were handled by the *karō*, or elders, who headed a huge bureaucracy. All these measures were designed so that, whatever the talents of its nominal head, the shogunate would roll on safely, like a well-oiled machine.

This was just as well. With few exceptions, most of the later shoguns were mediocre rulers—debauched, feeble-minded, or worse. Remembered as the most bizarre was the fifth shogun, **Tsunayoshi**. Although he undertook many reforms that improved the quality of life in Edo and was a patron of the arts, his virtues were eclipsed by his peculiarities. His proclivity for young boys and girls—lots of them— was the subject of mild criticism, but his Edict on Compassion for Living Things convinced the townspeople of Edo that he was out of his mind. After his young heir died, Tsunayoshi was much troubled by his inability to produce a replacement. His mother, **Keishō-in**, the hysterically religious daughter of a Kyoto grocer, was told by her spiritual adviser that Tsunayoshi was being punished for sins against animals in a former life; because he was born in the Year of the Dog, his debt was especially great toward this species. In atonement, Tsunayoshi built palatial dog shelters all over Edo and made the killing of a dog a capital crime.

Whatever Tsunayoshi's personal failings, his reign was culturally brilliant. In what is known as the Genroku period (1688–1704), urban culture flowered. At first it was not Edo, but the mature, self-assured cities of Ōsaka and Kyoto that took the lead. In Ōsaka, CHIKAMATSU created the puppet play *Sonezaki Shinjū*, about the double suicide of a prostitute and Tokubei, her shop-clerk sweetheart; this was the first widely successful play to treat the lives of the townfolk who made up Chikamatsu's audience. In literature, Iharu Saikaku's *Life of an Amorous Man* and *Life of an Amorous Woman* were the most outstanding examples of a genre called *ukiyo-zōshi*. *Ukiyo*, or "floating world," a term originally tinged with languid Buddhist melancholy, came to refer to the demimonde—the stylish world of the actor and the prostitute.

It was this *ukiyo* world that became the vanguard of culture, or, perhaps more accurately, of counterculture, especially in Edo. As the shogunate became increasingly bureaucratized, hundreds of thousands of officials and samurai retainers from the provinces poured into the city, leaving their wives and sweethearts back home. After the Genroku period, Edo overtook Ōsaka and Kyoto in size and cultural accomplishments, and it became inevitable that the pleasure quarters would be the center of city life; everyone was starved for female company. In Edo the **Yoshiwara** licensed quarter was the height of elegance. After the disastrous Furisode fire of 1657, the Yoshiwara was relocated outside the city boundaries, to the north of the Asakusa Kannon Temple, which became an entertainment district in its own right, a way station for those on their way to the Yoshiwara.

At first, the samurai dominated the Yoshiwara, but as time went on, it came to be considered the province of the townsmen, the countless unattached male artisans, laborers, and clerks who streamed into the shogun's city. In 1733, there were two men for every woman in Edo. Men of all classes brushed shoulders in the Yoshiwara not simply to satisfy carnal needs, but also because here was the one place that samurai and merchant alike could cast off the Confucian straitjacket of shogunate rules.

Samurai culture—KANŌ academy painting, Noh drama—had ossified under the influence of the shogunate. The townsmen of Edo—and not a few moonlighting samurai—seized upon the new arts of the Genroku period and injected their own exuberance and crudity into them. Naturally, the arts of Edo centered on love, especially the ephemeral love of the courtesan, and the pleasures of her world. Foremost was the ukiyo-e woodblock print, the quintessential art of Edo (see Art, p. 99); if Saikaku wrote about rakes and courtesans in *ukiyo-zōshi*, **Moronobu** (d. 1694) had the audacity to depict them, together, in *very* graphic detail. His guides to the Yoshiwara prostitutes, illustrating their specialties, were especially popular.

The Edo theater also revelled in *ukiyo* themes, focusing not on the timid passions of a Tokubei, the lovelorn clerk in *Sonezaki Shinjū*, but on the picaresque adventures of the Edo townsman. In *Sukeroku*, first staged in 1713, Sukeroku, lover of the Yoshiwara's top courtesan, flouts the law by wearing a headband of shogunal purple, and wreaks a just vengeance upon his villainous samurai rival. Plays like *Sukeroku* set the style for the **Edokko**, the scrappy "son of Edo," who idolized the dashing ruffian who is, at heart, brave and true, unlike the decadent samurai.

The Edokko also idolized himself. An Edokko was a third-generation Edo dweller, something which, as late as 1832, only one in ten inhabitants could boast of. The true-blue Edokko was a *tsū*, a connoisseur, a man (or woman) who had mastered the art of living and was an expert at understated elegance; he had to be, for the shogunate forbade obvious forms of display. If he was prohibited from wearing silk, he wore a hempen kimono with an elegant silk lining. *Edo komon*, a fabric painstakingly stenciled with microscopic dot patterns, was another subtle badge of wealth and taste. Tucked inside a sleeve, or dangling discreetly from his sash, were small accessories, *inrō* seal cases and netsuke toggles, which were concentrated masterpieces of the lacquerer's and sculptor's art. *Iki*, a word that combined the meanings of "chic," "generosity," and the "here-today-gone-tomorrow" worldly wisdom of the pleasure quarter, was an epithet, along with *tsū*, to which the Eddoko aspired. The samurai extolled frugality; the commoner found in the pleasure quarter a chance to escape frugality's strictures and thereby achieve a kind of heroism.

Compared with the cultural and economic vigor of Shitamachi, the life of the samurai in the High City was rigid and dull, regulated in all respects and governed by the Confucian virtues. When, in 1703, forty-seven samurai carried out a spectacular vendetta to avenge their lord's death, Edo was electrified; in 1706, the event was immortalized on the Bunraku stage, in the play *Chūshingura* (see Drama, p. 86). The stir created by this incident underscored how rare it was, in this age, for a samurai to uphold the warrior's code. With the coming of the Tokugawa peace, the samurai was little more than a civil servant, if he was lucky enough to have any employment at all. Indeed, since they were paid in rice, which fluctuated wildly in price, many low-ranking samurai lived in dire poverty. The shogunate, which had little understanding of economic problems, associated frugality with economic well-being.

It deeply disturbed the shogunate's more conservative advisors to see that the merchants, who in theory were at the bottom of the social hierarchy, were in fact conspicuously richer than many of the daimyo. Twice, in the 1790s and in the Tempō Reforms of the 1840s, austerity programs were initiated. These included not only economic measures, but moral ones as well. Artists and publishers who produced pornographic or satirical prints were censored and jailed. During the Tempō Reforms, the Kabuki theaters were moved from Ningyōchō, in the center of Edo, out to Asakusa, where a rundown theater district still remains. Both times, life soon returned to normal; attempts at reform had little effect except to expose the weakness of the shogunate, which in any event would soon fall.

To today's visitor, modern Tokyo seems like a slate wiped clean of its history. Even in the days of the shogunate, it was a city uncommonly prone to disasters. There were more than ninety serious conflagrations, a pattern that continued in the twentieth century with the terrible Kantō Earthquake of 1923 and the firebombing of 1945, each of which claimed 100,000 lives and leveled much of the city. The rare architectural survivor of old Edo, or even Meiji Tokyo, has succumbed to "progress." What endures instead is the character of the High City and the Low City, Shitamachi, each still worlds apart. The daimyo left the High City in 1868 to return to their home provinces, but a *sankin kōtai* of sorts continues with the legions of bureaucrats, politicians, businessmen, and foreigners who have taken their place. Shitamachi, on the other hand, still belongs to the fiercely proud Edokko, who have preserved something of the old city in their atmospheric (some might say shabby) working-class neighborhoods, shops, and festivals.

197

# TOKYO I. TRADITIONAL TOKYO (SHITAMACHI)

**Main Attractions:**
I:1  *** Asakusa Kannon Temple
I:1  ** Kappabashi (plastic food models)
I:2  ** Ueno Tōshō-gū (shrine)
I:2  *** Tokyo National Museum
I:2  ** Shitamachi Museum
I:3  * Akihabara (electronics district)
I:3  * Jimbōchō (booksellers district)

The northeast part of Tokyo, around Asakusa, Ueno, and Kanda, offers the best chance to see something of the city's past. Here are the remains of Shitamachi, haunt of the Edokko. Shitamachi is not beautiful; only a few neighborhoods, such as charming Yanaka, have escaped Tokyo's triple whammy: the 1923 Kantō Earthquake, the Allied bombings of World War II, and the relentless postwar remodeling of the city's face. Amid the multistory buildings, railroad tracks, and elevated highways, it takes intelligence and resourcefulness to envision the Edo of old. Even Asakusa Kannon, Shitamachi's symbol, and Kanda Myōjin, the area's most famous shrine, are both ferroconcrete reconstructions. It is not in physical monuments, but in traditions, upheld by the Edokko, that Shitamachi is at its most vital. It's no coincidence that two of Tokyo's most exuberant festivals, Asakusa's Sanja Matsuri and Kanda Myōjin's Kanda Matsuri, are firmly on the Edokko's turf. Each comes but once a year; busy every day, however, is Asakusa's Nakamise-dōri, with its shops, stalls, and crowds. Nineteenth-century ukiyo-e prints depict the same bazaar atmosphere that exists today.

Indeed, much of Shitamachi's charm lies in its various "bazaars." Since Tokyo's days as a castle town, merchants and craftsmen have been grouped by trade into neighborhoods. Shops in Inarichō sell Buddhist and Shinto altars; Asakusabashi specializes in toys and dolls. Postwar black markets followed the old pattern; Ueno's Ameyoko-chō began by trafficking in candy and American PX goods, Akihabara, the electronics mecca, by dealing in spare radio parts. One of the oddest wholesale neighborhoods is Kappabashi, which deals in restaurant supplies, including the plastic food models seen in the windows of many restaurants. And every book lover knows Jimbōchō, an area lined from end to end with stores selling books of every description.

The same principle seems to apply to institutions for religious and public edification. The grounds of Kan'ei-ji, a vast Edo-period temple town, is now Ueno Park, known for its complex of museums, including the Tokyo National Museum. The nearby Shitamachi Museum, with its portrayal of Edo-period life and reconstructions of Shitamachi shops and dwellings, is an ideal introduction to traditional Tokyo.

## I:1 ASAKUSA 浅草

*Take Ginza or Toei-Asakusa subway line to Asakusa station. A tsū will cruise up the Sumidagawa by sightseeing boat from Hama Rikyū* (II:3). The Asakusa Kannon Temple is the spiritual center of Shitamachi—not so much for any aura of sanctity that might cling to its incense-filled ferroconcrete hall as for the fervent pursuit of commercial success and good times that enliven its surroundings. This area also includes Kappabashi, Inarichō, Yoshiwara, and Kuramae/Ryōgoku.

---

**Half-day tour:** Hama Rikyū garden (II:3) — (0:30h cruise up Sumidagawa) — Asakusa—Nakamise-dōri—Asakusa Kannon Temple—(0:15h walk) — Kappabashi—(walk or subway)—Ueno (I.2)

**Lunch:** Komagata Dojō, Daikokuya, Miyako

**Note:** Sumida Kōen (park), along the Sumidagawa, is a famous cherry-blossom spot.

---

### Asakusa Sights

**\*\*\* Asakusa Kannon Temple (Sensō-ji)** 浅草寺 Asakusa Kannon is Tokyo's most venerable temple, founded by legend in A.D. 628 to enshrine a golden image of Kannon miraculously fished out of the Sumidagawa. Its popularity as a place of worship was only enhanced when, after the 1657 fire, authorities moved the Yoshiwara to a site not far north of the temple, and Asakusa became a way station for Yoshiwara-bound townsmen. The temple grounds were crowded with hawkers, street acrobats, and archery booths tended by women of easy virtue. Its popularity grew in the 1840s when the shogunate banished the Kabuki theaters to Asakusa, and attained its apex in 1890, with the completion of the Jūnikai, or Twelve Stories, then Tokyo's tallest building. Until the war, Asakusa was—as Shinjuku is now—a magnet for the city's youth, with its cinemas, musical shows, shops, and restaurants. Nakamise-dōri, the shop-packed central approach, still recalls Asakusa's heyday, but the sides and back of the temple grounds present an after-the-party scene of dingy shops, vacant theaters, and, by evening, deserted streets.

    **Kaminari-mon (Thunder Gate).** This landmark, depicted in famous ukiyo-e prints, burned in 1865 and was rebuilt only in 1955. It houses statues of Fūjin (right) and Raijin (left), gods of wind and thunder; their heads are old but the bodies are new. West of the gate is **Tokiwadō**, famous for *kaminari okoshi*, puffed millet-and-rice crackers that crackle thunderously when you bite them.

    ◆ **Nakamise-dōri** 仲見世通り "Inside shops street," so called because it lies within the temple precinct. The shops that crowd both sides of the stone-paved approach hawk wares from the kitschiest souvenirs to genuine gems of Edo craftsmanship. Some of the oldest establishments include Bairin-dō, a 200-year-old cracker shop just behind the Kaminari-mon, and Sukeroku, almost the last shop on the right, famous for its intricate miniature dolls.

    ◆ **Main Temple Compound.** Excavations show that a temple existed here as early as the 7th C, lending credence to the legend of its founding (see above). The sacred golden Kannon, a "secret image" hidden from view, is said to have survived the calamities that have destroyed the halls time and again, most recently in the air raid of 1945. The huge concrete main hall was built in 1958, and the pagoda, though one of the temple's most famous landmarks, was finished only in 1973. What gives these leaden structures life is the constant stream of worshippers, flapping pigeons, and coils of incense smoke from the giant censer in the main court. Inside the main hall is a fascinating group of enormous **votive paintings** donated in the 18th and 19th C by some of Edo's leading artists. The painting of an old hag on a moor is by ukiyo-e artist Utagawa Kuniyoshi. The great dragon on the ceiling is by Kawabata Ryūshi, and the angels and lotuses by Dōmoto Inshō, two prominent 20th-C painters. The immense red paper lanterns were donated by local geisha associations.

    A number of older structures stand in the cluttered grounds: On the east is the **Niten-mon** (gate, 1618) and Asakusa Jinja (see below). To the west are the **Yakushi-dō** (1649), a stone bridge (1618), and **Awashima-dō** (17th C), dedicated to a deity who cures feminine ailments and is a patron of womanly skills, such as sewing (on Feb. 8, a service for broken needles is held here). A **hexagonal chapel to Jizō**, built in the 15th or 16th C, is one of the oldest buildings in the city. A stone lantern at the north end of the grounds was built in 1146 to commemorate a visit by MINAMOTO no Yoshitomo.

    ◆ **Dembō-in (Abbot's Residence)** 伝法院 (3842-0181). Hrs: 10:00–15:00, but often closed. Apply for entry at the Sensō-ji office, near the pagoda. Dembō-in, founded in 1690, has a pleasant ENSHŪ-style **stroll garden**. It offers a charming view of the pagoda, reflected in the turtle-filled pond. The reception hall was built in 1777.

    ◆ **Asakusa Jinja** 浅草神社 (1649, ICP). This ornate shrine, brightly painted inside, is dedicated to the two brothers who fished the Kannon image out of the river and to their lord, who enshrined it—hence the popular name, **Sanja-sama**, the Shrine of the Three. Being consecrated to deified humans, it is in the Gongen style. This shrine holds the famous Sanja Matsuri in the 3rd week of May. **Benten-yama Shōrō (Belfry).** In the SE of the temple grounds hangs one of the 9 bells that tolled the hour in Edo. It was made famous in a haiku by BASHŌ: "Through clouds of blossoms/ Is that the bell of Ueno/ Or of Asakusa?" The bell still sounds at 6:00 a.m. and on New Year's Eve.

## Asakusa Shopping

Blocks on Nakamise are counted from Kaminari-mon.

**Bairin-dō** 梅林堂 (3841-2464). Hrs: 9:00–21:00, daily. Nakamise Block 1 on left. A 200-year history of selling *sembei* (rice crackers).

**Arai Bunsen-dō** 文扇堂 (3844-9711). Hrs: 10:30–18:00, daily. Nakamise Block 3 on left. An old fan shop.

**Iidaya** 飯田屋 (3841-3644). Hrs: 9:00–20:00, daily. Nakamise Block 4 on right. *Bangasa* (traditional oiled-paper umbrellas).

**\*\* Sukeroku** 助六 (3844-0577). Hrs: 10:00–18:00; clsd Th. Nakamise, 2nd from last shop on right. This toybox of a shop, founded in 1860, is renowned for its miniature hand-made dolls of Edokko.

**\* Hyakusuke** 百助 浅草2-2-14 (3841-7058). Hrs: 11:00–17:00; clsd Tu (W if Tu a NH). Two alleys east of Nakamise. Kabuki makeup, cosmetic brushes, and the fabled *uguisu no fun*, bush-warbler dung, for a smooth complexion (mix a small quantity with facial soap, lather, and rinse).

**\* Fujiya Tenuguiten** ふじ屋てぬぐい店 浅草2-2-15 (3841-2283). Hrs: 10:00–20:00; clsd Th (F if Th a NH). One alley east of Nakamise. Classic, hand-printed *tenugui* (kerchiefs).

**\* Yonoya** よのや (3844-1755). Hrs: 10:00–19:00; clsd W. On the side street to Denbō-in. A 300-year-old shop selling wooden combs and hair ornaments. Plain combs, all handmade, start at around Y3000.

**\* Adachiya** あだち屋 浅草2-22-12 (3841-4915). Hrs: 10:00–20:00, daily. In winter 10:00–20:00. Clsd Tu. On Hisago-dōri arcade NW of the temple. Authentic matsuri togs—*happi* coats, sashes, headbands, and straw sandals. The *momohiki*, ingeniously tailored, snug-fitting knickers, are very comfortable. In black or indigo, lined with cotton; large sizes. Y5–7000. Cotton sashes come in a variety of wonderful patterns and colors.

199

## \*\* Kappabashi かっぱ橋
*Near Tawaramachi subway station, between Asakusa and Ueno on the Ginza line.* Upon emerging, head west toward the building crowned by a Titanic bewhiskered chef. He marks the beginning of **Kappabashi-dōri**, an avenue lined from end to end with shops selling restaurant supplies and plastic food *sampuru*, the latter a capsule lesson in Japanese culinary customs. One will also find professional Japanese and Western kitchen equipment. Some shops appear to be holding a huge sale, but are in fact selling "Sale" banners. One warning: *All* the food you'll see here is fake. Don't come here on an empty stomach.

## Inarichō 稲荷町
*Between Tawaramachi and Ueno on the Ginza line.* A neighborhood with some 50 shops selling household Shinto shrines, Buddhist altars, and a panoply of accessories: for the altars, sacred images, vases, candlestands, censers, and the wooden tablets on which the names of the dead are written; for shrines, cedar trays, tiny white dishes for offerings of rice and salt, and images of the Inari fox. **Nabuya** なぶ屋 東上野6丁目 (2 blocks E, on the S side) is a maker of festival *mikoshi* and drums, founded in 1690.

## Exploring Yoshiwara
*Near Minowa or Minami-Senjū stations.* The Yoshiwara is now a tawdry area of massage parlors and love hotels, yet it was once not only the city's citadel of sex, but also the epitome of the culture of the Floating World, so dear to the Edokko. Not that life in the Yoshiwara was all flowers and willows: at **Jōkan-ji**, the "Disposal Temple," more than 11,000 Yoshiwara girls, average age 22, lie buried in unmarked graves. The shogunate regarded this region as its social dumping ground; toward Asakusa, it located the "untouchables," who disposed of dead horses from the daimyo estates, executed criminals, and worked with leather. As a lingering legacy, the region had an abattoir in the Meiji period and today has a thriving leather industry. The Yoshiwara was devastated by the 1923 earthquake, and the outlawing of prostitution in 1959 dealt its death blow.

**Ōtori Jinja** 鷲神社 *0:30h by Tōbu bus N from Kita-Senjū station.* This drab shrine bursts to life during the colorful Tori no Ichi market held on days of the Cock in November (see Calendar).

**Matsubaya** 松葉屋 (3874-9401). A former Yoshiwara brothel. 0:40h *oiran* (courtesan) shows at 19:00 and 21:20, daily. Y2000 w/drink.

## Exploring Kuramae, Asakusabashi, and Ryōgoku
**Torigoe Jinja** 鳥越神社 *Near Kuramae station, on the Toei-Asakusa line.* The concrete buildings are a disappointment, but the shrine is loved for its festivals, including the Dondo-yaki (Jan. 8) and Yo-matsuri in June.

**Toy District.** *Along Edo-dōri, between Kuramae and Asakusabashi stations.* Especially festive around the Doll Festival (Mar. 3), Boy's Day (May 5), in summer (fireworks), and New Year (calendars). Mingled in are shops for paper goods and fake flowers. **Ningyō no Nomura** 人形の野村 (3863-4711) has perhaps the most elegant selection of dolls. **Kyūgetsu** 久月 (3861-5511), founded in 1830, is one of the biggest doll shops in Japan. **Yoshitoku Taikō** 吉徳太閤 (3863-4419) is also a well-known doll shop.

**Yanagibashi (Willow Bridge).** This poetically named bridge spans the Kandagawa just before it flows into the Sumida. It was from here that pleasure seekers boarded boats bound upriver for the Yoshiwara. Eventually it became a pleasure quarter in its own right. The *funa-yado*, which still rent boats for outings on the river, seem out of place amid the concrete and grime.

**Kira-tei Ato** 吉良邸跡 *S of Ryōgoku station*. The site of the villa of Lord Kira, archvillain in the famous *Chūshingura* vendetta (see Drama, p. 86). The site is now a small park with tile-and-plaster walls, like those in daimyo estates. Exhibited inside are woodblock print scenes from *Chūshingura*, a small Inari shrine that stood in the estate, and the Head-washing Well.

**New Kokugikan (Sumo Stadium)** 国技館 (To reserve tickets, 3622-1100. Office, 3623-5111). *NW of Ryōgoku station*. Houses the **Sumo Museum**, a sumo hall of fame. During tournaments, sumo begins at noon, with bottom-ranked wrestlers; the real action is from 16:00–18:00. **Tickets:** Ask for *shōmen* (north) or *mukō-jōmen* (south) seats for the best view. The first floor is monopolized; visitors can get tickets on the upper balconies, from Y2–9500 (the cheap tickets, however, are quite far away; bring binoculars). Tickets sell out almost before they go on sale; large blocks are snapped up by the *chaya*, which then resell them at triple the price, right up to the day of a bout. The system is unofficially official — *chaya* stalls are built into the new stadium — but they won't tell you about them at the box office. You have to persuade the gatekeeper to let you in to negotiate with the *chaya* directly.

**Kyū Yasuda Teien (Garden)** 旧安田庭園 Hrs: 9:00–16:30; clsd NY. North of New Kokugikan. Pleasant stroll garden, built around 1850. Once owned by Yasuda Zenjirō, founder of the Yasuda *zaibatsu* (grandfather of Yoko Ono).

**Irei-dō** 東京都慰霊堂 Hrs: 9:00–16:00, daily. Adjacent to Yasuda Teien. This hall, dedi-cated to the 104,619 victims of the 1923 earthquake, stands where nearly 40,000 survivors

# Sumo

Sumo, with a history of 2,000 years and strong overtones of Shinto, is no mere sport, but a *kokugi*, or National Skill. Visitors should try to catch a glimpse, if only on televi-sion, of the pageantry and genuinely exciting sport in which near-naked behemoths clash with extraordinary speed and power, settling in seconds contests that make and break careers.

Sumo originated as a shrine oracle and offering, becoming a professional sport only in the Edo period; some shrines still hold sacred contests between a man and an invisible kami. A vestige of Shinto remains in the Shimmei-style roof suspended over the *dohyō* (ring). Wrestlers purify the *dohyō* by flinging salt over it, and women are forbidden to set foot in the ring. The *yokozuna* (grand champion) wears a special white belt of twisted rope, hung with the zigzag paper strips called *gohei*, seen in shrines.

The action takes place on a raised, hardened earth platform, in a straw ring only 4.55 meters in diameter. In each tournament, wrestlers are arbitrarily divided into *higashi* (east) and *nishi* (west); two wrestlers, one from each side, face off from behind two white lines drawn in the ground, 1.2 meters apart. After a great deal of earth-stomping, salt-flinging, and false starts to psych out the opponent, the two charge each other, often struggling for a two-handed grip on the opponent's belly band, the most popular tactic for gaining leverage. Legitimate moves include throws, lifts, tripping, shoving, and open-handed slaps to the upper torso; kicking and closed-fist punching are not allowed. The loser is the first to be forced out of the ring or to touch the ground with any part of his body other than the soles of his feet. There are no weight classes, and it is always cause for great excitement when a small but skillful wrestler overcomes a gargantuan rival.

The passions of sumo fans run especially high in Tokyo, where so many people come from the same outlying provinces as the wrestlers. The dream of becoming a sumo champion attracts strapping youths from poor rural areas, especially in Tōhoku, Hokkaidō, and Kyūshū, who are tough enough to withstand the grueling training and discipline. At age 15 or so a boy enters a *heya*, or "stable," run by a for-mer champion, where his early training includes menial chores such as cleaning, cooking, and scrubbing the backs of senior wrestlers in the bath. The prospect of graduating beyond this level is ample incentive for these underlings. In any case, ris-ing through the ranks is rewarded by privilege rather than money; only the upper ranks draw a salary. Many of the sumo stables are in Ryōgoku, near the New Kokugikan. One can usually peer in during practice, which begins around 8:00 a.m. and lasts through mid-morning.

Major tournaments (*bashō*) are held from the Sunday closest to the 10th of the month and continue for 15 days, closing on Sunday. Bashō are held in Tokyo in Jan., May, Sept.; in Ōsaka in Mar.; in Nagoya in July; and in Fukuoka in Nov. The Far East Network, on 810 kHz channel, gives simultaneous English broadcasts. The English-language papers and *Sumo World* magazine provide commentary.

sought refuge, only to perish in a superheated tornado whipped up by the infernos that engulfed the city. Paintings in the hall depict scenes of the earthquake, and the concrete pagoda behind it contains the bones of 58,000 victims. There is also a stone memorial to an estimated 2,000 Koreans slaughtered by mobs in the wake of the disaster. The Irei-dō is also dedicated to the 78,000 victims of the 1945 Allied bombing attacks, in which some 700,000 incendiary bombs were dropped on Tokyo.

## I:2. UENO　上野

*Take the Yamanote or Keihin Tōhoku line or the Ginza or Hibiya subway line.* Ueno Park, formerly the site of a large Tokugawa funerary temple, contains a museum complex that includes the Tokyo National Museum and Shitamachi Museum. The park adjoins two of the quainter neighborhoods in the city: Yushima, a district of traditional shops, and Yanaka, one of the few quarters in Tokyo to survive undamaged from before the Great Kantō Earthquake; with its temples, small museums, and shops, it offers the city's most charming walk.

---

**Walking Tour 1:** Ueno station — (0:03h) — Kan'ei-ji Kiyomizu-dō — (0:05h) — ** Ueno Tōshō-gū — (0:10h) — *** Tokyo National Museum — (0:05h) — Kan'ei-ji Main Hall — (0:10h) — Yanaka

**Walking Tour 2:** Ueno station — (0:05h via * Ameyoko-chō) — ** Shitamachi Museum — (0:10h via Shinobazu Pond) — * Yokoyama Taikan Gallery — (0:10h) — * Yushima Tenjin — (0:20h) — Kanda (II.3)

**Lunch:** Honke Ponta, Ikenohata Yabu Soba.

**Notes:** Try to visit the Tokyo National Museum on a rainless Thursday, when the Hōryū-ji Treasure House is open. Ueno Park is a noted cherry-blossom spot.

---

201

### Ueno Station　上野駅
Traditionally the gateway between Tokyo and northern Japan. The Tōhoku and Jōetsu Shinkansen lines pass through this station. The Keisei-Narita line from Narita airport terminates here. Tracks are numbered from west (Ueno Park side) to east:

2: Yamanote line toward Ikebukuro
3–4: Yamanote and Keihin lines toward Tokyo station
13–15: Tōhoku, Takasaki, Jōetsu and Shinetsu lines
19–20: Jōetsu Shinkansen to Niigata
21–22: Tōhoku Shinkansen

### Ueno Kōen (Park)　上野公園
*Exit Ueno station by Kōen-guchi or Shinobazu-guchi exits, both on the west side.* Ueno Hill once overlooked Edo Bay, in the days before landfill projects created the Shitamachi of the Edo townspeople. Because Ueno was situated at Edo's *kimon*, or "devil's gate" — the unlucky northeast direction — the second shogun, Hidetada, asked the eminent Tendai prelate, Tenkai, to build a temple here to protect the city (see Nikkō History, p. 242). **Kan'ei-ji,** as this temple was named, was conceived by Tenkai as an analog to Kyoto's protector, the great Tendai monastery of Enryaku-ji on Mt. Hiei. By the end of the 1600s, its precinct contained 36 halls and 36 subtemples, presided over by a huge main hall, which stood where the fountains now play, in the center of Ueno Park. This great hall and most of the others were destroyed in May 1868, when some 2,000 Tokugawa loyalists made their last stand at Ueno against a vastly superior imperial army. Afterward, the new Meiji government intended to build a hospital here, but was persuaded by a Dutch doctor to convert the grounds into a public park. The builders, however, seemed to cling to the idea of Ueno as a place of edification rather than of relaxation, with the result that the grounds are cluttered with museums, a zoo, and an arts university.

**Saigō Takamori Statue**　西郷像　Near the Shinobazu exit. This bronze statue of a casually attired, heavy-set, crew-cut samurai out walking his dog is a popular meeting place. It portrays Saigō Takamori, a Satsuma samurai who spared Edo from an all-out battle in 1868 through negotiations with the shogunate. He is one of the heroes of the Meiji Restoration — no matter that, a few years later, he began a civil war against the government he had helped found and ended up committing *seppuku* in battle. The statue was erected in 1898. Across the way is a chapel erected in 1882 for the repose of his foes, the Tokugawa samurai who were slain at Ueno in 1868.

**Kan'ei-ji Kiyomizu-dō**　清水堂　(1631, ICP). Built by Tenkai, who supposedly modeled it on Kyoto's Kiyomizu Temple, which it scarcely resembles. It enshrines an image of Kannon surrounded by dolls, given in thanks by parents who had their prayers for a child granted. The dolls are ceremonially burned on Sept. 25 to prevent overpopulation.

**Ueno Municipal Zoo (Dōbutsu-en)**　上野動物園　Hrs: 9:30–16:00; clsd M (Tu if M a NH), NY. An extensive zoo, best known for its pandas (not on view Friday).

**\* Kan'ei-ji Gojūno-tō (Five-Storied Pagoda)**　五重塔　(1639, ICP). Stands in the zoo grounds. An ornate structure, best seen from the approach to the Ueno Tōshō-gū.

See p. 228 for restaurants, p. 232 for hotels

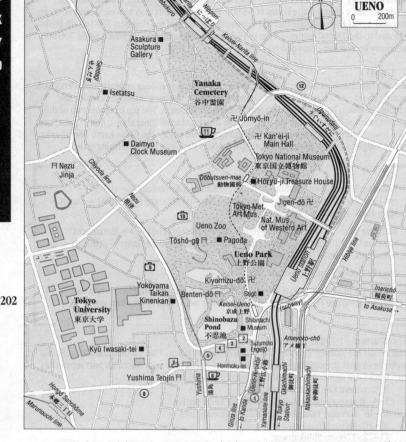

**\*\* Ueno Tōshō-gū (Shrine)** 上野東照宮 (ICP). Hrs: 9:00–17:30. In winter 9:00–16:30. Like the Nikkō Tōshō-gū (Kantō, p. 239), this is a shrine to Tokugawa Ieyasu. It was founded in 1627 within the Kan'ei-ji precincts. The present structure dates from 1651, at the time of Shogun Iemitsu's great Nikkō expansion project. It is in a similar opulent style, with interior paintings by KANō TAN'YŪ and others of the official painters' academy.

**\* Kokuritsu Seiyō Bijutsukan (National Museum of Western Art)** 国立西洋美術館 (3828-5131). Hrs: 9:30–17:00 (enter by 16:30); clsd M (Tu if M a NH), NY. This museum, housed in an influential (if not especially interesting) building by Le Corbusier, has a large collection of European art, notably Rodin sculptures and French Impressionist paintings.

**\* Jigen-dō** 慈眼堂 The founder's hall of Kan'ei-ji, dedicated to Tenkai. In the southeast of the enclosure stands the Koku-mon (ICP), formerly the gate to the abbot's quarters of Kan'ei-ji. It is pocked with bullet holes from the 1868 battle.

**\*\*\* Tokyo National Museum (Kokuritsu Hakubutsukan)** 東京国立博物館 (3822-1111/-7). Hrs: 9:00–16:30 (enter by 16:00); clsd M (except during NH and special shows), Tu if M a NH. Try to visit on Thursday, the only day of the week (barring rain) when the Hōryū-ji treasures are on view. This museum boasts the finest Japanese art collection in the world. Archeological materials, including superb *haniwa* clay tomb figurines are in the beaux-arts-style **Hyōkeikan** on the left. The oppressive **Main Building** (a prewar edifice) exhibits the main collection, which includes many of the most famous works in Japanese art. The exhibits give an excellent overview of Japan's art, period by period and genre by genre, although the conditions under which they are shown are scandalous: poor lighting, inadequate labels, and volumes of wasted space. The exhibits change frequently. The modern concrete **Tōyōkan** to the right of the entrance houses an excellent assemblage of art from other Asian countries. It has a cafeteria. Just outside the museum's main gate is the late Edo-period **Ikeda Mansion gate** (ICP), moved from the estate of the daimyo of Tottori.

   **\* Hōryū-ji Treasure House (Hōryū-ji Hōmotsuden)** 法隆寺宝物館 Open Th, closed if raining or humid. The objects displayed here, primarily of the Asuka and Hakuhō periods, are of the highest quality, rarity, and historical interest. They were donated to the government in 1876 by Hōryū-ji (Kinki, p. 399), founded in the 7th C by SHŌTOKU TAISHI and considered the birthplace of Japanese Buddhism. In the Meiji period, the temple became impoverished because of the seizure of its income-producing estates and, unable to properly house the treasures, gave part of its collection to the government in exchange for funds to carry out some repairs.

At the top of the stairs leading to the second-floor galleries is a splendid Asuka-period *kanjōban* canopy with pendant banners of gilt-bronze openwork depicting heavenly beings; it was used in ordination ceremonies. In the gallery to the left are numerous gilt-bronze statuettes, many of Kannon and Miroku, which were images for private worship; they are among the oldest Buddhist images in Japan and are probably of Korean origin. The statuettes display great individuality and charm. One remarkable group of small bronzes depicts Queen Maya, in the company of attendants, giving miraculous birth to Shaka; the infant, his palms pressed together in prayer, emerges from her sleeve. There are also many extraordinary Gigaku masks of the Asuka and Nara periods and a superb Tang-Chinese gilt silver ewer. The central gallery displays a magnificent pair of Tang mirrors bearing a vigorously rhythmic sea-and-mountain design. The remaining gallery exhibits paintings depicting the life of Shōtoku Taishi. One set of Heian-period screens, painted on silk that once adorned a pair of doors, depicts landscapes, buildings, and people; the screens are precursors of *Yamato-e* painting. Another, painted on hanging scrolls, is from the Kamakura period.

**Tokyo Metropolitan Art Museum** 東京都美術館 (3823-6921). Hrs: 9:00–17:00 (enter by 16:00); clsd 3rd M (Tu if M a NH), NY. This attractive, modern red-brick building designed by Maekawa Kunio stages temporary exhibitions by important contemporary Japanese artists.

∗ **Kan'ei-ji Hondō (Main Hall)** 寛永寺本堂 This quiet, neglected hall barely recalls the great temple that once stretched all the way to Shinobazu Pond. The original main hall, which stood in the center of Ueno Park, was destroyed in 1868. Behind the temple are the tombs of the fourth and fifth Tokugawa shoguns. Their mausoleums were destroyed in World War II, but the ornate gates still stand.

**Temple Quarter.** Those who continue from Kan'ei-ji on to Yanaka (see below) will pass through this quiet residential neighborhood with a number of temples. Most interesting is **Jōmyō-in** 浄名院, which claims to have 84,000 stone Jizō crowding its precinct.

203

### Shinobazu Pond and North Yushima

There is another side to Ueno, apart from its museums and temples. From Ueno station, instead of heading north into Ueno Park, turn down Ameyoko-chō, then circle back to visit the Shitamachi Museum. Afterward, stroll around Yushima, with its old shops and *rakugo* theaters, and pay a visit to the Yushima Tenjin Shrine. Hardy walkers might continue south past the love hotels to Kanda Myōjin and Yushima Seidō in Kanda (I:3).

∗ **Ameyoko-chō** アメ横丁 *Make a sharp left from Ueno station's Shinobazu exit.* Ameyoko is a famous alley crammed with some 400 shops for cut-rate goods, reminiscent of black markets, which in fact is how it got its start right after the war. The name has a dual meaning: in the beginning, the market traded primarily in food, in particular candy (*ame*), hence "candy alley"; later came an influx of American PX goods, hence "*Ame[rica]* alley."

∗∗ **Shitamachi Museum (Fūzoku Shiryōkan)** 下町風俗資料館 (3823-7451/7461). Hrs: 9:30–16:30 (enter by 16:00); clsd M (Tu if M a NH), NY. This is an excellent introduction to the fast-disappearing culture of Shitamachi. Exhibits include precise reconstructions of a merchant's counting house, a tenement, and a shop selling simple sweets called *dagashi*.

∗ **Shinobazu Pond and Benten-dō** 不忍池・弁天堂 *0:10h on foot from Ueno station.* This large pond, fringed with rushes and alive with waterfowl, was once an inlet of Tokyo Bay. It was built in imitation of the famous Benten shrine on Lake Biwa's Chikubujima near Kyoto. In 1670, causeways were built linking the island to the shore, and these became a lively scene of teahouses. In 1884, a racetrack was built around the pond, a subject often depicted in Meiji-era woodblock prints.

∗ **Yokoyama Taikan Kinenkan (Memorial Gallery)** 横山大観記念館 (3821-1017). Hrs: Th–Su 10:00–16:00; clsd M–W, and late June–mid-July, early Aug.–late Aug., and early Dec.–early Jan. A small collection of the paintings of Yokoyama Taikan (1868–1958), shown in his former home, a pleasant, traditional house with garden, such as one rarely sees in Tokyo. Taikan, a leading pioneer of *Nihonga* (modern Japanese-style painting), worked in traditional modes but broke with convention by bold use of shading.

**Kyū Iwasaki-tei (Former Iwasaki Mansion)** 旧岩崎邸 (ICP) (3813-2101). Hrs: M–F 10:00–11:30, 13:00–16:30; clsd Sa, Su, NH. By appointment only. On the grounds of the Supreme Court Legal Study Center. This house, built in 1896 for Iwasaki Hisaya, son of the founder of Mitsubishi, was designed by Josiah Conder. The grounds also contain a billiard hall and a Japanese wing with a scrap of garden. A fascinating view of how prewar tycoons lived.

∗ **Yushima Tenjin (Shrine)** 湯島天神 *0:05h walk from Yushima subway station.* This shrine to Tenjin, the Heian-period scholar Sugawara no Michizane, deity of scholarship (see Kyūshū, p. 480), may date from as early as 1355, though the present buildings are late 19th C. It stands on a bluff overlooking its surroundings and is Tokyo's only plum-blossom viewing spot of note, the plum being Tenjin's favorite flower. The heavily overburdened racks of *ema* (votive plaques) attest to its immense popularity with students, who pray for success on their entrance examinations. Especially charming in the early evening.

### Yanaka 谷中

This neighborhood, one of the few to escape the destruction of both the Kantō Earthquake and the firebombing, preserves a quiet, almost rustic atmosphere that has long made it a special favorite with Shitamachi lovers. With its old houses, temples, and small shops, it is a wonderful place to explore on foot. You can start from Nippori station and wend your way to Nezu station in about 2:00h (but expect to get lost).

**Yanaka Reien (Cemetery)** 谷中霊園　Stretching between Ueno Park and Nippori station is one of Tokyo's largest remaining cemeteries. Its lush, overgrown grounds are filled with tombs of all types.

\* **Asakura Chōsokan (Sculpture Gallery)** 朝倉彫塑館　(3821-4549). Hrs: 9:30–16:30 (enter by 16:00); clsd M, F, except if NH, then clsd day after. This is the charming traditional house of Asakura Fumio (1883-1964), a leading academic sculptor. The courtyard garden alone is worth the visit.

\* **Daimyo Tokei Hakubutsukan (Clock Museum)** 大名時計博物館　(3821-6913). Open Jan. 16–June 30, Oct. 1–Dec. 24. Hrs: 10:00–16:00; clsd M (Tu if M a NH). A fascinating museum of exquisite clocks built for the feudal lords. The hours are indicated by the Chinese characters for zodiac animals. The old Japanese hour was not constant, but instead was adjusted so that there would be equal numbers of hours day and night. A summer daytime hour might be nearly twice as long as the night hour. Although some compensation was built into the mechanism, the clocks still had to be adjusted frequently by professional clock-keepers.

\* **Isetatsu** いせ辰　谷中2-18-9　(3823-1453). Hrs: 10:00–18:00, daily; clsd Jan. 1. Beautiful little shop famous for Edo *chiyogami*, decorative paper with fine printed designs copied from samurai textiles.

\* **Nezu Jinja** 根津神社　*0:10h walk west of Nezu subway station (Chiyoda line)*. This shrine, one of Tokyo's most charming, claims to have been founded some 2,000 years ago by the legendary prince-hero Yamato Takeru, who passed through the wilderness that was Edo on his way north to conquer hostile tribes. Before the Meiji era, it was a syncretic establishment called Nezu Gongen. The main hall (ICP) was built in 1706.

## Ueno Rakugo Theaters

*Rakugo*, a humorous monologue by a sit-down comic, is the classic Shitamachi entertainment. Though clearly a knowledge of Japanese helps, it's fun to see the kimono-clad, fan-waving gentlemen perform their traditional style of delivery, peppered with mime and impersonations. (Foreigners risk ending up as part of the show.)

**Suzumoto Engeijō** 鈴本演芸場　(3834-5906). Hrs: 12:00–16:30, 17:00–20:40, daily; irregular schedule during NY. This is the oldest theater of its type in Tokyo, though it is now housed on the 3rd and 4th floors of a modern building. Features *rakugo* and *manzai* (comic dialogue), music, and magic tricks.

## Ueno Shopping

Ameyoko-chō for cut-rate goods. For fine traditional items, look around Yushima.

2 **Jūsanya** 十三屋　(3831-3238). Hrs: 10:00–19:00; clsd 1st and 3rd Su, NY. Across from the Shitamachi Museum. A 240-year-old shop for combs and hair ornaments carved from satiny boxwood. The shop is named *jūsan* (13) because *kushi* (comb) sounds like 9 (*ku* = suffering) and 4 (*shi* = death). But 9 plus 4, or 13, is not unlucky in Japan.

3 **Kyōya** 京屋　上野2-12-10　(3831-1905). Hrs: 10:00–18:00; clsd Su, NH, NY. Edo *sashimono*, small pieces of traditional furniture of exquisite workmanship and detailing. Among the more affordable items are letter trays and boxes. The ultimate small luxury is an *aibiki*, a cleverly collapsible seat used when kneeling on the floor. It's made of *kiri* (paulownia) for lightness, but the sliding joints are hardwood.

4 **Dōmyō** 道明　上野2-11-1　(3831-3773). Hrs: 10:30–18:30; Su and NH 10:30–17:00; clsd NY. A 300-year-old emporium for elegant *kumihimo*, or braided silk cords. Though now primarily a kimono accessory, *kumihimo* were used for wrapping scrolls, armor, and sword lacings, and other uses requiring strong, decorative cords.

7 **Haguro-dō** 羽黒堂　湯島4-6-11　(3815-0431). Yushima High Town Apts., 2F. Hrs: 10:00–18:00, daily; clsd NY, mid-Aug. A gallery for *nikuhitsu*, paintings of the ukiyo-e school. It was on these, in fact, and not the familiar woodblock prints, that many ukiyo-e masters lavished their best efforts. The proprietor, a veteran collector, also welcomes interested nonbuyers.

## Ueno Tea Breaks

6 **Tsuruse** つる瀬　湯島3-35-8　(3833-8516). Hrs: 8:00–21:00, daily; clsd NY. Yushima. Fresh Japanese confections molded into fruits, flowers, and other seasonal objects. A pleasant tea parlor serves sweet and savory dishes using sticky *mochi*, pounded glutinous rice.

11 **Tōrin-dō** 桃林堂　桜木1-5-7　(3828-9826). Hrs: 9:00–17:00; clsd NY. Quaint teahouse where one can rest over *matcha* (tea-ceremony tea) or *o-shiruko* (sweet bean broth). Tōrin-dō's specialty is candied fruit: grapefruit, angelica, kumquat, and eggplant.

## I:3 KANDA 神田

*Take the Yamanote or Chūō train line, or the Ginza subway line*. This quarter of Tokyo straddles the border between the High City and the Low City, and the differences between the two are quite palpable, at least to the perceptive observer. On the east, the Shitamachi side, are Akihabara, the famous discount electronics district, and the Kanda wholesale market. Ochanomizu, where the hills begin, became a university district after 1868, triggering the development of nearby Jimbōchō into a massive booksellers' quarter. The Kudan area, to the west, was connected with the castle.

**Walking Tour:** * Akihabara — (0:05h) — Kanda Ichiba wholesale market —
(0:10h) — * Kanda Myōjin — (0:03h) — * Yushima Seidō — (0:10h) — Nikolai
Cathedral — (0:10h) — * Jimbōchō

**Lunch:** Kandagawa Honten, Yabu Soba, Botan, Hisago

## * Akihabara 秋葉原 ✓

*Take the Hibiya subway or Sōbu line.* Akihabara, the Field of Autumn Leaves, ablaze not
with foliage, but with vast corridors of blinking signs, is to electronics what Las Vegas is to
gambling. In the space of a few blocks are crammed hundreds of shops, with annual sales of
Y30 trillion, or 10 percent of domestic sales in electronics. Though discounts here are actually no better than elsewhere, the range of selections — and the sheer sensation of being
here — is second to none. Adjacent is its counterpart in produce, the huge **Kanda Ichiba**.

### Akihabara Shopping

Discounts average 10 to 15 percent for new goods, 50 percent for used.

1 **Yamagiwa** ヤマギワ 外神田4-1-1 (3253-2111). Hrs: 10:00–19:00, Sa 10:00–19:30.
Lighting specialist, with a vast selection of lamps. Overseas voltages available.

2 **Laox** ラオックス 外神田1-2-9 (3253-7111). Hrs: 10:00–19:30; Su 10:00–19:00. Best
and biggest of the Akihabara shops. Tax-free shopping on 6–7F. Audio listening room.

e p. 228–229 for restaurants, p. 232–233 for hotels

205

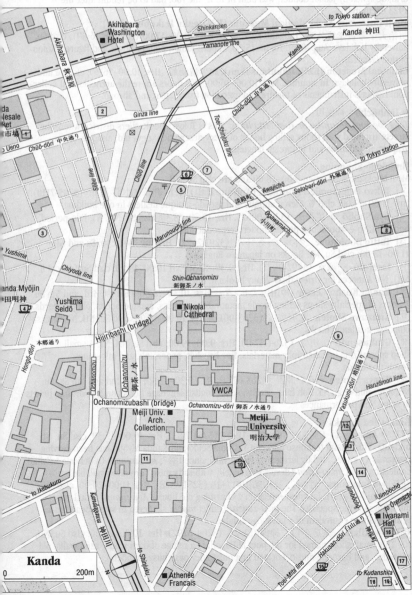

Kanda

## Ochanomizu 御茶ノ水

*Take the Chūō line or Marunouchi subway line to Ochanomizu or Awajichō; the Chiyoda line to Shin-Ochanomizu; or the Toei-Shinjuku line to Ogawamachi.* By the 1880s, five universities were established on this hill, including Meiji University. Southwest of the universities—at the bottom of the hill—was Jimbōchō, where booksellers were established to cater to the students; this area became the center of Tokyo's publishing industry. Today there are booksellers of all kinds, including shops that specialize in antique books and woodblock prints. The area has three wildly different religious landmarks: a Russian Orthodox church, a Confucian temple, and a Shinto shrine that holds one of Tokyo's most famous festivals.

* **Kanda Myōjin (Shrine)** 神田明神 *0:05h walk NE of Ochanomizu station.* This famous shrine, said to have been founded in 730, was located in Ōtemachi until Ieyasu moved it to its present site in 1616, designating it a guardian of Edo. The present structure is a 1934 concrete replica of its flamboyant, Momoyama-period Gongen-style predecessor. The Kanda Matsuri in mid-May is among Tokyo's most famous matsuri. The shrine was founded to placate the spirit of a 10th-C warrior, Taira no Masakado, who led a rebellion in Kantō and declared himself emperor, but was killed. His head was sent to Kyoto, but soon after local people spotted it drifting about, seeking its body; the hauntings stopped when they built a shrine for it. The head is still buried in Ōtemachi and the site is alleged to be cursed; not even the rapacious developers have been able to erect a building over the prime property it occupies.

* **Yushima Seidō** 湯島聖堂 Hrs: 10:00–16:30, daily. An austere Confucian temple founded in 1632 for the shogunate Confucianist, Hayashi Razan, who justified the Japanese feudal hierarchy in terms of neo-Confucian social doctrine. The Yushima Seidō was moved from Ueno to its present location by the Dog Shogun, Tsunayoshi, an ardent Confucianist. The main hall, which houses an image of Confucius, is open Sa, Su, NH.

**Nikolai-dō (Cathedral)** ニコライ堂 (ICP). This onion-domed Russian Orthodox cathedral, designed by Josiah Conder, was built in 1891; the roof had to be rebuilt after the 1923 earthquake.

206

**Meiji University Archeological Museum (Kōkogaku Hakubutsukan)** 明治大学考古学博物館 Daigaku Kaikan, 4F. Hrs: 10:00–17:00 (enter by 16:30); clsd Su, university holidays. Aug.–Sept. 10:30–15:30. Superb Jōmon pottery bowls and figures, Kofun-period *haniwa*.

**Criminal Museum (Keiji Hakubutsukan)** 刑事博物館 Hrs: 10:00–16:30; clsd Su and university holidays. In summer, M–F 10:00–16:00. Two floors above the archeological collection. Displays instruments of torture and execution from Japan and abroad.

## * Jimbōchō 神保町

*Take the Toei-Shinjuku or Toei-Mita lines.* This is Tokyo's booksellers district, where the streets are lined with shops selling books of every description: new, old, antique, pornographic, in Japanese and in foreign languages.

## Jimbōchō Shopping

Most bookstores are open 9:00–18:00 and are clsd Su, NH.

11 **Tokyo Ochanomizu Kottōkan (Antique Hall)** 東京御茶ノ水骨董館 (3295-7110). Hrs: 11:00–19:00; clsd W. Eleven antique and pseudo-antique dealers in one building.

12 **Ōya Shobō** 大屋書房 (3291-0062). Hrs: 10:30–18:30; clsd Su, NH, NY. Edo-period books, ukiyo-e woodblock prints, modern reproductions.

13 **Tuttle Bookstore** タトルブックストア (3291-7072). Hrs: 10:30–18:30; Sa and NH 11:00–18:00; clsd Su, NY. Books on Japan, in English.

14 **Issei-dō** 一誠堂 (3292-0071). Hrs: 9:30–18:30; NH 10:00–18:00; clsd Su (except if NH), NY. A mecca for Orientalists. Many books in English.

16 **Kanda Kosho Center** 神田古書センター Hrs: 10:30–18:30; clsd 1st, 3rd, and 5th Su. 7 floors of specialty shops selling movie memorabilia, comics, antique books, old postcards.

17 **Kitazawa Shoten** 北沢書店 (3263-0011). Hrs: 10:00–18:00; clsd Su, NH, NY. English-language academic books.

18 **Gyokusendō** 玉川堂 (3264-3741). Hrs: 9:00–19:00; clsd Su, NH, NY. A small shop specializing in calligraphy materials: fine brushes, paper, ink, and ink stones. Lovely postcards.

19 **Wanya Shoten** わんや書店 (3263-6771). Hrs: 9:30–17:30; clsd 2nd and 4th Sa, Su, NH, Apr., mid-Aug., NY. Noh fans, scripts, some English-language books on Noh drama; tickets to some Noh performances.

## Kanda Tea Breaks

4 * **Amanoya** 天野屋 外神田2-18-15 (3251-7911). Hrs: 10:00–17:30; clsd Su, NH, mid-Aug. This quaint teahouse between Yushima Seidō and Kanda Myōjin has been serving *amazake* (a sweet, slightly fermented rice drink) since 1847; *kuzumochi* (a delicate jellylike confection) and *miso-oden* (devil's tongue jelly with salty miso) are also available.

6 ** **Takemura** 竹むら 神田須田町1-19 (3251-2328). Hrs: 11:00–20:00; clsd Su, NH, mid-Aug., NY. Japanese sweets in a charming old house. *Age-manjū* (fried sweet dumplings) is the specialty. The *awa-zenzai* (millet *mochi* slathered in sweet bean paste) is the Japanese equivalent of a hot fudge sundae.

15 ** **Rihaku** 茶房李白 神保町2-24 (3264-6292). Hrs: 10:00–20:00; clsd Su, NH, NY. This small shop, named for the poet Li Po, offers a refuge of dark wood, sand walls, old ceramics, and baroque music. Located in a quiet alley near busy Jimbōchō.

**Kitanomaru Kōen (Park) and Kudan** 北の丸公園・九段
*Near Takebashi (Tōzai line) or Kudanshita (Tōzai or Toei-Shinjuku line) station.* The northern enclosure of Edo Castle, Kitanomaru, was flanked by a hill so steep that it had to be broken into *kudan*, or nine steps. After 1868, Kitanomaru was taken over by the imperial palace guard, and in 1969 it became a public park. The pleasant grounds contain several national museums. The west moat, **Chidorigafuchi Suijō Kōen** 千鳥ヶ淵水上公園, is open to recreational rowboats. It is one of Tokyo's best cherry-blossom spots. This area has several edifices dedicated to martial virtues: Yasukuni Jinja, the national shrine to Japan's war dead, and the Budōkan martial arts hall.

\* **National Museum of Modern Art (Kokuritsu Kindai Bijutsukan)**
東京国立近代美術館 (3214-2561). Hrs: 10:00–17:00 (enter by 16:30); clsd M (Tu if M a NH), NY. *Walk uphill from Takebashi station, into Kitanomaru Park.* Works by important artists from the Meiji period onward. The collection contains little contemporary art, but visiting shows are often very fine.

\* **National Museum of Modern Art Crafts Gallery** 工芸館 (3211-7781). Hrs: same as above. *0:05h walk from main museum.* Housed in a 1910 neo-Gothic brick building (ICP), former headquarters of the palace guard. The collection gives an overview of modern crafts descended from elite artisan traditions such as lacquer, porcelain, tea ceremony wares, and damascene.

**Science and Technology Museum** 科学技術館 (3212-8471). Hrs. 9:30–16:50 (enter by 16:00); clsd NY. In an aging, 5-story pentagonal building in Kitanomaru Park. Pretty low-tech, but try the robots.

**Nippon Budōkan** 日本武道館 (3216-5100). Octagonal hall built in 1964 for the Tokyo Olympics martial arts competitions; frequently used for rock concerts.

\* **Yasukuni Jinja (Shrine of Peace for the Nation)** 靖国神社 NW of Kitanomaru Park. State Shinto shrine founded in 1869 to deify those Japanese (and some non-Japanese), now numbering 2.5 million people, who gave their lives in the wars fought by modern Japan (see Shinto, p. 29). The 15-meter-high bronze torii dates from 1887. The shrine is in the Shimmei (Ise) style. An interesting little museum houses memorabilia, including photos and objects associated with kamikaze pilots from World War II. Soldiers headed into battle with the parting words, "Let's meet at Yasukuni," where their souls would supposedly return to be worshiped in eternal glory. A mother was supposed to retrieve her son's ashes stoically. Nine A-class war criminals, including Tōjō Hideki, are among those enshrined here. Not surprisingly, the Japanese Valhalla is subject to perennial controversy.

**Kudan Tea Break**
\* **Kudan Kaikan Beer Garden** 九段会館ビール園 Hrs: mid-May–Aug. 17:00–21:00 (last order 20:30); clsd in rain. On the roof of the Kudan Kaikan Hotel. Panoramic sunset views of Tokyo. Relaxed atmosphere.

**Exploring Kōraku-en Area**
**Koishikawa Kōraku-en (Garden)** 小石川後楽園 (3811-3015). Hrs: 9:00–17:00 (enter by 16:30), daily; clsd NY. *Take the JR Chūō line or the Tōzai or Yūrakuchō subway lines to Iidabashi, or the Marunouchi subway line to Kōrakuen.* Built in 1629, this is the oldest daimyo garden in Tokyo. Though much reduced and hemmed in by tall buildings, it preserves the character of a stroll garden. The garden was on part of the estate of the Mito Tokugawa, one of the *go-sanke*, or three great collateral branches of the Tokugawa House. The garden was completed by the second Mito lord, Tokugawa Mitsukuni, who was an eclectic (and the subject of the TV samurai soap, *Mito Kōmon*). His epitaph reads: "He honored Shinto and Confucianism, and he stood against Shinto and Confucianism. He revered Buddhism and Taoism, and he stood against Buddhism and Taoism." Mitsukuni gathered a group of scholars to write a definitive history of Japan. This group later became a hotbed of anti-Tokugawa radicalism, even though its founder was a grandson of Tokugawa Ieyasu. The garden, as eclectic as its builder, contains a small Confucian temple and a Shinto shrine to the Indian goddess Benten; there are miniatures of the causeway on China's West Lake as well as Arashiyama's Togetsu Bridge, Kiyomizu Temple, and other famous scenes of Japan. The garden's name, Kōraku-en (Garden of Pleasure Last), alludes to an ancient saying by a Chinese statesman, Fan Zhongyan, that "a gentleman should be the first to worry about the world's troubles and the last to enjoy its pleasures."

**Tokyo Dome** 東京ドーム (3811-2111). *By Kōrakuen station.* Tokyo's high-tech indoor baseball stadium (home astroturf of the Yomiuri Giants) was completed in 1988. It is aptly nicknamed Big Egg for its huge, curving roof fashioned from Teflon-coated glass panels. This soaring translucency is supported by a .3 percent elevation in indoor air pressure.

**Kagurazaka** 神楽坂 This is one of the few places in the High City that retains an atmosphere of its past. Kagurazaka was assigned to low-ranking direct retainers of the shogun. Unlike the great daimyo estates, it became a real community, with family houses and shops. When the shogunate fell, many of the residents remained. Some shops, such as the *tabi* maker **Minoya** (3260-7724), have been in business for over a century. Kagurazaka even has a small geisha quarter dating from the end of the Edo period. Secluded teahouses and restaurants are still found in the stone-paved back streets; turn into the alley across the street from the popular **Bishamon shrine** in the center of Kagurazaka.

# TOKYO II. ESTABLISHMENT TOKYO

**Main Attractions:**

| | |
|---|---|
| II:1 | *** Tokyo Imperial Palace |
| II:1 | ** Idemitsu Art Museum |
| II:2 | ** Ginza Yon-chōme Crossing |
| II:2 | ** Riccar Art Museum |
| II:2 | *** Kabuki-za (theater) |
| II:3 | ** Tsukiji (fish market) |

When Japan's first rail line, from Yokohama to Shinbashi Station, was completed in 1872, it ensured that this area would become the center of modern Japan — its window on the world. Not far from the station, the Shinbashi geisha quarter thrived. More important to the area's later history, the modern Ginza came into being. The same year the railroad was built, the mayor of Tokyo hired an English architect to rebuild the Ginza's main street — part of the old Tōkaidō — in brick. Although the brick buildings had a reputation for being moldy and damp, and they gradually disappeared, Ginza became the premier center for sightseers and shoppers; it was the symbol of Japan's experiment with "civilization and enlightenment."

In 1912, the railway was extended — the tracks roughly following the outer moat of what had been Edo Castle — and Tokyo station was opened. The land between the outer and inner moats, Marunouchi ("within the moat"), belonged to the Mitsubishi Corporation, which had purchased it in 1890. It had lain fallow — people derisively called it Mitsubishi Meadow — but when Tokyo station was built facing onto the open land, it quickly escalated in value and became the center of Japan's financial world, along with Hibiya and Yūrakuchō, immediately to Marunouchi's south. It was here that the government built the Rokumeikan to entertain elite foreign guests, the Imperial Hotel, and Japan's first Western-style public park, Hibiya Kōen. To the extreme east, by Tokyo Bay, a short-lived foreign quarter was built at Tsukiji. In 1935, Tokyo's great fish market was moved there, where it remains an early-morning sightseeing treat.

In establishment Tokyo, the railroad tracks define the old boundary between the castle and the Low City. Today the tracks divide the world of officialdom and finance in Marunouchi, Hibiya, Yūrakuchō, and Kasumigaseki from the centers of commerce, shopping, and pleasure in Ginza and Nihonbashi. Our description begins at Tokyo station, the bridge between the two faces of establishment Tokyo.

## Tokyo Station　東京駅

Served by Shinkansen (bullet train), urban train lines, Marunouchi subway line. Almost every visitor traveling to or from Tokyo by rail will pass through this station. Tracks are numbered from west to east. The most important lines are:

- 1–2: Chūō line to Shinjuku
- 3–4: Keihin-Tōhoku and Yamanote lines toward Ueno
- 5–6: Yamanote and Keihin-Tōhoku lines toward Shinagawa
- 9–10: Tōkaidō main line
- 14–19: Shinkansen lines

**Marunouchi (West) side:** Old, red-brick building facing the Imperial Palace. Here you'll find the Marunouchi subway line, and, deep underground, the JR NEX (p. 5), Yokosuka line and Sōbu line. Also located here are the Tokyo Station Hotel, Hato tour bus pier, and the lost-and-found.

**Yaesu (East) side:** Modern building facing Nihonbashi and Ginza. (Yaesu is a corruption of the name of Jan Joosten, the Dutch mariner who was given an estate here by Tokugawa Ieyasu.) Located here are the **Travel Service Center** (to exchange Rail Pass vouchers) and the **prefectural information offices** in the Kokusai Kankō Kaikan and Daimaru Department store.

## II:1 PALACE SIDE

This is the world of Japanese officialdom, dominated by the Imperial Palace and the adjoining business centers of Marunouchi, Hibiya, and Yūrakuchō. From Hibiya, government buildings extend along the palace moat toward Akasaka.

---

**Walking Tour:** Old Tokyo Station — (0:10h) — Ōte-mon Gate of ** Imperial Palace — East Garden — (0:10h) — Nijūbashi — (0:10h) — ** Idemitsu Art Museum — (0:10h) — Ginza (II:2)

**Lunch:** A Point, Shokudō Wan

**Notes:** Imperial Palace clsd M and F; Idemitsu Art Museum clsd M. Rent-a-cycle, Su only, 9:00–17:00; behind the police box in the Imperial Palace plaza.

---

## Marunouchi 丸ノ内

*Walk out the west side of Tokyo station, or take the Marunouchi, Toei-Mita, Tōzai, or Chiyoda subway line to Ōtemachi.* Literally meaning "within the moat," Marunouchi was the site of the mansions of the shogun's senior retainers. After the Meiji Restoration, it became a parade ground for the army, which Mitsubishi purchased cheaply at a time when the center of Tokyo's business district was in Nihonbashi. When the red-brick Tokyo station was built, Marunouchi experienced a building boom that has made it Japan's economic citadel. The area remains the city's financial center.

**Old Tokyo Station.** Marunouchi side of Tokyo station. This red-brick building, said to be a copy of Amsterdam station, was completed in 1914. It was designed by Tatsuno Kingo, a disciple of the British mentor of Meiji- and Taishō-period architects, Josiah Conder.

**✳✳✳ Tokyo Imperial Palace (Kōkyo)** 皇居 In the days of the Tokugawa shoguns, this was the largest castle in the world, with an outer wall 16 km long and 5 m thick, breached by 11 gates. A maze of inner moats and walls made it virtually impregnable. In 1868, it became the Imperial Palace. The area within the inner moat, 6.4 km in circumference, was deemed sufficient for the emperor's protection. The site of the shogun's palace is now the public East Garden. The Imperial Palace grounds in the western enclosure are open only on January 2 and the emperor's birthday; this compound was occupied by high shogunate officials, and is now entered by the bridge called Nijūbashi. The palace was rebuilt after being bombed in World War II. On the west, closed to the public, are the parklands of Fukiage, which served as a firebreak between old Edo, with its countless fires, and the castle. The northern enclosure, Kitanomaru, is now a public park (I:3).

**◆ Imperial Palace East Garden (Kōkyo Higashi Gyoen)** 皇居東御苑
Hrs: 9:00–16:00 (enter by 15:00); clsd M, F, NY. Enter by Ōte-mon, Hirakawa-mon, or Kitahanebashi-mon. This park consists of the Honmaru (inner enclosure) and the Ninomaru (second enclosure), once the very center of the shogun's palace. The recommended entrance is the **Ōte-mon** 大手門, which was the principal gate; rebuilt in 1967, it is an impressive example of the defensively designed *masugata* gate (see Castles, p. 46). The immense stones, brought 100 km from the Izu Peninsula, were fitted to prevent slippage in an earthquake. The path continues past some modern buildings into the Ninomaru, which now contains the East Garden, an attractive stroll garden originally designed in 1630 by KOBORI ENSHŪ. At the north end is a 19th-C tea arbor, **Suwa no Chaya**. To the west, separated from the Ninomaru by a bridge and truncated moat, is the **Honmaru**, which contained the shogun's palace halls, including a grand thousand-mat audience hall and the *Ō-oku*, which housed his many ladies (the Hirakawa-mon was for their use). Nearly all of these buildings were destroyed in fires shortly before the Meiji Restoration (1868). At the north end of the Honmaru are the foundations of the castle donjon, which was black and 51 m high, the tallest building in Edo; it burned in 1657 and was never rebuilt. Instead, the **Fujimi Yagura** (Mt. Fuji View Tower), a subsidiary turret that still stands at the south end of the Honmaru, served in its place. The imperial Gagaku orchestra gives concerts at the Tōka Music Hall, an ugly octagonal structure built in 1966.

**◆ Nijūbashi (Bridge)** 二重橋 *A kilometer to the SW of the Ōte-mon.* When the Imperial Palace was built, this bridge became its principal entrance. The double-arched stone bridge was completed in 1888 on a German design. It is now one of Tokyo's most familiar sights. Visible above it is the **Fushimi Yagura**, another of the castle's surviving turrets.

**Sakurada-mon (Castle Gate).** *SW of Nijūbashi.* On a snowy day in 1860, the shogunal minister (*tairō*) Ii Naosuke was setting out from his mansion (where the National Diet Building now stands) to the castle, when he was cut down before this gate by a band of xenophobic samurai who were enraged by his treaty with the Americans. The assassination severely weakened the shogunate, which collapsed in 1868.

## Hibiya and Yūrakuchō 日比谷・有楽町

*Take the Hibiya, Yūrakuchō, Chiyoda, or Toei-Mita line to Hibiya or Yūrakuchō station; the two stations are connected.* The heart of the business district; this is mainly a place for chores. Many airline offices and travel agencies are near the Imperial Hotel. A stop at the Tourist Information Center (TIC) is in order for newcomers. From here, one has only to duck under the tracks to Ginza; if it is early evening, the route will be thick with the aroma of *yakitori*, broiling skewers of chicken, billowing from numerous stalls huddled beneath the tracks.

**✳✳ Idemitsu Bijutsukan (Art Museum)** 出光美術館 (3213-9402). Kokusai Bldg., Teigeki side entrance, 9F. Hrs: 10:00–17:00 (enter by 16:30); clsd M (Tu if M a NH), NY. A superb collection of Chinese and Japanese ceramics, Zen paintings, Chinese bronzes, and Southeast Asian and Persian objects. The galleries are pleasant and offer a good view of the city. There is a Japanese-style tea room.

**Hibiya Kōen (Park)** 日比谷公園 After 1868, the abandoned daimyo estates here became an army parade ground, which in 1903 was turned into Japan's first formal Western-style park. Its proximity to the establishment centers made it a favorite protest site in the 1960s. From its earliest days as a park, it attracted large numbers of illicit lovers, bums, and loiterers, and it is notorious for Peeping Toms — seasoned hands in dark clothes with binoculars.

**Takarazuka Theater** 宝塚劇場 (3591-1711). Hrs: variable. Famous for its all-female cast, featured in lavish, romance-filled productions appealing to Japanese women.

## Hibiya Shopping and Services

**Tourist Information Center (TIC)** 有楽町1-6-6 (3502-1461). Hrs: M–F 9:00–17:00; Sa 9:00–12:00. JNTO-staffed. Maps and information in English.

**International Arcade** インターナショナルアーケード Under the tracks near the Imperial Hotel is this dingy passage crammed with shops selling things tourists want. For used kimono, try Hayashi Antique Kimono (3591-9826). Hrs: 10:00–18:00, daily; clsd NY.

**American Pharmacy** 有楽町1-8-1 (3271-4034). Hrs: 9:00–19:00; Su, NH 10:00–19:00; clsd NY. American brands. Some English spoken.

## Exploring Government Buildings

Follow Uchibori-dōri along the periphery of the castle moat. One can continue west to Akasaka or north to Kitanomaru Park.

**Kokkaigijidō (Diet Building)** 国会議事堂 (1936). This stiff, Western-style statehouse is one of the more oppressive structures in Tokyo. The building stands on the site of the Ii mansion (see Imperial Palace, Sakurada-mon). Visiting Hrs: M–F 9:00–17:00.

**Saikō Saibansho (Supreme Court)** 最高裁判所 (1974). A fortresslike pile of granite designed by Okada Shinichi. It conveys an impression of Japanese justice (which has no jury trials) as operating behind closed doors.

**\*\* Kokuritsu Gekijō (National Theater)** 国立劇場 (3265-7411). This concrete version of an *azekura* (log cabin) storehouse is a showcase for traditional theater arts. Kabuki is presented in the main theater, Bunraku in the small theater. The Engei Hall is an intimate theater for *rakugo*, *manzai* (Japanese vaudeville), and recitals. See Tokyo Theaters for schedule.

**Wacoal Kōjimachi Building** ワコール麹町ビル (1984). A steel-clad building with a cyclopean porthole eyeballing the imperial palace, designed by Kurokawa Kishō, a prankster among leading Japanese architects. The story circulating among Tokyo architects is that late Emperor Hirohito gazed out of his window one morning and was startled to find the structure staring back at him. "What," he intoned, "is *that*?"

210

## II:2 NIHONBASHI AND GINZA

This is the side of establishment Tokyo that grew out of the old Shitamachi. Nihonbashi's prosperity continued into the early Meiji era; here one still finds the main Tokyo branches of Mitsukoshi and Takashimaya department stores, the headquarters of the Bank of Japan, and many prestigious traditional shops. The main action, however, has shifted to Ginza; by evening, Nihonbashi and Kyōbashi are shut down.

---

**Walking Tour:** Mitsukoshi Dept. Store — (0:02h) — Nihonbashi bridge — (0:03h) — \* Kite Museum — (0:05h walk) — Nihonbashi station — (0:25h walk or subway) — \*\* Ginza Yon-chōme crossing — (0:10h) — \*\* Riccar Art Museum — (0:15h via Miyuki-dōri) — \*\*\* Kabuki-za (try to catch the late afternoon show).

**Lunch:** Munakata, Mimiu, Ōmatsuya, etc.

**Notes:** Museums clsd M. Check Kabuki-za schedule.

---

## Nihonbashi and Kyōbashi 日本橋・京橋

*Take the Ginza or Tōzai subway line. This area is only a few minutes' walk east of Tokyo station.* Nihonbashi, "the bridge of Japan," was the terminus of the five highways maintained by the shogunate, and was the place from which all distances were measured. It thus became the center of commerce in Edo; the gleaming white warehouses that lined the banks of the river, spanned by the Nihonbashi, were the subject of the first print in Hiroshige's famous *Fifty-three Stations of the Tōkaidō* series. Neighboring Kyōbashi, the "Kyoto bridge," was so named because it was the first bridge on the journey to the old capital. The Nihonbashi bridge itself — the present one was rebuilt in 1911 — now spans a putrid canal in the shadow of an overhead expressway.

**Bank of Japan** 日本銀行 Constructed in 1896 on the site of a shogunate silver mint, moved here from Ginza in 1800, this is the first full-scale Western-style building designed by a Japanese architect, Tatsuno Kingo, a student of the influential Josiah Conder. It was modeled on the neoclassical Berlin National Bank.

**\* Kite Museum** 凧の博物館 日本橋1-12-10 (3271-2465). Taimeiken Bldg., 5F. Hrs: 11:00–17:00; clsd Su, NH, mid-Aug., NY. A delightful little museum of Japanese kites from various regions.

**\* Tokyo Stock Exchange** 東京証券取引所 (3666-0141). Hrs: M–F 9:00–16:00. *NE of Nihonbashi station.* View the trading floor of one of the world's largest stock exchanges from a second-floor gallery. Best Hrs: 9:00–11:00 and 13:00–15:00.

**\* Bridgestone Museum of Art** ブリヂストン美術館 (3563-0241). Bridgestone Bldg., 2F. Hrs: 10:00–17:30 (enter by 17:00); clsd M, NY. Between Nihonbashi and Kyōbashi stations. One of the best collections in Japan of Western art and Western-style Japanese paintings.

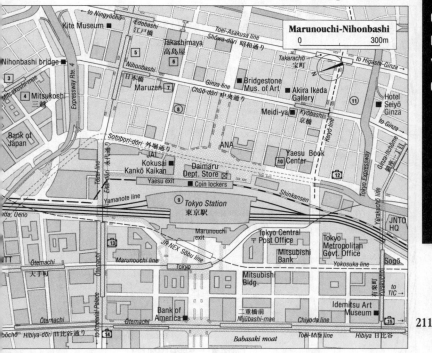

Marunouchi-Nihonbashi

0        300m

## Nihonbashi Shopping

**2 Ebiya Art Co., Ltd.** 海老屋美術店  日本橋室町 3-2-18 (3241-1914). Hrs: 10:00–18:00; clsd 2nd and 4th Sa, Su, NH, NY. This antique store is a "purveyor to the Imperial Household," but don't let that frighten you away. The shop's door stands open, the proprietor is friendly, and inexpensive, tasteful items are available as well.

**3 Kiya** 木屋  日本橋室町 1-56 (3241-0111). Hrs: 10:00–18:00; Su, NH 11:15–17:45; Jan.–Feb. clsd Su, NH, NY. By Mitsukoshi-mae station. Hand-forged Japanese cutlery and carpenter's tools, plus top-quality imported cutlery.

**4 Mitsukoshi Department Store** 三越(本店) (3241-3311). Hrs: 10:00–18:30; clsd M (except if NH), NY. July and Dec. 10:00–19:00. Mitsukoshi began in 1673 as a kimono shop, the Echigoya, founded by the family that went on to build the Mitsui commercial empire. An innovative place, it was the first store in Japan to display its wares and employ women as shop assistants. Today, however, it feels less like an innovator than a venerable establishment. Bears a resemblance to London's Harrods.

**5 Haibara** 榛原  日本橋 2-7-6 (3272-3801). Hrs: 9:30–17:30; Sa 9:30–17:00; clsd Su, NH, NY. Founded 1806. The elegant window displays of this famous paper shop contrast smartly with the dark, heavy appearance of the exterior. Handmade *washi* for calligraphy, letters, decorative prints, and stationery.

**6 Takashimaya Department Store** 高島屋 (3211-4111). Hrs: 10:00–18:30; clsd W (except if NH), NY. July and Dec. 10:00–19:00. The main Tokyo branch of another venerable business, which began as a Kyoto kimono shop.

**7 Maruzen Bookstore** 丸善 (3272-7211). Hrs: 10:00–18:30; clsd Su, NY. Founded in 1869 as Japan's first Western bookstore. English-language books, guidebooks, and crafts.

**10 Yaesu Book Center** 八重洲ブックセンター (3281-1811). Hrs: 10:00–19:00; clsd Su, NY. Carries 300,000 titles on its first 4 floors, including foreign books. Reading room (small fee charged) on the 4th floor.

## Ginza  銀座

*Take the Marunouchi, Ginza, or Hibiya subway line.* Ginza means "Silver Mint," for it was here, on reclaimed land, that the shogunate minted its coin from 1612 to 1800. After a fire razed the area in 1872, it acquired a fireproof streetfront of red-brick buildings and tree-lined alleys, becoming the first Westernized quarter in Tokyo; for people of fashion, it was synonymous with the latest in Western, particularly Parisian, culture. Although Roppongi and Aoyama have replaced it at the forefront of fashion, Ginza still smells of money and success; tucked away on the back streets are hundreds of tiny hostess bars to which successful businessmen and politicians repair at night. Ginza also has the top department stores, boutiques, and contemporary art galleries.

**\*\* Ginza Yon-chōme Crossing** 銀座四丁目 At the intersection of the two broad avenues, Chūō-dōri and Harumi-dōri; the streets are closed to traffic on weekends and holidays. On one corner stands the Wakō Clock Tower, a Ginza landmark that first appeared in 1894 (the present one dates from 1932). Across the way is Mitsukoshi, king of Ginza department stores.

212

Ginza
0      50m

One fashionable side street is the tree-lined Namiki-dōri, where Gucci, Louis Vuitton, and the like attract window shoppers. Miyuki-dōri has one of Ginza's first genuine cafés, Fūgetsudō, and at its east end, the Gallery Center Building (conventional art galleries).

**San'ai Building** 三愛ビル (1963). Designed by Hayashi Shōji of Nikken Sekkei. This 12-story glass cylinder pioneered the use of light as an architectural material. Each floor is divided by a layer of fluorescent lighting, and the tower is capped by a luminous cylinder. Contains fashion boutiques.

✱ **Sony Building** ソニービル (1966). Designed by Ashihara Yoshinobu. The tall, narrow front of this building is covered with glass units—TV screens, in fact—which flash a variety of changing light patterns. The building displays Sony products.

**Gallery Ueda Ginza** ギャラリー上田銀座 銀座6-6-7 (3574-7553). Asahi Bldg., B1. Hrs: 10:30–18:30; clsd NH, NY. This is one of Tokyo's top galleries for contemporary art, including Japanese and Korean, and is recommended as a starting point for a tour of other galleries, many of which are in the Ginza and Kyōbashi areas (see p. 191). Inquire here for the illustrated directory to Tokyo's contemporary art galleries.

✱✱ **Riccar Bijutsukan (Art Museum)** リッカー美術館 銀座6-2-3 (3571-3254). Riccar Bldg., 7F. Open only during exhibitions. Hrs: 11:00–18:00 (enter by 17:30); clsd M (Tu if M a NH), NY. *0:05h walk from Yūrakuchō station, or 0:10h from Ginza Yon-chōme crossing.* An outstanding collection of ukiyo-e woodblock prints, amassed by the now-bankrupt Riccar Sewing Machine Company. Shown in a small, pleasant gallery. Apply a few days in advance to see prints that are not on view. One room illustrates the technique of printmaking, and there is also a library.

**Shizuoka Press and Broadcasting Building** 静岡新聞放送東京支社 (1967). This black, cylindrical shaft with dark-glassed office units cantilevered off it looks like a fragment of one of architect Tange Kenzō's megastructure fantasies.

✱ **Shiseidō The Ginza** 資生堂ザ・ギンザ (3572-2121). Hrs: 11:00–20:00, Su 11:00–19:00. Trendy concrete-and-glass building that embodies Japan's largest cosmetic company's philosophy of integrating beauty, health and culture. Here you'll find Shiseidō cosmetics and accessories, skin-care and hair salons, an art gallery and a French restaurant. Across the street is a Shiseidō-operated health-food café with picture windows for people-watching.

✻ **Toto Ginza Pavilion** Toto銀座パビリオン (3573-1010). Hrs: 10:00–18:00, daily. Showrooms for bathroom-fixture maker Toto offer an intimate glimpse of Japanese life. See the microprocessor-controlled shower stalls, the latest twist in self-cleaning toilet bowls. For Y17,000 you can own a sound-camouflage device that simulates the roar of a toilet flushing.

**Ginza Pocket Park** 銀座7-9-15 (3573-1401). Hrs: 10:30–19:00; clsd W (except if NH), NY. Not a patch of greenery, but a shiny, modern building with an art gallery, architecture-magazine library, and model living spaces designed by Tokyo Gas Co.

✻✻✻ **Kabuki-za (Theater)** 歌舞伎座 (3541-3131). Opened in 1889, the present ''Japanese baroque'' building, with its curved front gable, dates from 1925. English program notes and earphone system are available. Tickets can be reserved up to 2 weeks in advance. Tickets are from Y2000 (to see one act from the upper gallery). See Tokyo Theaters for schedule.

**Shinbashi Enbujō** 新橋演舞場 (3541-2211). Founded in 1925 as a performance stage for Shinbashi geisha; today, a comfortable theater used for performances of Kabuki, Japanese dance, and plays from the Meiji period to the present.

**Nakagin Capsule Tower Building (Apartments)** 中銀カプセルタワービル One of Tokyo's modern architectural landmarks, designed by Kurokawa Kishō in 1972, at the height of the Metabolist movement. It consists of 140 box units bristling off two concrete elevator shafts. Each prefabricated unit has a built-in bed, bathroom, closet, desk, and even audio equipment.

✻ **Tokyo P/N** (5568-0461). 1-5-13 Shinbashi. Hrs: 11:00–22:00, daily. Pronounced ''Tokyo Paan.'' This Matsushita Electric showroom, opened in 1991, is a cyberpunk Disneyland. Futuristic amusements (a virtual reality cycling route), state-of-the-art recording studio.

## Ginza Shops and Services

4 ✻ **Kyūkyodō** 鳩居堂 (3571-4429). Hrs: 10:00–19:30; Su, NH 11:00–19:00; clsd NY. Branch of the Kyoto store established in 1663. Elegant paper goods, calligraphy implements, incense, and exquisite incense games and incense accessories.

6 **Jena** イエナ (3571-2980). Hrs: 10:30–19:50; Su 12:00–18:30; clsd NH, NY. Books and newspapers in English.

8 **K. Mikimoto & Co., Ltd.** ミキモト (3535-4611). Hrs: 10:30–18:00; clsd W, NY. The founder of this world-famous shop invented the cultured pearl in 1893. Prices are high, but so is the quality.

9 **Wakō (Department Store)** 和光 (3562-2111). Hrs: 10:00–17:30; Sa 10:00–18:00; clsd Su, NH, early Aug., NY. The dignified building, crowned by the famous clock tower, is the last prominent relic of prewar Ginza. Carries expensive imported merchandise. Wakō is owned by Hattori, the parent company of Seikō.

10 ✻✻ **Mitsukoshi (Ginza Branch)** 三越(銀座) (3562-1111). Hrs: 10:00–19:00; clsd M (except if NH), NY. This department store, for many the epitome of Ginza shopping, may well surpass the main Nihonbashi store in fame. Christian Lacroix, Tiffany on 1F.

13 **Ryūzen-dō** 竜善堂 (3571-4321). Hrs: 10:30–19:00; clsd 1st and 3rd Su, NY. Tea ceremony accoutrements: bowls, whisks, kettles, lacquered boxes, charcoal baskets, dishes used for the tea ceremony meal, and so forth.

14 **Matsuzakaya** 松坂屋 (3572-1111). Hrs: 10:00–19:00; clsd W (except if NH), NY. This large department store was originally a Nagoya kimono shop, established in 1611. Its Kyoto-made kimono fabrics are Matsuzakaya originals. Fine selection of combs, hair ornaments.

22 **Wan'ya Shoten** わんや書店 銀座8-7-5 (3571-0514). Hrs: 10:00–18:00, clsd 1st and 3rd Sa, Su, NH, mid-Aug., NY. Noh-related materials. Noh tickets can be purchased here.

23 **Hakuhinkan Toy Park** 博品館 (3571-8008). Hrs: 11:00–20:00, daily. Tokyo's answer to F.A.O. Schwarz. Restaurants and a cinema are on the top floor.

## Ginza Tea Breaks

11 ✻✻ **Budō no Ki** ぶどうの木 銀座5-8-5 (3574-9779). Hrs: 10:00–22:00; Su 10:00–20:30; clsd NY. Elegant and pricey dessert restaurant. Mousses, crepes, sorbets.

15 ✻ **Lion Beer Hall** ライオン(ビアホール) (3571-2590). Hrs: 11:30–23:00; Su and NH 11:30–22:30; clsd NY. Ginza's classic beer hall has a quasi Frank Lloyd Wright interior. Lively. Hearty fare to go with the beer.

17 ✻ **West** ウエスト 銀座7-3-6 (3571-2989). Hrs: 9:00–1:00 a.m.; Sa 9:00–11:00, Su, NH 12:00–21:00; clsd NY. A classic *meikyoku* (famous tunes) kissaten; subdued interior and a cabinet full of Western classical albums, which are played according to a daily program.

## Farther Afield: Ningyōchō 人形町

*Take the S exit from Ningyōchō station.* Ningyōchō (Puppet Town) got its name from the presence of puppet theaters and puppet makers. Until the 1840s, when they were moved to Asakusa, Edo's Kabuki theaters were also located here. Untouched by the fires of World War II, it is one of the most atmospheric Shitamachi quarters. Here and there, one can still spot an early 1920s shop with a copper facade. Recently, trendy shops have started moving in.

**Suiten-gū (Shrine)** 水天宮 This popular shrine was established by the lords of Kurume, which has Japan's head Suiten-gū shrine, a guardian of children and childbirth. Pregnant women still visit the shrine for a special pregnancy belly-band and dog amulet, dogs being noted for the ease with which they bear offspring. The buildings are recent.

✻ **Kurita Bijutsukan (Museum)** 栗田美術館 浜町2-17-9 (3666-6246). Hrs: 10:00–17:00; clsd NY. A small, attractive museum exhibiting Arita porcelain from the superb Kurita collection in Ashikaga (north of Tokyo).

**Ningyōchō Shopping**

**Ubukeya** うぶけや 人形町3-9-2 (3661-4851). Hrs: 9:00–19:00; clsd Su, NH, NY. *2 blocks W of Ningyōchō station.* Since 1793. A tiny, distinguished shop for Japanese cutlery: knives, scissors, gardening shears, tweezers.

**Kotobukidō** 寿堂 人形町2-1-4 (3666-4804). Hrs: 9:00–21:00; clsd Su. *Between Ningyōchō station and Suitengū.* Since 1883. Divine *kogane-imo*, bean sweets shaped like tiny baked yams, fragrant with cinnamon.

**Yanagiya** 柳屋 人形町2-11-3 (3666-9901). Hrs: 10:30–19:00; clsd Su, NY; NH 10:30–18:00. *Between Ningyōchō station and Kurita Museum.* Tokyo's best *tai-yaki*, fish-shaped pancakes stuffed with bean jam, hot off the griddle.

**Iwai Shōten** 岩井商店 人形町2-10-1 (3668-6058). Hrs: 8:00–20:00; clsd Su, NH, NY. Near Yanagiya. This small shop is stacked high with *tsuzura*, trunks of woven bamboo covered with lacquer. Items range from letter boxes to full-size *tsuzura* (custom-made).

## II:3 SHINBASHI AND TSUKIJI

East Shinbashi, toward Tsukiji, was the domain of the Shinbashi geisha, who rose to prominence through the patronage of Meiji parvenus. The streets near the Shinbashi Enbujō theater are filled with the exclusive restaurants where the geisha entertain; some geisha still arrive in rickshaws. Shinbashi recalls something of its heyday, but this is less the case with Tsukiji, which in the Edo period was claimed by various daimyo villas for its bay frontage. Today, however, Tsukiji is overwhelmingly plebeian, with its gargantuan wholesale fish market; the market was long a fixture in central Nihonbashi—a short stroll from the shogun's kitchens—but was removed to Tsukiji in 1935. One relic of former days is Hama Rikyū (Detached Palace), just south of Tsukiji across an inlet.

214

**Morning Tour:** Tsukiji — (0:07h walk) — ** Tsukiji Wholesale Market (8:30–9:30 a.m.) — (0:15h walk) — * Hama Rikyū — (0:35h by boat) — Asakusa (I:1)

**Lunch:** Edogin Sushi, Sushi Iwa

**Notes:** Market clsd Su. Hama Rikyū clsd M.

**Tsukiji** 築地

**** Tokyo Chūō Oroshiuri Shijō (Central Wholesale Market)** 東京中央卸売市場
Clsd Su. *A short taxi ride from Ginza, or 0:07h on foot from Tsukiji station on the Hibiya subway line.* Sushi was once called *Edomae* (front of Edo) — in other words, taken from Tokyo Bay. It would take a brave soul to eat anything that has been pulled out of Tokyo Bay's muck today, but Tokyo's fleet, having fished in waters around the world, still comes home to Tsukiji, the world's biggest fish market. The market employs 15,000 people who work at its 1,200 wholesale shops or related enterprises. Boats arrive through the night. The wholesaler's auction commences around 5:00 a.m. and lasts an hour. Then 3,000 wheelbarrows are mobilized to trundle the fish to the wholesale shops. Later, the city's retailers and restaurants arrive to buy the day's supplies, with the liveliest activity between 8:30 and 9:30; this is the best time for tourists to visit. Dress to wade through fishy puddles.

* **Hama Rikyū (Hama Detached Palace Garden)** 浜離宮 Hrs: 9:00–16:30 (enter by 16:00); clsd M, NY. *0:10h walk from Tsukiji, or 0:15h from Shinbashi station.* This large garden was part of a shogun's villa; its tidepool lake was a wildfowl hunting preserve. The villa burned and was not restored until 1869, when it was turned over to the government. Ulysses Grant and his wife stayed here on their famous visit to Japan in 1879. The slightly unkempt grounds are attractive and contain a carefully reconstructed tea pavilion.

**By boat to Asakusa.** 0:35h trips operate from 9:50–sunset. Board at a pier in the NE corner of Hama Rikyū. The Sumidagawa, a turgid, odoriferous flow contained by walls of concrete, still cuts its swath through the history of the city. Numerous sluice gates in the banks are a reminder that Edo was a city of moats and canals, and each bridge has its own story. This river is Tokyo's heart and bowels; a fascinating, if not exactly scenic, journey.

**West Shinbashi** 西新橋

While east Shinbashi caters to wealthy patrons, west Shinbashi supplies the simpler needs of ordinary commuters. This area, however, has a touch of Edokko style that newer commuter centers lack. One of the city's most charming red-lantern pub quarters is around **Karasumori Jinja**, a concrete shrine behind the New Shinbashi Building. The soft light of lanterns casts a nostalgic glow over the narrow alleys, and when the local shamisen minstrel makes his evening rounds, it's almost like a scene out of an old Mizoguchi movie.

* **Ōkura Shūkokan (Art Museum)** 大倉集古館 (3583-0781). Hrs: 10:00–16:00 (enter by 15:45); clsd M, NY. On the grounds of Hotel Ōkura. This is Japan's first private museum, opened to the public in 1917. The heavy, Chinese-style building houses a superb collection of Chinese and Japanese art amassed by Ōkura Kihachirō, an industrial tycoon who founded the Imperial Hotel (his son founded the Hotel Ōkura). Important pieces: the 13th-C scroll painting, *Zuishin Teiki Emaki* (The Imperial Guard Cavalry), attributed to Fujiwara Nobuzane and full of the humorous Japanese style that began to assert itself in the Kamakura period; a ceramic plate with a cartoon of Jurōjin, the deity of wisdom, by OGATA KENZAN and his

painter brother, KŌRIN; a Kamakura-period lacquered box with a fan design; a Heian-period statue of Fugen Bosatsu riding an elephant.

**∗ Japan Sword** 日本刀剣 虎の門3-8-1 (3434-4321). Hrs: 9:30–18:00; clsd Su, NH, NY. *On Sakurada-dōri, at the foot of the road to Hotel Ōkura.* The upstairs gallery of this well-known Japanese sword dealer exhibits some finer articles in a museumlike setting. The shop also carries armor and sword accessories.

**∗ Matsuoka Bijutsukan (Art Museum)** 松岡美術館 (3437-2787). Matsuoka Tamurachō Bldg., 8–9F. Hrs: 10:00–17:00; clsd M, NY. *Near Onarimon subway station.* This private museum has one of Japan's best collections of Chinese ceramics, especially of Yuan and Ming blue-and-white porcelains; one vase was acquired for a record price at a Christie's auction. The museum also exhibits Buddhist statuary, including a fine Northern Chi stone Shaka.

## Farther Afield: Shiba Kōen (Park) 芝公園

This land was once a city of temples around Zōjō-ji, the great mortuary temple of the Tokugawa shoguns. Modern times have been unkind to the area. Zōjō-ji was demolished by wartime bombing, and the shoguns were evicted from their tombs during the construction of Tokyo Tower (the 333-meter-tall TV tower is worth avoiding).

**Zōjō-ji** 増上寺 Ieyasu appointed this a Tokugawa mortuary temple when he entered Edo in 1590. His son Hidetada and six later shoguns were buried here in ornate mausoleums. The rebuilt Daimon (Great Gate) marked the pilgrim's approach to the majestic Sanmon (Main Gate, 1622, ICP). The only other surviving edifices are the gates to two mausoleums, Tai-tokuin Reibyō Sōmon (1632, ICP) and Yushōin Reibyō Nitenmon (1717, ICP).

**The Toleman Collection** 芝大門2-2-18 (3434-1300). Hrs: 11:00–19:00; clsd Tu, NY. Japanese antiques and modern print gallery housed in a beautifully refurbished Japanese house. The American owners say if you get lost, "Call from the phone near the Zōjō-ji Daimon, and a friendly crowd will come to get you."

**Keiō University** 慶応大学 Founded by Fukuzawa Yukichi, a samurai-born scholar of the West who is considered the father of modern Japan (he has replaced SHŌTOKU TAISHI on the Y10,000 bill). Its new library (Keiō Gijuku Toshokan Shinkan, 1981) by architect Maki Fumihiko is praised for its design.

## Farther Afield: Takanawa and Shinagawa 高輪・品川

**Sengaku-ji** 泉岳寺 Lord Asano and his 47 retainers, who avenged their lord's death in Japan's most spectacular vendetta (immortalized in the play *Chūshingura*, see Drama, p. 86), are buried here. The temple has a fine two-storied gate (1836). On the right of the grounds is the well where the loyal 47 washed the head of their enemy, Lord Kira, before lay-ing it on their lord's grave. On the left are the retainers' graves; even today, incense burns perpetually before them. A nearby hall displays their personal effects.

**∗ Hatakeyama Kinenkan (Art Museum)** 畠山記念館 白金台2-20-12 (3447-5787). Hrs: Apr. 1–Sept. 15, 10:00–17:00 (enter by 16:30); clsd M (Tu if M a NH). Oct. 1–Mar. 15, 10:00–16:30 (enter by 16:00); clsd M and Dec. 6–Jan. 7. *0:05h on foot from Takanawadai station.* Adjoins the elegant Hannya-en restaurant, former villa of Hatakeyama Issei, the wealthy Meiji industrialist who amassed the museum collection. A choice group of Chinese and Japanese art, noted especially for RIMPA art, Noh masks and robes, and tea ceremony utensils. The objects are shown a few at a time in one of the pleasantest settings in Tokyo.

**∗ Hara Bijutsukan (Art Museum)** 原美術館 北品川4-7-25 (3445-0651). Hrs: 11:00–17:00; W 11:00–20:00; clsd M (Tu if M a NH), NY. Kita-Shinagawa is the closest station. Tokyo's only museum of contemporary art, located in the Hara family's Bauhaus-era home. Works by leading artists from the United States, Europe, and Asia. There's a daily program of video art (call for details), and an annual spring exhibition of young artists.

# TOKYO III. CONTEMPORARY TOKYO

**Main Attractions:**

The 1964 Tokyo Olympics and its symbol, master architect Tange Kenzō's revolutionary, mollusk-like Yoyogi National Stadium, ushered in the New Japan. The bullet train, express-ways, Tokyo's vast subway network, and international hotels were constructed for postwar Japan's debut. This quarter of Tokyo, fanning out east from the stadium, is the center of Japanese aspirations in art and fashion. At the foot of Yoyogi National Stadium, suburban teenagers resurrect the American past — first the fifties, now the sixties — with a precision that the original eras probably never had. Nearby Harajuku and Omotesandō provide the sartorial embellishments for this crowd. Aoyama is the purveyor of fashions to older sophisticates; its boutique street is called "Killer-dōri." Aoyama Gochōme, south of Omote-sandō, is where affluent Japan contemplates its traditional roots; besides Antīku-dōri (antique-street), there are the Nezu Art Museum and Tessenkai, a contemporary Noh theater. The spiritual center and great meeting place of cosmopolitan Tokyo is Roppongi Crossing, a congested intersection in the shadow of one of Tokyo's great elevated expressways. Although Roppongi is Tokyo at its most Americanized—there is even a "little Beverly Hills"—the Japanese avant-garde is also much in evidence. Lest one think this area is all new, it's worth pointing out the monuments of its recent past as the center of Japanese militarism: the Defense Agency, the Meiji Shrine (to the Emperor Meiji), Nogi Jinja (to General Nogi), and Tōgō Jinja (to Admiral Tōgō).

## III:1 ROPPONGI 六本木

*Take the Hibiya line to Roppongi station. Nogizaka station, on the Chiyoda line, is a good place from which to walk toward Roppongi Crossing. Roppongi is a short taxi ride from Akasaka, but through heavy traffic.* Roppongi is Tokyo's party town, an open, on-display kind of place of bars and restaurants with wrap-around windows and stage-set interiors framed in neon and brass. Unlike Ginza or Akasaka, it's highly accessible. Roppongi's cosmopolitanism arose spontaneously, in the most unlikely of soils: the headquarters of the Imperial Japanese Army. Roppongi (Six Trees) got its name from six resident daimyo with the Chinese character for "tree" in their names. After 1868, their estates were taken over by the army. These in turn were requisitioned by the American Occupation, and Roppongi began its transformation into an international entertainment quarter.

**Walking Tour:** Nogizaka station (Chiyoda line) — (0:10h walk via Gaien Higashi-dōri) — ** Roppongi Crossing — (0:05h) — * Wave — (0:10h) — * "Little Beverly Hills" — (0:05h) — * Axis Building

**Note:** This area is best enjoyed in the evening.

216

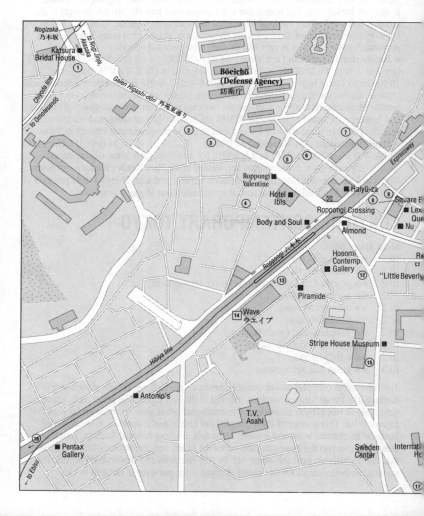

**Nogi Jinja** 乃木神社 A shrine to General Nogi Maresuke, hero of the Russo-Japanese War. On the grounds stands the house where, in 1912, when the EMPEROR MEIJI died, Nogi and his wife committed suicide to follow him in death. His testament suggests that Nogi, a modern general cut from samurai cloth, was troubled by the decline of samurai ethics in a rapidly westernizing Japan.

**Piramide.** Four-story courtyard building clad in steel-blue tile, with a glass pyramid in the center. Shops and restaurants seem to have an Italian theme.

**\*\* Roppongi Kōsaten (Crossing)** 六本木交差点 At night, this grimy intersection becomes a sea of faces from all over the world.

**"Little Beverly Hills."** Down a palm-lined alley are the Hard Rock Café, Tony Roma's, and Spago's, all bathed in the soft glow of neon. A Japanese fantasy: L.A. without the crime.

### Roppongi Shopping

**Forum Building.** Bigger-than-life-size black panthers prowl this building filled with boutiques, wine bars and clubs (Neojaponesque, Live House Tropic of Cancer).

**The Garden.** A Haagen-Dazs ice cream parlor marks the entrance to this patio garden development. Take an ice cream break and watch the goings-on at the wedding hall and upscale Chinese and French restaurants in the complex.

**\* Ark Hills.** Large development containing the ANA Tokyo Hotel, Suntory Concert Hall, TV Asahi, and a slew of restaurants. The architecture is a bit stiff, but dramatic.

10 **\* Axis Building** アクシス 六本木5-17-1 Most shops clsd M. This building contains shops specializing in well-designed objects. In B1 are Bushi (modern lacquered furniture), Kissō (contemporary Japanese tableware, restaurant), Nuno (avant-garde designer fabrics), OHS (hardware); 1F has Living Motif (designer housewares); 2F has Yamagiwa (lighting fixtures); 3F has À Tantôt (French cuisine), Lapis (graphic arts). 4F has galleries.

14 **\* WAVE** ウエイブ 六本木6-2-27 (3408-0111). Hrs: 11:00–22:00; Su 11:00–20:00; clsd 1st and 3rd W, and NY. Sound waves are what this building mostly deals in, with its vast stock of records, cassettes, computerized record reference system, 200-hit-song headphone library, and recording studios on the top floors. It also offers video, art books, and Cine Vivant, an art-film cinema. A holographic Jizō Bosatsu guards the back door.

217

230 for restaurants, p. 234 for hotels

### Roppongi Nightlife

**J Theater** (3475-0693). 7-4-8 Roppongi. Hrs: 20:00–6:00 a.m. Stylish young people flock to this upscale karaoke bar to croon favorite tunes to taped instrumental accompaniments. Cover: Y2000 (men), Y1500 (women).

**Roppongi Valentine** 六本木7-14-1 (3478-5068). Roppongi Hōshō Bldg., 4F. Hrs: 19:00–1:00 a.m.; F and Sa 18:00–4:00. Soul and blues. Cover: Y2000–2800.

**Body and Soul** 六本木7-14-12 (3408-2094). Izumi-Sōken Bldg., 3F. Hrs: 19:00–2:00 a.m.; clsd Su (M if Su a NH). Small and smoky club featuring some of the best jazz musicians in town. Cover: Y2200–2800.

**Cine Vivant** (3403-6061). WAVE Bldg., B1. Non-Japanese art films. Late show from 21:00.

**Haiyū-za** 俳優座 六本木4-9-2 (3470-2880). Tokyo's best contemporary theater. Also has a popular bar and **Cinema Ten** (3401-4073), featuring European films; late show at 22:00.

**Square Building** スクエアービル A department store for nightlife, filled from top to bottom with clubs and discos for every taste.

**Lexington Queen** 六本木3-13-14 (3401-1661). Hrs: 18:00–midnight, daily. An old standby. Visiting celebrities are sometimes dragged here, but the usual crowd is a bunch of wide-eyed foreigners, mostly models.

**Nū** (3479-1511). 3-12-6, Roppongi Plaza Bldg., 6F. Hrs: 18:00–wee hours. A disco arranged so you can actually carry on a conversation. Playful, Gaudiesque decor. Reasonable cover: weekdays Y1500 (men), Y1000 (women).

**Roppongi Pit Inn** (3585-1063). 3-17-7 Roppongi. Hrs: 18:30–23:00; clsd NY. Related to the famed Shinjuku jazz club, this version serves up fusion and ethnic. Cover: Y2500 w/drink.

Roppongi

0    100m

> **Tour 1:** Akasaka-Mitsuke station — ✶✶ Suntory Art Museum — (0:05h walk) —
> Myōgon-ji — (0:10h walk) — ✶✶ Sōgetsu Kaikan — (0:07h walk) — Aoyama Itchōme
> station — (subway) — Omotesandō — (0:05h walk through ✶✶ Aoyama Gochōme) —
> ✶✶ Nezu Art Museum — (0:10h walk via Kottōhin-dōri) — Omotesandō station.
>
> **Tour 2:** Omotesandō station — (0:15h walk) — ✶✶ Ōta Art Museum — (0:10h walk
> via ✶✶ Takeshita-dōri) — Harajuku station — (0:10h walk) — ✶✶✶ Meiji Jingū —
> (0:25h via Inner Garden) — ✶✶✶ Yoyogi Stadium — (0:20h walk) — ✶ Tobacco and
> Salt Museum (III:3)
>
> **Lunch:** Tsutsui, Mexico Lindo, Nagaura Soba, Moti, La Granata, Zakuro
>
> **Notes:** Museums clsd M. Try to visit Yoyogi Park on Su.

## Akasaka 赤坂

*Take the Ginza or Marunouchi lines to Akasaka-Mitsuke, or Chiyoda line to Akasaka sta-*
*tion.* With the establishment in the Meiji period of the National Diet, nearby Akasaka, with its
exclusive geisha quarter, became a favorite enclave of Japan's politicians. Today the geisha
have been joined by bar hostesses, but the exclusivity remains; every evening, black limousines shoehorn their way into the narrow streets where the elite restaurants are. There are,
to be sure, many bars and clubs where tourists can go, but on the whole, Akasaka nightlife is
a closed world. During the day, Akasaka offers the excellent Suntory Art Museum and the
Sōgetsu Kaikan, headquarters of the avant-garde flower-arrangement school and a bastion of
218 contemporary Japanese culture.

**Akasaka Prince Hotel.** An Akasaka landmark, this pleated tower of glacial white was
designed by Tange Kenzō in his corporate mode of the 1980s. Hidden behind it is the elegant
old wing, built in 1928 for Prince Yi of Korea, which was then a Japanese colony.

**Sannō Hie Jinja** 山王日枝神社 This famous Tokyo shrine is a branch of the Hiyoshi
Shrine near Kyoto, the guardian shrine of sacred Mt. Hiei. It is thought that Edo was the site
of an estate of the great parent shrine from early times, for a Hie Jinja already existed here
when Ōta Dōkan built Edo Castle in the 15th C. Dōkan enlisted the shrine to guard his castle,
and the practice was continued by the Tokugawa. Look for monkey images on the torii; the
monkey is the messenger of the shrine's kami. The concrete halls are unremarkable, but the
shrine museum has some fine swords donated by various Tokugawa and a pair of deity figures that were once mounted upon the floats of the shrine's Sannō Matsuri.

✶✶ **Suntory Bijutsukan (Museum of Art)** サントリー美術館 (3470-1073). Suntory Bldg.,
11F. Hrs: 10:00–17:00; F 10:00–19:00; clsd M (except if NH), NY. Visible from Akasaka-Mitsuke
station. Serene gallery exhibiting a fine collection famous for genre screens and decorative
arts, such as ceramics, lacquerware, costumes, and tea utensils. Interesting loan shows also.

## Along Aoyama-dōri, toward Omotesandō

**Myōgon-ji (Toyokawa Inari)** 妙巌寺 This oddity, with its banks of red lanterns, highly
visible on Aoyama-dōri, has a Shintō torii and is popularly called an Inari (rice deity) shrine,
but is officially a Zen temple. Its deity was regarded as a Buddhist manifestation of Inari.

✶✶ **Sōgetsu Kaikan** 草月会館 赤坂7-2-21 (3408-1126). Headquarters of the avant-
garde Sōgetsu flower-arrangement school, currently headed by Teshigahara Hiroshi, best
known abroad for his film *Woman of the Dunes*. The entire complex offers an impressively
incestuous view of Japan's contemporary art establishment. Tange Kenzō designed the mirrored glass building. The lobby, with granite forms by Isamu Noguchi providing a setting for
flower arrangements on a heroic scale, is pure theater. The **Sōgetsu Art Museum** (6F)
shows flower arrangements, the eclectic collection of the late founder, Teshigahara Sōfū, and
sometimes work by contemporary artists from Japan and abroad (Hrs: 10:00–17:00; clsd Sa,
Su, NH, NY, and between exhibits). **Lessons:** Beginner classes given in English, Tu 10:00–
12:00, for Y4500. Write to Foreign Liaison Office, Sōgetsu School, 7-2-21 Akasaka, Minato-ku,
Tokyo 107 (fax 3405-4947). Indicate name, nationality, address, phone, and course desired.

## Akasaka Tea Break

**Toraya** 虎屋 赤坂4-9-22 (3408-4121). Hrs: 8:30–20:00; Su and NH 8:30–17:30. On
Aoyama-dōri, between Akasaka-Mitsuke and Sōgetsu Kaikan. Famous maker of *yōkan* (sweet
bean jelly) and fresh, soft confections, which can be savored in the tearoom.

## Minami-Aoyama 南青山

*Take the Ginza line to Gaien-mae, or the Ginza, Nagatachō, or Chiyoda line to Omote-*
*sandō.* This mainly residential region is favored by artists, designers, and others in the
vanguard of contemporary culture. A prime area for shopping and absorbing what's going on.

✶ **Zenkoku Dentōteki Kōgeihin Sentā (Japan Traditional Craft Center)**
全国伝統的工芸品センター　南青山3-1-1　(3403-2460). Hrs: 10:00–18:00; every other
W 10:00–17:00; clsd Th., early Aug, NY. *One block from Gaien-mae station.* The second-
floor gallery carries an excellent selection of officially designated traditional crafts from all
over Japan.

* **Tepia** (5474-1171). 2-8-4 Kita Aoyama. Hrs: 10:00–18:00; Sa-Su, NH 10:00–17:00. Enter 1:00h before closing. Clsd M (except if NH, then clsd Tu). A building dedicated to "the future of human communications," sponsored by a consortium of high-tech companies. The imposing granite-and-marble structure is one of architect Maki Fumihiko's more successful recent efforts. Outside, a group of waterfalls and rivulets flowing over black and white marble terraces, forms a serene and inviting prelude to the interior. The ground floor houses a walkthrough exhibit of futuristic living — virtual-reality concerts, an HDTV garden, aromacological ventilation. The third-floor galleries are devoted to avant-garde art. Two restaurants, Jack Rose (moderate) and Makie (expensive). Private health club in basement.

* **Watari-um** ワタリウム (3402-3001). 3-7-6 Jingumae. Hrs: 11:00–19:00; clsd M. Small museum of modern and contemporary art, often of established Western artists. Interesting building designed by Mario Botta. Exquisite shop for books and gifts, with a quiet cafe tucked in one corner.

* **Spiral Building** スパイラルビル (1985). Cool, geometric forms by architect Maki Fumihiko. Galleries and performance space on first floor. French restaurant is a popular brunch spot. Trendy gift items in upper-level boutique.

** **Aoyama Gochōme** 青山五丁目 This tree-lined street is filled from end to end with trendy boutiques — Comme des Garçons, Issey Miyake (regular, Permanente, Pleats), Emporio Armani, Sonia Rykiel, Yōji Yamamoto — housed in elegant buildings by such architects as Andō Tadao (From First, Corezoné) and Uchida Shigeru. It's an impressive showcase of affluence and style. A prime area for watching people (and their gorgeous foreign cars).

* **Tessenkai Noh Institute** 銕仙会能研究所 南青山4-21-29 (3401-2285). *A few minutes' walk SE from Omotesandō station.* Tessenkai, an offshoot of the Kanze school of Noh, takes the attitude that Noh is not merely a cultural fossil, but a living dramatic form, alive with meaning even for contemporary audiences. It actively draws a younger audience and has constructed a stunning theater: tatami seating and an antique wooden stage, mellow with age, contained in an austere concrete hall. Tatami can be hard to sit on, so arrive early for a comfortable spot. See Tokyo Theaters for schedule.

** **Nezu Bijutsukan (Art Museum)** 根津美術館 (3400-2536). Hrs: 9:30–16:30 (enter by 16:00); clsd M, day after NH, between exhibitions, and Aug. *0:05h walk S of Omotesandō station.* Superb Japanese and Chinese art collection, including two of the most famous paintings in Japanese art, *Nachi Waterfall* (NT), a late Kamakura-period painting based on the idea of a natural landscape (the sacred Nachi waterfall) as a Buddhist mandala, and OGATA KŌRIN's *Iris Screen* (NT). The wooded grounds contain five excellent tea arbors, which can be seen by applying at the museum office; reservation advised.

**Antīku-dōri (Antique Street)** アンティーク・ストリート Lined with antique shops and high-fashion boutiques. Not great for bargain hunters, but there's much to look at. Most shops are closed Su.

### Minami-Aoyama Shopping

2 **Zenkoku Dentōteki Kōgeihin Sentā (Japan Traditional Craft Center)** (3403-2460). Hrs: 10:00–18:00; clsd Th, early Aug., NY. Excellent selection of traditional crafts.

9 **Issey Miyake Permanente and Pleats.** (3423-1408). Tessenkai Bldg., 1F and B1. Hrs: 11:00–20:00, daily; clsd NY. Permanent collection by order only. Pleats features the popular line of pleated clothes.

11 **From First Building** フロムファースト A red-brick building filled with boutiques by designers, avant-garde and otherwise.

**Yōji Yamamoto** (3409-6006). Hrs: 11:00–21:00; clsd NY. Avant-garde fashion. Spacious, minimalist spaces designed by architect of Roppongi's Wave building.

12 **Karakusa** からくさ 南青山5-13-1 (3499-5858). Hrs: 11:00–18:00; clsd Su, NH, clsd early–mid-Aug., NY. Specializes in sets of blue-and-white old Imari porcelain dishes.

### Minami-Aoyama Tea Break

102 **Yokku Mokku** ヨックモック 南青山5-3-3 (5485-3330). Hrs: 10:00–19:00, daily; clsd NY. Across from Tessenkai. Coffee and cakes in a gleaming, blue-and-white tile building. Patio in warm weather.

### Omotesandō, Harajuku, and Yoyogi Park 表参道・原宿・代々木公園
*Take the Ginza, Hanzōmon, or Chiyoda subway line to Omotesandō; the Chiyoda subway line to Meiji Jingūmae; or the Yamanote line to Harajuku station.* Stone lanterns at Omotesandō station flank Omotesandō, the broad avenue leading to the Meiji Shrine, thronged not with pilgrims, but with youthful worshippers of fad and fashion. Even more crowded is Takeshita-dōri, a cramped alley filled with fly-by-night boutiques selling cut-rate fashions, T-shirts, and sunglasses.

**Hanae Mori Building** ハナエモリビル (1978). An Omotesandō landmark, the Tange Kenzō mirrored-glass headquarters of the internationally famous couturier Hanae Mori. Chic shops and restaurants on the ground floor.

**Laforet** ラフォーレ (3475-0411). Hrs: 11:00–20:00. A boutique-choked building directed at the adolescent crowd. Laforet Museum on 5F stages exhibits and performances.

** **Ōta Kinen Bijutsukan (Art Museum)** 太田記念美術館 (3403-0880). Hrs: 10:30–17:30 (enter by 17:00); clsd M and 25th–end of each month. A superb ukiyo-e woodblock

219

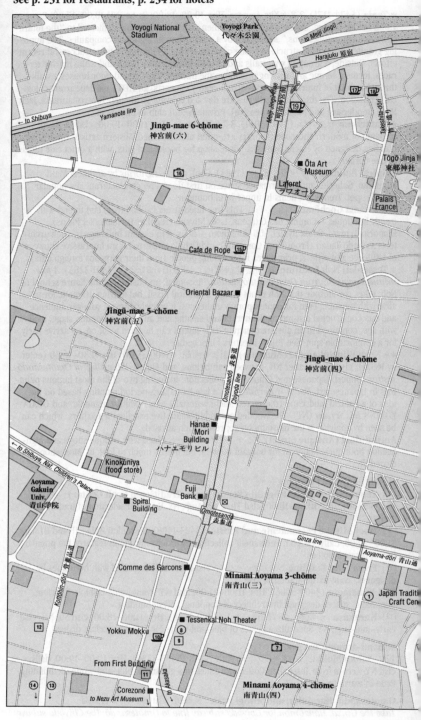

220

print and painting collection, shown a few at a time in an intimate, beautiful space. One of the best of Tokyo's smaller private art museums.

**★★ Takeshita-dōri** 竹下通り This cramped alley of cheap boutiques and coffee shops is the fashion center for young Japanese.

**Tōgō Jinja** 東郷神社 A Meiji-period shrine to Tōgō Heihachirō, admiral of the Japanese fleet that defeated the Russians in the Straits of Tsushima. Flea market on 1st and last Su of each month.

**★★★ Yoyogi National Stadium** 国立屋内総合体育館 A pair of dramatic structures designed by Tange Kenzō for the 1964 Tokyo Olympics, these are landmarks of contemporary architecture. The shell-like structures made daring use of steel-suspension roofing. Quipped one architecture critic: "Every time Tange designs a building, somebody ends up with a doctorate in structural engineering." The interiors should not be missed.

**Aoyama to Harajuku**

0    100m

Jingū-mae 2-chōme
神宮前(二)

■ Bar Radio

Yamamoto Kansai
Boutique

laura ashley ■

oyama Bell
ommons
青山ベルコモンズ

■ Tepia

Cemetery

to Akasaka-Mitsuke →
to Sōgetsu Kaikan →

*** **Meiji Jingū (Shrine)** 明治神宮 The
EMPEROR MEIJI (1852–1912), who reigned
over Japan's astonishing transformation into a
modern world power, is enshrined here with
his empress, though he was buried near Kyoto.
An enormous torii of Taiwanese cypress spans
the approach to the shrine compound. The
halls are built of unadorned wood. The shrine
was first completed in 1920 with state funds
and became a mecca for militarists. Destroyed
by the 1945 air raid, it was rebuilt in 1958
from private donations. In the thickly wooded
grounds is the ◆ **Nai-en** (Inner Garden),
famous for its late spring irises, and the
**Treasure Museum**, which exhibits photos,
memorabilia, and belongings of the emperor
and empress (Hrs: 9:00–16:30; clsd 3rd F.
Nov.–Feb. 9:00–16:00; clsd 3rd F).
* **Sword Museum (Tōken Hakubutsukan)**
日本刀剣博物館 代々木4-25-10
(3379-1386). Hrs: 9:00–16:00; clsd M, NY.
*About 500 m NW of Meiji Jingū.* This
museum, run by the Society for the Preservation of Japanese Art Swords, is devoted to
Japanese swords, which are admired as much
for their brilliant beauty as for their cutting
edge. About 30 blades are shown, along with
exquisite accessories (*tsuba*) and armor.

### Omotesandō and Harajuku Tea Breaks
15▷ **Café de Ropé** カフェドロペ
(3406-6845) Hrs: 11:00–23:00, daily. The
"people-watching" café on Omotesandō.
17▷ * **Suzuki** 寿ず木 (3404-8007). Hrs:
11:00–20:00; Su and NH 11:00–19:00; clsd NY.
In the Luceine Complex, near Takeshita-dōri.
*Namagashi* (soft confections) served in a
Japanese-style tearoom.
18▷ **Luceine** ルセーヌ (3470-1852). Hrs:
11:00–20:00; clsd NY, mid-Aug. A spacious café
with European decor and classical music.
19▷ **Stage Y2** ステージワイトウー
神宮前1-13-12 (3478-1031). Hrs: 9:00–
23:00; Su, NH 9:00–22:00. Right by Meiji
Jingū-mae station is this fashionable café-bar.
The terrace is open during the warmer
months. Reasonably priced food.
**Bar Radio** バーラジオ 神宮前2-31-7
(3405-5490). Villa Gloria, B1. Hrs: 19:00–
2:00; clsd Su, NH. A dark, intimate architectural gem, paneled in tawny wood and iron.
Designed by Sugimoto Takashi. Excellent,
expensive drinks.

221

## III:3 **SHIBUYA**　渋谷

*Take the Yamanote line, or the Ginza or Hanzōmon subway line.* Shibuya, a commuter center handling over a million passengers a day, might seem to belong to "commuter Tokyo," with Shinjuku and Ikebukuro. But Shibuya lacks the inhuman scale of these giants, and has also imbibed something of the trendiness of nearby Harajuku and Minami-Aoyama. This town-in-itself offers something for everybody, with an abundance of shops, bars, restaurants, and street scenes that are lively and accessible. Exciting things are happening here.

**Walking Tour:** Shibuya station — (0:05h walk) — ∗ Bunkamura (0:10h walk via Spain-dōri) — ∗ Tobacco and Salt Museum — (0:20h walk) — ∗∗∗ Yoyogi Stadium (III:2)

**Lunch:** Chōtoku, Charlie House, Temmi, Reikyō, Seiryū Mon

**Shibuya Station**　渋谷駅  Served by Yamanote line, Ginza and Hanzōmon subway lines, private Tōkyū-Tōyoko and Shintama lines, Keiō-Inogashira line. Shibuya (Astringent Valley) lies lower than other parts of the city, with the odd result that the subway is on the station's 3rd floor. The Tōkyū-Tōyoko line is on the 4th floor, the Yamanote line is on the 2nd floor.

**Hachikō Plaza**　ハチ公像  On the west side of Shibuya station is Tokyo's most famous meeting place, centered on a bronze statue of an Akita dog named Hachikō. Hachikō came to the station every day for ten years, waiting in vain for a master who had died one day at work. Hachikō became admired throughout the land for his doggedness. The real Hachikō was stuffed and is now in the National Science Museum.

See p. 231 for restaurants, p. 234 for hotels

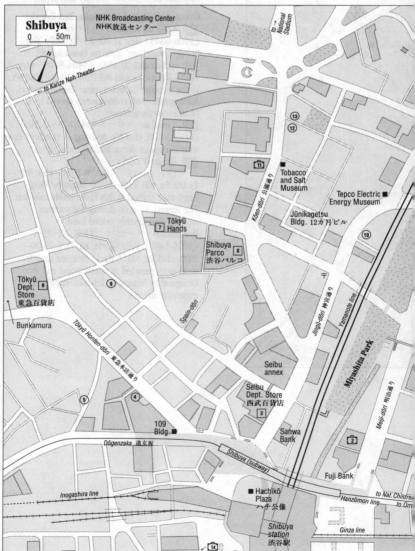

**Dōgenzaka** 道玄坂 Main road to the left from Hachikō Plaza. One of Edo's famous slopes, named for Dōgen, a bandit who would locate victims from atop a pine tree. When old age forced him to retire, he became a monk and lived in an arbor, Dōgen-an, along this road. The area to the north, Dōgenzaka Ni-chōme, is a tangle of narrow alleys crowded with restaurants, bars, and—at the top—a large congregation of love hotels. This charmingly seedy quarter was the birthplace of the striptease in Japan.

∗ **Bunkamura** 文化村 (3477-9911). 2-24-1 Dōgenzaka. Hrs: 10:00–19:00. Completed in 1989, this $160-million building houses concert halls, cinemas, art galleries, upscale boutiques and restaurants, including a branch of the famed Parisian roost, Les Deux Magots. Ogle the architecture and trendy denizens.

**Spain-dōri** スペイン通り This cramped, zigzagging pedestrian alley started out as a shortcut between the 109 Building and Parco, but acquired a life of its own after a local merchant decided to rebuild his shop in Castilian style. Others copied him and the alley was soon clogged with fantasy-hungry shoppers.

∗ **Tobacco and Salt Museum** たばこと塩の博物館 (3476-2041). Hrs: 10:00–18:00 (enter by 17:30); clsd M (Tu if M a NH), 1st Tu of June, NY. Yellow-brick museum run by Japan's formerly government-operated salt-and-tobacco monopoly. Interesting displays on the history of salt and tobacco production in Japan and abroad.

**Tepco Electric Energy Museum** 東京電力エネルギー館 (3477-1191). Hrs: 10:30–18:30 (enter by 18:00); clsd W (Th if W a NH), NY. This electric-company museum, resembling a seven-story incarnation of R2D2, is filled with colorful, well-assembled, interactive displays on every aspect of electricity, from its generation and properties to the latest consumer uses.

**National Children's Castle** こどもの城 (3797-5666). Hrs: 13:00–17:30; Sa, Su, NH 10:00–17:30; clsd M, NY. Late Apr.–late Sept., 10:00–18:00. *0:10h walk from Shibuya station.* This gleaming complex includes a swimming pool with underwater music and light-emitting course lines that pace one's speed, a video room for educational films and children's classics, and a music room with a Javanese *gamelan* orchestra.

**Kanze Nohgaku-dō** 観世能楽堂 松涛1-16-4 (3469-5241). *0:05h by taxi or 0:15h on foot from Shibuya station.* The Kanze school's Noh stage. See Tokyo Theaters for schedule.

223

## Shibuya Shopping

3 **Seibu Department Store** 西武 (3462-0111). Hrs: 10:00–19:00; clsd W, NY.

6 **Tōkyū Department Store** 東急 (3477-3111). Hrs: 10:00–19:00; clsd Tu (except if NH).

7 ∗ **Tōkyū Hands** 東急ハンズ (5489-5111). Hrs: 10:00–20:00; clsd 2nd and 3rd W (except if NH), NY. Eight-floor store selling merchandise for hobbies, crafts, home improvement.

8 ∗ **Shibuya Parco** 渋谷パルコ (3464-5111). Hrs: 10:00–20:30; clsd NY. A complex of buildings filled with boutiques: Commes des Garçons, Chanel, Issey Miyake (including Issey Miyake Stretch, his hit synthetic stretch material designs).

## Farther Afield: From Shibuya

∗∗ **Nihon Mingeikan (Japan Folk Art Museum)** 日本民芸館 (3467-4527). Hrs: 10:00–16:30; clsd M (Tu if M a NH), NY, and the ends of Mar., June, Sept. and Dec. *0:05h walk from Komaba station, 2 stops from Shibuya by Inokashira line.* The late Yanagi Sōetsu, founder of Japan's folk-art movement, collected the superb objects shown at this beautiful museum on his forays in the 1920s and 1930s through Japan, Korea, Okinawa, Taiwan, and other countries (see Crafts, p. 103).

∗ **Daikanyama** 代官山 *1 stop from Shibuya by Tōyoko line.* Many Tokyo fashion companies are located in this upscale pocket of suburban Tokyo, especially along Yamate-dōri. The street has some noted modern buildings, including the Hillside Terrace and Danish Embassy by Maki Fumihiko, and the BIGI Building by Andō Tadao.

∗ **Gotō Bijutsukan (Art Museum)** 五島美術館 世田谷区上野毛3-9-25 (3703-0661). Hrs: 9:30–16:30 (enter by 16:00); clsd M (except if NH), day after NH, Aug., NY. *From Shibuya, take the Tōyoko line to Jiyūgaoka, then change to Tōkyū Oimachi line and go 4 stations west to Kaminoge. 0:05h walk to the museum (map available at station).* One of Japan's foremost private collections, begun by Gotō Keita, founder of the Tōkyū railway empire. Most famous are the sections of the 12th-C *Genji Scrolls* (NT), shown during the first week in May for one week. Normal exhibits tend to be for specialists. Few English captions. Attractive building and grounds.

## Exploring Meguro

**Meguro Club Sekitei** 目黒クラブ石庭 下目黒2-1-6 (3494-1211). It's almost worth getting off at Meguro station—around dusk is best—just to see the Cinderella castle profile of Tokyo's most famous love hotel, looming like a mirage in the low-lying districts to the west. A short stay is Y8–13,000 (per couple). An overnight stay is Y12–20,000.

**Tokyo-to Teien Bijutsukan (Art Museum)** 庭園美術館 (3443-0201). Hrs: 10:00–18:00 (enter by 17:30); clsd 2nd and 4th W (Th if W a NH), NY. *0:05h on foot from Meguro station, at the south end of the National Park for Nature Study.* Loan exhibits only, but art deco lovers may want to see the splendid building, a former imperial prince's villa. The prince studied in France in the 1920s and commissioned Henri Rapin to design the interior.

# TOKYO IV. COMMUTER TOKYO

**Main Attractions:**

IV:1    \*\*\* Tokyo Metropolitan Government Office Building
IV:1    \*\* Kabukichō (Tokyo's steamiest nightlife)
IV:2    \*\* Seibu Department Store
IV:2    \*\* Rikugi-en (garden)

After World War II, Tokyo became a city of suburbs. Most of the people who work in Tokyo now live outside the Yamanote circle line. Many live in the neighboring prefectures of Chiba, Saitama, or Kanagawa, and commute through gargantuan hub stations on the Yamanote line, of which Shinjuku and Ikebukuro are the largest. Two million people pass through Shinjuku everyday, making it the busiest station — indeed the busiest place — in the world. On Sundays, the canyonlike streets between the cinemas and the department stores fill with pleasure-seekers in a form of ordered mass hysteria. At night comes a different sort of customer; besides thousands of bars, there is a startling variety of establishments to satisfy every sexual need. Both Shinjuku and Ikebukuro are also rapidly developing into major business centers. West Shinjuku is a futuristic spectacle of gleaming skyscrapers rocketing out of a flat expanse. Day or night, sleazy or supermodern, there is something more than a little frightening about it all. But go see it, and afterward escape to a saner part of town.

## IV:1 SHINJUKU 新宿

*Take the Yamanote or Chūō line, or the Marunouchi or Toei-Shinjuku subway lines.* The rail lines cleave Shinjuku into two parts, east and west, as different from each other as two city neighborhoods could be. West Shinjuku is an orderly, rectilinear, antiseptic arrangement of skyscrapers. East Shinjuku is a dense tangle of underground passages, department stores, cinemas, and the nightlife district Kabukichō.

224

### Shinjuku Station 新宿駅

The train tracks are numbered from east to west:

1–2: Saikyō line to Ōmiya (Tōhoku and Jōetsu Shinkansen)
3–4: JR NEX, Chūō main line to Matsumoto (CHŪBU IV:NE7)
5–6: Chūō line to Yotsuya, Kanda, Tokyo station
12–13: Yamanote circle line

**Subways:** The Marunouchi line (red) is at the north end of the station, on the east side. The Toei-Shinjuku line (lime green) is at the south end, on the west side.

**Private Commuter Lines:** The Odakyū line (to Odawara, Hakone) is on the west side, to the south. The Keiō line is on the west side. The Seibu-Shinjuku line (to Kawagoe) is separate, under the Shinjuku Prince Hotel; exit from the east and follow the tracks north.

**Station Department Stores:** The east side of the station building is a shopping complex called **My City**. The west side has the **Odakyū Department Store** and the **Keiō Department Store**.

### Nishi (West) Shinjuku

Site of the world's most expensive real estate. For years there were negotiations to move the City Hall here, and in the past decade, starting with the Keiō Plaza Hotel, dozens of corporations and hotels staked their bets on the area's future by erecting skyscrapers, giving Shinjuku a skyline visible for miles around. Their gamble has paid off: a few years ago the city government finally decided to make the move. As expected, the design of the new City Hall was awarded to Tange Kenzō, the senior statesman of Japanese architecture.

---

**Walking Tour:** Shinjuku Station — (0:05h) — Yasuda Insurance Building — (0:10h) — \* Century Hyatt — (0:05h) — \*\*\* Tokyo City Hall — (0:02h) — \* NS Building — (0:02h) — \* Shinjuku Washington Hotel — (0:05h) — Shinjuku Station

**Note:** Many of the buildings are lit up at night.

---

**Yasuda Kasai Museum of Art** 安田火災東郷青児美術館 (3349-3081). Hrs: 9:30–17:00 (enter by 16:30); clsd M (unless a NH, then clsd Tu), NY. Yasuda Kasai Bldg, 42F. Home to Van Gogh's Y5.8 billion *Sunflowers*. The painting, flanked by a Cezanne and a Gauguin, rests behind an unsightly security window. The gallery also shows paintings by late artist Tōgō Seiji (who was obsessed with appallingly kitschy female nudes).

\*\*\* **Tokyo Tochō (City Hall)** 東京都庁 (5320-7890). Observation floor hrs: 10:00–18:00; Sa, Su, NH 10:00–20:00; clsd M (except if NH, then clsd Tu), NY. This 48-story (243m) twin-spired behemoth, Japan's tallest building, was designed as an opulent monument to Japan's affluence by the studio of Kenzō Tange, granddaddy of Japan's postwar architects. Incensed citizens denounce the $1.1-billion structure as "tax tower." The complex fails as a public space, but the details — the textured granite and etched steel — are marvels of craftsmanship and design. The grid motif — suggestive of a silicon wafer — unifies the whole in spite of the mammoth scale. Whatever the flaws, this is one of the most audacious and beautiful skyscrapers in recent memory. A 55-second elevator ride lofts visitors to the observation floors, one in each of the two towers, for unsurpassed views of the city. Tokyo Bay is visible, and on clear days, Mt. Fuji.

✳ **NS Building.** Restaurant hrs: 11:00–22:00, daily. This commercial building is easy to spot by the rainbow-hued glass elevator shaft on the corner. Its cavernous, 30-story atrium is decorated with a 29m-high water-powered Seiko clock. Skywalks provide vertiginous access between two floors filled with all kinds of restaurants.

✳ **Shinjuku Washington Hotel.** With its port-hole like windows, white walls and curvaceous contours, this hotel looks like an ocean liner grown tall. The first hotel in Tokyo to use a computerized room-security system, the interior is fittingly high-tech. Stop in for a cup of coffee in the lounge overlooking the atrium and take in the scene.

## Nishi Shinjuku Shopping

5  **Yodobashi Camera** ヨドバシカメラ (3346-1010). Nishi-Shinjuku. Hrs: 9:30–20:30, daily. 20–50 percent discounts on a huge stock: this shop carries just about every model in production.

6  **Camera no Doi** カメラのドイ (3348-2241). Nishi-Shinjuku. Hrs: 10:00–21:00; Su, NH 10:00–20:30.

## Higashi (East) Shinjuku

Extending underground to Shinjuku San-chōme is a huge subterranean maze of shops and restaurants. Along the way are exits to Kinokuniya Bookstore and Isetan Department Store.

---

**Walking Tour:** Shinjuku Gyoen-mae station — ✳ Shinjuku Gyoen (Park) — (0:10h) — ✳ Suehirotei Theater — (0:05h) — Hanazono Jinja and ✳ Golden Gai alley — (0:05h) — ✳✳ Kabukichō — (0:05h walk via Subnade) — Shinjuku station

**Note:** This walk is most interesting in late afternoon and evening.

---

225

✳✳ **Kabukichō** 歌舞伎町 So named because there was once a plan to build a Kabuki theater here, this notorious quarter is a department store of Tokyo nightlife, from numerous little pubs to "No-pants Kissa," strip shows, and "soaplands" (see p. 125 for a note on nightlife).

✳ **Ichibankan and Nibankan** 一番館・二番館 歌舞伎町2-30 *200 m north of Yasukuni-dōri.* The names literally mean Building #1 and Building #2. These playfully abstract buildings designed by Takeyama Minoru have been widely acclaimed since they were erected in 1969 and 1970. Ichibankan is covered with black and white stripes; this was Takeyama's response to a building code that required the marks to warn low-flying aircraft. Nibankan is a cacophony of supergraphics that transform the building into a giant advertise-

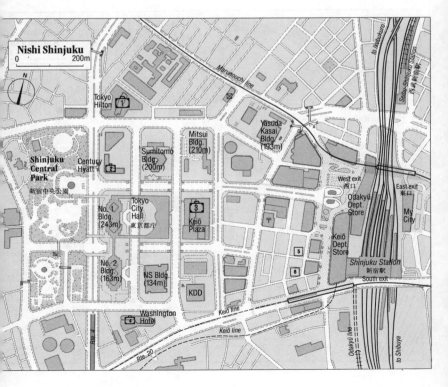

ment. The reflective glass cladding, opaquely geometric by day, transmits interior light at night to reveal the intimate world of pubs and cabarets inside.

**Sky Building No. 3** 第3スカイビル 大久保1-1-10 This condominium by Watanabe Yōji, assembled from steel units resembling mobile homes, gained notoriety for its rooftop water tank, a submarine-like form said to reflect the architect's nostalgia for his World War II navy days.

✽ **Golden Gai** ゴールデン街 From Kabukichō toward **Hanazono Jinja** is this lane filled with diminutive, ramshackle pubs frequented by artists and writers. A whiff of yesteryear.

✽ **Suehirotei** 末広亭 新宿3-6-12 (3351-2974). Hrs: 12:00–16:30, 17:00–21:30. 410-seat wooden theater for fast-talking *rakugo* comics, here performed by exponents of two leading schools.

✽ **Shinjuku Gyoen (Park)** 新宿御苑 Hrs: 9:00–16:30 (enter by 16:00); clsd M. The entrance is near Shinjuku Gyoen-mae station. This large park incorporates a hodgepodge of styles. The north end features a classical French garden. The south and west contain Japanese-style pond gardens. The **Taiwan-kaku** pavilion was built in 1927 by a Japanese architect living in Taiwan to commemorate Emperor Hirohito's wedding. It is a charming and faithful rendition of Chinese pavilion architecture; it's a shame it isn't in better repair.

✽ **National Noh Theater (Kokuritsu Nohgaku-dō)** 国立能楽堂 千駄ヶ谷4-18-1 (423-1331). Near Sendagaya station, south of Shinjuku Gyoen. This is the most beautiful of the national theaters, intimate, with gardens and rich use of satiny cypress wood. English-language guides to Noh and Kyōgen on sale. See Tokyo Theaters for schedule.

✽ **GA Gallery** GAギャラリー 千駄ヶ谷3-12-14 (3403-1581). 3-12-14 Sendagaya. Hrs: 12:00–18:00; clsd M, mid-Aug., NY. Designed by Suzuki Makoto and Futagawa Yukio, publisher of the internationally renowned *Global Architecture*. Has an excellent architectural book store and a stunning series of naturally lit rooms for exhibits of architectural drawings.

226 ✽ **Tokyo-to Taiiku-kan (Metropolitan Gymnasium)** 東京都体育館 (5474-2111). *By Sendagaya station on JR Chūō line*. The spaceship-like dome of the gymnasium dominates the vast, granite-paved plaza of this athletic complex designed by Maki Fumihiko. To the right, semiunderground, are the public facilities. Airy, light-filled and fully equipped, they are Tokyo's best bargain: A workout room (Hrs: 9:00–21:00; Y300 for first two hours), two Olympic-size pools (Hrs: 9:30–21:00 [enter by 20:00]; clsd 3rd M; Y400 for two hours), and an oval outdoor track (Y150 for two hours). Children half price. Buy magnetic admission cards at the entrance.

## Higashi Shinjuku Shopping

**Kinokuniya Bookstore** 紀伊国屋書店 (3354-0131). Hrs: 10:00–19:00; clsd 3rd W, NY. Subway exit B7 or B8. English-language books are on 6F.

**Camera no Sakuraya** カメラのサクラヤ (3341-3636). Hrs: 10:00–20:00; clsd NY. Yodobashi Camera's oldest and fiercest competitor; 20–60 percent discounts.

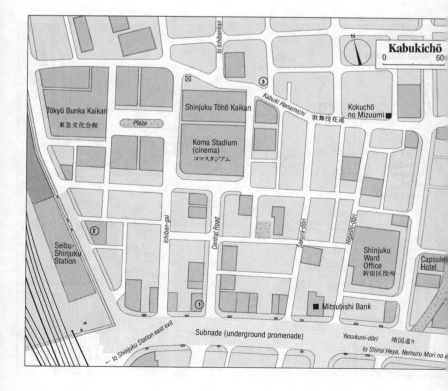

**Isetan** 伊勢丹 (3352-1111). Hrs: 10:00–19:00; clsd W (Th if W a NH), Jan. 1–3. Open daily July 1–15 and in Dec. Subway exits B3-5. This huge department store carries fashions ranging from Armani to Issey Miyake. The annex houses the men's department. Ticket outlet on 6F. Art gallery on 8F annex.

**Miyama Shōkai** ミヤマ商会 新宿3-32-8 (3356-1841). Hrs. 10:30–20:00; Su, NH 10:30–19:00; clsd NY. For new and secondhand professional-quality photographic equipment.

**Bingoya** 備後屋 若松町10-6 (3202-8778). 10–6 Wakamatsuchō. Hrs: 10:00–19:00; clsd M, mid-Aug., NY. About 2 km east of Shinjuku, out on Shokuan-dōri. Famous shop with a colorful stock of folk crafts from all over Japan.

### Shinjuku Nightlife

Shinjuku's nightlife centers on Kabukichō. Everything from bars, discos and restaurants to the rawest of sex shows. Shinjuku Ni-chōme has a concentration of gay clubs. By the tracks on the west side is a pungently atmospheric alley called *shomben-yokochō* (piss alley), packed with tiny pubs and *yakitori* shops. If you're looking for something more conventional, Shinjuku has numerous cinemas showing first- and second-run Japanese and foreign films. All the major hotels have discos.

**Shinjuku Pit Inn** 新宿ピットイン 新宿3-16-4 (3354-2024). Unryu Bldg., B1. Shows daily: 12:30–14:00 (Y800; Sa, Su, NH Y1300), 15:00–18:00 (M–F Y1300; Sa, Su, NH Y2500), 19:30–23:00 (Y2500), daily. Tokyo's top live-jazz club. Japanese and foreign musicians.

**Kokuchō no Mizu-umi (Black-Swan Lake)** 黒鳥の湖 歌舞伎町2-25-2 (3205-0128). 2-25-2 Kabukichō, Arao Bldg., B2. Hrs: 18:00–2:00 a.m., shows at 20:00, 22:30, 1:00; clsd Su. Drag-queen costume revue. Popular with women. Reservation advised. Cover: Y2500. Drinks and food from Y500.

**Shiroi Heya** 白い部屋 新宿5-10-1 (3354-3925). 5-10-1 Shinjuku, Daini Sky Bldg., BF. Hrs: 21:00–4:00 a.m., shows at 22:30, 1:30; clsd Su, NH. This well-established gay bar features beautiful "showgirls" and "hostesses." Cover: Y10,000.

**Nemuru Mori no Bijo (Sleeping Beauties)** 眠る森の美女 新宿2-15-10 (3341-1357). 2-15-10 Shinjuku, Daichi Tenko Bldg., 3F. Hrs: 20:30–3:30 a.m., shows at 22:30 and as they please; clsd Su, NH. "We've gathered the ugliest drag queens in Japan," the ladies here boast. Friendly. Cover: Y5000.

227

## IV:2 IKEBUKURO 池袋

*Take the Yūrakuchō or Marunouchi subway line, or the Yamanote line.* An aspiring Shinjuku, Ikebukuro somehow can't seem to make the grade, though it has all the right ingredients: the second heaviest flow of commuter traffic in Tokyo, a large sleazy quarter, and fashionable department stores. Rikugi-en, Tokyo's finest garden, is near Komagome, three Yamanote-line stations away.

### Ikebukuro Sights

**\*\* Seibu Department Store** 西武 (3981-0111). Hrs: 10:00–19:00, clsd Tu (except if NH), NY. East side of Ikebukuro station. More than just a department store, many consider this the most exciting cultural innovator in Tokyo. It was the first department store to have an art museum, and its cultural programs put on some of the best shows in town. It is a leading supporter of talented up-and-coming artists. One of Japan's leading graphic designers, Ishioka Eiko, created some of Seibu's fabulous posters. In fashion, the avant-garde Japanese designers are well represented. Studio Tech is a showcase of the latest consumer high-tech. The basement food markets are not to be missed.

**Sezon Bijutsukan (Museum of Art)** セゾン美術館 (5992-0155). Ikebukuro SMA-kan 1-2F. Hrs: 10:00–20:00 (enter by 19:30); clsd Tu. A major space for contemporary art, much of it by internationally famous artists.

**Sunshine City** サンシャインシティ *0:05h walk east of station.* This "complete city within a city" is a block of linked buildings including the 60-story Sunshine 60, Ikebukuro Prince Hotel, a shopping complex, and Bunka Sentā (Culture Center). It all stands on the site of notorious **Sugamo Prison**, which held Japan's wartime leaders, including Prime Minister Tōjō Hideki, who was hanged here.

**Ancient Orient Museum** 古代オリエント博物館 (3989-3491). Hrs: 10:00–17:00 (enter by 16:30); clsd M (Tu if M a NH), NY. Bunka Sentā, 7F. Located inside Sunshine City. Handsome exhibit of Near Eastern objects.

**\*\* Rikugi-en** 六義園 (3941-2222). Hrs: 9:00–17:00; clsd M (Tu if M a NH), NY. *0:08h walk from Komagome, 3 stations E of Ikebukuro on the Yamanote line.* The finest surviving example of an Edo-period stroll garden in Tokyo. It was begun in 1695 by Yanagisawa Yoshiyasu, comrade in debauchery of the Dog Shogun Tsunayoshi. Iwasaki Yatarō, founder of Mitsubishi, restored it around 1877. Its name means "six types of poem garden."

### Ikebukuro Shopping

**Seibu Department Store** (3981-0111). Hrs: 10:00–19:00, daily; clsd Tu, NY. See above.

**Parco** パルコ (5391-8000). Hrs: 10:00–20:30; clsd NY. Child of Seibu, this is the epicenter of Japanese fashion.

**BIC Camera** ビックカメラ 東池袋1-11-7 (3988-0002). 1-11-7 Higashi-Ikebukuro. Hrs: 10:00–20:00. Claims to have the lowest prices in Japan.

## Farther Afield: Toward Mejiro

\* **Eisei Bunko** 永青文庫　目白台1-1-1 (3941-0850). Hrs: 10:00–16:30 (enter by 16:00); clsd 1st, 3rd and 5th Sa, NH, mid-Aug., NY, and between exhibits. *Take the Yamanote line to Mejiro, then taxi or bus to Mejirodai 3-chōme, or take the Yūrakuchō line to Gokokuji station.* This small museum displays a few items at a time from one of the greatest private art collections in Japan, belonging to the Hosokawa. The Hosokawa were the lords of Kumamoto and are descended from one of the most distinguished and venerable families in Japan (see Castles, p. 49).

\* **Saint Mary's Cathedral** 聖マリア大聖堂 *Near Edogawa subway station, or 0:10h by bus or taxi from Mejiro station; across from Chinzan-sō restaurant.* Completed in 1964 to commemorate the centennial of Christianity's legalization in Japan, this stunning cathedral by Tange Kenzō is a contemporary to his world-famous Olympic Stadium in Yoyogi Park. The cathedral was designed to suggest a great bird with wings outstretched; the roof ridges meet in a cruciform. One should enter it to appreciate its soaring dimensions.

# DINING

### I:1 **Asakusa** (see p. 198)

\* **Miyako** 美家古　浅草2-1-16 (3844-0034). Hrs: 11:30–14:30, 17:00–20:00 (last order); clsd M, 3rd Su. *Two blocks E of Nakamise-dōri and one block N of Dembō-in-dōri.* Excellent Edo-style sushi. Moderate. No CC.

\* **Daikokuya** 大黒屋 (3844-1111). Hrs: 11:00–20:00; clsd M. *On Dembō-in-dōri, 2nd block W of Nakamise-dōri.* Famous for *tendon* (prawn tempura on rice). Y1200–1600.

**Asakusa Imahan** 浅草今半　浅草3-1-12 (3841-1114). Hrs: 11:30–22:00. (last order). *From N end of Nakamise-dōri, go one block E.* Sukiyaki and *shabu-shabu*. Sukiyaki lunch special, Y1500–3000. Full dinners Y6000–10,500. DC, MC, AX, V.

\* **La Flamme d'Or** ラ・フラーム・ドール　吾妻橋1-23-1 (5608-5381). 1-23-1 Azumabashi. Hrs: 11:30–22:00, daily. *Across the bridge from Asakusa.* You can't miss architect Philippe Starck's signature "golden flame" perched atop the mirrored glass trapezoid. Locals call it the Golden Poo-poo, but this Asahi Brewing Co. beer hall is no dump. Inside, abstract columns loom like giant thighs over exquisite Starck-designed tables and chairs. Eclectic nouvelle tapas-style dishes from Y850, beer from Y380.

\* **Miuraya** 三浦屋　浅草2-19-8 (3841-3151). Hrs: 12:00–22:00 (last order), daily Oct.–Mar.; clsd Aug. and W in Apr.–Sept. *700 meters NW of Asakusa temple.* Good *fugu* (see Cuisine, p. 115) and other seafood, in a jam-packed, three-story restaurant with chaotic service. Shitamachi atmosphere. About Y2600–5200 per person (reasonable for *fugu*). No CC.

\*\* **Komagata Dojō** 駒形どぜう　駒形1-7-12 (3842-4001). Hrs: 11:00–21:00; clsd NY. *Three blocks S of Asakusa station.* In a wonderful Shitamachi-style building. This place has been serving *dojō* (loach, a small eel-like fish) since Edo times. Try the *Dojō-nabe* (loaches simmered over charcoal) and *Yanagawa* (loaches with sliced burdock root in egg). Inexpensive. V, DC, MC.

\*\* **Minoya** みの家　江東区森下2-19-9 (3631-8298). Hrs: 12:00–14:00, 16:00–21:00; NH 12:00–21:00; clsd Th. *By Morishita subway stop (Toei-Shinjuku line).* Famous for *sakuraniku*, the mild and tender flesh of the horse. Try *ba-sashi* (raw, in thin slices served with garlic and soy), or sukiyaki, from Y1400. The atmosphere is pure Shitamachi. No CC.

### I:2 **Ueno** (see map, p. 202)

① \* **Honke Ponta** 本家ぽん多　上野3-23-3 (3831-2351). Hrs: 11:00–14:00, 16:30–20:00; clsd M (Tu if M a NH). Oldest *tonkatsu* shop in Tokyo, famous for its thick, tender cuts. *Katsuretsu*, Y2500. No CC.

⑤ **Ikenohata Yabu Soba** 池之端薮蕎麦　湯島3-44-7 (3831-8977). Hrs: 11:30–14:00, 16:30–20:00; NH 11:30–20:00; clsd W. Good *soba*, inexpensive. No CC.

⑧ **Echikatsu** 江知勝　湯島2-31-23 (3811-5293). Hrs: 17:00–21:00; clsd Su, NH, mid-Aug, NY. Sukiyaki restaurant in grand, traditional house. Reservations advised. Sukiyaki from Y6000; from Y8000; *shabu-shabu* from Y8000. AX, DC, V.

⑫ **Sasanoyuki** 笹乃雪　根岸2-15-10 (3873-1145). Hrs: 11:00–21:00; clsd M (Tu if M a NH). Near Uguisudani station. This tofu restaurant, the most famous in Tokyo, was founded by a tofu maker who was brought from Kyoto by Kan'ei-ji's imperial abbot. Set menus, Y1150–3750; special reserved menus, Y4–6000. No CC.

### I:3 **Kanda** (see map, p. 205)

③ \* **Kandagawa Honten** 神田川本店　外神田2-5-11 (3251-5031). Hrs: 11:30–14:00, 17:00–19:30 (last order); clsd Su, NH. Fabulous *unagi* restaurant. Lovely old-style house with gardens, friendly kimonoed waitresses. *Una-jū* (broiled eel on rice) from Y2500. No CC.

⑤ \* **Yabu Soba** 薮蕎麦　淡路町2-10 (3251-0287). Hrs: 11:30–19:00; clsd M, NY, end of Jan., mid-Aug. The most famous (and expensive) *soba* in Tokyo. Elegant setting. *Kamo namba* (with duck), Y1400; *seiro soba* (plain), Y600. No CC.

⑦ \* **Botan** ぼたん　須田町1-15 (3251-0577). Hrs: 12:00–21:00 (enter by 20:00); clsd Su, NH. Since 1898. Chicken sukiyaki cooked over charcoal. Wonderful old building. From Y6000. No CC.

⑨ **Hisago** ひさご　神田小川町3-2 (3294-0141). Hrs: 11:30–14:00, 17:30–22:00; clsd 1st Sa, Su, NH. Cosy folk interior and inexpensive meals, popular with students. V.

## II:1 Hibiya, Yūrakuchō (see p. 209)

⑨ **A Point** ア・ポイント (3216-4808). Tokyo Station, Yaesu south exit. Hrs: 10:00–22:00; clsd Su, NH. International deli cafeteria. Create-your-own sandwiches, Y450.

\* **Shokudō Wan** 食堂湾　内幸町2-1-4日比谷中日ビル (3503-2671). 2-1-4 Uchisaiwaicho, Hibiya Nakanichi Bldg, 1F. Hrs: 11:30–23:00; clsd Su, NH. Near Kasumigaseki station, across from SW corner of Hibiya Park. Excellent, inexpensive food in a lovely, wood-paneled space. Shared tables. Lunch set menus from Y800. *Omakase* course, Y3000.

\* **Robata** 炉端　有楽町1-3-8 (3591-1905). Hrs: 18:00–23:00; clsd Su. *Follow the train tracks from Imperial Hotel toward Yūrakuchō; this small pub is on the left.* Country atmosphere, home-style cooking. About Y4500 per person. No CC.

## II:2 Nihonbashi, Kyōbashi (see map, p. 211)

① \*\* **Tenmo** てん茂　日本橋本町4-1-3 (3241-7035). Hrs: 12:00–14:00, 17:00–20:00 (arrive by 19:00); Sa 12:00–14:00; clsd Su, NH. Atmospheric shop serving tempura since 1885. The present owner-chef is considered one of Tokyo's foremost tempura masters. Set menu, Y6–10,000 per person. No CC.

⑧ \* **Munakata** むなかた　日本橋3-1-17 (3281-3288). Hirose Bldg., B1. Hrs: 11:30–15:30, 17:00–22:00; clsd NY. Charmingly presented and affordable mini-*kaiseki*. From Y2500. Branch in Mitsui Urban Hotel in Ginza. AX, DC, V.

⑪ \* **Mimiu** 美美卯　京橋3-6-4 (3567-6571). Hrs: 11:30–20:30; Su, NH 11:30–20:00; clsd Su. Branch of famous Ōsaka *udon* noodle shop. *Udon-suki* (*nabe* with seafood, chicken, vegetables, and *udon*), Y4000. No CC.

## II:2 Ginza (see map, p. 212)

① \* **Tokyo Hanten** 東京飯店　銀座5-1-10 (3572-1686). Hrs: 11:30–15:00, 16:00–23:00; Sa 11:30–15:00, 16:00–21:30; NH 11:30–21:30; clsd Su, NY. Authentic Shanghai cuisine in an authentic atmosphere. Best way to order is to ask for a recommendation. À la carte from Y2000. AX, DC, MC, V.

229

② **Naokyū** 直久 (3571-0957). Tōshiba Bldg. Hrs: 11:00–21:00; Su, NH 11:00–20:00. *Ramen* noodles from Y350. No CC.

③ \*\* **Ōmatsuya** 大松屋　銀座5-4-18 (3571-7053). I.N. Bldg., 2F. Hrs: 11:30–14:00, 17:00–22:00; clsd Su, NH, mid-Aug., NY. The interior of the shop is from a 17th-century house. *Soba* at lunch; dinner features *sumiyaki*, charcoal-broiled chicken, prawns, scallops. Set menu, including fabulous, dark Yamagata *soba*, Y4500. AX, V.

⑤ \*\*\* **Jirō** 次郎　銀座4-2-15塚本素山ビル (3535-3600). Tsukamoto Motoyama Bldg., B1. Hrs: 11:30–14:00, 17:00–20:30; Sa 11:30–14:00; clsd Su, NH. Fabulous sushi. The day's selection of fresh fish, only the best the season and market have to offer, is spread out on beautiful plain wooden trays. Every detail, from the hand-grated *wasabi* to the crispness of the *nori* has been attended to with the care of a true master. Y15–20,000 per person. No CC.

⑫ \* **Ōshima** 大志満 (3574-8080). Ginza Core Bldg., 9F. Hrs: 11:00–21:00 (last order); clsd 2 days in Feb. and Aug. Serves *Kaga-ryōri*, the cuisine of the Japan Sea region around Kanazawa, which many consider the finest in Japan. At lunch, try the *bentō*, from Y1800. *Teishoku*, from Y2800, *Kaga kaiseki* from Y6000. V, DC, MC.

⑫ \* **Shabusen** しゃぶせん (3572-3806). Ginza Core Bldg., B2F. Hrs: 11:00–22:00 (last order 21:30). *Shabu-shabu teishoku* from Y3800. AX, DC, V, MC.

⑯ **Ten'ichi** 天一　銀座6-6-5 (3572-1698). Hrs: 11:30–21:30; Su 12:00–21:00. A famous tempura establishment, long popular with foreigners. Lunch from Y5700, dinner from Y8000. *Tendon* (prawn tempura on rice), Y3400, served until 16:00. AX, DC, V.

㉑ \* **Munakata** むなかた (3574-9356). Mitsui Urban Hotel, B1. Hrs: 11:30–16:00, 17:00–22:30; Sa, Su, NH 11:30–22:30. Their exquisite mini-*kaiseki*, starting at Y2800, is a good introduction to the pleasures of Japanese haute cuisine. AX, DC, V.

㉖ **Ginnotō Hirai** 銀の塔ひら井　銀座4-13-6 (3541-6395). Hrs: 12:00–20:00; clsd Tu (W if Tu a NH). Two blocks E of Kabuki-za. Great beef stew; gratin (for two or more). From Y1600–2000. No CC.

## II:3 Shinbashi, Tsukiji, Shiba (see p. 214)

\* **Edogin** 江戸銀　築地4-5-1 (3543-4401). Hrs: 11:00–21:30; clsd Su. Tsukiji sushi shop famous for oversized, extremely fresh toppings on its sushi. Plebeian atmosphere. Y2–5000 per person. AX, DC, V.

\*\* **Sushi Iwa** 寿司岩　築地2-15-12 (3541-0655). Hrs: 11:00–22:00; clsd Su, NH. Near Tsukiji, on Harumi-dōri. Sushi *moriawase* from Y2000. Saturdays, reserve for their wonderful *sushi kaiseki*, Y4200. AX, DC, V, MC, CB.

\*\*\* **Sushi Tatsu** 寿司辰　新橋2-15-5 (3501-0545). Hrs: 17:00–23:00; clsd Su, NH. Near Karasumori Jinja, W of Shinbashi station. Closet-sized shop—barely seats six—serving superb sushi. The fish is laid out on bright green cryptomeria fronds in a wooden tub. About Y7000 per person. No CC.

\*\* **Shinbashi Ōtomo** 大友　新橋2-9-17 (3501-9405). Hrs: 11:30–13:30, 17:00–21:30; clsd Su, NH, and Sa in July–Aug. Near Karasumori Jinja. Since 1937. Dedicated to fine Japanese cuisine at affordable prices. The menu—handwritten on a paper-thin sheet of wood—changes daily. Lunch, Y900. *Omakase* dinner from Y8000. DC, AX, V, MC.

**\*\*\*Daigo** 醍醐　愛宕2-4-2　(3431-0811). Hrs: 12:00–15:00, 17:00–21:00; clsd Th. Near Atagoyama, Onarimon station. Reservations. Originated as a branch of a *ryōtei* in Hida-Takayama. Serves a *kaiseki-shōjin* (Buddhist vegetarian) fusion. Lunch from Y12,000, dinner from Y14,000. AX, DC.

### III:1 Roppongi (see map, p. 216)

① **\*\*Feu** 馮　南青山1-26-16　(3479-0230). Hrs: 11:30–14:00, 17:30–22:00; clsd Su, NH, mid-Aug., NY. Nouvelle cuisine restaurant with a pleasant interior of light wood furniture and a brick wall covered with copper pans. Chefs work in full view, turning out colorful palettes of tiny morsels. Lunch Y1900–4200, dinner from Y8000. AX, DC, V, MC.

② **Torichō** 鳥長　六本木7-8-2　(3401-1827). Hrs: 17:00–23:00; Su, NH 17:00–20:00. The elegant interior compensates for the mediocre *yakitori*. Y5200 per person. AX, DC, V, MC.

③ **Inakaya** 田舎家　六本木7-8-4　(3405-9866). Hrs: 17:00–5:00 a.m., clsd NY. Reservations advised. An exceptionally theatrical *robatayaki* place, with a huge selection of fish, meats, and vegetables. All cooked to order over charcoal by robust, loud youths in *happi* coats. About Y10,000 per person. AX, DC, V, MC.

④ **\*Aux Six Arbres** オーシザーブル　六本木7-13-10　(3479-2888). Hrs: 12:00–14:00, 18:00–22:00; clsd Su. Quiet, elegant French restaurant. Lunch Y2500–5000, dinner from Y9300. AX, DC, V.

⑤ **\*Torigin** 鳥ぎん　六本木4-12-6　(3403-5829). Hrs: 11:30–14:00, 17:00–0:30 a.m.; clsd Su. Simple *yakitori*. English menu, friendly atmosphere. Sets from Y1000. No CC.

⑥ **Yotarō** 与太呂　六本木4-11-4　(3405-5866). Hrs: 17:30–22:00 (last order); clsd Su, open NH. Contemporary interior, but the proprietor is full of old-fashioned warmth. Tempura and *taimeshi* (rice cooked with a whole sea bream). Dinner sets from Y9000. AX, V, DC.

⑥ **Daikan Kamado** 代官かまど　六本木4-11-4　(3403-5364). Roppongi Bldg., 1F. Hrs: 17:00–1:30 (last order); Su, NH 17:00–24:00. Elegant farmhouse-style restaurant with dark wood interior and a huge *kamado* (clay stove). Meat, fowl, and fish *nabe* dishes of all types; set menus from about Y8000. AX, V, MC, DC.

⑦ **Nambantei** 南蛮亭　六本木4-5-6　(3402-0606). Hrs: 17:00–23:00, clsd NY. *Yakitori*: set course from Y3100, single skewers are Y210. Cosy atmosphere; efforts made to reassure the foreigner. AX, DC, MC, V.

⑧ **Roppongi Shokudō** 六本木食堂　六本木3-10-11　(3404-2714). Hrs: 10:00–14:00, 16:15–19:00; Sa 10:00–14:00; clsd 1st and 3rd Sa, Su, NH. Budget eating in a classic Japanese-style cafeteria.

⑨ **Gonin Byakushō (Five Farmers)** 五人百姓　六本木3-10-3　(3470-1675). Square Bldg., 4F. Hrs: 11:30–14:00, 17:00–22:00 (last order); Su, NH 12:00–22:00. Food is grilled around a huge clay oven; countrified atmosphere. *Robatayaki* and regional specialties from all over Japan. Lunch from Y900, dinner from Y4000. AX, DC, MC, V.

⑩ **\*\*Kissō** 吉左右　(3582-4191). Axis Bldg., B1. Hrs: 11:30–14:00, 17:30–21:00; clsd Su. Light, elegant *kaiseki*-style meals. Lunch Y1200+, dinner from Y9600. AX, DC, MC, V.

⑪ **\*\*Fukuzushi** 福ずし　六本木5-7-8　(3402-4116). Hrs: 17:30–20:00; clsd Su. Great sushi. Lunch *moriawase* Y2500, dinner about Y10,000 per person. AX, V, DC, MC.

⑫ **\*Tong Fu** 東風　六本木6-7-11　(3403-3527). Hrs: 11:30–14:30, 17:00–3:00 a.m. Trendy restaurant-bar featuring natural Chinese cuisine. Y7500+ per person. AX, V, DC.

⑬ **\*Moti** モティ　六本木6-2-35　(3479-1939). Hama Bldg., 3F. Hrs: 11:30–23:00 (22:00 last order), daily. Good Indian food. From around Y2000. AX, DC, V, MC.

⑮ **\*Borsalino** ボルサリーノ　六本木6-8-21　(3401-7751). Hrs: 18:00–22:30; clsd M. Excellent Milanesan cuisine served in a sleek, black-and-white setting.

⑯ **\*\*Jūjū** 十十　西麻布3-24-20　(3405-9911). Hrs: 11:30–5:00 a.m.; Su, NH 17:00–2:00 a.m. Near Kasumichō Crossing. Korean barbecue with a modernist esthetic. Set dinners from Y5000 (by reservation). AX, V, DC, MC.

⑰ **\*Les Choux** レシュー　六本木5-11-28　(3452-5511). Hrs: 12:00–15:00 (last order), 17:30–22:30 (last order). Cosy French restaurant. Lunch, Y1500, dinner from Y6500. AX, DC, MC, V.

⑱ **\*\*Nagasaka Sarashina** 永坂更科　麻布十番2-8-12　(3585-1676). Hrs: 11:00–20:30, daily. In Azabu-Jūban, a shopkeepers' quarter SW of Roppongi. Supplier of *soba* to the shogun, this shop is known for its ultra-refined, ultra-thin *gozen soba*. Excellent sashimi and yakitori too. From Y650. V, DC.

### III:2 Akasaka (see p. 218)

**\*Tsutsui** 津つ井　赤坂5-5-7　(3584-1851). Hrs: 11:00–15:00, 17:00–21:00, Sa 12:00–21:00; clsd Su, NH. Southwest of TBS and the Akasaka subway station. This friendly little place serves Japanese-style Western food. Downstairs has tables; upstairs, tatami. The popular *ainoko* (half-and-half) *bentō* is Y2000. Beefsteak *domburi* is Y2500. AX, DC, V, MC.

**Mexico Lindo** メヒコリンド　赤坂2-20-7　(3583-2095). Daini Seikō Mansion Bldg. Hrs: 11:30–14:00, 17:00–23:00 (last order 22:00); NH 17:00–21:00 (last order); clsd Su. South of Akasaka station. From Akasaka Twin Towers, walk toward Roppongi, take first right. Best Mexican food in town. Set menus from Y5000. AX, V, MC.

**Nagaura Soba** 長浦そば　(3581-0954). Akasaka Tōkyū Hotel, B1. Hrs: 11:30–21:00, clsd Su. This shop claims to have revived a genuine old-style *soba* made at a Zen temple in Owari (Aichi prefecture). Pleasant folk-art interior. From Y600. No CC.

∗ **Hayashi** はやし　赤坂2-14-1 (3582-4078). Sannō Kaikan Bldg., 4F. Hrs: 11:30–14:00, 17:30–23:00; clsd Su. East from Akasaka station. Stunning old farmhouse interior. Serves the cuisine of Hida, a mountainous region in central Japan. Food cooked over charcoal. Set menus from Y6000. AX, DC, V, MC.

∗ **Moti** モティ　赤坂3-8-8 (3582-3620). Hrs: 11:30–22:00; Su, NH 12:00–22:00. Near Akasaka-Mitsuke station. Popular Indian restaurant; tandoori cuisine. Set menus from Y2500. AX, DC, V, MC.

**La Granata** ラグラナータ　赤坂TBS会館 (3582-3241). TBS Kaikan Bldg., B1. Hrs: 11:00–14:00, 17:00–21:30 (last order), daily. Open between lunch and dinner as a café. Trattoria atmosphere, serving un-Japanized Italian food. Lunch is inexpensive, dinner expensive. AX, DC, V, MC.

∗ **Zakuro** ざくろ　赤坂TBS会館 (3582-6841). TBS Kaikan Bldg., B1. Hrs: 11:00–23:00, daily; clsd NY. Famous *shabu-shabu* restaurant; pleasant folk-art decor. *Bentō*, Y2500–2800, sukiyaki, Y9800. AX, V, DC, MC.

**III:2 Aoyama, Harajuku** (see map, p. 220)

① **Brasserie Shūshū** ブラッセリー・シュシュ　南青山3-3-15 (3404-4633). 3-3-15 Minami Aoyama. Hrs: 11:30–22:00 (lunch until 14:30), daily. Inexpensive French food in a slightly fancy setting. Lunch-steak set menu Y900. Full-course menus Y1500–3000.

③ **La Patata** ラパタータ　神宮前2-9-11 (3403-9665). Shiobara Gaien Bldg., 1F. Hrs: 12:00–14:00, 18:00–22:30; clsd M. Italian provincial cooking in a casual setting. Lunch, Y1100 (no lunch on Tu), dinner from Y5000. AX, DC, V, MC.

④ **Mominoki House** モミノキハウス　神宮前2-18-5 (3405-9144). Hrs: 11:00–22:00 (last order); clsd Su. Good natural foods restaurant. The master speaks some English and is happy to help explain the extensive, eclectic menu. Inexpensive to moderate. No CC.

⑤ **Ghee** ギー　神宮前2-18-7 (3401-4023). Hrs: 11:30–14:00, 17:30–22:00; Su, NH 12:00–16:00, 17:00–20:00; clsd NY. Tasty curries: beef, chicken, and vegetarian. Pleasant postmodern interior. Inexpensive. No CC.

⑥ ∗ **Tompo** 東ぽ　神宮前3-24-9 (3405-9944). Hrs: 18:00–24:00; clsd 1st and 3rd Su. Home-cooked Chinese food by friendly Beijing native. Tiny place. From Y2000. No CC.

⑧ ∗∗ **Isshin** 一心　南青山4-21-29 (3401-4611). Sugimoto Bldg., 2F, 3F. Hrs: 11:30–14:30, 17:00–22:00 (last order); clsd Su. Nouvelle cuisine in elegant space blending fresh flowers and black lacquer surfaces. Attentive service. Lunch, Y2100, dinner set menu, Y13,000. MC, AX, DC, V.

⑬ **Daini's Table** ダイニーズテーブル　南青山6-3-14 (3407-0363). Hrs: 17:00–midnight; clsd NY. Near Nezu Art Museum. Shanghai-style nouvelle cuisine in a gorgeous Chinoiserie setting. Dinner course from Y7000. AX, DC, V, MC.

⑭ ∗∗ **Bindi** ビンデ　南青山7-10-10 (3409-7114). Apartment Aoyama, B1. Hrs: 12:00–14:00, 18:00–23:00 (last order); clsd Su, NH. *Walk down Kottōhin-dōri, cross under expressway, turn R and go 2 blocks; shop is on R.* Home-style Indian cooking by a charming Indian couple. Lunch, Y600, dinner set menu Y2300. No CC.

**III:3 Shibuya** (see map, p. 222)

① ∗ **Chōtoku** 長徳　渋谷1-10-5 (3407-8891). Hrs: 11:30–21:00; clsd M (Tu if M a NH). Handmade *udon* noodles, made from the finest ingredients. Photo-album menu. Choice of *shōyu-* (soy sauce) or miso-flavored stock. Folk decor, classical music. AX, V, DC, MC.

④ **Kujiraya** くじら屋　道玄坂2-29-22 (3461-9145). Hrs: 11:30–22:00; clsd 1st and 3rd M, mid-Aug, NY. Tokyo's only whale-meat restaurant; barbecue, sukiyaki, sashimi, fried. Moderate. DC, CB, MC, V, AX.

⑤ **Reikyō** 麗郷　道玄坂2-25-18 (3464-8617). Hrs: 12:00–14:00, 17:00–0:30 a.m. (last order); clsd Th. In a low, red-brick, "medieval" building. Excellent Taiwanese cuisine, English menu. Extremely crowded at times. About Y2-3000 per person. No CC.

⑨ **Seiryū Mon** 青龍門　宇田川町32-7 (3496-7655). 32-7 Utagawachō, Chitose Bldg. Hrs: 11:30–15:00, 17:30–23:30; F, Sa, day before NH, open to 2:00 a.m. Folksy Taiwanese restaurant popular for its bargain lunches: soup, shumai, main dish and rice for Y780 or Y880.

⑩ **Tenmi** 天味　神南1-10-6 (3496-7100). Hrs: 11:30–14:00, 17:00–21:30 (last order); Su, NH 11:30–18:00; clsd 2nd and 3rd W. Natural-food restaurant. Inexpensive. No CC.

⑫ **Charlie House** チャリーハウス　神南1-15-11 (3464-5552). Hrs: 11:30–14:30, 17:00–20:30; clsd Su, NH. Handmade *ramen* noodles. The tiny shop is always packed with customers. Inexpensive. No CC.

⑬ ∗ **Sushi Bar Sai** すしバー彩　神南1-7-5 (3496-6333). Rambling Core Bldg., 2F. Hrs: 17:30–1:00 a.m.; Su, NH 16:00–22:00; clsd mid-Aug., NY. High-tech interior, with sushi to match: beef-sashimi sushi, tofu sushi. Expensive (about Y1000 per 2-piece order). Branch in Printemps Department Store, Ginza. AX, V, DC, MC.

∗∗∗ **Daikonya** だいこんや　猿楽町9-8 (3496-6664). Daikanyama Parkside Village, B1. Hrs: 13:00–14:30, 17:30–22:00; clsd Su. *600 m from Daikanyama station on Hachiman-dōri, turn L and go 100 m; shop is on R side of street.* Modern *kaiseki* in an intimate setting of skillfully contrasting concrete, wood, and red-lacquer surfaces. Lunch kaiseki bentō Y5000, dinner set menu Y8500, changes every month. AX, DC, V, MC.

## IV:1 Shinjuku (see map, p. 226)

① **Suzuya** すずや 歌舞伎町1-23-15 (3209-4480). Sugiyama Bldg., 2F. Hrs: 11:30–22:30; clsd NY. Roomy place, decorated with folk crafts. Wholesome, reasonably priced Japanese and Western-style food. A refuge from the madness outside. No CC.

② \* **Kirakuya** 喜楽家 歌舞伎町1-25-3 (3200-0009). 1-25-3 Kabukichō, Seibu Shinjuku Ekimae Bldg., 2F. Hrs: 17:00–3:00 a.m., daily. Chic modern Japanese interior. The youthful clients share seats at large tables. Chefs work behind a counter laden with heaping bowls. Eclectic offerings, from home-style cooking to squid-ink pasta. Choose from a pictorial menu. Try the junmai-zake (new sake). À la carte from Y350, set menus Y3400–4000.

③ **Tokyo Kaisen Ichiba** 東京海鮮市場 歌舞伎町2-36-1 (5273-8301). 2-36-1 Kabukichō. Hrs: 11:30–4:30 a.m.; Su, NH 11:30–23:00. Buy a fresh fish (500 grams per person) at the street-level fish market, and have the restaurant upstairs prepare it. Price per person to prepare: sashimi Y900, sautéed Y800, steamed Y600, fried Y700. Or order from the menu. Go with a group. Or try the inexpensive grilled fish and clams on the ground floor.

\* **Tatsukichi** 立吉 新宿3-34-16 (3341-9322). 3-34-16 Shinjuku, Ikeda Plaza Bldg., 5F. Hrs: 16:00–22:30; clsd Su, NH. *A few blocks from Shinjuku Station south exit.* An imaginative array of deep-fried, skewered meats, fish and vegetables, served at a bar. Bilingual pamphlet tells you what's what. Skewers from Y150. Special set menu, Y4000, by reservation.

**Tsunahachi** つな八 新宿3-31-8 (3352-1011). Hrs: 11:30–22:00, daily. An inexpensive tempura restaurant, popular with young people. Friendly, and they cook to your order at the counter. MC, DC, AX, V.

\*\* **Kyōbue** 京笛 (3348-2359). Tokyo Hilton, B1. Hrs: 17:00–24:00. Very elegant restaurant specializing in Kyoto-style *robata* — such unusual and elegant dishes as seafood in miso broth "stew" cooked on a piece of giant kelp over charcoal. Set menus from around Y5000, à la carte is less expensive. DC, AX, V, MC.

\*\*\* **Hiroshige** 広重 中野区新井2-6-5 (3386-0895). Hrs: 17:00–22:00; clsd Su, NH, NY. *Take JR Chūō line 3 stops W from Shinjuku to Nakano. Walk out N exit, go 2 blocks on Nakano-dōri, turn L, then R. Shop is on R.* A hideaway, worth seeking out if you are a dedicated student of Edo culture. This tiny, beautiful restaurant specializes in Edo *tateba-ryōri*, a refined version of the food served at teahouses along the old post highways. By reservation only (if possible, 7–10 days in advance). Set menu, Y9000. V.

## IV:2 Ikebukuro, Komagome (see p. 227)

**Misato** 味里 東池袋1-31-6 三昌ビル1 F (3981-0280). Hrs. 17:00–23:30 (last order); clsd Su, NH. *A 0:05h walk from Parco, in Higashi-Ikebukuro.* Known for saké from all over Japan. *Udon* noodle dishes; *nabe* from Y3500. AX, V, DC, MC.

**Chinzansō** 椿山荘 (3943-1101). Hrs: 12:00–21:30; clsd NY. A huge wedding palace and restaurant with large garden, across from St. Mary's Cathedral. Good and varied menu.

\*\* **Goemon** 五右エ門 本駒込1-1-26 (3811-2015). Hrs: 17:00–22:00; clsd M. *About 1 km from Rikugi-en.* Lovely Kyoto-style tofu restaurant. Set menus from Y4500. No CC.

# LODGINGS (TEL 03)

Choose a hotel near a central location, close to subways, shops, and restaurants. Prime areas: Tokyo station/Yūrakuchō (II:1), Ginza (II:2), Shinbashi (II:3), Akasaka (III:2). Next best: Kanda/Kudan (I:3), Roppongi (III:1), Aoyama (III:2). Tokyo hotels are heavily booked at all seasons, so reserve as far in advance as possible. Some of Tokyo's newest and best hotels are in Shinjuku, but using them means enduring the bedlam of Shinjuku station several times a day. Price categories are based on twin-room rates: (B) Budget, under Y5000 per person; (M) Moderate, Y5–8000 per person; (E) Expensive, Y8–12,000 per person; (D) Deluxe, over Y12,000 per person.

## I:1 Asakusa

\* **Mikawaya Bekkan** 三河屋別館 浅草1-31-11 (3843-2345). Fax 3843-2348. 1-31-11 Asakusa, Taitō-ku. Charming ryokan popular with foreign tourists. The inn is an oasis of quiet just half a block from Nakamise-dōri. Y10,000 w/2 meals (E).

## I:2 Ueno (see map, p. 202)

⑨ **Hokke Club Ikenohata** 法華クラブ池之端 (3822-3111). Fax 3822-3167. 2-1-48 Ikenohata, Taitō-ku. *0:05h walk from Yushima station, near Ueno Park.* Closed for rebuilding. Scheduled to open in spring, 1993.

⑩ **Suigetsu Hotel** (3822-4611) and **Ōgai-sō** 水月ホテル 池の端3-3-21 (3822-4611). Fax 3823-4340. 3-3-21 Ikenohata, Taitō-ku. Slightly ramshackle tourist ryokan and hotel on W side of Ueno Park. Geared to foreigners. S Y7200, Tw Y13,200 (M).

## I:3 Kanda (see map, p. 205)

⑧ \* **Tokyo YMCA Hotel** 東京YMCAホテル 神田美土代町7 (3293-1911). Fax 3293-1926. 7–1 Kanda-Mitoshirochō, Chiyoda-ku. New building opening in April, 1990. Forty rooms, including single, twin, and family rooms, all w/bath. Y8–25,000. Midnight curfew.

⑩ \*\* **Hilltop Hotel (Yamanoue)** 山の上ホテル (3293-2311). Fax 3233-4567. 1-1 Kanda-Surugadai, Chiyoda-ku. Smallest first-class hotel in Tokyo; cosy rooms with period furniture. The hotel is a favorite with writers working under deadline: the late Mishima Yukio was a regular. Well-ventilated with negative ions! S Y13–18,000, Tw Y21–27,000 (E).

**Diamond Hotel** ダイヤモンドホテル (3263-2211). Fax 3263-2222. 25 Ichibanchō, Chiyoda-ku. S Y10–12,500, Tw Y10–22,000 (E).

✱✱ **Hotel Kayū Kaikan** ホテル霞友会館　千代田区三番町8-1 (3230-1111). Fax 3230-2529. 8-1 Sanbanchō, Chiyoda-ku. Managed by Hotel Ōkura. The area, near Hanzōmon and Kudanshita stations, is perhaps too quiet, but service is efficient, rooms are spacious and pleasant, and the restaurants are fine. S Y12,500, Tw Y20,000 (E).

✱ **Kudan Kaikan Hotel** 九段会館　九段南1-6-5 (3261-5521). Fax 3221-7238. 1-6-5 Kudan Minami, Chiyoda-ku. A cosy older hotel, right by the palace moat. Convenient to Kanda and subways. S Y7800–9300, Tw 12,700–20,500, deluxe Tw Y21,000, J-style (triple occup) Y5800 per person (M).

✱ **Tokyo International Youth Hostel** 東京国際YH　飯田橋駅前 (3235-1107). Central Plaza, 18–19F, Iidabashi-ekimae, Shinjuku-ku. Convenient location right over Iidabashi subway station, near charming Kagurazaka. Spotless modern facility. Great views over the city. 21:00 curfew. Heavily booked in Feb. (entrance-exam month). Y3800 w/meals, Y3850 w/air conditioner (B).

## II:1–2. **Palace Side, Nihonbashi** (see map, p. 211)

12 ✱ **Yaesu Fujiya Hotel** 八重洲富士屋ホテル (3273-2111). Fax 3273-2180. 2-9-1 Yaesu, Chūō-ku. Good city hotel with an excellent location near Tokyo station. S Y11–12,500, Tw 20–30,000 (E).

13 **Tokyo Marunouchi Hotel** 東京丸ノ内ホテル (3215-2151). Fax 3215-8036. 1-6-3 Marunouchi, Chiyoda-ku. Location is the best thing about this hotel. Public areas are dim and seedy, service is good but limited. Rooms vary; superior twins are the best value. S Y12–19,000, Tw Y22–29,000 (E).

14 ✱✱ **Palace Hotel** パレスホテル (3211-5211). Fax 3211-6987. 1-1-1 Marunouchi, Chiyoda-ku. This hotel has the best setting in Tokyo, right by the Imperial Palace moat, visible from many of the rooms. Spacious rooms. S Y20–21,000, Tw Y26–52,000 (D).

15 ✱✱✱ **Imperial Hotel** 帝国ホテル (3504-1111). Fax 3504-1258. 1-1-1 Uchisaiwaichō, Chiyoda-ku. Deluxe, but soulless and impersonal. Excellent location for business travelers. S Y31–51,000 Tw Y36–56,000 (D).

233

## II:2 **Ginza** (see map, p. 212)

7 **Hotel Seiyō Ginza** ホテル西洋銀座 (3535-1111, in U.S. 1-800-447-3496). Fax 3535-1110. 1 Ginza, Chūō-ku. Luxurious 80-room hotel with lavishly appointed rooms and 24-hour pampering (guests are offered a startling choice of pillows). Unrated. Standard rooms Y40–72,000, suites Y85,000–280,000 (D).

18 **Ginza Nikkō Hotel** 銀座日航ホテル (3571-4911). Fax 3571-8379. 8-4-21 Ginza, Chūō-ku. JAL affiliate. S Y14–17,000, Tw Y25–30,000 (D).

19 ✱ **Shinbashi Dai-ichi Hotel** 新橋第一ホテル (3501-4411). Fax 3595-2634. 1-2-6 Shinbashi, Minato-ku. Location excellent, near hundreds of bars, restaurants, trains, and subways. Comfortable public spaces. Small rooms, but the location makes up for it. Handsome new annex. S Y9,500–11,000, Tw Y14,500–19,000 (E).

20 ✱ **Mitsui Urban Hotel** 三井アーバンホテル (3572-4131). Fax 3572-4254. 8-6-15 Ginza, Chūō-ku. Small but well-designed rooms, a cross between a little city hotel and business hotel. S from Y13,200, Tw from Y19,000 (E).

24 **Ginza Dai-ichi Hotel** 銀座第一ホテル (3542-5311). Fax 3542-3030. 8-13-1 Ginza, Chūō-ku. S Y17–19,000, Tw Y21–30,000 (M).

26 **Hotel Atami-sō** ホテル熱海荘　銀座4-14-3 (3541-3621). Fax 3541-3263. 4-14-3 Ginza, Chūō-ku. Good location near Kabuki-za. A mix of Western-and Japanese-style rooms, and some that have both tatami and beds. Rooms are pleasant, but you also pay for the location. Semi-double Y8990 (for 1), Y13,000 (for 2); Tw Y17,500–23,980 (E).

**Holiday Inn Tokyo** ホリディイン東京 (3553-6161). Fax 3553-6040. 1-13-7 Hatchōbori, Chūō-ku. A bit out of the way. S Y15,500–18,700, Tw Y26,000 (D).

## II:3 **Shinbashi, Shiba**

✱✱✱ **Hotel Ōkura** ホテルオークラ (3582-0111). Fax 3582-3707. 2-10-4 Toranomon, Minato-ku. The rooms may be a little past their prime, but the service is incredible. Intimate feeling. S Y27,500–33,000, Tw Y37–47,000 (D).

✱✱ **Hotel Pacific Meridien Tokyo** ホテルパシフィックメリディアン東京 (3445-6711). Fax 3445-5317. 3-13-3 Takanawa, Minato-ku. Meridien Hotel chain. Out of the way. S Y20,000+, Tw Y23,000+ (D).

✱✱ **Miyako Hotel Tokyo** 都ホテル東京 (3447-3111). Fax 3447-3133. 1-1-50 Shiroganedai, Minato-ku. Owned by the famous Miyako of Kyoto. Location is its main drawback. S Y20–22,000, Tw Y25–35,000 (D).

✱ **Shiba Yayoi Kaikan** 芝弥生会館 (3434-6841). 1-10-27 Kaigan, Minato-ku. Business-hotel class. Great harbor views. Twin rooms are a good value. Reservations accepted only on the day before or same day, so you have a fighting chance. S Y5700, Tw Y9100 (B).

**Takanawa Prince Hotel** 高輪プリンスホテル (3447-1111). Fax 3446-0849. 3-13-1 Takanawa, Minato-ku. S Y19,000, Tw Y23–30,000 (D).

**Tokyo Prince Hotel** 東京プリンスホテル (3432-1111). Fax 3434-5551. 3-3-1 Shiba-Kōen, Minato-ku. This famous hotel suffers from slipshod service and maintenance. S Y23,000, Tw Y24–33,000 (D).

**III:1 Roppongi** (see map, p. 216)

⑲ **Roppongi Prince Hotel** 六本木プリンスホテル (3587-1111). Fax 3587-0770. 3-2-7 Roppongi, Minato-ku. Urban resort hotel, designed by Kurokawa Kishō. S Y22,000, Tw Y24–28,000 (D).

⑳ **＊＊ ANA Hotel Tokyo** 東京全日空ホテル (3505-1111). Fax 3505-1155. 1-12-33 Akasaka, Minato-ku. Flagship hotel for the excellent ANA hotel chain, located in the enormous Ark Hills complex of shops and restaurants. S Y23,400, Tw Y31,500+ (D).

**III:2 Akasaka**

＊ **Akasaka Prince Hotel** 赤坂プリンスホテル (3234-1111). Fax 3262-5163. 1–2 Kioichō, Chiyoda-ku. Architecture by Tange. Sterile white, ultramodern. Some love it, others hate it. S Y23–35,000, Tw Y31–39,000 (D).

**Akasaka Shampia Hotel** 赤坂シャンピアホテル 赤坂7-6-13 (3586-0811). Fax 3589-0575. 7-6-13 Akasaka, Minato-ku. Business hotel. S Y8700, Tw Y14,800 (M).

**Akasaka Tōkyū Hotel** 赤坂東急ホテル (3580-2311). Fax 3580-6066. 2-14-3 Nagatachō, Chiyoda-ku. S Y19–24,000, Tw Y28,000–40,000 (D).

＊＊ **Capitol Tōkyū Hotel** キャピトル東急ホテル (3581-4511). Fax 3581-5822. 2-10-3 Nagatachō, Chiyoda-ku. Formerly the Hilton. Comfortable. Excellent location; back entrance is by Kokkaigijidō-mae subway stop. S Y24,500+, Tw Y34,500+ (D).

＊＊ **Hotel New Ōtani** ホテルニューオタニ (3265-1111). Fax 3221-2619. 4-1 Kioichō, Chiyoda-ku. Biggest hotel in Tokyo. S Y25–27,000, Tw Y30–48,000 (D).

**Hotel Yōkō Akasaka** ホテル陽光赤坂 赤坂6-14-12 (3586-4050). Fax 3586-5944. 6-14-12 Akasaka, Minato-ku. Business hotel. S Y8500–10,000, Tw Y15,000 (M).

**III:2 Aoyama, Harajuku** (see map, p. 220)

⑦ ＊ **Tokyo Aoyama Kaikan** 東京青山会館 南青山4-17-58 (3403-1541). Fax 3403-5450. 4-17-58 Minami-Aoyama, Minato-ku. Near Omotesandō. Hotel for teachers, but nonmembers can stay. Friendly. No English spoken. S Y5500, Tw Y9000 (D).

⑱ ＊ **Harajuku Trim** 原宿トリム 神宮前6-28-6 (3498-2101). Fax 3498-1777. 6-28-6 Jingūmae, Shibuya-ku. Business-hotel style. In-house sports facilities. S Y7700, Tw Y12–15,000 (M).

＊ **Asia Center** アジアセンター 赤坂8-10-32 (3402-6111). Fax 3402-0738. 8-10-32 Akasaka, Minato-ku. Good location in quiet residential area. Plain, has everything you need but nothing extra. S Y4500 w/o bath, Y5400 w/bath, Tw Y6000+ w/o bath, Y9200+ w/bath (B).

＊＊ **President Hotel** プレジデントホテル 南青山2-2-3 (3497-0111). Fax 3401-4816. 2-2-3 Minami-Aoyama, Minato-ku. Small city hotel with European fantasy decor, but very comfortable, with excellent service and location, 0:01h on foot from Aoyama Itchōme subway stop. S Y11,100, Tw Y15–22,200 (E).

**III:3 Shibuya** (see map, p. 222)

② **Shibuya Tōkyū Inn** 渋谷東急イン (3498-0109). Fax 3498-6189. 1-24-10 Shibuya, Shibuya-ku. Chain business hotel. S Y12,000, Tw Y17,600–18,600 (E).

⑪ **Shibuya Tōbu Hotel** 渋谷東武ホテル (3476-0111). Fax 3476-0903. 3-1 Udagawachō, Shibuya-ku. Pleasant but very small rooms. S Y11–12,700, Tw Y19–30,000 w/ tax, service (E).

⑭ **Hillport Hotel** ヒルポートホテル 桜ケ丘町23-19 (3462-5171). Fax 3496-2066. 23-19 Sakuragaokachō, Shibuya-ku. Most rooms are singles, for business travelers, and small for the price. 0:03h walk from Shibuya station. S Y11–12,900, Tw Y17,800–23,000 (E).

**IV:1–2 Shinjuku, Ikebukuro**

① ＊＊＊ **Tokyo Hilton International** 東京ヒルトン (3344-5111). Fax 3342-6094. 6-6-2 Nishi-Shinjuku, Shinjuku-ku. Luxurious accommodations and fine service. Kyōbue restaurant is excellent. S Y26–36,000, Tw Y32–42,000 (D).

② ＊＊ **Century Hyatt Tokyo** センチュリーハイアット (3349-0111). Fax 3344-5575. 2-7-2 Nishi-Shinjuku, Shinjuku-ku. Rooms are large and pleasantly furnished. Free shuttle to and from Shinjuku station. Sky pool, men's and women's sauna, pleasant restaurants w/decent food at decent prices. S Y21,000, Tw Y30–34,000 (D).

③ **Keiō Plaza Intercontinental Hotel** 京王プラザホテル (3344-0111). Fax 3345-8269. 2-2-1 Nishi-Shinjuku, Shinjuku-ku. Huge. South wing is newer, rooms are bright and nicely appointed, but service is poor and restaurants substandard. S Y21,000, Tw 26,000+ (D).

④ ＊ **Shinjuku Washington Hotel** 新宿ワシントンホテル (3343-3111). Fax 3342-2575. 3-2-9 Nishi-Shinjuku, Shinjuku-ku. Sleek design. S Y11,600, Tw Y 16–25,000 (E).

＊ **Kimi Ryokan** 喜美旅館 池袋2-36-8 (3971-3766). 2-1034 Ikebukuro, Toshima-ku. Rebuilt 1986. Recommended for budget travelers. Tradeoff is the location. Friendly owners; English spoken. S Y3800–4300, Tw Y6–7000 (B).

**Elegant Inn Yasuda** エレガントイン安田 世田谷区松原1-56-28 (3322-5546). Fax 3543-7232. 1-56-28 Matsubara, Setagaya-ku. *Take the Keiō line from Shinjuku 2 stations to Daitabashi, then walk 4 minutes.* Mr. Yasuda Hiroyasu has turned his home into a hospitable 16-room inn. The rooms are air-conditioned and come in Japanese and Western style. Bathrooms are shared. Mr. Yasuda speaks English and Chinese. S Y3800, Tw Y5600 (B).

**Four Seasons Hotel Chinzan-sō** フォーシーズンホテル 椿山荘東京 東京都文京区 関口2-10-8 (3943-2222). Fax 3943-2300. 2-10-8 Sekiguchi, Bunkyō-ku. Super luxurious newcomer geared to business travelers, 0:10h by car from Ikebukuro Station. S Y41–57,000, Tw Y45–59,000, Suites Y67–450,000 (D).

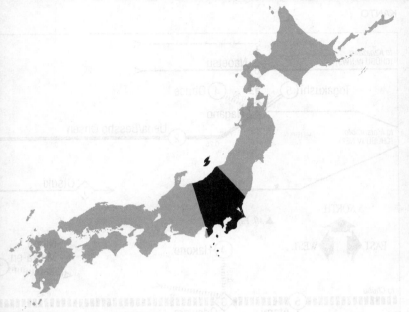

# Kantō

Although Tokyo is the epicenter of Japan's modernization, the surrounding regions of Kantō and eastern Chūbu (included in this chapter) contain numerous historical attractions, most of them within a few hours' train ride from the city. Foremost in interest are the medieval capital of Kamakura and the mausoleums of Tokugawa Ieyasu and Iemitsu at Nikkō. Other less frequented regions, such as Kawagoe, Nagano, and the Izu Peninsula, offer glimpses of a Japan that has all but vanished from Tokyo. The area's convenience to Tokyo is also its liability; see Seasons to find out about crowds.

## BEST ATTRACTIONS

I:N1    ✱✱✱ **Nikkō.** The ornate mausoleums of Tokugawa Ieyasu and Iemitsu. An excellent day or overnight trip from Tokyo (p. 239).

II:N3   ✱✱ **Sado Island.** Japan's fifth largest island offers unspoiled countryside and fishing villages (p. 246).

II:NW3  ✱✱ **Nagano.** Nagano's Zenkō-ji is one of Japan's most popular pilgrimage temples. Nearby is Togakushi, a scenic mountain area that was a center for *yamabushi* priests (p. 250).

IV:W2   ✱✱✱ **Kamakura.** Japan's military capital from the 12th to the 14th centuries, rich in temples, art, and history (p. 257).

IV:W6   ✱✱ **Izu Peninsula.** Mountains, ocean views, hot springs, and charming historical towns (p. 268).

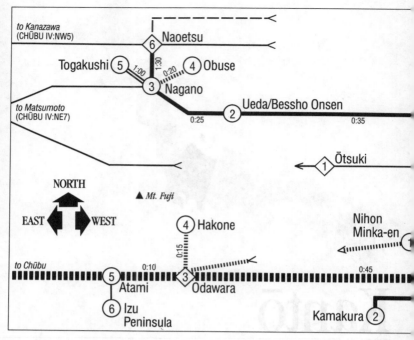

## Seasons

The south coast has a climate similar to Tokyo's, perhaps somewhat warmer in Kamakura and Izu, while the mountainous regions around Nikkō and eastern Chūbu are cooler and less humid, as is Sado Island. Niigata is in Japan's Snow Country, with very deep snowfall. Nikkō, Kamakura, and Hakone are extremely crowded during national holidays, the spring and fall season (weekends especially), and from July 20–Aug. 31; during these peak times, many resort hotels charge much higher rates. The Jōetsu Shinkansen, Chūō main line, and Shin'etsu line are all extremely crowded on weekends during the ski season.

### Average Temperature °C (°F)/Days of Rain or Snow

|  | January | April | July | October |
|---|---|---|---|---|
| Nikkō | 1.0 (33.8)/4 | 11.1 (52.0)/10 | 23.8 (74.8)/13 | 14.8 (58.6)/10 |
| Niigata | 1.8 (35.2)/22 | 10.4 (50.7)/12 | 24.2 (75.6)/11 | 15.4 (59.7)/14 |
| Nagano | −1.5 (29.3)/11 | 9.8 (49.6)/9 | 23.7 (74.7)/12 | 13.2 (55.8)/8 |
| Atami | 5.7 (42.3)/6 | 14.0 (57.2)/12 | 25.2 (77.4)/11 | 15.7 (60.3)/10 |

### Traveling

The main train lines into Kantō and eastern Chūbu radiate out of Tokyo, primarily from four stations: Asakusa, Ueno, Tokyo, and Shinjuku.

| Route | Starting Point | Line | Main Destinations | Continuing on to |
|---|---|---|---|---|
| I:N | Asakusa | Tōbu-Nikkō* | Nikkō | Tōhoku |
| II:NE | Ueno | Tōhoku Shinkansen | Utsunomiya | Tōhoku |
| II:N | Ueno | Jōetsu Shinkansen | Niigata, Sado | Tōhoku or Chūbu |
| II:NW | Ueno | Shin'etsu | Nagano | Chūbu |
| III:N | Shinjuku | Seibu-Shinjuku* | Kawagoe | |
| III:W | Shinjuku | Chūō | Fuji, Matsumoto | Chūbu |
| III:SW | Shinjuku | Odakyū* | Hakone | |
| IV:W | Tokyo | Yokosuka | Kamakura | |
| IV:W | Tokyo | Tōkaidō Shinkansen | Atami, Izu | Chūbu |

\* private lines

# SPECIAL INTERESTS

**Onsen:** Hot springs in this region offer the quintessential Japanese-style retreat from Tokyo. Highly developed and famous spas include the Hakone region and Atami. At Nozawa Onsen, north of Nagano, one can go "bath crawling" among a dozen public bathhouses. There are also many interesting rustic spas for those seeking a more peaceful venue. Some of the best: Oku-Nikkō and Oku-Kinu areas, Hōshi Onsen, Takaragawa Onsen, Ōsawa Onsen (Izu Peninsula). Jigokudani at Yudanaka Onsen, near Nagano, is famed for its bathing monkeys.
**Well-Preserved Towns:** Two easy day-trips from Tokyo are to Kawagoe, with its Edo-style merchant houses, and Nihon Minka-en, an excellent open-air museum of Japanese farmhouses. Matsuzaki has many tile-and-plaster houses typical of the Izu Peninsula. Unnojuku has a preserved stretch of an old post town.

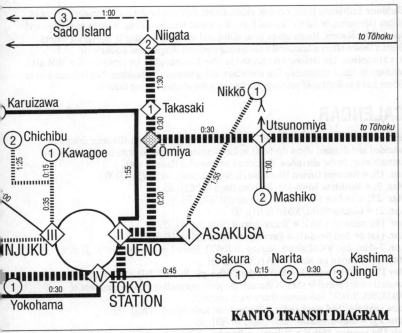

## KANTŌ TRANSIT DIAGRAM

237

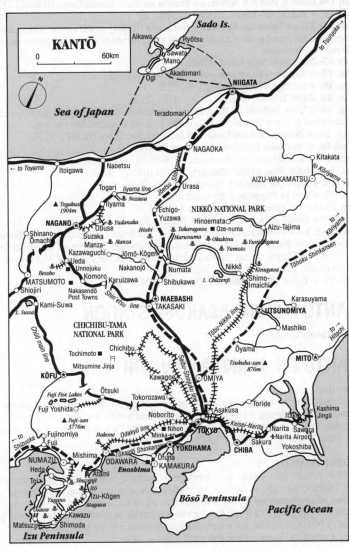

### KANTŌ

0        60km

*Sea of Japan*

NIKKŌ NATIONAL PARK

CHICHIBU-TAMA
NATIONAL PARK

*Sado Is.*

*Pacific Ocean*

*Bōsō Peninsula*

*Izu Peninsula*

**Outdoor Activities:** Japan's classic climb, up Mt. Fuji, can be done as a two-day trip out of Tokyo. Oze-numa, in Nikkō National Park, is a scenic marshy plateau. It offers easy hikes and spectacular flowers. Manza offers good skiing and aprés-ski soaking in hot-spring waters. Bessho Onsen offers a historical walk among medieval temples and countryside.

**Art Museums:** The Hakone Art Museum in Gōra is outstanding for ceramics. The MOA Art Museum in Atami combines a fine collection with a memorable building. The Hokusai-kan in Obuse has a collection of paintings attributed to the ukiyo-e master Hokusai.

# CALENDAR

**Jan. 14: ✱✱ Nakanojō no Tori-oi.** Nakanojō (II:N1). Ten 2-meter-diameter drums are pounded and dragged about the fields in the morning, in a rite to drive harmful birds and animals away. In the afternoon, the drums are paraded through town.

**Jan. 15: ✱ Nozawa Onsen Hi-matsuri.** Nozawa Onsen (II:NW5). F E

**Mar. 9: ✱ Kashima Saitō-sai.** Kashima Jingū (IV:E3). V

**Mar. 27: ✱ Yudate Shishi-mai.** Hakone (IV:W4). P

**Apr. 2: ✱ Gōhan-Shiki.** Nikkō (I:N1). E

**Apr. (Su nearest 10th): ✱ Tenzushimai.** Kōfu (III:W). P V

**Apr. (1st or 2nd Sa–Su): ✱ Furyūmono.** Hitachi (II). P V

**Apr. 7–May 26: ✱ Gokaichō.** Nagano (II:NW3). Every 7 yr (next in 1997). E V B

**May 17: ✱ Ennen no Mai.** Nikkō (I:N1). P B

**May 17–18: ✱✱ Grand Festival of the Tōshō-gū.** Nikkō (I:N1). On the 18th, armor-clad samurai escort portable shrines through the town, reenacting the enshrinement of TOKUGAWA IEYASU. *Yabusame* (horseback archery).

**June (usually 2nd weekend): ✱ Takigi Noh.** Sado Island (II:N3). P

**June 15: ✱ Tsuburosashi.** Sado Island (II:N3). P

**July (Su nearest 15th): ✱ Nobori no Bessho no Take.** Bessho Onsen (II:NW2). P V S

**July 15: ✱ Yudate Shishimai.** Hakone (IV:W4). P

**July 25–27: ✱✱ Yama'age Matsuri.** Karasuyama (II:NE1). At this remote village, three large floats are joined to form a Kabuki dance stage, on which a variety of performances are offered over three days.

**July 27–28: ✱ Noh.** Sado Island (II:N3). P

**Aug. 15: ✱ Nagatoro Funatama-sai.** Nagatoro (III:N2). V

**Aug. 16: ✱ Kiraigō.** Hikari-machi (IV:E). P B

**Aug. 23–24: ✱ Tsunabi Ningyō.** Ina-mura (II). P V

**Aug. 26–27: ✱✱ Yoshida no Hi-matsuri.** Fuji-Yoshida (III:W1). Sengen Jinja. Spectacular torch festival to honor the goddess of Fuji. The *mikoshi* is shaped like Mt. Fuji.

**Sept. 16: ✱ Tsurugaoka Hachiman-gū Matsuri.** Kamakura (IV:W2). P V

**Sept. 18: ✱ Menkake Gyōretsu.** Kamakura (IV:W2). P

**Sept. 21–22: ✱ Takigi-Noh.** Kamakura (IV:W2). P

**Oct. 5: ✱ Muku Jinja Ryūsei Matsuri.** Yoshida (III:N2). E V

**Oct. 15: ✱ Kawagoe Matsuri.** Kawagoe (III:N1). E V

**Oct. 15: ✱ Bun'ya Puppets.** Sado Island (II:N3). P

**Oct. 15–16: ✱ Chitochinton.** Sado Island (II:N3). P

**Oct. 17: ✱ Tōshō-gū Autumn Festival.** Nikkō (I:N1). V

**Dec. 2–3: ✱✱✱ Yo-matsuri.** Chichibu (III:N2). This festival celebrates the annual meeting of the male and female deities of two shrines. It is renowned for gorgeous, lantern-lit floats and fireworks. During the day, Kabuki and dance are offered on the floats. Main events are on the evening of the 3rd.

**Dec. 15: ✱ Teppō (Rifle) Matsuri.** Ogano (III:N2). P E

# KANTŌ I. FROM ASAKUSA STATION

**Prefectures:** Tochigi

# KANTŌ I:N. NIKKŌ AND VICINITY

**Traveling**

Nikkō well deserves to be one of the most popular day trips from Tokyo, but to beat the crowds, consider turning it into a three-day trip; spend a night, see Nikkō in the early morning, then push on into the interior of Nikkō National Park, to a region of wild mountains and onsen lodges.

## SHIMO-IMAICHI  下今市

*1:35h by private Tōbu-Nikkō line express from Asakusa; junction to Tōbu-Kinugawa line.* Visible to the right, as the train approaches the station, is a section of the famous **avenue of cryptomerias** lining the approach to the Nikkō mausoleum. The trees were planted over 20 years by a frugal daimyo who was unable or unwilling to offer a lavish gift. Some 13,000 trees survive. From Kami-Imaichi, one station to the west, you can walk along a stretch of the avenue and then catch a bus to Nikkō.

## N1 ✳✳✳ NIKKŌ 日光

*1:55h by private Tōbu-Nikkō line from Tōbu-Asakusa station in Tokyo. From Tokyo or Ueno station, 0:45–0:50h by Tōhoku Shinkansen to Utsunomiya, then 0:45h by JR Nikkō line.* The deep forests and mountains of Nikkō have been sacred for more than 1,200 years, ever since a holy man, Shōdō Shōnin, opened Futara-san ("two unruly mountains") to Buddhism. Later, the great Tendai priest Ennin (see Hiraizumi History, p. 169) converted the region into a Tendai preserve. In 1617, TOKUGAWA IEYASU was enshrined at the Tōshō-gū. His grandson IEMITSU completely rebuilt the shrine and, in 1653, was himself enshrined at the nearby Taiyūin-byō. Today, millions of tourists visit the two mausoleums, the most ornate and expensive buildings in Japan. Not a few visitors, admirers of Zen restraint, are shocked by their lavishness. But to dismiss the Nikkō shrines as an aberration would be to misunderstand the spirit of the age in which they were built.

### Calendar

**Apr. 2:** ✳ **Gōhan-shiki.** Rinnō-ji Sanbutsu-dō. *Yamabushi* priests try to force a group of men to eat an immense quantity of rice as a form of prayer for a prosperous year. At 9:30, 11:30, and 14:30.

**Apr. 13–17: Yayoisai.** Futara-san Jinja. 15 floats are festooned with great sprays of paper flowers.

**May 17:** ✳ **Ennen no Mai.** Rinnō-ji Sanbutsu-dō. (See Matsuri, p. 74.) Space for 400 only; first come first served.

**May 17–18: ✳✳ Grand Festival of the Tōshō-gū.** On the 17th, there is an exhibition of equestrian archery from 11:30–13:30. On the 18th, a "thousand-samurai" procession reenacts bringing Ieyasu's remains to Nikkō. Hrs: 11:00–14:00.

**July 31–Aug. 7: Tōhai-sai.** Futara-san Jinja at Chūzenji-ko. Pilgrims climb Nantai-san through the night. There are also Bon dances and lantern-floating on the lake.

**Oct. 17: Tōshō-gū Autumn Festival.** Thousand-samurai parade. Hrs: 10:00–14:00.

### Nikkō Sights

The sights begin at Shinkyō bridge, about 1 km (0:05h by bus) from Tōbu-Nikkō and Nikkō stations. Shrine and temple hours: Apr.–Oct. 8:00–17:00. Nov.–Mar. 8:00–16:00.

**Shinkyō (Sacred Bridge)** 神橋 (ICP). This arched red bridge spans the Daiyagawa at the spot where Shōdō Shōnin was carried across on the backs of two giant serpents in his quest to reach the summit of sacred Nantai-san. The bridge, built in 1636 for the exclusive use of the shogun and imperial envoys, was destroyed in a flood in 1902 and rebuilt in 1907. A fee is charged for the privilege of crossing (Hrs: 9:00–16:00). Across the road, at the base of the steps to Rinnō-ji, is a stone monument erected in 1648, bearing Lord Matsudaira Masatsuna's dedication of the famous cryptomeria avenue, planted by his order.

**✳✳ Rinnō-ji** 輪王寺 Founded by Shōdō Shōnin 1,200 years ago, this is now a Tendai temple. In 1654, the temple acquired an imperial abbot. The **Sanbutsu-dō** (1648, ICP), the largest hall at Nikkō, enshrines three huge gilt images of Amida Nyorai, Thousand-Armed Kannon, and Batō (Horse-Headed) Kannon, an unusual trinity that is the Buddhist manifestation of the three kami of Futara-san. The nine-ringed spire outside, **Sōrintō** (1643, ICP), was erected over a cache of buried sutras and is decorated with the Tokugawa crest. The **Hōmotsuden** exhibits some of the temple's considerable store of treasures.

**✳✳✳ Nikkō Tōshō-gū** 日光東照宮 This celebrated shrine-mausoleum is consecrated to Tokugawa Ieyasu, his predecessor, Toyotomi Hideyoshi, and his putative ancestor, the first of the governing shoguns, Minamoto no Yoritomo. (See Nikkō history, p. 242.) The practice of identifying a human as a kami and a *gongen* (avatar) is inherently syncretic. Nikkō is one of the rare places that preserves many temple structures — for example, the Niō gate, pagoda, sutra library, drum and bell towers — though it has officially been a Shinto shrine since the Meiji period.

The granite torii (1618, ICP) is one of the largest stone torii in Japan. The five-story pagoda (1818, ICP) is decorated with bright colors and has a peculiar shape: the first four stories are *wayō* ("Japanese" style), the uppermost is Zen style (see Buddhism, p. 39). The twelve "frog-crotch" struts on the first level contain carvings of the twelve Chinese zodiac animals. The Omote-mon or Niō Gate (ICP), at the top of a flight of stone steps, has two images of the Niō and a carving of a *baku*, a mythical creature who devours dreams. One must pay a fee to continue beyond this gate.

On the right side, beyond the Niō Gate, are three sacred storehouses (ICP), lacquered *azekura* (log cabin) structures containing sacred ritual objects. The upper storehouse has carvings of elephants, said to be based on sketches by KANŌ TAN'YŪ. On the left side of the path is the sacred stable, the only unpainted wood structure in the precincts. It is decorated with the famous **Three Monkeys** ("See no Evil, Hear no Evil, and Speak no Evil"), monkeys being guardian spirits of the horse, as well as chasers of evil spirits. Look for the numerous lanterns of stone, bronze, and iron, the gifts of many daimyo. The **Rinzō** (sutra library), to the left after the second torii, contains a revolving octagonal structure holding a 7,000-volume complete set of Buddhist scriptures; one spin is equivalent to reading them all.

On the next level are a bell tower and drum tower, one on each side of the approach. The bronze candelabrum by the bell tower and the revolving lantern by the drum tower were gifts of the Dutch government (the only European power that had

239

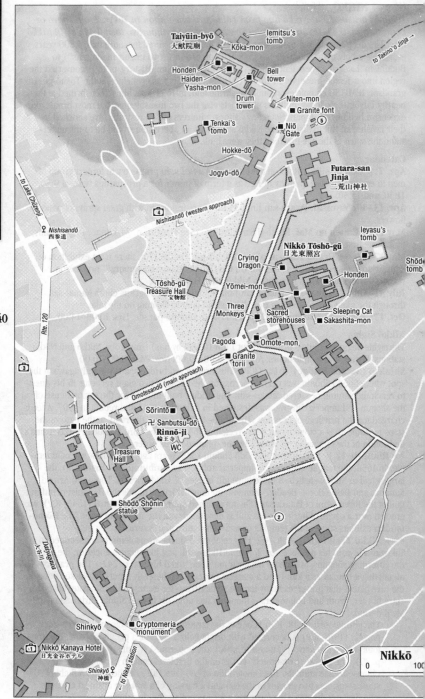

Taiyūin-byō
大猷院廟
Iemitsu's tomb
Kōka-mon
Honden
Haiden
Yasha-mon
Bell tower
Drum tower
Niten-mon
Granite font
Niō Gate
Tenkai's tomb
Hokke-dō
Jogyō-dō
Futara-san Jinja
二荒山神社
to Takino'o Jinja
⑤

Nishisandō (western approach) ④
Nishisandō
西参道
Ieyasu's tomb
Nikkō Tōshō-gū
日光東照宮
Shōd
tomb
Crying Dragon
Honden
Yōmei-mon
Tōshō-gū Treasure Hall
宝物館
Three Monkeys
Sacred storehouses
Sleeping Cat
Sakashita-mon
Pagoda
Omote-mon
Granite torii

Rte. 120
③

Omotesandō (main approach)
Sōrintō
卍 Sanbutsu-dō
Information
Rinnō-ji
輪王寺
WC
Treasure Hall
②
Shōdō Shōnin statue

Daiyagawa
大谷川
to Nikkō Station
Shinkyō
Cryptomeria monument
Nikkō Kanaya Hotel
日光金谷ホテル
Shinkyō
神橋
N
Nikkō
0          100

relations with the Tokugawa shogunate); the Tokugawa crests were cast upside-down on the lantern. Behind the drum tower is the **Honji-dō** (ICP), a large hall famous for its huge ceiling painting, the *Nakiryū* (Crying Dragon, ICP), which seems to emit a ringing cry when one claps one's hands at the spot directly beneath it.

The incredibly ornate ◆ **Yōmei-mon** (NT) marks the entrance to the next enclosure. Low-ranking samurai could go no farther, and high-ranking samurai were obliged to leave their swords outside. The gate is lavishly decorated: lions and dragons leap from every bracket, and mythical beasts, Chinese sages, immortals, and children adorn every surface. Look for tigers whose stripes are rendered by the natural grain of the timber. Most of the gate is painted white, with gold leaf covering the banks of bracketing. Of the 12 supporting columns, one was carved upside-down, a deliberate flaw calculated to mollify evil spirits who might otherwise be driven to paroxysms of jealousy by the gate's beauty. The gate is flanked by ornate, 220-meter-long fences and galleries (NT) enclosing the inner compound.

Inside the enclosure, on the left, is the **Jinyō-sha** (ICP), housing the three *mikoshi* (portable shrines) for the three kami (Ieyasu, Hideyoshi, and Yoritomo) enshrined at Tōshō-gū. The innermost gate, the ◆ **Kara-mon** (Chinese gate, NT), is an unusual structure with Chinese-style gables on all four sides. A mythical animal atop the front gable keeps watch over the grounds. Enter the inner area by the Sakashita-mon (ICP), to the right. The famous **Nemurineko** (Sleeping Cat, NT) carving is curled up in one of the open struts of the gallery. The innermost buildings are the ◆ **Haiden** (Oratory) and **Honden** (Main Hall), which are linked in the Gongen style (see Shinto, p. 27). The east antechamber of the Haiden was reserved for the shogun and the three Tokugawa collateral houses. The west antechamber was reserved for the imperial abbot of Rinnō-ji. Return to Sakashita-mon and exit. A long flight of stone steps leads up to the **tomb of Ieyasu**.

✳✳ **Futara-san Jinja** 二荒山神社 Hrs: 8:00–17:00; Nov.–Mar. 9:00–16:00. Founded in 782 by Shōdō Shōnin, this shrine is dedicated to the mountains Nantai (male), Nyotai (female), and their "child mountain," Tarō, all ancient centers of mountain worship. The shrine's bronze torii and colorful halls are ICP, but more famous are the **bake-tōro**, a demon lantern which bears sword scars inflicted by a frightened samurai, and the **Kōya-maki**, an ancient umbrella pine said to have been planted by KŌBŌ DAISHI. **Takino'o Jinja** (ICP), a branch shrine, is a 0:40h walk up a peaceful, stone-paved path.

✳ **Jogyō-dō and Hokke-dō** 常行堂・法華堂 Two halls on the path to Taiyūin-byō, belonging to Rinnō-ji and housing many Buddhist images removed from the Nikkō shrines during the Meiji period.

✳✳✳ **Taiyūin-byō** 大猷院廟 Mausoleum of Ieyasu's grandson, the powerful third shogun Iemitsu. Completed in 1653. Smaller but as ornate as the Tōshō-gū, it is set even more beautifully in a dense cryptomeria forest; while the Tōshō-gū is dazzling and overpowering, the Taiyūin-byō is considered more balanced and esthetically superior. The ornately carved **Niō Gate** marks the entrance. To the left are sacred storehouses similar to those at Tōshō-gū. To the right is a large granite font under a roof supported by 12 granite pillars. On the ceiling is a painting of a dragon gazing at its reflection in the water. Up the left stairs is the **Niten-mon**, a gate guarded on the outside by two of the Four Buddhist Guardian Kings and on the inside by the gods of wind and thunder. On the next level are a small drum tower and bell tower, and the **Yasha-mon**, a richly gilded gate housing four images of Yasha, or guardian spirits. The gallery extending to both sides is decorated with carvings of peonies. The final gate, **Kara-mon** (Chinese gate) and inner gallery contain exquisitely carved openwork of pines, bamboo, plum, and doves. The inner structures—**Haiden** (NT), **Ai no Ma** (connecting chamber, ICP), and **Honden** (ICP)—form a Gongen-style complex. The Kanō Yasunobu and Tan'yū paintings of Chinese lions in the Haiden are famous. The Honden houses a sumptuous lacquered altar containing a wooden image of Iemitsu. To the right of this complex, a break in the enclosure leads to the Kōka-mon, a Ming Chinese-style white plaster gate. Iemitsu's cast-bronze tomb stands beyond.

241

✳ **Tōshō-gū Treasure Hall (Hōmotsukan)** 東照宮宝物館 Hrs: 8:30–17:00; Dec.–Mar. 8:30–16:00. Shrine treasures.

## Nikkō Dining

The local specialty is *yuba*, a thin, soft "skin" skimmed from soybean milk. It is used in a variety of Buddhist vegetarian dishes.

② **Meiji no Yakata** 明治の館 (53-3751). Hrs: 11:00–20:00; clsd W (except in Aug., Oct.), NY. A pleasant complex of restaurants serving Western and some Japanese dishes, housed in a Meiji-period stone lodge. Trout Y1500, beefsteak Y2500.

⑤ **Futara Chaya** 二荒茶屋 (54-0535). Hrs: 9:00–16:00; Apr.–Oct. 8:00–17:00. Coffee and Japanese refreshments: *matcha* (tea-ceremony tea), *amazake* (sweet, slightly fermented rice drink), *konbu-cha* (kelp tea).

## Nikkō Lodgings (TEL 0288)

Pensions offer the best buys around Nikkō. Owners of the hard-to-find pensions will pick you up if you call from the station. (A dozen Nikkō pensions have formed an association; if one is full, they can refer you to another.)

① ✳✳ **Nikkō Kanaya Hotel** 日光金谷ホテル (54-0001; in Tokyo, 03-3271-5215). Fax 53-2487. 1300 Kamihatsuishi-chō, Nikkō-shi, Tochigi-ken. Classic resort hotel, in business since 1873. S Y6–25,000, Tw Y7–30,000. (High season rates apply July 20–Aug. 31, Oct. 1–Nov. 3, Dec. 30–Jan. 5, and weekends in Apr.–Nov.) AX, DC, V, MC.

③ **Pension Turtle** ペンションタートル (53-3168). 2-16 Takumi-chō. Near Tōshō-gū, on quiet street by river. Clean and comfortable. S Y3900–4900, Tw Y6800–8800. AX.

④ **Nikkō Pension** 日光ペンション (53-3636). 8-10 Nishisandō. Y8–9500 w/meals.

**Logettel St. Bois** ロヂテルサンボア (53-0082). 1560 Tokorono. On quiet hillside, 0:15h walk from station. Two Japanese rooms w/bath, Western Tw, and bunks. Y7500–8000 w/meals. AX, V.

**Pension Green City** ペンショングリーンシティ (53-4744). 1773 Kujira-chō. American Gothic. Y8500–10500 w/meals. AX, V, DC, MC.

**Pension Lambchop** ペンションラムチャップ (53-4359). 1541-12 Tokorono. The chef studied in Italy. Y7100 w/meals.

**Nikkō Daiyagawa YH** 日光大谷川YH (54-1974). 1075 Nakahatsuishi. Y3000 w/meals.

**Nikkō YH** 日光YH (54-1013). 2854 Tokorono. Y3700–3900 w/meals.

# Nikkō History: Tokugawa Ieyasu

**Tokugawa Ieyasu**        (1543–1616) Founder of the Tokugawa shogunate, which
                          ruled for 250 years. He is worshipped as "Gongen-sama" at
                          the Nikkō Tōshō-gū.

**Tokugawa Iemitsu**      (1604–1651) Ieyasu's grandson, who completed the consol-
                          idation of Tokugawa power. He totally rebuilt the Nikkō Tōshō-
                          gū and had himself enshrined nearby at the Taiyūin-byō.

**Priest Tenkai**         (d. 1643) Ieyasu's advisor on the establishment of the Tōshō-
                          gū shrines and the great temple complex at Ueno in Edo.

TOKUGAWA IEYASU is probably the single most important figure in Japanese history.
A man of incredible caution, with an almost superhuman ability to bide his time, he
knew how to take swift, sure action at the critical moments. He waited until he was
past the age of sixty, strengthening his position while his major rivals died, before he
saw his chance and seized supreme power. After a lifetime of patience, it is fitting that
his death became his crowning achievement. Ieyasu became a god, an avatar:
Gongen-sama, the protector of the realm (see Shinto, p. 27). His shrine, the **Nikkō
Tōshō-gū**, employed nearly every major artisan in the country and required over
23,000 man-days for gilding alone. In sheer ornateness, it remains unsurpassed.

Ieyasu was forced early to learn the lesson of patience. His father was a minor
lord caught between the powerful Imagawa and the Oda. When he became allied to
the Imagawa, he was obliged to hand over Ieyasu, then four years old, as a political
hostage. Before he could reach the Imagawa, however, Ieyasu was kidnapped by Oda
forces, and it was not until a truce two years later that he could be sent to his original
destination. He spent twelve years with the Imagawa; although he was well treated, he
was nevertheless a prisoner. At the age of eighteen, when he had already fought his
first battle, married, and fathered a child, he was finally able to return home.

Ieyasu's years as a hostage taught him to swallow his anger and move slowly. In
his instructions to his descendants, he says: "When excessive desires are harbored in
your heart, look back upon the days of extremity you have passed through. Bear in
mind that patience leads to a long life of security, while wrath is your own enemy. To
think much of your conquering and little of your stooping—that will fare ill with
you." A corollary of this worldly wisdom was not to quarrel with the powerful. In
1561, Ieyasu switched his allegiance from the Imagawa to ODA NOBUNAGA, even
though his own wife was from an Imagawa vassal family. In 1579, Nobunaga accused
her and her eldest son of disloyalty, and Ieyasu put them to death at Nobunaga's
command, for he was not a man to allow human feelings to stand in the way of his
rise to power.

Nobunaga was assassinated in 1582, and the role of hegemon fell to HIDE-
YOSHI, with whom Ieyasu fought briefly and inconclusively before they agreed to a
truce. In 1590, they joined forces and defeated the Hōjō, who controlled the Kantō
region. Hideyoshi offered to give Ieyasu eight provinces, including all of Kantō, in
exchange for the five provinces Ieyasu held in central Japan. Ieyasu knew that Hideyoshi's generosity was a ploy to weaken him by separating him from his ancestral fief,
removing him as far as possible from center stage—and a chance at supreme power.
Ieyasu, however, chose to see it as an excellent opportunity to increase his own
power base, unimpeded. He nodded agreement and said "Let's go piss on it." Posterity has dubbed them "the pissing pals of Kantō."

At Hideyoshi's suggestion, Ieyasu set up his new capital at Edo (Tokyo), a clump
of miserable hovels around a large rundown castle, sitting in the midst of a marsh.
He marched his bewildered retainers past the well-defended and heavily fortified
former Hōjō capital of Odawara, past Kamakura, into this most unpromising piece of
territory and set them to work dredging the land and constructing places to live (see
Tokyo History, p. 195). When Hideyoshi was seeking generals to lead the ill-fated
invasion of Korea in 1592, Ieyasu excused himself, saying he was still busy organizing
and building his new fief.

Then, in 1598, Hideyoshi died. Ieyasu was named to a council of daimyo that
was established to protect Hideyoshi's heir, HIDEYORI. Ieyasu's enthusiastic acquittal
of his duties aroused the enmity of other lords, particularly those in western Japan,
who saw that he was in fact seizing power for himself. In 1600, Ieyasu and his allies
defeated these lords in the decisive **Battle of Sekigahara**.

In 1603, Ieyasu became shogun, officially beginning an age of Tokugawa rule
that would continue uninterrupted for over 250 years. Although he passed on the title
to his son Hidetada in 1605, he continued to build his power, playing the same game

of political musical chairs that Hideyoshi had played with him, moving trusted daimyo into strategic fiefs and keeping potential rivals at a safe distance.

Ieyasu now began to enjoy his supreme position, the product of an entire lifetime of waiting. He "retired" to the seaside castle town of Shizuoka, where he could indulge his passion for falconry and concern himself with foreign affairs. His friendship with **Will Adams**, the English navigator who was shipwrecked on Japanese shores in 1600, is the stuff of legend as well as popular fiction (*Shogun*). Western visitors brought him gifts, including a Spanish clock, tortoise-frame spectacles, and a lead pencil, which are carefully preserved at the Kunō-zan Tōshō-gū near Shizuoka.

Yet Ieyasu was still playing a waiting game. Hideyoshi's son Hideyori, the last remaining threat to Tokugawa power, was ensconced in Ōsaka Castle. Not until 1614, when Ieyasu was absolutely sure of his strength, did he lay siege to Ōsaka. But in spite of all efforts, the great fortress proved impregnable. In the end, Ieyasu had to resort to a phony truce in order to take the castle and force Hideyori to commit suicide.

Now only one task remained. Ieyasu let it be known among religious circles that he was looking for advice on how to become a kami. He finally chose his long-time advisor, the Tendai Buddhist priest **Tenkai**, to guide him through the vagaries of Buddhist-Shinto syncretism that would allow him to be declared a human incarnation, or a *gongen* (avatar), of the Buddha. Ieyasu's predecessor, Hideyoshi, had provided a precedent by arranging to be deified at his shrine-mausoleum in Kyoto, known as Hōkoku-byō, or Toyokuni Jinja (Kyoto, p. 334). (The Tokugawa later tore it down.)

Since "Gongen-sama" was supposed to be "protector of the realm," Tenkai looked for a place to the north of the capital, to protect its unlucky direction. He settled on Futara-san, a syncretic holy mountain with both a Tendai temple and a shrine, a two-day journey north of the capital. Ieyasu approved the choice, sight unseen. Ieyasu's mausoleum was built between **Rinnō-ji**, the old Tendai temple, and **Futara-san Jinja**, the shrine. Nikkō is the Chinese-style pronunciation of Futara (Two Unruly Mountains). The sound Nikkō can also be written with characters that mean "sun light." Ieyasu's mausoleum was named Eastern Light Shrine (Tōshō-gū) in reference to this more complimentary meaning of Nikkō. Tenkai insisted that Ieyasu's old foe Hideyoshi also be enshrined — as a sort of consolation — as well as Ieyasu's putative ancestor, MINAMOTO NO YORITOMO. Tenkai also erected another Tōshō-gū at Ueno, on the north edge of Edo, so that "Gongen-sama" could protect the capital at close range.

When Ieyasu died in 1616, supposedly from overindulging in tempura, his cremated remains were enshrined on Kunō-zan, his favorite falconry spot (Chūbu, p. 277). The following year, in 1617, the Nikkō Tōshō-gū was completed, and Ieyasu's ashes were transferred there in a magnificent procession (reenacted during the annual Grand Festival in May).

IEMITSU, Ieyasu's worshipful grandson, totally rebuilt the Tōshō-gū, making it so ornate and costly that no other lord would ever be able to rival it. At Nikkō, Momoyama architecture reached its pinnacle — and last gasp. Iemitsu's rebuilding project is said to have cost 568,000 *ryō* of gold, 800 pounds of silver, and 1,000 *koku* of rice. An additional 1.69 million man-days of carpentry and 2.83 million man-days of cartage were required to build the shrine. Altogether, it cost perhaps $200 million in today's dollars. It was here that, every year, an imperial messenger came to confirm Ieyasu and his descendants as the legitimate temporal rulers of Japan. Iemitsu had his own impressive mausoleum, the **Taiyūin-byō**, built on the opposite side of Futara-san Jinja.

It was under Iemitsu that the Tokugawa shogunate achieved its ultimate form. The daimyo were compelled to keep their families at Edo; they themselves were required to spend alternate periods (six months to a year) there. Iemitsu forced them to spend enormous sums on their *sankin kōtai* processions to and from Edo, as well as on various public works. He brutally suppressed the Shimabara Christian uprising in 1638, and closed Japan to all European trade except one ship a year from Holland (see Nagasaki History, p. 483). He augmented Ieyasu's strict Code for Warriors, stipulating that marriages between daimyo families, and many other aspects of a lord's life, were to be regulated by the shogunate. Each daimyo had to put up with a *metsuke*, an official Tokugawa spy; in fact, the government was ridden with spies.

Under the Tokugawa system, the lessons of Ieyasu's early days were applied unflinchingly to all of Japan for 250 years. The gaiety of Nikkō belies the fact that nearly every aspect of ordinary life became constrained and grimmer, as people's duties and relationships, as well as their homes and belongings, came under the regime's strict, moralistic codes. Although the old Tokugawa order has disappeared, the mark it has left on the national character remains.

## CHŪZENJI-KO (LAKE) 中禅寺湖

*0:45h by bus from Nikkō station*, via the multiple switchbacks of **Iroha-zaka** (*i-ro-ha* = A-B-C... counting off the hairpin turns); this was originally the pilgrim's approach to sacred Nantai-san. Chūzenji-ko is a resort lake at the foot of the mountain. Nearby 97-meter-high **Kegon Falls** is one of Nikkō's famous attractions; an elevator bored through the cliff takes tourists down to an observation deck. **Futara-san Jinja**, on the lake shore, belongs to a group that includes the main shrine in Nikkō and the shrine at the summit of Nantai-san. The gate and halls date from 1705 (ICP). From July 31–Aug. 7, hundreds of pilgrims gather to make an ascent of Nantai, climbing through the night to reach the summit by dawn.

**Chūzenji-ko Lodgings** (TEL 0288)
∗ **Chūzenji Pension** 中禅寺ペンション (55-0720). Chūzenji-kohan, Nikkō-shi, Tochigi-ken. Lake view. Y8800–9500 w/meals. No CC.
**Hotel Kojōen** ホテル湖上苑 (55-0366). 2478 Chūgūshi, Nikkō-shi. Small lakeside ryokan. Open mid-Apr.–mid-Nov. Y8500–13,000 w/meals. AX, DC, V, MC.
∗ **Chūzenji Kanaya Hotel** 中禅寺金谷ホテル (55-0356; in Tokyo, 03-3271-5215). 2482 Chūgūshi. Old-fashioned lodge on the quiet north shore. Tw Y12–14,500. AX, DC, V, MC.
**Nikkō Prince Hotel** 日光プリンスホテル (55-0661; in Tokyo 03-209-8686). Fax 55-0669. 2485 Shōbugahama, Chūgūshi. Grander than the Kanaya, but less secluded. On the north shore of the lake. Tw only, from Y21,000. AX, DC, V, MC.

### Exploring Oku-Nikkō

# *By Yumoto-bound buses from Chūzenji-ko.* **Yumoto** (0:25h) is a small, pleasant onsen village. The nearby lakes are popular summer resorts, and there is cross-country skiing in winter. (Rentals at Kōtoku Cross-Country Ski-jō: 0288-55-0283; Y2500 for boots, skis, and poles.) **Marunuma Onsen** (0:40h by bus from Yumoto) is a lone rambling inn on the shore of a small, unspoiled lake. The bus road passes several gateways to Ozenuma and arrives at **Numata** (4:05h by bus from Marunuma, see next page). **Lodgings** (TEL 0288): In Yumoto, **Hotel Echigoya** (62-2325), a pleasant ryokan by a scenic marsh, with a beautiful wooden bath hall, Y9–15,000 w/meals; **Pension Tōge** (62-2571), a small ryokan-style pension with onsen bath, Y7400–8400 w/meals. At Marunuma: **Marunuma Onsen Hotel** (0278-58-2002), Japanese rooms only. Trout cuisine. Y1–20,000 w/meals.

### Exploring Okukinu and Yunishigawa Onsen

# *0:20h by Tōbu line from Shimo-Imaichi to Kinugawa, a tourist onsen, then 2:00h by bus (3 per day in summer, 2 per day in winter) to Meotobuchi Onsen.* **Meotobuchi** has a *rotemburo* and is the gateway to the Okukinu hot springs, a series of very rustic inns, reached on foot: **Hatchōnoyu** (1:10h from Meotobuchi), **Kaniyu** (0:15h from Hatchōnoyu), **Teshirozawa** (0:40h into the mountains from Kaniyu). From Kaniyu, one can hike to Marunuma in 4:00h (see Oku-Nikkō, above). **Yunishigawa Onsen**, 1:20h by bus (5 per day) from Kinugawa, is one of those inaccessible mountain regions that was supposedly a refuge of defeated 12th-century TAIRA warriors. There are three large, thatched-roof *minka* inhabited by putative descendants. **Lodgings** (TEL 0288): All the spas have inns. **Kaniyu** (96-0311) and **Teshirozawa** (96-0156) sound nice; clsd in winter; Y7–10,000 w/meals. Yunishigawa's **Bankyū Ryokan** (98-0111) is a farmhouse-style inn offering strange mountain food; Y16–20,000 w/meals.

**Easy Access To:**
**Jōmō-Kōgen** (KANTŌ II:N1): *0:30h by bus from Numata.*
**Aizu-Tajima** (TŌHOKU VI:W3): *2:20h by infrequent bus from Yunishikawa, changing at Kawaji Onsen.*

# KANTŌ II. FROM UENO STATION

**Prefectures:** Ibaraki, Tochigi, Gumma, Niigata, Nagano

**Calendar**
**Apr. (1st or 2nd Sa–Su):** ∗ **Furyūmono.** Hitachi (*2:00h by Jōban express from Ueno*). Magnificent floats: 15-meter-tall, multitiered puppet stages holding 25 hidden puppeteers and an orchestra.
**Aug. 23–24:** ∗ **Tsunabi Ningyō.** Ina-mura (*0:40h by Jōban express to Toride, then bus*). Atago Jinja. Mechanical puppets are sent flying along guidewires by *tsunabi* rockets, to the sound of drums and flutes.

# KANTŌ II:NE. NORTHEAST FROM UENO

## NE1 UTSUNOMIYA 宇都宮

*0:50h from Ueno by Tōhoku Shinkansen. Trains to Nikkō* (KANTŌ I:N1) *and buses to Mashiko pottery town.* 0:30h by bus from the station is **Ōya Kannon** 大谷観音, famous for its huge stone relief of Senju Kannon flanked by three images apiece of Yakushi, Shaka, and Amida (ICP); thought to date from the early Heian period (Hrs: 8:30–17:00; Jan.–Mar. and July, clsd 2nd and 4th Th). The temple is on the site of an old quarry (Hrs: 8:30–17:00).

**Calendar**
**July 25–27:** ∗∗ **Yama'age Matsuri.** Karasuyama (*1:30h by Karasuyama line from Utsunomiya to terminus*). See Calendar, p. 238.

244

**NE2 MASHIKO** 益子

*1:00h by bus from Utsunomiya station.* Though not the best pottery town to visit in Japan, Mashiko has become famous due to the presence of the internationally acclaimed potter Hamada Shōji (1894–1978), one of the pillars of the folk-art movement. Mashiko pottery today is mostly gas-fired commercial mingei ware. The town is spread out and hard to see on foot. The long main street is lined with all kinds of pottery shops. **Pottery fair:** Apr. 29–May 5, and early Nov.

**\*\*\* Mashiko Sankōkan (Reference Collection Museum)** 益子参考館 (0285-72-5300). Hrs: 9:30–16:30; clsd M (except if NH), Dec. 28–Jan. 4, and in Feb. *0:10h by car or 0:40h on foot from Mashiko station.* The eclectic pottery collection of Hamada Shōji, handsomely displayed in three old *kura*. The museum stands near the Hamada family's lovely thatched-roof farmhouse.

**Mashiko no Sato** 益子の里 A cluster of pleasant galleries and restaurants not far from the Sankō-kan.

**Shimaoka Tatsuzō** 島岡達三 (72-2225). By appointment. Mr. Shimaoka, a former apprentice of Hamada Shōji, is now the most prominent of Mashiko's best potters. His kiln is not far from the Sankō-kan.

**\*\* Higeta Hiroshi** 日下田博 (0285-72-3162). Hrs: 8:30–17:00; clsd Su, NH. Indigo dyeing, weaving, and stencil-dyed textiles.

**\* Tsukamoto Seitōsho** 塚本製陶所 (72-3223). Hrs: 8:30–17:30, clsd Th, NY. The largest pottery producer in Mashiko; showroom looks like a collection of tableware used in folk-style restaurants all over Japan. Visitors can observe every stage of production.

**Easy Access To:**
**\*\*\* Nikkō** (KANTŌ I:N1): *0:45h by train from Utsunomiya.*

# KANTŌ II:N. NORTH FROM UENO (JŌETSU SHINKANSEN)

**Main Attraction:** Sado Island (N3)

## N1 TAKASAKI 高崎

*1:10h by Shin'etsu line express or 0:50h by Jōetsu Shinkansen from Ueno.* Takasaki's **\* Gumma Prefectural Museum of Modern Art** 群馬県立近代美術館. is an outstanding building by architect Isozaki Arata. 0:35h by Jōetsu line express from Takasaki is **Shibukawa** 渋川 , gateway to a region of hot springs and ski resorts. Isozaki-designed **\* Hara Museum Ark** ハラ・ミュージアム・アーク is 0:20h from the station by bus. It's affiliated with the excellent Hara Art Museum in Tokyo. (Hrs: 10:00–16:30; clsd M (except if a NH, then clsd Tu). **Manza Onsen** 万座温泉, a good ski area with a rustic flavor and abundant hot springs, is 1:55h by express from Shibukawa (or 3:45h by express from Ueno) to Manza-Kazawaguchi, then 0:55h by bus.

**Calendar**

**Jan. 6–7: Daruma Market.** Takasaki, Shōrin-zan temple. Biggest in Kantō. Some 150 stalls sell the roly-poly red dolls, one of whose eyes is painted in by the buyer; the other one will be too, when prayers are granted.

**Jan. 14: \*\* Nakanojō no Tori-oi.** *0:45h by bus to Nakanojō's Ise-gū shrine, from Shibukawa station.* See Calendar, p. 238.

**Manza Lodgings** (TEL 0279)

**Manza Onsen Hotel** 万座温泉ホテル (97-3131). Fax 97-3595. Tsumagoi-mura, Agatsuma-gun, Gumma-ken. Modern resort hotel with a series of old-fashioned baths. Y15–18,000 w/meals. The Nisshin-kan annex 日進館 (97-3741) is an old-style inn; Y6500–8000 w/meals. No CC.

## JŌMŌ-KŌGEN/NUMATA 上毛高原・沼田

*0:20h by Jōetsu Shinkansen Toki express from Takasaki. Numata is 0:30h by bus from Jōmō-Kōgen, or 0:20h from Takasaki by the regular Jōetsu line.*

**\*\* Hōshi Onsen** 法師温泉 *1:00h by bus from Jōmō-Kōgen station, or 1:15h by bus from Numata station.* Guests can stay at the splendid, old-fashioned inn, **Chōju-kan** 長寿館 (0278-66-0005, fax 66-0003), deep in the mountains. Famous wooden bathhouse. Y13–26,000 w/meals. V, AX.

**\*\* Takaragawa Onsen** 宝川温泉 *1:10h by bus from Jōmō-Kōgen to Takaragawa Onsen Iriguchi, then walk 0:10–0:15h. There is also a direct bus, 0:45h, from Jōetsu line Minakami station.* The **Ōsenkaku** inn おう泉閣 (0278-75-2121, fax 75-2038), nestled in a green valley, has one of Japan's largest outdoor baths. The inn buildings range from old wooden structures to 5-story modern concrete. Y16–30,000 (depends on season). V, MC.

## \* # OZE-NUMA 尾瀬沼

*Main entry points are Hatomachi Tōge (2:20h by bus from Numata) and Ōshimizu (1:45h by bus from Numata). If coming from Oku-Nikkō* (KANTŌ I:N1), *change buses at Kamata (infrequent).* Oze is a very beautiful highland marsh surrounded by mountains. It is famed for a profusion of jack-in-the-pulpit which bloom May–June, and *nikkō-kisuge*, a bright yellow lily that blooms in July–August. Kilometers of raised boardwalks protect the terrain; the only drawback is the thousands of hikers who come when the flowers are at their peak. Still, Oze is a fine escape from Tokyo. Numerous huts provide tatami rooms, bedding, meals, and baths. To reserve: call in Tokyo (03-3451-1591); some huts can be reached directly: Chōzō-goya (0278-58-7100), Hiuchi-goya (0241-75-2059). Y6500 w/meals.

**Easy Access To:**
**Hinoemata** (TŌHOKU VI:W3): *0:50h by bus from Oze Numayama Tōge, which is a 1:30h hike from Ozenuma Hutte Kokuminshukusha.*

## NAGAOKA 長岡

*1:55h from Tokyo by Jōetsu Shinkansen. Change here for express trains to Toyama and Kanazawa* (CHŪBU IV:NW5). The \*\*\* **Shiritsu Kagaku Hakubutsukan** (Municipal Science Museum) 市立科学博物館 has Japan's finest flaming-Jōmon pottery collection. 0:15h walk from station. Hrs: 9:00–17:00 (enter by 16:30); clsd M, NY.

## N2 NIIGATA 新潟

*2:20h from Tokyo by Jōetsu Shinkansen. Change here for trains to Sakata, Akita, Hirosaki, and Aomori (see Tōhoku), or to Toyama and Kanazawa (see Chūbu).* A major industrial city on the Japan Sea coast. Gateway to Sado Island.

**Niigata Lodgings** (TEL 025)
\* **Bandai Silver Hotel** 万代シルバーホテル (243-3711). Fax 243-3720. 1-3-30 Bandai, Niigata-shi, Niigata-ken. Good city hotel run by ANA. S Y6500–7500, Tw Y10–16,000.
**Tōkyū Inn** 東急イン (243-0109). Fax 243-0401. 1-2-4 Benten. Business hotel. S Y6800, Tw Y12,000.
**Kaetsu Fujin Kaikan** 下越婦人会館 (266-6176). 425-2 Hakusanura 1-chōme. No English spoken. Y5800 w/2 meals.

246

## N3 \*\* SADO-GA-SHIMA (ISLAND) 佐渡島

*The port of Ryōtsu is 2:20h by ferry or 1:00h by hydrofoil from Niigata (both run 7 ferries and 10 hydrofoils per day in summer; in winter, 6 ferries and 3 hydrofoils per day). The hydrofoil fare is twice the second-class ferry fare. Akadomari is 2:00h by ferry from Teradomari, 2 per day from Apr.–Sept. Ogi, a more pleasant port than Ryōtsu, is 2:30h by ferry from Naoetsu. During storms, ferries will not cross rough seas.* Japan's fifth-largest island has a rather inhospitable image — remote, storm-battered, and associated with political exiles and prisoners worked to death in its gold mines. Yet it has a distinguished history and culture all its own. In the Nara period, the island was an independent province, with its own capital and state temple, Kokubun-ji, which still exists, not far from the original site. In the Middle Ages, Sado was the home in exile to such historical figures as Emperor Juntoku, Nichiren (see Kamakura History, p. 261), and ZEAMI, who left a legacy of Noh theater on the island. Today, there are 52 Noh stages on Sado. In addition to Noh, there is **Bun'ya**, an early puppet drama that survives nowhere else in Japan. It is livelier, if less refined, than Bunraku. Another Sado art form, now world famous, is **Ondeko**, the "demon drums of Sado."

During the Edo period, Sado came under the direct control of the shogunate, which mined gold and silver in the island's mountains, for some years a major source of the government's income. The old mines are now a big tourist attraction. More appealing, however, is Sado's tidy, well-preserved appearance: clusters of weathered gray houses surrounded by expanses of rice paddies stretching to the sea.

**Calendar**
In April and mid-October, there's a festival somewhere on the island every day. Avoid summer, when hordes of vacationers crowd the ferries and the minshuku.
**Apr. 1–Nov. 3: Okesa ballad-dance and Ondeko (Demon drums)**. At 20:00 daily at Okesa Kaikan in Ryōtsu, Sado Kaikan in Aikawa, Sado New Hall and Chūō Kaikan in Mano, and Niigata Kōtsu in Ogi (Okesa only).
**Apr. 14: Sannō Matsuri.** Niibo (near Ryōtsu), Hiyoshi Jinja. Horseback archery and Ondeko. Ondeko is also performed at various locales on the island from the 15th–16th.
**Apr. 28: Mano Performing Arts Festival.** Mano Kōen. Hrs: 10:00–15:30.
**Mid-June: \* Takigi Noh.** Usually during the 2nd weekend. Ushio Jinja, at Niibo-mura near Ryōtsu. Telephone 0259-22-3111 for details.
**June 15: \* Tsuburosashi.** Kusakari Jinja and Sugawara Jinja. Fertility festival by masked dancers. The male god wields a large wooden phallus as a female god dances provocatively, playing a simple instrument of two sticks, buzzed rythmically together.
**July 27–28: \* Noh.** Homma Noh stage near Ryōtsu. Hrs: 10:00–18:00.
**Aug. 14: Jizō Odori.** Mano Daiko-ji. Unusual Bon dance. Townspeople gently rock an image of Jizō Bosatsu on their backs while reciting the *nembutsu* and dancing.
**Aug. 21–23: Earth Celebration.** Ogi. A festival of (mainly non-Western) music, dance and

lectures by performers and scholars from around the world, organized by Kodō, the renowned percussion ensemble based on Sado. Phone 0259-86-2995 for information.

**Aug. 28–30: Ogi Minato Matsuri (Harbor Festival).** Ogi. Lion dances, Ondeko, and tub-boat races.

**Oct. 15: * Bun'ya Puppets.** Mano, Daijingū shrine. Sado's rustic puppet plays are performed at around 19:00.

**Oct. 16: * Chitochin-ton.** Shukunegi. Local version of the lewd *tsuburosashi* dance. Also lion dances and Ondeko.

**Oct. 19: Aikawa Matsuri.** Aikawa, Utō Jinja. This festival dates from 1615.

## Getting Around

Bus transport between main towns is frequent, but getting to the interesting sights is a problem. The **Sado Teiki Kankō (Scheduled Tour) Bus Free Jōsha-ken** is a 2-day pass (Y5,150) that allows unlimited use of all tour buses to get around to the main sights.

**Rentals:** In Ryōtsu, rent-a-car (and bicycles) at Sado Kisen Rent-a-car (0259-27-5195), Nippon Rent-a-car (3–4020). In Sawata, rent-a-cycle at Silver Village Sado.

## Sado Sights

**Ryōtsu** 両津 The dreary main port of Sado. In nearby Niibo is the **Homma Noh-butai** 本間能舞台 (0259-23-2888), an outdoor Noh stage built in 1885 for the leading Noh family on the island (see Calendar).

**Sawata** 佐和田 *0:45h from Ryōtsu by the Hon-sen bus line.* The main attraction here is **Myōshō-ji** 妙照寺 (*0:05h by Hon-sen bus from Sawata to Uenagaki, then walk 0:20h*), a beautiful temple where Nichiren lived for three years in the 13th C. It is now one of the head temples of the Nichiren sect.

> **Bun'ya Puppet Theater.** Silver Village Sado 文弥人形劇場シルバービレッジ佐渡 (52-3961). A small group that is keeping this art form alive.

> **Sado Hakubutsukan (Museum)** 佐渡博物館 (52-2447). Hrs: 8:00–17:00. Nov.–Mar. 8:30–16:00. Museum of Sado history, archeology, and folk performing arts. Housed in an early Meiji-period farmhouse.

247

**\*\* Aikawa** 相川 *1:10h from Ryōtsu by the Hon-sen bus line.* Once made wealthy by the gold from its mines, Aikawa is now one-tenth its former size. In addition to the mine-related sights listed below, visitors might be interested in **Mumyoi-yaki**, a high-fired ware made from the fine red clay found in the gold mines. **Recommended tour:** Walk or taxi to Doyū no Wareto, then walk back to town, stopping at the attractions. Walking time alone is 0:45h.

> ◆ **Gold Mine** 金山 Hrs: 8:00–18:00 (enter by 17:30). The most popular tourist trap on Sado. **Doyū no Wareto** 道遊ノ割戸 is the site of the first mine on Sado, where gold was discovered in 1601. The mountain was split in two by the digging. The later gold mine, **Sōda Yūkō**, was underground. Its interior is black with the smoke of oil lamps and scarred by digging tools. Mechanical dolls re-create early scenes of mining.

> **Mizukae Ninsoku no Haka** 水替人足の墓 Graves of the convict-laborers brought to Sado by the Edo authorities. The *mizukae ninsoku* were made to carry out the water that would pool in the mines. Working conditions were so harsh that most died within three to five years. In all, some 1,800 people perished. A priest erected this stone marker to console their souls.

> **Daian-ji** 大安寺 A temple founded in 1606 by the man who built and managed the Sado gold mines for the shogunate.

> **Aikawa Kyōdo Hakubutsukan (Museum)** 相川郷土博物館 (74-4312). Hrs: 8:30–17:00; clsd NY, Sa and Su in Dec.–Feb. In a red brick, Meiji-period building. Exhibits on gold mining.

**\* Mano** 真野 *0:50h from Ryōtsu or 1:05 from Ogi by bus. Service infrequent.* The center of government from Sado's earliest history to the Kamakura period. Most of Sado's early historical relics are scattered on the outskirts of this town.

> ◆ **Myōsen-ji** 妙宣寺 *0:15h walk from Takedabashi bus stop, on the route linking Ryōtsu and Mano.* In 1271, Endō Tamemori, who had accompanied Emperor Juntoku to Sado, converted to the Nichiren sect and founded this temple. It is noted for its 250-year-old pagoda and *kuri* (temple kitchen), which has a cavernous ceiling supported by smoke-burnished rafters. The road into Mano passes the site of **Kokubun-ji**, one of the national temples erected in the Nara period, as well as the present Kokubun-ji nearby.

> **Toki no Sato Kaiko-en/Mano Shiryōkan (Museum)** 朱鷺ノ郷懐古園真野資料館 Hrs: 8:00–18:00. *0:05h by bus from Shinmachi to Mano Goryō-iriguchi, then walk 0:10h.* An ugly modern museum with displays on Emperor Juntoku, Nichiren, and other local notables.

> **Mano Goryō** 真野御陵 *0:10h walk from Mano Shiryōkan.* Clsd. Jan.–Feb. This is the tomb of Emperor Juntoku, who was exiled here in 1222 by the Hōjō regents in Kamakura for participating in a rebellion that would have allowed him to exercise power. He spent 21 years on Sado and died here at age 46. The modest mausoleum, accompanied by a lone pine tree, stands in a beautiful grove.

**Hase-dera (Temple)** 長谷寺 *From Ryōtsu, Minami-sen bus to Hatano, change to Iwakubi-sen, get off at Hase bus stop.* Said to have been copied from the famous Hase-dera south of Nara in the early Heian period. This one also has a long flight of steps lined with peonies.

**Nashinoki Jizō** 梨ノ木地蔵 *From Mano, 0:20h by Akadomari-bound bus to Shizudaira bus stop, then 0:20h on foot.* This very popular Jizō cures sick children. Those who have been cured donate a small stone Jizō image—there are more than 3,000 in the precincts.

**Akadomari** 赤泊 *1:15h from Sawata, 3 buses per day; 0:40h from Ogi, 4 buses per day.* Daily ferries to Teradomari. An old port of Sado, said to have some charm.

**＊ Ogi** 小木 *By bus from Mano or Sawata. 2:40h by ferry from Naoetsu. Tour buses stop here.* In this area one can see the *tarai-bune*, round wooden tubs in which local women ride as they gather edible seaweed and shells.

>   **Kaiun Shiryōkan** 海運資料館 Hrs: 9:00–16:30; clsd NY. *0:03h walk from pier.* Maritime museum on Ogi's days as a major Japan Sea port.

>   **Rengebu-ji** 蓮華峰寺 *0:10h by Kobiei-sen bus from Ogi to Kobiei-iriguchi, then walk 0:10h.* A peaceful temple on a forested mountainside, founded in 807. The Main Hall (ICP) dates from the Muromachi period.

**＊＊ Shukunegi** 宿根木 *0:15h by bus west from Ogi.* One of the most charming fishing villages on Sado, with 200-year-old houses, their wood silver with age, packed close together. One house has a sharply angled corner resembling the prow of a ship—the handiwork of a ship's carpenter, people say. The village is encircled by trees, beyond which stretch rice paddies, brilliant green in summer. Village women bob about on *taruta* boats in the cove, gathering shellfish and seaweed.

>   ◆ **Ogi Minzoku Hakubutsukan (Museum)** 小木民俗博物館 Hrs: 8:30–17:00; clsd NY. A short distance out of Shukunegi, toward Ogi. Former school converted into an informal museum overflowing with old tools, household items, boats, clothing, and an intriguing group of old postcards of Sado *bijin* (beauties), local geisha from the not-so-distant past.

**Iwaya-san** 岩屋山 About 400 meters beyond the museum, toward Ogi, is a path on the left that leads through rice paddies to this cave temple filled with stone Buddhas, including seven carved in the cave wall; the locals confidently assert that they were made by KŌBŌ DAISHI himself.

## Sado Dining

**Ishihara** いしはら 両津市神明町 (27-2658). Hrs: 12:00–1:00 a.m. In Ryōtsu. Sushi sets Y700–1500.

**Amōre** アモーレ 両津市神明町 (23-2683). Hrs: 8:00–22:00. In Ryōtsu. Coffee in a restored Meiji-period lumber shop.

**Kadoya** かどや 真野町新町 (0259-55-2032) and **Taichi-an** 太一庵 真野町新町 (55-2031). Hrs: 11:00–17:30. Two *soba* shops in Mano, by the Shinmachi bus stop. Spring specialty is *soba* with whitebait (*shirauo*).

**Takeya Sushi** 竹家寿司 (86-2258). Hrs: 10:00–22:00; clsd 1st and 15th except in Aug. In Ogi. Excellent sushi. Friendly. Lunch, Y1600＋.

**Shichiemon** 七右衛門 小木町幸 (86-2046) and **Marugameya** 丸亀屋 小木町東 (86-2316). Hrs: 11:00–20:00; clsd 1st and 15th. In Ogi. Two *soba* shops known for excellent, old-style buckwheat noodles bound with mountain yam. *Ki-soba* (plain, fresh *soba*), Y400.

## Sado Lodgings (TEL 0259)

Numerous minshuku; about Y5800 w/2 meals.

**＊ Minshuku Ohana** 民宿お花 新穂村瓜生屋 (22-3028). Uriuya, Niibo-mura, Sado-gun, Niigata-ken. Near Ryōtsu, run by Mr. Ishii, who does *noroma ningyō*, stick puppets that are the Kyōgen of the puppet theater.

**Kokuminshukusha Senkaku-sō** 国民宿舎尖閣荘 (75-2226). Tassha, Aikawa-machi. Outside Aikawa; drives guests into town at night to see Okesa and Ondeko. Y6000 w/meals; also a ryokan (Y13,000＋) and YH.

**＊ Shōun-sō** 松雲荘 真野町新町 (55-2010). Shinmachi, Mano-machi. Part of this inn was built 70 years ago as the country house of a Meiji-period Minister of Agriculture, a Sado native. You can stay in the *chashitsu* (tearoom) by reservation. From Y8000 w/meals.

**Sado Pension** 佐渡ペンション (55-3106). Toyota, Mano-machi. Near beach. Y15,400–17,000 for two w/2 meals.

**＊＊ Akanashiya** 赤梨屋 (86-2058, fax 86-3751). Ogi-machi. Excellent family-run inn with great service and all the modern conveniences. The delicious meals are served one dish at a time. Beautiful cypress-paneled bathrooms. Y8000 w/meals.

**＊ Minshuku Takayama** 民宿高山 宿根木322 (86-3573). 322 Shukunegi, Ogi-machi. Has a farmhouse-style common room.

**Minshuku Shimizu-sō** 民宿清水荘 小木町強清水 (86-2538). Kyōshimizu, Ogi-machi. 1.5 km west of Shukunegi, near a pleasant cove with a beach. Will pick you up in Ogi.

**Minshuku Minatoya** 民宿港屋 藻浦 (26-2155). Futatsugame, Ryōtsu-shi. At the north tip of Sado. Beautiful location, run by an earthy couple. The husband is a *taiyū*, a Bun'ya puppet narrator.

## Easy Access To:

**Naoetsu (KANTŌ II:NW6):** *2:40h by ferry from Ogi.*

# KANTŌ II:NW. NORTHWEST FROM UENO (SHIN'ETSU LINE)

**Main Attraction:** Nagano (NW3)

## NW1 **KARUIZAWA**　軽井沢

*1:55 by limited express from Ueno station. All trains stop at Karuizawa, and most stop at Naka-Karuizawa.* Karuizawa, one of the first summer mountain retreats for Westerners and upper-class Japanese, looks like parts of America, full of golf courses and bungalows in the woods. And miles and miles of souvenir stands, fast-food joints, branches of Ginza emporiums, and shops selling blueberry jam and maple syrup. The center of town is for the hoi-polloi who come off the trains, the outskirts for wealthier people. Karuizawa is quite spread out, so inquire about fares before hopping into a taxi. The respected museum of contemporary art, **Seibu Takanawa Bijutsukan**　西武高輪美術館　is 0:10h by bus north of Naka-Karuizawa station (46-2020, Hrs: 10:00–18:00. Sept.–June clsd Th).

### Karuizawa Lodgings (TEL 0267)

✶✶ **Mampei Hotel**　万平ホテル　(42-2771). 925 Sakuranosawa, Karuizawa-machi, Nagano-ken. A classic resort hotel, built in 1894, the best in Karuizawa. Tw Y18–26,000.

✶✶ **Tsuruya Ryokan**　つるや旅館　(42-5555). 678 Kyū-Karuizawa, Karuizawa-machi. Rather graceful old inn with Japanese and Western rooms. Y8–25,000 w/meals.

**Karuizawa YH**　軽井沢YH　(42-2325). 1362 Kyū-Karuizawa, Karuizawa-machi.

## KOMORO　小諸

*0:20h from Karuizawa or 2:15h by limited express from Tokyo.* A former castle town and post station on the Hokkoku Kaidō (North-Country Highway). The castle's impressive gate stands behind the station. About 400 meters north, following the train tracks, is the **Kyū Komoro Honjin** (ICP), the remains of the Edo-period inn for important officials. Komoro's best attraction is the temple, ✶✶ **Nunobiki (Cloth-Pulling) Kannon**　布引観音　(*0:10h by bus to Ōkubo, then a 0:20h walk, or a Y1500 taxi ride out of town*). The temple got its popular name from a legend about an impious woman who was washing a cloth in the river when an ox caught the cloth in its horns and ran away. She chased it all the way to sacred Zenkō-ji in Nagano (NW3), and upon finding herself at the great temple, became a believer in the Buddha. The approach leads up a narrow ravine to the **Main Hall** (ICP), dramatically perched on a platform built over a rock ledge. The view over the valley is spectacular. The Honjin is on the route between the station and the temple.

### Exploring Unnojuku

*0:30h by bus from either Komoro or Ueda, by the bus linking the two towns. Get off at Moto-Unnojuku stop and walk about 0:05h south to the old post road (which runs parallel to the rail line).* This village boasts a 600-m stretch of road lined with more than 95 old houses, 55 of which date from the Edo period; they are noted for their *udatsu* (see Villages, p. 55).

## NW2 ✶ **UEDA/BESSHO ONSEN**

*2:30h by limited express from Tokyo to Ueda. Change here for the train to Bessho Onsen.* Ueda itself was a post town of the Hokkoku Kaidō. It has a few older houses, a castle ruin, museum, ruins of the Nara-period Shinano Kokubun-ji, and the present-day **Kokubun-ji**, which has a three-storied pagoda (ICP).

### Calendar

**July (Su nearest 15th):** ✶ **Nobori no Bessho no Take.** A rite for rain, said to have originated during a drought in the Muromachi period. Begins with a predawn procession up a mountain 3 km southwest of Bessho Onsen. Colorful banners on bamboo poles are unfurled as the sun rises, and the procession descends and marches through the town. Lion dances.

### Getting Around

The sights in Bessho Onsen can be visited along a 6-km walk that includes a section of a Kamakura-period highway and paths through the scenic countryside. Bessho Onsen station— (0:10h)—Jōraku-ji—(0:03h)—Anraku-ji—(0:05h)—Kitamuki Kannon—(0:40h)— Dōsojin—(0:45h)—Chūzen-ji—(0:20h)—Zenzan-ji/Dessin-kan.

### Bessho Onsen Sights

*0:30h from Ueda by tram to the terminus.* This spa, dating from around the 9th century, was chosen for the headquarters of Hōjō Yoshimasa, a Kamakura-period governor of the Shinshū region. A member of the Hōjō clan, de facto rulers of Japan, he brought the culture of Kamakura to this isolated mountain basin and built fine temples, some of which survive, leading people to call this area the "Kamakura of Shinshū."

✶ **Jōraku-ji**　常楽寺　Hrs: 6:00–18:00. The moss-covered stone pagoda (ICP) dates from the Kamakura period. The museum houses *ema* (votive pictures) by the ukiyo-e master, Hokusai.

✶✶✶ **Anraku-ji**　安楽寺　Hrs: 6:00–18:00. Its ◆ **octagonal pagoda** (NT) is the only one left

249

in Japan. Built in the Kamakura period, it is in the Sung Chinese style. The best view of the pagoda is from the steps leading up the hill behind it.

**Kitamuki Kannon (Temple)** 北向観音 Hrs: 6:00–18:00. This Kannon Bosatsu is popular because she answers prayers concerning *this* world rather than the next.

**Dōsojin** 道祖神 Male and female road guardian deities, carved in relief on stone. There were once many of these all over Japan, but especially in the Chūbu region. Some are openly erotic.

∗ **Chūzen-ji** 中禅寺 The Yakushi-dō (ICP), built in the early Kamakura period, is a thatched hall with features of Fujiwara-period architecture. The Yakushi Nyorai (ICP) inside is shown on request.

∗ **Zenzan-ji** 前山寺 Three-storied pagoda (ICP) of the Muromachi period. Adjacent is the **Shinano Dessin-kan** 信濃デッサン館 Hrs: 9:00–17:00. W. Displays sketches by modern Japanese artists. Nice coffee lounge.

## Ueda and Bessho Onsen Lodgings (TEL 0268)

**Mizuno Ryokan** 水野旅館 (22-1017). 4-13-19 Chūō, Ueda-shi, Nagano-ken. *0:20h on foot from Ueda station.* An inn of the old Hokkoku Kaidō. The inside has been refurbished and is very ordinary, but the owners are friendly. Y6000–10,000 w/meals.

**Hanaya Hotel** 花屋ホテル (38-3131). Bessho Onsen, Ueda-shi. A quaint two-story ryokan that looks like a Japanese castle. Fanciest inn here. Y12–25,000 w/meals.

**YH Ueda Mahoroba** YH上田まほろば (38-5229). Bessho Onsen, Ueda-shi.

## Exploring Nakasendō Post Towns

# Several former post towns lie along a quiet, walkable stretch of the old Nakasendō post highway. **Nagakubo**, 1:05h by bus from Ueda station, has a *honjin* (official's inn) said to date from the Momoyama period (not open). From here, the road climbs to a pass, where there is still an old teahouse, then descends along a stretch lined with red pines; in all, a 2:00h hike to **Ashida**. This village preserves a *honjin*, *waki-honjin*, and old inns. 0:30h beyond is **Motai**, a saké-brewing town; it still has many old saké warehouses, including one that is a museum. 0:30h further is **Mochizuki**, with many examples of Edo architecture. From Mochizuki, there are buses to Komoro (0:30h). **Lodgings** (TEL 02675): Kanamaru Tsuchiya Ryokan (6-1011), an old post-town inn in Ashida, Y6000–7000 w/meals. Yamashiroya (3-2014), in Mochizuki, Y5000–7000 w/meals.

## NW3 ∗∗ NAGANO 長野

*3:00h from Tokyo's Ueno station or 0:25h from Ueda, by Shin'etsu limited express. Or 3:12h by Chūō line limited express from Nagoya (CHŪBU IV) or 0:55h from Matsumoto (CHŪBU IV:NE7).* This city is dominated by the famous Zenkō-ji, one of the foremost pilgrimage temples in Japan. The magnificent main hall, swathed in billows of incense smoke and the steady drone of prayer, is alive with an aura of religious fervor that has vanished from most temples.

### Calendar

**Apr. 7–May 26 (once every 7 years):** ∗ **Gokaichō.** Zenkō-ji. A sacred replica of the legendary Buddha statue, said to have come from Korea in the 6th C, is revealed in a dramatic ceremony, attracting huge numbers of pilgrims. Next in 1997.

### Nagano Sights

∗∗∗ **Zenkō-ji** 善光寺 *The temple is located at the north end of a 1.6-km approach from the station. If you want to take a bus or taxi, get off at Dai-mon, just below the great Niō Gate, and walk the remaining 200 meters of the approach.* Millions of pilgrims visit this temple each year in the belief that one pilgrimage in a lifetime will ensure salvation. Their main object is to grope their way through a passage below the floor of the main hall, seeking to touch "the key of paradise." The mood, with hundreds of mostly aged, reverent pilgrims descending into the pitch-black tunnel, is a little awesome. Zenkō-ji is dedicated to a statue which, according to temple tradition, was the first Buddhist image to arrive in Japan, the gift of the king of Paekche in Korea. The image became an object of dispute between two feuding clans and wound up being dumped into a canal. At this point, history gives way to legend. A few years after this incident, one **Honda Yoshimitsu** is supposed to have found the golden image and taken it back to his native Nagano, where he built a temple for it. The temple was called Zenkō, from the "Chinese" reading of Yoshimitsu's name. He and his wife and son also came to be enshrined at Zenkō-ji. According to legend, these events occurred in the 7th C, though there is no record of a temple until the 9th C, and Honda Yoshimitsu's name doesn't come up until the Middle Ages. Historical veracity aside, the statue was so venerated that ODA NOBUNAGA absconded with it, and later TOYOTOMI HIDEYOSHI installed it at Hōkō-ji, the Great Buddha Hall he had built in Kyoto (see Kyoto, p. 334). Today, the image is never shown—it is believed that those who see it will go blind—but every seven years, an "exact copy" is revealed in a grand ceremony, which draws immense crowds of worshippers.

**Niō-mon.** This first gate of the approach was rebuilt in 1918 and houses a pair of Niō from the same time. The alleys parallel to the approach are lined with pilgrim's inns, separated into Jōdo and Tendai sect, the two official sects of this essentially nonsectarian temple. The approach continues to the immense **San-mon** (1750, ICP).

◆ **Hondō** (NT). Hrs: 4:30–16:30. In winter 6:00–16:00. The main hall, reconstructed in 1707, is unusual among temples because, like a shrine, the entrance is under the gable and the building is deeper than it is wide. The hall ranks among the largest wooden structures in Japan. Inside, worshippers rub a well-worn image of the rakan, **Obinzuru-sama**, who is said to cure any ailments corresponding to the spot rubbed on the statue. They then file to the right to grope through the dark passage seeking the "key of paradise" (it's really there).

**Daikanjin** 大勧進 (Zenkō-ji Tendai sect head temple). Hrs: 6:00–15:00. In winter 7:00–15:00. On west side of approach, just before the San-mon. The treasure hall displays a variety of paintings, documents, and sculpture: *Zenkō-ji Engi* scrolls illustrate the history of the temple.

**Daihongan** 大本願 (Zenkō-ji Jōdo sect head temple). Hrs: 5:30–16:00. On the west side of approach, just before Niō-mon. Daihongan is a convent which by tradition has an imperial abbess, the highest-ranking personage of the temple (hence Zenkō-ji's imperial chrysanthemum banners). There is a lovely courtyard garden and a mildly interesting treasure hall.

### Nagano Dining and Lodgings (TEL 0262)

Virtually every part of Japan claims fame for its *soba* (buckwheat noodles), but Nagano especially so. Many *shukubō* (temple lodgings) line the main approach to the temple; *shōjin-ryōri* (vegetarian cuisine) available. Reserve through Zenkō-ji (34-3591). Y7000 w/meals.

**Kitanoya** 北野屋　東之門町 (32-2492). Hrs: 11:00–19:00; clsd Tu (except if NH). Old *soba* shop, two short blocks east of the Niō-mon, on the southeast corner.

**Suki-tei** すき亭　妻科112-1 (34-1123). Hrs: 11:00–14:30, 16:00–20:30; clsd Su, mid-Aug., NY. Behind the Ken-chō (prefectural government office); serves Nagano's apple-fed beef. Nice wood interior. Sirloin Y4200, sukiyaki teishoku, Y1400–2600.

**Byakuren-bō** 白蓮坊 (32-0241). 453 Motoyoshi-chō, Nagano-shi, Nagano-ken. An excellent *shukubō*. Priest Wakaomi speaks a smidgen of English and is very kind. Chances are he'll take you up to the temple for morning services. Unique "temple"-style bath.

**Washington Hotel** ワシントンホテル (28-5111). 1177-3 Kamichitose-machi. Reliable business hotel chain. S Y6800+, Tw Y14,500.

**YH Kyōju-in** YH教授院 (32-2768). 479 Motoyoshi-chō. One of the Zenkō-ji *shukubō*.

### Exploring Hot Springs near Nagano

# Suzaka station (*0:15h from Nagano by the Nagano-dentetsu line*) is a gateway to some interesting hot springs: **Seni Onsen** (*0:30h by bus from Suzaka*), known for baths inside a natural cave, now part of the inn, Iwanoyu (0262-45-2453) Y18–27,000 for two w/meals; **Goshiki Onsen** (*0:55h by bus from Suzaka*), a lone inn with nice baths (42-2500) Y15,500 w/meals; 0:10h on foot from there is **Takayama Onsen**, one of the largest open-air baths in the region.

## NW4 * OBUSE 小布施

*0:20h by Nagano-dentetsu limited express from Nagano.* Obuse was the home of Takai Kōzan, a wealthy Edo-period merchant who became acquainted with the ukiyo-e genius Hokusai during a trip to Edo. At that time, Hokusai was nearly eighty and, though famous, quite poor due to a series of personal disasters. Kōzan became an important patron during Hokusai's remaining ten years of life. Hokusai visited Obuse on four occasions and stayed at Kōzan's house, painting for his host and other local clients. Many of the paintings are on display at the Hokusai-kan. (See Art, p. 99.)

\*\*\* **Hokusai-kan** 北斎館 (0262-47-5206). Hrs: 9:00–17:00. Nov.–Mar. 9:30–16:30; clsd NY. Enter 0:30h before closing time. This museum exhibits a large and varied collection of *nikuhitsu* (ukiyo-e painting) ascribed to Hokusai. Hokusai is most famous for his woodblock prints, but the breadth of his genius really appears in his paintings, which here include ukiyo-e beauties, still lifes, animals, legendary characters, and humorous sketches of the human figure. One of the most unusual exhibits is a pair of **festival carts** with ceilings designed and possibly painted by Hokusai. One is decorated with powerful, swirling waves, and the other with a dragon and phoenix. The colors are breathtakingly fresh and powerful.

\* **Kōzan-kan** 鴻山館 Hrs: 9:00–17:00. Nov.–Mar. 9:30–16:30. Dec.–Mar. clsd W, NY. Near the Hokusai-kan is this small museum housed in a *kura* on the former property of Takai Kōzan, Hokusai's patron in Obuse. Exhibits paintings by Kōzan, who was tutored by Hokusai.

\*\* **Ganshō-in** 岩松院 Hrs: 9:00–17:00. *2 km from station; taxi advised.* A Zen temple known for the spectacular Hokusai phoenix on the ceiling of the main hall.

### Obuse Dining

\* **Kurinoki Ouse-ten** 栗の木逢瀬店 (47-5740). Hrs: 9:00–18:00; clsd M. A chestnut confectioner since 1808, with a pleasant restaurant, next to the Hokusai-kan. *Matcha* (tea-ceremony tea) and light meals featuring rice steamed with chestnuts, from Y1000. Tsukuba lunch set Y1200. Also, fresh *amanatsu* (citrus), *budō* (grape), and *ringo* (apple) juice.

## YUDANAKA ONSEN 湯田中温泉

*0:40h by private Nagano-dentetsu express from Nagano to Yudanaka Onsen station, then 0:15h on foot.* Altogether, there are nine separate spas strung out along a 3.5-km stretch of the river. Farthest in is * **Jigokudani** (Hell Valley), famous for the wild monkeys that soak in the open-air baths to keep warm in the winter. Jigokudani's one inn, **Kōraku-kan** 後楽館 (0269-33-4376), is a rambling, old-fashioned place with an open-air bath for humans; the monkeys have their own bath in a nearby park. Address: Jigokudani Onsen, Yamanouchi-machi, Shimotaki-gun, Nagano-ken. Y9200–12,000 w/meals.

251

## NW5 ✳ TOGAKUSHI 戸隠

*1:00h by bus, via the "Birdline" scenic highway from Nagano station. Departures hourly, 8:00–18:00. The bus stops by the Niō gate and east gate of Zenkō-ji on the way. Road closed in winter. If you feel up to it, it's worth renting a car. Toyota Rent-a-Car (0262-27-1067) is 200 meters from Nagano station.* This mountainous region, popular with hikers and skiers, is connected with the Amaterasu (Sun Goddess) legend (see Shinto, p. 25). Togakushi means "door-concealing," and alludes to the local legend according to which the boulder that Amaterasu used to shut herself in a cave was concealed on this mountain. The three Togakushi shrines (outer, middle, and inner) are consecrated to Ame no Ōmoi Kane no Mikoto, the goddess who performed the ribald dance that tempted Amaterasu to tip aside the boulder and take a peek. One of the muscular gods seized the boulder and hurled it from southern Kyūshū, where these events occurred, to Togakushi, 800 km away. In historical times, Togakushi was a center for Shugendō, the syncretic mountain cult whose priests, the *yamabushi*, practiced austerities in the sawtoothed Togakushi range. With the Meiji-period purge of syncretic centers, however, Togakushi fell into ruin. The oldest hall left, the Hōkō-sha, dates only from 1861. But the dark groves of cryptomerias along the approach are eloquent reminders of Togakushi's past.

### Calendar

**Nov. 22–24: Togakushi Jinja Aki Matsuri.** On the 22nd and 24th, from 10:00, there are performances of a Kagura in which the Togakushi myths are reenacted in mime.

### Getting Around

The hourly bus from Nagano stops at all three shrines. Rent-a-cycle at Chū-sha.

### Togakushi Sights

252

Lower Togakushi, called **Hōkō-sha** 宝光社, looks somewhat abandoned, although there are some nice-looking inns nearby. The shrine, built in 1861, stands at the top of 200 stone steps. Middle Togakushi, or **Chū-sha** 中社, is where most of the *shukubō* (pilgrim's inns) and shops are. Twice monthly, evening performances of Dai-dai Kagura commemorate Ame no Ōmoi Kane no Mikoto's dance. Chū-sha is the base for winter skiing at Togakushi. About 2 km farther up the road is inner Togakushi, or **Oku-sha** 奥社. Near the bus stop, Oku-sha Iriguchi, is a small folk museum and a modest *ninja* museum. Continue through the cinnabar-red gate, **Zuishin-mon**, and up a steep, cryptomeria-flanked path, once lined with a hundred subtemples. The inner shrine, reached in 0:40h, is a disappointing concrete building — its predecessor was swept away by an avalanche in 1978 — but the magnificent cryptomerias that line the approach make the climb worthwhile.

### Togakushi Crafts

Togakushi baskets are hand-woven from a knotty scrub-bamboo. The distinctive *soba* baskets have a coarse herringbone-weave center surrounded by a finer weave.

### Togakushi Dining and Lodgings (TEL 0262)

There are many ryokan and *shukubō* around Hōkō-sha and Chū-sha.
**Iwatoya** 岩戸屋 (54-2038). Hrs: 8:00–19:00. In winter 9:00–18:00. A famous *soba* shop about 100 meters from Chū-sha shrine, on the left side of the main road.
✳ **Yokokura Ryokan** 横倉旅館 (54-2030, fax 54-2540). 3347 Chū-sha, Togakushi-mura, Kamiminochi-gun, Nagano-ken. Two-story thatched inn, which is also a kokuminshukusha and YH. Y5800–8000 w/meals. YH rate Y3600 w/meals. Pleasant coffee shop, Jūrin, next door.

## ✳ NOZAWA ONSEN 野沢温泉

*Take the Iiyama line from Nagano to Togari station, then a bus for 0:25h.* Popular ski resort and spa, with 13 free public baths, including a number of old wooden bathhouses; get a map from your inn or information center and go "bath crawling." Near the picturesque **Ōyu** bathhouse, housewives cook eggs and vegetables in near-boiling spring water to sell to tourists. There's also a European-style spa, **Kurhaus Nozawa** クアハウスのざわ (85-3184), which offers baths, steam rooms, and a hot-spring pool (Y1000; Hrs: 6:30–17:00; clsd Th. Nov.–Apr. 10:00–18:00.)

### Calendar

**Jan. 15: ✳ Nozawa Onsen Hi-matsuri.** Men born under the New Year's Chinese zodiac sign must defend — in vain — a small shrine from torch-wielding attackers. From 20:00.

### Nozawa Onsen Lodgings (TEL 0269)

**Nozawa Grand Hotel** 野沢グランドホテル (85-3151). Nozawa Onsen-mura, Shimotakai-gun, Nagano-ken. Y14–27,000 w/meals.
**Sakaya Ryokan** さかや旅館 (85-3118). Address as above. A pleasant tourist ryokan. Has a big wood-paneled bathhouse. Y14,000–22,000 w/meals.
**Minshuku Ōsawa-sō** 大沢荘 (85-2738). Address as above. Y6000 w/meals.

## NW6 NAOETSU 直江津

*1:30h by express train from Nagano. Ferries to Sado* (KANTŌ II:N3). *Trains to Kanazawa* (CHŪBU IV:NW5).

# KANTŌ III. FROM SHINJUKU STATION

**Prefectures:** Saitama, Yamanashi

# KANTŌ III:N. NORTH FROM SHINJUKU (SEIBU-SHINJUKU LINE)

## Traveling

The private Seibu-Shinjuku line leaves from beneath the Seibu Prince Hotel. All of these areas can be reached by direct trains—in some cases more conveniently—from Ikebukuro station as well.

### TOKOROZAWA 所沢
*By express, 0:35h from Seibu-Shinjuku station or 0:25h from Ikebukuro station. Junction to Seibu-Chichibu line to Chichibu (N2).*

### N1 ∗ KAWAGOE 川越
*Hon-Kawagoe station is 0:50h by Seibu line express from Seibu-Shinjuku station. Kawagoe-shi station is 0:45h from Ikebukuro by the Tōjō line express.* Kawagoe, a prosperous castle town, was known as "little Edo," a nickname that is even more appropriate today, for it is one of the few places left in Japan that retains the atmosphere of Edo and early Meiji Tokyo. Kawagoe preserves many heavy, fireproof, *kura*-style shops, in the style favored by wealthy Edo merchants; most were built after a fire in 1893 consumed the town. These splendid structures have clay-and-plaster walls a half-meter thick. Their tiny windows feature heavy shutters with interlocking edges, male and female, which can be sealed shut in a fire. The steep tile roofs are crowned by immense, fire-deflecting *onigawara* (devil tiles). Ordinary people, unable to afford such buildings, lived in shelters of the cheapest paper and wood, which today have all but vanished. The *kura*, however, remain in use as shops and dwellings. Also worth a visit is the temple, Kita-in, where Tenkai, the Tendai priest who was a close advisor to the first three TOKUGAWA shoguns, was abbot (see Nikkō History, p. 242).

253

## Calendar
**Oct. 14–15:** ∗ **Kawagoe Matsuri.** Hikawa Jinja. Full-scale matsuri held every other year features 17 floats, said to be replicas of the no-longer-used Kanda Matsuri floats in Tokyo. At night, the floats are rammed into each other.

## Getting Around
One can walk around the main sights in 2 to 3 hours. The densest concentration of *kura* occurs a few hundred meters north of Hon-Kawagoe station, along the main shopping street.

## Kawagoe Sights
∗∗ **Yamazaki Bijutsukan (Art Museum)** 山崎美術館 (0492-24-7114). Hrs: 9:30–16:30; clsd W (except if NH), last 2 days of month, NY. A small museum housed in several Edo-period *kura* adjoining **Kameya**, a prosperous confectioner that made sweets for the local lord. Exhibits modern Japanese paintings and old family treasures. Artistic sugar and rice-flour confections and cherry-wood candy molds are shown in a former sugar *kura*.
**Hattori Minzoku Shiryōkan** 服部民俗資料館 Hrs: 10:00–16:30; clsd M. A former clog and parasol shop, now an informal museum of old objects.
**Toki no Kane** 時の鐘 An Edo-style wooden bell tower, rebuilt in 1894. The great bronze bell booms at 6:00, 12:00, 15:00, and 18:00.
∗∗ **Kuratsukuri Shiryōkan (Museum)** 蔵造り資料館 (25-4287). Hrs: 9:00–16:30; clsd M (Tu if M a NH), last Fri. of every month. Three late 19th-C *kura*. One displays memorabilia from Kawagoe's castle town days. Another exhibits tools used to create the plaster ornamentation of the *kura*.
∗ **Ōsawa-ke** 大沢家 (1792, ICP). This private dwelling, formerly that of a kimono merchant, is one of the few Kawagoe buildings to predate the 1893 fire.
∗ **Kawagoe-jō Honmaru Goten** 川越城本丸御殿 (1848). Hrs: 10:00–16:30; clsd M (Tu if M a NH). A curved gable entrance and large reception room are all that remain of the lord's castle.
∗∗∗ **Kita-in** 喜多院 (22-0859). Hrs: 9:00–16:00; Apr.–Nov. 9:00–16:30; clsd NY, Feb. 2–4, Mar. 30, Apr. 6, Aug. 16. *0:10h walk from Hon-Kawagoe station.* Founded in 830 by priest Ennin (see Hiraizumi History, p. 169), Kita-in was the Tendai sect headquarters in Kantō. The temple is well worth visiting for its beautiful buildings and gardens. After a fire destroyed the temple, the ◆ **Kyakuden** (ICP) was moved here from Edo Castle by the third Tokugawa shogun, IEMITSU, as a gesture of friendship to its abbot, Tenkai. The building includes the room where Iemitsu was born. The **Shoin** (ICP) is decorated with paintings of artisans at work by KANŌ Yoshinobu. Included in the admission fee is the courtyard of the ◆ **Gohyaku** (500) **Rakan**.
∗∗ **Senba Tōshō-gū** 仙波東照宮 (ICP). Open Su, NH, Jan. 1–5, Apr. 17, Aug. 17. Tokugawa Ieyasu's remains and deified spirit passed through Kawagoe on their way from Kunō-zan in Shizuoka to Nikkō. This shrine was built to commemorate the event. Though smaller than the shrines at Nikkō and Kunō-zan, it too is quite ornate.

## Kawagoe Dining

**Kurazukuri no Chaya** くらづくり茶屋 (25-5252). Hrs: 11:00–18:00, daily. Pleasant teahouse. For a light meal, try their *seiro kura-meshi* ("pilaf"). Inexpensive.

**Imojū** 芋十 (22-0842). Hrs: 9:30–20:00; clsd W, NY. *Imo-sembei* (candied sweet-potato chips), a local specialty.

\* **Ichinoya** 市野屋 (22-0354). Hrs: 11:30–21:00; clsd M (Tu if M a NH). Famous for *unagi* (eel) dishes. Established 1832. *Unajū* from Y1950.

**Kotobuki-an** 寿庵 (25-1184). Hrs: 11:30–17:00; Sa, Su 11:30–20:00; clsd W (except if NH). *Wariko-soba* (five-flavor *soba*) Y1200.

## N2 CHICHIBU 秩父

*1:25h from Tokorozawa or 2:00h from Ikebukuro by Seibu-Chichibu line direct express to Seibu-Chichibu station. The Chichibu-tetsudō rail station, Ohanabatake, is a 0:05h walk away.* A world apart from Tokyo, this mountainous area, part of **Chichibu-Tama National Park**, is creased with countless valleys, rich in rural traditions.

### Calendar

**Aug. 15:** \* **Nagatoro Funatama-sai.** Nagatoro (*1:30h from Ikebukuro by Tōbu-Tōjō line express, or 0:25h by Chichibu-tetsudō line from Ohanabatake*). Festival of the water deity, with Bon elements. Decorated boats, lantern-floating, fireworks.

**Oct. 5:** \* **Muku Jinja Ryūsei Matsuri.** Yoshida-mura (*0:15h by Chichibu-tetsudō from Ohanabatake to Minano, then 0:25h by bus*). Giant flares of hollow pine logs and bamboo — said to have been introduced by 16th-C gunpowder experts — are shot to the cry *go-hōnō!* (sacred offering!); streaming colored smoke, they parachute back to earth. Thirty flares are sent up between 8:00–17:00.

**Dec. 2–3:** \*\*\* **Yo-matsuri.** Chichibu Jinja. See Calendar, p. 238. Don't plan on staying the night of the Yo-matsuri; inns are booked solid and prices inflated.

**Dec. 15:** \* **Teppō (Rifle) Matsuri.** Ogano-chō, Hachiman Jinja (*0:35h by bus from Seibu-Chichibu station*). Kantō hunters gather to pray for a good hunting season. At 15:00, two sacred horses race up the stone steps of the shrine as a hundred rifles are shot into the air. In the evening, Kabuki is performed on lantern-lit floats.

### Chichibu Sights

Rent-a-cycles near Seibu-Chichibu station. Chichibu itself is a rather drab working town with huge mills for concrete and silk textiles, though set in a pretty valley. Attractions in town include the ornate **Chichibu Jinja**, **Chichibu Matsuri Kaikan** (Yo-matsuri Festival Hall), and **Katō Kindai Bijutsukan** (Modern Art Museum).

\* **Kinshō-ji** 金昌寺 *0:20h by bus from Seibu-Chichibu station.* Chichibu has a popular version of the 88-temple Shikoku pilgrimage, and this temple, 34th on the circuit, is the most popular. The approach and grounds are lined with stone Jizō statues, and the Kannon-dō houses an Edo-period "Maria Kannon" of stone, nursing an infant; the form is startlingly Western.

\* **Mitsumine Jinja** 三峰神社 *0:25h from Ohanabatake station to Mitsumine-guchi, then 0:15h by bus to Ōwa. Cross the red bridge, and walk to the tramway. From the top, it's 0:15h on foot to the shrine.* The ornate shrine, sacred to Izanami and Izanagi, is an ancient center of mountain religion. Local belief holds that the messenger of the mountain kami is the mountain dog, which protects farmers' fields from wild beasts; dog statues guard the region's shrines.

\*\* **Tochimoto** 栃本 *0:40h by bus from Mitsumine-guchi station to Chichibu-ko (lake), then 0:20h farther by another bus.* This remote mountainside hamlet has a dozen minshuku among the old thatched farmhouses dotting the steep, terraced slopes.

### Chichibu Lodgings (TEL 0494)

**Kobushi** 甲武信 (55-0457), **Nishikawa** 西川 (55-0591), and **Asahi** 朝日 (55-0597) are three minshuku in Tochimoto. Address: Tochimoto, Otaki-mura, Chichibu-gun, Saitama-ken. Y5300–5500 w/meals.

# KANTŌ III:W. WEST FROM SHINJUKU (FUJI REGION)

## W1 ŌTSUKI 大月

*1:00h from Shinjuku by JR Chūō line limited express. Junction to Fuji-Yoshida, a gateway to Mt. Fuji and the Fuji Five Lakes.*

### \* FUJI-YOSHIDA 富士吉田

*0:45h from Ōtsuki; a few direct expresses from Shinjuku. By car, it's 1:00h from Gōra* (KANTŌ IV:SW4). This small town, situated on a plateau at the northeast foot of Mt. Fuji, was a center of the Edo-period Fuji cults.

### Calendar

**July 1: Fuji climbing season begins.** Rites at Komatake Jinja.

**Aug. 26–27:** \*\* **Yoshida no Hi-matsuri.** Sengen Jinja. See Calendar, p. 238. Main events on 26th, from 15:00 into evening.

## Fuji-Yoshida Sights

**\*\*\* Sengen Jinja** 浅間神社 (1615, ICP). Ornate shrine to the kami of Fuji. The deity seems to have been a composite of various mountain spirits and avatars, but after the Meiji Restoration, only the purely Shinto Konohanasakuya-hime (Flowers upon the Tree Blossoming Princess) was worshipped at the shrine. The main street to Sengen Jinja is lined with a few surviving Edo-period *oshi no yado*, pilgrim's inns run by professional proselytizer-guides called *oshi*. Each inn, set about 50 meters back from the street, has a garden with a waterfall, channeled from mountain streams. Here the pilgrims perform ablutions, change into white garb, and pray before proceeding to the shrine and then up the volcano. In the Edo period, women were not allowed on the mountain except once every 60 years; the rationale was that the mountain deity, a female, would become jealous.

**\*\* Oshino** 忍野 *0:15h by infrequent bus from Fuji-Yoshida*. This rural hamlet, dotted with thatched farmhouse minshuku, is a favorite for photographers of Fuji.

**Kawaguchi-ko** 河口湖 *0:07h by train from Fuji-Yoshida*. Famous resort lake, one of the Fuji Five Lakes. This is a gateway to the Fuji climb. Lots of picture-postcard views, but otherwise a bit dull. The Hyōketsu (ice caves) are rather interesting.

## Fuji-san 富士山

Climbing this celebrated peak is not a grand communion with nature; the whole point is to make the pilgrimage when everyone else does. From mid-July through mid-August, the main trails are as crowded as a Ginza sidewalk. The quick way up is to take a bus to a fifth station (trails are divided into ten stations), hike to the summit (4–5:00h), spend the night at a hut, and get up to greet the sunrise. The descent takes about half as long. To climb from the bottom would take about 10:00h. The upper part of Fuji is steep and covered with loose volcanic rubble. Wear sturdy hiking boots, and watch for falling rocks. The summit is at 3776 m, high enough to induce altitude sickness if you're not careful.

255

Fuji is officially open to climbers from July 1 to Aug. 26, though it is free of snow for some months longer. Buses to the fifth stations run from Apr. 7 to Nov. 10. Huts provide bedding and meals from June 30 to Aug. 26. Y4000 w/o meals, Y1000 extra per meal. Additional fifth-station lodges stay open (barring heavy snow), Apr. to Nov. Reserve through Fuji-Yoshida Shiyakusho Shōko-Kankō-ka, 1872 Shimoyoshida, Fuji-Yoshida-shi, Yamanashi-ken (tel: 0555-22-1111). The most popular bases are Gogōme on the north slope and Shin-Gogōme on the south slope. Buses: Kawaguchi-ko to Gogōme, 0:55h (July–Aug. 31); Fujinomiya or Mishima to Shin-Gogōme, 1:45h and 2:05h, respectively (July 20–Aug. 26).

## Fuji-Yoshida Dining and Lodgings (TEL 0555)

**Hanaya** はなや (22-2507). Hrs: 11:00–16:00; clsd 1st and 3rd W, NY. Near Sengen Jinja. *Yumori-udon*, homemade noodles served simply. Y300–600.

**Daikokuya** 大国屋 (22-3778). 583 Kamiyoshida, Fuji-Yoshida-shi, Yamanashi-ken. A minshuku and *oshi no yado* built more than 300 years ago. Y4700–5700 w/2 meals.

**Masu no Ie** 鱒の家 (84-2013). 195 Shibokusa, Oshino-mura, Minamitsuru-gun, Yamanashi-ken. Thatched minshuku at Oshino. Y7–10,000 w/2 meals.

## KŌFU 甲府

*1:50h by Chūō line limited express from Shinjuku. Junction to the Minobu line to Fuji.*

### Calendar

**Apr. (Su near 10th): \* Tenzushimai.** Suwa Jinja. The kami, embodied by a doll, is dressed in kimono and a red mask and taken to the shrine, where dances are performed in offering.

**Apr. (Sa–Su nearest 12th): Shingenkō Matsuri.** The great Sengoku-period warrior Takeda Shingen is commemorated with rites; at the end, 1,000 "samurai" fight a mock battle in the city streets.

### Easy Access To:

**\* Matsumoto** (CHŪBU IV:NE7): *1:40h by JR Chūō line limited express from Kōfu.*

**Fuji** (KANTŌ IV:SW6): *1:50h by JR Minobu line limited express from Kōfu.*

# KANTŌ III:SW. ODAKYŪ LINE

**SW1 \* NIHON MINKA-EN (JAPAN FARMHOUSE MUSEUM)** 川崎市立日本民家園 *0:20h by express or 0:30h by private Odakyū line local train from Shinjuku to Noborito, then 0:10h by taxi.* (044-922-2181). Hrs: 9:30–16:00 (arrive by 15:00 if possible); clsd M (Tu if M a NH), NY, Jan. 15, Feb. 11, July 1, and Nov. 23. An outstanding collection of farmhouses from various parts of Japan. This is the best place in the Tokyo area to view the distinctive rural architecture of Japan.

### Easy Access To:

**Odawara** (KANTŌ IV:W3): *1:15h by Odakyū line express from Noborito.*

# KANTŌ IV. FROM TOKYO STATION

**Prefectures:** Chiba, Ibaraki, Kanagawa, Shizuoka

# KANTŌ IV:E. AROUND NARITA

### Traveling

From Tokyo, the JR Sōbu line goes as far as Sakura (before branching off), the JR Narita line continues to Narita, and the JR Kashima line continues to Kashima Jingū. See p. 5 for information on getting between Tokyo and Narita Airport.

### E1 SAKURA 佐倉

*From Tokyo 0:45–1:00h by JR Sōbu line or Narita-bound private Keisei line, or 0:15–0:30h from Narita.* ✳✳✳ **National Museum of Japanese History (Kokuritsu Rekishi Minzoku Hakubutsukan)** 国立歴史民俗博物館 (0434-86-0123). Hrs: 9:30–16:30 (enter by 16:00); clsd M (if Su or M a NH, then clsd Tu), NY. *0:15h by bus or taxi from either station.* This huge modern museum features lavishly detailed models of tumuli, palaces, towns, and rural landscapes illustrating major historical periods.

### Calendar

**Aug. 16:** ✳ **Kiraigō.** Hikari-machi, Chiba-ken (*take Sōbu line express to Yokoshiba*). Kōsai-ji. Folk dramas, said to date from the Kamakura period, depicting Buddhist hell. Phone 0479-84-1661 for exact time.

### E2 NARITA 成田

256

*1:00h by Keisei-Skyliner express from Ueno station or 1:00h by JR Narita line express from Tokyo station. 0:20h by bus to Narita International Airport. (See also p. 5).* 0:15h on foot from Narita or Keisei-Narita stations is **Narita-san Shinshō-ji** 成田山 新勝寺, which attracts 12 million worshippers a year; Kabuki fans know it as the ancestral temple of Ichikawa Danjūrō. The temple is familiarly called O-Fudō-san, after its main image of Fudō Myō-ō (see Buddhism, p. 36), said to have been brought from Kyoto's Jingo-ji around 940. The temple was supposedly founded to assuage the spirit of TAIRA no Masakado, a rough warrior who led a rebellion in Kantō and declared himself emperor, before he was caught and beheaded (see Kanda Myojin, Tokyo, p. 206). Structures of interest: Niō gate (1830, ICP); pagoda (ICP); Shaka-dō (1858, ICP) to the left of the concrete Main Hall; Gaku-dō (ICP) hall for votive paintings; and Okuno-in (1701, ICP), the former main hall.

### Narita Lodgings (TEL 0476)

**Wakamatsu Honten** 若松本店 本町355 (22-1136, fax 24-1347). 355 Honchō, Narita-shi, Chiba-ken. Near Narita-san. Y12–20,000 w/meals.
**Ōgiya** 扇屋 幸町474 (22-1161, fax 24-1663). 474 Saiwaichō, Narita-shi. Near Narita-san. Y9000–20,000 w/meals.
**Umeya** 梅屋 仲町376 (22-0003). 376 Nakanochō, Narita-shi. Near Narita-san. Y10,000–15,000 w/meals.
**Holiday Inn Narita** ホリディイン成田 (32-1234, fax 32-0617). 320-1, Tokko, Narita-shi. *0:05h by car from the main airport terminal.* S Y14,000, Tw Y17–26,000.
**Narita Airport Rest House** 成田エアポートレストハウス (32-1212, fax 32-1209). 141 Furugome, Narita-shi. Inside the airport terminal building. S Y10,000, Tw Y16,000.

### SAWARA 佐原

*1:45h from Tokyo station by JR Ayame limited express. Or 0:30h by Narita line from Narita.* Sawara preserves rows of *kura*-style houses lining the banks of the Ōno River. The *soba* shop, **Koboriya Honten** 小堀屋本店 (ICP), dates from the late 18th century (Hrs: 11:00–18:30; clsd W). **Katori Jingū** 香取神宮 (*0:15h by bus from station*) has a Gongen-style sacred hall (1700, ICP) and is associated with Kashima Jingū (see below). Sawara and nearby **Itako** 潮来 (*0:15h by Kashima line or 0:35h by bus from Sawara*) are famous for their canals, now plied by sightseeing boats (Y1200 per person for 0:30–0.50h tides. In June, 0:50h rides only.

### Calendar

**Apr. (1st Sa–Su): Katori Jingū Otaue-sai.** Rice planting.
**Apr. 14–16: Katori Jingū Shinkō-sai.** Annual shrine matsuri. Once every 12 years (next in 2002), a colorful procession on the 15th takes the *mikoshi* on the river to Kashima Jingū and back.
**June:** Irises in bloom by the thousands along the canals.

### E3 KASHIMA JINGŪ 鹿島神宮

*2:10h from Tokyo by JR Ayame limited express, or 0:50h by JR Kashima line from Narita.* The most important shrine in Kantō, placed here in early times to "protect" Yamato from the still-untamed northeast of Japan. The shrine is sacred to Takemikazuchi, who with the deity of Katori Jingū (see above) secured Japan for Ninigi no Mikoto, grandson of the Sun Goddess and grandfather to Jimmu, the mythical first emperor (see Shinto, p. 26). In the Nara period, the FUJIWARA family adopted these two influential kami as clan deities, enshrining them at

Kasuga Taisha, the famous Fujiwara tutelary shrine in Nara. The colorful shrine festival,
* **Kashima Saitō-sai**, is held on Mar. 9. Hrs: 13:00–16:00.

# KANTŌ IV:W.WEST FROM TOKYO

**Main Attractions:** Kamakura (W2), Izu Peninsula (W6)

## W1 **YOKOHAMA** 横浜

*0:30h by JR Yokosuka line from Tokyo station, or 0:22h by Yokosuka line or private Keihindentetsu line from Shinagawa.* When the first Western ships docked at Yokohama in 1859, it was only a small fishing village, though blessed with an excellent harbor. It was close enough to Edo to suit foreign demands, yet far enough away to allow the Tokugawa government the pretense of keeping the foreigners at bay. The village has burgeoned into Japan's biggest port, second largest city, and major industrial zone, obliterating most traces of its recent past. Remnants of its treaty port days include a district of foreign residences and a Chinatown. The Sankei-en, a park built by a wealthy Yokohama merchant, contains fine examples of Sukiya-style architecture.

### Getting Around
The JR Negishi line runs from Yokohama station: 0:07h to Ishikawa-chō (Chinatown), 0:12h to Yamate (near Sankei-en). The line ends at Ōfuna, junction to the Yokosuka line to Kamakura and to the Tōkaidō line.

### Yokohama Sights
** **Chūkagai (Chinatown)** 中華街 *0:05h walk from Ishikawa-chō station. Y1000 by taxi from Sankei-en.* Today, Yokohama's Chinatown is home to 2,500 Chinese and some 100 shops. Nishimon-dōri, the street leading from the station, is lined with Chinese import shops; prices outside the gaudy Hairō-mon gate are cheaper than in the heart of Chūkagai. Shop at **Chūgoku Bōeki Konsu** on Saimon-dōri (Hrs: 9:00–17:00; clsd 2nd Sa, Su, NH). **Kōshō** 鴻昌　山下町 (681-1293) has good Cantonese food and fast service (Hrs: 11:30–20:00; clsd M).
** **Sankei-en** 三渓園 (045-621-0634). Hrs: outer garden 9:00–17:00; inner garden 9:00–16:00. *About Y1000 by taxi from Negishi station.* A fine, unusual collection of old villas, tea arbors, temple halls, and a farmhouse, brought from various parts of Japan and set in this landscaped park; the best are in the inner garden. ◆ **Rinshun-kaku** (1649), built by the lord of Kii (Wakayama), is a splendid Sukiya villa with panels painted by KANŌ SCHOOL artists. **Gekka-den** (1604) is a guesthouse built by TOKUGAWA IEYASU at Fushimi-jō in Kyoto. **Chōshū-kaku** (1623) is a strikingly irregular pavilion built by shogun IEMITSU at Kyoto's Nijō-jō. **Shunsō-rō** (ca. 1621) is a tea arbor built by the famous tea master Oda Urakusai (brother of ODA NOBUNAGA). There are also a lovely hall from Kamakura's Tōkei-ji, and a three-storied pagoda of the Muromachi period (all ICP).

## W2 *** **KAMAKURA** 鎌倉

*1:00h from Tokyo station by Yokosuka line (track 1, underground on Marunouchi side); or 0:50h from Shinagawa station (track 10). Kita-Kamakura station is one stop before Kamakura. On weekends and holidays, buy your return ticket upon arrival to avoid long lines later in the day.* This seaside town was the capital of Japan's first military government, the Kamakura shogunate (1185–1333). The period was dominated by strong-willed, single-minded warriors and priests, and it is their influence, often stern and ascetic, but also inspired, that colors the wealth of historical relics in this former capital. To the north, at Kita-Kamakura, are two of Japan's oldest Zen monasteries, Kenchō-ji and Engaku-ji. The center of Kamakura is Tsurugaoka Hachiman-gū, tutelary shrine of MINAMOTO NO YORITOMO, founder of the Kamakura regime. Among the common people, the cult of Amida, the "savior" Buddha, became widespread and inspired the Daibutsu, a 120-ton bronze image of Amida, now Kamakura's most famous sight. Religious art saw a revival of realism, led by the master sculptors of the KEI SCHOOL (see Art, p. 94); some of the finest works of this period are at the Kokuhōkan (National Treasure Hall). The hills surrounding Kamakura are riddled with thousands of *yagura*, or cave tombs. These date from the 12th–14th centuries and contain vaults for the cremated remains of warriors and priests, marked by tombstones shaped like five-level stupas (for samurai), or smooth and round on top (for priests).

### Calendar
**Jan. 1: Hatsumōde.** Tsurugaoka Hachiman-gū is thronged with New Year visitors. On the 4th, at 13:00, is *chōna-hajime*: the "first use of a carpenter's adze." On the 5th is the "first archery."
**Mid-Apr.: Sakura Matsuri.** A week (Sunday to Sunday) of festivities during cherry-blossom season. Shizuka no Mai, on the first day, commemorates Lady Shizuka's defiant dance (see Early Kamakura History, p. 261). On the last day, there is *yabusame* (horseback archery).
**Aug. 7–9: Bombori.** Hundreds of lanterns line the Hachiman-gū approach. Those who walk through the large straw hoop on the walkway are ensured a trouble-free year.
**Aug. 10: Fireworks festival** at Yuigahama Beach. From 19:30.
**Sept. 14–16:** * **Tsurugaoka Hachiman-gū Matsuri.** Purification rites at Yuigahama Beach on 14th. At noon on the 15th, three *mikoshi* exit the shrine. On the 16th, *yabusame*

from 13:00. Mounted archers charge down a shrine avenue at a full gallop and try to hit three targets in quick succession.

**Sept. 18: ✳ Menkake-gyōretsu.** The festival commemorates a legend about an outcast girl who became pregnant by Yoritomo. On his visits to her, he was accompanied by outcast men who wore masks to hide their identity. Today, men wearing grotesque masks, including one dressed as a pregnant woman, form a procession from Goryō Jinja to Gokuraku-ji. Childless women touch the masked "woman's" belly in the belief that they will become pregnant. The masks date from 1768. Begins at 13:00. Get there early.

**Sept. 21–22: ✳ Takigi (Torchlight) Noh.** Kamakura-gū. Apply for permission to attend by sending a self-addressed card between Sept. 1–8 to Kamakura-shi Kankō Kyōkai, 18-35 Onari-chō, Kamakura-shi, Kanagawa-ken.

**Nov. 1–3: Special showing of temple treasures** at Engaku-ji and Kenchō-ji, 9:00–16:00.

# Late Kamakura History:
# Nichiren and the Mongol Invasions

(see p. 261 for early history)

| | |
|---|---|
| **Nichiren** | (1222–1282) The impassioned evangelist who predicted the Mongol invasion but was exiled for his attacks on other Buddhist sects. |
| **Hōjō Tokiyori** | (1226–1263) The Kamakura regent. A follower of Zen, he founded Kenchō-ji and exiled Nichiren. |
| **Hōjō Tokimune** | (1251–1284) Tokiyori's son and regent during the two Mongol attacks. He was trained to military leadership by the Zen priest Mugaku and founded Engaku-ji. |
| **Mugaku** | (1226–1286) A Chinese Zen priest who survived the Mongol invasion of China. He sought refuge in Kamakura and became Tokimune's preceptor. |

In 1260, **Nichiren**, the fiery religious leader (see Buddhism, p. 38), sent a prophetic letter to the regent **Tokiyori** in Kamakura. In it, he predicted that the Mongol hordes pillaging the continent would invade Japan. He also wrote that if the entire nation did not abandon other sects and convert to his teaching, Japan's rulers would be vanquished and its people subjugated. For Japan, a nation of considerable religious tolerance, these were strong words. This was Japan's Age of Faith, however, and religious sentiment was hot. Buddhism was spreading from the aristocracy to the common people. In the 1240s, a single mendicant priest named Jōkō was able to raise enough funds from popular donations alone to cast the **Daibutsu**, a 12-meter bronze image of Amida Buddha. Nichiren was equally impassioned about his own brand of Buddhism, and had little good to say about any others: The Jōdo (Amidist) sect to which Jōkō belonged was denounced as the "path to hell," followers of Zen were "devils," Shingon would be the "ruin of the country," and the members of the Ritsu sect were "traitors." After receiving Nichiren's letter, Tokiyori, a Zen believer, exiled Nichiren to Izu.

It was Tokiyori's support of Zen that made Kamakura famous for Zen temples. His interest in this sect seems to have started after he met Dōgen, the founder of Sōtō Zen in Japan. Tokiyori became a student of **Rankei Dōryū**, a Chinese Rinzai Zen priest, for whom he built Kamakura's most prominent temple, **Kenchō-ji**, in 1253. Tokiyori even sent a priest to China to study building techniques and thus ensure that Kenchō-ji would be exactly like a Southern Sung Zen temple. In the following years, as Mongol armies swept across China, many Chinese Zen priests fled to Japan, where they found a home at Kenchō-ji.

In 1268, a letter arrived for Tokiyori's son and successor, the 18-year-old **Tokimune**. Addressing the "King of Japan," its author, Kublai Khan, demanded Japan become the Khan's tributary or face certain doom. The Japanese sent no reply. In 1274, the Mongols and their Chinese conscripts, sailing on Korean ships, attacked. After subjecting the islanders of Iki and Tsushima to assorted atrocities, the Mongols landed in northern Kyūshū, at Hakata Bay (see Kyūshū, p. 474). The local lords were helpless against the Mongol crossbows and engines of war, which included gunpowder bombs and huge catapults hurling fiery projectiles. All would have been lost had not a fierce storm decimated the Mongol fleet, forcing the Khan's soldiers to retreat to Korea.

Twice, representatives of the Khan came to Kamakura to repeat the demand for surrender; each time, Tokimune had them beheaded. Tokimune, like his father, was a firm believer in Zen. Tokimune is said to be the first commander to apply Zen principles to the art of war—what later would be called *bushidō*, the Way of the Warrior.

He invited the Chinese monk **Mugaku** to stay at Kenchō-ji. According to legend, while Mugaku was still in China, the Mongols raided his monastery, lopping off the shaved heads of terrified monks left and right. Mugaku remained in meditation, unperturbed by the possibility of imminent death; the Mongols, either puzzled or impressed, left him alone. In the few months between Mugaku's arrival and the Mongol attack, Mugaku is said to have used Zen principles to train Tokimune and his lieutenants to dedicate themselves singlemindedly to victory.

Tokimune commanded the construction of a huge wall to encircle Hakata Bay. It was nearly completed when, in 1581, the second Mongol armada, 150,000 strong, attacked. This was the largest sea-borne attack the world had yet seen. After more than fifty days of desperate fighting, Japanese forces were again near capitulation. Suddenly, another storm broke, blowing the invaders back out to sea, never to be seen again. To the Japanese, this twice-repeated miracle could only be a sign of divine will, and was called the kamikaze, or "wind of god." The suicide pilots of the last days of World War II adopted this name in hopes of similarly snatching victory from the jaws of defeat.

In 1282, Tokimune completed **Engaku-ji** to console the souls of the fallen, and appointed Mugaku as its first abbot. This temple owns a famous statue of Mugaku as well as Japan's finest Zen-style hall, the **Shari-den**. Tokimune died in 1282, on the day he took holy orders; his wife became a nun and founded Tōkei-ji, the "divorce temple," across the glen from Engaku-ji.

Nichiren's first prediction, that the Mongols would invade, had come true. And although Japan did not become a Mongol possession, the second part of the prediction was not entirely wrong; the Mongol invasion was one of the principal causes of the Hōjō downfall, fifty years later. Fearful of yet a third Mongol attack, the shogunate had to man Hakata Bay until after Kublai's death, in 1294. Added to this burden were signs of growing restlessness among the samurai, who clamored for recompense for years of bravery and sacrifice. Yet none was forthcoming, for the repulsion of the Mongol invasion had left no booty.

**Hōjō Takatoki**, who in 1311, at the age of eight, succeeded to the regency, exacerbated the problems by ignoring politics and devoting his time to dog fights. Sensing weakness, **Emperor Go-Daigo** rebelled (for a second time) in 1331 over a succession dispute (see Yoshino History, p. 411). The two Hōjō vassals who were sent to quell the disturbance, ASHIKAGA TAKAUJI and Nitta Yoshisada, both defected to Go-Daigo's side. Nitta Yoshisada marched on Kamakura in 1333. After five days of heavy fighting, Takatoki withdrew to Tōshō-ji and committed suicide with hundreds of followers; today the **Harakiri Cave** is all that remains of Tōshō-ji. Later, Ashikaga Takauji would establish a new shogunate at Kyoto, leaving Kamakura to fade into obscurity.

Nichiren, however, never had the pleasure of seeing the downfall of the hated Hōjō. Although released from Izu in 1263, he was arrested once more in 1271, almost executed, then exiled to the island of Sado, where he converted most of the population. In 1274, he was pardoned, perhaps in deference to the accuracy of his prediction. Nichiren wrote his greatest theological work in Kamakura, and the many Nichiren sect temples in the eastern part of town attest to his lasting influence. But in the end, Kamakura was nothing but a disappointment to him. After failing for a final time to get Hōjō Tokimune to accept his brand of Buddhism as the national religion, he and his followers retired to Mt. Minobu. It is said that Nichiren was bitterly disappointed when Tokimune managed to repel the Mongols a second time, confounding his prophecy yet again. He died soon thereafter, on November 21, 1282.

259

## Getting Around

There are three main areas: (1) Kita-Kamakura, (2) Central Kamakura, and (3) the Great Buddha Area. You can see the main attractions in a busy, well-planned day. Kamakura has some interesting hiking trails. Rent-a-cycle at the station and at Yamamoto Shōten on Komachi-dōri. Weekends and holidays, especially in spring and fall, are unbelievably crowded. Try to visit on a weekday. Kita-Kamakura is always quieter and more scenic; it is highly recommended for those seeking a contemplative atmosphere. *Exploring Kamakura*, by Michael Cooper (Weatherhill), provides a very nice historical guide to Kamakura. *Kamakura: Its History, Sights and Landmarks* (Japan Times) is not useful as a guidebook, but offers details on art and history.

## Kita-Kamakura 北鎌倉

★★★ **Engaku-ji** 円覚寺 Hrs: Mar. and Oct. 8:00–16:30; Apr. and Sept. 8:00–17:00; May– Aug. 8:00–17:30; Nov.–Feb. 8:00–16:00. The entrance is by Kita-Kamakura station. Engaku-ji was founded in 1282 by the regent Hōjō Tokimune, who built the temple for his Zen preceptor Mugaku, and to console the souls of warriors slain in the second Mongol attack the previous year. After entering the **Sō-mon**, the great **San-mon** (Main Gate, 1783) appears on the right. Directly behind the gate is the **Butsuden** (Buddha Hall), rebuilt in 1964. Its predecessor was destroyed in the Kantō Earthquake of 1923.

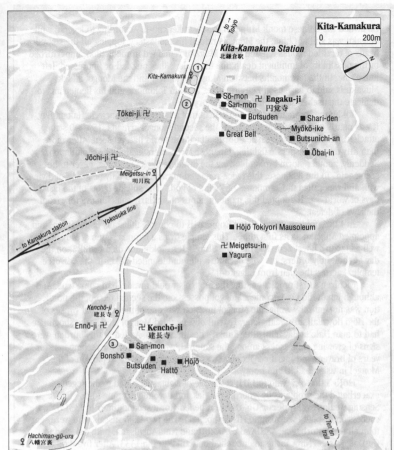

Up on the slope to the right, reached by stone stairs, is the temple's **Great Bell** (1301, NT), famous for its sonorous boom and beautiful shape.

> **Subtemples.** Engaku-ji formerly had 42 subtemples, of which 17 remain. Several can be seen in the upper part of the precincts. Follow the path left of the Butsuden, past a rectangular pond, **Myōkō-ike**. A short path to the left leads to **Shōzoku-in**, a subtemple founded by Mugaku and renowned for its ◆ **Shari-den** 舎利殿 (NT), or relic hall, considered the oldest extant example of a Sung-style temple hall. This famous structure, which unfortunately cannot be seen up close, exhibits the characteristic features of the Zen style (see Buddhism, p. 39). Its roof was originally gently sloped, but was redone with a thick layer of cypress, resulting in an atypically steep pitch. The hall's age is not known, but it is thought to have been brought to its present site from a Kamakura nunnery in the Muromachi period. Nearby is the pleasant **Butsunichi-an**, where one can rest over a bowl of tea. Opposite is the White Deer Cave, where a deer is said to have come to listen to Mugaku give the temple's inaugural sermon. At the top are the peaceful grounds of **Ōbai-in**, which was MUSŌ SOSEKI's subtemple. Engaku-ji's treasures are shown publicly from Nov. 1–3.

**∗ Tōkei-ji** 東慶寺 Hrs: 8:30–17:00. This was the famous Kakekomi-dera (Run-in Temple) founded in 1285 by the nun Kakuzan, widow of Hōjō Tokimune, as a refuge for abused wives. Kakuzan appealed for a law that allowed women to seek refuge at the convent and to obtain a divorce after spending three years here as a nun; until 1873, this was virtually the only way a woman could escape an unhappy marriage. In 1902, having outlived its function, Tōkei-ji became a regular Zen monastery with a male abbot.

> **Matsugaoka Hōzō** 松ガ岡宝蔵 Hrs: 10:00–15:00; clsd M. A museum and library on Tōkei-ji grounds, famed for its classic Zen texts, much of it donated by the Zen philosopher Suzuki Daisetz (1870–1966). It exhibits a lovely Muromachi-period ◆ **Suigetsu Kannon** (Kannon gazing at the moon's reflection on water) and a **lacquer box** (ICP) for the Catholic host. One room shows calligraphy. There is a cartoon illustrating the Zen teaching that anyone, even a vegetable, can achieve enlightenment.

**Jōchi-ji** 浄智寺 Hrs: 9:00–16:30. Founded in 1281, this Zen temple was ranked fourth among the Five Great Kamakura Zen temples. The Dongeden, on the right, houses a Sanzebutsu (Buddhas of the Three Worlds): Shaka (past), Amida (present), and Miroku (future). The grounds have an attractive air of age and neglect.

**Meigetsu-in** 明月院 Hrs: 9:00–16:30. In June 6:00–18:00. Worth a visit in June, when the wooded hillside grounds become a mass of pink, blue, and violet hydrangeas.

**\*\*\* Kenchō-ji** 建長寺 Hrs: 9:00–16:30. *0:15h walk from Kita-Kamakura station.* Head of the Five Great Kamakura Zen temples, completed in 1253 by regent Hōjō Tokiyori, who was an ardent student of Zen. He appointed the Chinese priest Rankei Dōryū as its first abbot. Kenchō-ji has burned many times, and many of its halls were destroyed in the Kantō Earthquake of 1923. The great **San-mon** (gate, 1754) houses 500 rakan statues (not on view). To the right is the **Bonshō** (NT), a great bell cast in 1255. The approach to the **Butsuden** (Buddha Hall, 1647, ICP) is lined with 700-year-old junipers, planted from seed brought from China by the founder. The Butsuden houses a large seated image of Jizō, containing a smaller Jizō which is credited with a miracle: it saved a condemned man from execution because he had hidden it in his topknot. The **Hattō** (1814), behind the Butsuden, is for public ceremonies. To the left, behind this hall, is a **Kara-mon** (Chinese Gate, ICP) and the **Hōjō** (Abbot's Hall), which has a famous **pond garden** in back, attributed to MUSŌ SOSEKI. The path continues into the hills, where it joins the Ten'en hiking course (see p. 264). On Nov. 1–3, Kenchō-ji shows its treasures, including a painting of Rankei Dōryū (1271, NT) and a portrait statue of Hōjō Tokiyori (ICP).

**Ennō-ji** 円応寺 Hrs: 9:00–16:00. Y100 donation in lieu of admission fee. Across the road from Kenchō-ji. This temple houses statues of the Ten Kings of Hell, presided over by **Emma-ō** (1251, ICP), who decide the fate of the dead. There are also images of **Jizō** and of **Datsueba**, the old hag who relieves all souls of their clothes on the banks of the Buddhist equivalent of the river Styx. Such depictions of hell and judgment became popular in the Kamakura period.

**Kenchō-ji to Central Kamakura:** *From Kenchō-ji bus stop, there are buses to Kamakura station via Hachiman-gū-ura (back of Tsurugaoka Hachiman-gū). The bus road goes through a Kamakura-period* kiritōshi, *one of seven passages hewn through the mountains for the various roads radiating out of Kamakura.*

# Early Kamakura History: Deceit and Betrayal—The Founding of the Kamakura Shogunate

| | |
|---|---|
| **Minamoto no Yoritomo** | (1147–1199) The first military ruler of Japan, founder of the shogunate capital at Kamakura, leader of the Minamoto clan, and the elder brother of Yoshitsune. |
| **Hōjō Masako** | (1157–1225) Yoritomo's wife, who wielded great power after his death as the "nun shogun." |
| **Hōjō Tokimasa** | (1138–1215) Masako's father and founder of a line of regents who governed from Yoritomo's death to the end of the Kamakura period. |
| **Shizuka Gozen** | The legendary lover of Yoshitsune. She was a famous *shirabyōshi* ("white rhythm"), a type of dancer who wore a male priest's white robe and carried drums or cymbals. They were popular at court in the 12th–13th centuries. |

**Hōjō Masako** has been called the strongest woman in Japanese history. When YORITOMO, heir to the leadership of the Minamoto clan, was exiled to Izu by TAIRA NO KIYOMORI and put in the custody of her family, she eloped with the proud young warrior, against her father **Tokimasa**'s wishes. Tokimasa was a man of discernment, however, and even though of Taira lineage himself, he decided to help Yoritomo against Kiyomori. Several other Taira families in eastern Japan followed his lead, and after the Minamoto victory (see Miyajima History, p. 449), he was second only to Yoritomo among the powerful men of Kamakura. The new military capital was established near the Minamoto tutelary shrine founded by Yoritomo's illustrious ancestor, Yoriyoshi, during his campaigns in northern Japan (see Hiraizumi History, p. 169). This shrine, **Tsurugaoka Hachiman-gū**, was moved a kilometer inland, where it became the center of the new capital.

Yoritomo was a calculating, able politician who bent the rest of Japan to his will; a famous portrait shows him an imperious, steely-eyed man. If he failed to set up a dynasty, it was perhaps because of want of family feeling. He was violently jealous of his younger half-brother YOSHITSUNE, who was a brilliant general and popular at court; just to hear Yoshitsune's name put him into a rage. Accusing Yoshitsune of subversion, Yoritomo issued an order for his capture, dead or alive.

It was some years before Yoritomo would see Yoshitsune's head, but his men were able to capture his brother's beloved, **Shizuka Gozen**. Masako commanded

Shizuka, the most skillful dancer of her time, to give an exhibition of her art to the assembled Kamakura grandees at Tsurugaoka Hachiman-gū. Though fearful for the fate of her lover and the child she was carrying—which Yoritomo ordered killed when it proved to be a boy—she danced with open defiance, singing of her love and anguish for the hunted Yoshitsune. Yoritomo was near apoplexy; only Masako could calm him down.

Masako was a formidable woman. During Yoritomo's rise to power, she wore a sword, and was said to have ridden into battle at times. Masako was not only Yoritomo's personal equal, she also had her powerful family behind her. Once when she discovered Yoritomo had a mistress, she had Hōjō vassals burn down the lady's house. Yoritomo, on the other hand, had little family left; in addition to persecuting and killing Yoshitsune, he had his remaining brother exiled and murdered as well. When Yoritomo was thrown from a horse and killed in 1199, he had few personal followers to protect **Yoriie**, his heir, a man who had few political talents and could not fend for himself.

Yoritomo had Yoriie marry a woman from the Hiki family, which now backed Yoriie's infant son to succeed him as shogun. Masako, along with her father and the powerful Hōjō clan, supported her younger son, **Sanetomo**. In 1203, the Hōjō invited the Hiki to settle their differences amicably over a banquet, but then treacherously slew the Hiki family members and the proposed heir, and razed their mansion on the site where Myōhon-ji stands today. Yoriie was soon disposed of as well (see Izu History, p. 269). Sanetomo became shogun, but in 1219, he was ambushed and killed on the front steps of Tsurugaoka Hachiman-gū by Kugyō, a younger son of Yoriie; Kugyō himself was quickly caught and killed, and Yoritomo's line was extinguished.

The office of shogun was given to an infant Fujiwara prince, brought from Kyoto. The Hōjō, whose power was now complete, governed as "regents" for this shogun (who was in turn supposed to be a kind of regent for the emperor in Kyoto). Masako had shaved her head and entered Jufuku-ji in 1199, after Yoritomo's death, inviting the priest **Eisai**, founder of the Rinzai Zen sect in Japan, to officiate there. Masako was called the "nun shogun," for she still wielded great power; when her father, Tokimasa, plotted against her in 1205, she promptly exiled him to Izu.

Masako died in 1225, at the age of sixty-eight. After her death, her brothers and their descendants continued to rule as regents for more than a century. Masako's interest in Zen was halfhearted; Eisai was asked mainly to perform Esoteric Buddhist rites in Yoritomo's memory and for the protection of the state. Her great-grandnephew, however, the fifth Hōjō regent **Tokiyori**, was an enthusiastic Zen believer and would begin founding the great Zen temples of Kita-Kamakura.

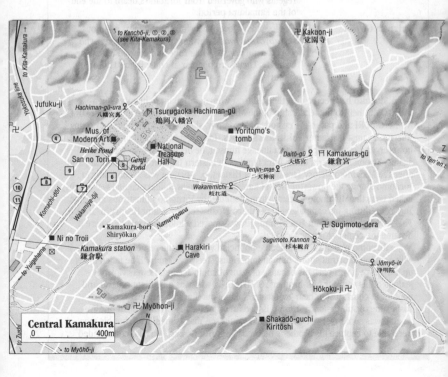

## Central Kamakura

To visit Tsurugaoka Hachiman-gū, exit by the east side of the station, then walk 0:10h on foot by one of two routes, **Komachi-dōri**, a bustling shop-lined street to the left (spanned by a red torii), or by **Wakamiya-ōji**, the historical approach. This avenue, spanned by three huge torii, was built by Yoritomo in 1182 as an offering for a safe delivery for the pregnant Masako. Between the second and third torii, a raised promenade down the center survives from the original approach. It is lined with cherry trees, which form a tunnel of blossoms in spring. The Hachiman-gū precinct begins at San no Torii (Torii No. 3).

**\*\*\* Tsurugaoka Hachiman-gū** 鶴岡八幡宮 This historic shrine was founded near Kamakura Bay in 1063 by Minamoto no Yoriyoshi as a branch of Kyoto's Iwashimizu Hachiman-gū, the tutelary shrine of his clan (see Hiraizumi History, p. 169). Yoriyoshi was on his way to quell a rebellion in northern Japan, and his successes precipitated the rise of the Minamoto as the foremost warrior clan in Japan. His descendant, Yoritomo, moved the shrine to its present site in 1180, atop a hill overlooking his headquarters.

The central approach crosses over a half-moon bridge that divides **Gempei Ike**, a pair of large, lotus-filled ponds. Masako supposedly conceived of building three islands in the larger, right-hand pond, and four islands in the smaller pond, for a symbolism of homonyms; *san* (three) also means birth, and *shi* (four) means death, hence the victorious Genji (Minamoto) and the defeated Heike (Taira). The ponds are planted with the appropriate Genji-white and Heike-red lotuses.

◆ **Hongū (Shrine Hall).** To the left of the steep stairs leading to the Hongū is an enormous **gingko tree**, nearly a thousand years old. It was here that, in 1219, Sanetomo was assassinated by his nephew, who ambushed him from behind the tree. The **Shimo Haiden**, an open hall at the foot of the stairs, is said to stand on the site where Shizuka Gozen danced before Yoritomo. The Hongū, rebuilt in 1828, is in classic Hachiman style, with covered galleries surrounding a pair of linked halls. Some of the shrine treasures are on view in the **Hōmotsuden** (Hrs: 9:00–16:00).

**\*\*\* Kokuhōkan (National Treasure Hall)** 国宝館 Hrs: 9:00–16:00; clsd M, NY. Special all-NT and ICP exhibition four times a year. Informative pamphlet in English. Some 2,000 treasures belonging to Kamakura temples are on view here, a few at a time, with exhibits changing monthly. The pieces mostly date from the Kamakura and Muromachi periods, and include many portrait statues of Kamakura-period lords and Zen priests, Jōdo-sect images of Amida, Jizō, and the Kings of Hell. The nude image of the goddess Benten (ICP) is a celebrated example of Kamakura realism (see Art, p. 94).

## Northeast Kamakura

The region just northeast of Tsurugaoka Hachiman-gū was the site of the various Kamakura shogunate headquarters. Nearby are Yoritomo's tomb and a number of temples in isolated, beautiful settings.

**Kamakura-gū** 鎌倉宮 *0:10h walk from Kokuhōkan, or 0:10h by bus to Daitō-gū bus stop.* This shrine was founded by the Meiji government in 1869 to memorialize Prince Morinaga (1308–1335), son of Emperor Go-Daigo (see Yoshino History, p. 411). Near the shrine is the cave where Morinaga, accused of plotting against the formidable general ASHI-KAGA TAKAUJI, was imprisoned. Takauji later had the prince executed, while Go-Daigo, who had been restored to power with Takauji's help, did nothing to save his son. The prince's grave is on a hilltop across the river.

**\* Kakuon-ji** 覚園寺 By guided tours (0:50h, Y300) only, at 10:00, 11:00, 13:00, 14:00, and 15:00. Clsd in rainy weather, Aug., and Dec. 20–Jan 7. *0:15h walk from Kamakura-gū.* This temple, located in a forested glen, was founded in 1296 as an ecumenical seminary. The **Jizō-dō** enshrines a Black Jizō statue (Kamakura period, ICP), who was burned black when he took the place of a soul burning in hell. The **Yakushi-dō** houses a Yakushi trinity (ICP) and Twelve Divine Generals. A path near the entrance to the precincts leads to the Ten'en hiking trail (see below).

**\* Zuisen-ji** 瑞泉寺 Hrs: 9:00–17:00. *0:15h walk from Kamakura-gū.* This secluded temple was founded at the close of the Kamakura period by the famous Zen prelate MUSŌ SOSEKI, who also founded or presided over major temples in Kyoto. Musō, one of Japan's legendary garden designers, created Zuisen-ji's ◆ **garden**, which was excavated and carefully restored in 1970 to its original state. This bare, naturalistic composition, consisting mainly of a "heart" pond and natural cliff face, is considered the most important garden of the Kamakura period. It lacks plants or rock arrangements; instead, the cliff was hewn to create a symbolic meditation cave.

**Harakiri Yagura** 腹切りやぐら This dank cave, marked by a stone memorial, is all that's left of Tōshō-ji, the temple where Takatoki, the last Hōjō regent, committed suicide along with some 870 followers in 1333, rather than be captured by the army of Nitta Yoshisada.

**Sugimoto-dera (Temple)** 杉本寺 Hrs: 8:30–16:30. This atmospheric temple is said to date from 734, making it the oldest in Kamakura. Steep stone steps climb to a thatched main hall, which houses three Kannon statues from the 12th–13th C. The grounds are full of mossy tombs.

**Shakadō-guchi Kiritōshi** 釈迦堂口切通 *0:15h on foot from the Sugimoto Kannon bus stop.* A dirt road leads up to a tunnel cut through the mountain in the Kamakura period. There are many *yagura* nearby.

**Hōkoku-ji** 報国寺 Hrs: 9:00–16:00. This small Zen temple has a pretty bamboo grove.

263

**Ten'en Hiking Trail** 天園ハイキングコース Perhaps the best place to start is Zuisen-ji. Just inside the temple gate, to the right, is the narrow Ten'en trail. The trail is quite pretty, although right in the middle it crosses a golf links, which momentarily breaks the spell. Along the way are several *yagura*, including **Hyakuhachi Yagura** (108 Cave Tombs), scattered in the area near the junction to the path leading down to Kakuon-ji. The hike to Kenchō-ji (Kita-Kamakura) takes 1:30h.

## Eastern Kamakura

∗ **Myōhon-ji** 妙本寺 *0:10h walk from station.* This large Nichiren temple dominates a quarter that abounds in Nichiren temples. Founded in 1274, it stands in a beautiful glen that was the site of a tragedy. In 1203, a succession dispute arose following the illness of the second shogun, Yoriie. Hiki Yoshikazu, a valued retainer of the Minamoto, put forward a claim for his 3-year-old grandson, Ichiman, the child of his daughter and Yoriie. The Hōjō responded by murdering Yoshikazu, Ichiman, and most other family members, and razing the Hiki mansion, which stood in this glen. All that was left of Ichiman was one of his tiny sleeves, which was buried in the Sleeve Mound, to the right of the temple's second gate.

∗ **Myōhō-ji** 妙法寺 *0:15h walk from Myōbon-ji.* This Nichiren temple has lovely, gardenlike grounds and an ancient, moss-covered flight of stone steps up the hill behind the temple. There is a nice view over Kamakura from the top of the hill.

## West of Tsurugaoka Hachiman-gū

∗∗ **Jufuku-ji** 寿福寺 *0:10h walk from station.* This temple's serene, maple-shaded stone approach, with a view of the main hall framed by the inner gate, is one of Kamakura's loveliest sights. Yoritomo had planned to build his headquarters here, on the site of his father's house, but gave up because one of his father's retainers had a small settlement there. In 1200, a year after Yoritomo's death, Masako built this temple, with Eisai, founder of the Rinzai Zen sect, as its first abbot. It is thus one of the earliest Zen temples in Japan. One can apply at the abbot's house, to the right, to enter its Main Hall and see a pair of Niō statues saved from Tsurugaoka Hachiman-gū during the Meiji-period "purge" of shrines. The path skirting the grounds leads to a pretty cemetery with the **tombs of Masako and Sanetomo.**

∗∗ **Zeniarai Benten** 銭洗弁天 *0:05h by taxi from station.* A very popular shrine to Benten, goddess of fortune, called "coin-washing Benten" because the spring at the shrine is supposed to ensure a 100 percent profit on the money washed in it. The shrine's origins go back to a dream Yoritomo had in which it was revealed to him that if he built a shrine at this spring, his new capital would prosper. The dream occurred at the hour of the snake, on the day of the snake, and in the year of the snake; as the snake is the messenger of Benten, it was obvious to whom the shrine was to be consecrated. The grounds, nestled in a gorge, are full of caves, running water, incense smoke, and countless subshrines, teahouses, and fortune tellers. The shrine is crowded on the Day of the Snake (every 12 days by the Chinese calendar), when the efficacy of the money washing is especially high. Look for offerings of eggs — a favorite food of snakes.

## Great Buddha Area

*From Kamakura station, 0:15h by bus to Daibutsu-mae, or 0:05h by Enoden private rail to Hase station.*

∗∗∗ **Kōtoku-in Daibutsu (Great Buddha)** 高徳院大仏 (NT). Hrs: Apr.–May and Sept.–Oct. 7:00–18:00. June–Aug. 7:00–18:00. Nov.–Mar. 7:00–17:00. Enter by 0:30h before closing. *0:10h walk from Hase station.* Though this is one of the most famous images in Japan, almost nothing is known about its origin. By popular account, Jōkō, an Amidist priest of the mid-12th C, raised funds to build a Great Buddha. It is thought that a wooden version was carved between 1238 and 1247. The bronze statue was completed in 1252, after repeated castings. It is 11.31 m tall without the pedestal. The image was originally housed in a huge hall, but the building was destroyed several times. In 1495, a tidal wave swept it away for good, leaving only foundation stones. The great bronze Buddha has sat in the open ever since. The image represents Amida, the merciful Buddha of the Western Paradise. In spite of its ungainly size, it is a masterpiece of proportion, designed not to be contemplated from afar, but to enfold and comfort the worshipper who kneels before it. Critics denounce it as top-heavy, but others point out that this is an ingenious way to achieve the proper balance between the head and the body.

∗∗ **Hase-dera** 長谷寺 Hrs: 7:00–17:00. Oct.–Feb. 7:00–16:40. *0:05h walk from Hase station.* By legend, this temple's 9-meter-tall gilded image of Kannon was carved from the same immense camphor tree as the celebrated Hase-Kannon in the mountains south of Nara (Kinki, p. 404). The twin was set adrift, and eventually washed ashore at Kamakura in 736, where this temple was founded for it. The earliest historical records of the temple, however, go back only to the Kamakura period. The famous Kannon image is housed in a modern, fireproof hall that displays the statue's size — it is among the largest wooden images in Japan — to good advantage. The temple grounds are filled with numerous stone Jizō dressed in red bibs; many are Mizuko-Jizō, offered recently by women to console their unborn children. (Abortion is a common form of birth control in modern Japan.)

## Enoshima 江ノ島

*0:25h by Eno-den private rail from Kamakura station.* Right by the station is **Ryūkō-ji**, a large Nichiren temple founded on the spot where, on September 13, 1271, Nichiren was saved from execution by a timely bolt of lightning, which knocked the blade from the executioner's hand. The temple is crowded with gong-beating worshippers from Sept. 11 to 13 in annual services commemorating the miracle. Nearby **Enoshima** is connected to the mainland by a causeway. This island is a famous place to view Mt. Fuji and is covered with atmospheric shrines and temples; one shrine is famous for its nude statue of the goddess Benten.

## Kamakura Shopping

The famous Kamakura-bori (Kamakura carving) is claimed to be nearly as old as the city itself, having originated as a form of decoration for Zen temple fixtures inspired by Sung Chinese carved lacquer. Designs such as Chinese cloud patterns, arabesques, camellias, and peonies are carved in a wood base, then coated with 7 to 8 layers of vermilion lacquer and given an antique burnish by sprinkling charcoal dust over the wet lacquer. To survive in the modern era, artisans turned to the carving of trays, tea caddies, hand mirrors, and furniture. Many Kamakura-bori shops are on Wakamiya-ōji. Komachi-dōri is the main shopping street.
**Kamakura-bori Shiryōkan** 鎌倉彫会館 (25-1502). Hrs: 10:00–16:00; clsd Su. Exhibits fine examples of Kamakura-bori, from the Kamakura period to the present, including Sung and Ming Chinese prototypes. Explanations in English. Small library.

⑤ **Hakuko-dō** 博古堂 (22-2429). Hrs: 9:00–17:30; clsd 2nd Su, NY, mid-Aug. At San no Torii. The finest Kamakura-bori, from this 28th-generation artisan line.

⑥ **Hasshō-dō** 八勝堂 (22-3778). Hrs: 8:00–18:00; clsd 2nd and 4th Tu (next day, if NH). Reasonable prices for quality work.

⑨ * **Yamago** やまご (22-1772). This shop on Komachi-dōri offers a superb selection of elegant bamboo utensils and flower baskets. Great gifts at affordable prices.

## Kamakura Dining

① **Yamamoto** やま本 (22-3310). Hrs: 10:30–17:00; clsd Tu, NY. A pleasant *soba* and *udon* noodle shop by Kita-Kamakura station. From Y380.

② * **Monzen** 門前 (25-1121). Hrs: 11:00–19:30; clsd NY. *Shōjin-ryōri* (see Cuisine, p. 117). *Obentō* from Y3000. Kaiseki from Y5000.

③ * **Hachinoki** 鉢の木 (22-8719). Hrs: 11:00–19:00; clsd M (Tu if M a NH), NY. *Shōjin-ryōri* near Kenchō-ji. From Y5000–11,700.

④ **Fudō Chaya** 不動茶屋 (22-7839). Hrs: 11:00–17:30; clsd Th (except if NH). Quaint teahouse on quiet lane near Jufuku-ji. Noodles and sweets (see Cuisine, p. 119). The garden contains a cave temple to Fudō.

⑩ ** **Isomi-tei** 磯見亭 (24-9127). Hrs: 11:00–19:00; clsd Th (W or F if Th a NH). Famous *soba* shop with lovely Japanese atmosphere. *Soba* from Y600.

⑪ ** **Tori-ichi** とり一 (22-1818). Hrs: 12:00–15:00, 17:00–20:00; clsd Tu. Famous for chicken dishes. Lovely setting. *Bentō* Y2500, *hako kaiseki* Y3500.

** **La Maree de Chaya** ラマレドチャヤ 葉山町鐙摺 (0468-75-6683). Hrs: 12:00–14:30, 17:30–21:30; clsd M (Tu if M a NH), NY. Near Zushi, one stop beyond Kamakura. An excellent nouvelle cuisine restaurant. In warm weather, ask for a table on the veranda overlooking the marina. Lunch menu Y5000; dinner Y8000 and Y10,000.

## Kamakura Lodgings (TEL 0467)

Being so close to Tokyo, Kamakura does not have much in the way of good lodgings. The beach resort of Zushi is one train stop to the east.

⑦ **Ushio Ryokan** 潮旅館 鎌倉市小町2-3-9 (22-7016). 2-3-9 Komachi, Kamakura-shi, Kanagawa-ken. Simple five-room inn on a quiet side street. Some English spoken. Y4500 w/o meals. No CC.

⑧ **Shangrila Tsurugaoka** シャングリラ鶴ヶ岡 鎌倉市雪ノ下1-9-29 (25-6363). 1-9-29 Yukinoshita. Simply furnished small hotel. Y6000 per person.

* **Kaihin-sō** 海浜荘 (22-0960). 4-8-14 Yuigahama. Fanciest ryokan in Kamakura; a mix of modern Sukiya style and Western fantasy. Y20–30,000 w/meals.

**Minshuku Yamakawa** 民宿山川 由比ヶ浜3-11-41 (22-0783). 3-11-41 Yuigahama. 0:05h walk from Yuigahama station on the Enoden line. No English spoken. Y6500 w/meals.

**Ajisai-sō** あじさい荘 (22-3506). 25-4 Sakanoshita. Cosy hotel run by a private-school association, open to nonmembers. Near Hase station and beach. Japanese rooms. Y4000 per person w/o meals, Y8000 w/meals.

**Kamakura Hotel Kagetsu-en (YH)** ホテル花月園 (25-1234). 27-9 Sakashita. Crowded, reservations a must. Ryokan rate is Y9600 w/meals. YH rate Y3800 w/meals.

## W3 ODAWARA 小田原

*0:45h by Kodama Shinkansen from Tokyo. By JR Tōkaidō line express, 1:05h from Tokyo station, or 0:25h from Ōfuna (junction to Yokosuka line). Or 1:15h by private Odakyū line express from Shinjuku.* Odawara was once a great castle town, but today most tourists merely pass through on their way to Hakone-Yumoto.

## W4 * HAKONE 箱根

*To Hakone-Yumoto, 1:30h by private Odakyū line direct express from Shinjuku station in Tokyo, via Odawara.* For the visitor who wants to spend a night out of Tokyo at a hot spring, Hakone is convenient, and not without its cultural attractions and scenic points. There are more than a dozen spas to choose from: Yumoto is the largest; Miyanoshita has the classic Fujiya Hotel; Dōgashima's inns are inside a gorge.

## Calendar

**Mar. 27:** \* **Yudate Shishi-mai.** Suwa Jinja, Sengokuhara (*0:40h by bus from Odawara*). A droll lion-dancer prances about a cauldron of boiling water, stirring it with a spray of bamboo and sprinkling the water over spectators as a charm against illness. From 11:00.
**July 15:** \* **Yudate Shishi-mai.** Miyagino Suwa Jinja (*0:45h by bus from Odawara*); see Mar. 27.
**Aug. 5: Torii-yaki.** Hakone. On Lake Ashi. From 19:30–21:00, rites in honor of the dragon deity of the lake. A pair of 15-meter torii is set afire. Fireworks and thousands of lanterns are set afloat.
**Nov. 3: Daimyo Procession.** Hakone-Yumoto. Reenacting the Odawara lord's procession.

## Getting Around

The main points of interest in Hakone form a loop: Hakone-Yumoto — (Hakone Tozan-tetsudō narrow-gauge rail, via several onsen and Hakone Open-Air Museum) — Gōra — (tramway) — Lake Ashi — (bus or boat) — Hakone Barrier — (old Tōkaidō) — Hatajuku — Hakone-Yumoto. Buses from Yumoto also cover all these sights.

## Hakone Sights

**Yumoto** 湯本 This onsen town is one of the most famous in Japan, and one of the oldest in the area. Today, it's crammed with tourists, souvenir shops, and hotels. For culture, one might visit **Sōun-ji**, a Rinzai Zen temple that was the mortuary temple of the Odawara Hōjō lords. HIDEYOSHI used it as his headquarters during the siege of Odawara Castle. **Shōgen-ji** is associated with the Soga brothers, Jūrō and Gorō, medieval heroes who often appear in Noh and Kabuki. The brothers are commemorated at this temple by the Jizō statues in the Soga-dō, a small hall said to have been built by Tora Gozen, Jūrō's mistress. At the west end of town is a stretch of stone pavement from the Tōkaidō. **Dining: Hatsuhana** はつ花 (5-8287). Hrs: 10:00–19:00; clsd Tu. *Soba.* **Shigure Chaya** 時雨茶屋 (5-7814). Hrs: 11:30–16:00; clsd W. *Soba.* **Tenzan Notenburo** 天山野天風呂 (5-7446). Hrs: 9:00–23:00, daily. Gimmicky: barbecue and onsen bath, Y2300.

**Tōnosawa** 塔の沢 *0:05 by rail from Yumoto.* Quiet spa just up river from Yumoto. Amida-ji, a thatched temple built in the Edo period, is 0:20h on foot from Tōnosawa station.
**Miyanoshita** 宮ノ下 *0:25h by rail from Yumoto.* Known as a luxury mountain retreat, with such famous hotels as the Fujiya Hotel and the Naraya Ryokan. A 0:25h walk away, by the riverside, is **Taikō no Iwaburo**, a bath cut into the rock that is said to be the one used by Toyotomi Hideyoshi during his Odawara campaign. **Dōgashima Onsen** 堂ガ島温泉, with two inns inside a gorge, can be reached only by private cable car or tram from Miyanoshita.
**Chōkoku no Mori Bijutsukan (Hakone Open-Air Museum)** 彫刻の森美術館 (2-1161). Hrs: 9:00–17:00, daily. Nov.–Feb. 9:00–16:00. Enter by 0:30h before closing time. *0:35h by rail from Yumoto; walk 0:03h.* Open-air museum exhibiting sculpture by eminent Western artists, including Rodin, Picasso, Arp, Noguchi, Moore, and Giacometti. There are also several indoor galleries displaying modern Japanese painting.
\* **Gōra** 強羅 *0:40h by rail from Yumoto.* An onsen resort near the summit of Sōun-zan, at the center of the Hakone region. Gōra is a pleasant, wooded area of resort villas and inns.
\* **Hakone Bijutsukan (Art Museum)** 箱根美術館 (0460-2-2623). Hrs: 9:00–16:00 (enter by 15:30); clsd Th (except if NH), NY. *From Gōra 0:03h by cable car to Kōen-ue.* A superb collection of Japanese and Chinese ceramics. The museum is surrounded by lovely, moss-carpeted grounds, shaded by bamboo and Japanese maples. (Affiliated with MOA Art Museum in Atami.)
**Cable Car.** Goes to the summit of Sōun-zan from Gōra terminal. A tramway (second longest in the world) continues down the other side to Tōgendai on the shore of Lake Ashi. On the descent, one can get off at Ōwaki-dani to view some sulfur-belching fumeroles. Buy a ticket to the bottom; it includes one free stop en route. From Tōgendai there are boats to Moto-Hakone and buses to Hakone-en.
\*\* **Moto-Hakone** 元箱根 *0:40h by bus from Yumoto.* One of the busiest tourist centers in the Hakone area. **Hakone Jinja**, popularly called Hakone Gongen, is a famous landmark, with its red torii out in the lake. The shrine was founded around 757, and until 1868 it was a center of the Shugendō cult. On the other side of the cove is a cryptomeria-lined stretch of the old Tōkaidō (see Villages, p. 53). Several hundred meters beyond it is the ◆ **Hakone Sekisho Shiryōkan** 箱根関所資料館, a museum on the Hakone barrier. (Hrs: 8:30–16:30. In winter 9:00–16:00. Enter by 0:30h before closing time.) Displays include a full-scale reproduction of the gatehouse. In the Edo period, travelers were required to carry permits and submit to *very* thorough searches at each barrier gate. The authorities, alert to the possibility of a rebellion by a daimyo, were especially on the lookout for firearms heading toward Edo and women leaving (the shogunate required wives of the daimyo to reside in Edo as political hostages); wax models depict a traveling lady being searched by a woman official employed for this purpose. The site of the infamous gate is near the museum.
\* **Hiking the Old Tōkaidō** 箱根旧街道 A stretch of the Hakone Kyū-Kaidō (old post road) can be hiked in 2:20h from Moto-Hakone to Sukumogawa, where one can catch a bus back into Yumoto. Sections of Edo-period stone pavement alternate with asphalt road (rather spoils the mood); the longest is a steep 1.9-km section from Moto-Hakone, which ends near tea-house **Amazake no Chaya** 甘酒茶屋; light meals and *amazake*, a sweet, slightly fermented rice drink, can be had here (Hrs: 7:00–17:30). Hatajuku is 1:00h away.

**\* Hatajuku** 畑宿 An old post town famous for *yosegi-zaiku*, attractive articles decorated with what looks like wood inlay, reminiscent of Middle Eastern designs. The geometric pattern is created by gluing variously colored woods together, then slicing them paper-thin. These are used to cover boxes, trays, and other items. Stacks of drying bundles stand in front of many Hatajuku houses. Yamada Kikujirō is the best-known *yosegi-zaiku* artisan. You can watch him at work at **Hata no Chaya** 畑の茶屋 (Hrs: 9:00–17:00, daily). From Hatajuku, you can catch a bus to Yumoto or Moto-Hakone: only 7 to 11 buses per day run this route, so check schedules in advance.

### Hakone Lodgings (TEL 0460)

1. **\* Bansuirō Fukuzumi** 万翠楼福住 (5-5531). 643 Yumoto, Hakone-machi, Ashigarashimo-gun, Kanagawa-ken. The inn has been in business since 1625, but the present building, a mix of Victorian and Japanese, is late 19th C. Y20–30,000 w/meals.

2. **\* Shunkō-sō** 春光荘 (5-5336). 554 Yumoto. Pleasant inn with thatched buildings and bamboo groves (also a modern wing). Arriving guests are served *matcha* in a tearoom. Y25–30,000 w/meals.

3. **Amayu-sō** あまゆ荘 (5-5676). 36 Yumotojaya. Large open-air bath. Y13–20,000 w/meals.

4. **\*\* Fujiya Hotel** 富士屋ホテル (2-2211). 359 Miyanoshita. Classic, gracefully aged resort hotel. A real period piece. Excellent service. S Y21,000, Tw Y23,000. Sa, Su, NH S Y24,000, Tw Y27,000.

5. **\*\* Naraya** 奈良屋 (2-2411). 162 Miyanoshita. A dark and elegant Meiji-era ryokan with unusual marble onsen bath. Y30,000+ w/meals.

6. **Gōra Kadan** 強羅花壇 (0460-2-3331, fax 2-3334). 1300 Gōra. This luxurious new ryokan built on the site of a nobleman's villa offers elegant, sukiya-style rooms with mountain views, splendid bath halls, indoor pool with jacuzzi, and excellent kaiseki cuisine. Small conference rooms. Rooms w/meals Y50–57,000 per person, w/private open-air bath Y60,000, cottage Y48,000, suite Y70,000. Unrated.

7. **Hakone Taiyō Sansō** 国民宿舎箱根太陽山荘 (2-3388). 1320 Gōra. A traditional onsen ryokan that is now a Kokuminshukusha. Y6500 w/meals.

267

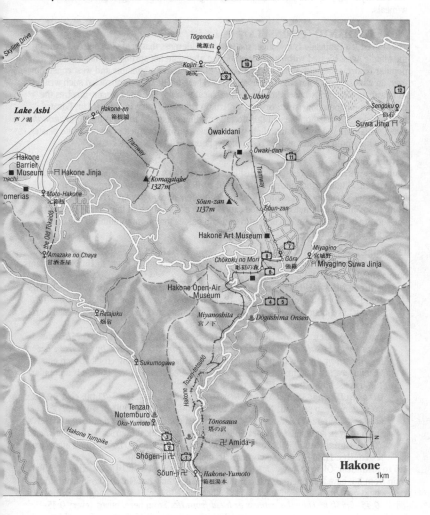

Hakone

0          1km

⑧ * **Gōra Hotel** 強羅ホテル (2-3111). 1300 Gōra. An older hotel, well-appointed and well-maintained. Japanese rooms w/meals, Y17,000 w/o bath, Y19,000 w/bath. Western rooms w/meals, Y13,000 w/o bath, Y15,000 w/bath. Slightly higher on Sa and day before NH.

⑨ **Pension Mori** ペンション森 (4-7667). 159-222 Moto-Hakone. By Lake Ashi. Y7700 w/meals.

⑩ **Lodge Fujimi-en** 国民宿舎ロッヂ富士見苑 (4-8675). 1245 Sengokuhara. Former drive-in ryokan, now a Kokuminshukusha. Overlooks Lake Ashi. Y6600 w/meals.

⑪ **Bangakurō** 萬岳楼 (0460-4-8588). Sengokuhara 1251. Partly thatched rustic inn. Wooden onsen baths filled with milky water. Y15–20,000 w/meals.

⑫ **Pension Hakone** ペンション箱根 (4-9849). 373 Sengokuhara. Sleek mini-hotel. Y8000 w/meals (Y8500 on weekends).

## W5 ATAMI 熱海

*0:55h by Shinkansen Kodama express, or 1:30h by Odoriko express, from Tokyo station.* This hustling onsen town is the gateway to the east coast of the Izu Peninsula. Its principal attraction is the lavish *** **MOA Bijutsukan (Art Museum)** MOA美術館 (84-2511). Hrs: 9:30–16:00 (enter by 15:30); clsd Th (except if NH), NY. Y1500. *0:10h by shuttle bus from station.* The fine collection of the late Mokichi Okada, founder of the World Church of Messianity, is housed in the most extravagant museum complex in Japan, with imposing buildings and landscaped grounds overlooking Atami Bay. Okada was "inspired by a belief in the spiritually elevating properties of great art viewed amidst an ideal natural setting." The wisteria-pattern ◆ Ninsei vase (NT) is always on view. The celebrated OGATA KŌRIN ◆ Red and White Plum screens (NT) are shown Jan.–Feb. A good copy is on view at other times. There is also a full-scale reconstruction of HIDEYOSHI's fabled gold teahouse.

**Atami Lodgings** (TEL 0557)

268 Atami is overpriced and tacky. The elegant ryokan below are at Izusan, *0:15h away by taxi.* ** **Hōrai** 蓬莱旅館 (80-5151). 750-6 Izusan Atami-shi, Shizuoka-ken. Beautiful inn with a spectacular cypress bathhouse overlooking the ocean. Y40–100,000 w/meals. ** **Tōrikyō** 桃李境 (80-2211). 824 Izusan. Elegant thatched cottages. Y25–60,000 w/meals.

## W6 ** IZU HANTŌ (PENINSULA) 伊豆半島

The rugged Izu Peninsula is no longer the remote wilderness that made it a place of exile in the Middle Ages. Blessed with balmy weather and abundant hot springs, Izu has become a popular resort, especially along the east coast. In the central mountains and west coast, however, an atmosphere of timeless isolation lingers. These idyllic regions attracted such writers as Kawabata Yasunari, whose semi-autobiographical novella, *The Izu Dancer*, inspires the more active Japanese tourists to tromp the "Izu no Odoriko" route in central Izu; Edward Seidensticker's translation puts all this nostalgia within grasp. South Izu is noted for *namako-kabe*, walls armored with diamond-shaped gray tiles, affixed by thick seams of white plaster. Gay as a harlequin's costume, they resist the typhoons that batter these coasts.

### Getting Around

Main gateways are Atami (east) and Mishima (central and west), both stops on the Kodama Shinkansen. Shimoda and Shuzen-ji are served by JR Odoriko expresses from Tokyo, via Yokohama, Ōfuna, Odawara, and Atami. JR Rail Pass holders have to pay the fare for the portion from Itō to Shimoda. Numazu, a limited express stop on the Tōkaidō line, has ferries to west Izu. Inquire in Tokyo about discounted round-trip passes that permit unlimited use of all trains and buses on Izu.

### Izu Sights

**Itō** 伊東 *0:22h by JR Odoriko express from Atami.* An old onsen town. In 1605, Will Adams built a ship here for TOKUGAWA IEYASU.

* **Ikeda Nijusseiki Bijutsukan (Art Museum)** 池田20世紀美術館 (45-2211). Hrs: 10:00–17:00, daily. July–Aug. 10:00–18:00. *0:30h by the Shaboten-Kōen bus from Itō station.* Twentieth-century art in a striking, stainless steel building. Major Western and some Japanese artists.

**Izu Kaiyō Kōen** 伊豆海洋公園 (51-1128 or in Tokyo, 03-573-2816). *0:25h walk from Jōgasaki Kaigan station, or 0:45h by bus from Itō, or 0:10h by bus from Izu Kōgen station.* Oceanside park with snorkeling and scuba diving (rocky beach entry). Visibility averages 20 m. Best season, mid-Sept.–Dec. The Picnical Course is a popular 1:30h coast hiking trail to Jōgasaki.

**Itō Area Dining: Amaya** 海女屋駅前店 (36-0036). Hrs: 11:00–21:00; clsd Tu. Near Itō station. Fresh seafood. *Teishoku* Y2000–3000, courses Y5000+. **Boranaiya** ばら納屋 (51-1247). Hrs: 10:30–17:00; clsd 1st and 3rd Th (next day, if Th a NH), NY. Open daily in summer. A 380-year-old house on the Picnical Course. *Sashimi teishoku* Y1400. **Hanafubuki** 花吹雪 八幡野磯道1041–53 (54-1550). Lovely small inn at Izu Kōgen. Hrs: 11:30–21:00 (last order): Teishoku Y2000–10,000.

**Itō to Shimoda.** Ōkawa Onsen 大川温泉 and Hokkawa Onsen 北川温泉 , about 0:30h by train from Itō, have free open-air baths on their beaches. Atagawa Onsen, 0:35h from Itō, is rather built up, but the Pension Atagawa isn't a bad place to stay (see Izu Lodgings). **Kawazu** 河津 *0:45–0:55h by Odoriko express or local from Itō.* From here, buses (every 0:35– 0:45h) head into mountainous central Izu, through to Shuzen-ji (2:00h; see Central Izu) Along the way, hiking paths follow the footsteps of the student in *The Izu Dancer* as he

# Izu History: The Opening of Japan

**Matthew Perry** (1794–1858) The American commodore who sailed into Edo Bay in 1853 demanding diplomatic relations with Japan. In 1854 he returned with his Black Ships and signed a Friendship Treaty with the Tokugawa shogunate.

**Townsend Harris** (1804–1878) First American consul to Japan. Harris spent two years in Shimoda trying to get the Japanese to negotiate a commercial treaty, which was finally signed in 1857.

**Henry Heusken** (1832–1861) Harris's Dutch interpreter.

Through most of Japan's history, mountainous Izu has been a backwater; its claim to fame was as a place of banishment. MINAMOTO NO YORITOMO was exiled by the TAIRA to the onsen town of **Shuzen-ji**. Later, his wife Masako sent their son, the second Kamakura shogun Yoriie, to Shuzen-ji, where he was murdered. Soon afterward, she shipped her meddlesome father here for a permanent hot-spring vacation (see Kamakura History, p. 261).

In 1853, **Commodore Matthew C. Perry** and his fleet of Black Ships arrived in Edo requesting trade and promising to return. Perry's message, backed by a show of America's naval strength, greatly alarmed the Japanese. They feared that, should he choose, Perry could blockade Edo, cutting off its food until the shogunate was forced to accede to American demands. Debate raged over how to deal with the determined barbarians, widening cracks in the already fractured government. Many advocated casting out the foreigners and forbidding all contact with them. But more practical men knew that Japan was no match for Western firepower.

269

Perry signed a treaty with the Japanese when he returned in 1854. Part of the treaty called for the opening of two coaling stations for foreign ships, one in far-away Hakodate, on the island of Hokkaidō, and the other at **Shimoda**, a safe harbor at the tip of the Izu Peninsula. Although Shimoda was only a day's sail from Edo, the mountainous peninsula provided a *cordon sanitaire* against the dangerous foreigners.

Late in 1854, Perry's chief rival, the Russian Admiral Putiatin, arrived in Shimoda aboard the *Diana*. While the Russian ship was anchored in the bay, Shimoda was hit by a great tidal wave that not only sank the *Diana*, but also destroyed most of the town. The surviving Russians moved to **Heda**, a lovely, well-protected fishing village, and with the help of the villagers built a new ship in the spring of 1855. After the Russians had sailed home, Edo ordered the villagers to build two more of the sleek, fast schooners. The shogunate, which had forbidden keeled, oceanworthy ships for more than 200 years, now found itself in need of the villagers' newly acquired knowhow.

By all accounts, the Russians and Heda villagers got along famously. The same cannot be said of **Townsend Harris** and the Japanese officials who were sent to deal with him in Shimoda. Harris arrived in 1856, two years after Perry's treaty, which included provisions for an American consul general in Shimoda, a provision which the Americans claimed could be invoked unilaterally, while the Japanese assumed it required mutual consent. The next two years were a constant trial for Harris, who had to haggle not only over where he should live, rates of exchange, and where to find servants, but also over whether he should be in Shimoda at all. Harris and **Henry Heusken**, his young Dutch interpreter, ended up in Gyokusen-ji, a temple in the hamlet of Kakisaki, even though Harris felt he was entitled to live in Shimoda proper, across the bay.

Although a man of some influence in America—he had helped found New York's City College—Harris was essentially a failed businessman. Already in his fifties, he decided to put his former life behind him and make his fortune in the Orient. He campaigned for a consular position in China, and when this proved unsuccessful, turned his attention to Japan, newly opened by Commodore Perry and with a vacant consul generalship—at least as the Americans understood it. After much lobbying by powerful friends, he received the appointment. Over the two years during which he languished in Shimoda, ranting at the officials and often ill, he must have regretted ever setting foot in Japan. But with grim determination, he persisted in his goal of an audience with the shogun in Edo, which was finally granted in December 1857. Soon afterward, in 1858, he negotiated a treaty opening Hakodate, Yokohama, Kōbe, Niigata, Shimoda, and Nagasaki to American traders, with Ōsaka and Edo to be added shortly. The treaty also included a "most favored nation" clause which, Harris explained, would dissuade more demanding nations like Great Britain from seeking more advantageous terms.

To modern-day Japanese visiting Shimoda, however, the genuine drama of Harris's historical role is eclipsed by the preposterous myth of his romance with a local geisha, **Okichi**. As with most myths, it contains an atom of truth. It seems that one of the endless haggles was over hiring women to attend to the two foreigners. Okichi and Ofuku, two professional women of Shimoda, were appointed to spend nights at Gyokusen-ji. Harris dismissed Okichi after three nights, supposedly because she had a suspicious rash. Presumably that was the end of it, but Okichi became an alcoholic and eventually drowned herself. Though Ofuku, who had a longer relationship with young Heusken, was later happily married to a local man, the myth persists that Okichi was stigmatized by her contact with a foreigner. What is interesting about the Okichi fiction is that she is so unabashedly viewed as a sacrificial lamb on the altar of international relations. A half-dozen films have immortalized her, and she has even been deified at Chōraku-ji as Okichi Kannon, portrayed in the nude. In the same vein, there is a memorial at Gyokusen-ji to the first cow slaughtered for meat in Japan, and wax mannequins of Harris and a demurely domestic Okichi serving him a glass of milk (a repulsive drink in Japan at that time, at least for healthy adults).

These are mild reflections of the tremendous internal conflict and culture shock Japan was experiencing. Perry and Harris, by prying open the doors of Japan, exposed its weak, vacillating government to fatal stresses. The Harris Treaty provided for extraterritoriality for foreign nationals and low tariff rates for goods, threatening Japan's already tottering economy; it set the precedent for a series of humiliating unequal treaties with Western nations. This not only sparked bitter resentment against foreigners—Henry Heusken was later assassinated in Yokohama—but against the Tokugawa shogunate, which had negotiated the Harris treaty without having it approved by the emperor. Within a decade, this resentment would explode in a full-scale rebellion that was to dramatically and irrevocably alter Japan's role in the world (see Hagi History, p. 460).

270

walked with a group of minstrels. Between Kawazu Nanadaru and Amagi-Tōge (pass), one can flag down the bus at any point. *Tochū-gesha* tickets allow you to get off and on along the way at no extra cost.

\* **Yugano Onsen** 湯ヶ野温泉 *0:15h by bus from Kawazu*. A rustic spa with inns crammed on terraces along the steep bank of the Kawazu River. One can still see the public bath where Kawabata's student discovers the entrancing little Izu dancer is a prepubescent girl.

\*\* **Kawazu Nanadaru** 河津七滝 Seven waterfalls in a scenic gorge, linked by an hour-long trail. The south fall, ◆ **Ōdaru** 大滝 , a beautiful 27-meter cataract, has a swimming hole and delightful onsen baths by the stream (bathing suits advised—it's very public). The other falls are upstream, but can be reached only by climbing up to the road and then back down into the gorge. **Shokei-daru** is considered the loveliest. A bronze Izu dancer poses beside it.

\*\*\* **Shimoda** 下田 *2:50h from Tokyo or 0:55h from Itō by Odoriko express*. This historic town became one of Japan's first treaty ports in 1854, when Commodore Perry returned to Japan with his Black Ships and forced an end to 220 years of seclusion. Two years later, Townsend Harris arrived as the first American consul general. Harris is remembered less for his diplomacy, however, than for his alleged affair with a local geisha, Okichi. Shimoda is compact and can be toured on foot in 2 to 3 hours. **Hōfuku-ji** 宝福寺 has an Okichi museum with "relics" and still shots from numerous film versions of her "life story." Her tombstone is in back of the temple. **Ryōsen-ji** 了仙寺 is the temple where Perry was lodged in 1854. Nearby is a pretty canal, lined with dusky houses, and **Chōraku-ji** 長楽寺 , a temple noted for its nude "Okichi Kannon" and sex museum. Nearby **Anchoku-rō** 安直楼 , a handsome *namako-kabe* sushi shop, was owned by Okichi in her final year. Other *namako-kabe* houses appear here and there; the finest is the **Suzukiya** (closed to public). 2 km (0:07h by bus) east of the station is the bayside **Gyokusen-ji** 玉泉寺 , the temple (now a museum) where Harris and Heusken lived for two years. A "Black Ship" cruises the bay. The tramway behind the station yields a view of Shimoda's dramatic site. (Oliver Statler's *Shimoda Story* is a lively account of Harris and the Japanese in those fateful years.)

**Shimoda Dining:** \* **Nakagawa** なかがわ (22-0310). Hrs: 11:00–22:00; clsd NY. Look for a big fish-shaped sign. Ground floor is a fish market, second floor has terrific seafood at low prices. *Teishoku* from Y1000. \* **Jashūmon** 邪宗門 (22-3582). Hrs: 10:00–20:00; late July–Aug. 10:00–22:00; clsd W. Café in a charming, 150-year-old *namako-kabe* cottage. The interior, built by a shipwright, has an interesting ceiling; the lavatory is a minor masterpiece. **Anchokurō** 安直楼 (22-0048). Hrs: 11:00–20:00, daily. Of Okichi fame. Sushi *moriawase* from about Y1300.

\*\* **"Margaret Line"** マーガレットライン Dramatic coastal route, served by buses between Shimoda and Matsuzaki; takes twice as long as the direct route, but worth the time and fare. One bus per hour from Shimoda, mid-morning to mid-afternoon. North of Mera, green mountains plunge into the sea, and tiny fishing villages huddle in the sheltered coves along the deeply crinkled coast.

✶✶✶ **Matsuzaki** 松崎 *2:20h by Margaret line bus, or 0:50h via Ōsawa Onsen, from Shimoda. 2:30h from Mishima, via Shuzen-ji, by bus. 1:20h by high-speed ferry from Numazu.* This charming port preserves some 200 houses with south Izu's distinctive tile-and-plaster *namako-kabe* walls. Surrounding hamlets, such as Yamaguchi, have photogenic clusters of *namako-kabe* buildings. In town, the best place to see them is the southwest corner (the Meiji-period town center). This quarter is also associated with Irie Chōhachi, an Edo-period artist who was a master of *kote-e*, the artistic application of wall plaster in a variety of rich tints to create frescoes and reliefs redolent of late Edo tastes. Chōhachi worked mostly in Matsuzaki and in Edo, where he trained as a KANŌ SCHOOL painter. Matsuzaki also has a sandy swimming beach, popular in summer. The Kokuminshukusha, at the north end of the beach, rents bicycles.

✶ **Jōkan-ji** 浄感寺 *Hrs: 9:00–16:00, daily.* Temple where Chōhachi spent his youth and old age. A large Chōhachi dragon glares from the ceiling in the main hall, and lovely angels in polychrome relief float high up on the walls.

✶✶ **Izu no Chōhachi Bijutsukan (Art Museum)** 長八美術館 (42-2540). *Hrs: 9:00–17:00 (enter by 16:30), daily.* This museum, exhibiting some 50 works of Chōhachi, is housed in a blindingly white structure crowned by an aluminum-and-glass cupola. It boasts a few modern *kote-e* works, which pale next to the delicate artistry of Chōhachi.

✶ **Iwashina Kyōdokan** 岩科郷土資料館 (ICP). *Hrs: 9:00–17:00, daily.* A former primary school built in 1881, a handsome example of Japanese-Western architecture. A second-floor room is decorated with cranes against sky-blue walls, attributed to a Chōhachi apprentice. Closed for repair until autumn 1992.

✶ **Ki'ichi-ji** 帰一寺 *0:10h by Ōsawa Onsen bus to Funata bus stop.* This peaceful Zen temple, founded in 1301, has a fine garden.

**Matsuzaki Dining:** ① ✶ **Mingei Sabō** 民芸茶房 (42-0773). *Hrs: 8:00–21:00.* Dockside restaurant cluttered with fishing decor. Fresh seafood. Sashimi *teishoku* Y1600. ② **Hōbai** 豊梅 北区373-1-1 (42-2315). *Hrs: 12:00–22:00; clsd NY. Okonomiyaki.* Old-fashioned atmosphere and an *irori* hearth. Inexpensive. ③ **Eiraku-dō** 永楽堂 宮内300-2 (42-0270). *Hrs: 8:00–20:00; clsd on 20th of each month, NY.* Riverside kissaten with an *irori* hearth.

271

✶✶ **Heda** 戸田 *From Matsuzaki, take a bus to Toi (0:55h), then change to one for Heda (0:35h). From Shuzen-ji, 1:00h by bus (5 per day) via a spectacular road. The ferry from Numazu is also very scenic; several boats per day (0:55h).* This fishing village is blessed with an enchanting bay and splendid view of Fuji. It has been saved from the tourist industry by its isolation and lack of hot springs. The **Zōsen Kyōdo-Shiryō Hakubutsukan** 造船郷土資料博物館 is a small museum on the 1854 *Diana* incident (*Hrs: 9:00–16:30; clsd W, NY. See Izu History*). Apart from this single museum, Heda offers only its lovely, pine-studded sandbar, sheltered swimming beach, and peaceful, undisturbed atmosphere.

✶ **Shuzen-ji Onsen** 修善寺温泉 *From Mishima, 0:30h by private Izu-Hakone rail or bus. From Tokyo, there is a direct JR Odoriko express (3 per day) via Mishima.* Buses to

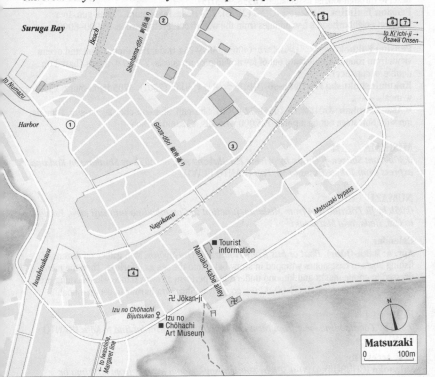

*Heda, Matsuzaki, Kawazu, Shimoda.* This most famous Izu spa was said to have been created by KŪKAI, who struck a boulder with his staff, causing hot, healing waters to gush forth. One can bathe in these very waters at * **Tokkonoyu**, an open-air bath carved in a boulder out in the river. **Shuzen-ji**, the temple, has a treasure hall of objects allegedly associated with the saint. Across the river is the **Shigetsuden**, a chapel founded by Hōjō Masako for her assassinated son, the second Kamakura shogun Yoriie.

### Izu Lodgings

**Hanafubuki** 花吹雪　八幡野磯道1041-53　(0557-54-1550). 1041-53 Yawatano-Isomichi, Itō-shi. At Izu Kōgen. Lovely small inn. Y13,500–16,500 w/meals.

**Pension Atagawa** ペンション熱川 (0557-23-2321). 1237-60 Naramoto, Higashi Izu-chō, Kamo-gun. Perched on a cliffside over Atagawa Onsen. Has an ocean view and *rotemburo*. Y8,100–11,200 w/meals.

**Fukudaya** 福田屋 (0558-35-7201). 236 Yugano, Kawazu-chō, Kamo-gun. Onsen. Kawabata stayed at this aged but atmospheric inn. Y8400+ w/meals. "Kawabata room," Y16,200.

** ** Minshuku Teppō** 民宿てっぽう (05583-5-7501). 175 Nashimoto, Kawazu-chō, Kamo-gun. Near Kawaino bus stop, just north of Kawazu Nanadaru. 200-year-old *namako-kabe* house in quiet hamlet. The owner's ancestor got rich making guns (*teppō*), and bought the house of a local headman. In the Edo period, firearms were severely restricted, but he was allowed to study gun-making in Edo as a reward for finding a special clay to build a new reverberatory furnace for the shogunate. Old furnishings. Meals cooked at the *irori*. Y7000 w/meals.

**Seiryū-sō** 清流荘 (0558-22-1361). 2-2 Kouchi, Shimoda-shi. Jimmy Carter slept here. Y27–53,000 w/meals.

**Ryokan Shimodaya** 旅館下田屋 (22-0446). 2-13-31 Shimoda-shi. Trim little ryokan, renovated since the days when Yoshida Shōin stayed here (see Hagi History, p. 460). Y7400–9000 w/meals.

**272**

④ * **Sankō-sō** 山光荘 (0558-42-1047). 280 Matsuzaki, Matsuzaki-chō, Kamo-gun. Beautiful old ryokan with *namako-kabe* and Chōhachi originals adorning the sill of its *kura*. Y8–15,000 w/meals.

⑤ **Kokuminshukusha Izu Matsuzaki-sō** 国民宿舎伊豆まつざき荘 (42-0450). Ena, Matsuzaki-chō. Good service and food. Rent-a-cycle. Y5100 w/meals.

⑥ **Sanyō-sō YH** 三余荘YH (42-0408). 73 Naka, Matsuzaki-chō. Has a pretty garden. Bus to Ōsawa Onsen and Shimoda stops in front.

⑦ ** ** Ōsawa Onsen Hotel** 大沢温泉ホテル (43-0121). 153-1 Ōsawa, Matsuzaki-chō. *0:10h by bus from Matsuzaki, in bucolic Ōsawa Onsen.* This marvelous inn, originally a samurai estate, retains its 380-year-old main building, *namako-kabe* storehouses (now guest rooms) and garden. The high-ceilinged wooden bath halls are floored with stone and have miniature gardens. There's a riverside *rotemburo* at the Ryokan Ōsawa-sō, across the river (Y400, closes 20:00). Y18–25,000 w/meals.

**Heda Minshukus.** Nearly every house on the waterfront is a minshuku. Y6000 w/meals. Reserve through tourist association (0558-94-3115).

**Pension Tsujihira** ペンションつじひら (2278). 278 Heda, Heda-mura, Tagata-gun. In a pleasant neighborhood a few minutes from the waterfront. Pretty garden. Y6900–8000 w/meals.

**Pension Fukuoka** ペンションふくおか (4063). 3879-254 Heda, Heda-mura. Fuji and ocean views from rooms. A little ways out of town. Will pick up guests. Y7500 w/meals (based on double occupancy).

**Kokuminshukusha Izu Heda-sō** 国民宿舎伊豆戸田荘 (2301). 3705 Heda-mura. Y5000 w/meals.

* **Asaba Ryokan** あさば旅館 (0558-72-0700). Shuzenji, Shuzenji-chō, Tagata-gun. Famous inn with Noh stage out on a pond. Y25,000 w/meals, Y32,000 w/ Noh.

## MISHIMA 三島
*0:30h from Shuzen-ji Onsen by private Izu-Hakone rail, or 1:05h by Shinkansen Kodama express from Tokyo. Buses to Mt. Fuji (KANTŌ III:W1).*

## NUMAZU 沼津
*0:05h by JR Tōkaidō line from Mishima. Junction to Gotemba line into Fuji area. Ferries to Ōse, Heda, and Matsuzaki.*

### Calendar
**Apr. 4: Baka-Odori.** *Boat or bus from Numazu to Ōse Myōjin.* Men gather on dozens of fishing boats to cast stones wrapped in straw bales into the sea as offerings. Then the men, dressed in comic masks and kimono underrobes, perform a rowdy dance while leaning precariously over the sides. Hrs: 7:00–12:00; go early to Shizu'ura harbor to get on a boat.

## FUJI 富士
*0:20h by Tōkaidō line local from Numazu. Junction to JR Minobu line to Kōfu (KANTŌ III:W1).*

### Easy Access To:
**Shizuoka** (CHŪBU I): *0:20-0:30h by Shinkansen Kodama express from Mishima or Atami; or 0:40–1:00h by Tōkaidō line express from Fuji or Numazu.*

# Chūbu

Alpine Chūbu, with its soaring peaks and inaccessible interior, lies between Japan's two great historical centers, the imperial capital of Kyoto and the shogun's city of Edo. Though rural and remote, it is crisscrossed with ancient highways and dotted with the sites of Japan's most famous battles. Hidden away in its isolated valleys are many of the best-preserved post towns and farm hamlets, while in cities such as Takayama and Kanazawa, there remain tangible traces of the old urban culture. Combined with beautiful natural scenery, these features make Chūbu one of the most rewarding places in Japan to visit.

## BEST ATTRACTIONS

| | |
|---|---|
| IV:NE3 | ✳✳✳ **Tsumago.** An almost perfectly preserved post town on the old Nakasendō road (p. 280). ✳✳ **Magome** (p. 279) and ✳✳ **Narai** (p. 282) also retain an Edo-period atmosphere. |
| IV:NE8 | ✳✳ **Kamikōchi.** Gateway to the Japan Alps, with Japan's finest hiking. Well-equipped mountain huts. Stunning in autumn (p. 285). |
| IV:NE7 | ✳✳ **Matsumoto.** Pleasant city framed by mountains, full of old-fashioned neighborhoods with a dash of sophistication. Famed castle. |
| IV:NE10 | ✳✳ **Tateyama-Kurobe Alpen Route.** A series of trams, buses, and trains over the Northern Alps. Ideal for those who hate to hike (p. 286). |
| IV:N1 | ✳✳ **Meiji Mura.** A museum-village of Meiji-era buildings, half-Japanese, half-Western, evocative of this schizophrenic phase of Japan's history (p. 287). |
| IV:N3 | ✳✳✳ **Takayama.** This "little Kyoto" preserves streets of Edo-period merchant houses, and is renowned for its festivals (p. 289). |
| IV:NW 3–4 | ✳✳✳ **Shirakawa-gō and Gokayama.** Two isolated farm hamlets famous for their magnificent, multistoried A-frame farmhouses (p. 296–297). |
| IV:NW5 | ✳✳✳ **Kanazawa.** The castle town of the Maeda, the richest daimyo of the Edo period, with a famed stroll garden and fine crafts to rival Kyoto (p. 298). |

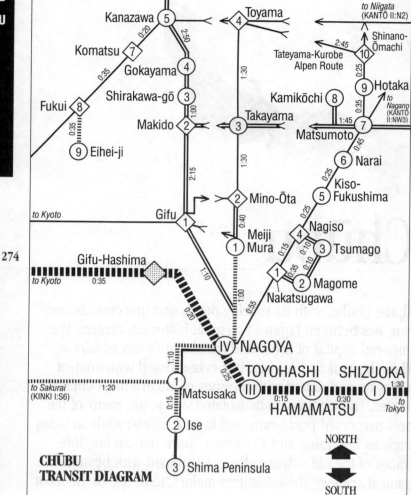

CHŪBU
TRANSIT DIAGRAM

NORTH

SOUTH

IV:NW6   **\*\* Noto Peninsula.** Rural scenes and fishing villages, and a wealth of history and old customs (p. 304).

IV:NW9   **\*\* Eihei-ji.** Japan's largest Sōtō Zen monastery, with miles of covered stairways and halls set on an extraordinarily beautiful forested mountainside (p. 306).

IV:S2   **\*\*\* Ise Imperial Shrines.** These elegant, elemental shrines, dedicated to goddesses of fertility and of the sun, have been rebuilt in fragrant cypress every 21 years, almost without interruption, since A.D. 690 (p. 307).

**Seasons**
In the high altitudes, fall comes early and spring late. Winters are cold and snowy; many mountain roads (for example, the road linking Matsumoto and Takayama) become impassable. Major tourist attractions such as Takayama and the Kiso post towns are spoiled by crowds from late spring to early fall. Mountain resorts and hiking areas are impossibly crowded from July 20–Aug. 31.

**Average Temperature °C (°F)/Days of Rain or Snow**

|  | January | April | July | October |
|---|---|---|---|---|
| Nagoya | 3.2 (37.8)/6 | 13.1 (55.6)/11 | 25.7 (78.3)/12 | 16.6 (61.9)/9 |
| Matsumoto | −1.2 (29.8)/5 | 10.2 (50.4)/8 | 23.2 (73.8)/12 | 12.5 (54.5)/8 |
| Kanazawa | 2.9 (37.2)/24 | 11.9 (53.4)/13 | 25.0 (77.0)/12 | 16.1 (61.0)/13 |

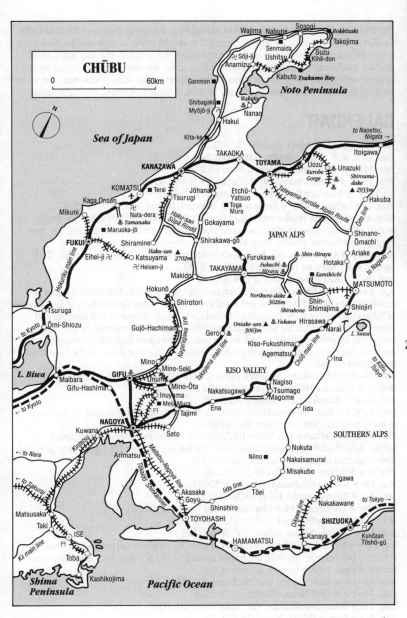

## Traveling

The central gateway for this area is Nagoya (IV), a major commercial city, though from Tokyo, the JR Chūō main line (KANTŌ III:W) to Matsumoto and the JR Shin'etsu line (KANTŌ II:NW) to Nagano offer excellent alternatives. Use the private Kintetsu line to Ise and Meitetsu line to Meiji Mura, and Meitetsu buses to the Shirakawa-gō area. Many points of interest, such as Kamikōchi, Shirakawa-gō, and Tsumago/Magome, can be reached only by bus or car.

# SPECIAL INTERESTS

**Onsen:** This is the place for those fantasizing about remote mountain spas, like Shirahone, Ariake, Nakabusa, Shirouma-yari (Japan's highest open-air bath), Fukuchi, and Shin-Hirayu. Kurobe Gorge has a series of rustic inns inside a river gorge. Utsukushigahara, Hirayu, and Yamanaka Onsen are pleasant onsen villages.

**Hiking:** Kamikōchi and Hotaka are gateways to the fine hiking trails of the Japan Alps. To the south is the hike over Norikura-dake, while to the north, the Tateyama-Kurobe Alpen Route provides access to other hiking trails. Hakuba is a base for the Northern Alps. The climb up sacred Haku-san is also popular.

**Skiing:** Happō-one, near Hakuba, has a gondola and many other lifts. There are several other ski areas nearby.

**Art Museums:** Kanazawa boasts many excellent museums on its traditional culture. Takayama is a "museum town" with numerous small museums, often with unique and charming collections. Matsumoto's Japan Ukiyo-e Museum is one of the best outside Tokyo.

The Tokugawa Museum in Nagoya exhibits objects from the vast collection of the TOKUGAWA. **Crafts:** Kanazawa, a must for anyone interested in elegant crafts, is renowned for Kutani porcelain, Kanazawa *yūzen* dyeing, *maki-e* lacquerware, and gold foil. The Kiso Valley towns produce handsome wood crafts. Takayama is famous for *shunkei-nuri*, translucent amber lacquer applied over wood. Seto is Japan's largest pottery town. Mino-Seki is noted for swordsmiths and cutlery. Paper (*washi*) is made by hand in Mino, Gokayama, and Etchū-Yatsuo.

# CALENDAR

**Jan. 1:** \* **Okina Matsuri.** Ago-chō (IV:S3). P

**Jan. 4–5:** \* # **Sakabe no Fuyu Matsuri.** Tenryū (III). P

**Jan. 14:** \* # **Niino Yuki Matsuri.** Niino (III). P

**Feb. 15:** \* # **Suikai Dengaku.** Ikeda-chō (IV:NW8). P

**L 1/18:** \* # **Nishiure Dengaku.** Misakubo (III). P S

**Mar. (Su before 15th):** \* **Ōagata Jinja Matsuri.** Ōagata Jinja (IV:N1). V S

**Mar. 15:** \*\* **Tagata Hōnen-sai.** Tagata Jinja (IV:N1). Near Meiji Mura. Famous fertility festival. Women praying for children cradle wooden phalluses in their arms, and the "god symbol" is a 3-meter phallus. From 14:00.

**Apr., May:** \* **Onbashira-sai.** Kami-Suwa and Shimo-Suwa (IV:NE6). Every 6 yrs. E S

**Apr. 5:** \* **Tejikara no Himatsuri.** Tejikara. F E

**Apr. 5–7:** \* **Kagura-sai.** Ise Jingū (IV:S2). P

**Apr. 14–15:** \*\*\* **Sannō Matsuri.** Takayama, Hie Jinja (IV:N3). This matsuri began as a supplication to the gods of plague and is patterned on the famed Gion Matsuri of Kyoto. Twelve of Takayama's twenty-three enormous wheeled carts, richly decorated with carvings and drapery, are displayed at the shrine and drawn through the town, escorted by townsmen dressed as Edo-period officials. Look for the amazing *karakuri* (mechanical puppets) atop the floats; they bow, mime, and perform complicated stunts to the delight of the huge crowd. Main events on 15th.

**Apr. 19–20:** \* **Furukawa Matsuri.** Furukawa (IV:N3). E V

**May 1:** \* **Takaoka Mikurumayama.** Takaoka (IV:NW4). V

**May 3–4:** \* **Kabuki.** Gero Onsen (IV:N2). P

**May 3–5:** \*\* **Tako-Gassen.** Hamamatsu (II). Hundreds of giant kites spar on the beach. At night, gorgeous floats are pulled through town.

**May 3–5:** \*\* **Seihaku-sai.** Nanao (IV:NW6). Three 20-ton floats with mechanical Kabuki dolls aboard are dragged about town. The festival, a prayer for a good crop, is said to have originated in 981 and acquired floats in 1473.

**May 5:** \* **Hikiyama.** Etchū-Yatsuo (IV:N3). V

**May 15:** \* **Jōhana Hikiyama.** Jōhana (IV:NW4). V

**May 24:** \* **Baka-bayashi.** Fukui (IV:NW8). P

**June 24:** \* **Izōnomiya Rice Planting.** Shima Peninsula (IV:S3). P S

**July 7–8:** \* **Abare Matsuri.** Ushitsu (IV:NW6). F E

**July 31:** \* **Gojinjo Daiko.** Nabune (IV:NW6). P E

**L 6/15:** \*\* **Ishizaki Hōtō-sai.** Nanao (IV:NW6). Twelve-meter-tall rectangular lanterns, colorfully painted with warriors, are hauled about by mobs of young men. Especially spectacular at night. Similar festivals abound in Noto.

**Aug. 13–16:** \* **Gujō Odori.** Gujō-Hachiman (IV:NW1). E

**Aug. 14–15:** \* **Ōmi Hōka.** Shinshiro (III). P B

**Aug. 15:** \* **Tokuyama Shikan-Mai.** Nakakawane (I). P

**Aug. 15:** \* **Kanko Odori.** Ise-shi (IV:S2). P

**Sept. 1–3:** \*\* **Owara Kaze no Bon.** Etchū-Yatsuo (IV:N3). A graceful dance performed for three days and nights to the music of strolling shamisen players. The dances are a prayer against typhoons that would destroy crops.

**Sept. 5:** \* **Sugō Matsuri.** Furukawa (IV:N3). P

**Sept. 26–27:** \* **Kokiriko Matsuri.** Gokayama (IV:NW4). P

**Oct. 3–4:** \* **Torch Festival.** Asama Onsen (IV:NE7). F

**Oct. 9–10:** \*\*\* **Hachiman Matsuri.** Takayama (IV:N3). Counterpart to the Sannō Matsuri (see Apr. 15). The floats wend their way through town on the afternoon and evening of the 9th. Main events on 10th.

**Oct. 14–19:** \*\* **Doburoku Matsuri.** Shirakawa-gō (IV:NW3). A harvest festival held at various shrines, with colorful processions of musicians and lion dancers. Everyone gathers at a shrine to drink *doburoku*, a milky-white, home-brewed saké.

**Nov. 2–3:** \* **Kabuki.** Gero Onsen (IV:N2). P

**Nov.–Jan.:** \* # **Hana Matsuri.** Tsuki (III). P S

**Dec. 24:** \*\* **Ise Ō-Kagura.** Kuwana, Masuda Jinja (IV:S). Acrobatic Kagura and lion dances, originally performed all over Japan for those who couldn't make the Ise pilgrimage. Hrs: 12:00–16:00.

# CHŪBU I. SHIZUOKA

**Tokyo to Shizuoka:** *1:30h by Shinkansen Kodama express.*
**Prefectures:** Shizuoka

## SHIZUOKA  静岡

TOKUGAWA IEYASU retired to this seaside castle town (see Nikkō History, p. 242). His first tomb was built atop Kunō-zan, a steep hill by the ocean.

**\*\*\* Kunōzan Tōshō-gū** 久能山東照宮 (ICP). Hrs: 9:30–17:00. In winter 9:30–16:00. *0:40h by bus to Nihon-Daira (noted for its view of Mt. Fuji) and then a tramway down to Kunō-zan.* The building is an ornate, cinnebar shrine-mausoleum with colorful carvings. The treasure house exhibits Ieyasu's tortoise-frame spectacles, Spanish clock, and lead pencil. Leave by the "main approach," a spectacular switchbacked staircase hewn into the side of Kunō-zan that faces the ocean. Catch a bus to the station at the base.

**\*\* Serizawa Bijutukan (Art Museum)** 芹沢美術館 Hrs: 9:00–16:30; clsd M (Tu if M a NH). Adjacent to Toro Iseki, a famous Yayoi excavation. This handsome stone museum displays works of the modern folk-textile artist, Serizawa Keisuke.

### Calendar

**Aug. 15: \* Tokuyama Shikan-Mai.** Nakakawane-chō (*0:30h by Tōkaidō line local to Kanaya, then 1:00h by Oikawa line*), Asama Jinja. Unusual Bon dance. Young men perform deer, monkey and horse dances around young girls dressed as *maiko* (apprentice geisha).

# CHŪBU II. HAMAMATSU

**Tokyo to Hamamatsu:** *2:00h by Shinkansen Kodama express.*

## HAMAMATSU  浜松

A former castle town and post station on the Tōkaidō, now noted for the production of motorcycles, Yamaha musical instruments, and *unagi* eels raised in the Hamana-ko, a large lagoon.

### Calendar

**May 3–5: \*\* Tako Gassen.** See Calendar, p. 276. Shuttle buses from the station ferry spectators to the festival site—but first pick up a lunch box at the station of Hamamatsu's famous broiled eel (*unagi bentō*).

**Aug. 13: Hōka Odori.** Rinkei-ji. Muromachi-period dance form, to an accompaniment of drums and flutes.

### Hamamatsu Lodgings (TEL 053)

**Mitsui Urban Hotel Hamamatsu** 三井アーバンホテル (455-1131). 137 Motoshiro-chō, Hamamatsu-shi, Shizuoka-ken. Business hotel. S Y5800, Tw Y10,800.

# CHŪBU III. TOYOHASHI

**Tokyo to Toyohashi:** *2:15h by Shinkansen Kodama express.*
**Kyoto to Toyohashi:** *1:35h by Shinkansen Kodama express.*
**Prefectures:** Aichi, Nagano

## TOYOHASHI  豊橋

The Iida line from Toyohashi wends its way into a remote mountainous region that preserves a distinctly rustic way of life. Of special interest to folklorists are the numerous vestiges of ancient matsuri forms found in villages along the way.

### Calendar

**Jan. 4–5: \* # Sakabe no Fuyu Matsuri.** Tenryū village (*2:30h by Iida line to Nakaisamurai*), Suwa Jinja. Oracle by boiling cauldron, sacred dances. (Tel: 0260-32-2001 for details).

**Jan. 14: \* # Niino Yuki Matsuri.** Niino (*3:00h by Iida line to Nukuta, then bus*), Izu Jinja. Performances from afternoon to dawn of Sarugaku, Dengaku. Fabulous masks.

**L 1/18: \* # Nishiure Dengaku.** *2:15h by Iida line to Misakubo.* Nishiure Kannon-dō. Ancient forms of Dengaku and Sarugaku Noh, said to have been introduced in 719. Performances go through the night. Hrs: 22:00–10:00.

**Aug. 14–15: \* Ōmi Hōka.** *0:35h by Iida line local to Shinshiro.* Nembutsu dances by three men with huge *uchiwa* (flat fans) on their backs, who visit temples and homes.

**End of Nov.–Jan.: \* # Hana Matsuri.** *1:30h to Tōei, then bus or taxi to festival site.* All-night Kagura (sacred dances) are performed in 11 rural hamlets. The earliest occurs at Tsuki village Nov. 22–23. Call the Hanamatsuri Kaikan for information: 05367-6-1610.

### Exploring Akasaka and Goyu

# Take the Meitetsu-Nagoya line local from Toyohashi to Goyu or Meiden-Akasaka stations. Two sleepy, rather well-preserved Tōkaidō post towns. A former Akasaka brothel depicted by Hiroshige is now the **Ōhashiya Ryokan** (05338-7-2450), Y7–12,000 w/meals. From Y8000 during mid-August and NY.

277

# CHŪBU IV. NAGOYA

**Tokyo to Nagoya:** *2:00h from Tokyo by Shinkansen Hikari express, slightly longer by Kodama express.*
**Kyoto to Nagoya:** *0:50h from Kyoto by Shinkansen Hikari express.*
**Prefectures:** Aichi, Nagano, Gifu, Toyama, Ishikawa, Fukui, Mie

## NAGOYA　名古屋

Major junction for train lines into the Chūbu region. Nagoya was one of the great castle towns of the Edo period and today ranks fourth in size among Japanese cities, but most of its cultural heritage was destroyed by severe bombing in World War II, leaving few attractions for the tourist. It is, however, a convenient place to make travel arrangements.

### Getting Around

Many shops and hotels are located around Sakae, 2 stops on the Higashiyama subway line from Nagoya station. The private Meitetsu line (to Meiji Mura, Inuyama) and Kintetsu line (to Ise, Nara) are convenient for excursions out of Nagoya; the stations are at the southwest end of Nagoya station. The Meitetsu bus terminal is on the 3F of the Meitetsu Melsa Building, the third department store south of Nagoya station.

### Nagoya Sights

**\*\* Nagoya-jō (Castle)** 名古屋城 Hrs: 9:30–16:30; clsd NY. *0:10h by bus from the station to Nagoya-jō Seimon-mae (main gate).* The original castle, built in 1609–1614, was one of the greatest fortresses in Japan. It was destroyed in World War II. Three turrets, one gate, and the stone foundations survive (all ICP). The rebuilt concrete keep houses ornate screens (many ICP) saved from the original castle. The grounds contain a reconstruction of a tea arbor built by ODA NOBUNAGA.

**\*\* Tokugawa Bijutsukan (Art Museum)** 徳川美術館 (935-6262). Hrs: 10:00–17:00 (enter by 16:30); clsd M (Tu if M a NH), NY. *0:20h by bus from the station to Shindeki-machi, then 0:03h walk.* Huge, superb collection of the Tokugawa family. The most famous objects are the 12th-C ◆ *Genji Monogatari* narrative scrolls (NT); however, they are shown only once every 5 years or so, and then only a few at a time.

**Atsuta Jingū (Shrine)** 熱田神宮 *0:06h by Meitetsu line to Jingū-mae, or Tōkaidō line local to Atsuta.* The second most important imperial shrine after Ise, it keeps the sacred sword, one of the three imperial regalia (mirror, jewel, and sword). The legendary hero Yamato Takeru carried the sacred sword when he set out to conquer eastern Japan (see Hiraizumi History, p. 169). The shrine is said to have been founded by his consort at the site of his tomb mound (which allegedly lies behind the shrine). The present shrine was formerly the sacred hall at Ise and was brought here after the 1953 rebuilding of Ise to replace the one lost in World War II. Reroofed with copper, unfortunately.

**\*\* Arimatsu** 有松 *0:25h from Nagoya station by Meitetsu-Nagoya line.* This village produces the refined, tie-dyed silk called Arimatsu-shibori. Many artisans still dwell in magnificent Edo- and Meiji-period houses, which stand in well-preserved rows along the old Tōkaidō (see Villages, pp. 54–55). Small museum.

### Nagoya Dining

Specialties: Chicken dishes. *Kishimen*, a fettucine-like noodle. *Moriguchi-zuke*, an impossibly long *daikon* radish pickled in saké lees and curled up in a neat spiral.
**\*\* Hasshō-kan** 八勝館　栄2-12-20 (221-1801). Hrs: 11:00–20:00 (last order); clsd Su, mid-Aug., NY. A *kaiseki* establishment of very high order. Y26,000+. No CC.
**Kishimen-tei** きしめん亭　錦3丁目 (951-3481). Hrs: 11:00–21:00; clsd Su, NY. Near Nishikidōri, not far from the Washington Hotels. Best place for *kishimen*. From Y530. No CC.
**Torikyū** 鳥久　駅南1-1-15 (541-1889). Hrs: 11:30–22:00; clsd Su, mid-Aug., NY. About 600 m east of the station. Famous chicken restaurant in Meiji-period building. *Kashiwa kaiseki*, sukiyaki, *mizudaki*. Set menus from Y5900. V.
**Toriei** 鳥栄　栄3-8-3 (241-5552). Hrs: 11:10–21:00; clsd on the 2nd, 12th, 22nd (open if a Su or NH), NY. Chicken restaurant in Sakae. Lunch set, Y670; *Teishoku*, Y2300; full course, Y4000. MC.

### Nagoya Lodgings (TEL 052)

**Nagoya Terminal Hotel** 名古屋ターミナルホテル (561-3751). Fax 581-3236. 1-1-2 Meieki, Nakamura-ku, Nagoya-shi. Near station. S Y8–10,000, Tw Y14–16,000. AX, DC, V, MC.
**Hotel Castle Plaza** ホテルキャッスルプラザ (582-2121). Fax 582-8666. 4-3-25 Meieki, Nakamura-ku. Near station. S Y7500–9500, Tw Y13–18,000. AX, DC, V, MC.
**Hotel Nagoya Castle** ホテル名古屋キャッスル (521-2121). Fax 531-3313. 3-19 Hinokuchi-chō, Nishi-ku. Castle view. S Y10–11,000, Tw Y18–32,000. AX, DC, V, MC.
**Dai-ichi (#1) Washington** 第1ワシントンホテル (951-2111). 3-18-28 Nishiki, Naka-ku. Near Sakae. S Y4500–6800, Tw Y8900–11,000. AX, DC, V, MC.
**Dai-ni (#2) Washington** 第2ワシントンホテル (962-7111). 3-12-22 Nishiki, Naka-ku. Near Sakae. S Y5300–7100, Tw Y11–13,000. AX, DC.
**Nagoya Yūbin Chokin Kaikan** 名古屋郵便貯金会館 (951-7611). 1-14-13 Higashi Sakura, Higashi-ku. Near Sakae. S Y4600, Tw Y9000. No CC.

# CHŪBU IV:NE. NORTHEAST FROM NAGOYA

**Main Attractions:** Magome (NE2), Tsumago (NE3), Narai (NE6), Kamikōchi (NE8), Tateyama-Kurobe Alpen Route (NE10)

### Traveling
This route mainly follows the JR Chūō line between Nagoya and Matsumoto, served by frequent expresses. From Tokyo, other direct limited express routes to Matsumoto are the Chūō line from Shinjuku station and the JR Shin'etsu line from Ueno station, via Nagano (KANTŌ II:NW).

## SETO 瀬戸
*0:30–0:45h by private Meitetsu-Seto line from Sakae station in the center of Nagoya to Owari-Seto station; service every 0:10–0:15h. From Tajimi, 0:55h by infrequent bus.* Seto, one of the oldest and most illustrious kiln districts in Japan, is today dominated by 24-hour semi-automated factories that produce one-sixth of Japan's everyday ceramics. Many distinguished potters are associated with the Akazu area. Seto is decentralized and tricky to get around; first visit the information booth near the station. Seto's pottery fair on the third weekend in Sept. attracts half a million bargain hunters.

**\*\*\* Aichi-ken Tōjiki Shiryōkan (Prefectural Ceramic Museum)** 愛知県陶磁器 資料館 Hrs: 9:30–16:30; clsd M (Tu if M a NH). *0:20h by bus from Owari-Seto station.* An extensive museum on Japanese ceramics and their history.

**\* Seto-shi Rekishi Minzoku Shiryōkan (Seto Historical Museum)** 瀬戸市歴史民族 資料館 Hrs: 10:00–16:30; clsd M, NH. Near Shin-Seto station. Pottery from the Jōmon period to the present, plus an important collection on traditional ceramic production.

**Seto-shi Tōjiki Center** 瀬戸市陶磁器センター Hrs: 9:00–17:00; clsd M. Works of Seto potters on view and for sale.

**\*\* Akazu-yaki Kaikan** 赤津焼会館 Hrs: 8:30–17:00; clsd Sa p.m., NH, NY. *0:20h by bus from Owari-Seto station.* Akazu-yaki, favored for tea ceremony ware, is famous for its glaze styles (see Crafts, p. 103). Modern Akazu-yaki is on display and for sale here.

## TAJIMI 多治見
*0:25h by JR Chūō main line express from Nagoya. Junction for JR Ōta line to Mino-Ōta (IV:N2). 0:55h by bus from Seto.* **\*\* Kokei-zan Eiho-ji** 虎渓山永保寺 *(0:10h by bus from Tajimi station or Y900 by taxi)*, a Rinzai Zen temple founded by MUSŌ SOSEKI, has a Muromachi-period Kaisan-dō and Kannon-dō (both NT) standing in a beautiful paradise-style garden. Located in a gentle canyon, it offers a lovely place to picnic. Tajimi is noted for the now extinct Mino ware, related to Seto ware, and the presently made Shino ware. Mino ware is exhibited at the **\* Gifu-ken Tōjiki Shiryōkan** 岐阜県陶磁器資料館 (0572-23-1191). Hrs: 9:30–16:30; clsd M, day after NH, NY. *0:10h by taxi from Tajimi station.*

## THE KISO VALLEY
The Japan of Hiroshige's woodblock prints still lives among the old **Nakasendō** post stations of the Kiso Valley. In villages such as Tsumago and Narai, dozens of Edo-period houses, mostly inns and shops catering to travelers, still line the single main street in tight rows. Today, many of the old inns are back in business as minshuku. The surroundings—dark stands of fine timber forests, steep mountains, rushing cascades—also remain little changed from Hiroshige's day. Visitors can retrace the footsteps of travelers of the Edo period on a quiet, beautiful stretch of the Nakasendō that still links Tsumago and Magome (see Villages, p. 53).

## NE1 NAKATSUGAWA 中津川
*0:55h by JR Chūō main line limited express from Nagoya. Buses for Magome leave every 0:50h from quay 3 in front of the station.*

## NE2 \*\* MAGOME 馬篭
*0:35h by bus from Nakatsugawa station. There are also buses from Nagiso station via Tsumago. Direct highway express bus from Nagoya, 1:55h.* Magome was rebuilt after an 1895 fire, but it remains evocative of an Edo-period post town. Not being as exactingly preserved, it doesn't have the movie-set look of Tsumago. Magome is the birthplace of the Meiji novelist Shimazaki Tōson (1872–1943), and there is a museum, **Tōson Kinenkan** 藤村記念館, on the site of his family home (Hrs: 8:30–16:45; Nov.–Mar. 8:30–16:15; clsd Tu–Th, Dec. 2). Tōson's heavily autobiographical novel, *The Family*, portrays life in Magome and Tsumago in the Meiji period (published in English by Columbia University Press). Magome's main street continues past many old houses that gradually thin out, and finally arrives at Magome Tōge (pass). The walk takes about 0:50h.

### \*\*\* Hiking the Nakasendō from Magome to Tsumago
The section between Magome Tōge (pass) and Tsumago is especially scenic. If time is short, we recommend taking a bus or taxi to the pass. Look for a path to the right from the paved

279

road after the lone teahouse, **Tōge no Chaya**. The 1:45h walk downhill to Tsumago goes by the site of a guardhouse set up in Tokugawa times to prevent the five types of regulated Kiso lumber from being smuggled out. The law was strict: "an arm for a branch" and "a neck for a tree." There is a pair of waterfalls, O-Taki (male) and Me-taki (female), and a teahouse nearby. About 500 m farther is a cluster of minshuku and, just beyond, a left fork in the road marked by a milestone indicating its distance, 79 *ri* (320 km), from Edo's Nihonbashi bridge. The path to the left leads to **Ōtsumago**, a quiet hamlet with a group of old houses. Tsumago proper is another half-hour further.

## ✓ NE3 *** TSUMAGO 妻籠

*From Nagiso (NE4), 0:10h by frequent bus, or 1:30h on foot by the old Nakasendō. From Magome, by bus, via the pass, or on foot by the old Nakasendō (see above).* Tsumago is a place where the clock has been turned back—about 100 years, to be precise—in efforts begun in 1968 to save the village from oblivion. Today, with strict, self-imposed rules that prohibit selling, renting, or destruction of the old houses, Tsumago is a living museum of old Japan. The *annaijo* (information office) issues an informative English pamphlet.

### Calendar
**Oct. 3: Hanauma Matsuri.** Three horses laden with colorful paper flowers are led about the village, accompanied by flutes and drums. At the climax people struggle to grab a flower off the horses' backs, to use as charms to repel insects.
**Nov. 23: Picture Scroll Parade.** People dress as Edo-period travelers and re-create scenes of the old Nakasendō.

### Tsumago Sights
*** **Terashita.** This part of Tsumago was built relatively late, in the mid-Edo period, and is the best preserved. Several Edo-period inns, like the Ikomaya and Matsushiroya, are still in operation. **Kami-Sagaya** was a middle-level inn; one can look inside to see the plain lodgings where commoners stayed. **Shimo-Sagaya** was a typical commoner's dwelling and is now a small museum. The **Enmei Jizō-dō** enshrines an image of a sleeping Jizō carved on a boulder, which was discovered in 1815 by a man fishing in the Araragigawa.
**Kōtoku-ji.** A Zen temple founded in 1583. The present Hondō was built in 1725. Its collection includes a palanquin on wheels, invented by a temple priest in the early 1800s and claimed to be the prototype of the rickshaw. The contraption once made a journey to Kyoto.
* **Masugata.** This sharp kink in the road was designed to protect the town from an attack. The comic Edo-period writer, Jippensha Ikku (*Shank's Mare*), lodged at the nearby Chōjiya.
**Nakamachi (Middle Town).** This area around the **Honjin** and **Waki-Honjin**, official Edo-period lodgings for high-ranking personages, was the high-rent district, so to speak. The road is wider, and houses have a broader street frontage (an indication of wealth or ability to avoid paying the higher taxes).
*** **Okuya Kyōdokan (Local Museum)** 奥谷郷土館 (57-3322). Hrs: 8:30–17:00; clsd Dec. 30–31. In the Edo period, Okuya served as the Waki-Honjin (secondary Honjin) of Tsumago. With the abolition of sumptuary laws, Okuya's Meiji-period master decided to rebuild using superb Kiso lumber that would have cost many a neck in the Edo period. The house was completed in 1877. As the most important house in Tsumago, Okuya played host to the EMPEROR MEIJI in 1881. Earlier, another imperial personage, Princess Kazunomiya, lodged there overnight on her way to wed the shogun. (Cartoonists of the day satirized this "unnatural" event—the first time in history that a shogun was able to wed a princess—as a marriage between a fox and mouse.) Memorabilia from Okuya's past are on display, but the main attraction is the magnificent house itself. The family is especially proud of the second-

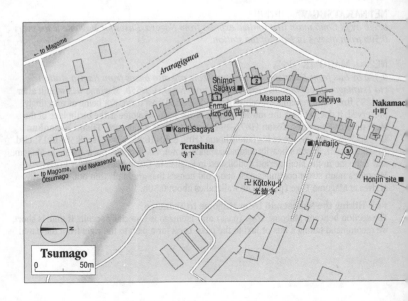

floor guest room where the Emperor Meiji stayed. Many rare woods were used in the room, and the privy is said to be an exact copy of one at Kyoto's Katsura Imperial Villa.

**Gokōsatsu (notice board).** Near the north end of Tsumago is a reconstructed notice board like those that once carried government edicts. Typical notices offered rewards of silver, perhaps even a family name, to people who informed on rebellious peasants or crypto-Christians. The government also admonished the people to live peaceably, and forbade gambling and slavery.

**Araragi and Urushibata** 蘭・漆畑 *0:15h and 0:25h, respectively, by bus from Tsumago (6 per day).* Araragi has been making *hinoki-gasa* (broad-brimmed hats of woven cypress wood strips) since the Edo period. Urushibata is a village taken over by lathe turners. The whole place is permeated with the fragrance of fresh wood shavings. Most of the souvenirs sold in Tsumago and Magome are made in these two villages.

### Tsumago Dining

Try *gohei-mochi*, a snack of pounded-rice dumplings on a skewer, smeared with a sweet paste of sesame, walnuts, and miso. As in other mountainous regions, *sansai ryōri* (see Cuisine, p. 116) is a mainstay of minshuku fare.

③ **Tawaraya Shokudō** 俵屋食堂 (57-2257). Hrs: 10:30–16:00; clsd W, late Dec.–Mar., mid-Aug. *Gohei-mochi* from the local housewives' association. Inexpensive.

④ **Kashiwaya** 柏屋 (57-3036). Hrs: 9:30–16:30; clsd Th (except if NH), July 23–24, mid-Aug., Dec.–mid-Mar. *Gohei-mochi*. Inexpensive.

⑤ **Ebiya** えび屋 (57-3054). Hrs: 8:00–17:00. Pleasant teahouse. Inexpensive.

⑥ **Yoshimuraya** 吉村屋 (57-3265). Hrs: 10:00–17:00; clsd Th (F if Th a NH), mid-Dec.–Dec. 31. Freshly made *soba* with *sansai*. Inexpensive.

⑦ **Sofu-tei** 蘇風亭 (57-2594). Hrs: 9:00–17:00. Real meals. *Sansai teishoku* Y850.

### Tsumago Lodgings (TEL 0264)

281

Numerous minshuku, many in old houses, charge about Y6000 w/2 meals (add Y1000 for single occupancy). Many have luxurious cypress-wood baths. Nearby Ōtsumago, a 0:30h walk along the Nakasendō, is quieter. Reservations advised.

① * **Ikomaya Ryokan** 生駒屋 (57-3013). Terashita, Tsumago, Nagiso-machi, Kiso-gun, Nagano-ken. A beautiful 200-year-old inn, one of the oldest in Tsumago. Y9500+ w/meals.

② * **Matsushiroya Ryokan** 松代屋 (57-3022). Address as above. Another historic inn. Y9000–12,000 w/meals.

⑧ * **Minshuku Daikichi** 民宿大吉 (57-2595). Koino, Tsumago. A newer house, but very pleasant. Excellent food and service. Y6000 w/meals.

**Minshuku Tsutamuraya** 民宿つたむらや (57-3235). Ōtsumago, Tsumago. Handsome old house with *irori*. Friendly. Y5700+ w/meals.

**Minshuku Kameyama** 民宿亀山 (57-3187). Ōtsumago. Y5700 w/meals.

**Minshuku Hanaya** 民宿花屋 (57-3106). Ōtsumago. 5700+.

### NE4 NAGISO 南木曽

*1:10h by JR Chūō line express from Nagoya. Some limited expresses don't stop here, in which case one needs to change to a local at Nakatsugawa* (NE1) *or Kiso-Fukushima* (NE5). *From Nagiso, it is 0:10h by bus to Tsumago.*

### NE5 KISO-FUKUSHIMA 木曽福島

*1:35h by JR Chūō main line limited express from Nagoya.* At Agematsu, one station before Kiso-Fukushima, the train passes Nezame no Toko, a stretch of river with low, sheer walls of eroded rock that was often depicted in ukiyo-e prints. Kiso-Fukushima, with its governor's

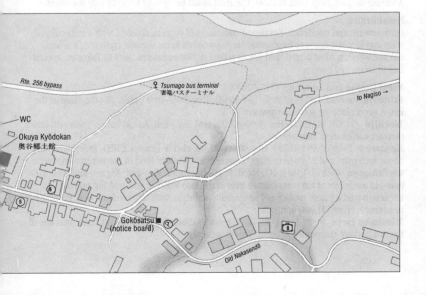

mansion and barrier gate, was the major post town of the Kiso Valley. It was also a base for the Ontake-san pilgrimage (see below); even today, there are throngs of white-garbed pilgrims at the train station. Suggested tour: take a taxi to the Kyōdokan; on the way, you'll pass the Yamamura Daikan Yashiki and Kōzen-ji, which you can visit afterward.

**Kyōdokan** 郷土館 Hrs: 8:30–17:00; clsd Wed. afternoons, NY. Travel gear, old documents, maps, and pictures from Kiso-Fukushima's post-town days.

**Kōzen-ji** 興禅寺 Hrs: 8:30–17:00. Zen temple established in 1434 which served as the funerary temple of Kiso's various lords and governors. It boasts the "largest dry garden in Japan," a product of countrified tastes, one might say. The cemetery contains a tomb of the 12th-C warrior Kiso Yoshinaka, a Minamoto general who was accused of treason by MINAMOTO NO YORITOMO and killed in an attack by MINAMOTO NO YOSHITSUNE; in Kiso, however, he remains a hero, and is commemorated on August 13 with a big torch festival.

**\*\* Fukushima Sekisho-ato** 福島関所跡 Hrs: 8:30–17:00; clsd NY. Across the river from Kōzen-ji. A reconstruction of the Kiso barrier gate, with interesting exhibits. Next door is the old **Takase House**, a prominent medicine-merchant's house.

**\*\* Yamamura Daikan Yashiki** 山村代官屋敷 Hrs: 8:30–17:00; clsd NY. A preserved portion of a mansion and garden of the governor of Kiso, now housing Edo-period memorabilia.

### Kiso-Fukushima Lodgings (TEL 0264)

**Minshuku Kurumiya** 民宿くるみや (22-2084). Shinkai, Kiso-Fukushima-machi, Kiso-gun, Nagano-ken. An old merchant's house in Kaminodan, a preserved section of the old Nakasendō. Y6000 w/meals.

**Kiso Ryojō-an YH** 木曽旅情庵YH (23-7716). 634 Shinkai. *0:25h by Ōhara bus to the end, then walk 0:03h*. In an old house. Popular.

### Exploring Ontake-san

This 3,063-m sacred volcano has been climbed by pilgrims since the late medieval period, and it remains a popular pilgrimage and hike. **Tanohara** (*1:40h by bus from Kiso-Fukushima*) is the main trailhead; from here, it's 3:00h to the summit. Ōtaki, below it, has several Ontake-related shrines. There's a hut at **Yukawa Onsen** (22-2005), above Kurosawa-guchi (*1:20h by bus from Kiso-Fukushima*), trailhead to the second of Ontake-san's trails. Lodges are open July–Sept. Y6800+ w/meals.

## NE6 \*\* NARAI 奈良井

*0:25h by local JR train from Kiso-Fukushima (NE5), or 0:45h by local train from Matsumoto (NE7). Trains are quite infrequent, so check schedules beforehand. A few buses also run to Narai.* Narai is another atmospheric old post town. It hasn't been restored like Tsumago—there's a train station, cars in the street, telephone poles—so it isn't as crowded or so thoroughly dependent on tourism for survival. The best-preserved section is about 0:15–0:20h south of the station (turn left). While walking along the street, formerly the Nakasendō, look for some of Narai's five public springs, which have provided water to travelers and villagers since the Edo period. Narai houses have ornamental notches, called *sarugashira* (monkey heads), which fit over the roof boards of the lower eaves at regular intervals.

**Hiranoya.** A saké brewer, with a huge globe of cryptomeria fronds hanging above the door, a mark of the trade.

**\*\*\* Tokuriya Kyōdokan** 徳利屋郷土館 Hrs: 9:00–17:00; clsd Tu (except if NH), Dec.–mid-Mar. A former high-class inn, now a museum. Lovely rooms.

**\*\* Kamidonya Shiryōkan** 上問屋史料館 Hrs: 8:00–17:00; clsd Jan.–Feb. Built 270 years ago, this house served as a station where travelers exchanged horses and palanquin bearers. Now a museum.

**\*\* Nakamura-tei** 中村邸 Hrs: 9:00–16:30; clsd M (Tu if M a NH). Dec.–Mar. 9:00–16:00. A former lacquer shop, built in 1830. The front could be opened up to display the wares.

### Narai Crafts

Lacquerware and woodcraft. Bentwood containers of cypress, finished with a rust-colored stain and lacquer, are very handsome. Among wooden items, *keyaki* (zelkova), a golden, oaklike wood, is most prized, and prices reflect it. **Matsuzakaya**, next to Tokuriya, specializes in lacquered combs.

### Narai Dining and Lodgings (TEL 0264)

**Echigoya Shokudō** 越後屋食堂 (34-3048). Hrs: 8:00–18:00, daily. Not the same as the inn. A good place for soba. Inexpensive.

**Tsuchiya** つちや (34-3102). Hrs: 9:00–17:00; clsd Dec.–Feb. An old house, converted into a pleasant coffee shop. Inexpensive.

**Kanameya** かなめや (34-3628). Hrs: 10:00–22:00; clsd W (except if NH). Refurbished old house with *irori* and beamed ceilings. Japanese and Western food. A bar at night. Moderate.

**\*\* Echigoya** 越後屋 (34-3011). Narai, Narakawa-mura, Kiso-gun, Nagano-ken. This 200-year-old inn is one of the most famous inns of the Kiso Valley. It survived the railroad era because it sold a patent medicine. Plain, traditional style, with top-notch service. Reserve well in advance. From Y11,000 w/meals.

**Minshuku Iseya** 伊勢屋 (34-3051). Address as above. This Edo-period house was one of the two portage companies in Narai. Y6500 w/meals.

## HIRASAWA 平沢

*0:25h by JR Chūō main line local train from Kiso-Fukushima (NE5), 10 per day. From Narai, Hirasawa is a 0:30h walk.* Hirasawa has long been known for lacquerware, which was made locally and sold to travelers on the Nakasendō. The main street is still lined with lacquer shops where one can view artisans at work (most shops clsd Su). The **Kiso Urushi Shiryōkan**, in the shop of Tezuka Manemon, near the station, displays and sells lacquerware and *akebi* vine baskets. The **Kiso Shikki Kaikan**, a 0:10h walk from the station, is a modern hall displaying the lacquer process and specimens of fine lacquerware (Hrs: 9:00–16:30; clsd M (Tu if M a NH). Dec.–Mar. 9:00–16:00).

## SHIOJIRI 塩尻

*2:10h by JR Chūō main line limited express from Nagoya; 0:10h from Matsumoto; or 2:55h by Chūō main line limited express from Tokyo's Shinjuku station.*

### Calendar

**Apr.–May:** * **Onbashira-sai.** This festival is held every six years, in the years of the tiger and monkey, at the Suwa Shrines in Shimo-Suwa and Kami-Suwa, 0:10h east of Shiojiri. The series of rites is said to have originated 1,200 years ago. Huge trees are felled, dragged down a mountain by hundreds of villagers, and erected amid great fanfare at the shrines (to symbolize a shrine rebuilding). Spectacular and rather dangerous. Next in 1992.

## THE JAPAN ALPS

The snow-capped crags of central Chūbu, soaring above lush forests and dark valleys, reminded Walter Weston, a 19th-century Englishman, of the Swiss Alps. Ever since, they have been known to the Japanese as their *Arupusu*. Weston, an avid mountaineer, was like a latter-day Shugendō holy man, who conquered peak after peak, "opening" them to alpinism. Today, his heirs assemble every year in Kamikōchi, on the first Sunday in June, to begin the hiking season officially with the Weston Festival. These mountains offer varied scenery and challenges to hikers of all abilities. A vast system of mountain huts, amply provisioned, with bunks, heat, hot meals, and supplies, makes it relatively easy for visitors from abroad to arrange a quick trek. Matsumoto is the main gateway to the region. Popular hiking bases include Kamikōchi, Shirahone Onsen, Hotaka, and Shinano-Ōmachi.

283

## NE7 ** MATSUMOTO 松本

*2:20h by JR Chūō line limited express from Nagoya. 3:10h by Chūō line limited express from Tokyo's Shinjuku station. Matsumoto is also connected by bus to Takayama (IV:N3), via Hirayu Onsen, or via Mt. Norikura. By Air: From Ōsaka, 2 flights per day with JAS.* This former castle town, located on a high plateau endowed with beautiful alpine scenery and numerous hot springs, is an excellent base for exploring central Chūbu. Matsumoto's importance in the region goes back at least to the Nara period, when it was the provincial capital. It became a castle town around the 13th century, and Matsumoto-jō, built in 1597, is one of the finest extant castles in Japan. The city today is an invigorating mix of tradition and modernity.

### Calendar

**Oct. 3–4:** * **Taimatsu (Torch Festival).** Asama Onsen, Misai Jinja.

### Getting Around

The center of town is a good size for walking. Pick up an English map at the station. Rent-a-cycles at station.

### Matsumoto Sights

** **Nakamachi-dōri** 中町通り *0:10h walk from station, en route to the castle.* This pleasant street boasts many handsome older buildings and fine craft shops, including Chikiriya and Chūō Mingei furniture. Stop in at **Hakari Shiryōkan** はかり資料館 (Hrs: 9:00–17:00; clsd M, NY), a small museum of weights and measures located in a beautiful turn-of-the-century house. Check out the tiny scale used to sex silkworm cocoons by weight.
*** **Matsumoto-jō** 松本城 (NT). Hrs: 8:30–17:00; clsd NY. *0:15h walk northeast of the station.* This is the oldest fully developed Japanese castle in existence, and is also among the most beautiful and well-preserved. The walls and moat date from 1504, and the six-storied *tenshukaku* was completed in 1597. Built to sustain actual warfare, it has a broad, deep moat, and its black walls are amply equipped with stone-dropping chutes and firing ports for arrows and guns. There is a splendid view from the top. Utility aside, Matsumoto-jō is an architectural beauty, with its balanced arrangement turrets, the striking pattern of black wood against white plaster, and unusual Tsukimi-yagura, or Moon-Viewing Turret, a pavilion with red railings, attached to the main keep. Near the main entrance to the grounds is the **Nihon Minzoku Shiryōkan**, a museum on local history, ethnography, and arts (admission included w/castle).
** **Matsumoto Mingeikan (Folk Art Museum)** 松本民芸館 (33-1569). Hrs: 9:00–17:00; clsd M (Tu if M a NH), NY. *0:15h by Utsukushigahara-Onsen bus from Matsumoto station to Mingeikan-guchi.* An excellent and charming private museum founded by the owner of Chikiriya Folk Craft Gallery in Matsumoto. Mainly Japanese and other Asian folk arts.

**\*\* Nihon Ukiyo-e Hakubutsukan (Art Museum)** 日本浮世絵博物館 Hrs: 10:00–17:00; clsd M, NY. *0:07h by taxi, west of Matsumoto station, or take the Matsumoto-dentetsu private line four stops to Ōniwa and walk 0:15h.* Woodblock prints from the vast collection of the Sakai family. Prints are shown 100 to 150 at a time, and there is an informative slide show on the basic technique of woodblock print-making. The beautiful building was designed by noted architect Shinohara Kazuo.

### Matsumoto Crafts and Shopping
**Chikiriya Kōgei-ten** ちきりや工芸店　中央 3 (33-2522). Hrs: 9:00–18:00; clsd W (except if NH), NY. Open daily in Aug. A reputable shop for regional handicrafts.
**Chūō Mingei Showroom** 中央民芸ショールーム　中央 4 (33-3536). Hrs: 9:00–18:00; clsd NY. Matsumoto's famous *mingei-kagu*, wild-cherry furniture influenced by traditional designs of Japan and the West.

### Matsumoto Dining
Local cuisine includes *sansai* (mountain greens) and not a few unusual sources of protein: horsemeat, locusts (*inago*), bee larvae (*hachinoko*), and pregnant snails (*tanishi*). Try *ba-sashi*, lean, tender raw horsemeat served with soy sauce and garlic.
**Mikawaya** 三河屋　中央 3 (32-0339). Hrs: 11:00–14:00, 17:00–21:00; clsd Su. Horsemeat restaurant with a long history.

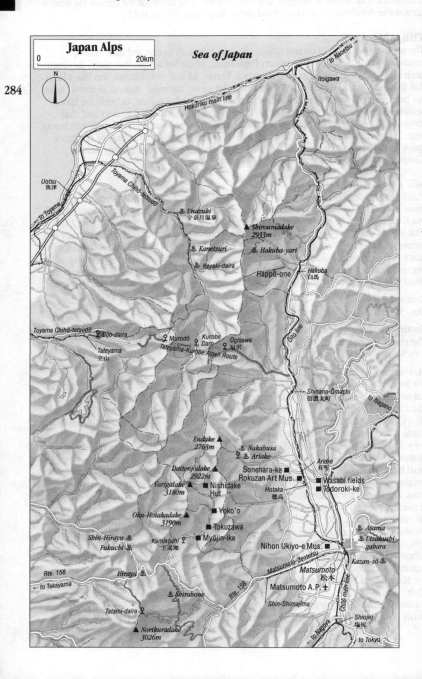

**Kisoya** 木曽屋　大手4-6-26 (32-0528). Hrs: 11:30–15:00, 16:30–21:00; clsd Tu (W if Tu a NH), mid-Aug., NY. *Dengaku* (vegetables, fish, tofu on skewers, charcoal-broiled with a thick coating of miso).

**Kura** くら　中央2 (33-6444). Hrs: 11:00–23:00; clsd 1st and 3rd W, NY. Sushi and tempura in a rambling, mud-walled *kura* storehouse.

**Delhi** デリー　中央2 (35-2408). Hrs: 11:00–23:30; clsd W. Curry in a beautiful *kura*.

**Taiman** 鯛まん　大手4 (32-0882). Hrs: 11:30–20:00 (last order); clsd 1st and 3rd W, NY. Famous French restaurant in an ivy-encrusted mock Tudor house furnished with Matsumoto's *mingei* furniture. Prix fixe menus from Y10,500.

## Matsumoto Lodgings (TEL 0263)

Utsukushigahara Onsen, a quiet village 0:20h by bus from Matsumoto station, has a pleasant, bucolic atmosphere. Nearby Asama Onsen is a booming spa of 600 inns.

＊**Ichiyama Ryokan** いちやま旅館 (32-0122). 2-1-17 Chūō, Matsumoto-shi, Nagano-ken. *Kura*-style classic inn. One wishes the food were more interesting. Y8000–10,300 w/meals.

＊**Marumo Ryokan** まるも旅館 (32-0115). 3-3-10 Chūō. This wooden inn by the river was built in 1888. Peaceful craft-filled café. Y6200 w/ breakfast.

**Tōkyū Inn** 東急イン (36-0109). 1-2-37 Fukashi. There is also a second one, the Daini Tōkyū Inn, which is more expensive, but also newer. S Y7800, Tw Y13,600.

**Green Hotel** グリーンホテル (35-1277). 1-5-11 Fukashi. Business hotel. S Y6500, Tw Y12,000.

**Matsumoto Tourist Hotel** 松本ツーリストホテル (33-9000). 2-4-24 Fukashi. S Y4600, Tw Y11,000+.

＊**Ryokan Sugimoto** 旅館すぎもと　美が原温泉 (32-3379). Utsukushigahara Onsen, Matsumoto-shi. A folk-theme ryokan serving daring but delicious meals. Y10,000+ w/meals.

＊**Katsura-tei** 桂亭　里山辺38 (32-7222). Utsukushigahara Onsen. Elegant ryokan in an old farmhouse, specializing in regional cuisine. Y13,600–23,000 w/breakfast, dinner an additional Y8000+.

＊**Kikunoyu** 菊ノ湯　浅間温泉 (46-2300). Asama Onsen, Matsumoto-shi. A comfortable "farmhouse" onsen ryokan. From Y18,000 w/meals.

## Easy Access To:

＊＊ **Nagano** (KANTŌ II:NW3): *0:55h by JR Chūō line limited express.*

## NE8 ＊＊ KAMIKŌCHI 上高地

*0:30h from Matsumoto by private Matsumoto-dentetsu Kamikōchi line to Shin-Shima-jima, then 1:15h by bus to Kamikōchi (by a harrowing mountain road).* Inaccessible Nov. 5–Apr. 30. This high valley offers some of the finest hiking in Japan. The peaks really soar, and the river really is clean, broad, and swift. Hotel development in Kamikōchi has been kept on a tight rein. This is an excellent hiking base, particularly if you want to do a short, 2- to 3-night circuit. Rental tents, gear, and provisions are also available. The area is incredibly crowded in summer. Fall is better, and the foliage is stunning, best in the first half of October. Views from the resort village are fine, and get even better if you hike upriver. The trail is level for several hours, with comfortable mountain huts along the way. (See Hotaka (NE9) for the hike between Kamikōchi and Ariake.)

## Kamikōchi Lodgings (TEL 0263)

Address: Kamikōchi, Azumi-mura, Minami-Azumi-gun, Nagano-ken.

＊**Kamikōchi Teikoku (Imperial) Hotel** 帝国ホテル (95-2001). Classic resort lodge run by the famous Imperial in Tokyo. Reserve well ahead. Tw Y25–41,000.

**Nishi-Itoya Sansō** 西糸屋山荘 (95-2206). Two-storied wooden inn, by bridge. Y10,600–18,100 w/meals.

**Mountain Huts.** At Myōjin-ike, *1:00h walk from Kamikōchi bus terminal*: **Sansō Yoshikiya** 山荘よしきや (95-2216) Y9–10,000 w/meals; **Myōjin-kan** 明神館 (95-2036) Y6–12,000 w/meals; **Kamonji-goya** 嘉門次小屋 (95-2418) Y5800 w/meals. About 1:00h farther is **Tokuzawa Lodge** 徳沢ロッヂ (95-2526); Y6–9000 w/meals. 1:10h beyond that is **Yoko'o Sansō** 横尾山荘 (95-2421), just before the trail turns up toward Hodaka and Yarigatake; Y7500 w/2 meals. Hot baths, all the comforts (except flush toilets). For other mountain huts, contact the tourist office at 0263-94-2301.

## SHIRAHONE ONSEN 白骨温泉

*0:30h from Matsumoto by private Matsumoto-dentetsu line to Shin-Shimajima, then 1:05h by bus (3 per day) to Shirahone Onsen. There is also one bus each day from Kamikōchi (1:00h).* This is a good base for the hike to the dormant volcano **Norikuradake** (3026 m), noted for its alpine flowers and panoramic views. The area is also rich in hot springs. Shirahone Onsen (white-bone hot spring, because the waters are white with minerals) has several inns with open-air baths.

## Hiking to Norikura and Tatami-daira

This is a more developed area than Kamikōchi. Shirahone Onsen — (0:20h by the road) — Awanoyu onsen inn — (3:00h) — Erizashi Tōge (pass) — (0:30h) — Reisen-goya hut — (0:30h) — Kuraigahara Sansō hut (bus road nearby) — (2:00h) — Kata no Koya hut (overnight) — (0:50h before dawn) — summit of Norikuradake at sunrise — (1:10h) — Tatami-daira (lodgings and buses to and from Hirayu Onsen, CHŪBU IV:N3).

**Shirahone and Norikura Lodgings** (TEL 0263)

\* **Yumoto Saitō Ryokan** 湯元斎藤旅館 (93-2311). Shirahone Onsen, Azumi-mura, Minami-Azumi-gun, Nagano-ken. A rambling inn, with some parts old, some new. Lots of atmospheric baths. Y13–23,000 w/meals.

**YH Ōishi-kan** YH大石館 (93-2011). Shirahone Onsen. Also a ryokan.

**Mountain Huts:** To reserve, call 93-2001; in summer 35-9711. **Kata no Koya** 肩ノ小屋 is open from June to mid-Oct. **Kuraigahara Sansō** 位ガ原山荘 is open from late Apr. through Aug. Y6200 w/meals. There are also two huts at Tatami-daira.

**Norikura Sansō** 乗鞍山荘 (0577-32-3191). Lodge by Tatami-daira bus terminal. Open July–Sept. Y8–13,000 w/meals .

**Easy Access To:**

\* **Hirayu Onsen** (CHŪBU IV:N3): *Buses Apr.–Oct. only. 2:50h from Matsumoto. 1:05h from Kamikōchi. 0:45h from Norikura.*

## NE9 \* **HOTAKA** 穂高

*0:35h by JR Ōito line local train from Matsumoto* (NE7). A popular base for mountaineers. Rent-a-cycle in front of Hotaka station. There are walking and cycling routes in the area; look for the numerous *dōsojin*, stone road-guardian couples, by the wayside. **Hotaka Jinja**, in front of the station, enshrines the kami of Mt. Hotaka. Continue east, across Rte. 147, to **Todoroki-ke** 等々力家 , the Edo-period *honjin* (official lodge) of the Matsumoto lords. Another 2 km east is \*\* **Gohōden Daiō Wasabi-den** 御法田大王ワサビ田 , the biggest *wasabi* field in Japan. *Wasabi*, the green "horseradish" served with sashimi and sushi, is planted in neat rows surrounded by clean water; here you can learn the history of *wasabi* and try some *wasabi* ice cream. Circle back along the Hotaka River toward town. The red-brick **Rokuzan Bijutsukan** 碌山美術館 (82-2094), a former chapel, houses works of the Rodin-style sculptor Ogiwara Morie (1879–1910), born in Hotaka (Hrs: 9:00–17:00; clsd M (Tu if M a NH), NH, NY. Nov.–Mar. 9:00–16:00). If you get hungry, there's a nice *udon* shop, **Inakaya** 田舎屋 , on the left side of the street leaving the station (Hrs: 9:00–20:00, daily).

A 0:45h walk NW of Hotaka station is the Edo-period house, **Sonehara-ke** 曽根原家 (ICP). This is closer to Ariake station, one stop north of Hotaka. Buses from Ariake take hikers to **Ariake Onsen** and **Nakabusa Onsen** (1:00h), deep in the mountains. From there, it's a 4-day hike to Kamikōchi via the famous Yarigatake (Spear Peak).

### Hiking between Ariake and Kamikōchi

Ariake— (1:25h by bus) —Nakabusa Onsen— (4:40h climb) —Enzan-sō hut— (2:00h) —Daitenjōdake hut— (3:00h) —Nishidake hut— (4:00h) —Yarigatake (3 huts) —(5:05h) —Yoko'o Sansō— (1:10h) —Tokuzawa Lodge— (2:00h) —Kamikōchi (NE8).

### Hotaka and Ariake Lodgings (TEL 0263)

**Azumino YH** あずみ野YH (82-4265). 4509 Kashiwabara, Hotaka-machi, Minami-Azumi-gun, Nagano-ken. Clsd Jan. 17–Feb. 7. *0:10h bus ride from Hotaka.*

**Sharomu Hutte** 舎ろ夢ヒュッテ (83-3838). 7958-4 Ariake, Hotaka-machi. *0:15h by bus then 0:10h walk.* Alpine-style pension. Rent-a-cycle. Y7500 w/meals.

**Pension Gohōden** ペンションごほーでん (82-6820). 3580 Hotaka, Hotaka-machi. *0:35h walk from station.* Farmhouse-style pension near the *wasabi* fields. Rent-a-cycle. Y7500 w/meals.

**Kokuminshukusha Ariake-sō** 国民宿舎有明荘 (35-9701). Nakabusa, Ariake, Hotaka-machi. Clsd late Nov.–Apr. Only inn at Ariake Onsen. 13 Japanese rooms. Y6500 w/meals.

**Nakabusa Onsen** 中房温泉 (35-9704). Nakabusa, Ariake, Hotaka-machi. Clsd late Nov.–Apr. Lone inn deep in the mountains. Has several open-air baths. Y10–18,000 w/meals.

## NE10 **SHINANO-ŌMACHI** 信濃大町

*1:00h by JR Ōito line local from Matsumoto* (NE7). Or *5:30 from Tokyo, or 4:20h from Nagoya, by direct express.* Gateway to the highly popular Tateyama-Kurobe Alpen Route. 0:05h on foot from Ōmachi station is the interesting \* **Shio no Michi Hakubutsukan (Salt Route Museum)** 塩の道博物館 , housed in a wonderful set of old *kura* once used to store the salt that was carried into the interior from the Japan Sea coast (Hrs: 9:00–18:00. Nov.–Apr. 9:00–17:00; clsd W).

## \*\* **TATEYAMA-KUROBE ALPEN ROUTE** 立山黒部アルペンルート

A series of buses, cable cars, tramways, and tunnels offers nonhikers spectacular mountain scenery, and also provides access to excellent hiking. Also accessible from Toyama (CHŪBU IV:N4), via Tateyama. The total trip is expensive (Y9850), and gets very crowded. Runs mid-May–Nov. 30. Reservations advised for July 20–Aug. 30 and Sept. 20–Oct. 20; call 0261-22-0804. The route: Shinano-Ōmachi— (0:40h by bus) —Ōgisawa— (0:15h by trolley bus through tunnel) —Kurobe Dam— (0:15h walk) —Kurobe lake— (0:05h by cable car) —Kurobe-daira (plateau) —(0:07h by tramway) —Daikan-bō— (0:10h by bus) —Murodō-daira— (0:05h by bus) —Bijo-daira (meadow) —(0:07h by cable car) —Tateyama— (1:00h by Toyama-tetsudō train) —Toyama.

### Hiking

The best access to trails is at Murodō. One recommended 3-day hike (stopping at mountain huts along the way) is to head north to **Keyaki-daira**, terminus of the Kurobe Gorge narrow-gauge rail line (CHŪBU IV:N4).

### Alpen Route Lodgings (TEL 0764)

**Ōgisawa Lodge** 扇沢ロッジ (0261-22-4444). Ōgisawa, Taira, Ōmachi-shi, Nagano-ken. Y8500–11,000 w/meals.

**Hotel Tateyama** ホテル立山 (65-3333). Murodō, Tateyama-machi, Nakaniikawa-gun, Toyama-ken. First class. Y17–27,000 w/meals.

**Raichō-sō** 雷鳥荘 (65-4596). Murodō-daira, Raichō-dai, Tateyama-machi. Y6–10,000 w/meals. Clsd late Nov.–mid-Apr.

**Lodge Tateyama Rempō** ロッジ立山連峰 (65-4594). Murodō-daira, Tateyama-machi. From Y6000 w/meals. Clsd Nov. 15–Apr. 25.

**Tateyama Kōgen Hotel** 立山高原ホテル (41-1220). Tengu-daira, Tateyama-machi. Y9250 w/meals.

**Kokuminshukusha Tateyama-sō** 国民宿舎立山荘 (42-3535). Midagahara, Tateyama-machi. Y5000 w/meals. Clsd Nov. 7–Apr. 27.

**YH Sugita** YH杉田 (82-1345). Tateyama. Clsd Jan.–Mar. Y3300 w/meals.

### HAKUBA 白馬

*1:40h from Matsumoto (NE7) or 0:35h from Shinano-Ōmachi (NE10) by JR Ōito line.* This is a major base for hiking and skiing in the Northern Alps. 0:35h by bus from Hakuba station is **Sarukura**, where there is a mountain hut, Sarukura-sō 猿倉荘 (0261-72-2279). Open June–Nov. From here, it is a 3:00h climb to **\*\* Hakuba-yari Onsen** 白馬鑓温泉 (2100 m), the highest hot spring in Japan; its open-air bath offers a splendid panorama of the peaks. There is a hut here, the Yari Onsengoya (72-2002), Y6800 w/meals. **Daisettsukei** (glacier) is a 1:40h hike from Sarukura. **Happō-one**, the main ski resort, is 0:05h by bus from Hakuba station.

287

### Easy Access To:

**Toyama** (CHŪBU IV:N4): *4:50h by Alpen Route to Tateyama, then 1:00h to Toyama by private Toyama Chihō-tetsudō line.*

# CHŪBU IV:N. NORTH FROM NAGOYA

**Main Attractions:** Meiji Mura (N1), Takayama (N3)

### Traveling

Most visitors to the popular mountain city of Takayama take the JR Takayama main line from Nagoya or Gifu, but if you have an extra day, we recommend visiting Meiji Mura and Inuyama, then intercepting the Takayama line at Mino-Ōta.

### N1 \*\* MEIJI MURA 明治村

*By bus: 1:20h from Meitetsu bus terminal in Nagoya; last departure at 11:35. By train: 0:25–0:40h by private Meitetsu line to Inuyama, change trains, then 0:20h by bus. Be sure to board the correct train in Nagoya; trains to various destinations use the same platform. The Meiji Mura counter at the Meitetsu bus terminal sells a package including round-trip fares and admission tickets. For a one-way ticket, ask for* katamichi dake, *or the clerks will automatically sell you the whole package.* (0568-67-0314). Hrs: 10:00–17:00, daily. Nov.–Feb. 10:00–16:00. This open-air "village" of buildings from Japan's Meiji and Taishō eras (1868–1912) is one of the most inspired and delightful architectural museums in the world. Perfect and not-so-perfect copies of Western architecture stand along-side traditional structures of the same period, bringing alive the contrasts, charm, and sheer audacity of Japan's astounding transformation.

Anyone who has spent some time traveling in Japan will realize that there are very few Meiji buildings left. Incalculable numbers were destroyed in World War II, and most of those that survived have been torn down to make room for postwar development. But one also suspects that most Japanese attached little sentiment to these Western-style buildings and Western things in general. Western culture was admired for its practical values more than its esthetic ones, and was diligently mastered to gain the respect of the West. With changing times, few were troubled that fine Meiji structures were being torn down to make room for something newer and more practical. Meiji Mura prompts one to reflect on the changes that have taken place in Japan, and on the direction they might take in the future.

### Calendar

The most crowded season is April–June (school kids).

**Jan. 1–5: Meiji no Oshōgatsu.** Visitors can play traditional New Year games with girls dressed up in Meiji-era kimono.

**Mar. (Su before 15th): \* Ōagata Jinja Matsuri.** Ōagata Jinja (*take Meitetsu Komaki line to Gakuden station, then walk 0:15h*). The distaff version of the famous Tagata Hōnen-sai.

**Mar. 15: \*\* Tagata Jinja Hōnen-sai.** Tagata Jinja (*take Komaki line to Tagata Jinjamae*). See Calendar, p. 276. Parade from 14:00.

## Getting Around

There's a little steam locomotive and an old Kyoto streetcar threading the park. On foot, one can race through in about 2:30h, though 3:00–5:00h is recommended. There's an excellent English pamphlet, but one should check it against the more frequently updated Japanese pamphlet.

## Meiji Mura Sights

Noteworthy traditional Japanese structures include an old Kabuki theater, public bathhouse, merchant houses, a martial arts hall, and the summer house of Meiji-period Japanophile Lafcadio Hearn. The park also has one of the world's architectural landmarks of the early 20th century, the famed Frank Lloyd Wright ◆ **Imperial Hotel**. The hotel was demolished in 1965, but the lobby was saved and the museum has spent more than 15 years and $25 million on reconstruction. Though it is actually a Taishō structure, the Imperial Hotel marked the end of Japan's first feverish phase of modernization. The hotel was completed just before one of Tokyo's greatest disasters, the Great Kantō Earthquake of September 1, 1923. It survived intact, but the rest of the city—the Tokyo of the Meiji era—was almost completely destroyed.

### ∗ Ōagata Jinja and Tagata Jinja　大県神社・田県神社

*One and 2 stops south of Meiji Mura-guchi station. Ōagata Jinja is not far from Gakudan station; Tagata Jinja is right by Tagata-Jinja-mae.* These shrines are consecrated to the two parent kami, Izanagi and Izanami (see Shinto, p. 24), represented by objects suggesting female and male genitalia, such as a cleft rock or knob-shaped branch. The shrine grounds are filled with similar offerings by people praying for children, wealth, or a good harvest. Such fertility shrines once played an important role in Japanese folk religion, but have decreased greatly in number since the Japanese began to adopt Victorian prudishness as part and parcel of their modernization effort.

## Meiji Mura Dining

**288**

**Ōi Gyūniku-ten**　大井牛肉店　(67-0318). Hrs: 11:00–15:30, daily. A former Kōbe beef shop, just inside Meiji Mura entrance. Sukiyaki cooked over charcoal. From Y3200, Y4,000.

## ∗ INUYAMA　犬山

*0:25h by private Meitetsu line express from Nagoya; if possible, continue one stop beyond to Inuyama Yūen. Walk 0:10h on the left bank of the river to the castle, perched atop a hill overlooking the river. The Meitetsu Hotel is just before the hill; Uraku-en is reached through the hotel parking lot.* Virtually all the local attractions were created by the Meitetsu Company, which runs not only Meiji Mura, but also Uraku-en, "Little World," Monkey Park, the Meitetsu Hotel, and boat rides on the Kiso River. Uraku-en and the genuine keep of Inuyama-jō are worth seeing; the rest can safely be skipped.

## Calendar

**Apr. (1st or 2nd Su): Inuyama Matsuri.** 13 Edo-period floats are dragged around town. Especially beautiful at night.

## Inuyama Sights

∗∗∗ **Uraku-en**　有楽苑　Hrs: 9:00–17:00, daily. Dec.–Feb. 9:00–16:00. This attractive park contains the ◆ **Jo-an** (1618, NT), one of the finest tea arbors in existence. Jo-an was built by ODA NOBUNAGA's brother Urakusai (1547–1621), a leading tea master. Inuyama was the home fief of the Oda family, which may be why Meitetsu purchased and moved Jo-an and **Shōden-in Shoin** (ICP), Urakusai's study, to Inuyama. Both structures originally stood in Shōden-in, a subtemple of Kyoto's Kennin-ji. The *shoin*'s interior is decorated with ink landscapes by KANŌ Sansetsu and Hasegawa Tōhaku, two preeminent painters of the Momoyama period. The Jo-an stands in back and is approached through a tea garden *roji*. It is a splendid example of the Sukiya style (see Villas, p. 65). Every detail—the grain of the ceiling board, the unusual printed wallpaper, the texture of the sand-and-straw plaster, and the layout of tatami, windows, and support columns—was carefully chosen to produce an atmosphere of naturalness and repose. Note the windows crisscrossed with vines; this feature, an invention of Urakusai's, is known as the *Uraku-mado*.

∗∗ **Inuyama-jō**　犬山城　(1601, NT). Hrs: 9:00–16:30; clsd Dec. 29–31. This small keep was built in a very early style and resembles a watchtower perched atop a two-storied foundation. The castle is still owned by descendants of its Edo-period castellans, the Naruse, senior vassals of the lords of Nagoya; it is the only privately owned castle remaining in Japan. The modest but beautiful structure is entirely utilitarian, with impressive foundations and support beams, all assembled without nails.

## N2 MINO-ŌTA　美濃太田

*From Inuyama, 0:40h (Y3500) by taxi, or hop over from the Meitetsu-Shinunuma station to Unuma station and take the JR Takayama main line 0:20h to Mino-Ōta. Or 0:30h from Gifu or 1:00h from Nagoya by Takayama main line express. Junction to the Nagaragawa line, an infrequent local train to Mino-Seki and places described under* CHŪBU IV:NW.

## Exploring Mino-Seki

*# 0:50h by train or 0:35h by bus from the Meitetsu Shin-Gifu station. Or 0:20h by Nagaragawa line train from Mino-Ōta (infrequent).* Seki is the best place to observe cormorant fishing (*ukai*) and is also noted for swordsmiths, who have been forging swords here since the Kamakura period. Today, Seki is a leading cutlery producer, but the town also has 20 swordsmiths, 17 sword-sharpeners, and 25 sword-ornament artisans. A public demonstration is held at the Nippontō Tanrenjō (23-3825) from 10:00–16:00 on Jan. 2, the 1st Su of each month, and 2nd weekend in Oct. during the Hamono (Cutlery) Matsuri. At other times, inquire at the Tourism Association (0575-22-3131). **Lodgings and Ukai: ✳✳ Adachi Minshuku U no Ie** 安立民宿鵜ノ家 (0575-22-0799). 78 Oze, Seki-shi, Gifu-ken. Owned by a cormorant fisherman. Guests can watch authentic *ukai* and dine on fresh *ayu* (see Cuisine, p. 116). Ask to stay in the beautiful old house, with its gardens and courtyard full of honking cormorants. From Y16,000 w/2 meals. *Ukai* only, Y4500 (w/box lunch). Reserve at 0575-22-2506.

## Exploring Mino

Adjacent to Mino-Seki. Mino is a paper-making town with an 800-year history, where a thousand households still produce *washi* by hand. The tradition is designated an Important Intangible Cultural Property. On a sunny day, one can see large boards with damp *washi* set out to dry. The Mino Hanamikoshi festival on Apr. 14–15 features *mikoshi* festooned with sprays of bright-pink Mino paper.

## GERO ONSEN 下呂温泉

*2:00h from Nagoya or 1:30h from Gifu by JR Takayama main line limited express.* An onsen town with a thousand-year history, now commercial and unattractive.

### Calendar

0:30h by bus or car from Gero are two public Kabuki stages, the Haku'un-za (built in 1891), which has a revolving stage, and the Hō'ō-za (1827). Local amateurs perform from the Kabuki Jūhachiban (18 plays of the Ichikawa family, see Drama, p. 87). Inquire at 05762-6-2387, 7-1354, or 5-3151 for exact schedule.

**May 3–4: ✳ Kabuki** at Hō'ō-za. From 13:00.
**Nov. 2–3: ✳ Kabuki** at the Haku'un-za. From 14:00.

289

## N3 ✳✳✳ TAKAYAMA 高山

*2:20h by JR Takayama main line limited express from Nagoya. 1:30h from Toyama (N4), on the Japan Sea coast, by much less frequent trains.* The highland city of Takayama, isolated by a barricade of mountains and cursed with poor farmland, nevertheless produced a distinct, elegant local culture that has earned it the nickname "little Kyoto." In the Nara period, Hida province was unable to produce enough rice to pay its taxes. Each village was obliged to send 10 artisans to the capital instead. Records show that Hida artisans worked on the great temples and palaces of Nara and were lauded for their skill. In the feudal period, Takayama became a castle town, and its lords built many temples and shrines. But in 1692, the Tokugawa shogunate, coveting the timber and mineral wealth of Hida for itself, reassigned the daimyo of Takayama to Tōhoku and took over the direct administration of the region. Bad government led to a series of peasant revolts, but the townspeople prospered and continued to develop superb crafts and architecture. Today, although the city has been modernized, the old culture remains much in evidence, in the splendidly preserved merchant houses, in magnificent spring and fall festivals, and in a wealth of detail—carved temple brackets, crafts, local saké, teahouses, and cuisine. A multitude of museums demonstrates the continuing vitality of this town, which today has a new source of wealth: the millions of tourists who have "discovered" Takayama.

### Calendar

**Apr. 14–15: ✳✳✳ Sannō Matsuri.** Hie Jinja. See Calendar, p. 276. Look atop the 12 festival floats for the amazing *karakuri* (mechanical puppets), which perform complicated stunts. On the 14th, there is a procession in the afternoon and evening. The 15th is the main day, with the floats gathering at the shrine in the morning. Draws about 200,000 people.

**Aug. 1–10: Ema-ichi.** A fair in which votive paintings of horses are sold. The *ema* are hung in entrances to homes, with the lucky horse "leaping inside."

**Oct. 9–10: ✳✳✳ Hachiman Matsuri.** Sakurayama Hachiman-gū. See Calendar, p. 276. Main events on the 10th.

### Getting Around

The information booth at the front of the station issues a useful English booklet (tel: 0577-32-5328; Hrs: 8:30–18:30). Takayama is a good size for exploring on a bicycle, though the attractions in the center of town can be seen on foot. Three rent-a-cycle shops near the station. The station (Ekimae) bicycle rental will store your bags for free.

### Takayama Sights

**✳ Asa-ichi (Morning Market).** Farm women from the surrounding country hawk fresh flowers and vegetables, homemade pickles, and toys every morning along the riverbank and in the open area in front of Takayama Jinya. Daily, 7:00–12:00.

**✳✳✳ Takayama Jinya** 高山陣屋 (32-0643). Hrs: 8:45–17:00; clsd NY. Nov.–Mar. 8:45–16:30. *0:10h walk from station.* This group of large whitewashed buildings is the only extant provincial government office of the Edo shogunate. It was the residence of the daimyo of Hida, but after he was "transferred" in 1692, Tokugawa governors took it over. The buildings were used for the local government office and courthouse until 1969. Visitors today enter the building by the main gate, formerly reserved for high officials. The raised floor allowed officials to dismount from their palanquins without touching the earthen floor of the vestibule. To the left is a series of **audience chambers**, but commoners had to kneel on the ground outside and make their appeals heard through the dark, slatted barrier erected along the veranda. By the garden in back stand the rice storehouses for the tax revenue of the shogunate; these are the oldest and largest extant in Japan. The **ornamental nail covers** on this side of the building, in the shape of floppy-eared rabbits, are said to symbolize the far-reaching ears of the shogunate. The adjoining building has a peculiar interior—half is tatami, bordered by a wooden veranda, and half is at ground level, covered with river cobbles. This was the **interrogation room**. Whips on the wall and some uncomfortable-looking pieces of

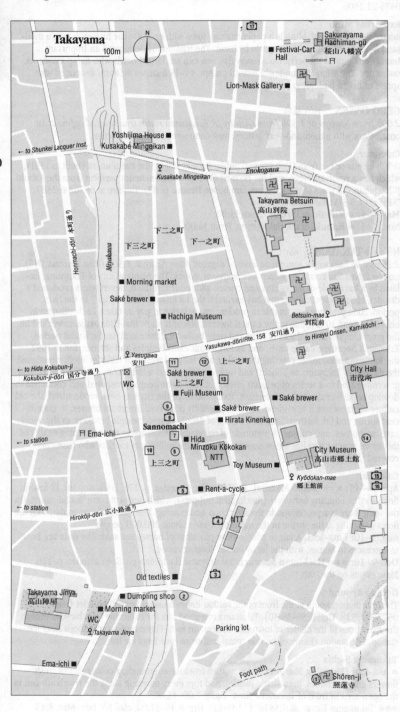

Takayama

0          100m

N

Sakurayama Hachiman-gū
桜山八幡宮
■ Festival-Cart Hall

Lion-Mask Gallery ■

← to Shunkei Lacquer Inst.

Yoshijima House ■
Kusakabe Mingeikan ■

Kusakabe Mingeikan

Enokogawa

Takayama Betsuin
高山別院

下二之町
Miyakawa
下三之町        下一之町

■ Morning market
Saké brewer ■

■ Hachiga Museum

Betsuin-mae
別院前

Honmachi-dōri 本町通り

to Hirayu Onsen, Kamikōchi →

Yasukawa-dōri/Rte. 158 安川通り

← to Hida Kokubun-ji
Kokubun-ji-dōri 国分寺通り

Yasugawa
安川
⑪   ⑫   上一之町
Saké brewer ■
上二之町   ⑬
■ Fujii Museum

WC

City Hall
市役所

⑨
⑧
Sannomachi
Ema-ichi
← to station

■ Saké brewer
■ Hirata Kinenkan
● Saké brewer

上三之町   ⑦
⑩        ⑥
■ Hida Minzoku Kōkokan
NTT
Toy Museum ■

City Museum
高山市郷土館
⑭

⑤  ■ Rent-a-cycle

Kyōdokan-mae
郷土館前
⑮
⑯

← to station
Hirokōji-dōri 広小路通り

④ NTT

Old textiles ■

③

Takayama Jinya
高山陣屋

● Dumpling shop ②
■ Morning market
WC
Takayama Jinya

Parking lot

Ema-ichi ■

Foot path

① Shōren-ji
照蓮寺

"furniture" are the only decor. Sketches illustrate how these implements were used. This chamber could accommodate all classes: Commoners were relegated to the river stones (very practical, easy to clean); more important persons got the veranda; and the highest enjoyed the comforts of tatami.

\* **Shōren-ji** 照蓮寺 Hrs: 8:30–18:00. Nov.–Mar. 8:30–17:00. This temple was brought here in 1961 from the Shōkawa Valley to save it from flooding by the Miboro dam. The Main Hall (1504, ICP) is claimed to be the oldest Jōdo Shin sect *hondō* in existence. The roof lines are considered especially fine. The temple serves *shōjin-ryōri* (vegetarian cuisine).

\*\*\* **Sannomachi** 三之町 A quarter famous for rows of handsome old merchant shops (see Villages, p. 54). Most buildings date from the mid-Edo period. Many shops sell local specialties such as saké in pottery bottles, *shunkei* lacquerware, and folkcrafts. To escape the crowds, walk east to Kami-Ichinomachi, an area of superb old saké and miso merchants' houses. Saké brewers display a large globe of cryptomeria fronds out in front. Traditionally, the fronds were picked at the beginning of the brewing cycle; by the time they had turned brown, the saké was ready to drink. Note that everything closes around 17:00.

**Hida Minzoku Kōkokan** 飛騨民族考古館 (32-1980). Hrs: 7:00–19:00. Dec.–Feb. 8:00–17:00. Archeological objects and old folkcrafts, displayed in an Edo-period physician's house. One block up is another folk-art museum, **Fujii Bijutsu Mingeikan** (32-0108). Hrs: 9:00–17:00; clsd NY. In July and Aug. 9:00–18:00.

\* **Hirata Kinenkan** 平田記念館 (33-1354). Hrs: 9:00–17:00. Ten generations of the Hirata family, makers of pomade and candles, collected the articles shown in a series of storehouses at the rear of the garden. The museum complex and collection present an attractive picture of the life of a prosperous Edo-period merchant.

\* **Kyōdo Gangukan (Toy Museum)** 郷土玩具館 (32-1183). Hrs: 8:30–17:00; clsd NY. A charming collection of over 2,000 folk toys of Japan.

\* **Takayama-shi Kyōdokan (City Museum)** 高山市郷土館 (32-1205). Hrs: 8:30–17:00; clsd M (except if NH), NY. Dec.–Feb. 8:30–16:30. A collection of folk art and historical material, housed in Meiji-period earthen storehouses. Of special interest are the 12 rough-hewn Buddhist images by Enkū, a 17th-C sculptor-monk who traveled about the countryside.

291

**Hachiga Minzoku Bijutsukan (Folkloric Art Museum)** 八賀民族美術館 (32-1238). Hrs: 9:00–17:00. Jan.–Mar. clsd W. Another old Takayama merchant family's art and memorabilia on view in several *kura*.

\*\*\* **Kusakabe Mingeikan (Folk Art Museum)** 日下部民芸館 (ICP) (32-0072). Hrs: 9:00–17:00. Dec.–Mar. 9:00–16:30; clsd NY. The Kusakabe were merchants and financiers to the Edo-period governor of Takayama. When their old house burned in 1879, they rebuilt in a grand style, using superb timbers that reflect the new freedom for merchants to build their homes in a manner commensurate with their wealth. The interior is dominated by a spacious earthen floor and a massive post-and-beam assembly supporting the soaring ceiling. The rafters conduct smoke to ceiling vents, diverting it from the second floor. The hearth was the center of daily life. Other rooms were used for business and sleeping quarters.

\*\*\* **Yoshijima-ke** 吉島家 (ICP) (32-0038). Hrs: 9:00–17:00. Dec.–Feb. 9:00–16:30; clsd Tu, NY. This magnificent saké-merchant's house is, with its neighbor, Kusakabe house, one of the finest traditional Japanese domestic dwellings in existence. It was built in 1905 in a similar style, but seems more elegant and warm.

**Sakurayama Hachiman-gū** 桜山八幡宮 The guardian shrine of Takayama, dedicated to the kami of war. It was founded over a thousand years ago. Its autumn festival is among the most famous in Japan.

\*\*\* **Takayama Yatai Kaikan (Festival-Cart Hall)** 高山屋台会館 (32-5100). Hrs: 8:30–17:00, daily. Dec.–Feb. 9:00–16:30. A hall housing four of the gorgeous *yatai*, or festival carts, for the Hachiman shrine festival. These *yatai*, among the finest in Japan, attained their present appearance by the early 1800s. They are fascinating examples of Edo-period flamboyance and craftsmanship.

\*\* **Shishi Kaikan (Lion-Mask Gallery)** 獅子会館 (32-0881). Hrs: 8:30–17:00, daily. A collection of 800 lion masks from all over Japan. The oldest dates from the Kamakura period, and another from 1577. *Karakuri ningyō*, ingenious Edo-period mechanical dolls, like those that ride on the Takayama festival floats, are also on display.

\* **Hida Kokubun-ji** 飛騨国分寺 *0:05h walk NE of station.* Founded in 746 as the state temple for Hida province. Noted for its Muromachi-period Main Hall (ICP), three-storied pagoda (1821), and main images of Yakushi Nyorai (ICP) and Shō Kanzeon Bosatsu (ICP).

\*\* **Hida Minzoku Mura (Hida Folklore Village)** 飛騨民俗村 (33-4714). Hrs: 8:30–17:00, daily. Clsd NY. *0:08h by bus or 0:15h by bicycle west of Takayama station.* Good illustrated pamphlet in English. An excellent open-air museum of Hida farmhouses. The "village" is comprised of two groups of buildings. The smaller, called Minzoku-kan, is based around Wakayama-ke (ICP), a fine, mid-18th-C *gasshō* farmhouse moved from the Shōkawa Valley (CHŪBU IV:NW2). Hida no Sato, 600 m southwest, is a larger collection of traditional dwellings. The farmhouses here exhibit regional crafts.

\# **Senkō-ji** 千光寺 (05777-8-1507). Hrs: 8:30–17:00. *0:15h by bus from Takayama toward Hirayu, get off at Machikata, then walk 0:50h.* This old mountain temple is noted for its collection of some 60 Buddhist images carved by the mysterious monk-sculptor Enkū during the years he lived here (ca. 1684–88).

## Takayama Crafts and Shopping

A **Garakuta-ichi**, a big sale of old junk, antiques, folkcrafts, is held on the 7th of the month, May–Oct.

**Shunkei Kaikan (Lacquer Institute)** 春慶会館 (32-3373). Hrs: 8:00–17:30. Dec.–Mar. 9:00–17:00. Somewhat out of the way; about 1 km NE of station. Extensive collection of Takayama's best-known craft, *shunkei-nuri*, objects made of beautifully grained woods coated with clear, amber-colored lacquer. Most pieces displayed are from the Edo period. The process is demonstrated here.

7 \* **Usagiya** うさぎ舍 (34-6611). Hrs: 8:30–18:00, daily. Exquisite plant-dyed fabrics. Be sure not to miss the gallery in back.

10 \* **Hida Sashiko** 飛騨さしこ 片原町60 (34-5345). Hrs: 8:30–17:00; clsd Su, Jan.– Mar. Sells *sashiko*, a decorative quilting of white thread on indigo cotton cloth, rescued from extinction by an old Takayama woman. Beautiful old-style shop.

11 **Fukudaya** 福田屋 (32-0065). Hrs: 8:30–20:00, daily. An established *shunkei-nuri* lacquerware shop.

13 \*\* **Hōkokusha** 芳国舍 (34-0504). Hrs: 8:00–20:00, daily. The Shibakusa porcelain made here since 1879 is nationally famous. Crisp designs are drawn in vivid colors against a pure white ground. The kiln 2 km west of the station can be visited during weekdays 8:00–17:00.

## Takayama Dining

Specialties: *hōba-miso*, a special seasoned miso broiled on a large brown leaf over a small clay brazier; *sansai-ryōri* (see Cuisine, p. 116); an elegant version of *shōjin-ryōri* (Buddhist vegetarian cuisine); *mitarashi-dango*, sticky rice dumplings broiled and dipped into a salty-sweet sauce, sold all over town from pushcarts and open-air stands.

1 \* **Kanenbō** 嘉念坊 (32-2052). Hrs: 11:00–18:00. *Shōjin-ryōri* served by the garden at Shōren-ji. Reservation advised. *Bentō* Y2500, *shōjin* course from Y5000.

2 \*\* **Suzaki** 洲さき 神明町 (32-0023). Hrs: 11:30–14:00, 17:00–18:30. Reservations. A 250-year-old establishment for *kaiseki*-style *sansai* cuisine, supposedly developed under the second daimyo of Takayama, a tea connoisseur. From Y9500. Lunchtime *bentō* from Y5000.

6 **Noguchiya** 野口屋 (33-7563). Hrs: 10:00–17:00, daily. Tofu cuisine. *Dengaku teishoku* Y750, tofu *teishoku* Y1000.

9 **Hidaji** 飛騨路 (33-4616). Hrs: 9:00–17:00, clsd Th. *Sansai bentō* from Y1800.

12 \* **Ebisu Honten** 恵比寿本店 (32-0209). Hrs: 10:00–20:00. Su 10:00–18:00. Beautiful old *soba* shop. *Soba* from Y630.

14 \*\* **Kakushō** 角正 (32-0174). Two seatings, at 11:30 and 13:30, clsd W, NY. Nationally famous *shōjin-ryōri* restaurant with a history dating back 150 years. Located in the former mansion of the official physician. Set menus, Y5000 and Y9000. Reservations advised. No CC.

\* **Suzuya** 寿々や 花川町24 (32-2484). Hrs: 11:00–20:00; clsd Tu, NY. Folk-art interior. *Sansai misodaki-nabe* Y1200, *sansai teishoku* Y1400, *yaki-miso teishoku* Y1000.

## Takayama Lodgings (TEL 0577)

Plenty of hotels and minshuku, but reservations essential during peak seasons. The station information booth can help out. Hirayu Onsen (see below) is an alternative well worth considering.

3 **Uenoya** 上野屋 (32–3919). 95 Kamininomachi. Friendly minshuku in prime area. Y6000 w/meals.

4 \*\* **Nagase Ryokan** 長瀬旅館 (32-0068). 10 Kami-Ninomachi, Takayama-shi, Gifu-ken. The oldest and best ryokan in town. Excellent location near Sannomachi. Eight of the 12 rooms have a private bathroom. Y13–25,000 w/meals. No CC.

5 **Saitō Ryokan** 斎藤旅館 上三之町 (32-1970). 2-25 Kami-Sannomachi. Old house on Sannomachi. Shared bathrooms. Y10–11,000. No CC.

8 \* **Ryokan Gōdo** 旅館河渡 (33-0870). 46 Sannomachi. Old Sannomachi house. Very friendly, good food and atmosphere. Y8000 w/breakfast. If you request it, they'll make a fine dinner for about Y2000 extra. No CC.

15 **YH Tenshō-ji** YH天照寺 (32-6345). 83 Tenshō-ji-chō. Temple.

16 \* **Minshuku Mitsui** 民宿三井 江名子町 (32-3864). 4359 Enako-chō. Nicely refurbished old house in farm country a few km outside the city. Call for a lift. Y6000 w/meals. Next door is **Minshuku Yamashita** 民宿山下 (33–0686). It's similar but somewhat grander.

17 \* **Takayama Kankō Hotel** 高山観光ホテル (32-4100). 280 Hachiman-machi. Large, comfortable modern ryokan. Some distance from town center. Y12–22,000 w/meals.

## Easy Access To:

\*\*\* **Shirakawa-gō** (CHŪBU IV:NW3): *1:25h to Makido* (CHŪBU IV:NW2), *then transfer to a bus to Ogimachi and Gokayama.*

## \* HIRAYU ONSEN 平湯温泉

*1:00h by Shinhotaka- or Norikura-bound bus east from Takayama.* A small hot-spring resort surrounded by mountains. O-Fudō-san, guardian deity of the hot spring, is 0:20h on foot beyond the Yumotokan Hotel. Free open-air bath nearby. 0:20h beyond Hirayu Onsen by Shinhotaka-bound bus is Fukuchi Onsen-guchi, a 0:10h walk from **Fukuchi Onsen**, the most

292

bucolic of the spas in this area. All the inns here have open-air baths. 0:10h farther on the same bus is **Shin-Hirayu Onsen**, a group of farmhouse hot-spring inns strung out along the mountain road.

**Hirayu Area Lodgings** (TEL 0578)
**Hotel Hirayu-kan** ホテル平湯館 (9-3111). 726 Hirayu, Kamitakara-mura, Yoshiki-gun, Gifu-ken. A deluxe resort ryokan arranged around a garden. Has a beautiful cypress bath hall and large outdoor bath. Y13–35,000 w/meals.
**Nakamura-kan** 中村館 (9-2321). Address as above. Fairly unpretentious, pleasant inn with an outdoor bath set in a garden. Y12–25,000 w/meals.
**Magokurō** 孫九郎 (9-2231). Fukuchi Onsen, Kamitakara-mura. Elegant farmhouse-style ryokan. Y15–18,000 w/meals.
**Seigaku-kan** 静岳館 (9-2410). Shin-Hirayu, Kamitakara-mura. Modest, cosy inn. Open-air bath. Y8–9000 w/meals.
**Kokuminshukusha Enkū-an** 国民宿舎円空庵 (9-2106). Shin-Hirayu. A hot-spring Zen temple inn. Y6000 w/meals.

**Easy Access To:**
✳✳ **Kamikōchi** (CHŪBU IV:NE8): *1:05h by bus, from Apr.–Oct.*

✳ **FURUKAWA** 古川
*0:15h by local JR train, or 0:30h by bus north from Takayama. Service none-too-frequent.* This old-fashioned town, though not so beautifully preserved as parts of Takayama, is quiet and pleasant.

**Calendar**
**Apr. 19–20:** ✳ **Furukawa Matsuri.** At 22:00 on the 19th, a mob of half-naked, intoxicated youths parade through town carrying a large drum with two drum beaters sitting astride. Lion-dancers chase bad fortune out of homes. On the 20th, 9 festival floats, similar to Takayama's, are pulled through town. Lodgings on the 19th are a necessity.
**Sept. 5:** ✳ **Sugō Matsuri.** Three types of humorous lion dances are offered at Matsuo Hakusan Jinja and Hakusan Jinja. Said to have been introduced 1,300 years ago, these dances are a famous folk performance of the region.

293

**Furukawa Sights**
✳✳ **Mishimaya** 三嶋屋 (3-4109). Hrs: 9:00–18:00; clsd W. Toward the center of town. A 220-year-old Japanese candle shop, where one can see candles being made from vegetable wax (animal tallow could not be used in a Buddhist temple). The wax is applied with bare hands, layer by layer, over a wick of *igusa*, the spongy core of tatami grass.
✳ **Okoshi Daiko Kaikan** 起こし太鼓会館 (3-5691). Hrs: 8:30–19:00; clsd W. Across the river, in a modern building. A display hall for the festival carts, drums, and videos of the Furukawa Matsuri.

**Furukawa Dining and Lodgings** (TEL 05777)
**Asahikan** 朝日館 (3-2847). Two blocks from Mishimaya is this charming little shop with a hearth. *Zōsui* (rice stew) Y400, Asahikan *teishoku* Y1500–2000, *yaki-miso teishoku* Y700.
✳ **Ryokan Tomoe** 旅館ともえ (3-2056). 10-27 Kanamori-machi, Furukawa-chō, Yoshiki-gun, Gifu-ken. One block from station, on the left side of main street. Friendly ryokan. The new wing (*shinkan*) is in traditional style, but with Western toilets. Y6200–10,000 w/meals. No CC.

**ETCHŪ-YATSUO** 越中八尾
*1:15h–1:35h by JR Takayama main line express or local from Takayama.* A former post town famous for handmade paper and the Owara Kaze no Bon festival. Production of Yatsuo-washi (paper) began around the Genroku era (1688–1704) to provide wrapping paper for patent medicines (made in nearby Toyama, N4).

**Calendar**
**May 5:** ✳ **Hachiman Jinja Reisai.** The town's six *hikiyama* (ornate floats) are paraded through the streets.
**Sept. 1–3:** ✳✳ **Owara Kaze no Bon.** See Calendar, p. 276. Extremely crowded; you may have to lodge in Toyama.

# **TOGA MURA** 利賀村
*1:30h by bus from Etchū-Yatsuo. Only 3 buses per day.* This isolated hamlet is the site of the 10-day **Toga International Arts Festival** in early August, featuring traditional and avant-garde international performers. Space is furnished in remodeled farmhouses and a stunning outdoor amphitheater designed by Isozaki Arata. Tickets by advance sale only. Inquire at 0763-68-2214 (in Japanese), or check the *Tokyo Journal*. Prepaid minshuku lodgings arranged by the Toga Chamber of Commerce (0763-68-2527). Daytime options are few. The main village, on the other side of a very long tunnel, has a farmhouse museum, Kitsutsuki the toymaker, and Sugawa Takao (0763-68-2715), a craftsman who makes *andon* (traditional lamps); Y3000 for a usably large one.

## N4 **TOYAMA** 富山

*1:40h by JR Takayama main line limited express from Takayama (N3). By Air: From Tokyo, 5 flights per day on ANA. Convenient air gateway for Gokayama (CHŪBU IV:NW4).*

### Calendar

**Aug. 7–8: Tatemon Matsuri.** Uozu (*0:30–0:50h by Unazuki-Onsen-bound Toyama Chihō-tetsudō*), Suwa Jinja. Ten enormous poles, hung with a pyramid of lanterns, are twirled about vigorously. This festival is a prayer to the sea god for a good catch.

### Toyama Dining and Lodgings (TEL 0764)

**✳✳ Ginrin** 銀鱗　根塚町813 (25-1133). Hrs: 11:30–22:00; clsd 2nd Th. *0:10h by taxi from station.* Superb fresh seafood. Y1500–5000. Lunch *teishoku* Y800–1500.
**Washington Hotel** ワシントンホテル (41-7811). 2-17 Honmachi, Toyama-shi, Toyama-ken. *0:07h walk from station.* Reliable chain business hotel. S Y6200+, Tw Y11,900+.

### Exploring Kurobe Gorge

1:05–1:30h by private Toyama Chihō-tetsudō to Unazuki Onsen, then switch to the narrow-gauge Kurobe-Kyōkoku-tetsudō, which threads a dramatic course through the deep Kurobe Gorge, linking several onsen inns along the way and arriving at Keyaki-daira in 1:30h.
**Lodgings: Miyama-sō** (0765-62-1634), at Kanetsuri Onsen, has open-air riverside baths and serves *sansai*. Y7000 w/meals. Clsd Dec.–Apr.

### Easy Access To:

**✳✳ Tateyama-Kurobe Alpen Route** (CHŪBU IV:NE10): *0:50h by Toyama Chihō-tetsudō.*
**✳✳✳ Kanazawa** (CHŪBU IV:NW5): *0:50h by JR Hokuriku main line limited express.*
**Naoetsu** (KANTŌ II:NW6): *1:50h by JR limited express. Ferries to Sado Island* (KANTŌ II:N3).

294

# CHŪBU IV:NW. NORTHWEST FROM NAGOYA

**Main Attractions:** Shirakawa-gō (NW3), Gokayama (NW4), Kanazawa (NW5), Noto Peninsula (NW6), Eihei-ji (NW9)

### Traveling

The Meitetsu express bus from Nagoya to Kanazawa, via Gifu and the Shōkawa Valley, runs once a day in each direction, pausing at sightseeing spots along the way. Fare is by distance (Y7180 for a pass permitting stops en route). Tel: 052-582-5151; reservations advised July 25–Aug. 15. Meitetsu Bus Schedule (July 1–Nov., 2nd Su):

| Nagoya | | Gifu | | Ogimachi | | Kanazawa |
|---|---|---|---|---|---|---|
| 8:30 | → | 9:41 | → | 14:09 | → | 17:32 |
| 18:15 | ← | 17:40 | ← | 12:11 | ← | 9:20 |

JR buses run on various parts of the route year round, and there's an infrequent train from Mino-Ōta (CHŪBU IV:N2) to Hokunō. A recommended way to enter the region is by bus or car from Takayama (CHŪBU IV:N3). For the intrepid, a rented car would be well worth the trouble. Nippon Rent-a-Car: Nagoya to Kanazawa for 24 hours with dropoff, Y22,880. Takayama to Kanazawa for 24 hours with dropoff, Y20,500. Plan to spend at least one night in the region at one of the farmhouse minshuku in Shirakawa-gō or Gokayama.

## NW1 GIFU 岐阜

*From Nagoya, 0:25h by JR Tōkaidō or Takayama main line express trains; or 0:30h by private Meitetsu-Nagoya main line. From Inuyama (CHŪBU IV:N1), 0:35h by Meitetsu train.* Gifu is a tourist trap, noted for *ukai* (cormorant fishing) and as a spa heavy on pink lights. Near Gifu Kōen (Park), 0:15h by bus from the station, is **Shōhō-ji**, noted for its 300-year-old, 13.5-m Buddha made of sutra-bearing paper. There is also a short tramway to **Kinkazan**, which has a concrete replica of Gifu-jō and panoramic view of mountains.

### Calendar

**Feb. 18: # Tanigumi Odori.** Tanigumi (*0:50h by Meitetsu Tanigumi line from Chūsetsu station in Gifu*), Kegon-ji. A type of rain dance in which male dancers carry big drums and wear a "phoenix tail" on a stand of 14-foot bamboo poles festooned with paper. Repeated Apr. 3, Aug. 15.
**Apr. 5: ✳ Tejikara no Himatsuri.** Tejikara Jinja (*from Meitetsu Shin-Gifu station, 0:10h by Meitetsu Kakamigahara line*). Pyromaniacal spectacle: 20m torches are doctored with gunpowder and lit by fuses, fireworks rain from portable shrines, and a platform is set alight and blown up with land mines. "If you get too close, your clothes will get charred," locals warn. Hrs: 18:00–21:00.
**May 11–Oct. 15: Ukai (Cormorant Fishing).** Nightly, except during full moons and after storms. Gifu claims a 1,200-year history of *ukai* (see Cuisine, p. 116), which is now a tourist spectacle, with spectator boats and dancing girls. You can arrange to attend through your inn or directly with the companies (reserve at 62-0104). Y2700–2900 per person. Pack a bentō.
**July (last Sa) and Aug. (1st Sa): All-Japan Fireworks Contest.**

**Gifu Shopping**
Gifu is famous for paper parasols and lanterns.
**Sakaida Eikichi Honten** 坂井田永吉本店　加納 (71-6958). Hrs: 9:00–17:00; clsd Su, NH. *0:10h walk SE of Meitetsu Shin-Gifu station.* Paper parasols.
**Ozeki Jihichi Shōten** 尾関次七商店　小熊町 (63-0111). Hrs: 8:30–17:00, clsd Su, NH. *0:05h on foot from Daigaku Byōin-mae 5 tram stops from Gifu station.* Makes and sells many varieties of lanterns.

**Gifu Lodgings** (TEL 0582)
**Nagaragawa Hotel** 長良川ホテル (32-4111). 51 Nagara-Ukaiya, Gifu-shi, Gifu-ken. Riverbank hotel run by Miyako Hotel chain. Long experience with foreigners. S Y8000+, Tw Y12–20,000. The elegant modern Japanese annex, **Kairan-tei**, is Y35–37,000 w/meals.
**Banshōkan** 萬松館 (62-0039). 2-18 Ōmiyachō. Traditional inn. Y20,000 w/meals.
**Gifu YH** 岐阜YH (63-6631). 4716-17 Kamikanoyama. Take the Romance Lift (*about 1.5 km NE of station*). Wooded surroundings.

**Easy Access To:**
✳✳✳ **Takayama** (CHŪBU IV:N3): *2:30h by JR Takayama main line limited express, 4 per day.*

## GUJŌ-HACHIMAN 郡上八幡
*2:45h by express bus from Nagoya; or 1:35h by express bus from Shin-Gifu station. Or 1:15h from Mino-Ōta by Nagaragawa line.* This isolated castle town is nationally famous for the month-long ✳ **Gujō Odori** (dance) in August. At mid-month, the height of Bon, the entire town erupts into a frenzy of all-night dancing. Local attractions, about 2 km northeast of the station, include **Omodakaya Mingeikan** (folk museum); the 5-story reconstructed castle; and **Jion-ji**, which has a "borrowed scenery" garden.

**Gujō-Hachiman Dining and Lodgings** (TEL 05756)
**Hirajin** 平甚 (5-2004). Hrs: 11:00–17:30; clsd W. Famous for *soba*.
**Yoshidaya** 吉田屋 (5-2178). An inn reputed to have the best cuisine in town. Seasonal dishes, like *ayu*. Y13–18,000 (Y15–18,000 during Gujō Odori). V, DC, CB.
**Mifuku Ryokan** 三富久 (5-2145). Sakyō, Hachiman-chō, Gujō-gun, Gifu-ken. Y12–18,000 w/meals.
**YH-Gujō Tōsen-ji** 郡上洞泉寺 (7–0290). 417 Ozaki. *0:20h walk from station.* Temple youth hostel serving wild greens and bamboo shoots. Y3250 w/meals.

## SHIROTORI 白鳥
*3:25h from Nagoya by Meitetsu bus.* The bus stops at **Hakusan Nagataki Jinja**, sacred to the *yamabushi* cult of **Haku-san**, one of the three most venerated mountains in Japan. The shrine, said to have been founded in 717, when the mountain was "opened," marks the beginning of a trail to the summit of Haku-san, 20 km northwest. Nearby is **Wakamiya Shūkokan** 若宮修古館 (ICP), house of the hereditary shrine priests; 2,000 objects relating to the Haku-san cult are on view (Hrs: 9:00–17:00; clsd Dec.–Mar.). Shirotori has a distinctive Bon dance, which peaks on Aug. 14–16.

## THE SHŌKAWA VALLEY
The river Shō flows north, out of the Ryōhaku mountains and into the Japan Sea. Hemming in the swift, winding river on both sides are steep mountains, not especially high, but formidable. In the 12th century, defeated TAIRA warriors fled here, where the vengeful MINAMOTO would never find them—or so the legend goes. People cite as evidence bits of regional dialect, the hamlets named Taira, and the courtly ballads and dances of the region. The Shōkawa Valley remained isolated until very recently, and today it is among the best-preserved rural regions in Japan. The villages of Shirakawa-gō and Gokayama in particular are famed for their magnificent A-frame farmhouses, built in a style called **gasshō-zukuri**, or "hands in prayer." Extended families of 30 or more members lived on the lower floors, while the upper floors were used to raise silkworms, which, especially in the Meiji era, provided the raw silk that fed Japan's booming textile mills.

In the Edo period, Shirakawa-gō and Gokayama lay in two different, enemy domains. Shirakawa-gō, in Hida, was ruled by the shogunate, while Gokayama lay in Kaga, domain of the greatest of the "outside daimyo," the Maeda of Kanazawa (see Castles, p. 49). But the mountains and untamed gorges offered a near-impenetrable barrier, so that in spite of Hida's proximity, the Maeda chose Gokayama for its top-secret production of gunpowder. Historical precedent also had something to do with it. In the 15th–16th centuries, Kaga was the scene of an extraordinary—victorious—peasant uprising. The peasants were led by the Ikkō (Single-Minded) sect, a militant branch of Jōdo Shin. Kaga became a "peasant's country," with low taxes and benevolent government, and continued to be so for nearly a century. In the late 16th century, Gokayama peasants began supplying gunpowder to the Ikkō armies throughout central Japan. But in 1580, ODA NOBUNAGA sent one of his generals to crush the Ikkō in Kaga, bringing this curious era to a bloody end (see Kyoto, p. 320). The "peasant's country," however, left a deep mark on the people of Kaga. Some suggest the shape of the *gasshō* houses was inspired by the religious devotion of these people, nearly all of whom continue to belong to the Jōdo Shin sect. The people of Gokayama also claim cultural differences—in dialect and festivals, for example—that set them apart from the villages of Shirakawa-gō.

295

# Gasshō-zukuri Houses

Building these houses was a major community endeavor. Professional carpenters were hired to do the ground floors, over which villagers would raise the roof. It took dozens of people several days just to tie down the thick layer of thatch. The magnificent dwellings standing today, however, do not give an accurate picture of the life of the average farmer. Most peasants lived in small, mean structures resembling a tent of thatch, such as one that is now used as a toolshed in Ainokura. Even residents of the large houses—village heads, their extended families and servants—found their quarters cramped. The ground floor was occupied by their daily work, and the upper floors were given over to silk cultivation, which became widespread in the Meiji period. The *gasshō* design proved exceptionally suitable for this; during different phases in their growth, silkworms require varying amounts of heat and light, which could be achieved by moving them from one floor to another.

## Calendar
A stay at a *gasshō-zukuri* minshuku is highly recommended, but be prepared for crowding in spring and summer.

**Sept. 26–27:** * **Kokiriko Matsuri.** Gokayama, Kaminashi, Hakusan-gū. Mournful, elegant local ballads and dances, said to have been transmitted by Taira nobles 800 years ago.

**Oct. 14–19:** ** **Doburoku Matsuri.** Shirakawa-gō. Harvest festival. 14–15th at Shirakawa Hachiman-gū. 16–17th at Hatogaya's Hachiman Jinja. 18–19th at Hatogaya's Iijima Hachiman. At 9:00, a colorful procession wends through the fields and village. At 15:00, lion dances and other performances are offered. Everyone gathers at the shrine to drink *doburoku*, a milky-white, sacred saké.

## Getting Around
Though the two main communities in the Shōkawa Valley are known as Shirakawa-gō and Gokayama, these names are not used for bus stops. The main stop in Shirakawa-gō is Ogimachi. In Gokayama, a scattered series of hamlets, we recommend Ainokura. Buses are expensive and infrequent; always check schedules in advance.

### NW2 MAKIDO　牧戸
*1:05h by bus from Shirotori, or 1:00h from Ogimachi. Or 1:25h by Nobi Co. bus from Takayama (CHŪBU IV:N3).* 0:25h by bus from Makido is the Miboro Dam; when the dam was built, a great many old farmhouses were submerged, though quite a few were saved and moved to other parts of Japan.

### NW3 *** SHIRAKAWA-GŌ (OGIMACHI)　白川郷(萩町)
*Ogimachi is the main bus stop, but most of the minshuku and sights are near Shirakawa Hachimangū-mae, 2 stops south. From Nagoya, 5:25h by Meitetsu or JR express bus. From Takayama (CHŪBU IV:N3), 1:25h by Nobi bus to Makido, then 1:00h by or Meitetsu bus to Ogimachi. From Kanazawa (NW5), 3:10h by Meitetsu bus via Gokayama; or 0:50h by JR Hokuriku line to Takaoka, then 0:50h by JR Jōhana line to Jōhana, then 2:00h by bus.* This much-photographed village has close to a hundred *gasshō-zukuri* farmhouses standing amid vegetable gardens and paddy fields. The modern buildings are regulated in size and construction so as not to clash. The narrow highway runs through the middle of the village.

** **Myōzen-ji**　明善寺 (ICP). Hrs: 7:30–17:00. The 170-year-old priest's residence of this Jōdo Shin sect temple is the largest *gasshō-zukuri* house in the village. Because of a priest's higher social status, the house was permitted to have massive beams and floors of fine lumber. The upper stories are crowded with dusty farm and sericulture tools. Take a close look at the ceiling to appreciate the skill and labor that went into raising the roof. Adjoining the house is the thatched-roof Main Hall, built 227 years ago (new inside). The belfry is also thatched.

** **Wada-ke**　和田家 (ICP). The Wada family dwelling, one of the largest and most beautiful houses in Ogimachi, is thought to be over 400 years old, making it one of the oldest in the region. It is not open to the public, but with its high hedges and gardens, it gives an idyllic picture of the life of a prosperous farmer.

* **Tenbōdai (Vista Point)**　展望台 *0:20h on foot from village center.* The classic, tourist-brochure view of Ogimachi is from this hilltop castle ruin. There's a big parking lot and restaurant up here, but the view is still worth the climb.

**Shirakawa-mura Gasshō no Sato**　白川郷合掌の里 Hrs: 8:30–17:00. Dec.–Mar. 9:00–16:00. Aug. 8:00–18:00. Clsd NY. *0:10h on foot from Ogimachi, via a suspension bridge and tunnel.* A park with real or reconstructed *gasshō-zukuri* houses, storage sheds, water mill, and craft workshops. The structures were moved from a nearby village abandoned in 1967.

**Haku-san Sūpā Rindō**　白山スーパー林道 This toll road offers a scenic shortcut to Kanazawa via Haku-san National Park (NW5), but only for those with access to a car. Hrs: June–

Aug. 7:00–18:00; Sept.–Nov. 8:00–17:00. Toll Y3400 (one-way), Y4800 (round trip). On the way is Chūgu Onsen, a rustic hot spring with 4 inns.

**Ogimachi Lodgings** (TEL 05769)
Inside, a *gasshō-zukuri* minshuku is much like other traditional houses. Meals are served by the *irori*. The smoky fire preserves the house, but can be rough on the eyes and throat. Broiled trout and *sansai* (mountain greens) are staples of the minshuku dinners. For help in making reservations, call Shirakawa-gō Kankō Annaijo (tourist information) at 6-1013. Minshuku are Y5,500 w/meals.
* **Yosobei** よそべい (6-1172). Ogimachi, Shirakawa-mura, Ōno-gun, Gifu-ken. In the most picturesque cluster of farmhouses, next door to Myōzen-ji. Delicious meals served on lacquer trays and bowls. Very friendly. A few others that looked especially nice were:
**Nodaniya** のだにや (6-1011), **Kidoya** きどや 001 (6-1077), **Furusato** ふるさと (6-1033). Address as above.

## NW4 *** GOKAYAMA 五箇山

Comprised of the scattered hamlets Nishi-Akao, Suganuma, Kaminashi, Shimonashi, and Ainokura. Ainokura is the best preserved, with the largest group of *gasshō-zukuri* houses. The river, which marks the border between Gifu and Toyama prefectures, twists and turns dramatically—at one stretch the highway crosses the river seven times in quick succession. One can understand why in former times, Gokayama and Shirakawa-gō, seemingly so similar, were in fact worlds apart. At many of the large houses, formerly the homes of local headmen, you will see cauldrons and implements used to make gunpowder in the Edo period. Gokayama is also noted for *washi* (paper).
* **Nishi-Akao** 西赤尾 *0:20h by bus from Ogimachi*. The finest *gasshō-zukuri* house here is * **Iwase-ke** (ca. 1720, ICP), open to the public (Hrs: 8:00–17:00). The house of the chief of gunpowder production, it is uncommonly elegant inside because it also served as lodgings for visiting domain officials. **Gyōtoku-ji**, the thatched-roof temple next door, has a small collection of works by leaders of the 20th-C folk-art movement Yanagi Sōetsu, Munakata Shikō, Kawai Kanjirō, and Bernard Leach, given during their visit in the 1920s. Hrs: 9:00–17:00; clsd Dec.–Apr.

297

* **Suganuma** 菅沼 *0:10h by bus from Nishi-Akao*. Two clusters of *gasshō-zukuri* houses. The one in neat rows is a youth center. The other, cradled in a crook of the highway, consists of some half-dozen thatched houses, one of which is a local museum. The Etchū-Gokayama YH is a 0:20h walk, across the river and up the road to the right.
** **Kaminashi** 上梨 *0:15h by bus from Suganuma*. A roadside cluster of *gasshō-zukuri* buildings that includes shops and restaurants, minshuku, a bathhouse called Gokayama Onsen, and ** **Murakami-ke** (ca. 1578, ICP, Hrs: 8:00–18:00). The lively master of this magnificent house finishes up his chat with local ballads, accompanied by ancient instruments called *sasara* (108 wooden clappers strung together which produce a buzz when snapped) and *kokiriko* (a pair of bamboo sticks lightly tapped together). Nearby is the shrine Hakusan-gū (ca. 1502, ICP). Across the river and up the hill are Rukei-goya, a prison cell for samurai convicts of Kaga, and the Haba-ke house (ICP; clsd to public).
**Shimonashi** 下梨 *0:10h by bus from Kaminashi*. A 0:01h walk from the bus stop, on the left-hand side of the uphill road to Ainokura, is the * **Goka-shi Kyōdo Kumiai** 五箇紙 協同組合 (Paper Cooperative), where visitors can see *washi* being made and, for a small fee, try their own hand at it. Attractive, inexpensive *washi* wallets, stationery, etc. on sale. Hrs: 8:00–17:00. May–Nov. clsd Tu. Dec.–Apr. clsd Su.
*** **Ainokura** 相倉 *0:05h by bus from Shimonashi to Ainokura-guchi, then a 0:03h walk*. An idyllic hamlet (marred only by the nearby parking lot). The 20 *gasshō-zukuri* houses (and a few unobtrusive modern dwellings) are crowded on the scenic shoulder of a

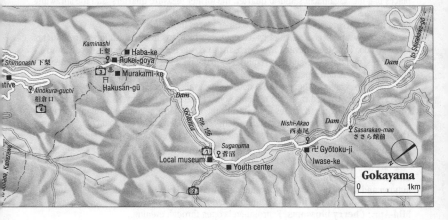

mountain. One of the old farmhouses is a local museum; another contains a very handsome display on paper-making.

## Gokayama Lodgings (TEL 0763)
Minshuku are about Y5000 w/meals. Add to addresses: Higashi-tonami-gun, Toyama-ken.
**In Suganuma:** ① **Minshuku Gorōbei** 民宿吾郎平 (67-3502). Suganuma, Taira-mura.
② **Etchū-Gokayama YH** 越中五箇山YH (67-3332). 24 Oze, Kamitaira-mura.
*Gasshō-zukuri* farmhouse in the mountains. Y3450 w/meals.
**In Kaminashi:** ③ **Yajibei** 弥次兵衛 (66-2639) and **Kitamura** 北村 (66-2321).
Kaminashi, Taira-mura. Bathe at Gokayama onsen next door.
**In Ainokura:** ④ **Yūsuke** 勇助 (66-2555). Ainokura, Taira-mura. Has a marvelous bath.
Other minshuku are **Rokuhei** (66-2731), **Shōshichi** (66-2206), **Sangorō** (66-2709),
**Goemon** (66-2154), **Nakaya** (66-2457), **Yomoshichi** (66-2377).

## JŌHANA   城端
*2:05h from Ogimachi (NW3) or 1:10h from Kanazawa (NW5) by Meitetsu bus. Or 0:50h by the JR Jōhana line from Takaoka.* Jōhana's wheeled festival floats, *hikiyama*, include lantern-festooned miniatures of famous Gion and Yoshiwara teahouses. The floats are normally on view at * **Hikiyama Kaikan** (Hrs: 10:00–17:00; clsd NY). A short walk away is **Zentoku-ji Jōhana Betsu-in**, a Jōdo Shin sect temple with an enormous gate which is "an exact copy" of the famous gate of its parent temple, the Higashi Hongan-ji in Kyoto. Zentoku-ji's art collection is in the small museum nearby (Hrs: 9:00–17:00).

### Calendar
**May 14–15:** * **Hikiyama**. Festival featuring Jōhana's floats.
**Sept 14–16: Mugiya Matsuri.** The melancholy *mugiya* ballad of Gokayama is performed here to preserve this ancient art form.

298

## TAKAOKA   高岡
*0:40h from Kanazawa (NW5) or 0:15h from Toyama (CHŪBU IV:N4) by JR Hokuriku main line express.* Takaoka is noted for its bronze casting, patronized by its feudal lords, a branch of the Maeda of Kanazawa. Takaoka's bronze Great Buddha (third largest in Japan, but no artistic marvel) and bronze bridge posts are town emblems. The century-old **Oigo Seisakusho** 老子製作所 (0766-63-6336) casts most of Japan's bronze temple bells. These require skilled handwork as well as sheer brawn, and it is impressive to see the huge molds, forging areas, and bells in various stages of production. Castings take place every few days. Visiting Hrs: 8:15–16:50; clsd Su, NH.

### Calendar
**May 1:** * **Takaoka Mikurumayama.** Gorgeous antique floats, famous for ornate wheels, lavish lacquerwork, and mechanical dolls.

## NW5 *** KANAZAWA   金沢
*0:45h from Toyama (CHŪBU IV:N4) or 2:45h from Kyoto by JR Hokuriku main line limited express. From Tokyo, it is almost as economical to fly to Komatsu Airport (NW7), 0:55h by bus from Kanazawa. JAL and ANA have 5 flights daily from Haneda Airport (flying time 1:00h), and ANA has 1 per day from Sapporo, Sendai, and Fukuoka.* Kanazawa was the castle town of the Maeda, lords of Kaga, Edo-period Japan's wealthiest domain (see Castles, p. 49). Its flourishing economy and culture made it one of the great cities of the land. Because it escaped bombing in World War II, Kanazawa is promoted as a town of traditional beauty, a second Kyoto. To be sure, progress has taken its toll. Nevertheless, Kanazawa is a very special place. From the top of a modern high-rise, one can still look down upon the glittering sea of tile roofs that is Kanazawa's hallmark. The aura of bygone times is palpable in places like the Nagamachi samurai quarter, the former pleasure quarters, and the sprawling temple towns. The famous garden, Kenroku-en, and the adjacent Seisonkaku villa evoke the life of the old privileged classes as do few other places in Japan.

Kanazawa preserves much of its old culture, which was markedly different from that of Kyoto or Edo. The Maeda invited Kyoto artisans to create tea ceremony bowls, lacquerware, dyed robes, paintings—everything required to maintain a life of taste and luxury. Under the Maeda, these arts developed a vitality and richness that contrasts with the delicacy and restraint of the capital. Whereas Kyoto houses have walls the color of sand and woodwork that suggests freshly stripped trees, the old mansions of Kanazawa boast walls of red ochre and cobalt blue and lacquered beams enhanced by the warm glow of gold leaf. Kutani porcelain, coveted by collectors around the world, epitomizes the Maeda taste for bold color and design. Though the Maeda no longer rule, the people of the city have proved equally enthusiastic and proud patrons. Kanazawa's arts, past and present, are exhibited in the city's many fine museums.

### Calendar
Autumn and spring offer the finest scenery and weather. Lodgings crowded July 25–Aug. 10.
**Jan. 6: Dezomeshiki.** Firemen's traditional laddertop stunts.
**Mid-Apr.: Cherry blossoms.** Kenroku-en is open through evening.

**May 15: Shinji (Sacred) Noh.** Ōno Minato Jinja. Ōno (*0:20h by bus from Kanazawa station*).

**June 12–15: Hyakumangoku Matsuri.** Main events on 14th. Costume parade and activities in various parts of town to honor Maeda Toshiie. Near Tenjinbashi and Asano Ōhashi (bridges), lanterns handpainted by Yūzen silk dyers are set adrift on the river.

**Aug. 1–3: Shinji (Sacred) Noh.** Saki Jinja, Kanaiwa (*0:20h by bus from Kanazawa station*).

**Aug. 1–2: Jongara Odori.** Nonoichi (*2 stops SW of Kanazawa by Hokuriku-tetsudō*). Villagers perform a traditional folk song and dance.

### Getting Around

The central area, around Kenroku-en, is compact enough to see comfortably on foot. For more far-flung areas, such as Teramachi or the eastern pleasure quarters, a bicycle is ideal. Rent-a-cycle near the station, Y1000/day. The listings below describe a circuit around central Kanazawa, starting at Ishikawa-mon. To get there, take a taxi or bus (#10 or 11) to Kenroku-en-shita (0:15h). Taxi with guide (no English spoken) is Y4740 per hour.

*Kanazawa: The Other Side of Japan* is a minutely detailed city guide in English by former resident Ruth Stevens; useful if you really want to delve into every corner of Kanazawa. Published by the Society to Introduce Kanazawa to the World; located in the Chamber of Commerce. Sold in bookstores in Tokyo and Kyoto, and in Kanazawa hotels.

### Central Area

Numerous museums, mingled with shrines and other attractions, are grouped around the old castle (now the Kanazawa University campus) and Kenroku-en.

\* **Ishikawa-mon (Castle Gate)** 石川門 (ICP). This imposing structure, merely a rear gate to the Maeda fortress, is an impressive reminder of the clan's wealth and power; Kanazawa is referred to as *hyakuman-goku no jōka-machi*, "castle town of one million *koku*" (about 5 million bushels of rice per annum). It overlooks a section of the inner moat, now filled in and turned into a road. In the grounds, the Sanjū-ken Nagaya-mon (ICP), a long barracks, is all that survived an 1881 fire.

299

\*\*\* **Kenroku-en** 兼六園 Hrs: 7:00–18:00. Oct. 16–Mar. 15 8:00–16:30. Detailed English maps are issued at the four entrances, near Ishikawa-mon, Seisonkaku, the Traditional Craft Museum, and the Prefectural government office. This large, splendid stroll garden was first built around 1670 but did not attain its present scale until 1837. It is a superb example of landscape art of the type that was in vogue among Edo-period daimyo (see Villas, p. 67). The name Kenroku-en means "garden combining six qualities," an erudite reference to a Chinese garden manual prescribing six desirable features of gardens: spaciousness, seclusion, human artifice, antique appearance, flowing water, and extensive views. The effect is impressive but mannered. No expense was spared in creating the pond, streams, and hills, in moving boulders, and in planting magnificent gnarled pine trees. A famous bipedal **stone lantern** stands with one foot in the water and the other on an islet. Water was syphoned from distant mountains to the garden's elevation—a massive engineering project that provided "flowing water" not only for the garden, but also for the castle in the event of attack. The **fountain** in the lower pond was a handy indicator of water pressure. One invasion the planners didn't foresee was the busloads of tourists who stampede through, led by a flag-waving, bullhorn-equipped guide. We advise going early (before 8:30), or late (after 16:30).

\*\*\* **Seisonkaku** 成巽閣 (ICP). Hrs: 8:30–16:30 (enter by 16:00); clsd W, NY. This sumptuous villa was built in 1863 for the mother of the 13th Maeda lord. Everything—the interiors, the gardens—reflects the Kaga penchant for richness and grandeur. Rooms are spacious, trimmed with ornate polychrome carvings and lacquered beams. The walls are covered with gold dust. The brilliantly colored second-floor rooms, in Shoin style, are quintessential Kaga taste (in Kyoto, one might see it in a brothel). The papered window facing Kenroku-en contains a pane of Dutch glass—an incredible novelty at the time. Display cases hold all kinds of imported 19th-C gadgets. The villa stands in a corner of Kenroku-en, with an entrance to and from the garden through the back.

\*\* **Ishikawa-kenritsu Dentō Sangyō Kōgeikan (Traditional Art Crafts Museum)** 石川県立伝統産業工芸館 (62-2020). Hrs: 9:00–17:00; clsd 3rd Th. In Dec.–Mar. clsd every Th, NY. Handsome, informative museum on the fine crafts of Kanazawa. An excellent English pamphlet provides historical background on 18 regional crafts, including Kutani porcelain, lacquerware, gold leaf, metal craft, and Yūzen dyeing. The step-by-step exhibits are self-explanatory. Some fine, present-day crafts are shown with price tags (but are not available for sale).

\* **Ishikawa-kenritsu Nohgaku-dō (Prefectural Noh Theater Culture Hall)** 石川県立能楽堂 (64-2598). Hrs: 9:00–17:00; clsd M (except NH). This is the only public Noh facility in Japan. The traditional stage (built in 1931) is loaned to local groups performing Noh, Kyōgen, traditional dance, and so on. It is used almost daily for practice and recitals. Visitors welcome.

\*\*\* **Ishikawa-kenritsu Bijutsukan (Prefectural Art Museum)** 石川県立美術館 (31-7580). Hrs: 9:30–16:30, daily; clsd NY and when exhibits are changed. An unusually fine museum. The core of its collection comes from the Maeda family; as one might expect, the quality is superb. The museum's collection of old Kutani porcelain is second to none, and large amounts of it are always on view. The life-size ◆ pheasant-shaped incense burner (NT) by Nonomura Ninsei is displayed in a room of its own. Exhibits change several times a year.

\*\* **Hanrō Honda Zōhinkan (Honda Museum)** 藩老本多蔵品館 (61-0500). Hrs: 9:00–17:00 (enter by 16:30), daily. Nov.–Feb. clsd Th, NY. The collection of the Honda family, hereditary senior vassals to the Maeda clan. The museum is on the former site of their upper estate. Honda Masanobu (1538–1616) was an intimate and trusted advisor of TOKUGAWA IEYASU; his son Masashige agreed to become the secretary general to the Maeda. The Honda family crest is a variation of the Tokugawa's triple *aoi* (hollyhock) leaf, awarded to Masanobu by Ieyasu. The collection includes many superb pieces of armor, equestrian equipment, bridal trousseaus, and colorful felt firefighting robes. One prized item is a lovely tea urn, Murasame no Tsubo, probably of south Chinese origin, which was awarded to Masashige by his lord.

\*\* **Nakamura Kinen Bijutsukan (Art Museum)** 中村記念美術館 (21-0751). Hrs: 9:00–16:00; clsd Tu, day after NH, NY. From the Prefectural Art Museum, there's a pleasant shortcut via a stairway. A fine collection, mostly of Japanese, Chinese, and Korean ceramics and tea ceremony utensils amassed by a wealthy saké brewer and tea enthusiast, Nakamura Eishun (1908–1978). This intimate museum was his residence. Old Kutani and Sung celadons seem always to be included in the exhibits, which change seasonally. The museum also owns paintings by SESSHŪ, OGATA KŌRIN, and SŌTATSU, and a lacquered box by HON'AMI KŌETSU. The small second-floor gallery often shows excellent recent work by Kanazawa artisans. The admission ticket includes a bowl of *matcha*, served next to a beautiful garden.

\*\*\* **Nagamachi** 長町武家屋敷 This neighborhood preserves the powerful earthen walls, twisting streets, and canals of its former days as a samurai quarter. Most of the houses are privately owned and have been rebuilt, but there remain some old gates, boasting Judas windows, behind which guards were once posted. Nagamachi was dealt its death blow when the Meiji Restoration left the samurai unemployed and destitute. ◆ **Nomura house** 野村家 , the only one open to the public, is a typical case. At first, the Nomura family tried to make a go of it by clearing their land and planting apple trees. But as the business became unprofitable, the family had to sell the property. The purchaser moved a fine old house from a nearby town to the site, and though they are not original, the house and its lovely garden evoke a feel for the past. Hrs: 8:30–17:30, Oct.–Mar. 8:30–16:30; clsd NY.

300

\* **Oyama Jinja** 尾山神社 Shrine to Maeda Toshiie, founder of the Maeda dynasty. Noted for its exotic gate (ICP), which has a masonry base with Western arches, crowned by a cupola with stained-glass windows, resembling a lighthouse. The unusual gate is said to have been built in 1875 with the help of Dutch teachers at the medical school and is a most appealing relic of early Meiji days. The shrine grounds contain a small pond garden.

\* **Ozaki Jinja** 尾崎神社 (ICP). This red-lacquer shrine, a very modest version of the Nikkō Tōshō-gū, is consecrated to TOKUGAWA IEYASU and was built by the fourth Maeda lord to demonstrate his loyalty to the shogunate. It was originally in the northern enclosure of the castle, probably for "protection"; if shogunate soldiers were to attack, they would have risked desecrating the shrine of their ancestral liege lord. The shrine has since been removed to its present site, a rather dreary and forsaken spot.

\*\* **Ōmichō Ichiba (Market)** 近江町市場 Kanazawa's central market, with a 300-year history. The long, covered arcade is choked with shops selling all kinds of things, especially fish. Busiest late in the afternoon.

**Shōen-ji** 照円寺 This temple has a wonderfully lurid set of ◆ Hell Scrolls (see Art, p. 95), shown for three days each at the spring and fall equinoxes. At other times, make an appointment to see them by calling 21-4785.

\*\* **Terajima Ōyūtei (Samurai House)** 寺島応養邸　大手町10-3 (62-3945). Hrs: 9:00–16:00; clsd Th, NH, NY. The 200-year-old house of a middle-ranking samurai. Though reduced to a third of its former size, the house and garden give an attractive picture of past life. There's an excellent English pamphlet providing details on the features of samurai dwellings. *Matcha* is served for a fee in the lovely tearoom.

### Teramachi and Western Pleasure Quarters 寺町・旧西廓

All castle towns have a temple quarter, situated to provide a first line of defense against invasion. Kanazawa's Teramachi stands out for its sheer magnitude—some 70 temples in all. They are located on the west bank of the river bordering the city on the west; a smaller temple town is located on the east bank of the river bordering on the east. These outskirts of town were also where the two major pleasure quarters were located. Nishi (West) preserves rows of former teahouses and brothels, many of which now operate as bars and restaurants.

\*\* **Myōryū-ji (Ninja-dera)** 妙立寺（忍者寺） Hrs: 9:00–16:30, Nov.–Mar. 9:00–16:00; clsd several days each month. By 0:20h tours only. Reserve at 41-2877; otherwise ring at the side entrance; there are usually a few places open on each tour. This Ninja temple is a tourist trap, but it's fun. The outwardly plain hall, built in 1659 as a temple of the Maeda daimyo, is a labyrinth inside, rigged with devices to protect the lord from *ninja* (spies). Stick close to the guide to see how it all works. There are numerous hidden passages, and fine bamboo shades and paper walls behind which men could stand guard without being seen. There's an emergency well, supposedly connected to the river and the castle. On the third floor, low windows give the building a two-storied appearance from outside. The elegant back rooms were for private entertainments (supplied by the nearby pleasure quarter). Other rooms were for defense. One has a high ceiling to allow free swordplay, and five escape routes. One tiny chamber with no escape route was a place to commit suicide. It was, disappointingly, never used.

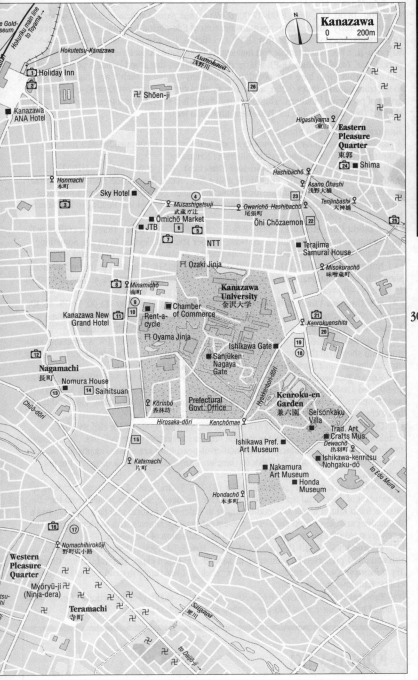

**Kanazawa**

0      200m

N

Hokuriku main line to Toyama

Hotel Gold-seum

Hokutetsu-Kanazawa

1 Holiday Inn
2

Kanazawa ANA Hotel

卍 Shōen-ji

Asanokawa 浅野川

26

Higashiyama 東山
**Eastern Pleasure Quarter** 東郭

24 Shima

Honmachi 本町

Sky Hotel

3

Hashibachō

Asano Ōhashi 浅野大橋

23

Tenjinbashi 天神橋

4 Musashigatsuji 武蔵ヶ辻

Ōwarichō Hashibachō 尾張町

Ōmichō Market 近江町市場

JTB

6
5

Ōhi Chōzaemon

22

25

NTT

7

卍 Ozaki Jinja

Terajima Samurai House

**Kanazawa University** 金沢大学

Misokurachō 味噌蔵町

8 Minamichō 南町

9

Kanazawa New Grand Hotel

11
10

Rent-a-cycle

Chamber of Commerce

21

Kenrokuenshita

20

卍 Oyama Jinja

Ishikawa Gate

19

18

12

**Nagamachi** 長町

Nomura House

14 Saihitsuan

13

Kōrinbō 香林坊

Sanjūken Nagaya Gate

**Kenroku-en Garden** 兼六園

Seisonkaku Villa

Chūō-dōri

Prefectural Govt. Office

Hirosaka-dōri

Kenchōmae

Trad. Art Crafts Mus.

Dewachō 出羽町

15

Ishikawa Pref. Art Museum

Hyakkenhon-dōri

Ishikawa-kenritsu Nohgaku-dō

to Edo Mura

Katamachi 片町

Nakamura Art Museum

Honda Museum

Hondachō 本多町

301

16
17

Nomachihirokōji 野町広小路

**Western Pleasure Quarter**

Myōryū-ji (Ninja-dera)

Saigawa 犀川

**Teramachi** 寺町

to Daijō-ji

\*\* **Daijō-ji** 大乗寺 *By bus, 0:25h from Kanazawa station, or 0:04h from Teramachi. Get off at Heiwa-machi and walk 0:25h.* The most impressive temple in Kanazawa is this Sōtō Zen sect monastary. The temple was founded in 1261, but the present buildings date from the early 1700s. The tombs of the Honda family (see Honda Museum) are here.

\*\* **Higashiyama and Eastern Pleasure Quarter** 東山・東郭
Counterpart to the Teramachi area. Higashiyama has fewer temples (only 50), but its geisha quarter is still active and is reputed to have the most artistically talented geisha in Kanazawa. One can occasionally spot a geisha in the early evening, on her way to a teahouse.
◆ **Shima** 料亭志摩 , an elegant former assignation house, is open to the public. Hrs: 9:00–17:00; clsd M and Dec. 15–Feb.

**\*\* Edo Mura** 江戸村

Hrs: 8:00–18:00. Oct.–Mar. 8:00–17:00. *0:40h by bus from Kanazawa station (departures every half hour)*. An attractive open-air museum of Edo-period buildings of the Kaga region. Of particular interest are a **Honjin** (ICP), an officials' inn and post station; **Yokoyama-ke/Kōraku-ji**, a combined temple and mansion built in classic Kaga style in the early Meiji period; and **Zaigō-Shōka** (ICP), a large merchant house that stood beside a post highway and was forbidden to have a second floor; it does anyway, but in such a way that it's impossible to tell from outside. Every 0:20h, a free van shuttles visitors to nearby **Danpū-en**, a smaller group of preserved buildings exhibiting Kaga crafts. It is of middling interest and can safely be skipped (but is included in the Edo Mura admission fee).

**Kanazawa Crafts and Shopping**

A visit to the Museum for Traditional Products and Crafts is recommended as a first stop for visitors interested in the fine craft traditions of Kanazawa.

**\* Yasue Kinpaku Kōgeikan (Gold-leaf Museum)** 安江金箔工芸館 (33-1502). Hrs: 9:30–16:30 (enter by 16:00); clsd Tu (W if Tu a NH), NY. At this unique establishment, you can view the traditional technique for making thin sheets of gold leaf. Kanazawa produces 90 percent of the world's output. Visitors are served tea with gold leaf floating in it; you can buy packets of gold leaf as a souvenir.

6 **\* Tsuda Ume Mizuhiki** 津田梅水引 十間町47 (62-4661). Here, the craft of making ornaments for wedding gifts from twisted paper string is elevated to an art. Something remarkable—a doll, an elaborate turtle or crane—is usually on view in this tiny shop.

9 **Nakaya** 中屋 (21-0118). Hrs: 8:30–18:00; clsd Su, NH. This late Edo-period medicine shop still sells traditional remedies, including the best-selling *kongentan*, an herbal cure-all. In business 400 years.

14 **\* Saihitsuan Yūzen Silk Center** 彩筆庵 (64-2811). Hrs: 9:00–12:00, 13:00–16:30; clsd Th, NY. A former Nagamachi samurai house converted into a center demonstrating Kanazawa Yūzen silk dyeing (see Crafts, p. 105). Do not photograph the artisans.

15 **Moroeya** 諸江屋 片町1-3-22 (63-7331). Hrs: 9:00–20:00; clsd W. A reputable Kutani porcelain shop. Visit the Prefectural Art Museum and train your eye before attempting to buy any. Among the most attractive items are copies of Old Kutani tableware.

19 **Kankō Bussankan** 観光物産館 (22-7788). Hrs: 9:00–18:00. Nov. 20–Mar. 20, 10:00–18:00; clsd Th. Restaurant Hrs: 11:00–20:00. A sterile but practical place to buy Kaga crafts and souvenirs. The second floor has an inexpensive Kaga-cuisine restaurant. The third floor has a crafts demonstration gallery (Hrs: 9:00–17:00).

20 **Uesaka** 上坂桐細工 小将町5-10 (31-2475). Hrs: 9:00–18:30; clsd NY. *Kiri* (paulownia) crafts. *Kiri* is a light wood that turns a lovely silvery gray with age. In Kanazawa, flower-and-bird designs of lacquer and mother-of-pearl inlay are applied against the wood to produce subtly elegant objects. *Hibachi* (braziers) are a classic item. Expensive, but not exorbitant.

22 **\*\* Ōhi Chōzaemon** 大樋長左衛門 (21-2397). Hrs: 9:00–17:00. Tenth-generation descendant of the official tea ceremony potter for the Maeda, who was invited from the famous Raku kiln in Kyoto. Ōhi-yaki is similar to Raku-yaki in form and lightness, but has a distinctive caramel-colored glaze. The present master experiments with modern forms. The lovely shop exhibits pieces for sale and has a fine collection of old pieces.

23 **Tsukuda** 佃 尾張町2-16-70 (31-2017). Hrs: 8:30–19:30. Elegant *tsukudani* (tiny fish and nuts) preserved by simmering in a sweet, soy-based glaze. The walnuts are divine. Try *shiramine* (walnuts encased in a wafer "shell"). *Gori* (tiny fish) and walnuts are the classic Kanazawa combination.

26 **Tawaraya** 俵屋 小橋2-4 (52-2079). Hrs: 9:00–18:00; clsd Su. Makers of *mizu-ame*, or liquid barley-sugar. This Edo-period shop is the quaintest in town.

# Kutani-yaki

By tradition, Kutani was first made in the late 1600s by Gotō Saijirō, who was sent to Arita (Kyūshū, p. 477) to steal the secrets of porcelain-making. Saijirō apprenticed himself to a master, even marrying into the family. After 10 years, he returned to Kaga (abandoning his wife) and began making porcelain, but production ceased, mysteriously, after one generation, leaving little evidence of what it looked like. Though its true provenance remains in dispute, there nevertheless emerged a distinctive Kutani type, characterized by a blue-black underglaze and overglaze enamels of green, yellow, blue, and aubergine. Characteristic designs consist of abstract patterns of textile and nature motifs, bearing an intriguing resemblance to Chinese ware of the late Ming and early Ch'ing. In the early 1800s, several artisans resurrected this type of "Old Kutani." Later, especially in the Meiji period, a gaudy red-and-gold ware, popular abroad, also became known as Kutani.

## Kanazawa Dining

*Kaga-ryōri*, the refined cuisine of Kanazawa, is considered by many to be the best in Japan. Like everything else, vis-à-vis Kyoto, it is full-bodied and rich. *Jibu-ni* is a poultry stew thickened with wheat gluten. *Ama-ebi* is a delectable sweet shrimp, served raw. *Kabura-zushi* is turnips and yellowtail, pickled in saké lees. *Buri* is mature yellowtail. *Gori* are tiny river fish. Good dining districts: Ōmichō market, Kōrinbō.

④ **Kotobukiya** 寿屋　尾張町2-4-13 (31-6245). Hrs: 12:00–14:00, 17:00–20:00; clsd Tu. Reservations. An extraordinary experience: Fine *shōjin-ryōri* (see Cuisine, p. 117) in a magnificent 120-year-old Kaga mansion. The beautiful food is served on exquisite old Wajima lacquer trays. Set courses: Y6–8000.

⑨ **Ōtomoro** 大友楼　尾張町2-27 (21-0305). Hrs: 11:00–14:00, 17:00–21:00. Reservation.

*Kaga-ryōri* by a descendant of the Maeda lord's chef. Lunch Y8000＋, dinner Y10,000＋.

⑬ *Nikorei* 似故礼 (61-0056). Hrs: 10:00–15:00. Teahouse in refurbished Nagamachi samurai home. *Matcha*, coffee.

⑰ *Terakiya* てら喜や　野町1-1-2 (42-2244). Hrs: 11:00–14:00, 16:00–21:30; clsd M, NY. Fish restaurant above a fish store; everything is impeccably fresh. Start with *tsukuri* (sashimi). Point at whatever appeals; the place is pretty casual. The *gori tsukudani* is delicious. A meal should run about Y2000–2500 per person.

⑱ *Takanoha* 鷹の羽 (21-2188). Kankō Bussankan, 2F. Hrs: 11:00–14:30, 16:30–22:00; clsd 1st, 3rd and 5th M, 2nd and 4th Su. A good place to try Kaga cuisine. Set menus, lunch Y1500＋, dinner Y6000＋.

## Kanazawa Lodgings (TEL 0762)

① *Holiday Inn Kanazawa* ホリディイン金沢 (23-1111). 1-10 Horikawa-machi, Kanazawa-shi, Ishikawa-ken. American-style comforts, English-speaking staff. Nice local seafood restaurant, Kita no Shōya. S Y9000, Tw Y14,000＋ (children under 12, free).

② **Kanazawa Miyako Hotel** 金沢都ホテル (31-2202). Fax 23-2856. 6-10 Konohana-machi. Convenient location by station. S Y9500, Tw Y17,000.

③ **Kanazawa Yūbin Chokin Kaikan** 金沢郵便貯金会館 (33-3381). 9-15 Tamagawa-chō. Post-office-subsidized hotel. Kaga cuisine dinner. Rooms S Y5000, Tw Y9000.

⑤ **Sumiyoshiya** すみよしや旅館　十間町54 (21-0157). 54 Jikken-machi. Pleasant business ryokan in a refurbished 200-year-old house. No English. The old wing (*honkan*) is cheaper and more atmospheric; the new wing (*shinkan*) rooms come w/toilet. Y8–15,000 w/meals.

⑦ ***Asadaya** 浅田屋 (31-2228). 23 Jikken-machi. A modern but very elegant inn, with superb cuisine and service. Y53,000＋ w/meals.

⑧ **Pension Raspberry** ペンションラズベリー　高岡町22-24 (23-0757). 22-24 Takaoka-chō. Popular with Western tourists. Y8500 w/meals.

⑪ *Kanazawa New Grand Hotel* 金沢ニューグランドホテル (33-1311). Fax 33-1591. 1-50 Takaoka-machi. Cosy city hotel. Excellent location near Kenroku-en, Katamachi. S Y10,000, Tw Y17,000＋.

⑫ **Kanazawa Pension** 金沢ペンション　長町3-8-4 (61-3489). 3-8-4 Nagamachi. Y8300–11,000 for two w/o meals.

⑯ **Minshuku Ikegame** 民宿いけ亀　野町2-1-16 (42-4821). 2-1-6 Nomachi. 80-year-old house; the owner is a fourth-generation chef. Meals are served on old Wajima lacquer and Kutani plates. Y5500 w/meals.

㉑ **New Grand Inn Kanazawa** ニューグランドイン金沢 (22-1211). 3-7 Kenrokumoto-machi. Excellent location. Business/tourist hotel run by the Kanazawa New Grand. S Y6200, Tw Y12,200.

㉔ **Minshuku Yōgetsu** 民宿陽月　東山1-13-22 (52-0497). 1-13-22 Higashiyama. Former geisha house. Y5500 w/meals.

㉕ **Kanazawa YH** 金沢YH　末広町37 (52-3414). 37 Suehiro-machi. *0:25h by bus from station to Suizokukan-mae.*

*Haku'unrō Hotel* 白雲楼ホテル (35-1111). Yuwaku Onsen. A classic hotel by Edo Mura (*0:40h by bus from Kanazawa*). The Sino-Hispanic building is built on the edge of a scenic gorge. The older wing has some beautiful Japanese rooms. Y24,000 w/meals.

*Takino-sō* 滝の荘　末町4-44 (29-0003). 4-44 Sue-machi. *0:20h taxi ride from town.* Charming country inn by a waterfall. Hot spring, mountain cuisine. Y10,000 w/meals.

## Exploring Haku-san National Park

Haku-san, the White Mountain, was "opened" to Buddhism by a *yamabushi* in 717 and is one of the most venerated mountains in Japan (see Shinto, p. 27). **Tsurugi** (*0:40h by Shiramine-bound bus (from pier 6, 3 per day) from Kanazawa*) has an ancient shrine to the mountain goddess. The bus continues onward to **Shiramine**, which has an old temple and a number of inns and hot-spring spas. From here, hikers and pilgrims climb the 12-km trail, reaching the desolate summit in the predawn hours in order to witness the sunrise.

303

## NW6 ** NOTO HANTŌ (PENINSULA) 能登半島

Noto is an excellent area for travelers who want to combine a bit of culture with an exploration of unspoiled rural life. The peninsula is large, over 70 km long. The west coast is more rugged, the east coast is more developed. Oku-Noto (Inner Noto, the cape) is the most beautiful part; plan to spend at least 2 nights (3 is ideal) to cover the region.

### Calendar

Somewhat crowded in summer. Nightly shows of Noto's famed Gojinjo Daiko from Mar. 15–Nov. 15 at Kasuga Jinja in Sosogi, and in Wajima on F, Sa.

**May 3–5: ** Seihaku-sai.** Nanao. See Calendar, p. 276.

**Mar. 1–7: Kisaragi Matsuri.** Wajima, Jūzō Jinja. Villagers aged 47–48 offer sacred rice and boughs in the middle of the night. After dumping their offerings at the shrine oratory, they flee home.

**L 6/15: ** Ishizaki Hōtō-sai.** Nanao. See Calendar, p. 276.

**July 7–8: * Abare Matsuri.** Ushitsu. Some 40 to 50 *kiriko*, 10-m lantern floats, are paraded about town. At night, huge torches are set ablaze. On the 8th, *mikoshi* are taken through sea and fire.

**July 31: * Gojinjo Daiko.** Nabune. Wild drumming by masked demons on the beach at night, commemorating a successful ploy to drive away an invasion by Uesugi Kenshin (see Tōhoku, p. 181). From 15:00 through the night.

### Getting Around

Kanazawa is the main gateway to Noto. JR trains run to Wajima and Suzu, but we recommend the Hokutetsu **Teiki Kankō (Scheduled Tour) Buses**, which visit the main sights and can be used like public buses. Plan ahead to avoid long waits: pick up a schedule at the Hokutetsu bus terminal by Kanazawa station. Departures: Daily at 9:10 and 11:50. Mar. 25–Nov. 30 also at 8:10. Prepaid reservations; cancel no later than 5 days before scheduled date. Tel: 0762-21-5011.

*Noto Peninsula, A Visitor's Guide* is a guidebook in English published by the Society to Introduce Kanawazawa to the World, Social Education Center, 3-2-15 Honda-machi, Kanazawa, Ishikawa-ken 920. Available in Tokyo at Maruzen and Kinokuniya.

### Noto Sights

**\* Kita-ke** 喜多家 (ICP). Hrs: 8:30–17:00. *0:45h from Kanazawa (0:30h stop).* A Maeda governor's house, built around 1720. There are four different entrances for persons of varying rank. Slatted windows enabled the officials to hear the petitions of commoners—who had to kneel on the ground outside—without being seen. Many fine objects are on display, and there is an exquisite garden.

**Chirihama (beach)** 千里浜 *0:20h from Kita-ke (0:15h stop).* The bus drives right into the sea on this beach of hard-packed sand. A novel experience. Rest house at the end of the beach.

**\*\* Myōjō-ji** 妙成寺 Hrs: 8:00–17:00, Dec.–Feb. 8:00–16:30. *0:20h from Chirihama (0:30h stop).* Just outside the gates are several regional farmhouses. Myōjō-ji, a Nichiren temple founded in 1293, has many fine structures, including a lovely five-storied pagoda; most date from the early 1600s, when Myōjō-ji was restored by the third Maeda daimyo in memory of his mother. The best view of the pagoda is from the *shoin* (study).

**\*\* Shibagaki** 柴垣 *A pleasant 0:20–0:25h walk from Myōjō-ji.* A picturesque fishing village with a sandy beach, boat harbor, a small shrine on a spit of land, and a scenic cycling path that hugs the jagged coast (but no rent-a-cycles). Good place to spend the night in a fisherman's minshuku.

**\* Ganmon** 巌門 *0:35h from Myōjō-ji (0:55h stop for boat ride).* Sea cliffs. **Fuku'ura**, just before Ganmon, is a quaint port with a wooden lighthouse built in 1876. The bus ride beyond Ganmon offers dramatic views over precipices. Ganmon can also be explored by a cycling path from Togimachi's Cycling Center (see lodgings).

**\* Sōji-ji** 総持寺 Hrs: 8:00–17:00. *0:50h from Ganmon (0:30h stop).* Sōtō Zen temple founded 1321. It is in the town of Monzen ("below the gate"). Attractive halls stand in lovely grounds. From Monzen, one can take a bus to Minatsuki, where there's a youth travel village, and from there hike along the coast to Ōzawa (about 2:00h). From Ōzawa, there are buses (once an hour) to Wajima.

**\*\*\* Wajima** 輪島 *0:35h from Sōji-ji to Wajima Shikki Shiryōkan.* The cultural heart of Noto, Wajima is famed for lacquerware, produced here for over a thousand years. The **\* Wajima Shikki Shiryōkan** (Lacquer Hall) 輪島漆器資料館 , a 0:10h walk from the station, exhibits old and new lacquerware along with the process of making it (Hrs: 9:00–17:00). Across the street is **Wajimaya Honten** 輪島屋本店 , a big lacquer store which presents a free **\* Gojinjo Daiko** performance at 20:30 (Apr. 10–Oct. 3 every F and Sa; almost daily in summer). Cross the river and walk toward the harbor to reach **Sumiyoshi Jinja**, guardian shrine of seafarers. Adjacent to the shrine is **\* O-Matsuri Yakata**, a small museum of floats used in local festivals. The shrine is the site of an **\* afternoon market** where you might buy some fresh seafood (ask your minshuku to fix it for dinner). The famous **Asa-ichi** (morning market) across the river is now an overpriced tourist trap. The area along the harbor and around the point is scenic. You will see many *ama*, or diving women, who gather seaweed and shellfish, cleaning and sorting their harvest by the harbor. A short way out of town, toward Sosogi, is the **\* Kiriko Kaikan** キリコ会館 , a hall displaying the beautiful lanternlike floats of Noto festivals (Hrs: 8:00–17:00. July 15–Aug. 31, 8:00–18:00).

**Hegurajima** 舳倉島 A sleepy little island of fisherfolk, reached by daily ferry from Wajima. Departs at 8:30, returns at 14:30 (during storms, ferry service may be suspended). Residents have banned cars from their scenic island. Many minshuku.

**✳✳ Senmaida (Thousand Paddies)** 千枚田 *0:30h from Wajima*. Noto's most famous sight are these terraced rice paddies stretching down to the sea. **Nabune** 名舟 (*0:05h from Senmaida*) is the site of Gojinjo Daiko (see Calendar).

**✳✳✳ Sosogi** 曾々木 *0:10h from Nabune (0:40h stop)*. This village is noted for a pair of magnificent houses, ◆ **Kami Tokikuni-ke** and **Shimo Tokikuni-ke** 上時国家・下時国家 (both ICP). Hrs: Apr.–Sept. 8:30–18:00; Oct.–Mar. 8:30–17:00. The locally powerful Tokikuni family claimed descent from a TAIRA noble who was exiled to Noto in 1185. Kami Tokikuni-ke was rebuilt in 1808. Though built like a farmhouse, with an immense thatched roof and cavernous kitchen, it shows definite aristocratic proclivities in the curved entrance gable, butterfly motifs (the Taira crest), and a room with a lacquered and gold-trimmed coffered ceiling, reserved for visitors of high court rank. A story, perhaps apocryphal, recounts the visit of a Maeda lord whose court rank was of insufficient elevation; the gold trim was covered before he was permitted to enter the room. Shimo Tokikuni-ke, built by a branch family about 200 years ago, is a humbler residence. Visitors can see ✳ **Gojinjo Daiko** nightly at Kasuga Jinja, from 20:00 (Mar. 15–Nov. 15, except on July 31–Aug. 1 and Aug. 17).

**✳✳ Rokkōzaki** 禄剛崎 *1:05h by local bus from Sosogi to Noroshi. (The tour buses also stop here, but they make a lot of unnecessary other stops en route.)* The scenic cape of Noto: lighthouse, YH, small shops, restaurants, and minshuku.

**✳ Kihē-don** 喜兵衛どん Hrs: 8:00–18:00. Dec.–Mar. 8:00–17:00. *0:40h from Noroshi (0:20h stop)*. A fine, late 19th-century farmhouse, now a museum of local history.

**Tsukumo-wan (Bay)** 九十九湾 *0:50h from Kihē-don (0:30h stop for boat ride)*. This small, islet-dotted cove is one of Japan's "hundred famous views," now somewhat marred by nearby development.

305

**Ushitsu** 宇出津 *0:40h from Tsukumo-wan*. Trains back to Kanazawa (2:30h by express).

## Noto Peninsula Lodgings

Hundreds of minshuku, Y5000 w/meals. A photographic guide (in Japanese) to area minshuku is available at the Ishikawa-ken Tourism Promotion Office in Tokyo.

**In Shibagaki: Minshuku Chiaya-sō** 民宿ちあや荘 (0767-27-1304). Shibagaki-machi, Hakui-shi, Hakui-gun, Ishikawa-ken. Friendly fisherman's minshuku, serving great seafood. Rise around 5:30 to see them bring in their catch. Guests are put into the modern annex, but you might ask for a room in the beautiful main house.

**Ganmon area: Togimachi Cycling Terminal** 富来町サイクリングターミナル (0767-42-2303). Satohongō, Togimachi, Hakui-shi. Bicycles for rent and lodgings. Bunks Y1960 per person; tatami Y2060 per person. Breakfast Y700, dinner Y1600. 18-km cycling path to Ganmon.

**In Wajima: Minshuku Hegura** 民宿へぐら (0768-22-1018). 91 Kamimachi, Fugeshimachi, Wajima-shi, Ishikawa-ken. A former lacquerer's lovely house. Good location near Sumiyoshi Jinja. **Minshuku Eifuku** 民宿永福 (22-0289). 139 Fugeshi, Fugeshimachi. **Minshuku Fumoto** 民宿ふもと (22-4852). 70 Onida, Sugiharamachi. **Pension Kurowassan (Croissant)** ペンションクロワッサン (22-1767). 86 Fugeshi, Fugeshimachi. Y8500 w/meals; seafood for dinner, and for breakfast, homemade croissants. **Hotel Yashio** ホテル八汐 (22-0600). Sodegahama, Fugeshimachi. A tourist ryokan with ocean views, Y15–30,000 w/meals.

**In Sosogi: Minshuku Yokoiwaya** 民宿横岩屋 (0768-32-0603). Sosogi, Machino-machi, Wajima-shi. 130-year-old house. **Sosogi Kajiyama YH** 曾々木梶山YH (32-1145). Address as above.

**In Noroshi: Minshuku Terai** 民宿てらい (07688-6-2038). He-61 Noroshimachi, Suzu-shi. Has a little art gallery.

**In Ushitsu: Minshuku Muroya** 民宿むろや (07686-2-0200). U-40 Ushitsu, Notomachi, Fugeshi-gun. Old house and garden.

## NW7 KOMATSU 小松

*0:20h by JR Hokuriku main line express from Kanazawa (NW5), or 0:10h by bus from Komatsu Airport, serving Kanazawa.* Kutani kilns are at Terai (0:15h by bus from the station). ✳✳ **Nata-dera** 那谷寺 (0:35h by bus from Komatsu station, or 0:10h from Yamashiro Onsen) is an interesting temple connected to the Shugendō cult of Haku-san. Hrs: 8:30–16:45. Dec.–Feb. 8:45–16:30.

## ✳ YAMANAKA ONSEN 山中温泉

*0:30h from Kanazawa by JR Hokuriku main line express to Kaga Onsen station, then 0:25h by bus.* An ancient and famous, yet quiet and pleasant, spa. There's a scenic walk by the riverside. The men's public bath, **Kikunoyu**, is an old yellow brick structure with a green copper, Japanese-style roof. Across the street is the main public bath and spa, **Fukushi Sentā** 福祉センター (Hrs: 7:00–22:30, Y250.)

**Yamanaka Onsen Lodgings** (TEL 07617)

**Kochō Ryokan** 胡蝶旅館 (8-1319). Yamanaka Onsen, Yamanaka-machi, Enuma-gun, Ishikawa-ken. Atmospheric 50-year-old wooden inn. Well-maintained. Nice garden. Gorge view. Y25–50,000 w/meals.

**Gomeikan** 五明館 (8-0002). Address as above. A Taishō-era inn, worse for wear but with handsome Kaga-style rooms, all looking onto lovely garden. Y14–20,000 w/meals.

## NW8 FUKUI 福井

*0:50h from Kanazawa (NW5), or 1:22h from Kyoto by JR Hokuriku main line limited express. Junction for the private Keifuku-dentetsu line to Eihei-ji (NW9).* **Mikuni**, 0:45h from Fukui by Keifuku-dentetsu, is an ancient port with a lovely temple, **Takidan-ji** (0:07h walk from station). At Hon-Maruoka, 0:35h by bus from Fukui, is **Maruoka-jō** (ICP), Japan's oldest castle keep, built in 1576; it is a small structure, built in an early style (see Castles, p. 46).

### Calendar

**Feb. 15: ✻ # Mizumi no Dengaku.** Ikeda-chō, Ukan Jinja *(bus from Fukui to Taniguchi, then 0:15h on foot)*. A Kamakura-period Dengaku and Noh-type dance. Call 0778-44-6111 for details.

**May 19–21: Mikuni Matsuri.** Mikuni. Rowdy, 300-year-old festival featuring floats with huge figures of samurai.

**May 24: ✻ Fukui Baka-bayashi (Idiot's Ballad).** Fukui, Homusubi Jinja. Dancers wearing antique masks dance crazily through town.

## NW9 ✻✻ EIHEI-JI 永平寺

*0:35h by private Keifuku-dentetsu line from Fukui.* Hrs: dawn–15:30, daily. Eihei-ji was founded in 1244 by Dōgen, founder of the Sōtō Zen sect in Japan, and today remains the leading monastery of the sect, with over 100 monks. The monastery centers around a remarkable compound of great halls, galleries, and courtyard gardens that stretch up a thickly forested mountainside to form a classic Zen temple *garan* (see Buddhism, p. 39). Go early (or in winter) to avoid the busloads of tourists who begin arriving around 9:30. Do not photograph the monks.

Enter by the large, modern building on the left; pay admission and proceed through the Sanshō-kaku (ceiling painted with flowers), the Shiden-dō, past the **Tosu** (lavatory) to the **San-mon** (Main Gate), rebuilt in 1749, an imposing structure housing images of the Shi-Tennō (Four Guardians). The cryptomeria-lined approach is used only by imperial messengers, who enter by the ornate **Chokushi-mon**, the gate bearing the imperial chrysanthemum crest. From the San-mon, head in a clockwise direction around the gallery. The next major hall is the **Sō-dō**, where monks meditate, eat, and sleep. This is one of three areas where monks are not permitted to speak; the other two are the lavatory and the bath. On the next level up is the central image hall, the **Butsuden** (1902), which houses a Three Worlds Trinity of Shaka flanked by Amida and Miroku (representing the Buddhas of the past, present, and future), a type of trinity transmitted from Sung China by Dōgen. At the top of the *garan* is the large **Hattō** (Dharma Hall, 1843) where debates, lectures, and services are held. The view over the roofs of the lower halls and galleys is memorable. The **Kuin**, or temple kitchen, is where meals are prepared by the monks. Hanging on the wall is a huge, blackened wooden pestle, a reminder to "keep grinding away."

### A Taste of Zen

Visitors can apply to receive Zen training by calling or writing at least 10 days in advance (phone 0776-63-3102). Trainees must arrive by 16:00, in time for bath, dinner, *zazen* meditation, and lectures in Japanese. The following day, one must rise at 3:30 a.m. for more lectures, *zazen*, breakfast, with checkout by 8:00 a.m. The fee is Y7000 for a night, w/2 meals.

### Eihei-ji Lodgings (TEL 0776)

**Eihei-ji Monzen Yamaguchi YH** 永平寺門前山口YH (63-3123). 22-3 Shihi, Eiheiji-chō, Yoshida-gun, Fukui-ken. Pleasant youth hostel, 0:15h on foot from the station. Y4600 w/meals.

**Kokuminshukusha Green Lodge** 国民宿舎グリーンロッジ (63-3126). 6-3 Shihi. 0:03h walk from the station. Y6500 w/meals.

### Exploring Heisen-ji

The beautiful, moss-carpeted grounds of this temple, and the beautiful country farms surrounding it, are 0:20h from Katsuyama, a terminus of the Keifuku line (0:55h from Fukui).

### Easy Access To:

**✻✻✻ KYOTO:** *2:15h from Fukui by JR Raichō limited express via west shore of Lake Biwa.*

**Maibara** (KYOTO VI:7): *1:15h from Fukui by JR limited express via eastern shore of Lake Biwa. Junction to Shinkansen express.*

# CHŪBU IV:S. SOUTH FROM NAGOYA

**Main Attraction:** Ise (S2)

**Prefectures:** Mie, Wakayama

## Traveling

Six JR expresses per day to Ise and Toba. The private Kintetsu line is more convenient. From Nagoya, departures every 0:20–0:30h from 6:30 to 22:40 (Y2120, reserved seating). From Kyoto, a direct express leaves at quarter past the hour, 7:15–18:15. From Ōsaka, departures every 20 minutes past the hour on weekends (slightly fewer on weekdays).

## KUWANA 桑名
*0:20h by Kintetsu or JR express from Nagoya.*

### Calendar
**Dec. 24:** \*\* **Ise Ō-Kagura.** Masuda Jinja (*take a bus from Kuwana station*). See Calendar, p. 276. Hrs: 12:00–16:00.

## S1 \* MATSUSAKA 松坂
*1:10h from Nagoya or 1:45h from Kyoto by Kintetsu express.* A quiet, former castle town famous for its beer-fed beef and enterprising merchants. In the ruined castle grounds are **Moto'ori Norinaga Kinenkan** 本居宣長記念館 and **Suzunoya Kyūtaku**, the museum and former home of a famous 18th-century scholar who led a protonationalist movement to restore the prestige of Shinto and native literature (Hrs: 9:00–16:00). Just outside the castle walls is **Gojōban Yashiki**, a lane lined with the homes of samurai assigned to the guard. **Uo-machi**, northeast of the castle, preserves the old homes of Matsusaka merchants. Nearby is the gate from the estate of one Matsusaka merchant family known the world over, the Mitsui.

307

### Matsusaka Dining (TEL 0598)
\*\* **Wadakin** 和田金 (21-1188). Hrs: 7:30–20:00; clsd 1st and 4th Tu, NY. Sukiyaki and *ami-yaki*, from Y7500. (Matsusaka Mingei, across the street, has a fine selection of regional crafts.)

\* **Kitamura** 北村 (21-1376). Hrs: 10:00–14:30, 16:30–21:00; clsd W, 3rd Th, NY. Since 1882. Steak from Y4500.

## S2 \*\*\* ISE 伊勢
*From Nagoya, 2:00h by JR limited express or 1:25h by Kintetsu limited express to Ise-shi station. Kintetsu also stops at Uji-Yamada station.* Ise Jingū, a pair of shrines consecrated to an agricultural divinity and to Amaterasu, the Sun Goddess, divine ancestor of the imperial line, are among the most important shrines in Japan. The mysterious sacred halls, set in the eternal twilight of a primal cryptomeria forest, produce an aura of sanctity that is uniquely Japanese. If you are interested in Shinto or architecture, Ise is a must.

### Calendar
**Jan. 1–3: Hatsumōde.** Ise Jingū is crowded for New Year.
**Apr. 5–7:** \* **Kagura-sai.** Ise Jingū. Kagura offered at the Kagura-den of the Nai-kū and Ge-kū, as well as Kagura, sacred music, Bugaku, and Noh from regions all over Japan.
**Aug. 15:** \* **Kanko Odori.** Shōgaku-ji. Bon dance by men wearing headdresses of white horsehair and skirts of straw. Exotic feel. Also at Izumo Jinja is nearby Tsu.
**Oct. 17: Ise Jingū Kan'name-sai.** One of the shrine's most important annual rites, in which food is prepared and offered to the deities. Rice, salt, vegetables, abalone, clay vessels, cloth, and fire, are all produced according to strict ancient procedures. The rites are secret and only a procession can be seen. There is a festival of folk songs and dances held at the same time.

### Ise's History and Architecture
The visitor to Ise may be astonished to learn that the celebrated shrine buildings—extolled as "temples to architecture"—cannot be seen. This is certainly disappointing, for the long gravel approach through the natural cathedral of towering cryptomeria only serves to heighten anticipation. The shrine buildings are enclosed by four layers of fencing, and visitors must content themselves with a glimpse of the heavy thatched roofs, bristling with wooden finials. Of all the great architectural and religious monuments in the world, these are surely the simplest and the most mysterious.

According to an early "history," the shrines were established in the 3rd century by a princess, Yamatohime, who was charged with finding a place to enshrine the sacred mirror of Amaterasu, the Great Heaven Illuminating Divinity, mythic ancestor of the imperial clan (see Shinto, p. 26). When she arrived at Ise, the goddess appeared to her and, expressing a liking for the area, directed that a shrine be erected here. By tradition, an imperial virgin was always chosen to serve as high priestess; the practice ended in the 14th century, during a time when the imperial court was split in two.

The **Nai-kū** (Inner Shrine) of Ise is consecrated to Amaterasu. The **Ge-kū** (Outer Shrine) enshrines Toyouke Ō-kami, the Abundant Food Great Divinity; according to record, this deity was moved to Ise in the 5th century from the Tamba region, northwest of Kyoto.

Perhaps the imperial clan, wishing to consolidate its influence, thought to boost Amaterasu's prestige through association with a local rice deity. There is little doubt that the worship of food deities, basic to early cultures, predated the cult of the Sun Goddess, which was a later development to bolster the ascendancy of the imperial clan. Significantly, the most important rites at Ise center on the production of rice.

The single most remarked-upon feature of the Ise shrines is the custom of rebuilding them every 20 years. This practice was initiated in A.D. 690 and has continued almost without interruption to the present (there was one 123-year hiatus during the war-torn 15th and 16th centuries). For this purpose, there is an identical plot of land next to the shrine, where an exact replica is built. A solemn ceremony transfers the divinity to the new shrine, and the old shrine is dismantled and distributed to shrines throughout the country that have petitioned for parts to repair their own buildings. Many other major shrines were rebuilt periodically, but only at Ise does the custom survive. The next rebuilding, the sixty-first, will be in 1993.

The shrines at Ise are considered to be pure statements of archaic native architecture. Although certain details are clearly foreign — for example, the Tang-style "flaming jewel" ornaments on the railings — architectural historians agree that the present form of the shrines was established by the 8th century. Even so, rebuilders must have occasionally taken liberties. From the Meiji period through the end of World War II, for instance, the Nai-kū was encrusted with heavy metal ornamentation; since 1953, the shrine has been restored to its pre-Meiji simplicity. By and large, Ise's architecture has remained nearly free of Buddhist influence throughout its long history.

The shrines are thought to resemble ancient granaries or storehouses. They are built of *hinoki* (cypress) from the Kiso forestry preserves. The unvarnished timbers are finished to draw out the perfection of the wood. The structures are three bays wide and two deep, with a raised floor. The supporting columns are embedded directly in the clean-swept, pebble-covered ground. The entrance is in the long side, in the central bay, a distinguishing feature of Ise architecture. The roof of heavy thatch swells richly. The eaves are straight, unlike the upcurved eaves of shrines that were influenced by temple design. The most distinctive ornaments are the *chigi*, suggestive of crossed bargeboards thrusting above the roof ridge, and the *katsuogi*, resembling logs weighing down the protective ridge cover. The *muchikake*, rows of long, slender pegs jutting out from the gabled ends, also probably represent elements that were once functional. These now-decorative features show that the Ise shrines are not literal representations of archaic rice storehouses. They are, rather, idealized storehouses, made abstract and perfect, and therefore timeless and sacred.

308

### Getting Around
Buses run every 0:10–0:20h between Ise-shi station, Uji Yamada station, Ge-kū and Nai-kū. Suggested tour: Station — Ge-kū — (bus from station to Sarudahiko Jinja) — walk via Oharai-machi — Nai-kū — Jingū Chōkokan — station. If you have time for only one shrine, see the Nai-kū.

### Ise Sights　伊勢神宮
∗ **Kawasaki**　河崎　*0:10h walk from station.* A 1-km stretch of old houses and warehouses along a canal. From the Edo period until the 1920s, the area thrived by supplying rice and fish to feed Ise pilgrims.
**Ise-shiritsu Kyōdo Shiryōkan**　伊勢市立郷土資料館 (24–2201). Hrs: 9:00–16:30; Oct.– Mar. 9:00–16:00; clsd M (except if a NH, then clsd Tu), NY. Local archeological and folkloric material displayed in the former post and telegraph office, a cute white building with red tile roof (built 1924). Videos of area festivals.

# The Ise Pilgrimage

Ise was originally barred to commoners because it was the shrine of the emperor. But when the fortunes of the imperial house plunged in the medieval period, the shrine became hard up for funds. Following the example of Buddhist temples, pros-elytizers were sent out to popularize Ise, setting up regional associations to support the shrine through offerings and encouraging members to make pilgrimages there. By the 15th century, it was widely believed that one pilgrimage in a lifetime would ensure salvation. During the Edo period, O-Ise Mairi became something of a national craze. Every community had an Ise Association that provided funds for one of its members, chosen by an annual lottery, to go on the journey. For most, this was a once-in-a-lifetime chance to travel. Considering the draconian restrictions on travel, it can only be supposed that the shogunate encouraged the pilgrimage as a harmless outlet for frustration. A busy pleasure quarter grew up around the shrines. On occasion, the pilgrimage took on staggering proportions, as a spontaneous Ise fever swept the country and millions dropped their work and hit the road with only the clothes on their backs, dancing, singing, and pilfering their way to Ise. This phenomenon occurred four times in the Edo period: in 1650, in 1705 (3,620,000 pilgrims recorded), in 1771 (2,700,000), and in 1830 (2,200,000).

✳ **Jingū Chōkokan (Museum of Antiquities)** 神宮徴古館 (22–1700). Hrs: Mar.–Oct. 9:00–16:30; Nov.–Feb. 9:00–16:00, clsd M. *0:10h by the bus running between Ge-kū and Nai-kū.* Neoclassical building housing paintings, documents, armor, weapons, and other objects donated to the shrines. Most interesting are ritual implements used in shrine ceremonies.

✳✳✳ **Ge-kū (Outer Shrine)** 外宮 Hrs: Mar.–Apr. and Sept.–Oct. 5:00–18:30. May–Aug. 4:00–19:30. Nov.–Feb. 5:00–17:30. *0:05h walk from station.* Consecrated to Toyouke Ō-kami, the Abundant Food Great Divinity. The main approach leads past a torii, the Anzaisho (imperial rest house), a second torii, and the Kagura-den (sacred dance hall). Beyond the Kagura-den, there's a left turn leading to three small shrines, Tsuchi no Miya (Earth Shrine), Kaze no Miya (Wind Shrine), and Taga no Miya, a shrine to the wild aspect of Ge-kū's goddess. Back beside the main approach is the ◆ **large, pebble-covered expanse**, the site of the next rebuilding in 1993. In the center is a tiny shed sheltering the **heart pillar**, a mysterious object that not only marks the center of the sacred hall but is also sacred in itself. The main shrine compound lies on a north-south axis, with the main gate on the south. The sacred area is delimited by ◆ **four concentric fences**, which cannot be penetrated by ordinary mortals. The fences are built of beautiful, plain cryptomeria boards, the inner more narrowly spaced than the outer, as if to indicate the tighter delimiting of sacred space. The ◆ **shōden** (sacred hall) of the Ge-kū is nearly identical to that of the Nai-kū, except in the cut of the *chigi* and the number of *katsuogi* (9 instead of 10). Among the secondary buildings, the most interesting is the **Mike-den**, in the NE corner of the outermost enclosure (visitors can peer through the fence), where offerings of food are made twice a day. The Mike-den is of *ita-azekura* construction; the wall planks are interlocked at the corners, log-cabin-style, a method considered more primitive than the *shōden*'s construction, in which wall planks are slid into grooves cut in the corner columns. It is thought that all the accessory structures were originally built in this manner.

✳✳ **Oharai-machi** おはらい町 *0:15h by Nai-kū–bound bus from station.* This last stretch of the pilgrim's path before arriving at Nai-kū is being restored to its Edo-period appearance. The famous Akafuku teahouse is here, as are many restaurants and shops.

✳✳✳ **Nai-kū (Inner Shrine)** 内宮 Hrs: Same as Ge-kū. *0:17h by bus from Ge-kū or station.* Consecrated to Amaterasu Ōmikami, tutelary deity of the imperial clan. Visitors first cross the **Ujibashi**, a 102-meter-long wooden bridge spanning the sacred Isuzu River. The view of encircling hills and forest is pure magic. Turn right and follow the main approach about 200 m to the next torii. Just beyond, on the right, is ◆ **Mitarashi**, where pilgrims descend to the river to perform ablutions (hampered by the seething mass of colorful carp). Continue along the path, past one of the two sacred stables, the Kagura-den, sacred rice and saké storehouses, and finally arrive at a flight of stone steps that ends at the outer gate of the *shōden*. A gauzy curtain conceals the view beyond. The sacred mirror, one of the three imperial regalia, is enshrined inside. To get an idea of the *shōden*'s appearance, look for the ◆ **Mishine no Mikura**, a small copy. (Head back the way you came about 100 m and take the path to the right. The structure stands about 50 m down, on the left.) The path continues back to the Uji bridge, passing the second sacred stable along the way. A white horse is "in residence" between 8:30–10:00; at 8:00 a.m. on the 1st, 11th, and 21st of each month, the sacred beast is presented at the shrine.

309

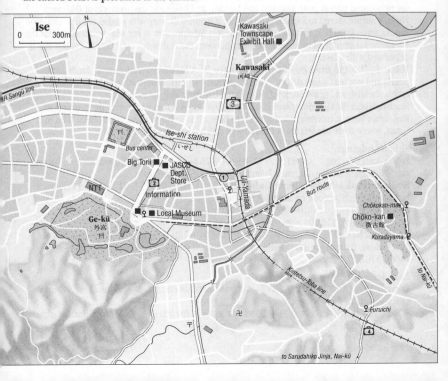

**O-Ise Mairi Shiryōkan** お伊勢まいり資料館 (24–5353). Hrs: 8:30–17:00. Edo-period Ise pilgrimages depicted using thousands of handmade paper figurines. Charming.

**Kongōshō-ji** 金剛証寺 *0:45h by bus from Nai-kū.* A serene old temple protecting the *kimon* (devil's gate, the unlucky northeast direction) of the Nai-kū. Its Momoyama-period Main Hall is an ICP.

## Ise Dining and Lodgings (TEL 0596)

Local seafood: *Ise ebi* (langoustines), *awabi* (abalone) and *sazae* (turban shell).

① \* **Kappō Daiki** 割烹大喜 岩ぶち2-1-48 (28-0281). Hrs: 11:00–21:00, daily. By Uji-Yamada station. Excellent seafood. Sushi *moriawase* from Y900, *kaiseki* from Y5000.

\*\* **Akafuku Honten** 赤福本店 (22-2154). Hrs: 7:00–17:00, daily. Venerable riverside shop selling famous *akafuku*, sticky rice paste filled with azuki bean jam. The tea water is still boiled in antique cauldrons. A dish of *akafuku* with bancha tea is Y200. For Y500 you can have it with *matcha* (tea-ceremony style) in an elegant room overlooking a garden.

**Sushiku** すし久 Hrs: 11:00–17:00. In Oharai-machi. Beautiful old-style restaurant with rooms overlooking the river. *Tekone sushi* Y800, *Hirazen* (various dishes including sashimi) Y1500.

② **Yamadakan** 山田館 (28–2532). Honmachi, Ise-shi, Mie-ken. Old-style inn with great location. Y8–9000 w/meals.

③ **Hoshidekan** 星出館 河崎2-15-2 (28-2377). 2-15-2 Kawasaki. Economical Inn Group ryokan, 0:07h walk from Ise-shi station. Natural foods. Y5000 w/meals.

④ \* **Asakichi Ryokan** 麻吉旅館 (22-4101). Nakanomachi. *0:10h by bus from station.* In Furuichi, an area once famed for teahouses, inns, and brothels that catered to Edo-period Ise pilgrims. This is the only establishment (now perfectly respectable) to survive from the early days. Rambling and cluttered, but friendly service. Y8–16,000 w/meals.

**Mie Kōsei-Nenkin Kyūka Center** 三重厚生年金休暇センター (39-1200). 1165-1 Ikenoue, Sahachi-chō. Subsidized resort with pool, tennis court. Y8000 w/meals.

**Jingū Kaikan** 神宮会館 (22-0191). Uji Nakanokiri-chō. Lodge run by the shrine; located near Nai-kū. Y6000 w/meals.

310

# S3 SHIMA HANTŌ (PENINSULA) 志摩半島

*Served by the Kintetsu line and frequent buses.* The countless coves along the peninsula's deeply indented coastline are dotted with islets and rafts of oysters (both the pearl and edible kind). Gourmets head for the oyster minshuku in **Matoya** (by bus from Shima-Isobe station).

## Calendar

**Jan. 1:** \* **Okina Matsuri.** Ago-chō, Anori (*0:50h from Uji-Yamada by Kintetsu to Ukata, then 0:25h by bus*). *Sanbasō* (felicitous dance) on the beach.

**June 24:** \* **Izōnomiya Otaue Shinji.** *0:40h by Kintetsu to Kamino-gō station, from Uji-Yamada.* A colorful planting festival for the sacred rice of the Ise shrines. Young men stampede through the paddies, then maidens plant the rice. Hrs: 11:00–14:30.

## Shima Hantō Sights

\* **Futamigaura** 二見浦 *0:10h by JR train or 0:25 by bus from Ise-shi station.* The beach-front walk from the station to the shrine (below) is less seedy than the main street. Japanese gather here to catch the sunrise, viewed between the celebrated **Meoto Iwa,** or "wedded rocks," two offshore boulders entwined in *shimenawa* (sacred ropes). The rocks represent the primordial parent gods, Izanami and Izanagi, and belong to the precincts of **Okitama Jinja,** a shrine sacred to Sarudahiko Ō-kami, a monkey divinity who guided the first emperor, Jimmu, from Kyūshū to Yamato. Also of interest is **Mishio-den,** a hut where sacred salt for the Ise shrines is produced by ancient methods between the end of July and Oct. 5; the last day is celebrated with a festival.

**Toba** 鳥羽 *0:15h from Ise-shi, by Kintetsu or JR.* A big tourist trap, famous for Mikimoto pearls and women "pearl divers" who are in fact, like their sisters all over Japan, diving for edible shellfish and seaweed. Boat rides in the bay can safely be skipped.

**Kashikojima** 賢島 *0:50h from Ise-shi by Kintetsu.* A resort with lovely views over **Ago Bay.** From here, a recommended route is to take a bus to **Nagiri** and **Daiō-zaki,** then to **Goza,** where there are ferries to Hamashima and back to Kashikojima.

## Shima Lodgings

**Iroha-kan** いろは館 大字江537-22 (05964-3-2024). 537-22 Ōaza Ei, Futami-chō, Watarai-gun, Mie-ken. A simple old inn at Futamigaura. Y8–15,000 w/meals.

**Kokuminshukusha Ise-Shima Lodge** 伊勢志摩ロッジ (05995-5-0225). 2165 Erihara, Isobe-chō. Fresh seafood on the table. Y5100 w/meals.

**Ikada-sō** 民宿いかだ荘 (05995-7-2035). Matoya, Isobe-chō, Shima-gun. Matoya oyster minshuku. Y12,000 w/meals.

\*\* **Shima Kankō Hotel** 志摩観光ホテル (05994-3-1211). Kashikojima, Ago-chō, Shima-gun. Deluxe; famous for its nouvelle cuisine. Y40,000 per person w/meals. Japanese-style annex, Y10,000 w/meals.

## Easy Access To:

**Yamato-Yagi** (KINKI I:S5): *1:20h by Kintetsu express via Muro-ji, Hase-dera, Sakurai.* Connections to Kyoto, Nara.

\* **Kumano** (KINKI I:S13): *0:15-0:20h by JR to Taki, the 2:05h by JR Kii line limited express.*

C
H
Ū
B
U

# Kyoto 京都

Kyoto is one of the most alluring cities in the world, though few would suspect it at first, judging from the characterless modernity around the railroad station. Yet, as one begins to explore its temples and old quarters, to stroll its riverbank and gaze at the encircling hills, an indelible impression begins to sink in — of the great weight of its history. Though time after time, real power has slipped away from its control, Kyoto rests on the enduring certainty that only here have people mastered the art of living. In the quiet backways of the city, one finds the elegant inns, exquisite gardens, and the shops and artisans that for over a millennium have made Kyoto the "Hana no Miyako," the Flowering Capital.

# TOURING KYOTO

Consider making Kyoto, not Tokyo, your base for seeing Japan. Kyoto's downtown is an hour's bus ride from Ōsaka International Airport. The city is compact and easy to navigate, and is guaranteed to make you feel you have truly come to Japan. Most of the important attractions lie nestled against the surrounding hills. Our coverage divides Kyoto into six parts:

(I) **Central Kyoto:** The area around Kyoto station and north to the Imperial Palace, bordered on the east by the Kamo River. Kyoto's subway, under Karasuma-dōri, forms its main axis. The shopping district is centered at the intersection of Shijō-dōri and Kawaramachi-dōri. Kyoto's nightlife straddles the river around Shijō-dōri; the west bank is Pontochō, one of the leading geisha quarters.

(II) **Eastern Kyoto:** Higashiyama, or Eastern Mountains, an area with many temples squeezed between the Kamogawa and the hills for which it is named. Gion, Kyoto's premier geisha quarter, is on the east bank of the river; geisha and *maiko* (apprentice geisha) can be seen here in early evening, walking in high clogs along Hanami-kōji.

(III) **Northeast Kyoto:** The guardian of Kyoto, majestic Hiei-zan, dominates the elegant villas and small rustic temples nestled in the valleys of this hilly district.

(IV) **Northwest Kyoto:** This area has many of Kyoto's finest Zen temples, including Ryōan-ji, famed for its rock garden, and the Golden Pavilion. It is also historically tied to the tea cere- mony. Many temples lie at the foot of the Northern Mountains, or Kitayama, by which name this area is often called.

(V) **Western Kyoto:** The mountains to Kyoto's west are several kilometers from the center of the city. Since the Heian period, this has been a retreat for Kyoto's courtiers, who have left sev- eral aristocratic old temples. The Togetsu-kyō bridge in Arashiyama is the focus for merry- makers on summer evenings.

(VI) **The Shores of Lake Biwa:** A good area for day trips from Kyoto, with many fine temples and matsuri (see p. 376 for transit diagram).

312

KYOTO

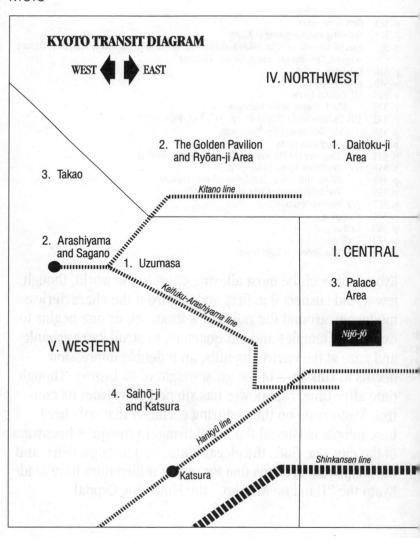

# BEST ATTRACTIONS

I:1   ✽✽✽ Tō-ji
I:1   ✽✽ Nishi Hongan-ji
I:2   ✽✽✽ Pontochō
I:3   ✽✽✽ Nijō-jō
I:3   ✽✽ Imperial Palace
II:1   ✽✽ Fushimi Inari Shrine
II:2   ✽✽✽ Sanjūsangen-dō (temple)
II:2   ✽✽ Kyoto National Museum
II:2   ✽✽ Kawai Kanjirō Gallery
II:2   ✽✽ Kiyomizu-dera (Temple)
II:2   ✽✽✽ Sannenzaka and Ninenzaka slopes
II:3   ✽✽✽ Gion/Hanami-Kōji ("Gion Corner" show)
II:4   ✽✽ Heian Jingū
II:5   ✽✽ Nanzen-ji
II:5   ✽✽ Philosopher's Walk
II:5   ✽✽✽ Ginkaku-ji
III:1   ✽✽✽ Shūgaku-in Imperial Villa (reservation required)
III:2   ✽✽ Hiei-zan (Enryaku-ji)
III:3   ✽✽ Sanzen-in
IV:1   ✽✽✽ Daitoku-ji
IV:2   ✽✽✽ Kinkaku-ji
IV:2   ✽✽✽ Ryōan-ji
V:1   ✽✽ Kōryū-ji
V:2   ✽✽ Tenryū-ji
V:2   ✽✽ Daikaku-ji
V:4   ✽✽✽ Saihō-ji (reservation required)
V:4   ✽✽✽ Katsura Imperial Villa (reservation required)

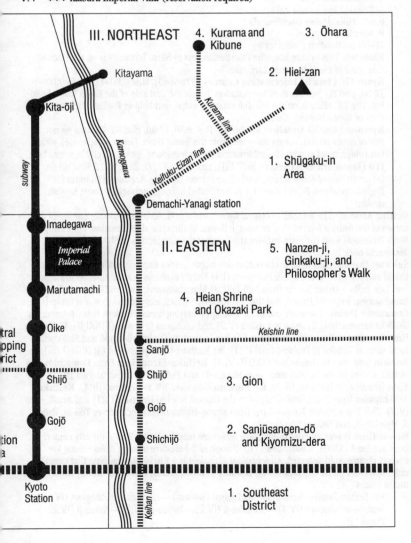

## Seasons

Early spring and late fall offer the best weather and scenery, but at these times Kyoto is crowded with millions of schoolchildren on field trips from all over Japan. Summer is hot and muggy. Winter — cold, clear, and quiet — is our favorite season for Kyoto.

## Average Temperature °C (°F)/Days of Rain or Snow

| January | April | July | October |
|---|---|---|---|
| 3.9 (39.0)/7 | 13.7 (56.7)/11 | 26.3 (79.3)/12 | 17.0 (62.6)/8 |

## Traveling and Navigating in Kyoto

A museum city with a millennium of history, Kyoto can easily baffle the visitor with its multitude of temples, palaces, and villas. To avoid being overwhelmed, we suggest you construct an itinerary consciously and selectively. Keep in mind that \*\*\* Uji and \*\*\* Nara are convenient day trips from Kyoto (see Kinki).

**Getting There:** 2:40h by Shinkansen Hikari express, or 4:00h by Kodama express from Tokyo Station. A highway bus departs at 23:00 from Tokyo station and arrives in Kyoto at 7:45; the fare is half the Shinkansen fare. From abroad, fly into Ōsaka International Airport. See Practical Advice for airlines serving Ōsaka. From Ōsaka Airport, it is 1:00h by a frequent and inexpensive express bus to Kyoto Station, Shin-Hankyū Hotel, Grand Hotel, Kyoto Hotel, and International Hotel.

**Kyoto Station:** The Shinkansen pulls up on the **Hachijō** side (south). Most of Kyoto lies to the north, on the **Karasuma** side, which is reached by an underpass on the east end, via the subway entrance, or by an overpass on the west side, via JR lines. See (I) and (II) for sightseeing areas easily reached from the station. The **Travel Service Center** is on the north side; exchange rail-pass vouchers and make JR reservations there. There are coin lockers on both sides of the station. The JR tracks from north to south are:

San'in 1, 2: San'in line
1: Tōkaidō line, Hokuriku line (eastbound)
2: Tōkaidō line (eastbound)
3: Kosei line
4: Tōkaidō line local
5: Tōkaidō line semi-local
6 & 7: Tōkaidō line (westbound)
8: Nara line
11–14: Shinkansen (bullet train)

**Kintetsu:** This private line offers the best access to Nara. Terminus is on the Hachijō side, west of the Shinkansen turnstiles.

**Kyoto TIC (Tourist Information Center)** (371-5649). Hrs: 9:00–17:00; Sa 9:00–12:00; clsd Su. Just north of Kyoto station. Follow the east side of the Kyoto Tower building. The TIC office is on the left. Information, maps, and help in English. Pick up a free copy of *Kyoto Monthly Guide*.

**Kyoto-shi Kankō Annaijo** (343-6655). Hrs: 8:30–17:00; clsd NY. Located on north side of Kyoto station, across the street from the Tower Hotel. Help (in Japanese) with bus routes, hotel and ryokan information and reservations. Pick up a city bus map here.

**JTB (Japan Travel Bureau)** (361-7241). Hrs: 9:30–17:30; Sa 9:30–12:30; clsd Su. On north side of Kyoto station, east of the station building. Arranges JTB tours for English-speakers. Reservations for JTB-affiliated lodgings, transport. Some English spoken.

**Getting Around:** The avenues of central Kyoto form a grid. Addresses usually consist of the names of the nearest intersecting avenues, followed by directional information. For example, Shijō Teramachi west (or nishi-iru) means "west of the intersection of Shijō-dōri and Teramachi-dōri."

**Subway:** One line runs from Kyoto station due north (under Karasuma-dōri) to Kitayama. Useful stops: **Gojō:** Near Higashi Hongan-ji (I:1) **Shijō:** Business center; junction to Hankyū line (see below) **Ōike:** Not far from Nijō-jō (I:3) **Marutamachi:** Imperial Palace (I:3). **Imadegawa:** Imperial Palace; bus line 59. **Kita-ōji:** Buses, easy access to north Kyoto (IV).

**Commuter Trains:** These are useful for getting to outlying areas. **Hankyū line:** Terminus at Shijō-Kawaramachi (I:2) stops at Katsura (V:3) and continues to Ōsaka (KINKI II). **Keihan line:** Terminus at Demachi-Yanagi; one line heads south to Ōsaka, via Sanjō and Shijō, with local stops at Tōfuku-ji, Fushimi Inari (II:1); the **Keihan-Uji line** goes to Uji (KINKI I:S); the **Keishin line** goes to Hama-Ōtsu (KYOTO VI:1). **Keifuku-Eizan line:** From Demachi-Yanagi station; serves NE Kyoto, with stops near Shisen-dō and Shūgaku-in Imperial Villa (III:1), Yase Yūen (tramway to Hiei-zan, III:2); the **Kurama line** forks NW to Kurama (III:4). **Keifuku-Arashiyama line:** From Shijō-Ōmiya (on the Hankyū line) to Uzumasa (V:1) and Arashiyama (V:2). This line joins the **Kitano Line** from Kitano-Hakubaichō which serves Tōji-in, Ryōan-ji, Myōshin-ji, and Omuro (IV:2).

**Buses:** There is now an English-language bus-route map for Kyoto. Within the city center, fares are fixed (Y180). A *kaisūken* (Y1000 book of 7 base-fare tickets) saves fishing for correct change; sold onboard. An *ichinichi jōshaken* is a Y1050 one-day pass that permits unlimited rides on all city buses. Sold at stations (Kyoto, Keihan-Sanjō, all subway stops). Two useful routes:

59: Keihan-Sanjō — Karasuma-Imadegawa (subway) — Horikawa-Imadegawa (IV:1) — Senbon-Imadegawa (IV:1) — Kinkaku-ji (IV:2) — Ryōan-ji (IV:2) — Ninna-ji (IV:2) — Utano YH

5: Kyoto Station—Shijō-Karasuma (subway)—Shijō-Kawaramachi—Keihan-Sanjō station—Okazaki Park/Heian Shrine (II:3)—Nanzen-ji (II:4)—Eikan-dō (II:4)—Ginkaku-ji (II:4)—Shisen-dō (III:1)—Shūgaku-in (III:1)

**Rent-a-Scooter or Bicycle:** Bicycles, Y900–1100 per day; scooters, Y2500–3000 per day (international driver's license required). **Nippon Rent-a-Car** (681-0311) for scooters and for bicycles (672-0662) is across from the Hachijō exit of Kyoto station. **Rent-a-Cycle Yasumoto** (751-0595) is near Keihan-Sanjō station. **Cycle House Daiko** (431-4522) is on the west side of the Imperial Palace.

**Taxis:** Most distances are short, which makes taxis very convenient. Y470 for first 2 km. **MK Taxi** (721-2237) offers excellent service and prices. For a small car, Y4300 for the first hour, Y1400 for each additional 0:30h. English-speaking drivers Y1000 per hour extra.

**Bus Tours:** Information on JTB bus tours in English available at hotels, TIC, and JTB. Less expensive are the **Teiki Kankō (Scheduled Tour) Buses** (in Japanese only) leaving from Kyoto station. Courses: **AS** (3:30h, Y3530, departs every 0:30–1:00h) covers Sanjūsangen-dō, Kiyomizu-dera, Heian Jingū, and Kinkaku-ji. **A** (5:00h, Y4000, departs every 0:30h) is the above plus Nishi Hongan-ji and Chion-in. **D** (7:00h, Y6630 w/lunch, departs 9:40) covers Tō-ji, Manpuku-ji and Byōdō-in (in Uji), and Sennyū-ji.

**Guidebooks to Kyoto:** *A Guide to the Gardens of Kyoto*, by Marc Treib and Ron Herman, is an intelligent and practical guide to the appreciation of Japanese gardens. *Kyoto: A Contemplative Guide*, by Gouverneur Mosher, is a classic that describes a small number of sights in great depth. *Historical Kyoto*, by Herbert Plutschow, offers a wealth of historical detail, but no practical information. *Old Kyoto: A Guide to Traditional Shops, Restaurants, and Inns*, by Diane Durston, is a wonderfully intimate guide to the artisans and culture of the city. All are available at Maruzen Bookstore (see Kyoto Shopping).

# SPECIAL INTERESTS

315

**Crafts:** See Kyoto Shopping for shops. The Dentō Sangyō Kaikan (II:4) gives an excellent overview of Kyoto's fine crafts, including Yūzen dyeing, Nishijin brocades, Kiyomizu-yaki porcelain, furniture, damascene, lacquer, dolls, and paper. Kawai Kanjirō House (II:2) is the lovely house, now a museum, of this highly influential folk-art potter. For more specialized interests, inquire with the TIC.

**Villas and Gardens:** See list of Best Villas and Gardens, p. 70. Other fine gardens: Shōren-in (II:3), Murin-an (II:4); Shisen-dō, Manshū-in (III:1); Sanzen-in (III:3).

**Relics of the Heian period:** Tō-ji, Shinsen-en, Imperial Palace (I); Kiyomizu-dera, Heian Jingū (II); Kamigamo Jinja, Hiei-zan, Sanzen-in (III); Ninna-ji (IV); Kōryū-ji, Daikaku-ji (V). Also, don't miss Daigo-ji and Uji (KINKI I:S1).

**Sculpture:** Tō-ji (I); Sanjūsangen-dō, Kyoto National Museum, Rokuharamitsu-ji (II); Senbon Shaka-dō (IV); Kōryū-ji (V).

**Ornate Screens:** Nishi Hongan-ji, Nijō-jō (I); National Museum, Chishaku-in, Nanzen-ji (II); Myōshin-ji (IV); Daikaku-ji (V).

**Zen:** Shōkoku-ji (I); Tōfuku-ji, Kennin-ji, Nanzen-ji (II); Daitoku-ji, Myōshin-ji (IV). Sōsen-ji (351-4270) Shimogyō-ku, Takakura Gojō-sagaru (*0:05h on foot east of Gojō subway station*) offers lecture in English and *zazen* at 18:00–21:00 on the 1st and 3rd M of each month.

**Tea Ceremony:** (See Villas, p. 66.) Ura Senke (IV:1) holds a demonstration on Thursdays. Kanō Shōjuan, a confectioner on Philosopher's Walk (II:5), offers a casual tea ceremony.

**Onsen:** Yase no Kamaburo Onsen has traditional steam baths inside round clay ovens. Take the Keifuku-Eizan line to Yase Yūen. You can reserve a steam bath (and meals and lodgings) at the inn (781-5126).

**Theaters:** Check *Kyoto Monthly Guide* for schedules. See Kyoto Calendar for events featuring traditional performing arts.

**Kanze Kaikan** (771-6114) (II:4). Noh theater used often by various schools. Kanze school regular performance from 10:30 on 4th Su of each month, except in July and October.

**Kongō Nohgaku-do** (221-3049). Shijō-Muromachi-agaru. Beautiful old Noh hall. Performance 4th Su of each month except in July and August. Mask and costume exhibition on last Sa and Su in July.

**Minami-za** (561-1155) (II:3). Kaomise all-star Kabuki program in December officially begins the Kabuki season in Japan.

**Gion Corner** (561-1119) (II:3). A professionally executed exhibition of Japanese performing arts designed for tourists. From Mar. 1–Nov. 29, 19:40 and 20:40, daily. Y2500.

# CALENDAR

There are more than 500 annual festivals in Kyoto. Only a selection of major matsuri are listed here. Many of the smaller matsuri are listed in the *Kyoto Monthly Guide*. For New Year, Aoi Matsuri, Gion Matsuri, Daimonji, and Jidai Matsuri, city hotels are booked far in advance.

**21st, each month: Kōbō-san Flea Market.** Tō-ji (I:1). Famous market where one can sift through mountains of junk looking for usable treasures. The market starts in the early hours, and bargaining is *de rigueur*. The year's first and last markets are especially lively.

**25th, each month: Tenjin-san Flea Market.** Kitano Tenman-gū Shrine (IV:1). Similar to the Kōbō-san market. In February, during the plum-blossom season, there's a tea ceremony given by *maiko* (apprentice geisha).

**Jan. 1–3: * Hatsumōde.** Fushimi Inari Shrine (II:1) draws a tremendous crowd for the New Year. Rokuharamitsu-ji (II:2) serves *obuku-cha* (fortune tea) of kelp and pickled plum. At Yasaka Jinja (II:3) are the year's first calligraphy and, on the 3rd, a "year's first card game" by ladies in Heian court robes.

**Jan. 8: * Hadaka Matsuri.** Yōkaichi (VI:5) Ⓔ

**Jan. 8: * Moriyama no Hi-matsuri.** Moriyama (VI:5) Ⓕ

**Jan. 15: * Tōshi-ya.** Sanjūsangen-dō (II:2). Hrs: 8:00–16:00. Famed archery contest in the 118-meter hall.

**Jan. 15: * Suichū Tsunahiki.** Mihama (VI:3) Ⓔ

**Feb. 2–3: * Setsubun.** (See Matsuri, p. 73). Mibu-dera (I:3) puts on Setsubun Kyōgen performances from 13:00, repeated 8 times, on both days. Rokuharamitsu-ji (II:2) has a demon chase and bean-throwing by *maiko* on the afternoon of the 3rd. Yasaka Jinja (II:3) has bean-throwing by *maiko* at 13:00 and 15:00. Yoshida Jinja (II:4) is famous for its demon chase at 19:00 on the 2nd, and a fire festival at 23:00 on the 3rd. Rozan-ji's (I:3) theatrical demon chase has a thousand-year history; from 15:00 on the 3rd.

**Mar. 15: * Sagano Taimatsu.** Seiryō-ji (V:2). Commemorates Shaka's death. From 14:00, performances of Nembutsu Kyōgen (Buddhist miracle plays). At 19:30, three immense torches are set ablaze to divine the coming harvest.

**Mid-Mar.: * Sagichō-sai.** Ōmi-Hachiman (VI:5) Ⓕ Ⓥ

**Apr. 1–30: * Miyako Odori.** Gion Kōbukaburenjo (II:3). Annual dance revue by Gion *maiko* and geisha. Holders of higher-priced tickets may attend a tea ceremony before the show.

**Apr. 12–14: * Sannō Matsuri.** Hiyoshi Taisha (VI:2) Ⓔ Ⓥ

**Apr. 14–15: * Taimatsu Matsuri.** Ōmi-Hachiman (VI:5) Ⓕ Ⓔ

**Apr. 14–16: ** Nagahama Hikiyama Matsuri.** Nagahama (VI:8). On the 14–15th, children perform Kyōgen and Kabuki on beautiful old floats.

**Early Apr.: Cherry Blossoms.** They last about one week. Best viewing: Imperial Palace Park (I:3), Maruyama Park (II:2), Heian Jingū (II:5), Philosopher's Walk (II:5), the Kamogawa in north Kyoto, Arashiyama (V:2), and Daigo-ji (KINKI I:S1).

**Apr. (2nd Su): * Yasurai Matsuri.** Imamiya Jinja (IV:1). A rite against plague, featuring dancers in demon costumes with flaming red hair. Large parasols are paraded through the steets to "collect" disease-causing spirits. The parasols are then taken to the shrine and exorcised. Spectators rush to get under the parasols as a charm against illness.

**Apr. 21–29: ** Mibu Kyōgen.** Mibu-dera (I:3). Hrs: 13:00–17:30. Pantomime Buddhist miracle plays, thought to be a form of Dengaku and Sarugaku folk theater, held every spring for the past 700 years. The plays are dedicated to Jizō Bosatsu, who is enshrined in the back wall of the stage; the gong player faces the image, with his back to the audience. The amateur actors (all male) wear elaborate robes and masks—some quite old—to portray a fantastic array of characters. The two most important plays are *Sai no Kawara*, about the riverbank in Hell where Jizō saves souls, and *Oketori*, the tale of a beautiful girl born with only three fingers on one hand, who draws water at a pond near Mibu Temple as a prayer to Jizō. Here she meets an old man; the two become lovers, but the man's pregnant wife dies of jealousy. The play ends here, but the audience knows the two wrongdoers repent. The young woman's role, one of the most difficult in the repertory, involves walking in a way that forms the Sanskrit character for Jizō. This and the symbolic pail she holds in her three fingers convey the play's message, of Jizō's infinite mercy. At the end of each day, a man twirls a staff to dispel evil spirits. On the final evening, the Yuwaki rite gives felicitous tidings for next spring's Mibu Kyōgen.

**May 1–3: * Senbon Emma-dō Kyōgen.** Senbon Emma-dō (IV:1). 650-year-old Buddhist mystery plays, similar to Mibu Kyōgen.

**May 5: Kurabe Uma.** Kamigamo Jinja (III:1). Horse races begun in 1093.

**May 5: Fujimori Sai.** Fujimori Jinja (south of Fushimi Inari, II:1). Acrobatic stunts performed on galloping horses. At 13:00, 15:00.

**May 15: ** Aoi Matsuri.** This rite originated in the 6th C as a supplication to the kami of Kamigamo Jinja, and took its present form in the Heian period, when imperial messengers were sent to offer the court's respects after a plague was divined to have resulted from neglect of the shrine. Aoi (hollyhock) leaves festooned the participants, in accordance with the god's decree. An imperial princess was chosen as the shrine priestess, and underwent purification rites at Kamigamo Jinja; today, this is reenacted on the first lucky day between May 1 and May 10. The matsuri was revived in 1884, and today consists of a procession of 500 people, horses, and 2 oxcarts carrying "imperial messengers." It leaves from Kyoto Imperial Palace (I:3) at

10:30 and arrives at Shimogamo Jinja (III:1) at 11:40 for a midday rest; Kagura and Kyōgen are offered at the shrine. At 14:00 the procession sets out once more, hugging the bank of the Kamogawa and arriving at Kamigamo Jinja (III:1) at 15:30. Here, there are further rites and horse races offered around 16:30. Best views are along the river and at Kamigamo Jinja.

**May 18: \* Kamigoryō-sai.** Kamigoryō Jinja. A procession starts in the morning from Shimogoryō Jinja on Teramachi-dōri and wends its leisurely way all over town. Costumed courtiers accompany colorful floats and an oxcart in a rite begun in 794 to placate the prince, posthumously made emperor, who was killed at Nagaoka-kyō (see Kyoto History, p. 319). Today, the emperors Go-Yōzei and Go-Mizuno'o are also placated.

**May (3rd Su): Mifune Matsuri.** Arashiyama (V:2). Decorated boats with people dressed as Heian courtiers, musicians, Kyōgen performers, and so on, drift about on the river.

**June 1–2: \* Takigi Noh.** Heian Jingū (II:4). Noh by torchlight in the front court of the shrine. Advance ticket sales.

**June 20: Takekiri-e Shiki.** Kurama-dera (III:4). A thousand years ago, a priest of Kurama defeated two evil serpents with the aid of Bishamon-ten, the Buddhist guardian enshrined at Kurama. In this curious matsuri, 8 priests, dressed in the robes and hoods of *yamabushi*, form two teams, and race to hack to pieces four thick lengths of green bamboo, symbolizing the serpents. The outcome is considered an oracle. From 14:00; the waiting seems interminable — then suddenly it's all over.

**July 14–17: \*\*\* Gion Matsuri.** Yasaka Jinja (II:3). Climax of this matsuri, which begins July 1. The Gion Matsuri began in the 9th C when halberds were carried to Shinsen-en pond south of the Imperial Palace and dipped in as a supplication to end a plague. The famous floats first appeared in the Middle Ages. The lead float is called Naginata-boko (Halberd Float) in reference to the festival's origins; it is the only one that still has a live child as its god. Today, there are 31 great *hoko* and *yama* floats, each built and maintained for centuries by the merchant blocks in central Kyoto (I:2), decorated with fabulous carvings and antique drapery, including Gobelin tapestries imported into Tokugawa Japan through Nagasaki. On the evenings of the 14th–16th, especially the 16th, central Kyoto is jammed with people in *yukata*, out to gaze at the lantern-festooned floats and listen to the music of gongs, drums, and flutes. On the morning of the 17th, the floats are hauled through the main streets, and, immmediately afterward, disassembled. Many shops in the central area are closed on the 17th.

317

**July 1: \* Mitoshiro Noh.** Kamigamo Jinja (III:1). Noh, Kyōgen, and dances are offered for the protection of the rice crop from insects. From 13:00.

**July 1–Aug. 31: Ukai (Cormorant Fishing).** Arashiyama (V:2). Hrs: 19:00–21:00. A seat on a spectator boat costs Y1000. (See Cuisine, p. 116, for background on *ukai*.)

**July 24: Hanagasa Gyōretsu.** Yasaka Jinja (II:3). Post-Gion matsuri festivities. Geisha and traditional troubadors perform.

**Aug. 1: Hassaku.** Gion (II:3). A Gion tradition. *Maiko* visit their teachers and the teahouses dressed in their best.

**Aug. 7–10: Tōki-ichi.** Gojō-dōri (II:2). Huge pottery market.

**Aug. 7–10: \* Rokudō-mairi.** Six Roads (States of Existence) Pilgrimage. As Bon drew near, the people of Kyoto made the rounds of six temples in Rokuhara to ensure the homecoming of souls. This quarter was a dumping ground for corpses — a suitable place to invoke wandering ghosts. Today, of the original six temples, only Rokuharamitsu-ji (II:2), Jizō-in, and Chinnō-ji continue the tradition. On these evenings, their grounds are aglow with lanterns. Incense hangs heavy in the summer night, gongs beat out a steady clang, and streams of people come to pray. Jizō-in is the smallest but the most colorful; its priest happily explains, with the aid of lurid old paintings, the horrors of Hell. At Chinnō-ji, people line up to ring its bell; its sound is guaranteed to reach the ears of the most far-off spirit wanderers. At 20:00 on the 8th–10th, Rokuharamitsu-ji has **Mantō-e**, pictures of a stupa and bodhi leaf formed on the ground by tiny oil lamps.

**Aug. 9–10: \* Rokusai Nembutsu Odori.** Mibu-dera (I:3). Acrobatic dances, lion dances, and pantomime, preserved and performed by various neighborhood amateur groups. Originated as rites to avert danger on "rokusai days," when evil demons are about. In the Heian period, Nembutsu dances, popularized by Kūya Shōnin (see Rokuharamitsu-ji, II:2), introduced a Buddhist element (sharing common origins with Mibu Kyōgen), and eventually the Rokusai Nembutsu became a Bon rite. Also performed later in August at other temples and shrines. Check *Kyoto Monthly Guide*.

**Aug. 13–16: O-Bon.** Many restaurants and shops are closed on these days.

**Aug. 14–16: \* Mantō-e.** Higashi Ōtani-byō Cemetery (II:3). 10,000 candle-lit lanterns welcome home the dead, transforming the cemetery into a magical galaxy of light.

**Aug. 15: \* # Hanase Hi-matsuri.** Hanase (III:4). A thousand torches are planted on an open field around an enormous central torch, or *matsuage*, made from the trunk of a cryptomeria. As a drum and gong sound a slow, mysterious beat, a score of village men light the small torches, which blossom and spread out on the dark field. When they are all ablaze, the men light lengths of twine and hurl them up at the mass of tinder atop the *matsuage*, some 70 feet above them, striving to set it alight before the small torches around them burn out. Success ensures a good harvest.

**Aug. 15–16: Matsugasaki Daimoku Odori.** Yūsen-ji. From 20:00. Staid Bon dance to the chant of *namu myōhō renge-kyō*, begun in the Middle Ages to console the victims of Hiei-zan warrior-monk raids on this Nichiren-sect village. The villagers are responsible for the *Myō Hō* fire of Daimonji.

**Aug. 16:** ✳✳ **Daimonji.** A rite to send off dead souls at the close of Bon (see II:5, Jōdo-in). Five huge figures, two for *dai* (Great), a *Myō Hō* (priest Nichiren's miraculous law), a boat (on which priest Ennin returned safely from China), and torii (for sacred Atago-san, near Arashiyama), are formed by bonfires on the hills surrounding Kyoto. All five fires are visible from Yoshida-yama and Funaoka-yama Park. We advise staking out a spot on these hills or atop a building in the north of the city. The fires are started at 20:00–20:20, and burn for half an hour. Later, there are Bon dances and a lantern-floating at Arashiyama.

**Aug. 16:** ✳ **Miyazu Tōrō-nagashi.** Ama no Hashidate (VI:3). Ⓥ.

**Aug. 23–24:** ✳ **Jizō-bon.** Jizō Bosatsu is the special guardian of children. A stall is set up in each neighborhood, and children gather to play before a stone Jizō. Adashino Nembutsu-ji (V:2) has a famous candle-lighting ceremony in its cemetery; reserve by sending a self-addressed postcard between June 15–July 31 to Adashino Nembutsu-ji, Toriimoto, Saga, Ukyō-ku, Kyoto.

**Aug. 24:** ✳ # **Hirogawara Hi-matsuri.** Hirogawara (III:4). Similar to Hanase Hi-Matsuri on Aug. 15.

**L 8/15:** ✳ **Kangetsu no Yūbe.** Daikaku-ji (V:2). Hrs: 17:00–21:00. The harvest moon, said to be the most beautiful of the year, is celebrated with a moon-viewing party. Dragon boats with dancers and musicians drift about on Ōsawa pond.

**Oct.–Dec.: Tō-ji** (I:1), **Ninna-ji** (IV:2), **Daigo-ji** and **Byōdō-in** (KINKI I:S1), show their treasures in the fall.

**Early Oct.:** ✳✳ **Mibu Kyōgen.** Mibu-dera (I:3). See Apr. 21–29. Popular demand in the Edo period resulted in the addition of autumn performances, consisting of just the most famous plays.

**Oct. 1–5:** ✳ **Zuiki Matsuri.** Kitano Tenman-gū (IV:1). Harvest thanksgiving. On the 4th, from 13:00, an unusual *mikoshi* made of vegetables makes the rounds.

**Oct. 9–10:** ✳ **Ōtsu Matsuri.** Ōtsu (VI:1) Ⓟ Ⓔ.

318 **Oct. 10: Bakuryō-ten.** Daitoku-ji Hōjō (IV:1). Rare chance to see the hall (NT), garden, and famed Muromachi paintings.

**Oct. 10:** ✳ **Ushi (Ox) Matsuri.** Kōryū-ji (V:1). The Tendai priest Ennin (794–864; see Hiraizumi History, p. 169) brought the Indian god Madara to Japan in exchange for a safe return from China. Later, when the priest Genshin (see III:3) visited Kōryū-ji, he had a vision of Madara riding an ox, attended by four *oni* (ogres), who were really the Four Directional Guardians (Shi-Tennō). Today, this scene is reenacted as Madara and the four *oni*, in peculiar paper masks, parade through grounds aglow with lanterns. Then Madara reads a very long *mantra*, with deliberate slowness. Nobody has any idea what it means, but if Madara makes a mistake, he has to read it all over again. The instant he finishes, the five rush into the temple hall, and spectators try to grab their masks. The festival ensures a good harvest.

**Oct. (2nd Su):** ✳ **Nijū-go Bosatsu Oneri Kuyō.** Sokujō-in (a subtemple of Sennyū-ji, II:1). Twenty-five children dressed as bosatsu enact Amida's descent to welcome souls into Paradise.

**Oct. 15–Nov. 11: Kamogawa Odori.** Pontochō Kaburenjō (I:2). Fall dance performance by the *maiko* and geisha of Pontochō.

**Oct. 22:** ✳ **Jidai Matsuri.** See also (II:4). Festival of the Ages, a procession of 2,000 people dressed in historical costume; from the Imperial Palace to Heian Shrine.

**Oct. 22:** ✳✳✳ **Kurama Hi-matsuri.** Kurama (III:4). Spectacular. Loin-clothed youths carry huge torches through the village in a rite said to have originated in a ceremony which brought the god of Yuki Jinja to Kurama. It now has the mood of a harvest festival and rite of passage. Long lines form at Demachi-Yanagi station on this night, but it's worth the wait and jam-packed train (cars and taxis are not allowed). To avoid the crowded return train, walk down the slope of the village, seeing the festival's quieter celebrations; continue for a few hundred meters to where taxis will be waiting.

**Nov.–early Dec.: Autumn Foliage.** Famous viewing spots: Tōfuku-ji (II:1), Shūgaku-in Imperial Villa (III:1), Ōhara (III:3), Takao (V:3), Sagano (V:2), Saihō-ji (V:4).

**Nov. 1–8: Special Exhibit.** A dozen temples show art and buildings normally not on view. The temples change every year, but usually several important ones are included.

**Nov. (2nd Su): Momiji Matsuri.** Arashiyama (V:2). Boat procession celebrating the autumn foliage. From 10:30.

**Dec. 1: Kencha-sai.** Kitano Tenman-gū (IV:1). Hrs: 10:00–15:00. Reenacts Hideyoshi's famous giant tea ceremony gathering.

**Dec. 1–26:** ✳ **Kaomise.** Minami-za theater (II:3). Kaomise literally means "face-showing"; the biggest names in Kabuki show up to do scenes from favorite plays. Opens the Kabuki season.

**Dec. 31:** ✳✳ **Okera Mairi.** Yasaka Jinja (II:3). People gather at this shrine to light a length of rope at a ritually pure fire; traditionally, the flame was taken home to light the New Year hearth fires. The ropes are twirled gaily to keep the flame burning. Immense crowds, with many people in their best kimono, fill Shijō-dōri, and geisha make the rounds to the Gion teahouses. Starting at midnight is *joya-no-kane*, 108 peals of temple bells to expiate the 108 "errors" of mankind: at Chion-in (II:3); also Kiyomizu-dera, Daitoku-ji, Tō-ji, Myōshin-ji, and Shinnyō-dō. Heian Jingū (II:4) has a Noh performance just after midnight.

# Kyoto History

## 1. A NEW CAPITAL AND A NEW BUDDHISM (784–894)

**Emperor Kammu** (767-806) Founder of Heian-kyō. Kammu became emperor through the influence of his father-in-law, a Fujiwara minister, for he had originally been passed over for the succession because of his mother's Korean commoner ancestry.

**Saichō** (767-822) Posthumously known as Dengyō Daishi. Founder of the Tendai sect of Buddhism and its headquarters at Enryaku-ji, on Hiei-zan.

**Kūkai** (774-835) Posthumously known as Kōbō Daishi. Founder of the Shingon sect of Buddhism and its headquarters temples Tō-ji, in Kyoto, and Kongōbu- ji, on Kōya-san. A great cultural hero.

In 794, **Emperor Kammu** officially inaugurated Heian-kyō, the Capital of Peace and Tranquility—a hopeful name, for the previous ten years had been anything but peaceful or tranquil. First, Nara had to be abandoned because the temples had become powerful enough to pose a direct threat to imperial authority. One priest, Dōkyō, had even attempted to usurp the throne (see Nara History, p. 392). A new capital was built at Nagaoka, a few miles west of Kyoto, but foul deeds and bad omens clouded the project. The Fujiwara official in charge was murdered and an imperial prince was blamed, exiled, and then secretly strangled. Shortly after, members of the court began dying of mysterious illnesses caused, the diviners said, by the prince's angry ghost. The troubles stopped after the ghost was promoted to emperor, but the haunted capital was abandoned and the court moved once again, this time to Heian-kyō. It was this city, so auspiciously named, that was destined to remain the imperial capital of Japan for more than a millennium.

Heian-kyō was modeled on Chang-an, the great capital of the Tang empire, and built on a site that fulfilled Chinese geomantic requirements: Mountains surround it to the north, east, and west, and two crystalline rivers, flowing north to south, bound it on east and west. Kyoto's streets were laid out in a grid. The original central avenue, the eighty-two-meter-wide Suzaku-ōji, lay where Senbon-dōri is today. At the south end, the entrance to the city was the gate called Rajō-mon (known in literature and cinema as Rashō-mon). At the northern end, approximately where Nijō-jō is today, stood the Imperial Palace. All that remains of it is the small pond of **Shinsen-en** garden. To avoid a replay of the Nara debacle, only two temples, the West Temple and the East Temple (Tō-ji), flanking the central avenue, were allowed to stand within the city itself. All the others had to be built outside the city limits.

Buddhism so permeated palace ceremonies, however, that its influence was nearly impossible to restrict. What was needed was a Buddhism free of the Nara taint. Just at this time, like a heaven-sent solution to the imperial court's quandary, two new types of Buddhism entered Japan. Tendai (T'ien-t'ai) and *mikkyō* (Esoteric Buddhism) were then prominent in Tang China, and intimations of their complex philosophies had begun to reach Japan in snippets of sutras and strange icons— multi-armed deities and mandala charts—that hinted at deep mysteries. Dismayed by the decadence and corruption of Nara Buddhism, two young monks, **Saichō** and Kūkai, joined a trading mission to China in 804 in hopes of bringing these teachings back to Japan.

Saichō spent his year abroad in south China, on Mt. T'ien-t'ai, headquarters of the sect, where he picked up an eclectic mix of teachings, including the Lotus Sutra, meditation, and bits of Esoteric ritual. When he returned to Japan in 805, he founded the Tendai sect atop **Hiei-zan**, a mountain northeast of Kyoto, where he had established a monastic community in his younger days. Tendai was embraced by the court, and its importance to the new city was given weight by its headquarters on the sacred mountain, guardian against the evil influences from the northeast, the most unlucky direction according to Chinese geomancy. However, though the court had broken with Nara, priests were still ordained there, a fact that did not suit Saichō at all. He petitioned for recognition as an independent institution. He was denied this, however, and it was only after his death that the court hastened to honor him and raised the temple on Hiei-zan to official status, giving it a new name, **Enryaku-ji**. This was the first schism in Japanese Buddhism. Ironically, Tendai itself became torn by schisms as later religious leaders seized on the various parts of the sect's eclectic teachings. Thus, Tendai gave rise to almost every other sect of Japanese Buddhism. An exception was Shingon, the sect introduced to Japan by Saichō's fellow seeker Kūkai.

Kūkai journeyed directly to the Tang capital of Ch'ang-an, then the most cosmopolitan city in the world. He was after the secrets of *mikkyō*, or Esoteric Buddhism, a complex and vast teaching developed by Indian sages, and so he sought out the priests who had translated *mikkyō* sutras from Sanskrit into Chinese. While Saichō had pursued an eclectic study, Kūkai devoted two years to becoming a master of *mikkyō*. He learned to read Sanskrit, which, it is said, inspired him to invent the *kana* syllabary for Japanese. He returned to Kyoto and founded the Shingon (Mantra) sect. For a time, he resided quietly at **Jingo-ji**, in the western hills of Kyoto. After Saichō's death, Kūkai came to prominence: No other priest possessed his genius or his complete mastery of *mikkyō* ritual, which no doubt endeared him to the ritual-loving court. In 823 Emperor Saga presented him with **Tō-ji**, the East Temple, where today a visitor can see the "state-protecting" mandala of statues supposedly carved and arranged by Kūkai himself. Kūkai was a cultural giant who gave Japan its own script, compiled its first dictionary, founded schools and seminaries, and undertook pilgrimages and public-works projects.

The life of the Heian court revolved around rituals. In addition to the Buddhist ceremonies, there were Shinto rites to propitiate the numerous kami of the Kyoto area. **Fushimi Inari Taisha**, south of Kyoto, sacred to the rice god, was a shrine of the first importance. It predates the city, and was the tutelary shrine of the Hata, an extremely influential Korean family that owned much of the land around Kyoto. In the seventh century the family built one of Kyoto's oldest temples, **Kōryū-ji**, to enshrine an image given by SHŌTOKU TAISHI. Kūkai diplomatically made Fushimi Inari the guardian shrine of Tō-ji. The **Kamo Shrines** were dedicated to the clan deities of the Kamo, another important immigrant family, which also gave its name to Kyoto's Kamo River. One of the most important festivals in Kyoto is the Aoi Matsuri, which took its present form in the ninth century as an imperial procession to appease the Kamo god who, angered by lack of attention, had caused a devastating storm. This was one of the first of the many annual observances for which Kyoto is famous.

As if numerous festivals weren't enough to keep them occupied, the Heian nobles were also obliged to observe all sorts of Shinto taboos. Many features of the palace were designed to ensure the ritual purity of its precious occupant, the emperor. The exquisite quarters of the empress and the imperial concubines were kept separate not so much to discourage amorous swains (who, judging by *The Tale of Genji*, had ample access to court ladies), as to ensure that the "unclean" activities of menstruation and parturition would not sully his majesty's enclosure. Because death was also unclean, an aging emperor could spare the court the trouble of elaborate purification rituals if he passed away somewhere else. Many Esoteric Buddhist temples on Kyoto's outskirts, such as **Ninna-ji** and **Daikaku-ji**, were originally the villas of emperors who had retired and become priests. Besides the complex dictates of Shinto and Buddhism, the court consulted Confucian moralists, Taoist astrologers, geomancers, and shamans. Immutable laws governed when members of the court could wash, cut their nails, travel, or leave their houses. To violate these taboos, as daily necessity forced the wretched commoners to do, was to invite disaster.

The reign of Kammu was the apogee of imperial power. Succeeding emperors, ensnared by webs of taboo and protocol, became ineffectual, and power migrated into the hands of their FUJIWARA ministers. The work of Kammu's time endured, however. The court at last had a secure home, and an eclectic mix of new faiths and new ceremonies filled the cultural vacuum left by the abandonment of Nara. In 894, exactly a hundred years after the city's founding, court minister Sugawara no Michizane put an end to official missions to China. Heian-kyō, presided over by the now all-powerful Fujiwara, was poised for a great cultural synthesis that was to produce one of the most peculiar and refined societies in the world (see Uji History, p. 387), but that also led to effeteness and decline, until warrior clans wrested power from the court late in the twelfth century (see Miyajima History, p. 449).

## 2. THE GOLD AND SILVER PAVILIONS (1334–1573)

**Musō Soseki** (1275–1351) Famous Zen prelate and garden designer. Advisor to Ashikaga Takauji.

**Yoshimitsu** (1358–1408) The strong third Ashikaga shogun, builder of the Golden Pavilion.

**Yoshimasa** (1436–1490) The eighth Ashikaga shogun, given entirely to esthetic pursuits at his Silver Pavilion.

In 1338, ASHIKAGA TAKAUJI, a talented general descended from the MINAMOTO, was named Shogun by the emperor whom he had helped put on the throne. To reach this pinnacle in his career, Takauji had twice betrayed his lords, first rallying to the cause of **Emperor Go-Daigo** against the Hōjō regents in Kamakura, and then turning against Go-Daigo when it became clear he could do better for himself than by relying on the largesse of the imperial court (see Yoshino History, p. 411). For this, Takauji is reviled as the greatest turncoat in Japanese history. To his credit, however, Takauji was a gifted politician in an age of petty squabblers, and though he failed in his lifetime to establish full control over Japan, he found time to foster cultural developments of profound importance. In this respect, he set the tone for the 200-year dynasty of Ashikaga shoguns who presided over warfare and calamity in the political arena, while nurturing a great artistic flowering.

Takauji's spiritual advisor was MUSŌ SOSEKI, the most eminent Zen priest of his time, who transformed the Rinzai Zen sect into a more diversified community that merged Zen with esthetic pursuits. Musō must have been either irreproachably holy or an adroit opportunist, for he first came to Kyoto at Go-Daigo's invitation to head the **Nanzen-ji** monastery, then stayed on to serve Takauji. Musō's great innovation was to consider gardens an aid to meditation, a revolutionary idea from which evolved the Zen rock garden. Two Kyoto gardens attributed to Musō are **Saihō-ji**'s famed Moss Garden and the garden of **Tenryū-ji**, which he advised Takauji to build at Go-Daigo's childhood villa to appease the deposed monarch's angry spirit. Musō persuaded the shogunate to fund the project by resuming trade with China under the direction of the Zen temples, whose priests could manage the language and had many contacts in China. This trade had a number of far-reaching consequences: It made the Zen temples very rich, and it introduced a stream of fresh cultural influences. Against the high standards of Chinese art, esthetic sensibilities were honed as they had not been since the Heian period.

Takauji and his son Yoshiakira were too busy fighting wars to engage much in the arts, but his grandson YOSHIMITSU, a strong ruler, decided it was time to enjoy the full fruits of victory. Takauji had paid the court nobility outward respect, but now Yoshimitsu set out to put them in their place. He built the shogunal headquarters in the Muromachi district (which lent its name to the period of Ashikaga rule), to the *north* — that is, "above" the Imperial Palace, an unprecedented statement of superiority to the emperor. Nearby he built **Shōkoku-ji**, granted it a monopoly on the China trade, and established there an academy of Chinese-style ink painting, from which later emerged nearly all of Japan's great painters, including SESSHŪ and the masters of the KANŌ SCHOOL.

Having quashed all remaining resistance to Ashikaga rule, Yoshimitsu abdicated in favor of his nine-year-old son, though of course he remained firmly in power, and built himself a lavish retirement villa, the famed **Golden Pavilion** (Kinkaku-ji). There he continued to support the arts, especially the Noh (see IV:2). Noh's chief exponent, the genius ZEAMI, a mere actor who became an intimate of the shogun, had many jealous enemies. After Yoshimitsu's death, he fell out of favor and eventually was exiled to Sado Island for ten years, where he left a living legacy of Noh.

The strong reign of Yoshimitsu was followed by a brief period of stability, but by the time of the sixth shogun, Ashikaga hegemony was crumbling. The seventh shogun, a young boy, died after two years and was succeeded by a younger brother, YOSHIMASA, then thirteen. Yoshimasa showed no acumen at all for governing. Instead, he tried to relive the halcyon days of his grandfather Yoshimitsu's Golden Pavilion and devoted his energies to resurrecting it. He built the **Silver Pavilion** (Ginkaku-ji), which was never actually covered in silver. Though elegant, Ginkaku-ji reeks of Zen restraint. Historian George Sansom denounced the Silver Pavilion as "an insipid structure that belies its name." Few today would agree with this assessment of the place that gave birth to the culture of the tea ceremony — its esthetic of restraint, its architecture, and its tradition of connoisseurship. The tastes of Yoshimasa's coterie were guided by three professional connoisseurs, Nōami, Geiami, and Sōami, who were trained in Chinese ink painting, but whose duties extended to such tasks as choosing the proper utensils for a moonlit tea ceremony. It was through their support that the Kanō School gained prominence and became the official painting academy, a position that it held for 400 years and that made its paintings ubiquitous in Kyoto.

Yoshimasa is considered a Japanese Nero who sat sipping tea at his exquisite villa while Kyoto's streets piled high with the corpses of victims of famine and war. Utterly uninterested in civil government, he left affairs of state to his ambitious wife, Hino Tomiko, and two families of hereditary vassals, the **Hosokawa** and the Yamana, who let the shogunate's economic base deteriorate (see Castles, p. 49). Debt amnesties were promulgated thirteen times during Yoshimasa's rule alone. Yoshimasa named his brother as his successor, then reneged when a son of his own was born. A succession quarrel ensued, the Yamana backing the child and the Hosokawa backing the brother. Their armies fought desultorily for eleven years, from 1467 to 1477, destroying nearly all of Kyoto's temples and villas in the process.

The **Ōnin War**, as this conflict was called, ended inconclusively. The Ashikaga grew steadily weaker, and soon after, new fighting broke out all over Japan. This was the beginning of the Sengoku Jidai (Period of the Country at War). In the disorder, Kyoto changed hands several times. Its aristocrats fled to the port town of Sakai, south of Ōsaka, and the castle-town of Yamaguchi (Chūgoku, p. 457), taking their culture with them. The emperors, who remained in Kyoto, went through lean times.

One emperor had to wait twenty years to be enthroned; another eked out a living by selling his calligraphy; a third lay unburied for six weeks after his death. The imperial court lived in ramshackle huts and subsisted on gruel. When the Jesuit priest Francis Xavier came to Kyoto seeking to convert the emperor to Christianity, he couldn't find the monarch and eventually returned to Yamaguchi in disgust.

Xavier's arrival, in 1549, marked the beginning of Japan's Christian Century, when Nagasaki, the port the Portuguese favored, became an important conduit for new cultural influences (see Nagasaki History, p. 483). After ODA NOBUNAGA marched into the imperial city in 1568, however, Kyoto returned to the center of the national stage.

## 3. NOBUNAGA AND HIDEYOSHI: THE GLITTERING MOMOYAMA PERIOD (1573–1615)

**Oda Nobunaga**  (1534–1582) The ruthless warlord who unified central Japan, paving the way for his successors. He is unfondly remembered for the destruction he wrought.

**Toyotomi Hideyoshi**  (1536–1598) Nobunaga's more politic successor, capricious but loved for his extravagance and generosity. He reunified Japan and rebuilt much of what Nobunaga had destroyed.

It was June 21, 1582. ODA NOBUNAGA was quartered, as was his habit, at Honnō-ji, a temple in central Kyoto. That morning he was entertaining courtiers, showing them his prized tea utensils. He had every reason to be content, holding, as he did, the greater part of central Japan, to which he had brought a sort of peace after a century of warfare. Just a few days earlier, he had dispatched Akechi Mitsuhide to the aid of his top lieutenant, TOYOTOMI HIDEYOSHI, who was fighting in western Japan against one of the last strongholds of resistance. In Kyoto there was talk that Nobunaga had been offered the title of Shogun, and more than a few observers must have wondered whether this fiercely independent warrior would accept.

Nobunaga's climb to power had not been easy; it had been achieved as much by sheer stubbornness and cruelty as by courage and military brilliance. Nobunaga's father, the de facto daimyo of Owari province, died in 1551, leaving his seventeen-year-old son to cope with internal dissension and hostile neighboring clans. Nobunaga, however, proved no easy prey. He quickly crushed a rival branch of the family. Hearing that his own brother was planning a revolt, Nobunaga feigned illness and lured him to the sickroom, where he was put to death. A greater danger came from the neighboring Imagawa clan, which was preparing to attack with a large army. Nobunaga gathered a band of low-ranking horsemen and footsoldiers to defend his territory. His advisers counseled caution, but Nobunaga, knowing a bold stroke was the only way to offset his disadvantage in numbers, launched a surprise attack and routed the Imagawa.

By 1568, Nobunaga had won several key battles. He next advanced on Kyoto, bringing with him the puppet shogun Ashikaga Yoshiaki. Yoshiaki tried to reward Nobunaga by making him vice-shogun, but Nobunaga refused. He would not be any man's servant. Nobunaga also knew he could not rest on empty honors so long as he had enemies in Japan. Once, when Yoshiaki put on an all-day Noh entertainment for him, Nobunaga walked out in a huff after the fifth act, complaining that Japan was not yet at peace and that he had work to do.

Nobunaga's ambition made him unusually open-minded about who might serve him. He befriended Hideyoshi, a common footsoldier of unusual abilities, raising him to the rank of daimyo. Nobunaga was also quick to exploit Western firearms, which had first arrived in Japan in 1542. In a famous 1575 battle with the powerful warlord Takeda Katsuyori, Nobunaga stationed his artillery behind wooden palisades and gunned down the attacking cavalry, inflicting heavy losses on the enemy while sustaining few casualties among his own men. Delighted by these Western innovations, he was quite hospitable to the Portuguese missionaries who were visiting Japan. A Jesuit named Luis Frois was invited to Kyoto, and Nobunaga seems to have enjoyed conversations with him. Nobunaga no doubt also enjoyed seeing the consternation this wrought among the Buddhist sects, most of which he heartily despised.

Indeed, of all the cruel acts that blemished his career, Nobunaga is especially remembered for the wanton destruction of temples and massacres of monks (who, often as not, were armed thugs). When the warrior-monks of Hiei-zan, themselves frequent terrorizers of Kyoto, gave quarter to his foes in 1571, Nobunaga put the great monastery to the torch and allowed no monk, woman, or child to escape the flames. His most tenacious enemy was the **Ikkō**, or Single-Minded, sect. When the monks of

Hiei burned down the sect's Kyoto headquarters in 1465, its leaders had taken their cause to the countryside. By the sixteenth century, the Ikkō sect had established numerous autonomous and well-armed religious domains, ruled by Ishiyama Hongan-ji in Ōsaka and commanding widespread support among the peasantry. The Ikkō followers had their own gunsmiths and a penchant for allying themselves with anti-Nobunaga lords. One by one, Nobunaga exterminated the Ikkō communities, massacring tens of thousands of peasants, but it took him until 1580 to finally control the sect (see Higashi and Nishi Hongan-ji, I:1).

During his final years, Nobunaga built Azuchi-jō on Lake Biwa, a fortress of unprecedented magnificence and scale (see Castles, p. 46). Nobunaga's position was still threatened by the Uesugi to the north and the Mōri to the west, but he felt secure enough to visit Kyoto in the early summer of 1582, entrusting the campaign against the Mōri to Hideyoshi. Hideyoshi was laying siege to the fortress at Bitchū-Takahashi (Chugoku, p. 440) and needed reinforcements, which Nobunaga sent under his trusted lieutenant Akechi Mitsuhide. It was a fatal error; that morning Mitsuhide, who perhaps nursed a grudge against Nobunaga or simply saw his chance to usurp power, turned his troops around, surrounded Honnō-ji, and set it to the torch. Nobunaga, seeing that all was lost, retreated to an inner chamber and there disemboweled himself.

Mitsuhide held Kyoto for thirteen days, until Hideyoshi sped back to Kyoto to defeat and execute him. With equal swiftness and decisiveness, Hideyoshi proceeded to complete the reunification of Japan. In 1585, the emperor rewarded Hideyoshi by naming him *Kampaku*, or Regent, an astoundingly high rank for the son of a common footsoldier. This was but the least of the amazing feats of this little monkey-faced man, whom historians have compared to Alexander and Napoleon.

Hideyoshi was generous and cunning, where Nobunaga had been cruel and impolitic. He rewarded loyal generals with fiefs, strategically placed to keep watch over less-trusted lords. Hideyoshi's famous Sword Hunt is also typical of the man: he confiscated swords from the peasantry and temples, claiming that the iron was needed to build a colossal Buddha in Kyoto, but his true intention was to permanently disarm the nonwarrior classes. Furthermore, Hideyoshi established a fixed social hierarchy, ensuring — ironically — that he would be the first and last ruler of premodern Japan to come from humble origins.

Just as he rebuilt the body politic of Japan, Hideyoshi reconstructed Kyoto, devastated by more than a century of war. Temples burned by Nobunaga were rebuilt, including that stronghold of the Ikkō sect, the great Hongan-ji, which later split into East and West. **Nishi Hongan-ji** has a Noh stage and the Hiunkaku Pavilion, both supposedly once part of the Juraku-tei, a luxurious palace Hideyoshi built in 1588. The Hideyoshi years are remembered for their extravagance and good times. A devotee of the tea ceremony, Hideyoshi was close to SEN NO RIKYŪ, Japan's most famous tea master, and had a portable tea arbor made of solid gold to take with him on his campaigns. In October 1587, Hideyoshi celebrated a military victory with a huge tea party at Kyoto's **Kitano Tenjin Shrine**, which was open to the entire populace of Kyoto, regardless of social station (see IV:1). The 1590 siege of Odawara was something of a carnival, and even the wives and concubines of the warriors were sent for. In his final year, he held a lavish cherry-blossom party at **Daigo-ji** (Kinki, p. 382); the subtemple, Sambō-in, was rebuilt and given a new garden, said to have been designed by Hideyoshi himself and made of fine rocks commandeered by the hundreds from other lords.

But in 1591, a dark cloud passed over Hideyoshi's life. His only son, the two-year-old Tsurumatsu, died, and Hideyoshi became despondent and megalomaniacal. He named his nephew Hidetsugu his heir, and gave him Juraku-tei. He himself moved to the fortified, luxurious **Fushimi-jō** south of Kyoto. Then, in 1593, a son, HIDE-YORI, was born to Hideyoshi's favorite concubine, Yodogimi. Hidetsugu was disowned, confined to Mt. Kōya, and eventually forced to commit suicide by the increasingly unstable Hideyoshi. In 1592 and 1597, Hideyoshi sent troops to attack Korea, with the ultimate goal of conquering China. Vast sums were spent, but the Japanese ultimately failed.

Hideyoshi died in 1598, when his son was only five. He entrusted Hideyori to a council of five elders, but in 1600, one of them, TOKUGAWA IEYASU, usurped power and defeated his rivals in the Battle of Sekigahara. In 1603, Ieyasu received the title of Shogun at **Nijō-jō** (see I:2). Hideyori was allowed to retain Ōsaka-jō, the great fortress built by Hideyoshi, until 1615, when the Tokugawa laid siege to the castle, forcing Hideyori and Yodogimi to commit suicide. Two and a half centuries of Tokugawa rule were to follow (see Nikkō History, p. 242). Power shifted to Edo, the Tokugawa castle town. Kyoto was never to regain the political center stage.

# KYOTO I. CENTRAL KYOTO

**Main Attractions:**

I:1 **\*\*\*** Tō-ji
I:1 **\*\*** Nishi-Hongan-ji
I:2 **\*\*\*** Pontochō (geisha quarter)
I:3 **\*\*\*** Nijō-jō
I:3 **\*\*** Nijō Jinya (inn for officials)
I:3 **\*\*** Kyoto Gosho (Imperial Palace)

**See p. 368–369 and 371–372 for restaurants, p. 372–375 for hotels**

324

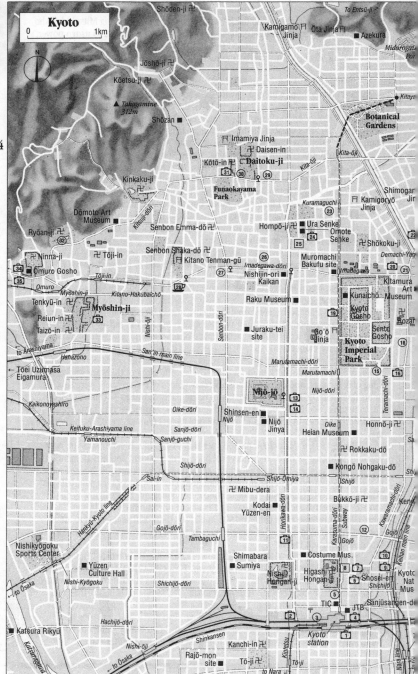

## I:1 STATION AREA

This gritty, unattractive area has long been out of step with the northern parts of the city; viewers of Kurosawa's movie *Rashomon*, which takes place a little west of Kyoto Station, will recall that in the late Heian period, the area had decayed into a semiwilderness inhabited by vagabonds. Three important institutions were, for one reason or another, exiled to this undesirable neighborhood. Tō-ji, founded at a time when temples were viewed with respectful suspicion, was one of only two temples grudgingly allowed within the city limits; today it is famous for its art treasures. Nishi Hongan-ji, which had been burned and chased out of Higashiyama in the previous century, was rebuilt here in 1591 because this was the only available land. The third outcast was Shimabara, the Edo-period licensed quarter, which was moved south to its present location in order to keep its wild courtesans and even wilder customers away from the center of the city.

---

**Tour 1:** Station (0:05h by taxi or bus, or 0:15h on foot) — *** Tō-ji

**Tour 2:** Station (0:05h on foot) — Higashi Hongan-ji — (0:15h on foot) — ** Nishi Hongan-ji — (0:10h on foot) — Shimabara

**Lunch:** Izusen, Manshige Porta-ten

**Notes:** Tō-ji flea market on the 21st of each month. Many shops for Buddhist implements and incense are near Hongan-ji.

---

*** **Tō-ji** 東寺 Hrs: 9:00–16:30 daily. *Brief taxi ride from Kyoto station, or take bus 17, or 0:15h on foot.* This great temple has imposing halls, serene grounds, history, and art treasures, yet because of its wrong-side-of-the-tracks location, most tourists ignore it. Tō-ji was founded in 794 as a guardian temple for Kyoto and in 823 became a theological university under KŪKAI (KŌBŌ DAISHI), founder of the Shingon sect. On the 21st of each month, a lively **flea market** is held around the temple grounds in his honor.

325

A distant cousin of Tibetan Buddhism, Shingon is the most exotic of the Japanese Buddhist sects; it draws on incantations, rituals, and a diverse pantheon of fierce-looking gods in the quest for enlightenment (see Buddhism, p. 36). Among the important tools of the sect is the mandala, a diagram depicting the universe as a kaleidoscope of Buddhist deities, centered around the cosmic Buddha, Dainichi Nyorai. In Tō-ji's lecture hall, one can see a mandala rendered in sculpture — 21 images, their gilt still glinting dimly, creating an awesome vision of the Shingon universe. Visitors are admitted via a gate at the north end of the wire-fenced enclosure.

◆ **Kōdō** 講堂 (1491, ICP). Lecture Hall housing the famous sculpture mandala devised by Kūkai for the protection of the new capital. The images (NT and ICP) are popularly believed to have been carved by his own hand in the early 9th C. There are three main groups of five images apiece: The central group is the Five Nyorai, with the cosmic Buddha, Dainichi at the center. On the right are their manifestations as Five Bosatsu, gentle-faced figures wearing crowns, symbolic of wisdom. On the left are their manifestations as Five Myō-ō, fearsome gods who destroy illusion; at its center sits Fudō Myō-ō, or O-Fudō-san, as he is popularly called, a much-venerated deity in Shingon temples throughout Japan. Tō-ji's is the oldest Fudō image in Japan. In addition, four scowling directional guardian kings stand in the corners and Bon-ten (Brahma) and Taishaku-ten (Indra), sit at the ends of the dais. The Bon-ten is an exquisite, multiheaded image of gentle countenances and voluptuous arms, seated upon a lotus supported by four geese.

**Kondō** 金堂 (1606, NT). A magnificent structure with a high ceiling supported by a system of tall columns and extensive bracketing, a rare example of the Daibutsu style of construction (see Buddhism, p. 38). Houses a Momoyama-period Yakushi trinity.

◆ **Pagoda** (1643, NT). This five-tiered pagoda, visible from trains pulling into Kyoto, is a symbol of the city. From a distance it is a picture of grace, but up close it is immense, towering almost 200 feet (making it the tallest pagoda in Japan). The present one, built by TOKUGAWA IEMITSU, is the sixth to stand here.

◆ **Hōmotsukan (Treasure Museum)** 宝物館 Hrs: spring and autumn 9:00–16:30. NW corner of the precinct. Objects from Tō-ji's impressive collection are on view for two months in spring and again in autumn. Tobatsu Bishamon-ten (NT), on 1F, is a 2-meter-tall wooden image of a guardian king, said to be from Tang China. He stands on a female "earth goddess," an iconographic form of Central Asian origin. On 2F are Edo-period copies of Tō-ji's celebrated Two Worlds Mandala (see Buddhism, p. 36).

◆ **Kanchi-in** 観智院 Hrs: 9:00–17:00, clsd on Wed. Y900 fee includes tea. A hidden gem, this is a fine example of the Shoin style as found in Esoteric temples (see Villas, p. 63). The Kyaku-den (1605, NT) is decorated with indistinct wall paintings of hawks and bamboo attributed to Miyamoto Musashi, the semilegendary swordsman and painter who supposedly hid in Kanchi-in for three years after felling a rival in a duel. An adjacent wing houses five rare Tang Chinese Kokuzō Bosatsu (ICP) seated on the lion, elephant, horse, garuda, and peacock, which are also commonly seen in Tibetan temples. The lovely *chaseki* (tearoom), entered through a simple garden, is intimate and subtly luxurious. It offers a superb setting for enjoying a bowl of *matcha*.

## The Hongan-ji Temples

Hongan-ji began as a chapel to Shinran, founder of the Jōdo Shin sect, built in 1272 at Ōtani (in Higashiyama) by his daughter (see Buddhism, p. 38). Opposed by rival Jōdo Shin temples, it grew slowly until the 15th C, when it acquired a charismatic abbot, **Rennyo**, who advanced the popularity and power of the sect so dramatically that in 1465, Tendai warrior-monks from Hiei-zan destroyed the Ōtani temple. Rennyo escaped to the Japan Sea coast, around Kanazawa, where his more fanatic followers seized regional power with the support of an armed peasantry (see Chūbu, p. 296). The militants built an immense headquarters in Ōsaka, the Ishiyama Hongan-ji, from which ruled pontiffs more powerful than many a warlord; even ODA NOBUNAGA was unable to vanquish them. Only after the head priest negotiated a surrender— the event which eventually led to the schism, dividing Hongan-ji into East and West—were the Ishiyama headquarters burned.

In 1591, HIDEYOSHI built a new sect headquarters at the present Nishi Hongan-ji, but in 1602, the brother of its abbot, who had dissented in the Ishiyama surrender, founded his own temple, the Higashi Hongan-ji, a few blocks east. It was built on land granted by the new shogun, TOKUGAWA IEYASU, who encouraged the schism to ensure against an overly powerful temple. The two temples head separate sects, but with their common origin, they look nearly identical. Each has a huge main hall, dedicated to Shinran and built to hold thousands of worshippers, and a smaller adjacent hall, dedicated to Amida, the Buddha worshipped by all Jōdo sects. Nishi Hongan-ji is renowned for its Momoyama art treasures.

✳ **Higashi Hongan-ji** 東本願寺 *0:05h on foot N of the station.* The huge Main Gate of this temple, facing Karasuma-dōri, is the first impression of the "real Kyoto" most visitors see as they drive into the center of town. The temple shows no important art treasures, but one noteworthy curiosity is the great coil of rope woven from the hair of women believers, donated to haul timbers for the 1895 rebuilding of the Great Hall.

**Kikokutei Garden (Shosei-en)** 渉成園 Hrs: 9:00–16:00 (entry by 15:30), when not in use for temple functions; inquire at the office, to the right of the temple gate. *0:05h on foot east of the temple.* TOKUGAWA IEMITSU granted this estate to the abbot of Higashi Hongan-ji. The large pond garden, now peaceful and neglected, is attributed to two famous Edo-period garden designers, Ishikawa Jōzan and KOBORI ENSHŪ.

✳✳ **Nishi Hongan-ji** 西本願寺 *0:05h by taxi or subway, or 0:10h on foot, from Kyoto station.* Tours of the Shoin M–F 10:00, 11:00, 13:30, 14:30; Sa 10:00 and 11:00. Apply (a few days in advance, if possible) at the Sampai-bu, to the left of the main hall. This temple owns some outstanding buildings of the Momoyama period, of which the ornate Shiro Shoin reception hall, two Noh stages, and Kara-mon can be easily seen. The breathtaking Hiunkaku Pavilion and Kuro Shoin are not shown to the general public. Because of HIDEYOSHI's patronage of the temple, the Noh stages, Hiunkaku, and Kara-mon are thought to have come from his Fushimi Castle.

◆ **Shoin** 書院 (NT). This building, the largest extant in Shoin style, consists of a group of rooms lavishly decorated with gilt, paintings, carved transoms, and exquisite metal fittings. On the way in, you will pass the Kokei no Niwa, a garden of sand and boulders set against cycad palms. The huge audience hall, Taimenjo, was gorgeously painted by Hasegawa Tōhaku with various subjects: cranes and flowers for the lower level, and Chinese themes for the raised level occupied by the most important personages. Behind (north) of the Taimenjo are the rooms of the Shiro Shoin, classic examples of the Shoin style: the raised section called Shimei no Ma, shows the standard arrangement of *tsukeshoin* (desk), staggered shelves, *chōdaigamae* (decorative doors), and *tokonoma* alcove (see Villas, p. 64). It is decorated with landscapes by, among others, the Hasegawa School. The Gan no Ma (Goose Room) has a carved transom of flying geese which, viewed from a certain angle, appear to fly against a silver moon.

◆ **Northern Noh Stage** (1581, NT). Thought to be the oldest Noh stage in existence. The ground around the stage is covered with cobblestones, said to enhance acoustics.

**Kuro Shoin (Black Study**, NT, not shown). A celebrated example of Sukiya-Shoin style, the Black Study is exquisitely subtle, decorated with ink landscapes and somber, natural woods, in contrast to the opulent public rooms of the Shiro Shoin.

**Hiunkaku (Flying Cloud Pavilion**, NT, not shown). Together with the Silver and Gold pavilions, this is counted among the three famous pavilions of Japan. It is delightfully irregular, with several roof styles combined at different levels. An opening in the floor allows visitors to enter by boat from the pond.

◆ **Kara-mon** (NT). "Chinese Gate" in the south wall of the precincts. A famous example of Momoyama ornateness.

**Costume Museum (Fūzoku Hakubutsukan)** 風俗博物館 (351-6750). Hrs: 9:00–17:00; clsd Su, June 1–14, Dec. 16–Jan 6. NE of Nishi Hongan-ji, Izutsu Bldg., 5F (sign in English). The mannequin displays are corny, but the costumes, from various historical periods of Japan and China, are quite interesting.

**Shimabara (Former Licensed Quarter)** 島原 *Bus 6 or 206 from Kyoto station or Shichijō-Horikawa (near Nishi Hongan-ji) to Shimabara-guchi; or 0:10–0:15h walk from Nishi Hongan-ji.* The name of this Edo-period pleasure quarter, which had a reputation for rowdiness, refers hyperbolically to the 1637 Shimabara Rebellion in Kyūshū (see Nagasaki History, p. 483). The area quieted considerably after prostitution was outlawed in 1958, and now the handful of remaining Shimabara courtesans are a cultural institution, seen during seasonal events such as New Year *mochi* (rice cake) pounding ceremony. Their elevated clogs are worn barefoot and produce a peculiar, erotic gait, and their broad sashes of luxurious brocade are tied in front. Their smiles, incidentally, will convince you that blackened teeth are charming. At the entrance to the quarter is the old gate, which was closed at night in the interest of public order. The **Sumiya** (1781, ICP), famous for its Sukiya style—especially the elaborate detailing on window screens and transoms—is probably the oldest building in Japan that was once used as a brothel (see Villas, p. 67). Both it and the nearby **Wachigaiya**, famous for its *fusuma* designs, are not open to the public. They are now exclusive teahouses with chaste entertainment.

### Exploring South Kyoto

**Jōnan-gū (Shrine)** 城南宮  Hrs: 8:30–16:30, daily. *South of Kyoto station; take bus 19 or 20 to Jōnan-gū, or Kintetsu train to Takeda station, where there's a free shuttle bus to the shrine.* This shrine stands on the site of an extensive villa occupied by the Heian emperors Shirakawa, Toba, and Go-Shirakawa. The grounds contain three beautiful modern gardens in the styles of the Heian, Muromachi, and Momoyama periods. On Apr. 29 and Nov. 3, Heian "courtiers" reenact a poetry party in the Heian-style garden.

**Kodai Yūzen-en** 古代友禅苑  (811–8101). Hrs: 9:00–17:00 (enter by 16:00); clsd NY. Museum of Yūzen silk dyeing. Near Ōmiya Takatsuji-dōri.

## I:2 CENTRAL SHOPPING AND ENTERTAINMENT DISTRICT

The Kamogawa is the center of modern Kyoto. On the east bank is Gion (II:3), with its geisha and cabarets. On the west bank is a solid conglomeration of bars, restaurants, department stores, and pachinko and video-game parlors. Each north-south street has its own unique flavor. Hugging the river bank is a cobblestone path, a favorite of lovers, that offers an entrancing view into the restaurants and bars along Pontochō, a charming, narrow alley parallel to the river. Kiyamachi, the next street west, runs along a picturesque, willow-lined canal and is another prime night spot. Kawaramachi-dōri is a broad, glittering boulevard, the hangout of teenagers and shoppers. Farther west are two covered shopping arcades, Kyōgoku and Shin-Kyōgoku, which feature a mix of venerable shops and souvenir stands catering to uniformed secondary-school field trippers. Nishiki-kōji, an atomospheric fish-and-produce market, runs west from here.

327

---

**Day Tour:** ＊ Nishiki-kōji—Shin-Kyōgoku—Upper Teramachi

**Night Tour:** ＊ Kiyamachi— (walk from Shijō to Sanjō) —＊＊＊ Pontochō

**Lunch:** Misoka-an Kawamichiya, Owariya, Chinchikurin, Ashoka

---

＊＊＊ **Pontochō** 先斗町  The second-ranked geisha district, after snobbish Gion across the river. It is said to have acquired its name in the 16th C from the Portuguese word for bridge. Many restaurants on the east side of the alley have *yuka*, wooden verandas over the river, a highlight of summertime Kyoto. Pontochō is a mix of cheap, casual spots and exclusive teahouses. In summer, from a *yuka* of the former type, one can often glimpse a geisha out on a *yuka* of the latter type. Two former teahouses with good *yuka* are Yamatomi (cheap) and Uzuki (expensive but not exclusive). The **Kaburenjō** theater at the north end is where Pontochō *maiko* perform the Kamogawa Odori in spring and fall (see Kyoto Calendar).

＊ **Kiyamachi** 木屋町  This street runs along the willow-lined **Takasegawa**, a transport canal built in the early 17th C which served as Kyoto's main commercial waterway until the Meiji period. The street's name, "wood-shop town," comes from the lumberyards that formerly stood along the canal. A wooden canal boat loaded with rice bales marks the site of a dock (behind the Kyoto Hotel). At the intersection with Sanjō-dōri is the Time's Building, a striking, concrete boutique building by architect Andō Tadao.

**Kawaramachi** 河原町  This is Kyoto's main street. Its intersection with Shijō-dōri forms Kyoto's busiest crossing, dominated by the Takashimaya and Hankyū department stores. On Kawaramachi you will find a great variety of shops, including the Maruzen bookstore, Yamato Folk Crafts, and an endless row of boutiques and cafés.

**Shin-Kyōgoku and Kyōgoku** 新京極・京極  Two shopping arcades, both called Kyōgoku, or "capital boundary," because they marked the easternmost limit of old Kyoto. This became Kyoto's commercial center in the Meiji era, and by Taishō (1912–1926), it had spilled over to Kawaramachi, all because land was available here, but not in the old city center. Though their facades are modern, many venerable shops do business here. Northern Kyōgoku has the wonderful Kyūkyodō paper and incense shop, and Honnō-ji, the historic temple where ODA NOBUNAGA was assassinated, since relocated to its present site. The street turns into **Teramachi** (temple town), a good place for antiques, old junk, and shops selling traditional items.

**Gokōmachi and Fuyachō** 御幸町・麸屋町  Only a few blocks from the glitter of Kyōgoku one finds rows of older, two-storied town dwellings. In the Edo period, these streets were lined with inns for traveling merchants, a few of which are still in operation, including the famed Tawaraya (House of Rice Sacks) and Kinmata, originally patronized by patent medicine salesmen from Lake Biwa. Nearby is Misoka-an Kawamichiya, a classic old *soba* shop.

* **Nishiki-kōji** 錦小路 Begins at the small shrine, Nishiki Tenman-gū, on Kyōgoku arcade. Kyoto's central market, the narrow, stone-paved, Brocade Alley, is a colorful tapestry of fish and produce. One can find dainty *kaiseki* cuisine decorations, like tiny baskets woven from kelp, and Japanese kitchen implements at the elegant Aritsugu. Fish shops close Sunday, many other shops on Wednesday.

**West Toward Karasuma.** *A 0:10h stroll through an area with the atmosphere of Kyoto's old merchant quarter.* Rokkaku-dō 六角堂 is a quiet, picturesque temple—supposedly founded by SHŌTOKU TAISHI—noted for its Rokkaku (Hexagonal) Hall and *heso-ishi*, or "belly-button stone," which was popularly said to mark the exact center of Kyoto. The temple is next to the tall, modern headquarters of Ikenobō, the flower-arrangement school founded in the Middle Ages. Near Sanjō-Karasuma intersection is the red-brick * **Heian Museum** 平安博物館, with displays on Heian-kyō, early shrines, copies of Heian-period paintings, and objects excavated from beneath the city (Hrs: 9:00–16:30; clsd M).

## Central Kyoto Tea Breaks

⑪ **Francois** フランソワ 四条小橋西詰南 (351-4042). Hrs: 9:30–23:00; Sa, 9:30–23:30; clsd NY. Fifty-year-old coffee parlor with classic interior.

⑯ **Tsukiji** 築地 河原町四条上ル一筋目入ル (221-1053). Hrs: 11:00–23:00, Sa, Su, NH 10:30–23:00. Classical music kissaten that was a favorite haunt of novelist Tanizaki Junichirō.

㉓ **Tanaka** タナカコーヒー先斗町店 (221-3809). Hrs: 11:00–7:00 a.m., daily.

㉖ **Surugaya** 駿河屋 三条河原町西入ル (221-0447). Hrs: 12:00–18:00, clsd W. Elegant Japanese-style sweet shop on the Sanjō arcade.

See p. 368–369 for restaurants, p. 373 for hotels

328

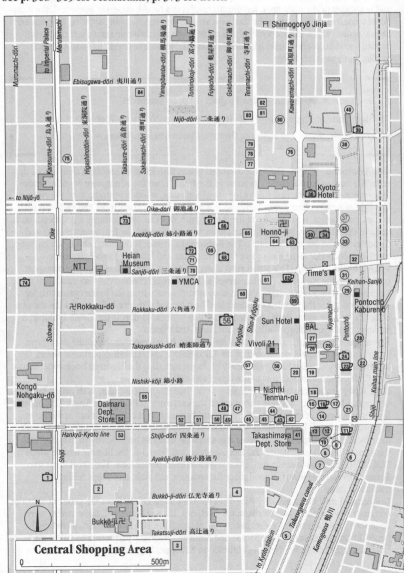

Central Shopping Area

0                    500m

## I:3 NIJŌ-JŌ AND IMPERIAL PALACE AREA

These two palaces, especially Nijō-jō, with its grand scale and sumptuously decorated audience halls, provide a marked contrast to the temples on Kyoto's perimeter.

---

**Tour:** ✻✻ Nijō Jinya — (0:02h on foot) — Shinsen-en — (0:07h on foot) — ✻✻✻ Nijō-jō — (0:20h on foot or 0:10h taxi) — ✻✻ Imperial Palace — ✻ Shōkoku-ji

**Lunch:** Owariya, Junshin-an, Honyara-dō

**Note:** The Imperial Palace is clsd Su.

---

✻✻✻ **Nijō-jō (Castle)** 二条城 *Subway to Oike, then walk 0:10h; or bus 9, 12, 50, 52, 61, 67.* Hrs: 8:45–17:00 (enter by 16:00); clsd NY. Hour-long tours throughout the day, in English and in Japanese. Except for its moat, surviving ramparts, and imposing gate, there is nothing very castlelike about Nijō-jō today. People come to see the ornate audience halls of the Ninomaru Palace. These were put in their present form for the 1626 meeting between Tokugawa Iemitsu and Emperor Go-Mizuno'o. The Tokugawa lavished the efforts of their finest craftsmen on these rooms, making them the most magnificent examples of the Shoin style (see Villas, p. 64). The inner residential quarters are small and modest, but the series of sumptuous audience halls were built to impress and cow both enemies and allies.

The design of Nijō-jō betrays the paranoia of Iemitsu. Behind the lavishly decorated *chōdaigamae* doors were secret, windowless rooms for bodyguards. The famous "nightingale floors" (*uguisu-bari*), which squeak loudly when trod upon, gave warning of

329

# The Emperor and the Shogun

In 1603, TOKUGAWA IEYASU came to Kyoto to receive, at his newly finished castle, Nijō-jō, the title of Shogun from Emperor Go-Yōzei. In theory he was a loyal subject of the emperor, charged with ensuring the peace of his majesty's realm. In reality, he had become the unchallenged military dictator of Japan since winning the Battle of Sekigahara in 1600 (see Nikkō History, p. 242). While formally submitting to the emperor, he and his descendants wasted few opportunities to remind their sovereign where power really lay. Ieyasu built Nijō-jō on the approximate site of the original Heian imperial palace — of which only the Shinsen-en pond remains — thereby symbolically claiming the position of supreme authority. Nijō-jō attained its present magnificence under Ieyasu's grandson IEMITSU, who rebuilt it for an audience in 1626 with Go-Yōzei's successor **Go-Mizuno'o**.

Iemitsu's sister had become Go-Mizuno'o's empress, reviving the classical tradition of powerful families marrying off their daughters to emperors. When a son was born, the Tokugawa pressured Go-Mizuno'o to abdicate in favor of the child. He resisted, however, and then the child died. In 1627, the emperor had another fight with the Tokugawa, over the assignment of "purple robes" to the abbots of Daitoku-ji and Myōshin-ji; humiliated, Go-Mizuno'o abdicated in protest in 1629 and, breaking tradition, left his throne to a daughter, who became the first reigning empress in more than 850 years (see Nara History, p. 392). After his abdication, Go-Mizuno'o's relations with the Tokugawa improved, and he was able to build a new imperial palace and the **Sentō Gosho**, or retired emperor's palace, for which the artistically gifted ex-emperor helped design a fine stroll garden. Go-Mizuno'o and his empress, known to history as Tōfukumon-in, restored many of Kyoto's temples and also built the **Shūgaku-in** villa as a country retreat (see III:1).

The Tokugawa's generosity was motivated by a desire to keep the emperor busy, contented, and in their debt. The Tokugawa governed with a free hand; after Iemitsu, no shogun bothered to even visit Kyoto. The emperor was confined to his palace and forbidden to meet with provincial lords. In the 19th century, however, Kyoto became a hotbed of proimperial, antishogunate activity. In 1822, Emperor Kōkaku, visiting the imperial villa at Shūgaku-in, became the first reigning emperor in almost two centuries who was allowed by the Tokugawa to leave the imperial palace. His procession, which covered only a few kilometers, was heartily cheered by the people of Kyoto. In the 1860s, Kyoto was the scene of numerous plots against the shogunate hatched by aristocrats and discontented samurai from Western Japan (see Hagi History, p. 460).

In 1863, Shogun **Iemochi**, trapped between foreign demands for an open Japan and the intransigent xenophobia of many of the daimyo, came to Kyoto, hoping for an imperial decree to break the deadlock. This unprecedented admission of weakness spelled the end of the shogunate. In 1868, Iemochi's successor, **Keiki**, officially returned his mandate to govern to the young EMPEROR MEIJI, in the Ōhiroma room of Nijō-jō. For a few months, Nijō-jō served as the seat of the new government.

intruders. But in fact, the Tokugawa were so powerful that they had no real need of a fortified castle in Kyoto. When the tower keep was struck by lightning in 1750, it was not rebuilt.

◆ **Ninomaru Palace.** From the great entrance gate, **Higashi Ōte-mon** (ICP), proceed to the Ninomaru compound through the **Kara-mon** (ICP), or "Chinese Gate," thought to have come from HIDEYOSHI's Fushimi-jō. Inside the gate is the entrance court—the earthen walls that surround it were originally for defense—and the carriage entrance, with its large *kara-hafu* eaves. This entranceway, the first of its kind, is the direct ancestor of the modern Japanese *genkan* where you take off your shoes. Behind the carriage entrance is the **Tōzamurai**, where callers waited to be received. The tour takes visitors through five successive halls arranged diagonally in the classic "warrior style." Each hall is named for its most important room—generally a Shoin-style audience room. (Only these will be described.) To give every hall a different mood, each was painted by a different KANŌ SCHOOL painter; the second and third, however, were both painted by the young KANŌ TAN'YŪ (1602–1674). Visitors could proceed only as far inside the compound as their trustworthiness and rank allowed. Each succeeding hall could be locked against the previous one. If guests were only to be met by a shogunal minister, they would be ushered to the **Shikidai no Ma**, famous for its pine screens by Tan'yū. There are also famous Tan'yū pines in the next important room, the **Ōhiroma**. This formal audience hall was used by the shogun to receive various daimyo. Seated in the raised *jōdan no ma* is a mannequin of the last Tokugawa shogun, announcing his resignation to the daimyo (see box). Note the doubly recessed coffered ceiling that emphasizes the shogun's superiority, and the decorative doors to his left, behind which bodyguards hid. The next formal audience room, the **Kuro (Black) Shoin**, was for audiences with those daimyo considered relatives of the shogun; the decoration is sumptuous but more understated than in the Ōhiroma; note the unusual double "staggered shelves" in the corner. The innermost hall, **Shiro (White) Shoin**, was the shogun's private quarters. It is decorated with ink landscapes, and provided a quiet, relaxed atmosphere; only women were allowed to attend the shogun here. On the way out, at the back of the Tōzamurai, is the **Chokushi no Ma**, where imperial messengers were received; contrary to what one might expect, the messenger sat in the raised portion of the room, and the shogun sat below.

**Garden.** Attributed to the famous designer, KOBORI ENSHŪ. This ostentatious garden, with its abundance of oversized, expensive rocks, and exotic cycad palms, was built for Emperor Go-Mizuno'o's 1626 visit. It was meant to be viewed from the Ninomaru Palace and also from a separate palace, just south of the garden, that was built for the emperor's private use and dismantled after his visit. The **Honmaru** (main castle enclosure) was surrounded by an inner moat; this is where the keep stood until 1750. The current buildings were donated by Prince Katsura in the late 19th C.

**Shinsen-en** 神泉苑 *0:07h on foot from Nijō-jō.* This rather tattered pond garden, once the playground of courtiers in dragon boats, is all that remains of the original Heian palace built in 794 (see Villas, p. 60). The palace grounds extended to Imadegawa-dōri, 2 km north. The pond was located at the south end of the palace, in accordance with Chinese geomantic rules. It lends its common name, O-ike, the "honorable pond," to the broad avenue that stretches east from the pond.

**\*\* Nijō Jinya** 二条陣屋 (ICP) (841–0972). *0:10h on foot from Nijō-jō.* One-hour tours at 10:00, 11:00, 14:00, 15:00, by reservation. Still owned by the founding Ogawa family, this elegant inn for visiting officials was built in the early Edo period and incorporated many ingenious devices to protect against the two scourges of that still unsettled time—fire and assassins. The building's sprinkler system, using water drawn from 12 interconnected wells, is only one of the features that saved it from the great fire of 1788, which destroyed most of central Kyoto, including part of Nijō-jō. Other features—trap doors, secret escape routes, hidden rooms with ladders or stairs that can be pulled up—ensured the security of its occupants.

**Mibu-dera (Temple)** 壬生寺 SW of Nijō-jō. This temple dedicated to Jizō is famous for Mibu Kyōgen (see Kyoto Calendar).

### Kyoto Imperial Park (Kyoto Gyoen)
*From the station, subway to Marutamachi or Imadegawa; from Nijō-jō, 0:10h by taxi.* This spacious public park includes the Kyoto Gosho (Imperial Palace) and the Sentō Gosho (Retired Emperor's Palace)—which share the grounds with baseball diamonds.

**Imperial Household Agency (Kunaichō)** 宮内庁 (075-211-1211). Near the central gate facing Karasuma-dōri. Issues permits to view the two palace compounds in the park, as well as the Katsura (V:4) and Shūgaku-in (III:1) imperial villas (you must be over 20). Tours M–F, and Sa a.m.; clsd Su, NH, Dec. 25–Jan. 5. Usually, you can see the Imperial Palace on the same day you apply. To visit the villas, advance reservations are essential: the Sentō Gosho requires but a few days, but Katsura and Shūgaku-in take two weeks or more (varies greatly with the season). To guarantee a reservation, we recommend telephoning up to three months in advance. (The office has some English speakers.) Someone must visit the office in person by a set time on the reserved day to receive a permit, and you must show your passport at the time of the tour.

**\* Sentō Gosho (Retired Emperor's Palace)** 仙洞御所 Tours (in Japanese only) at 11:00, 13:30. The Sentō Gosho is celebrated for its superb stroll garden. It is simpler than the gardens of Katsura or Shūgaku-in, but subtle and well-designed, offering ever-changing panoramas as one walks along the wooded shores of its lakes. The villa was built for retired emperor Go-Mizuno'o by the Tokugawa in 1630, and was designed by the emperor himself in collaboration with KOBORI ENSHŪ. The versatile Go-Mizuno'o, an adept in Zen, the tea ceremony, and flower arrangement, was also, as this garden shows, a masterful garden designer. One of its famous features is the lakeshore of smooth cobblestones, a gift of the daimyo of Odawara, who had them gathered from a beach near Mt. Fuji, wrapped individually in silk, and sent to Go-Mizuno'o.

**\*\* Kyoto Gosho (Imperial Palace)** 京都御所 Tours at 9:00, 11:00, 13:30, and 15:00; apply by 0:20h before at the Imperial Household Agency. Although the emperor left Kyoto for good soon after the Meiji Restoration (1868), each new sovereign returns here for his investiture. In the Heian period, when the palace was near Nijō-jō, this site was reserved for the estates of high court nobles. During the turbulent Middle Ages, the emperor was forced to live simply and move frequently. In the 14th C, the owner of the site, Tsuchimikado Higashi no Tōin, played host on and off to several emperors, and thenceforth his villa gained the status of one of several temporary "village palaces." After NOBUNAGA repaired it and HIDEYOSHI completely rebuilt it, this village palace came to be considered the permanent palace. It attained new magnificence when Emperor Go-Mizuno'o married Tokugawa Kazuko in 1620. The palace burned several times, and the present buildings date from 1855. The present ceremonial buildings are in fact based on the emperor's Shinden-style private living quarters and ceremonial halls, the only structures that were included in the village palaces (see Villas, p. 60). Originally, the public palace halls, where governmental functions were performed, resembled the Heian Shrine (II:4).

**Enclosure and Gates.** The five white bands on the walls of the enclosure signify imperial status; when you see similar lines on the walls of a temple or shrine, it indicates imperial favor. The unlucky northeast corner is inverted—making it a "noncorner"—and near it is placed a carving of a monkey, a divine messenger of the Hiyoshi shrine (at the eastern foot of Mt. Hiei) who chases away evil spirits. The great south gate, Kenrei-mon, is for the exclusive use of the emperor. The other gates are for various lower ranks, the lowest being the Seisho-mon, through which visitors today enter.

**Shishin-den.** With the Seiryō-den, this is one of the two most important halls in the palace. The great hall is reserved for the most imporant ceremonies, such as the enthronement of an emperor. A smaller hall, the Shunkō-den, houses the sacred mirror of the imperial regalia during the ceremony. The Shishin-den has a magnificent roof, with a foot-thick covering of cypress-bark shingles. The 18 steps in front of the Shishin-den represent the 18 court ranks allowed inside the palace. The steps are flanked by a cherry tree and an orange tree. The vast enclosure of raked white gravel before the Shishin-den, a sacred space called *yuniwa*, is also found in imperial shrines.

**Seiryō-den.** Usually not shown. This hall functioned as the emperor's living quarters in the Heian period, but has since become another ceremonial hall, associated with ancestor worship and some interesting-sounding fertility rites in which the emperor represents the "male principle" (see Shinto, p. 23).

**Ko Gosho (Small Palace) and Tsune Gosho (Everyday Palace).** The crown prince's ceremonial hall and an informal audience hall, respectively. The Gakumon-jo, north of the Ko Gosho, is an attractive Shoin-style room where the emperor would listen to scholars. Facing the Tsune Gosho is a stream that was the site of poetry contests. The contestants, ranged along the stream, had to race to complete a poem before a saké cup, floating on a tiny raft, drifted by. Success was rewarded with a drink from the cup. In a separate enclosure to the north is the empress's quarters (not open).

## Exploring around the Imperial Palace

**Kyoto Rekishi Shiryōkan** 京都歴史資料館 (241-4312). Hrs: 9:00–17:00; Sa 9:00–12:00; clsd 2nd, 4th Sa, Su, NH, NY. Small modern building with changing displays connected to Kyoto's history and a video library (in Japanese only) on Kyoto's festivals.

**Rozan-ji** 盧山寺 Hrs: 9:00–12:00, 13:00–16:00; clsd NY, Feb. 1. This temple, said to stand on the site of LADY MURASAKI's villa, has a handsome garden recently built in memory of the author of *The Tale of Genji*. The Main Hall is a Shinden-style hall brought from the Sentō Gosho. The cemetery contains tombs of many court personages. Setsubun festival (Feb. 3).

**Kitamura Bijutsukan (Art Museum)** 北村美術館 (256-0637). Hrs: Mar.–June, Sept.–Nov. 10:00–16:00; clsd M, day after NH. Private gallery of tea ceremony ware collected by Kitamura Kinjirō. Pleasant building and garden.

**\* Shōkoku-ji** 相国寺 (231-0301). Museum Hrs: 10:00–17:00 (enter by 16:30). Of the Gozan, or Five Great Zen Temples of Kyoto (actually six), this one remains the most serene and least spoiled by tourism. Shōkoku-ji was founded in 1392 by ASHIKAGA YOSHIMITSU, who established a painting academy within its precincts; SESSHŪ and KANŌ MASANOBU studied here (see Art, p. 95). The celebrated Golden and Silver Pavilions, built by Ashikaga shoguns, now belong to this monastery. The imposing Hattō was rebuilt in 1610 by TOYOTOMI HIDEYORI. The \* Jōtenkaku museum 承天閣美術館 exhibits painted screens (ICP) by Hasegawa Tōhaku and numerous other interesting art objects primarily connected with the Muromachi period and Ming China. The subtemple Jishō-in contains the tombs of several Ashikaga shoguns. Under renovation until 1995.

**\* Raku Bijutsukan (Raku Pottery Art Museum)** 楽美術館 (414-0304). Hrs: 10:00–16:00; clsd M, NY, mid-Aug. Graceful modern building adjacent to the old house where the Raku family still makes the famed ware (see Art, p. 97). Superb collection. A must for ceramics enthusiasts.

331

# KYOTO II. EASTERN KYOTO

**Main Attractions:**

**Higashiyama**, the district of the Eastern Mountains, lies east of the Kamogawa. Although in Heian times this area was not even considered part of the capital, it is Higashiyama's temples, shrines, and promenades that offer the quintessential images of Kyoto today. Higashiyama is also home to Gion, the most famous and elegant of Kyoto's geisha districts.

## II:1 SOUTHEAST DISTRICT

This is mainly an industrial district, but nestled in the quiet greenery of the eastern hills are some serene temples and one of the most popular shrines in the land, Fushimi Inari, famous for its tunnels of vermilion torii.

> **Half-day Tour:** * Sennyū-ji — (0:10h by taxi) — * Tōfuku-ji — (0:10h by taxi) — ** Fushimi Inari Shrine
>
> **Lunch:** The approach to Fushimi Inari is lined with shops selling broiled quail and sparrow.
>
> **Note:** Tōfuku-ji is famous for fall foliage, Fushimi Inari for New Year throngs.

**\* Tōfuku-ji** 東福寺 Hrs: 9:00–16:00, daily. *0:08h from Sanjō-Keihan to Tōfuku-ji station, or 0:15h on foot from Kyoto National Museum.* Tōfuku-ji was one of the five top-ranked Zen monasteries of Kyoto. It was founded in 1236 by FUJIWARA no Michiie in an attempt to revive his clan's waning fortunes. The temple's name takes a Chinese character from each of the two temples associated with the Fujiwara family's early glory—Tōdai-ji and Kōfuku-ji in Nara—and was built on the site of Hosshō-ji, which had been a Fujiwara family temple in Heian-kyō, during the height of the clan's power. Tōfuku-ji has often been ravaged by fire, most recently in 1881, but on the south end of its grounds are some of the oldest and finest Zen temple structures in Japan.

◆ **San-mon Gate** (1400, NT). This great temple gate, the oldest of its kind in Japan, is a beautiful and rare example of Daibutsu-style construction. The upper floor, open in November (maple-viewing season), houses statues of Shaka and the 16 Rakan, and is painted with clouds and angels ascribed to the painter Minchō (1352–1431).

◆ **Yokushitsu (Bath) and Tosu (Lavatory)** (early 15th C, ICP). Perhaps the most famous buildings of their kind, these two halls stand to the west of the San-mon. Zen monasteries include these among their principal halls because Zen practice extends to bodily as well as mental functions. The Yokushitsu, like most large baths before the Edo period, is a steam bath. Near the Tosu is the **Rokuhara-mon** (ICP), a gate that formerly stood in the Kamakura shogunate's Kyoto headquarters (see Rokuhara-mitsu-ji, II:2).

◆ **Hōjō (Abbot's Quarters).** Hrs: 9:00–16:00. Rebuilt in 1890. Has several fine modern gardens designed by Shigemori Mirei (1895–1975). Particularly memorable are two small gardens with an abstract checkerboard motif, one of thick moss and stepping stones, and the other of clipped shrubs.

**Ryūgin-an.** Usually open in fall. This subtemple supposedly has Japan's oldest *tatchū* architecture (see Villas, p. 63).

◆ **Tsūtenkyō.** North of the Hōjō. This picturesque Bridge to Heaven spans a gorge which is spectacular during the maple season. Across the bridge is the **\* Kaisan-dō** (Founder's Hall, Hrs: 9:00–17:00), which has a very pretty front courtyard garden. Both the hall and garden date from the late 17th C.

**Funda-in (Sesshū-ji).** Hrs: 9:00–17:00. This subtemple has a garden originally designed by the 15th-C painter SESSHŪ.

**Dōju-in.** Hrs: 9:00–16:30. A subtemple famous for its **Jūman Fudō** (ICP), the only authenticated work by the father of JŌCHŌ (see Art, p. 94). The grounds contain the grave of Oyuki Morgan, a Gion geisha who, while performing in the 1902 Miyako Odori, caught the eye of American millionaire George Morgan and eventually married him. The two encountered so much prejudice in America and Japan that they finally settled in Paris, where they lived until Morgan died in 1916.

**\* Sennyū-ji** 泉涌寺 Hrs: 9:00–16:30. *0:03h by taxi or 0:15h on foot from Kyoto National Museum; or 0:10h on foot from Tōfuku-ji. Bus 202, 207, 208.* This lovely, secluded Shingon temple has long ties to the imperial house. The temple was built in 1218 on the site of a 9th-C hermitage of KŪKAI, and received its name, Bubbling Spring Temple, when a spring miraculously welled up in the compound. The little Kannon Hall on the left, just inside the main gate, contains the **Yōkihi (Yang Kuei-fei) Kannon**, which by tradition was sculpted in Tang China after the famous *femme fatale* of Chinese history. The **Butsuden** (ICP) has a large dragon on the ceiling, painted by KANŌ TAN'YŪ. Part of the **Honbō** (Abbot's Quarters) was taken from the Kyoto Imperial Palace and donated by the EMPEROR MEIJI. Adjacent to and behind the abbot's quarters are 16 imperial mausoleums. Just north of Sennyū-ji is **Raigō-in**, a rustic subtemple with a garden; serves *matcha* tea.

**\*\* Fushimi Inari Taisha (Shrine)** 伏見稲荷大社 *0:10h from Sanjō-Keihan, or 0:02h from Tōfuku-ji by Keihan line.* This is the most famous of Japan's 40,000 shrines to Inari, the highly popular kami of rice, saké, and general prosperity. The shrine's origins are unclear, but it is associated with the Hata family, Korean immigrants who also built Kōryū-ji (V:1) and played a key role in founding Heian-kyō. In the 9th C, when KŪKAI chose the shrine to protect his new monastery, Tō-ji (I:1), the shrine was moved from the slopes of Inari-san to its present location at the base. Tō-ji's original pagoda was built with sacred timber from the mountain. The street leading from the station to the shrine is lively with shops selling household shrines, amulets, and old-fashioned candy and souvenirs. The street is fragrant with the aroma of broiled quail and sparrow, a tasty snack after a hike around Inari's precincts.

**Honden (Sacred Hall)**, 1494, ICP). A Nagare-style structure decorated with carvings and colorfully painted. To the right of the Honden is a Kagura stage, where worshippers can make a donation to have shrine maidens offer sacred dances.

◆ **Ochaya** (ICP). South of the Honden. A tea arbor from the Retired Emperor's Palace (Sentō Gosho, I:3), given to the shrine by Emperor Go-Mizuno'o in the 17th C. This fine example of the Sukiya-Shoin style is sometimes open to the public.

◆ **Inari-san.** The lushly wooded slope of Inari-san behind the main shrine is dotted with subshrines, linked by a maze of paths leading to the summit. Along the way are innumerable vermilion torii, offered by enterprises all over Japan, which stand so close together that they form a tunnel. It takes two hours to cover the whole mountain, but 15 minutes is sufficient to walk through the famous **thousand torii** near the base. Before each of the many subshrines are offerings of saké and pairs of stone foxes, the messengers of Inari. Inari's foxes are beneficent, but others are dangerous, magical creatures who, in the guise of beautiful women, play nasty tricks and lure the unsuspecting to their deaths. Good and bad alike, foxes adore fried bean curd. A sushi of fried bean-curd purses is called *Inari-zushi*. Families possessed by foxes find themselves eating inordinate amounts of food. Inari-san is ideal for an outing, and teahouses offer rest and refreshment, but picnickers should take precautions and pack for extra company!

## II:2 SANJŪSANGEN-DŌ AND KIYOMIZU-DERA AREA

A miniature capsule of Kyoto's history, this area contains monuments built by three great generals. Sakanoue no Tamuramaro (758–811), famous for his exploits in Tōhoku, built Kiyomizu Temple. TAIRA NO KIYOMORI oversaw the construction of Sanjūsangen-dō, and had his headquarters near Rokuharamitsu-ji, where there is a famous portrait of him as a priest. TOYOTOMI HIDEYOSHI was a great admirer of Kiyomori; both were outsiders who had succeeded by sheer force of personality. They are the two most eccentric, incandescent figures in Japanese history, and perhaps because of their very individualism, neither was able to establish a dynasty. Perhaps a sense of spiritual kinship led Hideyoshi to build so many of his personal monuments here: the Mimizuka, Toyokuni Jinja, Chishaku-in, Yōgen-in, and his Great Buddha temple, Hōkō-ji.

> **Half- to Full-day Tour:** Kyoto station — (0:10h by taxi or 0:20h on foot) — \*\*\* Sanjūsangen-dō — \*\* National Museum — (0:10h on foot) — \*\* Kawai Kanjirō House — (0:05h by taxi or 0:20h on foot) — \*\*\* Kiyomizu Temple — \*\*\* Sannenzaka — (0:20h on foot) — \*\*\* Gion (II:3)
>
> **Lunch:** Hagi, Okutan, Minoko, Hisago
>
> **Note:** The road from Kiyomizu to Yasaka Jinja, via the preserved areas of Sannenzaka and Ninnenzaka, has many restaurants and souvenir shops.

**\*\*\* Sanjūsangen-dō (Rengeo-in)** 三十三間堂 Hrs: Apr. 1–Nov. 15, 8:00–17:00 (enter by 16:40). Nov. 16–Mar. 31 9:00–16:00 (enter by 15:30). *Y470 by taxi from Kyoto station, or take bus 206, 208.* This temple was originally built by Taira no Kiyomori for the retired emperor Go-Shirakawa in 1164, before the two became enemies. Founded at a time when it was believed the world was entering Mappō, a Dark Age when salvation was attainable only through the mercy of Amida Buddha, the temple was dedicated to Kannon Bosatsu, the Goddess of Mercy, Amida's agent in this world (see Buddhism, p. 37). The temple burned in 1249 and was rebuilt in 1266. The hall is famed for its 1,001 Kannon statues, an awe-inspiring array expressing in finite sculpture the infinite compassion of Kannon.

The extraordinary ◆ **Main Hall** (1266, NT) is 118 meters "wide" and 18 meters deep. The long side has 33 bays of standard width, called *ken* — hence the temple's popular name, Sanjūsan (33) Ken Hall. This number corresponds to the 33 manifestations of Kannon. A simple calculation shows that 33 manifestations times 1,001 Kannons equals 33,033 Kannons to save all beings. This great capacity for mercy made Sanjūsangen-dō a favorite with pilgrims.

For an art lover, the pleasure of viewing this outpouring of faith is intensified by the excellence of the carving. When the hall was rebuilt in 1266, the great sculptor TANKEI (1173–1256), eldest son of the genius UNKEI, directed the sculpting of new images (see Art, p. 94). The principal image is a splendid, seated **Thousand-armed Kannon** (NT), wearing a "crown" of 10 heads, including the head and tiny image of Amida, of whom Kannon is a manifestation. The same convention is followed in the 1,001 smaller images (ICP). In the back corridor are 30 other Kei School statues, masterpieces of Kamakura vigor and realism. These include 28 "spirits attending Kannon" — many of Hindu origin, such as the flute-playing bird-man **Karurao** (Garuda, NT) and the gaunt holy man, **Basūsennin** (NT) — and **Fūjin and Raijin** (NTs), gods of wind and thunder.

Since the Edo period, Sanjūsangen-dō has been famous for archery contests, now held Jan. 15 and May 2, in which Japan's top archers compete to send arrows flying down the length of the hall's outer veranda to a target at the opposite end (where the posts are riddled with arrow punctures); the record of 8,133 bull's eyes by one man, set in 1686, still stands. The contests became so popular that a copy of the hall was built in Edo.

\* **Yōgen-in** 養源院 Hrs: 9:00–16:00; clsd Jan., Mar., Sept. 21. Adjacent to Sanjūsangen-dō. This temple was founded in 1594 by Toyotomi Hideyoshi for the deceased father of his favorite concubine, Yodogimi. The small temple has several door panels and walls painted by the early RIMPA SCHOOL genius TAWARAYA SŌTATSU. The pairs of lions, *kirin*, droll white elephants, and pines, painted on bare wood panels, are wonderful examples of Sōtatsu's unique and vivacious graphic style. The temple's famous Chi Tenjō (ceiling of blood) was built from boards stained by the blood of Tokugawa retainers who commited suicide during the siege of Fushimi-jō by Toyotomi forces.

\*\* **Kyoto National Museum (Kokuritsu Hakubutsukan)** 京都国立博物館 (541-1151). Hrs: 9:00–16:30 (enter by 16:00); clsd M, Dec. 26–Jan. 3. *Y430 by taxi from Kyoto station, or take bus 206, 208.* An outstanding collection, noted especially for its pictorial art, which is usually arranged in chronological sequence to illustrate the evolution of Japanese painting. Heian-period works dominate the sculpture section. The brick Meiji-era wing to the right is reserved for special exhibitions.

\* **Chishaku-in** 智積院 (541-5361). Hrs: 9:00–16:30 (enter by 16:00), daily. Directly across Higashiyama-dōri from the Kyoto National Museum. Chishaku-in stands on the site of an earlier temple founded by Hideyoshi in memory of his first son, Tsurumatsu, who died in infancy. The treasure house exhibits superb ◆ **Momoyama-period screens** (NT) of trees and flowering plants against gold grounds by Hasegawa Tōhaku and his son Kyūzō (see Art, p. 96). The admission fee includes the temple's pleasant garden, built in the 17th C.

**Myōhō-in** 妙法院 Directly N of Chishaku-in. The head temple of Sanjūsangen-dō. Except for a week in November, the only building on view is the **Kuri** (NT), the temple kitchen, with its soaring ceiling supported by an impressive matrix of rafters. It is said to have lodged Hideyoshi during the building of Hōkō-ji.

**Mimizuka (Ear Mound)** 耳塚 A grass-covered mound marked by a stone stupa. Toward the end of his life, Hideyoshi decided he wanted to conquer China, and sent, in 1592 and 1597, two preliminary expeditions to Korea. He was unsuccessful, but the ears brought back as war trophies instead of heads, which were too cumbersome, attest to the violence of these campaigns.

**Toyokuni (Hōkoku) Jinja** 豊国神社 *On the NW corner behind the National Museum, about 0:05h on foot N of Sanjūsangen-dō.* In 1598, foreseeing his imminent death, Hideyoshi erected this shrine to himself, where he was posthumously worshipped as a kami. A famous genre screen of Kyoto shows a great Bon dance in front of the mausoleum. The shrine was dismantled by Hideyoshi's successor, Tokugawa Ieyasu (see Nikkō History, p. 242) and was not rebuilt until 1880. The beautiful **Kara-mon** (Chinese Gate, NT) was brought, perhaps as a kind of revenge, from the Tokugawa-sponsored Konchi-in at Nanzen-ji (II:5). The treasure house contains possessions of Hideyoshi (Hrs: 9:00–16:30). Hideyoshi's tomb lies in a lonely spot atop Amida-ga-mine, a 0:15h climb due east of the National Museum.

**Hōkō-ji** 方広寺 Directly N of Toyokuni Jinja. This forlorn temple is all that remains of Hideyoshi's Great Buddha Temple, which housed an immense image that surpassed even the Nara Daibutsu. The pious project had its practical side: Seeking "iron for the Buddha," Hideyoshi confiscated the swords of the peasantry. The image was destroyed by an earthquake not long after completion. A crude wooden copy was housed here until 1973, when it burned. The sole

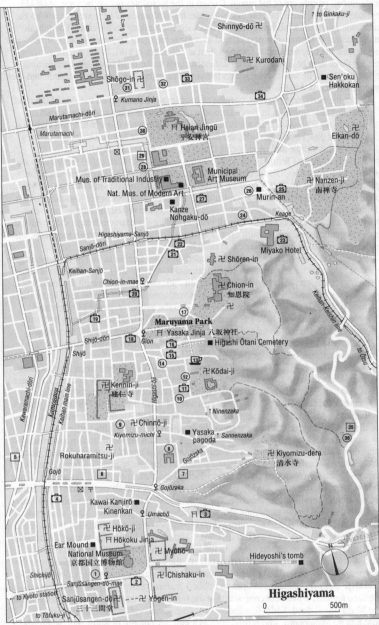

Higashiyama

0          500m

relic of Hideyoshi's temple is the enormous **bell** (4.4 m high, 2.8 m in diameter), cast by his son HIDEYORI; the inscription contained an insulting reference to the relative status of the houses of Toyotomi and Tokugawa, which Ieyasu used as an excuse to mount the siege of Ōsaka Castle and destroy all of Hideyoshi's progeny. Visitors can sound the bell for Y100.

**∗∗ Kawai Kanjirō Kinenkan (House)** 河井寛次郎記念館 (561-3585). Hrs: 10:00–17:00 (enter by 16:30); clsd M, Aug. 10–20, Dec. 24–Jan 7. *0:10h walk from Kyoto National Museum. Bus 16, 202, 206, 207 to Umachō, then walk 0:02h.* The beautiful home and studio of the late ceramicist Kawai Kanjirō (1890–1966), a leading figure in Japan's folk-art movement. Examples of his work and objects from his private collection are exhibited in the handsome house. In back is his climbing kiln, a multichambered, wood-fired kiln of a type that is now outlawed within city limits (too much pollution). The house is in **Gojō-zaka**, Kyoto's former kiln quarter, an area now known for its numerous pottery shops.

**∗ Rokuharamitsu-ji** 六波羅蜜寺 (561-6980). Hrs: 8:00–17:00. *0:10h on foot from Kawai Kanjiro House. Bus 16, 202, 206, 207 to Kiyomizu-michi bus stop, then 0:05h walk.* Though unimposing and a trifle shabby, this temple is worth a visit for its art and architecture. The **Main Hall** (ICP), built around 1363, is one of the oldest buildings in central Kyoto. The temple was founded in 963 by an early Amidist proselytizer, Kūya Shōnin, in what was then the village of Rokuhara. Taira no Kiyomori and the Kamakura shogunate built their Kyoto headquarters nearby. The temple's treasure house exhibits a marvelous ◆ **statue of Kūya Shōnin** (ICP) invoking Amida Buddha—tiny Amidas, one for every character of *Namu*

*Amida Butsu*, parade out of his mouth. Carved in the Kamakura period by a son of UNKEI, the statue vividly captures the holy man's intense, forward stride as he marches through the countryside, his sleeves billowing as he strikes the gong hanging on his chest. There is an equally famous ◆ **statue of a priest**, said to portray the aging Kiyomori, looking shrewd and cruel despite his holy vestments. Kiyomori died at Rokuhara in 1181, in the grip of a raging fever; for three days he lay naked in an unheated room in the dead of winter, complaining of the heat. Some say he was cursed; within five years his entire line would be exterminated (see Miyajima History, p. 449).

From the early Heian period, corpses of beggars were dumped on the side of the road past Rokuharamitsu-ji, in Toribeno, and a nearby crossroads came to be known as Rokudō no Tsuji, where the six roads of reincarnation were thought to begin (see Buddhism, p. 38). From Aug. 7–10, the **Rokudō Mairi** or Six Roads Pilgrimage, centers around this temple and neighboring Chinnō-ji (see Kyoto Calendar).

**\*\*\* Kiyomizu-dera (Temple)** 清水寺 Hrs: 6:00–18:30. *By taxi, 0:10h from Kyoto station, or 0:05h from Shijō-Kawaramachi. Bus 16, 202, 206, 207 to Kiyomizu-michi or Gojō-zaka bus stops, then 0:10h climb to the temple.* ◆ **Kiyomizu-michi** and **Gojō-zaka**, two narrow, uphill approaches to Kiyomizu-dera, are lined with vendors of Kiyomizu pottery and other souvenirs, sold to pilgrims and sightseers who have visited the temple for over a thousand years. The short climb is a small price to pay for the marvelous sight that awaits: the temple's magnificent main hall, built upon a towering scaffold against a green mountain, surveys the city below. The view is magical at twilight.

Kiyomizu is older than Kyoto; it was founded for priest Enchin in 780 by the famous general Sakanoue no Tamuramaro (see Hiraizumi History, p. 169). The site, near a sacred fall, gave the temple its name, Pure Water. In 798, Tamuramaro rebuilt the main hall using the ceremonial palace hall from the abandoned Nagaoka capital (see Kyoto History, p. 319). It was supposedly at this time that the temple acquired its celebrated profile. Affiliated with Nara's Kōfuku-ji, Kiyomizu was burned several times by hostile monks of Hiei-zan. It has since become an independent Shingon-Hossō sect temple, dedicated to Kannon and designated sixteenth on the famous Kansai pilgrimage of 33 Kannon temples (see Villages, p. 56).

◆ **Main Hall** (1633, NT). Rebuilt by TOKUGAWA IEMITSU. From here, a flight of stone steps leads down to **Otowa no Taki**, the sacred falls worshipped by Enchin. The water is said to be efficacious for all illnesses, and one can often see pilgrims standing beneath the falls. The path continues past several small halls to the **Okuno-in**, also built on a scaffold, with a splendid view of the Main Hall. Another trail leads to the three-storied pagoda across the gorge, from which one can see the entire temple.

**\*\*\* Sannenzaka and Ninenzaka** 三年坂・二年坂 This series of stone-paved roads, sloping downhill from Kiyomizu-dera toward Yasaka Jinja, is one of the most pleasant places in Kyoto. From Kiyomizu head down Kiyomizu-michi to Shichimiya Honpo, a famous vendor of *shichimi-tōgarashi* (seasoned chili powder) located at a fork in the path. To the right, down a flight of steps, is Sannenzaka, a slope lined with old houses and shops that has been designated an architecturally preserved zone. The walk to Yasaka Jinja takes a leisurely half-hour, if one isn't detained by the numerous shops and teahouses along the way. Many shops sell bamboo ware, folk crafts, and Kiyomizu-yaki, colorful porcelain and enameled stoneware that are a hallmark of Kyoto's elegant craft traditions. At the top of Ninenzaka, marked by another short flight of steps, take a short detour to the left to see the five-storied **Yasaka Pagoda** 八坂塔 (1440, ICP), a landmark of murky origins; the foundations are said to date from the Asuka period (538–645). The present pagoda is all that remains of a temple called Hōkan-ji.

**\* Kōdai-ji** 高台寺 (Usually not open to public.) Ninenzaka deposits you by the driveway to the Ryōzen Kannon, a huge concrete statue of the Goddess of Mercy that serves as a memorial to the World War II dead. Kōdai-ji, adjacent to Ryōzen-ji, was established for Hideyoshi's widow, Kita no Mandokoro, who retired here as a nun. Its Tamaya, or Spirit Hall, where she prayed for her husband's soul and is herself enshrined, is richly decorated with gold designs of flowers and musical instruments against a ground of black lacquer, renowned as Kōdai-ji *maki-e*. Higher up are two famous tea arbors brought from Fushimi-jō, **Shigure-tei** and **Kasa-tei**, the "umbrella arbor," said to be the first to employ a spokelike arrangement of ceiling rafters.

**\* Ishibe Kōji (Alley)** 石塀小路 A quiet stone-paved alley with many inns and traditional restaurants. If you walk all the way through and turn right, you will arrive at Yasaka Jinja.

### Kiyomizu Area Tea Break

13⃞ **Bashō-dō** 芭蕉堂 (561-0374). Hrs: 10:00–18:00, daily. Thatched cottage with mossy garden by Maruyama Park. Japanese sweets.

## II:3 GION AND ENVIRONS

A casual, open attitude is suitable to this area, because no matter where you wander, you'll find something interesting. Gion, Kyoto's famed geisha quarter, is enchanting in the early evening, when teahouses and restaurants light their lanterns, and the *maiko*, with white faces and shimmering kimono, appear on the street, hurrying to appointments. In the daytime, you might visit the great Chion-in Temple and Shōren-in's exquisite villa and garden, or browse along Shijō-dōri, with its shops of *maiko* accessories, or hunt for bargains among the antique shops on Shinmonzen-dōri.

**Walking Tour:** \* Yasaka Jinja — (0:02 on foot) — \*\*\* Hanami-kōji Street — Gion Corner — \* Kennin-ji — (0:10h on foot) — \*\* Shinbashi — Shinmonzen-dōri — \* Chion-in — (0:05h on foot) — \* Shōren-in

**Lunch:** Minoko, Takarabune, Izū, Yuranosuke

**Note:** Gion Corner (19:40 and 20:40; clsd winter). Maruyama Park for cherry blossoms, Miyako Odori geisha dances in April.

\* **Yasaka Jinja** 八坂神社 Every evening, the Kagura platform of this shrine is illuminated with hundreds of white paper lanterns, each emblazoned with the name of a Kyoto shop — Gion restaurants in particular. During the day, a steady stream of people come to pay their respects, dawdling on the way out at the few amusement booths near the colorful **Rō-mon** (gate, 1497, ICP). The shrine seems to have originated before the founding of Kyoto as the tutelary shrine of a local figure, and later became affiliated with the Tendai monastery on Hiei-zan. It was "purged" of Buddhist associations after the Meiji Restoration, but its syncretic past is evident from the architecture of the **Honden** (1654, ICP), a unique temple-like hall in which the space under the front eaves serves in place of an oratory. It sports a magnificent roof of cypress shingles.

**Maruyama Kōen (Park)** 円山公園 This public park offers a pleasant walk between Yasaka Jinja and Chion-in. The park is famous for nighttime cherry blossoms in April. During this period, and also on New Year's Eve, the park becomes a mob scene, crowded with revelers and refreshment stands. Teahouses and inns dot the grounds; Hiranoya specializes in *imobō*, a 300-year-old recipe for yams and dried cod. On the south side of the park is Chōraku-kan, a Meiji-period villa, now a coffee shop and ladies' hotel. Nearby stand large concrete storehouses for many of the disassembled Gion Matsuri floats. A path at the back of the park leads to the belfry of Chion-in, via a small Benten shrine and Anyō-ji, a temple on the site where Hōnen Shōnin, founder of the Jōdo sect, first preached faith in Amida to his followers, including Shinran, who founded the Jōdo Shin sect. To the south of the park is **Higashi Ōtani Cemetery**, with the graves of Shinran and thousands of Jōdo Shin sect believers, where there is a dazzling Mantō-e, "ten-thousand lamp ceremony," Aug. 14–16.

**Shijō-dōri in Gion.** From Yasaka Jinja, one finds the following unusual or elegant shops on the north side of the street: Kazurasei (*geiko* hair ornaments and make-up), Aizen-dō (incense), Maruta (kimono fabric), Kagizen (a sweet shop), and the Kyoto Craft Center. On the south, at the corner of Shijō-dōri and Hanami-kōji, are the red walls of the Ichiriki-tei (see below).

**Minami-za (Theater)** 南座 (561-1155). "Japanese baroque" theater on Shijō-dōri, by the Kamogawa. In December, Kabuki stars from Tokyo perform here in **Kaomise** (Face Showing). A stone monument on the west side of the theater proclaims this site as the birthplace of Kabuki, where a shrine dancer, Izumo no Okuni, first performed her sensational plays (see Drama, p. 89). The Minami-za is the sole descendant of six small playhouses that operated here in the Edo period, and is the oldest working theater in the country.

\*\*\* **Hanami-kōji** 花見小路 One of Kyoto's most beautiful streets, with rows of classic teahouses and restaurants, most dating from the 17th C. It is now an architecturally preserved zone. In the early evening one will certainly see *maiko* here. The side streets are also interesting, and there are several good restaurants here.

&#9670; **Ichiriki-tei** 一力亭 This is Japan's most famous teahouse, where *geiko* and *maiko* meet and entertain clients. The Ichiriki-tei's walls of red ochre and the slatted, fence-like structures along the lower halves of the wall — called "dog repellers" — are the epitome of Kyoto style. Ichiriki is the setting of Act 7 in the Bunraku and Kabuki play *Chūshingura* (Tale of the Forty-Seven Rōnin), where Ōboshi Yuranosuke, leader of the avenging samurai, pretends to become dissolute and to give up plans for a vendetta (see Drama, p. 86).

**Yasaka Kaikan** 八坂会館 (561-1119). At the south end of Hanami-kōji is a concrete monstrosity vaguely reminiscent of a Japanese castle. On the first floor is the \* **Gion Corner** show, a nightly précis of Kyoto's traditional arts: tea ceremony, koto music, flower arrangement, Bugaku (ancient court dance), geisha dances, and Bunraku. The performers are highly professional, and unless you have the means and the connections to experience each art form in its natural habitat, you shouldn't miss it. Shows Mar. 1–Nov. 29 (clsd Aug. 16) at 19:40 and 20:40; Y2500.

**Gion Kaburenjo** 祇園歌舞練所 (561-1115). South of Yasaka Kaikan. For the entire month of April, the Gion geisha hold the **Miyako Odori**, lavishly staged and sentimental dance revues by legions of *maiko*, with musical accompaniment by senior *geiko*. The dances were conceived by the mayor of Kyoto in 1872 to increase tourism and pick up the city's spirits after it lost its status as the capital.

\* **Kennin-ji** 建仁寺 Hanami-kōji ends at the back gate of this austere temple, which sits primly next to lively Gion. Kennin-ji was Japan's first major Zen temple, founded in 1202 by the priest Eisai, who had just returned from Sung China with the teachings of Rinzai Zen. Later, in the hierarchy of Kyoto's five top Zen temples, it ranked third. The present buildings

# The Geisha and the Townsman

Though **Yasaka Jinja**, or "Gion-san" as it is fondly known, lies at the east edge of the city, it is nevertheless the heart of Kyoto. The history of most of Kyoto's temples and palaces is a history of aristocrats and warriors. The townsman, however, has long kept a jealous hold on Gion-san and its summer festival, the Gion Matsuri. For a short period after the Ōnin Wars, the authorities tried to forbid the parade of floats, but the people defiantly held the festival anyway. Other seasonal events further confirm Gion-san's place at the hub of the Kyoto townsman's life. On New Year's Eve, Shijō-dōri becomes a river of humanity, as hundreds of thousands of people surge toward the shrine to receive a bit of purified fire on a piece of rope, and then push on to Chion-in to hear the great bell toll at midnight. In April, nearby Maruyama Park turns into a mass of cherry pink—both the blossoms and the faces of the inebriated revelers who turn out to see them.

In the Edo period, tourist-pilgrims freshly arrived from the nouveau-riche east to sample the delights of Kyoto culture would stop first at Gion-san to pray for prosperity in this world. If they were of the Jōdo persuasion, they would also visit Chion-in, the great Jōdo sect headquarters, to ensure their place in Amida's Western Paradise. West of Gion-san's gates, a different sort of paradise awaited them. The approach—what is now the east end of Shijō-dōri—became crowded with vendors of souvenirs and amusements; the Kabuki got its start here, by the riverbank, where the Minami-za theater stands today (see Drama, p. 89). Here was the first crack at the purse of the rich bumpkin from the east. It was here too that the Kyoto merchant, or more likely his dissolute son, could spend his money freely, without the authorities pawing his kimono and prying into his home, forbidding him the bright silks and fine timbers that were status symbols reserved for the samurai. In the pleasure quarters, money and style counted for more than one's social class.

By the early 19th century, the cultural life of Gion had become dominated by the **geiko**, as the geisha is called in Kyoto. The *geiko* is a part of the Japanese demi-monde, but she is not a prostitute. She is, rather, an accomplished artist who entertains clients with her conversation, dancing, and music, leaving the prostitute to take care of the simpler pleasures. The *geiko* of Gion and rival Ponto-chō, across the river, competed for the title of being the most skilled at the love ballad, acted out in dance and accompanied by the three-stringed *shamisen*. Because Gion was patronized by the future leaders of the Meiji Restoration—many Gion *geiko* married government ministers—Gion became slightly more prestigious than Pontochō, which had been patronized by the Old Guard. Since 1872, the competition has gone public: Every spring, the various *geiko* communities stage lavish dance shows—the Miyako Odori of Gion versus the Kamogawa Odori of Pontochō.

Most of the time, however, the *geiko* live behind closed doors, in a world of feminine accomplishments and feminine hierarchy, a world apart from men. They live together with their "mothers" and "sisters," speaking a special geisha language and conforming to a strict code of conduct. Apprentice *geiko* are called *maiko*. Their principal duty is to look charming, both for their clients and for the endless Kyoto travel posters and pamphlets on which they appear. The older *geiko*, on the other hand, is skilled at putting the shy Japanese male at ease and drawing him into conversation. *Geiko* and *maiko* never receive clients at their homes, but only on the neutral ground of an *ageya*, also called *chaya* (teahouse). If you spot a *geiko* or a *maiko* walking though Gion or Pontochō, she is most likely on her way to or from a teahouse.

Fronting proudly on the corner of Shijō-dōri and Hanami-kōji are the elegant, red-ochre-stained walls of Japan's most famous *chaya*, the Ichiriki-tei. South, on Hanami-kōji, stand rows of teahouses and inns that easily evoke the atmosphere of earlier times. Not so the part of Gion just north of Shijō-dōri, where teahouses are giving way to cabarets. Around 8:00 p.m., this area becomes filled with bar and cabaret hostesses in tight-fitting cocktail dresses, scrambling to get to work. Here, as in so many other apects of Japanese life, the traditional and the modern exist side by side.

date from 1596. Interiors can be seen only by applying in writing to the temple. Kennin-ji holds a tea ceremony conducted in the early Zen monastic style, uninfluenced by the later elaborations of Shukō and SEN NO RIKYŪ.

✱ **Shinbashi** 新橋 Gion north of Shijō-dōri has become an interestingly sleazy area where old teahouses are giving way to cabarets and bars. But hugging the banks of the willow-lined Shirakawa, a few blocks north of Shijō-dōri, is ◆ **Gion-Shinbashi**, an architecturally preserved zone, with rows of beautiful teahouses.

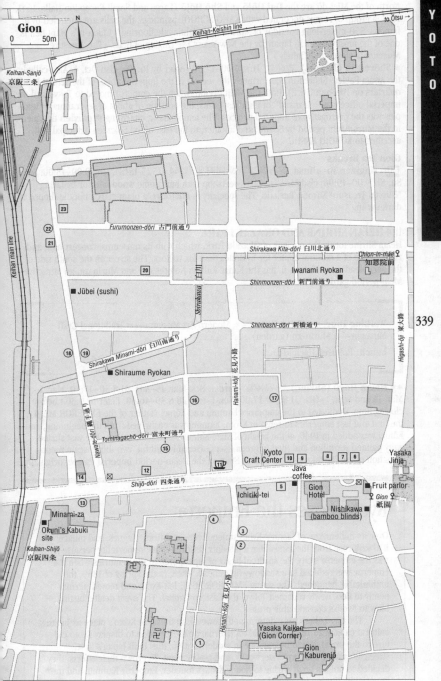

**Shinmonzen-dōri** 新門前通 A street of antique and curio shops; stores tend to be open 10:00–18:00, with many closed Monday. The street is lined with traditional merchant houses, which adds to the fun of poking around. An association of ''English-speaking'' shops displays a special sticker. Ezōshi is a friendly shop for Japanese woodblock prints. One street north is **Furumonzen-dōri** (Old Gatefront Street), which leads to the main gate of Chion-in.

\* **Chion-in (Temple)** 知恩院 *0:05h on foot from Chion-in-mae bus stop (bus 201, 202, 203, 206). 0:15h on foot from Yasaka Jinja via Maruyama Kōen.* Headquarters of the Jōdo sect, located on the site where its founder, Hōnen Shōnin (1133–1212), lived and taught his doctrine of faith in Amida Buddha (see Buddhism, p. 37). The temple was founded by a disciple, Genchi. The imposing **San-mon** (1619, ICP) is the largest temple gate in Japan. The **Miei-dō** (Founder's Hall, 1639, ICP), where an image of Hōnen is worshipped, is also a massive structure, glittering inside with gilded pillars and pennants, with room for hundreds of worshippers. The smaller **Amida Hall** to its west enshrines the principal image of Amida.

North of the Miei-dō are the **Dai Hōjō** and **Shō Hōjō** (Large and Small Reception Halls, 1641, ICP), a group of rooms decorated with KANŌ SCHOOL paintings; the halls are encircled by a famous, 550-meter-long corridor of squeaking "nightingale flooring." Chion-in's giant bell is one of the most famous in Japan for the New Year's Eve ringing of bells. (The Treasure Museum is closed indefinitely.)

✳ **Shōren-in (Temple)** 青蓮院 Hrs: 9:00–17:00 (enter by 16:30); clsd Oct. 4. Also called the Awata Palace, Shōren-in was formerly the temple of the imperial abbot of the Tendai headquarters on Hiei-zan (III:2). Until the Meiji period, when the emperor moved to Tokyo and the imperial office was "cleansed" of Buddhist taints, the position of abbot of several major temples was the prerogative of imperial princes. The temple has a charming ◆ **garden** designed in the Muromachi period by Sōami, and another, to the east of the Sokaden principal hall, ascribed to KOBORI ENSHŪ.

**Gion Tea Breaks**

🍵 **Kagizen Yoshifusa** 鍵善良房  祇園町北側264  (525-1818). Hrs: 9:00–18:00; Sa, Su, NH 9:00–19:00; clsd M. A famous sweetshop with handsome wood interior by Living National Treasure Kuroda Tatsuaki. The specialty is *kuzukiri*, a plant-starch noodle dipped in dark syrup.

## II:4 HEIAN SHRINE AND OKAZAKI PARK

Heian Shrine forms the nucleus of Okazaki Park, which with its museums, concert hall, and zoo is more of a cultural center for Kyotoites than for visitors. The street on the south side of the park, leading to Nanzen-ji, has the Kanze Kaikan Noh theater and Murin-an, an attractive Meiji-period garden.

340

**Walking Tour:** ✳✳ Heian Shrine—✳ Modern Art Museum—✳ Traditional Craft Museum—✳ Murin-an (garden)

**Lunch:** Rokusei, Hachiki-an

✳✳ **Heian Jingū (Shrine)** 平安神宮 Garden Hrs: Mar. 15–Aug. 31 8:30–17:30. Mar. 1– Mar. 14 and Sept. 1–Oct. 31 8:30–17:00. Nov. 1–Feb. 28 8:30–16:30. Enter by 0:30h before closing time. Dedicated to the emperors Kammu and Kōmei (father of the EMPEROR MEIJI), the first and last emperors to reign in Kyoto; Kammu was enshrined from the beginning, and Kōmei was added in 1940, at the height of State Shinto-based nationalism. The vast shrine, gaily painted vermilion and tiled in green, is a reasonably faithful, two-thirds scale reconstruction of the Daigoku-den, or Hall of State, of the Heian-period Imperial Palace, originally

# Kyoto Loses the Emperor

Over its millennium of history, Kyoto suffered repeated fires, plagues, and pillage; yet it always rose from the ashes, like a phoenix, assured of its immortality because it was the emperor's city, the spiritual heart of Japan, even in the centuries when the emperor was reduced to a shadowy figurehead. Then, in the spring of 1869, the unthinkable happened: The young EMPEROR MEIJI left Kyoto and moved permanently to Edo, newly renamed Tokyo, the Eastern Capital. The event dealt a lasting blow to Kyoto's considerable pride.

The city fathers were determined, however, to preserve Kyoto's place as Japan's cultural capital. In 1872, they held an international exposition to display Kyoto culture to the world. Not to be outdone in modernization, they built Japan's first streetcar system, modern waterworks, and power plant. To crown their efforts, they decided to build a great shrine to honor Kyoto's founder, Emperor Kammu, and the imperial institution in general.

The site chosen was significant. Here, in 1077, the retired emperor Shirakawa built a temple and actually governed as a "cloistered emperor," defying the power of the FUJIWARA. He erected a nine-storied pagoda as a symbol of his authority to greet travelers entering the city from the east. Shirakawa was the first in a series of retired emperors who tried to restore power to the imperial house; their hopes were dashed by the TAIRA and MINAMOTO warrior clans in the following century (see Miyajima History, p. 449).

In 1895, on the site of Shirakawa's pagoda, long crumbled to dust, the Heian Shrine was built to commemorate Kyoto's 1,100 years of imperial glory. Interestingly, in an era of nationalist State Shinto, the shrine was built in the foreign, Tang Chinese style of the original Heian imperial palace. The shrine's main festival, the **Jidai Matsuri** (Festival of the Ages, Oct. 22), is a long costume parade of people dressed as the courtiers and heroes from Kyoto's history.

located on the site of Nijō-jō (I:3). Behind the shrine is a spacious ◆ **pond garden** of the type supposed to have been favored in the Heian period. Unlike typical Kyoto gardens — Zen gardens in particular — it makes lavish use of flowering plants. A central focus of the garden is the Taihei-kaku, a Chinese-style bridge with a center pavilion, reminiscent of the *tsuridono* (fishing pavilion) of a Heian villa.

✳ **National Museum of Modern Art (Kokuritsu Kindai Bijutsukan)** 国立近代美術館 (761-4111). Hrs: 9:30–17:00 (enter by 16:30); F 9:30–20:00 (enter by 19:30); clsd M (Tu if M a NH), NY. Beautiful building designed by Maki Fumihiko. Fine permanent collection of contemporary ceramics on top floor. The museum's excellent galleries are often lent to major traveling art exhibits.

**Municipal Art Museum (Shiritsu Bijutsukan)** 市立美術館 (771-4107). Hrs: 9:00–17:00 (enter by 16:30); clsd M (Tu if M a NH), NY. Small collection of modern Japanese-style painting. The museum is often used for loan shows and local exhibits.

✳ **Municipal Museum of Traditional Industry (Dentō Sangyō Kaikan)** 伝統産業会館 (761-3421). Hrs: 9:00–17:00 (enter by 16:30); showroom 13:00–16:30; clsd M (Tu if M a NH), NY. Admission free. Pleasant modern galleries offering excellent displays, demonstrations, and sales of Kyoto crafts — a highly recommended introduction. The basement contains a reconstruction of a typical Kyoto townhouse interior.

✳ **Murin-an** 無鄰庵 Hrs: 9:00–16:30 (enter by 16:00); clsd NY. Near entrance to Nanzen-ji. Murin-an was the villa of the leading Meiji-period statesman, Yamagata Aritomo (see Hagi History, p. 460), who purchased the land from nearby Nanzen-ji. Its pleasant, quiet garden, built in 1896, is naturalistic in style, with stream-laced lawns enclosed by a high wall of trees which part at the far end to let in the "borrowed scenery" of the Higashiyama hills.

### Exploring Kurodani and Yoshida Jinja

North of Okazaki Park is a range of green bluffs, graced by the pagodas of two temples popularly known as Kurodani and Shinnyō-dō. For those tired of the showcase atmosphere of Kyoto's famous temples, these shady heights, with their incense-filled temple halls, graveyards, and tranquil walkways, offer a glimpse of a different Kyoto. **Kurodani**'s main halls are open, and visitors are free to roam the large, hillside cemetery, with a pretty, three-storied pagoda (1633, ICP) at the summit; there's a wonderful sunset view from here. **Shinnyō-dō**, north of Kurodani, is lovely in autumn. A short distance NW is **Yoshida Jinja**, on wooded Yoshidayama. In the 14th and 15th C, its hereditary priests, the Yoshida family, descendants of an ancient clan of diviners, developed a system whereby Shinto was the root of Buddhism, and enshrined all "eight million" kami of Japan in hopes of establishing itself as the head of all shrines; the system was broken up after the Meiji Restoration. The main shrine hall, Saijōsho Daigen-gū (1484, ICP), is an unusual octagonal structure with a thatched hip-and-gable roof. It is now the guardian shrine of nearby **Kyoto University**.

## II:5 NANZEN-JI, GINKAKU-JI, AND PHILOSOPHER'S WALK

For many people, this area is the essence of Kyoto: Nanzen-ji, the classic Zen temple, and Ginkaku-ji, a jewel of medieval villa design and garden art. The two are linked by a tranquil canalside path, Philosopher's Walk, named for Nishida Kitarō (1870–1945), a professor at nearby Kyoto University, who attempted a fusion of Western and Eastern philosophies. Like Kant, Nishida seems to have had an unvarying morning walk, which took him along the cherry-lined canal. Nishida was influenced by European higher mathematics and was also deeply interested in the philosophies of Hegel, William James, Henri Bergson, and others. At the same time, Nishida practiced Zen meditation, and was a lifelong friend of the modern Zen philosopher Suzuki Daisetz. Perhaps, then, it was no accident that Nishida's walk took him near two of Kyoto's most renowned Zen temples.

**Walking Tour:** ✳✳ Nanzen-ji — ✳ Eikan-dō — Nyakuōji Jinja — ✳✳ Philosopher's Walk (Sen'oku Hakkokan, Antoku-ji, Hōnen-in) — ✳✳✳ Ginkaku-ji — Hakusason-sō

**Lunch:** Okutan, Kōan, Omen, Osaidokoro, Daigin

**Note:** In mid-April, Philosopher's Walk is enveloped in an ethereal cloud of cherry blossoms.

✳✳ **Nanzen-ji** 南禅寺 *0:10h from Heian Shrine or 0:05h from Murin-an on foot; or take bus 5 to Eikan-dō-mae, then 0:05h on foot.* This celebrated Zen temple is located amid shady pine groves at the foot of Higashiyama. In this serene spot, retired emperor Kameyama built a villa which was converted into a Zen temple in 1291, at his behest. Its second abbot expanded it into a full monastery and gave it its name. Chinese tradition dictated that the top Zen temples should be five in number, the Gozan. The members of the Kyoto Gozan frequently changed, but as of 1380, Nanzen-ji ranked first. Later, when Shogun ASHIKAGA YOSHIMITSU wanted to include the newly founded Shōkoku-ji among the five, Nanzen-ji was promoted to a special status, above the five temples; therefore when one talks about Kyoto's Five Great Zen Temples, one sometimes means six. In the 15th C, Nanzen-ji, like most of Kyoto, was destroyed in the Ōnin Wars. Today, none of its halls predates the late 16th C. Scattered about the precincts are subtemples, elegant ryokan and the famous

Nanzen-ji tofu restaurants. Just north of the temple, along the road toward Eikan-dō, are Okutan, a tofu restaurant, and Kōan, which serves Buddhist vegetarian cuisine.

◆ **San-mon** (Gate, 1628, ICP). Hrs: 8:00–17:00. Nov.–Mar. 8:30–17:00. The massive, two-story temple gate was built to console those fallen in the 1615 siege of Ōsaka Castle (see Kyoto History, p. 323). The second floor, which offers a splendid view, houses a Shaka trinity, 16 Rakan, and wall paintings of heavenly beings. In the Kabuki play *Sanmon Gosan no Kiri*, Ishikawa Goemon, a Japanese Robin Hood, hides in this gate until he is captured and boiled to death; the iron cauldron baths once common in Japan are called *Goemon-buro*.

**Tenju-an** 天授庵 (Subtemple). Hrs: 9:00–17:00, in spring and fall only. Noted for its pleasant gardens.

◆ **Konchi-in** 金地院 (Subtemple). Hrs: 8:30–17:00 (enter by 16:30). Around 1600, Konchi-in's abbot Sūden, an influential figure who mediated between the shogunate and Kyoto's temples, restored this temple and built the **Tōshō-gū** (1628, ICP), a shrine to TOKUGAWA IEYASU, on the low rise to the south. Unlike its florid namesake, the Nikko Tōshō-gū, it is coated entirely in black lacquer, giving it a rather ominous aspect. The Tōkaidō highway entered Kyoto not far from here, and the shrine was probably intended to remind travelers arriving in the imperial city of the shogun's authority. From the Tōshō-gū, proceed through the small gate to the right, to the **Hōjō** (abbot's quarters, ICP); this hall, moved from Fushimi-jō, is decorated with KANŌ SCHOOL paintings. The famous ◆ **garden**, completed in 1632, is one of the few authenticated works by the great garden master, KOBORI ENSHŪ. It consists of a large quadrangle of raked white sand with two arrangements of boulders and gnarled pine trees, said to suggest a tortoise and crane, symbols of immortality. The one horizontal and the other vertical, they are tensely balanced. Rising behind the quadrangle is an embankment of lush, clipped shrubbery, a signature of Enshū's style. The large, flat stone embedded in the garden supposedly afforded a place to meditate and at the same time pay homage to Ieyasu.

◆ **Hōjō (Nanzen-ji Abbot's Quarters)** 方丈 (NT). Hrs: 8:30–16:30. Nov.–Mar. 8:30–17:00. The Hōjō consists of two buildings, the Dai Hōjō, originally part of the Imperial Palace, and the Shō Hōjō, formerly in Fushimi-jō. Both were given to Nanzen-ji in 1611. The halls contain paintings by the Kanō School masters MOTONOBU, EITOKU, and TAN'YŪ. The **main garden**, south of the Dai Hōjō, is a composition of raked white gravel, large boulders, and bold vegetation, enclosed by an earthen wall and "borrowing" the scenery of nearby temple roofs and hills (see Villas, p. 64).

**Nanzen-in** 南禅院 (Subtemple). Hrs: 8:30–17:00 (enter by 16:30). South of the Hōjō, beyond the aqueduct that cuts through the Nanzen-ji precincts. This subtemple is built on the site of the original temple founded by the retired emperor Kameyama. The present buildings were built by Tokugawa Tsunayoshi's mother, Keishō-in, in 1703 (see Tokyo History, p. 195). The quiet, peaceful garden centers on a "heart" pond, said to be descended from a Kamakura-period garden by the famous Zen prelate MUSŌ SOSEKI, who served as one of Nanzen-ji's early abbots.

✳ **Nomura Bijutsukan (Art Museum)** 野村美術館 Hrs: 10:00–16:30; clsd M, June 10–Sept. 10, Dec. 5–Mar. 10. A modern Japanese-style building on the left side of the road linking Nanzen-ji and Eikan-dō. Features tea ceremony wares, including a tea scoop made by HIDEYOSHI and an Oribe incense box in the shape of an owl.

✳ **Eikan-dō (Zenrin-ji)** 永観堂 Hrs: 9:00–17:00 (enter by 16:00). *A short walk N of Nanzen-ji.* An enjoyable temple. The lower grounds are more a public park than temple garden, and the entire precincts are charmingly shabby. It was founded in 856 as a Shingon temple, but at the end of the 11th C it was converted into an Amidist temple by the priest Eikan—hence its popular name. The temple halls are built against the mountainside and linked by long, covered corridors and stairways. The **Main Hall** enshrines a famous image, the **Mikaeri Amida**, an unusual statue of Amida looking over his shoulder. Although art experts think differently, temple lore ascribes the image to Eikan. According to legend, the statue joined the *nembutsu* dance Eikan was leading. When the flabbergasted Eikan stopped dancing, Amida looked at him over his shoulder and told him to get a move on!

✳✳ **Philosopher's Walk (Tetsugaku no Michi)** 哲学の道 This canalside path winds through a quiet residential neighborhood, with occasional imperial tombs and temples, peaceful sanctuaries favored as mortuary temples by poets and artists. In the Heian period, this area, Shishigatani, was the scene of a plot against TAIRA NO KIYOMORI; the plot failed, but Kiyomori's harsh punishment of the conspirators augured the doom of the house of Taira. In mid-April, when the cherry trees that line the canal erupt into bloom, this may be the most beautiful spot in Kyoto. The walk is described from south to north, but is just as easily followed in reverse. The walk is level and takes half an hour from Nyakuōji Jinja to Ginkaku-ji.

**Nyakuōji Jinja** 若王子神社 *0:05h on foot, NE of Eikan-dō.* In 1160, Emperor Go-Shirakawa founded this small shrine as a branch of the Kumano Shrines (see Kinki, p. 415).

◆ **Kanō Shōju-an** 叶匠寿庵 若王子町2-1 (751-1077). Hrs: 9:00–16:30; clsd W, NY. A lovely Japanese confectionary shop, done tastefully in a modern style, with barewood furniture and Tamba pottery floortiles. One can rest over a bowl of *matcha* in the tearoom. The service is gracious, and when the shop is not crowded, they will even perform a simple tea ceremony for you.

Philosopher's Walk
0     100m

Jōdo-in 卍

Ginkaku-ji
銀閣寺 卍

5  4
Hakusason-sō
白沙村荘

Ginkaku-ji-mae ♀ 3

N

Bobby Soxer ■
(coffee, pizza)

Hōnen-in
法然院

Shishigatani canal

Reizei ■
Emperor
mausoleum

Anraku-ji
安楽寺 卍

Shishigatani-dōri

Shirakawa-dōri
白川通り

Shirakawa
白川

Notre
Dame
Women's
College

♀ Kamimiyanomae-chō

♀ Shinnyō-dō-mae

Philosopher's Walk 哲学の道

Sen'oku
Hakkokan
泉屋博古館

Miyanomaechō  ■ Kōun-ji
Nyakuōji
(coffee) ■

♀ Higashi-
Tennōchō  卍 Chōshō-in
Kanō
Shōju-an

to Nyakuōji
Jinja

Eikan-dō
永観堂

♀ Eikan-dō-mae

Nomura
Art
Museum ■

Lake Biwa aqueduct

to Okazaki Park

2
1 Chōshō-in
(tofu)
Nanzen-ji
南禅寺  Hōjō

Junsei
(tofu)  San-mon

Tenju-an 卍

■ Yachiyo
Ryokan
卍 Konchi-in   Nanzen-in 卍

◆ **Sen'oku Hakkokan** 泉屋博古館
(771-7227). Hrs: 10:00–16:00 (enter
by 15:30); clsd Su, NH, July–Aug., and
Dec.–Feb. A few minutes W of Kōun-ji,
a large temple hall visible from Philosopher's Walk. This handsome museum,
frequented by few people, exhibits the
magnificent Sumitomo collection of
ancient Chinese bronzes, one of the
best in the world. It also has a fine
group of Chinese paintings, shown for
two weeks in May and October.

**Anraku-ji** 安楽寺 Open only Sa, Su,
and NH in Apr., May, 2nd week in June,
Oct., and Nov. Hrs: 9:30–16:00. A
secluded little temple, built in memory
of Anraku and Juren, two monks who
were followers of Hōnen Shōnin,
founder of the Jōdo sect. They converted two of Emperor Go-Toba's
ladies-in-waiting, who fled the palace
and became nuns. Rumors arose that
the two monks' intentions were not
entirely honorable, and the furious
emperor exiled Hōnen and executed
the monks. The lush, still temple
grounds contain their stupa-shaped
tombs and the graves of the ladies, Pine
Beetle and Bell Cricket.

343

◆ **Hōnen-in (Temple)** 法然院 Hrs:
6:00–16:00, daily. The main hall, with
its famous Momoyama screens (ICP), is
open Apr. 1–7, and Nov. 1–7. Founded
in 1680 by an abbot of Chion-in (II:3)
on the site of a chapel where Honen
and his two followers, Anraku and
Juren, performed a 24-hour cycle of
prayer. The grounds are loveliest in fall,
when maples spread a crimson canopy
over the stone steps, raked white sand,
and beds of moss. The graveyard contains the tomb of the novelist Tanizaki
Junichirō (1886–1965).

**\*\*\* Ginkaku-ji (Jishō-ji)** 銀閣寺 Hrs: 8:30–17:00 (enter by 16:30). In winter 9:00–
16:30. *Bus 5, 17, 203 to Ginkaku-ji-mae; or 0:10b by taxi from Shijō-Kawaramachi.* In
1482, the eighth Ashikaga shogun YOSHIMASA retired here, at his newly completed
Higashiyama villa, built on the site of an old Amidist temple. As this was barely five years after
the ruinous Ōnin War, Yoshimasa was never able to cover its famous Silver Pavilion in silver
leaf. Like his grandfather YOSHIMITSU, who built the Golden Pavilion (IV:2), Yoshimasa
aspired to promote a cultural flowering at his villa. Here, Yoshimasa gathered a circle of connoisseurs and patronized Murata Shukō, who created the tea ceremony; the temple has
Japan's oldest tea room (see Villas, p. 64–65). Yoshimasa's **Higashiyama Culture** was one of
the Muromachi period's cultural apexes. Ginkaku-ji itself, with its blend of aristocratic refinement and Zen asceticism, is considered the epitome of Higashiyama style. Of the original 12
buildings, the Silver Pavilion and Tōgu-dō are the only important structures to survive.

◆ **Garden.** The grounds are entered by a carefully composed approach, first through a formal corridor of tall hedges, then around a bend to a gate. Beyond is a second gate and wall with a bell-shaped window, framing the first glimpse of the garden proper. It is one of the most interesting — and strangest — gardens in Kyoto, a combination of an abstract dry garden and a lushly planted pond garden. Originally, the garden and pavilion were modeled on the celebrated garden of Saihō-ji (V:3), with its complex pond, pavilion, and boulder arrangement in the upper garden, called Cha no I, or Tea Well. The dazzling white flattened cone and sea of sand appeared much later, in the early Edo period; it is said that they were for moon viewing, but a rival theory suggests that the cone developed from piles of sand kept on hand to rake over the bare ground. The pavilion, the pond, and the pines in the background provide interesting contrasts that accent one's progress through the garden. It is thought that Yoshimasa designed the garden with the help of the son or grandson of Zen'ami, a famous "rock-placement artist" who founded a dynasty of professional gardeners. Zen'ami was from the *kawaramono*, or "riverbank people," a pariah class. In the Muromachi period, however, talented members often attained recognition in the highest circles, something that became unthinkable in later periods.

◆ **Ginkaku** (Silver Pavilion, ca. 1489, NT). The first floor is in the residential Shoin style, while the second is in the Zen style, with bell-shaped windows. It houses an image of Kannon. This pavilion is said to be a copy of the no-longer-extant Ruriden pavilion of Saihō-ji.

◆ **Tōgu-dō** (NT). Apply in writing for permission to view the interior. This building, which adjoins the Hondō (Main Hall), was Yoshimasa's residence and private chapel. Its northeast chamber is the famous **Dōjin-sai**, Japan's oldest tearoom — the first to have the canonical 4¹/₂ tatami mats — as well as the very first example of *shoin* architecture.

**Jōdo-in.** Not open to public. This little Jōdo temple, all that remains of a large, Tendai Amidist temple of the Heian period, is responsible for the oldest and most famous of the five Daimonji bonfires (Aug. 16). The annual rite is said to have begun as a Bon rite for the victims of epidemics and famine that decimated Kyoto, even as Yoshimasa enjoyed himself at his Silver Pavilion. A trail, starting north of the temple, leads to the huge *dai*, a character meaning "great," near the top of Nyoigadake hill behind Ginkaku-ji.

**Hakusason-sō** 白沙村荘 Hrs: 10:00–17:00. Built as a villa in 1916 by the painter Hashimoto Kansetsu, it has a pleasant garden and is now a museum of the artist's work.

# KYOTO III. NORTHEAST KYOTO

**Main Attractions:**

The theme of these wooded mountains and scenic valleys is the gradual decline and collapse of Japan's Heian-period Golden Age (see Uji and Miyajima Histories, pp. 387 and 449). Widespread pessimism was caused by the belief in Mappō, "the decline of the Buddhist law," which was supposed to begin in 1052; only by turning one's back on this world and depending on the Amida's mercy could one be saved. Like many other Japanese sects, Amidism originated at Enryaku-ji, the Tendai headquarters on Hiei-zan, the mountain dominating northeast Kyoto. As FUJIWARA power declined at the end of the Heian period, Hiei's warrior-monks wreaked havoc as they swarmed into the city to battle other sects or extort political concessions from the court. Retired emperor Shirakawa said there were three things he couldn't control: "the waters of the Kamo River, the dice of the *sugoroku* game, and the bonzes of the mountain." The Heian period came to a close in 1185 when the TAIRA were defeated in battle and exterminated. KIYOMORI's daughter, the empress KENREIMON-IN, was allowed to take the tonsure and retire to Ōhara, today an hour's bus ride from Kyoto. Her hermitage at Jakkō-in is a short walk from Sanzen-in, one of the earliest temples associated with the belief in Amida.

## III:1 SHŪGAKU-IN AREA

This area is noted for three outstanding Sukiya-style villas and gardens, the product of a small aristocratic circle, which reflect the vitality of Kyoto culture in the early Edo period.

**Tour:** ✱✱ Shisen-dō — (0:15h on foot) — ✱✱ Manshū-in — (0:10h on foot) — ✱✱✱ Shūgaku-in (by reservation) — (0:15h by taxi) — ✱ Entsū-ji — (0:10h by taxi) — ✱ Kamigamo Jinja

**Lunch:** Old and New, Heihachi-jaya, Azekura

**Notes** This is a recommended tour for those interested in gardens and Sukiya architecture. Bus 5 is fairly convenient. Shisen-dō's clipped azaleas bloom in May; Shūgaku-in has superb autumn foliage.

** **Shisen-dō (Temple)** 詩仙堂 Hrs: 9:00–17:00; clsd May 23. The villa of Ishikawa Jōzan (1583–1672), a littérateur of the early Edo period. Originally a retainer of TOKUGAWA IEYASU, Jōzan quarrelled with him over the 1615 siege of Ōsaka-jō and was forced to take the tonsure and retire to Kyoto. He built his "temple"—really a pleasant villa—in 1636, and devoted himself to the gentler arts. The villa is named Poets' Hall after the KANO TAN'YŪ paintings of the thirty-six classical poets that decorate the walls of one of the chambers. As befits Jōzan's independent spirit, both villa and garden are quite unlike any other. The garden is renowned for its superbly composed view from the veranda: clipped azaleas with a foreground of white raked sand and background of wild forest. The harmony achieved between the dark interior and the bright garden is delightful. The stillness is occasionally broken by the sound of the *shishi-odoshi*, a bamboo device that fills with water until it tips over, spilling the water and rebounding with a resounding clack—ostensibly to chase away marauding wild boars. Next to Shisen-dō is **Nobotoke-an** 野仏庵 a group of five tea arbors in various styles. Hrs: 11:00–16:00. Admission fee includes tea.

** **Manshū-in (Temple)** 曼殊院 Hrs: 9:00–17:00. Although well known for its superb Sukiya-style buildings and garden, this villa-cum-temple is usually peaceful, with few visitors. The temple was originally established by Saichō on Hiei-zan. When it was moved here in 1656, it was completely rebuilt under the guidance of its abbot, Prince Yoshihisa. He was the son of Hachijō-no-miya Toshihito, the architect of Katsura Imperial Villa (V:3), of which Manshū-in is strongly reminiscent. The **Daishoin** (Great Shoin, ICP), which enshrines an image of Amida, is noted for its exquisitely crafted door handles in such shapes as scrolls, fans, and gourds. The main rooms of the **Kojoin** (Small Shoin, ICP) are even finer examples, but are not shown to the public. Both *shoin* are elegantly roofed with cypress shingles. The adjoining **tea arbor** (ICP) is in the "eight-window" style of KOBORI ENSHŪ. The lovely garden employs white sand to suggest ponds and rivulets, dotted by islands of rock, moss, and plants, and blends with its natural backdrop.

345

*** **Shūgaku-in Rikyū (Imperial Villa)** 修学院離宮 1:30h tours (in Japanese only), M–F 9:00, 10:00, 11:00, 13:30, and 15:00; Sa 9:00, 10:00, and 11:00; clsd 2nd and 4th Sa, Su, NH, day after NH, Dec. 25–Jan. 5. By reservation through the Imperial Household Agency (I:3). This magnificent, parklike estate at the foot of Hiei-zan was the life work of the retired

# Emperor Go-Mizuno'o and Kyoto's Artistic Revival

Ever since the fall of the Taira, the imperial court had lived in relative penury. The court's fortunes changed in 1620, after Emperor Go-Mizuno'o married TOKUGAWA Kazuko, the daughter of the second shogun Hidetada. Her bridal procession from Edo was an exercise in extravagance that cost seven times the annual income of the imperial household. In 1624, she was elevated to Empress, and became known as **Tōfukumon-in**. At first, his in-law's efforts to meddle in affairs of the throne estranged Go-Mizuno'o from the shogunate, but he eventually made peace with them and received a generous stipend. For the first time in more than four centuries, the court was able to live in some style.

The imperial couple and their Tokugawa patrons set about rebuilding Kyoto, much of which had been burned during the preceding centuries of disorder. The palace was rebuilt, the older buildings were donated to Daikaku-ji and Ninna-ji, and many other temples, such as Kiyomizu-dera and Nanzen-ji, were rebuilt from scratch. The emperor and empress patronized HON'AMI KŌETSU and the artisans of Nishijin, and were themselves accomplished in the gentler arts. Tōfukumon-in gave land for Sen no Sōtan's tea ceremony school. Go-Mizuno'o supported the Ikenobō school of *rikka* flower arrangement and favored the *sencha* infused tea ceremony imported from China by the monks of Mampuku-ji (Kinki, p. 389). He shared *sencha* with Shogun Ietsuna and his uncle, Prince Hachijō-no-miya Toshitada, builder of the famed Katsura Villa. The Hachijō-no-miya family produced many other noted examples of the Sukiya-Shoin style such as the Kuro Shoin of Nishi Hongan-ji, built by an abbot who was married to Toshitada's daughter (see Villas, p. 67).

Go-Mizuno'o himself designed the exquisite retreat at **Shūgaku-in**, his life work. The retired emperor and Tōfukumon-in made periodic excursions to this collection of delicate "teahouses" amid rice paddies, parklands, and ponds, to enjoy a few days in its restful, expansive atmosphere, cultivating a life of arts and leisure. Go-Mizuno'o continued to visit his beloved villa until he was well into his eighties. Near Shūgaku-in are several smaller but very fine Sukiya villas of the same era. The *sukiya shoin* of **Manshū-in** was built by a son of Toshitada who took the tonsure and retired to this peaceful mountain villa-temple. **Shisen-dō** was built by a former Tokugawa retainer, who also nominally became a monk and took up an aristocratic life of poetry and art.

emperor, Go-Mizuno'o (see box). Shūgaku-in is divided into three levels, called the "three teahouses," not because they were specifically intended for tea, but to reflect their informal, Sukiya-style construction. These sufficed for brief stays of a few nights, but were never intended for permanent residence. The original villa designed by Go-Mizuno'o included only the lower and upper levels. The middle level was part of a nunnery for one of Go-Mizuno'o's daughters. The three complexes were originally linked only by rustic footpaths between paddy fields, in harmony with the Sukiya ethic of understated simplicity. In 1884, however, under the influence of the imperial restoration and modern ideas of monumentality, each teahouse was surrounded by walls and joined by stately paths symmetrically flanked by dwarf pines.

**Shimo no Ochaya (Lower Teahouse).** Go-Mizuno'o would rest here upon arrival, after a journey by oxcart that took several hours. The L-shaped **Jugetsukan** pavilion was restored in 1824. The small garden is naturalistic and full of motion, laced with rivulets and tiny cascades. It is noted for two stone lanterns, a "Korean lantern," and a strikingly modern "sleeve-shaped" lantern, which has a rectangular base with a square bite taken out of it; it is also called Crocodile Mouth.

**Naka no Ochaya (Middle Teahouse).** The middle villa was built in 1668 for Akenomiya Teruko, a daughter of Go-Mizuno'o who retired as a nun, and remained part of the Rinkyū-ji convent until it was returned to the Imperial Household in 1885. The **Rakushiken** hall was moved here from Teruko's living quarters at the Imperial Palace. The adjoining ◆ **Kyaku-den** was formerly Tōfukumon-in's dressing room there. It has an exquisite *chigaidana* (staggered shelving); it is considered, with those at Sambō-in Temple and Katsura Imperial Villa, one of the three most beautiful. The low paper doors below the shelves are painted with scenes of Yūzen silk dyers at work, and one set of cedar doors is painted with Gion Matsuri floats, including the ever-popular Boat Float, a theme that belongs to the popular genre-screen tradition and reflects the cultural affinity between Kyoto's aristocrats and wealthy townsmen (see Art, p. 98). Another set of doors is painted with fat, lifelike carp, which, according to lore, swam away each night until the famous painter, Maruyama Ōkyo, painted nets over them — complete with holes and tatters. The "Christian stone lantern" in the garden has a tiny image at its base of the Virgin Mary in the guise of Jizō Bosatsu, dating from the days of the Christian persecutions (see Nagasaki History, p. 483).

**Kami no Ochaya (Upper Teahouse).** The approach to the uppermost pavilion is by a pine-lined path, surrounded by paddy fields. To the left, a large embankment of terraced, clipped hedges echoes the terraces of the rice paddies. The final approach cuts sharply up a stone stairway, narrowly hemmed in by hedges that gradually become lower and more open. At the top, just as one reaches the ◆ **Rin'un-tei** pavilion, the view explodes into a vast panorama. This dramatic view is the masterpiece of Shūgaku-in. It is said that Go-Mizuno'o composed the view with painstaking care, building a clay model to help him design the dam and lake to provide the perfect middleground that would link the distant hills and the foreground into a coherent whole. It is easily the most spectacular use of the "borrowed scenery" (*shakkei*) technique in Japanese garden history (see Villas, p. 68).

**The Lake.** The path around the lake is expertly designed to offer an ever-changing, beguiling series of views. The two islands in the lake are joined by the pavilion-like **Chitose-bashi** (Eternity Bridge). There is a story that this bridge was a gift to the villa in 1824; the donor's generosity to the imperial house so alarmed the shogunate that the poor man was ordered to commit suicide. The ◆ **Kyūsui-ken** tea arbor, located on the northern island, was already in place as an informal retreat before the official construction began. Its paper-thin shutter of red wood is designed to shed a warm, crimson light at sunset, and can be lifted at other times of the day to take in the view.

✳ **Entsū-ji** 円通寺 Hrs: 10:00–16:00. *Taxi or 0:20h walk from Kitayama station.* This Zen temple was originally a villa of Emperor Go-Mizuno'o. After the completion of Shūgaku-in, this villa passed through various hands until in 1678 it became a nunnery. Go-Mizuno'o was fascinated by the possibilities of the *shakkei* or "borrowed scenery" technique, which is used so impressively at Shūgaku-in (see above). At Entsū-ji, Hiei-zan, the spiritual protector of Kyoto, provides the backdrop for a meditative lawn-and-rock garden. A trimmed hedge, some low brush, and slender trees establish an effective middle ground that serves both to block out the characterless suburbs between the temple and the mountain, and to draw Hiei-zan into the garden's composition.

## The Kamo Shrines

The upper Kamo shrine, Kamigamo Jinja, and the lower Kamo shrine, Shimogamo Jinja, both on the banks of the Kamogawa, share a story: One day, the goddess of Shimogamo was bathing in the river when a red arrow came swimming toward her.... By and by a son, the Thunder God, was born, and was enshrined at Kamigamo Jinja. Historical records show that the Kamo Shrines were already established in the 7th C, and were the tutelary shrines of the Kamo, a wealthy local family of Korean origin (see Kyoto History, p. 319). During the Heian period, these shrines, like the Ise Shrines, had an imperial priestess — an institution with shamanistic origins — and were rebuilt every 21 years until 1863. Their Nagare-style architecture became the most typical shrine style in Japan (see Shinto, p. 28). The Kamo Shrines are famous for their innumerable festivals, many of archaic form, and most of all for the Aoi Matsuri (May 15). This festival existed by the 7th C, and in the Heian period became an elaborate procession from the Imperial Palace.

**＊ Shimogamo Jinja** 下鴨神社 *Bus 1, 4, 14, 54, 205.* This shrine, possibly the oldest in Kyoto, is set in a large wood, at the fork where the Kamogawa is joined by a tributary, the Takanogawa. The stately Honden and Gonden (temporary shrine) are NT.

**＊ Kamigamo Jinja** 上賀茂神社 *In the north of Kyoto, 0:10h walk from Kitayama.* This is the more beautiful of the two shrines, with its sylvan setting and emerald lawns. Mysterious cones of white sand stand before the Honden and Gonden (NT).

**Ōta Jinja** 大田神社 *0:10h walk east of Kamigamo Jinja,* via a pretty street with a clear-running stream and earthen walls belonging to the traditional, prosperous-looking houses of families with hereditary connections to Kamigamo Jinja. In May, around the time of the Aoi Matsuri, the pond in front of this tiny shrine becomes a mass of purple iris.

**Azekura** 愛染倉 Hrs: 9:00–17:00; clsd M. A short distance east of Ōta Jinja. This early 18th- and 19th-C Yamato house was moved to this pleasant locale in 1967. It is now a lovely *soba* shop. The grounds contain a folklore museum.

## III:2 HIEI-ZAN

Hiei is historically the most important monastery mountain in Japan. In former days it was a temple city, with thousands of subtemples. Although today only about about 70 remain, it is still a pleasure to walk in the shade of its forest and discover some solitary temple. One cannot truly understand Kyoto's history—or Japan's—until one has seen Hiei-zan.

---

**Tour 1:** Kyoto station — (1:10h by bus) — ＊＊ Enryaku-ji — (0:10h by tramway) — Yase Yūen station — (0:15h by bus) — Ōhara — (0:40h by bus) — Central Kyoto

**Tour 2:** Enryaku-ji — (0:10h by cable car) — Hiyoshi Taisha (VI:2) — (0:10h on foot) — Sakamoto station — (0:15h by train) — Mii-dera — Hama-Ōtsu — (0:30h by Keihan line) — Kyoto

---

347

**＊＊ Enryaku-ji** 延暦寺
Hrs: 9:00–16:30 (Sai-tō and Yokawa close at 16:00 and 15:30). Dec.–Feb. 9:30–16:00. *1:10h by express bus from Kyoto station, via Shijō-Ōmiya, Keihan-Sanjō station, and Imadegawa-dōri. From Yase Yūen station, 0:10h by cable car and tramway (once every 0:30h), then 0:40h on foot to the Konpon Chū-dō.* The headquarters of the Tendai sect, built to guard Kyoto's "unlucky" northeast direction, Enryaku-ji was founded in 806 by Saichō (see Kyoto History, p. 319). As one can see from all the different rituals performed in the halls on the mountain, Tendai embraces a variety of practices. These gave rise to nearly all the subsequent major sects of Japanese Buddhism. The founders of the Jōdo, Jōdo Shin, Nichiren, and Zen sects all began their careers here. Angered by such affronts to its authority, Enryaku-ji's warrior-monks often raided offending temples or even the city itself; the great monastery that was supposed to protect Kyoto instead became its scourge. These raids persisted for hundreds of years. In 1571, the ruthlessly efficient ODA NOBUNAGA burned the entire monastery, massacring virtually every soul on the mountain. HIDEYOSHI and the TOKUGAWA helped rebuild the main halls, but while Enryaku-ji is still impressive, it is but a shadow of itself in former times, when it could boast of 3,000 subtemples.

**Tō-tō (East Tower or Precincts).** The Konpon Chū-dō and Jōdo-in, the most important halls of Enryaku-ji, are here. It is also more visited than the Western Precincts (Sai-tō).

◆ **Konpon Chū-dō (Fundamental Central Hall)** 根本中堂 (NT). This is the very heart of the Tendai faith, built on the site of Saichō's first hermitage, a small hall dedicated to Yakushi Nyorai, the Buddha of Healing. The present hall, of much vaster size, was last rebuilt in 1642. The great hall is enclosed by a cloister. Such features as the copper roof and the curved "Chinese" gable over the entrance show that it was built after the Momayama period. The interior is divided into an outer worship hall, for laypeople, and an inner hall, with a deeply sunken stone floor, for initiates. The main image of Yakushi is flanked by Nikkō and Gakkō Bosatsu, the Four Directional Guardians, and the Twelve Divine Generals. The chrysanthemum crests incorporated into the lantern grids recall Enryaku-ji's connection with the imperial house; until 1868, the abbot was always a high-ranking aristocrat, often an imperial prince.

**Kaidan-in (Ordination Hall,** ICP). *W of the Konpon Chū-dō.* The battles (both verbal and armed) between Enryaku-ji and Nara Buddhism arose over Saichō's demand that he be allowed to establish an independent ordination platform. Until then, all Buddhist priests were ordained under the auspices of Nara's Tōdai-ji. Permission was granted in 827, after Saichō's death. Wars with the Nara temples led Enryaku-ji to keep an army of monks, making it a potent political force. The present ordination hall, built in 1604, has the bell-shaped windows and the curved "Chinese" gable that became extremely common in the Momoyama period.

**Jōdo-in (Pure Land Hall)** 浄土院 *0:15h on foot NW; walk along the road or adjacent path to the tiny chapel, Sannō-in, then follow the path to the right.* This peaceful, well-kept temple contains three halls: one houses a concealed image of Amida supposedly carved by Saichō himself, the second a statue of Saichō, and the third, the one in the back surrounded by a stone fence, is Saichō's tomb.

**Mudōjiga-dani** 無動寺谷 *0:25h on foot from Konpon Chū-dō.* Although this is part of the Eastern Precinct, it is about a kilometer south of the rest and is often called the "southern mountain." The main hall is dedicated to the fierce deity Fudō Myō-ō. In both Tendai and Shingon, Fudō—literally "the unwavering"—gives support to monks who undergo austerities, such as those undertaking the most difficult of Tendai's "three difficult practices." In this ordeal, one must walk 30 km a day for 800 days, 60 km a day for 100 days, 84 km a day for 100 days, and then, entirely foregoing food and sleep, meditate for two weeks.

**Sai-tō (Western Precinct)** 西塔 *A pleasant, 0:15h walk by road or mountain trail NW of Jōdo-in.* This area, devoid of parking lots and tour buses, has a decidedly more spiritual atmosphere.

**Benkei no Ninai-dō (The Halls that were Benkei's Burden,** 1595, ICP). Two halls connected by a bridge, which Benkei, a superman warrior-monk (YOSHITSUNE's sidekick), supposedly carried over his shoulders. In the **Jōgyō-dō** (Forever Walking Hall), monks circumambulate a statue of Amida, chanting "Save me, Amida Buddha." In the **Hokke-dō** (Lotus Sutra Hall) monks alternately walk, chanting the Lotus Sutra, and sit meditating on it. The Lotus Sutra, based on Shaka's last sermon, is considered in Tendai to contain the highest level of truth. (Tendai recognizes many levels of truth.)

**Shaka-dō (Hall,** ICP). Down a flight of steps from the Ninai-dō, at the bottom of the valley, is the main hall of the Western Precinct. The oldest structure on Hiei-zan, this hall was brought here by HIDEYOSHI's order from Mii-dera, the rival Tendai monastery at the eastern foot of Hiei (see VI:1). Dating from the Kamakura period, the hall is in the Wayō style favored by old Tendai and Shingon temples (see Buddhism, p. 36). The hall houses a concealed image of Shaka "carved" by Saichō, and statues of the Four Directional Guardians.

348

See p. 375 for hotels

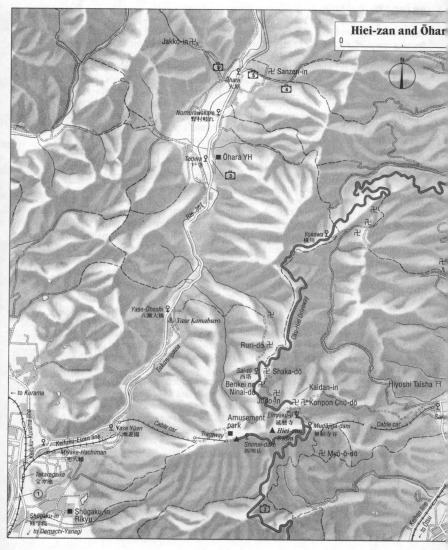

**Sōrin-tō (Spire,** ICP). A *sōrin-tō* is the nine-ringed metal spire that crowns a pagoda. Pagodas were reliquaries; here, the *sōrin-tō* itself performs this function, covering a vault containing 23 sutra scrolls buried by Saichō.

**Ruri-dō** (ICP). *800 m north of Sōrin-tō.* This "lapis-lazuli hall" from the Muromachi period was the only building on Hiei to escape NOBUNAGA's armies in 1571.

**Yokawa.** *Almost 4 km NE of the Western Precinct; 1:30h on foot, or 0:10h by very infrequent bus.* The third of Enryaku-ji's precincts, this is the most isolated. There is little to see, except perhaps the **Hihōkan** (Treasure Hall), which is open only in the spring and fall. Although Tendai believers had always worshipped Amida as one of many aids to salvation, Genshin (942–1017), who founded Yokawa, made it a center of exclusive Amida worship (see Sanzen-in, III:3).

**Sakamoto and Hiyoshi Taisha** (see VI:2). *0:11h by cable car from near the Konpon Chū-dō.* Sakamoto, "the foot of the hill," was the base of the pilgrim's approach to Hiei. Nearby stands Enryaku-ji's guardian shrine, Hiyoshi Taisha, which, although it developed under the strong influence of Enryaku-ji, in fact predates the temple. The monks of Hiei would carry the *mikoshi* (portable shrines) of Hiyoshi Taisha when they attacked Kyoto.

## III:3 ŌHARA

This pretty country village is famous for its two Amidist temples, Sanzen-in and Jakkō-in, and the *Ōhara-me* (Ōhara wenches), who dressed in rustic garb and carried firewood on their heads, which they sold, until recently, in Kyoto. Today they roam Ōhara under the auspices of the local tourist association.

---

**Day Trip:** Central Kyoto — (0:40h by bus) — Ōhara — (0:05h on foot) — ** Sanzen-in — (0:25h on foot) — * Jakkō-in

**Lunch:** Suigetsu Chaya. Also numerous teahouses around the temples.

**Note:** Sanzen-in's autumn foliage draws large crowds.

---

**** Sanzen-in (Temple)** 三千院 Hrs: 8:30–17:00 (enter by 16:30). Dec.–Feb. 8:30–16:30 (enter by 16:00). *0:40h by bus "Kita 6" from Demachi-Yanagi station, or 0:35h by bus 13, 14, or 15 from Kita-ōji station, or 0:40h from Sanjō-Keihan by bus 17 (all via Yase Yūen station at the base of Hiei-zan); get off at Ōhara bus stop and walk 0:05h east.* Sanzen-in's Amida Hall, standing in grounds shaded by lofty cryptomeria and carpeted by moss, is one of Kyoto's loveliest sights. Its radiant autumn foliage attracts large crowds, but it is perhaps most sublime in winter, under the silent cover of snow. The Amida Hall was first built in 985 by Genshin, a retired vice-abbot of Enryaku-ji. During his years of study at the Yokawa district of Hiei, Genshin came to believe that the unlearned masses, for whom monastic discipline was an impossibility, could attain salvation by praying wholeheartedly for Amida's Pure Land Paradise. He called his Amida Hall the Ōjō-Gokuraku-in, the Temple of Rebirth in Paradise, and created in it such a vision of unearthly beauty as to evoke intense yearning for the Pure Land. Genshin considered this an extension of Tendai teachings, but in later times, Hōnen Shōnin preached the supremacy of faith in Amida, which led to schism and the founding of the Jōdo sect (see Buddhism, p. 37). In the late 15th C, Ōjō-Gokuraku-in was joined with Sanzen-in, a *monzeki* (imperial) temple originally located on Hiei, whose status is indicated by the five white bands on its outer walls.

**Kyaku-den.** The reception hall of Sanzen-in's imperial abbot. The present building dates from the 16th C. The adjoining **Shinden** enshrines a Fudō Myō-ō (ICP) encircled by flames, and a Guze-Kannon (ICP). The sliding screens were painted by leading artists of the Meiji and Taishō periods.

◆ **Amida Hall (Ōjō Gokuraku-in,** ICP). This hall enshrines the statue of Amida (ICP), thought to be the original sculpted by Genshin himself. The hall was rebuilt in 1148, with an unusual ceiling, shaped like the inverted floor of a boat, to accommodate the statue. Amida's gorgeous halo has small images of his various manifestations embedded in an arabesque pattern. The two kneeling attendants, Kannon and Seishi, were carved about 100 years later. The Amida is an early example of the multiblock construction that would later be used by JŌCHŌ and the KEI SCHOOL to mass-produce Amidist images. The ceiling and walls are covered with paintings, barely visible through the centuries' accumulation of incense smoke, of heavenly beings and the 25 bosatsu who attend Amida as he descends to welcome souls into his Pure Land.

* **Jakkō-in** 寂光院 Hrs: 9:00–17:00 (enter by 16:30). Dec.–Feb. 9:00–16:30 (enter by 16:00). *0:20h on foot W of Ōhara bus stop.* Jakkō-in claims to have been established by SHŌTOKU TAISHI in 594 as a funerary temple for his father emperor Yōmei (for whom Hōryū-ji was also built), and later joined Hiei's Tendai sect. It is renowned from *Tales of the Heike* as the isolated nunnery where Empress KENREIMON-IN, daughter of TAIRA NO KIYOMORI, was forced to retire in 1185, at the age of 30. Her son, the child emperor Antoku, and the entire Taira clan had perished that year in the naval battle at Dan no Ura (see Miyajima History, p. 449). Although she too tried to drown herself, she was saved against her will, and lived out her life at Jakkō-in, praying for the soul of her son. In the "Ohara Gokō" chapter, the most pathetic in the tale (also adapted into a Noh play), the retired emperor

Go-Shirakawa visits her, and the two grieve over the glory that has passed. Jakkō-in's intimate garden fits the description given in the epic. The Main Hall (17th C) contains the Amidist deity Jizō Bosatsu, flanked by images of Kenreimon-in and Awanonaishi, her faithful lady-in-waiting. The hall once contained 60,000 tiny images of Jizō, the savior of dead children.

## III:4 KURAMA AND KIBUNE

The road to Kurama winds through a narrow, wild valley, much of it startlingly unspoiled. Taira no Kiyomori thought Kurama Temple a suitably remote place of exile for the young MINAMOTO NO YOSHITSUNE; the youth, however, often slipped away from his sutra studies to learn martial secrets from a mysterious mountain *tengu* (see below). This early training no doubt enabled Yoshitsune to engineer the defeat of the Taira clan, establishing his half-brother, YORITOMO, as shogun. Today, Kurama offers a quaint scene of inns and teahouses lining the approach to the temple. The active traveler may want to visit the temple, then hike over the mountain to Kibune Jinja, in the adjacent valley, where one can rest at a country inn before returning to Kyoto.

---

**Day trip:** Kyoto — (0:30h by train) — Kurama — (0:30h walk) — ✳ Kurama-dera — (0:35h walk) — Kibune Jinja — (0:30h walk) — Kibune-guchi station — (0:30h by train) — Kyoto

**Lunch:** Beniya at Kibune, and various inns at Kurama

**Note:** October 22 ✳✳✳ Kurama Fire Festival

---

350 ✳ **Kurama-dera (Temple)** 鞍馬寺 Hrs. 9:00–17:00 (enter by 16:30). Oct.–May 9:00–16:30 (enter by 16:00). *0:30h by Keifuku line to Kurama from Demachi-Yanagi station; or 0:50h by Hirogawara-bound bus 32 from Keihan-Sanjō station. From the temple gate, to the left of the station, it is a 0:03h cable-car ride (bypassing Yuki Jinja) or 0:30h hike to the top.* Kurama Temple was founded in 770 and dedicated to Bishamon-ten, the most popular of the Four Directional Guardians of Buddhism, who guards the dangerous northern direction. In 796, the temple was charged with protecting the new capital to the south. Kurama is associated with *tengu*, a winged creature with a man's body; by legend, it was a *tengu* who taught Yoshitsune his awesome martial skills. There are two types of *tengu*: one has a red face and phallic nose, the other has a bird's beak. They dress as *yamabushi* and folklorists think they are Buddhist manifestations of the mountain god worshipped in primitive Shinto (see Shinto, pp. 23, 27). Many of the details of the Yoshitsune legend — his faithful retainer Benkei, his parting with Shizuka at Yoshino, and his escape through Tōhoku — have close links to the *yamabushi*. The *tengu*, like the *yamabushi* themselves, were sometimes viewed as men who practiced austerities to augment their personal power, rather than to achieve enlightenment.

**Yuki Jinja.** *A 0:05h climb from the Niō-mon (gate).* This shrine, founded in 940, was, like Kurama Temple, assigned to protect the capital. The shrine's deity was brought from the imperial palace by young men carrying burning trees, an event said to be the origin of Kurama's famous fire festival. The **Haiden** (oratory, 1610, ICP) is an unusual hall cleft in two by a stone stairway.

**Main Hall.** Farther up, past the top of the cable-car station. This concrete hall enshrines a Bishamon-ten (ca. 10th–12th C, ICP) flanked by Senju Kannon and Maō-san (the deity of the planet Venus). To the left is a small hall housing a *tengu* statue.

**Reihōkan (Treasure Hall).** Hrs: 9:00–16:30 (enter by 16:00); clsd M. To the left of the Main Hall. The natural history collection displays *tengu*'s fingernails (which the caption explains are fossilized shark teeth). On the third floor are Heian and Kamakura statues, including a fine Bishamon-ten (1127, NT), shown holding his usual pagoda, but also shading his eyes, the better to keep watch over Kyoto. From here, it is a 0:15h walk to the **Maō-den** (Inner Sanctum), then a 0:10h descent to Kibune Jinja.

**Kibune Jinja** 貴船神社 *0:30h by Keifuku line to Kibune-guchi, one stop before Kurama, then 0:30h (uphill) on foot. Or 0:25h hike from the Main Hall of Kurama Temple.* Kibune Jinja, sacred to a water deity, was charged with protecting the source of the Kamogawa, one of Kyoto's principal rivers. In times of drought, prayers were offered here. As rivers flow out of mountains, irrigating the rice paddies, so the kami of water, mountains, and fertility are typically worshipped at mountain shrines. Kibune Village, in a pretty, riverine valley, has inns which in summer put out dining platforms over the river, a genteel and effective way to obtain relief from the heat.

## Exploring Hanase and Hirogawara

*About 1:00h by bus 32 north of Kurama.* The road winds over a pass and down into the hamlet of **Hanase**, where one can still see a few thatched-roof houses, and **Daihizan Bujō-ji**, a magnificent mountain temple founded 800 years ago (Hrs: 9:00–15:30, enter by 15:00; clsd Nov. 20–Mar. 30 and on rainy days). From the weathered Niō gate (ICP), it is a 0:30h climb to the top, through primeval forest. The Main Hall (1345, ICP) is dramatically perched on scaffolding. Beyond Hanase, the road hugs the river to **Hirogawara**, a slightly larger village. On Aug. 15 and 24, respectively, Hanase and Hirogawara hold electrifyingly beautiful fire festivals. (See Calendar. Lodgings or car a must.)

# KYOTO IV. NORTHWEST KYOTO

IV:1    **\*\*\*** Daitoku-ji
IV:2    **\*\*\*** Kinkaku-ji
IV:2    **\*\*\*** Ryōan-ji
IV:2    **\*\*** Myōshin-ji
IV:2    **\*\*** Ninna-ji

This district, called Kitayama, or Northern Hills, was a great center of Kyoto's medieval culture (see Kyoto History, p. 320). It contains some of Japan's finest temples, many on lush and expansive estates. Often, however, these oases are linked by busy thoroughfares, unpleasant to walk; prudent use of taxis or buses will help make a tour more enjoyable. See map, p. 324.

## IV:1 DAITOKU-JI AREA

The beautiful, cloistered world of the great Zen monastery, Daitoku-ji, is the historical focus of this part of Kyoto. Here, the temple's close associations with the tea ceremony, wealthy burghers, and artisans gave rise to Kamigata culture, the light, elegant style of Kansai. Those with a little extra time can trace its evolution by including the Ura Senke tea ceremony center, the Nishijin brocade weaver's district, the Kitano Temman-gū Shrine, and Kōetsu-ji in a tour of the area.

---

**Tour:** Ura Senke — (0:10h on foot) — Nishijin — (0:07h by bus) — \* Kitano Tenman-gū Shrine — (0:10h by bus) — **\*\*\*** Daitoku-ji — (0:05h by taxi) — \* Kōetsu-ji

**Lunch:** Sushi Tora, Ikkyū, Izusen

**Note:** On the 25th of each month, there's a large flea market at Kitano Tenman-gū.

351

---

\* **Ura Senke and Omote Senke.** Sen no Sōtan established his tea ceremony school on this property in the early 1600s; it was subsequently divided between two of his sons.
     **Omote Senke** 表千家 Not open to the public. This branch is associated with "daimyo's tea," as one is reminded by its gate, an imposing structure given by the Wakayama branch of the TOKUGAWA family. It owns two famous tea arbors, **Zangetsu-tei** and **Fushin-an** (very difficult to see).
     **Ura Senke** 裏千家 Now the most famous tea ceremony school in Japan, Ura Senke popularized the *wabi* tradition and today requires two large computers, located in its modern headquarters, to keep track of its followers. Of all the tea ceremony schools, it has been the most innovative. In the Meiji period, it invented a style using chairs for the benefit of Westerners. The current master has opened branches abroad. His son recently married the emperor's niece, indicating either that Japan is becoming more egalitarian, or that the Ura Senke is becoming more exclusive. By applying in writing (connections help), you can sometimes see the old estate. It includes the tiny **Konnichi-an** tearoom (rarely shown), constructed by Sōtan in the two-mat configuration that Sen no Rikyū liked, the **Yūin-an** tea arbor, and some of Japan's finest tea gardens. An altar contains a statue of Rikyū, said to be the fateful one that led to his death (see box). Ura Senke has a tea ceremony demonstration Thursdays at 13:30 and 15:00 (except in Jan. and Aug.) in its modern headquarters; call 451-8516 by noon on the day you wish to attend. The building also houses a museum. Next door is **Hompō-ji**, a Nichiren temple with a garden by Hon'ami Kōetsu.

**Nishijin** 西陣 Kyoto's famous brocade-weaving district was established here after the Ōnin Wars, and took its name from the Nishi-jin (Western Barracks), the headquarters of the Hosokawa armies. During the Ōnin Wars, the weavers, along with many Kyoto townsmen, had fled to the port of Sakai, south of Ōsaka. The Chinese and Indian textiles flowing into Sakai introduced exotic motifs into Nishijin weaves. Today, Nishijin remains synonymous with sumptuous brocades, considered among the world's finest — it supplies the Vatican — but quality is succumbing to commercialism. The **Nishijin-ori Kaikan** (Textile Hall) 西陣織会館 , a 7-story gallery-store near the Horikawa-dōri and Imadegawa-dōri intersection, gives a good idea of the present state of the art (Hrs: 9:00–17:00; Dec. 29–Jan. 4, 10:00–16:00). The Nishijin district, east and south from the Textile Hall, preserves the aura of an old artisan quarter. Most of the work is done on some 3,000 looms hidden behind the wood-slatted facades of the aging houses.

\* **Senbon Shaka-dō (Daihō'on-ji)** 千本釈迦堂 Hrs: 9:00–17:00 (enter by 16:00), daily. *Bus 203 to Kamishichiken, then 0:05h on foot.* This temple's **Main Hall** (1227, NT) is one of the oldest structures to survive in Kyoto. The Treasure Hall houses some breathtaking sculpture, including a sublime group of ◆ **Six Kannon** (NT) by TANKEI.

\* **Kitano Tenman-gū (Shrine)** 北野天満宮 *Bus 203.* This famous shrine is dedicated to Sugawara no Michizane (845–903), a court scholar and minister who was exiled to Kyūshū and later deified as Tenjin, the god of scholarship, after a series of disasters was blamed on his angry spirit (see Kyūshū, p. 480, and Shinto, p. 27). The spacious grounds are planted with many plums, Michizane's favorite flower, and there is a big bronze statue of his servant, the ox. The ◆ **Shrine Hall** (NT), rebuilt in 1607, is in the Gongen style (see Shinto, p. 29). Its cypress-thatched, multigabled roof is particularly beautiful. Kitano Tenman-gū is famous for its flea market, held on the 25th of each month; on these days (barring rain), the Treasure House exhibits the famous ◆ **Tenjin Engi Scrolls** (1219, NT), depicting the Michizane legend. On October 1, 1587, HIDEYOSHI held a huge tea gathering on the shrine grounds that was open to the entire city. The event, reenacted on Dec. 1 every year, helped to establish the tea ceremony among the townsmen, and marked SEN NO RIKYŪ's ascendancy.

### Kitano Tea Break

[28] **Awamochi-tokorosawaya** 粟餅所沢屋 (461-4517). Hrs: 9:00–17:00; clsd Th and 26th of each month. Across Imadegawa-dōri from Kitano Tenman-gū. Famous for *awamochi*, sticky rice and millet cakes. Try *awa-zenzai* (*awamochi* in hot sweet bean sauce).

**\*\*\* Daitoku-ji** 大徳寺 Subtemple Hrs: 9:00–16:00 (enter by 15:30). The main grounds are always open. Separate admissions charged by subtemples. *Bus 1, 12, 61, 204, 205, or 206 to Daitoku-ji-mae.* Unlike most of Kyoto's large Rinzai Zen monasteries, Daitoku-ji, founded as a small temple in 1319 by Daitō Kokushi, did not form close ties with the ASHIKAGA shoguns or the Kyoto Zen establishment. Thus, when Daitoku-ji was destroyed in the Ōnin Wars (1467–1477), its abbot Ikkyū (1394–1481) rebuilt the temple with funds raised from an outside source—the wealthy merchants of Sakai. It was through this connection that Daitoku-ji became the leading center of the tea ceremony (see Villas, p. 66). In the 16th C, Daitoku-ji gained the support of NOBUNAGA and HIDEYOSHI, both avid tea practitioners; Hideyoshi chose the temple for Nobunaga's funeral rites and encouraged his vassal lords to build subtemples. With the support of these lords and the artistic contributions of SEN NO RIKYŪ, Furuta Oribe, KOBORI ENSHŪ, and other leading tea men, dozens of subtemples were built. Today, the 24 that remain occupy the greater part of the monastery, dwarfing the formal *garan*. These subtemples, 8 of which are regularly open to the public, are Daitoku-ji's great attraction, with their superb art, buildings, and gardens. There is no better place to experience the creative power and diversity of Zen culture.

**352**

**The Garan.** The formal arrangement of seven main halls prescribed for Zen temples is near the east entrance. The halls were rebuilt in the late 16th to early 17th C. In 1589, Sen no Rikyū rebuilt the upper part of the San-mon (Main Gate), and placed inside it the offending statue that is said to have driven Hideyoshi to order his suicide. At the north end is the Kara-mon (Chinese Gate, NT), which serves as the front gate to the ◆ Hōjō (Abbot's Quarters, NT). The Hōjō is open on Oct. 10, when it airs its famous paintings.

**Ryūgen-in** 竜源院 (Subtemple). Hrs: 9:00–17:00. South of the San-mon. The **Hōjō** (ICP), dating from Ryūgen-in's founding in 1502 by three daimyo, is one of the oldest extant examples of a Zen abbot's residence. Ryōgen-in has five attractive gardens, and a memorial to LADY MURASAKI, author of *The Tale of Genji*.

**Kōrin-in** 興臨院 (Subtemple). Founded in the Muromachi period, the buildings and fine dry garden were recently reconstructed from old texts. Visit by appointment (491-7636).

**Zuihō-in** 瑞峰院 (Subtemple). Founded as his funerary temple in 1535 by Ōtomo Sōrin, an important daimyo in Kyūshū who later converted to Christianity. The garden, designed in 1961 by Shigemori Mirei, incorporates a cruciform rock arrangement.

**Sangen-in** 三玄院 (Subtemple). By reservation (492-5039). Founded in 1589 by three powerful daimyo of western Japan, Ishida Mitsunari, Asada Yukinaga, and Mōri Tadamasa. Sen no Rikyū's grandson, Sōtan, is said to have trained here. It has a lovely garden.

◆ **Daisen-in** 大仙院 (Subtemple). This has one of Japan's most famous gardens, a powerful, concentrated composition of vertically thrusting rocks, white sand, and sparse vegetation. Created in the Muromachi period by the temple's founder, Kogaku Zenshi—probably in cooperation with his friend, the painter Sōami—this small garden is a three-dimensional rendition of Sung-style landscape paintings (see Villas, p. 62). Try to view this garden seated on the veranda during a lull in the constant crowds that gather here. The **Hōjō** (NT) is an important structure showing some key evolutionary stages in Japanese *shoin* architecture, including a precursor of the *tokonoma* alcove. The interiors are decorated with ink landscapes by Sōami, as well as early KANŌ SCHOOL works by MOTONOBU and Yukinobu.

◆ **Kōtō-in** 高桐院 (Subtemple). Founded in 1601 by Hosokawa Tadaoki (1563–1645), one of the most powerful daimyo in the land and a disciple of Sen no Rikyū; a stone lantern, which now serves as his tombstone, was given by Rikyū, and the Ihoku-ken hall is said to have come from Rikyū's residence. Kōtō-in is entered by a carefully composed maple-canopied approach, preparing the visitor for the exquisite natural beauty, steeped in the *wabi* spirit, of the inner gardens and buildings. The south garden is set in a sparse maple grove, with clean-swept ground and a single stone lantern. On the west side is a *roji*, or tea garden, with stepping stones leading to a two-mat tea arbor, Shōkō-ken, said to have been used at the Great Kitano Tea Party. The Hosokawa graves stand in the grounds; among them is a memorial to Gracia, Tadaoki's wife, who was not only the

# Rikyū, Hideyoshi, and Townspeople's Culture

In 1587, noticeboards were set up all over Kyoto inviting the entire populace—nobles, samurai, commoners, and even foreigners—to a huge outdoor tea ceremony at Kitano Tenman-gū. Nearly 800 tea arbors were set up in the wooded precincts, and everyone was welcome to attend so long as they dressed simply; obvious displays of wealth were forbidden. The mastermind behind this extraordinary occasion was TOYOTOMI HIDEYOSHI, and the tea master in charge was SEN NO RIKYŪ. The Great Kitano Tea Party was perhaps the finest hour in their unusual relationship.

Both Hideyoshi and Rikyū embodied their era. It was an age of great social mobility, when men could rise to the pinnacles of power and influence, as they had, on the strength of their talent. Rikyū, the son of a wealthy Sakai merchant, perfected a tea ceremony of humbleness and simplicity from what had originally been a luxurious diversion of the rich and powerful. In Rikyū's *wabi* tea, all were equal under the teahouse roof, and though often an exclusive and expensive affair, ideally the tea ceremony was an exercise of the heart, not of the purse (see Villas, p. 66). The Great Kitano Tea Party was, in its way, the ultimate realization of this ideal. For Hideyoshi, who esteemed *wabi* tea as much as he adored extravagant display, it perfectly expressed his ebullient and contradictory nature.

The relationship between the two men was governed by mutual respect—Rikyū even lived for a time in a tea arbor within Hideyoshi's Juraku-tei palace—but inevitably feelings between the warrior and the artist were often strained. Nobody knows for certain why Hideyoshi forced Rikyū to commit suicide in 1591; the most commonly told story is that when Rikyū rebuilt the gate of Daitoku-ji, he placed a statue of himself in its upper floor. Hideyoshi, who often visited the temple, entered through the gate on the assumption that he was walking beneath images of buddhas and saints. When he found out he had put himself "below" Rikyū, he was beside himself with rage.

353

After Rikyū's death, his disciples, such as Furuta Oribe and KOBORI ENSHŪ, both daimyo, turned the tea ceremony in an aristocratic direction, allowing class distinctions back into the tea arbor. It was left to Rikyū's grandson, **Sen no Sōtan** (1578–1658), to revive the *wabi* tradition. Sōtan was given a property in the northwest of the city, which after his death was divided among two sons who formed the Omote Senke (Anterior House of Sen) and Ura Senke (Posterior House of Sen). (A third son started yet another school.) The property lies near Daitoku-ji, and even today the heirs of these hereditary schools are required to spend six months in training at the monastery. During the Edo period, Rikyū's descendants, especially those of the Ura Senke, continued to be patronized by Kyoto's townsmen; this benefitted them greatly in modern times. From the Meiji period, the tea ceremony became closely tied to middle-class aspirations, and today Ura Senke boasts more than two million students.

Among Sōtan's close friends was fellow free spirit HON'AMI KŌETSU (1557–1637). This multitalented genius invented his own form of the tea ceremony and founded an art colony at Takagamine, around the family temple now called Kōetsu-ji. Kōetsu was a follower not of Zen but of the Nichiren Buddhist sect, and his ties were to Kyoto's merchants and craftsmen, who were Nichiren followers and had formed tightly knit autonomous guilds, the *machi-shū*, during the decades of anarchy following the Ōnin Wars. The *machi-shū*'s days of autonomy were long over, but they still dominated craft centers such as Nishijin, where Kyoto's exquisite weaving and dyeing is done even today. Kōetsu, himself descended from a line of sword appraisers, combined traditional arts and crafts with the new tea esthetic, creating unique ceramics, lacquerware, and metalwork; his calligraphy is particularly exquisite. His artistic followers and descendants—TAWARAYA SŌTATSU, OGATA KŌRIN, OGATA KENZAN— became known as the RIMPA SCHOOL. They too came from the craft tradition. Sōtatsu began his career as a fanmaker, while Kōrin was a textile designer, and Kenzan a potter. These artists shaped the **Kamigata style**, the elegant sensibilities of townsmen's culture in Kyoto and Ōsaka, which still leaves its mark on the decorative tastes of the city.

most famous Catholic woman in Japan, but a daughter of Akechi Mitsuhide, Oda Nobunaga's assassin. She was killed during a battle by her husband's order so that she would not be captured by his enemies. Tadaoki, who had astutely followed three winners—Nobunaga, Hideyoshi, and Ieyasu—was awarded a large fief at Kumamoto in Kyūshū, which his descendants held until the Meiji Restoration (see Castles, p. 49).

**Kohō-an** 孤蓬庵 (Subtemple). Request permission by postcard, and pay Y1000. This subtemple's gardens and tea arbor, designed by Kobori Enshū, are among the finest at Daitoku-ji. The temple has in its custody the **Kizaemon Tea Bowl**, a Korean Ido bowl that is the most famous piece of crockery in Japan. It acquired a reputation for being cursed—a succession of owners suffered from boils—and the last owners, the Matsudaira lords of Matsue, deposited it here for safekeeping.

**Shinju-an** 真珠庵 (Subtemple). Usually closed. Founded by Ikkyū; the south and east gardens are attributed to Murata Shukō, Japan's first tea master.

**Imamiya Jinja** 今宮神社 A charming shrine directly NW of Daitoku-ji. Hard by its eastern side entrance are **Ichiwa** and **Kazariya**, a pair of shops famous for *aburimochi*, grilled rice dumplings doused in sweet, sticky brown sauce, made from a 700-year-old recipe. (Hrs: 10:00–17:00; clsd W). The shrine is famous for the Yasurai Matsuri, 2nd Su in Apr.

### Takagamine
Rustic neighborhood about 2 km north of Daitoku-ji.

**Shōzan** しょうざん Hrs: 9:00–17:00 (enter by 16:30); clsd NY. A large, wooded complex with a garden, restaurants, weaving and dyeing studio, amusement park, and swimming pool.

∗ **Kōetsu-ji** 光悦寺 Hrs: 8:00–17:00; clsd Nov. 10–13. This Nichiren-sect temple was originally a family chapel of HON'AMI KŌETSU, the artistic genius who founded an artisan colony here in 1615. The lushly wooded grounds look out across a valley to the high hump of Mt. Takagamine, covered with stands of arrow-straight Kitayama *sugi* (cryptomeria). Kōetsu was an ardent tea man who invented his own style, and the grounds are dotted with tea arbors based on his designs. The superb **bamboo fence** that curves along the path, also Kōetsu's design, is the temple's most famous feature. The Treasure House exhibits an eclectic sampling of the exquisite work of Kōetsu and his followers, including a copy of a famous lacquered inkstone box (see Art, p. 97).

354 **Jōshō-ji** 常照寺 Hrs: 9:00–17:00. Associated with Yoshino Taiyū, a top-ranking Shimabara courtesan famed for her artistic skills and her love affair with essayist Haiya Jōeki (1610–1691), a disciple of Hon'ami Kōetsu. The circular windows often seen in teahouses are called Yoshino *mado*. The temple grounds are lovely in the cherry blossom season. On the 3rd Su in April, a procession of Shimabara *taiyū* commemorates Yoshino Taiyū's death.

∗ **Shōden-ji** 正伝寺 Hrs: 9:00–17:00. *0:05h NE of Takagamine by taxi.* A very secluded temple with a small meditational **garden** of raked white sand and clipped azalea bushes, against a background of forests framing the peak of Hiei-zan; it is a noted example of the "borrowed scenery" technique. The **Honden** (ICP), moved here from Fushimi-jō, contains ink landscapes by KANŌ SANRAKU.

## IV:2 THE GOLDEN PAVILION AND RYŌAN-JI AREA
This area has many famous temples, spaced at half-kilometer intervals along Kitsuji-dōri. Kinkaku-ji has one of Kyoto's most familiar landmarks, the Golden Pavilion, and Ryōan-ji its most celebrated garden, the rock-and-sand rectangle that is the archetype of the Zen garden.

**Walking Tour:** ∗∗∗ Kinkaku-ji — (0:20h) — ∗∗∗ Ryōan-ji — (0:10h) — ∗∗ Ninna-ji — (0:10h) — ∗∗ Myōshin-ji — (0:10h) — ∗ Tōji-in

**Lunch:** Seigen-in, Vingt-et-un

∗∗∗ **Kinkaku-ji (Rokuon-ji)** 金閣寺 Hrs: 9:00–17:30. Oct.–Mar. 9:00–17:00. *Bus 59 to Kinkakuji-mae; or 204 or 205 to Kinkakuji-michi.* In 1397, the third Ashikaga shogun, Yoshimitsu, ceded his title to his 9-year-old son, Yoshimochi, and retired to his new pleasure villa among the northern hills, built on the grounds of an old aristocratic retreat.

◆ **Kinkaku.** The Golden Pavilion is the first sight that greets the visitor today, its reflection shimmering in the spacious pond stretched out before it. Yoshimitsu's original plan was to cover the upper stories with gold leaf. It seems, however, that he was able to gild only the top level, and even this had long peeled away by 1950, when a mad acolyte burned the priceless pavilion to the ground. Mishima Yukio's novel *The Golden Pavilion* contains a fictional account of this strange incident. The pavilion was rebuilt exactly—the original had been carefully measured and studied—and today, the top two floors are gilded, fulfilling Yoshimitsu's original plan. What startled visitors in Yoshimitsu's day, however, was not the gold covering so much as the pavilion's novel design. Yoshimitsu welcomed guests on the first floor, built in the Shinden style derived from Heian palaces. It has a roofed dock attached, for his pleasure boat. The second floor, where he entertained important guests, resembles a temple hall, and enshrines Kannon Bosatsu. The topmost level, where Yoshimitsu gathered with his intimates, has the bell-shaped windows, paneled doors, and other features of the Zen style, yet enshrines a Jōdo-style Amida with 25 bosatsu.

◆ **The garden.** Also eclectic. Originally part of an estate belonging to the Saionji court family, it was patterned by Yoshimitsu after a Jōdo paradise garden, but with carefully composed views from the pavilion of rocks and plantings, giving it elements

# The Eclecticism of Kitayama Culture

The Kamakura period was an era of stern warriors and single-minded Zen priests, who prefered the austere halls of Kamakura. Meanwhile, the Kyoto court maintained the earlier style of *shinden* palaces, with their elegant halls and broad covered corridors. (Something of this sumptuous tradition can be sensed at Ninna-ji's reconstructed Omuro Gosho.) When the ASHIKAGA shoguns returned the capital to Kyoto in 1334, these two cultural streams began to merge. Emperors took a greater interest in Zen — Myōshin-ji was founded by an emperor, for example — and Zen priests such as MUSŌ SOSEKI, Ashikaga TAKAUJI's spiritual advisor, remodeled several old Heian aristocratic gardens. In 1397, with the completion of shogun YOSHIMITSU's Golden Pavilion at Kinkaku-ji, this trend achieved a genuine synthesis.

Yoshimitsu's **Kitayama Culture**, which took its name from the northern hills around Kinkaku-ji, was influenced by Ming Chinese culture and even more profoundly by that of the already defunct Sung dynasty (920–1280), the roots of Zen culture. Besides collecting rare Chinese celadons and textiles, Yoshimitsu was keenly interested in Sung painting. He started an impressive painting collection and founded a painting academy at Shōkoku-ji (I:3). (See Art, p. 95.)

Yoshimitsu's greatest cultural contribution was his patronage of the Noh, the art form that achieved the greatest fusion of Zen esthetics with older Japanese traditions. When he was nineteen, Yoshimitsu first saw the young Noh actor ZEAMI perform with his father, KAN'AMI. Yoshimitsu took Zeami as a lover and became a dedicated patron of Noh. Under Zeami, Noh shed its earlier farcical elements and became serious drama, which should be imbued, according to the treatise Zeami wrote, with *yūgen*, a blend of mystery and spontaneity. After his retirement, Yoshimitsu had the pleasure of seeing Zeami perform on the Noh stage at Kinkaku-ji.

355

The supreme pleasure, however, came near the end of Yoshimitsu's life. In 1408, he entertained the emperor at Kinkaku-ji, becoming the first shogun to receive so exalted a guest. Now the merging of the worlds of emperor and warrior received something akin to official recognition. Yoshimitsu's pavilion was a perfect marriage between the old aristocratic traditions and the newer Zen culture. The overall structure takes its cue from the water pavilions often portrayed in Sung painting, but much of its detail follows native traditions: the first floor is in the Heian-period Shinden style; the second floor is built like an Amida Hall. Only the third floor has the cusped *katō-mado* windows which are part of the Sung-inspired Zen style.

After Yoshimitsu's death, other arts came to bear the stamp of this eclectic approach. The emblem of later Muromachi eclecticism is the Silver Pavilion (II:5), the product of the fervent adoration of Yoshimitsu by his grandson, the shogun YOSHIMASA. An even better example of the direction in which later Muromachi culture was headed was the minimalist rock-and-sand garden of Ryōan-ji, inspired by ink paintings or perhaps by the Zen riddles called *kōan*.

of a Zen meditation garden. It is said to have been deeply influenced by the Moss Garden designed two generations earlier by Musō Soseki. Seventy years after they were built, Yoshimitsu's villa and temple complex were destroyed in the Ōnin Wars, leaving only the Golden Pavilion. Among the rebuilt structures in the precincts are the Sekka-tei tea arbor used by Emperor Go-Mizuno'o and the Kyōhoku-rō, a Meiji reconstruction of Yoshimitsu's residence.

**Dōmoto Bijutsukan (Art Museum)** 堂本美術館 Hrs: 10:00–17:00 (enter by 16:30); clsd M, NY, Mar. 25–31, Sept. 25–31. *Bus 59 to Kinugasa.* The museum, which has an unusual white stucco facade, contains works in both Western and traditional Japanese styles by Dōmoto Inshō (1891–1975); his screens can be found in many Kyoto temples.

∗ **Tōji-in** 等持院 Hrs: 8:00–17:00. Enter 0:30h before closing time. *Bus 59 to Ritsumeikan, then walk 0:10h. Or Keifuku train to Tōji-in station, then walk 0:07h.* Tōji-in was founded in 1341 by ASHIKAGA TAKAUJI, and became a funerary temple of the Ashikaga shoguns. Rebuilt in 1818, the temple has an air of elegance. The beautiful pond garden was originally designed by MUSŌ SOSEKI, but with its lush plantings, brilliant in autumn, it retains almost no evidence of his influence. A small hall enshrines statues of the Ashikaga. Around the time of the Meiji Restoration, the Ashikaga, both as bad rulers and as persecutors of the nationalist hero, Emperor Go-Daigo (see Yoshino History, p. 411), were unpopular historical figures. In 1863, a mob carried off three of the statues' heads and dumped them in the Kamo River (they were later recovered), and until recently, people would pay to beat the statues.

∗∗∗ **Ryōan-ji** 竜安寺 Hrs: 8:00–17:00; arrive early to avoid the constant crowds. *Bus 59 to Ryōanji-mae.* The ◆ **Abbot's Garden** of Ryōan-ji is considered the supreme example of an abstract Zen garden. It consists of a rectangle of raked white gravel on which are arranged 15 rocks, devoid of all vegetation save for a few splashes of moss, the whole enclosed by a mottled earthen wall. Its origins are as mysterious as its meaning, its creator and age unknown. In spirit, it is a work of the late Muromachi period, when the eclecticism of Kitayama culture crystallized into statements of Zen philosophy, rendered in painting, tea ceremony, and gardens. The garden was probably constructed shortly after the Ōnin Wars, but the event went unrecorded, perhaps because it was considered insignificant. Indeed, it was not until the 1930s that it was "discovered" and became world-famous. A taped voice tells visitors that the garden might represent "islands in the sea" or "a tigress swimming with her cubs," but its true meaning, if it exists at all, seems intended to be grasped only through concentrated meditation (see Villas, p. 63). Unfortunately, the garden is frequently crowded, making it difficult to appreciate it as it was meant to be seen, in solitude.

Ryōan-ji stands on the site of a Heian nobleman's estate, from which there remains a large pond, Kyōyōchi. The path behind the temple leads to a quiet spot with several Heian-period imperial tombs and a view of Kyoto. The estate was taken over by Hosokawa Katsumoto (1430–1473), a powerful deputy to the Ashikaga who was a principal combatant in the Ōnin Wars; his death brought an end to the conflict.

**\*\* Myōshin-ji** 妙心寺 Garan Tour and Subtemple Hrs: 9:00–16:00 (enter by 15:40). *Take the Keifuku-Kitano line to Myōshin-ji station, near the north gate of the precincts, or JR San'in line from Kyoto station to Hanazono station, 0:05 on foot from the south, main gate.* Myōshin-ji was founded in 1337 with the help of Emperor Hanazono. It was treated with antipathy by the ASHIKAGA shoguns and was burned to the ground during the Ōnin Wars. Afterward, under the patronage of the powerful Hosokawa family and, later, the TOYOTOMI and TOKUGAWA, it expanded, becoming a labyrinth of subtemples. Unlike Daitoku-ji (IV:1), which has a similar history, Myōshin-ji did not recognize "worldly pursuits" such as the tea ceremony and so does not have the many exquisite tea arbors and *roji* gardens found at Daitoku-ji. Nevertheless, it owns a considerable store of treasures, most concealed behind the earthen walls of its 47 subtemples.

**The Garan.** Frequent tours. The formal seven structures are at the south end of the precincts. The **Hattō** (Lecture Hall) is famous for its enormous dragon, painted by KANŌ TAN'YŪ; its fiercely staring eyes follow you all around the hall. Also inside the Hattō is a bell (NT) from a neighboring temple bearing an inscription dated 698, making it the oldest documented bell in Japan. It was cast near Fukuoka, in Kyūshū, and is mentioned in Yoshida Kenkō's 14th-C classic, *Essays in Idleness*. The tour also visits the **Yokushitsu** (steam-bath), built by the uncle of NOBUNAGA's assassin Akechi Mitsuhide.

◆ **Taizō-in** 退蔵院 (Subtemple). Hrs: 9:00–17:00. West of the San-mon gate. The great painter KANŌ MOTONOBU, who once lived here, is credited as the designer of this temple's fine **dry garden**, which depicts a stream flowing between cliffs and exhibits the strong influence of landscape painting (see Villas, p. 62). Nearby is a modern garden designed by Nakane Kinsaku that makes bold use of hide-and-reveal techniques. Viewing it from below, one detects a reference to the older garden in the placement of boulders along the stream bed. Taizō-in owns the famous painting, *Catching a Catfish with a Gourd* (NT), by the Zen artist Josetsu, a teacher of SESSHŪ's. The original is in the Kyoto National Museum; a copy is displayed here (see Art, p. 95).

**Keishun-in** 桂春院 (Subtemple). Hrs: 8:00–17:00. Founded in 1632, this subtemple contains a Sōan-style tea arbor—unusual for Myōshin-ji—tucked into the northeast corner to escape detection.

**Daishin-in** 大心院 (Subtemple). Founded by the Hosokawa in 1492; modern garden by Nakane Kinsaku.

**Reiun-in** 霊雲院 (Subtemple). Usually closed, but often included in special openings in Nov. The **Gokō no Ma** (Imperial Visit Room) was built onto the main building around 1543 for this occasion, and is one of the oldest *shoin* in existence. It looks out onto a fine little dry garden, believed to have been built for the same occasion.

**Shunkō-in** 春光院 (Subtemple). Usually closed. This subtemple owns the bell of Namban-ji, the "southern barbarian temple" built by 16th-C Jesuits in central Kyoto (see Nagasaki History, p. 483). The bell is inscribed with a cross and dated 1577. The church itself is said to have resembled the Silver Pavilion.

**Tenkyū-in** 天球院 (Subtemple). Usually closed. Has rooms decorated with gorgeous screens (ICP) by KANŌ SANRAKU and Sansetsu.

**\*\* Ninna-ji** 仁和寺 Hrs: 9:00–17:00 (enter by 16:30). In winter 9:00–16:30 (enter by 16:00). *Bus 59 to Omuro-Ninna-ji, immediately before the temple gate.* This wonderfully spacious temple was founded in 886 with retired emperor Uda as its first abbot; it was popularly known, after the area, as the Omuro Gosho (Palace). Ninna-ji thus became the first of Kyoto's *monzeki*, a temple that by custom drew its abbot from the imperial or highest court families. (*Monzeki* were disestablished in the Meiji period, but the walls of these temples still boast the five white bands that signify imperial status.) In April, the late-blooming *Omuro-zakura*, a dwarf, double-petaled variety of cherry, draws crowds.

Ninna-ji burned in the Ōnin Wars and was only partly restored in the massive rebuilding of Kyoto undertaken by Emperor Go-Mizuno'o and the TOKUGAWA in the 1630s (see III:1). The **Niō gate** (ICP) and **five-storied pagoda** (ICP) date from this time. The **Kondō** (Main Hall, NT) and **Mie-dō** (Founder's Hall, ICP), at the north end of the precinct, were originally the Shishinden and Seiryūden, the two principal halls of the imperial palace, given to Ninna-ji at the time, for the imperial palace was also being rebuilt. The Kondō houses an **Amida Nyorai** (888, NT). The Miei-dō, a graceful, square building with a cypress roof and a flaming jewel on top, is dedicated to KŌBŌ DAISHI. The **Reihōkan** (Treasure House) houses the temple treasures, mainly Esoteric Buddhist art of China and Japan (open Oct. 1–15, 9:00–16:00; enter by 15:30).

◆ **Omuro Gosho** 御室御所 In its own enclosure in the SW corner of the precincts. In the 1630 rebuilding, the Tsune Goten from the imperial palace was placed here, on the site of Emperor Uda's original villa. They were rebuilt after a fire in the Meiji period. The front court boasts a pine tree that has been trained horizontally to an amazing length. Although the halls are influenced by the Shoin style, their broad verandas, covered corridors linking the several buildings, and reticulated shutters (*shitomido*) all belong to the Heian-period Shinden style (see Villas, p. 60). The lovely garden dates from the Edo period, as do two tea arbors, one in the OGATA KŌRIN style (not open to the public).

# KYOTO V. WESTERN KYOTO

**Main Attractions:**

Western Kyoto is to Japan's literature what eastern Kyoto is to its religious history; a stunning number of Japan's literary classics were written, composed, or set in this outskirt of the city. The area is quite scattered, but Sagano, with its many charming little temples, rustic scenery, and literary allusions, is perfect for a relaxed walk.

357

### V:1 UZUMASA
The name of this crowded suburb is a Japanese-style wordplay combining the names of SHŌTOKU TAISHI and the Hata clan, who together founded Kōryū-ji in the 7th century. This, Kyoto's oldest temple, enshrines a sublime statue of Miroku Bosatsu, which no art lover should miss.

---

**Tour:** ✲✲ Kōryū-ji — (0:05h walk) — ✲ Eiga Mura (Movie Village) — (0:10h by train) — Arashiyama (V:2)

**Lunch:** Tarumiya

---

✲✲ **Kōryū-ji** 広隆寺 Hrs: 9:00–17:00. Dec.–Feb. 9:00–16:30; clsd NY. *From Shijō-Ōmiya or Arashiyama stations, take the Keifuku-Arashiyama line to Uzumasa station, or 0:10h on foot from Katabira-no-tsuji station. Kōryū-ji's faded cinnebar-red Niō gate faces the street.* Kōryū-ji, one of Japan's oldest temples, was founded in 622 by the Hata clan, which had emigrated from the Korean kingdom of Silla in the 4th C and is credited with bringing many crafts to Japan, especially sericulture. Although the clan's name is written with a different Chinese character, *hata* can mean "loom," and the shrine immediately behind Kōryū-ji is dedicated to the kami of the silk cocoon and weaving. The temple's statue of Miroku Bosatsu, perhaps the best-loved image in Japan, became the first National Treasure. Hata Kawakatsu, a high official, received the statue from his friend, Shōtoku Taishi, and built this temple for it, which was moved to its present location in 794, at the founding of Heian-kyō.

**Kōdō (Lecture Hall,** 1165, ICP). The first hall, to the right after the main gate. The oldest surviving structure at Kōryū-ji. It houses a superb Amida Nyorai (NT), flanked by Jizō Bosatsu and Kokuzō Bosatsu (ICP), all of the 9th C.

◆ **Reihōkan (Treasure Hall)** 霊宝館 A modern building at the north end of the grounds. Houses Kōryū-ji's stupendous collection, including the famed ◆ **Miroku Bosatsu** (NT). The burnished wood sculpture, thought to have been carved in Silla (Korea), sits cross-legged, his right hand raised gently to his cheek. He smiles pensively, lost in thought, seeking ways to save all sentient beings. The philospher Karl Jaspers called it "the purest, fullest and most eternal expression of human existence freed from attachment." Miroku is depicted as a youth, who is at the present only a bosatsu, but is destined to become the Nyorai of the Future (see Buddhism, p. 34). In Korea, Miroku became the patron deity of troupes of boys formed to undergo rites of passage. The head of each troupe, a particularly promising boy, was considered an incarnation of Miroku. Many similar images, usually only a few inches tall, have been found both in Korea and in the many locales in Japan that were settled by Korean immigrants. Other fine statues owned by the temple are the gilded and bejeweled "crying" Miroku Bosatsu (6th C, NT), also Korean; a lovely, eight-armed Fukūkenjaku Kannon (8th C, NT); a Senju Kannon (ca. 9th C, NT); and a group of the Twelve Generals (11th C, NT).

◆ **Keigū-in (Chapel,** 1251, NT). To the east end of the precincts is this small, octagonal hall of lovely simplicity, dedicated to SHŌTOKU TAISHI, who was, nominally, the founder of Kōryū-ji. (He seems to have died just before the temple was founded.) The veneration accorded the prince probably contributed to the longevity of this chapel.

**∗ Tōei Uzumasa Eigamura (Movie Village)** 東映太秦映画村 Hrs: 9:00–17:00 (enter by 16:30). In winter 9:30–16:00 (enter by 15:30); clsd Dec. 21–Jan. 1. *0:05h on foot from Kōryū-ji.* Always mobbed with children, this film studio does give some impression of an Edo-period town, including a Kabuki theater and geisha teahouses. One hall has a jukebox-like display of excerpts from Japan's great movie classics, but today the Tōei Company, like most of Japan's moribund film industry, is largely reduced to making "samurai soaps" for television.

**Rokuō-in** 鹿王院 Hrs: 9:00–17:00. *SW of Rokuō-in station on the Keifuku line, 2 stops before Arashiyama.* This secluded Zen temple has a lovely dry garden that "borrows" Arashiyama for its background. Lodgings for women (see Kyoto Lodgings).

## V:2 ARASHIYAMA AND SAGANO

The scenic beauty of Arashiyama and Sagano has attracted princes, poets, and writers since the Heian age. A stroll among these verdant lanes and bamboo groves, hoary temples and country retreats, is a stroll through Japan's literary history. Here one finds allusions from *The Tale of Genji, Tales of the Heike, Essays in Idleness,* the saga of the Northern and Southern dynasties, and the arbor where BASHŌ wrote *Saga Diary.* Today, crowds of tourists trace the worn pathways, savoring the gentle scenes vibrant with ancient poetry.

**Walking Tour:** ∗∗ Tenryū-ji — (0:05h) — Nonomiya — (0:15h) — ∗ Jōjakkō- ji — (0:05h) — ∗ Rakushisha — (0:05h) — ∗ Nison-in — (0:05h) — ∗ Giō-ji — (0:15h) — ∗ Nembutsu-ji — (0:25h) — ∗ Shaka-dō — (0:15h) — ∗∗ Daikaku-ji

**Lunch:** Nishiki, Togetsu-tei, Izusen

**Note:** Avoid Sa, Su, NH in spring and autumn. Rent-a-cycle at all of the stations, Y800 per day.

**Arashiyama** 嵐山 *0:20h by Keifuku-Arashiyama line from Shijō-Ōmiya station, or 0:20h from Kitano-Hakubaichō by Keifuku-Kitano line (change at Katabira-no-tsuji), or 0:20h by JR San'in line from Kyoto station to Saga.* Arashiyama, the "storm mountain," rising above the south bank of the Hozu River, is celebrated for its restless beauty. In spring, the slopes are enveloped in clouds of cherry blossoms, which the Emperor Saga — who took his name from Sagano, the area north of the river — transplanted from the sacred groves of Mt. Yoshino. In early summer, the summit is veiled in misty rain. In autumn, the mountain spreads a brilliant brocade of foliage. Winter finds it still, brooding, the bare trees stark against snow.

**Togetsu-kyō (Moon-Crossing Bridge)** 渡月橋 Just S of the Keifuku station. This long wooden bridge, now reinforced with concrete, is an Arashiyama landmark that has existed since the Heian period, when it was located somewhat upstream. The name is said to have been given by Emperor Kameyama, founder of the Southern or Daikaku-ji line to which Emperor Go-Daigo belonged (see Tenryū-ji).

**Hōrin-ji** 法輪寺 0:05h on foot from the south end of the bridge, on the slopes of Arashiyama. Has a small pagoda and a good view.

**Hozu Rapids Boat Ride.** Pole boats take tourist on a 2:00h, 16-km ride of the mild rapids of the Hozugawa to Arashiyama, through a fairly unspoiled canyon. The rides begin in Kameoka *(0:50h from Kyoto station or 0:25h from JR Saga station by "Torokko" tourist train).* Departures 9:00, 10:00, 11:00, 12:00, 14:00, and 15:30. Dec.–Mar. 9 at 11:15, 12:45, 14:15 and 2:15. Y3400.

**∗∗ Tenryū-ji** 天竜寺 Hrs: 8:30–17:30 (enter by 17:00). Oct.–Mar. 8:30–17:00 (enter by 16:30). *0:02h on foot from the Keifuku station.* In 1338, soon after ASHIKAGA TAKAUJI's foe, Emperor Go-Daigo, had died at Yoshino (see Yoshino History, p. 411), Takauji's Zen preceptor, MUSŌ SOSEKI, dreamed that the aggrieved emperor had turned into a golden dragon rising out of the river at Arashiyama. Musō reported this omen and advised Takauji to build Tenryū-ji, the Heavenly Dragon Temple, to placate Go-Daigo's angry spirit. (The dragon — a benevolent creature in the East — is a Chinese symbol for the emperor.) The new temple was built on the ruins of an imperial villa where Go-Daigo was raised, and Musō, a brilliant garden designer, refurbished its old, Heian-period ◆ **pond garden**, subtly injecting Zen acuteness into the languid scenery. The garden's focal point is a group of seven vertical rocks at the back of the pond, suggesting a monochrome, Sung Chinese landscape painting (see Villas, p. 62, and Art, p. 95). Musō urged Takauji to finance the temple through trade with Yuan-dynasty China, which was carried out by means of the famous Tenryū-ji Ship.

Tenryū-ji, at its founding, ranked first among the Five Great Zen Temples of Kyoto. At its height, it commanded 150 subtemples within vast precincts stretching almost to Uzumasa (V:1). But after the Ōnin Wars, which destroyed all its buildings, Tenryū-ji fell into ruin. The present halls date from the Meiji period; about all that remains from the original temple is the garden, considered one of the finest and historically most important in Kyoto.

**Nonomiya Jinja** 野宮神社 *0:05h walk from the back exit of Tenryū-ji.* To this rustic little "shrine in the fields" came imperial princesses who were appointed priestesses to Ise, for purification rites. In *The Tale of Genji*, Genji seeks out the Lady Rokujō here: "The shrine gates, of unfinished logs, had a grand and awesome dignity for all their simplicity.... With heart unchanging as this evergreen / This sacred tree, I enter the sacred gate." The estranged lovers part in tears. The scene was adapted for the Noh play *Nonomiya*. The Japanese find this a romantic spot and stop here by custom when touring Sagano.

**Ōkōchi Sansō** 大河内山荘 Hrs: 9:00–17:00. *0:10h walk from Nonomiya Jinja, via a beautiful bamboo grove.* The pleasant gardens and tea arbors of a villa built by Ōkōchi Denjirō, a samurai movie star of the 1920s. Nice view of Kyoto.

∗ **Jōjakkō-ji** 常寂光寺 Hrs: 9:00–16:30. *0:05h walk from Ōkōchi Sansō.* During the Momoyama and Edo periods, the Fuju-Fuse sect, radical followers of Nichiren (see Buddhism, p. 38) who refused to have any dealings with nonbelievers, was severely persecuted by the authorities. This temple was originally the refuge of the Fuju-Fuse priest Nichisada. The current abbot, known as the "antilitter priest," decided to open his temple free of charge when other Kyoto temples closed their gates to protest a proposed tax on temple admission fees. Situated on the hillside is a lovely Edo-period Tahō-tō (pagoda, ICP), symbol of the Lotus Sutra, the name of which Nichiren believers invoke.

∗ **Rakushisha** 落柿舎 Hrs: 9:00–17:00, clsd NY. *0:05h walk from Jōjakkō-ji.* This rustic hermitage, the "fallen persimmon hut," was inhabited by a haiku poet, Mukai Kyorai (1651–1704), a leading disciple of Bashō. Bashō wrote the *Saga Diary*, one of his final works, while staying here. Evoking "the breathless heat of a Kyoto summer," he wrote: "The sixth month — / Clouds are resting on the peak / At Arashiyama" (translation and quote from Donald Keene, *World Within Walls*).

**Nison-in** 二尊院 Hrs: 9:00–16:30 (enter by 16:00). *0:05h walk from Rakushisha.* This attractive temple gets its name, Two-Image Temple, for its two statues of Shaka and Amida (ICP); Shaka enlightens humans in this world, and Amida saves them in the next. The temple was founded by Emperor Saga in 841 (see Daikaku-ji, below). It is best known as the place where FUJIWARA Teika (1161–1240) compiled the anthology *Hyakunin Isshu* (A Hundred Poems by a Hundred Poets), which is so well known that it forms the basis of a popular card game. The Misono-tei tea arbor contains several paintings by KANŌ EITOKU.

359

∗ **Giō-ji** 祇王寺 Hrs: 9:00–17:00; clsd NY. *0:05h on foot from Nison-in.* This peaceful, thatched hermitage, in a garden of moss and maples, stands in memory of Giō, a dancer celebrated for her skill and beauty, who was the mistress of TAIRA NO KIYOMORI. In the *Tales of the Heike* it is told how she helped another dancer, Hotoke, gain an audience with Kiyomori. To her sorrow, Kiyomori soon became infatuated with Hotoke and sent poor Giō away. Before she left Kiyomori's palace, Giō scrawled a sad poem on the *shōji* about the ephemerality of happiness in this life and then retired here as a nun with her mother and sister. Hotoke later read the poem and, realizing that her own happiness would also be brief, left Kiyomori, shaved her head and joined Giō. The hall that stands today was built in the Meiji period; the garden is famous for its fall color. Nearby **Takiguchi-dera** (temple) 滝口寺 recalls another unhappy love affair, this one between Yokobue, a lady-in-waiting of Kiyomori's daughter, Empress KENREIMON-IN, and Takiguchi Nyūdō, a retainer of Kiyomori. *Tales of the Heike* recounts how the young man renounced the world and became a monk. The distressed lady eventually took holy orders herself, but, burdened by grief, soon died. Takiguchi redoubled his prayers and became known as the Saint of Kōya.

∗ **Adashino Nembutsu-ji** 化野念仏寺 Hrs: 9:00–17:00 (enter by 16:30). In winter 9:00–16:30 (enter by 16:00). *0:15h walk from Giō-ji.* Adashino, "haunted field," was a dumping ground for corpses, and this temple was said to have been founded by KŪKAI to console their abandoned souls. A century ago, thousands of stone Buddha grave markers were gathered from the surrounding countryside and placed in the precincts, where they stand, row upon row, in attendance on Amida, whose mercy in the afterworld is invoked by the *nembutsu*. Most of the stones are thought to date from the 14–16th C. In spite of the throngs of tourists, the temple has visual appeal and considerable poignancy. "If man were never to fade away like the dews of Adashino, never to vanish like the smoke [of cremations] over Toribeyama, but linger forever in the world, how things would lose their power to move us!" wrote the 14th-C priest Kenkō in *Essays in Idleness*. A scale model of the 1st-C stupa at Sanchi in central India is also in the precincts. This temple is renowned for **Jizō Bon** on Aug. 23–24, when the cemetery fills with flickering candles to beckon home the kinless ghosts.

∗ **Shaka-dō (Seiryō-ji)** 清涼寺 Hrs: 9:00–16:00 (enter by 15:30). *0:25h walk from Nembutsu-ji.* This large temple, with its prominent, two-storied gate, barren grounds, and huge main hall, is lacking in charm, but makes up for it in historic interest. It is famous for a peculiar sandalwood image of **Shaka Nyorai** (NT). Tradition ascribes it to Katsuma Bishu, "a celebrated Hindu sculptor," and credits Chōnen, a Chinese priest, for bringing it to Japan in 987. Art historians believe it was carved by a rather unskilled sculptor working in south China in the Sung period. Its characteristic form, with symmetrically draped robes, and ropelike rows of hair, is called the Seiryō-ji style. The image is highly venerated, and is shown publicly only on the 8th and 19th of each month. The Reihōkan houses several other important images, and is open Apr.–May, and Oct.–Nov.

∗∗ **Daikaku-ji** 大覚寺 Hrs: 9:00–16:30 (enter by 16:00). *0:10h walk from Shaka-dō.* This temple was the birthplace of one of the most wrenching incidents in Japanese history. It

was originally the retirement villa of the 9th-C Emperor Saga, who took his name from this area. During the 13th C, Emperor Go-Saga (Saga II) also retired as abbot here, giving the succession to his eldest son. Go-Saga, however, so doted on a younger son—known to posterity as Emperor Kameyama—that he eventually forced the elder son to resign in favor of this son, to whom he also willed Daikaku-ji and its landed estates. After Go-Saga's death, the two sons quarreled, and a compromise was worked out whereby the senior line and the junior, "Daikaku-ji," line alternated on the throne. The fourth junior-line emperor, Go-Daigo, broke this compromise, attempted rebellion, and finally fled with the imperial regalia south to Yoshino (see Yoshino History, p. 411). In 1392, after 60 years of desultory fighting, the last Daikaku-ji emperor, Go-Kameyama, was tricked by ASHIKAGA YOSHIMITSU into returning the imperial regalia to the senior line, on the understanding that the alternate rule would con-

tinue. This agreement was not honored. Go-Kameyama fled once in protest back to Yoshino, but in the end he agreed to retire here at the Saga Gosho (palace).

Daikaku-ji retains many of the architectural features of a *shinden* palace (see Villas, p. 60), with its spacious halls, covered corridors, small courtyard gardens, and broad veranda overlooking scenic Ōsawa Pond, which Emperor Saga had modeled on China's Lake Tungting. The Momoyama-period *shinden* was donated by Emperor Go-Mizuno'o from the quarters of his consort Tōfukumon-in. It is decorated with copies of KANŌ SANRAKU screens of peonies on a gold ground. The **Seishinden** or Kyaku-den, built in the Shoin style, has a series of connected chambers, all gorgeously decorated. The main objects of worship at this Shingon temple are wooden images of the **Godai Myō-ō** (Five Great Myō-ō), thought to date from the 12th C. In 818, supposedly on the advice of the Shingon sect founder, KŪKAI, Emperor Saga donated copies in his own hand of the *Hannyashin-kyō* (Prajnaparamita Sutra) as a prayer to end a plague. These are enshrined in the **Shinkyō-den**. The Hōmotsukan (Treasure House) displays the original *shinden* screens and two of the Myō-ō statues.

### Exploring Kiyotaki and Atago-san

The narrow road past Adashino Nembutsu-ji was the pilgrim's approach to sacred **Atago-san** (924 m), the highest mountain near Kyoto. The mountain has long been venerated as Kyoto's guardian against conflagrations. The road continues to the hamlet of **Kiyotaki**, a cluster of teahouses and pilgrim's inns (one is now a tiny museum) on the banks of the Kiyotaki, the Clear Cascade River. In the *Saga Diary*, Bashō evoked its cool torrent: "Clear cascades—/ Into the waves scatter/ Green pine needles." From here, it is a 2:00h steep climb to the shrine at the summit of Atago, which Wake no Kiyomaro, founder of Jingo-ji in Takao (V:3), established in 781. Takao itself is a 1:00h hike from Kiyotaki village, up the Kiyotaki River.

## V:3 TAKAO

The ancient mountain retreat of Takao, extolled for its autumn foliage, was an early breeding ground for Esoteric Buddhism. In the late Nara period, the courtier Wake no Kiyomaro foiled the priest Dōkyō's plot to usurp the throne (see Nara History, p. 392). Disgusted by the corrupt Nara temples, Kiyomaro retired to this mountain hideaway. Jingo-ji, which he and his son established here, became a sanctuary for clerics similarly disillusioned by Nara Buddhism, including Saichō and KŪKAI, both of whom had returned from studying in China, but had not yet founded the Tendai and Shingon sects (see Kyoto History, p. 319).

---

**Tour:** Arashiyama— (0:30h by parkway) —∗∗ Jingo-ji— (0:20h on foot) —Saimyō-ji— (0:10h on foot) — ∗ Kōzan-ji

**Lunch:** Togano Chaya, Takao Chaya

**Note:** The Arashiyama-Takao Parkway (Y1000 toll) is recommended; it is scenic, and also less crowded than the public road. Buses to Takao are infrequent.

362

---

∗∗ **Jingo-ji** 神護寺 Hrs: 9:00–16:00; clsd NY. *0:30h by taxi from Arashiyama, or 1:00h on foot from Kiyotaki (V:2), or 1:00h by bus 8 from Shijō-Ōmiya station.* The temple is a 0:30h walk from the road; descend into a ravine, cross the Kiyotakigawa, and climb up a long flight of stone steps on the opposite side. Jingo-ji, with its Esoteric statues and dramatic setting on a precipitous mountainside, has an air of mystery. The precincts begin at the Rō-mon (gate). Past the gate is the Shoin, where temple treasures are shown May 1–5; just beyond is Jingo-ji's famous bell (875, NT).

The **Kondō** (Main Hall) houses the main image of **Yakushi Nyorai** (NT), dimly visible in the dark hall. It is thought to have come from the Wake family temple and been moved here after Kiyomaro's death. This powerful, brooding masterpiece of Esoteric Buddhist sculpture was carved from a single block of wood. Some distance up a hill to the right of the Kondō is Kiyomaro's grave.

Jingo-ji has many typical Esoteric Buddhist elements (see Buddhism, p. 36). The temple owns a famous Two Worlds Mandala (NT). The Womb Mandala depicts Five Kokuzō Bosatsu (Bosatsu of Wisdom) above and Five Myō-ō below, an arrangement echoed by the halls: directly north of the Kondō is a **Tahō-tō** pagoda that represents the Lotus Sutra and houses gorgeous, feminine **Godai Kokuzō Bosatsu** (NT, not on view); south of the Kondō, in the **Godai-dō** hall, are their wrathful counterparts, the **Godai Myō-ō**. Past the Bishamon-dō hall is the **Daishi-dō**, a chapel enshrining an image of Kōbō Daishi, as Kūkai was called posthumously. This exquisitely simple old hall is the only one to survive the Ōnin Wars, and was restored in the 16th C. The best views are farther south at the **Jizō-in** hall near a precipice where worshippers write prayers on clay saucers and hurl them, frisbee-fashion, over the edge. Today, most people skip the prayer and throw them for fun; saucers sold on premises.

According to *Tales of the Heike*, Jingo-ji became the home of the remarkable monk Mongaku. Originally, Mongaku had been a warrior in the imperial service who became infatuated with the lady Kesa Gozen and pressured her to help him kill her husband. In high Japanese style, she tricked Mongaku into killing her instead of her husband in order to escape forever Mongaku's unwanted affections. He did penance, standing under the icy torrent of Nachi waterfall (Kinki, p. 415) while praying to Fudō Myō-ō, and ended up as a monk in the service of Jingo-ji. When the temple fell into disrepair, the zealous Mongaku crashed a party thrown by Emperor Go-Shirakawa and demanded funds. Exiled to Izu for his insolence, he met and became the spiritual advisor of MINAMOTO NO YORITOMO. When Yoritomo became Shogun, Go-Shirakawa was finally forced to pay up. After Yoritomo's death, Go-Shirakawa, who had not forgiven Mongaku, exiled the monk to remote islands.

**Saimyō-ji** 西明寺 Hrs: 8:00–17:00; clsd mid-Aug., NY. *0:20h walk from Jingo-ji, across a red bridge.* This pleasant little temple on the banks of the Kiyotakigawa was originally a subtemple of Jingo-ji. Its main image of Shaka (ICP) is similar to one at Seiryō-ji (V:2).

∗ **Kōzan-ji** 高山寺 Hrs: 8:30–17:00 (enter by 16:30). *0:10h on foot from Saimyō-ji, or right by Togano'o bus stop.* This temple, set in a primeval cryptomeria forest, became affiliated with Jingo-ji in the Heian period. Mongaku (see above) entrusted the rebuilding of Kōzan-ji to his disciple Myō-e (1173–1232), who received approval for the project from Emperor Go-Toba in 1206. This priest made Kōzan-ji a Kegon (Nara sect) temple, but, as his main concern was to oppose the new Amidist sects (see Buddhism, p. 38), his approach was to embrace several of the more conservative teachings. He taught Go-Toba the Shingon doctrine, and was a good friend of Eisai (1145–1215), who established the Rinzai Zen sect. In Kegon, Shingon, and Zen, one attains nirvana through *jiriki*, one's own power; Myō-e believed each person must aspire to become a Buddha, without relying on the mercy of Amida.

The **Sekisui-in** hall (NT), with its graceful roof lines, austere detailing, and simple *kaerumata* (frog-crotch struts), is one of the finest remaining examples, albeit much altered, of Kamakura residential architecture. Displayed here are copies of Kōzan-ji's *Chōju Giga* (Pictures of Frolicking Birds and Animals, late 12th C, NT), humorous ink sketches of animals and humans parodying human society. These strangely modern illustrations are now kept at the Tokyo National Museum (see Art, p. 95). The temple also owns a narrative picture scroll, *Legends of the Kegon Sect* (NT), and *Priest Myō-e Meditating in the Trees* (NT). Myō-e, unlike Eisai and his Zen brethren, preferred to meditate outdoors. The two priests were good friends and when Eisai returned from China he presented Myo-e with Japan's first tea plants suitable for making *matcha* (see Villas, p. 65); the original tea plantation has been reconstructed on the slopes above the Sekisui-in.

## V:4 SAIHŌ-JI AND KATSURA

The southwest of Kyoto, with its factories and apartment blocks, is not a tourist area in general, but it contains two gardens that were important milestones in garden history. Prior arrangements are necessary to see them, but they are well worth the trouble. The Moss Garden at Saihō-ji contains what is considered Japan's first dry garden. The Katsura Imperial Villa, built 300 years later, has one of the earliest and finest stroll gardens, and its buildings are masterpieces of world architecture.

363

**Lunch:** Juntei, Kinsuitei (in spring)

**Note:** Both Saihō-ji and Katsura are three-star attractions, not to be missed if you can get a reservation.

**Matsuno'o Taisha (Shrine)** 松尾大社 Hrs: 9:00–17:00. Nov. 30–Mar. 9:00–16:30. *1.5 km south of Arashiyama's Togetsu Bridge, by a pleasant road.* This shrine, established in 701 by the Korean Hata family (see Kōryū-ji, V:1), is one of Kyoto's oldest shrines. Stacked high in the quiet grounds are barrels of saké offered by brewers, who venerate the shrine's kami. The shrine's 9th-C images of its kami are among the earliest statues of Shinto gods; they are now housed in the Kyoto National Museum (see Art, p. 93).
**\*\*\* Saihō-ji** 西芳寺(苔寺) *1 km south of Matsuno'o Taisha. 0:45h by bus 73 from Kyoto station, or 0:40h by bus 63 from Sanjō-Keihan station. Shown from 13:00; tours last 1:30h.* By reservation. You must be 18 or older. Write to Saihō-ji so that your letter arrives 5–30 days in advance of the desired date. Enclose a postcard self-addressed to your hotel (JTB or your hotel may be able to help). Address: Saihō-ji, 56 Kamigatani, Matsuo, Nishikyō-ku, Kyoto. Visitors are required to either copy or chant sutras, or sit in Zen meditation; if you have a preference, you might ask the temple to reserve an appropriate day for you. After arriving promptly and paying your Y3000 donation, your hour of religious discipline begins, after which you may view the garden. The garden is most radiant in early summer, after the rains, but its autumn foliage is not to be scorned either.

Entering this garden is a remarkable experience, like stepping into an enchanted forest. MUSŌ SOSEKI, who considered gardens an aid to meditation, designed this one in 1339 for his own use, on the remains of an older Jōdo paradise garden (see Villas, p. 60–62). It has changed greatly since his time, and though the full intention of his original design is not clear, the garden today has two distinct levels. The lower level preserves the character of the old paradise garden, with its dark, tranquil pond recalling Amida's Pure Land across the Western Ocean. The pond's convolutions form the character *kokoro*, or "spirit," which in Zen refers to the enlightened mind. More than a hundred varieties of moss spread a luxuriant carpet over the grounds. The moss and the groves of luminous maples capture the mystery and enchantment of a dream forest. Ironically, the moss for which the temple is so famous began to grow only in the early Edo period, 300 years after Musō designed the garden, by which time the temple had been flooded and burned several times. One-quarter of the way around the pond, on the right, stands the **Shōnan-tei** (ICP), a fine *sōan* tea arbor. SEN NO RIKYŪ's son Shōan repaired and lived in it after his father's suicide. This is the only pre-Meiji building on the grounds. After circling the pond, the path climbs a wooded slope and enters the second level of the garden, which centers on a moss-covered jumble of boulders, a "waterless waterfall" which is considered a seminal *kare sansui*, or dry garden. Beside it stands a chapel to Musō. Farther along the path lies a large, flat-topped boulder upon which Musō is supposed to have meditated while viewing the pond below.

**Ike no Taiga Bijutsukan (Art Museum)** 池大雅美術館 (381-2832). Hrs: 10:00–17:00 (enter by 16:30); clsd W. This small, shabby museum near Saihō-ji exhibits an extensive group of ink paintings and calligraphy by Ike no Taiga (1723–1776), a master of the "literary school" of painting (see Art, p. 100).

**Take no Tera (Jizō-in)** 地蔵院(竹の寺) Hrs: 9:00–17:00. Dec.–Mar. 9:00–16:30. Near Saihō-ji. MUSŌ SOSEKI's chief disciple restored this temple founded for the Hosokawa family. It burned in the Ōnin Wars; today the temple has a dry garden called the 16 Rakan, believed to be from the Edo period.

**Suzumushi-dera (Bell Cricket Temple)** 鈴虫寺 Hrs: 9:00–17:00. Near Saihō-ji. A country temple famous for its specially bred *suzumushi* (bell crickets), whose melodious cries can be heard year round.

**\*\*\* Katsura Rikyū (Imperial Villa)** 桂離宮 *0:15h on foot from Hankyū Katsura station, or Y1000 by taxi from Kyoto station.* Reservations necessary: see Imperial Household Agency (l:3) for details. Tours at 10:00 and 14:00, subject to change. Clsd 2nd and 4th Sa, Su, NH. Tours begin promptly. In 1600, in the months before the famous TOKUGAWA victory at Sekigahara, the daimyo Hosokawa Yūsai, sole custodian of the *Kokin Denju* (Secrets of the Kokinshū), was under siege by anti-Tokugawa forces. The castle was on the verge of falling when Emperor Go-Yōzei intervened and effected a truce, rescuing Yūsai so that he could continue to teach the secret tradition to the emperor's younger brother, known to history as Hachijō-no-miya Toshihito (1579–1629). The *Kokin Denju* was a collection of secret readings of characters, the ancient names of certain plants, and other minutiae pertaining to the 10th-C *Kokinshū*, one of Japan's most important poetry collections. It was, in short, a bunch of trivia. Nevertheless, from the time of Toshihito, it was considered so important that only members of the imperial family could see it, although Yūsai and many of his predecessors in the tradition were commoners. Prince Toshihito had for a time been a commoner himself, after he was adopted as an heir by TOYOTOMI HIDEYOSHI. When Hideyoshi had a child of his own, Toshihito was restored to his princely rank and later allowed to start the Hachijō-no-miya family. Toshihito was a politic man, and served as a liaison between the imperial family and the TOKUGAWA; in return for his services, he received the Katsura estate from the second shogun, Hidetada. The estate was well chosen for the literary Toshihito, as it was the site of FUJIWARA NO MICHINAGA's Katsura Mansion, where parts of *The Tale of Genji* are thought to have taken place. Katsura has been called the last word in Japanese estheticism, built as it was by aristocrats who would order battles stopped for the sake of poetry. Indeed, some modern critics have called Katsura Rikyū the epitome of Japanese culture. Since the 1930s, international architects have found in it a confirmation of many modern esthetic creeds, including its harmony of interior and exterior spaces, its simplicity, and the elegant fusion of its form and function.

◆ **The Garden.** More or less completed by Toshihito in 1620, this is among the earliest full-fledged stroll gardens, large-scale landscaped compositions with ever-changing vistas of islands and serpentine ponds, sometimes framed by hedges, at other times accented by a stone lantern (see Villas, p. 67). Katsura's designers pondered every detail, every stone, giving particular thought to the way the garden would unfold. The garden path, which circles the lake in a clockwise direction, is famous for its imaginative and playful stone pavement, which acts as a barometer of formality. In contrast to the "formal" villa approach of cut stone (seen at the end of the tour), the garden path progresses from a "semiformal" pavement, combining cut and irregular stones, to an "informal" series of natural stepping stones, called "jumping stones." Of the walkway's 1,716 stones, these last are the most important, because they function as devices to present the garden's carefully planned views to best effect; at strategic points, "jumping stones" were placed to force viewers to watch their step, so that upon arriving at the next place, they would see the garden from an entirely new perspective.

◆ **Shōkin-tei (Pine Zithern Pavilion).** Katsura's most famous tea arbor. It is built in the eight-window style of KOBORI ENSHŪ, who was a friend of Toshihito. Enshū is credited as the inventor of the stroll garden, and although modern scholars think it unlikely that Enshū himself designed Katsura's garden, it can be supposed that it profited from his influence, and perhaps even his advice. The Shōkin-tei looks out upon a miniature view of Amanohashidate. The real Amanohashidate is a pine-studded sandbar that spans a bay on the Japan Sea coast; it lay within the domain of Toshihito's wife's family. More important, as one of Japan's three famous views, it was mentioned in the *Kokinshū* and other poetry collections. Ardent student of poetry that he was, Toshitada designed Katsura's garden for poetry parties where host and guests would, while boating on the lake or resting in one of the tea arbors, compose *waka* poems and exchange linked verses replete with erudite allusions; for this reason, the garden itself is rife with literary references.

**Shōka-tei (Flower Viewing Pavilion).** This open pavilion is situated at the highest point in the garden. A thicket of trees was placed between the Shōka-tei and the Firefly Lantern down in a small hollow so that the lantern would imitate the flickering of fireflies; this is but one of many garden details that allude to descriptions in *The Tale of Genji*. West of the Shōka-tei, stands **Onrin-dō**, the memorial chapel of the Hachijō-no-miya family. It was built by Toshihito's son Toshitada (1619–1662), whose name is a compound of the names of his father and their benefactor, the shogun Hidetada.

In addition to Katsura, he and his family built many of Kyoto's finest *sukiya* apartments (see III:1). Toshitada married a daughter of Japan's wealthiest *tozama daimyō* family, the Maeda (see Castles, p. 49), and was able during the 1640s to rebuild his father's villa in a lavish style, which today can be seen to best advantage from the Shōka-tei.

◆ **Main Villa.** Only the rightmost part belonged to Toshihito's original estate; the adjoining buildings were added by Toshitada. Toshitada adopted a son of Emperor Go-Mizuno'o, Yasuhito, and during his second visit to the villa, Gomizuno'o was in fact the guest of his own son. Yasuhito remodeled the villa for the visit, and it was at this time that it attained its present form. The stunningly beautiful ensemble of halls, joined under four connected roofs, is described as "geese in formation," alluding to its diagonal placement and light, effortless appearance. This arrangement maximizes fresh air and views onto the garden. Bamboo laths cover the space under the verandas, permitting additional ventilation. Both the floors and the eaves of each section are on slightly different levels, achieving an overall cascade effect. The ground bordering the buildings consists of bands of bare earth, pebbles, stepping stones, and moss, providing a transitional element between the human order of the buildings and the naturalness of the garden; the pebbles also serve as rain gutters. The interiors, unfortunately not shown, are considered the epitome of Sukiya-Shoin style. A *shoin*, literally a study, is so called because its desks and shelves are built into the walls. Katsura's *shoin* are called *sukiya* because they borrow from the vocabulary of tea huts. The structural elements are slender, light, natural timbers, and the rooms are intimate in size, constructed with daily life, albeit a leisurely life, in mind. The rightmost part, the **Old Shoin**, was built by Toshihito, who was particularly fond of the Moon Viewing Platform that faces out on the pond. The **Middle Shoin** was added by Toshitada, as was the small Musical Instruments Room, under an adjoining eave, and a veranda for watching *kemari*, the court kickball game. The Miyuki Goten (Imperial Visit Temporary Palace), also called the **New Shoin**, is where retired emperor Go-Mizuno'o and his Tokugawa consort Tōfukumon-in stayed in 1658 and 1663. The New Shoin's Katsura Shelf, a wildly unorthodox *chigaidana* that merges with a *tsuke-shoin* or built-in desk, is probably Japan's most famous shelf. The New Shoin is also famous for its exquisitely designed door pulls.

**Geppa-rō (Moon Wave Pavilion).** Built by Toshihito and named in reference to a verse by the Chinese poet Po Chu-i (Hakurakuten). This pavilion is built in a rustic style, with bamboo rafters and a lovely, unadorned ceiling. Po Chu-i (772–846) was the only Chinese poet to become known in Japan during his own lifetime, and he had a strong influence on Heian poetry from about the time that the *Kokinshū* was compiled. Another of Katsura's tea arbors, Kokin Denju no Ma (Room of the *Kokin Denju*), was given in 1912 to the Hosokawa of Kumamoto (Kyūshū, p. 494) in appreciation of Hosokawa Yūsai's role in preserving and transmitting the *Kokin Denju* to Toshihito. As you leave the villa you will pass by the **Miyuki Mon**, the Imperial Visit Gate used by Go-Mizuno'o during his visit. After exiting, notice the superb Katsura Fence of bamboo, reminiscent of fences used in tea gardens, but on a much larger scale; it encircles the entire garden.

### Exploring Tai-an
*Take Hankyū line to Ōyamazaki.* The grounds of Myoki-an temple contain **Tai-an** (NT), a celebrated two-mat *sōan* tea arbor, the only one extant ascribed to SEN NO RIKYŪ. It can be seen by application (961–0103); Ryūzaki, Ōyamazaki, Ōyamazaki-chō, Otokuni-gun, Kyoto-fu.

# SHOPPING

## SHOPS BY TYPE
See listings by area, below, for details on individual shops.

**Antiques:** Many antique shops are on Shin-Monzen-dōri, Teramachi-dōri, and Sanjō-dōri near the Miyako Hotel. **Bamboo ware:** Takano Take Kōgei-ten (I:2). **Books and prints:** Maruzen (I:2) for books in English, Ezōshi (II:3) for woodblock prints. **Ceramics:** Tachikichi (I:2), Ambiente (I:2), Manju-dō (II:2), Tōjiki Kaikan (II:2). The Gojō-zaka area (II:2) has many pottery shops. **Crafts in general:** Maronier (I:2), Maruzen (I:2), Yamato Mingeiten (I:2), Kyoto Craft Center (II:3). **Culinary:** Nishiki-kōji (I:2) is a colorful market alley. Takashimaya (I:2) has the best basement food market. Tsunenobu (I:2) for cutlery, Aritsugu (I:2) for fine traditional Japanese kitchen ware, Ippō-dō (I:2) for tea. **Department stores:** Takashimaya (I:2), Hankyū (I:2), Daimaru (I:2). **Dolls:** Matsuya (I:2), Tanakaya (I:2). **Fashion:** Inexpensive, trendy clothes in Shin-Kyōgoku and Kyōgoku arcades. Takashimaya has the best designer boutiques. The Times Building at Sanjō-Kiyamachi (I:2) is filled with avant-garde boutiques. **Flea markets:** 21st of each month at Tō-ji (I:1). 25th of each month at Kitano Tenman-gū (IV:1). Junk, antiques, bonsai trees, food. Old kimono are among the better buys. Not particularly cheap, but some bargaining allowed. **Furniture:** Maeda Heihachi Shōten (I:2) for split-bamboo hanging screens, Miyazaki (I:2) for handcrafted furniture, Miura Shōmei (II:3) for Japanese-style lighting fixtures, Izawaya (II:3) for small articles of furniture (*sashimono*). **Hair ornaments and jewelery:** Cloisonné and *zōgan* (damascene, metal inlay) at Kyoto Craft Center (II:3), combs and hairpins at Jūsanya (I:2), geisha makeup at Kazurasei (II:3). **Incense:** *Nioi-bukuro*, tiny, brocade-covered sachets, make great gifts— portable, inexpensive, elegant, exotic. Ōno Kungyoku-dō (I:1), Kyūkyodō (I:2), Toyota

Aisan-dō (II:3). **Lacquerware:** Hatsusegawa Ryū-an (I:2), Asobe (I:2), Monju (II:3), Zōhiko (II:4). **Paper, stationery:** Handmade paper at Yamato Mingeiten (I:2), Morita Washiten (I:2), Mine (I:2), Kakimoto (I:2). Elegant paper at Kyūkyodō (I:2). Kyoto fans at Miyawaki Baisen-an (I:2). Ink and brushes at Kobai-en (I:2). Parasols and lanterns at Kasagen (II:3). Hiyoshiya (IV:1) has the large parasols used in outdoor tea ceremonies. **Textiles:** Kimono textiles at Erizen (I:2), Ido Kotobukiya (I:2), Murata (II:3). Antique fabric at Konjaku Nishimura (II:3), Chingireya (II:3). **Miscellaneous:** Custom nameplates at Shimizu Sue Shōten (I:2), pewter at Seika-dō (I:2), brooms at Naitō Shōten (I:2).

## SHOPS BY AREA

### I:1 Station Area (see map, p. 324)

⁸ **Ōno Kungyoku-dō** 負野薫玉堂　堀川通西本願寺前 (371-0162). Hrs: 9:00–18:00; clsd 1st and 3rd Su. Across from Nishi Hongan-ji. In operation since 1594; a dark, unpretentious store with high-quality incense.

### I:2 Central Shopping Area (see map, p. 328)

² **Morita Washiten** 森田和紙店　東洞院仏光寺上ル (341-1419). Higashi-Tōin Bukkō-ji north. Hrs: 9:30–17:30; Sa 9:30–16:30; clsd Su, NH, first of each month, NY. *Washi* from everywhere in Japan. Paper knickknacks. No CC.

³ **Hatsusegawa Ryū-an** 初瀬川柳庵　高辻柳馬場角 (351-0983). Takatsuji Yanaginobanba. Hrs: 10:00–17:00; clsd Su, NH, NY. Three blocks S of Shijō-dōri. By appointment. Lacquerware with contemporary flair. No CC.

⁴ **Maeda Heihachi Shōten** 前田平八商店　寺町仏光寺上ル (351-2749). Teramachi Bukkō-ji north. Hrs: 9:00–17:00; clsd Su, NH, NY. *Misu-sudare*, fine split-bamboo hanging screens trimmed in brocade.

**366**

¹³ **Hankyū Department Store** 阪急デパート (223-2288). Shijō Kawaramachi SE corner. Hrs: 10:00–19:00; clsd Th. Mostly clothing.

¹⁸ **Matsuya** 松屋　河原町四条上ル (221-5902). Kawaramachi Shijō north. Hrs: 11:00–20:30; clsd M, NY. Fine Kyoto dolls.

¹⁹ **Maronier** マロニエ　河原町四条上ル東側 (221-0117). Kawaramachi Shijō north. Hrs: 11:00–20:30; clsd M, NY. Contemporary crafts for daily use, by Kyoto artisans. AX, V.

²⁰ **Fukuda Shōkadō** 福田松花堂 (221-2009). Hrs: 9:30–20:00 (to 18:00 on F); clsd. W. This small shop carries fans of elegantly plain paper.

²⁶ **Maruzen** 丸善 (241-2161). Kawaramachi Takoyakushi. Hrs: 10:00–19:00; Su, NH 10:00–18:30; clsd W. Books in English on 3F. On 5F, fine selection of Japanese handcrafts, traditional and contemporary. Tobe porcelain, wood and bamboo crafts. V.

²⁷ **Yamato Mingeiten** やまと民芸店　河原町蛸薬師上ル (221-2641). Hrs: 10:00–20:30; clsd F, NY. Next to Maruzen. Good selections of *washi*, pottery, glass, baskets, and textiles. The shop operates a nearby craft gallery. AX, V, MC, DC.

³² **Naitō Shōten** 内藤商店　三条大橋西詰北側 (221-3018). Hrs: 8:00–20:00; clsd NY. Handmade Japanese brushes and brooms.

⁴¹ **Takashimaya Department Store** 高島屋 (221-8811). Shijō Kawaramachi SW corner. Hrs: 10:00–19:00; clsd W. Best in Kyoto. All major credit cards.

⁴² **Erizen** ゑり善　四条河原町西入ル (221-1618). Shijō Kawaramachi NW corner. Hrs: 10:00–19:00; clsd M, NY. Elegant kimono textiles including cotton *yukata* fabric (summer).

⁴⁵ **Jūsanya** 十三や　四条寺町東入ル (211-0498). Shijō Teramachi east. Hrs: 11:00–21:00, daily. Boxwood hairpins and combs.

⁴⁹ **Tsunenobu** 常信　四条御幸町西入ル (221-3745). Shijō Gokōmachi west. Hrs: 10:00–19:00; W 10:00–18:00; clsd 2nd and 3rd W. Cutlery shop, founded in 1631 by a swordsmith.

⁵⁰ **Ido Kotobukiya** いど寿屋　四条御幸町西入ル (223-0008). Shijō Gokōmachi west. Hrs: 10:00–18:00; clsd W, NY. Okinawan Bingata textiles and kimono accessories.

⁵¹ **Tachikichi** たち吉　四条富小路角 (211-3141). Kawaramachi Tomi-kōji. Hrs: 10:00–19:00; clsd W. Shop founded in 1752; carries pottery in every price range. AX, DC, V.

⁵² **Tanakaya** 田中弥　四条柳馬場東入ル (221-1959). Shijō Yanaginobanba. Hrs: 9:30–18:00; clsd W. Kyoto dolls. Excellent workmanship, and consequently expensive. Also carries Noh masks.

⁵³ **Asobe** アソベ　四条高倉 (211-0803). Shijō Takakura. Hrs: 9:30–18:00; clsd W, NY. Lacquerware for daily use. Inexpensive.

⁵⁴ **Daimaru Department Store** 大丸 (211-8111). Shijō Takakura. Hrs: 10:00–19:00; clsd W, NY. Conservative in taste and high in quality.

⁵⁵ **Aritsugu** 有次　錦小路御幸町西入ル (221-1091). Nishiki-kōji Gokōmachi west. Hrs: 9:00–17:30; clsd Su, NH, NY. Fine traditional Japanese kitchen ware—cutlery, copper pans, cypress tubs. This shop once supplied the imperial palace. No CC.

⁶⁰ **Ambiente** アンビエンテ　寺町三条下ル (221-1578). Teramachi Sanjō south. Hrs: 11:00–18:00; clsd W, NY. Well-designed tableware in traditional Japanese pottery styles, but suitable for Western tables.

⁶¹ **Iseya** 伊勢屋 (221-2021). Teramachi Sanjō south, Ichibeh Bldg., 1F. Hrs: 11:00–20:00. Contemporary crafts, from housewares to toys.

⁶⁴ **Mine** 峯　河原町三条上ル西入ル (231-1017). Hrs: 12:00–21:00; clsd Tu, NH. One street north and west from Kawaramachi Sanjō. Small craft shop with *washi* stationery.

65 **Kyūkyodō** 鳩居堂　寺町姉小路角 (231-0509/0510). Teramachi Sanjō north. Hrs: 10:00–18:00; clsd Su, NY. Just walking into this shop for elegant Kyoto paper goods and incense is a sensual experience. Brushes, ink and inkstones, incense and incense games.

70 **Miyawaki Baisen-an** 宮脇売扇庵　六角通富小路西入ル (221-0181). Rokkaku-dō Tomi-kōji. Hrs: 9:00–17:00; clsd NY. Elegant Kyoto fans. AX, V, MC.

77 **Takano Take Kōgei-ten** 高野竹工芸店　寺町二条南入ル (211-8694). Teramachi Nijō south. Hrs: 9:30–19:00; clsd NY. Bamboo handwork: baskets, tea utensils. No CC.

78 **Seika-dō** 清耀堂　寺町二条下ル (231-3661). Teramachi Nijō south. Hrs: 10:00–18:00; clsd Su, NH, NY. Pewter crafts have a long history in Japan; this is the only pewter specialist in Kyoto. Tea utensils and custom work. All major credit cards.

79 **Shimizu Sue Shōten** 清水末商店　寺町二条下ル (231-4838). Teramachi Nijō south. Hrs: 9:00–19:00; clsd Su, NH. Custom *kanban*, elaborate nameplates carved in wood. Small items can be finished in 10 days. Bring a Japanese speaker to interpret. No CC.

81 **Kakimoto** 柿本　寺町二条上ル (211-3481). Teramachi-Nijō. Hrs: 9:00–18:00; clsd Su. Handmade paper.

82 **Ippō-dō** 一保堂　寺町二条北 (211-3421). Teramachi Nijō north. Hrs: 9:00–19:00; clsd Su, NY. Famed tea shop, in business since 1717. Classic building, filled with tea crocks.

83 **Kobai-en** 古梅園　寺町二条上ル (231-1531). Teramachi Nijō north. Hrs: 9:00–17:30; clsd Su, NH. Ink from the venerable Nara shop, as well as brushes and paper.

84 **Miyazaki** 宮崎　夷川通堺町 (231-6337). Ebisugawa-dōri, Sakai-chō. Hrs: 9:00–18:00; clsd M. Finest Kyoto-style handcrafted furnishings.

## II:2 Sanjusangen-dō/Kiyomizu Area (see map, p. 335)

5 **Suisō-dō** 翠草堂　河原町五条上ル (361-0557). Kawaramachi Gojō north. Hrs: 9:00–19:30, clsd Su, NH. This shop makes custom-designed insignia seals (*inkan*). Each is a work of art.

6 **Manju-dō** 萬珠堂　五条大橋東3丁目 (541-0101). Gojō Ōhashi Higashi 3-chōme. Hrs: 10:00–18:00; clsd 1st and 3rd Th. Good-quality Kiyomizu-yaki.

7 **Tōjiki Kaikan** 陶磁器会館　五条東大路東入ル (541-1102). Hrs: 9:30–17:00; clsd NY. Located at the bottom of Kiyomizu-michi. Kyoto stoneware and porcelain. AX, DC, V, MC.

## II:3 Gion (see map, p. 339)

5 **Monju** 文珠　四条花見小路東入ル南側 (525-1617). Shijō Hanami-kōji east. Hrs: 10:00–19:30; clsd Th, NY. Lacquerware for daily use. Moderate prices.

6 **Kazurasei** かづら清　祇園町北側 (561-0672). Hrs: 9:30–19:00; clsd 1st, 3rd, and 5th W. Hair ornaments, *maiko* makeup, cosmetic brushes, and rouge packaged in clam shells.

7 **Kasagen** かさ源　祇園町北側 (561-2832). Hrs: 9:30–21:00, daily. Shijō in Gion, north side. Japanese parasols and paper lanterns. No CC.

8 **Miura Shōmei** 三浦照明　祇園町北側 (561-2816). Hrs: 9:30–20:00; clsd Su, NH, NY. Shijō in Gion, north side. Elegant Japanese-style lighting fixtures, traditional and contemporary.

9 **Toyota Aisan-dō** 豊田愛山堂　祇園町北側 (551-2221). Hrs: 10:00–19:00; clsd W, 4th Th, NY. Shijō-dōri in Gion, north side. Wide selection of incense and censers.

10 **Kyoto Craft Center** 京都クラフトセンター　祇園町北側 (561-9660). Hrs: 10:00–18:00; clsd W. Shijō-dōri in Gion. Contemporary crafts with an even mix of traditional and modern designs. Many small, usable, and affordable items that would make excellent gifts.

12 **Murata** むら田　祇園町北側 (531-0105). Hrs: 9:40–19:00; clsd M, NY. Craft kimono textiles, fine *tsumugi* (pongee), *kasuri*, and regional weaves.

14 **Izawaya** 井沢屋　四条南座前 (525-0130). Hrs: 10:30–21:00, daily. Across from Minami-za theater. Kyoto fabric accessories and a selection of finely made small articles of furniture (*sashimono*). All major credit cards.

20 **Ezōshi** 絵草子　新門前縄手東入ル十六五ビル1F (551-9137). Shinmonzen-dōri, Tōrokugo Bldg., 1F. Hrs: 10:00–18:00, daily. Antique woodblock prints. AX, V, MC, DC.

21 **Konjaku Nishimura** 今昔にしむら　縄手古門前 (561-1568). Nawate Furumonzen-mae. Hrs: 10:00–18:30; clsd W, NY. Antique fabric shop patronized by tea connoisseurs.

23 **Chingireya** ちんぎれや　縄手三条南入ル (561-4726). Nawate Sanjō south. Hrs: 9:00–20:00; clsd NY. Antique textiles, obi, kimono, and fragments. Wallets made from old indigo-dyed cloth. All major credit cards.

## II:4 Heian Shrine, Okazaki Park (see map, p. 335)

29 **Zōhiko** 象彦　岡崎景勝寺町 (761-0212). Hrs: 9:00–17:00; clsd Su, NH. Near Kyoto Kaikan. Kyoto lacquerware, elegant and traditional. Good for the expensive, fine wares; other stores offer better deals on the cheaper wares. AX, V, MC, DC.

35 **Higashiyama Sansō** 東山山荘　東山ドライブウェイ (581-3510). Short ride from Miyako Hotel. By appointment; clsd Su. Warehouse of antique furniture, porcelain, lacquerware, and bridal kimono.

## IV:1 Daitoku-ji Area (see map, p. 324)

25 **Hiyoshiya** 日吉屋　寺之内通堀川東入ル (441-6644). Teranouchi Horikawa east. Hrs: 7:00–19:00. Near the Ura Senke and Omote Senke tea ceremony schools. Parasols — the large kind used in outdoor tea ceremonies — can be ordered for Y55,000 and Y80,000.

# DINING

*Kyō-ryōri*, the cuisine of Kyoto, is the most refined and subtle in Japan. This is the place to try elegant *kaiseki*, vegetarian Buddhist *shōjin-ryōri,* and tofu dishes (see Cuisine, p. 116–117).

## I:1 **Station Area** (see map, p. 324)

③ * **Manshige Porta-ten** 萬重ポルタ店　京都駅地下　(343-3920); clsd 3rd Th, NY. In station basement complex. Branch of famous old Nishijin *ryōtei.* Mini-*kaiseki* Y3500.

⑤ * **Izusen** 泉仙　烏丸七条下ル　(343-4211). Hrs: 11:00–20:00; clsd Th, NY. Near TIC. Branch of famous *shōjin-ryōri* (vegetarian Buddhist cuisine) restaurant. *Bentō* Y1800, *teppachi* set from Y3000.

⑫ ** **Finlandia** フィンランデイヤ　五条柳馬場西北角　(351-7689). Gojō Yanaginobanba west. Hrs: 12:00–14:30, 17:00–21:30; Su, NH 12:00–21:00; clsd M. Wonderful Finnish restaurant with clean, pale wood interior. Elk meat in juniper cream sauce and smoked trout are excellent. Full dinner Y4800–8500. AX, V, CB, MC, DC.

## I:2 **Central Shopping Area** (see map, p. 328)

⑤ ** **Kitamura** 北村　木屋町仏光寺上ル　(351-7871). Hrs: 17:00–23:00; NH 17:00–22:00; clsd Su. Elegant versions of home-style Kyoto cuisine. There's a *kaiseki* section, but the culinary wonders are at the counter, presided over by the young master. Try tofu gratin and soft, fresh *mochi tarako-ae* (pounded glutinous rice with a scarlet sauce of cod roe. We recommend leaving the choice of dishes up to the master; just tell him how much you want to spend per person (Y6–12,000 would be reasonable), and mention any likes or dislikes. Excellent *yuka* in summer. *Kaiseki* Y9000+. No CC.

⑥ * **Kanoko** かのこ　西石垣四条下ル　(351-2081). Hrs: 15:30–21:00 (last order); clsd 4th W. Old beef shop. Sukiyaki, *oil-yaki, shabu-shabu* (order in advance). Generous portions. *Yuka* in summer. From Y3200. No CC.

⑦ * **Hanayama Daikichi** 花山大吉　四条河原町南二筋東入ル　(351-7775). Hrs: 12:00–21:30; clsd M (except if NH, then clsd Tu). Tasty curries and homemade cakes at this natural-food restaurant. Nonsmoking only. Curry from Y700.

⑧ **Tsukimura** 月村　西木屋町四条下ル　(351-5306). Hrs: 17:00–21:30; clsd M. A *nomiya* in the alley south of Hankyū Department Store. A place to meet local foreigners. Good *kamagohan* (rice casserole) Y1500.

⑨ * **Chinchikurin** 珍竹林　西木屋町通四条下ル　(351-9205). Hrs: 11:30–22:00; clsd W. *Kamameshi* (rice casserole) Y950, *zōsui* (rice stew) Y800, *teishoku* from Y1200. Charming folk-art interior. No CC.

⑩ **Takasebune** 高瀬舟　西木屋町四条下ル　(351-4032). Hrs: 11:00–21:30; clsd M (Tu if M a NH), NY. Y700 tempura *teishoku* is one of the best deals in town. Good sashimi also. Old building with atmosphere. No CC.

⑫ **Morishige** 森繁　西木屋町四条下ル　(351-1702). Hrs: 12:00–14:00, 16:00–22:00; clsd M (except if NH), NY. Inca cuisine: "Kapakku" and "Inca" stew from Y2500.

⑭ **Shirukō** 志る幸　河原町四条上ル一筋目東入ル　(221-3250). Hrs: 11:30–20:30; clsd W. *Rikyū-bentō* of Kyoto delicacies, Y2300.

⑮ * **Kurokawa** 黒川　河原町四条上ル一筋目東入ル　(241-1434). Hrs: 18:00–1:00; clsd Tu, NY. *Nomiya* with home-style cooking. Try the *iromeshi* (rice casserole), Y800 w/miso soup. Other dishes displayed on the counter. Expect to spend about Y4000 per person.

⑰ * **Maruman Sushi** 丸万寿司　西木屋町四条上ル　(221-0927). Hrs: 17:00–0:30; clsd M, NY. Cozy shop with excellent sushi. *Moriawase* Y1500.

㉑ * **Yamatomi** 山とみ　四条先斗町上ル　(221-3268). Hrs: 12:00–23:30; clsd Tu, NY. Casual former Pontochō teahouse with popular summer *yuka*. *Teppin-age*, a kind of *fondue bourgignon*. Also good *bentō*. English menu. Set menus are about Y2500.

㉒ **Maeda** 前田　木屋町四条上ル　(223-5725). Kiyamachi Shijō north, Kiyamachi 50 Bldg., 2F. Hrs: M–Sa 18:00–22:30, Su 17:00–22:00. Artsy-folksy saké bar-restaurant featuring brews from all over Japan. À la carte, Y500–2300. V, DC, CB.

㉕ **Yagenbori Kiyamachi-ten** 薬研彫木屋町店　河原町蛸薬師東入ル　(221-5903). Hrs: 12:00–14:00, 16:00–23:00; clsd NY. Country cuisine. *Zōsui* (rice stew), Y1800; *wappa bentō*, Y3000; mini-*kaiseki*, Y4500; Yagenbori course (a sampling of adventurous dishes: trout sashimi, loach pot, mustard tofu) Y6000; *shabu-shabu* Y5000. AX.

㉘ ** **Uzuki** うづき　先斗町三条下ル　(221-2358). Hrs: 17:00–23:00 (last order 22:00); clsd 2nd and 4th W. A former Pontochō *chaya*, now an elegant *kaiseki* place, open to all, no reservation needed. Set menu from Y5000 (Y8000 for *yuka* seating).

㉙ * **Torisei** 鳥せる　先斗町三条下ル二筋目角2F　(255-5566). Hrs: 17:00–1:00, daily. Near Pontochō Kaburenjō. Trendy *yakitori* bar. Set menus from Y2500.

㉚ **Fable Table** (252-5151). Royal Hotel, B1. Hrs: 17:30–23:20 (last order), daily. Japanese and Western food served with beer from around the world. Bilingual menu. The large, trendy interior (lots of stonework) is fun to look at, and the mood is relaxed. À la carte Y350-750.

㉛ **Matsuzushi** 松ずし　木屋町三条下ル　(221-2946). Hrs: 14:00–19:00; clsd Th, NY. Reputed to have the best sushi in town. From Y5000. No CC.

㉝ \*\***Agatha** 阿雅左　木屋町三条上ル遊里香ビル2F　(223-2379). Kiyamachi Oike south. Hrs: 17:00–midnight, daily. Charcoal-broiled skewers. Cross-cultural menu and interior. English spoken. Courses from Y2200. Also try their soup (spinach and chicken meatballs in broth) and the tofu with chilied cod roe in butter sauce. V, DC, MC, AX.

㉟ \***Bloomer 55** 木屋町御池下ル (255-3424). Kiyamachi Oike-sagaru, Ueba Bldg., 3F. Hrs: 17:00–midnight; clsd Tu. Casual, sports-motif wine-bar restaurant run by a jovial chef who trained in France but serves whatever he feels like making. Menu in French. Be prepared for friendly banter. À la carte Y800–3500.

㊲ \*\***Agatha** (Northern branch) 阿雅左（北店）　木屋町御池下ル上羽ビル2F (255-2279). Hrs: 17:00–midnight, daily. A clone of the popular main branch (see above).

㊳ **Ōiwa** 大岩　木屋町二条下ル (231-7667). Kiyamachi Nijō south. Hrs: 17:00–22:00; Su, NH 16:00–22:00; clsd W, NY. *Kushiage* (deep-fried skewered meats and vegetables) in a pleasant, renovated *kura*. *Teishoku* (7 skewers) Y1200, full course (up to 30 skewers, stop when you're full) about Y5000. No CC.

㊵ \*\***Ebisugawa-tei** 夷川亭 (222-1511). Hrs: 12:00–21:30 (dinner from 16:00). At Fujita Hotel. Three steakhouses in a beautiful riverside villa with garden. Ōmi offers a European influenced menu. Chidori is Japanese style surf and turf. Kura serves steak *kaiseki*. Prix fixe Y9,500–20,000. AX, V, CB, DC, MC.

㊸ **Edogawa** 江戸川　新京極四条上ル花遊小路 (221-1550). Hrs: 11:00–21:00, daily. Modern, roomy shop for *unagi* (eel) cuisine. *Una-don* from Y1200, *bentō* Y2100, *okimari* (light set menu) from Y4000. CB, MC, V, AX.

㊻ \***Ashoka** アショカ　寺町四条 (241-1318). Kikusui Bldg., 3F. Hrs: 11:30–14:30, 17:00–21:00; Su and NH, to 20:30; clsd 2nd Tu. Good North Indian cuisine (tandoori dishes) with elegant decor, friendly service. Lunch Y1300; dinner from Y2500. AX, V, CB, MC, DC.

㊼ **Kimura Sukiyaki-ten** キムラすき焼店　寺町四条上ル西側 (221-0506). Hrs: 12:00–20:00; clsd M (except if NH, then Tu), NY. Popular sukiyaki shop in the Teramachi-Kyōgoku arcade. From Y2800.

㊿ **Izumo** 井津茂　寺町蛸薬師下ル (221-5425). Hrs: 15:00–22:00; Sa, Su 13:00–22:00; clsd Th. On Teramachi north of Nishiki-kōji. Fresh and inexpensive sushi.

58 \*\***Okina-tei** 翁亭　河原町蛸薬師西入角 (221-0250). Hrs: 11:30–21:30, no set holiday. Sukiyaki since 1872 (oldest sukiyaki shop in Japan). Atmospheric and cozy. Sukiyaki from Y4500, full-course menu from Y6500. AX, V, MC, DC, CB.

59 **Yōmenya** 洋麵屋　河原町三条下ル京宝ビル3F (223-0301). Kyōhō Bldg., 3F. Hrs: 11:00–21:30 (last order), daily. Serves a variety of pasta, from Y700.

69 \*\***Misoka-an Kawamichiya** 晦庵河道屋　麩屋町三条上ル (221-2525). Hrs: 11:00–19:30 (last order); clsd Th, NY. The most famous *soba* shop in Kyoto. *Soba* from Y800. *Hōkōro-nabe*, a version of Mongolian hotpot with tofu, chicken, *soba*, Y3200/person. AX, V.

71 **Ueda** うえだ　富小路三条上ル (221-4909). Hrs: 11:00–15:00, 17:00–19:30; 2nd and 3rd Sa 17:00–20:00; clsd Su, NH. *Udon* and *soba* in an old house. *Yakizakana* (broiled fish) *teishoku* Y630+, *oroshi-soba* Y650. No CC.

75 \*\***Owariya** 尾張屋　二条車屋町下ル (231-3446). Hrs: 11:00–19:00; clsd W, NY. A quaint *soba* shop in business since 1465 (so the *noren* proclaims). Specialty is *Hōrai-soba*, stacked in small lacquer trays and eaten with a variety of condiments, Y1500. No CC.

76 \*\***Anda** アンダ　河原町二条下ル SSSビル (221-2289). Kawaramachi Nijō south, SSS Bldg., B1. Hrs: 17:00–22:00; clsd Su. New style kaiseki restaurant with creative and delicious food. The contemporary stone and wood interior is marvelous. Only two tables. Most customers sit at the two long counters. Fixed course menu from Y12,000.

80 \*\***Yamamoto** 山本　新烏丸二条上ル (231-4495). Hrs: 11:30–13:30, 17:00–22:00; clsd 2nd and 4th Su, NY. One block E of Teramachi's Ippō-dō tea shop. Exquisite *tonkatsu* (pork cutlet). Lunch *hire teishoku* Y2750; *rōsu teishoku* Y2550. No CC.

## I:3 North of Oike-dōri, Palace Area (see map, p. 324)

15 \*\***Junshin-an** 純心庵　丸太町麩屋町西角 (256-3825), branch (231-4624). Marutamachi Fuyachō. Hrs: 12:00–14:00, 17:00–22:00 (last order); clsd Tu and 1st of each month. Innovative beef cuisine. Simple set menu Y5000; steak *kaiseki* Y5–10,000 (2 days advance notice). AX, V, DC, CB, MC.

17 \*\***Hachiki-an** 八起庵　川端通丸太町上ル東側 (761-5470). Kawabata Marutamachi north. Hrs: 11:30–14:00, 17:00–22:00; clsd M, NY. Specialist in chicken. *Iori bentō* (lunch) Y2800; *omakase* course Y8000+; *mizudaki* Y8000. MC, MC, AX, DC, V.

18 **Torisei** 鳥せゐ　河原町丸太町上ル西側 (222-2554). Kawaramachi Marutamachi north, on west side. Hrs: 17:00–midnight; clsd M, NY. *Yakitori*, three skewers from Y360. Also try one of their raw dishes and the *soboro* (ground chicken) over tofu or eggplant. No CC.

21 \***Honyaradō** ほんやら洞　今出川寺町西入 (222-1574). Teramachi Imadegawa. Hrs: 9:00–22:00; clsd 1st W. Popular student hangout with good and inexpensive natural food. Lunch set Y500, dinner Y600.

## II:2 Sanjūsangen-dō/Kiyomizu Area (see map, p. 335)

① **Warajiya** わらじや　七条大和大路西入ル (561-1290). Hrs: 12:00–14:00, 16:00–19:00; Sa, Su, NH 12:00–19:00; clsd Tu. *Uzōsui course* Y5060 includes *matcha*, appetizers, a delicate smoky broth of eel, and *uzōsui* (eel and rice "stew"). Unusual and fine flavor. Delightful old house near National Museum. CB, V.

⑧ **Ashiya Steak House** 芦屋ステーキハウス　清水4-172-13 (541-7961). Hrs: 17:30–22:00 (last order); clsd M, NY. Just off Higashiyama-dōri near Kiyomizu-zaka. Handsome Japanese house converted into a *teppanyaki* restaurant by its American owner, Bob Strickland, and his Japanese wife, who do an admirable job of making you feel welcome in Kyoto. The clientele is mostly foreign, the food is inconsistent. Prix fixe dinner Y12,500–20,000. Fish dinner Y9000. DC, AX, V.

⑨ **Tonchinkan** とんちんかん　安井神社南鳥居前 (561-7250). Hrs: 12:00–20:30 (last order); clsd M, NY. Southeast of Kennin-ji. Unusual and delicious Japanese-style pork dishes. Courses Y3–4000. No CC.

⑩ Hisago ひさご　下河原町八坂鳥井前 (561-2109). Hrs: 12:00–20:30; clsd M, NY. *Soba* and *donburi* dishes with good reputation; near Yasaka Jinja. From Y330.

⑫ **Hagi** 波ぎ　高台寺畔 (531-4551). Hrs: 11:00–15:00; clsd Tu. Just N of east entrance to Ishibe-kōji. Teahouse with beautiful garden, classical music. Dainty seasonal Kyoto dishes. *Hagi teishoku* Y1400. No CC.

⑭ **Minoko** 美濃幸　祇園下河原清井町 (561-0328). Hrs: 11:30–20:00 (last order); clsd 2nd and 4th W. Just S of Yasaka Jinja. Excellent *chabako bentō* (order by 14:30) Y3000, lunch *kaiseki* Y8000, dinner Y12,000+. V, CB, MC, DC.

⑰ * **Hiranoya Honten** 平野屋本店　円山公園内知恩院南門前 (561-1603). Hrs: 10:30–20:00, daily. In Maruyama Park. Charming teahouse, specialists in *imobō*, a simmered dish made from yams and dried cod. Made for 300 years, this humble concoction was a delicacy in land-locked Kyoto and was served on festival days. *Imobō teishoku* Y2000, *shōjin kaiseki* Y4800, *kaiseki* Y6000. No CC.

370

## II:3 Gion (see map, p. 339)

① ***Takeuma** 竹馬　祇園町南側570-7 (525-1156). Hrs: 17:00–22:00; clsd M. Tiny, barlike shop with superb *Kyō-ryōri* by a master who apprenticed at the famed Kitchō. Reserve a day in advance so the master has time to devise a menu. (Let him know if you don't drink alcoholic beverages.) Full dinners from Y12,000. No CC.

② **Jūnidanya** 十二段家　祇園花見小路四条下ル (561-0213). Hrs: 12:00–14:00, 17:00–21:00 (last order); clsd Th. On Hanami-kōji. Beef *shabu-shabu* in informal farmhouse setting, Y5000. Multi-course dinner Y10,000+. AX, DC, V, MC, CB.

③ **Yuranosuke** 由良之助　花見小路四条 (541-5371). Hrs: 12:00–15:00, 16:00–22:00; clsd 1st and 3rd W, NY. On Hanami-kōji. Elegant interior, friendly service. Named for the hero of *Chūshingura*. *Kamagohan* (rice casserole) lunch set Y4500, *Kyō-zukushi* (mini-*kaiseki*) lunch Y10,000, *tenshin* Y4000. Dinner set from Y10–18,000.

④ * **Yagenbori Hanamikōji-ten** 薬研彫　花見小路四条一筋下ル西入ル (525-3332). Hrs: 12:00–14:00, 16:00–22:30 (last order). Elegant farmhouse interior and country cuisine. Not for the fainthearted: they have a penchant for cooking live fish at the table. Prix fixe dinner Y9000+. AX, DC, V, MC.

⑬ **Matsuno** 松乃　四条南座東 (561-2786). Hrs: 11:30–20:30; clsd W (except if NH). *Unagi* on Shijō, in Gion. Nice interior, English menu. *Teishoku* Y6–12,000. No CC.

⑮ **Takarabune** たから舟　祇園富永町 (561-6040). Hrs: 12:00–14:00, 16:00–21:00; clsd Tu. Excellent home-cooked semi-Western dishes in a pleasant little shop. Chicken sauté, sandwiches. Moderate. No CC.

⑯ * **Izū** いづう　八坂新池清本町 (561-0750). Hrs: 11:00–23:00; clsd Tu, NY, open NH. Famous Kyoto-style sushi shop, in business since 1781. *Saba sugata-zushi* (whole pickled mackerel pressed onto a bed of rice) Y3000, *moriawase* Y2200, *chirashi* Y2200. No CC.

⑰ **Yassan** 安参　祇園町北側347 (541-9666). Hrs: 18:00–23:00; clsd Su, 3rd Sa. Specializes in beef cuisine: set appetizer of raw choice cuts of tongue, heart, filet, and tripe, followed by a choice of *nikomi* (stewed oxtail) or *yakiniku* (grilled meat). Prix fixe Y7000+.

⑱ **Kappa** かっぱ　縄手通富永町上ル (531-2322). Hrs: 18:00–2:00; clsd 1st, 2nd, 3rd M. Cramped, friendly *robata* place on Nawate-dōri. Inexpensive. No CC.

⑲ * **Hokusai** 北斎　縄手通四条上ル白川畔 (561-7121). Hrs: 12:00–21:00 (last order); clsd NY. *Goryō nabe*: vegetables with beef, duck or chicken, grilled on a hoe blade over charcoal. The presentation is charming. Set dinner from Y4100. AX, DC, CB, V, MC.

㉒ * **Sugiharu** すぎ春　縄手通三条下ル (541-0333). Hrs: 17:00–21:00; clsd Th, NY. On Nawate-dōri near Sanjō station. Old-style building; the *zashiki* area in the rear is nicer than the bar. Chicken (sashimi, *yakitori*, fried) from Y650 per order, *nabe* Y3500.

## II:4 Heian Shrine Area (see map, p. 335)

㉔ **Maruta** まる多　岡崎円勝寺町91 (751-7851). Hrs: 12:00–14:30 (last order), 17:00–19:30 (last order); clsd M, NY. Near Miyako Hotel. *Kaiseki* by reservation; run by friendly couple. Elegant and original. Lunch from Y10,000, dinner from Y12,000. No CC.

㉖ * **Hyōtei** 瓢亭　南禅寺草川町 (771-4116). Hrs: 11:00–19:00 (enter by); clsd 2nd and 4th Tu, NY. Good *kaiseki*, beautifully presented; careful service. Genuine *sukiya* architecture and gardens. Lunch Y15–20,000, dinner Y20–30,000 (w/o tax and service). *Asagayu* (rice porridge breakfast): July–Aug. 8:00–10:00, Y5000; Dec.–Mar. 15, 11:00–14:00, Y10,000. AX, DC, V.

㉘ **Le Relais Okazaki** ルルレオカザキ 岡崎東山二条東 (761-1326). Hrs: 11:00–21:00 (last order); clsd twice a month. Classical Franco-Japanese. Prix fixe menu: lunch from Y3500, dinner from Y7000. DC, V, CB, AX, MC.

㉚ *✱ **Rokusei** 六盛 平安神宮西横水北側 (761-6171). Hrs: 11:30–15:00, 17:00–21:00; clsd M. Modern Kyoto-style shop catering to tourists, but the food is good, and beautifully presented. *Teoke bentō* Y2800–6000. DC, V.

㉛ ✱ **Shōgo-in Kawamichiya** 聖護院河道屋 聖護院御殿西門前 (771-7531). Hrs: 11:00–20:00; clsd Tu, NY. Fish, vegetables, and noodles, simmered in clay casseroles. Rambling old buildings, gardens. *Yōrō-nabe* Y2900, *soba kaiseki* Y4000. V.

㉜ **Time Paradox** タイム・パラドックス 聖護院東町16-2 (751-6903). Hrs: 17:00–24:00, clsd Th, NY. An American-style natural foods restaurant. Good soups, salads, Sicilian pizza, and gratin. Foreigners' hangout; menu in English. A la carte Y1000–3200. V, DC, MC.

㊱ ✱✱ **Higashiyama Sansō** 東山山荘 東山ドライブウェイ (581-3510). Hrs: 17:00–20:00 (last order); clsd Su. *A short taxi ride from the Miyako Hotel.* Secluded villalike restaurant offering excellent *shabu-shabu* and pretty surroundings. Sensitive to the comfort of foreign guests; owner Emiko Takeda spent 8 years in America and speaks excellent English. Mrs. Takeda also sells antiques, shown on request. Reservations needed. Full dinner Y9330 (w/tax, service). AX, V.

## II:5 Nanzen-ji to Ginkaku-ji (see map, p. 343)

① ✱ **Okutan** 奥丹 南禅寺福地町 (771-8709). Hrs: 10:30–17:30 (last order); clsd Th, NY. By Nanzen-ji, often crowded. Vegetarian *yudōfu* set Y3000. Beautiful garden. No CC.

② ✱ **Kōan** 壺庵 南禅寺福地町 (771-2781). Hrs: 11:00–16:30 (last order); clsd W, NY. Near Nanzen-ji. Good *shōjin-ryōri*. *Tenshin* Y3300, *yudōfu* Y2700, *honzen* (full course meal) Y4400+. No CC.

③ ✱ **Omen** おめん 浄土寺石橋町74 (761-8926). Hrs: 11:00–22:00; clsd Th, NY. Near Ginkaku-ji. Noodle shop with beautiful folk-art decor. *Omen*, plump white noodles in a basket, dipped into a broth garnished with blanched, julienne vegetables and toasted sesame seeds, Y900. No CC.

④ ✱ **Osaidokoro** お菜ところ 浄土石橋町37 (771-5157). Hrs: 11:00–19:00; clsd M. Charming old house, set slightly back from the road to Ginkaku-ji. *Bunjin bentō* Y2200, *osōzai teishoku* Y1400, *yudōfu teishoku* Y1200. Sweets. No CC.

⑤ ✱ **Daigin** 大銀食堂 左京区浄土寺東田町60 (751-7890). Hrs: 11:00–20:00; clsd Th, NY. A great *shokudō* (cafeteria) on the road that leads to the Ginkaku-ji approach. Cheap, easy (wax models), and popular.

✱✱ **Ryōzanpaku** 梁山泊 百万遍西南入ル (771-4447). Hyakumanben nishi-minami iru (SW). Hrs: 17:00–22:00; clsd Su, NH, NY. Fresh, seasonal cuisine, especially fish. *Kurogomadōfu* (black sesame tofu) is a specialty. Very handsome interior, with bare wood, wetted-down stone floor, and even cryptomeria fronds in the toilet. Set menu Y10,000 (or set your own price limit, or order à la carte). AX, DC, V.

## III Kita-Shirakawa, Shūgaku-in

✱ **Old New** オールドニュー 一乗寺向畑町53 (722-9333). Kita-Shirakawa Kitayama south. Hrs: 11:00–1:00 (last order), daily. Stunning modern space designed by Sugimoto Takashi, divides into three parts: Casa (Italian), Bar Old/New, and Kirara, with *udon* noodles from Sanuki (on Shikoku) and very nice *kaiseki*-style *omakase* course Y5000, Y7000; *kirara-nabe* (noodles in a stew) Y1500+ (lunch), Y2500–7000 (dinner). V, MC, DC, AX.

① ✱ **Yamabana Heihachi-jaya** 山ばな平八茶屋 山端川岸町8 (781-5008). Hrs: 11:00–20:00 (last order); clsd W. Country roadside inn on road to Yase. Blanched carp sashimi and *tororo* (gooey grated yam) over barley-rice. Guests can use the clay steam bath. Lunch (to 14:00) Y2600–6000. Dinner Y10,000. MC, DC, V.

✱ **Azekura** 愛染倉 上賀茂岡本町30 (701-0161). Hrs: 9:00–17:00; clsd M. East of Kamigamo Jinja. Fine *udon* and *soba* in a 19th-C farmhouse brought from Nara prefecture. From Y600, expensive for *soba*, but you pay for the quality and wonderful atmosphere.

**Beniya** べにや 貴船町17 (741-2041). Hrs: 11:00–20:00, daily. Clsd in winter. Kibune teahouse with platforms built over the river. *Ayu* and *sansai* in summer, *botan-nabe* (wild boar stew) in winter. Expensive. DC, V.

## IV Northwest Kyoto (see map, p. 324)

㉓ ✱✱ **Hatakaku** 畑かく 上御霊前通烏丸西入 (441-0610). Hrs: 12:00–closing (enter by 19:00); clsd M, NY. Near Kuramaguchi subway stop. Beautiful old house with garden. Winter specialty, *botan-nabe* cooked over a charcoal fire in a sunken hearth. The wild boar meat used here is delicate and not at all heavy. Set menu Y7000. V, CB, MC, DC.

㉖ ✱ **Toriiwarō** 鳥岩楼 五辻通智恵光院西入ル (441-4004). Itsutsuji-dōri, Chiekō-in nishi-iru. Hrs: 12:00–21:00; clsd Th, NY. In elegant old house, moved from Gion to Nishijin. Chicken *mizutaki* dinner Y4500.

㉗ ✱ **Sushi Tora** 寿司寅 今出川千本西入ル (462-0615). Sembon Imadegawa west. Hrs: 9:00–19:30; clsd Th, NY. An unpretentious shop with very good Kyoto-style sushi. *Oke-zushi* from Y1000–1300. No CC.

371

㉙ **Ikkyū** 一久 大徳寺門前20 (493-0019/1919). Hrs. 12:00–18:00; clsd NY. Reservations. By Daitoku-ji. Kyoto's foremost *shōjin-ryōri* establishment, in operation for more than 500 years. Set menus, Y7000, Y10,000, and Y12,000 (w/o tax, service). No CC.

㉚ * **Izusen (Daitoku-ji branch)** 泉仙 大徳寺店大慈院内 (491-6665). Hrs: 11:00–15:00; Th 11:00–15:00; clsd NY. Located in Daiji-in subtemple of Daitoku-ji. *Shōjin-ryōri* sets from Y3000. No CC.

㉜ **Seigen-in** 西源院 (462-4742). Hrs: 10:00–17:00, daily. This subtemple of Ryōan-ji serves *yudōfu* Y1500, and *shōjin-ryōri* Y3300. No CC.

## V Western Kyoto (see map, p. 361)

**Tarumiyama** 垂水山 太秦垂箕山町 (861-0660). Hrs: 12:00–21:00; clsd Tu, NY. Near Kōryū-ji on Tarumiyama-chō, by Katabira-no-tsuji station. *Yudōfu* set Y4000. No CC.

① ** **Nishiki** 錦 嵐山中ノ島公園内 (871-8888). Hrs: 11:00–19:00; clsd Tu. In Arashiyama. Very good *Kyō-ryōri*, prepared with originality and charm, in a pleasant riverside teahouse. Menus change monthly. Prix fixe Y3800–9000. Private room reserved if you order the Y5800+ menu. V, MC, DC.

② * **Togetsu-tei** 渡月亭 嵐山中尾下町 (871-1310). Hrs: 10:00–19:00, daily. This old-fashioned teahouse offers a riverside view of Arashiyama. Fresh, light *yudōfu* in an elegant cypress tub with a special compartment for lumps of charcoal to keep everything warm. *Take bentō* Y2700, *tofu ryōri* Y3–4,000, *kaiseki* Y10,000+. V.

③ *** **Kitchō** 吉兆嵯峨店 (881-1101). Hrs: 11:30–13:00, 16:00–19:00; clsd 2nd and 4th W. Reservations. This is one of Japan's most famous *ryōtei*, located in a beautiful house in Arashiyama. The cuisine emphasizes the fresh, natural flavors and textures of the finest seasonal foods, prepared with disarming simplicity, and the presentation is second to none. Service, however, is haughty. Lunch Y47,000, dinner Y50,000, *bentō* Y20,000. AX, V.

⑦ * **Izusen (Sagano branch)** 泉仙嵯峨野店 鳥本六反町11 (881-7016). Hrs: 11:00–17:00; clsd Tu, NY. Buddhist vegetarian cuisine. Set menu from Y3000. No CC.

⑧ * **Hiranoya** 平野屋 嵯峨鳥居本仙翁町16 (861-0359). Hrs: 11:30–21:00, daily. A delightful, thatched-roof teahouse in a narrow river gorge, on the road to Kiyotaki. *Ayu* cuisine (summer), Y15,000; *yudōfu* (fall-spring), Y4500; *botan-nabe* (wild boar, winter), Y10,000. No CC.

**Takao Chaya** 高雄茶屋 (872-3810). Hrs: 9:00–17:30. Teahouse in grounds of Jingo-ji. *Yudōfu*, sukiyaki Y3500, *bentō* Y1800. No CC.

**Togano Chaya** とが乃茶屋 (861-4206). Hrs: 10:00–17:00; clsd Th, Dec. 15–Mar. 10. A teahouse overlooking a river, across from Kōzan-ji. Cold *sōmen* noodles and broiled *ayu* in summer. Moderate. No CC.

**Juntei** 旬亭 西京区樫原鳴谷50 (391-7191). Hrs: 12:00–20:00; clsd 1st and 3rd W, NY. Set in a large bamboo grove near Katsura Rikyū. Special *takenoko* (bamboo shoot) cuisine mid-March–mid-May. *Kaiseki* from Y8000, sukiyaki, *yosenabe* from Y3500, lunch *yudōfu* Y3000, mini-*kaiseki* Y6000. AX.

** **Kinsuitei** 錦水亭 長岡天神2-15-15 (951-5151). Hrs: 11:30–21:30. *Near Nagaoka Tenjin on the Hankyū line.* Famed for *takenoko* (bamboo shoot) cuisine, available only mid-Mar.–May (reservation a must). The setting is uncommonly picturesque: a series of thatched pavilions on the shore of a large pond. The land was given by an imperial prince in the Meiji period so that he would always have a place to enjoy the unparalleled bamboo shoots of Kyoto. Novices may find the craze for the delicate, fresh flavor of new bamboo shoots hard to fathom, but gastronomes consider it the quintessence of Kyoto spring. The set menu serves several types of shoots prepared in a variety of ways. You can also order *koi no amedaki*, a steak of roe-filled carp simmered in a rich, dark, sweet sauce that is the perfect foil for the ethereal bamboo. Prix fixe dinner from Y12,000. DC, V, AX, MC.

# LODGINGS (TEL 075)

Hotels are heavily booked in spring and autumn (esp. Saturday), and around New Year, the Aoi Matsuri (May 15), Gion Matsuri (July 14–17), Daimonji (Aug. 16), and Jidai Matsuri (Oct. 22). The most convenient areas to stay are around Shijō-Kawaramachi (I:2) and Gion (II:3). Northeast Kyoto (III) and Sagano (V:2) are inconvenient, but offer a quieter atmosphere. Kyoto offers many excellent ryokan in all budget ranges. Price class is generally based on twin room rates: (B) Budget, under Y5000 per person; (M) Moderate, Y5–8000 per person; (E) Expensive, Y8–10,000 per person; (D) Deluxe, over Y10,000 per person. **Temple Lodgings:** Expect to rise early, around 5:00–6:00 a.m. Temples have curfews generally around 21:00. To avoid confusion, apply by postcard, and indicate whether or not you will be taking meals (evening, breakfast). Bring your own pajamas, toothbrush, and towel.

## I:1 Station Area (see map, p. 324)

① * **Hotel Keihan Kyoto** ホテル京阪京都 (661-0321). Fax 661-0987. 31 Nishi Sannōmachi, Higashi-Kujō, Minami-ku. By station. S Y7500–8000, Tw Y15,100–16,000 (M).

② ** **Kyoto Grand Hotel** 京都グランドホテル (341-2311). Fax 341-3073. Higashi-Horikawa Shiokōji sagaru, Shimogyō-ku. Top class, but not much else in the neighborhood. Shuttle bus to station. S Y12–17,000, Tw Y19–26,000 (E).

372

4 ✻ **Kyoto Century Hotel** 京都センチュリーホテル (351-0111). Fax 343-3721. Higashi-Tōin-dōri, Shiokōji sagaru, Shimogyō-ku. S Y9000–12,500, Tw Y15,500–23,000 (E).

6 **Kyōka** 京花旅館 下珠数屋町通東洞院東入ル (371-2709). Shimojuzuyamachi-dōri Higashitōin Higashi-iru, Shimogyō-ku. Near Higashi Hongan-ji. Economical inn group. Rooms are nice and large. Y3600 per person (B).

7 **Matsubaya** 松葉屋 上珠数屋町通東洞院西入ル (351-3727). Kamijuzuyamachi-dōri, Higashitōin Nishi-iru, Shimogyō-ku. Economical inn group. Every room looks out onto the central courtyard. Tiny bit of English spoken. Y4000 per person. No meals (B).

9 ✻ **Yuhara Ryokan** ゆはら旅館 下京区木屋町通正面上ル (371-9583). 188 Kagiya-chō, Kiyamachi-dōri Shōmen agaru, Shimogyō-ku. A favorite with foreigners. Charming family-run ryokan. Y3500 per person, Y4000 w/breakfast (B).

10 ✻ **Hiraiwa** 平岩旅館 二宮町通上ノ口上ル早尾町314 (351-6748). 314 Hayao-chō, Ninomiyamachi-dōri Kaminokuchi agaru, Shimogyō-ku. Part of economical inn group. Geared for foreign tourists. S Y3500, Tw Y6000. No dinner. 14 rms, plus 7 in the annex (B).

11 ✻ **Kyoto Tōkyū Hotel** 京都東急ホテル (341-2411). Fax 341-2488. Horikawa-dōri Gojō sagaru, Shimogyō-ku. By Nishi Hongan-ji. S Y11,000, Tw Y19–27,000 (E).

## I:2 **Central Shopping Area** (see map, p. 328)

1 ✻✻ **Karasuma Kyoto Hotel** からすま京都ホテル (371-0111). Fax 371-2424. Karasuma-dōri, Shijō-sagaru, Shimogyō-ku. Fine city hotel, heart of the business district, close to subway. S Y8500, Tw Y14,800 (M).

24 ✻ **Kiyamachi Hotel 196** 木屋町ホテル 196　東木屋町蛸薬師 (221-0196). Fax 255-7908. Higashi Kiyamachi Takoyakushi, Nakagyō-ku. Tiny city hotel with sleek, modern decor. Prime location. S Y6500, Tw Y17,500 (M).

34 **Kyoto Royal Hotel** 京都ロイヤルホテル (223-1234). Fax 223-1702. Kawaramachi Sanjō agaru, Nakagyō-ku. Central location. S Y8–9500, Tw Y13,500–20,000 (E).

36 **Kyoto Hotel** 京都ホテル (211-5111). Fax 221-7770. Kawaramachi-Oike, Nakagyō-ku. Central location. S Y8750, Tw Y15,100 (E).

39 ✻✻ **Hotel Fujita Kyoto** ホテルフジタ京都 (222-1511). Fax 256-4561. Nijō-Ōhashi Nishizume, Nakagyō-ku. Excellent riverside location, pleasant atmosphere. Fine restaurants. The Japanese rooms are the best; Y24,000. S Y9500–14,000 (low and high season); Tw Y17–26,000. Riverside rooms, with wonderful view, Y3000 more (E).

43 **Kyoto Central Inn** 京都セントラルイン (211-1666). Fax 241-2765. Shijō-Kawaramachi Nishi-iru, Shimogyō-ku. Not great, but acceptable because of its superlative location. S Y6000, Tw Y9350 w/o tax (B).

48 ✻✻ **Kinmata** 近又旅館 御幸町四条上ル (221-1039). Fax 231-7632. Gokōmachi Shijō agaru, Nakagyō-ku. Wonderful family-run inn, now nearing two centuries in business (founded 1801). Red-ochre walls, beautiful interiors. The master is a fiend for detail; he's put a different *andon* (lamp) in every room and built a stunning cypress bath. Seasonal Kyoto cuisine; Western breakfast available. One room w/Western toilet. Kinmata was originally an inn for patent-medicine peddlers from the Ōmi region. In the entryway, there's a noticeboard with Edo-period ryokan laws forbidding gambling, prostitutes, and badly dressed guests, and admonishing prompt payment of bills. Even today, one shouldn't just walk in; get an introduction if possible, and always reserve by the previous day. 7 rms. Y25–35,000 per person w/meals, Y12–15,000 w/breakfast, Y10,000 w/o meals (E).

56 ✻ **Tani House Annex** 御幸町六角南西角 (255-0716, fax 492-5489). Gokōmachi Rokkaku, SW corner, 2-3F. The friendly young proprietors own the LAX boutique on the ground floor. Two clean and bright tatami rooms, each with kitchenette and private bathroom, air conditioning. Y6000 for two persons, Y7500 for three.

63 ✻ **Hotel Alpha Kyoto** ホテルアルファ京都 (241-2000). Fax 211-0533. Kawaramachi Sanjō agaru, Nakagyō-ku. Comfortable business hotel (small rooms), superb location. S Y7510, Tw Y15,030. (M).

66 ✻✻✻ **Tawaraya** 俵屋旅館 (221-5566). Fax 211-2204. Fuyachō Oike sagaru, Nakagyō-ku. 300-year-old establishment, generally acknowledged to be the finest ryokan of all. Elegant, successful blend of traditional and modern. Reservations necessary; booked months in advance during peak seasons and on weekends. The more expensive ground-floor rooms with garden verandas are best. Y33–55,000 w/meals (dbl. occ.). Room only, w/o meals, Y35–90,000 (D).

67 ✻✻ **Hiiragiya** 柊屋旅館 (221-1136). Fax 221-1139. Fuyachō Oike-kado, Nakagyō-ku. Not as flawlessly elegant as the Tawaraya, but still beautiful and luxurious. 33 rooms, ground floor w/gardens. 5 rms w/o baths. Y26–80,000 per person w/meals (dbl. occ.) (D).

68 ✻✻ **Sumiya** 炭屋旅館 (221-2188). Fax 221-2267. Fuyachō Sanjō sagaru Nakagyō-ku. New wing lacks charm, but the old wing, especially first-floor rooms with gardens, is beautiful. This is a tea connoisseur's inn; each room is different. Two tea ceremony rooms. Y30–80,000 per person (dbl. occ.). Tawaraya is superior at the high range, but if you don't mind sharing the bathroom, Sumiya's lower-priced rooms, such as "Kōetsu" and "Tsuki," are better (D).

72 ✻ **Pension Tomy Rich Inn** ペンショントミーリッチイン　富小路通三条上ル (255-0137). Fax 225-1730. Tominokōji-dōri Sanjō-agaru, Nakagyō-ku. Mini-hotel with bright, trim rooms. A very good deal. Y4700 w/ breakfast (dbl. occ.) (B).

73 **Hotel Gimmond Kyoto** ホテルギンモンド京都 (221-4111). Fax. 221-8250. Oike-dōri Takakura Nishi-iru, Nakagyō-ku. English spoken. Offers a 30 percent discount to guests introduced by the TIC. S Y6500, Tw Y10,000 (M).

74 ✳ **Sanjō Karasuma Hotel Kyoto** 三条烏丸京都ホテル (256-3331, fax 256-2351. Sanjō Karasuma Nishi-iru, Nakagyō-ku. Small city hotel (154 rooms) opened in 1989. Good location. Restaurant and the large public baths have garden views. S Y8000, Tw Y13–16,000. All major credit cards.

I:3 **Palace Area** (see map, p. 324)

13 ✳✳ **Kokusai Hotel (International Hotel Kyoto)** 京都国際ホテル (222-1111). Fax 231-9381. 284 Nijō-Aburanokōji, Nakagyō-ku. Right by Nijō-jō (but not convenient to much else); still one of the best hotels in Kyoto. Nice garden and roof bar; beer garden in summer. S Y9500–14,000, Tw Y16–28,000. Castle-side rooms are a little more expensive; Japanese rooms Y20,000 (D).

14 ✳✳ **ANA Hotel Kyoto** 京都全日空ホテル (231-1155). Fax 231-5333. Nijō-jō-mae, Horikawa-dōri, Nakagyō-ku. Near Nijō-jō. Large rooms with views. Part of the excellently managed ANA chain. S Y10–16,000, Tw Y18–26,000 (E).

16 **Uno House** 宇野ハウス 新烏丸丸太町下ル (231-7763). Fax: 256-0140. Shin-Karasuma Marutamachi sagaru, Nakagyō-ku. Good location by palace. Budget inn in a family house. Tw Y1,500 per person (shared rms); some private rooms (B).

19 ✳ **Heian Kaikan** 平安会館 烏丸上長者町通上ル (432-6181). Fax: 431-7949. Karasuma-dōri Kamichōja-machi agaru, Kamigyō-ku. Hotel/wedding hall on west side of Imperial Palace; has a lovely garden. S Y7550, Tw Y1500 (M).

20 ✳ **Nashinoki** 梨の木旅館 今出川寺町西入ル2筋目上ル (241-1543). Teramachi Imadegawa agaru Nishi-iru Futatsujime agaru, Kamigyō-ku. Just north of the Imperial Palace. Bright, pleasant little ryokan with Japanese-style rooms. Y4650 per person (B).

22 **Senzuru Bekkan** 千鶴別館 下鴨宮崎町 (781-1222). Fax: 721-3278. Miyazaki-chō, Shimogamo, Sakyō-ku. Near Shimogamo Jinja, Imperial Palace. Rambling, rather rundown inn with lovely large garden. Rooms w/bathrooms. From Y8000 w/meals (M).

374

II **Higashiyama** (see map, p. 335)

2 **Kyoto Park Hotel** 京都パークホテル (525-3111). Fax 551-4350. 644-2 Sanjūsangen-dō Mawari-chō, Higashiyama-ku. Near Kyoto National Museum. S Y9000–12,000, Tw Y17,000–24,000 (E).

3 ✳ **Mishima** 宿坊三嶋 渋谷通東大路東入ル上馬町539-3 (551-0033). Fax: 531-9768. 539-3 Kamiumamachi, Shibutani-dōri, Higashi-Ōji Higashi-iru, Higashiyama-ku. Economical inn group. Ryokan run by a shrine; modern. Every room has a toilet. S Y4000, D, Y7000 (B).

4 ✳✳ **Seikōrō Ryokan** 晴鴨楼旅館 (561-0771). Fax: 541-5481. Tonya-chō Gojō sagaru, Higashiyama-ku. Near Sanjūsangen-dō. Fine ryokan built in 1831; also has a new wing. Y20–70,000 per person w/meals (D). New big bath open for the guests.

11 ✳ **Uemura** うえむら旅館 下河原石塀小路 (561-0377). Ishibe-kōji, Gion-Shimogawara, Higashiyama-ku. Tiny ryokan with lovely, old-fashioned rooms in Ishibe-kōji. Y12,500 w/meals (E).

15 ✳ **Hatanaka** 畑中旅館 (541-5315). Fax: 551-0553. Yasaka Torii-mae, Gion-Shimogawara, Higashiyama-ku. Just south of Yasaka Jinja. A "modern" ryokan, bland outside, but with some elegant woodwork inside. Run like a small hotel rather than a traditional inn. Shining marble Western toilets, wooden baths, superb location. Can handle English. Y25–30,000 per person (dbl. occ.) w/meals (D).

16 **Ladies' Hotel Chōrakukan** レディスホテル長楽館 円山公園 (561-0001). Fax: 561-0056. Gion-Maruyama Kōen, Higashiyama-ku. By Maruyama Park. A Meiji-era villa that lodged the Rockefellers and Russian crown prince. A newer wing is now a ladies' hotel. Japanese and Western rooms, shared bath and toilet. Little English, but willing to try. Y5150 per person (B).

18 ✳ **Kyoto Gion Hotel** 京都祇園ホテル (551-2111). 555 Gion-machi Minami gawa, Higashiyama-ku. A small city hotel in the heart of Gion. Small rooms, but clean and pleasant. S Y8200–9200, Tw Y14,000–15,200 (w/o tax and service) (M).

19 ✳ **Shiraume** 白梅旅館 縄手通四条上ル新橋 (561-1459). Fax: 531-5290. Shin-bashi, Nawate-dōri Shijō-agaru, Higashiyama-ku. Ryokan with charming canalside location in Gion-Shinbashi. Ask for 1st floor room looking onto the garden. Y14,000 w/breakfast, Y20–25,000 w/2 meals, shared bathroom (E).

20 ✳ **Iwanami Ryokan** 岩波旅館 新門前東大路西入ル (561-7135). Shinmonzen Higashi-ōji Nishi-iru, Higashiyama-ku. Excellent location. Traditional inn, a little dark. Long experience with foreigners. 8 rooms (5 w/Western toilets) Y8000 w/breakfast (M).

21 ✳ **Pension Higashiyama** ペンション東山祇園 白川筋三条下ル梅宮町474-23 (882-1181). Fax 862-0820. 474-23 Umemiya-chō, Shirakawa-suji Sanjō sagaru, Higashiyama-ku. Opened 1985; minihotel with picturesque and convenient location by Shirakawa canal. Lots of foreigners. Y3900 per person (B).

22 **Higashiyama YH** 東山YH 三条白川橋五軒町112 (761-8135). 112 Shirakawabashi-goken-chō, Sanjō-dōri, Higashiyama-ku. Large and institutional, but well-situated. Rent-a-cycle. Y4200 w/meals (B).

23 ✳✳ **Miyako Hotel** 都ホテル (771-7111). Fax 751-2490. Sanjō Keage, Higashiyama-ku. An old favorite—rambling, a trifle worn, but well-maintained, and with excellent service. We recommend the lovely Japanese wing, which offers ryokan atmosphere with the privacy and full services of a hotel. S Y13–17,000, Tw, from Y19,000 (D).

25 ** **Yachiyo** 八千代旅館 (771-4148). Fax 771-4140. 34 Nanzenji Fukuchi-chō, Sakyō-ku. Near Nanzen-ji. The atmospheric former villa of an Ōsaka magnate. 25 rooms, most with garden. The back faces a noisy road; ask for a room toward the front. Tw Y13,000 (cheapest twin room, w/o bath, toilet, meals). Average, Tw Y20–50,000 w/2 meals (Japanese or Western breakfast); no-meal rate available (D).

27 * **Kyoto Traveler's Inn** 京都トラベラーズイン 岡崎円勝寺町91 (771-0225). Fax 771-0226. 91 Okazaki Enshōji-chō, Sakyō-ku. Near Nanzen-ji. Friendly hotel with Japanese and Western rooms. Some English spoken. The new rooms in front are in the best shape (but are close to the road). S Y5000, Tw Y9000, all w/bath. Can negotiate a discount in off-seasons (B).

33 * **Three Sisters Inn (Rakutō-sō)** 洛東荘 岡崎道丸太町北入西 (761-6336). Fax 761-6338. Okazaki Kurodani-mae, Sakyō-ku. A Kyoto inn that has catered to an exclusively foreign clientele for years. Quiet location, convenient to Higashiyama. Shared bathrooms. Prices are moderate to expensive. They'll try to accommodate your budget (M).

34 **Hotel Sunflower Kyoto** ホテルサンフラワー京都 (761-9111). Fax 761-1333. 51 Higashi Tennō-chō, Okazaki, Sakyō-ku. A bit shabby, but an excellent location for Higashiyama sightseeing. Rent-a-cycle. For Y6900 per person: room, breakfast. The Japanese rooms are better. S Y9000, Tw Y14,500–17,000 (M).

## III **Northeast Kyoto** (see map, p. 348)

2 **Hiei-zan Kokusai Kankō Hotel** 比叡山国際観光ホテル (701-2111). Fax 711-5527. Hiei-zan Ipponsugi, Sakyō-ku. Mountain resort hotel, cool in summer. Tw Y12–30,000 (M).

3 **Minshuku Nodaya** 民宿野田家 (744-2534). 196 Todera-chō, Ōhara, Sakyō-ku. Y6500 w/meals.

4 **Jōrenge-in** 宿坊浄蓮華院 (744-2408). 407 Raigōin-chō, Ōhara, Sakyō-ku. Temple lodging. Vegetarian cuisine. Y5500 w/meals.

5 **Minshuku Hatanaka** 民宿畑中 (744-2756). 59-1 Shōrinin-chō. Y6000 w/meals.

6 **Minshuku Chadani** 民宿茶谷 (744-2952). Fax 744-2953. 160 Kusao-chō Ōhara, Sakyō-ku. Home-grown rice and vegetables, pheasant and *botan nabe* in winter. Y5500 w/meals.

*** **Miyama-sō** 美山荘 花背大悲山 (746-0231). Fax 746-0233. Daihizan, Hanase, Sakyō-ku. Luxurious hideaway in Hanase village. *Tsumikusa-ryōri* (mountain cuisine). A very fine ryokan in delightful surroundings; lovely bath overlooking the river. Y30,000 w/meals (D).

**Mujin Kissa-ten** 無人喫茶店 広河原大花町 (746-0353). Ōhana-chō, Hirogawara, Sakyō-ku. An "unmanned coffee shop" in the countryside, which provides lodging. Call ahead if you want to arrange for meals. Y2500 w/futon, no meals; Y5500 w/meals (B).

## IV **Northwest Kyoto** (see map, p. 324)

24 **Myōken-ji** 妙顕寺 寺之内堀川東入ル (431-6828). Teranouchi-dōri, Horikawa Higashi-iru, Kamigyō-ku. Popular, sometimes crowded with tourists. About Y4000 w/breakfast.

31 **Tani House** 谷ハウス 紫野大徳寺町8 (492-5489). Fax 252-3277. 8 Daitokuji-chō, Murasakino, Kita-ku. By Daitoku-ji. Popular with foreigners. Charming old house, but can get overcrowded. Y1500 per person (B).

33 **Myōshin-ji Subtemples:** Myōshin-ji, Hanazono, Ukyō-ku. **Daishin-in** 妙心寺大心院 (461-5714), Zen gardens, Y4000 w/breakfast. **Tōrin-in** 妙心寺東林院 (463-1334), Y4000 w/breakfast.

34 **Pension Utano** ペンション宇多野 鳴滝本町110-5 (463-1118). Fax 463-7859. 110-5 Narutaki Honmachi, Ukyō-ku. Toward Sagano. Y7500 w/meals per person (B).

35 **Utano YH** 宇多野YH 太秦中山町29 (462-2288). Fax 462-2289. 29 Nakayama-chō, Uzumasa, Ukyō-ku. Between Ninna-ji and Hirosawa Pond. Convenient for seeing northwest Kyoto and Arashiyama. Rent-a-cycle. Y3350 w/meals (B).

## V **Sagano** (see map, p. 361)

4 **Minshuku Saga no Sato** 民宿嵯峨の里 嵯峨天竜寺北造路町46-2 (881-9387). 46-2 Kitatsukurimichi-chō, Tenryū-ji, Saga, Ukyō-ku. In front of Tenryū-ji gate. Former movie star's house. Y8500–14,000 w/meals (B).

5 **Pension Furusato** ペンション古郷 嵯峨天竜寺立石町1-4 (882-1817). 1-4 Tateishi-chō Tenryū-ji, Saga, Ukyō-ku. Former ryokan. Y8800 w/meals (B).

6 **Minshuku Tsujimura** 民宿辻村 嵯峨天竜寺瀬戸町17 (861-3207). 17 Setogawa-chō, Tenryū-ji, Saga, Ukyō-ku. In beautiful large house. Near bamboo groves of Nonomiya Jinja. Y5000 w/o meals (B).

**Rokuō-in** 鹿王院 嵯峨北堀町24 (861-1645). 24 Kitahori-chō, Saga, Ukyō-ku. Zen temple with lovely gardens, takes women guests only. Y4500 w/breakfast.

375

# KYOTO VI. THE SHORES OF LAKE BIWA

**Prefectures:** Shiga, Fukui, Kyoto-fu

This area is ideal for day trips out of Kyoto. There are numerous superb temples and matsuri that tend to be overlooked by tourists. Near Ōtsu are such historically famous temples and shrines as Mii-dera and Hiyoshi Taisha. Ōmi-Hachiman's old town and canal trips make for a pleasant outing, and Hikone's castle is one of the finest in Japan. Starting with Mii-dera (and Hiei-zan), the area around Lake Biwa has dozens of *mikkyō* temples with fine Esoteric Buddhist art and *wayō* architecture. Ishiyama-dera, the three temples of the Kotō Sanzan, Chōmei-ji, and the temples of Obama are but a few. See Kinki map, p. 383.

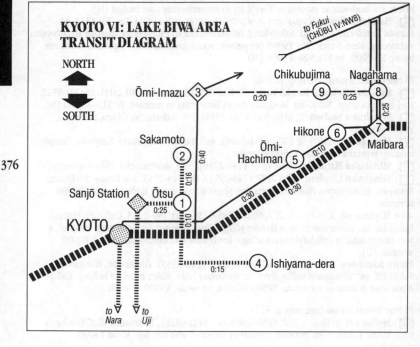

**KYOTO VI: LAKE BIWA AREA TRANSIT DIAGRAM**

NORTH

SOUTH

## VI:1 * ŌTSU  大津

*From Kyoto, 0:25h by private Keihan line from Keihan-Sanjō station to Hama-Ōtsu, with frequent connections to Mii-dera, Sakamoto (VI:2), and Ishiyama-dera (VI:4). Alternatively, 0:10h by JR Tōkaidō line from Kyoto station to Ōtsu station.* The bustling city of Ōtsu lies at the southeastern foot of Hiei-zan and is rich in temples and shrines historically associated with the great Tendai headquarters, Enryaku-ji (III:2). Ōtsu-e, naive, humorous votive paintings on folk religious themes, were sold here to Edo-period pilgrims. *Oni no nembutsu,* a comical demon beating on a gong and chanting the *nembutsu* (Hail Amida Buddha!) is a classic.

### Calendar

**Apr. 12–15: * Sannō Matsuri.** Hiyoshi Taisha (VI:2). A famous matsuri featuring the shrine's notorious and gorgeous *mikoshi.* On the 12th, the *mikoshi* are taken down from the mountain. On the 13th, at 20:00, there is a violent "fight festival." On the 14th, from 14:00, the *mikoshi* are put on boats in the lake.

**Oct. 9–10: * Ōtsu Matsuri.** Ōtsu. 13 splendid floats draped with Gobelin tapestries. *Karakuri ningyō* (mechanical puppets) appear on the evening of the 9th; floats go around the town on the 10th.

### Ōtsu Sights

**\*\*\* Onjō-ji (Mii-dera)** 園城寺（三井寺） Hrs: 8:00–17:00; clsd NY. *0:01h by Keihan train, then 0:05h on foot.* Mii-dera, as this temple is popularly known, was founded in 774 as a branch of Enryaku-ji, the great Tendai monastery on Hiei. By the 10th C, it had become the center of a powerful faction, and posed a threat to Enryaku-ji's authority. All monks affiliated with Mii-dera were expelled from Hiei, and the temple was razed time and again by the Enryaku-ji monks. At its greatest, Mii-dera contained 859 buildings. Though much reduced, it is still magnificent, with many fine halls standing peacefully in a cryptomeria forest. It remains the headquarters of the Tendai Jimon sect, with strong ties to Shugendō, the cult of mountain ascetics.

    **Niō-mon** (ICP). A Muromachi-period gate given to the temple by TOKUGAWA IEYASU. On its right is a refectory (ICP), also of the Muromachi period.

✻ **Kōjō-in and Kangaku-in.** Subtemples renowned for their superb *shoin* (NT). Not open to the public: those wishing to see them should apply by phoning 0775-22-2238. (Kangaku-in's *shoin* is reproduced at New York's Metropolitan Museum of Art).

✻ **Kondō** (NT). Rebuilt in the Momoyama period by HIDEYOSHI; an impressive structure with sweeping eaves and mighty columns. The shed next to it, **Akaiya** (ICP), shelters a spring-fed pool, from which comes the popular name, Mii-dera, Temple of the Three Wells.

**Reishō-dō.** Houses a huge bell (ICP) which was deeply gouged on its sides, supposedly when the legendary warrior-monk Benkei threw it down from the top of Hiei-zan. The **Issai-kyō-zō** (Sutra Library, ICP) contains an elaborate, octagonal sutra repository. The **Taishi Gobyō-sho**, second only to the Kondō in importance, houses a hidden image (NT) of Shinra Zenshin, founder of Mii-dera. The **Kannon-dō**, dedicated to Nyoirin Kannon (ICP), is the 14th temple on the 33-temple Kannon pilgrimage and is popular with worshippers.

✻ **Enman-in** 円満院 Hrs: 9:00–17:00. *100 m from the Niō Gate of Mii-dera.* A temple with many imperial connections. The **Shinden** (ICP) was moved from the Imperial Palace in 1641 and is a fine example of Momoyama Shoin-style architecture. The panels are decorated with KANŌ SCHOOL paintings. The temple also has a noted garden ascribed to the Muromachi-period painter Sōami and a museum of old Ōtsu-e.

## VI:2 ✻ SAKAMOTO 坂本

*0:20h by bus or 0:16h by train from Hama-Ōtsu; the bus stops in front of Hiyoshi Taisha. There is a cable car to the top of Hiei-zan, where one can visit Enryaku-ji and descend by tramway to Kyoto. A recommended circuit, in either direction.*

✻✻ **Hiyoshi Taisha (Shrine)** 日吉大社 *0:15h walk from Sakamoto station.* Also known as the Sannō Shrine, this is an ancient shrine to the guardian of Enryaku-ji and the kami of sacred Mt. Miwa south of Nara. It has numerous branches throughout Japan, including Hie Jinja, near Tokyo's Akasaka. The shrine deity's messengers are the wild monkeys inhabiting the slopes of Hiei-zan. HIDEYOSHI was the last to rebuild the shrine's main structures. Tradition holds that he was a special patron of the shrine, partly because his childhood name was Hiyoshi, partly because he resembled — and was called — "the monkey".

The shrine was the center of a syncretic sect of Shinto that attempted to pair the deities of Enryaku-ji's Tendai Buddhism with the kami of native Shinto. The shrines became especially important when TOKUGAWA IEYASU was interred and deified at Nikkō according to its rites. The large torii at the entrance to the shrine is in the Sannō syncretic style, bearing a distinctive triangular, gablelike ornament. The two main shrine buildings (NT) —**Nishi (West) Hongū** and **Higashi (East) Hongū** —incorporate the hip-and-gable (*irimoya*) roof commonly seen in temples. Nearby are branches of many of Japan's important syncretic shrines, including Usa Hachiman, protector of Nara's Tōdai-ji, and Hakusan, an important *yamabushi* mountain. The Tōshō-gū branch shrine was built by the priest Tenkai, who oversaw the founding of the Nikko Tōshō-gū (see Nikkō History, p. 242). A concrete storehouse contains the famous **mikoshi** of the shrine's Sannō Matsuri. These were borne on the shoulders of the brigand-monks of Hiei-zan during their forays into Kyoto to extort favors from the imperial court; because the *mikoshi* were sacred, no one dared stand in their way.

### Ōtsu Shopping and Dining

**Ōtsu-e no Mise** 大津絵の店 (24-5656). The Hashimoto brothers are the last remaining painters of Ōtsu-e. Their shop is near the Kannon-dō of Mii-dera.

✻ **Tsuruki** 鶴喜 (78-0002). Famous 250-year-old *soba* shop. *Al dente soba* in a charming old shop, near the stone torii over the lantern-lined approach to Hiyoshi Taisha.

## VI:3 ŌMI-IMAZU 近江今津

*0:40h by JR Kosei line express or 1:15h by local from Kyoto. Junction for buses to Obama and boats to Chikubujima (VI:9). Fukui (CHŪBU IV:NW8) is 1:00h by JR Hokuriku main line limited express from Ōmi-Imazu.*

### Calendar

**Jan. 15:** ✻ **Suichū Tsunahiki.** Mihama (*0:40h from Obama by train*). Near-naked youths have a tug of war in the winter sea.

**Mar. 2: Mizu-okuri.** A fire festival at Jingū-ji to "send" water via a legendary underground stream to Tōdai-ji, in Nara, where it is "received" 10 days later in the famous Omizutori rite.

**Aug. 16:** ✻ **Tōrō-nagashi.** Miyazu Bay, at Amanohashidate. On the last day of Bon, 15,000 lanterns are set adrift as fireworks burst overhead.

### Exploring Obama

*1:00h by bus from Ōmi-Imazu.* This port, an early back door for continental culture, is known as the Nara of the Sea for its wealth of ancient temples and art. An excellent Teiki Kankō bus tour departs from Obama station, daily Mar. 20–Nov. 4, and Su and NH until Nov. 30. Starts at 9:00, ends at 15:25 (Y1580 plus temple fees). Of special interest are **Myōtsū-ji**, a beautiful mountain temple noted for its Hondō (1258, NT) and pagoda (1270, NT), and **Jingū-ji**, a rare syncretic temple in which a kami is worshipped alongside Buddhist images. **Dining:** Sushimasa (52-0875), sushi from Obama's famous seafood. **Lodgings** (TEL 0770): Fukuki (52-3077), Y12–20,000 w/meals. Pension Seagull (53-0296), Y10,000 w/meals. Obama also has a YH and Kokuminshukusha.

## Exploring Amanohashidate

*By JR from Obama. From Kyoto, 3:00h by special limited express, or 3:30h by Kyoto Kōtsu express bus, which offers all-day tours that include Ine.* This pine-covered sandbar stretching across Miyazu Bay like a "heavenly bridge" is designated by tradition as one of Japan's Three Famous Views. Its delicate, poetic beauty is shattered by the pervading commercialism. The traditional view of Amanohashidate is from across the bay, at Kasamatsu Kōen; you're supposed to turn your back to the scenery, bend over, and look from between your legs.
**Lodgings** (TEL 07722): Genmyō-an (2-2171), fine inn with superb view and good cuisine, from Y25,000. Amanohashidate YH (7-0121), Y3200 w/meals; and YH Amanohashidate Kankō Kaikan (7-0046), Y4600 w/meals, both near Kasamatsu Kōen.

Ine, a fishing village on the Tango Peninsula, is famous for its fishermen's houses, built out over the water on stilts. Their boats are kept under the houses. Festival on the bay, July 27–28.

### Easy Access To:
**San'in Coast:** *1:20h from Amanohashidate to Toyo'oka, then switch to JR San'in line. From Toyo'oka, 1:35h by limited express to Tottori* (CHŪGOKU I:N1), *3:45h to Matsue* (CHŪGOKU II:N4).

## VI:4 * ISHIYAMA-DERA 石山寺

*0:40h from Kyoto via Hama-Ōtsu by Keihan line.* Hrs: 8:00–17:30 (enter by 17:00). In winter 8:00–16:45 (enter by 16:15). A beautiful mountain temple, founded in the 8th century by the priest Rōben. Rōben dreamed that he should pray to Ishiyama's Kannon for the discovery of gold needed to gild the Great Buddha in Nara. Soon after, gold was found in northern Japan, and Rōben converted his Ishiyama hermitage into a temple. It later became a Shingon temple. The **Main Hall** (NT), built on stilts, is a Fujiwara-period structure, replete with the musty atmosphere of Esoteric Buddhism. The **Tahō-tō** (NT), built in 1190 by MINAMOTO NO YORITOMO, is the oldest stupa of its type in Japan. Tradition holds that in the Heian period, LADY MURASAKI wrote parts of *The Tale of Genji* while staying here. From Mar. 1–June 30 and Aug. 1–Nov. 25, the temple holds an exhibition of articles connected with the famous writer. There is said to be a 4–5:00h mountain trail from here to Daigo-ji (Kinki, p. 382); hikers go at their own risk.

## SHIGARAKI 信楽

*1:05h by bus from Ishiyama station.* One of the Six Ancient Kilns. Today, most of the kilns churn out uninspired commercial ware, though some may find the battalions of *tanuki* (fat badgers sporting drunken grins) not uncharming. A few kilns, such as Sawa Kiyotsugu's (0748-82-3056), still make traditional ware that a pottery enthusiast might find worth investigating. Traditional Shigaraki-yaki receives a natural ash glaze, ranging from ochre to charred olives and browns, and has glassy-white particles—highly prized—that bubble out on the surface. **Shigaraki-yaki Shiryō Bijutsukan** 信楽焼資料美術館, about 1 km SW of town center, exhibits Shigaraki-yaki from all periods, including the work of contemporary potters (Hrs: 10:00–17:00; Dec.–Feb. 10:00–16:00; clsd F, NY).

## VI:5 * ŌMI-HACHIMAN 近江八幡

*0:40h from Kyoto by JR Tōkaidō line.* The attractions are near the castle hill, 1.5 km north of the station. This lakeside castle town was built by Toyotomi Hidetsugu, the nephew and ill-fated adopted heir of TOYOTOMI HIDEYOSHI (see Kyoto History, p. 323). In the Edo period, the town was famous for its merchants; houses of these prosperous traders still stand.

### Calendar
**Jan. 8: * Moriyama no Hi-matsuri.** Moriyama (*4 Tōkaidō line local stops west of Ōmi-Hachiman*), Katsube Jinja. Fire festival of 16 enormous torches shaped like snakes.
**Mid-Mar.: * Sagichō-sai.** Held on a F–Su in mid-March. Twelve floats are paraded about by men dressed as women. At 20:00 on the 2nd day, the floats are burned at Himure Hachiman-gū as celebrants dance around the bonfire.
**Apr. 14: * Taimatsu Matsuri.** Huge drums are beaten, and giant torches burned at Himure Hachiman-gū at 20:00.
**Aug. (1st Su): Isaki no Saotobi.** Isaki-dera (temple). A log is placed like a pirate's plank off the edge of a cliff; people dive off it into Lake Biwa, some 10 meters below.

### Ōmi-Hachiman Sights
**** Kyōdo Shiryōkan (Local Museum)** 郷土資料館 (32-7048). Hrs: 9:00–16:30; clsd W p.m., Th, NY. *Near Kobatamachi bus stop, 0:07h from the station.* The museum is in the Meiji-period Western-style residence of an Ōmi merchant near a street lined with Edo-period dwellings. Exhibits include decorative Ōmi roof tiles. The adjoining Edo-period
◆ **merchant's house** has attractive displays on the Ōmi townsman's life.
** Himure Hachiman-gū** 日牟礼八幡宮 Pretty shrine at the base of the castle hill. The *ema* hall has a copy of the shrine's Annan Tokaisen no Ema (1648, ICP), "Votive painting of a Vietnam-bound ship," supposedly donated by the family of a ship captain who was locked out

of Japan when the country closed its doors to the outside world. In the Edo period, the shrine was supported by Ōmi merchants, who donated many of the stone lanterns on the grounds.

**\* Zuiryū-ji** 瑞龍寺 Hrs: 9:00–17:00. *On the castle hill, 0:04h by tramway.* Nichiren sect temple founded by Zuiryū-in, half-sister of Hideyoshi, in memory of her son Hidetsugu. This *monzeki* (temple with an imperial abbot) was moved from Kyoto in 1963 to promote the tramway. Visible to the east is the low hill where ODA NOBUNAGA'S **Azuchi Castle** stood. To see the magnificent lake view from the back of the temple hall, one must pay an entrance fee.

**\*\*\* Suigō-meguri (Canal Trip)** 水郷巡り *Boat landings are 0:20h on foot from the Hachiman-gū.* Wooden boats, powered by oar, ply Ōmi-Hachiman's peaceful canals, first developed by Hidetsugu for his castle's defense and to transport goods from Lake Biwa. The reed-fringed waterways and surrounding mountains are quite beautiful—ideal for moon viewing. Groups of up to six can reserve rides (2:00h for Y8750 per group) through the local canal preservation association (32-2564).

**\*\* Chōmei-ji** 長命寺 Hrs: 8:00–17:00. *0:25h by bus from station, then a 0:30h climb up steep stone steps; taxis go to the top.* This beautiful Tendai temple, on a bluff overlooking the lake, is said to have been founded by SHŌTOKU TAISHI. At the top of 808 stone steps are the Main Hall (1524, ICP), three-storied pagoda (1597, ICP), bell tower (ICP), and Goma-dō hall. Its *wayō* ("Japanese") architecture is typical of Tendai temples in the Lake Biwa region. As the 31st temple of the Kansai 33-temple Kannon pilgrimage, it is frequented by pilgrims.

### Ōmi-Hachiman Dining and Lodgings (TEL 0748)

Ōmi is famed for its rich, marbled beef and pungent *funa-zushi*, made from fermented carp.
**\* Ōmi Nishikawa** 近江西川 (32-2336). Hrs: 11:00–19:00 (last order); clsd Th. A well-known Ōmi beef restaurant. Sukiyaki Y5000, *shabu-shabu* Y5000, *teppan-yaki* Y6000.
**Kanekichi** かねきち 駅前 (33-3055). Hrs: 11:00–14:00, 16:00–20:30; clsd Tu, NY. Near station. Restaurant run by Ōmi's top beef dealer. From Y4000.
**Shiga Kōsei Nenkin Kyūka Center** 滋賀厚生年金休暇センター (32-3221). Kitanoshō, Ōmi-Hachiman-shi, Shiga-ken. Pleasant Social Security agency recreational lodge near canals. Y7500 w/meals.
**Mizugahama Pension** 水ガ浜ペンション (32-4440). Chōmeiji-chō, Mizugahama. Lakeside resort (*0:25h by bus toward Kokumin Kyūkamura*). Y6800 w/meals.
**Ōmi-Hachiman Kokumin Kyūkamura (People's Vacation Village)** 近江八幡国民休暇村 (32-3138). Okinoshima-chō. Resort located on a secluded cove. Y6700 w/meals.
**Kanshū-ji YH** 勧修寺YH (32-2938). 610 Maruyama-chō. Temple near Chōmei-ji. Y4000 w/meals.

379

## YŌKAICHI 八日市

*0:15h from Ōmi-Hachiman or 0:35h from Maibara by Ōmi-tetsudō line.* 0:35h by bus from the station is **Eigen-ji** 永源寺, a lovely Rinzai Zen temple (included on the Kotō Sanzan bus tour, see below). At Minokuchi, 0:30h by Ōmi-tetsudō line from Yōkaichi, is **Daichi-ji** 大池寺, which has a noted garden with a magnificent topiary hedge, attributed to KOBORI ENSHŪ. Yōkaichi's **Shōfuku-rō** 招福楼 (0748-22-0003) is counted among the best *chakaiseki* restaurants in Japan. From Y20,000, by reservation. Clsd 1st and 3rd M, NY.

### Calendar
**Jan. 8: \* Hadaka Matsuri.** New Year's naked festival: youths compete in a temple hall at Hōtoku-ji for a suspended ball. 20:00.
**Sept. 1: Imokurabe.** Hino (*0:20h by Ōmi-tetsudō line from Yōkaichi*), Nakayama Kumano Jinja. "Yam comparing" festival from the 12th C. East and West teams compare yams. If West wins, the harvest will be good; West always wins.

## VI:6 \* HIKONE 彦根

*0:50h from Kyoto or 0:06h from Maibara by JR Tōkaidō line express.* Hikone was the castle town of the Ii family, trusted advisors to the TOKUGAWA shoguns. The main avenue from the station leads to **\*\*\* Hikone-jō** 彦根城, built in 1603 as the first bulwark of defense against possible attack by the anti-Tokugawa daimyo of the western provinces. (Hrs: 8:30–17:00.) The three-storied keep (NT), overlooking Lake Biwa, is small but beautifully proportioned. Several turrets and gates also survive. The **\* Hikone-jō Hakubutsukan** (museum) 彦根城博物館 in the castle grounds exhibits the fine collection of the Ii, including a photographic reproduction of the famous *Hikone Byōbu* (screen, NT) (Hrs: 9:00–16:30). Adjacent to the castle are **Genkyū-en** 玄宮園, an Edo-period stroll garden, and **Rakuraku-en**, the former villa and garden of the Ii, now a ryokan.

### Hikone Lodgings (TEL 0749)
**Rakuraku-en** 楽々園 (22-4560). 3-44 Konki-machi, Hikone-shi, Shiga-ken. Former Ii villa. From Y18,000 w/meals.
**Hikone Prince Hotel** 彦根プリンスホテル (26-1111). 1453 Matsubara-chō. Lakeside resort hotel. Tw Y15–25,000.

## Exploring Kotō Sanzan

The hills flanking the east shore of Lake Biwa shelter three beautiful, ancient temples, each on its own sacred mountain. They were founded in the Nara period, but became Tendai temples affiliated with Enryaku-ji on Hiei-zan. **Saimyō-ji** has an image-filled Main Hall (NT) and three-storied pagoda (NT) of the Kamakura period; the mandala-painted interior of the pagoda should not be missed. **Kongōrin-ji's** Main Hall (1288, NT) contains an impressive array of images. **Hyakusai-ji** owns an exquisite Nara-period bronze of Miroku Bosatsu and has a beautiful modern pond garden. A **Teiki Yūran (Scheduled Tour) Bus** runs Su and NH from Apr. 1–Oct. 20, and daily from Oct. 21–Nov. 30; board at Maibara station (10:10), Hikone Prince Hotel (10:15), or Hikone station (10:25). The tour covers all three temples, plus Eigen-ji (see Yōkaichi, preceding page), ending at Maibara station at 17:10. Y5250 w/lunch and entrance fees.

## VI:7 MAIBARA 米原

*3:20h from Tokyo or 0:30h from Kyoto by Shinkansen Kodama express. Junction to JR Hokuriku and Tōkaidō main lines.* On May 3, at 14:00, one can see the charming **Nabe-kaburi Matsuri**, a procession of eight little girls wearing paper pots over their heads. The festival, originating in the Heian period, is a prayer to the deity of rice.

## VI:8 NAGAHAMA 長浜

*0:10h by local or 0:25h by the frequent Kinomoto-Jizō-bound bus from Maibara. Boats to Chikubushima (VI:9).* Nagahama was the first fief of TOYOTOMI HIDEYOSHI.

### Calendar
**Apr. 14–16: ** Hikiyama Matsuri.** See Calendar, p. 316.

## 380  VI:9 CHIKUBUSHIMA 竹生島

*Boats operate mid-Mar.–Nov. 0:25h from Nagahama, departing at 10:45 and 13:15; Su and NH at 9:00; returning at 12:45 and 15:15 (Y2920). 2:30h from Hama-Ōtsu, Su and NH only, departing at 10:30, returning at 14:00 (Y3200). 0:35h from Hikone, departing 10:00–14:30, returning 11:35–16:15 (Y3240). 0:20h from Ōmi-Imazu, Apr. 21–Nov. 30; departing hourly 10:10–14:10, returning 12:25–16:50 (Y2380).* This small island is the site of **Hōgon-ji**, a temple founded in the Nara period. TOYOTOMI HIDEYORI, the son of Hideyoshi, dedicated it to Benzai-ten, goddess of fortune. The buildings, originally part of Hideyoshi's Fushimi-jō, were transferred here in 1602. These include the Kara-mon (Chinese gate, NT) and Kannon-dō (ICP), and the *maki-e*-lacquered Funarōka (ICP) and Honden (NT) of the adjacent **Tsukubusuma Jinja**.

### Easy Access To:
**Ōmi-Imazu** (KYOTO VI:3): *0:35h by bus from Nagahama to Kinomoto, then 1:00h by another bus.*
**Ōmi-Shiozu**: *1:00h by bus from Kinomoto. Junction for the JR Hokuriku main line to Fukui (CHŪBU IV:NW8).*

# Kinki

This region is the cradle of Japanese civilization. It is here in ancient Yamato that the imperial clan first emerged into recorded history. The imperial capitals of Nara and Kyoto produced the great monuments of Japanese culture. No other region has so much history packed into so little space. For travelers with a deep interest in early and classical Japan, it offers an almost unlimited number of sites to visit.

## BEST ATTRACTIONS

I:S1    ✱✱ **Daigo-ji.** A great Shingon temple. Its famous Sambō-in subtemple was rebuilt by HIDEYOSHI (p. 382).

I:S1    ✱✱✱ **Uji.** The phoenix hall of Byōdō-in is one of the masterpieces of Japan's art and architecture (p. 386).

I:S3    ✱✱✱ **Nara.** Capital from 710 to 784, the golden age of Buddhism in Japan. It remains a city of magnificent temples, famous for its Great Buddha and Buddhist art treasures (p. 390).

I:S4    ✱✱✱ **Hōryū-ji.** A temple filled with art treasures, founded by SHŌTOKU TAISHI in the 7th century. It has the oldest wooden buildings in the world (p. 400).

I:S8    ✱✱ **Murō-ji.** The "Women's Kōya," where women were allowed to worship. This mountain temple preserves some of the oldest and finest Esoteric Buddhist temple halls and art (p. 404).

I:S11    ✱✱ **Asuka.** Tomb mounds and strange carved rocks amid rice paddies — Yamato Japan's birthplace (p. 406).

I:S13    ✱✱ **Yoshino.** This ancient mountain sanctuary, renowned for cherry blossoms, was the headquarters of the mysterious *yamabushi*. In the 14th century, Emperor Go-Daigo escaped to Yoshino and established his "southern court" here, in one of the stranger episodes of Japanese history (p. 410).

II:S1    ✱✱✱ **Kōya-san.** On this remote, holy mountain, Japan's great saint, KŌBŌ DAISHI, waits for the Buddha of the Future, surrounded by a huge graveyard filled with the tombs of the great figures of Japanese history (p. 419).

IV    ✱✱✱ **Himeji.** Himeji-jō, the White Egret castle, is the largest and most beautiful castle in Japan (p. 424).

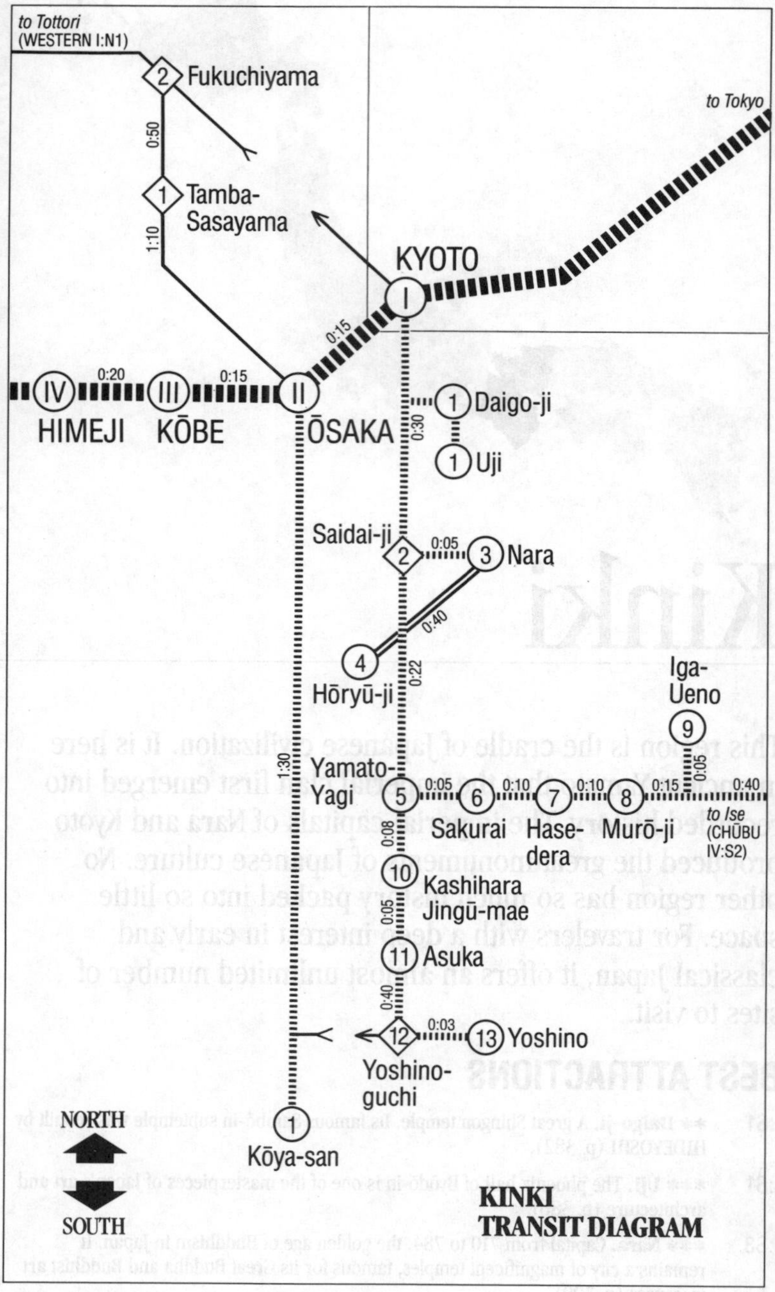
to Tottori
(WESTERN I:N1)
2 Fukuchiyama
0:50
1 Tamba-Sasayama
1:10
to Tokyo
KYOTO
I
0:15
IV
0:20
III
0:15
II
HIMEJI
KŌBE
ŌSAKA
1 Daigo-ji
0:30
1 Uji
Saidai-ji
2
0:05
3 Nara
0:40
4
Hōryū-ji
0:22
Iga-Ueno
9
0:05
1:30
Yamato-Yagi
5
0:05
6
0:10
7
0:10
8
0:15
0:40
Sakurai
Hase-dera
Murō-ji
to Ise
(CHŪBU IV:S2)
0:08
10
Kashihara Jingū-mae
0:05
11 Asuka
0:40
12
0:03
13 Yoshino
Yoshino-guchi
NORTH
SOUTH
1
Kōya-san
KINKI
TRANSIT DIAGRAM

**Seasons**

Cherry-blossom season is early April, fall foliage from mid-October through November. In spring and autumn many temples show treasures and buildings that are normally not on view (including the *** Shōsō-in Exhibit in Nara). Tourists, including hundreds of thousands of students on school trips, pour into Nara at this time, so be sure to book hotels well in advance. Winter, although cold, is often sunny, and many tourist sites are almost deserted.

**Average Temperature °C (°F)/Days of Rain or Snow**

| | January | April | July | October |
|---|---|---|---|---|
| Ōsaka | 5.6 (42.1)/6 | 14.5 (58.1)/11 | 27.0 (80.6)/10 | 18.3 (64.9)/8 |

**Traveling**

Kinki is criss-crossed with many private lines, such as the Hankyū, Kintetsu, Nankai, and Keihan lines. These are often faster and cheaper than JR trains; for example, the recommended line from Kyoto to Nara is Kintetsu.

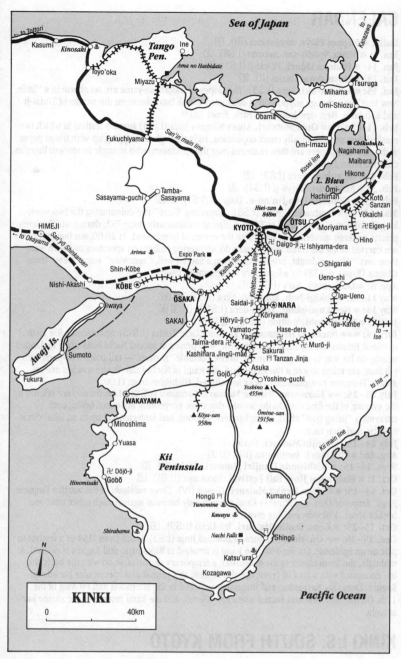

# SPECIAL INTERESTS

**Archeology:** The excavated site of Heijō (Nara) Palace is open to the public. Asuka, the birthplace of the Yamato state, is dotted with strange carved rocks, temple foundations, and *kofun* (mound tombs). Cycling paths through the countryside allow one to explore the countless ruins (don't miss the Kashihara Archeological Museum). Japan's largest *kofun* is in Sakai.

**Well-Preserved Towns:** Iga-Ueno is an isolated castle town that was the birthplace of the poet BASHŌ and a center for the *ninja*, the acrobatic spies of the Edo period. Imai-chō, near Yamato-Yagi, is the best-preserved merchant town in Japan.

**Onsen:** Hot springs are mostly found at the southern tip of the Kii Peninsula. Kawayu Onsen has open-air baths dug in the river cobbles. Yunomine Onsen is an ancient spa on the Kumano pilgrimage. Katsu'ura, a big spa town, is famous for sea-cavern baths.

**Buddhist Art:** Kinki is superb for Buddhist art. There are many national treasures at such lesser-known temples as Hōkai-ji, Shōrin-ji (Sakurai), Taima-dera, and at such Nara temples as Shin-Yakushi-ji, Jōruri-ji, Hokke-ji, and Akishino-dera.

# CALENDAR

**Daily:** \* **Puppet Plays.** Awajishima (III). P

**Jan. 1:** \* **Miwa Nyōdō-sai.** Sakurai (I:S6). F

**Jan. 14:** \* **Hadaka Odori.** Hōkai-ji (I:S1). E

**Jan. 14:** \* **Doya-doya.** Ōsaka (II). E

**Jan. 15:** \*\* **Yamayaki.** Nara (I:S3). The slopes of Wakakusa-yama are set ablaze in a "little New Year" rite, though supposedly it originated with a battle between the monks of Tōdai-ji and Kōfuku-ji. Best view from Nara Park. From 18:00.

**Feb. (1st Su):** \*\* **Onta Matsuri.** Asuka Niimasu Jinja (I:S11) Fertility festival in which two masked dancers graphically enact copulation, right through to mopping up with tissue paper at the end. The papers are then scattered over the spectators, who struggle to retrieve them as charms. From 14:00.

**Feb. 3:** \* **Setsubun.** Nara (I:S3). P

**Feb. 3:** \* **Setsubun.** Hōryū-ji (I:S4). P

**Feb. 23:** \*\* **Godairikison Jin'nō-e.** Daigo-ji (I:S1). F E

**Mar. 12:** \*\*\* **Omizutori.** Nara (I:S3). "Receiving Water" rite culminating the two-week-long Shuni-e rites, performed at Tōdai-ji almost continuously since 752, during which eleven priests undergo austerities to exonerate the errors of humankind. At 20:00, ten huge torches are carried along the veranda of Nigatsu-dō, showering embers on specators to "burn away their sins." After midnight, priests draw from a sacred well, "receiving" water "sent" from Obama (Kyoto, p. 378) by a legendary subterranean river.

**Apr. 8:** \* **Otaimatsu.** Nara (I:S3). F

**May 11–12:** \* **Takigi-Noh.** Kōfuku-ji, Nara (I:S3). P V

**May 14:** \* **Nerikuyō-shiki.** Taima-dera (I:S11). P V B

**July 7:** \* **Kaeru-tobi.** Yoshino (I:S13). P B

**July 14:** \*\*\* **Nachi no Hi-matsuri.** Kumano Nachi Taisha (I:S13). Spectacular fire festival to honor Jimmu, the mythical first emperor, who prayed at sacred Nachi Falls when he landed nearby on his way to conquer Yamato. Twelve portable "shrines" — tall poles festooned with gilt fans, are taken to join a thirteenth god, the kami of Nachi Falls. Twelve torches are set ablaze. Dengaku rice-planting dances are offered. Highlights from 11:00.

**July 24–25:** \*\* **Kozagawa Mifune Matsuri.** Kozagawa (I:S13). Lion dances are offered on the evening of the first day. On the second day, three gorgeously bedecked boats, each carrying a "living god" child, flying banners, ribbons, and lanterns, sail up to an islet, circle it twice, and then race.

**July 24–25:** \* **Tenjin Matsuri.** Ōsaka (II). V

**Aug. 16:** \* **Hi-Odori.** Awajishima (III). P F

**Sept. 14–15:** \* **Kishiwada Danjiri Matsuri.** Ōsaka (II). E

**Oct. 1:** \* **Hachiman Jinja Fall Festival.** Hirokawa (II:S1). P

**Oct. 14–15:** \*\* **Mega Kenka Matsuri.** Himeji (IV). Three *mikoshi* of the warlike Empress Jingū, Emperor Ōjin, and Hime Ō-kami are viciously battered against each other until one breaks apart. A bloody, exciting event.

**Oct. 23–25:** \* **Ueno Tenjin Matsuri.** Iga-Ueno (I:S9). V

**Dec. 15–18:** \*\* **On-Matsuri.** Nara, Wakamiya Jinja (I:S3). Dates from 1134 as a festival to placate an epidemic. On the 16th, the kami is invoked at Wakamiya, and Kagura is offered. At midnight, the kami moves to the *o-tabisho*, a temporary shrine of wood with the bark still on, decorated with a roof of green boughs. Against this primal and spectacular backdrop, Kagura, Dengaku, Sarugaku, and Bugaku are offered in the afternoon and evening of the 17th. On the 18th, Noh and sacred sumo are offered, and the kami returns to the shrine late at night.

# KINKI I:S. SOUTH FROM KYOTO

**Main Attractions:** Daigo-ji (S1), Uji (S1), Nara (S3), Hōryū-ji (S4), Asuka (S11), Yoshino (S13)

**Prefectures:** Kyoto-fu, Nara, Wakayama

**Traveling**
(See p. 314 on getting to Kyoto.) To visit Nara and points south, the private Kintetsu line is best. For a Tokyo-based round-trip excursion to this area, there's the 8-day Yamatoji Free Kippu, good for unlimited travel on JR and Kintetsu trains in this region, including the base round-trip fare from Tokyo to Kyoto.

With Kyoto, this region is Japan's richest repository of history and culture. Basically, the farther south one goes, the more ancient the history. To do a historical tour in chronological order, one might start out in Asuka and head north to Hōryū-ji, Nara, Uji, and finally Kyoto.

## S1 \*\* DAIGO-JI 醍醐寺
*3:30h by bus from Keihan-Sanjō station to Sampō-in-mae.* This Shingon temple was founded by a holy man, Rigen Daishi, in the late 9th century, and expanded by Emperor Daigo (who took his name from this temple) after it became an imperial temple in 907.

384

It was badly damaged in the Ōnin Wars (1467–1477) and was restored by HIDEYOSHI, who chose the sacred slopes in the temple precincts as the site for his cherry-blossom expedition in 1598. At this time, the abbot Gien appealed to him to rebuild the ruined temple. Hideyoshi accepted, taking special pains with Sambō-in, the imperial subtemple where he had stayed. Because Hideyoshi died in the same year, the restoration was completed by his son HIDEYORI.

Daigo-ji offers a study in contrasts. The vast precincts are divided between two areas, Shimo (Lower) Daigo, a level expanse with large buildings at the base of a mountain, and Kami (Upper) Daigo, a scattering of small halls at the summit. Socially, it is a temple with close ties to the imperial house; before the Meiji Restoration, Daigo-ji had five imperial sub-temples (*monzeki*). On the other hand, it was Hideyoshi's plebeian dash and vigor that make Sambō-in, with its gardens and architecture, the most important stop on a tour of Daigo-ji.

### Calendar

**Jan. 14: ✱ Hadaka Odori.** Hōkai-ji (1.5 km south of Daigo-ji). A famous Naked Dance to mark the end of a 2-week New Year rite. 19:00.

**Feb. 23: ✱ Godairikison Jin'nō-e.** Festival of the deity who prevents disasters. At 9:00, a bonfire of votive sticks is lit at Kami-Daigo. At 13:00, at Shimo-Daigo, there is a strength contest in which participants try to see how long they can hold two giant ricecakes weighing a total of 150 kg.

**Apr. (2nd Su): Taikō Hanami Gyōretsu.** Costume parade reenacts the famous cherry-viewing party of Hideyoshi, who was popularly known as the Taikō (the Retired Regent).

### Daigo-ji Sights

**✱✱✱ Sambō-in (or Sampō-in)** 三宝院 Hrs: 9:00–17:00. In winter 9:00–16:00. Directly on the left after Daigo-ji's first gate. The five white stripes on the surrounding wall signify Sambō-in's former status as an imperial subtemple. Sambō-in was founded in 1115, but its present form dates from the rebuilding undertaken in 1598 by Hideyoshi, who is said to have personally directed the design of the buildings and garden; as such, Sambō-in is the most complete example of the fabled general's tastes. 385

    **First Building.** Consists of three reception rooms (ICP) noted for paintings by KANŌ SANRAKU (1559–1635); many of the painted screens at Sambō-in are attributed to him. The antechamber, **Aoi no Ma**, has screens depicting Kyoto's Aoi Matsuri. The inner room was reserved for imperial messengers, who entered by the **Chokushi-mon** (NT) in the south wall of the enclosure. The gate, said to be from Hideyoshi's Juraku-tei Palace, bears his paulownia and 12-petaled chrysanthemum crests — similar, but not identical, to those of the emperor.

    ◆ **Garden.** A showcase of Hideyoshi's bravado and wealth, this garden is a crazy-quilt of raked sand, moss, a complicated pond with islands and bridges, an abundance of fine garden rocks, and luxuriant plantings, all intricately arranged to draw and delight the eye. It contains elements of the Muromachi meditation garden, meant to be viewed from a single vantage point, but beckons one to walk through it, presaging the Edo-period stroll garden (see Villas, p. 67). Of the nearly 800 stones in the garden the most famous is the **Fujito**, a large rectangular stone standing upright to the left of the earth-covered bridge. The stone, said to be stained with the blood of a man killed by treachery during the Genpei Wars, forms the basis of the Noh play *Fujito*. The abbot Gien is said to have been offered a choice between the stone and a thousand *koku* of rice — enough to feed a thousand men for a year.

    ◆ **Omote Shoin** (NT). The main building facing onto the garden, this Momoyama-period structure combines the Shinden style of Heian-period palaces, seen in its broad, encircling veranda and portion built over water, with the medieval Shoin style, seen in such elements as the *tokonoma* alcove and staggered shelves of the *jōdan no ma* (see Villas, p. 64). This last room has ceiling beams placed at right angles to the way the tatami is laid, contrary to convention; this is said to be one of Hideyoshi's idiosyncrasies.

    **Junjōkan** (ICP). The next building from the Omote Shoin was moved from Yariyama, halfway up to Kami-Daigo, where it had been built for Hideyoshi's cherry-blossom excursion. Meant for parties, the rooms look out on a garden with moss beds in the shapes of a gourd and circles — a saké flask and cups.

    **Goma-dō** (Main Hall, ICP). Standing farthest east, on a rise, this hall houses an image of Miroku (1192, ICP) by KAIKEI, flanked by portraits of Rigen Daishi, founder of Daigo-ji, and KŪKAI, founder of the Shingon sect.

    ◆ **Shinden** (ICP). The return route detours to the right, toward the entrance to this hall, reserved for the most exalted personages; its northeast room contains the Daigo Shelf, a decorative *chigaidana* famous as one of the "three great shelves." Attached to this hall is the Shōgetsu-tei, a tea arbor of the late 15th–early 16th C.

**✱✱✱ Hōjuin (Treasure House)** 宝聚院 Open Apr. 1–May 25 and Oct. 1–Nov. 25. Hrs: 9:00–16:00; clsd Nov. 1. Modern building, across the main approach from Sambō-in. It exhibits objects from Daigo-ji's huge and superb collection, mostly documents and items relating to the temple's history and to Esoteric Buddhism.

**✱✱✱ Shimo-Daigo.** From Sambō-in, the temple's famous cherry-lined main approach leads to the huge **Niō-mon**, main gate to the Shimo-Daigo complex. The buildings of Shimo-Daigo were begun in 926, including the famous pagoda, the only structure to survive the Ōnin Wars.

**Kondō** (Main Hall, Kamakura period, NT). To the left of the central avenue. This hall was originally at Negoro-dera, a powerful Shingon temple in Kii (Wakayama) that had rebelled against Hideyoshi and been defeated. The hall was given to Daigo-ji as part of the spoils. It probably came with its main images, a Yakushi trinity of the late 12th C, decorated with *kirikane* (delicate frets of gold).

◆ **Five-Storied Pagoda** (951, NT). This is the oldest building in Kyoto prefecture, and one of only two Heian-period five-storied pagodas extant in all of Japan. The interior, not shown, is gorgeously painted with Shingon mandalas, among the oldest color paintings of their type in existence.

✱✱ **Kami-Daigo.** The avenue through Shimo-Daigo continues, passing a pretty little Benten shrine on a pond, to the foot of the 0:45h climb to Kami-Daigo. About halfway up, a small sign marks **Yariyama**, the rather precarious site of Hideyoshi's cherry-blossom party.

◆ **Daigo-Sui** (Spring). The white-clad pilgrims who climb to Kami-Daigo always pause first to drink from this sacred spring, which gave the temple its name. By legend, when Rigen Daishi came here, the mountain kami appeared to him in the form of an old man. A spring came bubbling out of the ground. The old man bent to drink it and exclaimed: "Ah, the taste of *daigo*!" *Daigo* is a kind of ambrosia, an Indian sweet made from an extract of milk, which was a metaphor for the ultimate of Shaka's teachings as contained in the Lotus Sutra. To the left of the spring is the **Seiryō-gū Haiden** (1434, NT), a graceful, cypress-thatched prayer hall to the dragon-god of the spring. After drinking and praying, pilgrims climb the stone steps on either side of the waterfall to pray at the **Juntei-dō**, a hall to Kannon (No. 11 on the Kansai 33-temple pilgrimage).

**Yakushi-dō** (1124, NT). A narrow path leads to the right from the Juntei-dō to this hall, the oldest at Kami-Daigo. Its light, elegant *kaerumata* (frog-crotch struts) are considered among the "best three" in Japan.

**Godai-dō.** Farther uphill from the Yakushi-dō is this chapel (rebuilt 1938), dedicated to the Five Myō-ō, fierce deities of Esoteric Buddhism. In front of the hall is a modern bronze statue of En no Gyōja, the 7th-C holy man who invented Shugendō, a syncretic mix of native mountain worship and Buddhism. It became affiliated with the Shingon and Tendai sects. The Shingon branch, founded by Rigen Daishi, has its official headquarters at Daigo-ji. Between 1868 and 1945 Shugendō was outlawed, but today one can occasionally see its priests, the *yamabushi*, wearing boxy little black hats and baggy trousers, at Kami-Daigo (see Shinto, p. 27). At the very summit is the **Nyoirin-dō** (1608, ICP), one of the first halls founded, and the **Kaisan-dō** (Founder's Hall, 1608, ICP), housing an image of Rigen Daishi. A 5:00h hiking trail links Kami-Daigo and Ishiyama-dera (see Kyoto, p. 378); use at your own risk.

✱✱ **Hōkai-ji** 法界寺 Hrs: 8:30–17:00. In winter 9:00–16:00. *1.5 km south of Daigo-ji; taxi advised. Otherwise, short bus ride to Ishida, then 0:15h walk, or 0:30h on foot from Daigo-ji.* This quiet temple was the villa of an 11th-C court noble named Hino Sukenari. In 1051, he built a simple Amida Hall on the grounds, as was the fashion of his time. Today, this **Amida-dō** (NT) is, along with the famous Phoenix Hall at Byōdō-in, one of the most precious relics of the Fujiwara period. The interior walls and ceiling are covered with faded wall paintings of angels and flowers. Its main image, a great gilded statue of **Amida** (NT) seated in meditation, is very similar to the one at Byōdō-in, and is attributed to the school of JŌCHŌ. The flamelike halo, with billowing robes of angels worked into its design, is exquisite. The smaller Yakushi-dō (ICP) enshrines a Yakushi Nyorai (Buddha of Healing) popularly known as the "Milk Yakushi" because it grants an easy delivery and a plentiful supply of milk to the women who pray to it.

## S1 ✱✱✱ UJI 宇治

*0:20h by JR Nara line from Kyoto station, or 0:35h–0:40h from Kyoto's Keihan-Sanjō station by Keihan-Uji line to Ōbaku station (Mampuku-ji) or to Uji station (Byōdō-in).* Uji lies on the ancient road linking Nara and Kyoto, at an important river crossing. A stone marker by the **Uji Bridge** indicates that the first bridge was erected here in 646. In the Heian period, the misty beauty of the Uji River enticed many courtiers to build their country villas along its banks; the Phoenix Hall of Byōdō-in remains from those days, a miraculous survivor of the medieval battles that often erupted at the bridge. Six centuries removed from the Phoenix Hall is Mampuku-ji, the Ming Chinese-style headquarters of the Ōbaku Zen sect. It is marvelous to think of these two essentially Chinese temples surviving in the Japanese countryside.

### Calendar

**June 5: Agata Matsuri.** Agata Jinja, near the south gate of Byōdō-in. At midnight a silent god-procession leaves the shrine.

**Mid-June–Aug. 31: Cormorant fishing (ukai)** on the Uji River. See p. 116.

### Uji Sights

✱✱✱ **Byōdō-in** 平等院 Hrs: 9:00–17:00. Dec.–Feb. 9:00–16:00. *From Uji station, cross the Uji Bridge and walk 0:10h.* The Phoenix Hall, built in 1053, is all that remains of the villa-temple of the Heian nobleman, Fujiwara no Yorimichi. The most splendid survivor from the halcyon Fujiwara era, it is one of the most famous buildings in Japan. (It adorns the 10-yen coin.) Nearly all the other original halls were burned in 1336 by the army of Kusunoki Masashige (see Yoshino History, p. 411).

386

# Uji History: Fujiwara Elegance and Pessimism

**Fujiwara no Michizane** (966–1027) The most powerful of the Fujiwara regents, Michizane was supposed to be one of the models for the Shining Genji.

**Lady Murasaki** (ca. 1000) A court lady who wrote *The Tale of Genji*, often called the world's first novel.

**The Shining Genji** The amorous hero of *The Tale of Genji*.

**Fujiwara no Yorimichi** (992–1074) Michizane's son, builder of the Byōdō-in.

"If you have any doubts about Paradise, just go worship at the temple at Uji!" advises an ancient children's song, referring to the Phoenix Hall at Uji's **Byōdō-in**. The structure, capped by two phoenix finials, itself resembles a huge phoenix, hovering over its garden pond. Inside the hall, the elaborately carved flaming halo, the musicians frolicking on the walls, the coffered ceiling embedded with mirrors, all bespeak a heavenly grace. In the midst of this elegance sits the sculptor JŌCHŌ's masterpiece — a huge yet tranquil Amida Buddha, in beatific meditation, all its benign energies focused inward.

The era that gave birth to this magnificent phoenix, the Fujiwara period (894–1185), was an apogee of refinement and elegance, both in art and in human relations. Like Jōchō's Amida, however, the Fujiwara world was closed and inward-looking. Trade and diplomatic missions to China ceased in 894. The flood of influences from Tang China, then in decline, was reduced to a trickle. The Heian court set about creating an intensely self-occupied culture. The world outside Japan, outside the Heian capital, indeed outside the Kyoto court itself, was of little account. Commoners who decided to "go worship at the temple at Uji" had to do so from across Byōdō-in's pond, contenting themselves with a glimpse of Amida's smile through a small window. Only the "good people," the aristocrats, were allowed inside. Entering the Phoenix Hall, they could meet Amida's gaze, and stare up at the heavenly musicians.

Today, any tourist can enter the Phoenix Hall, but to spiritually "enter" the hermetic Fujiwara world, we must turn to its great chroniclers, the Fujiwara women. While men exerted themselves in politics, producing reports and histories in stilted Chinese prose, women wrote diaries and novels relating, in free-flowing Japanese, incidents from their private lives. Excluded from the study of Chinese characters, women used a simple system of writing called *kana*, which was invented by the Shingon Buddhist saint KŪKAI. Kūkai studied Indian sutras written in the phonetic Sanskrit alphabet, which inspired him to create the analogous *kana* so that Japanese of little education, such as women and peasants, could read something of the Buddhist canon. Heian court ladies, however, found other uses for the *kana*. In the tenth century, **Sei Shōnagon** wrote a witty and gossipy collection of epigrams concerning court life called the *Pillow Book*. Almost a generation later, LADY MURASAKI, a court lady in the service of the empress, wrote *Genji Monogatari* (The Tale of Genji), possibly the world's first novel, and still one of its finest.

*Genji Monogatari* portrays an age when women, eyebrows plucked and teeth blackened, lived in a dimly lit indoor world, separated from all men but their fathers, brothers, husbands — and lovers. Affairs were usually begun by clandestine exchanges of poetry, and poetic incompetence could easily spell the end of a budding romance. The mixing of perfumes was a complicated science; in the dark of the night, lovers identified one another more by scent than by facial features. A woman's figure, already obscured by darkness, was concealed beneath twelve layers of robes, each inner layer protruding beyond the one above it for a pleasing effect. The colors of the sleeves had to be carefully orchestrated; the wrong combination could lead to an unendurable loss of face.

"The Shining Genji," the tale's hero, impatiently seeks out these gentle ladies who, like colorful gift packages, lie hidden away in secret places, yearning to be discovered. Although the son of an emperor, Genji was born to a low-ranking mother and was reduced to the status of a commoner by being made a member of the GENJI (MINAMOTO) clan. Despite his nonroyal status, his beauty, charm, loyalty, and sensitivity not only overwhelm the highest-ranking ladies, but in time, bring him high political responsibility.

It is known that Lady Murasaki belonged to a collateral branch of the Fujiwara family, and that she was a lady-in-waiting to an empress at court, but the year of her death, and even her real name, are unknown. Posterity calls her by a teasing nickname, "Murasaki," the name of a principal heroine of *The Tale of Genji* who is

387

endowed with many qualities that may have been lacking in the author herself.

The writer Murasaki was no doubt a shy spectator rather than a participant in the great romances of the court. Still, she was able to observe the great men of the age and to draw a composite portrait of them in her hero. Minamoto no Tōru (822-895), a famous courtier who originally owned the property at Byōdō-in, may have been the inspiration for the Shining Genji's name. The brilliant and stylish Fujiwara no Korechika, who was banished to Dazaifu in Kyūshū after he plotted an unsuccessful coup, might have been the basis for the character's charm as well as his sad period of exile. Korechika's illustrious uncle, the regent Michinaga, is thought to have been the model for Genji's later years as a man of responsibility, power, and passion. Murasaki's diary records that she once had to bolt her door—no easy thing to do—against Michinaga, who was drunk and lustful.

Michinaga was the most powerful of a long line of regents who ruled by marrying off Fujiwara daughters to child emperors. As soon as an emperor produced an heir by a Fujiwara lady, he was forced to retire in favor of his son; emperors were not allowed to attain the maturity needed to wield power themselves. Michinaga himself was "father-in-law to two emperors, grandfather to a third, grandfather and great-grandfather to a fourth, and grandfather-in-law to a fifth," Ivan Morris observed in *The World of the Shining Prince*.

Although there were occasional political murders, executions were unheard of in this Buddhist-influenced court. Michinaga, while keeping a tight grip on power, meted out comparatively mild punishments to his enemies. His nephew Korechika, for example, was sent into exile for only a year. Both political affairs and affairs of the heart were carried out with a since-unequaled standard of tact, delicacy, and humanity—partly, perhaps, because of the incestuousness of political and sexual relations.

388

After the heyday under Michinaga, the Fujiwara's fortunes deteriorated, partly because of the spiritual pessimism connected with the doctrine of Mappō. Buddhism teaches that history is a decline in five stages, and Mappō, the Decline of the Law, is the last, most decadent stage. During Mappō, the world is in such spiritual disorder that it is impossible to attain enlightenment by one's own efforts. Many came to believe that the only way to salvation was faith in Amida Buddha (see Buddhism, p. 37). Learned priests predicted that this dreaded age would start in 1053.

In that year, Michinaga's son, **Fujiwara no Yorimichi**, began work on the Hall of Amida at Byōdō-in, the name he had given the Uji villa when he had turned it into a temple the previous year. Here Yorimichi, the most powerful man of his time, prayed for salvation until his death in 1071. Of the dozens of Amida Halls built by aristocrats in the late Heian period, few survive today. **Hōkai-ji** (p. 386) has a simpler, though quite beautiful, Amida Hall that was probably more typical of the time. **Jōruri-ji** near Nara has the only extant hall with nine Amida images.

Reflecting the times, the last ten chapters of *The Tale of Genji*, which treat the generation following Genji, describe a state of subtle spiritual malaise. Called the Uji chapters, they center on Kaoru, thought by the world to be Genji's son, but actually the shameful fruit of Genji's wife's infidelity. Genji, now dead, knew this dreadful secret, but bore the insult uncomplainingly, taking it as retribution for his unfilial and incestuous relations with his own father's consort. Human relationships, as well as the Buddhist law, have gone awry.

Kaoru possesses Genji's sensitivity but does not have Genji's boldness and therefore loses in love. He secretly keeps a mistress, Ukifune, at Uji—the very name of which has depressing overtones in Japanese. In the end, he finds out that she has been seduced by his best friend, Niou. He is willing to forgive her, but Ukifune, unable to face the two of them, throws herself into the Uji River. (Memorials all over Uji mark where these events "occurred.") Grief leads the already devout Kaoru to study Amidist doctrine with added diligence. Meanwhile, unknown to the world, Ukifune has survived her suicide attempt and is studying to be a nun. After some time, Kaoru hears of her whereabouts, but before he can take her back to his palace, she takes the tonsure. The novel ends inconclusively, on a pessimistic note.

A few years before Fujiwara Yorimichi's death, Emperor Go-Sanjō, who happened not to have a Fujiwara mother, was nevertheless able to ascend the throne. Succeeding emperors, such as Shirakawa and Toba, after "retiring" into priesthood, managed to govern almost independently of the Fujiwara. They wielded great power as "cloistered emperors," ruling from temple-villas. Eventually, however, power fell to two great warrior clans, the Minamoto and the TAIRA. These two clans fought for power in an unprecedentedly bloody manner (see Miyajima History, p. 449). Even worse, when final victory went to the Minamoto in 1185, the capital was moved from Kyoto to Kamakura, ending the brilliance of the Heian period and the Fujiwara hold on power (see Hiraizumi History, p. 169). It seemed as if Mappō had truly arrived. Although Kyoto was the Heian capital, not a single building remains inside the city from that era. Only the villas and temples to its south—Daigo-ji, Hōkai-ji, Jōruri-ji, and Byōdō-in—remain to tell the story of the Fujiwara splendor.

◆ **Hō'ō-dō** (Phoenix Hall, 1053, NT). The graceful hall, its wings outstretched like a phoenix in flight, mirrored in a pond representing the Western Ocean, is an architectural realization of the imagined Pure Land Paradise of Amida Buddha. Such worlds, based on the idioms of Tang Chinese palaces, were depicted in mandala paintings meant to inspire believers to greater faith. With the coming of Mappō, the situation became desperate; those with the means built full-scale replicas of the scenes depicted in the mandalas. Many of these replicas were built in Uji. The Hō'ō-dō was the most elaborate and literal of all. Although the wings have no practical function, they are esthetically brilliant, giving the hall its transcendent beauty. The phoenix finials on the roof and the hall's shape itself led the people of later periods to call it the Phoenix Hall.

◆ **Amida Statue** (NT). Amida Nyorai is depicted meditating in his Pure Land: the hands rest in his lap, knuckles pressed together in the meditation mudra as he gazes down at the worshipper. A window in the front lattice of the hall allowed humbler people a glimpse of Amida's face from across the pond. This statue is the only authenticated work of the great sculptor JŌCHŌ (d. 1057), who perfected the *yosegi* technique (see Art, p. 93). Here, it was put to masterful use to achieve a gentleness and grace that belie the statue's great bulk. Amida's brilliant halo of roiling golden clouds, in which Dainichi Nyorai and 12 bosatsu hover, dates from the Edo period (6 of the bosatsu, however, are originals). The interior of the hall was lavishly decorated to represent the heart of Amida's Paradise. One can easily imagine its mirrors, gold leaf, lacquer, and mother-of-pearl, softly aglow in a candle-lit service. The ceiling beams are painted with floral motifs, and hanging high on the walls are the sublime ◆ **Bosatsu in the Clouds** (NT), 52 small sculptures of dancing and music-making bosatsu riding on tiny clouds, also the work of Jōchō and his school. A glorious canopy, exquisitely carved and covered in gold leaf, its coffered ceiling once inlaid with mother-of-pearl, hangs above Amida. The lacquered rails and sides of the dais were also once inlaid with mother-of-pearl. The doors and wooden walls were brilliantly painted with scenes of Raigō: Amida in the company of 25 bosatsu descending to receive the souls of the faithful into the Pure Land. There are nine different paintings, because Amida's Paradise has nine different ranks. The paintings now on the doors are copies; the originals are in the Treasure House. Some of the delicately engraved metal fittings also date from the Fujiwara period.

389

**Kannon-dō** (hall, ICP). Rebuilt in the Kamakura period. Stands on the riverbank site occupied by the *tsuridono* ("fishing pavilion") of the original Fujiwara villa. Until the 16th C, one side projected out over the Uji River. The hall enshrines a Jūichimen Kannon (ICP), flanked by Jizō Bosatsu and Fudo Myō-ō, all carved in the Fujiwara period.

◆ **Hōmotsukan** (Treasure House). Open Apr. 10–May 31 and Sept. 15–Nov. 3. Hrs: 9:00–16:00. Houses the Phoenix Hall's original phoenix finials (NT); Raigō door panels (NT), among the most important examples of early Yamato-e painting; and the original great bronze bell (NT), with marvelous reliefs of mythical beasts and heavenly beings. (It is one of Japan's Three Famous Bells; the others are at Jingo-ji and Mii-dera.) A copy hangs in the belfry opposite the Treasure House.

＊ **Ujigami Jinja** 宇治上神社 Across the river from the Byōdō-in. A series of bridges via the center island leads to Uji Jinja; Ujigami Jinja is a short distance northeast. The Nagare-style **Honden** (Main Hall, NT) was built in the Heian period and is the oldest shrine building in Japan. Its delicately carved *kaerumata* (frog-crotch strut) is considered one of Japan's Three Best Kaerumata. The **Haiden** (Oratory, NT) dates from the Kamakura period.

＊＊ **Mampuku-ji** 万福寺 Hrs: 9:00–16:30. *0:05h walk west of Ōbaku station.* This unusual monastery, built in the style of Ming China, is one of the most attractive temples in Japan. After the fall of the Ming dynasty to the Manchus, a high priest of the Ōbaku Zen sect, Ingen (1592–1673), left Fukien, in southern China, and went to Nagasaki in 1654, where he was warmly welcomed by the many members of the sect in its Chinese community. Ingen attracted the attention of retired emperor Go-Mizuno'o and Shogun Ietsuna who, making an exception to the exclusion-of-foreigners policy, invited him in 1661 to establish Mampuku-ji amid the tea hills of Uji. The temple was built in Ming Chinese style and, until the mid-1700s, every abbot was Chinese. During the period of isolation under the Tokugawa, Mampuku-ji seemed terribly exotic to the Japanese. An 18th-century haiku captures these feelings:

> Once you leave the gate,
> You're back once more in Japan—
> A tea-picking song!

(trans. Donald Keene)

Mampuku-ji follows the same general plan as other Japanese Zen temples, with the major halls arranged along an axis, and other halls on both sides, connected by cloisters. The famous Chinese atmosphere comes from decorative details such as the subdued red color of the buildings, the railings with the *manji kuzushi* (broken swastika) pattern, moon windows, tile floors, tasseled Chinese lanterns, and the sharply uptilted eaves and dolphin finials of the roofs. Notice the *trompe l'oeil* "light and shadow" painted on the eave brackets. The halls were built of imported teak. At Ingen's invitation, a Chinese sculptor came to do most of the religious images, which have foreign features rendered with vigorous, almost grotesque realism, very unlike those of typical Japanese temple images. Many artistic influences came into Edo Japan through Mampuku-ji: the *sencha* infused tea ceremony was popularized here; Ingen's dry-brush calligraphy was greatly admired; and Chinese literati painting, with its rough brushstrokes, influenced the Nagasaki school of painters and Japanese literati (*bunjin*) painters. Even in Japan today, the *sencha* ceremony uses *bunjin*-style scrolls or Ingen's style of calligraphy, while the traditional *matcha* ceremony makes use of the older painting and calligraphy traditions. The Ōbaku Zen sect, the last major Buddhist sect to enter Japan, is an offshoot of Rinzai Zen, but it is a great deal more eclectic. It incorporates elements of the Jōdo sect, such as the *nembutsu* (repeated invocation of Amida Buddha), bits of Esoteric ritual, and even Tibetan lamaism. Mampuku-ji has over 500 branches in Japan.

**Sō-mon** (Outer Gate, ICP). This small gate has a distinctly Chinese-style roof, crowned with dolphins. Inside, on the right, is the **San-mon** (Main Gate, ICP), bearing a tablet with the temple's full name, Ōbaku-san Mampuku-ji, in Ingen's hand.

**Tennō-den** (Heavenly Kings Hall, ICP). Houses a fat, jolly Hotei, guarded by the Four Directional Kings. Hotei was a great Chinese priest who was considered an incarnation of Miroku, the Bosatsu of the Future.

◆ **Daiyūhō-den** (Main Hall, ICP). Enshrines a statue of Shaka flanked by two disciples, Ananda and Kushida. Against the walls are 18 Rakan, grimacing in thought or gesticulating in argument. They have distinctly Chinese or even Indian features.

**Refectory.** To the right of the Daiyūhō-den. A large wooden fish hangs in front; it is beaten to announce meals and services. Mampuku-ji is famous for its "Chinese" vegetarian cuisine, *fucha-ryōri*, which you can sample by reserving a week in advance (Y3000 per person, minimum party of 4), or more simply by visiting the restaurant outside the temple gate (see below).

**Maisa-dō.** A small hall dedicated to the "founder" of the *sencha* ceremony, an informal style of serving steeped tea which was introduced at Mampuku-ji in the 17th C. The hall is open on Sunday and the 16th of every month for a public tea ceremony.

◆ **Hōzō-in** 宝蔵院 (Subtemple). Hrs: 9:00–16:00. *0:05h north of the Sō-mon.* More than the other Zen sects, Ōbaku emphasized study of the sutras. Ingen brought to Japan a "complete" set of the Buddhist sutras, the *Issaikyō*. A Japanese disciple named Tetsugen, or Iron Eyes, was determined to have them printed. After many tribulations, he was finally able to complete the 60,000 wooden blocks. At this subtemple of Mampuku-ji, you can see craftsmen tirelessly making impressions from the blocks in the old way. Asked if he doesn't get bored, one elderly printer retorted: "The Buddha lives in these scriptures. Skipping around is not allowed!"

**Uji Dining**

∗ **Haku'un-an** 白雲庵 (0774-31-8017). Hrs: 11:00–17:00; clsd NY. Across from Mampuku-ji's main gate. Pretty garden; beautifully presented *fucha-ryōri* courses (see Cuisine, p. 116). Y4400–7500 per person.

# Uji and Tea

Tea was imported as a kind of medicine from Tang China, but it wasn't until the 12th century that it was cultivated in Japan, from seed brought by Zen monks. One of the earliest places where tea was grown was Uji, with its mild climate and gentle hills. Uji tea was reserved for the most exalted persons and is still ranked the nation's best. Through the Middle Ages, tea was powdered and drunk in the fashion of the tea ceremony, and it was only in the 17th century that the now common *sencha* (steamed, rolled green tea) was introduced by the Chinese priests of Mampuku-ji. Today, Uji's souvenir candies and noodles are bright green with tea. In June, the new tea is offered in a ceremony at Agata Jinja.

## S2 SAIDAI-JI 西大寺
*0:30h by Kintetsu express from Kyoto. 0:50–1:00h by JR Nara line. Junction for trains to Kashihara* (S10). *See "West Nara" (p. 396) for nearby sights.*

## S3 ∗∗∗ NARA 奈良
*0:35h by Kintetsu express or 1:00h by JR Nara line local from Kyoto. Limited expresses leave on the hour and half-hour from 8:00–20:00 (except at 9:30, 13:30, 19:00). From Ōsaka, take the Kintetsu from Namba station or JR Kansai main line from Ōsaka station. If coming by car from Kyoto, you can stop at Uji on the way (driving time from Kyoto to Nara, over 1:00h.)* Nara was Japan's capital for a mere 74 years, from 710 to 784. Yet during this brief interlude, moved by a fervent belief in Buddhism and the unity of the state, Japan embarked on a glorious age that produced some of the world's finest religious monuments and art. Although the town of Nara, long left behind by the mainstream of history, never developed the elegant traditions and amenities of Kyoto, then again, nothing in Kyoto can touch the age and splendor of Nara's temples, the classical halls and sublime images that speak of an age of faith and the bright hopes of a young civilization.

## Calendar

**Jan. 15: ✳✳ Yamayaki.** See Calendar, p. 382. At 18:00.

**Feb. 3: ✳ Setsubun.** At Gangō-ji Gokurakubō, from 12:00, Saitō Goma-e (firewalking). At Kōfuku-ji, from 19:00, large and small demons are chased around the Tō-Kondō by Bishamon-ten. At Kasuga Taisha 3,000 lanterns are lit at 18:00. Bugaku is offered at 20:00.

**Mar. 12: ✳✳✳ Omizutori.** See Calendar, p. 382. Torches at Nigatsu-dō from 19:30. At 2:00 a.m. on the 13th, 14th and 15th, the priests draw from the sacred well and perform a vigorous Tartar Dance with a 2-meter-long torch to purify the water.

**Mar. 13: Kasuga Matsuri.** Kasuga Taisha. A sacred horse is presented at the shrine, and a graceful, ancient sacred dance, called *Yamato-mai*, is offered.

**Apr. 8: Kanbutsue (Shaka's Birthday).** Tōdai-ji. A small hall decked with flowers is built, and inside, *amacha* (sweet tea) is poured over an image of the infant Shaka (a copy of a famous NT).

**Apr. 8: ✳ Otaimatsu.** Shin-Yakushi-ji. A beautiful torch ceremony with prayers against sickness offered to Yakushi. From 19:00.

**Apr. (2nd Sa, Su): Ōchamori.** Saidai-ji. Hrs: 9:00–16:00. By reservation. A peculiar tea ceremony in which participants must help one another drink from giant tea bowls.

**May 5: Bugaku.** Manyō Botanical Gardens. Hrs: 13:00–16:00.

**May 11–12: ✳ Takigi Noh.** Torchlight performances at Noh's birthplace, Kasuga Taisha and Kōfuku-ji. This performance originated with Sarugaku offerings in the Heian period. Since the Muromachi period, the main Noh schools have performed here every year (except during World War II). Performances of *Okina* and *Sanbasō* from the afternoon of the 11th at Kasuga Taisha, followed by a series of Noh plays at Kōfuku-ji.

**May 19: Uchiwa-maki.** Tōshōdai-ji. Temple priests hurl fans into a crowd of people, who struggle to retrieve them; they are believed to be effective against illness.

**June 17: Yuri Matsuri (Lily Festival).** Isakawa Jinja. Lilies from Mt. Miwa are offered at the shrine, and four shrine maidens dance, holding the flowers, to ward off disease.

**Aug. 7: Daibutsu Ominugui.** Tōdai-ji. Yearly cleaning of the Great Buddha by priests of the temple.

**Aug. 14–15: Mantōrō.** Kasuga Taisha. Repeat of Feb. 3.

**L 8/14–16: Full Moon.** Tōshōdai-ji flings open its main hall doors at night and illuminates the magnificent images inside. Crowded but special. At Sarusawa Pond, the Unemi-sai commemorates a Nara court lady who, having lost the emperor's favor, drowned herself in the pond. Musicians in dragon boats glide across the pond, and a giant fan of flowers is set afloat as the full moon rises.

**Oct. 8–10: Zuhiko Jinja Fall Festival.** At 19:00 on the 8th, there's a sacred dance using Muromachi-period masks and robes. On the 9th and 10th, at 13:00, shrine sumo (not like sport sumo) is offered.

**Oct (2nd Su): Ōchamori.** Saidai-ji. Repeat of April Ōchamori.

**Oct.–Nov.: Tsunokiri.** Antler-cutting of the sacred deer at Kasuga Taisha. The bucks are lassooed and their antlers carefully sawn off by a shrine priest. On Su and NH from mid-Oct. to early Nov. (canceled in rain).

**Oct.–Nov.: ✳✳✳ Shōsō-in Treasures.** On view at the Nara National Museum for two weeks, from the end of Oct. to early Nov.

**Nov. 3: Bugaku.** Manyō Botanical Gardens. Hrs: 13:00–16:00.

**Dec. 15–18: ✳✳ On-Matsuri.** Wakamiya Jinja. Main events on 17th. See Calendar, p. 382.

391

## Getting Around

Nara's main sights center around a vast park filled with roaming deer, pleasant to tour on foot. It takes 0:30h to walk from the Kintetsu station across the park to Kasuga Taisha. The JR Nara station is a 0:15h walk from the Kintetsu station. If you plan to tour by taxi, it's better to arrange it in Kyoto, where you'll be able to get an English-speaking driver. MK Taxi in Kyoto has reasonable rates; 075-721-4321.

**Suggested Visit:** On day one, see Kōfuku-ji, National Museum, Tōdai-ji, Kasuga Taisha, Shin-Yakushi-ji. On day two, see Yakushi-ji, Tōshōdai-ji, Hōryū-ji, Chūgū-ji, Hokki-ji, Jikō-in.

**Bus Tours:** Teiki Kankō (Scheduled) Bus tours cover areas otherwise hard to combine: B (7:00h): Tōdai-ji, Kasuga Taisha, Hōryū-ji, Jikō-in, Yakushi-ji, Tōshōdai-ji (Y5870, dep. 9:00, 9:45). C (5:30h): Hōryū-ji, Chūgū-ji, Jikō-in, Yakushi-ji, Tōshōdai-ji (Y5080, dep. 9:10, 9:10, 10:10). D-1 (7:00h): Hokke-ji, Heijō Palace Site, Akishino-dera, Saidai-ji, Akahada Kiln, Yamato Bunkakan, Gansen-ji, Jōruri-ji (Y5300, dep. 9:25). D-2 (2:30h): Gansen-ji, Jōruri-ji (Y2000, dep. 9:05, 14:05). Tours start and end at JR Nara and Kintetsu-Nara stations. In Japanese only.

## Resources

*Historical Nara*, by Herbert Plutschow (Japan Times). This is a good companion historical guide, but has no practical information.

**Rekishi Kyōshitsu.** Hrs: 10:00–closing (enter by 17:30); clsd M. Kintetsu-Nara station 4–5F. A fine mini-museum that explains Nara's history through pictures, models, and video. Captions are in Japanese, but there is a detailed handout in English.

**Free English-speaking student guides** (0742-26-4753).

# Nara History: Imperial Nara and the Rise of the Great Temples

**Fujiwara no Fuhito**     (659–720) He engineered the move to Nara, and built Kasuga Taisha and Kōfuku-ji.

**Emperor Shōmu**     (701–756, r. 724–748) Fuhito's grandson. He presided over the casting of the Great Buddha.

**Empress Kōken**     (718–770) Daughter of Shōmu. She reigned twice, the second time as Empress Shōtoku (not to be confused with Shōtoku Taishi). Because of her conduct, she would be the last empress to reign for 800 years.

**Priest Dōkyō**     (d. 772) Faith healer and lover of Empress Kōken, who gained such influence over her that he was almost able to usurp the throne.

The founding of Nara in 710 marked a coming of age for the Japanese. For centuries, Japan had looked to its closest neighbor, Korea, for cultural inspiration, but around the sixth century, the Japanese and their Korean ally, the Paekche kingdom, lost a series of wars with rival Korean kingdoms that were backed by the armies of Tang China. These defeats had a twofold effect: The Japanese lost interest in Korea, and they became intrigued with China. In 701, shortly before the founding of Nara, the first embassies were sent to Tang China, and it was the symmetrical grid plan of Ch'ang-an, the splendid Tang capital, that was adopted for Nara.

The new capital measured 4.8 by 4.3 kilometers, with an immense palace compound at the north end. Gleaming tile roofs and brilliant red columns replaced the modest wooden dwellings of earlier times. To give appropriate distinction to the city and its ruler, it was decreed that there should be National Literature: Two huge (and half-fabricated) histories, the *Nihon Shoki* and the *Kojiki*, were written, and more than 4,000 poems extolling the native landscape, especially around Nara and the Yamato heartland, were compiled in the *Manyōshū* (Collection of Myriad Leaves). But the essence of culture, and the vehicle for the arts of civilization, was Buddhism, which flourished in Japan of the Nara period.

Buddhist glory reached its height in the reign of **Emperor Shōmu** with the completion of the **Great Buddha** of Nara, an epoch-making event for Japan. Shōmu had declared himself "a slave of the Three Buddhist Treasures," which sounds humble, but was by implication a statement that he was Buddha's chosen representative to unite and rule Japan. In 743, after a smallpox epidemic and a rebellion put him in a shaky position, Shōmu ordered the construction of the colossal bronze Buddha, an ultimate symbol of imperial sovereignty. An equally colossal temple, **Tōdai-ji**, was built to house the image and was declared the head of a national network of state temples, called Kokubun-ji, which Shōmu had ordered built in every province some years earlier. The casting of the Great Buddha, after many attempts, drained Japan's copper and gold supply; millions of conscripted peasants labored on it.

In 752, the temple, which rivaled the greatest Tang monuments, was inaugurated in the most splendid ceremony ever witnessed in Japan. An Indian priest, assisted by Chinese and Japanese priests, painted in the eyes of the image. Dignitaries from throughout the Buddhist world attended. Rich gifts were presented, many of which are preserved in the **Shōsō-in** imperial repository. Among the thousands of objects are cut-glass bowls from Persia. (Glass vessels would not be seen again until the arrival of Portuguese traders in the 1500s.)

Although Shōmu presided over the inauguration of Tōdai-ji, it was his grandfather, the FUJIWARA patriarch, FUHITO, who had laid the groundwork, encouraging the move to Nara and establishing **Kōfuku-ji** and **Kasuga Taisha**, the clan temple and shrine, as protectors of the new capital. At court, he further bolstered his clan's power by relentlessly marrying off his daughters to emperors, a practice his descendants were to continue for centuries. Incest was not of great concern; both Emperor Shōmu's mother and his consort, Empress Kōmyō, were daughters of Fuhito. In 737, however, smallpox killed many of the Fujiwara, depriving the clan of its abundant supply of marriageable daughters and capable sons. In the ensuing decades, the weakened Fujiwara found their position threatened by the very religious institutions they had helped to foster.

The magnificence of Tōdai-ji was achieved at the price of ruining the economy. The peasants, as always, shouldered the heaviest burden. One rebellious prince even stirred the peasants to revolt but was caught and killed. Nara's great Buddhist temples were the worst oppressors. They owned immense tax-free estates, squeezed their serfs, and became increasingly avaricious. The struggle with the temples came to a head in the person of a priest named **Dōkyō**, who brought Shōmu's daughter, **Empress Kōken**, under his sway. A Japanese Rasputin, Dōkyō healed the empress and wound up in her bed. A contemporary song went:

> Don't be contemptuous of monks because of their robes.
> For under their skirts are garters and hammers.
> When the hammers erect themselves,
> The monks turn out to be awesome lords.
> (trans. Kyoko M. Nakamura in *Historical Nara*)

Dōkyō hammered out a niche of power for himself as "priestly grand minister of the state," but he was after greater glory. He claimed that the guardian kami of Tōdai-ji, enshrined at Usa Hachiman in Kyūshū, had pronounced through an oracle that he, Dōkyō, should be made emperor. The court, its suspicions aroused, sent a messenger to Usa to check this report and received the reply that Dōkyō could not become emperor because he was not of imperial lineage. Thereafter, Dōkyō's influence waned. The empress died in the following year, and Dōkyō was promptly banished.

Alarmed by the power of the temples, the Fujiwara made two decisions: one, that women (who were susceptible to handsome priests), could not ascend the throne, and two, that the capital must be moved elsewhere, away from Nara's ambitious temples. Under **Emperor Kammu**, a new capital was founded at Heian-kyō (see Kyoto History, p. 319), where the Fujiwara were destined to preside over the culturally brilliant Heian period.

After the imperial court left, Nara's temples and shrines remained a potent force, historically and culturally. Kasuga Taisha and Kōfuku-ji remained the Fujiwara tutelary shrine and temple; they were to play an important part in the development of Buddhist-Shinto syncretism (see Shinto, p. 27), the KEI SCHOOL of sculpture, and the Noh theater. The priests continued to meddle in political affairs, with sometimes disastrous consequences, as when in 1180 TAIRA NO KIYOMORI's son, Shigemori, burned Nara's temples to the ground for backing the MINAMOTO. After the Minamoto victory, YORITOMO sponsored a massive rebuilding which left its own distinctive legacy of artistic and architectural masterpieces.

393

**Around Nara Park**
**\*\*\* Kōfuku-ji** 興福寺 Hrs: 9:00–17:00, daily. As the tutelary temple of the Fujiwara, Kōfuku-ji's fortunes followed the family's ups and downs. When the court moved to Nara, the temple moved with them. During the height of Fujiwara power, Kōfuku-ji received numerous halls as gifts from the court. And when the Fujiwara backed the Minamoto in the 12th C, the temple was burned to the ground by a Taira general. Though much reduced, the grounds today contain several outstanding structures rebuilt in the Middle Ages. The lovely **Hokuen-dō** (North Octagonal Hall, 1208, NT), built in memory of Fujiwara no Fuhito, and the **Tō-Kondō** (East Golden Hall, 1415, NT) are considered to be faithful to their Nara-period originals. The three-storied pagoda and landmark five-storied pagoda (1426) are also NT.

◆ **Kokuhōkan** (National Treasure Hall) 国宝館 Hrs: 9:00–17:00. There is an excellent booklet in English and French. This museum exhibits images formerly housed in Kōfuku-ji's halls, and is noted for masterpieces of the Nara and Kamakura periods. Renowned images include the large, strikingly beautiful **bronze head of Yakushi** (685, NT) discovered beneath the central image in the Tō-Kondō in 1937; the sublime **Ashura** (8th C, NT), a dry-lacquer three-faced, six-armed demon who has become a gentle-faced guardian of the faith; and **Muchaku and Seshin** (NT) by UNKEI, remarkable imaginary portrait statues of the two Indian founders of the Hossō sect (who look very Japanese).

**\*\*\* Nara Kokuritsu Hakubutsukan (National Museum)** 奈良国立博物館 (22-7771). Hrs: 9:00–16:30 (enter by 16:00); clsd M (except if M a NH, then clsd Tu), NY. Superb holdings, mostly pertaining to the Asuka, Hakuhō, and Nara periods. The modern wing used to have a fine and instructive exhibit of Buddhist art, but it now seems uncurated. The Shōsō-in treasures are shown here in autumn. The exhibits in the old wing are more diverse and somewhat more specialized. The underground corridor connecting the two wings contains a display of photographs of famous Nara-area Buddhist images. **Hassō-an**, a reconstructed Furuta Oribe tea arbor, can be seen by applying at the museum office M–Sa morning.

**\*\* Neiraku Bijutsukan (Art Museum)** 寧楽美術館・依水園 (22-2173). Hrs: 10:00–16:30. June–Sept. and Dec.–Mar. clsd Tu. A choice collection of early Chinese bronzes (mostly Yin and Chou), mirrors from the Warring States to Tang periods, and an abundance of Chinese, Japanese, and Korean ceramics. Admission includes the **Isui-en**, a Meiji-period stroll garden which "borrows" the great roof of Tōdai-ji and the slopes of Wakakusa-yama for a backdrop—certainly one of the best views of Tōdai-ji. *Matcha* and sweets are served on the veranda. At lunch, they serve *Mugitoro Gozen* (barley and rice with grated yam) Y1100, or *Unatoro Gozen* (with eel) Y2200.

**\*\*\* Tōdai-ji** 東大寺 Hrs: Mar. 8:00–17:00. Apr.–Sept. 7:30–17:30. Oct. 8:00–17:00. Nov.–Feb. 8:00–16:30. The temple of the Great Buddha is the summation of the Nara court's ambition. Emperor Shōmu probably heard of a Great Buddha near the Chinese Sui dynasty capital of Loyang and, desiring to centralize power on the Chinese model, conceived of the project as a symbol of his authority over a unified, Buddhist Japan. It was completed in 752. Three decades later, the imperial court abandoned Nara, and though Tōdai-ji remained the supreme authority in Buddhist affairs, its age of glory had passed. In later periods, various disasters befell the temple. In 855, the Great Buddha's head fell off in an earthquake. In 1180, the temple was burned by Taira no Shigemori. Minamoto no Yoritomo rebuilt it, entrusting the task to the priest Chōgen. The temple was burned again in the 16th-C civil wars. A TOKUGAWA-sponsored rebuilding was not completed until the early 1700's and included only the central buildings. The handful of surviving original structures and objects rank among the most precious treasures of Japanese culture. They include the bronze lantern before the Daibutsu-den, the clay Guardian Kings in the Kaidan-in, the Shōsō-in treasures, and the inner sanctum of the Hokke-dō.

◆ **Nandai-mon** (Great South Gate, NT). An imposing structure dating from the Kamakura-period rebuilding. Its style of construction comes from South China in the Sung period and was introduced to Japan by Chōgen. Called Daibutsu style, its main feature is the use of extremely long columns supporting extensive planar bracketing (see Buddhism, p. 38). The gate houses a pair of tremendous ◆ **Niō** (NT), masterpieces of Kamakura sculpture carved by UNKEI and KAIKEI. On the opposite side is a trim pair of Koma-inu (ICP), or "Korean Dogs."

**Foundations of Tōdai-ji's two pagodas.** Located 150 m on either side of the main approach. Tōdai-ji had two huge pagodas, 300 feet tall, each standing in its own enclosure. A full-scale reconstruction of the golden spire that crowned the pagodas gives an idea of their colossal dimensions; it stands outside the southeast corner of the Daibutsu-den enclosure.

◆ **Daibutsu-den** (Great Buddha Hall, NT). The largest wooden structure in the world (47.5 m high, 57 m wide, 50 m deep) is enclosed by a vast cloister. The original was half again as large. In the center court stands a copy of the famed \* **Bronze Lantern** (NT); the reliefs of four heavenly musicians embody the voluptuous *joie de vivre* of the Nara court. The great hall was rebuilt in 1709 and is not faithful to the original; in particular, the curved "Chinese" gable in the center of the lower eave was probably introduced in the Edo period. Beneath it is a window which, viewed from afar, frames the Buddha's face.

◆ **Daibutsu** (Great Buddha, NT). This famed image has been repaired so extensively that it is impossible to discern its original appearance. Though one might not be stirred by it artistically, its size is impressive. The image is of Rushana (Vairocana), the cosmic Buddha, whose infinite manifestations appear as buddhas and bodhisattvas in all worlds to save all beings. A surviving fragment of a petal from the Great Buddha's lotus seat shows delicate etchings of arrays of buddhas, depicting this vision of worlds within worlds, populated by a hierarchy of Vairocana's envoys.

**Kaidan-in** (Ordination Hall) 戒壇院 Houses Japan's first ordination platform, built for the mass ordination ceremony conducted by Ganjin (see Tōshōdai-ji, p. 397). It contains the celebrated clay ◆ **Shi-Tennō** (NT), life-size images of the Four Directional Guardians. These marvelous statues date from Tōdai-ji's founding. The finely modeled features are stern yet wise, typical of the era's preference for gentle refinement over the grotesque. The hall and surrounding yard have been handsomely renovated.

◆ **Shōsō-in** (Imperial Repository, NT). This large "log cabin" on stilts housed the fabulous collection of personal effects of Emperor Shōmu and religious regalia used in Tōdai-ji's inauguration, bequeathed to the temple by Shōmu's widow, Empress Kōmyō. The simple but ingenious *azekura* construction, among the oldest architectural forms in Japan, has kept the 1,200-year-old treasures in an astounding state of preservation. The timbers would swell with humidity, sealing the building against moisture, and shrink with dry weather, allowing fresh air to circulate. Today, the treasures have been removed to a fireproof concrete building. Many objects were gifts of foreign dignitaries, and form a catalog of the art of the Silk Route, from Persia to Tang China. The annual Shōsō-in exhibition (see Calendar) should not be missed. The enclosure is open to the public during this period and for a few days in spring (call 26-2811 for information).

**Tegai-mon** (NT). This gate in the NW corner of the precincts is one of the few structures dating from the founding of Tōdai-ji. It is said to cure the diseases of all who walk by it. The Shunjō-dō hall houses a famous Kamakura-period **portrait statue of priest Chōgen** (NT) on view July 5 only. The **Shōrō** (Belfry, NT), a Daibutsu-style structure dating from the Kamakura period, contains the great bell (NT) that was used in the inauguration of Tōdai-ji. It still booms out every evening.

◆ **Nigatsu-dō** 二月堂 (Edo period, ICP). Elevated on stilts, this hall provides a splendid view of the Daibutsu-den. It is called Second Month Hall after its famous rite, Omizutori, originally held in the second lunar month (see Calendar). A shed, Akaiya (Kamakura period, ICP), shelters the sacred Wakasa well.

◆ **Hokke-dō** 法華堂 (or Sangatsu-dō, NT). The inner sanctum of this small hall was built around 748. A hall of worship was added in the 9th C, and the two halls joined under one roof around the 13th C, giving the structure its singular and lovely roof line. The hall houses one of the supreme collections of Nara-period statuary. The main image is a dry-lacquer **Fukūkenjaku Kannon** (NT), a multi-armed, aloof being who foreshadows Esoteric Buddhist images of the following period (see Buddhism, p. 36). The clay images of ◆ **Nikkō and Gakkō** (NT), hands pressed together in prayer, are realistic yet expressive of a remote, spiritual purity. There are also two dry-lacquer images of Bon-ten and Taishaku-ten (NT); clay images of the female divinities Kisshō-ten and Benzai-ten (ICP) in the guise of court ladies; the Shi-Tennō (NT); and a pair of Kongō Rikishi (NT), hard to miss with their flaming hair, beards, and Central Asian armor. Behind the altar is a colored clay image of the lightning-wielding Shukongōshin (NT); it can be seen only on Dec. 16.

**Kaisan-dō** (Founder's Hall, Kamakura period, NT). Houses a portrait statue of **Rōben**, the first abbot of Tōdai-ji. The image is on view Dec. 16.

**Tamukeyama Hachiman-gū** (Shrine). A branch of Kyūshū's Usa-Hachiman, enlisted as Tōdai-ji's guardian shrine (see Kyūshū History, p. 469). The present hall dates from the Edo period. The grounds contain a subshrine, Sumiyoshi Jinja, which has a Kamakura-period Main Hall (ICP) and an 8th-C *azekura* storehouse (ICP).

**\*\* Kasuga Taisha (Shrine)** 春日大社 This celebrated shrine was founded in 709 by Fujiwara no Fuhito for the Fujiwara clan deity of Kashima Jingū (Kantō, p. 256), which was named the guardian of the new capital at Nara. Three other kami were also placed here, each in its own shrine. By one legend, Kasuga Taisha became affiliated with Kōfuku-ji when a priest dreamed that its kami appeared as a bosatsu and expressed a wish to become the guardian of the temple. Thus the shrine had early associations with Shinto-Buddhist syncretism. Later, the sacred deer, messengers of the Kasuga deities, appeared in mandala paintings of the shrine (see Art, p. 93). Their descendants still roam Nara Park.

The 1,300-meter-long shrine approach begins at Ichi no Torii. Worshippers over the centuries donated the thousands of stone lanterns lining the way and the bronze lanterns crowding the shrine cloister. The four shrines of the **Honden** (NT), built in Nagare style, are said to be faithful to their Heian-period form, though they were rebuilt every 20 years (a total of 57 times) until the Edo period.

Kasuga Taisha is a birthplace of dramatic arts: Gagaku and Bugaku, ancient court music and dances imported from Tang China, are still performed in shrine festivals. Noh drama was developed by KAN'AMI, a priest of the shrine, and his son, ZEAMI. The adjacent **Wakamiya Jinja**, consecrated to the child of a Kasuga kami, is renowned for the On-Matsuri, in which many ancient entertainments are offered to the kami. The **Hōmotsuden** (Treasure Hall) 宝物殿 exhibits objects given to the shrine or used in its ancient rites, including a pair of huge Gagaku drums and Bugaku masks. Hrs: 8:30–16:30. Nov.–Mar. 9:00–16:00.

395

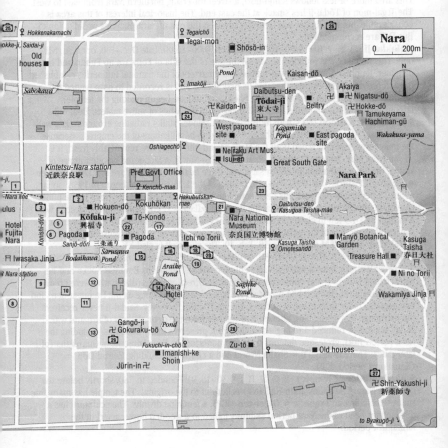

**South of Nara Park**

✦✦ **Shin-Yakushi-ji** 新薬師寺 Hrs: 8:30–17:30. In summer 8:30–18:00. Temple to the Buddha of Healing, built in 747 by Empress Kōmyō as an offering for the recovery of Emperor Shōmu. Once vast, the grounds have been reduced to a single city block. The ◆ **Main Hall** (8th C, NT), a building of classical purity, was formerly the refectory, the original Main Hall having been lost to lightning. Nara-period *oni-gawara* (demon tiles) survive on the roof. Inside the hall, faded paintings of the Buddhist pantheon can be discerned on the pillars. The main image of ◆ **Yakushi Nyorai** (NT), a wooden sculpture of the early Heian period, resembles a comic-book character. The halo of leaves and flames has a unique, archaic flavor; the miniature images in it represent Yakushi's other manifestations. Arrayed around Yakushi are the ◆ **Jūnishinshō** (11 are NT), clay images of twelve divine generals embodying Yakushi's twelve vows. They are protectors of Yakushi's Eastern Paradise.

**Byakugō-ji** 白豪寺 Hrs: 9:00–17:00. *0:10h walk SE of Shin-Yakushi-ji.* Fujiwara-period Amida Nyorai (ICP) and Kamakura-period Emma-ō (ICP). In the autumn, the precincts are abloom with bush clover.

✦ **Zu-tō** 頭塔 This 120-meter-high stupa mound of a Nara-period priest has three levels, each one covered with stone reliefs of Buddhist images, particularly Nyorai trinities.

✦✦ **Imanishi-ke Shoin** 今西家書院 (ca. Muromachi?, ICP) (23-2255). Hrs: 10:00–16:00 (enter by 15:30); clsd Th, Aug. 10–20, Dec. 21–Jan. 10. This lovely house belonged to Fukuchi-in, a nearby temple, but came into the possession of the Imanishi, wealthy saké brewers. Domestic structures of this period are rare. Here you can sit and drink coffee or tea in a quiet room beside a garden.

✦✦ **Jūrin-in** 十輪院 Hrs: 9:00–17:00; clsd Aug. 22–24, NY. This beautiful little temple was once part of Gangō-ji. The lovely Kamakura-period Main Hall (NT) is noted for its elegant *kaerumata* (frog-crotch struts). The temple is unique in Japan for its inner altar, a stone chamber (ICP) with reliefs of Jizō, Shaka, and Miroku Bosatsu.

✦ **Gangō-ji and Gokuraku-bō** 元興寺(極楽坊) Hrs: 9:00–17:00. Founded by Soga no Umako, Gangō-ji is among the oldest temples in Japan. It originally stood on the site of present-day Asuka-dera (S11) and was transferred to Nara in 718, where it became an official temple. All that remains of the original is the Zenshitsu hall (NT). Gangō-ji became an early center of Amidism in the 8th C when priest Chikō was directed in a dream to abandon scholarship and rely on faith in Amida alone. His quarters, thereafter called Gokuraku-bō (Paradise Quarters), developed into a separate temple. Its Main Hall (NT) dates from the Kamakura period. The Treasure Hall houses a famous miniature pagoda (8th C, NT).

**West Nara** (see map, p. 402)

This area more or less follows Ichijō-dōri, a street traversing northern Nara from east to west. The Tegai-mon of Tōdai-ji lies smack at the east end. The historical interest of this area is considerable, but visit it after you have already seen the rest of Nara. Bicycles or Teiki Kankō Bus D-1 are recommended.

✦ **Hokke-ji** 法華寺 Hrs: 9:00–16:30. Oct.–Feb. 9:00–16:00. Late Dec.–Feb. open Su, NH only. This nunnery was founded in 745 on the site of the villa of Fujiwara no Fuhito and his daughter, Empress Kōmyō, and was named headquarters of the national nunneries established in each province. The empress became its first abbess and is recorded to have tended the destitute and dying with her own hands. She is said to have begun making the temple's famous dog amulets, which the nuns still make from the ashes of votive tablets. Hokke-ji's ✦ **Jūichimen Kannon** (NT), with lotus leaves on slender stalks radiating around it, is a well-known early Heian image; each of the faces is said to be a likeness of the empress. Because the image was kept concealed until the Meiji period, the colors are remarkably fresh; it is shown from Mar. 20–Apr. 7, June 6–8, and Oct. 25–Nov. 8. A lacquered wooden image of Yuima, the great Mahayana Buddhist sage, and three heads of buddhas are ICP. Lovely garden.

✦ **Heijō-gū Palace Site** 平城宮跡 Excavation of the 1.25 sq km site began in 1958; so far about 25 percent of the work has been completed. The excavated sites are open to the public. One of the discoveries made was that the imperial palace was enclosed by an enormous wall, 5 m high and 4.5 km in circumference. The **Shiryōkan**資料館(museum), 500 m west of the site, exhibits models of the palace and artifacts recovered from the site. Museum Hrs: 9:00–16:00; clsd. M (Tu if M a NH), Dec. 18–Feb. 19. The site itself is clsd NY, F.

✦ **Saidai-ji** 西大寺 Hrs: 8:30–16:30. *0:05h walk SW of Kintetsu-Saidai-ji station* (S2). The Great Western Temple was built as a counterpart of Tōdai-ji by Empress Kōken and her priest friend Dōkyō. It was consecrated to the Four Directional Guardians, who were credited with quelling a rebellion. It had two Main Halls, each nearly as large as the Daibutsu-den, and two pagodas taller than those of Tōdai-ji. Unlike Tōdai-ji, however, Saidai-ji never received the patronage that would have allowed it to recover from the depredations of fire and war. Today, it is much reduced and neglected, though it preserves many treasures, including the Nara-period **Jaki**, grotesque demons trampled underfoot by Four Directional Guardians (of later date). There is also a fine Shaka Nyorai and a charming, childlike Zenzai Dōji (Kamakura period, ICP).

✦ **Akishino-dera** (Temple) 秋篠寺 Hrs: 9:30–16:30. Founded in 780, shortly before the court left Nara. The dainty Main Hall (NT) is faithful to the original. The temple has many fine statues, including an exquisite ◆ **Gigei-ten** (ICP), a feminine divinity. The sculpture has a dry-lacquer head of the Nara period skillfully joined to a wooden body carved in the Kamakura period.

**\*\* Yamato Bunkakan (Art Museum)** 大和文華館 (45-0544). Hrs: 10:00–17:00 (enter by 16:00); clsd M (except if a NH, then clsd Tu), NY. *Take the Kintetsu line to Gakuen-mae, then walk 0:10h.* The museum houses the superb Asian art collection of Ōita Torao, late president of Kintetsu, and puts on many fine shows. There is a dazzling exhibition, usually in autumn, of its NT and ICP. Well-known pieces include the Matsu'ura Screen (see Art, p. 98) and a *Nezame Monogatari* narrative scroll of the Heian period.

## Nishinokyō

*Two stops south of Saidai-ji by a Kintetsu local train.* Two extremely important temples, Yakushi-ji and Tōshōdai-ji, are a 0:05h walk from Nishinokyō station.

**\*\*\* Yakushi-ji** 薬師寺 Hrs: 8:30–17:00. This temple was founded at Fujiwara-kyō around 690 as an offering to the Buddha of Healing during an illness of Empress Jitō (see Hōryū-ji History, p. 400). It was transferred to Nara in 718 and is the most important repository of Hakuhō-period art and architecture. Its famed bronze Yakushi trinity and Shō-Kannon are pivotal works in Japanese art history (see Art, p. 91). The Kondō and West Pagoda were recently rebuilt in wood, at enormous expense and with as much fidelity to the originals as possible. With their crisply uptilted eaves and bright coats of paint, they seem gaudy now, but they are expected to acquire the patina and more gracefully set roof lines of their 1,200-year-old companions.

◆ **Kondō**. Houses the temple's principal images, the 8th-C bronze ◆ **Yakushi trinity** (NT), especially famous for the attendants, **Nikkō and Gakkō**, figures of breathtaking majesty, grace, and movement. Yakushi Nyorai is seated on a rectangular dais decorated with grapevines (a West Asian motif) and twelve barbarians, troll-like cavemen symbolizing Yakushi's twelve vows to save all beings (often represented by twelve divine generals). The **Kōdō** (Lecture Hall), an early Edo-period hall, houses a bronze Yakushi trinity (ICP) similar to the one in the Kondō.

◆ **Tōin-dō** (1285, NT). Houses a sublime bronze ◆ **Shō-Kannon** (early 8th C, NT). The hall also houses the ◆ **finial of the East Pagoda** (NT), a bronze openwork masterpiece of Hakuhō lyricism, showing slender heavenly musicians against a "water design," and a copy of the famous Nara-period **painting of Kisshō-ten** (NT), a feminine deity who grants fortune to followers of Buddha.

◆ **East Pagoda** (NT). This unusual and beautiful pagoda was built in 730, but it is considered the supreme example of the earlier Hakuhō style. It has three stories, with intermediate eaves (*mokoshi*) which give it the appearance of having six stories. The uneven eaves are proportioned to achieve an overall effect of lightness and balance. Its bronze finial is now in the Tōin-dō.

**Bussoku-dō.** Behind the west pagoda is this small hall containing a stone engraving of Buddha's footprint (753, NT), and a stone tablet (NT) bearing a Japanese poem written with Chinese characters used purely as phonetic symbols (*manyō-gana*) the earliest known example of its type.

**Treasure House.** Open Oct. 8–Nov. 10 and Jan. 1–15. Exhibits the famous Kisshō-ten painting and Shinto statues (NT) of Hachiman (Emperor Ōjin), Empress Jingū (his "mother"), and Nakatsu-hime (his consort), who were enlisted as divine protectors of the temple after a fire in 974. These are among the earliest works portraying Shinto kami as humans. **Hachiman Jinja** (1603, ICP), where they were enshrined, stands outside the South Gate.

**\*\*\* Tōshōdai-ji** 唐招提寺 Hrs: 8:30–16:30 (enter by 16:00). This is one of the most beautiful monasteries in Japan and, next to Hōryū-ji, the most impressive for the antiquity and integrity of its extant halls and images. The temple, named "Invited from Tang Temple," was founded by the Chinese priest Ganjin (688–763), who introduced the Ritsu sect. Around 735, Emperor Shōmu, disturbed by the lack of proper training of the clergy, directed two priests to travel to China and invite a master of monastic discipline to Japan. The two priests, who spent years searching, finally found their man in Ganjin, abbot of a great Chinese monastery. Five attempts to make the hazardous crossing failed, and an eye disease left him blind, but Ganjin finally arrived in Nara in 754. Soon after, he presided over a huge ordination ceremony at Tōdai-ji. In 759, the court gave the aging priest the land to build Tōshōdai-ji, where he spent his remaining years. Ganjin's reforms were aimed against the easy, splendor-loving ways of Nara Buddhism, and the sculpture at Tōshōdai-ji, done by Chinese sculptors who came with Ganjin, reflects this reaction. Gone is the gentle and seductive warmth of Nara art; in its place are images infinitely more aloof and unfathomable, demanding disciplined meditation. These presaged the Esoteric Buddhism that would dominate the Heian period (see Buddhism, pp. 34–36, and Art pp. 92–93).

◆ **Kondō** (NT). This magnificent classical hall, supreme example of Nara architecture, stands majestically at the head of the main approach. The front columns feature a slight entasis (swelling). The hall houses a large, dry-lacquer image of **Birushana** (NT), the Cosmic Buddha; the halo is studded with a thousand tiny Buddhas representing his infinite manifestations. On the right is a large standing Yakushi Nyorai, and on the left a 5-m-tall Senju (Thousand-armed) Kannon. Smaller images flanking Birushana are Bonten and Taishaku-ten, and the Shi-Tennō stand at the corners (all Nara period, NT). The image-filled hall was regarded as the abode of the Buddha; worshippers prayed outside.

◆ **Kōdō** (NT). Directly behind the Kondō. Moved from Heijō Palace, this is the only example left of Nara palace architecture. The roof is hip-and-gable, possibly the result

397

of later repairs (Nara architecture favored the plain hipped roof). The hall was used for lectures and assemblies, and houses an image of Miroku Nyorai (1287, ICP).

**Auxiliary buildings.** To the west are the Belfry and Kaidan, a three-tiered stone ordination platform built in 1284. To the east are the two-storied Korō (drum tower, NT) of the Kamakura period, and the long hall Higashimuro (Kamakura period, ICP), containing monks' quarters. Behind this hall are two *azekura* storehouses (8th C, NT), small versions of Tōdai-ji's famous Shōsō-in imperial repository.

◆ **Shin-Hōzō** (Museum). Open Mar. 18–May 20, Sept. 15–Nov. 5. Hrs: 8:30–16:00. This modern building to the east of the main halls houses many temple treasures. Highlights include a magnificent headless wooden standing Buddha (ICP) with richly swelling thighs and sharply chiseled robes exhibiting a major advance in wood sculpture technique, and a Dainichi Nyorai (Birushana).

**Ganjin's Tomb and Mie-dō.** In NE corner of precincts. The Mie-dō enshrines a celebrated ◆ **statue of Ganjin** (NT), said to have been carved just before his death. The serene portrait of the blind old priest is one of the earliest and greatest works of realism in Japanese art. Shown June 5–7, the anniversary of Ganjin's death.

## Walks and Explorations Near Nara

The hills around Nara offer rustic mountain scenery and are littered with ancient temples and stone buddhas.

**Gansen-ji** 岩船寺 **and ** Jōruri-ji** 浄瑠璃寺 *These two temples are on the Kasagi-bound bus route from Kintetsu Nara station; service is infrequent. To see just the temples, Teiki Kankō bus tours D-1 or D-2 are recommended.* Gansen-ji has a three-storied pagoda (1382, ICP) and a Fujiwara-period image of Amida (ICP) (Hrs: 8:00–18:00). A 2-km hiking path (1:00h) lined with ancient stone buddhas links Gansen-ji to Jōruri-ji (Hrs: 9:00–17:00. Dec.–Feb. 10:00–16:00. Clsd NH). This lovely and extraordinary temple is thought to have been founded in 1047 as a temple to Yakushi Nyorai; Jōruri is Yakushi's Eastern Paradise. In 1178, the three-storied pagoda (NT), where the Yakushi image is now housed, was moved from a temple in Kyoto. It faces westward across a pond to the ◆ **Main Hall** (1107, NT), which represents Amida's Western Paradise. The hall houses Nine Amidas (NT), each representing one of the nine stages of nirvana. Such arrays were popular in the Fujiwara period, but Jōruri-ji has the only surviving example. The boulder in the center of the pond is said to represent the present world, poised midway between the paradises of Yakushi and Amida.

**Enjō-ji** 円成寺 Hrs: 9:00–17:00. *From JR Nara station, 0:40h by Yagyū-bound bus to Nin'niku-zan, then 0:05h walk.* This isolated mountain temple, said to have been founded in 756, is popularly called Dainichi-ji because of its famous Dainichi Nyorai (ICP), sculpted by the young UNKEI. The Muromachi-period Hondō (ICP) also houses the main image of Amida (ICP). The temple pond is all that remains of a Heian-period paradise garden. Two shrines in the precincts, Kasuga-dō and Hakusan-dō, both NT, were built in 1228. From Enjō-ji, one can hike the **Takisaka Michi**, a 10-km (3:00h) trail to Nara, near Shin-Yakushi-ji. Parts of this path are stone-paved and lined with stone buddhas. Food is available near Enjō-ji and at an old teahouse en route.

## Nara Crafts and Shopping

*Narazuke* (Nara pickles) are Nara's single contribution to the culinary arts. Typically *uri*, a member of the melon family, is pickled in saké until it is a crisp, translucent brown. A few too many at lunch may make it hard to stay awake during the afternoon! *Sumi* (ink) and brushes, introduced with Buddhism, are famous.

1 * **Genrin-dō** 玄林堂　高天町 (63-0255). Hrs: 9:00–17:30; clsd Su, NH, NY. A venerable *sumi* maker. By appointment. (See Kobai-en, below.)

4 **Honda Seishi-en** 本田青篶園　東向商店街 (22-5297). Hrs: 9:30–18:00, clsd NY. Modern copies of Shōsō-in lacquerware. Y10,000 and up.

9 * **Kobai-en** 古梅園　椿井町 7 (23-2965). Hrs: 9:00–17:00; clsd Su, NH. This 14th-generation *sumi* maker, supplier to the imperial household, employs the ancient, painstaking process of collecting soot from tiny lamps of rapeseed oil. During the cooler months, visitors can visit the old-fashioned premises by appointment.

10 **Fujita Unkō-tei** 藤田芸香亭　西寺林町 (22-2082). Hrs: 11:00–18:30; clsd Th. Lacquerware.

11 **Monjuan** 文珠庵　西寺林町16 (22-4269). Hrs: 10:00–18:00; clsd Th (except if NH), NY. Antiques.

21 **Nagano Rokumeisō** 永野鹿鳴荘 (22-3893). Hrs: 10:00–17:00, daily. Beautiful black-and-white souvenir photos of Nara's treasures.

23 **Mori** (26-2063). Hrs: 8:00–17:00; clsd Tu (except if a NH), NY. Famous *narazuke* shop by Tōdai-ji's South Gate.

## Nara Dining

5 **Japanned** 小西町2-1 (22-1661). Hrs: 12:00–23:00; clsd Tu. Postmodern comes to Nara in this cheerfully trendy café-bar. Light food.

6 **Shizuka** 志津香　小西町 (22-8029). Hrs: 11:30–20:00; clsd Tu (M if Tu a NH). Cramped shop popular for *kamameshi* (rice casserole). *Teishoku* Y1400.

8 * **Ryōzanpaku** 梁山泊　西城戸町 (26-2523). Hrs: 17:00–23:30; clsd Su, NY, Bon. *Robata-yaki*. Extensive menu of seasonal specialties. Moderate.

(12) **Hirasō** 平宗　今御門町21 (22-0866). Hrs: 11:00–20:00; clsd M (Tu if M a NH). Take-out *kakinoha-zushi*, a delicious sushi of pickled mackerel wrapped in persimmon leaves. This is a time-honored method of preserving fish in the Yamato interior. Y750 per order.

(13) **Harishin** はり新　中新屋町15 (22-2669). Hrs: 11:30–15:30; clsd M (Tu if M a NH). *Bentō* Y2500 in a place reminiscent of an old post-town inn.

(17) ** **Yanagi Chaya** 柳茶屋　奈良公園興福寺隣 (22-7460). Hrs: 11:30–18:00; clsd W (Th if W a NH), except by reservation. An elegant teahouse, nearly 200 years old, with semi-private rooms arranged around lovely gardens. *Kaiseki* set menu from Y6000.

(19) **Umanome** 馬の目　荒池畔 (23-7784). Hrs: 11:30–15:00, 17:30–20:30; clsd Th, Su and NH evenings, and Aug. 1920s farmhouse with antique interior. Lunch: *sōzai teishoku* of 4–5 dishes, Y3500–4500; dinner (by reservation), Y15,000.

(22) * **Tō no Chaya** 塔の茶屋 (22-4348). Hrs: 11:30–18:30 (bentō until 16:00); clsd Tu. Quaint teahouse serving *chagayu* (rice gruel made with tea) in antique lacquer bowls. *Chagayu bentō* (Y2500) comes with soup and a dozen morsels of regional specialties.

(28) **Ukimidō** 浮見堂　高畑大道町1247 (26-4366). Hrs: 9:00–20:00; clsd 2nd and 4th F (except if NH), NY. Teahouse owned by a Japanese-American couple.

**Kusa-no-e** 草ノ戸 (33-3017). Hrs: 11:00–20:00; clsd W (except if W a NH, then clsd Th). A Yamato farmhouse east of Nishinokyō station. A nice *bentō* for Y2000.

**Ryūō-an** 龍王庵　唐招提寺南大門西側 (33-9676). Hrs: 10:00–18:00. Kissaten near Tōshōdai-ji.

## Nara Lodgings (TEL 0742)

(2) ** **Kasuga Hotel** 春日ホテル (22-4031). 40 Noboriōji-chō, Nara-shi. A ryokan. From Y15–20,000 w/meals.

(3) * **People's Inn Hanakomichi** ピープルズイン花小路　小西町23 (26-2646). 23 Konishi-chō. Business hotel with Japanese and Western rooms. Room Y5600 per person, Y11,000 w/meals.

(7) * **Hotel Fujita Nara** ホテルフジタ奈良 (23-8111). Fax 22-0255. 47-1 Shimosanjō-chō. Pleasant first-class hotel. Low season: S Y7–8000, Tw Y12,500–16,000. High season: S Y9–10,000, Tw Y14–18,000.

(14) ** **Nara Hotel** 奈良ホテル (26-3300). Fax 23-5252. 1096 Takabatake-chō. Famous old hotel with Japanese-Edwardian interior; now with a brand-new wing. Tw Y14,800–26,000.

(15) * **Kotton Hyakupāsento** 古っぽん100%　菩提町1122–21 (22-7117). 1122-21 Bodaiji-chō. Mini-hotel with cheery white clapboard exterior. Japanese or Western rooms. Y7500 w/meals per person.

(16) ** **Kikusuirō** 菊水楼 (23-2001). 1130 Takabatake-chō. Sumptuous old inn. Y30–60,000 w/meals.

(18) ** **Ryokan Edosan** 旅館江戸三　奈良公園 (26-2662). 1167 Takabatake-chō. Sukiya-style cottages in a grove on the edge of Nara Park. Built over 70 years ago; memorable atmosphere and fine cuisine. Nonflush plumbing (Tanizaki Junichirō would have approved). Y13–15,000 w/meals.

(20) **Aoba Chaya** 青葉茶屋　奈良公園 (22-2917). 1169 Takabatake-chō. Ryokan. Getting shabby, but nice location in Nara Park. Y10–13,000 w/meals.

(24) **Wakasa Ryokan** わかさ旅館　押上町14 (22-2228). 14 Oshiage-chō. Y6600–13,900 w/meals.

(25) **Nara YH** 奈良ユースホステル (22-3148). 1716 Hōren-chō. Fancy institution; members only. Y3250 w/meals.

(26) **Hotel Yamato Sansō** ホテル大和山荘 (26-1011). Fax 26-1016. 27 Kawakami-chō. Up a scenic drive starting near the Shōso-in. A hotel-ryokan fusion. Nice views; open-air bath. Y13,000 per person w/meals, Tw (w/o meals) Y12–15,000.

**Temple lodgings:** (27) **Shin-Yakushi-ji** 新薬師寺宿坊 (22-3736). 1352 Takabatakefuku-chō. Y4900 w/breakfast. (29) **Gangō-ji Gokurakubō** 元興寺極楽坊 (23-1378). 11 Nakanoin-chō. Clsd NY. Y4500 w/breakfast.

## KŌRIYAMA 郡山

*0:05h by Kintetsu-Kashihara line express from Saidai-ji (S2) to Yamato-Kōriyama, or 0:05h by JR line from Nara; the two stations are about 1 km apart.* Kōriyama had one of the few castles in the Yamato area; the ruins are just west of the Kintetsu tracks. About 0:15h west by bus from the Kintetsu station is the **Minzoku Hakubutsukan** (Folklore Museum); it has several fine preserved houses (Hrs: 9:00–17:00 (enter by 16:30); clsd M (Tu if M a NH), NY). On a nearby hill is **Yata-dera** 矢田寺, a rustic temple founded in 673. It has a popular Jizō statue which is celebrated on the 3rd Su in April with a procession of Jizō, demons, and bosatsu. Hydrangeas on the grounds bloom profusely in June. Temple lodgings at Kokuminshukusha Daimon-bō (07435-3-1445), and subtemples Nenbutsu-in (3-1522), Kita Sōbō (3-1531), and Minami Sōbō (2-3871). Y5000 w/2 vegetarian meals.

## S4 *** HŌRYŪ-JI 法隆寺

*From Kintetsu-Nara station, 0:55h by Ōji-bound bus, or 0:40h by Hōryū-ji-bound bus, get off at Hōryū-ji-mae. From JR Nara station, 0:12h by Kansai main line to Hōryū-ji. By taxi from Nara, 0:40h, Y4000.* Hrs: 8:00–17:00. Nov. 20–Mar. 10, 8:00–16:20. This most precious of Japan's temples contains the oldest wooden structures in the world and is a repository of early Buddhist art, heavily continental in influence, charming and archaic—exotic even to the Japanese. Hōryū-ji was founded in 607 as a seminary for SHŌTOKU TAISHI's followers, but many scholars now believe the first temple was destroyed in a fire and rebuilt in 710. Nevertheless, the architecture and art are considered to be true to the late Asuka period, the age of its founder.

## Calendar

**Feb. 3: ∗ Shuni-e.** At 20:00, in the Saien-dō, red, blue, and black *oni* (demons) appear with torches, as gongs and drums beat inside the hall. Taishaku-ten (one of the Four Guardian Kings) appears and drives them away.

**Apr. 11–May 5: Yumedono no Hibutsu.** Showing of the Guze Kannon.

**Oct. 22–Nov. 3: Yumedono no Hibutsu.** Showing of the Guze Kannon.

## Getting Around

The JR station is 0:04h by bus or 0:10h on foot from the temple. There are rent-a-cycles at the station.

# Hōryū-ji History: Shōtoku Taishi and the Flowering of Japanese Buddhism

| | |
|---|---|
| **Shōtoku Taishi** | (572–621) Viewed as the father of Japanese Buddhism and the Japanese state. An enduring culture hero. |
| **Nakatomi no Kamatari** | (614–669) Founder of the Fujiwara family. |

400

When SHŌTOKU TAISHI's mother was seized with birth pangs, she fled to the stables to avoid polluting the imperial palace with the act of childbirth. The infant's unusual entry into the world, distantly echoing the Nativity of Christ, marked the beginning of a brilliant career. According to legend, the young prince could speak as soon as he was born and read the Chinese classics at an early age. From childhood, he was deeply interested in the Buddhist scriptures and studied them with a Korean monk. Thanks to his talent and family connections—his father was Emperor Yōmei, his mother a Soga—he was appointed regent in 593. Shōtoku promulgated reforms that began the transformation of Japan into a nation-state with a culture that could impress visitors from abroad. In 600, the Japanese sent their first official embassy to China. However, it was not Shōtoku's statecraft but his genuine devotion to Buddhism that gives him the stature of a beloved saint. Until recently, his portrait graced the face of the 10,000-yen bill, Japan's highest denomination.

Shōtoku declared Buddhism the state religion of Japan. For the imperial house and its supporters, Buddhism pointed the way toward breaking the power of the clans. The emperor was to be the Buddha's agent in Japan, with a hierarchy of court officials serving him; even the kami were his servants. These were radical reforms for a land which was still a chaotic confederacy of jealous, bickering clans. Attitudes about government must have been basic indeed, judging by the famous Constitution of Seventeen Articles, a document believed to reflect Shōtoku's ideals. Article three enjoins: "When the Lord speaks, the Vassal listens." In anticipation of initiating diplomatic relations with China, Shōtoku created a system of court ranks and wrote two histories of Japan with his mentor, **Soga no Umako** (see Asuka History, p. 407), so that Japan could no longer be scorned for backwardness. Shōtoku sponsored the building of important state temples such as Shitennō-ji, which was situated near Naniwa (Ōsaka) Bay so that its splendid pagoda would be the first landmark sighted by arriving Chinese envoys.

No place, however, is more intimately associated with Shōtoku Taishi than the hallowed temple of **Hōryū-ji.** Hōryū-ji is located in the village of Ikaruga, birthplace of Shōtoku's favorite consort, where the prince retreated in his later years to study the sutras. On the grounds of his palace there, he founded a small seminary for his followers and commissioned TORI BUSSHI to sculpt an image of Yakushi Nyorai, Buddha of Healing, in memory of his father, Emperor Yōmei. After Shōtoku's death at age forty-nine, Tori was commissioned to create a splendid bronze Shaka trinity, which is housed alongside the Yakushi in the Kondō (Image Hall). It was said that this bronze bore a likeness to Shōtoku, and people believed the prince had been reborn as a Buddha. The man who created these immortal works was of Korean descent and is the earliest artist in Japan whose name is on record (he signed his pieces).

Hōryū-ji became the center for a cult of Shōtoku. Nearly a century after his death, the **Yumedono,** or Hall of Dreams, was erected on the spot where he was said to have dreamed of an old man who explained the meanings of some knotty scriptural passages. This hall became the focus of Shōtoku worship. As the cult spread, images of the infant Shōtoku, hands pressed together in prayer, became associated with fertility and the harvest. Although the prince's memory is venerated to this day, his progeny did not escape persecution. Shōtoku's son Yamashiro was named crown prince, but this was opposed by Soga no Emishi and his son Iruka, who had succeeded to the Soga clan leadership after Umako's death. The problem was that Yamashiro did not have a Soga mother. Yamashiro retreated to Hōryū-ji, and Iruka, worried that the prince would foment a rebellion, sent troops to crush him. The prince and his family, finding themselves besieged, committed suicide in the pagoda of Hōryū-ji, bringing the Shōtoku line to an abrupt end. Soon after, the Soga began openly to aspire to imperial power. They built moated palaces, took to calling themselves by royal titles, and employed fearsome Kyūshū aborigines as bodyguards.

At this juncture, **Nakatomi no Kamatari**, chief of one of the clans ousted a generation earlier by Soga no Umako, was in "retirement," secretly hatching a plot with Prince Naka no Ōe to overthrow the Soga. The two met over a game of kickball at Tōnomine, a mountain near Asuka, and took to studying Chinese texts together, which allowed them to meet frequently without arousing suspicion. In 645, they made their move. Iruka was murdered in the presence of the empress, and she was forced to abdicate. Naka no Ōe became crown prince. Kamatari was awarded a new family name, FUJIWARA, "Wisteria Grove," after the place where he and Naka no Ōe had supposedly strolled while "studying" together. The Fujiwara would remain the most powerful court family for the next five hundred years.

In 646, the government announced the **Taika Reform**, an ambitious group of edicts that in theory made all of Japan the property of the emperor, who would appoint governors to administer the provinces. One of the first tasks of the Reform was to establish a permanent capital. There were short-lived attempts to build a city at Naniwa (in Ōsaka) and at Fujiwara-kyō (near Asuka). The influence of Shinto, which in the past had proscribed permanent capitals, was clearly on the wane. Empress Jitō, who reigned at Fujiwara-kyō, was the first ruler to follow Buddhist custom and be cremated.

401

Fujiwara-kyō, though carefully planned, proved unsatisfactory; perhaps it was too small to accommodate a growing Chinese-style bureaucracy. After only fifteen years, a decision was made to move the capital north to a much larger site with better links to the provinces, over which the court was now trying to establish firm governance. This was Heijō-kyō, better known as Nara.

## Hōryū-ji Sights

**\*\*\* Sai-in (West Temple).** This is the temple founded by Shōtoku Taishi. It is the most famous part of Hōryū-ji. When first built, it was laid out in continental style, with the main halls aligned on a north-south axis, the pagoda taking precedence. The Kondō housed an image of Yakushi Nyorai dedicated to the memory of Shōtoku's father, Emperor Yōmei, and a Shaka dedicated to Shōtoku. After a fire around 670, the halls were rebuilt, probably in 710, and the ground plan altered to place the Kondō and pagoda on an equal footing, side by side, perhaps as a way of paying homage to Shōtoku Taishi. It is this complex that is the present West Temple.

The first gate, **Nandai-mon** (NT), was rebuilt in the Muromachi period. The approach leads to the **Chū-mon** (Middle Gate, ca. 710, NT), which houses two **Kongō Rikishi** (NT), guardians of the Buddhist universe. It is built into the cloister surrounding the main halls. The columns of the Chū-mon and cloister show entasis, a gentle swelling in the middle to produce an illusion of perfect parallelism. The layout of the *garan* is brilliantly balanced: the pagoda is approximately twice as tall as the Kondō, and the two structures occupy approximately the same volume of space. The east side of the cloister is one bay longer, to accommodate the Kondō. The back of the cloister was extended, probably in the late 10th C, to incorporate the belfry, sutra repository, and Dai-Kōdō (lecture hall).

◆ **Pagoda** (NT). Each floor is smaller than the one beneath it, so that the topmost has half the dimensions of the first; the effect is an impression of stability and an illusion of greater height. The ornamental cloud brackets and broken-swastika motif on the railings are characteristic of Hōryū-ji; these motifs are rare in Japanese temples, and are seen primarily in the few that received direct continental influence, such as Mampuku-ji (S1). The support posts beneath the eaves, decorated with climbing dragons, were added in the Edo period; after a thousand years, the deep eaves of the roof had begun to sag precariously. The pagoda houses ◆ **scenes from the life of Shaka**, sculpted in clay. On the north, disciples mourn Shaka's death; on the west, they divide Shaka's relics; on the south is the world of Miroku, Buddha of the Future; on the west is the famous debate between Yuima and Shaka's disciple, Monju. Yuima was a great lay philosopher of Mahayana doctrine who, instead of withdrawing to a monastery, chose to live among ordinary people. Likewise, Shōtoku Taishi chose to remain in government in order to promulgate Buddha's teaching throughout the land.

◆ **Kondō** (Image Hall, NT). This hall has an unusually steep hip-and-gable roof. Echoing the pagoda, its upper story is much smaller than the first, and the eaves are very deep; it too has the cloud brackets and broken-swastika ornamentation. The splendid paintings of Buddhist deities on the interior walls had been compared to the Ajanta cave paintings in India; they were destroyed by fire in 1949. The walls now bear reproductions. The Kondō houses a large podium representing Mt. Sumeru, the central mountain of the Buddhist cosmos. Upon it are the famous bronze images of ◆ **Yakushi** (date unknown, NT), thought to be a copy by the Tori school of sculptors, and ◆ **Shaka Trinity** (623, NT) by Tori Busshi. They are stylistically very similar to the stone statuary of Chinese Northern Wei; the flat folds and frontal orientation suggest an effort to reproduce a stone relief in bronze, without exploiting the more plastic capabilities of the latter. Nevertheless, their idealized purity and benevolence (that archaic smile!) make them most appealing. The **Shi-Tennō** (Four Directional Guardians, NT), the oldest in Japan, also show an archaic stiffness. The west and central canopies (Hakuhō period, ICP) over the main images are decorated with charming heavenly musicians.

**Dai-Kōdō** (Lecture Hall, NT). Rebuilt in 990. Houses a fine wooden Yakushi trinity (NT) of the same period.

**\*\*\* Daihōzōden (Treasure Hall)** 大宝蔵殿 Treasures accumulated by Hōryū-ji over the centuries are shown in this musty museum. The ◆ **Kudara (Paekche) Kannon** (NT) is of obscure origin and unique in Japanese art. The wooden image is curiously elongated to create an impression of gentle omniscience. The Yumetagae (Dream-changing) Kannon (NT) is a small Nara-period bronze with sunny features who changes bad dreams into good. Tamamushi-zushi (altar, NT) is named for inlays (long rotted away) of the iridescent wings of *tamamushi* (jewel beetle); the right panel is painted in lacquer with a barely discernible scene of Shaka (in a previous life) plunging from a cliff so that a starving tigress could feed on his corpse. Tachibana Shrine (NT) contains a bronze Amida trinity; each figure sits on a long-stemmed lotus.

**\*\*\* Tō-in (East Temple).** Completed in 739 on the site of Shōtoku's residence to appease his soul for the extermination of his family. The ◆ **Yumedono** (NT), or Hall of Dreams, is the oldest octagonal hall in Japan. It is said to stand on the site of Shōtoku Taishi's chapel and study, where a golden figure would appear to him in his dreams to explain the meaning of some difficult sutras. The hall houses a famous image, the ◆ **Guze Kannon** (NT), which became the focus for a cult of Shōtoku. The image was concealed under layers of wrapping until 1884, when it was brought to light by Ernest Fenellosa, the pioneering scholar of Japanese art. It can be seen dimly in the dark hall Apr. 11–May 5, and Oct. 22–Nov. 3.

**\*\*\* Chūgū-ji** 中宮寺 Hrs: 9:00–16:15. Oct. 1–Mar. 20, 9:00–15:45. This nunnery was the residence of Shōtoku's mother and houses (in an uninspired modern hall) a celebrated ◆ **Miroku Bosatsu** (NT), a time-burnished image of the Bosatsu of the Future sitting crosslegged, pondering ways to save humanity. The slight, ethereal figure, exuding unbounded innocence and compassion, is one of the most affecting works of religious art. It is remarkably similar to an image at Kōryū-ji in Kyoto (p. 357), but though the Kōryū-ji statue is acknowledged to be Korean, this image is claimed to be of Japanese origin. The nunnery also shows a copy of the **Tenjukoku Mandala** (NT), an embroidered tapestry said to have been ordered by Shōtoku's widow, Tachibana no Iratsume. It depicts the prince in paradise.

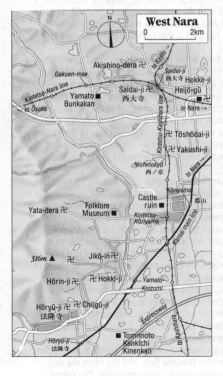

## Nearby Attractions

**\*\* Hōrin-ji** 法輪寺 Hrs: 8:00–17:00. *0:15h on foot from the Tō-in.* Said to have been founded in 622 by Yamashiro no Ōe, eldest son of Shōtoku Taishi. Its small size suggests that it was a family temple. The temple was arranged like the present Hōryū-ji. The pagoda was destroyed by lightning in 1944, but the Treasure House has a choice collection of sculpture, including an archaic-style wood **Kokuzō Bosatsu** (7th C, ICP) and late Heian-period images of Kisshō-ten, Shō-Kannon, Bishamon-ten, and Jūichimen Kannon.

**\*\* Hokki-ji** 法起寺 Hrs: 8:00–16:30. *0:10h on foot from Hōrin-ji.* This small walled temple, standing amid rice paddies, was established in 638 by Yamashiro no Ōe. Its layout is the mirror-image of Hōryū-ji. The dainty, three-storied ◆ **pagoda** (NT) is said to have been completed in 706, making it possibly the oldest wooden structure in the world. Like the Hōryū-ji pagoda, it has cloud brackets.

**\*\* Jikō-in** 慈光院 (0743-53-3004) Hrs: 9:00–17:00. In summer 8:30–17:00. *0:20h on foot from Hokki-ji.* A Zen temple with lovely thatched *shoin* (ICP) and the tea arbor Kōrin-an (ICP), looking out on a beautiful dry garden and distant view of the Yamato plain. Buildings and garden were designed by an Edo-period tea man. *Matcha* is included with the Y800 admission. *Soba* available; also, by reservation, special *bentō* (Y5000) and *shōjin-ryōri* (Y2500, Y5000, and Y8000).

**\*\* Tomimoto Kenkichi Kinenkan (Memorial Gallery)** 富本憲吉記念館 安堵村東安堵 (0743-57-3300). Hrs: 10:00–17:00 (enter by 16:30); clsd Tu (except if NH), Aug. 1–9, Dec. 21–Jan. 4. *0:10h by taxi from Hōryū-ji.* A collection of porcelains by Tomimoto Kenkichi (1886–1963), a leading member of the folk-art movement (see Crafts, p. 103). The pieces are exhibited in his studio, a traditional Yamato house. Tomimoto worked not in the "folk craft" stoneware of his better-known colleagues, Hamada Shōji and Kawai Kanjirō, but in porcelain, often decorated with overglaze enamels, gold, and silver. Special exhibition Oct.–Dec.

## Hōryū-ji Dining and Lodgings (TEL 07457)

① **Hanagaran** 花伽藍 (4-5547). Hrs: 8:30–18:00. Tearoom and gallery near the foot of the approach to Hōryū-ji. *Teishoku* Y1000.

② **Ryokan Ukawaya** 旅館卯川屋 (4-2136). 1308 Hōryū-ji, Ikaruga-chō, Nara-ken. Simple inn near Hōryū-ji. Y7–12,000 w/meals.

## S5 YAMATO-YAGI 大和八木

*0:22h by Kintetsu express from Saidai-ji (S2), or 0:45h by limited express from Kyoto. Junction to the Kintetsu line to Ise (Chūbu, p. 307) via Sakurai, Hase, and Murō-ji.*

**\*\*\* Imai-chō** 今井町 *One stop S of Yamato-Yagi, at Yagi-Nishiguchi, then 0:10h walk; from the station, head south, then west, crossing two sets of tracks and the river. Just across the bridge is the northeast corner of Imai-chō.* This astonishingly well-preserved merchant town developed as a fortified, self-governing community in the mid-16th C, centered around Shōnen-ji, a temple of the militant, virtually autonomous Jōdo Shin sect. The sect was one of ODA NOBUNAGA's sworn enemies (see Kyoto History, p. 322); he would have destroyed the town had not an Imai merchant, a member of his tea circle, intervened. The townsmen, in return, had to agree to tear down the walls and moat encircling Imai (traces can still be seen). Even without these defenses, however, the tightly knit community prospered. It was said that "seven-tenths of Yamato's gold is in Imai."

Today, after 400 fire-free years, Imai's original plan remains intact. The rectangular town is formed of row upon row of white-plastered, tile-roofed merchant houses, in neat blocks slightly staggered for defense; 80 percent of the buildings date from the Edo period. Of the eight most valuable houses (ICP), seven are open to the public (Hrs: 10:00–12:00, 13:00–17:00, admission charged). The grandest, **Imanishi-ke**, is open only Apr. 15–May 14 and Oct. 15–Nov. 14; Hrs: 9:00–17:00. These houses are classic *machiya* (see Villages, p. 54). Imai-chō has no tourist facilities.

## S6 \* SAKURAI 桜井

*0:05h from Yamato-Yagi (S5) by Kintetsu line; or 0:30h from Nara (S3) by JR Sakurai line.* The town itself is of little interest, but the surrounding area is rich in cultural relics. Tanzan Jinja is an excellent gateway to the Asuka plain (S11).

### Calendar

**Jan. 1:** \* **Miwa Nyōdō-sai.** Ōmiwa Jinja. People gather to receive a bit of purified New Year's fire to take home.

**Apr. 18: Hanashizume.** Sai Jinja. Lilies are offered at the shrine in a 2,000-year-old festival to avert disaster and clean the air.

**Nov. (2nd Su): Kemari.** Tanzan Jinja. Men in court costume reenact the kickball game at which Nakatomi no Kamatari and Naka no Ōe met. From 11:00.

### Sacred Mt. Miwa

**\*\* Miwa Myōjin (Ōmiwa Jinja)** 三輪明神 *0:07h by bus from Sakurai station, or 0:10h on foot from JR Miwa station.* Considered the oldest shrine in Japan, established around the 2nd century B.C., long before the arrival of the imperial clan in Yamato. The handsome structure in the shrine court is the Haiden (ICP), or oratory; there is no hall to house the kami because the kami dwells on the mountain itself; according to an ancient legend, it appears in the form of a snake.

403

\* **Sai Jinja** 狭井神社 *0:05h on foot by a pleasant path from Miwa Myōjin*. This quiet shrine is said to stand on the site of the palace of Jimmu, the mythical first emperor of Japan. There is a sacred medicinal well on the grounds. One can apply at the shrine office to climb sacred Mt. Miwa (2:00h round trip). The trail is steep and rough, with lush greenery and rushing streams. At the summit are large boulders and trees roped off by *shimenawa*, an example of the ancient Shinto archetype of delimiting sacred objects or spaces without constructing a shrine to house them in.

\* **Kanaya no Sekibutsu** 金屋石仏 *0:10h on foot S of Miwa Myōjin*. A pair of large stone reliefs of a standing Shaka Nyorai and Miroku Nyorai, thought to date from the Kamakura period. Beneath the small concrete shelter is a mysterious sarcophagus of red stone.

### Toward Tōnomine and Tanzan Jinja

\*\* **Shōrin-ji** 聖林寺 Hrs: 9:00–17:00. *0:10h by Tōnomine/Tanzan Jinja bus; get off at Shōrin-ji-mae, walk 0:05h*. The temple has sublime \* **Shō-Kannon** (NT), a masterpiece of 8th-C sculpture.

\*\*\* **Tanzan Jinja** 談山神社 Hrs: 8:30–16:30. *Near the summit of Mt. Tōnomine, 0:25h by bus from Sakurai station, then 0:15h on foot. From here, a 1:30h walk (highly recommended) leads to Ishibutai, in Asuka* (S11). Tanzan Jinja enshrines Nakatomi no Kamatari, founder of the great FUJIWARA family. Tanzan means Mt. Conversation, and it was supposedly here that Kamatari and Naka no Ōe met over a game of kickball; they later plotted the downfall of the Soga clan and promulgated the epoch-making Taika Reform of 646 (see Hōryū-ji History, p. 400). Kamatari's son had his father's grave moved to the mountain and had a 13-story pagoda erected. The present, Sung Chinese-style pagoda (1532, ICP) is a dainty structure, strikingly lovely, with 13 cypress-shingled roofs. The grounds are brilliant with foliage in autumn. The famous kickball game is reenacted on the second Sunday in November.

### Sakurai Lodgings (TEL 07444)

**Kaika-rō** 皆花楼　本町 (2-2016). Honmachi, Sakurai-shi, Nara-ken. *0:03h walk from Sakurai station*. Simple, traditional ryokan. Y6000 w/meals.

## FROM SAKURAI TOWARD ISE

### S7 \* HASE-DERA 長谷寺

*0:15h by local Kintetsu train from Yamato-Yagi* (S5), *then 0:20h on foot via an atmospheric road lined with inns and shops*. Hrs: Apr.–June 8:00–17:00. July–Sept. 8:30–17:00. Oct.–Mar. 9:00–16:30. Hase has been considered an abode of souls of the dead since antiquity, and a temple was founded here around 686. In 727, Emperor Shōmu ordered a Kannon statue installed here. According to legend, the location of a sacred camphor tree was revealed to a priest, Tokudō Shōnin, in a dream, and a huge image of Jūichimen (Eleven-headed) Kannon was carved from it in three days. Tokudō Shōnin founded western Japan's 33 Kannon Temple Pilgrimage, and Hase-dera became popular with Heian court ladies and gentlemen on their way to worship at the Kumano shrines to the south (see Villages, p. 56). Today, pilgrims follow their footsteps, mounting the interminable covered staircase up the mountainside; though it is gently graded, climbing it is an act of penance. In spring, peonies line the way. At the top is the Kannon Hall, built on stilts. Inside is the image of Kannon (ICP), an 8-m gilded colossus; the present one was carved in 1538. The veranda offers a wonderful view out over the valley.

### S8 \*\* MURŌ-JI 室生寺

*0:25h from Yamato-Yagi* (S5) *by Kintetsu local and some expresses to Murōguchi-Ōno station, then 0:20h by bus. From Hase-dera, the easiest way is by taxi (under Y2000)*. Hrs: Mar. 1–Apr. 10 and Oct. 1–Nov. 30 8:00–16:30 (Su and NH 8:00–17:00). Apr. 11–Sept. 30 8:00–17:00. (Su and NH 8:00–18:00). Dec. 1–Feb. 8:00–16:00. This Shingon temple, with its exquisite halls and images, all intact from the early Heian period, is one of the most precious relics of Esoteric Buddhism in Japan. On the way to Murō-ji from the station, pause by **Ōno-dera** 大野寺 *(0:05h on foot from the station)* to see its 11.5-m image of Miroku carved into a cliff face.

Murō-ji's origins are as misty as the forested mountain slope on which it stands. Though popular tradition holds that KŪKAI founded it, this is in fact not so. It seems that quite early, a temple was built here in syncretic affiliation with the shrine of a dragon deity, a rain god that is still enshrined at **Ryūketsu Jinja** 竜穴神社 , or Dragon Hole Shrine, about 1 km upstream along the Murōgawa. Toward the close of the Nara period, the temple was enlarged and became associated with Nara's Kōfuku-ji, supposedly after prayers were successfully offered here for the recovery of the crown prince—the future Emperor Kammu. The remote mountain retreat attracted reclusive holy men and became a center of Esoteric teachings. It wasn't until 1694, however, that it formally became a Shingon temple when Shogun Tsunayoshi's mother, Keishō-in (see Tokyo History, p. 195), a compulsive builder of temples, ordered Murō-ji to separate from Kōfuku-ji. It was at this time too that it became known as the "Women's Kōya," because unlike Kōya-san (KINKI II:S1), women were allowed within its precinct.

Cross the arched bridge, pay admission at the abbot's quarters, and proceed through the large Niō gate. The Kamakura-period Miroku-dō on your left houses a Miroku Bosatsu (ICP) and a seated image of ◆ **Shaka Nyorai** (NT), masterpieces of early Heian art. The carved wooden images display a remote dignity, but there is great lyrical beauty in the sharply chiseled, eddying folds of the robes. On the next level up is the ◆ **Kondō** (NT), also of the early Heian period, although the front part, on stilts, was added in the Edo period as an Esoteric Buddhist *gejin* (see Buddhism, p. 36). The hall houses a **standing Shaka** (NT), flanked on the left by Monju (ICP) and a superb **Jūichimen Kannon** (NT), and on the right by Yakushi (ICP) and Jizō (ICP), all of the Heian period. In front are smaller images of the Jūnishinshō (12 divine generals, Kamakura period, ICP). The images have beautifully painted haloes of wood. The back wall is painted with a **Taishaku-ten Mandala** (NT), showing Taishaku-ten (Indra) surrounded by other divinities of the *ten* class. Behind the Kondō and to the right is a memorial stupa to Keishō-in. Directly ahead is the Kamakura-period **Hondō** (NT), housing an image of **Nyoirin Kannon** (NT). Just behind it is Murō-ji's famous ◆ **five-storied pagoda** (late 8th–early 9th C, NT), the smallest and most beautifully proportioned in Japan. From here, it is a steep climb up 400 stone steps to the **Mie-dō** (Kamakura period, ICP), the inner sanctuary of Murō-ji, where Kūkai is enshrined.

### Murō-ji Dining and Lodgings
∗ **Pension Mahoroba** ペンションまほろば　榛原町下井足 (07458-2-5603). Shimoidani, Haibara-chō, Uda-gun, Nara-ken. *Near Haibara station, between Hase-dera and Murō-ji stations.* The house is new, but the old gate and living room hearth set an antique tone. First-floor rooms look onto lovely gardens. Y7500 w/meals (no bath), Y9500 w/meals (w/bath).
∗ **Hashimotoya** 橋本屋 (07459-3-2056). Murō, Murō-mura, Uda-gun. Old inn by the Murō-ji bridge. *Sansai-ryōri.* Y11–14,000 w/meals; *teishoku* lunch, Y2000.

### S9 ∗ IGA-UENO　伊賀上野
*To Iga-Kanbe station, 0:40h from Yamato-Yagi (S5), or 0:40h from Ise/Uji-Yamada (CHŪBU IV:S2) by Kintetsu express. By JR, 1:00h from Nara to Iga-Ueno station. Iga-Kanbe and Iga-Ueno stations are linked to Ueno-shi station, nearest Ueno Park, by a rather infrequent local service. By taxi, Ueno Park is 0:05h from Iga-Kanbe, or 0:10h from Iga-Ueno.* This small provincial castle town was the hometown of the celebrated haiku poet MATSUO BASHŌ (1644–1694) and the infamous *ninja*, acrobatic spies of Japan's medieval era. Bashō, born into a poor samurai household, was raised as a companion to the local daimyo's son, with whom he first began writing haiku. The young lord, however, died at the age of 23. The heartbroken Bashō left Iga-Ueno and dedicated his life to raising haiku to the status of true literature. He traveled widely, usually in the guise of a pilgrim, and wrote haiku-studded accounts of his travels that have become classics of Japanese literature.

### Calendar
**Oct. 23–25:** ∗ **Ueno Tenjin Matsuri.** Sugawara Jinja. There is a parade on the 25th of *mikoshi*, floats, the Seven Lucky Gods, and 100 demons, wearing fascinating old masks. Dates from the late 1500s.

### Iga Ueno Sights
Many of Iga-Ueno's attractions are in Ueno Kōen, a park centered around Iga-Ueno's reconstructed castle.
∗ **Basho Ōu Kinenkan** 芭蕉翁記念館 Hrs: 8:30–17:00; clsd M, Th p.m., day after NH. A modern museum exhibiting items connected with Bashō. On the north side of the grounds stands the Haisei-den, an octagonal, two-storied folly (built 1942) modeled on the figure of Bashō dressed as a pilgrim (the upper roof is his broad-brimmed hat).
∗∗ **Ninja Yashiki** 忍者屋敷 Hrs: 9:00–17:00; clsd NY. A house formerly belonging to an Iga *ninja* clan. Local girls (in incongruous rose-pink *ninja* outfits) demonstrate the uses of various deadly *ninja* gadgets that are on display. Touristy, but fun. Iga and nearby Kōga were two leading centers of *ninjutsu* (*ninja* arts). Included in the admission is the nearby **Oni-gyōretsu Hozonkan** 鬼行列保存館, a former rice storehouse exhibiting masks and costumes used in the Tenjin Matsuri (see Calendar). Of the 100 masks, most date from the Edo period, but some go back to the Momoyama period.
**Basho Ōu Seika** 芭蕉翁生家 Hrs: 8:30–17:00, clsd Tu, NY. This is the house where Bashō was born in 1644.
∗∗ **Old Town.** Several streets south of the tracks, there are several old samurai houses.
**Minomushi-an** 蓑虫庵 Hrs: 8:30–17:00; clsd day after NH, NY. All his life, Bashō favored living in tea arbors; this one was built for him by his biographer and disciple, Hattori Tohō.

### Iga Crafts
**Iga-Shigaraki Kotō-kan** 伊賀信楽古陶館 Hrs: 9:00–17:00; clsd NY. Right by Ueno-shi station. Gallery of Iga-yaki and the similar Shigaraki-yaki, a burnt-looking earthenware, fired repeatedly to produce heavy ash glazing. The second-floor museum shows old Iga-yaki and Shigaraki-yaki (admission charged).
**Iga Kumihimo Center** 伊賀くみひもセンター (23-8038). Hrs: 9:00–17:00; clsd M, NY. *2km S of Ueno-shi station on Ginza-dōri.* Iga-Ueno produces 90 percent of Japan's *kumihimo*, complex braided silk cords that were used on armor, swords, and sutra scrolls. Today, *kumihimo* is used as a decorative cord to fasten the *obi* (sash) of a kimono.

**Iga-Ueno Dining and Lodgings** (TEL 0595)

\* **Wakaya** わかや (21-4068). Hrs: 10:30–15:00; clsd M, NY. Charcoal-grilled *dengaku*, tofu broiled with miso. Y500 per serving.

\* **Kanaya** 金谷 (21-0105). Hrs: 11:00–21:00; clsd M (except if a NH), NY. A famous old restaurant serving Iga beef dishes. Sukiyaki, butter-yaki, or *teppan-yaki*. From Y6400.

\* **Honjin Konnyakuya** 本陣こんにゃく屋 (23-3011). Hrs: 11:00–15:00; clsd M, NY. Cuisine of *konnyaku*, a rubbery-textured starch, prepared in an amazing variety of ways. By reservation. Course, Y3–4000.

**Kitamuraya** 北村屋 相生町2789 (21-0266). 2789 Kajimachi, Ueno-machi, Mie-ken. Family ryokan. Y6000 w/breakfast, Y8500 w/2 meals.

**Easy Access To:**

\*\*\* **Nara** (KINKI I:S3): 1:00h by JR express from Iga-Ueno.

\*\*\* **Ise** (CHŪBU IV:S2): 1:30h by Kintetsu express from Iga-Kanbe.

# FROM YAMATO-YAGI SOUTH TO YOSHINO

## S10 \* KASHIHARA JINGŪ-MAE 橿原神宮前

*0:30h by Kintetsu express from Saidai-ji (S2), or 0:50h by limited express from Kyoto. Junction for the Kintetsu Minami-Ōsaka line to Taima-dera.* A base for exploring the Asuka region. Bicycles can be rented here and dropped off in Asuka (see below for details). Lodgings and eating facilities are better here.

\*\* **Nara Prefectural Archeological Museum (Kenritsu Kashihara Kōko Hakubutsukan** 奈良県立橿原考古博物館 (4-1101). Hrs: 9:00–17:00 (enter by 16:30); clsd M (also Tu if M a NH), NH (except during special exhibition), NY. *0:15h walk from station, or 0:03h walk from Unebi-Goryō-mae station (one stop north of Kashihara).* An excellent museum on the material excavated from sites in the district. Large *haniwa*, bronzes, and other artifacts (real and reproductions) are displayed in bright, airy surroundings.

\*\* **Kashihara Jingū (Shrine)** 橿原神宮 *0:10h walk from station.* A spacious shrine built in 1889 to enshrine Japan's first emperor, the mythical Jimmu, who is said to be buried in the nearby tumulus (as determined in 1863). The timbers for the impressive buildings were taken from the Imperial Palace in Kyoto. This is among the most attractive State Shinto shrines (see Shinto, p. 29). A pleasant place to end the day after touring the nearby sights. Grand festivals Feb. 11, Apr. 3.

## S11 \*\* ASUKA 飛鳥

*From Kyoto or Nara, take the Kintetsu express to Kashihara-Jingū-mae (S10), and transfer to a local to Asuka, 2 stops south. Or walk down from Tanzan Jinja in Sakurai (S6).*

> Among Yamato's clustered hills
> It is close-by Ama no Kaguyama
> That I climb and stand to view the land.
> Here and there curls of smoke rise from the plain
> And gulls take wing from the lakes, endlessly—
> Yes, a sweet country it is
> This dragonfly isle, this land of Yamato.
>
> —Emperor Jomei (A.D. 593–641)

The Asuka plain, the heartland of Yamato, remains one of the most poetically lovely and historically beguiling places in Japan. In this one small area, amid paddy fields and farm villages, one can witness the great transformation that took place in Japan in the seventh century.

### Calendar

Asuka is at its loveliest in late September, when the golden paddy fields are fringed with scarlet *higanbana* (amaryllis) and the wooded ways are purple with bush clover.

**Feb. (1st Su):** \*\* **Onta matsuri.** Asuka Niimasu Jinja. See Calendar, p. 382. At 13:00.

### Getting Around

There is a well-maintained cycling/walking path. Rent-a-cycle shops near Asuka station: Manyō Rent-a-cycle 万葉レンタサイクル (074454-3500) with dropoffs at Kashihara and Asuka-dera, large bicycles available, reservations advised on spring and fall weekends; Asuka Rent-a-cycle 明日香レンタサイクル (074454-3919), dropoff at Kashihara. In Kashihara: Asuka Cycling Center 飛鳥サイクリングセンター (07442-7-2141), dropoffs at Oka-dera and Asuka stations.

**Walking or Cycling Course:** The Asuka cycling route can be done as a day trip or overnight excursion out of Kyoto or Nara. The approach we recommend is via **Tanzan Jinja**, 0:25h by bus from Sakurai. From the shrine, continue uphill to a pass. The road forks: the right fork is the short way down and takes about an hour. The left fork is a detour that goes by some highland farmhouses and an emperor's tomb. Either way, continue straight and you will come out at the Ishibutai *kofun*. From here, take a bus to Oka-dera or Asuka stations and rent a bicycle.

# Asuka History: Soga no Umako and the Dawn of the Yamato State

**Soga no Umako**   (d. 626) Soga clan chieftain and counselor to the emperor.

By legend, Kyūshū is where the divine ancestors of the first emperor, **Jimmu**, touched down from heaven, but it is the Asuka plain, with its gentle mountains and golden fields, that is palpably the cradle of Japanese civilization. Here, Jimmu's wanderings ended; here, he settled, died, and lies buried in one of the ancient mounds, now tree-covered, that dot the plain. Amid the paddy fields lie exposed the foundations of Japan's earliest temples and palaces, and boulders sculpted in now meaningless shapes of beasts and semi-humans. A stone sepulcher, its nameless occupant long vanished, lies heaved out of the ground, like some discarded prehistoric refrigerator.

Asuka was not an actual city like Nara or Kyoto. In the days of the early emperors, a palace was a flimsy affair, which had to be abandoned when it became defiled by the death of its occupant. The art of government was embryonic; the emperor ruled by worshipping the gods of rival clans. The imperial clan claimed its mandate from a divine ancestress, the Sun Goddess, ruler of the High Plain of Heaven. Later, in imitation of China, an elaborate history was written. Jimmu's conquest of Yamato was set in 667 B.C., and the life spans of the early emperors reached biblical lengths. More reliable calculations place Jimmu, if he ever existed, in the third or fourth century A.D.

Eventually imperial power grew, to judge by the increasing size of the burial mounds, or *kofun*. Placed on the *kofun* were *haniwa*, baked clay figurines of men and women, horses, and houses, which perhaps replaced a cruel practice of burying servants with their master. It is thought that the *kofun*, now overgrown with vegetation, were once starkly geometrical monuments paved with pottery cylinders. The supposed *kofun* of Jimmu lies behind **Kashihara Jingū**, the shrine that is consecrated to him.

At the beginning of the fifth century, **Paekche**, a Korean state allied to Japan and continually desperate for Japanese military aid, sent a gift of scribes who carried with them the Thousand Character Classic and other rudiments of Chinese learning. There also arrived a steady stream of Korean and perhaps Chinese settlers, most of whom seem to have been master artisans. Their contribution to the developing culture of Japan was profound, and these immigrants were accorded positions of high rank. They were promoted by the imperial clan because they helped to strengthen the power of the emperor vis-à-vis the indigenous clans. By the ninth century, fully one-third of the nobility claimed descent from the continent. The **Takamatsuzuka Kofun** in Asuka contains frescoes similar to those found in Korean tumuli. The cardinal directions in the *kofun* are indicated by mythical beasts specified by Chinese geomancy (directional magic).

But by far the most powerful—and disturbing—gift of the Koreans was a small gilded image of the Buddha that the king of Paekche sent with a message urging the Japanese to adopt this "most excellent" of doctrines. It would be some time before the Japanese could claim profound understanding of Buddhism, but one thing was quickly recognized: Unlike the native belief in a diverse body of local kami commanding splintered loyalties, Buddhism espoused a single, hierarchical system under a central, omnipotent deity. It could be a powerful tool for unifying the nation and strengthening the throne. Iname and his son **Umako**, heads of the **Soga clan**, pressed for adoption of the new religion, which did not prevent them from committing several murders to further the cause. After bitter fighting, the Soga won in 587. Their rivals, the Mononobe and Nakatomi clans, were vanquished.

To his credit, Umako did not seize the throne for himself. Instead he established his niece, who was of imperial blood, as **Empress Suiko**, and contented himself with ruling from behind the throne. This set an important precedent in Japanese history: The emperor (or empress) reigned, but a Soga (or, in later periods, a FUJIWARA, MINAMOTO, ASHIKAGA, or TOKUGAWA) ruled. Under the reign of Umako's niece and his grandson, the prince regent SHŌTOKU, Japan embarked on a period of advancement that was among the most remarkable in its history (see Hōryū-ji History, p. 400).

Soga no Umako is believed to have been buried in **Ishibutai**, an exposed *kofun* with the largest known crypt of any tomb in Asuka. Not far from it is what remains of Gangō-ji, or **Asuka-dera**, one of the first temples built by Umako. It shelters a time-ravaged bronze Buddha, the oldest extant Buddhist image made in Japan.

## Asuka Sights

**\*\*\* Takamatsuzuka Kofun** 高松塚古墳 (NT). When excavations of this tomb in 1972 revealed sophisticated paintings on the interior walls, it triggered an antiquities boom in Japan. The 1,300-year-old paintings, which still retain their rich colors, depict a miniature universe, with star charts of gold leaf and cinnabar on the ceiling, and a sun, moon, and courtly attendants on the walls. These are executed with a finely modulated brush technique and composed in a way that indicates a strong debt to Tang Chinese tomb painting. The four directional beasts—a blue dragon, white tiger, red bird, and black snake-entwined tortoise—are painted on the four walls according to Chinese geomantic rules. The actual chamber is hermetically sealed and cannot be seen, but nearby a mini-museum exhibits an excellent full-scale reproduction. Open Apr.–May and Oct.–Nov. Hrs: 9:00–16:30 (enter by 16:00); clsd M (if M a NH, then clsd Tu), NY. Jan. 16–Feb.

**\*\* Kibi no Himemiko Hinokuma no Haka (Tomb) and Saru-ishi (Monkey Stones)** 吉備姫王桧隈墓 Tomb of the grandmother of Naka no Ōe, leader of the Taika Reform. On the grounds are four strange monkey-men of stone (7th C) of mysterious origins and meaning.

**\* Oni no Setchin and Oni no Manaita** 鬼の雪隠・鬼の俎 Demon's Privy and Chopping Board, local names for an upturned stone *kofun* chamber carved out of a single block of granite and a flat cut stone that formed its floor.

**Tombs of Emperor Temmu and Empress Jitō** 天武・持統天皇陵 Empress Jitō became the first ruler to be cremated according to Buddhist rites. Her ashes were interred alongside the coffin of her husband, who reigned before her.

**\*\*\* Kame-ishi (Turtle Stone)** 亀石 This large, carved stone (7th C) resembling a somnolent, friendly turtle lies beside a path through the paddy fields. One theory is that the stone was a boundary marker; another is that it has directional meaning.

**\* Tachibana-dera (Temple)** 橘寺 Hrs: 8:00–17:00, daily. Originally a nunnery, said to stand on the site of SHŌTOKU TAISHI's birthplace. The Taishi-dō houses a Muromachi-period image of Shōtoku at age 35 (ICP). West of the main hall is the curious **Nimen-seki** (two-faced stone, ca. 7th C), with a face carved on each side; one theory holds that the stone depicts the dichotomy of good and evil.

**\*\*\* Ishibutai** 石舞台古墳 Hrs: 9:00–17:00. This exposed stone *kofun* chamber, the largest found in Asuka, is thought to be the tomb of Soga no Umako. The chamber can be entered. The largest boulders weigh about 75 tons.

**\* Oka-dera (Temple)** 岡寺 Hrs: 8:00–17:00. This temple was founded in the late 7th C by Gien. It was the training temple of Dōkyō, the infamous would-be usurper of the Nara throne (see Nara History, p. 392). The main image, a 4.5-m Nyoirin Kannon (9th C, ICP), is the largest clay image in Japan.

**Purported Site of the Itabuki Palace** 伝板蓋宮跡 Soga no Iruka was chopped to pieces in front of the empress at this palace (see Hōryū-ji History, p. 400). The name, Itabuki, or "board roofed," suggests that at the time, shingled roofs, instead of thatch, were a novelty.

**\*\* Sakabune-ishi (Saké Press Stone)** 酒船石 This flat boulder is carved with oval and circular indentations linked by narrow channels. One theory is that it was used to brew saké or to press oil; another is that these formed some kind of watering mechanism for a garden. Excavations have uncovered channels to carry water to the boulder from higher ground.

**\*\*\* Asuka-dera (Angō-in)** 飛鳥寺 Hrs: 8:00–17:30. Oct.–Mar. 8:00–17:00. The first true temple in Japan, founded by Soga no Umako in the late 6th C. Korean workmen from Paekche helped to build it, and excavations show it had a central pagoda surrounded by three main halls; a similar temple has been excavated near Pyongyang. The original temple, Gangō-ji, followed the court to Nara, where it still exists, but left behind its **Great Bronze Buddha** (ICP), a 4.8-m image of Shaka cast by TORI BUSSHI in 609. It is the oldest extant Buddhist image in Japan. Numerous fires and poor repairs have left it badly disfigured.

408

Asuka

0        300m

* **Asuka Niimasu Jinja** 飛鳥坐神社 A shrine of considerable antiquity; its hereditary priest family, the house of Asuka, claims to be in its 87th generation. The shrine preserves strong vestiges of once-widespread phallic cults. Natural phallic-shaped stones line the approach, and its Onta Matsuri, a rice-fertility festival, is famous for its explicitness.

*** **Nara Kokuritsu Asuka Shiryōkan (National Center for Asuka Material)** 奈良国立飛鳥資料館 (3561). Hrs: 9:00–16:00 (enter by 16:00); clsd M (except if M a NH, then clsd Tu). Excellent museum on excavations of the many palaces, temples, and tombs of the Asuka region. Of special interest: **Shumisen**, a three-tiered rock with reliefs suggesting mountains, thought to represent Mt. Sumeru; it may have been used as a fountain. Another stone carving, depicting a male and female figure embracing, is also thought to be a fountain. There's a model of an ancient water clock like one excavated recently.

* **Masuda no Iwafune (Stone Ship of Masuda)** 益田岩船 Most easily reached from Oka-dera station. A mysterious 7th-C monolith, 11 m long and 4.7 m high, with a flat top bearing two square holes.

### Kashihara and Asuka Dining and Lodgings

There are many hotels and restaurants around Kashihara station.

① **Saka no Chaya** 坂之茶屋 (074454-3129). Hrs: 11:00–16:00. Dec.–Feb. open Su only. Near Oka-dera. *Sōmen* or *nyūmen* (cold or hot vermicelli) and *warabi-gohan* (rice with ferns) are served here. Inexpensive.

② **Kashihara Oak Hotel** 橿原オークホテル (07442-3-2525). 905 Kumechō, Kashihara-shi, Nara-ken. Business hotel. S Y5500, Tw Y10,000.

③ **Kashihara-shi Cycling Terminal Chirin-sō** 橿原市サイクリングターミナル千輪荘 (07442-7-3196). 855-2 Nishimachi, Kashihara-shi. Rent-a-cycles available. Y2500 w/o meals, Y4000 w/2 meals. Y300 surcharge for air conditioning.

④ **Pension Asuka** ペンション飛鳥 (074454-3017). 17 Koshi, Asuka-mura, Takaichi-gun. Cosy mini-hotel. Tennis courts. Right near Asuka station. Y8000 w/meals.

409

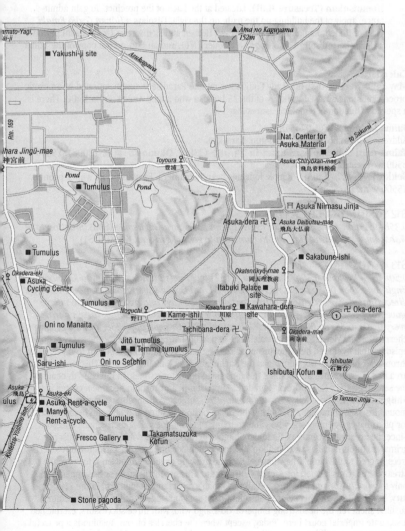

## * TAIMA-DERA 当麻寺

*From Kashihara-Jingū-mae, 0:15h by Kintetsu local (Abenobashi-bound) to Taima-dera station.* Hrs: 10:00–17:00. The origins of this temple seem to go back to a family temple of the local Taima clan, which embraced Buddhism early on. It is the only temple that preserves two pagodas from a style popular in the 7th and 8th centuries. The temple is famed for the **Taima Mandala**, a depiction of Amida's paradise, which by legend was woven in one night by Lady Chūjō in 763; it is one of the world's oldest surviving mandala. In the 12th century, the mandala became widely venerated due to the belief that the world was entering Mappō; it was one of the inspirations for the Byōdō-in at Uji (S1).

**Nakanobō.** This hall, just inside the main gate, on the left, has a lovely *shoin* (ICP) and garden with a view of the east pagoda. Nearby is the Bonshō (NT), or Indian Bell, of the 8th C, one of the oldest bells in Japan.

◆ **Kondō** (1184, ICP). Houses a **Miroku Butsu** (NT), Buddha of the Future, flanked by exotic, bearded **Shi-Tennō** (ICP), all of the late 7th C (except the Kamakura-period Tamon-ten). The three original Shi-Tennō, sculpted from lacquer, have dignified human features and a Central Asian flavor. The **Kōdō** (Lecture Hall, ICP) houses images of Amida and Jizō (ICP).

◆ **Hondō, or Mandala-dō** (NT). This was originally a much smaller hall of the Nara period, but in the 12th C the special veneration of the Taima Mandala prompted the temple to erect a larger structure over it. The nearby Kondō and Kōdō had to be rearranged to make room. The original hall, **Naijin**, enshrines a 16th-C copy of the ◆ **Taima Mandala** (the original is in special storage). The floating palaces and musicians in the foreground are reminiscent of Indian and Silk Road art. The hexagonal *zushi* (altar) is of the 8th C (repaired in the Kamakura period).

◆ **East and West Pagodas** (NT). Three-storied pagodas from the 8th C. The especially pretty west tower employs three-step bracketing to give it the appearance of added height.

**Hōmotsukan (Treasure Hall).** Located at the back of the precinct. To gain admittance, apply at the building up the path, on the right. Displays a *Hōnen Gyōjō Emaki* (Life of Hōnen, Kamakura period, ICP), a Heaven and Hell screen (Muromachi period), a Heian-period sutra box of *maki-e* lacquer (NT), and an Edo-period copy of the Taima Mandala.

### Calendar

**May 14:** * **Nerikuyō-shiki.** Lady Chūjō's ascent into Paradise is commemorated by an exotic procession along a raised walkway of the 25 bosatsu who attend Amida. From 16:00. There is a special exhibition of temple treasures May 14.

**Taima Lodgings** (TEL 074548)
Address: Taima-chō, Kitakatsuragi-gun, Nara-ken.
**Taima-dera Subtemples: Sainan-in** 西南院 (2202), **Okuno-in** 奥院 (2008). Y5500–6500 w/vegetarian meals.
**Sekkō-ji** 石光寺 (2031). Temple lodgings near Taima-dera. Famous for its winter peonies. Y5500 w/meals.

## S12 YOSHINO-GUCHI 吉野口

*0:35h–0:45h by Kintetsu local or express from Kashihara-Jingū-mae (S10). Junction to JR Wakayama line toward Hashimoto (junction to get to Kōya-san, KINKI II:S1).*

## S13 ** YOSHINO 吉野

*0:50h from Kyoto or 0:30h from Saidai-ji (S2) by Kintetsu limited express to Kashihara-Jingū-mae, then 0:45h by express to Yoshino. From Ōsaka (Abenobashi station), 1:20h by direct limited express. Buses (infrequent during the day) and taxis to Yoshino village leave from Yoshino-Jingū-mae, one stop before Yoshino. From Yoshino, there's a tram every 0:20h, 6:55–20:00 (Y260, or Y460 round trip). Or walk up, 0:25h.* Yoshino is Japan's cherry-blossom viewing spot par excellence and a most attractive stage for the many historic episodes that occurred here. Japan's mythical first emperor Jimmu is reported to have passed through Yoshino after worshipping at the Nachi Falls (see Kumano, p. 415). This mountainous area had been deemed an abode of the gods since prehistoric times. In the late 7th century, the semi-legendary En no Gyōja "founded" Kimpusen-ji, and Yoshino became a center for the **Shugendō sect**, whose followers, the *yamabushi*, subjected themselves to severe trials in the mountains (see Shinto, p. 27). During the Heian period, Yoshino and Kumano became sites for pilgrimages by emperors, who came to thank the kami for aiding their august ancestor. Since the area was a center of Buddhist-Shinto syncretism, these doubled as Buddhist pilgrimages. Imperial villas were built in Yoshino, which became famous for its 100,000 cherry trees, sacred to the kami. The village of Yoshino grew up around Kimpusen-ji to serve the stream of pilgrims headed for sacred **Ōmine-san**. This mountain fastness has appealed not only to *yamabushi* and pilgrims, but also to Japan's most famous fugitives. In the 12th century, YOSHITSUNE and his beloved Shizuka Gozen sought refuge here. In the 14th century, Yoshino sheltered the headstrong Emperor Go-Daigo who, with three successors, established a separate imperial court here. Today, except when the cherries bloom, Yoshino is a peaceful mountain village, still beautiful, still remote, wrapped in memories of long-dead heroes.

# Yoshino History: Loyalty to the Emperor—But Which One?

**Emperor Go-Daigo** (1288–1339) The last emperor to try to rule directly. He was foiled by his ambitious general, Ashikaga Takauji, and forced to flee to the hills of Yoshino, where for fifty years his descendants reigned as "southern emperors," while the throne in Kyoto was occupied by a "northern emperor."

**Ashikaga Takauji** (1305–1358) A general of the Kamakura shogunate, Takauji crossed over to Go-Daigo's cause, helping to overthrow Kamakura, then drove Go-Daigo from Kyoto and established the Ashikaga shogunate, which lasted 200 years.

**Kusunoki Masashige** (d. 1336) Go-Daigo's stalwart follower. His deeds of bravery and cunning, mostly legendary, served as a model of loyalty during World War II.

There are certain events in a nation's history that penetrate to the core of its contradictions, that are still the subject of political debate centuries later. The French argue to this day about the Revolution of 1789; for Japan, the attempt of a fourteenth-century emperor to reestablish direct imperial rule was a topic of heated dispute until recent times.

In the late thirteenth century, a quarrel over the imperial succession resulted in a compromise whereby the descendants of two brothers agreed to reign alternately (see Kyoto, p. 360). In 1318, **Go-Daigo**, of the junior line, became the seventh emperor to ascend the throne under this system—which, however, he came to repudiate. His wish to have his own descendants monopolize the throne was part of a larger plan to get rid of the hated Kamakura shogunate, which had arranged this compromise. By toppling Kamakura, Go-Daigo believed he could take power out of the hands of the warriors and restore it to the court. At the beginning of his reign, he took the name Go-Daigo, meaning Daigo II, after the Heian emperor Daigo (885–930) who had also been a strong proponent of direct imperial rule. Instead of achieving his objectives, however, Go-Daigo needlessly subjected Japan to sixty years of sporadic conflict.

Go-Daigo, although intelligent and strong-willed, seems to have been neither wise nor gallant. His opponent, ASHIKAGA TAKAUJI, a brilliant general and able administrator, seems quite the superior personality. Nevertheless, in the *Taiheiki*, an epic of this period, and in the writings of nationalist scholars of subsequent centuries, Go-Daigo came to be portrayed as a noble sovereign unjustly robbed of his imperial prerogatives. (Go-Daigo's 1334 Kemmu Restoration was seen by Meiji loyalists as the precedent for their own movement in 1868.) His followers, especially **Kusunoki Masashige**, were idealized as selfless heroes dedicating their lives to the imperial institution against impossible odds. Ivan Morris, in *The Nobility of Failure*, suggests that what made Kusunoki Masashige the ultimate Japanese hero was his sincere and utter devotion to a cause that was doomed from the start. During World War II, Go-Daigo and Kusunoki Masashige were held up as chief exemplars by Japan's militarists, who marched millions off to die for the sake of the emperor.

Go-Daigo began plotting against Kamakura soon after his accession, but it was not until 1331, when one of his trusted advisors betrayed his plans, that the shogunate felt the need to take direct action against the emperor's sacred person. Go-Daigo fled to a monastery south of Kyoto, on Mt. Kasagi. It was here, according to the *Taiheiki*, that he had the famous dream in which he was invited to sit under a tree, on a throne facing south. Go-Daigo interpreted this to mean that he would be able to restore imperial rule, and that his mainstay in this enterprise would be someone named Kusunoki (camphor tree), written with a Chinese character combining "south" and "tree." A well-known warrior—something of a bandit—named Kusunoki Masashige was summoned to Mt. Kasagi, where he immediately swore fealty to Go-Daigo.

Not long after, the renegade emperor, with his hair ignominiously unkempt and his clothes a shambles, was brought back to Kyoto, a captive of Kamakura forces. Before his capture, however, Go-Daigo had commissioned Masashige to save his cause. While the emperor was escorted into exile on the remote Oki Islands in 1332, Masashige and Go-Daigo's son, **Prince Morinaga**, continued to resist. The bandit-warrior and the prince showed such resourcefulness that the two Kamakura generals sent to subdue them, Ashikaga Takauji and Nitta Yoshisada, decided to defect to the imperial cause. In 1333, Nitta Yoshisada sacked Kamakura, forcing the Hōjō regent to retreat to a cave and commit suicide with hundreds of followers. Go-Daigo, in the meantime, had escaped from Oki. Joined by loyalist warriors on the Japan Sea coast,

411

he triumphantly entered Kyoto, where he set about turning his dream into reality.

Go-Daigo's reign was a disaster. In his enthusiasm for an imperial revival and his blindness to political realities, he and his aristocratic coterie failed to give his warrior supporters their due. The fatal error was in the treatment of Takauji, who, as the emperor's most powerful general, wished to be invested with the title of Shogun. Go-Daigo, however, intended to reserve this office for a member of the aristocracy. In 1335, Takauji left the capital against Go-Daigo's orders, ostensibly to quell a small rebellion of Hōjō supporters in Kamakura. Nitta Yoshisada was sent to chastise him, but was beaten instead. Seeing his chance, Takauji returned to Kyoto with a large army. Go-Daigo was forced to flee once more, this time to Mt. Hiei, where his son, Prince Morinaga, was abbot of Enryaku-ji. Morinaga and Masashige mounted a counterattack three days later. Takauji withdrew to Kyūshū, where he raised more support. The following year, in 1336, Takauji and his army landed near Kōbe; at the Minato River crossing he engaged in a decisive battle with Kusunoki Masashige.

Masashige, knowing that his own small band could not win this battle, had proposed a strategic withdrawal into the hills, evacuating the capital, to give him time to regroup his forces and retake Kyoto later. Go-Daigo, however, was loath to quit his palace once again and refused to permit this. Unable to defy his lord, Masashige loyally marched into battle, knowing it would be his last. After fighting long and hard, he was forced to commit suicide at a nearby farmhouse. A song, "Aoba shigereru Sakurai no," popular with the Japanese army in World War II and subsequently banned by the Allied Occupation, recounts the parting of Masashige and his ten-year-old son Masatsura:

412

> Here is the precious sword
> That his Majesty bestowed upon me many years ago.
> Now I am giving it to you.
> In Memory of this, our last farewell.
> Go Masatsura, back to our village.
> Where your aging mother waits.

(trans. Ivan Morris, The Nobility of Failure)

The victorious Takauji set up a member of the senior line as emperor and from him received the long-coveted title of Shogun. Go-Daigo, after a brief period in captivity, escaped with the imperial regalia and what was left of his supporters and set up a rival "southern court" in the mountain fastness of Yoshino. He died in 1339, pining for Kyoto and clutching the sword of the regalia. The Namboku-chō (Northern and Southern Courts) period continued for another fifty years, through three successions. Kusunoki Masatsura, obedient to his father's last instructions, tried to retake Kyoto in 1347; but after some initial successes, he too was slain. At various times, the southern court controlled Kamakura, Kyūshū, and other parts of Japan, but the cause was doomed to failure. The last southern emperor was tricked into returning the imperial regalia to the northern line and spent the remainder of his life at a villa south of Kyoto.

The Kemmu Restoration was a fiasco, but as a symbolic event it had lasting repercussions. It shattered the polite myth of a divine, infallible emperor presiding over his family, the Japanese people. First, there was the distressing fact of *two* emperors, each with an incontrovertible claim. Worse, Go-Daigo was clearly not only fallible, but at times reprehensible — as when in 1335, at the height of his power, he allowed his loyal son, Prince Morinaga, to be executed by Takauji. But the greatest violence to the myth was in Go-Daigo's shabby treatment by Takauji, who not only went unpunished, but achieved the ultimate worldly success.

In the Meiji period, the southern party became national heroes. Shrines were dedicated to Go-Daigo and Masashige. In 1911, there was a national controversy over a school textbook that treated the Northern and Southern lines as equal. At the request of the government, the EMPEROR MEIJI, himself a descendant of the Northern line, issued a decree recognizing the Southern line as the truly legitimate one.

In the 1950s, a shopkeeper claiming descent from Go-Daigo asked the Japanese public if *he* shouldn't replace the emperor, but on the whole, the debate quieted down with the end of World War II. Yoshino itself is one of the few lingering legacies. **Yoshino Jingū**, a State Shinto shrine at the foot of Mt. Yoshino, enshrines Go-Daigo. The southern court's palace is said to have stood behind the great temple hall, Zaō-dō. Go-Daigo's mausoleum is near **Nyoirin-ji**, where he prayed in his final, bitter years. Its wooden door bears a famous farewell poem by Kusunoki Masatsura, who scratched it there with the butt of his arrow on his way to battle. His topknot, recovered later, is entombed in a nearby mound. Masashige and Masatsura are considered exemplars of the ideal samurai, who unflinchingly accepts — if only to please his lord — a painful, even futile, death. Like the cherry blossom which, just as it attains its fullness of beauty, is scattered by the wind, the most glorious death was to fall in the prime of life. Every spring, Yoshino is enveloped in a cloud of blossoms from tens of thousands of mountain cherry trees, the most celebrated in Japan.

## Calendar

**Apr.: Cherry-Blossom Viewing.** There are three major sets of trees, the Lower, Middle, and Upper Thousand, which bloom in progression. The Lower Thousand reach their peak around April 10, the Middle around April 15, the Upper around April 20–25 (may be the least crowded). Accommodations must be reserved many months in advance.

**July 7: \* Kaeru-tobi.** Reenacts the fable of a man who was turned into a frog for his lack of faith in the Buddha; having repented, he was restored to human form by a *yamabushi* on Yoshino. A fellow dressed as a giant frog has to lumber about town. From 14:00.

## Getting Around

To walk from Yoshinoyama tramway station to Kimpu Jinja takes about 1:20h. The village straggles along a sharp mountain ridge; its one main street is not hard to find.

## Yoshino Sights

**Yoshino Jingū** 吉野神宮 *0:20h walk from Yoshino Jingū station.* This State Shinto shrine dedicated to Emperor Go-Daigo was erected in 1889.

**\*\*\* Kimpusen-ji** 金峯山寺 Hrs: 9:00–17:00. Pilgrims worship here before making the hazardous journey to Ōmine-san. During the Meiji-period campaign to purge Shinto of Buddhist influence, Kimpusen-ji nearly went out of business, but recently Shugendō has experienced a bit of a revival. The first gate, Kuro-mon, spans the road. Go through and keep to the right to stay on the official temple approach, which passes through a large bronze torii (ICP) and the Niō-mon (1455, NT). Note the syncretism.

◆ **Zaō-dō** 蔵王堂 (1455, NT), the large main hall, is one of several "second-largest" wooden buildings in Japan, after the Great Buddha Hall in Nara. The hall enshrines a massive image of **Zaō Gongen** (the avatar of Yoshino) apocryphally ascribed to En no Gyōja and shown once every 60 years. In keeping with Shugendō's back-to-nature philosophy, the massive columns retain the shapes of tree trunks. There is a motley collection of sculpture and temple documents displayed in the dim interior.

413

West of the Zaō-dō, down a flight of steps, is the site of the southern court palace. One can continue down into a valley with a small shrine to Noten Ō-kami, a manifestation of Zaō Gongen who protects one's head. Pilgrims come to drink from a health-bestowing

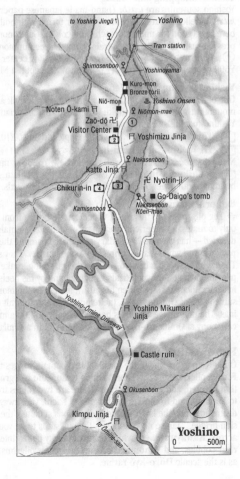

spring and offer eggs to the god's messenger, a serpent. The practical-minded shrine boils the eggs and presents them as edible mementos to visitors.

**\*\*\* Yoshimizu Jinja** 吉水神社 Hrs: 8:00–17:00. This shrine, like nearly every other on Yoshino, was formerly a Shugendō temple. The \* **Shinden** (ICP) is worth visiting for its charming Shoin-style architecture (see Villas, p. 64) and dramatic situation, perched on tall railings on a steep incline (excellent view of blossoms). By tradition, this building was used by Go-Daigo and, earlier still, as the hiding place of Yoshitsune and Shizuka. The shrine collection, attractively displayed, includes paintings, documents, arms and armor, lacquerware, and musical instruments connected with its history. Two pretty screens ascribed to KANŌ SCHOOL artists (allegedly given by HIDEYOSHI during his blossom-viewing party here) are displayed Apr.1–May 31 and Oct. 1–Nov. 30.

**Katte Jinja** 勝手神社 Shizuka Gozen's dance before YORITOMO in Kamakura is famous (see Kamakura History, p. 261). According to local legend, she also danced at this small shrine for her captors who had seized her at Yoshino soon after her final parting from her lover, YOSHITSUNE.

**\*\* Nyoirin-ji** 如意輪寺 Hrs: 8:00–17:00. Kusunoki Masatsura, son of the hero Masashige, is said to have inscribed a poem and the names of his men on the temple door before he led them to their last battle. The mausoleum of Go-Daigo is in the precincts. The items in the Hōmotsuden (Treasure Hall) are of interest for their historical connection to the southern court, rather than for their artistic merit.

**\*\* Chikurin-in (Temple)** 竹林院 Hrs: 7:00–17:00. The entrance to this temple is spanned by a four-story white roadside inn (the temple runs a ryokan). The pleasant pond garden is said to have been designed by the great tea master, SEN NO RIKYŪ.

**\*\* Yoshino Mikumari Jinja** 吉野水分神社 (ICP). Hrs: 7:00–17:00. *0:30h on foot from Chikurin-in.* This is the shrine of the water kami of Yoshino. Built in 1604 by TOYOTOMI HIDEYORI, the linked halls are beautiful examples of Momoyama-period style.

414   **Kimpu Jinja** 金峯神社 *0:20h on foot from Mikumari Jinja.* This simple shrine standing in the twilight shadow of great cryptomerias is on the Shugendō pilgrimage route to Ōmine-san. The mountain is barred to women; on the trailside, just beyond the shrine, is a stone post with the inscription *nyonin kekkai* (limit for female persons).

### Yoshino Shopping and Dining

Yoshino souvenirs are *washi* (hand-made Japanese paper) from villages nearby, and Yoshino *kuzu*, a delicate starch used in cuisine or mixed with boiling water to make a soothing, thick beverage (good for upset stomachs and colds). Gastronomes should try *kakinoha-sushi*, pressed sushi of pickled mackerel wrapped in persimmon leaves (don't eat the leaf).

① **Yakko** やっこ (2-3117), in front of the visitor center, has very good *kakinoha-zushi*, Y600 per serving. Hrs: 9:00–17:00; clsd W (except if a NH or in Apr.).

### Yoshino Lodgings (TEL 07463)

One of the pleasures of Yoshino is a brisk morning walk along the winding village road and mountain trails. For a minshuku, call the tourist association (2-3014). Address: Yoshinoyama, Yoshino-machi, Yoshino-gun, Nara-ken.

② **Tōnan-in** 東南院 (2-3005). Temple lodgings. Y10,000 w/meals.

③ **YH Yoshinoyama Kizō-in** ユースホテル吉野山喜蔵院 (2-3014). Also a temple inn. Nice Japanese rooms, some with a good view. Y3250 w/meals.

④ \* **Chikurin-in** 竹林院 (2-8081). Temple ryokan. Ask for a room in the *honkan* (old building) with a view of the garden. Y15–35,000 w/meals.

### Exploring Ōmine-san

\# The pilgrimage to this peak, which can be begun from either Yoshino or Kumano, is open only to males; an American woman who attempted to make the pilgrimage—she finally desisted—has assumed legendary proportions among the locals. Today Boy Scouts, backpackers, and white-clad pilgrims make the journey. They start in the early morning hours. The *yamabushi*, at a certain stage in their training, make the round trip every day. Every pilgrim must endure such trials as being hung by his heels over a sheer cliff (to realize his insignificance and strengthen his faith), as well as the more usual cold-water ablutions. Five subtemples of **Ōminesan-ji**, the temple near the summit of Ōmine-san, provide simple lodgings. The pilgrimage season is begun officially at 2:00 a.m. on May 3 in a "door opening" ceremony at Ōminesan-ji, and ends on Sept. 22 in a similar "door closing" ceremony.

## FROM YOSHINO TO KUMANO

Ōmine-san is but one of the formidable mountain ranges that separate Yoshino from Kumano. For nonpilgrims, the way from Yoshino to Kumano is a grueling 5:00h bus ride through beautiful, rugged, and isolated terrain. There are two routes from Yoshino: from Yamato Kamiichi to Kumano, and from Gōjō to Shingū and Nachi, via Kawayu Onsen. The former is the most dramatic, while the latter includes diversions such as "the world's longest pedestrian suspension bridge," Tanise no Tsuribashi; the bus stops to let you make the truly vertiginous walk across. **Kawayu Onsen**, which features murky baths, intermittently scalding, dug right into river cobbles, and **Yunomine**, an ancient spa for pilgrims, are both near Hongū (see below), as is the scenic **Doro-kyō** ravine.

## \* KUMANO 熊野

When the future emperor Jimmu landed near present-day Ōsaka on his quest to conquer Yamato, he met stiff resistance from the locals. Beating a strategic retreat, he decided to approach Yamato via Kumano, where he enlisted the support of its three kami, now enshrined at the **Hongū**, **Shingū**, and **Nachi** shrines. In the late Heian period, these kami became avatars of buddhas: Hongū as Amida in the Western Paradise, Shingū as Yakushi in the Eastern Paradise, and Nachi as Kannon in the Southern Paradise (see Shinto, p. 27). Nachi has the most dramatic setting, overlooking the sea and the 130-m \*\*\* **Nachi no Taki**, the waterfall depicted as a syncretic Shinto-Buddhist nature mandala in the famous painting, *Nachi Waterfall* (see Art, p. 93). Of the three shrines, Nachi came to be considered the most important because Kannon is the bosatsu specially assigned to save souls in the present era. The best way to visit the shrine is to take the bus 0:10h from Nachi station to Daimon-zaka, then climb 0:20h by the old pilgrim's approach, a stairway of mossy stones, through primal forest. Near Nachi shrine is **Seiganto-ji**, the starting point of the 33 Kannon Temple Pilgrimage (see Villages, p. 56). In the Middle Ages, when the head priests of Fudarakusan-ji (in Katsu'ura) reached a certain age and rank, they were sealed inside small boats and set adrift in the currents off the Kii Peninsula; it was confidently believed that they would reach Fudaraku, Kannon's Southern Paradise.

### Calendar

**July 14: \*\*\* Nachi no Hi-matsuri.** Kumano Nachi Taisha (Shrine). See Calendar, p. 382. Spectacular fire festival. Highlights from 11:00.

**July 24–25: \*\* Kozagawa Mifune Matsuri.** Kozagawa-chō, Kōchi Jinja (take JR Kii line to Koza station, then walk 0:20h to Furata). See Calendar, p. 382.

**Oct. 15–16: Kumano Hayatama-sai.** Shingū. Commemorates the god of Shingū's arrival on a ship borne by the Black Current. Highlight is a fleet of boats sailing up the Kumano River.

### Kumano Lodgings

**Ryokan Kameya** 旅館かめや (07354-2-0002). Kawayu Onsen, Hongū-chō, Higashimuro-gun, Wakayama-ken. A creaky older inn. *Honkan* (old wing) rooms face the river. Y10–15,000 w/meals.

**Azumaya** あづまや (07354-2-0012). Yunomine Onsen, Hongū-chō. A venerable ryokan. Y13–20,000 w/meals. V.

**Sonshō-in** 尊勝院 (07355-5-0331). Nachi-san, Nachi-katsu'ura-chū, Higashimuro-gun. Seiganto-ji. Y6000 w/Buddhist meals.

**Hotel Urashima** ホテル浦島 (07355-2-1011). Nachi-Katsu'ura-chō. Katsu'ura onsen inn famed for hot-spring bath inside what was originally a natural seaside cavern. Y14–55,000 w/meals.

**Hotel Nakanoshima** ホテル中ノ島 (07355-2-1111). 1179-9 Katsu'ura, Nachi-Katsu'ura-chō. This resort inn stands on its own island, with open-air baths by the sea. Y15–35,000 w/meals.

### Easy Access To:

**\* Matsusaka** (CHŪBU IV:S1): *3:05h by limited JR express from Katsu'ura. Change to JR or private Kintetsu train to \*\*\* Ise* (CHŪBU IV:S2).

**Shirahama Onsen** (KINKI II:S1): *1:30h from Katsu'ura by JR Kii line limited express.*

# KINKI II. ŌSAKA

**Tokyo to Ōsaka:** *3:00h by Shinkansen Hikari express to Shin-Ōsaka.*
**Kyoto to Ōsaka:** *To Umeda station: 0:40h by private Hankyū express from Kawaramachi-dōri. To Temmabashi/Yodoyabashi: 0:40–0:45h by private Keihan limited express from Keihan-Sanjō. Note: Umeda station is connected to JR Ōsaka station.*
**Ōsaka International Airport:** *For international flights, see Practical Advice. 0:25h by airport express bus from Shin-Ōsaka station, or 0:30h from Umeda station. 1:00h by airport express bus from Kyoto station.*
**Prefectures:** Ōsaka-fu, Hyōgo, Wakayama

## \* ŌSAKA 大阪

From the earliest times, Ōsaka has been Japan's major port and center of commerce. Naniwa-kyō, Japan's first known capital, was situated here, close to the ports for continental trade. In the feudal period, the tax-rice wealth of the nation flowed into the city. During the reign of the TOKUGAWA shoguns, Ōsaka marched to its own cultural drum, giving birth to Bunraku, the puppet theater that inspired Japan's greatest dramatist, CHIKAMATSU, to write his masterpieces. Ōsaka emerged from the ashes of World War II as an ugly industrial jumble of factories and cheap housing. With the affluence of the past decade, however, the city has begun to cast off its grimy cloak. The new Ōsaka is an increasingly attractive, invigorating city filled with exciting architecture and trendy restaurants and clubs. In addition to the abundance of hedonistic pleasures, there are several superb museums, a fantastic aquarium, and the National Bunraku Theater, which alone merits a visit to the city.

### Calendar

**Jan. 9–11: Tōka Ebisu.** Imamiya Ebisu shrine. Merchants throng this shrine dedicated to the god of prosperity.

**Jan. 14: \* Doya-doya.** Shitennō-ji. A huge naked festival. 15:00.

**Apr. 22: Shōryō-e.** Shitennō-ji. Commemorates SHŌTOKU TAISHI with impressive nighttime Bugaku performances.

**June 14: Otaue Shinji.** Sumiyoshi Jinja. From 13:00. Young shrine maidens plant rice in the sacred paddies of one of Japan's historically most important agricultural shrines.

**June 30–July 2: Aizen Matsuri.** Shōman-in, near Shitennō-ji. Boisterous festival where *yamabushi*, mountain priests, build a sacred fire.

**July 24–25:** ∗ **Tenjin Matsuri.** Ōsaka's great riverborne matsuri. On the night of the 25th, festival boats with drum-beaters aboard sail up past Temmabashi. Fireworks.

**Sept. 14–15:** ∗ **Kishiwada Danjiri Matsuri.** Kishiwada *(0:25h south of Namba station on the Nankai line)*. A famous "fight" festival. Large floats are crashed into each other, as people riding on them try to invade rival floats.

**Nov. 22–23: Shinnō Matsuri.** Sukuna-Hikona Jinja. Originated in 1822 when, during a cholera epidemic, medicine of tiger bones, packaged inside paper tigers, was given to worshipers at this shrine. Today, paper tigers are handed out as amulets against disease.

### Getting Around

Subways form a grid. Useful lines, north–south: **Midōsuji** (center, Umeda to Namba) and **Tanimachi** (east side, Temmabashi to Tennōji); east–west: **Keihan** (Temmabashi to Yodoyabashi), **Sennichimae** (Tanimachi to Namba). The No. 7 subway to the Expo '90 site is Japan's first magnetic-levitation train line. Ōsaka is an easy day trip from Kyoto.

### Ōsaka Sights

**Ōsaka Station Area.** The area around the station, known as Umeda, is situated on the northern fringe of old Ōsaka. It is choked with new hotels, stores, offices, and countless bars and eateries catering to commuters and people attracted by the glitter. The area east of Higashi-Umeda subway stop is **Sonezaki**, a name familiar to drama fans from the Bunraku masterpiece *Sonezaki Shinjū*, written when this was a lonely wood where two lovers could flee and end their lives together. The **Ohatsu Tenjin shrine** nearby commemorates the unhappy heroine of the play (see Drama, p. 84).

**Nakanoshima.** Near Yodoyabashi station. An island in the river with many early Western buildings and bridges. South of Nakanoshima is Semba, the heart of Ōsaka's old merchant community.

∗∗∗ **Ōsaka Shiritsu Tōyō Jiki Bijutsukan (Museum of Oriental Ceramics)** 大阪市立東洋陶磁美術館 (223-0055). Hrs: 9:30–17:00 (enter by 16:30); clsd M, day after NH, NY. On Nakanoshima, near Nagahama station. Superb museum of Chinese, Korean, and Japanese ceramics from the collection of the defunct Ataka *zaibatsu*. Lovely building.

∗ **Teki-juku** 適塾 北浜3-3-8 Hrs: 10:00–16:00; clsd Su, M, NH, NY. Across the street from the east exit of Yodoyabashi station. A fine old residence and school of Ogata Kōan (1810–1863), an early student of Dutch medicine. Among his pupils was Fukuzawa Yukichi, a famous thinker and educator of the early Meiji period.

∗ **Ōsaka-jō (Castle)** 大阪城 Hrs: 9:00–17:00 (enter by 16:30). July 15–Aug. 31, 9:00–20:30 (enter by 20:00). *0:15h walk from Temmabashi station.* In 1583, TOYOTOMI HIDE-YOSHI built Ōsaka-jō, the most formidable fortress in Japan, on the ruins of Ishiyama Hongan-ji, headquarters of the bellicose Ikkō sect (see Kyoto History, p. 322). It was by deceit that TOKUGAWA IEYASU breached the castle walls in 1615 and wiped out Hideyoshi's heirs. When the shogunate fell in 1868, the keep was burned by retreating Tokugawa loyalists. The present concrete keep was erected in 1931. The powerful walls include an immense stone, 11 m long and 5.1 m high, given to Hideyoshi by Katō Kiyomasa (see Kyūshū, p. 493). Original structures include the **Ōte-mon** (Great Outer Gate), five parapets, several arsenals, and a wellhouse (all ICP). The keep exhibits objects related to the house of Toyotomi and Ōsaka history.

∗∗ **Ōsaka International Peace Center** (947-7208). Hrs: 9:30–17:00 (enter by 16:30); clsd M (except if M a NH, then clsd Tu), day after NH, last day of each month, NY. *S of Ōsaka Castle. Take Chūō subway line to Morinomiya.* Probably the only public museum in Japan to openly confront Japan's aggression in Asia during World War II. Exhibits on atrocities in China, as well as the firebombing of Ōsaka.

∗∗ **Fujita Art Museum (Bijutsukan)** 藤田美術館 (351-0582). Open Mar.–May, Sept.–Nov. Hrs: 10:00–16:00 (enter by 15:30); clsd M (Tu if M a NH). *0:10h walk from Kyōbashi station on the Keihan line.* The important Chinese and Japanese art collection of Baron Fujita, shown in an old *kura* on his former estate. Many RIMPA tea ceremony objects.

∗∗ **Namba** 難波 Major rail junction, 4 stops S of Ōsaka/Umeda station. A lively area filled with department stores, theaters, and restaurants, Namba is one of Japan's most pleasant night towns. **Dōtonbori**, on the south bank of the canal, has an open, friendly atmosphere presided over by the giant mechanical king crab of the Kani Dōraku crab restaurant. Tucked away in the stone-paved alleys behind the Nakaza Theater on Dōtonbori is the ∗ **Mizukake Fudō (Hōzen-ji)** 水かけ不動, a tiny popular temple. **Soemon-chō**, across the canal, is much more exclusive; at night — the only time it's active — it's crawling with limousines and taxis that will stop only for drunken salarymen.

∗∗∗ **National Bunraku Theatre (Kokuritsu Bunraku Gekijō)** 国立文楽劇場 (212-2531). Between Nipponbashi and Tanimachi-kyūchōme subway stations. Bunraku from around 11:00 and 16:00 (sometimes 15:00) in January, April, June (lecture program), July, August, November. English program notes, earphone guide. See Drama, p. 84.

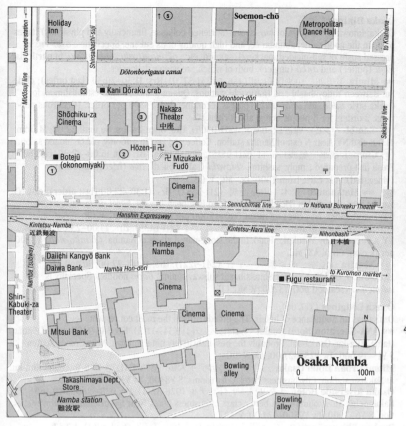

Ōsaka Namba

0          100m

\*\*\* **Kaiyūkan (Ōsaka Aquarium)** 海遊館 (576-5500). Hrs: 10:00–20:00 (enter by 19:00). Admission Y1950. Children age 7–12, Y900; ages 4–6, Y400. Avoid the weekend crush. *From Ōsaka or Shin-Ōsaka station, take Midōsuji subway line to Honmachi, then Chūō line to Ōsaka-kō, walk 0:05h.* Superb aquarium at Ōsaka Harbor, designed by U.S. architect Peter Chermayeff and built at a cost of $133 million. Sharks, rays, schools of fish and an awesome whale shark churn in a 1.4 million gallon central tank. Smaller tanks on the periphery represent zones of the Pacific "Ring of Fire," such as the Aleutians, Monterey kelp forests, Panama Bay, the Great Barrier Reef, and the Japan Sea. The path wraps like a corkscrew around the central tank, down to the "sea floor" at a depth of 30 meters. How volcanoes affect these ecological niches is not made clear, but this is still a wonderful aquarium. Food available at the adjacent Harbor Village development.

\* **Shitennō-ji** 四天王寺 Hrs: 8:00–16:30. Oct.–Mar. 8:30–16:00. *0:07h walk from Shitennō-ji-mae on the Tanimachi subway line.* One of Japan's oldest temples, founded by SHŌTOKU TAISHI in 593. The temple is dedicated to the Shi-Tennō (Four Directional Guardians), who were credited with his clan's victory over rival, anti-Buddhist clans (see Asuka History, p. 407). The present temple, rebuilt in concrete, preserves only its original layout, called the Kudara (Korean Paekche) style, one of the earliest formal temple plans in Japan; the main halls are aligned on a north-south axis and enclosed within a cloister. The **Kokuhōkan** (National Treasure Hall) exhibits NT documents and other objects.

\* **Shiritsu Bijutsukan (Municipal Museum of Fine Arts)** 大阪市立美術館 (771-4874). Hrs: 9:30–17:00 (enter by 16:30); clsd M, NY. In Tennōji Kōen (park). *0:05h walk from Abenobashi or Tennōji stations.* An excellent museum of East Asian art, including a Hakuhō bronze and 21 works by OGATA KŌRIN.

**Senri Expo Park** 万博記念公園     *From Kyoto, 0:30h by Hankyū express to Ibaraki-shi, then 0:15h by bus to Nihon Tei-en-mae. From Ōsaka Umeda station, take the Hankyū Senri line to Yamada, or Midōsuji line to Senri-Chūō, then bus or taxi to the park.* Hrs: 9:00–17:00 (enter by 16:00). Clsd W (Th if W a NH). This large, rather strange park was the site of the 1970 Ōsaka Expo. Two interesting museums (see below). Food and drink are available at **Nihon Tei-en**, a serene modern garden with several restaurants and coffee shops.

\*\* **Kokuritsu Minzokugaku Hakubutsukan (National Museum of Ethnology)** 国立民族学博物館 (876-2151). Hrs: 10:00–17:00 (enter by 16:30); clsd W (Th if W a NH), NY. In Senri Expo Park. Huge collection from around the world. Quality is uneven, but the dramatic presentation and use of technology make this museum outstanding. Extensive video library of festivals and rituals, including a few with English narrative. The memorable building was designed by Kurokawa Kishō.

\*\* **Nihon Mingeikan (Japan Folk Art Museum)** 日本民芸館 (877-1971). Hrs: 10:00–17:00 (enter by 16:00); clsd W (Th if W a NH), NH, NY. In Senri Expo Park. One of the best folk-art museums in the country.

## Ōsaka Dining

Ōsaka, known as the town of *kui-daore* (surfeited collapse, financially and physically), takes pride in the good value, abundance, and high quality of its cuisine. Specialties: *oshi-zushi*, pressed sushi of salt-pickled mackerel, salmon, etc.; *okonomiyaki*; *nabemono*, in particular *fugu* (puffer) and *ankō* (angler), both of which are winter delicacies.

** **Mimiu** 美美卯 中央区白の町4-6-5 (231-5770). Hrs: 11:30–20:30 (last order); clsd Su. Between Yodoyabashi and Honmachi stations. Quaint teahouse-style establishment for Ōsaka-style *udon*; the *udon-suki* (pot) is recommended; Y3300 per order. (Generous portions: 2 orders for 3 people is just about right.) V.

① **Bambi** バンビ 難波駅50M北 (211-0305). Hrs: open 24 hrs; Su until 22:00; M from 11:00; clsd NY. Near N exit of Namba station. Coffee and jazz in a roomy, old fashioned salon.

② **Gimpei** 銀平 難波1-6-11 (211-9515). Monzō Bldg., B1. Hrs: 16:00–22:30; clsd Su. Fresh fish prepared simply: sashimi, *shioyaki* (salt-broiled), *age* (fried), *sunomono* (vinegared). À la carte from Y600. DC, MC, V, CB.

③ ** **Matsumoto** 松本 中座西側 (211-5652). Hrs: 11:30–22:00 (last order); clsd NY. Namba. Not elegant, but friendly, and the food is superb. Try the *karei no kara'age* (crisp-fried sand dabs). No prices on menu. Y10–15,000 per person. AX, MC, V, CB.

④ **Sumō Chaya Shiten** 角力茶屋 難波1-1-7 (211-8125). Hrs: 14:00–23:00; clsd M, NY. A cozy shop by Mizukake Fudō, in the stone-paved alleys of Namba. *Chanko-nabe* Y3300 per person. CB, V, AX, MC.

⑤ **Nishiya** にし家 心斎橋筋一丁目 (241-9221). Hrs: 11:00–22:00; Su and NH 11:00-21:00; clsd W, NY. Near Shinsaibashi subway station. *Udon* noodles. Specialty is *udonchiri* (seafood pot) Y3200. V, MC, CB.

## Ōsaka Lodgings (TEL 06)

Ōsaka has an abundance of hotels. The Umeda area is the most convenient.

** **ANA-Sheraton Hotel Ōsaka** 全日空シェラトン (347-1112). Fax 348-9208. 1-3-1 Dōjima Hama, Kita-ku, Ōsaka-shi. Probably the best deluxe city hotel in town. Near Umeda station. S Y15–19,000. Tw Y25–32,000. AX, V, DC.

**Mitsui Urban Hotel Ōsaka** 三井アーバンホテル大阪 (374-1111). 3-18-8 Toyosaki, Kita-ku. At Nakatsu station. City/business hotel. Cozy rooms. S Y8300, Tw Y17,000.

**Ōsaka Riverside Hotel** 大阪リバーサイドホテル (928-3251). Fax 928-3260. 5-10-160 Nakanochō, Miyakojima-ku. A better class of business hotel. Near Sakuranomiya subway station. S Y6–7000, Tw Y9500–12,000. V, MC.

**Ryokan Ebisu-sō** 旅館えびす荘 浪速区日本橋1-7-33 (643-4861). 1-7-33 Nipponbashi-nishi, Naniwa-ku. *0:08h walk from Nipponbashi subway station.* 16-room inn. Y4200 per person. AX, V, MC.

**Shin-Ōsaka Seni City Hotel** 新大阪センイシティーホテル (394-3331). 2-2-17 Nishimiyahara, Yodogawa-ku. *0:08h on foot from Shin-Ōsaka station, 0:20h by car to airport.* Business hotel. S Y4600, Tw Y7600 (no bathroom), Y8300 (w/bathroom). All major credit cards.

**Airport Hotel** エアポートホテル 大阪空港ビル3 F (855-4621). Airport Bldg., 3F. Five minutes from the boarding gate. S Y10,800, Tw Y17,600. All major credit cards.

# KINKI II:N. NORTH FROM OSAKA

**N1 * TAMBA-SASAYAMA** 丹波篠山

*1:10h by Fukuchiyama express (only 9 per day) from Ōsaka station to Sasayama-guchi, then 0:15h by bus or taxi to Hon-Sasayama.* This small castle town, located on a bucolic, isolated plain, preserves many older buildings and clearly retains the outlines of an Edo-period castle town. Nearby Tachikui is known for Tamba-yaki folk pottery.

## Calendar

**Mid-Apr. Sa: Noh.** Offered outdoors at Kasuga Jinja.

**Aug. 4–5: Gion Matsuri.** Sasayama's version of the Kyoto festival.

**Mid-Sept. Sa: Noh.** By moonlight at Kasuga Jinja.

**Oct.: A month of matsuri:** Events include: "frog dance" Dengaku on the 4–5th; *mikoshi*, giant drums and puppets on the 8th; lion dance on the 11th.

**Mid–Oct. Sa–Su: Pottery Fair.** Tachikui.

## Sasayama Sights

** **Old Merchant Quarter.** By Hon-Sasayama bus terminal (rent-a-cycles available). A 500-meter stretch of road lined with Edo-period merchant houses. The pottery and Noh museums are on this street.

*** **Tamba Kotō-kan (Old Tamba Pottery Museum)** 丹波古陶館 (2-2524). Hrs: 9:00–17:00; clsd M (Tu if M a NH), NY. In a wonderful group of old rice *kura*. Seven hundred years of Tamba-yaki, explained in an English pamphlet. New Tamba ware is sold here and at the shop next door.

**\*\* Nohgaku Shiryōkan** 能楽資料館 (2-3513). Hrs: 9:00–17:00; clsd M (Tu if M a NH), NY. A unique museum dedicated to the Noh theater. In addition to fine masks, robes, and instruments, there is a cutaway model of a Noh stage showing the large crocks placed beneath the floor for acoustical effect.

**\* Castle Ruin and Buke-yashiki.** Only the stone walls and outer moat are intact. Along the south moat and one street west of the castle moat are several thatched-roof *buke-yashiki* (samurai houses) — modest structures, but atmospheric.

**\* Sasayama Rekishi Bijutsukan (Historical Art Museum)** 篠山歴史美術館 (2-0601). Hrs: 9:00–16:30; clsd W (Th if W a NH), NY. Exhibits fine decorative screens, personal effects of the local daimyo, and Ōjiyama-yaki, a fine porcelain made at a short-lived local kiln.

**\*\* Tachikui** 立杭窯本 *Very infrequent bus from Aino station (local stop on Fukuchiyama line); or Y2500 by taxi from Sasayama-guchi station.* Many kilns are near Shikenjō-mae bus stop. This attractive rural area is famous for **Tamba-yaki**, a simple, brown-black stoneware that has been made here for 700 years. The pottery is still made by local farmer-potters, and wood-fired climbing kilns are much in evidence. Sturdy, unpretentious, and affordable everyday ware.

**Sasayama Dining and Lodgings** (TEL 07955)

In Kyoto, Tamba legumes, chestnuts, and beef are much prized. These and other specialties, such as wild boar, are served at local inns.

**\* Jinyōrō** 濘陽桜 (2-0021). Shimo-Nikaimachi, Sasayama-chō, Taki-gun, Hyōgo-gun. An old ryokan with excellent cuisine; beef or *inoshishi* (boar) by reservation. Western rooms available. Y12–15,000 w/meals. AX, V, MC.

**Kokuminshukusha Sasayama-sō** 国民宿舎篠山荘 (2-1127). 474-1 Kawaramachi. Y6000 w/meals.

## N2 FUKUCHIYAMA 福知山

*Junction to JR San'in line. 2:00h from Ōsaka by JR Fukuchiyama line express. 1:30h from Kyoto by JR San'in line limited express.*

## KINOSAKI ONSEN 城崎温泉

*1:15h from Fukuchiyama or 2:40h from Kyoto by JR San'in line limited express.* A small hot-spring town centered around a pretty, willow-lined canal. The town features seven public baths with varied "theme" decor. The baths are open 6:00–23:00. There is also a fine temple, **Onsen-ji**, halfway up the tramway.

**Kinosaki Lodgings** (TEL 079632)

**\* Nishimuraya** 西村屋 (2211). Fax 4456. Kinosaki-chō, Kinosaki-gun, Hyōgo-ken. A slick, slightly sterile modern ryokan, but all the rooms look out on the garden, and there's much lovely woodwork. From Y24,000 w/meals. V, MC, DC.

## KASUMI 香住

*0:25h from Kinosaki by express train.* 0:05h by bus from the station is **Daijō-ji**, a temple famous for its numerous screens (ICP) by Maruyama Ōkyo (1733–1795) and his disciples (see Art, p. 100).

**Easy Access To:**
**Tottori** (CHŪGOKU I:N1): *0:50h by JR San'in line limited express from Kasumi.*

# KINKI II:S. SOUTH FROM ŌSAKA: KŌYA-SAN

## SAKAI 001 堺

*0:10h by JR Hanwa line local from Tennōji station in Ōsaka. To connect with the Nankaitetsudō line to Kōya-san (S1), continue one stop south to Mikunigaoka. The Nintoku mausoleum and city museum are near Mozu station, two stops farther south.* Sakai's early importance is attested to by the **\*\* Nintoku Tennō-ryō**, alleged to be the tomb of Japan's sixteenth emperor. The triple-moated, keyhole-shaped mound is the world's largest tomb. In the medieval period, Sakai was a port made wealthy by overseas trade, and had strong cultural ties to Kyoto. SEN NO RIKYŪ, the great tea master, came from a Sakai merchant family. The **\*\* Sakai-shi Hakubutsukan** (City Museum) 堺市博物館 , just south of the Nintoku tumulus, is a handsome museum with outstanding exhibitions (Hrs: 9:30–17:15; enter by 16:30; clsd M (except if NH), day after NH) NY.

## S1 \*\*\* KŌYA-SAN 高野山

*1:30h by private, Nankai-tetsudō Kōya-gō limited express from Ōsaka's Namba station. Departures at 9:20, 9:50, 13:15, 14:15. From central Kinki take the JR Wakayama line to Hashimoto (0:40h by local from Yoshino-guchi, KINKI I:S12), then 0:45h by Nankai line to Kōya-san. Final ascent by cable car.* The monastery atop this wild mountain is the holy of holies of Shingon Buddhism. It was founded in 816 by KŪKAI (posthumously known as KŌBŌ DAISHI). Kūkai established the Shingon sect and performed so many miracles that he is the most venerated figure in Japanese history (see Kyoto History, p. 319). By legend, a local kami, disguised as a hunter, ordered his two hunting dogs to lead Kūkai to this hidden vale. (The two dogs, one white, the other black, are often depicted.) By the Edo period, there were a thousand temples on the mountain. Today, only 123 remain, but the majestic primordial groves, the burning lamps, and the drone of mantras, are timeless.

More than a million pilgrims visit Kōya-san every year to worship at its Okuno-in, or inner sanctuary, where the faithful believe Kūkai sits, not dead, but in deep meditation, awaiting the coming of Miroku, the Buddha of the Future. Many of Japan's historical greats—at least one of their teeth or perhaps a lock of hair—lie buried here in a vast necropolis, waiting with the Daishi; burial on Kōya has through the centuries been a status symbol for Japanese of all religious sects. If you want to really experience Kōya-san, spend the night in a temple inn, eat some of the famous Kōya-dōfu, and attend early morning services.

### Calendar

**L 3/21: Shōmieku.** Commemorates Kūkai's entry into his final meditation. Rites at Okuno-in at 8:00 and at the Mie-dō at 12:00.

**Aug. 13: Bon.** A hundred thousand candles line the Okuno-in approach.

### Getting Around

From the cable-car station, the town center is 0:20h by bus via Nyonin-dō. Taxis take the longer but more scenic route via Dai-mon (bypassing the Nyonin-dō). Kōya-san divides into two easily walked parts: the area in town around the Garan and Kongōbu-ji, and the Okuno-in area. The Kankō Kyōkai (Tourism Association) rents bicycles.

### Garan and Kongōbu-ji Area

The *garan*, a complex of sacred halls (frequently rebuilt), is the site of Kūkai's original monastery and seminary. The nearby Kongōbu-ji is the head temple of the Kōya-san Shingon sect. Treasures from the various temples form the fabulous collection of the Reihōkan Museum.

420

**Dai-mon (Great Gate).** The immense main gate to Kōya, built in 1705, faces west. On clear days, one can see as far as Awajishima and Shikoku.

**\*\*\* Garan (Central Compound)** 伽藍 Kūkai's original *garan* consisted of the Kondō (Main Hall), the Dai-tō (Great Pagoda) and the Sai-tō (West Pagoda). The Dai-tō corresponds to the *Taizōkai* (Womb) Mandala, while the Sai-tō depicts the *Kongōkai* (Diamond). Roughly, the first represents the world of action, the latter the world of wisdom, and the Kondō represents their union; it is a fundamental tenet of Shingon that these are two aspects of a single reality (see Buddhism, p. 36). Later, other halls were added by various historical figures as acts of piety and symbols of their power.

> **Kompon Dai-tō** (Fundamental Great Pagoda). This immense vermilion-and-white *tahō-tō*, rebuilt in concrete and wood in 1937, is the symbol of Kōya-san. It houses a simplified *Taizōkai* Mandala: a statue of Dainichi Nyorai surrounded by the four directional nyorai—Ashuku, Hosho, Amida, and Fukujoku—at the cardinal points.

> **Mie-dō** (ICP). W of Kompon Dai-tō. "The hall of the honorable shadow," second only to the Okuno-in in holiness, it contains a venerated portrait of Kūkai painted during his lifetime. Only the highest priests of the sect are allowed to see it. The pine tree growing in front of the hall is said to have descended from a tree in whose branches Kūkai found the *vajra* that he had hurled across the sea from China in order to determine the site of his future monastery. NW of this hall is the **Sai-tō** (West Pagoda), relegated to a minor position.

> ◆ **Fudō-dō** (NT). SE of Kompon Dai-tō. Rebuilt in 1197, this is the oldest of the monastery buildings. It is said to preserve features of Heian-period *shinden* (palace) architecture. Fudō, the fierce deity enshrined here, helps acolytes combat a wavering will and is especially revered by followers of the Shingon sect.

> The **Kondō** (Main Hall) was rebuilt after a disastrous 1931 fire. The **Tō-tō** (East Pagoda) was first built by Emperor Toba, even though the Kompon Dai-tō served as the eastern pagoda according to Kūkai's original plan. The colorful **Shisha Myōjin-sha** is a shrine principally dedicated to the mountain kami and her son, the hunter who led Kūkai to Kōya.

**\*\*\* Kongōbu-ji** 金剛峯寺 Hrs: 8:00–17:00. Nov.–Mar. 8:30–16:30. Kongōbu-ji was the name Kūkai gave to the entire mountaintop complex, but it now refers to this temple, headquarters of the Kōya-san Shingon sect. The temple was founded in 1593 by HIDEYOSHI in memory of his mother, and though rebuilt in 1863, it contains the original Momoyama-period ◆ **screens** by KANŌ MOTONOBU, TAN'YŪ, and Tansai. The Yanagi no Ma (Willow Room) is where the regent Hidetsugu, on his uncle Hideyoshi's orders, committed *seppuku*, supposedly while viewing the same Tansai screens that are there today. Visitors are served free tea and sweets near the Banryū-tei, a modern rock garden that is "Japan's largest." The kitchen, on the way out, contains huge ovens capable of feeding thousands. The large, wooden barrels on the roof of the main hall and kitchen are kept filled with water to douse fires.

**\*\*\* Reihōkan (Treasure Hall)** 霊宝館 Hrs: 8:00–17:00 (enter by 16:30). Nov.–Mar. 8:30–16:30 (enter by 16:00); clsd Jan. Rotating exhibits of Kōya's incredible art treasures, exhibited in two buildings, one old and one new. The most famous paintings, such as Eshin's *Amida Raigō Triptych*, a late-Heian *Death of the Buddha*, and *Red Fudō*, are rarely shown. The Two Worlds Mandala known as the Blood Mandala is said to have been painted with pigments mixed with blood from TAIRA NO KIYOMORI's head. A set of *vajra* (ICP) are believed

to have been brought back from Tang China by Kūkai. Some of the lifelike statues of the
♦ Hachi Dōji (NT), eight boy attendants of Fudō, are attributed to UNKEI. Documents include letters (NT) of MINAMOTO NO YORITOMO and YOSHITSUNE.

∗ **Kongōsanmai-in** 金剛三昧院 This beautiful subtemple was built in 1223 by Hōjō Masako in memory of her husband, Minamoto no Yoritomo. Its Tahō-tō (pagoda, ca. 1223, NT) is particularly graceful. The Kyōzō (Sutra Repository, 1223, ICP) is of *azekura* construction.

∗ **Tentoku-in** 天徳院 Every lord in Edo-period Japan built a subtemple on Kōya. This one was built by the Maeda (see Castles, p. 49) and has a beautiful garden attributed to KOBORI ENSHŪ (not authenticated).

∗∗ **Tokugawa Reidai (Mausoleums)** 徳川霊台 (1643, ICP). Dedicated to TOKUGAWA IEYASU and his son Hidetada, these halls were built by his grandson IEMITSU in a restrained version of the Nikkō Tōshō-gū. Unlike at Nikkō, Ieyasu is not styled here as a kami—perhaps out of deference to Kōbō Daishi. Because Ieyasu was born in the year of the tiger, there is a tiger carved under the curved gable of his mausoleum; Hidetada's has a rabbit. The interiors, not shown, are richly painted.

**Nyonin-dō (Women's Hall)** 女人堂 The bus from the cable-car station reaches Kōya-san by the Fudō Slope, one of seven traditional approaches to the holy mountain. Until 1873, women were forbidden to enter the precinct; a substitute worship hall was built for them at each of the seven entrances. This is the only one left. (In fact, there seem to have been secret "women's paths" that led quite deeply into the precinct.)

## To the Okuno-in

Pilgrims walk through a cemetery of more than 200,000 tombs, but their destination, the Okuno-in, is not considered to be Kōbō Daishi's tomb. Rather, according to Shingon belief, the Daishi is still alive, a Buddha in his own body, in deep meditation inside the hall. Every day, food is offered to him at 5:40 and 11:00 (priests traditionally did not eat after noon). Believers consider that while they live, the "Daishi walks beside them." Japanese of all sects and historical periods have wished to be buried near the Daishi, to ensure their own salvation.

∗∗∗ **Okuno-in Cemetery.** *There are two paths to the Okuno-in: We suggest taking a taxi or bus to the Okuno-in bus stop, and from there walking the path through the new cemetery to the Okuno-in. Afterward, take the longer (2 km) traditional approach back to town.* This necropolis reads like a *Who's Who* of Japanese history. The new cemetery is dominated by memorials erected by famous corporations such as Toyota and Kirin Beer for their employees. Leave New Japan by taking the first path to the left, which joins the main approach, flanked by the tombs of the rich and powerful of Old Japan, mostly daimyo. To the left of the path, look for unusual "houses" of stone, the mausoleums (ICP) of the Echizen Matsudaira (relatives of the Tokugawa). Also along this path are the "tombs" of TAIRA NO KIYOMORI, TOYOTOMI HIDEYOSHI, ODA NOBUNAGA, and Hōnen Shōnin, founder of the Jōdo sect. Lord Asano and his 47 faithful retainers, of *Chūshingura* fame, as well as Kabuki actor Ichikawa Danjūrō, are also here. Many tombs are *gorintō*, or "five-ringed towers," representing the five elements (from top to bottom: void, wind, fire, water, earth). Each element is represented by a different geometric shape and marked with a different Sanskrit letter.

∗∗∗ **Okuno-in (Inner Sanctum)** 奥ノ院 Hrs: 8:00–17:00. Nov.–Mar. 8:30–16:30. After passing a rest hall and temple offices, the path abuts on seven bronze statues, mostly of Jizō, the bosatsu who saves souls in purgatory; one prays to them by dousing them with water. The path then crosses a bridge, which marks the beginning of the inner compound of the Okuno-in. The first hall is the **Tōrō-dō** (Lantern Hall), which though modern, houses two oil lanterns that supposedly have been burning continuously since the Heian period; one was given by Emperor Shirakawa, the other by a poor woman who sold her only possession, her hair, in order to buy the lamp. To the left of the Tōrō-dō is an enclosure for imperial tombs. Directly behind is the **Okuno-in** itself, a closed, wooden hall. Pilgrims can pray—and visitors can peer—at the entrance gate of Kukai's mausoleum. The return route, along the older, longer approach (keep to the right) takes you to Ichi no Hashi bridge.

∗ **Shōjōshin-in** 清浄心院 The first subtemple on the right, after crossing Ichi no Hashi to leave the cemetery. This temple is similar to Kongōbu-ji in the grandeur and completeness of its Momoyama-period design. Lovely garden.

## Kōya-san Lodgings (TEL 0736)

Fifty-three subtemples (including those described above) are inns, called *shukubō*, and a stay (2 nights is ideal) is not to be missed. They're like a fine old ryokan except that you'll be served by monks. The *shōjin-ryōri* (vegetarian cuisine) is excellent and will include *goma-dōfu* (sesame tofu) and *Kōya-dōfu*, a spongy, freeze-dried tofu, supposedly invented here. Guests rise around 5:30 for morning services. Prepaid reservation through JTB or Kankō Kyōkai (56-2417). Y7–10,000 w/meals. Some favorites:

**Yōchi-in** 桜池院 (56-2003). 293 Kōyasan, Kōya-chō, Ito-gun, Wakayama-ken. Beautiful grounds and old buildings.

∗ **Shinnō-in** 親王院 (56-2227). 144 Kōyasan. Long experience with Western guests.

**Tentoku-in** 天徳院 (56-2714). 370 Kōyasan. Guests can stay in a tea arbor.

**Kongōsanmai-in** 金剛三昧院 (56-3838). 425 Kōyasan.

**Shōjōshin-in** 清浄心院 (56-2006). 566 Kōyasan.

**Sainan-in** 西南院 (56-2421). 249 Kōyasan. New buildings. Deluxe rooms, Y10,000.

**Easy Access To:**

** **Yoshino** (KINKI I:S13): *0:45h by Nankai line to Hashimoto, then 0:40h by JR Wakayama line local to Yoshino-guchi.*

## Exploring the Southwest Coast of Kii Peninsula

Fine coastal scenery, but trains are slow and infrequent. There are lodgings of all types for the summer crowds. Cape **Hinomisaki** is famous for **America Mura**, a village of returned Japanese emigrés. There's a small museum of their memorabilia. A short walk from Gobō station is the temple, **Dōjō-ji**, famous in Noh and Kabuki (see Drama, p. 87); the legend of the bell is reenacted April 27. **Shirahama Onsen** (*0:15h by bus from Shirahama station*) is a hot-spring resort with white sand beaches and an excellent museum of ukiyo-e prints.

### Calendar

**Oct. 1:** * **Hiro Hachiman Jinja Fall Festival.** Hirokawa (*0:45h by local from Wakayama to Yuasa*). Dengaku dance miming planting and harvest. Lion, demon, and crocodile dancers appear at the end.

**Easy Access To:**

* **Kumano** (KINKI I:S13): *1:40h to Nachi, or 1:55h to Shingū by JR Kuroshio limited express from Shirahama.*

# KINKI III. KŌBE

**Tokyo to Kōbe:** *3:15h by Shinkansen Hikari express.*
**Kyoto to Kōbe:** *From Kyoto station, 0:35h by Shinkansen, or 1:10h by JR San'yō main line express. From Shijō-Kawaramachi, take the private Hankyū line 0:45h to Jūsō, change to Hankyū-Kōbe line and ride 0:40h to Sannomiya station.*

422 **Kōbe to Shanghai:** *The Jian Zhen, operated by the China-Japan International Ferry Co. (078-392-1021), has twice-monthly service between Shanghai and Kōbe. The trip takes 48:00h. Fares: Y20,700 (communal, sleeping on futon), Y22,500–28,800 (2nd-class bunk or tatami room), Y39,150 (1st class, more spacious bunks), Y100,800 (stateroom). Best way to arrange is through JTB (visa included; allow 7 days). Geared to Japanese groups.*
**Prefectures:** Hyōgo

## KŌBE 神戸

Though Kōbe has been an important port since the 8th century, it remained little more than a cluster of fishing villages until 1858, when the shogunate agreed to open it to foreign traders. For tourists, its interest lies in various relics of Japanese-Western encounters. Wedged between mountains and the sea, Kōbe is one of the prettiest Japanese cities.

### Getting Around

Sannomiya station, served by both JR and Hankyū, is the center for shopping and dining. An English map is available at the Kōbe Kōtsū Center building at Sannomiya, and at the Tourism Office in Shin-Kōbe station.

### Kōbe Sights

** **Kōbe-shiritsu Hakubutsukan (City Museum)** 神戸市立博物館 (391-0035). Hrs: 10:00–17:00 (enter by 16:30); clsd M (except if NH), day after NH, NY. *0:07h on foot south of Sannomiya station.* This museum is noted for its collection of *namban* art—paintings by Japanese artists who were influenced by the Western art introduced by 16th- and 17th-C Portuguese and Spaniards. Five *namban* screen exhibitions annually.

* **Takenaka Daiku Dōgukan (Carpentry Tools Museum)** 竹中大工道具館 (242-0216). Hrs: 9:30–16:30 (enter by 16:00); clsd M (Tu if M a NH), Bon, NY. This handsome museum is a tribute to the Japanese carpenter's craft, with displays on history, techniques, and tools. **Ijin-kan (Foreigners' Houses)** 異人館 Hrs: 10:00–17:00. Apr.–Oct., houses are open 1:00h longer. About 30 of the original 270 Western residences survive, mostly in **Kitano-chō**, now a chic boutique neighborhood. Several have been opened to the public, including (by "given name") Uroko no Ie, Kazamidori no Yakata (ICP), Shiroi Ijinkan (ICP), and Rhine no Yakata. A walking map of the area is available at the houses. There is also the **Perushia Bijutsukan** (Persian Art Museum) ペルシャ美術館 (222-0081), and Rose Garden and Kitano Alley, two buildings by noted Ōsaka architect Andō Tadao.
**Port Island.** *0:10h by tram from Sannomiya.* An artificial island in Kōbe Harbor, with amusement parks, public housing, and the luxurious Portopia Hotel. Frank Gehry fish.
* **Goshikizuka Kofun** 五色塚古墳 Hrs: 9:00–17:30; clsd Su. *0:35h from Sannomiya by San'yō-dentetsu to Kasumigaoka, then 0:05h on foot.* A restored 4th- or 5th-C keyhole tumulus crowned by a ring of cylindrical *haniwa*.

### Kōbe Dining

Eclectic offerings. Kitano-chō is Kōbe's international dining center. Tor Road and Motomachi are popular shopping and dining areas.

① **Ikariya** いかりや 中央区北長狭通り1-21-15 ニューアンカービル1・2階 (331-0967). New Anchor Bldg., 1F. Hrs: 15:00–22:30, Su 12:00–22:00, clsd Th. A classic place to savor famed Kobe beef, cooked on a grill. Abalone (*awabi*) steak also available. From Y5000.

③ **Hong Kong Sarō** 香港茶楼　北長狭通3-2-2 (391-5454). Hrs: 11:00–20:00; clsd W. Near Sannomiya station. Dim sum from Y300 per dish.

④ **Akaman** 赤まん　北長狭通2-11 (331-0831). Hrs: 14:30–21:00; clsd W. Near Sannomiya. Cheap and delicious *gyōza* (Peking ravioli), 7 for Y220.

⑤ **Tōtenkaku** 東天閣　山本通3-14-18 (231-1351). Hrs: M-F 11:30–14:00, 17:00–21:00; Sa, Su 11:30–21:00; clsd NY. Tor Road. Peking cuisine in an old house. Lunch special (11:00–14:30) Y5000. DC, CB, V, MC.

⑦ **Gaylord** ゲイロード　磯上通明治生命ビル　(251-4359). Meiji Seimei Bldg. Hrs: 11:30–14:30, 17:00–21:30. Sa, Su, NH 11:30–21:30. Three blocks S of Sannomiya on Flower Road. Excellent Indian food. Tandoori dishes recommended. Full courses Y3000+. DC, V.

### Kōbe Lodgings (TEL 078)

② **Kōbe Washington Hotel** 神戸ワシントンホテル (331-6111). Fax 331-6651. 2-8-2 Shimoyamate-dōri, Chūō-ku. Kōbe-shi, Hyōgo-ken. Business hotel. S Y9–10,000, Tw Y17,000.

⑥ **Oriental Hotel** オリエンタルホテル (331-8111). Fax 391-8708. 25 Kyōmachi, Chūō-ku. This famous city hotel was the grande dame of old Kōbe. New building. S Y12–14,000, Tw 23–25,000.

⑧ **Portopia Hotel** ポートピアホテル (302-1111). Fax 302-6877. 6-10-1 Nakamachi, Minato-chō, Chūō-ku. S Y12,500–14,000, Tw Y22–24,000.

**Ryokan Takayama-sō** 旅館高山荘　有馬温泉 (904-0744). 400-1 Arima-chō, Kita-ku. At Arima Onsen, one of the oldest recorded spas in Japan (*0:40h by bus from Sannomiya station*). Economical inn group; manager speaks English. Under renovation. To reopen in fall, 1992.

### Exploring Awajishima

*1:10h by ferry from Kōbe (22 per day).* The largest island in the Inland Sea nearly forms a land bridge between Kōbe and Shikoku, especially now that the Ōnaruto Bridge has been completed on the Shikoku end. Vacationers go for the beaches, fishing, and seafood. Culturally, Awajishima is famous for *ningyō jōruri*, the puppet drama that gave birth to the Bunraku theater. Half-hour performances daily (except NY) at 10:10, 11:10, 13:10, and 15:10 at the Awaji Ningyō-za in Fukura. **Lodgings:** There are 200 minshuku on the island. (Ask Hyōgo prefectural tourism office in Tokyo for help.) The resortlike Minami Awaji Kokumin Kyūkamura (People's Vacation Village, 0799-52-0291) in Fukura is Y7300 w/meals (Y8300 during holidays).

423

### Calendar
**Aug. 16:** ✳ **Hi-Odori.** Awajishima, Sumoto. Each household visits its ancestral graves and performs dances, twirling torches to the music of drums and bells.

### Easy Access To:
**Shikoku Island:** *0:40h by bus from Fukura via the Ōnaruto Bridge.*

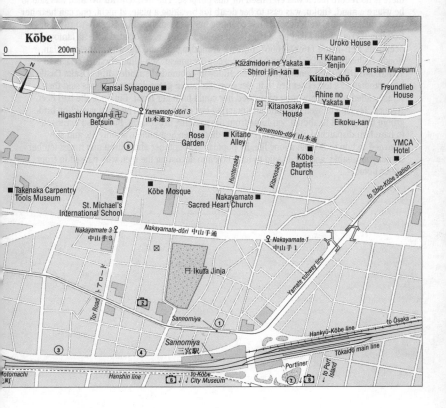

# KINKI IV. HIMEJI

**Tokyo to Himeji:** *3:50h by Shinkansen Hikari express.*
**Kyoto to Himeji:** *0:50h by Shinkansen Hikari express.*
**Prefectures:** Hyōgo

### *** HIMEJI 姫路

The castle of Himeji, known as the White Egret, is simply the most spectacular extant castle in Japan. Even visitors with limited time should make an effort to see it.

### Calendar

**Oct. 14–15:** ** **Mega Kenka Matsuri.** See Calendar, p. 384. Matsubara Hachiman Jinja (*0:10h by Sanyō-dentetsu line from Himeji to Shirahamanomiya, then 0:05h on foot*).

### Himeji Sights

** **Hyōgo-kenritsu Rekishi Hakubutsukan (History Museum)** 兵庫県立歴史博物館 (0792-88-9011). Hrs: 10:00–17:00 (enter by 16:30); clsd M (except if M a NH, then clsd Tu). *800 m north of the station; 0:05h by bus.* A handsome building designed by Tange Kenzō, at the northeast corner of Himeji-jō. Before visiting the castle, you should examine the museum's splendid exhibits on Japanese castles, particularly Himeji-jō. The museum also displays a wonderful group of puppet heads from Awajishima, the Inland Sea island that was the birthplace of *ningyō jōruri* (puppet drama). Video of *ningyō jōruri* shown regularly.

*** **Himeji-jō** 姫路城 (NT). Hrs: 9:00–17:00 (enter by 16:00). *0:05h by bus or 0:15h on foot from station.* In 1601, Ikeda Terumasa, a trusted son-in-law of TOKUGAWA IEYASU, was awarded this castle, an old structure which had been fortified by TOYOTOMI HIDEYOSHI. The castle watched over strategically vital land and sea routes in western Japan. Ieyasu was especially concerned about the many lords in western Japan who were hostile to him, and feared that they might rally around Hideyoshi's son HIDEYORI, who was ensconced in Ōsaka Castle. Terumasa added twenty new turrets and the five-storied keep, which took nine years to complete. Much of the work was paid for by the shogunate. Built at a time when great castles served not only as actual fortresses, but also as palatial seats of government, Himeji-jō achieves the ultimate marriage of Momoyama form and military function (see Castles, p. 46).

Its turrets are an elegant alternated layering of curved gables (*kara hafu*) and pointed gables (*chidori hafu*), punctuated now and then by cusped windows (*katōmado*). The keep is crowned by a pair of dolphins, charms against fire. The walls of the labyrinthine approach to the donjon are riddled with loopholes, round or square for the rifle, long and narrow for the bow. Other standard features of a castle, such as *ishi-otoshi*, or rock-chutes, are much in evidence. At the base of the main tower there once stood a mansion, where the lord of the castle lived in times of peace.

The castle is rich in legends. The southwest citadel is called the *harakiri* citadel, though there is no record that it was ever used for this purpose. The well, **Okiku no Ido**, was said to be where a maid, Okiku, was cast to her death for breaking a plate; at night, one can hear her voice echoing in the well, despairingly counting her lord's dishes. The **Keshō-yagura**, or Boudoir Turret, of the Nishi no Maru (Western Enclosure), is associated with its famous occupant, **Sen-hime** (1599–1666), Ieyasu's granddaughter and the wife of the castellan, Honda Heihachirō Tadatoki, who had succeeded Terumasa. Sen-hime's first marriage, to TOYOTOMI HIDEYORI, ended in disaster: Hideyori committed suicide within Ōsaka Castle as her grandfather's forces set fire to it. Her own life was in grave danger, and it is said that Ieyasu called out that any man who saved her could have her hand. But once she had been rescued, Ieyasu changed his mind and married her off to Honda. The jilted would-be bridegroom threatened to abduct Sen-hime from the wedding procession, but Ieyasu arranged to have him dispatched, permanently. Honda died when Sen-hime was only 35, and she returned to Edo to live out a long life. By popular account, her short-lived marriages left her sexually insatiable, and she is said to have taken to accosting the men who passed in front of her home.

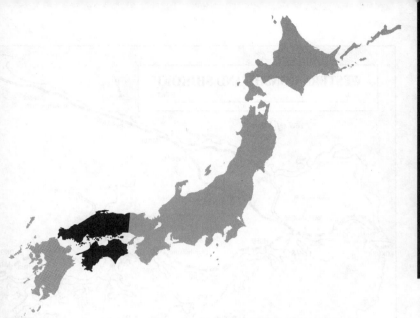

# Chūgoku and Shikoku

Chūgoku (western Honshū) and Shikoku are marked by great diversity. Though this chapter is organized from east to west, the actual geographical and cultural division is from north to south. Facing the Japan Sea is the isolated San'in, "in the shadow of mountains," a region with a mysterious past and gloomy skies. The bright, aggressively industrial San'yō coast on the south, facing the Inland Sea, was the major corridor for historical events and the flow of cultural influences from the continent. Against the backdrop of the industrialized San'yō coast are islets of the Inland Sea, where life moves with the pace of bygone times. Shikoku, the smallest of Japan's four main islands, is the site of the famous eighty-eight-temple circuit in honor of the great Buddhist saint, Kūkai.

## BEST ATTRACTIONS

I:S6   ✷✷ **Kotohira Shrine.** This shrine on Shikoku is visited by seafarers throughout Japan. Nearby Zentsū-ji, the birthplace of Kūkai, is crowded with pilgrims (p. 435).

II   ✷✷✷ **Kurashiki.** Handsome Edo-period rice warehouses—now stuffed with art instead of rice—are grouped around a willow-lined canal (p. 438).

II:N2   ✷✷ **Fukiya.** An isolated ghost town in beautiful surroundings (p. 440).

II:N5   ✷✷ **Izumo Shrine.** Perhaps the oldest shrine in Japan, it is a cypher left by the ancient Izumo tribe, children of the unpredictable storm god, Susano'o (p. 443).

III:S1   ✷✷ **Tomo no Ura.** A dazzling little fishing port (p. 445).

III:S4   ✷✷ **STS Inland Sea Cruise.** This excessively commercial but convenient operation takes you to Ōmishima, home of the greatest collection of armor in Japan (p. 446).

IV:S1   ✷✷✷ **Miyajima.** The celebrated Itsukushima Jinja, its vermilion pavilions reflected in the waters of the Inland Sea, is one of the most exquisite sights in Japan (p. 449).

VI:N4   ✷✷ **Hagi.** A beautiful old San'in castle town known for its tea pottery. Cradle of the Meiji Restoration (p. 459).

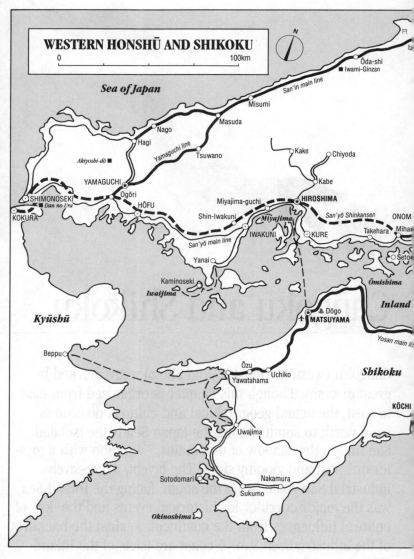

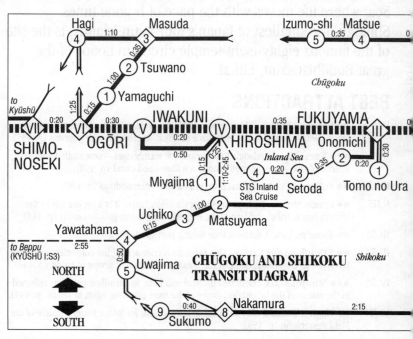

## Traveling

The San'yō Shinkansen is fast, but trains along the San'in coast and in Shikoku are slow. The Yakumo-gō express from Okayama (via Kurashiki) to Izumo is the speediest way to get to the San'in. The Seto Ōhashi bridge provides rapid access by train and road to Shikoku Island. There are also ferries from Kasaoka, Onomichi, and Hiroshima. The STS company runs a convenient cruise of the Inland Sea. Exploring the Inland Sea using local ferries is rewarding but time-consuming; you must be willing to juggle the chaotic ferry schedules. Most ferries don't let passengers near the bow of the boat, limiting your view. Hydrofoils, while costlier, offer better views. To visit remoter areas, such as Izumo or Kōchi, much time can be saved by flying, which is almost as cheap as taking limited express trains.

## Resources

For Inland Sea explorers, Donald Richie's classic travel account, *The Inland Sea*, is the perfect companion. Pack a copy, since you'll have plenty of time to read while waiting for ferries.

# SPECIAL INTERESTS

**Well-Preserved Towns:** Uchiko, on Shikoku, has a street of fine wax-merchants' houses. Tsuwano and Bitchū-Takahashi are small, old-fashioned castle towns. Iwakuni, another castle town, is famous for its beautiful "Brocade Sash Bridge." Yamaguchi preserves fine temples and shrines from its heyday as the largest and most cultured city of Japan's Sengoku period. Iwami-Ginzan was the site of one of Edo Japan's great silver mines. Iwaishima is an isolated Inland Sea island with mazelike stone walls.

**International Villas:** The Okayama Prefectural Government has created a half-dozen of these little inns in remote and scenic areas: beautifully renovated farmhouses at the rural hamlets of Hattōji and Koshihata, a new but traditional-style inn at the well-preserved village of Fukiya, and sleek, architect-designed villas at Shiraishi Island, Ushimado, and Yahata Onsen. The inns are a delight, and will lure you into wonderful regions that you might not have thought to visit. All have tasteful decor, fully equipped kitchens (no meals provided), and modern bathroom facilities. The villas are reserved for non-Japanese and their Japanese friends. (They tend to be filled with resident foreigners on weekends. Ideal for families with children.) Guests bring groceries (rice and coffee are provided at each villa) or dine at nearby restaurants. By reservation only, Y3000 per person. Once you stay in one, you become a 2-year member, and the price drops to Y2500. For information and reservations, contact Okayama Prefectural Government International Exchange Section, 2-4-6 Uchisange, Okayama City 700 (tel: 0862-24-2111, fax 0862-23-3431).

**Archeology:** The Kibi Plain, near Kurashiki, and Yakumo Village near Matsue, ancient strongholds of two non-Yamato tribes, are dotted with tumuli and ruins of Nara-period temples. Kibi has a scenic cycling route.

**Crafts:** Tottori, Kurashiki, and Izumo have fine folk-craft museums. Imbe, near Okayama, makes the famed Bizen pottery. Hagi's pinkish, Korean-style ware is prized for the tea ceremony. Yamaguchi has a charming lacquerware. Tobe-yaki, made near Matsuyama on Shikoku, is a sturdy, handsome folk porcelain.

### Seasons

The climate is as varied as the geography. The San'in coast has more precipitation and is generally cloudy, whereas the San'yō coast and Shikoku enjoy clear, mild weather.

**Average Temperature °C (°F)/Days of Rain or Snow**

|  | January | April | July | October |
|---|---|---|---|---|
| Matsue | 3.8 (38.8)/20 | 12.5 (54.5)/11 | 25.2 (77.4)/11 | 16.2 (61.2)/11 |
| Hiroshima | 4.3 (39.7)/7 | 13.3 (55.9)/10 | 25.6 (78.1)/11 | 17.0 (62.6)/6 |
| Matsuyama | 5.3 (41.5)/7 | 13.9 (57.0)/11 | 26.2 (79.2)/10 | 17.7 (63.9)/8 |
| Kōchi | 5.6 (42.1)/5 | 15.4 (59.7)/12 | 26.2 (79.2)/13 | 18.4 (65.1)/9 |

# CALENDAR

**Jan. 2, 3, 5:** \* **Bugaku.** Miyajima (IV:S1). P
**Feb. (3rd Sa):** \*\* **Saidai-ji Eyō.** Okayama(I). One of the largest naked festivals in Japan. Hundreds of men struggle for a wooden ball in the temple hall as they are doused with water. Midnight.
**L 3/3:** \* **Hina-nagashi.** Tottori (I:N1). V
**Apr. 7:** \* **Aofushigaki no Shinji.** Miho (II:N4). E S
**Apr. 15:** \* **Hiwatari.** Miyajima (IV:S1). F E
**Apr. 16–18:** \* **Jin-Noh.** Miyajima (IV:S1). P
**May 3:** \* **Farmer's Kabuki.** Shōdoshima (I:S2). P
**May 14–16:** \* **Izumo Taisha Daisairei.** (II:N5). P S
**L 5/5:** \* **Ōyamazumi Jinja Otaue-sai.** Ōmishima (III:S4). P S
**June (1st Su):** \*\* **Hana-taue.** Chiyoda (IV). Famous rice-planting festival. Sacred dances are offered in the morning. From 14:30, dozens of young women in traditional farming clothes plant rice seedlings as the men play drums and flutes.
**July 23–24:** \*\* **Warei Jinja Matsuri.** Uwajima (IV:S5). One of the most spectacular festivals on Shikoku. Hundreds of boats fill the harbor to accompany the *mikoshi* arriving by ship. The *mikoshi* are carried upriver by youths. Festivities include bullfights, torch races, and fireworks.
**L 6/17:** \*\* **Kangen-sai.** Miyajima (IV:S1). Decorated sacred boats sail through the famous torii, as sacred music and dances are performed. Lantern-lit boats at night.
**Aug. 12–15:** \*\* **Awa Odori.** Shikoku, Tokushima (I:S4). A festival said to have originally celebrated the completion of Tokushima's castle at the end of the 16th century. Dancing revelers and musicians playing *shamisen* and gongs engulf the town for four nights. Exceedingly popular with tourists; reserve hotels months in advance (YH recommended).
**Aug. 14–16:** \* **Shiraishi Odori.** Shiraishi (II). P
**Aug. 16:** \* **Sha'ara Bune.** Okinoshima (II:N4). V
**Aug. 31:** \* **Itsukushima Jinja Jūshichiya Matsuri.** Abu-machi (VI:N4). P F V
**Sept. 24–25:** \* **Sada Goza-kae Shinji.** Kajima (II:N4). P S
**Sept. 28:** \* **Izumo Kagura.** Daitō (II:N4). P
**Sept. (2nd Sa):** \* **Nishi-Chūgoku Senbatsu Kagura Kyō-en Taikai.** Kakei (IV). P
**L 9/9:** \* **Ōyamazumi Jinja Nukiho-sai.** Ōmishima (III:S4). P S
**Oct. 10:** \* **Farmer's Kabuki.** Shōdoshima (I:S2). P
**Oct. 11–18:** \* **Aki Matsuri.** Shōdoshima (I:S2). P E
**Oct. 28–29:** \*\* **Uwatsuhiko Jinja Matsuri.** Shikoku, Uwajima (IV:S5). Rustic matsuri, famous for Yatsushika Odori, in which 8 male deer-dancers search for a female. Giant *ushi-oni* (ox-demons) chase away bad spirits.
**Nov. 3:** \* **Mishō Hachiman-sai.** Mishō (IV:S5). P
**Nov. 15:** \* **Hiwatari.** Miyajima (IV:S1). F E
**L 10/11–17:** \* **Kamiari-sai.** Izumo Taisha (II:N5). S
**Dec. 3:** \* **Morotabune Shinji.** Miho (II:N4). S
**Dec. 31:** \* **Chinkasai.** Miyajima (IV:S1). F E V

# CHŪGOKU I. OKAYAMA

**Tokyo to Okayama:** *4:00h by Shinkansen Hikari express.*
**Kyoto to Okayama:** *1:10h by Shinkansen Hikari express.*
**Prefectures:** Okayama, Tottori, Kagawa, Tokushima, Kōchi

**∗OKAYAMA** 岡山
A major city on the Inland Sea. Okayama is noted for the large landscape garden, Kōraku-en, built by its feudal lord. Nearby excursions include the ancient pottery center of Bizen and the Kibi plain. Ports near Okayama serve the Inland Sea and Shikoku.

## Calendar
**Feb. (3rd Sa): ∗∗ Saidai-ji Eyō.** See Calendar, preceding page. From midnight, at Saidai-ji *(0:20h by train to Saidai-ji station or 0:30h by bus from Okayama station)*.

## Getting Around
Main attractions form a walkable loop: Orient Museum—Prefectural Art Museum—Prefectural Museum—Kōraku-en—Castle—Hayashibara Art Museum; about 4:00h. You can purchase a combined admission ticket for all of these except the Orient Museum. The Nishikawa Greenway Park is a lovely canalside promenade. **Rent-a-car:** The highway to Kibi, Takahashi, and Fukiya (II:N1–2) is not too difficult to drive. Main roads are indicated by romanized signs. Japaren ジャパレン (32-2421), a block from Okayama station, rents S-class cars with unlimited mileage for about Y5000 per day.

## Okayama Sights
**∗∗ Orient Bijutsukan (Orient Museum)** 岡山市立オリエント美術館
(32-3636). Hrs: 9:00–17:00 (enter by 16:30); clsd M (Tu, if M a NH), NY. Handsome museum of ancient Near Eastern art. Displays emphasize how the culture of the Near East was transmitted to Japan via the Silk Route.

**∗ Okayama-kenritsu Bijutsukan (Pref. Museum of Art)** 岡山県立美術館 (25-4800).
Hrs: 9:00–17:00 (enter by 16:30); clsd M (except if a NH, then clsd Tu), NY. Paintings by SESSHŪ, fabled swordsman Miyamoto Musashi, and other fine works of art are exhibited in this new building designed by Okada Shinichi.

**∗ Okayama-kenritsu Hakubutsukan (Prefectural Museum)** 岡山県立博物館
(72-1149). Hrs: 9:00–18:00; clsd M (Tu if M a NH), NY. Oct.–Mar. 9:30–17:00. Archeological materials from the Kibi Plain, Bizen pottery, and art, including fragments and copies of a Kamakura-period scroll depicting Kibi no Makibi's trip to China.

**∗∗∗ Kōraku-en** 後楽園 Hrs: 7:30–18:00. Oct.–Mar. 8:00–17:00. Large stroll garden built in 1686 by the Okayama daimyo, whose black castle (a reconstruction) looms in the background. This garden has many visually appealing details, including patches of rice paddies and tea bushes to provide a pastoral touch. The broad expanses of lawn may be more recent, introduced under the influence of Western ideas.

**Okayama-jō** 岡山城 Hrs: 9:00–17:00; clsd NY. In counterpoint to the White Egret Castle of Himeji, the black Okayama-jō was nicknamed the Crow Castle. Only two turrets survive. The ferroconcrete reconstruction of the keep is faithful to exterior details.

**∗∗ Hayashibara Bijutsukan (Art Museum)** 林原美術館 (23-1733). Hrs: 9:00–17:00 (enter by 16:30); clsd NY and one week every two months. The museum stands behind an Edo-period gate removed from the Okayama daimyo's mansion. A fine collection of Chinese and Japanese art, much of it the former property of the Okayama daimyo. Especially noted for lacquer, swords, Noh costumes, and Chinese bronzes.

429

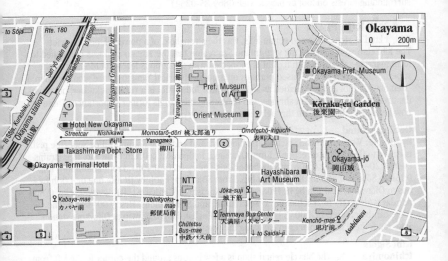

**Okayama Dining and Lodgings** (TEL 0862)

Shops and restaurants are concentrated near Omotemachi and the Tenmaya Bus Center (many shops clsd Tu).

① **Miyoshino** 三好野 駅前町 (25-2251). Hrs: 11:00–21:00. Try *matsuri-zushi*, seafood and vegetables arranged on a bed of vinegared rice. Y1000.

② **Itchō** 一丁 表町1-1-26 (23-1648). Hrs: 9:00–20:00; clsd Tu (except if NH), NY. Sushi from Y900. No CC.

③ **Okayama-ken Seinen Kaikan YH** 岡山県青年会館YH (52-0651). 1-7-6 Tsukura-chō, Okayama-shi, Okayama-ken.

④ **Okayama Yūbin Chokin Kaikan** 岡山郵便貯金会館 (23-8100). 1-13 Kuwata-chō. S Y4800, Tw Y9000.

⑤ ✴✴ **Okayama Tōkyū Hotel** 岡山東急ホテル (33-2411). Fax 23-8763. 3-2-18 Daiku. S Y8300–14,000, Tw Y17,500.

⑥ ✴ **Okayama Kokusai Hotel** 岡山国際ホテル (73-7311). Fax 71-0292. 4-1-16 Kadota Honmachi. S Y8500–13,500, Tw Y16,500–36,000.

## ✴ IMBE 伊部

*From Shinkansen stations Okayama or Aioi, take the JR Akō line to Imbe (0:40h–0:45h, infrequent). Teiki Kankō bus tour: In Japanese, Y3300. Mar.–Nov. on weekends, NH. Okayama station (10:30) — Bizen Osafune sword museum — Fujiwara Kei Kinenkan — Morishita Museum — Shizutani Gakkō — Bizen Tōgei Kaikan and kilns — Okayama station (17:00). Reserve at Okayama-ken Kankō Bus, 0862-24-0888.* This 700-year-old pottery village is famous for **Bizen-yaki**, a high-fired, unglazed ware that has long been prized by tea masters. It is typically a burnished rust or charred blue-gray, speckled or dripping with molten ash. Wood-fired climbing kilns remain widely used, as only they can produce the desired effects. Because the quality of a piece depends so much on "kiln accidents," Bizen-yaki is expensive. Good Bizen ware is outnumbered by the mediocre. Many studios, *kamamoto* (larger kilns), and shops line the street that forms a T-junction with the main street from the station. Stop in at the gallery of "living national treasure" Yamamoto Tōshū.

✴✴ **Bizen Tōgei Bijutsukan (Ceramics Museum)** 備前陶芸美術館 (0869-64-1400). Hrs: 9:30–17:00 (enter by 16:30); clsd M (Tu if M a NH), NY. This handsome gray building is visible from the station. Its tasteful displays of excellent Bizen-yaki, old and new, supplemented by a pamphlet in English on the ware's history and characteristics, make an excellent introduction. Pick up a map of local kilns and shops.

✴✴ **Fujiwara Kei Kinenkan (Memorial Gallery)** 藤原啓記念館 (67-0638). Hrs: 10:00–16:30; clsd M, Dec. 20–Jan. 10. *0:10h by taxi from station.* A museum exhibiting the work of the late Fujiwara Kei, a Bizen potter who was a Living National Treasure.

✴✴✴ **Shizutani Gakkō** 閑谷学校 (67-1436). Hrs: 9:00–17:00. Oct.–Mar. 9:00–16:00; clsd Dec. 28–31. *0:20h by taxi (about Y5000 round trip) from Imbe or 0:10h from Yoshinaga station on the JR San'yō main line. Only 1–2 buses per day.* An unusual Edo-period school for commoners established by the Lord of Bizen in 1670. Nestled in a stunning mountain valley, the main complex of the lovely campus is surrounded by a superb wall of pale stone (ICP). Directly in line with the main gate is the Seibyō (Confucian shrine), and Shizutani Jinja (ICP). The **Kōdō** (Lecture Hall, NT), is a templelike structure with bell-shaped windows and a soaring roof of burnt-red tiles, reminiscent of Bizen-yaki.

✴✴ **Hattōji Village** 八塔寺 *0:30h by bus (only 2–4 per day) from Yoshinaga station.* This isolated hamlet is situated on a high mountain plateau in a region of great natural beauty. Visitors can stay at the International Villa (see p. 428) and explore ancient temples in the surrounding forests on foot or bicycle (tel: 0869-85-0254).

## ✴ # THE KIBI PLAIN

Kibi, a land of rice plains and gentle hills, was the stronghold of a powerful, ancient tribe. The Kibi clan so dominated the vital Inland Sea region that the Yamato clan was compelled to form marriage alliances with it. Kibi is connected with the famous legend of Momotarō, the superboy born of a peach, based perhaps on a quasi-historical Yamato prince who conquered "demons" in Kibi and was deified as **Kibitsuhiko**. Today, Kibi is a rural backwater, but abundant relics — tumuli, ancient shrines, and temples — attest to its former importance. These are now linked by a bicycle path through the scenic countryside.

### Getting Around

**By bicycle:** We recommend starting at Ichinomiya and ending at Kokubun-ji or Sōja (the path is easier to find in this direction). From Okayama, Ichinomiya is 0:12h by JR Kibi line (trains every 0:20–0:40h), or 0:30h by Sōja-bound bus (every 0:20–0:40h). From Kokubun-ji it is 0:15h to Sōja or 0:45h to Okayama by bus. From Sōja, it is 0:40h by JR Kibi line or 1:00h by bus to Okayama, or 0:15h by JR Hakubi line to Kurashiki (CHŪGOKU II). Rent-a-cycles (Y800 per day w/dropoff) near Ichinomiya, Kokubun-ji, and Sōja stations. Hrs: 9:00–18:00. The route can be covered in 4:00–5:00h. Pick up an English-language map at Okayama station. Take food; there are no places to eat along the way.

### Kibi Sights

**Ichinomiya** 一宮 The bicycle rental shop is a few houses around the corner to the left from the station. A 0:05h walk from the station is **Kibitsuhiko Jinja** (late 17th C, ICP), which has a large pond garden. Look for the cycling path (has a white railing); head west on it.

**\*\*\* Kibitsu Jinja** 吉備津神社 This shrine, sacred to the deified hero Kibitsuhiko, was ranked for centuries among the most important shrines in the nation. Set on a wooded hillside, its twin gables are visible from a distance. A pine-lined approach leads to the Main Gate (ICP). The ◆ **Main Hall** (NT), rebuilt by ASHIKAGA YOSHIMITSU in 1425, is unique; the oratory and inner sanctum, usually two separate halls, are joined under one roof, crowned by two dormer gables perched side by side. The deep, uplifted eaves and gables create an effect of unusual grace and grandeur. The **south gate** (ICP) leads to a long staircase. Near the bottom, turn right to the ◆ **Okama-den** (1612, ICP), or Cauldron Hall, a building modeled on an ancient kitchen. It contains a cauldron of steaming water that groans if a petitioner's request is to be granted. The sound is supposedly emitted by the head of a demon slain by Kibitsuhiko, which is buried beneath it. Divinations are performed every morning, except on Monday. Outside the precincts stand a few old inns and teahouses, reminders of the shrine's popularity with pilgrims in former times.

**Koikui Jinja (Carp-Devouring Shrine)** 鯉喰神社 *About 2.5 km west of Kibitsu Jinja, across the Ashimori River.* This nondescript place is connected to a story about a demon who transforms himself into a carp to escape Kibitsuhiko, but winds up being devoured by him. The path follows the river, but at the second bridge, diverges left, away from the river. About 1 km farther is **Tsukuriyama Kofun** 造山古墳 , the fourth largest tumulus in Japan. It now looks like a small, tree-covered hill surrounded by a narrow moat.

**Kokubun-niji Ato** 国分尼寺跡 *About 0:20h by bicycle from Tsukuriyama Kofun.* Stone foundations of the national nunnery established in each province during the Nara period. Nearby are the **Kenritsu Kibiji Kyōdokan** (Archeological Museum, Hrs: 9:00–16:30; clsd M, NY) and **Kōmorizuka Kofun**, an excavated 5th or 6th-C tomb.

**\*\* Bitchū Kokubun-ji** 備中国分寺 This temple was established in the 8th C as the "national temple" of Kibi province under Emperor Shōmu (see Nara History, p. 392). The present structures were rebuilt on an adjacent site in the 19th C. Its five-storied pagoda (ICP), soaring above the rice paddies and farmhouses, is Kibi's most charming sight.

**Sōja** 総社 Bicycles can be dropped off near Sōja station. Hōfuku-ji, a Zen monastery 3 km northwest of Sōja station, is where the young SESSHŪ, a novice of the temple, was punished for doodling on his sutra scrolls by being tied to a pillar. Using his toes, he painted a vivid rat out of the puddle of his tears. It was so realistic that it gave the priests a great fright; and this is how his artistic talent was recognized.

431

### Exploring Okayama Environs

**Yahata Onsen** 八幡温泉 *1.5 km south of Fukuwatari station, which is 0:30h from Okayama by JR Tsuyama line express.* The reason to come here is to soak in the hotspring waters at Takebe International Villa (see p. 428), which boasts magnificent bathhouses and two outdoor baths (tel: 08672-2-2500).

**Ushimado** 牛窓 *1:00h by bus from Okayama station.* The quiet charm of this ancient Inland Sea port is being shattered by recent resort development, but one can still enjoy the lovely view from Honren-ji, a temple that housed traveling Korean and Chinese envoys. For an even better view, stay at the Ushimado International Villa (see p. 428; tel: 086934-4218).

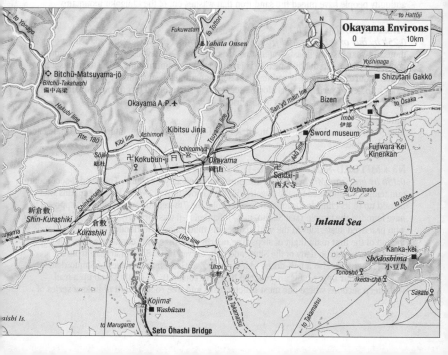

# CHŪGOKU I:N. NORTH FROM OKAYAMA: TOTTORI AND THE SAN'IN COAST

## N1 TOTTORI 鳥取

*2:45h by the JR Tsuyama/Inbi line Sakyū limited express from Okayama, 4 per day. From Fukuchiyama (KINKI II:N2), 2:20h by San'in line limited express, originating in Kyoto.* Tottori is a major city on the San'in coast.

### Calendar
**L 3/3: * Hina-nagashi.** An ancient form of the Doll Festival; bad fortune is exorcised by setting tiny red-and-white dolls strapped onto a woven basket adrift on the river.

### Tottori Sights
**\*\* Tottori Mingei Bijutsukan (Folk Art Museum)** 鳥取民芸美術館 Hrs: 10:00–17:00; clsd W (Th if W a NH), NY. *0:05h on foot from the station.* A small, attractive museum with a fine ceramics collection. Adjoining the museum are a good craft shop and restaurant. The odd, cylindrical "chapel" in front has gathered within it many stone reliefs of Jizō that served as gravestones for children.

**\* Kannon-in Tei-en** 観音院庭園 Hrs: 9:00–17:00. *0:10h by bus from the station.* A fine 17th-C garden composed of a large pond, wooded hill, and the idiomatic crane-tortoise islets. A "dry waterfall" across the pond gives the garden a focus and depth.

**\* Jinpūkaku** 仁風閣 (ICP). Hrs: 9:00–17:00 (enter by 16:30); clsd M, day after NH, NY. *0:05h by bus from station.* A handsome French Renaissance-style villa built in 1907 for the crown prince (the future Emperor Taishō).

**\* Sakyū (Sand Dunes)** 砂丘 *0:20h by bus from station.* This is Tottori's most famous attraction, because of its uniqueness in Japan. The 2-km-wide, 16-km-long expanse of wind-patterned yellow-brown sand fringed with twisted pines, stark against the Japan Sea, is best at sunrise and sunset. The dunes are the setting for Teshigahara Hiroshi's film, *Woman of the Dunes.* Tour buses congregate at one end, but the loudspeakers make such a racket that you have to walk a long way to get out of earshot.

### Tottori Dining
**Takumi Kappō-ten** たくみ割烹店 (0857-26-6355). Hrs: 11:30–20:30; clsd W. Next to the Folk Art Museum. Fresh seafood, prepared in local fashion. *Kisetsu-ryōri,* Y10,000.

## N2 KURAYOSHI 倉吉
*0:40h by JR San'in line limited express from Tottori.* This pleasant small town is the gateway to Misasa Onsen, a famous hot-spring resort, and to Mitoku-san Sanbutsu-ji. Attractions include **Dōzogun,** an area of back streets with old *kura* and a traditional soy-sauce brewery (*near Meiji-machi bus stop, 0:10h from station*). Nearby is **Mingei** 民芸 (0858-23-1822), a cozy craft shop for colorful local papier-mâché toys (Hrs: 9:00–17:30; clsd Th, NY). The **Kurayoshi Hakubutsukan/Rekishi Minzoku Shiryōkan** 倉吉博物館/歴史民俗資料館 is a handsome museum of art, local history, and ethnography (Hrs: 9:00–17:00 (enter by 16:30); clsd M (Tu if M a NH), day after NH, NY. *0:10h walk from Meiji-machi bus stop*). Its collection of preindustrial iron-forging and casting tools is unusually complete and well-preserved. Iron technology was especially important in the San'in region, where since antiquity people have mined the sand iron that washes out of the Chūgoku mountains.

## MISASA ONSEN 三朝温泉
*0:25h by bus or 0:15h by taxi from Kurayoshi station.* Misasa Onsen, a spa with a thousand-year history, boasts waters that are truly "hot"—they have the highest radium content in Japan. (In the hills nearby is Japan's largest uranium mine.) The town has a bust of Marie Curie, discoverer of radium, and holds an annual festival in her honor. One can enjoy a soak at a variety of inns along a scenic river surrounded by green mountains, or in the free open-air riverside baths by the bridge in the center of town.

### Calendar
**May 3–4: Ōtsunahiki.** Misasa Onsen. A tug-of-war between huge, interlocking "male" and "female" ropes.

## N3 \* MITOKU-SAN SANBUTSU-JI 三徳山三仏寺
*0:15h by bus from Misasa Onsen.* Treasure hall open all year round. This Tendai-sect mountain temple is renowned for the Nageire-dō, the Throw-In Hall, which legend explains was heaved up to its cliffside location by En no Gyōja, the 7th-century mystic who is supposed to have founded the temple (see Shinto, p. 27). Sanbutsu-ji was formerly a temple of *yamabushi,* who practiced austerities in the wild, dangerous mountains. The Hondō (Main Hall) stands at the top of the first main flight of steps. The nearby **treasure hall** contains a fine, gilt wood **Zaō Gongen,** patron deity of the Shugendō cult, carved in 1168 by an artisan from the capital. There are also a half-dozen older, rustic Zaō Gongen and images of Shinto deities. The spectacular upper halls are reached by a very rough, 0:30–0:40h climb up a trail with steep sections where one must clutch chains and tree roots. The trail links a series of

halls, the most important of which are the **Monju-dō** (ca. 16th C, ICP), **Jizō-dō** (ca. 15th C, ICP), and the famed ** **Nageire-dō** (ca. 12th C, NT), an architectural marvel which has clung to the rock face for more than 800 years. There is a fire festival on the last Su in Oct.

### Misasa and Mitoku-san Lodgings (TEL 0858)
* **Ōhashi Ryokan** 大橋旅館 (43-0211). Misasa Onsen, Tōhaku-gun, Tottori-ken. Rambling old inn along the river. Mixed baths built from natural boulders. Y15–30,000.
* **Temple Lodgings at Sanbutsu-ji:** By reservation. The temples also serve a lunch of mountain greens and pink-fleshed trout, from Y2500. **Shōzen-in** ·正善院 (43-2668) is friendly and has a lovely garden; Y8000 w/meals. **Rinkō-in** 輪光院 (43-2667) is Y5000 w/meals.

### Easy Access To:
* **Matsue** (CHŪGOKU II:N4): *From Kurayoshi, 1:40h by San'in line limited express.*
*** **Kurashiki** (CHŪGOKU II): *From Kurayoshi, 1:05h to Yonago, then change to the Yakumo express to Kurashiki and Okayama.*

# CHŪGOKU I:S. EASTERN AND CENTRAL SHIKOKU

**Main Attraction:** Kotohira (S6)

### Traveling
We have split Shikoku into two sections, east/central, and west. From the Shinkansen, the best access to the east/central regions is from Okayama, and to the west, from Hiroshima. See CHŪGOKU IV:S for a description of western Shikoku.

### S1 KOJIMA 児島
*0:25h by JR Seto Ōhashi line from Okayama.* Starting point for the Seto Ōhashi bridge to Shikoku Island. Leapfrogging from islet to islet, the bridge's six spans add up to 12.3 km, making it the world's longest double-decker bridge. For good views, take the JR Marine Liner train. You can also cross by bus and get off at Yoshima for a boat ride around the base of one of the spans.

### S2 * SHŌDOSHIMA 小豆島
*0:40h by jetfoil or 1:20h by ferry from Okayama harbor, or 0:35h by JR train from Okayama to Uno, then 1:30h by ferry to Tonoshō, on the W side of Shōdoshima. From Takamatsu, 0:35h by hydrofoil or 1:00h by ferry.* Shōdoshima is an interesting detour for Shikoku-bound travelers. The second-largest Inland Sea island abounds in scenic coves, beaches, mountains, and rustic villages and ports. The mood is somewhat spoiled by a fake Parthenon (to go with Shōdo's olive groves), and peacock and monkey parks, but there are also sights of genuine historical interest, such as the 88 temples of its popular, 150-km version of the Shikoku pilgrimage circuit, and the Ōsaka-jō Chikujō Zanseki, the quarry that provided the granite for Ōsaka Castle. Other areas worth exploring are Cape Jizōzaki, the panoramic mountain road up to the eroded formations at Kankakei, and Utsukushinohara, the roof of Shōdo, with a sweeping view of the Inland Sea.

### Calendar
Beaches and minshuku are crowded in August.
**May 3:** * **Farmer's Kabuki.** Shōdoshima's traditional farmer's Kabuki is performed at Rikyū Hachiman-gū in Tonoshō.
**Oct. 10:** * **Farmer's Kabuki.** Kasuga Hachiman-gū, Ikeda-chō.
**Oct. 11–18:** * **Aki Matsuri.** Festival of the Hachiman shrines in every town on this island. Drum beating by skillful drummers is the main event.

### Getting Around
Motorscooters are Y3000 per day (w/insurance) from Ryōbi Rent-a-Bike 両備レンタバイク (62-6578), located near the pier. Hrs: 8:30–17:00.

### Shōdoshima Lodgings (TEL 0879)
There are also numerous minshuku and youth hostels.
**Kokuminshukusha Shōdoshima** 国民宿舎小豆島 (75-1115). 1500-4 Ikeda-chō, Shōzu-gun, Kagawa-ken. *0:25h by bus from Tonoshō to Kokuminshukusha-mae, then 0:05h walk.* Splendid views. Y5600 w/meals. No CC.
**Uchinomi-chō Cycling Terminal** 内海町サイクリングターミナル (82-1099). Uchinomi-chō, Shōzu-gun. At Sakate port, on the waterfront. Y4600 w/meals. No CC.

### S3 * TAKAMATSU 高松
*From Okayama, 1:00h by JR Seto Ōhashi line. 10:30h by JR sleeper train from Tokyo. From Shōdoshima (S2), 0:35h by hydrofoil or 1:00h by ferry. ANA and JAS have daily flights to Takamatsu from the major cities.* This city is a gateway to Shikoku Island. Near the ferry dock stand the surviving turrets of Takamatsu's castle, which once kept watch over traffic in the Inland Sea. Sights in and around the city include the Edo-period stroll garden at Ritsurin Kōen, Shikoku Farmhouse Village, and Kotohira-gū (S6), one of the most popular shrines in Japan.

433

## Calendar

**Aug. 25: Nembutsu Odori.** Takinomiya Tenman-gū (*0:45h by Kotohira-gū-bound tram to Takinomiya, then 0:05h*). Conch-blowing *yamabushi* are followed by a parade of dancers chanting the *nembutsu*.

## Takamatsu Sights

**✱✱✱ Ritsurin Kōen** 栗林公園 Hrs: sunrise–sunset. *0:10h by bus from station to Ritsurin-Kōen-mae.* Former estate of the daimyo of Takamatsu. The north part of the park is a botanical garden. The south part is a superb large-scale stroll garden, full of ponds and artificial hills. The **Kikugetsu-tei** (Chrysanthemum Moon Pavilion), situated at the edge of the large pond, is a fine example of *sukiya* architecture, where visitors can enjoy a bowl of *matcha* (Hrs: 8:30–16:00).

**✱✱ Sanuki Mingeikan (Folk Art Museum)** 讃岐民芸館 Hrs: 8:45–16:00; W 8:45–15:00; clsd NY. Near the entrance to Ritsurin Kōen. An excellent museum on the folk art of Sanuki (the old name for this province), including roof tiles, dark-gray with a satin sheen of mica, molded into spectacular demon tiles and other ornamental and symbolic forms. The museum sells the rustic local pottery, Mimaya-yaki (slate gray, unglazed ware) and Kōzai-yaki (orange medicinal teapots).

**Yashima** 屋島 *0:20h east of Takamatsu by Koto-den tram.* This promontory overlooking the Inland Sea is one of the famous battle sites of the 12th-century Genpei war (see Miyajima History, p. 449). Ruins of the last TAIRA refuge can be seen amid decaying tourist hotels. The temple **Yashima-ji**, said to have been founded by the Chinese priest Ganjin in 754, offers nice views (see Art, p. 92).

**✱✱✱ Shikoku Mura** 四国村 Hrs: 8:30–17:00; Nov.–Mar. 8:30–16:30. *0:05h on foot from Yashima station.* An outstanding open-air museum of traditional Shikoku architecture, including a vine suspension bridge, an open-air village Kabuki theater from Shōdoshima, an unusual circular sugar mill, a paper-making hut, and farmhouses. There's a pleasant pair of restaurants near the entrance, one a farmhouse specializing in Sanuki *udon*, and the other a Western-style building brought from Kōbe.

434

## Takamatsu Dining and Lodgings (TEL 0878)

**✱✱✱ Maimai-tei** まいまい亭 東田町18-5 (33-3360). Hrs: 11:30–14:00, 17:00–23:00; clsd NH, NY. Authentic and extraordinarily good Sanuki cuisine in an intimate and unpretentious shop with a lovely natural wood interior. Master Matsuoka makes many of the utensils, such as lacquer steaming boxes for the succulent *anago-meshi* (Y1000). À la carte from Y300. Courses (by reservation): *kaiseki* Y4000, *setouchi* Y6000, and *shōjin* Y7000. V.

**✱ Zeniya** ぜにや 瓦町2-10-21 (33-0808). Hrs: 17:00–23:00; clsd Su, NY, mid-Aug. Open daily in Dec. Reasonably priced *fugu* (see Cuisine, p. 115). Dinner from Y2800. V.

**Takamatsu Grand Hotel** 高松グランドホテル (51-5757). Fax 21-9422. 1-5-10 Kotobuki-chō, Takamatsu-shi, Kagawa-ken. Run by ANA; near pier and Takamatsu station. S Y7–7500, Tw Y12,500–13,500. AX, DC, V, MC.

**✱ Hotel Kawaroku** ホテル川六 (21-5666). 1-2 Hyakken-chō. Best ryokan in town; Japanese and Western rooms. Good food and service. Accustomed to foreign guests. Y13–15,000 w/2 meals. S Y6000, Tw Y10,000. AX, DC, V, MC.

**Washington Hotel** 高松ワシントンホテル (22-7111). 1-2-3 Kawaramachi. Cozy business hotel in a lively part of the city. S Y7150, Tw Y13,000+. AX, DC, V, MC.

## S4 TOKUSHIMA 徳島

*1:20h by JR limited express from Takamatsu; also numerous ferries from Ōsaka and flights on ANA and JAS from major cities.* The least interesting of Shikoku's main cities, Tokushima is worth a special trip only during the Awa Odori festival. **Jūrobei Yashiki** 十郎兵衛屋敷 川内町 (*0:25h by bus from the station*) is the house of a 17th-century local hero, Jūrobei. He was a rice inspector for the fief, which had to import rice illegally because the domain's economy was based on salt and indigo. When the shogunate found out, Jūrobei, rather than implicate his lord, took full blame and was executed. This story inspired CHIKAMATSU to write a puppet play. A 0:30h scene (with taped narration) is performed here on most weekends (call 65-2202 for schedule).

## Calendar

**Aug. 12–15: ✱✱ Awa Odori.** See Calendar, p. 428. Battalions of dance groups perform for the stands of paying spectators, but the real fun is out in the streets. The youth hostel rents outfits, gives lessons, and arranges for bus transport. Hotels are booked months in advance.

## Tokushima Lodgings (TEL 0886)

**Tōkyū Inn** 徳島東急イン (26-0109). 1-24 Motomachi, Tokushima-shi, Tokushima-ken. New and relatively elaborate member of this chain. Close to station. S Y7600, Tw Y13,200.

**Awa Kankō Hotel** 阿波観光ホテル (22-5161). 3-16-3 Ichiban-chō. Established older city hotel. Rebuilt in 1989. Y13,000 w/meals.

**Tokushima YH** 徳島YH (63-1505). 7-1 Hama, Ōhara-machi. *0:30h by bus from station.* This hostel is near a beach.

## Exploring South of Tokushima

**# Hiwasa**, a fishing village, has a scenic beach park, Ōhama Kōen, where sea turtles come to lay eggs in late July–mid-August. In the *umigame* (sea turtle) matsuri on July 21, the turtles are given saké to drink and set free. Lodgings at **Kokuminshukusha Umigame-sō** (08847-7-1166), on the beach. The train line ends at Kaifu, from which buses head to Muroto Misaki (S7).

# TAKAMATSU TO KŌCHI

## MARUGAME 丸亀

*0:25h by JR express from Takamatsu.* The town has a genuine castle keep (ICP), picturesque viewed from afar, and is a major producer of *uchiwa*, flat fans, a craft plied by the poor Marugame samurai, who sold them to Kompira pilgrims arriving by sea.

## Exploring Shiwaku Islands

**#** This group of scenic islands was known as the home of master mariners and pirates who terrorized the Inland Sea and occasionally fought in major battles that altered the course of Japanese history. Of the 50 Japanese crewmen who accompanied the 1860 shogunate mission to ratify the Harris treaty in Washington, D.C., 35 came from these islands. **Honjima**, 0:35h by ferry from Marugame, is noted for old houses, art treasures, historical sites and buildings. There are several minshuku on the island.

## S5 * ZENTSŪ-JI 善通寺

*0:35–0:40h by JR Dosan line express from Takamatsu.* This temple, though architecturally undistinguished, is famous as the birthplace of KŪKAI, and is a headquarters of the Shingon sect (see Kyoto History, p. 319). Kūkai is said to have founded the temple in 813. The temple, No. 75 on the Shikoku pilgrimage, is usually thronged with pilgrims. **Temple lodgings** (Zentsū-ji Shukubō) 善通寺宿坊 (0877-62-0111) are Y4,300 w/meals; 21:00 curfew, 5:30 service, 6:00 breakfast, 7:00 checkout (Oct.–May, the schedule is a half-hour later).

435

## S6 ** KOTOHIRA 琴平

*0:45h by JR Dosan line express from Takamatsu, or 1:05h by private Koto-den line via Ritsurin Kōen in Takamatsu.* Kotohira-gū, or **Kompira-san**, as it is affectionately called, is a very popular pilgrimage shrine dedicated to Ōkuninushi no Mikoto, the god of Izumo, and to the 12th-century retired emperor Sutoku, who died in exile in Shikoku. It originated, however, as a syncretic temple to Kompira Daigongen, a deity derived from Kumbhira, the Indian crocodile god of the Ganges. Kompira-san came to be worshipped as a guardian of seafarers and was much revered by the people of the Inland Sea. The long, stone-paved stairway leading to the shrine is Japan's most impressive *monzen-machi*. It is lined with a colorful assortment of old inns and shops (see Villages, p. 56). After the Meiji Restoration, Kotohira-gū became a Shinto shrine, but its architecture betrays its syncretic past.

## Calendar

**Oct. 9–11: Kotohira-gū Matsuri.** Kompira-san's biggest matsuri. Lantern parades, dragon dance, offerings of Kagura, and a *mikoshi* procession.

## Getting Around

If the 0:40h climb to the top is daunting, there are palanquin bearers for hire (Y4,500 one way, Y5,500 round trip).

## Kotohira Sights

**Sayabashi.** An unusual covered bridge. From here, there's a back path that joins up with the main approach via the Kabuki theater.

*** **Kyū Kompira Ōshibai** 旧金毘羅大芝居 (ICP). Hrs: 9:00–17:00; clsd Tu. This marvelous building is the only complete Edo-period Kabuki playhouse left in Japan. It was built in 1835 and has two *hanamichi* ramps, a revolving stage, and dressing rooms. The door is small to keep gate-crashers out. Originally located in the center of town, it was used as a movie theater until 1965.

* **Shrine Museum** 金刀比羅宮博物館 Hrs: Oct.–Mar. 9:00–16:00; Apr.–Sept. 8:00–16:00. In two parts: the Gakugei Sankōkan houses a large, excellent *ema* (votive painting) and old tools; the Hōmotsukan exhibits a Jūichimen Kannon (ICP), a *Tale of Genji* screen by Tosa Mitsumoto, and other fine paintings.

** **Shoin** 書院 (ICP). Hrs: 9:00–16:00. This building was formerly the reception hall of the shrine, dating from the Edo period. It contains two handsome *shoin* and screen paintings by Maruyama Ōkyo and Itō Jakuchū (see Art, p. 100).

* **Asahi no Yashiro (Sunrise Shrine)** 旭社 Built in 1837, the ornately carved hall was originally dedicated to Kompira Daigongen. It is now consecrated to Amaterasu Ōmikami, the Sun Goddess.

** **Ema-dō** 絵馬堂 A pavilion hung with numerous *ema* (votive pictures), wonderful miniature ship models, and old photos, all offered by pilgrims. The Gohonsha (Main Hall) stands nearby.

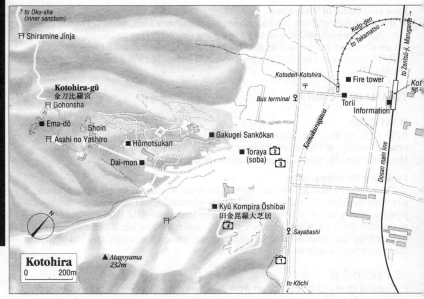

↑ to Oku-sha
(inner sanctum)

Ⓗ Shiramine Jinja

Kotohira-gū
金刀比羅宮
Ⓗ Gohonsha

■ Ema-dō     Shoin
Ⓗ Asahi no Yashiro
            ■ Hōmotsukan
Dai-mon

▲ Atagoyama
   232m

Kotohira
0        200m

Kotoden-Kotohira

〒

Bus terminal  ♀

Koto-den
to Takamatsu

■ Fire tower
              Torii
   Information

to Zentsū-ji, Marugame ↓

Kot
琴

■ Gakugei Sankōkan
     ■ Toraya  [2]
        (soba)  [3]

■ Kyū Kompira Ōshibai
  旧金毘羅大芝居
     [4]

♀ Sayabashi

[1]

to Kōchi

Kamakuragawa

Dosan main line

## Kotohira Lodgings (TEL 0877)

Address: Kotohira-chō, Nakatado-gun, Kagawa-ken.

[1] **Kadan** 花壇 (75-3232). A rambling mix of old and new. Y13–40,000 w/meals. AX, DC, V.

[2] **Shikishima-kan** 敷島館 (75-5111). Still preserves its old pilgrim's inn facade, but the rooms are in a characterless modern wing. Y13–18,000 w/meals. AX, DC, V, MC.

[3] **Bizenya** 備前屋 (75-4131). Like the Shikishima-kan. Y12–16,000 w/meals. No CC.

[4] **YH Kotohira Seinen no Ie** YH琴平青年の家 (73-3836). Y3,000 w/meals.

## Exploring the Dosan Line to Kōchi

# **Iyadani** (*1:00h by bus from Ōboke station*) is alleged to be one of those refuges for the TAIRA clan after their defeat in 1185. The mountains, terraced fields, and weathered villages are lovely. There is a famous vine suspension bridge at Iyadani. At Ōtaguchi is **Buraku-ji**, which has a main hall (NT) built in 1151. At Ōtoyo is **Jōfuku-ji YH** (0887-74-0301/2), a temple with *sansai* cuisine and a bath heated by firewood.

## S7 * KŌCHI 高知

*From Takamatsu (S3), 2:35h by JR limited express. From Ōsaka, the ferry is cheapest and not much slower than the train. By Air, ANA has 5 flights per day from Tokyo, 17 per day from Ōsaka.* Castle town of the old province of Tosa, which Ki no Tsurayuki described in the 10th-century *Tosa Diary* as a remote outpost accessible by sea, due to the impenetrable mountain range across central Shikoku. Kōchi has a subtropical atmosphere, with palm-lined streets and hot-blooded locals. Tosa was among the fiefs that led the overthrow of the Tokugawa shogunate. One of its heroes is Sakamoto Ryōma (1835–1867), a swashbuckling swordsman and arms-runner who helped negotiate the alliance between the two powerful clans, Satsuma and Chōshū, that toppled the shogunate (see Hagi History, p. 460). His immortality was ensured by his murder at age 31. Numerous statues and portraits depict Ryōma in a Napoleonic pose, his right hand thrust into the breast of his rumpled kimono.

## Calendar

Almost every day of the week there is an open-air market somewhere in Kōchi. The biggest one is on Sunday, along the palm-lined avenue leading to the castle.

**Aug. 9–11: Yosakoi Matsuri.** Thousands of Kōchi people hit the streets in *yukata*, wielding wood clappers and singing.

## Getting Around

Kōchi has an easy east-west, north-south tram system, intersecting at **Harimaya-bashi**, a red bridge over a now nonexistent river, made famous in a song taunting a bald priest who is discovered buying a lady's hair ornament at a shop near the bridge.

## Kōchi Sights

** **Kōchi-jō** 高知城 (ICP). Hrs: 9:00–16:30. The five-storied keep was rebuilt in 1753. The castle houses a historical museum in which Sakamoto Ryōma figures prominently. The first floor was the lord's living quarters, an unusual feature (see Castles, p. 47).

** **Chikurin-ji** 竹林寺 Hrs: 8:30–17:00. *0:20h by bus to Goshikidai*. This pretty temple, No. 31 of the Shikoku pilgrimage, is said to have been founded in 724. The Treasure House contains a fine group of Fujiwara- and Kamakura-period sculpture (all ICP). The Main Hall (ICP) and garden are said to date from the Muromachi period.

### Fighting Dogs and Long-Tailed Fowl

Kōchi is famous for the *Tosa-ken*, a dog that resembles the mastiff and is esteemed for its fighting ability. Champions are awarded ornate "aprons," just like a sumo wrestler, and given the same ranks. The dogs can be seen at the **Tosa Tōken Center** 桂浜土佐闘犬センター at Katsurahama, a beach resort 0:30h by bus from Kōchi; demonstration fights are held if more than 30 spectators gather (Hrs: 8:00–17:00). The *Onagadori*, or long-tailed fowl, supposedly was bred to provide feathers to adorn the standards of the Tosa daimyo's procession. But the really long feathers — 4 meters and more — did not appear until around 1920. Breeders have since produced 10-meter tails (the cause is a recessive gene that keeps tail feathers from molting). Only the most docile cocks become show birds since they must be kept in narrow boxes to preserve their tails. The best place to see them is the **Nagaodori Center** 長尾鶏センター 南国市篠原 (0888-64-4931), 0:15h by taxi toward Kōchi airport. Hrs: 9:00–17:00.

### Kōchi Dining and Lodgings (TEL 0888)

Tosa cuisine features seafood dishes that go well with saké. *Katsuo no tataki* is fresh bonito, barely broiled over a pine-needle fire, sliced and served with garlic, *shiso*, and citrus. *Saba no sugata-zushi* is sushi made from a whole pickled mackerel. *Sawachi* is a platter heaped with the above. *Shutō* is salt-pickled bonito entrails, which are consumed with saké.

\* **Tosa-han** 土佐藩 帯屋町1-2-2 (21-0002). Hrs: 11:30–22:00. Well-known for Tosa cuisine. Pleasant folk-art decor. *"Mini" Sawachi* is Y6000 for two.

**Chūnagon** 中納言 本町1-1-16 (22-2266). Hrs: 8:00–19:00; clsd NY. Pleasant place for *bentō*, *rāmen* (Chinese noodles), and other light fare. Inexpensive.

**Washington Hotel** ワシントンホテル (23-6111). 1-8 Ōtesuji, Kōchi-shi, Kōchi-ken. Excellent location, reliable business hotel. S Y6800, Tw Y13,000+. AX, DC, V.

**Sansui-en Hotel** 三翠園ホテル (22-0131). 1-3-35 Takajōmachi. Large ryokan on former Tosa lord's estate; preserves the old guards' barracks (ICP). Y12–25,000 w/meals. DC, V, MC.

**Hotel Takasago** ホテル高砂 駅前町2-1 (22-1288). 2-1 Ekimae-chō. Small ryokan that has seen better days; still serves good local cuisine. Y12–20,000 w/meals. V.

### Exploring Muroto Misaki

# This cape SE of Kōchi is noted for dramatic cliffs. On the way, there's the stalactite cave, **Ryūgadō**, a big tourist attraction; inside is a prehistoric pot which over time has become cemented onto the rock. Nearby is a bizarre, European-style "castle." **Aki** (*1:00h by bus from Kōchi*) is an old-fashioned town with an old-fashioned pottery kiln, Uchiharano. It was also the hometown of Iwasaki Yatarō, founder of Mitsubishi; you can visit the thatched house where he was born in 1834. At Muroto is **Higashi-dera YH** (08872-2-0366), a temple on the Shikoku pilgrimage circuit.

### Calendar

**May 3: Kiragawa Onda Matsuri.** Muroto. Onda Hachiman-gū. A women's festival, with Sarugaku, sword dances, and other folk performances by women. The women struggle for possession of a "god child" doll, said to ensure the winner's fertility.

**Oct. 15: Hachiōji-gū Fall Festival.** Muroto. Youths carry *mikoshi* along the beach and leap with it into the pounding surf.

### S8 NAKAMURA 中村

*2:15h by JR express from Kōchi (S7). Junction for buses to Sukumo (S9).*

### S9 SUKUMO 宿毛

*0:40h by bus from Nakamura, or 1:55h from Uwajima (CHŪGOKU IV:S5). 3:00h by ferry from Saeki on Kyūshū.* A fishing village with a scenic natural harbor. **Hamada no Tomariya** (ICP, *0:15h by bus from Sukumo bus center*) is a curious little hall built on high posts that served as a kind of meetinghouse for local youths from the late Edo period to the 1920s.

### Sukumo Lodgings (TEL 0880)

\*\* **Sukumo YH** 宿毛YH 橋上町神有196 (64-0233/0162). 196 Kamiari, Hashigami-chō, Sukumo-shi, Kōchi-ken. A farmhouse in a lovely valley, run by a natural-food enthusiast who grows his own rice and vegetables and makes his own miso and tofu. He even has a charcoal kiln. If you let him know your arrival time at the bus center, he'll come pick you up. Y3600 w/meals. Apr.–Nov. Y2800.

### Exploring Okinoshima

# *1:45h by ferry from Sukumo (S9), departs at 6:30, 14:00; returns at 8:30, 16:15.* This remote island, also called Hahajima, has a picturesque fishing village built up on terraces and fortified against typhoons with stone walls. There's not much to do here except fish, swim, and enjoy the unspoiled atmosphere. The island has three ryokan and a minshuku.

437

# CHŪGOKU II. KURASHIKI

**Tokyo to Kurashiki:** *4:30h by Shinkansen to Shin-Kurashiki station; 9 direct Hikari expresses per day. Otherwise, take the Shinkansen to Okayama* (CHŪGOKU 1) *and switch to a local or limited express train to Kurashiki station, which take 0:12–0:17h.*
**Prefectures:** Okayama, Shimane

## *** KURASHIKI 倉敷

Kurashiki, a bustling, industrial city, has one tiny but immaculately preserved section of its old rice-merchant quarter, which prospered in the Edo period. Old Kurashiki today consists of dozens of the characteristic whitewashed, black-tiled *kura*, or rice storehouses, centered around a willow-lined transport canal. What makes them especially attractive is that many have been converted into museums, shops, teahouses, and inns, injecting contemporary vitality into these relics of traditional Japan.

### Calendar

Avoid visiting on Monday, when most museums are closed, and on spring and autumn weekends and national holidays, when tourism is at its height.

**Oct. (3rd Sa–Su): Achi Jinja Fall Festival.** Dancers wearing comical masks lead the *mikoshi* procession. At Kurashiki's Kompira-gū, there's a demon procession.

### Kurashiki Sights

*From Shin-Kurashiki station, 0:15h by bus or taxi (abut Y2500). From Kurashiki station, a 0:10h walk. Ask for* unga no iriguchi *(entrance to the canal area)*. This area of concentrated picturesqueness abounds in museums, Bizen pottery shops, restaurants, and inns. Some of the back streets offer quieter scenes. From Achi Jinja, there is a good view of Kurashiki's tiled roofs.

**** Ōhashi-ke (House)** 大橋家 (ICP) (22-0007). Hrs: 9:00–17:00; clsd M (except if NH), NY. This fine house was built in 1796 by the Ōhashi, prominent members of Kurashiki's merchant community. The family claims a samurai lineage, however, and their house is said to retain features of samurai dwellings. A detailed explanation is provided in English.

***** Ōhara Bijutsukan (Museum of Art)** 大原美術館 (22-0005). Hrs: 9:00–17:00 (enter by 16:30); clsd M (except if NH), NY. This art museum, with its prominent neoclassical facade, was the first in a series of the museums that have transformed Kurashiki into a museum town. This one was founded in the 1920s by Ōhara Keisaburō, scion of the Kurabō textile company, who amassed Japan's first publicly shown collection of Western art, including El Greco's *Annunciation* and many works of the French Impressionist school. Several adjoining *kura* display a fine collection of Japanese folk art and ancient Chinese art. Each of the folk-art potters—Hamada Shōji, Bernard Leach, Kawai Kanjirō, and Tomimoto Kenkichi—has a room of his own, as does the textile artist Serizawa Keisuke and the woodblock-print artist Munakata Shikō. The Chinese collection includes Northern Wei stone sculptures and Tang objects. Behind the main museum is the **Ōhara New Art Museum**, a contemporary building displaying Japanese and Western modern art.

**Kurashiki Kōkokan (Archeology Museum)** 倉敷考古館 (22-1542). Hrs: Mar.–Nov. 9:00–17:00 (enter by 16:30); Dec.–Feb. 9:00–16:30 (enter by 16:00); clsd M (except if NH), NY. This dim, dusty museum, a converted Edo-period *kura*, has local prehistoric pottery and some pre-Columbian Peruvian pottery.

**Kurashiki Bijutsukan (City Art Museum)** 倉敷美術館 (25-0017). Hrs: Mar.–Nov. 9:00–17:00, daily. An overwhelming assortment of ornate European marbles and some not uninteresting Mediterranean and West Asian antiquities.

**** Kurashiki Mingeikan (Folk Art Museum)** 倉敷民芸館 (22-1637). Hrs: 9:00–17:00; Dec.–Feb. 9:00–16:15; clsd M (except if NH), NY. Folk art, primarily from Japan, of excellent quality and charmingly displayed. Worth visiting if you have an interest in folk art or have never visited a *mingeikan* before.

**** Nihon Kyōdo Gangukan (Japanese Toy Museum)** 日本郷土玩具館 (22-8058). Hrs: 8:00–17:00; clsd NY. This is a wonderful museum, with room after room of traditional Japanese toys. One room is devoted to toys from around the world. Adjoining the museum is a toyshop, which is as interesting as the museum itself.

**Ivy Square** アイビースクエア This compound is the renovated red-brick Meiji-period factory of Kurabō textile industries, source of Mr. Ōhara's wealth.

**Kojima Torajirō Memorial Hall** 児島虎次郎記念館 (22-0005). Hrs: 9:00–17:00 (enter by 16:45); clsd M (except if NH), NY. Shows the Western-style paintings of Kojima Torajirō (1881–1929), the Kurashiki-born artist who helped Ōhara build his European painting collection.

**Kurabō Memorial Hall** 倉紡記念館 (22-0011). Hrs: 9:00–17:00 (enter by 16:45), daily. This museum documents the history of Kurashiki and the Kurabō mills. One can see what Kurashiki looked like in early times and then glimpse the future in some surreal remnants from the textile exposition at Expo '70 in Ōsaka.

### Kurashiki Dining

Most coffee houses and restaurants around the canal close by early evening; hotel and ryokan dining facilities stay open later.

② **El Greco** エルグレコ (22-0297). Hrs: 10:00–17:00; clsd M, NY. Popular café.

③ **Kamoi Sabō** カモ井茶房 (22-0606). Hrs: 9:00–18:00; clsd M (Tu if M a NH). Good, moderately priced meals. Dec.–Mar., try *nuku-sushi*, a steamed rice-and-fish dish, Y800.
⑤ **\*\* Ryokan Kurashiki** 旅館くらしき (22-0730). Hrs: 12:00–14:00, 16:00–20:00. Excellent *kaiseki* and Inland Sea *nabe* dishes, from Y8000. The *kaiseki* lunch is Y5000+.
⑥ **Kōhīkan** コーヒー館 (24-5516). Hrs: 10:00–17:30; clsd M (Tu if M a NH), NY. Open daily in Mar. and Aug. The Ryokan Kurashiki's excellent coffee house.

## Kurashiki Lodgings (TEL 0864)
Reservations urged during the height of the spring and fall tourist seasons and on weekends.
①̄ **\* Kurashiki Kokusai (International) Hotel** 倉敷国際ホテル (22-5141). Fax 22-5192. 1-1-44 Chūō, Kurashiki-shi, Okayama-ken. A cozy business hotel with interesting modern architecture and modern folk-art decor. S Y7500, Tw Y12–17,000. Cheaper rooms w/sofabed available; also Japanese rooms, Y16,000 for 2 persons.
④̄ **\* Ryokan Tsurugata** 旅館鶴形 (24-1635). 1-3-15 Chūō. A good ryokan in a house built in 1744. Run by the Kokusai Hotel. Adjoining restaurant. Y15,700–35,000 w/meals.
⑤̄ **\*\* Ryokan Kurashiki** 旅館くらしき (22-0730). 4-1 Honmachi. A lovely inn with excellent food, usually good service, and familiarity with foreigners. Like Kurashiki itself, it is a mixture of indigenous and international, small and very comfortable. The building was a sugar-merchant's house, and has been beautifully refurbished, with exquisite attention to detail. From Y18–30,000 w/meals.
⑦̄ **Kurashiki Tokusankan** くらしき特産館　本町8-33 (25-3056). 8-33 Honmachi. Minshuku in a 230-year-old house; it's not in the best repair, and one might prefer the *shinkan* (new wing) down the street. Y5200 w/meals, Y4200 w/o meals.
⑧̄ **\* Kurashiki Ivy Square** 倉敷アイビースクェア(ホテル) (22-0011). 7-2 Honmachi. Hotel built into Ivy Square, with quaint, European-style decor. S Y9100, Tw Y14,200–17,000. Cheaper rooms w/o bath available; S Y6800, Tw Y10,800–12,000.
⑨̄ **Kurashiki YH** 倉敷YH　向山1537-1 (22-7355). 1537-1 Mukōyama. *0:15h walk from attractions.*

439

## Washūzan 鷲羽山
*1:10h by bus from Kurashiki station.* This promontory is reputed to offer one of the finest views of the Inland Sea.

## \* Shiraishi 白石
*0:30h from Kurashiki on JR San'yō main line to Kasaoka, then 0:25–1:00h by ferry.* This island, with its quiet fishing villages and farms, seems of a bygone era. There's a marvelous International Villa (see p. 428) at the island's apex, overlooking a small beach and the shimmering Island Sea Waters. The shadowy silhouette of the Nippon Steel Mills on the horizon lend a touch of surrealism. Note, the villa can be reached only by a 500m walk from the ferry dock (tel: 08656-8-2095). **\* Shiraishi Odori**, on Aug. 14–16, is a Bon dance to console victims of the 12th-C Genpei War.

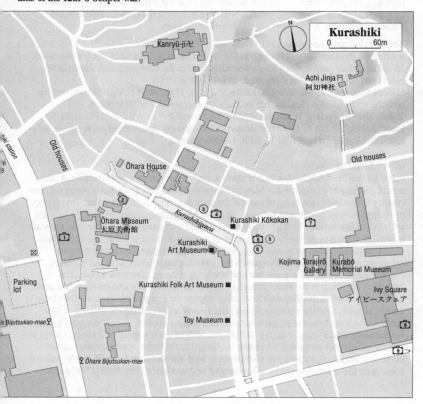

C
H
Ū
G
O
K
U

# CHŪGOKU II:N. NORTH TO IZUMO

**Main Attractions:** Fukiya (N2), Izumo (N5)

**Traveling**
The JR Yakumo limited express (7 per day) from Okayama (CHŪGOKU I) via Kurashiki to Matsue and Izumo, is fast and convenient.

## N1 ✳ BITCHŪ-TAKAHASHI 備中高梁
*0:40h by JR express from Kurashiki, or 0:30h from Sōja (Kibi Plain) by local JR Hakubi line. Most Yakumo expresses stop here.* This tiny former castle town is in an isolated, mountainous region of great scenic beauty. Takahashi itself has a number of attractions including the beautiful garden at Raikyū-ji and the highest mountain fortress in Japan. At the north end of town are many old merchant houses, willow-lined canals with little shrines built over them, and a street of samurai houses.

### Calendar
**Aug. 14–16:** Bitchū Matsuyama Odori. Two Bon dances introduced in the Edo period, one for "samurai" and one for "townsmen."

### Bitchū-Takahashi Sights
✳✳✳ **Raikyū-ji** 頼久寺 Hrs: 9:00–17:00. When KOBORI ENSHŪ (1579–1647), the famed tea master and garden designer, was appointed governor of this town, he lived at this temple and is said to have designed its garden in 1604. In fact, there are very few documented Enshū gardens, but this one is worthy of the story. Finely composed, with borrowed scenery and a bold, wavelike topiary hedge, it's a daring and masterful work, one of the finest gardens outside Kyoto.

440 ✳ **Shōren-ji** 松連寺 A Nichiren sect temple, noted for its stone-walled terraces. None of the individual halls is remarkable, but the entire effect, viewed from below, is pleasing and unusual.
✳✳ **Bitchū-Matsuyama-jō** 備中松山城 (ICP). *0:20h by car to parking lot, then 0:15h on foot.* This castle, the highest in Japan, became famous in the Sengoku period. Although the present keep was rebuilt in 1683, it retains the features of a medieval-style *yamajiro* (mountain castle) in its inaccessibility, invisibility, and austerity. It is the highest fortress in Japan (see Castles, p. 46). In 1582, HIDEYOSHI, acting as ODA NOBUNAGA's lieutenant, laid siege to this castle, which was held by Shimizu Muneharu, a vassal of the Mōri clan. Near victory, Hideyoshi arranged with the Mōri to take the castle peacefully, sparing its garrison in exchange for Shimizu's suicide. On June 22, word reached Hideyoshi that Nobunaga had been assassinated in Kyoto. Hideyoshi kept this news from the Mōri; the following morning the hapless Shimizu committed *seppuku* and Hideyoshi's forces took the castle. Hideyoshi then sped back to Kyoto, and within a short time became the supreme lord of the land (see Kyoto History, p. 322). Today, few people visit this historic site, leaving the ruined castle to stand in tomblike tranquility. A caretaker admits visitors to the keep.

### Bitchū-Takahashi Lodgings (TEL 0866)
✳ **Aburaya Ryokan** 油屋旅館 (22-3072). 38-1 Honmachi, Takahashi-shi, Okayama-ken. An old inn, plain outside, but with a lovely carp pond in the courtyard, and atmospheric rooms and views. Somewhat overpriced. Y13–18,000 w/meals.
**Midori Ryokan** みどり旅館 栄町1336 (22-2537). 1336 Sakae-chō. An old wooden inn near the station. Looks pleasant, but we make no guarantees. Y6500 w/meals.
**Takahashi-shi Cycling Terminal** 高梁市サイクリングターミナル (22-0135). 2281-3 Matsubara-chō. *0:20h by bus from station to Wonderland amusement park.* Simple lodgings with bicycles for rent. Clsd Tu. Y4500–4800 w/meals.

## N2 ✳✳ FUKIYA 吹屋
*0:50h by bus from Bitchū-Takahashi station. Only 3 per day in each direction. A car would enable you to explore the beautiful surroundings.* This remarkably preserved, fascinating village lies in the heart of some of the most beautiful country in Japan. Fukiya once prospered from its copper and *bengara*, or red ochre, a mineral used to stain the wooden grillwork of fine houses. Its single main street is lined with handsome, plaster- and tile-walled houses, most built in the late Edo to early Meiji periods. Rich mine owners commissioned expert carpenters from Kyoto and Ōsaka to build them. But then the copper mine was exhausted and the demand for *bengara* waned, forcing the villagers to abandon Fukiya. The fine houses stood empty for years, but now are being restored. The ✳✳✳ **Kyōdokan** 郷土館 , the house of the junior branch of the *bengara*-rich Katayama family, is a superb, handsomely detailed dwelling with interesting displays on *bengara* production. The shrine at the end of town, near the old schoolhouse, has a stone fence bearing the emblem of Mitsubishi, which made one of its early fortunes from Fukiya copper. The old *bengara* mill and ✳✳ **Sasaune Kōdō** (copper mine) 笹畝坑道 , with its narrow-gauge rail intact, 1.8 km outside the village, can be visited. Admission is charged to the mine; open all year. Another interesting attraction, located just 4 km away, is ✳✳✳ **Hirokane-tei** 広兼邸, a 170-year-old house built like a fortress by a local copper and *bengara* baron. Hrs: 8:30–17:00 daily.

**Fukiya Lodgings** (TEL 0866)

** **Fukiya Sansō** 吹屋山荘 (29-2727). 693 Fukiya, Nariwa-chō, Kawakami-gun, Okayama-ken. A beautifully refurbished Meiji-period house with gardens, a teahouse, cypress baths, flush toilets. Minshuku-style accommodation, Y4500 w/o meals. Meals are served at the restaurant across the street. *Sansai* Y800–2000, *botan-nabe* Y3000, breakfast Y500. Clsd Dec.–Mar.

** **Fukiya International Villa** (29-2222). 836 Fukiya. Outside, this inn suggests a pair of old storehouses. Inside, it's a judicious blend of traditional Japanese and modern Scandinavian. Fireplace, great bath. Four Western- and one Japanese-style room. See p. 427.

## N3 YONAGO 米子

*2:15h by JR Yakumo express from Kurashiki. 0:50h by JR San'in main line limited express from Kurayoshi (CHŪGOKU I:N2). Yonago airport, one of two serving this vicinity, is 0:25h by bus from the station. JAS has 5 flights per day from Ōsaka. ANA has 2 flights per day from Tokyo.* This large town is a gateway to the San'in coast, the side of western Honshū that faces the Sea of Japan.

### Exploring Daisen

*0:50h by bus from Yonago, then 0:15h on foot to* **Daisen-ji**, an ancient Tendai temple on the slopes of Daisen, a smooth volcanic cone looming over the coast, popular with hikers and skiers. A few subtemples offer lodgings: **Dōmyō-in** (0859-52-2038), **Seikō-an** (52-2303) are about Y6500 w/meals; they also serve vegetarian *shōjin-ryori* (Y4500), as does **Renjō-in** (52-2506), where the novelist Shiga Naoya stayed. He set the ending of his novel, *A Dark Night's Passing*, in this region.

## N4 * MATSUE 松江

*2:40h by JR Yakumo express from Kurashiki. 1:20h by JR San'in line limited express from Kurayoshi. Airports at nearby Yonago and Izumo.* The descendents of Matsudaira Naomasa, a grandson of TOKUGAWA IEYASU, ruled Matsue during the Edo period. Lafcadio Hearn, the 19th-century Japanophile, taught English at Matsue Middle School for seven months in 1890. He later wrote of his experiences and impressions of the region in many books, including *Glimpses of Unfamiliar Japan*. Matsue's main attractions are its castle and Hearn's house by the castle moat. The street where the house stands still has its old wall and one samurai residence, open to the public. Sadly, this is the only part of Matsue that still evokes the town that so charmed Hearn.

### Calendar

**Apr. 7: * Aofushigaki no Shinji.** Miho, Miho Jinja (*1:15h by bus from Matsue station*). This matsuri commemorates the mythological event in which Ōkuninushi ceded Japan to Amaterasu's grandson (see Shinto, p. 25). Right afterward, Amaterasu's messenger, Kotoshironushi no Mikoto, vanished in the sea; this legend is reenacted as two boats decorated with sacred green boughs race out on the sea. Followed by Kagura and sumo.
**Sept. 24–25: # * Sada Goza-kae Shinji.** Sada Jinja (*0:30h by bus from Matsue*). On the 24th, the gods' straw-mat seats are changed to new ones. On the 25th, there are offerings of sacred dances and a famous sacred Noh based on mythology and forms borrowed from Kyoto in the 17th C. It is considered to be the origin of Izumo Kagura (see Izumo Calendar, p. 443).
**Dec. 3: * Morotabune Shinji.** Miho Jinja. Related to the Aofushigaki no Shinji (see above). At this matsuri also, two boats race in the bay. Upon their return, there's a ritual reenactment of Ōkuninushi no Mikoto surrendering the land.

### Getting Around

Rent-a-cycles at Matsue and Matsue Onsen stations, and at Matsue Seinen (Youth) Center. The main sights clustered around Matsue castle can be seen comfortably on foot. The main attractions provide pamphlets in English.

### Castle Area

** **Matsue-jō (Castle)** 松江城 (ICP). Hrs: 8:30–17:00. Preserves the genuine castle keep and stone fortifications. In 1875, the castle was sold for 90 dollars to a wrecker, but a local group campaigned successfully to save it. The six-storied keep, completed in 1611, houses a well. The white, Western-style **Kyōdokan** is a museum of local history.
* **Koizumi Yakumo Kyūtaku (Lafcadio Hearn Residence)** 小泉八雲旧居 Hrs: 9:00–12:30, 13:30–16:30; clsd W, Aug. 13–16, NY. Faces the northern castle moat. This former samurai dwelling was the home of Lafcadio Hearn, or Koizumi Yakumo, as he was legally renamed upon becoming a naturalized Japanese. Next door is the **Koizumi Yakumo Kinenkan** (memorial hall), where various items connected with him are exhibited.
* **Tanabe Bijutsukan (Museum)** 田部美術館 Hrs: 9:00–17:00; clsd M, NY. Next to Hearn's house. Exhibits the tea-utensil collection of the late Tanabe Chōemon, a former governor of Shimane prefecture. The quality is uneven, but the items are handsomely displayed in a modern building designed to suggest elements of a tea arbor and garden.
**Buke-Yashiki (Samurai House)** 武家屋敷 Hrs: 8:30–17:00. Adjacent to Tanabe Bijutsukan. The very modest, 240-year-old residence of a middle-rank samurai, filled with items used in daily life.

441

**\*\* Meimei-an** 明々庵  Hrs: 9:00–17:00. A noted tea arbor built in 1779 by Matsudaira Fumai (1751–1818), daimyo of Matsue, which was relocated to its present site and beautifully restored. The new grounds are faithful to such details as the waiting area with its bench and dry lavatory—stones arranged to suggest a toilet. Fumai was the foremost exponent of the aristocratic daimyo tea ceremony. Unlike the egalitarian *wabi* tea hut, this arbor has both a low entrance and a tall entrance, reserved for guests of high rank (see Villas, p. 65). Visitors today can enjoy *matcha* in a nearby house. **Kanden-an** (ICP), an even finer Fumai tea arbor, is 0:20h by car NE of the town center (Hrs: 9:30–16:00; clsd Th, except by reservation).

## Yakumo Mura

This scattered village 5 km south of Matsue (*0:25h by bus or 0:15h by taxi*) was the center of government and culture in ancient Izumo province.

**\*\* Yaegaki Jinja** 八重垣神社 (21-1148). Hrs: 9:00–17:00. This site is said to be the home of the deities Susano'o and Kushinada-hime, the lovely maiden whom he rescued from the dragon Yamata no Orochi (see Shinto, p. 25). The divine couple and several other kami are portrayed in rare and delicate \* **wall paintings** (ca. 12th C, ICP), once concealed inside the shrine but now shown in the concrete Hōmotsuden. The popular shrine is connected with marriage and sells erotic amulets for marital harmony and fertility.

**\*\* Kamosu Jinja** 神魂神社  Hrs: 9:00–17:00. *0:20h from Yaegaki Jinja or 0:15h from Fudoki no Oka, on foot.* This shrine's Honden (1346, NT) is the oldest extant example of a Taisha-style shrine (see Shinto, p. 26). The interior is decorated with richly colored wall paintings.

**\*\* Fudoki no Oka Shiryōkan (Archeological Museum)** 風土記の丘資料館 (23-2485). Hrs: 9:00–17:00 (enter by 16:30); clsd M, NY. *0:25h walk from Yaegaki Jinja. From Matsue, 0:20h by bus to Fudoki no Oka Iriguchi then 0:05h on foot.* This museum is near numerous *kofun* and the ruins of the Nara-period Kokubun-ji. It exhibits many interesting objects, including fine *haniwa* horses, a whimsical deer, and egg-shaped clay whistles (Yayoi period), similar to ancient Chinese whistles, found in Japan only along the Japan Sea coast.

442

## Matsue Lodgings (TEL 0852)

Many visitors stay at Tamatsukuri Onsen, 0:30h by bus from Matsue. One of the most famous hot springs on the Japan Sea coast, its name, "jewel-making," comes from the *magatama* (comma-shaped jewel) carving guild located there from prehistoric times.

\* **Minami-kan** 皆美館  末次本町 (21-5131). Suetsuguhon-machi, Matsue-shi, Shimane-ken. An elegant old inn, noted for its regional cuisine. The guest rooms face onto river and garden. Y16–32,000 w/meals.

**Washington Hotel** 松江ワシントンホテル (22-4111). 2-22 Higashihonmachi, Matsue-shi. *0:05h by taxi from Matsue station.* Reliable business hotel. S Y5900+, Tw Y10,000+.

**Young Inn Matsue** ヤングイン松江  魚町5 (22-2000). 5 Uomachi. Small budget inn. S Y3200, Tw Y5600, triple Y8400 w/o bath.

**Chōraku-en** 長楽園  玉湯町 (62-0111). Tamayu-chō, Yatsuka-gun, Shimane-ken. Tamatsukuri Onsen. Modern, tastefully appointed ryokan with pretty gardens and a huge *rotemburo*. Y15–18,000 w/meals.

**Kasui-en Minami** 佳翠苑皆美  玉湯町 (62-0331). Tamatsukuri Onsen. Address as above. Large, farmhouse-style ryokan. Y15–30,000 w/meals.

## Exploring Oki Island

# *The islands are reached by ferry from Sakai or Shichirui, both near Mihonoseki, northeast of Matsue, or by air from Ōsaka, Yonago, and Izumo airports.* These wind-swept islands of rolling green meadows and sheer cliffs have been a place of exile for political prisoners since the Nara period. The most famous inmate was the 14th-century emperor

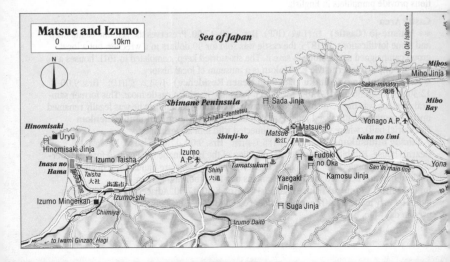

Go-Daigo, who was packed off to Oki for rebelling against the Kamakura shogunate (see Yoshino History, p. 411). Oki remains a remote place, with unspoiled scenery and a rustic way of life. **Dōgo**, the largest, north island, is known for Ushitsuki, a kind of bull sumo. **Dōzen**, a cluster of smaller islands to the south, has spectacular cliffs. On August 16, the last day of Bon, the villages of Nishinoshima build * **Sha'ara Bune**, large straw boats, beautifully decorated, and set them adrift to escort spirits back across the sea. There are many inns, minshuku, Kokuminshukusha, and YHs.

## SHINJI 宍道

*0:15 from Matsue by JR San'in line*. This former post town is known for **Yakumo Honjin** (ICP), a 250-year-old inn for the daimyo of Matsue that preserves its gorgeous interiors and gardens. It is now part of a superb ryokan, one of the most memorable in Japan. One fine *shoin* room came from the Matsudaira mansion, given in lieu of payment of a debt; another was built for a crown prince—who, as it happened, only stayed for lunch.

### Calendar
**Aug. 6: Tanabata.** Daitō-chō (*0:25h by Kisuki line from Shinji*). Major performance of Izumo Kagura.
**Sept. 28: * Izumo Kagura.** At Suga Jinja (*0:20h by bus from Izumo-Daitō*). See Izumo Calendar, below. From 15:00.

### Shinji Lodgings (TEL 0852)
** **Yakumo Honjin** 八雲本陣 (66-0136). 1335 Shinji-chō, Yatsuka-gun, Shimane-ken. Reserve; specify *honkan* (old wing) or they'll put you in the *shinkan* (new wing), which is nice enough and air-conditioned, but not nearly as elegant as the old wing. Their specialty is *kamo no kaiyaki*, slices of wild duck and vegetables simmered on an abalone shell over a charcoal brazier. Y14,000 w/meals; Y16,000 w/duck. Meal only, from Y8500.

443

## N5 ** IZUMO-SHI 出雲市

*0:20h from Shinji by JR San'in line. 7:00h from Kyoto or 5:00h from Shimonoseki* (CHŪGOKU VII) *by JR San'in line limited express. From Okayama* (CHŪGOKU I), *3:20h by JR Yakumo express. From Hiroshima* (CHŪGOKU IV), *4:30h by express bus. From Tokyo or Ōsaka, it is almost as cheap to fly: by JAS 2 per day from Tokyo, 4 per day from Ōsaka, to Izumo Airport, near Shinji*. The famous Izumo Taisha is in the nearby village of Taisha. Izumo-shi is the more convenient place to rent a car and find lodgings.

### Calendar
The Izumo region is noted for **Izumo Kagura**, a series of colorful and theatrical dances that depict Shinto myths. Most popular is one in which Susano'o rescues Kushinada-hime from the coils of the lustful dragon, Yamata no Orochi (Shinto, p. 25).
**Jan. 3: Kitchō to Bannai.** Taisha village. Procession of men wearing Izumo Kagura masks and costumes, and carrying tall banners in a prayer for prosperity and fortune.
**May 14–16: * Izumo Taisha Daisairei.** Many formal rites, including a performance of Izumo Kagura.
**L 10/11–17: * Kamiari-sai.** Izumo Taisha. One of the most noted Shinto rites in Japan. During this period, the "8 million" kami of Japan are said to gather here. At 19:00 on the first day, priests and pilgrims gather at Inasa no Hama to greet the kami, who come from across the sea. Fires burn on the beach, and people clutch small *gobei* to pick up some of the powerful vibes. At 20:00, a lantern procession escorts the kami to the shrine. Unfortunately, the mood is spoiled by TV crews.

### Izumo Sights
** **Izumo Mingeikan (Folk Art Museum)** 出雲民芸館　知井宮町　Hrs: 9:00–17:00; clsd M, NY. *0:05h on foot from Chimiya station, one stop west of Izumo-shi*. Japanese folk art beautifully displayed in a wonderful old house, formerly the estate of a village headman. A good selection of local crafts are on sale, including indigo-dyed textiles, *washi*, and Shusai pottery.
**Nagata Somemono Kōba** 長田染工場　上成橋東 (21-0288). *0:15h on foot from station, near Jōneibashi (bridge)*. Virtually the last shop still making the paste-resist indigo-dyed fabrics that were once the pride of an Izumo bride's trousseau. Brides-to-be still place orders, but usually only for a *furoshiki*, a large square cloth emblazoned with the family crest and good luck motifs—cranes, tortoises, pines, and moneybags.
*** **Izumo Taisha (Shrine)** 出雲大社　*0:30h by bus from Izumo-shi station to Seimon-mae (by a large, wooden torii); or 0:25h by private Ichibata line from Izumo-shi to terminus, then 0:10h on foot, along the pine-lined main approach*. According to mythology and semihistorical records, this was the first shrine in Japan to have a permanent hall. In a highly symbolic episode of Japan's creation myth, Amaterasu Ōmikami's wild brother, Susano'o, was exiled from the High Plain of Heaven, and settled in Izumo (see Shinto, p. 25). His descendant, the good-natured **Ōkuninushi no Mikoto**, came to rule over the inhabitants of Japan. When messengers from Amaterasu asked him to cede the land to her grandson, Ninigi no Mikoto (whose own grandson Jimmu was destined to be Japan's first

emperor), Ōkuninushi agreed. This so pleased Amaterasu that she had a shrine built for him. The original structure was reportedly modeled on the emperor's palace and was enormous—according to one highly improbable theory, it stood atop immense stilts nearly 100 m tall. The shrine has been rebuilt at least 25 times, most recently in 1744, and though no doubt much reduced, is still the largest shrine in existence, measuring 24 m from the ground to the tips of its *chigi*. As for Ōkuninushi, he remains the most popular kami of industry, fortune, and above all, marriage. It is this last aspect that accounts for the unique custom of invoking the Izumo god by clapping four times—twice for oneself and twice for one's mate or desired mate—rather than just twice, as is the practice at all other shrines. It also accounts for the huge number of weddings that take place here, especially during the auspicious tenth lunar month, when the 8 million kami gather. See Shinto, p. 26, for details on the shrine's construction, called *Taisha-zukuri*, a style seen throughout the Izumo region.

**Haiden** (Oratory). The first structure beyond the main torii. It has an immense *shimenawa* of twisted straw—the largest in Japan—hanging above the entry.

**Shinko-den** (Treasure House) 神祜殿 Hrs: 8:00–16:30. Modern building to the right of the Haiden. Exhibits shrine treasures and objects used in shrine rituals, such as rubbing sticks for making sacred fire.

◆ **Honden** (Sacred Hall, NT). This great hall stands in the center of a double enclosure that cannot be entered. A special feature of Izumo Taisha is the **Jūku-sha**, two long structures on either side of the compound, with 19 mini-shrines to lodge the kami of Japan, all 8 million of them, when they gather at Izumo in the tenth lunar month (see Calendar).

**Shōkokan** (Former Treasure Hall). Hrs: 8:00–16:30. In NW corner of the grounds. An old wooden building that houses a large collection of folk images of Daikoku, a popular version of Ōkuninushi, depicted as a jolly figure standing on two bales of rice with a sack slung over his shoulder. He is often with Ebisu, his son and look-alike, who holds a plump sea bream. The two kami are among the Seven Lucky Gods of Japanese folk religion.

**Inasa no Hama (Beach)** 稲左ノ浜 *0:20–0:30h on foot from Izumo Taisha*. A popular swimming beach, with powdery white sand. When the 8 million kami arrive in Izumo, this is where they land.

**∗∗ Hinomisaki** 日御碕 *0:30h by bus from Taisha station; the bus stops in front of Izumo Taisha on the way*. This scenic cape has a noted shrine, **Hinomisaki Jinja** (1644, ICP), a pair of graceful, Momoyama-style halls sacred to Amaterasu and Susano'o. The cape boasts Asia's tallest lighthouse, a majestic white structure soaring dramatically above plunging cliffs. Around the point is **Owashihama**, a hamlet hugging a stony beach facing a lovely, isle-dotted cove. A little farther on is **Uryū**, on a dramatic, partially enclosed cove filled with fishing boats. Minshuku lodgings are available at both places.

## Exploring the North Shore of Shimane Peninsula

# This coast is reputed to be unspoiled, beautiful, and dotted with fishing villages in which parturition huts (presumably long out of use) still stand; traditionally, childbirth was considered impure.

## Izumo Dining and Lodgings (TEL 0853)

Izumo is famous for its *soba*, a dark, brawny noodle cooked al dente and served in stacking containers called *warigo*. This comes with a pitcher of broth which should be poured over the *soba*.

**Arakiya** 荒木屋 (53-2352). Hrs: 10:00–19:00; clsd M (except if NH). Famous 170-year-old *soba* shop, a few minutes' walk from the pine-lined approach to Izumo Taisha.

**Izumo-shi Cycling Terminal** 出雲市サイクリングターミナル (23-1370). Enya-chō, Izumo-shi, Shimane-ken. *0:10h walk from Izumo-shi station*. Y3600–3800 w/meals.

**Takenoya Ryokan** 竹野屋旅館 (53-3131). Taisha-chō, Hikawa-gun. Near the shrine; best ryokan in Taisha. From Y13,000 w/meals.

**Hinodekan** 日の出館 (53-3311). Taisha-chō. 100-year-old inn near the shrine. Y10,000–15,000 w/meals.

**Ebisuya YH** えびすやYH (53-2157). Taisha-chō. Near Taisha-mae station. Y3250 w/meals, nonmembers, Y3750.

## Exploring Iwami-Ginzan

# *0:30h by bus from Oda station, which is on the JR San'in line*. The silver mines of Iwami, the biggest in Japan's history, were discovered by the Ōuchi of Yamaguchi (CHŪGOKU VI:N1) in the Sengoku period, and subsequently witnessed many bloody battles waged over the fantastic wealth the mines yielded. The mines eventually came under the Tokugawa shogunate and remained important into the Meiji period (silver was one of Japan's major exports), supporting a town of 200,000. Today, the much-shrunken town preserves many Edo-period houses. The gatehouse of the Edo-period governor's mansion contains a museum on Iwami's history. Scattered about the countryside are numerous shrines and temples from Iwami's heyday, including Rakan-ji, with its 500 statues of rakan.

## Easy Access To:

**∗∗ Hagi** (CHŪGOKU VI:N4): *3:25h by JR San'in line express from Izumo*.

# CHŪGOKU III. FUKUYAMA

**Tokyo to Fukuyama:** *4:45h by Shinkansen.*
**Kyoto to Fukuyama:** *1:55h by Shinkansen.*
**Prefectures:** Hiroshima, Ehime

**FUKUYAMA** 福山
A former castle town and junction for buses to Tomo no Ura and trains to Onomichi, where one can catch a ferry to Setoda and connect with the STS Inland Sea Cruise. Fukuyama-jō, a concrete reconstruction with a museum, stands by the station.

# CHŪGOKU III:S. SOUTH FROM FUKUYAMA

**Main Attractions:** Tomo no Ura (S1), STS Inland Sea Cruise (S4)

## S1 ** TOMO NO URA 鞆の浦
*0:30h by bus or Y3500 by taxi from Fukuyama.* Tomo no Ura, a little gem of a fishing village, has been a famous scenic spot since the Nara period, when it was mentioned in the *Manyōshū* poetry collection. Throughout history it has been an important center for the Inland Sea trade, and was a refuge for the last ASHIKAGA shogun Yoshiaki after he was chased out of Kyoto by ODA NOBUNAGA. During Tokugawa times, Korean embassies, which sailed through the Inland Sea on their way to Edo, would rest a few days here, enjoying the view. Three islands, Sensuijima, Kōgōjima, and Bentenjima—the last adorned by a quaint red pagoda—offer a Chinese-style landscape when framed in the windows of the emissaries' lodgings, the Taichōrō. By this hospitality, their Japanese hosts wished to stress that they were as civilized as China, to whom both the Koreans and Japanese looked for cultural inspiration.        445

### Calendar
**May 1–31: Tai-ami.** Sea bream are caught by the traditional method of using several boats to drag a large net. Once every weekday, twice on Su, NH. The sea bream, or *tai*, is an auspicious fish that is always served at weddings and celebrations.

### Getting Around
Rent-a-cycles at the ferry landing. Hrs: 9:00–16:30. Y100 for 2:00h.

### Tomo no Ura Sights
**\*\*\* Taichōrō (Wave-Facing Pavilion)** 対潮楼 Hrs: 7:00–18:00; Dec.–Feb. 7:00–17:00. Located behind and above the public ferry landing. This temple hall was built at the end of the 17th C by the shogunate to house the Korean delegation that periodically came to pay its respects at Edo. The priest will show you the memorabilia the Koreans left, and then open the shutters to disclose the renowned view. (He also has a collection of foreign coins and bills; contributions welcome.) Nearby is **Empuku-ji**, also with a nice view, built on the remains of a castle that played an important part in the 14th-C wars between the northern and southern courts.

**\*\* The Old Town.** Tomo preserves rows of fine old houses. There is a distillery that makes Tomo's own patent medicine, *okagame hōmeishū*, and nearby is a former inn, the **Shichikyō-ochi-iseki**, which played a role in the Meiji Restoration. A few workshops around town still make nails used for building wooden ships, these being a traditional Tomo specialty.

**\*\* Temple and Shrine Quarter.** Along a street in the northeast corner of town stretch Tomo's religious buildings, an easy walking or bicycle circuit. North to south:

**Ankoku-ji** 安国寺 Originally named Kinhō-ji, it was renamed Ankoku-ji under the system of national Rinzai Zen temples (all named Ankoku-ji) that ASHIKAGA TAKAUJI tried to establish. Its Shaka-dō (13th C, ICP) is said to be one of the oldest examples in the country of a Zen-style hall (see Buddhism, p. 39).

**Nunakuma Jinja** 沼名前神社 Rebuilt in concrete. The Noh stage, said to have come from HIDEYOSHI's Fushimi-jō, is of interest.

**Hōsen-ji** 法宣寺 Growing on the grounds of this temple is the Tengai no inn. (Halo Pine), which has one branch that has been trained along poles to a length of over 35 meters.

### Tomo no Ura Lodgings (TEL 0849)
**\*\* New Kinsui Kokusai Hotel** ニュー錦水国際ホテル (82-2111). TELEX 6434-72. Sensuijima, Tomo-chō, Fukuyama-shi, Hiroshima-ken. Expensive but pleasant. The owner-manager, Kitamura Hiroko, speaks English. The only hotel on Senseijima; guests take a 0:05h ferry ride to cross to the quiet, wooded island. From Y20–24,000 w/meals. AX, V.
**Keishōkan** 景勝館 (82-2121). 421 Tomo. Pleasant, modern ryokan with good views. From Y12,000 w/meals. DC, V, AX.
**Taizankan** 対山館 (83-5045). 629 Tomo. Small waterfront inn. From Y13–20,000 w/meals. No CC.

## S2 * ONOMICHI 尾道
*0:20h by JR train from Fukuyama, or 0:50h by taxi from Tomo no Ura. A block from the railway station is the ferry to Setoda (S3), where one catches the STS Inland Sea Cruise (S4).* Onomichi was the home of the elderly couple in Ozu Yasujirō's film *Tokyo Story*, but

today it evokes little of the charm of 40 years ago. Besides an interestingly seedy-looking bar quarter (opposite end of the long shopping arcade from the station), the city offers an official "temple tour" around the hills behind the town. (Ask for information at the Kankō Annaijo). Onomichi has been an important center on the Inland Sea since ancient times, and has several fine temples. **\*\*\* Senkō-ji** is an old Shingon temple with a good view, reached from the top of a tramway. **Saikoku-ji** boasts a huge pair of straw sandals hanging from its Niō Gate. **\*\*\* Jōdo-ji**, which claims to have been founded by SHŌTOKU TAISHI, was rebuilt by ASHI-KAGA TAKAUJI, who stayed here during his retreat from Kyoto. It has a beautiful Tahō-tō and Main Hall (both NT), a tea arbor (ICP) from Fushimi-jō, and an extensive treasure house.

## S3 \* SETODA (IKUCHIJIMA)　瀬戸田
*0:35h by ferry from Onomichi to the port of Setoda, on the island of Ikuchijima.*
**\*\*\* Kōsan-ji**　耕三寺 Hrs: 8:00–17:00. A Setoda boy, Kanemoto Kōzō, made his fortune by monopolizing the steel-tubing industry. He built this assortment of full-scale replicas of famous Japanese temples and shrines over a 30-year period from 1935. Officially a Jōdo Shin temple, Kōsan-ji was dedicated to his mother, who is worshipped here as a manifestation of Kannon Bosatsu. The precincts include the villa he built to comfort her in her old age. A rather unctuous guide takes you through Mother's House: "This is where she took her bath," etc. The replicas have been drawn from the Kyoto Imperial Palace, Nikkō, Hōryū-ji, Shin-Yakushi-ji, Murō-ji, Shitennō-ji, Hōkai-ji, Byōdō-in, and Ishiyama-dera, making it a kitsch capsule history of Japanese architecture. Separate admission fees are needed for the Senbutsu-dō (Thousand Buddha Cave), a sort of Buddhist version of Dante's *Inferno*, as well as the treasure house, which has some respectable pieces. Nearer Setoda harbor, **Kōjō-ji**, founded in 1403, has a three-storied pagoda (NT).

### Setoda Dining and Lodgings (TEL 08452)
**Setoda Suigun**　瀬戸田水軍 (7-3003). STS-owned restaurant down the road from Kōsan-ji.
**Minshuku Setoda Pony**　民宿瀬戸田ポニー (7-0120). 970 Fukuda, Setoda-chō, Toyota-gun, Hiroshima-ken. Y5500–10,000 w/meals.

## S4 \*\* STS INLAND SEA CRUISE
This hydrofoil tour is *very commercial*, but it does make it easy to see the loveliness of the Inland Sea. The tour runs from **\*\*\* Miyajima** (CHŪGOKU IV:S1) to Setoda and back once daily between Mar. 1 and Nov. 30. Allow time to see Kōsan-ji on Setoda. The fare is Y6380 one way. The current schedule is:

| Miyajima | | Hiroshima | | Ōmishima | | Setoda |
|---|---|---|---|---|---|---|
| 8:30 | → | 9:00/9:10 | → | 10:20/12:25 | → | 12:45 |
| 17:40 | ← | 17:20/17:10 | ← | 16:00/14:35 | ← | 14:15 |

## Calendar
**L 5/5: \* Ōyamazumi Jinja Otaue-sai.** This is among the most important rice-planting festivals in Japan: Three *mikoshi* are paraded, followed by offerings of Kagura and *hitori-sumō*, a humorous event pitting a man against the kami.
**L 8/21–22: Ōyamazumi Jinja Ubuzuna Tai-sai.** *Mikoshi*, lion dances, and *yakko* (lackey), dance.
**L 9/9: \* Nukihosai.** Harvest rites, including *hitori-sumō*.

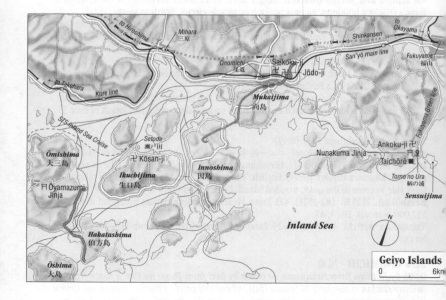

### \*\*\* Ōmishima 大三島

*In addition to the STS route, one can take a hydrofoil from Onomichi (0:40h), Mihara (0:30h), or Takehara (0:20h).* The attraction of this island is the curious **Ōyamazumi Jinja** 大山祇神社 , a shrine on a flattish island in the middle of the sea, worshipped by semi-pirates and dedicated to the Great God of Mountains. While pondering this paradox, visit the treasure halls, which contain over half of the NT armor in Japan.

Ōyamazumi Jinja has received imperial donations since prehistoric times; because of its long history, there are few clues to the shrine "mystery." Intriguingly, the Great Mountain God's messenger is a kind of eel (*unagi*) that is hatched in mountain streams and then swims out to sea, where it lives all its adult life; this could signify either that the shrine was moved from a mainland mountain, or at least that the kami comes down from one of them (see Shinto, p. 23–24). Strengthening this kami's claim on his mountain realm is a little museum (near the treasure halls) with rocks donated from every mine in Japan. The museum gives the sea its due; it also exhibits one of late Emperor Hirohito's marine biology research boats.

From the end of the Heian period until the time of HIDEYOSHI, these, the **Geiyo Islands**, were the base of the Murakami *suigun* or "navy," semi-pirates who charged ships on the Inland Sea tolls and "protection" money. They helped the GENJI army get from Yashima to Dan no Ura, where the Genji defeated the HEIKE (see Miyajima History, p. 449). This is one reason why Ōyamazumi Jinja has so much Heian-period arms and armor. The shrine was destroyed when it took the losing southern side during the Namboku Wars (see Yoshino History, p. 411). The present buildings date from 1427. Hideyoshi, on his way to conquer Shikoku in 1585, put an end to the Murakami "navy," which by that time also operated as *wakō* pirates, terrorizing the coastal cities of China and Korea.

◆ **Kokuhōkan (National Treasure Hall) and Shinyōden.** Hrs: 8:00–17:00. Two buildings housing the celebrated shrine collection. Includes the oldest arms and armor from Japan's historical period, much of it connected with great figures: the armor of MINAMOTO NO YOSHITSUNE and YORITOMO; Benkei's blade; the long sword that felled Kusunoki Masashige; a sword and copper water pitchers offered by Taira no Shigemori. One suit of armor has brocade patterns also seen in the Shōsō-in at Nara, and another was fitted for a woman, said to be a daughter of the Ōhori family, hereditary priests of the shrine. A splendid Tang Chinese mirror was donated by Empress Saimei, who died in 661; the gift of such a mirror, highly valued as an emblem of power (a mirror forms part of the imperial regalia), is evidence of the high status enjoyed by the shrine. There is also a necklace of *magatama*, the comma-shaped jewel that is also part of the imperial regalia.

Food is available at **Ōmishima Suigun** 大三島水軍 , an STS-owned restaurant.

### Exploring Takehara
# *1:00h by JR train from Onomichi, changing trains at Mihara, or 0:20h by jetfoil from Ōmishima.* Takehara was a prosperous Edo-period salt-producing town that retains several wealthy townsmen's dwellings, now part of a nationally preserved architectural zone.

### Exploring Mitarai
# *0:45h by hydrofoil or 1:40h by ferry from Takehara (8 per day).* On the STS tour you get only a glance at this once-important island port as you go by; it is said to have several well-preserved townsmen's houses.

# CHŪGOKU IV. HIROSHIMA

**Tokyo to Hiroshima:** *4:30–5:15h by Shinkansen Hikari express.*
**Kyoto to Hiroshima:** *1:30–2:00h by Shinkansen Hikari express.*
**Prefectures:** Hiroshima, Ehime

### \* HIROSHIMA 広島

Hiroshima was an important port from early times, and in the Edo period it was the castle town of the Asano. In the modern period, it served as a major military base in wars with China and Russia, and during World War I and World War II. It was chosen from among several cities as the target of the world's first atomic bomb attack at 8:15 a.m., August 6, 1945. The Peace Memorial Park contains monuments and museums that soberly and eloquently memorialize and record the suffering of the victims. Hiroshima has been completely rebuilt, and has regained its position as the region's most important city.

### Calendar
**June (1st Su):** \*\* **Hana-taue.** Chiyoda (*1:30h by bus from Hiroshima, or 0:40h by JR Kabe line, then 0:20h by bus to Yae*). One of Japan's most colorful rice-planting rites. Sacred dances are offered in the morning, then from 14:30, dozens of young women in traditional farm clothing plant seedlings as the men play drums and flutes.
**Aug. 6: Peace Ceremony.** Peace Memorial Park. A-bomb attack memorial services at 8:15 a.m. Those who died in the previous year from effects of A-bomb injuries are added to the roll of victims. At night 10,000 lanterns are set afloat on the city's waterways.
**Sept. (around 3rd weekend):** \* # **Nishi-Chūgoku Senbatsu Kagura Kyōen Taikai.** Kake (*1:35h by JR Kabe line from Hiroshima*), Kake Shōgakkō (primary school). Selected performances of Izumo-style Kagura. For information, call 08262-2-1221.

447

## Hiroshima Sights

**\*\*\* Heiwa Kinen Kōen (Peace Memorial Park)** 平和記念公園 *0:10h by taxi or 0:15h by Gion Ōhashi-bound streetcar from the front of the station to Genbaku-Dōmu-mae (A-Bomb Dome).* The park is on a delta island in the Odagawa. The museum, cenotaph, and eternal flame in the center of the park were designed by architect Tange Kenzō, and the two Peace Bridges by American sculptor Isamu Noguchi.

◆ **Genbaku Dōmu (Atom Bomb Dome)** 原爆ドーム The old industry promotion hall, it was one of the few buildings near the epicenter that was not completely flattened, although the steel frame melted and fused. It is the only bomb-damaged building allowed to remain standing in Hiroshima.

**The Cenotaph** contains a roll of victims (several thousand names are still added every year), and is situated so that it frames the A-Bomb Dome.

◆ **Heiwa Kinen Shiryōkan (Peace Memorial Museum)** 平和記念資料館 Hrs: 9:00–18:00, Dec.–Apr. 9:00–17:00; enter 0:30h before closing time; clsd NY. About 200,000 people were killed by the Hiroshima bomb and its aftereffects. Victims such as the one who left his shadow on a hospital wall had little time to feel pain, but many who survived the initial destruction suffered from radiation sickness. Those receiving the heaviest doses spewed blood from all orifices and were dead within 10 days. Less severe cases lost their hair, suffered inflammation, bleeding, sperm loss and menstrual difficulties. Many victims developed keloids, large, ugly scars caused by radiation, and a significant percentage later developed cancer. The many infants born with abnormally small heads are viewed by survivors as a symbol of their suffering. Many non-Japanese, including 25,000 Korean forced laborers, also perished.

**\* Fudō-in Kondō** 不動院金堂 (1540, NT). *0:20h by bus north of station*. This is the largest medieval Zen-style Buddha Hall; built for the funerary temple of Hiroshima's daimyo.

**\* Shukkei-en** 縮景園 Hrs: 9:00–18:00. Oct.–Mar. 9:00–17:00; clsd NY. Reconstructed after the war, this pleasant stroll garden was built in 1620 for the lord of Hiroshima.

**Hiroshima-jō (Castle)** 広島城 Hrs: 9:00–17:30. Oct.–Mar. 9:00–16:30; clsd NY. Originally built by the Mōri clan in 1589, it is a postwar reconstruction. Local history museum.

## Hiroshima Dining and Lodgings (TEL 082)

Hiroshima is famous for its *kaki* (oysters). Winter is the season to enjoy them.

① **Suishin** 酔心 立町6–7 (247-4411). Hrs: 11:10–22:00 (order by 21:00, on Su by 20:40); clsd W (Th if W a NH), mid-Aug., NY. *Kamameshi*, a rice casserole cooked with various ingredients: *kaki, matsutake* (pine mushrooms), *tai* (sea bream), *ebi* (shrimp). From Y670. DC, V, MC.

② **Kakifune Kanawa** かき船かなわ 平和大橋 (241-3493/241-7416). Hrs: 11:00–14:00, 17:00–22:00 (last order 21:00). Clsd Su Apr.–Sept.; clsd 1st and 3rd Su Oct.–Mar. Oysters in a converted boat restaurant, docked by Heiwa Ōhashi. Lunch from Y3000, dinner Y6000. V, DC.

③ **\*\* ANA Hotel Hiroshima** 広島全日空ホテル (241-1111). Fax 241-9123. 7-20 Nakamachi, Naka-ku, Hiroshima-shi. Fine city hotel. S Y9500–11,000, Tw Y18–21,000 w/tax. AX, DC, V, MC.

④ **Minshuku Ikedaya** 民宿池田屋 中区土橋町 (231-3329). 6-36 Dobashi, Naka-ku. Good location near Peace Park. Member of economical inn group. Y4500 per person.

⑤ **Maruko Inn Hiroshima** マルコーイン広島 中区銀山町7–8 (242-0505). 7-8 Kanayama-chō, Naka-ku. Centrally located hotel. Small rooms. S Y7700, Dbl Y9–13,600, Tw Y11,300–17,000.

⑥ **Yayoi Kaikan** 弥生会館 (263-8411). 3-2-15 Futabanosato, Higashi-ku. Business-hotel type. *0:03h on foot from station* S Y4600, Tw Y7500. No CC.

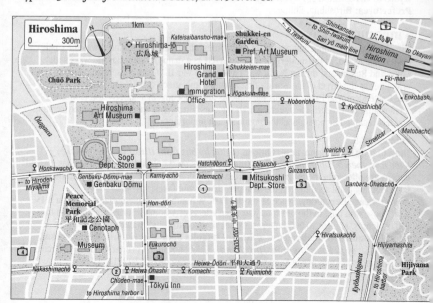

# CHŪGOKU IV:S. SOUTH FROM HIROSHIMA (MIYAJIMA AND WESTERN SHIKOKU)

## S1 ✳✳✳ MIYAJIMA 宮島

*0:22h by high-speed boat from Hiroshima pier (5 km by taxi from station, ask for Seto-Naikai Kisen Hiroshima Sanbashi). From Genbaku-Dōmu-mae, 0:50h by streetcar to Hiroden-Miyajima, then 0:15h by frequent ferry to Miyajima. From Hiroshima station, 0:25h by JR San'yō line to Miyajima-guchi, transfer to ferry pier. Ferry Hrs: 6:00–22:00.*
Though this famous island is cluttered with many unnecessary "attractions," it is still worth a trip just to see Itsukushima Jinja, the celebrated shrine that gives the island its name, Shrine Island. Miyajima was considered so sacred that ordinary people were forbidden to set foot on it; instead, worshippers approached by boat through the great torii out in the water. Numerous deer, messengers of the kami, roam about freely. The shrine is breathtaking at night when, as often happens, someone makes an offering to have the lanterns in the galleries lit.

### Calendar

**Jan. 2, 3, 5:** ✳ **Bugaku.** Itsukushima Jinja. Ancient court music and dances. The shrine is mobbed with people paying their New Year visit.

**Apr. 15:** ✳ **Hiwatari.** Gunmonji-dō (*on Misen, 0:20h from top of tramway*). Shingon priests burn wooden tablets with prayers written on them, and then walk barefoot over the embers, followed by hundreds of pilgrims. Starts at 13:30.

**Apr. 16–18:** ✳ **Jin-Noh.** Noh plays on Itsukushima Jinja's famous open-air stage. Open seating. Hrs: 9:00–16:00.

**L 6/17:** ✳✳ **Kangen-sai.** Itsukushima Jinja. See Calendar, p. 428. Lantern-lit boats at night.

**Sometime in Aug.:** **Tamatori-sai.** Itsukushima Jinja. Loinclothed youths gather at high tide under the torii and fight to retrieve a huge ball hanging from a high tower.

**Nov. 15:** ✳ **Hiwatari.** Repeat of April 15.

**Dec. 31:** ✳ **Chinkasai.** Itsukushima Jinja. People come for purified New Year's fire.

# Miyajima History: The Rise and Fall of the Taira

**Taira no Kiyomori** — (1118–1181) Ruthless patriarch who raised the Taira clan to supreme power, but whose pride and despotism spelled its fall.

**Minamoto no Yoritomo** — (1147–1199) Exiled in boyhood by Kiyomori, he grew up to vanquish the Taira and become shogun.

In 1146, TAIRA NO KIYOMORI, then a vigorous man of twenty-eight, became governor of Aki, a province facing the western Inland Sea. Seeking to profit from trade with China, he set about dredging channels and developing the Hiroshima area. Nearby he built a sanctuary on Itsukushima (Miyajima) to gain the protection of the island's three sea goddesses for his clan. As the Taira rose to great power, the shrine grew splendid, rivaling the palaces of the capital in magnificence

That a clan whose power base was hundreds of miles from the capital should come to rule the court, however briefly, reflects profound changes in the political structure of Japan. This came about through the court's habit of farming out superfluous descendants of the imperial family to provincial manors, where they were assigned the dirty work of defending the court's interests. Two clans that became prominent through their military services were the MINAMOTO and the TAIRA. Over time, these provincial clans became more attached to their own land and correspondingly less loyal to the throne. But the court, contemptuous of mere warriors, failed to see the danger.

In 1156, a dispute arose between **Emperor Go-Shirakawa** and retired emperor Sutoku. The patriarch of the Minamoto clan sided with Sutoku, but his son Yoshitomo and Taira no Kiyomori backed Go-Shirakawa. In the ensuing battle, the pro-Sutoku forces lost. Kiyomori ordered Yoshitomo to behead his own father, an appalling sentence he finally could not bring himself to carry out, and instead left to a retainer. Dozens of others were executed; the streets of Heian-kyō ran with blood for the first time since its founding. Punishment by exile and other niceties were put aside as the fight between the two warrior clans escalated. Four years later, Yoshitomo rebelled against Kiyomori, but was defeated. Yoshitomo perished with most of his kinsmen, but his three small sons, YORITOMO, Noriyori, and YOSHI-TSUNE, were spared, so that their prayers might succor the ghosts of the dead. Little did Kiyomori dream they would grow up to avenge their clan.

With the Taira victory in 1160, the military class for the first time became undisputed masters of Japan. Kiyomori, however, was not a rough soldier, but a man with close affinities to the court. Indeed, it was whispered that his real father was the late cloistered emperor Shirakawa, who had presented his pregnant concubine to Kiyomori's father. Now that there was no one to oppose him, Kiyomori built a palace at Rokuhara (Kyoto, p. 333) and had the court confer upon him the highest ranks, though many courtiers grumbled at the unprecedented honors being given to this rustic upstart. To expand his influence, he pressed his numerous daughters upon powerful members of the court, including the FUJIWARA regent. The court was further humiliated by a grandson of Kiyomori's who set his thugs upon a nobleman's entourage when it failed to move out of his way. In 1171, Kiyomori succeeded in pairing his daughter, known to history as KENREIMON-IN, with the eight-year-old Emperor Takakura, whom Kiyomori had maneuvered onto the throne. Not surprisingly, it took some time to produce an heir, but a son was born in 1178. Two years later, Takakura was persuaded to abdicate, and the infant, Kiyomori's grandson, became Emperor **Antoku**. Kiyomori's power was absolute.

The Taira tutelary shrine at Itsukushima naturally flourished. It was here that Kenreimon-in, pregnant with the emperor-to-be, came to pray for a safe delivery. Kiyomori spent vast sums on the shrine. Its palatial pavilions were built out over the waters of the Inland Sea, and a huge torii was erected out in the bay so that worshippers approaching by boat could see its sweeping wings and galleries reflected in the sea, like a vision of Paradise. The Taira lavished splendid gifts on the shrine, including masks for Bugaku court dances and a famous set of **Lotus Sutra scrolls** copied by members of the family and exquisitely illustrated and adorned. In 1180, Kiyomori planned to take his son-in-law, the abdicated Emperor Takakura, on a pilgrimage to Itsukushima to pay homage to the Taira tutelary gods. This latest act of hubris further enraged the court.

450

Cloistered emperor Go-Shirakawa, Kiyomori's old protector, had intended to strengthen imperial power and instead saw the court in a weaker position than ever. Now his son, Prince Mochihito, called on the only Minamoto remaining in the capital, the seventy-five-year-old Yorimasa, to back his candidacy for the throne and end the tyranny of the Taira. Badly outnumbered, Yorimasa fought valiantly at Uji Bridge and then retreated to nearby Byōdō-in to commit suicide. But farther east, in Kamakura, Minamoto no Yoritomo, now grown to manhood, heeded the call to arms and began a revolt that eventually spread over the land.

Meanwhile, Kiyomori dragged the court, with the emperor and abdicated emperors in tow, to his stronghold near present-day Kōbe. But they raised such a fuss that he had to let them return to Kyoto half a year later. In the winter of 1181, Kiyomori contracted a raging fever and lay stark naked for several days in an unheated apartment at his Rokuhara palace before he died. In his final moments, Kiyomori commanded his sons to forego prayers for his soul and instead bring Yoritomo's head to his grave. But with Kiyomori gone, there was no strong leader for the clan.

Raising the banner of Prince Mochihito, Yoritomo began to advance on the capital. For two years, the Minamoto and Taira armies grappled in central Japan, with the Taira only slowly losing ground. Suddenly, in the summer of 1183, they found themselves in the capital in danger of being trapped between Minamoto troops coming from the east and south. Worse, the troublesome cloistered emperor, Go-Shirakawa, had slipped out of their custody and was now safe atop Mt. Hiei, where he gave the Minamoto cause his imperial stamp of approval. The Taira hastily burned their buildings in Rokuhara and, taking the child emperor and the imperial regalia, fled west, where they were still powerful.

For a time, they held out at Yashima on Shikoku, friendly Taira territory where Kiyomori's father had once been governor. Their long mastery of the Inland Sea gave them confidence. But by bold ploys Yoshitsune, Yoritomo's brilliant younger brother, forced the Taira to put to sea and sail west, past Itsukushima to Shimonoseki, at the western limit of the Inland Sea. It was there, at **Dan no Ura**, that the Taira turned and awaited the fateful battle. It came on April 25, 1185. The two navies, each with four to five hundred ships, clashed out in the straits, where at first the current favored the Taira. But midway the tide turned, and the Taira, who had prospered by the sea, were now betrayed by it. When it became clear that all was lost, Kiyomori's widow grasped her grandson, the child-emperor Antoku, and leaped into the sea. Kenreimon-in, with her weeping ladies, followed, but was dragged from the waters alive.

Kenreimon-in, the former empress and last of the Taira, was taken to Kyoto, where she took the tonsure and retired to the tiny nunnery of Jakkō-in in Ōhara (Kyoto, p. 349), there to spend the rest of her life praying for her son and slaughtered kin. The shrine at Miyajima, however, continued to prosper, for although the Taira were gone, the sailors of the Inland Sea continued to seek its protection. In 1587, TOYOTOMI HIDEYOSHI, a great admirer of Kiyomori, built the Senjōkaku Hall overlooking the shrine. The disaster of the Taira is immortalized in the epic ballad known as *Tales of the Heike* and in countless works of literature and drama. And at Dan no Ura, people say that a strange species of local crab, the *Heike-gani*, with hideous faces sketched on their carapaces, are reincarnations of the drowned Taira warriors.

## Getting Around

Maps in English at tourist office in the JR ferry building. Bicycles for rent by the pier, but the main sights can be seen on foot in about 3:00h.

## Miyajima Sights

**\*\* Senjōkaku** 千畳閣 (ICP). This "pavilion of a thousand mats" was built in 1587 as an offering to Itsukushima Jinja by Toyotomi Hideyoshi. The vast hall is built of rough timbers and hung with numerous large *ema* (votive paintings). The nearby pagoda dates from 1407.

**\*\*\* Itsukushima Jinja** 厳島神社 (NT). Hrs: 6:00–sunset. Miyajima was considered the sacred island of sea deities as early as the 6th C. The massive vermilion **torii** standing out in the bay is in the Ryōbu style of syncretic Shinto-Buddhist sanctuaries, which Itsukushima was before 1868; the present torii was rebuilt in 1875 (see Shinto, p. 27).

With its symmetrical wings, galleries, and open-air Bugaku stage, Itsukushima Jinja reflects the influence of Tang palace design and Buddhist paradise halls. Near the west corner is an arched bridge, Soribashi, used by imperial messengers. Nearby is a ◆ **Noh stage**, stunningly built out over the water, which was donated by Mōri Motonari, the most powerful lord of western Honshū; he initiated the annual Jin-Noh in atonement for polluting the island with his battles. The shrine is most spectacular viewed at high tide on a dark evening when the lanterns hanging in the covered galleries are often lit with candles. To arrange to have the candles lit, make a reservation and pay Y10,000 at the shrine office (44-2020).

**\*\*\* Itsukushima Jinja Hōmotsukan (Treasure Hall)** 宝物館 Hrs: 8:00–17:00. The glory of the collection is the ◆ **Heike Nōkyō** (NT), illuminated sutra scrolls, 33 in all, copied and offered to the shrine by members of the Taira clan in 1164 and 1166. Of these, Langdon Warner wrote: "Hardly another monument exists which so adequately expresses that delicate and lavish 12th-century culture. ..." The great 17th-C artist, TAWARAYA SŌTATSU, helped restore these scrolls and may have been profoundly influenced by them. A few of the scrolls are shown, usually in autumn; superb, hand-drawn copies are always on view. There's also a painted cypress fan (NT), thought to have been offered by ex-emperor Takakura or Kenreimon-in, fine Bugaku masks (ICP), armor (NT) of Minamoto no Yoritomo, and a large votive painting, *Yamauba (the Mountain Hag) and Kintarō* (ICP), by Rosetsu.

**Daigan-ji** 大願寺 Established in 1201 as one of Itsukushima Jinja's affiliated temples, dedicated to Benzai-ten, the goddess of music. Contains Kamakura-period Buddhist images (ICP).

**\* Rekishi Minzoku Shiryōkan (History and Folklore Museum)** 歴史民俗資料館 Hrs: 8:30–17:00; clsd NY. In a mid-19th-C merchant's house.

**\*\* Momiji-dani (Maple Valley)** 紅葉谷 A pleasant glen dotted with teahouses and inns, ablaze with maples in mid-November. 0:15h on foot up the valley is the tramway to Misen.

**(Mt.) Misen** 弥山 *0:15h by two-stage tramway (return trip gets badly backed up after the fire festivals)*. Hrs: Mar.–Nov. 8:00–17:00. May, Aug., Sept. 8:00–17:30. Dec.–Feb. 9:00–16:20. The Shingon temple near the summit was once syncretically affiliated with Itsukushima Jinja. Hiking trails offer views of the Inland Sea.

## Miyajima Lodgings (TEL 0829)

1 **\*\* Iwasō** 岩惣 (44-2233). Miyajima-chō, Saeki-gun, Hiroshima-ken. An elegant old ryokan with a new annex. Ask for the older wing. Y20–40,000 w/meals. AX, V.

2 **Miyajima Grand Hotel** 宮島グランドホテル (44-2411). Address as above. Japanese and Western rooms; well-appointed. From Y16,000 w/meals. AX, V.

3 **Kokuminshukusha Miyajima Lodge** 国民宿舎宮島ロッジ (44-0430). Address as above. *0:25h on foot from pier*. Rooms with bath and toilet, Y6700+ w/meals. No CC.

## Easy Access To:

**\* Iwakuni** (CHŪGOKU V): *0:20h by JR San'yō line from Miyajima-guchi*.
**\*\* STS Inland Sea Cruise** (CHŪGOKU III:S4): *Board at Miyajima pier at 8:40*.

451

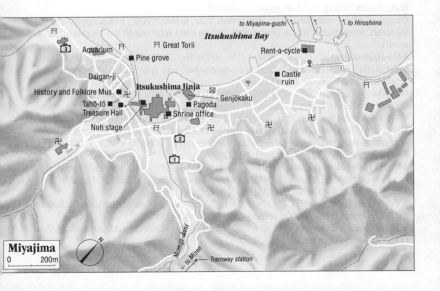

## WESTERN SHIKOKU

### S2 ✳ MATSUYAMA　松山

*1:10h by hydrofoil from Hiroshima (some via Kure), or 2:45h by regular ferry, via Kure. 2:50h by JR limited express from Takamatsu (CHŪGOKU I:S3). By air: frequent flights on ANA, 1-2 daily on JAL, from Tokyo and Osaka. 0:15h by bus from airport to city. See* CHŪGOKU I:S *for descriptions of eastern and central Shikoku.* This bustling Inland Sea port town has one of the finest surviving feudal castles in Japan and Dōgo Onsen, a celebrated spa which is said to have attracted SHŌTOKU TAISHI and received mention in the 8th-century poetry anthology, *Manyōshū*. More recently, Natsume Sōseki chose it as the setting for his novel *Botchan*.

### Getting Around

The private Iyo-tetsu line's Matsuyama-shi station is closer to the city attractions than the JR Matsuyama station. The convenient and simple streetcar serves both stations and goes to Dōgo Onsen via Ōkaidō, Mitsukoshi Department Store, the ANA hotel, and the castle.

### Matsuyama Sights

✳✳✳ **Matsuyama-jō**　松山城　(ICP). Hrs: 9:00–17:00; clsd Dec. 31. *Reached by tramway from a souvenir-cluttered station 300 m north of Ōkaidō tram stop.* Sprawled over the top of the 130-m-high mountain is an extensive and beautiful complex of surviving turrets, *tenshūkaku*, and high stone walls, first built in 1603 by Katō Yoshiaki. Many of the present structures were rebuilt in 1854 after a fire, but are considered to be faithful to the original style. With its broad views and grand scale, this is among the most evocative of Japanese castles. At the foot of the castle hill stands the late-19th-C Western villa of the former castle lord.

### Dōgo Onsen　道後温泉

452

*0:20h by tram from Matsuyama station.*

✳✳✳ **Dōgo Onsen Honkan**　道後温泉本館　Hrs: 6:30–22:00 (enter by 21:00), daily. A majestic old public bathhouse, built in 1894. 1F: large, crowded, public baths. 2F: common lounge. 3F: private rooms, including a Botchan Room in honor of the character in Natsume Sōseki's novel, *Botchan*, who frequented the spa. The bottom price gets you into the friendly bathhouse crowds, the top price nets a private room, tea, and access to the "imperial bath." The Yūshinden is a luxurious, Shoin-style suite built for an imperial visit in 1899.

✳✳ **Isaniwa Jinja**　伊佐爾波神社　(ICP). *0:05h on foot from Dōgo Onsen station, up an impressive flight of stone steps.* This quiet hilltop shrine to Hachiman, the god of war, was built in 1667 and is a fine, colorful example of Hachiman-style shrine architecture.

✳✳ **Ishite-ji**　石手寺　*0:05h by bus E of Dōgo Onsen station.* This temple, No. 51 of the Shikoku pilgrimage, is distinguished by its fine Kamakura-period architecture, including the Niō Gate (NT), with Niō statues ascribed to the KEI SCHOOL, main hall, pagoda, and bell tower (all ICP). The temple's name means Stone Hand, and alludes to a legend about a local lord who was born clutching a stone. The inscription on the stone explained that the infant was the reincarnation of an impious man who repented his sins and was granted a choice of his next life on earth; he chose to be reborn a great lord so that he might serve the people.

### Matsuyama Crafts and Shopping

Iyo-kasuri is a type of indigo-dyed *ikat* textile. Tobe-yaki is a sturdy porcelain decorated with freely brushed cobalt-blue designs on a white ground. Tobe village, 0:50h by bus from Matsuyama, is sprawling and not rewarding to visit, except perhaps by specialists.

**Baizan**　梅山　(33-6388). Matsuyama ANA Hotel, 3F. Hrs: 11:00–20:00; clsd M (except if NH). Stocks Tobe porcelain from the 100-year-old Baizan kiln.

**Mingei Iyo Kasuri Kaikan**　民芸伊予かすり会館　(22-0405). Hrs: 8:00–17:00; Dec. 31– Jan. 1 8:00–15:00. Demonstration and sales center for Iyo-kasuri.

### Matsuyama Dining and Lodgings (TEL 0899)

Ōkaidō　大街道, near Mitsukoshi Department Store, is Matsuyama's best shopping and dining street. Most tourists stay in Dōgo Onsen, but we don't recommend it—it's overpriced and tawdry.

**Shin-Hamasaku**　新浜作　三番町4　(33-3030). Hrs: 11:00–15:00, 16:30–21:30 (last order 20:00), daily. Pleasant and roomy restaurant with folk decor. Inland Sea specialties. *Teishoku* from Y1000–2000. No CC.

**Goshiki**　五志喜　三番町　(33-3838). Hrs: 11:00–21:00, daily. Five-color *sōmen* (vermicelli) noodles. In business since 1722. From Y1000. Try it with tempura. No CC.

✳ **Ehime Kyōsai Kaikan**　愛媛共済会館　(45-6311). 5-13-1 Sanbanchō, Matsuyama-shi, Ehime-ken. Clean and pleasant business-type hotel. An excellent deal, with a good location near trams, shopping streets. Japanese and Western rooms. S Y4900 w/bath, Y4200 w/o bath, Tw Y6400 (for one), Y9300 (for two). No CC.

✳✳ **ANA Hotel Matsuyama**　松山全日空ホテル　(33-5511). 3-2-1 Ichibanchō. Excellent location by tram stop and Mitsukoshi, with nice night views of the castle and the French-style villa. S Y7800–12,000, Tw Y14–28,000. AX, DC, V, MC.

✳ **Funaya Ryokan**　ふなや旅館　(47-0278). 1-33 Yunomachi, Dōgo, Matsuyama-shi. Best in the Dōgo Onsen. From Y24,000 w/meals. AX, DC, V, MC.

✳ **Shinsen-en YH**　神泉園YH　(33-6366). 22-3 Dōgohimezaka Otsu, Matsuyama-shi. Near Dōgo Onsen. Y3800 w/meals.

## S3 * # UCHIKO 内子

*1:00h from Matsuyama, or 0:25h from Ōzu by the Matsuyama-Uwajima express bus. Get off at Chiseibashi stop. From here, head away from the bridge, veer left immediately onto a street leading away from the river. At the second intersection, you should see an old Western-style bank building on the right corner. The road straight ahead is Yōkaichi.* Though most of Uchiko today is utterly ordinary, there's a kilometer-long lane, Yōkaichi, which is lined with late Edo- and early Meiji-period dwellings and is now an architecturally preserved zone. The old houses of Uchiko were the estates of wealthy merchants dealing in *rō*, a vegetable wax that was an important Meiji-period export item. These houses have walls of lovely pale sand colors, protected by gray tiles. Windows and doors are covered with wood laths and trimmed with ornate carvings in wood and plaster.

**\*\*\* Yōkaichi** 八日市 A gently inclined road lined with old buildings. **Amazake Chaya** is a teahouse selling *budō* (grape) and *yuzu* (citrus) juice, and *amazake* (mild, sweet saké). The shop makes miso, soy sauce, and sweets in the old factory across the street. Upstairs is a gallery with displays about the brewing of soy sauce. **Nagaike Mingei-ten** is a tiny shop selling delightful folk crafts. Young Mr. Nagaike makes delightful little brushes of a brown tree bark fiber once used for raincapes. ◆ **Hon Haga-tei**, the finest house in Uchiko (not open), was built in 1884 by a wax merchant and boasts a wealth of ornamental detail. Naka Haga-tei and Kami Haga-tei, branch houses of Hon Haga-tei, are nearby.

**\*\*\* Kami Haga-tei** 上芳我邸 Hrs: 9:00–16:30; clsd M. A complete wax-merchant's house. The storehouse contains tools to make *rō* (wax). There's a fantastic kitchen, courtyard garden, and gracious living quarters. The upper floors are handsomely renovated and house a gallery and a pleasant coffee shop.

**\*\* Ōmori Rōsoku (Candlemaker)** 大森ローソク (43-0385). Hrs: 9:00–17:00; clsd M. Turn right at the stone lantern near the top of Yōkaichi street, just before Kōshō-ji. Mr. and Mrs. Ōmori make *wa-rōsoku*, Japanese candles, in the traditional way, applying layer upon layer of the vegetable wax over a wick of wound *igusa* cores (the white, spongy core of tatami straw). Candles in all sizes are on sale, along with cakes of pure *rō*, like those sold in Uchiko's heyday, and attractive iron candlestick holders.

453

**\* Uchiko-za (Theater)** 内子座 Near JR Uchiko station. A rare, old-style theater, built in 1915 and reopened Oct. 1985.

### Uchiko Dining and Lodgings (TEL 0893)

**\* Inariya** いなりや (44-2218). Hrs: 10:00–14:00, 16:00–22:00, daily. A friendly place with folk decor. *Rāmen* noodles, *bentō*, and (by reservation) *irori-yaki*—freshwater fish and vegetables broiled over coals. Y1500–3000.

**Uchiko Sports Inn** 内子スポーツイン (44-2245). 3-5 Uchiko Daba, Uchiko-chō, Kita-gun, Ehime-ken. *0:05h taxi ride from town center.* Pleasant and simple modern facility. Japanese rooms. Y7100 w/meals.

## \* ŌZU 大洲

*Ōzu-Honmachi is 1:20h by express bus from Matsuyama or Uwajima, or 0:25h from Uchiko, or 1:00h by JR Yosan main line limited express from Matsuyama or Uwajima. From the station, walk, take a taxi, or bicycle to Ōzu-Honmachi.* From Ōzu-Honmachi walk toward the river, then turn right onto the street just before the bridge. There are many old-fashioned (early Western) stores, several antique shops and confectioners. At the far end are rows of houses dating from the late Edo to early Meiji periods.

**\*\*\* Garyū-sansō** 臥竜山荘 Hrs: 9:00–17:30; Nov.–Mar. 19, 9:00–16:30; clsd Tu, NY. This exquisite Sukiya-style villa with gardens and tea huts was built by a wealthy importer in 1907. It is situated on a steep, wooded bank overlooking the river, on land that once belonged to the local daimyo.

### Ōzu Lodgings (TEL 0893)

There is a youth hostel by the castle, and a kokuminshukusha by the river, near Garyū-sansō. **Aburaya Ryokan** 油屋旅館 (24-3125). Honmachi 2-chōme, Ōzu-shi, Ehime-ken. Ōzu's oldest and best is this inn by the river, just off the shop-lined street in the old town. Serves *ayu* fish and *bentō* lunches by reservation. Y8–12,000 w/meals. No CC.

## S4 YAWATAHAMA 八幡浜

*1:15h from Matsuyama (S2) or 0:50h from Uwajima by JR Yosan line limited express. 2:55h by ferry from and to Beppu (KYŪSHŪ I:E3) and Usuki (KYŪSHŪ I:E6).*

## S5 # UWAJIMA 宇和島

*From Matsuyama (S2), 1:30h by JR Yosan main line limited express, or 3:00h by express bus, via Uchiko and Ōzu. From Kōchi (CHŪGOKU I:S7), 3:40–4:00h by indirect train, changing at Kubokawa; from Sukumo (CHŪGOKU I:S9), 1:55h by express bus. The latter route offers some of the best coastal scenery in Shikoku. From Beppu (KYŪSHŪ I:E3), 3:15h by direct ferry via Yawatahama.* Uwajima's temple quarter and old neighborhoods are rather charming, and the town claims a bit of sophistication because its Edo-period lords were descended from the senior branch of the great Date clan of Sendai (see Castles, p. 49). A type of bull sumo seen here is also seen in Korea, Okinawa, and Japan Sea Islands such as Oki and Tsushima.

### Calendar

Many local festivals feature *ushi-oni*, or ox-demons, part of a curious bovine cult.

**July 23–24:** ** **Warei Jinja Matsuri.** See Calendar, p. 428. At Warei Jinja (*0:05h walk north of station, across river*).

**Oct. 28–29:** ** **Uwatsuhiko Jinja Matsuri.** See Calendar, p. 429.

**Nov. 3:** * **Mishō Hachiman-sai.** Mishō (*0:45h by bus from Uwajima*). Rustic festival with *ushi-oni* and deer dances.

### Getting Around

Bicycles for rent at the Kankō Kyōkai (Tourism Office, 22-3934), across the street from the station.

### Uwajima Sights

* **Uwajima-jō (Castle)** 宇和島城 (1601, ICP). The keep is small but genuine. The promontory on which it is located was once surrounded by sea-water moats.

** **Date Hakubutsukan (Museum)** 伊達博物館 (22-7776). Hrs.: 9:00–16:30; clsd M (Tu if M a NH), NY. Noted items include a portrait of Hideyoshi (ICP) and an ornate suit of armor that belonged to Munetada, 7th Date lord. The museum prides itself on the superb condition of its collection.

**Tensha-en (Garden)** 天赦園 Hrs: 8:30–17:00. Oct.–Mar. 8:30–16:30. The Date lord's stroll garden is now a rather ragged public park. Noted for its wisteria arch.

** **Temple Quarter.** Most of the old temples are along a quiet canal on the east side of town. From the bright red bridge, about 0:15h on foot south of the station, are **Seigō-ji** 西江寺, a Zen temple with a pleasant dry garden; **Tōkaku-ji**, with the tombs of several Date lords; **Dairyū-ji**, an old Zen temple with other Date tombs; and **Uwatsuhiko Jinja**, a simple shrine to the guardian kami of Uwajima.

** **Taga Jinja** 多賀神社 Hrs: 8:00–17:00. Y600. Fertility shrine with a notorious sex museum — everything from woodblock print "pillow books" and erotic Buddhas to flesh magazines and onsen souvenirs. The quantity is staggering.

**Tōgyūjō (Bullfight Ring)** 闘牛場 (25-3511). *Tōgyū* is a kind of shoving match between two bulls. Bouts are held on Jan. 2, 3rd Su in Mar. and Apr., 3rd Su of May, July 14, and the 3rd Su in Nov. In addition, there are frequent demonstration bouts put on for tour groups, though these exhibitions are rather lifeless. In a real tournament, dozens of bulls are kept sparring all day, to the enjoyment of rowdy locals. Rules and ranks are similar to sumo, and the bulls themselves are quite docile outside the ring. They are pampered and fed raw eggs to make them burlier.

### Uwajima Dining and Lodgings (TEL 0895)

*Tai-meshi* is sea bream sashimi mixed with egg yolk and soy sauce and poured over hot rice. *Fukumen* is gelatinous noodles topped with flaked fish and vegetables. *Satsuma-jiru* is a broth of puréed baked white fish, garnished with scallions and citrus peel. *Fuka yuzarashi* is blanched slices of shark, served with a tangy mustard and vinegar sauce.

* **Gansui** 丸水 (22-3636). Hrs: 11:00–21:00; clsd M (Tu if M a NH), NY. Well-known restaurant serving local dishes, as well as more familiar dishes. *Tai-meshi* Y1600. No CC.

** **Kiya Ryokan** 木屋旅館 (22-0101). 2-8-2 Honmachi Oite, Uwajima-shi, Ehime-ken. The best reason to stay overnight in Uwajima. Wonderful family-run inn built in the Meiji period, it is genuine and has a touch of class. A few inconveniences (no bath/toilet with rooms), but worth it. Superb local cuisine. From Y10,000 w/meals. No CC.

**Marujū Ryokan** 丸重旅館 (22-0586). 1-4-10 Marunouchi. Right at the foot of the castle. An old-style wooden inn with garden, in decent repair. Y5700 w/meals. No CC.

**Uwajima YH** 宇和島YH (22-7177). Atago Kōen. Clsd Jan. 24–27. Members, Y3600 w/meals, nonmembers, Y4300.

### Exploring Sotodomari

# *From Uwajima or Sukumo, 0:45h by express bus to Mishō, then change to a bus heading for Sotodomari, Nakadomari or, more frequently, for Kajima Tosenjō-mae (Kajima ferry pier).* This tiny fishing village is known for its extensive stone walls and terraces.

**Lodgings:** Minshuku Ishigaki-sō (0895-82-0421). Y6000 w/meals.

# CHŪGOKU V. IWAKUNI

**Tokyo to Iwakuni:** *5:40h by many Shinkansen Hikari expresses to Shin-Iwakuni station. Or switch at Hiroshima to the JR San'yō line and take it 0:50h to Iwakuni station.*
**Prefectures:** Yamaguchi

* **IWAKUNI** 岩国
*0:20h by JR San'yō line from Miyajima-guchi* (CHŪGOKU IV:S1). The focal point of Iwakuni is Japan's most famous bridge, the Kintai-kyō (Brocade Sash Bridge). The western side of the bridge, the former samurai quarter, preserves vestiges of an Edo-period castle

town. It has been turned into a large park, containing museums, samurai houses, and a reconstructed castle. There is a naval base in Iwakuni, shared by the U.S. Navy and Japanese Self-Defense Forces. June 1–Aug. 31, there is *ukai* (cormorant fishing) on the Nishikigawa (Hrs: 18:30–21:00).

## Getting Around
The main attractions are about equidistant between Iwakuni station (San'yō line) and Shin-Iwakuni station (Shinkansen); it's about 0:15–0:20h by bus from either station, or a Y1200 taxi ride. About once an hour there's a JR Gantoku line train from Iwakuni station to Nishi-Iwakuni (0:05h).

## ✱✱✱ Kintai-kyō (Brocade Sash Bridge) 錦帯橋
This beautiful bridge, first built in 1673, is put together without nails. Its five linked arches form an undulating span—likened to a "brocade sash"—across the river. While locals can walk across for free, visitors have to pay a small toll. Originally, only samurai could use the bridge, which separated their quarter from the townsmen's; commoners, if they had business in the samurai quarter, had to take a small boat. The bridge was rebuilt in 1953 after it was destroyed by a typhoon, and, though reinforced with steel, is otherwise faithful in every detail to the old bridge. The complex joinery is a marvel of engineering.

## Samurai Quarter
The lord of Iwakuni, Kikkawa Hiroie, received this fief of 60,000 *koku* from his distant relatives, the powerful Mōri lords of Hagi (see Castles, p. 49). Hiromasa built Iwakuni Castle in 1608, but in 1615, the TOKUGAWA proclaimed the edict: "One realm, one castle." Since his castle was a subsidiary to the Hagi castle of the Mōri, Hiromasa was forced to tear it down. He moved his headquarters off the castle hill and down to the samurai quarter, where the family managed to preserve the compound intact through the turbulence of the Meiji era.

✱✱ **Kikkō Kōen (Park)** 吉香公園  This area contains the remains of the Kikkawa residence and several beautiful samurai houses. Near the Kintai-kyō is Kagawa Nagaya-mon, the residence gate of one of Iwakuni's castellans. The Kin'unkaku is a restored pavilion scenically perched beside a canal. The Chōkokan contains various Kikkawa documents, and the Mekata House, which can be viewed from the outside, is an exquisite samurai dwelling.

✱✱ **Nishimura Hakubutsukan (Museum)** にしむら博物館  Hrs: 9:00–17:00, daily. Contains over 6,000 pieces of arms and armor; very much worth a look.

✱ **Iwakuni-jō** 岩国城  Hrs: 9:00–16:45; clsd NY. Reached by cable car (or on foot). This is a reconstruction built in 1962. A large well situated behind the present structure marks the site of the original castle, which was built to be unobservable from below. The present castle juts out proudly over Iwakuni; on a clear day, it offers good views of the Inland Sea.

✱ **Momiji-dani Kōen** 紅葉谷公園  This public ground, noted for fall color, contains several temples, including the Kikkawa funerary temple, **Tōsen-ji**. At the back of the park is a small hexagonal pavilion.

455

## Townspeople's Quarter
About 1 km from Iwakuni station, on the north bank of the river, are some old merchant houses and a market. Not far from the station is the **Shirohebi (White Snake) Jinja**, a shrine to Benten, the goddess of wealth and music, whose messenger is a white snake; much fuss is made over the albino snakes that dwell near the shrine.

## Iwakuni Lodgings (TEL 0827)
It is best to try to get lodgings close to the famous bridge.

1 **Yamane Ryokan** 山根旅館
1丁目4-8 (41-0368).
1-4-8 Iwakuni, Iwakuni-shi, Yamaguchi-ken. Unpretentious and friendly. Y8–9000 w/meals.

2 **Hangetsu-an** 半月庵
1丁目17-27 (41-0021).
1-17-27 Iwakuni. An old wooden inn, now a kokuminshukusha. Y7000 w/meals.

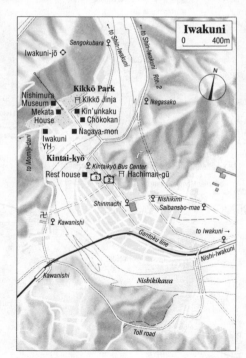

## Exploring

# Southwest on the San'yō line from Iwakuni is the town of **Yanai**, with many old merchant houses, including Kunimori-ke (ICP). Board a bus here to **Murotsu** and **Kaminoseki**, two old port towns that were important to the Inland Sea trade; each has a set of old merchant houses (Murotsu even has an old brothel). To really get away from it all, take the ferry from Kaminoseki to **Iwaijima** (Celebration Island). A tiny fishing village nestles precariously against the slopes of this small island. At night, preferably during the full moon, climb the cobblestone steps of the village and explore the maze of stone walls. With your back to the sea, look for the small shrine above and to the left of the village. The shrine, charming at night if the lanterns are lit, is known for its Kagura. At present, there are plans to build a nuclear power plant on Iwaijima—less than 100 km from Hiroshima—over the protests of the majority of the residents. **Lodgings:** In Kaminoseki, Minshuku Miura-sō (0820-62-1466). On Iwaijima, Minshuku Kunihiro (0820-66-2053) is very pleasant.

# CHŪGOKU VI. OGŌRI

**Tokyo to Ogōri:** *6:10h by Shinkansen: not all trains stop here.*
**Prefectures:** Yamaguchi, Shimane

## OGŌRI 小郡

Junction to the JR Yamaguchi line which cuts across Honshū with stops at Yamaguchi, Tsuwano, and, on the north coast, Izumo (CHŪGOKU II:N5) and Tottori (CHŪGOKU 1:N1). This rail line passes through some lovely countryside.

## # HŌFU 防府

456  *0:15h by JR San'yō line local train east of Ogōri.* For art connoisseurs, this town offers a number of treats. SESSHŪ's *Four Seasons Landscape Scroll* (NT), one of the most famous paintings in Japan, is on view at the ** **Mōri Hontei** 毛利本邸 , a fine Meiji-era villa built by Mōri Motonori (1830–1896), a prominent figure in the Meiji Restoration (see next page; Hrs: 9:00–16:00; clsd M, NY). The **Matsuzaki Tenjin** shrine owns a famous *Tenjin Engi* narrative scroll (ICP). The shrine's festival on Nov. 15 is a boisterous affair.

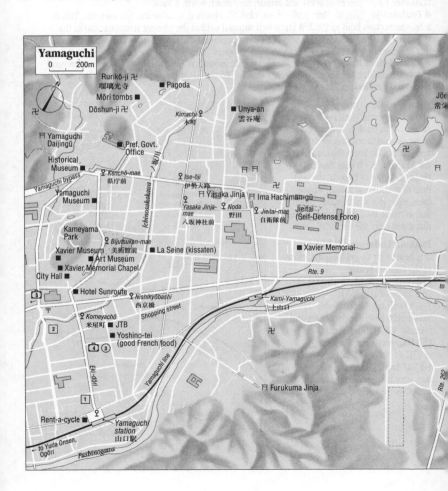

# CHŪGOKU VI:N. NORTH FROM OGŌRI

**Main Attraction:** Hagi (N4)

## N1 * YAMAGUCHI 山口

*0:14h from Ogōri by JR Yamaguchi line express.* This small castle town was founded in the 14th century by Ōuchi Hiroyo, who was awarded the lands of westernmost Honshū by ASHIKAGA TAKAUJI. Lord Hiroyo patterned his new city on Kyoto, and his successors transformed it into one of the most prosperous and cultured cities in Japan. When the Ōnin Wars (1467–1477) devastated Kyoto, many aristocrats and literati sought refuge in Yamaguchi, bringing with them the refinement of the capital. In 1550, the Jesuit Francis Xavier, on his way to Kyoto to seek an imperial audience, stopped for two months in Yamaguchi. Xavier was welcomed by Lord Ōuchi who, it is said, assumed that the priest, having arrived from India, belonged to some new sect of Buddhism. The indefatigable missionary took to the city streets to deliver harsh sermons reviling Japanese vices (idolatry, infanticide, and sodomy—the last a conspicuous habit of samurai and monks). When Xavier finally reached Kyoto, he found the city in ruins and was unable to locate the emperor. He returned to Yamaguchi, impressed anew with the splendor of the provincial city. Not long after Xavier's visit, Lord Ōuchi was assassinated, and the province came under the rule of Ōuchi vassals, the Mōri, who moved the seat of power to Hagi (N4). In 1863, the Mōri domain, Chōshū, revolted against the TOKUGAWA shogunate, and Yamaguchi, being more secure than Hagi, once again became the provincial capital (see Hagi history, p. 460). Chōshū forces fired on European vessels in the Straits of Shimonoseki (with disastrous results for Japan). Later, progressive advisors persuaded Lord Mōri Motonori to take the lead in surrendering his domain to the emperor. The gate of the Mōri mansion stands in front of the prefectural office.

**Calendar**

457

**July 20–27: Gion Matsuri.** Yasaka Jinja. A copy of the famous Kyoto festival. Performances of the stately Sagi-mai (egret dance).

**Getting Around**

Rent-a-cycle at the station, Y800 per day.

### Yamaguchi Sights

**\* Xavier Kinen Seidō (Memorial Chapel)** ザビエル記念聖堂 Hrs: Dec.–Feb. 9:00–17:00. Mar.–Nov. 8:30–17:30. This church is in hilly Marugame Park. It was built in 1952 to commemorate the 400th anniversary of Francis Xavier's visit.

**Yamaguchi-kenritsu Bijutsukan (Prefectural Art Museum)** 山口県立美術館 Hrs: 9:00–16:30; clsd M, NY. Modern museum of regional art.

**Rekishi Minzoku Shiryōkan (Historical Museum)** 歴史民俗資料館 Hrs: 9:00–17:00; clsd M, day after NH, NY. Contains interesting historical material.

**\*\* Yamaguchi Daijingū** 山口大神宮 Lord Ōuchi established this lovely branch of the Ise Shrines in 1520, at a time when incessant warfare had halted the periodic rebuildings at Ise (see p. 307). This one was built in similar style, with outer and inner sanctuaries. The shrines once enjoyed great popularity as the Ise of the West, but nowadays the elderly priestess can barely scrape together funds in the hope of some day rebuilding them.

**\*\*\* Rurikō-ji** 瑠璃光寺 This temple's ◆ **five-storied pagoda** (1404, NT) was built by Ōuchi Moriharu to console the soul of his older brother, Yoshihiro, who died fighting the armies of ASHIKAGA YOSHIMITSU. The beautiful pagoda is set in a pretty park. Each roof is slightly steeper than the one below it, giving the pagoda an especially striking appearance. Off to one side is an interesting little museum that compares it to the 40 other five-storied pagodas in Japan. In the same parklike area are graves of the Mōri lords and the temple, **Tōshun-ji**, which has an impressive gate and beautiful Kannon Hall.

**Yasaka Jinja** 八坂神社 This is the site of the famous Sagi-mai (egret dance) of the Gion Matsuri in July, which also fled here from Kyoto in the 15th–16th C.

**\*\* Ima Hachiman-gū** 今八幡宮 (1503, ICP). Shrines commonly have a gate, an oratory, and a main hall where the god resides. This shrine represents a local variant, in which all three buildings are attached under a complicated set of roofs, creating a very beautiful structure.

**Ichinosakakawa** 一ノ坂川 This small river flowing through town has one section that is quite pretty. In spring it is lined with blossoming cherry trees, and on summer evenings it is aglow with large fireflies, called *Genji-botaru* (a smaller species is called *Heike-botaru*).

**\*\* Jōei-ji** 常栄寺 Hrs: 8:00–17:30; daily. *0:10h by taxi, NE of the station.* This temple was originally Ōuchi Masahiro's villa, but he later converted it into a temple for his mother. Behind the main hall is a ◆ **garden** attributed to the painter SESSHŪ. It consists of a large pond surrounded by expanses of lawn in which he arranged boulders in a Zen-style dry landscape. Sesshū sailed to China with an Ōuchi trading ship and spent the latter half of his life in the Yamaguchi region. He and his disciples lived at **Unya-an**.

### Yamaguchi Shopping

1 **Mihoridō Uirō** 御堀堂ういろう (22-1248). Sells the local *uirō*, a steamed rice-paste confection; at the second-floor kissaten, you can sample it with coffee or tea.

2 **Kuwahara** 桑原 道場門前 (22-1790). Near the station. Sells lacquerware and Ōuchi *ningyō*, pairs of small, spherical dolls of finely painted lacquer (for the Doll Festival).

## Yamaguchi Dining and Lodgings (TEL 0839)

*Chōshū soba* and *soba-zushi*, bundles of the buckwheat noodle rolled up inside dried laver, are the local specialities. There are many inns at Yuda Onsen, 0:10h by bus from the station.

③ **Yamabuki** 山吹 駅通2-13-9 (22-1462). Hrs: 11:00–19:00; clsd on 1st and 15th of each month, mid-Aug., NY. An old *soba* shop. Inexpensive.

**Tokyo-an** 東京庵 (22-1561). Hrs: 11:00–23:00; clsd Th (except if NH), NY. Yuda Onsen. *Chōshū soba*. Inexpensive.

④ **Fukuya Ryokan** 福屋旅館 駅通2-1-3 (22-0531). 2-1-3 Eki-dōri, Yamaguchi-shi, Yamaguchi-ken. Popular with young travelers. Y5500 w/meals.

⑤ ** **Matsudaya Hotel** 松田屋ホテル (22-0125). 3-6-7 Yuda Onsen, Yamaguchi-shi. This wonderful ryokan features a "Meiji bath" and a teahouse where the antishogunate clique plotted the Meiji Restoration; the teahouse furnishings include an oversized seat for the hero of Satsuma, Saigō Takamori. Excellent regional cuisine. From Y18–50,000 w/meals.

## # AKIYOSHI-DŌ (GROTTO) 秋芳洞

*1:05h by bus from Yamaguchi, or 1:15h by bus from Higashi-Hagi.* Hrs: 8:30–16:30, daily. Third largest limestone cavern in the world. The one-way route through the cavern deposits you at some distance from the entrance. **Akiyoshi-dai** *(0:25h by bus from the grotto)* is a rolling grassland bristling with limestone upthrustings.

## N2 * TSUWANO 津和野

*From Ogōri, 1:05h by JR Yamaguchi line limited express. On Apr. 29–May 5, July 20–Aug. 31, and Su and NH in May and Sept.–Nov., you can take SL Yamaguchi, one of the last steam locomotives running in Japan. It takes 2:00h each way. It departs from Ogōri at 10:30, and returns from Tsuwano at 12:30. From Masuda (N3), 0:30h by limited express. From Higashi-Hagi (N4), 1:30h by express bus.* This tiny former castle town is squeezed picturesquely into a narrow valley. Though it is basically just a quiet country town, Tsuwano offers pleasant scenery, a dramatic castle ruin, and an old samurai school, which produced some leading figures of Meiji Japan, including Nishi Amane (1829–1897), the country's first Western-style philosopher, and Mori Ōgai (1862–1922), one of the earliest and most famous modern Japanese writers. On a darker note, Tsuwano was one of the places where the Nagasaki Christians who revealed themselves to a Western missionary in the early Meiji period were exiled and tortured (see Nagasaki, p. 486).

### Calendar

Tsuwano's quiet charm is shattered on spring and fall weekends by busloads of tourists. Tonomachi's canals are filled with blooming irises in early June.

**July 20, 24, 27: Sagi-mai.** Yasaka Jinja. The graceful egret dance of Kyoto's Gion Matsuri was transmitted to this backwater via Yamaguchi. The Sagi-mai later vanished from Kyoto, and was reintroduced from Tsuwano only in 1955.

### Getting Around

Bicycle rentals in front of station. Y800 per day.

### Tsuwano Sights

**Maria-sei-dō (Chapel of St. Mary)** マリア聖堂 This tiny chapel was built in 1948 by a German priest in memory of Japanese Catholics who perished in Tsuwano between 1865 and 1873. The site of the chapel is called Otome Tōge (Virgin Pass) and has a view of the town.

* **Yōmei-ji** 永明寺 This Sōtō Zen temple founded in 1420 has a handsome, thatched hall, a pretty garden, and Mori Ōgai's tomb.

*** **Tonomachi** 殿町 *0:10h on foot from the station.* Tonomachi is a street lined with whitewashed, black-tiled walls that once enclosed samurai estates. A few old gates are all that remain of Tsuwano's samurai houses. The shallow canals that flow at the bases of these walls are filled with colorful carp.

458

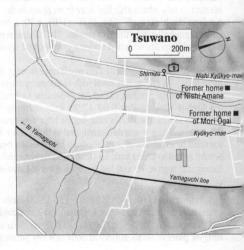

Tsuwano
0          200m
N

Shimizu
Nishi Kyūkyo-mae
Former home of Nishi Amane
Former home of Mori Ōgai
Kyūkyo-mae
to Yamaguchi
Yamaguchi line

**✽✽ Yōrōkan** 藩校養老館跡  Hrs: 8:30–17:00. A school for samurai youth during the late Edo period. It was an innovative school in its time, and had Dutch studies in its curriculum. Photos of its most famous graduates, Nishi Amane and Mori Ōgai, are displayed.

**Kyōdokan** 郷土館  Hrs: 8:30–17:00. This local history museum has a small exhibit on the exiled Christians.

**✽ Taikodani Inari** 太鼓谷稲荷  A gaudy vermilion shrine up on the hillside, best seen from a distance. The stone steps ascend through a tunnel of 2,000 small red torii.

**✽✽✽ Tsuwano-jō Ato (Castle Ruins)** 津和野城跡  *By tramway, then 0:15h walk*. The crumbling stone walls snake along a sharp ridge, which offers splendid views over Tsuwano and the surrounding valleys.

**Tsuwano Dining and Lodgings** (TEL 08567)

*Sansai* (mountain greens) and carp are the local specialties.

① **Shinobu** 忍  (2-0308). *Sansai teishoku* from Y1500.

② **Shōin-tei** 松韻亭  (2-1661). Garden restaurant inside one of Tono-machi's samurai gates. *Sansai bentō* Y1500.

③ **✽ Meigetsu** 明月旅館  (2-0685). Tsuwano-chō, Kanoashi-gun, Shimane-ken. The best traditional ryokan in town. Specializes in carp cuisine. Y8000–17,000 w/meals.

④ **Minshuku Wakasagi no Yado** 民宿若さぎの宿  (2-1146). Address as above. Friendly and eager to help. Y6000 w/meals. No CC.

⑤ **Tsuwano Rojji** 津和野ロッジ  (2-1683). Address as above. Y5500 w/meals.

## N3 **MASUDA** 益田

*0:35–0:40h by JR Yamaguchi line express or local from Tsuwano. Or 2:10h from Izumo (CHŪGOKU II:N5) or 0:55h from Higashi-Hagi (N4) by JR San'in line express.* This seaside town is noted for two small gardens at the temples **Mampuku-ji** and **✽✽ Ikō-ji**, said to have been designed by the great painter SESSHŪ; both 0:10h by bus from the station. Sesshū's tomb is at **Taiki-an**.

459

### Calendar

**Dec. (1st Su): Iwami Kagura.** Kenmin Kaikan. Vigorous Izumo-type sacred dances miming a variety of mythological tales.

**Sept. (last Sa): Ino Kagura.** Misumi-chō *(0:25h by express, 0:50h by local from Masuda)*. Hachiman-gū. Izumo Kagura with gorgeous masks, robes, much posturing.

### Masuda Lodgings (TEL 0856)

**Shimadaya** 島田屋  (22-0020). 3-15 Honmachi, Masuda-shi, Shimane-ken. A ryokan rebuilt in an elaborate modern style aimed at the wedding business. Y10–25,000 w/meals.

**Araisokan** 荒磯館  平原町1019  (27-0811). 1019 Nishihirahara-chō, Masuda-shi. Two train stops E of Masuda. Shabby onsen ryokan with rooms and baths built right over the pounding surf. Y7000+ w/meals.

## N4 **✽✽ HAGI** 萩

*Express buses are best: 1:25h from Ogōri, 1:30h from Tsuwano, or 1:10h from Akiyoshi-dō. All buses stop at Hagi Bus Center and Higashi-Hagi station. By JR San'in line express, 1:10h from Masuda or 1:45h from Shimonoseki (CHŪGOKU VII) to Higashi-Hagi.* Hagi was for 260 years the castle town of the Mōri lords of Chōshū, one of the richer domains in Edo Japan (see Castles, p. 49). The Mōri were "outside lords" who were accorded respect but were not trusted by the Tokugawa shogunate, and so when the Mōri moved to Hagi in 1601, they chose their site with care. Hagi is protected on two sides by the forks of the Aibagawa river and on the remaining north side by the sea. The castle, now in ruins, is further fortified by moats and a defensive checkerboard of samurai dwellings. The remains of these *buke-yashiki*, with their earthen walls, old gates, and orchards of bright, yellow-orange citrus are Hagi's most famous sight.

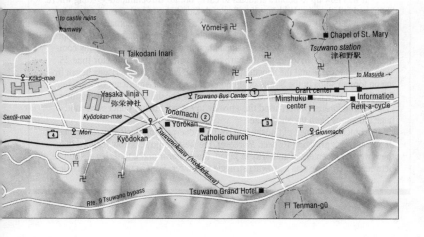

**Calendar**

**Aug. 3: Jinkō-sai.** Sumiyoshi Jinja. Boat-shaped floats.

**Aug. 13: Lantern lighting.** Daishō-in.

**Aug. 15: Lantern lighting.** Tōkō-ji.

**Aug. 31: * Itsukushima Jinja Jūshichiya Matsuri.** At Abu-chō *(0:20h by JR San'in line from Higashi-Hagi to Nago)*. The shrine is on a small island near the station. Gagaku boats go out on the Japan Sea at sunset, while bonfires burn and 500 lanterns are set adrift. Prayers are offered for safety at sea.

# Hagi History: The Plotters of the Meiji Restoration

**Yoshida Shōin**  (1830–1859) A Hagi samurai and educator who preached national unity through reverence for the emperor. Though his life was marked by failure, he was an inspiring teacher who nurtured the leaders of the Meiji Restoration, including Kido Kōin (1833–1877), Itō Hirobumi (1841–1909), and Yamagata Aritomo (1838–1922).

**Yoshida Shōin** lay dead on the execution grounds of Temmachō prison. Itō Hirobumi and Kido Kōin, two of Shōin's former students, rescued the body of their revered teacher at no small risk to their own safety and gave it a decent burial.

Shōin had been destined to be a teacher; at the age of six, his uncle died and he succeeded to the hereditary position of headmaster of the Chōshū domain's military science school at Hagi. He was a precocious student, and for most of his short life he was obsessed with the great problem of his day—how to save Japan from the encroachments of the Western powers. Though Shōin was not the first to promote loyalty to the emperor as an instrument of national unity, he was among the most vocal in expressing this view. "Revere the Emperor and Expel the Barbarians!" was the rallying cry of these new nationalists. However, they well knew that to accomplish the goal of an independent and strong Japan, they would need to study the West, to learn its military science and ways of thought.

Shōin often risked his life to pursue these seemingly contradictory goals. In 1854, determined to experience conditions in the West, he and a companion traveled to Shimoda, where the American commodore had come to conclude the Kanagawa Treaty (see Izu History, p. 269). Because leaving the country was then a capital offense, the two waited until nightfall to steal a fishing boat and row out to Perry's flagship. Shōin, a man of letters, was not very good at handling the oars; it was close to dawn by the time they wearily boarded the *Powhattan* and requested passage to America. The Americans, not wishing to contravene Japanese law, sent them back to shore, where they were arrested and carted off to an Edo prison.

After some months in prison, Shōin was returned to Hagi under house arrest; his unlucky friend had meanwhile died in jail. In Hagi, Shōin opened a small school for young samurai, where he lectured on politics, on revering the emperor, and on the importance of Western science. He developed a passionate hostility for the shogunate, and when, in 1858, he heard that a shogunate official was trying to convince the emperor to approve Harris's Open Port Treaty, he became enraged and determined to kill the man. Ever the man of words, Shōin talked so much about his plot that he was arrested before he even left Hagi. Some months later, he was executed.

It was now up to Shōin's students to carry on. Itō Hirobumi, succeeding where Shōin had failed, smuggled himself to England. Kido Kōin, of higher samurai rank, acted as a liaison between the low-ranking radical loyalists and domain officials. By this time, the court, encouraged by its xenophobic supporters, had refused to approve the Open Port Treaty—which the shogunate honored anyway—and haughtily commanded the shogunate to "expel the barbarians," setting the deadline for June 25, 1863. The day came and the shogunate did nothing, but Chōshū garrisons began firing on foreign ships in the Straits of Shimonoseki. A fleet of American, British, French, and Dutch ships retaliated, bombarding the Chōshū forts and seizing their cannon. The foreign powers used this episode to extract further concessions and a huge indemnity from the shogunate.

Ironically, the men of Chōshū had, by their courage and decisiveness, earned the Westerner's grudging respect. Moreover, the Western powers now realized that there were two centers of authority in Japan, the emperor and a tottering shogunate, between which there was a growing struggle for power. Even as the smoke was clearing, England, perceiving that the future lay with Chōshū and the southern Kyūshū province of Satsuma—both long-time enemies of the shogunate—began supplying them with arms.

In the spring of 1865, a mixed militia of peasants and samurai, trained in Western methods by two of Shōin's students, staged a coup d'état against the Chōshū government. The following year, they forced the larger shogunate army, which had come to chastise them, to sue for peace. The old order was collapsing; not only had a single domain defied the shogun, but an army of mixed social classes had humiliated the samurai. In 1867, Tokugawa Yoshinobu, a candidate of the proimperial Mito clan, became shogun. Yoshinobu tried for a while to restructure the feudal system, but when in the autumn of 1867 forces led by Satsuma and Chōshū seized the palace and announced an "imperial restoration," he accepted it to avoid bloodshed. In the same year, the emperor died, leaving his teenage son as successor. As if to give Japan a clean slate, the new era of Meiji was proclaimed on January 25, 1868. Not long afterward, the young EMPEROR MEIJI was bundled off from Kyoto to Edo, which was soon renamed Tokyo, the new capital of Japan.

It was primarily the young samurai of Chōshū and Satsuma who effected the astonishing transformation of Japan. The brilliantly successful mixed militia of Chōshū became the model for the imperial army. This work was undertaken by **Takasugi Shinsaku** and **Yamagata Aritomo**, a former student of Yoshida Shōin who would become a prime minister. **Kido Kōin**, who with Itō Hirobumi had buried Shōin's body and, while fighting the shogunate, had cut a dashing figure, was responsible for many of the early measures aimed at turning feudal Japan into a modern state. **Itō Hirobumi**, who had studied in Europe, would become Japan's leading statesman and frame its first modern constitution—modeled, ominously, on that of Bismarck's Germany.

In the first decade of the Meiji era, the new government had to pacify outraged samurai and poverty-stricken peasants who were in rebellion all over Japan. At the same time, the architects of the new Japan, Shōin's protégés among them, unremittingly pursued reform. Given his belief in meritocracy, Shōin would have welcomed universal education, instituted in 1872, which not only gave the children of poor samurai and peasants hope for self-improvement, but was also a prerequisite for an industrially and militarily strong nation. And indeed, the army and navy quickly made use of railways, steamships, and modern artillery, all products of Western learning. Shōin might have felt however, that it was imprudent to fling Japan wide open to Western customs and political institutions—and even Westerners themselves—as the Meiji government did.

These drastic changes had little effect on the remote town of Hagi, where so many of the Meiji Restoration's leaders were born. Ironically, the considerable attraction of this, the cradle of modern Japan, is its feudal atmosphere. At **Tōkō-ji**, the Mōri, lords of Chōshū, lie buried in majestic mausoleums attended by legions of mossy stone lanterns. Amid the old citrus orchards stand the little **Village School Beneath the Pines** of Yoshida Shōin and the dwellings of his students—Itō Hirobumi's humble thatched house and Kido Kōin's finer samurai home. For many Japanese, the main object of a visit is to honor Shōin's spirit at **Shōin Jinja**. Plaques from the local Lion's Club, a wax museum recounting Shōin's quixotic life story, and the fanfare of tour buses rather shatter the atmosphere appropriate to a deified hero, but they do attest to the reverence in which he is still held.

461

## Getting Around

Bicycles and motorbikes are ideal for exploring the town; for rent at Hagi Rent-a-cycle (2-1195) near Higashi-Hagi station, and at many other sites around town. Several other rent-a-cycle shops are nearby. Taxi courses (4-person cab; no English); the 2:00h course covers the main parts of town and costs Y7410; the 3:00h tour includes Myōjin Ike and Kasayama, and costs Y11,120. We recommend visiting the east side of the river to get acquainted with the great men of Hagi before exploring the scenic samurai quarter to the west.

## East of the River

**\*\*\* Tōkō-ji** 東光寺 Hrs: 8:30–17:00, daily. An Ōbaku Zen temple of rustic loveliness. The majestic, austere tombs of five Mōri lords (the third lord and all the odd-numbered generations that succeeded him) stand behind this temple, up a stone pathway flanked by nearly 500 moss-covered stone lanterns offered by their vassals, standing like an eternal honor guard for their dead lords.

**\*\* Shōin Jinja** 松陰神社 Established in the Meiji period in honor of Yoshida Shōin. Nearby is Shōin's old home and **Shōka Sonjuku**, the Village School Beneath the Pines, where Shōin taught more than 60 future national leaders. The **Yoshida Shōin Rekishikan** (History Hall) depicts Shōin's eventful life in wax: Shōin at age 11 lecturing eruditely to Lord Mōri, Shōin and his companion rowing out to Perry's boat, Shōin in jail. Hrs: 9:00–17:00, daily.

\* **Itō Hirobumi Kyūtaku** 伊藤博文旧宅  The humble, thatched-roof childhood home of Itō Hirobumi, a peasant's son adopted into the house of a poor samurai. He was elected prime minister four times and drafted Japan's Meiji Constitution.

## Samurai Quarter and Castle

\*\*\* **Kumaya Bijutsukan (Art Museum)** 熊谷美術館  Hrs: 8:30–17:30. Dec.–Feb. 9:00–17:00; clsd NY. The collection of the Kumaya family, special merchants to the Mōri lords, displayed in three storehouses on the grounds of their 1768 home (ICP). The collection includes a pair of screens with a fan design, a variety of literati paintings, old Hagi tea bowls, and Japan's oldest piano, said to have belonged to Franz von Siebold, a German physician at Nagasaki.

\*\* **Kikuya-ke Jūtaku** 菊屋住宅  (ICP). Hrs: 9:00–17:00, daily. The 17th-C house of the wealthy Kikuya family, special merchants to the lord of Hagi.

\* **Kido Takayoshi (or Kōin) Kyūtaku** 木戸孝允旧宅  Hrs: 9:00–17:00, daily. The family house of Kido Kōin. His father was the clan physician, and in contrast to the homes of Itō Hirobumi or Takasugi Shinsaku, this residence is that of a well-to-do family.

**Takasugi Shinsaku Kyūtaku** 高杉晋作旧宅  Still a private residence. The small, ordinary samurai dwelling of Takasugi Shinsaku (1839–1867), founder of the famous Chōshū civilian army that defeated the shogun's army. He died of tuberculosis at age 29.

\*\* **Ishii Chawan Bijutsukan (Tea Bowl Museum)** 石井茶碗美術館 (2-1211). Hrs: 9:00–11:30, 13:00–17:00; clsd Tu (except if NH), Dec. 20–31, Jan. 6–31. An outstanding group of tea bowls, including Korean Kōryo-dynasty bowls, collected by Ishii Kigensai, a scholar of Hagi-yaki.

\*\*\* **Horiuchi** 堀内  This area, "within the moat," was once occupied by the high-ranking samurai vassals of the Mōri lords. It is now an architecturally preserved zone. This beautiful neighborhood is a maze of earthen walls, interrupted here and there by an imposing samurai mansion gate.

462

\* **Hagi-jō Ato (Castle Ruins)** 萩城跡  Standing on the low terrain at the foot of the castle hill is the Nagaya (ICP), a guardhouse. Within the castle grounds, there's little to see.

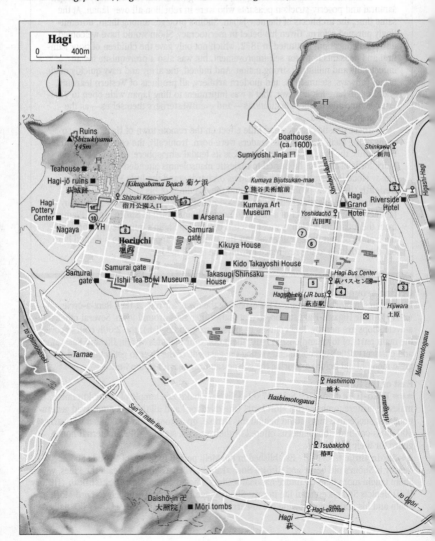

## Other Sights

**\*\* Daishō-in** 大照院 *0:15h by bus from Higashi-Hagi.* Like the more popular Tōkō-ji, this was a funerary temple of the Mōri lords, with the same magnificent rows of stone lanterns and peaceful grandeur. The first two lords, and all the even-numbered generations, are buried here together with their wives.

**Hagi Hansharō** 萩反射炉¹ *1.2 km from Higashi-Hagi, on the coast road to Myōjin Ike.* A brick forge built in 1858 by the Hagi clan to manufacture guns and ship parts.

**Myōjin Ike** 明神池 *0:15h by bus from Higashi-Hagi.* A saltwater lagoon where the Mōri lords used to go pleasure-boating. The lagoon is filled with sea bream, ray, mullet, and other species usually found in the open sea. On the other side of the lagoon is Kasayama, a diminutive extinct volcano, which offers a view of the island-dotted Japan Sea.

## Hagi Crafts

Hagi-yaki, a pinkish beige stoneware for which this town is renowned, ranks among the most highly esteemed tea ceremony wares. It was first made in the early 1600s by Korean potters who were captured during HIDEYOSHI's Korean campaign and established in Hagi by Lord Mōri Terumoto. It is considered to be the closest in style to Ido ware, Korean rice bowls that first captivated the Momoyama tea masters. Hagi-yaki ripens to its full beauty with use, its pale, rather hard tones deepening and softening as tea seeps into the porous crazing. Today, tourism and the pottery boom have combined to spawn a myriad of mediocre artisans who turn out worthless junk. About ten to twenty kilns still fire with wood.

[1] **Sakagama** 坂窯元　椿東中の倉 (2-0236). The 16th-C founder of this kiln, the Korean potter Yi Kyung, supposedly made tea bowls for Hideyoshi himself.

[5] **Harada Chōju-en** 原田長寿園　東田町38 (2-0861). Central Hagi, near Ishii Chawan Bijutsukan. Shop carrying wares by a variety of Hagi potters.

[11] **Tamamura Shōgetsu** 玉村松月 (2-2132). Elegant shop by Hagi-jō showing works by Hatano Zenzō, a noted potter.

463

## Hagi Dining

[6] **Hyakumangoku** 百万石　下五間町49 (2-2136). Hrs: 11:00–21:30; clsd Tu, NY, 3 days per month. *Kura*-style shop. Seafood. *Isohama teishoku* (super-fresh sashimi), Y2800.

[7] **Fujita Soba-ten** 藤田屋そば店　熊谷町59 (2-1086). Hrs: 11:00–19:00; clsd 2nd and 4th W, NY, mid-Aug. *Seiro-soba* in stacking containers, Y600.

[10] **Hananoe Satei** 花江茶亭　萩城跡内 (5-1750). Open early Mar.–Nov. Hrs: 9:30–16:00, Sa and Su 9:00–16:30, daily; clsd on 17th of every month. By Hagi-jō. For *matcha* (tea-ceremony tea) from Hagi bowls. Set in charming garden.

## Hagi Lodgings (TEL 08382)

[2] **Minshuku Higashi-Hagi** 民宿東萩　新川南3064-1 (2-7884). 3064-1 Shinkawaminami. Y6000 w/meals.

[3] **Minshuku Furusato** 民宿ふるさと　土原2-260 (2-6645). 2-2 Hijiwara. Y6000 w/meals.

[4] **Tomoe Ryokan** 常茂恵旅館 (2-0150). 608 Hijiwara, Hagi-shi, Yamaguchi-ken. This Hagi inn was rebuilt and upgraded in 1990. We hope it has kept up its former high standards, but leave it unrated pending a visit. Y28–65,000, all rooms with bath.

[8] **\* Hokumon Yashiki** 北門屋敷　堀内210 (2-7521). 210 Horiuchi. Spacious inn reminiscent of the samurai mansions that once surrounded the neighborhood. Y20–60,000 w/meals. CB.

[9] **Hagishizuki-sō** 萩指月荘 (2-7580). 485-2 Ōaza Horiuchi. Beachside ryokan. Y7300 w/meals.

## Easy Access To:

**\*\* Izumo** (CHŪGOKU II:N5): *3:05h by JR San'in line limited express.*

to Masuda
Hagi Hansharō (forge)

Miwa kiln

[1]

Hagi Honjin
Onsen-iriguchi
萩本陣温泉入口

ry Hall

Tōkō-ji
東光寺

Shōin Jinja

Mōri tombs ■

Itō Hirobumi House

Shōin Jinja-mae
松陰神社前

# CHŪGOKU VII. SHIMONOSEKI

**Tokyo to Shimonoseki:** *5:20–6:40h by Shinkansen to Shin-Shimonoseki station.*
**Kyoto to Shimonoseki:** *2:40–3:50h by Shinkansen to Shin-Shimonoseki station.*
**Pusan (Korea) to Shimonoseki:** *15:30h from Pusan by ferry. Departures daily at 17:00 (in both Pusan and Shimonoseki), arriving at 8:30. For information and reservations: Ōsaka (06-345-2245), Shimonoseki (0832-24-3000), Pusan (463-3165).*
**Travel Advisory:** The Travel Service Center in Shimonoseki, where one can exchange Rail Pass vouchers, is closed on Sunday and national holidays.
**Prefectures:** Yamaguchi

## SHIMONOSEKI 下関

*The Shinkansen station, Shin-Shimonoseki, is 0:20h by bus from the regular JR Shimonoseki station.* Most people linger here only because they have to wait for the ferry to Pusan, Korea.
**Sumiyoshi Jinja** 住吉神社 Hrs: 9:00–16:00; Dec. 8–14. *0:05h by car from Shin-Shimonoseki.* Sea guardian shrine with a national-treasure Honden.
**∗ Akama Jingū (Shrine)** 赤間神宮 Hrs: 9:00–17:00. *0:10h by bus from Shimonoseki station.* Enshrines child-emperor Antoku, who perished in 1185 in the battle of Dan no Ura, in the Straits of Shimonoseki (see Miyajima History, p. 449); the shrine overlooks the waters where the cataclysmic naval encounter took place. There are tombs of TAIRA warriors, and the **Hōichi Hall**, connected with *Miminashi Hōichi* (Earless Hōichi), a blood-curdling ghost story about a blind lute player who loses his ears to the ghost of a Taira warrior. A small museum on the Genpei War displays paintings by Tosa Mitsunobu depicting Antoku's life story. On Apr. 23–25, the shrine holds the **Sentei-sai** in memory of Antoku and the TAIRA. A procession of courtesans commemorates the Taira ladies who sold themselves into prostitution in order to pay for rites for their dead kin.
**Shimonoseki Suizoku-kan (Aquarium)** 下関水族館 Hrs: 9:00–17:00. In Aug., 9:00–18:00. One of the largest and best aquariums in Japan.
**Kōzan-ji** 功山寺 Hrs: 9:00–17:00. July–Aug. 9:00–18:00. *0:20h by bus from Shimonoseki (past the aquarium), then 0:10h on foot.* The **Butsuden** (NT) of this temple was built in 1327 and is a fine example of a Zen-style hall (see Buddhism, p. 39). The temple stands near an area called Furue-shōji, which preserves some earthen walls and gates from the time when this area, Chōfu, was a castle town.

### Shimonoseki Dining and Lodgings (TEL 0832)
Shimonoseki is the *fugu* (puffer) capital of Japan (Cuisine, p. 115).
**Nakao** なかを 赤間町中央通 (31-4129). Famous *fugu ryōtei*. Full course Y15,000＋.
**Torafugu** とらふぐ 駅近く (23-1129). Near Shimonoseki station. A less fancy *fugu* restaurant. Full course from Y5600.
**Shimonoseki Grand Hotel** 下関グランドホテル (31-5000). 31-2 Nabe-chō, Shimonoseki-shi, Yamaguchi-ken. S Y5600, Tw Y9,200＋.
**Kokuminshukusha Kaikan-sō** 国民宿舎海関荘 (23-0108). Mimosusogawa-chō Hinoyama. Y4900–5100 w/meals.
**Shimonoseki Hinoyama YH** 下関火の山YH (22-3753). 3-47 Mimosusogawa-chō Hinoyama.

### Easy Access To:
**Kokura** (KYŪSHŪ I): *0:10h by Shinkansen.*

464

# Kyūshū

Kyūshū, the southernmost of Japan's four main islands, has never been at the center of Japan's history. But its role as the great gateway, where foreign influences, from prehistoric continental cultures to the Portuguese galleons, first arrived in Japan, gives it great historical interest and variety. Though few major monuments survive, countless lesser ones—tumulus clusters, mysterious stone buddhas, Korean pottery villages, remote crypto-Christian refuges, the ruins of a Dutch trading post—testify to its volatile and fascinating history. These, and Kyūshū's "southern" mood, haunting volcanic landscapes, and hard-drinking, warm-hearted people, offer attractive contrasts to other parts of Japan.

## BEST ATTRACTIONS

I:E4     **∗∗ Yufuin.** A pleasant, self-consciously rustic spa on a highland plateau, not far from the famous and sleazy hot-spring town of Beppu (p. 473).

II:E1     **∗∗ Dazaifu.** The Yamato court's outpost in Kyūshū. Sugawara no Michizane, the Heian-period scholar, was exiled here; there is now a famous shrine where his mollified ghost is worshipped as Japan's god of learning (p. 479).

III:W1     **∗∗ Nagasaki.** The one port in Edo-period Japan where foreign trade was permitted. This quaint, romantic city has a beautiful harbor, a distinctive cuisine, and an eclectic architecture. The second atomic bomb was dropped at nearby Urakami in August, 1945 (p. 482).

IV:W1     **∗∗ Yanagawa.** This old castle town preserves many canals; small tour boats glide past quaint old houses and shrines (p. 491).

V:E3     **∗∗ Takachiho.** A mountain village in a beautiful setting that claims to be where imperial ancestor Ninigi no Mikoto descended to earth. Primordial history is replayed in the theatrical Takachiho Kagura (p. 497).

VI:W1     **∗∗ Chiran.** A base for Kamikaze fighters in World War II, this quiet village amid tea fields was founded by samurai farmers who built beautiful gardens (p. 500).

VI:W2     **∗∗ Ibusuki.** A spa with a Mediterranean mood, where one can be buried in steaming sand or romp in a jungle bath (p. 501).

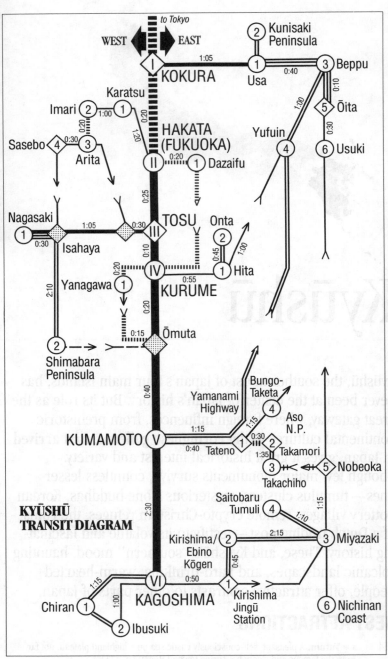

466

## Seasons

Kyūshū is significantly warmer than Honshū. Cherry blossoms arrive in early April. Southern Kyūshū tends to be hard hit by typhoons in September.

### Average Temperature °C (°F)/Days of Rain or Snow

|           | January      | April        | July         | October      |
|-----------|--------------|--------------|--------------|--------------|
| Ōita      | 5.5 (41.9)/5 | 13.8 (56.8)/10 | 26.0 (78.8)/11 | 17.6 (63.7)/7 |
| Hakata    | 5.7 (42.3)/11 | 14.2 (57.6)/11 | 26.7 (80.1)/11 | 17.8 (64.0)/7 |
| Nagasaki  | 6.4 (43.5)/12 | 15.0 (59.0)/12 | 26.5 (79.7)/12 | 18.8 (65.8)/6 |
| Kumamoto  | 4.9 (40.8)/7 | 15.1 (59.2)/11 | 26.8 (80.2)/13 | 17.9 (64.2)/6 |
| Kagoshima | 7.0 (44.6)/10 | 16.1 (61.0)/12 | 27.2 (81.0)/12 | 19.6 (67.3)/8 |

## Traveling

The Shinkansen terminates at Hakata (Fukuoka). Trunk lines within Kyūshū are the JR Nippō main line (east coast) and JR Kagoshima main line (west coast). Cross-island trains are slow, with infrequent service. The private Nishitetsu line from Fukuoka to Dazaifu, Kurume,

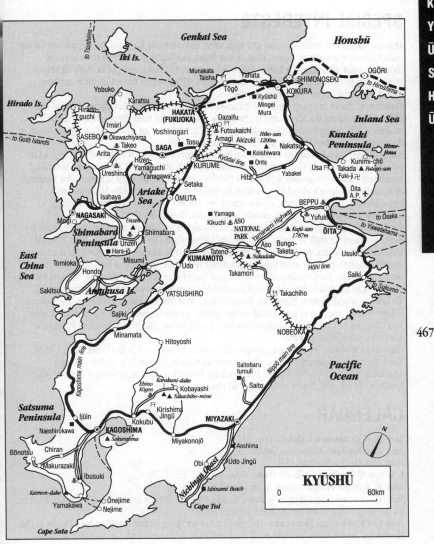

Yanagawa, and Ōmuta, is efficient. In Aso National Park and southern Kyūshū, a car is useful. Visitors from Tokyo or Ōsaka might consider flying, which is comparable in cost to taking the train.

| | | By Limited Express* | | By Air** | |
|---|---|---|---|---|---|
| Tokyo to: | Ōita | 7:50h | (Y27,260) | 1:30h | (Y25,250) |
| | Hakata (Fukuoka) | 6:10h | (Y21,300) | 1:40h | (Y25,350) |
| | Nagasaki | 9:00h | (Y23,510) | 1:45h | (Y29,100) |
| | Kumamoto | 8:10h | (Y23,150) | 1:35h | (Y27,300) |
| | Kagoshima | 11:15h | (Y24,950) | 1:45h | (Y29,500) |
| | Miyazaki | 11:15h | (Y24,640) | 1:30h | (Y27,900) |
| Ōsaka to: | Ōita | 4:40h | (Y16,300) | 0:55h | (Y12,900) |
| | Hakata (Fukuoka) | 3:20h | (Y14,310) | 1:05h | (Y14,400) |
| | Nagasaki | 5:50h | (Y16,510) | 1:10h | (Y17,750) |
| | Kumamoto | 5:00h | (Y16,050) | 1:05h | (Y15,800) |
| | Kagoshima | 8:05h | (Y17,850) | 1:05h | (Y18,450) |
| | Miyazaki | 8:05h | (Y17,540) | 1:00h | (Y16,300) |

*Not including waiting time between transfers.
**Add 1:00h for travel time from airports to city centers.

**By Ferry to Kyūshū: Ōsaka–Beppu:** 13:00–16:00h by overnight steamer; 3 per day in each direction, calling at Kōbe en route. One also stops at Matsuyama, and one at Takamatsu. Call Kansai Kisen: Tokyo (03-274-4271); Ōsaka (06-572-5181). **Hiroshima–Beppu:** Daily, at 21:00; takes 5:30h (from Beppu, daily departure at 15:00). **Yawatahama–Beppu:** 5 boats per day in each direction; takes 3:00h. **Yawatahama–Usuki:** 9 boats per day in each direction; takes 2:50h.

# SPECIAL INTERESTS

**Onsen:** Yufuin is a stylishly rustic spa with some exceptionally fine ryokan. Beppu, one of the most famous spa towns in Japan, is an onsen Reno. Aso National Park has several rustic mountain spas with open-air baths. Takeo has a great, old-fashioned public bath. At Ibusuki, visitors can be buried in geothermally heated sand. Ebino Kōgen has an idyllic rotemburo. Remote Yakushima has *rotemburo* by the sea.

**Outdoors:** There are easy climbs of Yufuin-dake, various peaks in Aso National Park, and Ebino Kōgen. Along the Yamanami Highway are trails into the Kujū range, including one to a mountain hot-spring lodge with an open-air bath. Yakushima, an island national park south of Kagoshima, is famous for its primeval cryptomeria forests.

**Antiquities:** Dazaifu has the ruins of the Yamato court's outpost, which was built like a Chinese fortress; there is a fine historical museum there. Yoshinogari is a new excavation of a settlement contemporaneous with Queen Pimiko's kingdom. Saitobaru is famous for hundreds of *kofun* which have yielded fine *haniwa* figurines. The Kumamoto City Museum has reproductions of many painted *kofun* chambers. Usuki's stone buddhas were made by unknown sculptors. Kunisaki Peninsula is an ancient Tendai Buddhist preserve.

**Crafts:** Kyūshū crafts are dominated by Korean-influenced pottery, much originally made by Korean potters brought to Japan by Hideyoshi's generals in the 16th century. Arita is world-famous for porcelain, while Karatsu's elegant, Korean-style stoneware is prized for the tea ceremony. Satsuma-yaki, a porcelain-like enameled stoneware, is made at Naeshirokawa village, near Kagoshima. Earthy folk pottery is made at Koishiwara and Onta. Kurume, famous for Kurume-gasuri textiles, also produces handmade paper and *rantai-shikki* (lacquerware).

**Well-Preserved Towns:** Hitoyoshi, Bungo-Taketa, and Obi are old castle towns. The pottery village of Onta, located in a beautiful, remote valley, preserves many water-powered mortars and climbing kilns. Sakitsu, on Amakusa Island, and Bō no Tsu, on the Satsuma Peninsula, are picturesque fishing ports.

**Christian Kyūshū:** In addition to Nagasaki, where Christian relics are major tourist attractions, there are numerous remote islands such as Hirado, the lovely Gotō Islands, and Amakusa, where crypto-Christians practiced the forbidden religion in secrecy for 250 years. These areas are now dotted with memorial chapels.

# CALENDAR

**Jan. 3:** * **Tamaseseri.** Hakata (II). E

**Jan. 7:** * **Usokae, Onisube.** Dazaifu (II:E1). F E

**Jan. 7:** * **Oniyo.** Kurume (IV). F

**L 1/7:** * # **Ten'nen-ji Shujō Onie.** Takada (I:E1). F E B

**May 3:** * **Nishi Hongū-taisai.** Takachiho (V:E3). P S

**July 10–12:** ** **Gion-daiko.** Kokura, Yasaka Jinja (I). Drums mounted on floats are beaten all day long as the floats are dragged through town.

**July 1–15:** ** **Gion Yamagasa.** Hakata (II). An energetic matsuri, said to have begun in the Kamakura period when a priest quelled an epidemic by prayers and a procession of altars dedicated to the victims who had not been properly mourned (and who therefore might become harmful spirits). Today, illuminated mountain-shaped floats covered with large dolls of historical figures are erected in the streets. The festival starts on the 1st, but the highlight is on the 15th, when 28-man teams carry the 750-kg floats and race over a 5-km course; from Kushida Jinja at 4:59 a.m.

**July 13–15:** * **Tobata Gion Yamagasa.** Kokura (I). E V

**July (near 20th):** * **Soga-don no Kasayaki.** Kagoshima (VI). F

**July (3rd Su):** * **Pēron Boat Races.** Togitsu (III:W1). E

**July (4th Su):** * **Pēron Boat Races.** Nagasaki (III:W1). E

**July 28:** ** **Onda Matsuri.** Aso Jinja (V:E1). Large drums herald the approach of *mikoshi*, accompanied by shrine maidens swathed in white who present a mysterious appearance. The *mikoshi* are paraded around so the kami can "see" the area under its protection, and sheaves of rice stalks are thrown on the *mikoshi* to predict the harvest. Lion dances are performed.

**Aug. 13–15:** * **Chankoko Odori.** Gotō Islands (II:W4). P

**Aug. 14–17:** * # **Himejima Bon Odori.** Himejima (I:E2). P

**Aug. 15:** * **Urabon-e.** Nagasaki (III:W1). V B

**L 7/26–28:** * **Chinese Ura Bon.** Nagasaki (III:W1). V B

**L 8/1:** ** **Usudaiko Odori.** Saito, Shimozuru (VI:E4). An ancient folk performance of the region. Youths wear costumes with three tall, banner-festooned poles protruding above their backs and beat large drums strapped to their chests while dancing. The sound of the drums is supposed to drive insects out of the fields. Also performed at the Kofun Matsuri, Nov. 1.

**L 8/15:** * **Jūgoya Sorayoi.** Chiran (VI:W1). P F

**Sept. 22–23:** * **Higashi Hongū-taisai.** Takachiho (V:E3). P S

**Sept. (late):** * **Yame Tōrō Ningyō.** Yame (IV). P V

**Oct. 1:** * **Kaijō Jinkō Sai.** Munakata Shrine (I). P V

**Oct. 7–9:** *** **Okunchi.** Nagasaki, Suwa Jinja (III:W1). This splendid matsuri was supported by the Edo-period authorities in an attempt to dampen interest in the forbidden Christianity. Dutch and Chinese traders were invited to participate, giving the festival its famous dragon dance and "Dutch" minstrels. Other quarters built whimsical floats and deco-rated parasols, some of which are now 200 years old. During the three days, the exotic and exciting crash of Chinese gongs is heard all over town.

**Oct. 9–11: ✳ Usa Jingū Hōjōe.** Usa (I:E1). 🆅

**Oct. 14: ✳ # Kebesu Matsuri.** Kunimi-chō (I:E2). 🄵 🄴

**Nov. 2–4: ✳✳ Karatsu Kunchi.** Karatsu (II:W1). Features fourteen unusual lacquered floats in the shapes of giant helmets, lion heads, mythical beasts. On the 3rd, the floats are pulled across the sandy beach. During the three days of this boisterous event, the town is enveloped in the matsuri spirit; people prepare feasts and throw open their houses.

**Nov. 3: ✳ Yo-Kagura Kōkai Matsuri.** Takachiho (V:E3). 🄿 🅂

**Nov. 18: ✳✳ Myōken-sai.** Yatsushiro (V). A lively matsuri with processions of sacred horses and a giant lacquered tortoise with a serpent's head, of distinctly Chinese appearance, repre-senting a mythical beast who crossed the sea from China carrying a bosatsu on its carapace. Lion Bugaku and other sacred dances are offered.

**Nov.–early Feb.: ✳✳ Takachiho no Yo-Kagura.** Takachiho (V:E3). The theatrical 33-dance Iwato Kagura cycle, based on ancient Shinto myths, is performed by masked dancers from late afternoon to noon the following day in farmhouses in the area. Of all the famous genuine folk performances, this is one of the most accessible.

# Kyūshū History: The Puzzling Origins of the Japanese

469

**Queen Pimiko** (died ca. 250) A priestess-queen who, according to Chinese records, ruled over a Japanese kingdom, probably in northern Kyūshū. Also known as Himiko.

**Emperor Jimmu** The mythical first emperor of Japan, who set out from Kyūshū to conquer the Yamato region (Kinki). The *Kojiki* has him reigning from 660–585 B.C., but this was a fiction invented so that the Japanese could claim a history almost as ancient as China's.

**Empress Jingū** (4th C?) The mythical Japanese empress who established a colony on the southern tip of Korea. She gave birth to Emperor Ōjin, deified as Hachiman, the god of war.

The Sun Goddess and ruler of heaven, **Amaterasu**, ordered her grandson **Ninigi** to govern Japan, which was still inhabited by immortal gods. She gave him the three imperial regalia—the mirror, the sword, and the *magatama* jewel—and he descended, alighting on the summit of Kyūshū's **Mt. Takachiho** (VI:E2). (See also Takachiho, V:E3.) Ninigi married Konohanasakuya-hime (Flowers-upon-the-tree Blossoming Princess), the beautiful daughter of a local god. But when he was offered her ugly older sister as well, he sent her back to her father who, deeply shamed, cursed Ninigi's offspring with lives "as brief as the flowers upon the trees." Thus the race of mortals—the Japanese people—was born. Local legend holds that Ninigi and his immediate descendants are interred in the **Saitobaru Burial Mounds** (VI:E4). Ninigi's grandson, however, left Kyūshū, and, at the age of forty-five, crossed the Inland Sea and conquered Yamato, the area around Nara and Ōsaka; he became the first emperor, **Jimmu** (see Asuka History, p. 407).

The Japanese are not as racially homogeneous as is commonly supposed. Regional and individual types vary greatly. Some have the characteristics of Southeast Asians, others of the Ainu, yet others of Koreans. Some Japanese blood-protein studies show close similiarity with Chinese and Koreans, while others indicate the Japanese are closest to Mongols living around Lake Baikal in Soviet Central Asia. Most newborn Japanese babies have the "Mongol spot" on the small of their backs, a bruiselike mark that fades with age; the trait is found as far away as Eastern Europe, wherever the Mongols invaded. It is clear that immigrants, bringing with them advanced arts, crossed the 200 kilometers of sea between Korea and Kyūshū; probably the ancestors of the imperial house were among them.

Archeological findings, especially pottery, provide the best record of the various waves of foreign influence that washed over Kyūshū. From about 10,000 B.C., cooking vessels and female figurines—the oldest pottery yet discovered in the world—were being produced in a style totally unlike any on the Asian mainland (see Art, p. 100). The Jōmon, or Rope Pattern, people, so-called for the designs on their pots, were primarily hunters and gatherers, but toward the end of this culture's heyday—about 300 B.C.—the Jōmon people in Kyūshū seem to have taken up rice cultivation. These farmers may or may not have been the antecedents of the people who made the new Yayoi pots (200 B.C.–A.D. 400). By conquest or diffusion, Yayoi cul-ture spread north from Kyūshū, until today only the culture of the Ainu of Hokkaidō retains certain aspects of the Jōmon people. Recent studies of Jōmon and Ainu teeth strongly indicate that the two groups are related.

Yayoi pottery resembles some of the early mainland Asian styles, but it is fired at higher temperatures, more spare in ornamentation, and more symmetrical than Jōmon pottery. Most likely the culture was the result of foreign immigrants — perhaps invaders — mixing with Jōmon people. Numerous elaborate bronze implements, such as the bell-like *dōtaku*, prove that the Yayoi were in constant contact with the mainland, as far away as China. A tributary seal, thought to be the one recorded as having been presented to a Japanese ruler by the Later Han court in A.D. 57, was found by a farmer near Hakata (II) in 1753. Its stamp declares it is a gift to "the King of Na in the Land of Wa [Japan]."

By the first few centuries A.D., the Yayoi tribes had formed small kingdoms. A third-century Chinese chronicle describes a **Queen Pimiko** who ruled a kingdom in northern Kyūshū, possibly like the one discovered at **Yoshinogari**. Pimiko, whose name can mean "sun priestess" or "princess," was probably a shamaness. There are remains of an archaic shamanistic cult in Okinawa, Tōhoku, and Korea, and an imperial priestess resided at Ise until the fourteenth century (see Shinto, p. 26). The description of Pimiko's subjects fits the more recent Japanese rather well:

> ... It is their general custom to go barefoot. Respect is shown by squatting down. They are much given to strong drink. They are a long-lived race, and persons who have reached 100 are very common. All men of high rank have four or five wives; others two or three. The women are faithful and not jealous. There is no robbery or theft, and litigation is infrequent.
>
> (trans. by G. Sansom in *Japan: A Short Cultural History*)

The account also describes customs relating to ritual purity, and even mentions the *hachimaki*, a cloth headband still worn by cramming students and laborers.

Around A.D. 250, Japan entered the Kofun period (ca. 250–538), named for the huge mounds in which local rulers of the time were buried. The Chinese chronicle describes Pimiko's burial rites: "A great mound was raised over her, more than a hundred paces in diameter, and over a hundred of her male and female attendants followed her in death." The *kofun* were tributes to the power of these rulers. Each kingdom vied with the others to import continental technology and use it to conquer their neighbors. Buried along with the ruler were mirrors, *magatama*, and swords — like the imperial regalia Ninigi brought with him from heaven — and, later, also large amounts of gilt-bronze horse trappings. This has led some scholars to suggest that Asiatic "horse-riders" crossed via Korea and, by virtue of superior military technology, became rulers of Japan. If so, the Japanese and the people of Lake Baikal may indeed share common ancestors.

By the fourth century, most of these independent kingdoms seem to have become vassals of the imperial line, the mythical Jimmu's descendants, who ruled from Yamato. There, near Ōsaka, are two of Japan's largest *kofun*, said to be those of the powerful emperors Ōjin and Nintoku, considered to be historical, if murky, figures. The tomb of Nintoku is a vast, keyhole-shaped mound surrounded by moats; it surpasses the Great Pyramid in volume, if not in height (Kinki, p. 419). Unlike Pimiko, the dead emperor was not attended by live victims, but by *haniwa*, clay models of servants and warriors — which, intriguingly, wear what is almost certainly Central Asian armor.

Connections with the continent — that is, Korea — became more explicit with the legend of **Empress Jingū** who, although pregnant with the future **Emperor Ōjin**, accompanied her husband to Kyūshū to subdue the troublesome Kumaso around Kumamoto (V). When he died in battle she took the helm, finished off the Kumaso, and went on to conquer Korea. There, if Japanese histories are to be believed, the colony of **Mimana** was established in 369. During three years of campaigning, Jingū staved off labor by binding a stone to her pregnant belly; the legend has Ōjin conscious inside her womb, directing battle operations. On her return to Japan, she finally gave birth, near Hakata.

During the next two hundred years, traders sailed back and forth to Korea, bringing to Japan not only new merchandise, but skilled immigrants — silk weavers, artisans, scribes, and Buddhist priests. Many Korean immigrants, such as the **Hata** and **Kamo** families, became attached to the Yamato court (see Kyoto History, p. 319). On the sacred isle of Okinoshima, about fifty kilometers offshore, sailors praying for safety at sea left a treasure trove of offerings on the island, now kept at **Munakata Taisha** (I). These included mirrors, jewels, and, interestingly, horse trappings, all of which were left exposed on open rock ledges for over a thousand years.

In the sixth century (traditionally 534), during the dawn of Japan's recorded history, the Yamato court lost its Korean colony. Over the next century, the Japanese tried to take it back, but in the middle of the seventh century they were badly beaten by a rival Korean kingdom and its Tang Chinese allies. The legend of Jingū and Ōjin seems to have coalesced at this time. Jingū may have been a powerful shamaness, and was probably not Ōjin's real mother. They entered into a family relationship, along with Ōjin's "wife," when they became identified with the three kami of an important clan of Korean origin located around the town of **Usa** in eastern Kyūshū (I:E1). The name of this influential region, Yahata, can be read in the "Chinese" manner as "Hachiman," the name given to this warrior trinity. It was hoped that Usa's Hachiman Shrine (Usa Jingū), newly fused with important imperial ancestors, would protect Japan against a possible invasion from a now united and powerful Korea.

The Japanese also strengthened the military defenses of **Dazaifu** (II:E1), the Yamato state's military and administrative headquarters in Kyūshū. In the seventh century, Emperor Tenji (Naka no Ōe in Hōryū-ji History, p. 400) came to Dazaifu to direct the final disastrous effort in Korea. There he built **Kanzeon-ji**, dedicated to the memory of his mother but also intended as a guardian temple against the Koreans. From about this time, embassies stopped at Dazaifu on their way to and from China. By the ninth century, however, Dazaifu had declined in importance to the point where it served as a place of exile, most infamously for the Heian minister **Sugawara no Michizane**, who was later deified as Tenjin.

Kyūshū remained Japan's gateway to the continent, the first place to absorb its novelties—and to bear the brunt of its attacks. In the thirteenth century, huge Mongol armadas sailed twice into Hakata Bay in an attempt to conquer Japan (see Kamakura History, p. 258). In the sixteenth century, Portuguese weapons and priests landed in **Kagoshima** (VI). Soon after, **Nagasaki** became Japan's first major trading port with the West (see Nagasaki History, p. 483). In 1592 and 1597, HIDEYOSHI tried to invade Korea from a point near **Karatsu** (II:W1), with disastrous results. Kyūshū's feudal lords, however, were able to kidnap skilled Korean potters; even today Kyūshū remains unexcelled in this craft (see Crafts, p. 103).

471

# KYŪSHŪ I. KOKURA

*Tokyo to Kokura: 5:40–6:15h by Shinkansen Hikari express.*
*Kyoto to Kokura: 3:00–3:40h by Shinkansen Hikari express.*
**Prefectures:** Fukuoka, Ōita

### KOKURA(KITA-KYŪSHŪ) 小倉
*Junction to JR Nippō line.* The **Chūō Toshokan** (library), designed by Isozaki Arata (see Tokyo, p. 193), is 0:15h on foot from the south exit of the station; it houses a nice historical museum. Nearby is the rebuilt Kokura Castle and the Shiyakusho (city hall), which offers a remarkable, 360-degree view from the top: to the NE, the straits of Shimonoseki and historic **Dan no Ura**, site of the 12th-century TAIRA defeat, to the NW, the immense complex of Nippon Steel. The stunning **Kita-Kyūshū Municipal Art Museum** 北九州市立美術館 , also by Isozaki, is 0:20h by taxi from the station (Hrs: 9:30–17:30 (enter by 17:00); clsd M, NY).

### Calendar
**July 10–12: ✽✽ Kokura Gion-daiko.** Yasaka Jinja. See Calendar, p. 468.
**July 13th–15th: ✽ Tobata Gion Yamagasa.** Hachiman Jinja. Features enormous pyramids of lanterns.

### Kokura Lodgings (TEL 093)
**Kokura Washington Hotel** 小倉ワシントンホテル (531-3111). 1-8-9 Kaji-chō, Kokura Kita-ku, Kita Kyūshū-shi. Reliable business hotel. S Y6200, Tw Y10,200. AX, DC, V.
**Tōkyū Inn** 小倉東急イン (521-0109). 8-5 Konya-chō, Kokura Kita-ku. Chain business hotel.

## KOKURA TO HAKATA

### Kyūshū Mingei Mura (Folk Art Village) 九州民芸村
*Take JR Kagoshima line local 4 stops to Yabata, then Tajiro-bound bus 0:40h to Jizō-mae.* (093-652-8833). Hrs: 10:00–17:00; clsd W, NY. This trim, well-run artisan commune is a blend of old and new, from handweaving and thatched farmhouses to glassblowing and the brick Yōbikan café/gallery.

### ✽✽ Munakata Taisha (Shrine) 宗像大社
*0:45h from Kokura or 0:35h from Hakata by JR Kagoshima line local to Tōgō, then 0:10h by taxi or 0:15h by bus to Jinja-mae.* Hrs: 8:00–20:00. Munakata Taisha is the shrine of **Okinoshima**, a sacred island 50 km off the coast, which has been worshipped since antiquity as the guardian of sea traffic. The shrine became nationally important between the 5th and 9th centuries, when official envoys to Korea and China, embarking from nearby ports, prayed here for safety. Starting in 1954, archeologists have discovered a wealth of objects offered by early mariners; because of the island's sanctity, these were left undisturbed on open rock ledges for more than a millennium. Of the objects found, 315 are NT. The ✽ **Shinpōkan** (Treasure House) exhibits remarkable fine gilt-bronze horse

trappings, a miniature gilt-bronze loom and *koto*, perhaps from China or Korea, a gold ring, tricolor pottery, and crude stone figures of boats, horses, and men. The displays are nicely augmented by photos and models of the sites.

On Oct. 1 is the \* **Kaijō Jinkō-sai**, the shrine's festival for safety at sea. There's a huge, colorful flotilla on the 1st. On the 2nd–3rd, *yabusame* (archery) and sacred dances are offered.

### Exploring Takehara Kofun
*From Hakata, 1:15h by JR bus to Fukumaru, then 0:05h by Shimizuguchi-bound bus.* At Wakamiya-chō is this well-known painted tomb chamber from the 6th C, which appears to depict a man leading a horse off a boat. Hrs: 9:00–17:00; clsd M.

# KYŪSHŪ I:E. THE EAST COAST OF KYŪSHŪ

**Main Attraction:** Yufuin (E4)

### Exploring Hiko-san
*1:30h from Kokura, or 0:40–1:00h from Hita by Hita-Hikosan line, then 0:30h by bus to Buzenbō-mae (get off two stops before, at Bessho-chūshajo, to see the Kyū Kameishi-bō garden).* Hiko-san was the center of Shugendō in Kyūshū until the Meiji Restoration (see Shinto, p. 27). Kyū Kameishi-bō, a former temple, still has its garden, attributed to SESSHŪ, who resided here for three years. There is also a Treasure House, temporarily closed.

### Exploring Yaba-kei
#*0:40h by JR Nippō line limited express to Nakatsu, then 0:30h by bus to Ao no Dōmon. It is 0:25h farther to the cycling terminal.* This quietly scenic area is threaded by a pleasant, 22-km cycling path, a paved-over railroad track. Attractions include **Ao no Dōmon**, Japan's most famous hand-chiseled tunnel, carved over the course of 30 years by a mendicant monk to save the local people from a treacherous, cliff-hugging trail. It has since been widened to accommodate modern traffic. **Rakan-ji** is an old temple on a rocky hill; the tramway up takes 0:05h, but the 0:25h walk is much more scenic. At the top is a hall set in a cliff and covered with rice scoops, a symbol of fortune, scribbled with wishes. Inside are the 500 Rakan seated around an image of Shaka. All the way at the end of the cycling path is **Kamio-ke** (ICP), a thatched Kyūshū *minka* built in 1771. The road through Yabakei continues to Hita (KYŪSHŪ IV:E1).
**Lodgings:** The modern Yabakei Cycling Terminal (09795-4-2655) rents cycles. Rooms there are Y4500 w/meals. YH/Ryokan Yamakuniya (2-2008) is Y3500 w/meals.

### E1–E2 \* USA AND KUNISAKI HANTŌ (PENINSULA) 宇佐・国東半島
*Usa is 1:05h by JR Nippō line limited express from Kokura. To tour the Kunisaki Penin-sula, we advise taking a Teiki Kankō Bus Tour from Beppu or Ōita. Tours last 5:00–7:00h and cost Y5000. Course A leaves Ōita station daily at 8:30, stops by Beppu station at 9:00, and finishes around 17:00. It can get crowded.* Usa and the Kunisaki Peninsula are an ancient center of Buddhism—based, it is thought, around a clan of Korean origin. Though almost nothing is known about it, the fact that Usa Jingū, the shrine to the continental war god, Hachiman, became protector of the great Nara temple, Tōdai-ji, points to an unusual degree of influence. Saichō, founder of the Tendai sect, stopped in Usa on his return from China in 805 and established nearby Kunisaki, Land's End, as a Tendai sanctuary. Temples were built among its jagged, cave-riddled peaks, where monks practiced austerities. Many were destroyed, however, by the 16th-century Christian daimyō, Ōtomo Sōrin. Stone buddhas and the Heian-period Fuki-ji remain, and the rustic scenery has a forlorn beauty and an undeniable aura of antiquity.

### Calendar
**L 1/7:** \* # **Ten'nen-ji Shūjō Onie.** Takada (*0:10h by bus from Usa, then 0:25h by bus and 0:40h on foot to Ten'nen-ji*). An ancient rite, introduced in 718. At 18:00–23:00, *oni* (demons) dance. Finally, two wild, torch-wielding *oni*, manifestations of Fudō and Aizen Myō-ō, scatter "*oni's eye*" ricecakes and chase people who pick them up, showering them with disease-preventing sparks.
**Aug. 14–17:** \* # **Himejima Bon-Odori.** Himejima, off Kunisaki Peninsula coast (*0:25h by ferry from Imi harbor*). Famous Bon dance, noted for pre-Buddhist dance forms.
**Oct. 9–11:** \* **Usa Jingū Hōjō-e.** Usa. Forty to fifty sacred boats sail down the river to the sea in this rite begun around 720 for those slain in a battle between the Yamato state and the local Hayato clan. Originally, live sea creatures were released to appease their spirits.
**Oct. 14:** \* # **Kebesu Matsuri.** Kunimi-chō (*1:20h by bus from Usa*). Late-night festival. Mobs of demon-masked youths charge a fire; they're repeatedly driven off by 10 guardians, but finally break through and leap into the flames.

### Usa and Kunisaki Sights
\*\* **Usa Jingū (Shrine)** 宇佐神宮 *From Usa station, 0:10h by bus, then 0:15h on foot.* This famous shrine is consecrated to the mythical Emperor Ōjin, his "mother," Empress Jingū, and his consort, Hime Ō-kami (Nakatsu-hime). These deities were identified with Hachiman, god of war, who became a defender of the nation. There are 25,000 branch

shrines throughout Japan. The vermilion **Honden** (NT) is a classic example of the Hachiman style (see Kyūshū History, p. 469, and Shinto, p. 28).

**Futago-ji** 両子寺 Hrs: 8:30–17:00. Near the summit of Futago-san, in the center of Kunisaki Peninsula. A pair of troll-like stone Niō guard the approach. From the main hall, steps lead to the Okuno-in, a hall built against a cliff and enshrining the temple's main image, a Jūichimen Kannon, and Futago Daigongen, male and female avatars of the mountain. In back, there is a small cave with candle-lit images of Fudō. A teahouse by the parking lot serves *dango-jiru teishoku*, a lunch of soup with dumplings, said to be good for fertility.

**Zaizen-ke Bochi** 財前家墓地 Stone tombs (1321, ICP) of the Zaizen family; the tombs, known as Kunisaki pagodas, are shaped like five-tiered stupas (for the five elements), but have a nine-ringed spire on top, like a pagoda.

**Maki Ōdō** 真木大堂 Hrs: 8:30–18:00. In winter 8:30–19:30. Nine Heian-period statues (ICP), including an image of Dai'itoku Myō-ō riding a bull.

**Kumano Magaibutsu** 熊野磨崖仏 Two large reliefs carved into a natural rock face, one of Fudō Myō-ō and the other of Dainichi Nyorai (ICP). They are the largest of their kind in Japan and are thought to date from the late Heian period. The long, rough stairway of natural stones leading to the images was supposedly thrown together in one night by a demon.

**\*\* Fuki-ji** 富貴寺 Hrs: 8:30–16:30; clsd rainy days. The small, graceful **Main Hall** (NT) dates from the 11th C, making it the oldest structure on Kyūshū. It houses a fine wooden image of Amida (ICP) of the late Heian period, and the walls are decorated with much-faded frescoes depicting Amida's Paradise—a Chinese-style palace and hosts of music-making bosatsu.

## E3 BEPPU 別府

*1:45h by JR Nippō line limited express from Kokura. By ferry: from Ōsaka, overnight ferries depart three times daily (takes 13:00–16:00h). From Hiroshima, one ferry per day (takes 8:30h).* Beppu, Japan's most famous hot-spring town, is thoroughly dreadful, full of touts, garish signs, and the dregs of Japanese popular culture—a combination some may find fascinating. Beppu's main sightseeing attraction, a series of "hells," bubbling mudpots and steaming ponds, embellished with crocodiles and jungle plants, are a time-consuming tourist trap. If you are seeking a peaceful hot-spring hideaway, change here for a bus to Yufuin.

**Takegawara Onsen** 竹瓦温泉 *About 0.5 km from Beppu station, near the beach.* One of several places along the beach where visitors can be buried in steaming sand.

**Suginoi Palace (Hotel)** スギノイパレス Admission Y1800 (Su, NH Y1700). Beppu-style culture. Among the innumerable offerings of Beppu's grande dame is a giant public bath complete with slides, fish tanks, miniature Thai pavilions, and jungle plants. There's also a collection of old Japanese art and curios in the Suginoi Museum.

**Myōban Onsen** 明礬温泉 *1-km walk up a narrow road from Hoshu Jizō "hell," on the bus route to Yufuin.* A small spa with thatched huts built over steam vents to collect *yunohana* (flowers of sulfur), which is sold as a kind of bath salt.

### Beppu Dining and Lodgings (TEL 0977)

**Fugumatsu** ふぐ松 北浜3-6-14 (21-1717). Hrs: 11:00–22:00, daily. *Fugu* (puffer) restaurant; full course from Y6000.

**Beppu Shōwa-en** 別府昭和園 (22-3211). TELEX 7734-35. 217-8 Minami Tateishi, Beppu-shi, Ōita-ken. As resort ryokan go, this one, with traditional decor and garden, isn't bad. Y20–50,000 w/meals.

**\* Sakaeya** 民宿サカエヤ 鉄和井田之組 (66-6234). Idonikumi, Ida, Kannawa. Very popular minshuku in a lovely traditional house. The meals are cooked with geothermal energy. Y8000 w/meals.

**Ryokan Kanna-en** 神和苑 (66-2111). Kannawa, Beppu-shi. Large garden; sprawling, old-fashioned buildings; and open-air baths. Y17–35,000 w/meals.

## E4 \*\* YUFUIN 湯布院

*1:00h by bus from Beppu. 0:50h from Ōita (E5) or 1:05h from Hita (KYŪSHŪ IV:E1) by JR Kyūdai main line.* This countrified hot-spring town, on a beautiful highland plateau, is the fashionable alternative to Beppu. On the shore of Kinrin-ko, a small lake 0:25h on foot east of the station, there's a charming thatched-roof public bathhouse (Y100). Nearby Bussen-ji is an atmospheric, thatched-roof temple. The **Sueda Bijutsukan** (Art Museum) 末田美術館 is a strange, charcoal-colored, clapboard building exhibiting modern sculpture; the setting is perhaps more interesting than the art (Hrs: 9:00–18:00, daily). The **Yufuin Mingei Mura** (Folk Art Village) 民芸村 is a showcase for artisans making lathe-turned toys, blown glass, hand-forged steel blades, etc. (Hrs: 8:30–17:30, daily.) Majestic **Yufuin-dake** can be climbed from Higashi-Tozan-guchi (on the Beppu-Yufuin bus route) in 2:00h, round trip. Yufuin hosts one of Japan's best new **film festivals** for 4 days in late August. Call 0977-84-3111 for information.

### Yufuin Dining and Lodgings (TEL 0977)

Address: Yufuin-chō, Ōita-ken.

**\*\*\* Tamanoyu** 玉の湯 (84-2158). One of the most delightful inns in Japan. Refined handcraft theme, from *yukata* sashes to the dinner plates and *kasuri* quilts. Relaxed atmosphere and superb, innovative cuisine. Y23–38,000 w/meals. **Budōya**, a folk-style restaurant run by Tamanoyu, serves *kaiseki bentō* for Y1800, *torinabe* (chicken pot) for Y2400 (Hrs: 11:30–20:30). The Coffee Corner serves excellent coffee and desserts (Hrs: 8:00–22:00).

**\*\* Kamenoi Bessō** 亀の井別荘 (84-3166). Farmhouse-style ryokan located on sprawling grounds. Y20–32,000 w/meals.

**\*\* Sansō Yamashige** 山荘山重 (84-3650). Very charming thatched inn with garden and lovely bathhouse. Only 2 rooms, both w/bath and toilet. Y9000+ w/breakfast.

**Pension Yufuin** ペンションゆふいん (85-3311). Western style. Y7800 w/meals.

**Oyado Nakaya** お宿なか屋 (84-3835). Y7–9000 w/meals.

**Easy Access To:**
**\* Kumamoto** (KYŪSHŪ V): *6:00h by Yamanami highway express bus, via Aso National Park. Very scenic.*

## E5 ŌITA  大分

*1:40–1:50h by JR Nippō line limited express. Junction to the JR Kyūdai line to Yufuin, Hita, and Kurume (KYŪSHŪ IV), and to the JR Hōhi line to Bungo-Taketa, Aso, and Kumamoto (KYŪSHŪ V).*

### Ōita Lodgings (TEL 0975)

**\*\* Ōita Nishitetsu Grand Hotel** 大分西鉄グランドホテル (36-1181). Fax 32-4125. 1-4-35 Maizurumachi, Ōita-shi. A comfortable first-class hotel by the river, 0:05h by car from station. S Y7500–9000, Tw Y15–18,000.

**Daiichi Hotel** 第1ホテル (36-1388). 1-1-1 Funaimachi. Near station. S Y6350, Tw Y8800.

## E6 \* USUKI  臼杵

*2:20–2:40h from Kokura or 0:40h from Beppu by JR Nippō line limited express. 2:50h by ferry from Yawatahama (CHŪGOKU IV:S4).* Usuki is famed for its ancient stone Buddhist images. The town itself, established as a castle town by Ōtomo Sōrin, a great 16th-century Christian daimyo, has a pleasant, old-fashioned air.

**\*\*\* Usuki Sekibutsu (Stone Buddhas)** 臼杵石仏 Hrs: 8:30–17:00, daily. *0:15h by bus from station, then 0:05h on foot.* More than 60 stone Buddhist images were carved out of the cliff some time during the late Heian to early Kamakura periods. Of the numerous carvings found in the mountains of northeast Kyūshū, these are the most extensive and of the highest artistic quality. Some of the images, including a head of Dainichi Nyorai, retain their original coloring. Almost nothing is known about who carved these images, or why.

**Easy Access To:**
**Nobeoka** (KYŪSHŪ VI:E5): *1:40h by JR Nippō line limited express.*

# KYŪSHŪ II. HAKATA (FUKUOKA)

**Tokyo to Hakata:** *6:40h by Shinkansen Hikari express.*
**Kyoto to Hakata:** *3:50h by Shinkansen Hikari express.*
**By Air:** *From Tokyo, 1:40h (ANA, JAL, JAS). From Ōsaka, 1:05h (ANA, JAL). International service from Pusan, Seoul, Hong Kong.*
**Prefectures:** Fukuoka, Saga, Nagasaki

## HAKATA (FUKUOKA)  博多（福岡）

This large, commercial city was the gateway to the continent early in Japan's history. Dazaifu, to the south, the preeminent historical attraction of this area, was a fortified government outpost of the Nara and Heian courts. In the 13th century, Mongol armadas sailed into Hakata Bay and twice attempted to invade Japan. The Japanese fought desperately and both times were saved by violent typhoons (see Kamakura History, p. 258). The city's two names originated in the feudal era: Hakata, on the east, was the merchants' town, while Fukuoka, on the west, across the Nakagawa, was the castle lord's town. Today, Fukuoka is poised to reclaim its historic place as gateway to Asia, with plans for international air service and major conference facilities.

### Calendar

**Jan. 3: \* Tamaseseri.** Hakozaki Jinja (*0:20h by bus from Hakata station*). Half-naked youths vie for a large ball thrown by the priest. Afternoon.

**May 3–4: Hakata Dontaku.** This big matsuri supposedly got its name from the Dutch *Zontag* (Sunday), and began as a procession of Hakata merchants' paying their New Year visit to the daimyo in Fukuoka. The city resurrected it in 1961 as a Golden Week event.

**July 1–15: \*\* Gion Yamagasa.** See Calendar, p. 468. The festival starts on the 1st, but the highlight is on the 15th, when 28-man teams carrying the 750-kg floats race over a 5-km course, starting from Kushida Jinja at 4:59 a.m. On the 12th, there are practice sessions. On the 13th, the floats are gathered in the center of town, near Tenjin.

### Getting Around

The center of town lies between the JR Hakata station and Nishitetsu-Fukuoka station, where one boards the private Nishitetsu line to Dazaifu, Kurume, and Yanagawa. The two stations are linked by subway; get on near the south exit of Hakata station and take it to Tenjin station, which is about 100 meters north of Nishitetsu-Fukuoka station.

## Fukuoka Sights

\* **Shōfuku-ji** 聖福寺 *1 km north of Hakata station, near Gion subway stop*. This is the oldest Zen temple in Japan, founded in 1195 by the priest Eisai upon his return from China. Eisai went on to found important Rinzai Zen monasteries in Kamakura and Kyoto. Shōfuku-ji itself is a small, neglected version of a Kamakura temple, set down in the middle of a modern city. The grounds contain tea hedges where Eisai supposedly planted Japan's first tea.

**Kushida Jinja** 櫛田神社 *300 m west of Gion subway stop*. This shrine displays the largest Gion Yamagasa float (see Calendar); it depicts the legendary hero Kintarō and the tragic Empress Kenreimon-in.

\* **Fukuoka-shi Hakubutsukan (City Museum)** 福岡市博物館 (845-5011). Hrs: 9:00–17:00 (enter by 16:30); clsd M, NY. *0:10h walk from Nishijin station*. Opened in Oct. 1990. Exhibits include a replica of the Gold Seal of Na, which was recorded in Chinese annals as having been given to a Japanese king in A.D. 57. A seal fitting the description was unearthed in a paddy field by a peasant in the 17th C. It is a NT and is housed in Tokyo.

\* **Fukuoka-shi Bijutsukan (Art Museum)** 福岡市美術館 Hrs: 9:30–17:30 (enter by 17:00; clsd M, NY. *0:10h by subway to Ōhori Kōen from Hakata station*. Noted collection of Japanese art in a handsome museum designed by Maekawa Kunio. The museum stands by **Ōhori Kōen**, a pretty park built from the castle moat and modeled on China's West Lake. The castle grounds contain a reconstructed gate and turret.

**Genkō Kinenkan (Mongol Invasion Memorial Hall)** 元寇記念館 (651-1259). Hrs: 10:00–16:00, daily. *Near JR Yoshizuka station*. A huge bronze statue of the priest Nichiren glowers near the hall. Nichiren, who prophesied the Mongol invasion, took credit for the *kamikaze* typhoons that sank their fleet. The dingy hall houses a Mongol helmet, armor, and weapons recovered from the battle. It's worth a visit for history buffs. To the west of Hakata are ruins of the wall built around Hakata Bay to stave off the Mongol attack.

**Twin Dome City.** Huge baseball arena–amusement park complex to be completed in the spring of 1993. Isozaki Arata, a local boy who is now Japan's best-known architect, has designed an 80-meter-high, 200-meter-diameter arena styled on Rome's Colosseum.

475

## Fukuoka Dining and Lodgings (TEL 092)

Tenjin Chika-gai, beneath the Nishitetsu-Fukuoka station, is a chic, underground arcade. Nakasu, the river island halfway between Hakata station and Tenjin, is a major dining and nightlife district. Shunkō-bashi, at the south end of Nakasu island, is lined at night with carts selling cheap, tasty meals.

\*\* **Shin-Miura** 新三浦 石城町21-12 (291-0821). Hrs: 12:00–20:00 (last order); clsd 1st and 3rd Su, NY, mid-Aug. This establishment has been serving *kashiwa no mizudaki* since 1910 (see Cuisine, p. 114). Full courses from Y9000. Branch in Tenjin Bldg. Basement (721-3272). Hrs: 11:00–20:30; clsd 2nd Tu, NY, mid-Aug. Course from Y4000.

\*\* **ANA Hotel Hakata** 博多全日空ホテル (471-7111). 3-3-3 Hakata Ekimae, Hakata-ku, Fukuoka-shi. Close to Hakata station. Best in town. S Y9800, Tw Y17,000. AX, DC, V.

\* **Mitsui Urban Hotel** 三井アーバンホテル (451-5111). 2-8 Hakata Ekimae, Hakata-ku. Near Hakata station. S Y6200, Tw Y11,080–13,980. AX, DC, V, MC.

**Maruko Inn Hakata** (461-0505). 3-30-25 Hakata ekimae, Hakata-ku. Near Hakata station. One of the better budget inn chains. S Y5000–7800, D Y6800–8800, Tw Y8800–15,000. Weekly and monthly rates available.

\*\* **Il Palazzo Hotel** (716-3333). 3-13-1 Haruyoshi, Chūō-ku. Beautiful 66-room hotel designed by Aldo Rossi. S Y11,000, Tw Y15,000.

\* **Nishitetsu Grand Hotel** 西鉄グランドホテル (771-7171). 2-6-60 Daimyō, Chūō-ku. Established. By Nishitetsu-Fukuoka station. S Y11,500, Tw Y17–25,000. AX, DC, V, MC.

**Kyūshū Kaikan Garden Palace** 九州会館ガーデンパレス (713-1112). 4 Tenjin, Chūō-ku. 0:05h on foot from Nishitetsu-Fukuoka station. S Y6300, Tw Y11,400.

**Tokyo Daiichi Hotel Fukuoka** 東京第1ホテル福岡 (281-3311). 5 Nakasu, Hakata-ku. S Y6–7500, Tw Y9–16,000.

# KYŪSHŪ II:W. WEST FROM HAKATA

## Traveling

Public transport around this region is a patchwork of train lines, none of which is especially frequent. Check timetables when making plans.

## W1 \* KARATSU 唐津

*1:10h by the subway/Chikuhi line from Hakata station. The line is semiprivate, and Rail Pass holders have to pay the subway portion separately*. Karatsu, which means "China Port," is today a sleepy seaside town. But in early times, it was a thriving center of trade with the continent. It is not far from Nagoya, the fortress from which HIDEYOSHI launched his futile invasion of Korea. Karatsu has long been renowned for its earthy but elegant pottery, similar to Korean wares, which were made here even before the late 16th-century influx of Korean potters who were captured and brought back to Japan by Hideyoshi's generals. Karatsu is a popular summer resort, with its white sand beach at Niji no Matsubara.

## Calendar

Nov. 2–4: \*\* **Karatsu Kunchi.** See Calendar, p. 469.

## Getting Around
Rent-a-cycle at Karatsu station, near Yōyōkaku ryokan, and at the YH. About Y1000/day. It takes 2:00–3:00h to see the main sights in town.

## Karatsu Sights
**\*\*\* Hikiyama Tenjijō (Festival Float Exhibition Hall)** ひき山展示場 Hrs: 9:00–17:00; clsd 1st Tu and W in Dec, NY. Displays the remarkable, lacquered papier-mâché floats for Karatsu's Kunchi festival. The oldest dates from 1819, the most recent from 1876. The most unusual and well-known are the two lion mask floats, with nostrils large enough to accommodate one's head, and the whimsical, bright-red sea bream.

**\* Karatsu-jō** 唐津城 Hrs: 9:00–17:00 (enter by 16:30); clsd NY. The rebuilt keep occupies a commanding site overlooking town and sea. The castle houses a museum on Karatsu's history, and exhibits Old Karatsu pottery.

**\*\* Niji no Matsubara** 虹ノ松原 A grove of twisted black pine trees, 1 km wide and stretching for 5 km along a white sand beach. The pines were planted by order of the lord of Karatsu to provide a windbreak for the agricultural plain extending inland. The road through the middle of the grove is a cyclists' favorite. Here and there stand the ruined shells of prewar resort lodges, built for China traders who used to summer here.

## Karatsu Crafts
Karatsu stoneware is strongly influenced by Korean Yi-dynasty wares. E-garatsu (picture Karatsu) is decorated with freely brushed, simple designs of grasses, flowers, and birds, in iron underglaze against a soft gray ground. Mishima Karatsu is made by incising the surface with a small punch and filling the depressions with white slip.

**\*\*\* Nakazato Tarōemon Kiln** 中里窯陳列館 (2-8171). Hrs: 8:30–17:30; clsd NY. *0:05h by bicycle from the station*. The 13th-generation master of this kiln is one of the most highly regarded potters in Japan today. A handsome gallery exhibits and sells pieces turned out by his apprentices, as well as signed masterpieces. Also on view are works of the late master, Living National Treasure Nakazato Muan. Videos show the techniques employed in making Karatsu-yaki. Nearby are work areas where visitors can observe various stages of production.

**\*\*\* Ryūta-gama** 隆太窯 見借 (4-3503). Hrs: 9:00–17:00; clsd Nov. 2–4, NY. *In an idyllic valley, 0:15h by car from town*. Founded by Nakazato Takashi, a younger son of Nakazato Muan, this kiln offers an interesting contrast to the main house. The workshop, house, and gallery are in an updated traditional style. The younger Nakazato combines the best traditional techniques with a fine esthetic sensibility and an independent spirit. Gallery at Yōyōkaku Ryokan.

## Karatsu Dining and Lodgings (TEL 09557)
**Takeya** 竹屋 中町1884-2 (3-3244). Hrs: 12:00–19:00; Su, NH 12:00–18:30; clsd 1st, 3rd, and 5th Su. *Unagi* in a venerable building. *Unajū*, Y1500.

**\*\* Yōyōkaku** 洋々閣 (2-7181). 2-4-40 Higashikaratsu, Karatsu-shi, Saga-ken. Atmospheric old inn, close to the beach, and comfortable with foreign guests. Extensive gardens, good food and service (special dinner during Kunchi). The master speaks excellent English and is a mine of information on the area. Y13–35,000 w/meals.

**Kokuminshukusha Niji no Matsubara Hotel** 国民宿舎虹ノ松原ホテル (2-5181). 4 Higashikaratsu. Y5300 w/meals.

**Niji no Matsubara YH** 虹ノ松原YH (2-4526). 4108 Kagami. Y3200 w/meals.

## Exploring Higashi-Matsu'ura Peninsula
Buses are infrequent, but this would make a good day trip out of Karatsu. **Yobuko** is a charming fishing village with a morning market (*0:35h by bus from Ōteguchi bus terminal in Karatsu*). Farther out are the ruins of **Nagoya-jō**, a great castle from which HIDEYOSHI directed his abortive invasions of Korea. (Hideyoshi himself never went to Korea.) **Nanatsu-gama** sea caves are a locally famous scenic attraction, but perhaps of lesser interest to foreign visitors. On Aug. 15, there is **Kaichū Tsunahiki** in Yobuko; a half-meter-thick, 30-meter-long rope is engaged in a tug-of-war in the sea. Hideyoshi is said to have begun the festival to raise the spirits of his men.

## Exploring Iki and Tsushima
# *Iki is 1:05h by ferry from Yobuko, or 2:20h–2:35h from Hakata. Izuhara on Tsushima is 4:15h by direct ferry from Hakata, or 4:40h via Gōnoura, on Iki. The islands are also served by flights from Hakata and Nagasaki.* These two islands, lying along the ancient sea lanes between Japan and Korea, offer seascapes, clean beaches — quiet even in summer — and a slightly exotic Korean tint to the local culture. Iki is a compact island of gently sloping hills and fine beaches. Tsushima is a mini-archipelago with steep, forested mountains and beautiful Aso Bay, dotted with islets. Tsushima's main port, Izuhara, is a former castle town with remains of stone walls from samurai houses and Banshō-in, the funerary temple of its castle lord. 0:50h away by bus, at Shiine, is a cluster of storehouses roofed with stone slabs, something seen nowhere else in Japan.

## W2 \* IMARI 伊万里
*1:00h by bus or JR Chikuhi line from Karatsu*. Imari-yaki is the most famous name in Japanese porcelain, though it was not made in Imari but in nearby Ōkawachiyama and Arita. Export ware was shipped out from the port of Imari to the rest of Japan. From Nagasaki, Imari ware eventually reached Europe on Dutch ships.

# Imari/Arita Porcelain

The Japanese have long prized porcelain and have imported it from China and Korea since the 12th century, but it was not until 1615, when **Ri Sanpei**, a Korean captive of the **Nabeshima** daimyo, discovered kaolin near present-day Arita, that they were able to make it themselves. The timing was fortunate, for Ming China was collapsing, and European traders were looking for a new source of the "China ware" that sold so profitably in the West. The Nabeshima domain established a porcelain monopoly and set up a community of Korean artisans, which it kept under tight guard to keep other clans from stealing the valuable secrets. Porcelain was produced in two areas, **Ōkawachiyama** and **Arita**. At Ōkawachiyama, pieces were biscuit-fired, then decorated with underglaze blue, covered with slip, and fired again at 1300°C to vitrify the clay. The resulting ware included completed blue-and-white ware, and incomplete pieces destined for further decoration. The latter were transported under armed samurai escort to Akae-machi near Kami-Arita, where the clan kept its specialists in *akae*, the colorful overglaze enamels that were so difficult to perfect and apply. *Akae* formulas were strictly guarded among 16 families, which passed the secrets from father to son. When the *akae* artisans were finished, the pieces were returned to Ōkawachiyama for a third firing. Arita still produces the gamut of wares made in the past, from the exquisitely refined **Iro-Nabeshima** and **Kakiemon** to gruesomely gaudy export wares (see Crafts, p. 103).

**Calendar**
**Oct. 22–24: Ton-ten-ton Matsuri.** A lively "fight" festival dating from the Muromachi period. In the late afternoon on the 24th, a portable shrine and a float are locked together and dropped into the river. The first to reach the shore is the winner.

### *** Ōkawachiyama 大川内山

*0:15h by bus or ¥3000 round trip by taxi from Imari station.* Hemmed in on three sides by precipitous crags, Ōkawachiyama was a virtual prison for the Korean potters brought here to make porcelain for the Nabeshima domain. A rebuilt barrier gate near the entrance and a reconstructed feudal porcelain factory at the **Nabeshima Hanyō Kōen** (park) evoke early conditions. A more affecting relic of the past is the mound of gravestones of the 880 Korean descendants who worked and died here. Standing by itself is the tomb of Ri Sanpei. Today, the village bristles with the tall brick chimneys of the 20 kilns still in operation. The narrow main street winds uphill past shops and studios crammed together. The **Tenjikan** (community showroom), on the right as one enters Ōkawachiyama, has maps and examples of wares from all the kilns. A good one to visit is **Seizan** (09552-3-2366), on the right toward the upper end of the main street. There are no restaurants or inns here, but there is a campground beyond the upper end of the village. There is a porcelain fair Apr. 1–5.

### W3 ✳ ARITA (TEL. 0955) 有田

*0:20h by infrequent train or 0:40h by bus from Imari. 0:40h (¥2300) by taxi from Ōkawachiyama to Kami-Arita.* This sprawling porcelain-making town, near where Ri Sanpei made his historic discovery of kaolin, is the birthplace of Japanese porcelain. Though it lacks the compact charm of Ōkawachiyama, it is an important place for anyone with an interest in ceramics. It holds a porcelain fair Apr. 29–May 5.

**Getting Around**
To get around Arita on foot would take most of a day. Walk or take a taxi to the Kyūshū Ceramic Museum, then take a taxi to the kaolin quarry (or train to Kami-Arita) and walk the 4 km back into town, visiting shops and the other museums along the way.

**Arita Sights**
**✳✳✳ Kyūshū Tōji Bunkakan (Kyūshū Ceramic Museum)** 九州陶磁文化館 (43-3681). Hrs: 9:00–16:30; clsd M, NY. *0:08h on foot from Arita station.* This fine museum is an excellent introduction to the ceramic art of Kyūshū, especially the development of porcelain, with exhibits on the technical evolution of ceramics, characteristic examples of noted wares (in particular, Iro-Nabeshima, Kakiemon, Karatsu, Ko-Imari, export wares, and early European copies), and modern pieces. The museum has a free taped guide in English.
**✳✳ Izumiyama Jisekiba** 泉山磁石場 *0:13h on foot from Kami-Arita station.* Kaolin is still obtained at this quarry discovered by Ri Sanpei in 1615.
**Rekishi Minzoku Shiryōkan (Historical Museum)** 歴史民俗資料館 Hrs: 9:00–16:30; clsd NY. Right by the quarry. Displays a model of a wood-fired climbing kiln and pottery shards excavated in Arita.
**✳✳ Arita Tōji Bijutsukan (Ceramic Art Museum)** 有田陶磁美術館 (42-3372). Hrs: 9:00–16:30; clsd M, NH, NY. *0:15h walk from Kami-Arita station.* A converted stone storehouse with an interesting collection of Arita porcelains from all periods, including Ko-Imari, Nabeshima, and Kakiemon.

**\* Tōzan Jinja** 陶山神社 *0:15h on foot from Kami-Arita station*. The blue-and-white porcelain torii, ablution basin, and guardian dogs of this shrine were donated by the Arita townsmen in 1888. Nearby is a memorial to Ri Sanpei.

**\*\*\* Imaizumi Imaemon** 今泉今右衛門 (2-3101). Hrs: 9:00–17:00; clsd 1st Su, NY. *0:10h on foot from Tōzan Jinja*. Now in its 13th generation, this exalted *akae* family decorated the prized **Iro-Nabeshima**, one of the finest porcelains ever made. In feudal times, its use was restricted to the Nabeshima daimyo and other lords who received it as gifts. The delicate-toned enamels over underglaze blue depict flowers, birds, textile prints, and objects, often arranged in abstract patterns of startling modernity. Part of the old Imaizumi house is now a showroom/gallery. Next door is a more extensive three-storied museum. Serious students might apply in advance for permission to view work areas, where artisans still sit on tatami, painstakingly casting pieces and brushing on glazes and enamels in a process which, the present master boasts, "hasn't changed since the Edo period."

**\*\*\* Sakaida Kakiemon** 酒井田柿右衛門 (3-2267). Hrs: 9:00–17:00; clsd NY. *0:20h on foot from Arita station*. The founder of this world-famous kiln pioneered the use of overglaze enamels around 1646. The ware is famed for its persimmon-red enamel which, by tradition, the founder of this kiln achieved by dint of sleepless toil. He was awarded the name Kakiemon, from the word *kaki*, or persimmon. The ware has no underglaze; instead, enamels— *kaki* red, yellow, green, and black—are applied over *nigoshi*, an opaque glaze "the color of water in which rice has been washed." The delicately brushed designs of birds and flowers are restrained and pictorial. Since Kakiemon ware was not restricted to clan use, it found its way to Europe by the late 17th C, where it was greatly admired and was much imitated. The showroom of Kakiemon XIV and a museum of old Kakiemon ware, located on pretty grounds, are open to the public.

**\*\* Gen'emon** 源右衛門 (2-4164). Hrs: 8:00–17:30; clsd NY. *0:05h by taxi from Arita station*. The present master of this 360-year-old kiln is a rather innovative and commercial-minded soul who likes to experiment with traditional designs applied to modern tableware, lamps, cufflinks, etc. In addition to offering an interesting contrast to other Arita kilns, the Gen'emon kiln grounds and gallery are so handsome as to be quite rewarding in themselves.

478

### Arita Dining

**Kibun Sushi** 紀文ずし 赤絵町1574 (2-2535). Hrs: 11:00–21:00; clsd 1st and 3rd Su. Friendly shop near Imaizumi Imaemon. Inexpensive to moderate.

## TAKEO ONSEN 武雄温泉

*0:14h by express train from Arita*. This is a good place for visitors to the Arita area to stay. Legend has it that Empress Jingū bathed here on her way to invade Korea. Don't miss the old **public baths** 公衆浴場. The exterior is modern but inside it's a classic—wood-paneled halls with stone-paved baths fed by hot springs. Public bath hours: 6:30–0:00.

### Calendar

**Sept. (Su closest to 23rd): Kose no Ara Odori.** A chance to see *menfuryū*, a famous regional dance by masked drummers.

### Takeo Onsen Lodgings (TEL 0954)

**Nakamasu Ryokan** なかます旅館 (22-3118). Onsen-dōri, Takeo-shi, Saga-ken. Trim, modern inn. From Y12,000 w/meals.

### Easy Access To:

**\*\* Nagasaki** (KYŪSHŪ III:W1): *From Takeo, it is a 0:30h bus ride to Ureshino Onsen, then a scenic 0:25h bus ride over mountain tea plantations to Sonogi on the coast, where you can board a JR train to Nagasaki.*

## W4 SASEBO 佐世保

*0:30h by express train from Arita*. This harbor town and naval base (for both U.S. and Japanese forces) is a gateway to Hirado and the Gotō islands.

## HIRADO 平戸

*From Sasebo, take a 0:30h bus ride to Kashimae, then board the sightseeing boat through Kujūkushima, "99" pine-studded islets, to Hirado, a 1:00h ride. 8 boats per day in each direction. Or 1:20h by infrequent local train from Sasebo to Hirado-guichi, then 0:15h by bus.* The quaint port of Hirado, nestled at the tip of Hirado Island, was a way station for such historical figures as KŪKAI and Francis Xavier. In the early 1600s, Dutch traders set up offices here, but were ordered by the shogunate to move to Nagasaki's Dejima in 1641. The ruins of the Dutch settlement are one of Hirado's attractions. Hirado was ruled for 700 years by the Matsu'ura, whose rebuilt castle offers a nice view. The **Matsu'ura Museum**, formerly the lord's villa, displays "southern barbarian" screens and memorabilia, as well as a copy of the famous *Matsu'ura Screen* (NT). The spire of the **Xavier Memorial Chapel**, at the head of the bay, juts above the nearby Buddhist temple. Hirado's scenic, remote interior is scattered with relics of crypto-Christians, descendants of Xavier's converts. On Aug. 18 are Hirado Jan-gara Bon dances by dancers wearing deep straw hoods and beating drums and gongs.

**Hirado Lodgings** (TEL 0950)
**Kokuminshukusha Oranda-kan** 国民宿舎オランダ館 (22-3939). 493 Kawauchimachi, Hirado-shi, Nagasaki-ken. Y6000 w/meals.

# # GOTŌ ISLANDS (RETTŌ)  五島列島

*Air service from Nagasaki airport to Arikawa and Fukue on NKA (reserve through ANA). Fukue is 3:25h by ferry from Nagasaki. Arikawa is 2:40h by ferry from Sasebo (2 boats per day). Narao, at the south tip of Nakadōri island, is 2:55h by ferry from Nagasaki.* This offshore archipelago of some 150 islands is a place of forlorn beauty. It is divided into Shimo (south) and Kami (north) Gotō. During the Edo period, many crypto-Christians fled here, where they could practice their faith in relative safety.

**Fukue Island (Shimo-Gotō)** 福江  Since its first missionary contact in 1561, this island has had a long crypto-Christian tradition. Its most famous church is the red-brick **Dōzaki Ten-shudō**, built in 1874 beside a beautiful inlet. The countryside is verdant, and there are several fjord-like inlets on the SW side. Fukue city has a friendly morning market and the remains of **Ishida-jō**, built by the thirtieth Gotō lord. He began building the castle in 1848 because for-eign ships were entering Japanese waters with increasing frequency. Five years after completion, the castle was destroyed in the Meiji Restoration, but the pleasant garden of the lord's villa has survived and is open to visitors. There's also a **Buke-yashiki** (Samurai House) and a **Ming Chinese-style hexagonal well**, built by a *wakō* boss. (*Wakō* were pirates who raided the Chinese and Korean coasts. The coastal population of these countries sometimes moved inland en masse to avoid their depradations.) On sale in the city are the island's gremlin-faced Baramon kites.

**Kami-Gotō** 上五島 **Nakadōri**, the spindly main island of the Kami-Gotō cluster, has a half-dozen little Catholic chapels built in memory of its crypto-Christians. Near Arikawa, the main port, is a pleasant beach, Hamaguri-hama. **Wakamatsu Seto**, a "mini-Inland Sea" between Nakadōri and Wakamatsu islands, is breathtaking. One can usually hitch a ride on a fishing boat from Gōnokubi across to Wakamatsu, where there are three small inns.

479

**Calendar**
**Jan. 16: Hetomato.** Fukue. A 4-m long, 350-kg giant straw sandal is paraded around by loinclothed youths and offered at the shrine. Afterward, they blacken one another with soot and kick a straw ball around.
**Aug. 13–15:** * **Chankoko Odori.** Fukue. An unusual, well-known Bon dance in which men wear decorated hats, colorful costumes, and play drums and gongs; has a "southern" flavor.
**L 7/15: Ōmondē.** Bon dance similar to Chankoko Odori. On Sago no Shima, a tiny island west of Fukue, reached by ferries from Kaizu or scenic Tanna no Ura.

**Gotō Dining and Lodgings**
The fresh seafood and sushi in Fukue is excellent. Places to try: **Matsukiyo** (0959-72-4847); **Yase** (72-1688); **Benten Sushi** (72-3512); **Kanō** (72-3542).
**Hama-sō** 浜荘 (0959-72-2273). 7-7 Sakaechō, Fukue-shi, Minami Matsu'ura-gun, Naga-saki-ken. In Fukue. A harborside ryokan where you can fish from your window. Y8000 w/meals.
**Hashiguchi Ryokan** 橋口旅館 (0959-40-2525). 163 Wakamatsugō, Wakamatsu. Friendly family-run inn. Y6000 w/meals.

# KYŪSHŪ II:E. SOUTHEAST FROM HAKATA

### E1 ** DAZAIFU  太宰府
*0:20–0:30h by private Nishitetsu train from Nishitetsu-Fukuoka station; some direct trains, otherwise change at Futsukaichi, served by both locals and expresses.* Dazaifu was the southern outpost of the Yamato government. It was from here that the Japanese launched armies in the 6th century to defend their Korean colony, Mimana, and their ally, the Paekche Kingdom (Kudara in Japanese) against a rival Korean kingdom, Silla, and Tang China. Later, the Nara court appointed governors to Dazaifu to administer all of Kyūshū and to host foreign envoys. Dazaifu became a splendid, smaller version of Nara, and an appointment to the governorship carried power and prestige. But in the Heian period, as the court became less concerned with provincial and foreign affairs, the Dazaifu post offered an excuse to remove political foes from Kyoto. The most famous exile was Sugawara no Michizane, who "governed" from Dazaifu for two years before succumbing to grief. The Dazaifu Tenman-gū was later built to console his deified spirit. The shrine has since taken on a life of its own so that today the town of Dazaifu thrives around the approach to the shrine, while the ruins of the ancient government headquarters lie amid fields and groves.

**Calendar**
**Jan. 7:** * **Usokae and Onisube.** Dazaifu Tenman-gū. From 19:00, people form a circle, and in pitch darkness hand around wooden *uso* (bullfinches) in hopes of getting a lucky gold

one. Later, the *uso* are burned; *uso* also means "falsehood," so the rite expiates the lies told during the past year. At 21:00, smoky fires are lit to drive demons from the Onisube hall.

**Aug. 25: Sentōmyō.** Dazaifu Tenman-gū. A thousand candles illuminate the grounds to placate Michizane's soul.

**Sept. 25: Sentōmyō.** Repeat of Aug. 25 rite.

## Getting Around

The Dazaifu Tenman-gū is a short walk from Nishitetsu-Dazaifu station, and the Kannon-ji/Tofurō area is about 0:25h on foot from the station. We recommend renting a bicycle at the Tourist Center across from the station ticket window.

## Dazaifu Sights

**\*\*\* Dazaifu Tenman-gū (Shrine)** 太宰府天満宮 *0:10h walk from station.* This shrine is dedicated to Tenjin, the deified Sugawara no Michizane, kami of scholars. The present head priest claims direct descent from Michizane. The precincts are planted with numerous flowering plums. The famous **Flying Plum** that followed Michizane into exile stands on the right before the shrine. On the left is a plum given by the mother of the Taishō emperor as a prayer for his "recovery" (he was mentally frail). The Momoyama-style **Honden** (ICP) was rebuilt in 1583. The unpainted inner sanctum housed Michizane's tomb until the Meiji period, when it was forbidden for shrines to contain graves, and the tomb was replaced by a statue. (At the same time, the Buddhist Niō in the gate were replaced by archers.) To the right of the grounds is the **Hōmotsukan** (Treasure House) with a collection devoted to Michizane, including many personal relics, an Edo-period picture scroll of the shrine's festival, and an unillustrated text of the *Tenjin Engi*, an account of Michizane's life and deification. Behind the hall is a museum of Hakata clay dolls depicting Michizane's life. At the rear right corner of the shrine is a stone tub full of *umeboshi* (pickled plum) pits donated by devotees; supposedly if you split a plum seed, you can see Tenjin.

**480**

**\*\* Kōmyō Zenji** 光明禅寺 Hrs: sunrise–17:00. This Zen temple was established in the Kamakura period as a companion to Dazaifu Tenman-gū. It has a beautiful garden, formed of swirling white sand and cloudlike islands of moss, dotted with boulders and shaded by maples.

**\*\*\* Kyūshū Rekishi Shiryōkan (Historical Museum)** 九州歴史資料館 (923-0404). Hrs: 9:30–16:30 (enter by 16:00); clsd M, NY. A large, very interesting collection of objects from the Jōmon, Yayoi, and Kofun periods, along with many local Buddhist relics, excellently displayed.

**\*\*\* Kanzeon-ji** 観世音寺 *0:15h on foot from Tenman-gū.* Kanzeon-ji was founded by Emperor Tenji in memory of his mother, Empress Saimei, when he came to Dazaifu in 663 to send an army to the aid of Paekche. The temple was completed in 746, and was one of only three in Japan to have an ordination platform. All that remains from this time is a great bell

# Sugawara no Michizane (845–903)

Sugawara no Michizane was, by legend, an unsurpassed scholar of Chinese, as well as a great poet and calligrapher. He chose as his symbol the plum blossom, a gentlemanly flower then newly imported from China. Michizane became a favorite of Emperor Uda, who appointed him Minister of the Right. Alarmed that someone outside their family should be given so much power, the FUJIWARA plotted to have him lead the hazardous embassy to China. When he refused, they dispatched him to "govern" Dazaifu. As he tearfully quitted the capital for the last time, he bid farewell to his beloved plum: "If the east wind blows this way/ Oh blossoms of the plum tree/ Send your fragrance to me!/ Never forget the Spring/ Even though your master is no longer there!" According to legend, the loyal plum tree uprooted itself and flew to Dazaifu to join its master.

Michizane died two years later, some say of homesickness. An ox, drawing the funeral cart, collapsed in grief on the way to the cemetery, and it was decided that Michizane's remains should be buried on the spot. In the years that followed, disasters befell the people who had brought about Michizane's downfall. An ominous black thundercloud approached the imperial palace and struck a Fujiwara official dead. The incident left the emperor (Uda's son, who had conspired against Michizane) so shaken and ill that he had to retire. A priest dreamed that Michizane's vengeful spirit was behind the wave of disasters. Seeking to assuage it, Michizane's old foes promoted the angry ghost to Minister of the Left; later, he was deified and a splendid shrine, the Kitano Tenman-gū, was built in Kyoto in his honor. Michizane's mausoleum at Dazaifu was turned into a shrine as well. Michizane's deified spirit, known as **Tenjin**, worshipped here and in 10,000 subshrines across Japan, has since granted protection to poets, calligraphers, and millions of Japanese students praying for success in their high school and college entrance examinations.

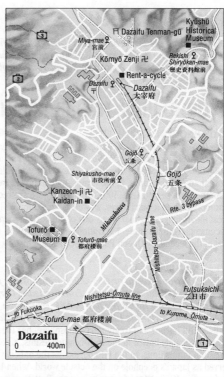

Dazaifu

0    400m

(NT), one of the oldest in Japan. The ◆ **Treasure Hall** contains an important group of sculptures (Hrs: 9:00–17:00). Most impressive is the Tobatsu Bishamonten (10th C, ICP), standing on the shoulders of an earth goddess, an unusual form said to come directly from Central Asian iconography. Positively rare is the 11th-C Daikoku (ICP), familiar as one of the Seven Lucky Gods, but depicted here in his original form as a Central Asian war god. Kannon is represented by three enormous statues (ICP), including the largest Batō (Horse-headed) Kannon in Japan, a fierce manifestation with a horse's head emerging from the top of its head. One of the Bugaku masks (12th C, ICP), called Ryū-ō, has a demon clinging to its head and resembles Indonesian masks.

**Kaidan-in** 戒壇院 This temple adjacent to Kanzeon-ji stands on the site where the priest Ganjin performed his first ordination ceremony after arriving in Japan (see Kinki, p. 397). The Main Hall houses a late-Heian Rushana Buddha (ICP).

✳ **Tofurō (Tower of the City)** 都府楼 *500 m from Kanzeon-ji*. Like Taga-jō near Sendai in Tōhoku, this was an outpost of the Yamato government against independent and rebellious tribes, such as the Kumaso in south Kyūshū. Dazaifu was also used as a staging area for military adventures in Korea (see Kyūshū History, p. 469). When Japan's ally Paekche capitulated to Silla and Tang China, the Japanese, fearing an invasion, fortified the area even more strongly. As the government headquarters of Kyūshū, Dazaifu was built on a rectilinear plan, similar to Nara, but at about half the scale. The foundation stones of the Tofurō, which was the heart of Dazaifu, show the outlines of several buildings arranged axially within a surrounding wall. A small museum occupies the southeast corner of the site (Hrs: 9:00–16:30; clsd M, mid-Aug., NY).

### Dazaifu Lodgings (TEL 092)
Most tourist lodgings are at nearby Futsukaichi Onsen.

 ⬠1 **Kokumin Nenkin Hoyō Sentā Dazaifu** 国民年金保養センター太宰府 (925-5801). 1775 Dazaifu, Dazaifu-shi. *0:25h on foot from Dazaifu station*. Lodge run by Social Security Agency. Y5500 w/meals.

 ⬠2 **Dazaifu YH** 太宰府YH (922-8740). 1553-3 Dazaifu, Dazaifu-shi. *0:10h on foot from Dazaifu station*. Y4500 w/meals.

### Exploring Koishiwara
# *2:00h by bus from Fukuoka Bus Center (in Tenjin station), then 0:15h on foot*. This pleasant little village is noted for its Korean-style folk pottery, similar to that of Onta (KYŪSHŪ IV:E2), which lies across the mountain ridge. At Sarayama ("Plate Mountain") is an engaging exhibition hall, the **Kōgeikan**, as well as the showrooms of several potters (clsd M). Yanase Masato's kiln is a good one to visit. Pottery fairs around May 5, Oct. 10.

### Easy Access To:
**Kurume** (KYŪSHŪ IV): *0:20h by Nishitetsu limited express from Futsukaichi.*

# KYŪSHŪ III. TOSU

**Tokyo to Tosu:** *6:40h by Shinkansen Hikari express from Tokyo to Hakata, then 0:25h by JR Kagoshima line limited express. About once an hour, there are through expresses from Hakata to Nagasaki, via Tosu, Saga, Hizen-Yamaguchi, and Isahaya.*
**Prefectures:** Saga, Nagasaki

# KYŪSHŪ III:W. NAGASAKI AND SHIMABARA

**＊YOSHINOGARI** 吉野ヶ里
*Take JR Nagasaki line local 3 stops W of Tosu to Mitagawa, then 0:10h by bicycle (loaned for free), 0:15h on foot, or 0:05h by taxi (Y490).* Phone: 0952-53-5910. Hrs: Oct.–Mar. 9:00–17:00; Apr.–Sept. 9:00–18:00. This major archeological site has yielded the remains of more than 350 dwellings, 2,500 graves, and countless weapons, pottery and other objects from the Yayoi period (B.C. 300–A.D. 300). There are reconstructions of pit dwellings, storehouses, and a watchtower, as well as an exhibit hall. The settlement was enclosed by a great moat, suggesting that it was one of the northern Kyūshū kingdoms described in Chinese documents from that time. Excavations in the late 1980s raised the possibility that this was the seat of the legendary Queen Pimiko (see Kyūshū history, p. 469).

**W1 ＊＊ NAGASAKI** 長崎
*2:25–2:50h from Hakata or 1:55–2:20h from Tosu by JR Nagasaki line limited express. By Air: see also Kyūshū introduction. From Haneda (Tokyo) 7 flights per day by ANA, JAL, or JAS. From Ōsaka, 4 flights per day by ANA. From Naha (Okinawa), one flight per day by ANA. Nagasaki Airport is 1:00h by express bus from Nagasaki station.* Nagasaki, famous for
482  its beautiful harbor and treaty-port atmosphere, has the most exotic history of any city in Japan. Intimately linked to the 16th-century Jesuits, it became the scene of bloody anti-Christian inquisitions. In the Edo period, as the only city open to foreign trade, Nagasaki served as Japan's peephole on the outside world. When Japan finally ended its 220 years of seclusion in 1858, Nagasaki was among the first open ports. Ironically, this city, which has had longer contact with the West than any other in Japan, was chosen as the target for the atomic bomb attack of August 9, 1945.

## Calendar
**Apr.–May (weekends): Kite Flying.** Inasayama. A long tradition. Kite designs were borrowed from Chinese kites and old European nautical banners. The string is coated with glass, and rivals attempt to cut one another down.
**July (3rd Su): ＊ Pēron Boat Races.** Togitsu (*0:35h by bus from Nagasaki*). Said to be more authentic than the famous Nagasaki Pēron.
**July (4th Su): ＊ Pēron Boat Races.** A custom of Chinese origin. Dragon boats from each city ward race between Dejima pier and Matsugaebashi. Spectator boats ply the harbor.
**L 7/26–28: ＊ Ura Bon.** Chinese-style observances at Sōfuku-ji.
**Aug. 9: Peace Memorial Services.** Peace Park.
**Aug. 13–15: ＊ Urabon-e.** Chinese-flavored Bon observances. Lantern-floating on the 15th.
**Oct. 7–9: ＊＊＊ Okunchi.** See Calendar, p. 469. The best viewing may be at Yasaka Jinja (Oct. 7, 10:00–13:00). On the 7th festivities go on all day and into the evening. Activities on the 8th are sparse (early a.m. only), and on the 9th, end by noon. Performances at Suwa Jinja are closed to tourists.
**Oct. 14–15: Takengei.** Autumn festival of Wakamiya Inari Jinja. Two youths dressed as male and female foxes perform stunts atop 10-m bamboo poles.

## Getting Around
Nagasaki has a convenient streetcar system serving all the main sights. All rides are Y100, and a one-day pass costs Y500. Hired taxes are about Y8960 for 3 hours.

---

# Nagasaki History: The Christian Century

| | |
|---|---|
| **Francis Xavier** | (1506–1552) An important Jesuit who introduced Christianity to Japan. The charismatic priest gained several converts among the Japanese, whom he regarded as the "best race yet discovered." |
| **Amakusa Shirō** | (1622–1638) The tragic young hero of the Shimabara Rebellion, who died with 40,000 peasants and samurai in the abortive uprising. His fight against repressive authority and grinding poverty made him a popular postwar hero. |

Japan's Christian Century began around 1542, when Portuguese sailors were blown ashore at Tanegashima, and ended in 1639, when 40,000 peasants, led by Japanese Christians, were massacred in the Shimabara Rebellion. It was in this period, the most eventful in the history of premodern Japan, that the town of Nagasaki came into being, and that its role as Japan's window on the West was decided.

**Francis Xavier**, a founding member of the Society of Jesus, was a zealous evangelist intent on spreading Christianity to Asia. In 1549, he arrived in Kagoshima, the first missionary to set foot in Japan. Xavier was welcomed there and at Yamaguchi (Chūgoku, p. 457), a thriving city of 400,000, where the rulers listened politely to the teachings of this "new sect of Buddhism"—a natural confusion, for Xavier had arrived from India. Because, as another missionary put it, "everything depends on the rulers," Xavier concentrated on gaining converts among the noble and the powerful, calculating that commoners would follow their example. From Yamaguchi he proceeded to Kyoto, where he sought to convert "Japan's King." Kyoto was in such disorder, however, that he could find neither emperor nor shogun, much less gain an audience with either. After some weeks, he returned in disgust to Yamaguchi.

In spite of all the misunderstanding and confusion with which Xavier's message was greeted, Christianity couldn't have arrived in Japan at a better time. The Japanese, their civilization disrupted by seventy years of civil war and anarchy, yearned for something new. The warlords were especially eager for any innovation that could give them an advantage over their rivals. By the time Xavier arrived, the Portuguese arquebuses introduced at Tanegashima seven years earlier had been successfully copied and were being made all over Japan. Firearms forced the development of the great castles, and made possible the reunification of Japan, bringing a century of warfare to a close (see Castles, p. 45).

Xavier died soon after he departed Japan for China in 1551, but the Portuguese followers he left behind had gained six converts among the daimyo by 1579. First to convert, in 1563, was a minor daimyo in northwest Kyūshū, **Ōmura Sumitada**, who thereby reaped a large financial reward: A share of the trade from the Portuguese ships, which anchored at Nagasaki, the new port he established with Portuguese help in 1571. Though blessed with a fine natural harbor, Nagasaki lies on a remote peninsula, hemmed in by mountains. Its inaccessibility made it less than ideal for domestic trade, but the Portuguese were more interested in the fact that it was easy to defend. Indeed, in 1579, Ōmura had to fight off neighboring warlords who coveted Nagasaki's profits. Afterward, he handed over part of the municipal administration to the Jesuits, reckoning they would help defend the city if they had a stake in it.

Nagasaki quickly grew into an exciting—and profitable—carnival of East-meets-West. The Portuguese were called **nambanjin** (southern barbarians), and as uncomplimentary as this name may sound, a feverish enthusiasm grew up in Japan for *namban* things and their *namban* names: tobacco (*tabako*), card games (*karuta*), bread (*pan*), and *tempura*, that quintessentially Japanese dish of deep-fried fish, said to have been named for the Portuguese word for cooking (*tempero*) or temple (*templo*). Nagasaki's *kasutera* (Castilla) spongecake is still one of its famous specialties. The Jesuits introduced the first movable metal-type printing press, which they used to print Bibles and *Aesop's Fables*. Although *namban* bathing habits, or the lack of them, were a subject of criticism, *namban* dress became a fad. Genre screens depicted a Nagasaki populated by Portuguese and Japanese dressed up in high ruff collars, capes, and voluminous pantaloons. The screens also show the bay filled with *namban* ships. The Portuguese in fact traded not in Western goods, but in Chinese silk and Japanese silver, which was immensely profitable because Ming China and Japan had broken off official trade relations.

The Jesuits, meanwhile, obtained several audiences with Japan's most powerful lord, ODA NOBUNAGA, and in 1576 even established a church in Kyoto, which was commonly known as the "namban temple." Nobunaga, in his quest to unite Japan, had fought the Tendai warrior monks and militant Ikkō sect, and he now welcomed the Christians in order to check the power of the monks. Nobunaga himself had no interest in converting, but many powerful lords and fashionable members of Kyoto artistic circles became Christians. Several of tea master SEN NO RIKYŪ's disciples, including Furuta Oribe, were Christians. (It is said that certain aspects of the tea ceremony were borrowed from the Catholic sacrament.) **Hosokawa Gracia** (the inspiration for Mariko in *Shogun*), the wife of a powerful daimyo, may be the most romanticized upper-class Christian because of her tragic death (see Castles, p. 49). In 1582, Ōmura Sumitada and two other Christian daimyo sent a mission of young Japanese Christians to Rome, where they were received by the pope and made a very favorable impression.

By the time this delegation returned home in 1590, however, the position of Christianity in Japan had changed drastically. Three years earlier, HIDEYOSHI, who had reunified the country and become de facto ruler, had become alarmed at the extent of Jesuit influence over the Christian daimyo in Kyūshū and had ordered the missionaries expelled. (Hideyoshi was not indisposed toward Christianity in principle; it was even said that he might have converted had the religion not prohibited polygamy.) Nagasaki was taken out of Jesuit hands and became an imperial city under the direct rule of Kyoto. But the first anti-Christian edict was not seriously

483

enforced. Portuguese traders were still welcome, and Nagasaki continued to prosper.

The fortunes of both traders and Christians, while outwardly expanding, were, however, in danger. Increasingly severe persecutions alternated with unofficial tolerance. In 1596, a Spanish galleon that was shipwrecked in Shikoku had its cargo impounded. The captain tried to get it back by threats; he boasted that with a fifth column of Christian converts — an astounding 400,000 by 1605 — Spain could easily invade Japan. Hideyoshi heard of this and was not amused. **The Twenty-six Martyrs**, mostly Spanish Franciscans and Japanese laymen who were on the ship, were taken from Shikoku, paraded through Ōsaka, Sakai, and Kyoto, and then to Nagasaki's Nishizaka Hill, where they were crucified.

**Will Adams**, the British navigator, arrived in 1600 on a Dutch ship, and through his special relationship with TOKUGAWA IEYASU, the Dutch started trading at **Hirado**, north of Nagasaki, in 1609. The British trade began in 1613. The Japanese soon perceived that these "red hairs" disliked the Catholics and were more interested in trade than in religion. In 1614, Christianity was banned and all missionaries — except about forty who went into hiding — were deported, along with Christian daimyo who refused to apostatize. Soon, the Christians of Nagasaki and neighboring provinces, even children, were being burned in straw raincoats, branded on the genitals, forced to rape their mothers, boiled in the "hells" of **Unzen**, and compelled to undergo many other tortures the authorities devised to make them recant their faith. From 1629, suspected Christians were forced to step on *fumi-e* (treading pictures) of the Virgin Mary and Infant Jesus.

The shogunate became obsessed with controlling foreign influence, and trade with the outside world suffered. By 1641, the Spanish and Portuguese had been excluded, and all Japanese wives and mixed-blood children of foreigners were deported. Japanese living abroad were forbidden to return. The only Europeans allowed in Japan were the Dutch, who were restricted to a tiny artificial island in Nagasaki harbor called **Dejima**, a state of affairs that would last until 1855.

The event that precipitated Japan's 220 years of seclusion was the **Shimabara Rebellion** (1637–1638), an uprising by impoverished Christians and peasants in Shimabara and the Amakusa Islands south of Nagasaki. When the persecutions started, the devout from the Christian provinces of Kyūshū, including many samurai, fled to the most remote, outlying districts around Nagasaki, where Christian settlements already existed. Here they lived in poverty, but they could at least practice their religion in relative safety. Amakusa was always an impoverished district, notorious in the Meiji period for the coal ships that carried its young girls to brothels in China and Southeast Asia. It was because of this desperate poverty, as well as the persecution of Christianity, that the rebellion erupted in 1637. A Shimabara man, forced to watch his Christian daughter being tortured by a local official, became enraged and murdered the man, sparking an uprising that quickly escalated. Some 40,000 rebels, led by the valiant Christian youth **Amakusa Shirō**, occupied Hara-jō and won a succession of stunning victories against local daimyo armies. Alarmed, the shogunate sent a force of 120,000 to besiege the castle. The Dutch, in a test of loyalty, were ordered to bombard the Christian fortress. After eighty days, the defenders set fire to the castle, and virtually all of them perished in the flames.

The Shimabara Rebellion sounded the death knell of Japan's Christian Century, but **Kakure Kirishitan** (crypto-Christians) continued to practice in secret, in spite of periodic inquisitions and government rewards for their arrest. These families kept crosses hidden in their homes, along with portraits of Mary and Jesus disguised as Kannon and Jizō Basatsu. In the 1850s, when Japan emerged from two centuries of seclusion, thousands of crypto-Christians were discovered in Hirado, Gotō, Shimabara, Amakusa, and Urakami (on the fringe of Nagasaki, at the epicenter of the A-bomb). They still preserved garbled, uncomprehended fragments of the Latin Mass. Tragically, many of these people were arrested and sent to other parts of Japan until the anti-Christian laws were repealed in 1872.

Throughout the Edo period, Nagasaki, even without its Christians, remained an exotic city. In 1638, Nagasaki's Shinto guardian, Suwa Jinja, began its **Okunchi** festival, to which the Nagasaki Chinese contributed the famous dragon dance. The Chinese also built Chinese-style Ōbaku Zen temples, **Kōfuku-ji** and **Sōfuku-ji** (see Buddhism, p. 40). Nagasaki's *shippoku-ryōri* is a hybrid of Japanese and Chinese cuisines. Although contact with the Dutch on Dejima was restricted, in 1720, Shogun Tokugawa Yoshimune lifted the ban on Dutch books, and Japanese flocked to Nagasaki to study European arts and sciences, including medicine, military science, and the manufacture of armaments. Vanishing-point perspective entered Japanese art. Kyūshū specialties such as Satsuma cut glass and distilled *shōchū* liquor developed because of the Dutch presence.

In 1859, Nagasaki once again became an open port. Today, Nagasaki preserves its unique blend of native, Chinese, and European influences, against as stunning a natural backdrop as any city in Japan.

### Near the Station

**Twenty-six Martyrs Memorial (Nijūroku Seijin Junkyōchi)** 二十六聖人殉教地
*0:05h on foot from station.* This memorial wall, erected in 1962, depicts the 6 Spanish friars and 20 Japanese Christians who were crucified here in 1597. Among them were two young boys, 13-year-old Antonio, son of a Nagasaki Chinese, and 12-year-old Ibaraki Luis, who might have been spared had he renounced his faith. Instead, he chose to die on the cross, crying out "Jesus" and "Mary." The 26 were canonized in 1862.

**Suwa Jinja** 諏訪神社 *0:06h by tram from the station to Suwa Jinja-mae.* This shrine was established around 1555 as the guardian shrine for the fledgling city. From around 1624, local authorities strongly supported temples and shrines to counter the influence of Christianity, and in 1638 Suwa Jinja began its Okunchi festival, which has become Nagasaki's greatest annual event.

### Teramachi and Stone Bridges

Nagasaki's temple street is one of the best places for a stroll. The street parallels Nakajimagawa, a picturesque stream spanned by many arched stone bridges, each of which marked an approach to a temple in Teramachi.

** **Meganebashi** 眼鏡橋 (ICP). Spectacles Bridge, a double-arch which, reflected in the water, suggests a pair of spectacles. It was built in 1634 by the second abbot of Kōfuku-ji; the Chinese-style bridge introduced the stone arch into Japan.

*** **Kōfuku-ji** 興福寺 Hrs: 8:00–17:00. This lovely temple, with its lawns and cycad palms, was founded in 1620 by the Chinese of Nagasaki. It is the oldest Ōbaku Zen temple in Japan. Before it could be built, the Japanese conducted a thorough check to ascertain that it wasn't really a Christian institution in disguise. Ōbaku Zen became the last Buddhist sect to enter Japan, and in 1654 the shogunate invited Ingen, an eminent Chinese priest, to found the sect's headquarters at Mampuku-ji, near Kyoto (see Kinki, p. 389). The main hall, Daiyūhō-den (ICP), was rebuilt in 1893 by carpenters from southern China. It contains an image of Shaka. The Kyū Tōjin-Yashiki Mon (ICP), a simple, solid gate standing to the west, was once one of the gates to Nagasaki's Chinatown. Near it is the Sankō Kaijo no Mon, a gate used for a Chinese meeting hall. A gate and hall from the Nagasaki Confucian temple were also moved here after the rest of it was destroyed in a fire in 1959. The roof tiles on the belfry show a parade of demons facing out, and Daikoku, a god of fortune, facing in. Kōfuku-ji was patronized by Nanjing Chinese, which soon prompted Chinese residents from other provinces to support temples of their own.

*** **Sōfuku-ji** 崇福寺 Hrs: 8:00–17:00. This Ōbaku Zen sect temple was founded in 1629 by a priest from Fukien at the request of the Fukien Chinese in Nagasaki. Built by Chinese carpenters, it reflects the temple architecture of southern China in the late Ming dynasty. The San-mon (1849, ICP) is an exotic Dragon Palace gate. At the top of the stairs is the Dai-Ippō-mon (NT), which was built in China in 1694 and reassembled in Japan. The main hall, Daiyūhō-den (1646, NT) houses a Chinese-style Shaka trinity with 18 disciples. To the right, in front, is a giant cauldron in which Sōfuku-ji's abbot boiled porridge for 3,000 famine victims in 1682. The Maso-dō, a Chinese shrine to the sea goddess, stands in the rear right corner of the compound.

### Maruyama 丸山

The Shianbashi streetcar stop is near the site of **Shianbashi**, the "should I or shouldn't I?" bridge that once marked the entrance to the **Maruyama pleasure quarter**. Along with Edo's Yoshiwara and Kyoto's Shimabara, this was one of Tokugawa Japan's licensed quarters. Maruyama was created in 1642, and by 1681 it had 766 women, including many courtesans of great artistic ability. They were among the few Japanese permitted to visit the Dutch and Chinese settlements, and not a few became involved in highly lucrative smuggling. Toward Maruyama Kōen (park) is **Fukusaya**, an old-fashioned *kasutera* cake shop. The road continues past the park and ends at the gates of **Kagetsu**, a former top-class brothel famous for having entertained such figures as Sakamoto Ryōma and Takasugi Shinsaku, two samurai who were in the vanguard of the Meiji Restoration. They and other political reformers journeyed to Nagasaki to learn Western technology and purchase guns. Kagetsu is now a *shippoku* restaurant and is not open to casual visitors.

### The Old Foreign Settlements

* **Site of Old Chinese Settlement (Tōjin Yashiki Ato)** 唐人屋敷跡 In 1689, the shogunate ordered all Chinese living in Nagasaki and nearby regions to move to a walled compound in the southeast corner of the city. Though their movements were, in theory, as restricted as those of the Dutch on Dejima, the Chinese were in fact able to come and go with some freedom, visiting their temples and stopping at teahouses on the way. Today, only two wooden halls, Tengo-dō and Kannon-dō, remain from the Chinese compound. The neighborhood, with its winding, narrow streets and pungent marketplace, is evocative.

**Shinchimachi**, full of Chinese restaurants and replete with Chinatown atmosphere, was a landfill area built for Chinese warehouses after a fire in 1698 destroyed an older warehouse district. The Chinese community's festivals, music, and dances were practiced freely, with lasting impact on Nagasaki culture. Nagasaki today has 700 Chinese residents, among which 80 families have been here since before the war.

* **Dejima Shiryōkan** 出島資料館 (21-5117). Hrs: 9:00–17:00; clsd M, NY. This museum, housed in a Western-style clubhouse built for the Meiji-period Western community, exhibits

485

relics of the Dutch in Nagasaki. The yard contains a 1/15 scale model of Dejima, where the Dutch lived. The museum stands close to the site of Dejima, which is no longer an island. (A city plan to restore Dejima is currently hampered by local landowners.)

**Oranda-zaka.** Stone-paved "Holland Hill" retains a few weathered clapboard houses occupied by Westerners in the late 19th C.

**\*\* Kōshi-byō/Chūgoku Rekidai Hakubutsukan (Confucian Temple/Chinese History Museum)** 孔子廟　中国歴代博物館 Hrs: 8:30–17:00. This gaudy, yellow-tile-roofed Confucian temple was founded in 1893. It includes a handsome new \* **museum**, which exhibits objects on loan from the Chinese National History Museum in Beijing; well worth seeing.

**Rekishi Minzoku Shiryōkan (Historical Museum)** 歴史民俗資料館 Hrs: 9:00–17:00; clsd M. The former Hong Kong-Shanghai Bank, now housing local historical relics, including a room devoted to the early telegraph lines. In 1871, a cable was laid between Shanghai and Nagasaki, which was thereby electronically linked to London, but until the connection to Yokohama and Tokyo was completed two years later, telegrams had to be forward by footrunners.

**\* Ōura Tenshu-dō (Church)** 大浦天主堂 (NT). Hrs: 8:00–18:00. Dec.–Feb. 8:30–17:00. Admission charged. This church was completed in February 1864 to serve foreigners in Nagasaki. A month later, a dozen Japanese from Urakami visited the church and expressed a desire to look inside. To the astonishment of its French priest, Bernard Petitjean, they revealed themselves to be Christians, members of a group who had practiced their faith secretly and at great peril for nearly 250 years. Christianity was still outlawed for Japanese, and when the authorities got wind of this, they rounded up some 3,000 crypto-Christians in Urakami and exiled them to remote parts of Japan. Hundreds perished of exposure and torture by 1872, when the anti-Christian law was repealed.

**\*\* Grabā-en (Glover Park)** グラバー園 Hrs: 8:00–18:00 (enter by 17:40). Dec.–Feb. 8:30–17:00 (enter by 16:40). An open-air museum of Western residences in Meiji-period Nagasaki. The **Glover House** (ICP) was built in 1863 by Thomas Glover (1838–1911), a Scotsman who supplied the Chōshū army in western Japan with arms, enabling them to topple the Tokugawa shogunate (see Hagi History, p. 460). He also helped smuggle Itō Hirobumi and Inoue Kaoru to England, built Japan's first railroad, and helped construct its first steamship. Glover married a Maruyama geisha; such romances in the Nagasaki foreign community pro-

486

vided the inspiration for Madame Butterfly—an entirely fictitious figure. A true tragedy was the case of Glover's son, who during World War II was unjustly accused of spying by the Japanese military and committed suicide. Other fine houses in the park are the **Alt House** and the **Ringer House** (ICP). The houses, built by Japanese workmen from Japanese lumber and roof tiles, are ever so slightly exotic. The grounds are beautifully maintained, but the hillside escalators give them an unfortunate amusement-park veneer. On the way out is the **Kunchi Shiryōkan**, which exhibits floats, dragons, and videos from the Okunchi festival.

## Northern Nagasaki

The Nagasaki bomb, which detonated at 11:02 a.m. on August 9, 1945, was a plutonium bomb with three times the explosive power of the Hiroshima bomb. The bomb fell short of its intended target, the Mitsubishi Shipyards, and instead exploded over Urakami, the village of the crypto-Christians (see Ōura Tenshu-dō, preceding page). Nearly 150,000 people, out of Nagasaki's population of 210,000, died of the blast and its aftereffects.

**\*\* Heiwa Kōen (Peace Park)** 平和公園   *0:10h by streetcar from the station to Matsuyama-chō, then 0:05h on foot.* Walk through **Chūshinchi Kōen**, where a black stone column marks the epicenter. The park has been planted with 500 cherry strees, on ground that people feared would remain barren for decades. The **Kokusai Bunka Kaikan** (International Culture Hall) 国際文化会館  houses records and relics of the attack on floors 2–4 (Hrs: 9:00–18:00, Dec.–Feb. 9:00–17:00; clsd NY).

**Urakami Tenshu-dō** 浦上天主堂  This church was erected for the Urakami Christians. It took nearly 33 years to build, and was completed in 1925. The church was destroyed by the atomic bomb, which also claimed 8,500 parishioners. It was rebuilt in 1958. Headless stone statues of saints, scorched by the atomic fire, stand along the path to the church.

**Nyoko-dō/Nagai Kinenkan** 如己堂  The two-mat hut of Nagai Takashi, a hero of the atom bomb attack. Dr. Nagai, an assistant professor at the Nagasaki University of Medicine, lost his wife and was himself seriously injured, but he devoted himself to treating victims until his own death in 1951, caused by the aftereffects of the explosion. He kept a detailed record of his patients' stories of the attack; it was discovered by accident in 1970.

487

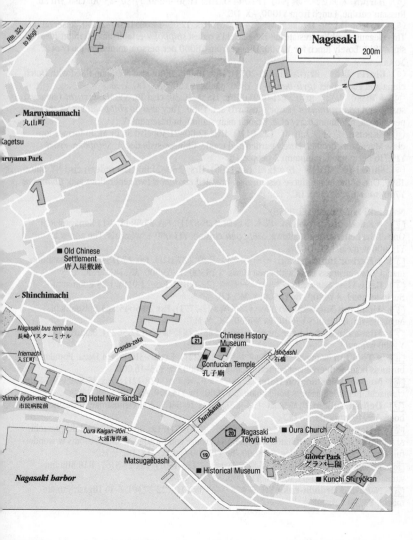

## Views of Nagasaki

**Inasayama** 稲佐山 *0:10h by bus from the station, then 0:05h by tramway*. This mountaintop park offers a splendid view over Nagasaki. At the foot is the **Inasa Kokusai Bochi**, one of two foreigners' cemeteries in Nagasaki.

**Port Cruise** 長崎港めぐり From Ōhato terminal, 0:50h sightseeing cruises at 10:15, 11:40, and 15:10, and in August, at night. In winter, at 11:40 only.

## Nagasaki Shopping

Koga-ningyō, clay dolls depicting exotic foreigners—Chinese and Europeans—are a folk toy of Nagasaki. *Kasutera* is a type of spongecake introduced by the Portuguese. *Bekko*, or tortoise shell, a famous Nagasaki product, is made from sea turtles (we advise you not to buy, since some of it comes from endangered species). Shopping areas: **Hamanomachi Arcade**, starting at Kuroganebashi contains Nagasaki's main fish market. **Kajiyamachi**, leading to Teramachi, has numerous temple-accessory shops, restaurants, and craft shops.

[11] **Kawabe-dō** 河辺堂　油屋町 (22-3863). Hrs: 10:00–20:00; clsd 1st and 3rd Th, NY. A selection of local folk crafts.

[12] **Morimoto Hataten** 森本ハタ店　鍛治屋町 (22-6781). Hrs: 6:00–20:30, daily. Maker of Nagasaki kites patterned on European nautical flags.

[13] **✳ Fukusaya** 福砂屋 (21-2938). Hrs: 8:30–20:00; clsd 2nd Th, NY. Famous *kasutera* shop; claims it got its recipe directly from the Portuguese, 15 generations ago.

## Nagasaki Dining

*Shippoku-ryōri* is a Japanized version of Chinese cuisine, with a few dishes of allegedly Portuguese origin mixed in. Appetizers are laid out on a *shippoku*, a low, round red table. The banquet begins with *ozōni*, a soup with ricecakes, after which guests drink saké and partake of the various dishes (usually requires 4 or more diners). *Champon*, like chop suey, is a Chinese-inspired noodle dish doused in fish, clams, vegetables, and egg. *Sara-udon* is a drier version. Cheap, filling, and ubiquitous.

① **Sakamotoya** 坂本屋 (26-8211). Hrs: 11:30–14:00, 17:30–19:00, daily. This ryokan serves *shippoku*; minimum party of 2. Lunch Y3000, dinner Y6000. AX, DC.

⑥ **Harbin** ハルビン　興善町 (22-7443). Hrs: 11:30–14:30, 17:30–23:00; clsd 3rd Su. Russian cuisine. Lunch from Y1000. AX, DC.

⑧ **✳✳ Ichiriki** 一力　諏訪町 (24-0226). Hrs: 12:00–14:00, 17:00–22:00. Reservation. This elegant, rambling restaurant is Nagasaki's oldest *shippoku* establishment, in business since 1813. Lovely lunch for Y2500. Dinner from Y8000 per person, minimum party of 2. No CC.

⑨ **Ginrei** 銀嶺　鍛治屋町 (21-2073). Hrs: 10:00–21:00; clsd NY. Shop filled with Dutch china and glass. Beef (*gyū-bentō*) is Y800, paella is Y600. AX, DC, V, MC.

⑩ **✳ Yossō** 吉宗　浜町 (21-0001). Hrs: 11:00–20:30; clsd Tu, NY. *Mushizushi* (steamed sushi) and *chawanmushi* (savory custard) set, Y980. They also do *shippoku* for Y4–6000 per person, minimum party of 2. Branch near station, in basement. V.

⑭ **Kagetsu** 花月　丸山町 (22-0191). Hrs: 12:00–21:30; clsd Su or M. In former top-class Maruyama brothel. Lovely garden and exotic, Chinese-style decor. *Shippoku-ryōri* Y19,716 per person, minimum 2 people. DC.

⑲ **Shikai-rō** 四海楼　松ヶ枝町 (22-1296). Hrs: 9:30–21:00 (last order); clsd NY. Since 1899. One of the best Chinese restaurants. Invented *champon* two generations ago. *Champon* Y700, *sara-udon* Y600. DC.

## Nagasaki Lodgings (TEL 0958)

[2] **✳ Sakamotoya Ryokan** 坂本屋旅館 (26-8211). Fax 25-5944. 2-13 Kanayamachi. One of the better ryokan in town. *Shippoku* cuisine. Y13,000+ w/meals. The annex is Y13,000 w/meals. AX, DC, MC.

[3] **✳ Harbor Inn Nagasaki** ハーバーイン長崎 (27-1111). Fax 27-1154. 8-17 Kabashimamachi. Cozy business hotel with great views. S Y5500, Tw Y9500. AX, DC, V, MC.

[4] **Belle View Nagasaki** ベルビュー長崎 (22-0019). Fax 22-0116. 1-25 Edomachi. Business hotel. S Y4800, Tw Y8500. V, MC, CB.

[5] **Ajisai Inn Nagasaki** あじさいイン長崎 (22-7771). Fax 20-5645. 4-1 Ebisumachi, Nagasaki-shi. Central. S Y5000, Tw Y9000. DC, V, MC.

[7] **Minshuku Siebold-tei** 民宿シーボルト邸　桜馬場町 (22-5623). Sakurababa. Y4900 w/meals.

[15] **✳ Tōei Inn Nagasaki** 東映イン長崎 (22-2121). Fax 26-3105. 7-24 Doza. Popular business hotel with excellent central location. S Y7000, Tw Y13–16,000.

[16] **Nagasaki Washington Hotel** 長崎ワシントンホテル (28-1211). Fax 25-8023. 9-1 Shinchimachi. Reliable business hotel chain. S Y7500, Tw Y15,000. AX, DC, V, MC.

[17] **Dejima Kaikan** 出島会館 (24-4702). Fax 26-5465. 2-11 Dejimamachi. Business-type hotel. Y5940 w/meals. No CC.

[18] **✳ Hotel New Tanda** ホテルニュータンダ (27-6121). Fax 26-1704. 2-24 Tokiwamachi. At foot of Oranda-zaka. Affiliated with the ANA group; comfortable, if small, rooms w/wonderful harbor views, good service. S Y8000, Tw Y15,800 (w/tax). AX, DC, V, MC.

[20] **✳ Nagasaki Tōkyū Hotel** 長崎東急ホテル (25-1501). Fax 23-5167. 1-18 Minamiyamatemachi. S Y9800–11,500, Tw Y16,000. AX, DC, V, MC.

[21] **Nagasaki Oranda-zaka YH** 長崎オランダ坂YH (22-2730). 6-14 Higashiyamatemachi. Y3200 w/meals.

## W2 * SHIMABARA PENINSULA  島原半島

*2:10h by express bus from Nagasaki via JR Isahaya station to Unzen. From Unzen it is 1:00h further to Shimabara. Additional buses from Isahaya serve the same scenic route.*
This peninsula, dominated by the steaming volcano **Unzen**, became the scene of terrible persecutions of Japanese Christians in the early 17th century, which culminated in the Shimabara Rebellion in 1637 (see Nagasaki History, p. 483). Today the area is dotted with little chapels—and chapel-shaped drive-ins—commemorating this history.
**Note: In 1991, the volcano Unzen erupted violently, forcing evacuation of surrounding areas. Mudslides and lava have caused heavy destruction as far away as Shimabara. At the time of this revision, this area is not recommended for visitors.**
** **Unzen Onsen** 雲仙温泉 *2:10h by express bus from Nagasaki.* Unzen Onsen is a village of hot-spring hotels which was developed in the late 19th C as a hill station for China traders. Get off at Shinyu to pick up information at the Visitor Center and walk among the boiling ''hells'' where 17th-C Japanese Christians who refused to apostatize were scalded to death. Lush vegetation and twisted pines growing about the steaming vents and mud pots give it a gardenlike atmosphere; the boiling pools themselves, in spite of their macabre history, are not that awesome.
**Hiking:** From behind the Fukiya Hotel a 2-km trail leads to Ikenohara meadow and Unzen Golf Course, the oldest public golf links in the country. Nestled in a green vale against the towering bulk of Unzen, it is also the prettiest spot in the park. The trail continues to Nita Tōge and Myōken-dake; it is perhaps easier to find the trail walking down from Nita Tōge.
* **Nita Tōge (Pass)** 仁田峠 *0:20h by bus from Unzen Bus Terminal.* Views of the Shimabara coastline and Amakusa Islands. There's a tramway and trail up **Myōken-dake**, a volcanic crag with azalea-covered slopes. From there it's a 1:00h climb to **Fugen-dake**, or a 4:00h loop including Fugen shrine.
**Shimabara** 島原 *0:40h from Unzen Onsen, or 1:10h by train from Isahaya. Ferry from Ōmuta and Misumi. The bus terminal is by the pier. Pick up maps and information inside.* While Shimabara is associated with a fascinating chapter of Japanese history, there are only a few things to see. **Shimabara-jō** (*0:15h by bus from pier, get off at Ōte*), has a rebuilt keep housing a collection of Christian relics, many excavated from the castle area, including some crypto-Christian Maria-Kannon images. 0:05h on foot NW of the castle park is a *buke-yashiki* (samurai house) of the mildest interest. It adjoins a street lined with old stone walls and open canals, giving a faint impression of former days.
**Hara-jō** 原城 *0:45h by bus from Shimabara pier.* In 1637, 37,000 rebel Christians— warriors, peasants, women, and children—took refuge in Hara-jō, abandoned some years earlier when its lord moved to Shimabara. Under the inspired leadership of a 14-year-old youth, Amakusa Shirō, they held out for 80 days against a shogunate army of 120,000 before falling on February 28, 1638. This event prompted the shogunate to expel all missionaries, conduct a brutal purge of Japanese Christians, and close off Japan for the next 220 years. Hara-jō is now a grass-covered ruin.

489

**Unzen Lodgings** (TEL 0957)
Address: Unzen, Obama-chō, Minamitakaki-gun, Nagasaki-ken.
** **Unzen Kankō Hotel** 雲仙観光ホテル (73-3236). A survivor of Unzen's hill station days. Plenty of character and high standards of comfort and service. S Y6–15,000, Tw Y10–18,000. Japanese rooms (very nice) are Y12,000 per person w/meals. AX, DC, V, MC.
* **Kyūshū Hotel** 九州ホテル (73-3234). A large, modern, and comfortable tourist ryokan, looking onto the hells. Y16–20,000 w/meals. AX, DC, V, MC.
* **Hotel Tōyōkan** ホテル東洋館 (73-3243). Deluxe modern ryokan. Y13–18,000 w/meals.
**Kaseya** かせや旅館 (73-3321). Small, simple ryokan. Y7–8000 w/meals. No CC.

**Exploring Amakusa**
# *The suggested way to see the west coast of Amakusa is to take the ferry (1:20h) from Mogi, 0:15h by taxi from Nagasaki. A 4-day Amakusa bus pass from Kumamoto is Y3700.*
Amakusa, a stronghold of early Japanese Christians, was and still is one of the poorest parts of Japan. Until the 1920s, local families regularly sold their daughters to coal ships, which crowded them into stinking holds and carried them to brothels in Southeast Asia. Comprised of two main islands, it is the west coast, facing the China Sea, that remains most beautiful and forlorn. From Mogi, ferries cross to **Tomioka**, which has a castle ruin and tiny local museum with Maria-Kannon images and a photo of a slave buyer. **Takahama** has a high-grade kaolin quarry by an old headman's house, where villagers were once required to gather to trample on Christian images. **Myōken-ura** has spectacular sea cliffs and a swimming beach. At **Ōe**, a crypto-Christian village, there's a tatami-floored chapel built in 1933 by a French priest. The picturesque fishing village **Sakitsu** has another chapel and the **Ryokan Minatoya** (09697-9-0380) across the bay (Y6000 w/meals). **Hondo**, the main town, has the **Kirishitan-kan** (Hrs: 8:30–17:00), a museum of Christian relics, including Amakusa Shirō's famous war banner (ICP).

**Easy Access To:**
**Ōmuta:** *0:50h by high-speed boat from Shimabara. Here, switch to the JR Kagoshima line to Kumamoto (KYŪSHŪ V) or Hakata (KYŪSHŪ II), or to the private Nishitetsu line to Yanagawa (KYŪSHŪ IV:W1).*
**Misumi:** *1:00h by ferry or 1:30h by sightseeing boat from Shimabara via the Amakusa Five Bridges. From Misumi, there are direct trains to Kumamoto (KYŪSHŪ V).*

# KYŪSHŪ IV. KURUME

**Tokyo to Kurume:** *6:40h by Shinkansen Hikari express to Hakata, then 0:30–0:40h by JR express from Hakata station. Or 0:30h from Nishitetsu-Fukuoka station by Nishitetsu limited express.*
**Prefectures:** Fukuoka, Ōita

## KURUME 久留米
This town is of interest for students of folk crafts. In addition, the **Ishibashi Bunka Center**, built by the Bridgestone Tire Company, has an art museum, affiliated with the Bridgestone Museum in Tokyo, and a Japanese garden (*0:05h by bus from Nishitetsu-Kurume station.* Hrs: 10:00–17:00; clsd M, NY). 0:05h on foot from the JR station are the lovely grounds of **Bairin-ji**, the funerary temple of Kurume's daimyo. Nearby, on the riverbank, is the **Suiten-gū**, head of the many Suiten-gū shrines all over Japan dedicated to the child-emperor Antoku (see Miyajima History, p. 449).

### Calendar
**Jan. 7: ✳ Oniyo.** At Tamatare-gū Shrine (*take Nishitetsu from Kurume to Daizen-ji*). Six 12-meter torches are set ablaze to burn away bad luck.
**May 5–7: Suiten-gū Spring Festival.** Suiten-gū.
**Sept. (late): ✳ Yame Tōrō Ningyō.** Yame village, Miyanochō Hachiman-gū. Puppet plays on a bright, lantern-festooned float-stage. Begun in 1744.

### Getting Around
The JR and Nishitetsu stations are 0:10h apart by bus. Many artisans work in Hirokawa and Yame, 0:40h by Nishitetsu buses 30, 31, 32. The Annaijo at the JR station has a bilingual map.

490 **Kurume Crafts**
Call the workshops in advance of your visit.
**✳✳ Moriyama Kasuri Kōba** 森山かすり工房 広川町新代 (09433-2-0023). Hrs: 9:00–11:30, 13:00–16:00; clsd Su, NH. *0:05h on foot from Kawase bus stop, in Hirokawa.* Kurume-gasuri, the most famous of the many *kasuri* textiles in Japan, is perhaps the only one credited to a historical figure, a farm girl named Inoue Den, who was born in 1788. According-ing to a story familiar to any Japanese child, Den noticed some worn spots on a piece of indigo cloth and thought to imitate them by tie-dyeing the threads before weaving the cloth. The truth of this story can be doubted, since *kasuri* has been imported from Okinawa since the 16th C, but every Japanese "invention" has to have its Japanese inventor. The result of her weaving, at any rate, was successful; it resembled large splashes of frost on the blue. This classic pattern has since diverged into pictorial and colored patterns as well. Moriyama Torao, a Living National Treasure, goes by the tradition handed down over four generations. At his workshop, threads are hand-tied, dyed in genuine indigo, and handwoven (see Crafts, p. 105). A bolt runs around Y150,000. Mr. Moriyama says the best way to prevent fading is to soak it in soy milk.
**✳ Yamaguchi Seishijo** 山口製紙所 宮野288-1 (09432-4-5539). Hrs: 8:00–12:00, 13:00–17:00; clsd Su, NY. *0:20h on foot from Yame Eigyōjo bus stop.* Papermaking was introduced to this village in the late 16th C by a priest from Gokayama (Chūbu, p. 297). This workshop, a small, family-run affair, still uses enormous, wood-fired cauldrons to boil the mulberry fibers (see Crafts, p. 107).
**✳ Inoue Rantai Shikki** 井上藍胎漆器 小頭町6-23 (39-5454). Hrs: 8:00–17:00; clsd Su. In front of Honmachi Yon-chōme bus stop, in central Kurume. *Rantai-shikki* is made by coating a bamboo basket-weave with layers of contrasting colored lacquer—dark amber over yellow, black, and red—and then polishing it to bring out the texture of the bamboo weave. Items are handsome, functional, and reasonably priced.
**Giemon** 儀右ヱ門館 日吉町12-12 (33-7233). Hrs: 8:30–17:30; clsd Su, NH, NY. *0:05h walk from Mutsumon bus stop, in central Kurume.* Kurume-gasuri fashions.

### Kurume Dining and Lodgings (TEL 0942)
**✳✳ Tanaka Unagiya** 田中うなぎ屋 国鉄駅前通 (34-3000). Hrs: 11:30–19:30; clsd Su, NY. *0:03h on foot from JR Kurume station.* An atmospheric old shop said to have been patronized by the daimyo. Succulent *unagi no seiro-mushi* (broiled eel steamed on a bed of rice) from Y1600. No CC.
**✳ Gojō Ryokan** 五条旅館 (32-2205). 2-25 Nishitetsu Ekimae, Tōrihigashi-chō, Kurume-shi, Fukuoka-ken. By Nishitetsu-Kurume station. Good ryokan, friendly proprietor. Y7000–12,000 w/meals. No CC.
**Hotel New Plaza** ホテルニュープラザ (33-0010). 16-1 Mutsumon-chō. A business hotel, *0:05h walk from Nishitetsu-Kurume station.* S Y6000, Tw Y10,200. AX, DC, V, MC.
**Kurume Grand Hotel** 久留米グランドホテル (38-1231). 13-14 Hiyoshi-chō. Central. S Y6200, Tw Y13,600. AX, DC, V, MC.

### Exploring Akizuki
**#** *0:40h by Nishitetsu-Amagi line from Kurume to Nishitetsu-Amagi, 0:10h walk to bus center, then 0:25h bus ride.* Akizuki is a pleasant village with a village museum, another museum called the Kiyo Bunko, which exhibits tea utensils, and the remains of the old castle, now a school. The road up to the village crosses an old stone bridge, similar to the Spectacles Bridge of Nagasaki.

# KYŪSHŪ IV:W. WEST FROM KURUME

## W1 ✱✱ YANAGAWA 柳川

*By Nishitetsu-Ōmuta line express, 0:20h from Kurume, or 1:00h from Hakata, or 0:15h from Ōmuta.* Yanagawa is a tranquil old castle town laced with canals and former moats. The stone-banked waterways are lined with old houses, drooping willows, and cascades of flowering shrubs. Stone steps lead down to the water, where in times past people unloaded goods and used the water for their daily needs. Wooden boats, poled along by Japanese gondoliers, take tourists through quiet, murky waterways where the charm of old Japan lingers.

### Calendar
**Jan. 20: Kōwaka-mai.** Setaka, Ōe Tenman-gū. Kōwaka-mai, a military dance from the Muromachi period, survives only here. Three men perform tales from the *Nihon Shoki* and ancient epics.
**May 3–5: Funabutai.** Suiten-gū. Plays and matsuri music performed on boats on the canal.
**Oct. 9–11: Mihashira Jinja Autumn Festival.** Daimyo processions.
**Nov. 1–3: Hakushū Matsuri.** In honor of the poet Kitahara Hakushū. Evening boat festival with fireworks.

### Getting Around
The canal boat dock is 0:05h on foot from Nishitetsu-Yanagawa station. Bicycles can be rented nearby.

### Yanagawa Sights
**✱✱✱ Canal Trip** 水郷めぐり (0944-72-8647). Hrs: from 9:00; clsd mid-Feb. Board in front of Shōgetsu Ryokan; Y1200 to cover a 4-km course in 1:10h. The boats go through a water lock, built into the stone embankments of the old castle moat. The sluice gates controlled water levels to create a formidable defense network. A local ditty proclaims, "Three years for Yanagawa, three months for Kumamoto; Saga and Arima before breakfast," referring to famous Kyūshū castles and how long each one would take to capture. Here and there along the canal are picturesque old storehouses, where goods were loaded from barges. The canalside vegetation is spectacular in spring.
**✱✱✱ Ohana** お花 (旧立花家別邸) Hrs: 9:00–18:00, daily. The Meiji-period European-style villa of the Tachibana, former lords of Yanagawa. Now a museum. Ohana preserves its large **pond garden**, modeled on the islet-studded bay of Matsushima in Tōhoku. Attached to the villa is the Japanese-style former residence of the lord, now used by the adjoining inn.

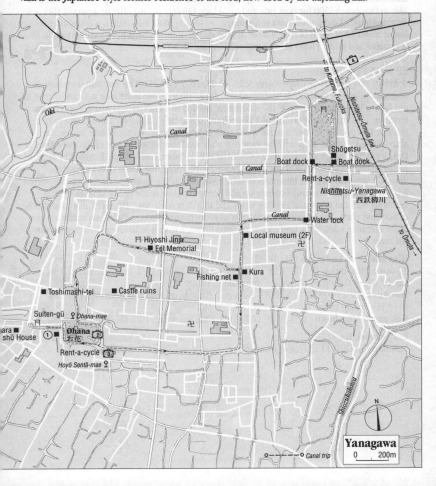

\* **Suiten-gū** 水天宮 A quaint shrine built on the canal. It is sacred to Emperor Antoku (see Miyajima History, p. 449).

\*\* **Toshimashi-tei** 戸島氏邸 Open daily, during daylight hours. The early 19th-C tea arbor and garden of Yanagawa's lord.

**Hakushū Seika** 北原白秋生家 Hrs: Nov.–Jan. 9:00–16:30. Feb.–Mar. and Oct. 9:00–17:00. Apr. and Sept. 9:00–17:30. May–Aug. 9:00–18:00. Clsd NY. The house where Kitahara Hakushū (1885–1942), an influential poet, was born. Hakushū published nearly 200 books, ranging from modern *tanka* poetry and *belles-lettres* to immensely popular children's poems.

### Yanagawa Dining and Lodgings (TEL 0944)

*Unagi* and peculiar fish from the Ariake Sea are Yanagawa specialties.

1️⃣ **Rokuki** 六騎 (72-0069). Sweets and light meals. *Unagi seiro mushi* (eel steamed on rice), Y1450.

2️⃣ \*\* **Ohana** お花 (73-2189). Shinhoka-machi, Yanagawa-shi, Fukuoka-ken. Dining Hrs: 11:00–21:00, daily. Ryokan in good modern taste. Antiques decorate hallways and private dining rooms in the old villa. The baths are fed by hot springs. Dine like a daimyo on local haute cuisine. Dinner from Y4500, by reservation. Ryokan rate, Y17,000 w/meals. AX, DC, V.

3️⃣ **Yanagawa Hoyō Center** 柳川簡易保険保養センター (72-6295). 10-1 Yashiro-chō, Yanagawa-shi. Publicly run spa and lodgings. Tatami rooms only. About Y6000 w/meals; discounts for larger groups staying in one room.

4️⃣ **Runowāru YH** ルノワールYH 瀬高町下庄栄町 (0944-62-2423). Shimonosho Sakaemachi, Setaka-chō, Yamato-gun, Fukuoka-ken. *0:15h by bus from Nishitetsu-Yanagawa station*. Cosy old house. Y3500 w/meals.

# 492 KYŪSHŪ IV:E. EAST FROM KURUME

### Traveling

This route is on the JR Kyūdai line, which traverses northern Kyūshū from Kurume to Ōita (KYŪSHŪ I:E5). Trains are infrequent, only 3 expresses per day.

### E1 HITA 日田

*0:55h by JR Kyūdai line express from Kurume. 1:50h from Ōita (KYŪSHŪ I:E5) or 1:00h fron Yufuin (KYŪSHŪ I:E4) by JR Kyūdai line express.* Hita is a sleepy, rather old-fashioned country town noted for hot springs and *ukai* (cormorant fishing) on the river, mid-May to October; Y3500 for boat ride and meal (see Cuisine, p. 116). The best part of Hita is a neighborhood of old houses near \* **Shimaya** 嶋屋 豆田町 (24-0851), a delightful tea-house about 1 km north of Hita station. Try the *dagojiru teishoku*, a hearty country soup of vegetables and pork, Y1000 (Hrs: 10:00–17:00; clsd M, NY).

### E2 \* ONTA 小鹿田

*0:45h by bus from Hita (departures 9:25, 11:55, 16:00, 17:45).* This tiny pottery village is so beautiful and so thoroughly traditional that it's worth a detour by anyone with an interest in old Japan. The village is deep in the mountains, nestled in a narrow, forested gorge. The bus terminus is in front of the **Onta-yaki Tōgeikan** (open daily), a display hall of Onta-yaki, a genuine folk pottery with distinctive spoke patterns made by skittering a blade across the glaze-dipped surface. It's nearly the twin of a ware made on the other side of the mountains at Onta's kindred village of Koishiwara (KYŪSHŪ II:E1); the original village, founded by Korean potters, split in two some 300 years ago. From the Tōgeikan, the single street meanders downhill, following a clear mountain stream, along which one can see a dozen water-powered *kara-usu* (Korean mortars) bobbing up and down to pulverize the yellow clay. The village resounds with the rhythm of gushing water and thudding *kara-usu*. On sunny days, hundreds of pots and plates are set out to dry in front of every house. If you're lucky, you might see one of the climbing kilns being fired. Yama no Soba Chaya, a teahouse in lower Onta, serves *sansai soba*.

### Hita and Onta Lodgings (TEL 0973)

**Tōsuien Minshuku** 民宿陶遂園 上野展望台横 (24-4122). 2 Tenbōdai Yoko, Ueno, Hita-shi, Ōita-ken. Calls itself a "pottery minshuku." Y7000 w/meals.

**Yorozuya** よろづや旅館 (22-3138). Sumi-chō, Hita-shi. Pleasant modern ryokan by the river. Hot-spring baths. Y10,000 w/meals. AX, V, MC.

**Sakamoto Minshuku** 坂本民宿 (29-2312). Onta Sarayama, Hita-shi. Y4500 w/meals.

### Easy Access To:

**Nakatsu** (KYŪSHŪ I:E): *1:45h from Hita by bus (4 per day) via Yabakei.*

# KYŪSHŪ V. KUMAMOTO

**Tokyo to Kumamoto:** *6:40h by Shinkansen Hikari express to Hakata, then 1:35–1:40h by JR Kagoshima main line limited express to Kumamoto.*

**By Air:** *From Tokyo, 5 flights per day with ANA or JAS. From Ōsaka, 5 flights per day with ANA. From Nagoya, 2 flights per day with ANA. From Naha (Okinawa), 1 per day with ANA. Kumamoto airport is 0:50h by bus from Kumamoto station, or 1:00h from Aso National Park* (E1).

**Prefectures:** Kumamoto, Miyazaki, Ōita.

## ✳ KUMAMOTO 熊本

Few would call Kumamoto a beautiful city, but it has a brash candor that can be engaging. Perhaps this comes from being an outsider. In ancient times, Kumamoto was the territory of the Kumaso, a southern tribe that liked to make trouble for the Yamato state. In the Edo period, Kumamoto became the domain of the Hosokawa family (see Castles, p. 49), but their more flamboyant predecessor, Katō Kiyomasa, is a man closer to the Kumamoto native's heart. Even today, Kumamoto impresses one as a provincial stronghold of stubborn energy. The modern city is a chaos of concrete buildings, softened by irrepressible growths of greenery. Kumamoto's celebrated castle, Suizen-ji Park, and Honmyō-ji, the gorgeous mausoleum of Katō Kiyomasa, head the list of tourist attractions.

### Getting Around

Kami-Kumamoto station, one train stop N of Kumamoto station, is closer to Kumamoto-jō and Honmyō-ji, but has no information booth. Both stations are served by streetcar lines to the castle and Suizen-ji Kōen. Kōtsū Center, near the castle, is the bus terminal.

### Kumamoto Sights

**✱✱ Honmyō-ji** 本妙寺 Museum Hrs: 9:00–16:30; clsd M, NY. *0:05h by streetcar from Kami-Kumamoto station to Honmyō-ji-mae, then walk 0:15h.* This Nichiren temple was founded by the great 16th-C warlord Katō Kiyomasa (1562–1611), who is interred here in an ornate, Momoyama-style mausoleum. The tomb stands at the top of a steep flight of steps, at the same level as the keep of Kumamoto-jō, where the spirit of Kiyomasa could watch over his proudest accomplishment (though it must have distressed his ghost to see his son exiled and his fief turned over to the Hosokawa). To the right is a museum of Kiyomasa's belongings, including a drum from the Korean campaign, in which he served as one of HIDEYOSHI's generals, and his tall helmet, filled with thousands of twisted papers bearing the inscription *Namu Myōhō Renge-kyō*, the mantra of the Nichiren sect. Kiyomasa, a master civil engineer, is fondly remembered for building many bridges and canals in his province.

**✱ Shimada Bijutsukan (Art Museum)** 島田美術館 (352-4597). Hrs: 9:00–17:00; clsd W, NY. A pleasant private museum with a collection on Kumamoto culture. It is noted for its paintings by Miyamoto Musashi, a fabled master swordsman and painter (famous in America

493

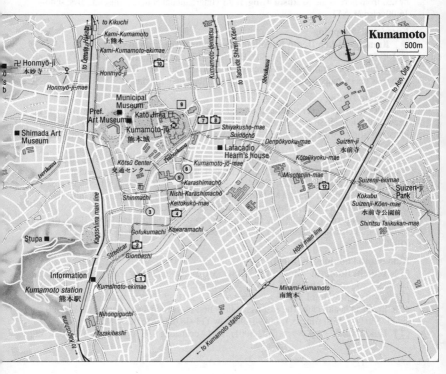

as the author of *The Book of Five Rings*). The Musashi of legend is suspected to be a composite of several historical figures. He spent his later years in the service of the Hosokawa and is a favorite hero of Kumamoto.

**\*\*\* Kumamoto-jō (Castle)** 熊本城 Hrs: 8:30–17:30. Nov.–Mar. 8:30–16:30; clsd NY. *0:15h by streetcar from Kumamoto station to Kumamoto-jō-mae*. Kumamoto-jō was one of Japan's greatest fortresses, and though the donjon is a reconstruction — it was destroyed in 1877 during the Satsuma Rebellion — the castle is well worth visiting for its fortifications and surviving structures. Katō Kiyomasa, who completed the castle in 1607, is considered Japan's greatest castle architect. Kiyomasa was one of TOYOTOMI HIDEYOSHI's most powerful allies, and though he fought against the Toyotomi in the Battle of Sekigahara (1600), he built Kumamoto-jō as a refuge for Hideyoshi's son HIDEYORI (to no avail, for Hideyori perished in the 1615 siege of Ōsaka-jō). The remarkable walls, a hallmark of Kiyomasa's engineering, are equipped with stone-dropping vents and overhanging eaves called *musha-gaeshi* (warrior repulsers). These can be seen on the eleven surviving turrets (ICP). Of the original three keeps, two have been rebuilt. One houses part of the **Naminashi-maru** (ICP), the exquisite boat on which Kiyomasa's successors, the Hosokawa, made their periodic journeys to Edo.

**\*\* Kumamoto-kenritsu Bijutsukan (Prefectural Art Museum)** 県立美術館 (352-2111). Hrs: 9:30–16:30; clsd M, NY. A modern, red-brick building on the west side of the castle, by a playing field. A large part of the museum is devoted to loan exhibits. In spring and/or fall, the museum shows pieces from the famous Hosokawa collection of Tokyo's Eisei Bunko Museum. Of special interest are the full-scale models of *kofun* burial chambers, painted with geometrical shapes unique to the Kumamoto region.

**Kumamoto Hakubutsukan (Municipal Museum)** 熊本博物館 (324-3500). Hrs: 9:00–16:30; clsd M, NH, NY. Near Art Museum. Building designed by Kurokawa Kishō. Exhibits on city history, planetarium.

**\*\* Suizen-ji Kōen** 水前寺公園 Hrs: 7:30–18:00. In winter 8:30–17:00. *0:30h by street-car from Kumamoto station to Suizen-ji Kōen-mae*. The garden is best visited early in the day, before tour buses start arriving. Though marred by a public park atmosphere, the garden of Suizen-ji distinguishes itself by its bold design. The pond and swirling, lawn-covered artificial hills — dominated by a miniature Mt. Fuji — represent the 53 stations of the Tōkaidō. The garden was part of a temple founded in 1632 by Hosokawa Tadatoshi, but was later converted into a pleasure park. The tea-arbor-cum-souvenir-shop, **Kokin Denju no Ma**, was moved in 1912 from Kyoto's Katsura Villa to commemorate Hosokawa Yūsai's role in transmitting the *Kokin Denju* tradition to the imperial house (see Kyoto, p. 365). Although in scandalously poor repair, it offers the best view of the garden. You can order a bowl of *matcha* and examine the rather shabby KANŌ SCHOOL screens inside.

**\* Tatsuda Shizen Kōen (Nature Park)** 立田自然公園 Hrs: 8:30–16:30; clsd NY. *0:25h by bus from Kōtsū Center*. This natural park contains the remains of Taishō-ji, a Hosokawa funerary temple. The temple has a nice tea arbor and a grave of Hosokawa Gracia (1563–1600), one of the most famous women of Japan's feudal era. Gracia was a devout Catholic, and her name was mentioned often in Jesuit letters. She was killed on her husband's order to avoid her capture by an enemy. (James Clavell modeled Mariko, in *Shogun*, after her.) 0:15h by taxi from here is the **Kokusai Mingeikan** (International Folk Art Museum; Hrs: 9:00–16:00; clsd M, NY).

## Kumamoto Shopping

9 **Kumamoto-ken Dentō Kōgeikan (Prefectural Traditional Crafts Hall)** 熊本県伝統工芸館 (324-4930). Hrs: 9:00–17:00; clsd M (Tu if M a NH), NY. A showcase of Kumamoto crafts such as damascene, Shōdai pottery, and Obake no Kinta, a toy ghost who rolls his eyeballs and sticks out his tongue at the tug of a string.

## Kumamoto Dining

The best way to get a feel for Kumamoto character is to spend an evening dining on *ba-sashi* (raw, tender horseflesh seasoned with soy sauce and garlic) and *karashi-renkon* (deep-fried lotus root stuffed with miso-mustard paste), washed down with *kuma-shōchū* (distilled spirits).

3 **Misumi Kobijutsu-ten** 三角古美術店 中唐人町15 (352-3798). Hrs: 10:00–23:00; clsd Tu, NY. A Meiji-era bank that has been turned into a coffee shop. Antiques sold.

5 **\* Sanbun Rihaku** さんぶん李白 花畑町7-10産業文化会館(326-3563). Hrs: 11:00–22:00; clsd 2nd and 4th M. Novices might feel more comfortable in this folk-style restaurant. Good local cuisine, plus numerous other items. Moderate.

6 **\* Mutsugorō** むつ五郎 花畑町12-11 (356-6256). Kumamoto Green Hotel, B1. Hrs: 17:00–24:00 clsd Su, mid-Aug., NY. A tiny pub serving excellent Kumamoto specialties. From Y1000.

## Kumamoto Lodgings (TEL 096)

1 **Daiichi Hotel** 第一ホテル (325-5151). 356 Motoyama-chō. *0:05h walk from station*. Japanese-style rooms cheaper. S Y5000, Tw Y8400. CB.

2 **\*\* New Sky Hotel** ニュースカイホテル (354-2111). 2 Higashi Amidaji-chō. Run by ANA. Excellent health club. The east wing offers first-class rooms (no singles), D Y15,000, Tw Y17–20,000. West wing: S Y7800–11,000, Tw Y13–18,000. AX, DC, V, MC.

4 **Hokke Club** 法華クラブ (322-5001). 20-1 Tōrimachi. Y8500 w/meals. AX, DC, V, MC.

494

7 * **Kumamoto Hotel Castle** 熊本ホテルキャッスル (326-3311). 4-2 Jōtōmachi.
S Y8500–10,500, Tw Y15–19,500. AX, DC, V, MC.

8 **Hotel Ōkus** ホテルオークス (322-1711). 6-8 Kamitōri. Near castle. S Y6500,
Tw Y12,000. AX, DC, V, MC.

10 * **Chitose Hotel** 千歳ホテル 京町1 (354-1851). 1 Kyōmachi. Cozy modern ryokan
close to castle. Good meals. Also semi-Western rooms. Y10,000 w/2 meals. AX, DC, V, MC.

11 **Kumamoto-shiritsu YH** 熊本市立YH (352-2441). 5-15-55 Shimasaki-chō,
Kumamoto-shi. Near Shimada museum. Y2600 w/meals.

12 **Suizen-ji YH** 水前寺YH (371-9193). 1-20-20 Hakuzan. Y2500 w/breakfast.

## YATSUSHIRO 八代

*0:30h by JR Kagoshima main line express south from Kumamoto. Junction to JR Hisatsu
line to Hitoyoshi.* This castle town was the place of retirement of Hosokawa Tadaoki (see Castles, p. 49). About 0:10h by bus from the station is the castle ruin and **Shōhinken**, the
castellan's villa and garden, built in 1688. **Sakai Shunichi** kiln (09653-3-2859) is noted for
Kōda-yaki, an incised celadon in the Korean tradition (*0:10h by taxi from the station*).

### Calendar
**Nov. 18: ** Myōken-sai.** Yatsushiro Jinja. (See Calendar, p. 469).

### Exploring Hitoyoshi
# *1:00h by JR Hisatsu line express from Yatsushiro.* An old castle town and spa. Wooden
boats take tourists down the Kuma River for a moderately exciting, 18-km run (Y2700, takes
2:30h). This remote region was ruled for some 700 years by the Sagara clan, who were given
their fief by MINAMOTO NO YORITOMO. Temples and statues of artistic and historical value
are scattered about. Aoi Aso Jinja, south of Hitoyoshi station, is noted for **Usu-daiko**, a dramatic drum dance performed on Oct. 9–11.

### Easy Access To:
* **Ebino Kōgen** (KYŪSHŪ VI:E2): *1:40h from Hitoyoshi by JR Ebino-gō express to
Kobayashi, then transfer to a bus.*

### Exploring the Utase Boats at Sajiki
# *0:50h by JR Kagoshima main line local from Yatsushiro, then 0:15h by bus to Sajiki
harbor.* This is one of the last places in Japan with *utase-bune*, multisailed fishing boats. The
long, narrow boats, operated by husband-wife teams, are set perpendicular to the wind and
swept sideways, against the tide. They drag a broad net hanging off the bow, stern, and masts.
On a sunny, not too windy day, the full-blown sails are a glorious sight. From March to May,
and July 20 to Nov. 30, tourists can charter a boat with room for 12 for Y40,000, lunch
included. Phone Mr. Kusuyama Masanori (0966-82-3241), preferably a week in advance.
Sajiki is not far from **Minamata**, which drew world attention in the 1960s when residents
were stricken with illnesses and severe birth defects caused by eating fish tainted by mercury-
laden effluents from a local factory.

# KYŪSHŪ V:E. EAST FROM KUMAMOTO

**Main Attraction:** Takachiho (E3)

### Exploring Kikuchi and Yamaga
# *NE of Kumamoto city; served by buses.* Kikuchi has a rather good farmhouse museum
village (*minka mura*); nearby is Funayamajō (096886-2012), a pleasant farmhouse
restaurant. Yamaga has a famous **Bon dance** on Aug. 15–16, performed by women wearing
ornate paper lanterns on their heads.

## E1 TATENO 立野
*0:40h by JR Hōhi line express from Kumamoto. Gateway to Aso National Park. Junction to
Minami Aso Tetsudō, a charming little train into southern Aso NP (E2).*

## * ASO NATIONAL PARK 阿蘇国立公園
*From Kumamoto by JR Hōhi line express (infrequent), 0:40h to Tateno (junction to
Minami Aso line), 1:05h to Aso town. Slightly longer by express bus from Kumamoto
station/Kōtsū Center. From Kumamoto Airport, 1:00h by express bus to Aso. From Beppu
(KYŪSHŪ I:E3), 2:40h by Yamanami highway bus, via Yufuin. From Ōita (KYŪSHŪ I:E5),
by JR Hōhi line express, 2:00h to Aso and 2:25h to Tateno, via Bungo-Taketa (E4). From
Takachiho (E3), 1:30h by bus (approx. hourly) by a very scenic backcountry route.* This
park contains the world's largest caldera, one of the world's most active volcanoes, grassy
highlands, and countless hot springs. Like other national parks, it includes areas of shameless
development and heavy tour-bus infestation. The loveliest parts of Aso—missed by most
tourists—are not the designated sights in the center, but the rolling farm country on the
southwest slopes of Aso-zan. Here, tucked away in scenic valleys, are rustic hot springs no
onsen lover should miss.

495

## Calendar
**July 28:** ✳✳ **Onda Matsuri.** Aso Jinja. See Calendar, p. 468.
**Sept. 25: Aso Tanomi Shinji.** Aso Jinja harvest festival. A variety of activities throughout the day; Kagura, horse races, *yabusame* (horseback archery), sumō.

## Getting Around
Public trains and buses within the park are infrequent. You might consider renting a car; park highways are broad and well-maintained. Toyota Rent-a-Car (09673-2-0100) and Nippon Rent-a-Car (2-0615) are both at Uchinomaki Onsen, one stop west of Aso.

## Aso Town
This dreary town has little to recommend it, but one can pick up information and rent a car. The one place of interest is **Aso Jinja** (*0:15h by bus from the station or 0:10h on foot from Miyaji, one local train stop east*). By tradition, the shrine was founded as early as 282 B.C., and its hereditary priest claims to be the 90th in an unbroken line. The shrine deities were associated with the Aso clan, hereditary rulers of what is now Kumamoto prefecture, and the shrine has enjoyed high status throughout its history. The present structures date from 1835. **Daikanbō** (*0:30h by bus from Aso station*) offers a sweeping view of the park.

## ✳✳ Naka-dake 中岳
*0:40h by bus from Aso to Aso-zan Nishi tramway station; departs approximately once an hour between 8:45 and 15:30.* The scenic bus route from Aso passes **Komezuka**, a trim volcanic cone shaped like an inverted rice bowl, and **Kusa Senrigahama**, a pretty meadow in the crater of Mt. Eboshi; the volcano museum across the road is not worth a stop. The bus terminates at Aso-zan Nishi, where there's a tramway up **Naka-dake**, to the brink of a 100-meter-deep caldera. Thick clouds of vapor rise from the sickly green lake at the bottom. From this vantage point, you can see the rim of the outer crater of Aso, 128 km in circumference and 125 m deep. From the caldera, there's a trail up Naka-dake, Taka-dake, and down to Sensui-kyō, a volcanic gorge. (From Sensui-kyō, it's 0:15h by bus to Miyaji station.) This trail takes 5:00–6:00h over rough ground. There's also a trail to Jigoku Onsen; 1:50h.

496

## E2 TAKAMORI 高森
*0:30h by Minami Aso line local train (5 per day), or 0:40h by bus (11 per day) from Tateno (E1).* At Aso-Shimoda station, one can catch a bus or taxi to ✳✳ **Tarutama Onsen and Jigoku Onsen**, where there are two rambling old inns. If you're hesitant about plunging headlong into a thoroughly Japanese environment but still want to enjoy the scenery, there's a pleasant pension village; the pension owners will pick you up in a van from Tochinoki bus stop (*0:10h by bus from Tateno*). There's another pension village near Takamori. From Takamori, there are buses to Aso and Takachiho (E3).

## Aso and Takamori Dining and Lodgings (TEL 09676)
✳ **Dengaku no Sato** 田楽の里 (2-1899). *Head out Rte. 265 from Takamori toward the Kokumin Kyūkamura.* Skewered tofu, yams, vegetables, and still-twitching trout are broiled over *irori* coals, slathered with sweet miso, and broiled again. The restaurant is in a transplanted *gasshō-zukuri* farmhouse; touristy but fun. Y1440 for a complete *dengaku* meal.
**Pension Orange Beer** ペンションおれんじびーる (7-1890). 4635-5 Kawayō, Chōyō-son, Aso-gun, Kumamoto-ken. Near Tochinoki stop. A lodge-style place that does a lawn barbecue in warmer months. Trim, neat rooms. Y7500 w/meals. AX, DC, V.
✳ **Yamaguchi Ryokan** 山口旅館 垂玉温泉 (7-0006). Tarutama Onsen, Chōyō-son. *0:20h from Shimoda station.* Rustic mountain onsen in a very pretty area. Sprawling inn with bungalows. Y6,500–10,500 w/meals. No CC.
✳ **Seifū-sō** 清風荘 地獄温泉 (7-0005). Jigoku Onsen, Chōyō-son. Just beyond Yamaguchi Ryokan. A smaller, 80-year-old wooden inn with a new wing. Open-air baths. Wild boar or pheasant cuisine in colder months. Y6000–12,000 w/meals. No CC.
**Minami-Aso Kokumin Kyūkamura** 南阿蘇国民休暇村 (2-2111). Nakajima, Takamori-machi, Aso-gun. National Vacation Village. Local cuisine. Y5500–9000 w/meals.
**Pension Flower Garden** ペンションフラワーガーデン (2-3021), **Pension Cream House** ペンションくりーむはうす (2-3090), **Pension Wonderland** ペンションワンダーランド (2-3040), all in Takamori. About Y6900 w/meals.

## ✳ YAMANAMI HIGHWAY やまなみハイウエイー
*Mar.–Nov., daily sightseeing express buses cover the highway from Kumamoto to Yufuin and Beppu (KYŪSHŪ I:E4–3) via Aso; 9 per day, most departing 8:00–9:30. Travel time from Kumamoto to Beppu, 4:00–6:45h depending on length of stop in Aso. Some courses include Unzen, and Nagasaki. The major operator is Kyūshū Kokusai Kankō Bus (096-357-3900).* The rolling grasslands and mountains stretching from Aso almost to Beppu offer some of the finest natural scenery in Kyūshū. The excursion is marred only by the taped chatter and canned music on the buses.

## Exploring Hot Springs on the Yamanami
# *Take a local highway bus (tour buses don't stop en route).* 1:10h from Aso, at Kujū Tozan-guchi is **Chōjabaru Onsen**, a small resort situated on a plateau at the foot of Kujū-zan. Lodgings at the **Kujū Highland Hotel** (09737-9-2111), from Y8000 w/meals. Trails head into the Kujū range; **Hokke-in Onsen** (0974-77-2810), a 1:30h hike from Kujū Tozan-guchi, is an isolated inn with open-air baths and fabulous views, Y6000 w/meals.

## E3 ** TAKACHIHO 高千穂

*From Takamori* (E2), *1:10h by bus via a beautiful, unfrequented road to Takachiho Bus Terminal. From Kumamoto, 2:40h by four express buses per day. From Nobeoka* (KYŪSHŪ VI:E5), *1:25h by bus or 1:25h by private Takachiho railway.* Ninigi no Mikoto, the grandson of Amaterasu Ōmikami (the "Sun Goddess"), is said to have landed on a mountain called Takachiho, in Kyūshū (see Kyūshū History, p. 469). The villagers of this mountain fastness claim that this is the place, no matter that there is a more plausible Mt. Takachiho farther south. Though this Takachiho can point to no such Olympian peak in its vicinity, it does have a wealth of place names famed in Japanese mythology—Kunimigaoka (Land Surveying Bluff), Takamagahara (High Plain of Heaven), and Ama no Iwato (Boulder Door of Heaven), the very cave in which Amaterasu hid, depriving the world of light. A quick-witted goddess performed a ribald dance that set the company of gods to laughing so uproariously that Amaterasu was compelled to come out and see what the fun was about. This dance is said to be the original Kagura, and at Takachiho, the repertory has been expanded to include 33 mimed dances relating the famous deeds of the gods. When frost whitens the tips of the stubble in the harvested paddies, villagers gather in farmhouses to watch the tales unfold through the night.

### Calendar

**May 2–3:** * Nishi Hongū-taisai. Ama no Iwato Jinja. Iwato Kagura is performed 9:30–12:00 on the 3rd.

**Sept. 22–23:** * Higashi Hongū-taisai. Ama no Iwato Jinja. Iwato Kagura is performed on the morning of the 23rd.

**Nov. 3:** * Yo-Kagura Kōkai Matsuri. Ama no Iwato Jinja. Iwato Kagura from 10:00–22:00.

**End Nov.–early Feb.:** ** Takachiho no Yo-Kagura. See Calendar, p. 469. Anyone is welcome to attend these all-night performances at local farmhouses. Call by the previous day; inquire about details and an appropriate offering of money or saké at Ama no Iwato Jinja's shrine office (0982-74-8239). Hrs: 6:00–17:30.

497

### Getting Around

Local buses are infrequent. One painless way to see the sights is to take a regular tour bus from the bus terminal. **A Course** (Y1660, 3:00h) departs at 8:50 and 13:10, and visits Unkaibashi (a scenic bridge), Ama no Iwato Jinja, Takachiho-kyō, Kunimigaoka, Kagurayado (thatched houses converted into inns and restaurants), Takachiho Jinja. **B Course** (Y1150, 2:00h) departs 9:50, 14:10, and covers the same course, minus Ama no Iwato Jinja.

### Takachiho Sights

* **Takachiho Jinja** 高千穂神社 *0:10h on foot from the bus terminal.* The grounds are surrounded by magnificent cryptomeria trees. A short program of *** **Iwato Kagura** 岩戸神楽 is performed here for tourists every evening from 20:00–21:00. The shrine is pretty at night, and the Kagura is well presented. During the intermission, one of the men sings a haunting folksong. The final piece is a congenially lewd mime of the amorous play of Izanagi and Izanami, the parent gods.

** **Takachiho-kyō (Gorge)** 高千穂峡 *0:05h by bus from bus terminal, or 0:20h on foot from Takachiho Jinja.* Takachiho-kyō is a scenic little gorge, best viewed from a rented rowboat (an exorbitant Y600 per 0:30h). The sheer walls are broken by rock formations and beautiful cascades.

** **Ama no Iwato Jinja (Nishi Hongū)** 天岩戸神社 *0:20h by bus from the bus terminal.* The shrine oratory, a small open pavilion, faces Amaterasu's cave, which is on the hill across the river. This is an unusual example of an archaic shrine type, in which the kami resides in a natural object rather than in a sacred hall. Worshippers perform ablutions with water or by passing huge loops of vine over the body. The large tree standing in the grounds is girt by a sacred rope and has a role in the shrine rituals because it is recorded that it was this tree, rather than the more commonly used *sakaki*, that provided a branch of berries held by the goddess who lured Amaterasu out of her cave. On top of the hill across the river, in a beautiful, lonely spot, is Higashi Hongū, the eastern half of this shrine, consecrated to the violent aspect of Amaterasu. You can pay about Y18,000 to have a performance of Iwato Kagura offered at the shrine.

** **Ama no Yasugawara** 天ノ安川原 *0:10h on foot from Ama no Iwato Jinja, upstream along the river.* This sacred cavern, beautifully situated beside a clear, rushing river, is where

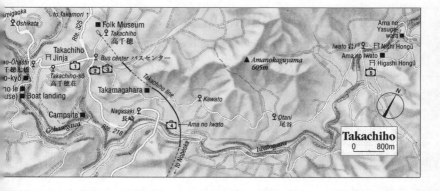

the gods congregated to mull over ways to coax Amaterasu out of her cave. The mouth of the cavern is littered with hundreds of tiny cairns; each little stone tower is supposed to invest its builder with the energies of this divine gathering.

∗ **Kunimigaoka** 国見が丘 *0:20h by bus from bus terminal*. This "land surveying bluff" is the kind of place from which the ancient gods might have gazed upon the surrounding countryside.

**Takachiho Lodgings** (TEL 0982)

① **YH and Ryokan Yamatoya** YH旅館大和屋 (72-2243). 1148 Mitai, Takachiho-chō, Nishiusuki-gun, Miyazaki-ken. Good location. YH rate, Y3500 w/meals. Ryokan rate, Y6000–12,000 w/meals. Recommended.

② **Ryokan Kaminoya** 旅館かみの家 (72-2111). Mitai. Economical inn group. Y5–6500 w/meals.

③ **Imakuni Ryokan** 今国旅館 (72-2175). Mitai, Minami-machi. Y8–20,000 w/meals.

④ **Takachiho YH** 高千穂YH (72-3021). 5899-2 Mitai. Near Ama no Iwato station.

⑤ **Iwato Furusato YH** 岩戸ふるさとYH (74-8254). 6333 Iwato. Also a ryokan.

## E4 ∗ BUNGO-TAKETA 豊後竹田

*1:55h from Kumamoto or 0:50h from Aso by JR Hōhi line express (infrequent), or 1:10h from Ōita (KYŪSHŪ I:E5). By bus, 0:50h from Aso or 1:30h from Ōita by bus.* This quaint little castle town is worth visiting as much for its attractions as for the spectacular train ride.

**Getting Around**
The easiest way to see the town is to take a bus to the castle, 2 km east of the station, (or a taxi all the way to the top), and then walk back through town.

**Bungo-Taketa Sights**

498

∗∗∗ **Oka-jō Ato (Castle Ruin)** 岡城跡 *0:10h by bus to Oka-jō Iriguchi, or 0:35h on foot from the station*. Though not one splinter of Oka-jō remains, this is a truly impressive fortress by virtue of its unassailable position atop a steep ridge, with rivers on either side. The powerful stone walls straggle for over a mile along the ridge. The site of the Honmaru (main keep) offers a breathtaking view of the surrounding mountains, as far as Aso and Kujū-san. The castle well, 73 meters deep, can still be seen. By local legend, this well was actually a secret exit. The castle's lord, though poor, devised a trick to make it seem as though he commanded a considerable force: His men would enter openly by the gate, slip out through the well, and then circle around to enter by the gate once more.

∗ **Kirishitan Dōkutsu (Crypto-Christian Cave)** キリシタン洞窟 Walking back to town from the castle, take a left just past Hirose shrine. Walk about 100 meters. Turn left toward a wooded area at the foot of a cliff (there are signs in Japanese pointing the way). In 1590, there were perhaps 15,000 Christians in this area. After Christianity was banned, it is thought that believers constructed this odd little cave as a safe place in which to conduct secret Masses.

∗∗ **Chikuden-sō** 竹田荘 Hrs: 9:00–16:00; clsd M, NY. From the crypto-Christian cave, return to the quiet lane, turn left, and follow it past the crumbling adobe walls of a few old samurai houses. Continue straight ahead, past the inn, Chikuden Saryō, up on the left. A little farther, on the left, is the gate of the 200-year-old home of the literati painter Tanomura Chikuden. Especially charming is the *kura* in the corner, which has a tea arbor and its own little tea garden.

∗ **Rekishi Shiryōkan (History Museum)** 歴史資料館 (63-1923). Hrs: 9:00–16:30; clsd M, NY. Continue along the same road from Chikuden-sō. The museum, a modern white building, is on the right. It is noted for a bronze Western-style bell (ICP), carrying the inscription "Hospital Santiago 1612." Records show there was a Jesuit hospital by that name in Shimabara (KYŪSHŪ III:W2). Many of Chikuden's paintings are also on view.

**Bungo-Taketa Dining and Lodgings** (TEL 0974)

∗ **Chikuden Saryō** 竹田茶寮 (63-3261). 2420 Taketa, Taketa-shi, Ōita-ken. A rambling country inn noted for local cuisine. It features dishes such as *enoha* (a pink-fleshed, troutlike fish) and sweet-cooked carp. *Bentō* Y1700, lunch *kaiseki* Y4000. Rooms w/meals from Y10,000. The charming tea cottage, Binbō-tei, is Y13,000 w/meals.

**Travel Inn Yoshitomi** トラベルイン吉富 (62-3185). 134 Tamachi, Taketa-shi. A tiny business hotel with a folk-craft theme. S Y4330, Tw Y7640.

# KYŪSHŪ VI. KAGOSHIMA

**Tokyo to Kagoshima:** *6:40h by Shinkansen Hikari express to Hakata, then 4:20–5:00h by JR Kagoshima main line limited express.*
**By Air:** *From Tokyo, 1:50h by 8 direct flights per day on ANA, JAS, JAL. From Nagoya, 1:15h by 3 flights per day on ANA. From Ōsaka, 1:10h by 6 direct flights per day on ANA or JAS.*
**Prefectures:** Kagoshima, Miyazaki

## KAGOSHIMA 鹿児島

This "Naples of the Orient" has a splendid setting, facing across a bay toward the restless hulk of Sakurajima, one of the world's most active volcanoes, but the city itself is not very attractive. Badly bombed in World War II, it retains few traces of its dynamic history. The main sightseeing attraction is Iso Tei-en, a garden built by the Shimazu, lords of Kagoshima, who ruled the Satsuma domain for 700 years. The Shimazu are among the most famous and colorful daimyo in Japanese history. It was they who welcomed Francis Xavier when he landed here in 1549. Under the TOKUGAWA regime, the Shimazu were treated as "outside lords." When the shogunate began to falter, Satsuma, allied with Chōshū, brought about the Meiji Restoration in 1868 (see Hagi History, p 560). Ōkubo Toshimichi and Saigō Takamori, two of the "three giants" of the Meiji Restoration, were Satsuma samurai. Ironically, "the Great Saigō," the most beloved of Meiji heroes, led a bloody rebellion in 1877 against the state he had helped to found. The figure of Saigō, a hefty, bull-headed, crew-cut man with large eyes, is seen everywhere in the city. There is also a famous bronze statue of him in Tokyo's Ueno Park.

## Calendar
**Mid-July:** * **Soga-don no Kasayaki.** Held on a Sa near the 20th. A rite for the Soga brothers, medieval heroes long venerated in this martial province. From 20:00, loinclothed youths sing about the Soga around a bonfire of old parasols on the banks of the Kotsukigawa.

## Getting Around
City maps in English can be picked up at the Kankō Annaijo, to the left of the bus quay at Nishi-Kagoshima station. Streetcars from Nishi-Kagoshima go to Tenmonkan in the main shopping and business area and to Kagoshima-eki-mae (terminus, near harbor). Main bus depots are Nishi-Kagoshima station and the Yamagataya Department Store, near Tenmonkan. Hayashida buses (to Kirishima/Ebino Kōgen, E2) leave from in front of the Takashimaya Department Store, also near Tenmonkan.

## Kagoshima Sights
** **Iso Tei-en (Garden)** 磯庭園 Hrs: 8:30–17:30. Nov.–Mar. 15, 8:30–17:00. *0:20h by bus 1 from station*. The glory of this former feudal lord's garden and *sukiya* villa is the view of Sakurajima, across the bay. The garden and villa were built in 1660 by the 19th lord of Satsuma.

499

* **Shōko Shuseikan** 尚古集成館 Hrs: 8:30–17:30. Nov–Mar 15, 8:30–17:00. Just outside Iso Tei-en. This stone building erected in 1855 was Japan's first Western-style factory. It was built by Lord Shimazu Nariakira, on the advice of Saigō, Ōkubo, and other young samurai. Nariakira, convinced that the Western challenge could be met only with the aid of Western technology, also experimented with reverberatory blast furnaces (needed to cast cannons) and photography, and built several naval vessels. Some of the items manufactured here — cannon, gunpowder, glass, ceramics — are exhibited along with personal effects of the Shimazu family.

**Tsurumaru-jō Ato (Castle Ruin)** 鶴丸城跡 *0:10h walk from Kagoshima station*. Stone walls and moat of the castle, built in 1602. In the grounds is the ** **Reimeikan** 黎明館, a museum of regional history, from the Stone Age to the present (Hrs: 9:00–16:30; clsd M, 25th of the month, NY). Of special interest are items on the Nansei (southwest) islands, including videotapes of festivals. There are also displays on St. Francis Xavier and the arrival of the Portuguese, and on the leaders of the Meiji Restoration, notably Saigō Takamori. Nearby is the **Nanshu-bochi**, a cemetery for 2,023 Satsuma samurai who died — many by suicide — in the Satsuma Rebellion, including the tomb of Saigō himself. A memorial hall displays information about his life. Farther up, on the road to Shiroyama, is the cave where Saigō killed himself.

*** **Sakurajima** 桜島 *0:15h by ferry, departures every 0:10–0:15h from Sakurajima Sanbashi pier (0:05h on foot from Kagoshima station, or 0:15h by bus from Nishi-Kagoshima)*. This beautiful, ominous volcano erupts almost daily with an audible rumble, pelting Kagoshima with a fine rain of ash. Tombstones on Sakurajima have corrugated tin roofs to keep off the volcanic debris. Lava fields can be seen 0:10h on foot from Sakurajima-kō (the dock). But far more spectacular is the view from the * **Yōgan Tenbodai** on the southeast side of the volcano (*0:30h by bus from the dock*). This observation platform faces out over the jagged coast and a bridge of lava created by a cataclysmic eruption in 1914, which linked this former island to the mainland. Sakurajima *daikon*, monster turnips weighing up to 45 kg, grow in the fertile volcanic soil. Tour buses make the rounds; they depart daily at 9:30 and 13:30 from the dock (3:00h, Y1700). Bicycles can be rented by the dock for Y300 per hour. It takes 4:00h to circle the volcano.

## Kagoshima Crafts
Satsuma-yaki is a famous stoneware, typically covered with a finely crazed, soft ivory glaze and richly decorated with overglaze enamels and gold. It was made by artisans captured in HIDEYOSHI's Korean campaign, who were trying to create a porcelain-like ware. Closer to folk pottery is Kuro-Satsuma, a glossy olive-black (supposedly a degenerate celadon), represented by the classic *kuro-joka*, a *shōchū* vessel resembling a flattened teapot. For quality wares, visit **Naeshirogawa** (*0:10h by bus from Higashichiki or Ijuin stations on the JR Kagoshima line, or 1:00h by bus from Izuro in Kagoshima*). Descendants of the original Korean artisans still live in this quiet country town. The lord of Satsuma settled them here in the 17th century, giving them low-ranking samurai status to protect them from their Japanese neighbors; when the Meiji government abolished social classes, they were exposed to abuse. Naeshirogawa straggles along a country lane, and many kilns are discreetly tucked away behind hedges and bamboo groves. There's also an old cemetery with Korean tombstones.

** **Chin Jukan** 沈寿官 (74-2358). Hrs: 8:30–17:00; clsd 1st and 3rd M, NY. *50 m from Miyama bus stop*. The delightful gallery, museum, studio, and garden of the 14th-generation descendant of Chin Tōkichi, who is credited with inventing white Satsuma ware. Some of the contemporary work is quite affordable.

**Araki Tōyō** 荒木陶窯 (74-2733). Hrs: 8:30–17:00; clsd NY. A short distance from the main road. This kiln produces attractive, modern designs in olive and black.

**Sameshima Satarō** 鮫島佐太郎 (74-2450). Hrs: 8:00–17:00, daily. The only potter who still makes pure Kuro-Satsuma folk ware. Very small stock.

## Kagoshima Dining

Satsuma cuisine is one of the most distinctive in Japan. Most shops have local dishes such as *tonkotsu* (stewed pork), *kibinago* (sardine sashimi), *satsuma-age* (deep-fried fish sausage stuffed with sweet yams), *satsumajiru* (a stewlike miso soup), *saké-zushi* (rice, fish, and vegetables marinated in saké). The preferred drink is *shōchū*, a 120-proof distilled liquor made from sugarcane or yams. The best dining district is around Tenmonkan, near the Hayashida Hotel.

**Satsumaji** さつま路 東千石町6-29 (26-0525). Hrs: 11:30–22:00; clsd Aug. 13–15, NY. Five blocks from Hayashida Hotel. Folk interior. *Satsuma teishoku*, a sampler of local dishes, from Y2500. No CC.

**Nanakusa** 七種 東千石町9-20 (24-7793). Hrs: 11:30–14:00, 17:00–22:00; clsd Su, NY. Cheap, popular lunch *teishoku*, Y500. Home-cooking at night; dinner, Y2500. No CC.

## Kagoshima Lodgings (TEL 0992)

∗∗ **Shigetomi-sō** 重富荘 (47-3155). 31-7 Shimizu-chō, Kagoshima-shi. Near Iso Tei-en. Former villa of a Shimazu brother, now an elegant ryokan with spacious, landscaped grounds and views of Sakurajima. Outdoor *okariba-yaki* (hunt barbecue, but with beef and chicken). From Y15,000 w/meals. AX, DC, MC.

∗ **Hayashida Hotel** 林田ホテル (24-4111). Fax 24-4553. 12-22 Higashi Sengoku-chō. Modern hotel in heart of the shopping and business district. S Y7800, Tw Y13,000. AX, DC, V, MC.

500 **Shiroyama Kankō Hotel** 城山観光ホテル (24-2211). Fax 24-2222. 41-1 Shinshōin-chō. S Y9000+, Tw Y16,000+. AX, DC, V, MC.

**Silk Inn Kagoshima** シルクイン鹿児島 (58-1221). 19-30 Uenosono-chō. 0:03h walk from Nishi-Kagoshima. Cozy business hotel with hot-spring baths. S Y4500, Tw Y8000. No CC.

# KYŪSHŪ VI:W. SATSUMA PENINSULA

**Main Attractions:** Chiran (W1), Ibusuki (W2)

## Traveling

Public transport is slow and infrequent. One good option is to take the regular Teiki Kankō (tour) bus: **A-5** departs Nishi-Kagoshima station at 10:10, and covers Chiran, Bōnotsu, Kaimondake, and ends at Ibusuki's Jungle Bath (17:35); **B-11** departs Ibusuki at 10:10, and covers Kaimondake, Chiran (0:45h stop), Tarumizu (across the bay, best sunset views of Sakurajima), Sakurajima lava fields, and ends in Kagoshima at 17:45. Both tours are about Y3500. If you wish to drive, the main roads are not too difficult once you've found your way out of Kagoshima onto the Ibusuki Skyline highway. Rent-a-car in Kagoshima: Japaren ジャパレン (57-3900) is cheapest; Nippon 日本レンタカー (58-3336), Toyota トヨタレンタカー (50-0100), Nissan 日産レンタカー (51-4123).

## W1 ∗∗ CHIRAN 知覧

*1:15h by bus from Yamagataya Bus Center in downtown Kagoshima (0:15h by streetcar from Nishi-Kagoshima station). Departures about once an hour. Or 0:40h by bus from Makurazaki, at the tip of the Satsuma Peninsula. By car: Drive south on the Ibusuki Sky-line, get off at the Chiran exit and drive west about 10 km.* The "samurai lane" of this country town is one of the most attractive and important preserved areas of samurai dwellings and gardens in Japan. Chiran was one of Satsuma's 113 *fumoto machi*, administrative centers established at the bases of old castles that were destroyed because of the "One Province, One Castle" decree of TOKUGAWA IEYASU. The Tokugawa also prohibited samurai from farming, but Satsuma, being so far away and an "outside" domain to boot, pretty much ignored that decree. Chiran's samurai took up tea cultivation as a profitable yet suitably genteel occupation. The gardens of Chiran are said to be styled after Kyoto gardens, but some features, such as the stone walls, show Okinawan influence. Though they didn't have a castle, young Chiran samurai were still obliged to harden their bodies and train in the martial arts every night. That these gardens have survived so well is due, one likes to think, to the Chiran samurai's prowess with the pruning shears.

## Calendar

L 8/15: ∗ **Jūgoya Sorayoi.** Harvest moon festival. Young boys in loincloths, straw skirts, and peculiar straw hoods sing and stamp the ground to ensure a good harvest. Spectators are not allowed to make sounds.

## Getting Around

From Nakagōri bus stop, cross the bridge to the *yakuba* (town hall), where you can pick up tourist pamphlets, including an informative leaflet in English. If coming by car, park at the lot near the second signal. Across the street is the town hall. From the town hall, cross the main street, follow the river for one block and turn left; the houses are on this one lane.

## Chiran Sights

**\*\*\* Samurai Houses and Gardens of Chiran.** Hrs: 8:00–17:30, daily. The stone walls topped by thick, clipped hedges lining the samurai lane were initially designed with defense in mind, as were the stone barricades that prevented enemies from charging headlong through the gates of the houses. A toilet was always built by the gate, ostensibly for the convenience of guests, but also to permit the master to eavesdrop on conversations outside. The gardens are situated in the northeast corners of the estates to take advantage of the "borrowed scenery" of the mountain to the east.

◆ **Saigō Keiichirō** 西郷恵一郎 All the classic landscape garden idioms are present: the mountain in the left corner, represented by the tallest rock and yet taller clipped hedge behind it, the dry waterfall of rocks spilling out to the sea of dry sand. The mountain is said to suggest a crane, and the low-lying boulder a tortoise.

◆ **Hirayama Soyo** 平山ソヨ The garden of a high-ranking retainer, built between 1751–1772. This one achieves a sweeping, panoramic effect while retaining overall unity.

**Hirayama Ryōichi** 平山亮一 This garden, built in 1780, is composed entirely of clipped shrubs—azaleas against a hedge of darker vegetation, shaped like a distant mountain. On the way in is a stone trough supposedly used to wash blood-smeared swords and other weapons after a battle.

**Futatsuya Minka** 二つ屋民家 An old thatched house, considered unusual because two quarters have been linked irregularly to give it a somewhat complicated roof.

**Sata Tamiko** 佐多民子 Another classic landscape garden, but perhaps less interesting than the Saigō garden.

**Sata Naotada** 佐多直忠 A finely composed landscape garden making excellent use of borrowed scenery.

◆ **Mori Shigemitsu** 森重堅 At the far end of the lane, by the foot of the old castle hill. This house, built around 1741 by a high-ranking Chiran retainer, is of special importance because both house and garden have been preserved intact. The large, whitewashed storehouse near the gate has a roof tied on with ropes, which could be removed in case of fire. The house has a special entrance reserved for visits by members of the Shimazu family. The garden has a pond and uses the castle hill for its background.

**Tokkō Ihinkan** 特攻遺品館 Hrs: 8:00–17:00. *0:15h on foot from the town hall*. Chiran was a base for kamikaze operations during World War II, and this is a museum of kamikaze memorabilia.

## Chiran Dining and Lodgings (TEL 0993)

**Taki-an** 高城庵 (83-3186). Hrs: 10:00–17:00; clsd 3rd F. Near the T-junction at the end of the samurai lane, on the left. A pleasant little place run by an elderly lady. Serves hand-cut *udon* and *soba* noodles and fresh mandarin orange juice. Looks out on a nice garden.

**Tomiya Ryokan** 富屋旅館 (83-4313). 104 Kōri, Chiran-chō, Kawanabe-gun, Kagoshima-ken. Y6000–7000 w/meals.

## W2 \*\* IBUSUKI 指宿

*1:00–1:15h by train from Nishi-Kagoshima, or 1:30h by bus*. This well-known hot-spring resort has a relaxed, Mediterranean ambiance.

**\*\* Tennen Sunamushi-buro (Steaming Sand Bath)** 天然砂蒸し風呂 Hrs: 8:30–21:00. Nov.–Mar. 8:30–20:00. *0:05h by bus or 0:20h on foot from Ibusuki station, by the beach*. Y510, *yukata* included. Change into a *yukata* and walk out to the beach, where cheerful old ladies will bury you up to your neck in steaming hot sand. Afterward, wash off in the shower and take a relaxing soak in the public bath.

**\*\*\* Jungle Bath** ジャングル浴場 Hrs: 7:00–22:00, daily. Y620. In the gargantuan, rather rundown Ibusuki Kankō Hotel's Health Center. A variety of tiled baths in a vast greenhouse filled with jungle plants. Semi-mixed bathing; a women's section is available.

**\*\* Iwasaki Bijutsukan (Art Museum)** 岩崎美術館 Hrs: 8:00–17:30, daily. Next to the Ibusuki Kankō Hotel. A museum of late 19th-century to contemporary art (mainly of French and Western-style Japanese painters), housed in a stunning building designed by Maki Fumihiko, one of Japan's foremost contemporary architects.

## Ibusuki Lodgings (TEL 0993)

**\* Hotel Shūsuien** ホテル秀水園 (23-4141). 5-27-27 Yunohama, Ibusuki-shi, Kagoshima-ken. A modern ryokan with good service, ocean views, tasteful decor, and lovely baths. Y20–50,000 w/meals. DC, V, MC.

**Ginshō** 旅館吟松 (22-3231). 5-26-27 Yunohama. Low, rambling inn in "traditional" style, built right on the beach. Y15–30,000 w/meals. AX, V, DC, MC.

**Ibusuki Kankō Hotel** 指宿観光ホテル (2-2131). 3755 Jūni-chō. Resort hotel to make Japanese honeymooners think they're in Hawaii. Jungle bath. Y10–15,000 w/meals. DC, V, AX, MC.

**Ibusuki Royal Hotel** 指宿ロイヤルホテル (23-2211). 4232-1 Jūni-chō. More restrained than the Kankō Hotel. Y10–20,000 w/meals. AX, DC, V, MC.

**Kokumin Kyūkamura (People's Vacation Village)** 指宿国民休暇村 (22-3211). 10445 Higashikata. *0:20h by microbus from station*. Resort facilities. Y6500 w/meals. No CC.

**Tamaya YH** 圭屋YH (22-3553). 5-27-8 Yunohama. Across from sand baths. Ryokan type.

501

## YAMAKAWA 山川
*0:07h by train from Ibusuki. 0:15h by bus from the station is Yamagawa-kō (harbor), where you can catch a ferry across the bay to Nejime or Ōnejime.*

### Exploring the West Coast of Satsuma Peninsula
# From Ibusuki, the JR line continues west, hugging the south shore of the peninsula, to the deep-sea fishing port of **Makurazaki** (*1:20h from Ibusuki, or 0:40h by bus from Chiran*). On the way, you'll pass the perfect cone of **Mt. Kaimon**. The harbor and fish market of Makurazaki is extremely lively during the peak bonito season (April–May). On sunny days, *katsuobushi*, woody brown filets of bonito, are set out to dry in the sun. **Bōnotsu** (*0:25h by bus from Makurazaki*) is an idyllic fishing village set in a cove. This village was a port of trade with China from the 6th century on. When in the early 17th century the Tokugawa shogunate closed all ports except Nagasaki to foreign trade, the Satsuma domain continued to use Bōnotsu to conduct a secret trade via Okinawa. There are old neighborhoods and a historical museum. **Fukiage-hama** (*1:10h by bus from Makurazaki*) is a long, white sand beach with a quiet hot-spring village and *tai-ami* (sea-bream netting) in the fall. **Lodgings:** Kurahama-sō (0993-67-0073), 150-year-old house on the waterfront in Bōnotsu, Y5500 w/meals. At Fukiage, Fukiaga-hama YH (0992-92-3455), a small, pleasant house.

### Exploring Southwest Islands
# Adventurous travelers with time may be tempted by the subtropical coral islands trailing off the southern tip of Kyūshū. Ferries depart from Kagoshima pier; air service is available from Kagoshima airport.

**Tanegashima.** *1:35h by jet foil from Kagoshima.* The historically famous island where Portuguese castaways introduced firearms into Japan in 1543 (see Nagasaki History, p. 483).

**Yakushima.** *1:43h by daily jet foil from Kagoshima.* A mountainous, rainy, subtropical island, part of Kirishima-Yaku National Park, famous for virgin forests of Yaku *sugi* (cryptomeria). There are open-air hot-spring baths amid tide pools at Hirauchi, 1:20h from Miyanoura dock. **Lodgings:** Hotel Yakushima (09974-2-0175), Kokuminshukusha Yakushima Onsen (7-2011).

**Iojima.** *5:00h by ferry from Kagoshima (8 per month).* An exotic desolation of sulfur, volcanoes, spectacular open-air hot springs, and wild peacocks.

**Amami Ōshima.** *12:00h by ferry from Kagoshima, 25:00h from Ōsaka.* Nase is the main harbor. This is the largest of the Amami group of islands, which once belonged to the Ryūkyū Kingdom (Okinawa). Known for Ōshima-tsumugi, a hand-woven, expensive silk pongee. White sand beaches and coral seas.

**Tokunoshima.** *15:40h by ferry from Kagoshima.* Coral seas, resorts.

**Okinoerabu.** *18:20h by ferry from Kagoshima.* Tropical flower plantations and caves.

**Yoron-tō.** *20:20h by ferry from Kagoshima or 4:20h from Naha (Okinawa).* A small, flat coral atoll. Beach resorts.

502

# KYŪSHŪ VI:E EAST FROM KAGOSHIMA

### E1 **KIRISHIMA JINGŪ STATION** 霧島神宮駅
*0:50–1:20h from Nishi-Kagoshima or 1:20–1:40h from Miyazaki by JR Nippō line express or local. Junction for buses into the Kirishima/Ebino Kōgen region.*

### E2 * **KIRISHIMA/EBINO KŌGEN** 霧島・えびの高原
*The simplest of the many routes into the park is to take an express bus departing once or twice an hour from Kagoshima (Nishi-Kagoshima station or Tenmonkan): 2:05h to Hayashida Onsen via Kirishima Jingū, with a few continuing on to Ebino Kōgen. From Hayashida Onsen, it is 2:30h by another express bus via Ebino Kōgen and Kobayashi to Miyazaki (E3). From Kumamoto (KYŪSHŪ V) or Miyazaki, take the JR Ebino-gō express train to Kobayashi, and change to a bus to Ebino Kōgen.* This beautiful highland of volcanoes, pocked with multihued caldera lakes, offers good hiking, superb scenery, and an abundance of hot springs. There are two major tourist centers: Hayashida Onsen, a developed spa, and Ebino Kōgen, a mountain resort in a scenic setting, with good access to hiking trails. This area is intimately connected with Japanese myths of creation. Takachiho no Mine, a tall volcano in the southeast side of the park, is where Ninigi no Mikoto, grandson of Amaterasu Ōmikami, the Sun Goddess, landed on his mission to rule Japan (see Kyūshū History, p. 469.)

* **Kirishima Jingū (Shrine)** 霧島神宮 *1:35h by bus from Kagoshima, or 0:15h by bus from Kirishima Jingū station.* Dedicated to Ninigi no Mikoto. The shrine is said to have been founded in the 6th C. The present buildings date from 1715. It is in a pretty grove of cryptomeria, but offers little else to see. On L 2/4, the shrine conducts its **Otaue-sai**, a humorous rice-planting festival with masked dancers.

**Takachiho-gawara** 高千穂川原 *0:45h by bus from Kirishima Jingū station.* This was the original site of Kirishima Jingū. From here, the steaming caldera of **Takachiho no Mine** (1574 m) can be reached in a 1:30h climb; thrust into the cairn at the summit is a halberd, called Ama no Sakaboko, said to have been planted by Ninigi upon his landing there. From Takachiho-gawara one can hike northwest to Karakunidake and Ebino Kōgen via several smaller peaks (4:00h).

**★★★ Ebino Kōgen** えびの高原 *0:20h by bus from Hayashida Onsen, or 2:20h by express bus from Kagoshima*. This volcanic plateau, called Shrimp Meadow, is covered with pampas grass that turns shrimp-red in September, a phenomenon attributed to chemical reactions with the sulfurous fumes billowing constantly from the fumeroles that dot the slopes. In early summer, wild azaleas splash the mountainside with magenta. There are easy hikes around the "hells" and tiny crater lakes.

**★★★ Karakunidake** 韓国岳 *1:00h climb from Ebino Kōgen*. This dramatic volcano towering above Ebino Kōgen offers a splendid view. You may not be able to see Karakuni (Korea), but on a clear day you will be rewarded with a view of Sakurajima.

**★★ Ebino Kōgen Rotemburo** えびの高原露天風呂 *1.5 km from the Ebino Kōgen bus terminal*. The Kobayashi-bound bus stops right in front. These boulder-lined open-air baths, surrounded by trees and tall grass, are among the most idyllic hot-spring baths in Japan. There are a few simple cabins on the site where you can stay for a small fee (see Lodgings).

## Kirishima/Ebino Kōgen Lodgings
**★ Gajōen** 雅叙苑　妙見温泉 (0995-77-2115). 4230 Shuku Kubota, Makizono-chō, Aira-gun, Kagoshima-ken. Onsen inn with a rustic theme at Myōken Onsen, on the route from Kagoshima airport. Marred by the ugly hotels across the river. Y15,000 w/meals.

**★ Ebino Kōgen Hotel** えびの高原ホテル (0984-33-1155). Suenaga, Ebino-shi, Miyazaki-ken. The *honkan* (main wing) is a pleasant lodge right at the foot of Karakunidake. Mountain cuisine. Tw Y7-25,000.

**Kokuminshukusha Ebinokōgen-sō** 国民宿舎えびの高原荘 (0984-33-0161). Suenaga, Ebino-shi. Onsen bath. Y5609 w/meals.

**Ebino Kōgen Rotemburo**. 1208 Ōji Suenaga, Ebino-shi. In summer, reserve by mail. Basic tatami-matted cabins; Y1500 per person; Y610 futon rental.

## E3 MIYAZAKI　宮崎
*2:00h by bus from Ebino Kōgen (4 per day). 2:30h by express bus (Y2700) or 2:20h (Y3500) by JR Nippō line express from Kagoshima. 5:30h from Kokura* (KYŪSHŪ I) *by JR Nippō line express. By air: 1:30h from Tokyo, or 1:00h from Ōsaka (ANA). By ferry: 16:30h from Ōsaka, 14:00h from Kobe.* Typical southern Japanese city—humdrum buildings softened by lush greenery and palm-lined boulevards. North of Miyazaki is Saitobaru (E4), with some 380 *kofun* (mound tombs) dating from the 5th–6th centuries.

**Getting Around**
Buses to various sights stop at Tachibana-dōri San-chōme, 0:05h on foot from Miyazaki station; walk 500 meters west to a major intersection, turn left at Yamagataya Department Store, and walk one block. Buses to Miyazaki Jingū and Heiwa-dai Kōen stop on the right. The main bus terminal, called Miya-kō City, is near Minami-Miyazaki station.

**Miyazaki Sights**
**Miyazaki Jingū (Shrine)**　宮崎神宮 *0:10h by bus from Tachibana-dōri San-chōme*. State Shinto shrine to the mythical first emperor, Jimmu, built in the Shimmei (Ise) style. Quiet wooded grounds.

**★ Heiwa-dai Kōen (Peace Park)**　平和台公園 *0:15h by bus from Tachibana-dōri San-chōme. 600 meters north of Miyazaki Jingū*. The peace tower in this park was built in 1940 with the help of the Burmese. Near it is a flower garden dotted with copies of *haniwa*, the clay tomb figurines excavated in quantity from Saitobaru (E4). Though a little ramshackle, they give a picture of the varieties of *haniwa* and how they might have appeared in the open, as it is surmised, arranged on top of the burial mounds. A small hall in the center of the garden displays a *haniwa* torch that served as the starting point for the 1964 Olympic flame. There is also a "make your own *haniwa*" workshop.

**Miyazaki Dining and Lodgings** (TEL 0985)
The local warm-weather dish is *hiyajiru* (cold soup), made of broiled white fish, ground with sesame, thinned with a stock, and chilled. It is served with minced cucumber, *shiso* (beefsteak leaf), and crumbled tofu, and poured over hot rice.

**★ Kuretake** 呉竹本店　橘通西3-2-10二幸ビル地下 (24-2818). Nikkō Bldg., basement. Hrs: 17:00-22:00 (last order); clsd Su, NY. Near Washington Hotel. *Hiyajiru* and other local dishes are arranged in large bowls on the counter, so you can order by pointing. *Hiyajiru* with rice, Y600.

**Washington Hotel** ワシントンホテル (28-9111). 3-1-1 Tachibana-dōri Nishi, Miyazaki-shi. Cozy business hotel; near nightlife district. S Y5900, Tw Y10,900.

**YH Miyazaki Fujin Kaikan** YH宮崎県婦人会館 (24-5785). 1-3-10 Asahi. Y3000 w/meals.

## E4 ★ SAITOBARU KOFUN-GUN (TUMULI)　西都原古墳群
*1:10h by bus from Miya-kō City (in Miyazaki)*. This is one of the most famous archeological sites in Japan, with more than 300 burial mounds from the 5th–6th centuries, most rather small. The *kofun* are in various shapes—round, square, keyhole—and are thought to have been built by a powerful local clan; one tradition holds that they were relatives of the imperial clan. The park doubles as a beautiful garden, enhancing the mysterious atmosphere. Two of the tombs can be entered. Excavations have uncovered large numbers of gilt-bronze horse

503

trappings and unusual *haniwa*, such as "the child-possessing *haniwa*," a house with smaller houses sprouting from each of its four sides. There is a model at the **Saitobaru Shiryōkan** museum. (Hrs: 9:00–16:30; clsd M, day after NH, NY.) The original is in the Tokyo National Museum.

**Calendar**
L 8/1: ✶✶ **Usudaiko Odori.** Saito, Shimozuru (*0:13h by bus from Saitobaru*). See Calendar, p. 468.

### E5 NOBEOKA 延岡
*1:15–1:30h from Miyazaki or 3:35h from Beppu* (KYŪSHŪ I:E3) *by JR Nippō line limited express. Nobeoka is the junction to Takachiho* (KYŪSHŪ V:E3).

### E6 NICHINAN KAIGAN (COAST) 日南海岸
*There is a train to this region, but to see the seascapes and attractions, take a bus or car along Rte. 220, which hugs the coast. Buses and car rentals at Miyazaki station.* This 60-km stretch of coast is anchored at either end by heavily trafficked tourist attractions, Aoshima and Toi Misaki. We suggest skipping these two places and concentrating on the beautiful coast between, with its stretches of "devil's washboard" eroded rock formations, white sand beaches, offshore islets, and cliffs that plunge hundreds of feet to the ocean.

**Aoshima** 青島 *0:30–0:40h from Miyazaki, by train or bus.* Hard to miss: a wall of hotels blocks the view of the beach, while aggressive parking attendants block the road trying to wave cars into their lots. The reason for the excitement is a minuscule islet fringed by "devil's washboard" eroded basalt and lush with subtropical flora. The far side is unspoiled and quiet. Aoshima is connected with the legend of Umisachi (Luck of the Sea) and Yamasachi (Luck of the Mountain), two sons of Ninigi, the god who landed on Mt. Takachiho (see Kyūshū History, p. 469). The two decide one day to trade roles, but Yamasachi loses Umisachi's precious fishhook. Umisachi is furious, and Yamasachi must find the hook. His quest takes him to the Dragon King's undersea palace, where he falls in love with a Sea Princess. The Dragon King assembles his subjects and finds the fishhook caught in the throat of a sea bream. Yamasachi joyfully returns to land, climbing ashore at Aoshima.

✶ **Udo Jingū (Shrine)** 鵜戸神宮 *1:20h by bus from Miyazaki.* After Yamasachi (see above) returns to land, the two brothers quarrel, but Yamasachi subdues Umisachi with the two magic jewels and dagger he received from the Dragon King. Yamasachi marries the beautiful Sea Princess. But when she gives birth, he secretly spies on her and sees her in her true form, as a huge crocodile. Angry and ashamed, she returns to the sea, but sends a younger sister to nurse the child, Ugayafukiaezu no Mikoto. Udo Shrine is dedicated to this child, who becomes the father of Japan's mythical first emperor, Jimmu. The shrine occupies a wonderful location by a sea cliff, inside a large cavern. Most visitors spend their time aiming clay balls at a small hole on the back of Kame-iwa, a turtle-shaped boulder among the rocks below which is supposed to fulfill one's wishes.

✶✶ **Obi** 飫肥 *1:10h by JR Nichinan line from Miyazaki, or two stops from Aburatsu town, on the coast.* Obi was the castle town of the Itō, a poor daimyo family. After his father had lost the castle to the Shimazu of Kagoshima, Itō Suketaka won it back ten years later as a reward for his valor in HIDEYOSHI's Kyūshū campaigns against the Shimazu. **Yoshōkan**, the Itō's Meiji-period villa, has a rather dilapidated garden. The local history museum exhibits Itō memorabilia and an interesting collection of "god masks" from a nearby shrine (Hrs: 9:30–17:00; clsd NY). The **Matsuomaru**, a probably not-too-faithful reconstruction of the residence of the Itō lord's principal wife, is now rented out as a reception hall (with all the modern conveniences). The most interesting part of the building is an old-fashioned *mush-iburo*, or steam bath, with a large clay stove sheltered by a "Chinese-style" gable. Above the Matsuomaru is the site of the early castle, which offers a pleasant view and is surrounded by cryptomerias, for which Obi is famous. If one follows the curve of the street below the main castle gate, there's a neighborhood of old stone walls and gates from former samurai dwellings. Nearby stands the old clan school, a smallish wooden building.

**Ishinami Kaigan** 石波海岸 A beautiful cove with unspoiled white sand beach and Minshuku Kyūkamura, a group of old farmhouse-minshuku (open only in summer). Just off the southern end of this cove is **Kōjima**, inhabited by wild monkeys (famous for the discovery by anthropologist Itani Junichirō of simian culture; mother monkeys were teaching their offspring how to wash sweet potatoes).

**Toi Misaki (Cape)** 都井岬 *2:50h by bus from Miyazaki.* Scenic, but the tip is covered with shabby tourist hotels, and the roads are full of tour buses and people stopping to feed the "wild" horses.

#### Nichinan Lodgings (TEL 0987)
**Daiichi Hotel** 第一ホテル (23-9111). 1-16 Iwasaki, Nichinan-shi, Miyazaki-ken. S Y5000, Tw Y9000.
**Hotel Yamashiro** ホテル山城 (25-3505). Obi Ekimae, Nichinan-shi. By Obi station. S Y4400, Tw Y8000.
**Nichinan Kaigan YH** 日南海岸YH (27-0113). 2348 Kumaya, Nichinan-shi. Good views.

504

# Okinawa

Okinawa, with its warm tropical beauty, sugarcane fields, luminous coral seas, and white beaches, is publicized as Japan's Hawaii. But the real fascination of these islands lies in their unique culture and history, distinct in almost every way from their Japanese cousin. Poor in natural resources, the Okinawans became skillful mariners. They assimilated and combined the influences of China, Japan, and Southeast Asia to create an entrancing culture. Though the outward signs of old Okinawa are vanishing, there is still a different mood here, a mood set by the Okinawan *jabisen*, heard everywhere, wafting over the soft breezes from some unseen source—a radio or, at night, a *karaoke* bar. The lilting South Asian rhythms, gay yet with a melancholy undercurrent, are a world apart from mainland Japan, and bespeak a different ethnic personality—slower, warmer, less compulsively punctual and punctilious. The music entices the traveler to seek out the real Okinawa behind the beach-resort facade.

## BEST ATTRACTIONS

| | **Naha.** Living Okinawan culture—music, dance, crafts and cuisine—and at Shuri, the ruins of the royal city (p. 511).

|| **Kumejima.** Beautiful, unspoiled island famous for exquisite silk pongee (p. 520).

|| **Taketomi.** This tiny island has Okinawa's best-preserved village, abloom with tropical flowers (p. 523).

|| **Iriomote.** Most of the island is unspoiled jungle, protected as a national park. Excellent scuba diving (p. 524).

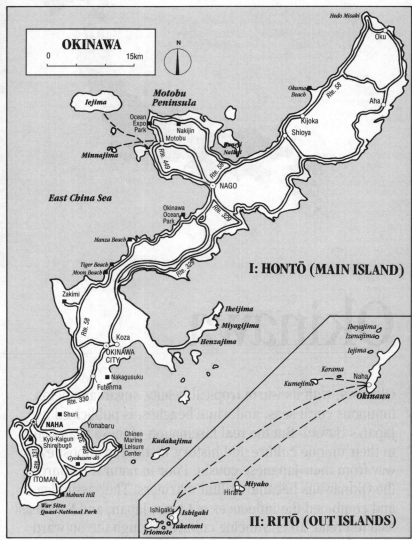

## Seasons

The high season, July 20–August 31, is scorchingly hot and crowded; reservations for transport and hotels are essential. Winter, spring and fall are better for traveling. But bear in mind the May rainy season and typhoons (July–Oct.). Famous resorts such as Manza Beach are booked solid months in advance from April to September. Between November and March, the seas are cooler but visibility improves for scuba divers, and many hotels offer discounts. What to bring: sunglasses, hat, sunscreen, umbrella, mosquito repellent, swimsuit, beach sandals, snorkeling equipment. Be careful not to step onto sea urchins.

## Average Temperature °C (°F)/Days of Rain

|  | January | April | July | October |
|---|---|---|---|---|
| Naha | 16.0 (60.8)/12 | 20.8 (69.4)/10 | 28.2 (82.8)/10 | 24.1 (75.4)/9 |

## Traveling

Naha is served by domestic flights from Sapporo, Sendai, Tokyo, Ōsaka, Fukuoka, and major cities in Kyūshū, as well as by international flights from Guam, Taipei, Hong Kong, and Manila. ANA and JAL offer special discounted airfare and hotel packages, usually of short duration. In addition, there are ferries from Tokyo, Ōsaka, Hakata, Kagoshima, and Keelung (Taiwan).

For interisland travel, Nansei Kōkū (SWAL) 南西航空 (098-857-4961) flies small prop planes from Naha to Ishigaki, Miyako, Shimoji, Kume, and Yoron (Kagoshima prefecture). There is also ferry service between the islands. If time is limited, you must check plane/ferry timetables in advance and plan accordingly. The ferries in the Yaeyama Islands are particularly chaotic; if all else fails, you can try to charter a boat. Since public transport can be inconvenient, consider renting cars or scooters. Road signs on the main island are in English, and the outer islands are small and fairly uncomplicated.

| Flights to Naha | Travel Time | One-Way Fare* |
|---|---|---|
| From Tokyo, 8–10/day (ANA, JAL) | 2:30h | Y34,900 |
| From Nagoya, 4–6/day (ANA, JAL) | 2:10h | Y32,750 |
| From Ōsaka, 3–4/day (ANA, JAL) | 2:00h | Y29,100 |
| From Fukuoka, 4–5/day (ANA, JAL) | 1:35h | Y23,100 |

| Ferries to Naha | Travel Time | Fares | Phone |
|---|---|---|---|
| From Tokyo, 3–5/mo. | 48:00h | Y19,670–49,180 | 03-3273-8911 (Tokyo) |
| | | | 098-861-1811 (Naha) |
| From Tokyo, 3–6/mo. | 44:00h | Y19,670–49,180 | 03-3281-1831 (Tokyo) |
| | | | 098-868-1126 (Naha) |
| From Ōsaka, 5–7/mo. (W, Sa) | 33:40h | Y15,450–38,620 | 06-531-9271 (Ōsaka) |
| | | | 098-868-2191 (Naha) |
| From Ōsaka, 4–5/mo. (Sa) | 39:20h | Y15,450–38,620 | 06-538-0051 (Ōsaka) |
| | | | 098-868-1126 (Naha) |
| From Hakata, 6–9/mo. | 27:30h | Y12,970–32,450 | 092-271-5315 (Hakata) |
| | | | 098-868-1126 (Naha) |
| From Kagoshima, 8–11/mo. | 20:00h | Y11,850–29,610 | 0992-26-1652 (Kagoshima) |
| | | | 098-868-1126 (Naha) |

| To/From Taiwan | Departures | Travel Time | 2nd Class | Cabin Class |
|---|---|---|---|---|
| From Naha | Friday (20:00) | 35:30h | Y15,600 | Y21,900 |
| From Keelung | Monday (20:00) | 36:30h | Y15,600 | Y21,900 |

*Phone*: Arimura Sangyō Co. In Tokyo, 03-3562-2091. In Naha, 098-868-2191. In Keelung, 032-248151.

| Interisland Air Routes (SWAL) | Travel Time | One-Way Fare* |
|---|---|---|
| Naha-Kume, 7/day | 0:35h | Y5360 |
| Naha-Miyako, 6/day | 0:45–1:00h | Y10,950 |
| Naha-Ishigaki, 8/day | 0:55h | Y14,710 |
| Miyako-Ishigaki, 2/day | 0:30–0:35h | Y5360 |

507

| Interisland Ferries | Travel Time | Base Fare | Phone |
|---|---|---|---|
| Naha-Kume, 1/day | 1:45h | Y2680 | 098-868-2686 |
| Naha-Zamami (Kerama), 3/day | 1:50h | Y1750 | 098-868-4567 |
| Naha-Miyako, 4–10/mo. | 10:00–10:30h | Y3810 | 098-868-1126 or |
| | | | 098-868-2191 |
| Naha-Ishigaki, 4–10/mo. | 13:30–17:30h | Y5250 | 098-868-1126 or |
| | | | 098-868-2191 |
| Miyako-Ishigaki, 4–10/mo. | 5:30h | Y1850 | 098-868-1126 or |
| | | | 098-868-2191 |

*10 percent discount on round trip, if return is within 10 days of departure.

**Car Rental in Naha:** Japaren ジャパレン東町20-2 (861-3900) Y5500+ for 6:00h, Y10,500+ for 24:00h. Kūkō (Airport) Rent-a-car 空港レンタカー 山下町1-1 (859-1111) Y5000+ (6:00h), Y8,500+ (24:00h), Y14,500+ (48:00h), Y5000 for each additional day plus Y1500 per day insurance. Nippon/Hertz 日本レンタカー 西1-19-1 (868-4554), Nissan/Avis 日産レンタカー 久茂地2-15-12 (867-4123), Toyota トヨタレンタカー 奥武山町16 (859-0100).

### Resources

*Okinawa by Road* is a detailed road atlas to Okinawa's main and outer islands, with illustrations and text on towns and attractions. Published by Kume Shobō, Jingū-mae, Shibuya, Tokyo (03-405-8510). Sold at Naha Airport and at bookstores in Okinawa and Tokyo. *Okinawa: The History of an Island People*, by George H. Kerr (Charles E. Tuttle, 1958), is substantial and excellent.

# SPECIAL INTERESTS

**Well-Preserved Towns:** Traditional Okinawan houses were built of wood, open to the breezes, and surrounded by tall hedges and fine stone enclosures. Their bright roofs of red tile contrast smartly with thick seams of white mortar, crowned by *shīsā* (lions). Such houses are becoming rare. Some of the best-preserved areas include Taketomi, Kumejima and, on the main island, villages such as Kijoka.

**Crafts:** Naha's Tsuboya pottery, lacquerware, and glass, hand-blown from recycled bottles, are attractive, but the glory of Okinawa is its textiles, which have a bright, open beauty that belies their history as a burdensome tax (see Okinawa History). In certain areas fine textiles are still handwoven with extraordinary fidelity to tradition. Most employ simple weaves, with stripes, plaids, and *kasuri* designs, using plant dyes. Bashōfu, a linenlike plantain fabric, once worn by commoners, is produced at Kijoka. Minsā-ori, *ikat*-patterned sashes, are woven on Taketomi. Two fine textiles once reserved for "tribute," Miyako-jōfu, a fine, indigo-dyed ramie, and Kumejima-tsumugi, a silk pongee dyed with plants and iron-rich mud, are still woven on Miyako and Kumejima. Bingata, the aristocrat of Okinawan textiles, is made by applying rice-paste resist with stencils and then filling in the designs with bright colors. It is made in Shuri. The yellow in Kumejima-tsumugi and Bingata comes from the bark of the *fukugi*, a tree used for hedges. The dye was reserved for royalty.

**Performing Arts:** Early visitors to Okinawa remarked on the islanders' fondness for singing and dancing, and until only a few decades ago workers in remoter areas carried their *jabisen* into the fields. Though Okinawan dance is said to be influenced by Noh and Kabuki, its affinity to Southeast Asia is more obvious, especially in the tonal scale and rhythms of the music, and in the supple, expressive hand gestures of the dancers. The vast repertory ranges from the mesmerizing court dances by Bingata-clad beauties and haunting love ballads to lusty, rhythmic jigs of the country folk. There are also dances based on karate *kata*. (The Okinawans practiced karate for self-defense because they were forbidden to carry weapons.) Dances are performed at matsuri and in excellent professional dance theaters in Naha.

**Cuisine:** Okinawan cuisine combines characteristics of Chinese and Japanese cuisine. The staple is pork, and virtually every part of the pig is used. Sauces are rich compared to mainland Japanese cuisine, but the food is arranged attractively in the Japanese manner. Typical dishes: *rafutei* (chunks of pork simmered until very tender with miso, soy sauce, *awamori*, and sugar), *ashite-bichi* (stewed pigs' feet), *nakami no suimono* (pork tripe soup), *mimigā* (julienned pork ear with cucumber, dressed with vinegar), *goya champurū* (sautéed bitter melon), *jīmāmi-dōfu* (peanut tofu), *Ryūkyū-soba* (a broad noodle served in rich, pork broth). *Awamori* is a strong distilled rice liquor that mellows with age; *shīkwāsa* is citrus juice.

**Beach Resorts:** Since Okinawa reverted to Japan in 1972, Japanese companies have been building deluxe beach resorts on the finest white sand beaches and islets. Generally, they offer high standards of accommodation but are very expensive, resort equipment is often in poor condition, and beach use is often restricted. Not the best value, at Y15,000 or more per person per day. Better resorts: Manza Beach (main island), Eef Beach (Kumejima).

**Scuba Diving:** Iriomote's Manta Way and Kerama's fantastic coral reefs offer some of the best diving in Asia. Rental gear, boats, and guides operate on each of the islands (cost is about Y10,000 per day, all-inclusive). PADI or NAUI certification accepted. Look under listings for details.

508

# CALENDAR

Okinawans still observe nearly all matsuri by the lunar calendar, and many localities jealously guard these important religious rites against becoming tourist spectacles. Ask for permission before taking pictures. The Okinawan matsuri cycle has special features: *Tantoi* (seed selection) is in L 9–10. *Taue* (rice planting) is during L 12–1. *Mugi no Ho* (prayer for rich harvest) is in L 2. In L 5, *Hārī* boat races bring the blessings of the spirit world across the sea. The rice harvest is in L 6. (See p. 75 for a lunar calendar conversion chart.)

**L 1/20: ✻✻ Juriuma.** Naha (I). A parade that enabled women of the pleasure quarter, dressed in their finest, most colorful *bingata* kimono, to see their kin. Distinctive song and dance with hobby horses.

**May 3–4: ✻✻ Hārī.** Naha (I). Dragon-boat races. Excited spectators often plunge into the sea to urge on their team.

**L 5/4: ✻✻ Hārī.** Itoman (I) and Ishigaki (II) are good places to watch the boat races.

**L 6: ✻✻ Yaeyama Hōnen-sai.** Ishigaki (II). Held for two days, starting on the first "lucky day." On the 1st day are sacred rites; saké, Mishagpashi song and Maki dance are dedicated to the kami. Offerings of pole dances and lion dances. The 2nd day features processions, a women's tug-of-war, and many other lively games and performances.

**L 6: ✻ Ōtsunahiki.** Yonabaru (I). Around L 6/26. P E

**L 7/13–15 ✻✻ Eisā.** Bon dances throughout Okinawa. Koza, near Okinawa city (I), has one that's big and easy to see. Vigorous, rhythmic dances by drum-beating young men.

**L 7/14–16: ✻ Angamā.** Ishigaki (II). P B

**L 7/15: ✻ Kuichā Yuichā.** Miyako (II). P

**L 7/16: ✻ Angamā.** Taketomi (II). P B

**L 7: ✻✻ Unjami Matsuri.** (First day of the Boar after L 7/15). Shioya (I) has an especially colorful version of this widely observed rite. A group of priestesses gathers to call the gods from across the sea, for the prosperity and safety of the village. Then men in dugout boats race to nearby islands to spread the blessings. There's a dance called Usudēku, performed by women in kimono; they dance in a circle while beating drums. Usudēku is thought to be a very ancient Ryūkyūan form. Kijoka is a good place to see it.

**L 8: ✻ # Hōnen Matsuri.** Taramajima, Miyako (II). Sa–M between L 8/1–15. P

**L 8–L 9: ✻ Setsu Matsuri.** Iriomote, Sonae (II). For 3 days, at Tsuchi no toi day. P E

**L 8/15: ✻✻ Itoman no Tsunahiki.** Itoman (I). Immense male and female ropes are interlocked and engaged in a tug-of-war to predict the harvest. There are two teams, east and west; if west wins, it will be a good year; if east wins, it will be an unlucky year. From 17:00.

**L 9: ✻ Yūkui.** Miyako, Ikemajima (II). On a lucky day at the end of the month. P S

**Oct. 10: ✻✻ Naha Ōtsunahiki.** Naha (I). Two enormous ropes, male and female, one meter thick and 100 meters long, are interlocked in a tug-of-war involving thousands of people and lasting for hours. Since Naha isn't agricultural, its tug-of-war wasn't really an annual rite. Today it commemorates the day American bombing destroyed Naha in 1944.

**L 10: ✻✻ Tantoi.** Taketomi (II). From Ki no esaru day, continues for 10 days. This is a festival for the harvest. On days 7 and 8, there are offerings of dances and Kyōgen, nearly 40 in all.

**L 11/15–19: ✻ Izaihō.** Kudakajima (I). In the year of the horse (next in 2002). P S

# Okinawa History

Okinawa, the Rope on the Sea, is the southern half of the 1,300-kilometer chain of islands dangling from Kyūshū almost to Taiwan. The main island in the chain—the heart of its culture and history—is also called Okinawa. Geography has dramatically determined the fate of its people. Okinawan language and folk traditions are closely related to those of Japan, but since the fourteenth century, the Okinawans have been profoundly influenced by China. After a few centuries of relative prosperity, however, Okinawa found itself in the difficult position of being a vassal of both China and Japan, or to be exact, the **Satsuma** domain of Kagoshima which ruled—and taxed— the islands from 1609 to 1879. After nearly three centuries of exploitation by Satsuma, Okinawa received semi-colonial treatment from the new Japanese government. During World War II, Okinawa paid the price for Japan's aggressive war in Asia with some 150,000 civilian dead. Ironically, because they were treated with suspicion by the mainland Japanese, most Okinawans had been until 1944 only minimally involved in the war effort. This tragic history is oddly at variance with the enchanting beauty of the land itself and the charm and gentle refinement of Okinawan culture.

There is overwhelming evidence for a common prehistory for the Japanese and Okinawan peoples, at least as far south as Okinawa island, where pottery from Japan's prehistoric Jōmon and Yayoi cultures has been unearthed. Japanese language and the various Okinawan dialects, although mutually unintelligible, are closely related. One linguist estimates that they diverged 1,500–2,000 years ago. Another scholar, noting that *nishi* means "west" in Japanese and "north" in Okinawan, suggests that they are both related to Japanese *inishi*, "the past," implying that Japanese origins lie to the west, and Okinawan origins to the north—that is, in Kyūshū, where the ancestors of each people crossed from Korea and then split apart.

Perhaps the most intriguing evidence of a common origin is the shamanistic cult of priestesses, called *noro*. Originally a virgin whose cult was associated with the purity of the hearth—most rural villages have a sanctuary for the *noro*'s three sacred hearth stones—the *noro* often had considerable political power. *Noro* priestesses, descendants of King Shō En, governed the sacred islands of Iheyajima and Izenajima until the nineteenth century; in Japan, there was a virgin priestess of royal birth at Ise up until the fourteenth century. Both the Ise priestesses and Okinawa's *noro* are reminiscent of Queen Pimiko, a Japanese priestess-queen of the third century, and point to a tradition of shamanesses among the common ancestors of the Japanese and the Okinawans (see Kyūshū History, p. 469). The curved *magatama* jewel of the Japanese imperial regalia is also the symbol of the *noro*'s office.

Okinawa is first mentioned in Japanese annals in 753, but it is in the late twelfth century that Okinawan history truly begins. A local *anji*, or chieftain, named Shunten united the main island, building his castle at present-day Shuri. Shunten was supposed to be the offspring of a MINAMOTO warrior exiled by the TAIRA and an Okinawan *anji*'s daughter. However improbable this legend, there were undoubtedly Japanese visitors to Okinawa at the time; Shunten's son is credited with adapting the Japanese *kana* writing system for the Okinawan language. The Eiso dynasty, which followed Shunten's, received tribute from the neighboring islands of Amami, Kerama, and Kume.

In 1316, Okinawa split into three kingdoms: southern, central, and northern. In 1372, Chūzan, the central kingdom, entered into formal relations with Ming China, and by 1383 all three kingdoms had sent tribute. This began Okinawa's long role, lasting until 1872, as a tributary of China. The Chinese called the islands Liuqiu, pronounced Ryūkyū in Japanese. These tribute missions were actually lucrative opportunities for trade, and it was not long before the "thirty-six families," a group of Chinese merchants, came to settle at Chūzan's Kume Village (now a quarter of bustling Naha), bringing with them Chinese customs. Okinawa's best families began sending their sons to study in China.

Okinawa's first great age began in 1429, when Shō Hashi reunited the island. The Ming emperor confirmed him as King of the Ryūkyū. It was during Shō Hashi's dynasty that Okinawa's Chinese-style cuisine, clothing, architecture, and music developed. The three-stringed *sangen* arrived from China in 1437, where it evolved into the Okinawan *jabisen*. (The snake-skinned *jabisen* later entered Japan and became the cat-skinned *shamisen*, which transformed Japanese drama and music in the seventeenth century. See Drama, p. 89.) Chinese stone-cutting techniques and knowledge of the stone arch, as yet unknown in Japan, enabled the Okinawans to build arched stone bridges, the eerie, "turtle-backed" Okinawan tombs, and the magnificent castles that dot the landscape.

A more exotic accent entered Okinawa through its trade with Malaysia and Indonesia. Malay-style turbans became fashionable among the aristocrats, and Southeast Asian textile techniques such as *ikat*, tie-dyeing, and stencil-dyeing (all of Indian

509

origin) profoundly influenced Okinawan crafts. Even today, the Okinawans are known as consummate weavers of *kasuri* (*ikat*), and the bright, stencil-dyed *bingata* is the Okinawan "national costume." In turn, these techniques became important in Japan.

Shō En, an able minister of the first Shō dynasty, rebelled in 1470 and established the second Shō dynasty, which built **Shuri Castle** and the **Tamaudon Royal Tombs.** His son, Shō Shin, compelled the local chieftains to give up their arms and live as nobles in Shuri. Here, trying to outdo each other in finery, they created a demand for objects of lacquer, silk, gold, and silver. Okinawa's new courtly culture also produced the *Omoro Sōshi*, compiled in 1532, a body of incantations, legends, and poems of the *noro* cult that forms the earliest comprehensive record of Okinawan traditions.

In 1523, the Ming dynasty and Japan's ASHIKAGA shogunate ceased direct trade relations. This marked the beginning of Okinawa's most prosperous age, as the major trade intermediary between them. It was during this period, in 1554, that the Ming Chinese chose to compliment Okinawa by presenting a tablet upon which it proclaimed Okinawa *shurei no kuni* (nation of propriety). A grand ceremonial gate, **Shurei Mon**, was built for the tablet; its postwar reconstruction remains the tourist symbol of Okinawa. Okinawan students had long studied in Peking and the trading port of Ch'uang-chou; in 1572, Okinawans also began to study at Kyoto's Zen temples (which were engaged in trade).

Toward the end of the sixteenth century, European ships began to cut deeply into the trade between China and Japan, with dire economic results for Okinawa. The arrival of the Europeans also set in motion a chain of events leading to Japan's reunification and a heightened Japanese interest in the islands to the south. Kyūshū's Satsuma domain, which held a "title" to Okinawa granted centuries earlier by the Kamakura shogunate, had long profited from the Okinawan trade. Fearful that the Tokugawa might block this activity, Satsuma laid a trap to gain control of the islands for good.

510

Satsuma asked the Okinawan king to pay his respects to Japan's new shogun, TOKUGAWA IEYASU. Having benefited from a century of disorder in Japan, the Okinawans underestimated the threat of a now-unified Japan, and the king refused. Ieyasu, who saw a chance to allow the restless and warlike Satsuma clan to let off steam, gave permission for a punitive expedition. In 1609, Satsuma sent a force of 3,000 to Okinawa, which captured its king and destroyed Shuri Castle. After two years, the king was returned home—in shame—but from then on Okinawa was, in fact if not in name, a colony of Satsuma. It was never to regain its independence.

Besides exacting heavy taxes, Satsuma used Okinawa's tribute missions to China, which had enabled the poor nation to prosper, for its own profit. An eminent Okinawan compared the Satsuma policy to cormorant fishing. The birds are put on a leash, with a tight ring around their necks; they catch the fish, but can't eat them. During the 260 years that Okinawa lived under Satsuma, it became much poorer, but in some ways it advanced. **Sai On**, the greatest statesman in Okinawan history, instituted agricultural reforms. These, together with the introduction of sugarcane and sweet potatoes, enabled the Okinawans to cultivate more land and stave off the famine that Satsuma's harsh policies threatened to engender. The Yaeyama and Miyako islands, having few resources other than painstaking labor, became known for fine textiles. Miyako-jōfu, a *kasuri* cloth made from ramie fiber, was first woven in 1583 as a gift to the king at Shuri; from the seventeenth century on it was sent as tribute to Satsuma, and became known in Japan as Satsuma-jōfu. Okinawa's Tsuboya pottery and the final forms of its distinctive dance and music developed at this time.

Satsuma, anxious to preserve its trading connection with China, was at pains to maintain the illusion of Okinawa as an independent Chinese tributary. Speaking Japanese was forbidden when the Chinese traders called at Naha. To show off their "foreign" vassal state, Satsuma ordered the Okinawans to dress in a Chinese style during their periodic embassies to the shogun's court at Edo. After the fall of the shogunate, however, the Meiji government was determined to remake the Okinawans into Japanese. In 1879, the Japanese annexed the islands and established Okinawa prefecture. They made its king a Japanese marquis and moved the capital from Shuri, with its royal associations, to nearby Naha. Like Satsuma before it, however, the government continued to tax Okinawa out of all proportion to its ability to pay. The only solution it cared to offer for Okinawa's poverty was to encourage emigration. By 1907, some 10,000 Okinawans were living abroad, many in Hawaii and the Americas. The government did, however, introduce widespread public education—in Japanese.

In spite of being treated as second-class citizens, the Okinawans did their best to assimilate, only to be caught between the "hammer and anvil" of American invading forces and fanatical Japanese defenders in 1944. During the last year of the war, the outer islands of Japan—including Okinawa and Iwo Jima—were riddled with tunnels, and preparations were made to fight a war of attrition with invading American forces. Naha was wiped out in American bombing attacks that began in October

1944. American forces landed, without resistance, at Kadena on April 1, 1945, and after mopping up northern Okinawa, closed in on the Japanese stronghold in the south. After ninety days of bitter fighting, the Japanese forces were dislodged from Shuri Castle and slowly pushed to the southern edge of Okinawa, to the cliffs of Mabumi, where virtually the entire Japanese command committed suicide. Japanese authorities had made no provision for civilian safety; to the contrary, some Japanese soldiers murdered Okinawans for food or shelter. Civilians fled to caves and tombs in the countryside. As the Americans advanced, many died rather than surrender to the "demons" who, they had been warned, would torture and kill prisoners. When the Battle of Okinawa ended, more than 250,000 people—Japanese, Americans, and Okinawans—were dead. Over half were Okinawan civilians, amounting to one-eighth of the island's population. Much of Okinawa's cultural heritage, including Shuri Castle and the treasures of the Shō royal family, were pulverized in the fighting.

After the war, it was Okinawa, not mainland Japan, that became an American possession. Many farmers saw their land taken, with little compensation, and paved over for military bases. Realizing that independence was not possible, the large majority of Okinawans wanted reunification with Japan. Education continued to be in Japanese; young Okinawans were forgetting their native dialects. The long and bitter sacrifice Okinawans had made in adapting to Japanese language and customs would hardly be repaid by quasi-colonial status as an American military outpost. Finally in 1972, Okinawa reverted to Japan. But the remaining presence of American bases and attitudes of the mainland Japanese are lingering sources of tension. In a recent controversy over requiring Japanese students to sing *Kimigayo*, the anthem of imperial Japan and still the unofficial national anthem, it was noted that the song was sung in virtually no Okinawan school.

511

# OKINAWA I. HONTŌ (MAIN ISLAND)

**Tokyo to Naha:** *See* p. 507.
**Prefecture:** Okinawa

The main island, or *hontō*, of Okinawa, though greatly modernized, remains the cultural center of the Okinawan archipelago. The old trading port of Naha is now a bustling city, short on sightseeing attractions, but a good place for shopping and dining. The main cultural relics are at nearby Shuri, the royal city destroyed in the war, and at the magnificent castle ruins of Nakagusuku and Nakijin. To the south are many memorial sites from the Battle of Okinawa. The large beach resorts are on the central west coast. Motobu Peninsula has some interesting museums from the 1975 Ocean Expo. Villages such as Kijoka, Oku, and Aha, in the north, and offshore islets such as Minnajima, Iheyajima, and Izenajima give a glimpse of traditional Okinawan life. The pristine and scenic northeast coast has a fine road with no public transport; the area is completely undeveloped.

## Traveling

There are tourist information desks at the airport and near the bus terminal in Naha; these offer assistance with hotels, car rental, sightseeing (some English spoken). There is a good public bus service between main towns, radiating out of the Naha Bus Terminal. If you can afford it, however, rent a car; the highways are well marked in English (side roads less so), and there is a detailed road atlas in English, *Okinawa by Road* (see p. 507).

## ** NAHA　那覇

Naha, the modern capital of Okinawa, is a chaotic jumble of pale concrete, sweating under the tropical sun. Yet this homely city, rebuilt over wartime rubble, remains an impressive repository of Okinawan culture. It has the best Okinawan cuisine, theaters of Okinawan dance and music, and attractive traditional crafts such as Tsuboya pottery, Ryūkyū lacquerware, and varieties of the famed textiles. In nearby Shuri, the old royal city, some of the monuments destroyed in the war have been restored amid lush, serene surroundings that evoke the gentle refinement of a vanished world.

## Calendar
L 1/20: ** **Juriuma.** Tsuji district. See Calendar, p. 508.
May 3–4: ** **Hārī.** Asa (new port). See Calendar, p. 508.
May 17: **Nanmin-sai.** Festival of the Naminoue-gū.
Oct. 10: ** **Naha Ōtsunahiki.** Kokusai-dōri and Ōnoyama-Kōen. See Calendar, p. 508.

## Getting Around
Downtown Naha is 0:15h by bus from the airport, 0:15 from Naha-kō (south harbor), or 0:10h from Tomari-kō (north harbor). Taxis start at Y360 (Y1200 for 0:30h). Makishi bus stop on Kokusai-dōri is served by buses 1, 9 and 13 to Shuri, and 17 to Himeyuribashi (near Tsuboya) and Shuri.

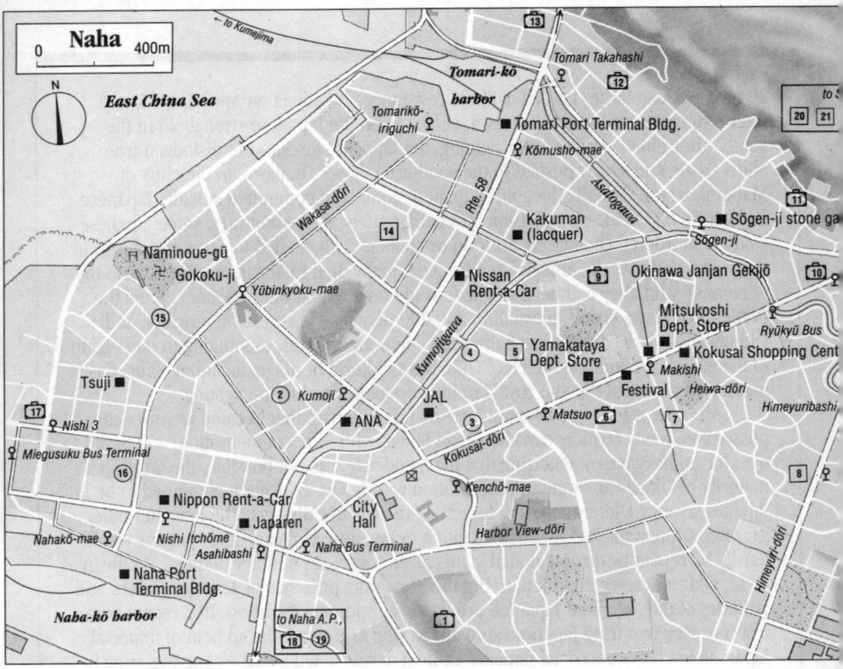
Naha
0
400m
N
East China Sea
to Kumejima
Tomari Takahashi
Tomari-kō
barbor
Tomarikō-iriguchi
Tomari Port Terminal Bldg.
Kōmusho-mae
Asatogawa
Rte. 58
Wakasa-dōri
Kakuman
(lacquer)
Sōgen-ji stone ga
Sōgen-ji
Naminoue-gū
Gokoku-ji
Yūbinkyoku-mae
Nissan
Rent-a-Car
Okinawa Janjan Gekijō
Mitsukoshi
Dept. Store
Ryūkyū Bus
Kokusai Shopping Cent
Kumojigawa
Yamakataya
Dept. Store
Makishi
Festival
Heiwa-dōri
Tsuji
Kumoji
JAL
ANA
Matsuo
Himeyuribashi
Nishi 3
Miegusuku Bus Terminal
Kokusai-dōri
Kenchō-mae
Nippon Rent-a-Car
City
Hall
Japaren
Harbor View-dōri
Nahakō-mae
Nishi Itchōme
Asahibashi
Naha Bus Terminal
Himeyuri-dōri
Naha Port
Terminal Bldg.
Naha-kō barbor
to Naha A.P.,



**Rent-a-cycle:** Okinawa Ringyō 沖縄輪業 松山1-4-1 (868-0404), near Matsuo bus stop. Naha is one place you don't want to drive a car: parking is scarce, it's easy to get lost, and rush-hour traffic is a nightmare. Bus lanes on main avenues are closed to cars M–Sa 7:00–9:00 and 17:30–19:30.

**Naha Sights**

**Naminoue-gū** 波の上宮 *0:10h by bus from Kenchō-mae, or 0:10h on foot from Naha-kō.* The Shrine Above the Waves, an unremarkable postwar reconstruction with pleasant grounds, perches on a promontory overlooking the ocean. It was the head shrine of the Eight Shrines of Okinawa, established in 1461. The shrine is sacred to the three gods of Kumano (see Kinki, p. 415), guardians of the adjacent Gokoku-ji, which was the premier temple of the Ryūkyū Kingdom, where the king prayed for the well-being of his realm. Just below the shrine is the **Kōshi-byō** 孔子廟, a Confucian temple with pretty stone walls, a red gate, and a peaceful courtyard. Just south of this area is **Tsuji** 辻, Naha's former licensed quarter, now a district of cabarets, sleazy hotels, and some fine traditional restaurants.

** **Kokusai-dōri** 国際通り A mile-long avenue which developed after the war into Naha's main shopping street, a favorite nighttime stroll for tourists. It is lined with every conceivable kind of shop, from dinner-theaters and craft shops to American diners and New Wave boutiques. The best areas are between the Kokusai (International) Plaza Hotel and Mitsukoshi Department Store. The Festival Building was designed by leading contemporary architect Andō Tadao.

*** **Heiwa-dōri** 平和通り This market street, forming a T-junction with Kokusai-dōri near Mitsukoshi Department Store, is the other face of Naha. The narrow, labyrinthine alleys are lined with produce stalls, pungent with exotic, South Asian aromas. Walls and roofs of older houses sprout weeds, and tiny, gnarled grannies with their silken white hair twisted in a neat Okinawan topknot scurry about their shopping.

*** **Tsuboya** 壺屋 Located in the neighborhood across from McDonald's on Himeyuri-dōri. Nice walk from Heiwa-dōri. This quaint pottery community was established in 1682 from three older kilns and remains home to some 20 workshops for traditional pottery. Hamada Shōji, the famous folk-art potter, was deeply influenced by his visits to Tsuboya in the 1920s and 1930s. Tsuboya turns out a wide range of everyday items, from teacups to ornate funerary urns with flaming, roof-shaped lids and bright splashes of glaze. *Shīsā* (lion roof ornaments) are virtually a symbol of Okinawa. Classic designs include crescent-shaped wine flasks and *kara-kara*, awamori servers with funnel-shaped mouths and curved spouts. Tsuboya is compact and fun to explore, with its open-doored workshops and walls embedded with broken pottery.

**Tsuboya Tōki Kaikan (Pottery Center)** 壺屋陶器会館, on the second floor over a parking space near the entrance to Tsuboya, shows and sells pottery from all of the kilns (Hrs: 9:00–18:00; Su, NH 9:30–18:00; clsd mid-Aug., NY).

**Sōgen-ji Sekimon** 崇元寺石門 (ICP). A rebuilt section of arched stone gates to the memorial temple of all the Ryūkyū kings. The temple is thought to have been built in the early 16th C.

*** **Shuri** 首里

*0:25h by bus from Makishi bus stop on Kokusai-dōri; get off at Ikehata.* The 500-year-old royal city of the Ryūkyū Kingdom was described in the 1930s as a "dream city" by Yanagi

Sōetsu, founder of Japan's folk-art movement. Tragically, it was destroyed by heavy bombing in the Battle of Okinawa. (Shuri had been appropriated as headquarters for Japanese military command.) Parts of the exterior walls and gates have been restored. Note: There are almost no restaurants in the area.

**\*\* Okinawa-kenritsu Hakubutsukan** (Prefectural Museum) 沖縄県立博物館 (884-2243). Hrs: 9:00–17:00; clsd M, NH, NY. *0:02h walk from Ikehata bus stop.* This modern museum stands on the site of the mansion of the Shō family, descendants of the Ryūkyū king. Across the street is a large pond, Ryūtan, built in 1427 for dragon-boat races to entertain the envoys of the Chinese emperor. Exhibits include the Bankoku Shinryō bell (ICP), a model of Shuri Castle, and textiles, pottery, and historical and folklore material, giving a fine overview of Okinawan history and culture.

**Benzaiten-dō** 弁財天堂 A charming chapel to the goddess of music, wealth, and jealousy, on an islet connected to the shore by a stone bridge (ICP). The hall was first built in 1502 to house Buddhist sutras from Korea, but was destroyed by Satsuma troops in 1609. It was rebuilt in the 17th C, and destroyed again in 1945.

**\* Engaku-ji Ato** 円覚寺跡 Site of the memorial temple of the second Shō dynasty kings; built in 1492 by a Japanese priest and based on the great Kamakura Zen monastery of the same name. Until 1944, it was a magnificent complex with the classic seven halls, designated NT. The low stone bridge, **Hōshō-kyō** (ICP), and **Sō-mon** gate were rebuilt after the war.

**\* Kankai-mon** 歓会門 A splendid reconstruction (1949) of the Shuri castle gate, with high walls of superb Okinawan masonry work. First built in the late 15th–early 16th C.

**Sonohiyan Utaki Seki-mon** 園比屋武御嶽石門 (Restored 1957, ICP). This small stone gate and wall built in Chinese style was erected in 1519 to enclose a sacred precinct of the high priestess of Okinawa. The king would pray here for safety on the road before traveling.

**Shurei Mon** 守礼門 A ceremonial gate on the main approach to Shuri Castle; rebuilt after the war. The graceful structure of wooden columns with a double roof of tile was first built 450 years ago to display a tablet inscribed "Land of Propriety," sent by the Chinese emperor. It is considered the symbol of Okinawa, hence the busloads of tourists posing before it with costumed Okinawan beauties.

513

**\*\*\* Tamaudun** 霊御殿 (ICP). Hrs: 8:30–18:00. Oct.–Apr. 8:30–17:30. *0:05h on foot from Shurei Mon.* The stone mausoleum of the second Shō dynasty was built in 1501 to entomb King Shō En. The compound is enclosed by two limestone walls, and standing sentinel at various points are unusual stone lions. The mausoleum consists of three chambers. The center chamber was where the body was left to putrefy before the bones were washed and interred. The left chamber was for the permanent interment of kings and queens, and the right chamber for princes and princesses. Severely damaged in the war, the tombs have been handsomely restored.

**\*\* Nihon Mingeikan** (Okinawan Branch of the Japan Folkcraft Museum) 日本民芸館 (885-0248). Hrs: May–Sept. 8:30–18:00. Oct.–Apr. 8:30–17:30. *0:10h on foot from Shurei Mon.* A small collection of Okinawan textiles and pottery, charmingly displayed in a 100-year-old Okinawan house moved from Ishigakijima. The textiles, on loan from the Nihon Mingeikan in Tokyo, were collected by Yanagi Sōetsu, founder of the Japanese folk-art movement.

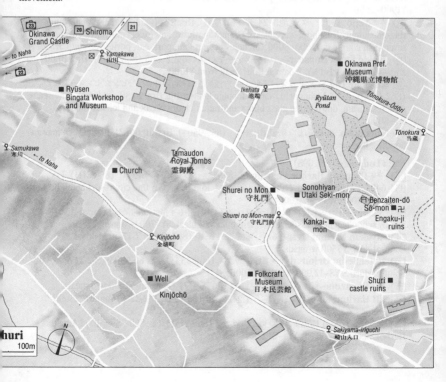

* **Kinjōchō Stone-paved Road** 金城町 In 1522, a stone-paved road was build to cover the 10 km from Shuri Castle to Naha harbor. This 200-m stretch is all that remains. With its quiet houses and vine-covered walls, it recalls something of bygone Okinawa.
* **Ryūsen** 竜泉 (886-1131). Farmhouse-style building in which Ryūsen fabric (like Bingata but made by a different technique) is displayed and sold. Workshop on third floor. A tea room on the ground floor provides a welcome rest spot.

## Ryūkyū Dance Theaters
**Okinawa Janjan Gekijō** 沖縄ジャンジャン劇場 牧志2-1-1 (862-4488). No set schedule. Ryūkyū theater, dance, folk music, etc., at this theater on Kokusai-dōri.

## Naha Crafts and Shopping
[5] **Aosa Kōgeikan** 青砂工芸館 久茂地3-17-5 (868-9338). Hrs: 9:00–20:00; clsd Su, NY. Gallery carrying high-quality traditional and modern Okinawan glassware, textiles, ceramics and lacquerware.

[7] **Yohena Shōten** よへな商店 牧志3-3-7(863-2832). Hrs: 10:30–20:00; clsd 2nd and 4th Su, NY. Heiwa-dōri. Ryūkyū-gasuri textiles.

[8] **Tsuboya Tōki Kaikan (Pottery Center)** (866-3284). Hrs: 9:00–18:00; Su, NH 9:30–18:00; clsd NY. Sells wares from all the kilns. See Tsuboya, p. 512.

[14] ** **Bembō** 紅房 松山2-21-20(868-1867). Hrs: 8:30–18:00 (enter by 16:30 to view workshop); clsd Su, NY, and Oct. 10. Fine Ryūkyū-shikki (lacquerware). Okinawan lacquerware has a distinctive appearance; it is gayer than mainland Japanese lacquer and more lyrical than Chinese lacquer, with painted designs, shell inlay, and carved-lacquer "appliqués." The lacquer is kept liquid by exposure to sunlight; this bleaches it, resulting in brilliant, clear tones that are a characteristic of Ryūkyū-shikki. Bembō was founded in 1931 as a shop committed to preserving traditional forms as well as developing new ones suitable to modern life; here one can choose from a wide variety of wares, from elegant stacking boxes to sophisticated contemporary tableware.

[20] **Shiroma Bingata Kenkyūjo** 城間紅型研究所 (885-9761). Hrs: 8:00–17:00; clsd Su, NY. In Shuri, east of the Okinawa Grand Castle Hotel. The leading Bingata workshop. Excellent workmanship, but not geared to casual visitors.

[21] ** **Nadoyama Kōgeikan** 名渡山工芸館 (884-0614). Hrs: 8:30–17:30; clsd Su, NY. A small Bingata workshop in Shuri, where artisans once catered to the royal court. There are about a dozen Bingata shops left in the neighborhood. One can watch artisans stencil rice-paste resist on the cloth and apply dyes for background and shading (a special characteristic of Bingata). The gallery salesroom shows old Bingata alongside the new.

## Naha Dining
Naha offers the finest Ryūkyū cuisine as well as the cheapest steaks in Japan.

(2) **Yotsutake Kumeten** 四竹久米店 久米2-22-1 (866-3333). Hrs: 11:00–22:00, daily. Ryūkyū dance show with dinner, from Y5000.

(3) ** **Yūnangī** ゆうなんぎい 久茂地3-3-3 (867-3765). Hrs: 12:00–15:00, 18:00–24:00; clsd Su. A *nomiya*, friendly and boisterous. Try some *awamori*, the pungent Okinawan distilled brew. *Rafutei, Goyā-champurū* (sautéed bitter melon), local fish. Fixed courses, Y1900–2600.

(4) ** **Ayajō** 綾門 久茂地3-24-5 (861-7741). Hrs: 17:00–22:30, daily. A charming, relaxed shop with Tsuboya-ware plates, Okinawan music, and excellent Ryūkyū cuisine. The seven-dish course is Y3500–5000 (includes peanut tofu, pork ear, pork tripe soup, *rafutei*).

(15) **Jackie Steak House** ジャッキーステーキハウス 辻2-5-5 (868-2408). Hrs: 10:00 a.m.–4:00 a.m.; clsd NY, 2 days at Bon. Steak from Y1000.

(16) **Sam's By The Sea** サムズバイザシー 西町2-4-5 ナハショッピングセンター10F. (862-6660). 2-4-5 Nishimachi, Naha Shopping Center, 10F. Hrs: 16:30–midnight. American-style restaurant, down to the glass buoys and rattan chairs. Steak and lobster dinners, Y3–8000.

(19) **Naha Soba** 那覇そば 奥武山26-7 (857-9504). Hrs: 10:00–21:30, daily. Okinawan noodles. Inexpensive.

## Naha Lodgings (TEL 098)
[1] ** **Okinawa Harbor View Hotel** 沖縄ハーバービューホテル (853-2111). Fax 834-6403. 2-46 Izumizaki,'Naha-shi, Okinawa. Run by ANA. A fine city/resort hotel, best in Naha. S Y9000, Tw Y13–20,000.

[6] **Yashio-sō** 八汐荘 松尾1-6-1 (867-1191). 1-6-1 Matsuo. Near Kokusai-dōri. Hotel run by schoolteachers' association. Plain but convenient. SY5700 w/o meals.

[9] **Ryokan Narumi** 旅館なるみ 牧志2-17-46 (867-2138). 2-17-46 Makishi. Near Kokusai-dōri. Y5500 w/meals.

[10] **Hotel Seibu Orion** ホテル西武オリオン (866-5533). Fax 862-9039. 1-2-21 Asato. On Kokusai-dōri. S Y8–12,000, Tw Y15–17,000.

[11] **YH Tamazono-sō** 玉園荘 安里54 (867-5377). 54 Asato. Y1900 w/o meals.

[12] **YH Harumi-sō** YH 晴海荘 泊2-22-10 (867-4422). 2-22-10 Tomari. Y3600 w/meals.

[13] * **Naha Tōkyū Hotel** 那覇東急ホテル (868-2151). Fax 868-7895. 1002 Ameku. Harbor view. S Y9000, Tw Y14–21,500.

514

17. \* **Pacific Hotel** パシフィックホテル (868-5162). Fax 868-8876. 3-5-1 Nishi. Comfortable. S Y7700, Tw Y11,800.

18. **Naha YH** 那覇YH 奥武山51-3 (857-0073). 51 Ōnoyama-chō. Y3600 w/meals.

22. \* **Okinawa Miyako Hotel** 沖縄都ホテル (887-1111). Fax 886-5591. 40 Matsukawa. Near Shuri. S Y12,500, Tw Y14-20,000.

23. \* **Okinawa Grand Castle** 沖縄グランドキャッスル (886-5454). Fax 887-0070. 1-132-1 Yamakawa-chō, Shuri. S Y11,000, Tw Y15-21,000.

## \* SOUTHERN OKINAWA (NANBU)

*One convenient way to visit the sites of the Battle of Okinawa is by Teiki Kankō (scheduled) bus tour from Naha. Ryūkyū Bus* 琉球バス *牧志3-15-15 (098-863-3636) departs from Kokusai-dōri, across from the Seibu Orion Hotel. Course A (10:00–16:00, 13:00–18:00, Y3600) includes the Imperial Navy HQ, Himeyuri no Tō, Peace Museum, Mabuni Hill, Gyokusen-dō cave.* The southern part of Okinawa has always been among the more populated areas of the island. Here, amid sugarcane fields, you will see many of the traditional turtle-backed tombs. It was inside such tombs that civilians and soldiers, fleeing from the north, attempted to find shelter during the most brutal fighting of the Pacific War.

### Calendar

**L 5/4: \*\* Hārī races.** Itoman. See Calendar, p. 508.

**L 5/4: \* Haryū-sen.** Yonabaru (*0:30h by bus 30, 37, 38, 39, or 40 from Naha*). Hārī boat races in Yonabaru harbor.

**L 6 (near the 26th): \* Ōtsunahiki.** Yonabaru. A harvest festival featuring a tug-of-war between titanic, interlocking male and female ropes. The ropes are carried about during the day; riding upon them are people dressed as historical and legendary foes, such as Gosamaru and Amawari (see Nakagusuku, next page). The tug-of-war starts around 16:30 and is over in about 10 minutes.

**L 8/15: \*\* Itoman no Tsunahiki.** Itoman. Immense male and female ropes are interlocked in a tug-of-war. Hrs: 17:00–17:30.

**L 8/16: \* Usudēku.** Itoman-Komesu. Circular dance by women beating drums.

**L 11/15–19: \* Izaihō.** Kudakajima. Held every 12 years, in the year of the horse (next in 2002). All island women age 30 and over gather at the *noro* shrine and live as white-robed priestesses for 5 days. They perform dances, sing from the *Omoro Sōshi* (see Okinawa History), initiate women participating for the first time, have a tug-of-war, and conduct processions.

515

### Southern Okinawa Sights

**\*\*\* Kyū Kaigun Shireibugō (Imperial Navy HQ)** 旧海軍指令壕 *0:30h by bus 33 or 95 from Naha to Tomigusuku-Kōen-mae, then 0:10h on foot.* Hrs: 8:30–17:00. An astonishing series of tunnels and chambers, 30 m underground and cold as a tomb, which served as the final headquarters of the Imperial Japanese Navy on Okinawa. The total length of the tunnels was 1,550 m, of which 225 m have been repaired and opened to the public. In these grim quarters, 4,000 men committed suicide on June 13, 1945, many by exploding grenades. The explosives have left scars on the walls.

**Itoman** 糸満 *0:40h by bus 32, 33, 34 or 35 from Naha, or 0:45h from Tomigusuku.* This town, today Okinawa's largest fishing port, was the stronghold of the Southern Mountain Kingdom in the 14th C. Coming from Naha via Rte. 331, look on the left, just before the rotary in the town center, for the torii of the **Hakugin-dō**, guardian shrine of Itoman. The small, red-roofed shrine is built against a cavern of coral rock. Continue to the rotary and turn left, then right after the first traffic light, and go about 50 meters. On the left is the \* **Kōchi bara monchū no haka**, the 300-year-old stone crypts of the Kōchi family, a prominent branch of the royal family. The crypts (rebuilt after the war) entomb more than 2,500 people.

**\*\*\* Okinawa War Sites Quasi-National Park** 沖縄戦跡国定公園 *Bus 82, 83 or 85 (infrequent) from Itoman, or tour buses from Naha.* This area was the scene of the bloodiest fighting in the Battle of Okinawa, which claimed more than 250,000 lives. One-eighth of the Okinawan civilian population perished. Many were caught between the relentless onslaught of the Americans and the suicidal resistance of the Japanese forces, while many others were driven to the cliffs on the south, where they leaped to their deaths.

**Himeyuri no Tō** ひめゆり塔 *0:15h by bus from Itoman.* On June 19, 1945, 190 senior high school girls and their 14 teachers, trapped by the American advance, put on their school uniforms, sang their school song, and committed suicide en masse on these grounds. Made famous in novels and movies, this memorial park is now among the biggest tourist draws. Adjacent is a memorial to 50 doctors, nurses, and other medical personnel who remained in the midst of the fighting and were killed.

**Konpaku no Tō** 魂魄ノ塔 *0:20h from Itoman to Komesu bus stop, then 0:15h on foot through cane fields.* This memorial site at the edge of a sea cliff is dedicated to 35,000 unknown war dead, whose remains were interred here in the winter of 1946 by the local villagers.

◆ **Mabuni no Oka (Mabuni Hill)** 摩文仁ノ丘 *0:15h on foot from Kenji no Tō bus stop.* Site of the fiercest battle of the war; tens of thousands of soldiers and civilians died on this beautiful bluff overlooking the sea. It is now a memorial park, strewn with monuments, including one from each of 30 prefectures in Japan.

◆ **Heiwa Kinen Shiryōkan** (Peace Memorial Museum) 平和記念資料館 (098-997-2874). Hrs: 9:00–16:30; clsd M, NY. *0:15h on foot from Kenji no Tō bus stop*. Relics, photographs, testimonials, and other exhibits on the Battle of Okinawa. There is a pamphlet in English, and a booklet of testimonials of war survivors, translated into English.

** **Gyokusen-dō** (Cave) 玉泉洞 (098-949-7421). *0:50h by bus 54 from Naha by Maegawa line to Gyokusen-dō-mae, then walk 0:05h; or 0:50h by Fusato line bus 51 or 52 to Aragusuku, then walk 0:15h (however, the Maegawa line runs only 4 per day, while the Fusato line departs every half hour)*. Hrs: Apr.–Oct. 9:00–17:30; Su, NH 9:00–18:00; Nov.–Mar. 9:00–17:00. A 4-km cavern, 800 m of which are open to the public. The cave contains subterranean rivers, waterfalls, the largest grotto in Asia, and an abundance of formations. The exit from the cave is designed to deposit you by the Habu Kōen (Snake Park).

**Chinen Hantō** (Peninsula) 知念半島 *1:00h by bus 37 or 38 from Naha*. A scenic region of sugarcane fields and seascapes. This extremity of the island is connected with Okinawan creation myths about divine strangers who came from across the sea, bringing new grains, fruits, and agricultural methods to the barren island.

**Seifuā Utaki** 斎場御嶽 *0:15h on foot from Kudeken bus stop*. Once the most venerated shrine on the island, located on a promontory facing sacred Kudakajima (see below). The precincts were forbidden to men, and the Ryūkyū kings, who until the 18th C were required to worship here, could go only as far as the first flight of steps. There are no buildings left, but there are caves, six boulders, and the remains of a sacred hearth. Nearby are two sacred springs, held to be the site of the first rice planting in Okinawa.

**Chinen Marine Leisure Center** 知念海洋レジャーセンター (098-948-3355). Hrs: 9:00–18:00, daily. Oct.–Apr. 9:00–17:00. Across the highway from Seifuā Utaki, down by the shore. Marine sports facility. Glass-bottom boats, and boats to Kudakajima and the uninhabited beach island of Komakajima.

**Chinen-jō Ato** (Castle Ruin) 知念城跡 *0:15h on foot from Chinen bus stop, 2 km southwest of Chinen Leisure Center*. An ancient castle site, now overgrown with banyans. A fortress was last built here 500 years ago, from which there remain two fine arched gateways.

* **Kudakajima** 久高島 *0:20h by motorboat from Chinen Leisure Center*. A flat, narrow island, 5 km off the tip of Chinen Peninsula. This is the island where in mythology Amamikiyo, the mother goddess of Okinawan creation myths, made a gift of five grains to the people of Okinawa. Except for the small village at the southwest end, the island is a green carpet of sugarcane, fringed with windbreaks of *fukugi* trees. Parts of the village, away from the harbor, are rather atmospheric. There's a shrine, not especially old, where the famous Izaihō festival is held (see Calendar). The road heading out along the north coast of the island hugs a sea cliff, with steps cut into it leading down to a series of freshwater springs.

## * CENTRAL OKINAWA

This is the most developed part of Okinawa, with heavily traveled highways, major American military bases, and popular beach resorts. It also has two of the most important cultural relics outside of Naha: the Nakagusuku castle ruin and the lovely Okinawan house, Nakamura-ke.

### Calendar

L 7/13–15: ** **Eisā Taikai.** Koza (on the outskirts of Okinawa City). See Calendar, p. 508.

### Central Okinawa Sights

**Futenma** 普天間 *0:45h by bus 21, 22, 23, 24, 25, 26, 31, or 77 from Naha bus terminal*. Near a large American military base. In the center of town, right near the bus stop, is **Futenma Gongen**, one of the Eight Ryūkyū Shrines founded in 1461–69. There is a sacred cave behind the hall.

*** **Nakamura-ke** (House) 中村家 (ICP). Hrs: 9:00–17:30. *0:15h by bus 58 from Futenma on the Nakagusuku-bound bus, or 0:10h on foot from Nakagusuku*. A well-preserved mid-18th-C farm estate, with typical Okinawan features like the stone enclosure and evil-spirit barrier facing the entrance. The main house and animal sheds are arranged around a stone-paved courtyard. In the center stands a raised storehouse with walls sloping steeply outward to thwart rats. The pig pens, in a rear corner, are of remarkably fine masonry. The inner part of the house is still occupied by descendants of the Nakamura family.

*** **Nakagusuku** (Castle Ruin) 中城城跡 Hrs: 9:00–17:30. In summer 9:00–18:00. *0:20h by bus 58 from Futenma*. (Ignore the dreadful "museum" in the castle park grounds.) The largest castle ruin in Okinawa, covering an area of 13,300 square meters and commanding a sweeping view of the coast. Built around 1450 on the foundations of an older fortress, Nakagusuku's marvelous stonework, all that remains, exemplifies Okinawan masonry skills, which far surpassed those of the mainland Japanese. There are three compounds, each enclosed by high stone walls, with terraced walkways on the inside to accommodate the defenders. Arched passages link the compounds. The castle was destroyed in 1458 in the Amawari Rebellion. During a period of succession strife at the Shuri court, the lord of Nakagusuku, Gosamaru, learned that the northern lord, Amawari, was plotting against the king. Gosamaru, intending to block Amawari's attack on Shuri at Nakagusuku, began mobilizing troops. Amawari, hearing of these activities, convinced the king it was Gosamaru, not he, who was fomenting rebellion. The king sent his forces against Nakagusuku, and Gosamaru committed suicide rather than take up arms against his king.

**Okinawa City** 沖縄市 *1:10 by bus 21, 22, 23, 24, 25, 26, 31, 63, 77, or 90 from Naha*. A city that grew up around Kadena Air Force Base (prewar population 7,000; postwar, 100,000). If you want pizza, steak, a swinging nightlife, or Army-Navy surplus, this is the place. The **Tuttle Bookstore** (3-3520) at Plaza House Shopping Mall is the best place to pick up English-language books on Okinawa. The **Moromi Mingeikan** 諸見民芸館 exhibits folk crafts from all over the Okinawan islands (Hrs: 9:30–17:30). **Kankō Tōgyū** (Bullfight Exhibition) at the Okinawa-shiei Tōgyūjō 市営闘牛場 .This type of bovine sumo, in which bulls are pitted against each other in a shoving match, is found along sea lanes from Okinawa north to such places as Uwajima in Shikoku and the Oki Islands.

**Zakimi-jō Ato** 座善味城跡 *1:20h by Yomitan-line bus 28 or 29 from Naha to Zakimi, then walk 0:10h*. A fine castle ruin, said to have been built around 1420 by Gosamaru (see Nakagusuku, preceding page). The two main compounds, walls, and arched stone gate remain. The **Yomitan-sonritsu Rekishi Minzoku Shiryōkan** (History and Folklore Museum) stands in the grounds (Hrs: 9:00–16:30; clsd M, NH, NY).

**Moon Beach**. *1:20h by bus 20 from Naha, or 1:10h from Nago*. Hrs: 9:00–18:00. A white sand beach hemmed in by the Moon Beach Resort Hotel. Glass-bottom boats, snorkeling, windsurfing.

**Tiger Beach**. *1:30h by bus 20 from Naha; adjacent to Moon Beach*. Hrs: 9:00–22:00. Hotel and restaurant facilities, barbecue, glass boats. Beach admission, Y400.

**Manza Beach**. *1:35h by bus from Naha, get off at Ota stop*. Hrs: 9:00–18:00 in summer, 9:00–17:00 in winter. Presided over by the Manza Beach Hotel, a deluxe resort hotel with pool, beaches, marine sport facilities. Beach admission, Y600. Manzamō, a lawn-covered promontory across the cove from Manza Beach, is famous for its views.

**Okinawa Kaichū-Kōen (Ocean Park)** 沖縄海中公園 *1:30h by bus 20 from Naha*. Hrs: 9:00–18:00. Comprised of the narrow, white-sand Imbu Beach, an oceanic exhibition hall, museum of shells, underwater observatory, glass boats, and an elaborate swimming pool.

517

### Exploring Yokatsu Shotō

A group of islets off the Yokatsu Peninsula, northeast of Okinawa City. Henzajima (taken over by oil refineries) is joined to Yakena, on the peninsula, by a 5-km road built right on the shallow seabed. One can continue across to Miyagijima, and then by bridge to **Ikeijima** *(0:30– 0:45h by minibus from Yakena)*, which has a quiet, atmospheric village, fields, and sandy swimming beaches. Lodgings at 2 minshuku and the Ikeijima Health Center.

### Central Okinawa Lodgings

\* **Hotel Moon Beach** ホテルムーンビーチ (098-965-1020). Fax 965-0555. 1203 Maeganeku, Onna-son, Kunigami-gun. Tw Y16–25,000.

\*\* **Manza Beach Hotel** 万座ビーチホテル (098-965-1211). Fax 966-2210. 2260 Seragaki, Onna-son. Luxury resort hotel operated by ANA. Popular with honeymooners: Tw Y26– 36,000. Room w/meals (dbl. occ.).

**Kokuminshukusha Nagoura-sō** 国民宿舎名護浦荘 (0980-53-2813). 1732 Kise, Nago-shi. Right by Okinawa Kaichū-Kōen. Y5000 w/meals.

## MOTOBU HANTŌ (PENINSULA) 本部半島

The major attraction of this rural peninsula is the Expo Park, on the site of the 1975 World Exposition. It has several fine museums of Okinawan culture. The port town of Motobu is the jumping-off point for visits to several small and interesting offshore islands.

### Motobu Hantō Sights

**Nago** 名護 *2:30h by bus 20 or 21 from Naha. Junction for buses to points in Motobu and northern Okinawa*. The most pleasant area of town is around the **Hinpun Gajumaru**, a 250-year-old banyan at the southeast end of town. Not far from it is the old castle hill, noted for its cherry blossoms, which bloom in January. Toward the west end of town is the **Shiyakusho** (City Hall), a striking pinkish structure with wings of terraced, gazebo-like units draped in bougainvillea. The roof recalls the traditional Okinawan red-tile roof. It was designed by Team ZOO of Tokyo. Food is available at **Hotel Ōkura** ホテルおおくら (52-2250), which offers Okinawan cuisine in a cafeteria setting. (No connection with the famous Tokyo hotel.) **Shinzan Shokudō** 新山食堂 (53-3354) has good "Nago soba" (noodles). Both are near the Hinpun Gajumaru banyan tree.

**Motobu** 本部 *0:55h by bus 65, 66, 70, 76, or 93 from Nago*. Ferries to Iejima from Motobu-kō (harbor) and to Minnajima from Toguchi-kō.

\*\* **Iejima** 伊江島 *0:35h by ferry from Motobu-kō (car toll is very expensive)*. Rent-a-cycles and scooters at Mitsuba (098049-2039), by the pier. The town by the ferry dock is quite plain, but the rest of the island is covered with rippling waves of sugarcane (plus two airstrips and an American military base). **Gushukuyama** is an odd hill rising like the crown of a sombrero in the center of otherwise flat Iejima; climb 0:10h from the parking lot to the summit for a terrific view. The north shore of Iejima ends abruptly in sheer cliffs, dropping down to tide pools filled with colorful baby tropical fish. **Nyateiya-gama**, a seaside cave toward the southwest, has a window looking onto the sea. It was used as a shelter during the war. 0:10h on foot from the pier is a memorial to **Ernie Pyle**, the famous World War II correspondent, who was killed here in April 1945 while covering the Battle of Okinawa. It stands on a patch of lawn amid a few hibiscus, with the hot sun beating down. There are several ryokan, and there is camping at the Youth Travel Village (see Motobu lodgings). **Minami Shokudō**, right near the pier, has excellent seafood; *teishoku* Y1000 (Hrs: 10:30–20:00).

\* **Minnajima** 水納島 *0:30h by ferry from Toguchi-kō (only 2–4 per day)*. This tiny, unspoiled coral atoll has a protected sandy beach and two minshuku.

\*\* **Kaiyō Hakurankai Kinen Kōen (Ocean Expo Park)** 海洋博覧会記念公園 *2:30h by direct bus 93 from Naha (3 per day, Su, NH only), or 0:45h by bus 70 from Nago, to Kinenkōen-mae*. (0980-48-2741) Hrs: 9:30–18:00; clsd Th (F if Th a NH). In summer 9:30–19:00. Museums close 0:30h earlier than the rest of the park.

    **Oceanic Cultures Pavilion.** Excellent exhibits of boats, houses, folk art, and videos of the cultures of Oceania.

    ◆ **Okinawa-kan.** A museum of Okinawan culture. Mysterious masks used in sacred rites (Angamā masks with faces of an old man and woman, representing spirits of the dead who return at Bon, and Mayuganashi masks with mother-of-pearl eyes and teeth embedded in a black face, representing gods from beyond the sea), photos of festivals, dioramas of traditional fishing methods, objects from the Ryūkyū Kingdom and from World War II.

    ◆ **Okinawan Village.** A most attractive cluster of reconstructed traditional Okinawan houses of various types, including the house of a *noro* (priestess), with a shed housing three sacred hearthstones.

    **Aquarium.** Designed by the distinguished architect Maki Fumihiko from a frame of precast, modular pieces. Its huge Black Current tank seethes with various species of large sharks, rays, and schools of pelagic fish such as tuna and bonito. In a separate pool, outside, is a rare American manatee.

**518**

    Other attractions include the Aquapolis, a rusting, futuristic "floating city" built off-shore; Dream Center, shaped like the Tower of Babel, housing a high-tech botanical park; and Emerald Beach and Expoland, an artificial white sand beach (free admission) and amusement park, north of Expo Park.

\*\* **Nakijin Castle Ruin** 今帰仁城跡 *1:00h by bus 66 from Nago, or 0:20h by bus 65 or taxi from the Expo Park. From Nakijin-gusuku-ato Iriguchi bus stop, walk 0:15h*. This is the ruin of a great castle, built in the 14th C by a local baron who founded the short-lived North Mountain Kingdom that ruled the northern part of Okinawa. Though the small, rough-cut stones show less technical skill than contemporary castles to the south, the great scale and design of the fortress are impressive. The entrance has a flat rather than arched ceiling, and is flanked by guardhouses with small windows. The innermost enclosure contained the lord's residence and commands a breathtaking view extending north to the islands of Iheya and Izena, and to the northeast, beyond Cape Hedo, to the Amami and Yoron Islands. Three shrines were built in the inner courtyard for *noro* (priestesses), who conducted rituals while facing the sacred island of Iheya.

    Not far from Nakijin Castle, on the road to Nakijin village, stand windbreaks of Ryūkyū pines, said to have been planted on the order of Sai On (1682–1761). Sai On, one of the greatest statesmen in Okinawan history, undertook extensive economic reforms, including innovative land conservation and reforestation programs. In 1952, the U.S. Civil Administration translated and distributed his writings. Continue east along the north coast of the Motobu Peninsula, past **Haneji Naikai**, a scenic, isle-dotted cove, to rejoin Rte. 58.

### Exploring Izenajima and Iheyajima

\# Two unspoiled islands north of the Motobu Peninsula. Izenajima (*1:30h by ferry from Motobu-kō*) is a small, round island covered with sugarcane fields, and is said to have a gardenlike beauty. Izena was the birthplace of King Shō En, founder of the second Shō dynasty. Iheyajima (*2:00h by daily ferry from Motobu-kō*) is a long, narrow island, the northernmost of the Okinawan archipelago. Until the 19th C, later than any other Okinawan island, Iheya was ruled by *noro* priestesses, descended from the sister of King Shō En. The island has a Kumayā-gama (Hiding Place), the cave where, in Japanese creation myths, the Sun Goddess hid herself (see Shinto, p. 25). Iheya remains sacred to the *noro* cult.

### Motobu Peninsula Lodgings (TEL 0980)

**Ieson Seishōnen Ryokō Mura (Youth Travel Village)** 伊江村青少年旅行村 (49-5247 in summer). 2439 Higashiemae, Ie-son, Kunigami-gun. Iejima. Campground located in a shady grove with a secluded beach. Tent rental Y1500.

**Minshuku Uema** 民宿上間 (49-3040). 501 Kawahira, Ie-son. On Iejima.

**Minshuku Yafuso** 民宿屋富祖 (47-3615) and **Minshuku Ōshiro** 民宿大城 (47-3646). Minnajima, Motobu-chō, Kunigami-gun.

## * NORTHERN OKINAWA

Okinawa's backcountry is underpopulated and unspoiled, with a dramatic coastline and an occasional village that recalls the charm of old Okinawa. Bus service is limited to a few a day; this is where it is really worth having a car.

### Calendar

**L 7: ** Unjami Matsuri.** Shioya (*0:40h by bus 67, 73, or 74 from Nago*). See Calendar, p. 508.

### Northern Okinawa Sights

**\*\*\* Kijoka** 喜如嘉 *1:00h by bus 73 or 74 from Nago*. This village is renowned for Bashōfu, a linenlike textile made from plantain fibers, once worn by commoners but now so rare it is designated an Important Intangible Cultural Property. The cloth is still woven at Mrs. Taira's famous **Bashōfu Orimono Kōbō** 芭蕉布織物工房 (0980-44-3202; Hrs: 8:00– 17:30; clsd Su, NH, NY). From the Daini-Kijoka bus stop, head north on Rte. 58, and look for a driveway on the right with a hand-painted sign (in Japanese) pointing the way. Visitors who call ahead can observe the women making Bashōfu. The sheaths of plantain stalks are boiled, scraped, and separated into individual fibers, which are tied end to end in long strands. These are spun, reboiled, and dyed, often by *kasuri* methods, using natural indigo and *tekachi* (hawthorn) brown. The dyed thread is rinsed in a sour rice solution, boiled again, and is finally ready for weaving, which is done entirely by hand. Production is necessarily limited, but it is possible to buy Bashōfu here (at about half to a third its retail price in Tokyo). Afterward, head back to Rte. 58, turn left, go back past the bus stop, and take the first left. Follow the road, crossing a creek, and veer right at a fork to get to the heart of Kijoka village, where there are still some Okinawan-style houses, each with a grove of plantains.

**\*\*\* Hedo Misaki** 辺戸岬 *0:50h by bus 68 or 69 from Hentona (just N of Okuma Beach) to Hedo Misaki-iriguchi, then 0:15h on foot; the coast drive is spectacular*. The northern cape of Okinawa Island is stunning, with green lawns extending to the edge of a 100-meter cliff, plunging down to surf breaking over coral reefs. The bus route rounds the cape and terminates 5 km down the road, in the hamlet of **Oku**, which has a cluster of red-roofed Okinawan houses.

519

### Exploring the Northeast Coast

One needs a car to continue south along the new highway, which offers wide-open views of an almost unspoiled coastline. Along the way are several small fishing villages on pristine white sand beaches with wooden dugouts pulled ashore. The hamlet of **Aha**, huddled on a terraced hillside by the road, is about the last place on the island to preserve thatched houses.

### Northern Okinawa Lodgings

**Villa Okuma** ヴィラ奥間 (0980-41-2222). 913 Okuma, Kunigami-son, Kunigami-gun, Okinawa-ken. *0:55h by bus 67 from Nago*. This private JAL-owned beach resort uses cottages from a former American army base; perhaps the regimented schedule of this place is a legacy of its past. Swimming is permitted only 9:00–18:00, no snorkeling without a license, the barbecue patio closes after dinner, and a picket fence keeps lazy people from trying to walk a beeline from the bungalows to the beach. It is, however, the best hotel in this part of the island. Rate per person, w/meals, Y13–25,000 (low and high season rates).

**Oku Ryokan** 奥旅館 (0980-41-8128). 36 Oku, Kunigami-son, Kunigami-gun, Okinawa-ken. An older house at Oku, with very simple facilities. They're very friendly and go out of their way to accommodate foreigners—which means, unfortunately, that if you want local dishes, you'll have to make a special request. Y3500 w/meals.

# OKINAWA II. RITŌ (OUT ISLANDS)

**Main Attractions:** Kumejima, Taketomi, Iriomote

In modern times, Okinawa's traditional culture has not fared well, having first been forced to conform to Japanese colonial policy, and then, in desperate straits after the war, left to the mercy of the American Occupation. The worst damage to native culture was on the main island. The *ritō*, or out islands, by contrast, were left comparatively untouched until recently, and it is among them that the visitor will find the unspoiled fishing villages and coral seas, the folk songs, dances, and festivals that recall the Okinawa that was. Kumejima and Taketomi preserve many old houses. These two islands and Miyako are still renowned for fine textiles, which were paid in lieu of rice tax in the days of the kingdom. The *ritō* are also a scuba diver's paradise; Kerama has superb coral reefs, while at Iriomote's Manta Way, one is almost guaranteed a close view of manta rays. But time is running out. The once-pristine reefs and beaches are being bulldozed to make way for vast resort hotels catering to tourists more interested in a pseudo-Hawaii than in the delicate, precious heritage of the islands.

### Traveling

See Okinawa introduction. Nansei Airlines (SWAL) flies from Naha Airport to most of the islands. Ferry schedules are complicated. Anyone planning a trip to the *ritō* should purchase the indispensable *Okinawa Ritō Jōhō* 沖縄離島情報 , a ferry schedule (in Japanese) updated twice a year, published by Sōei Shuppan Company (03-3260-2889), Chiyoda Bldg. Ichigaya Den-chō 2-37, Shinjuku-ku, Tokyo.

## \* KERAMA  慶良間

*35 km west of Naha. 1:00h by ferry to Tokashiki, or 1:30h to Zamami, from Naha's Tomari-kō. Or by chartered Cessna flights from Naha airport to Fukachi island by Kōkyō Airlines* 公共航空 *(57-8443).* This cluster of beautiful islets offers the best scuba diving in Japan (coral reefs, many sea snakes). Zamami Island 座間味 is the recommended base for diving and sightseeing (many minshuku operate sightseeing boats). Kerama was taken by American troops only days before the invasion of the Okinawa main island.

### Kerama Diving and Lodgings (TEL 098)
**Coral Divers** コーラルダイバーズ (987-2930). 878 Zamami, Zamami-son, Shimajiri-gun, Okinawa-ken. Scuba gear rental and diving boats.
**Minshuku Hama** 民宿浜 (987-2013). 97 Zamami. Y6500 w/3 meals.
**Minshuku Takatsuki** 民宿高月 (987-2247). 878 Zamami. Y5500 w/3 meals.

## \*\* KUMEJIMA  久米島

*0:35h by Nansei Airlines from Naha (5–8 per day), or 1:45h by a ferry every other day from Naha's Tomari-kō. The airport is near Nakadomari, the main (and uninteresting) town.* Much of this island is stunningly beautiful, with its expanses of sugarcane divided by windbreaks of Ryūkyū pines, accented here and there by a red tile roof. In the quiet back lanes of Nakazato village, local women dye and weave the famous silk Kumejima-tsumugi. The Eef Beach Hotel has a fine beach, marine sports facilities, including scuba diving on Kumejima's barrier reef; it runs day trips to Sky Holiday Reef, a pristine sandbar.

### Getting Around
From the airport, it's 0:10h by bus to Nakadomari. Rent-a-cycles at Nakadomari and Eef Beach Hotel. A 3:00h taxi tour around the island costs about Y9000. Rent-a-car in Nakadomari is about Y4800 for 6:00h. Rent-a-scooter, Y800 per hour.

520

### Kumejima Sights
**\* Goeda no Matsu (Five-branched Pine)** 五枝ノ松 *0:05h by bus or 0:20h on foot from Nakadomari.* This naturally growing Ryūkyū pine looks like the work of a master gardener.
**\*\*\* Uezu-ke** 上江洲家 (ICP). Hrs: 8:00–17:00, daily. *0:10h on foot from the pine tree, or 0:05h by bus from Nakadomari to Nishime stop.* This splendid house, built about 280 years ago, is the oldest in the Okinawan islands. It has the classic, bent entrance passage of hedges, stone walls, and barriers to keep out evil spirits. The smoke-blackened interior is built in Shoin style, reflecting the high status of the Uezu family, who were stewards of the manor. The storehouse exhibits family treasures.
**\*\* Hamakawa-ke** 浜川家 Hrs: 8:30–17:00, daily. This is a pleasant, century-old house with a garden. This family's proudest possession is a "unicorn's horn" given to an ancestor 10 generations ago by King Shō Kei as a reward for helping the islanders survive a famine.
**\* Chinbei-donchi** 君南風殿内 *0:10h by bus from Nakadomari.* This simple hall standing on a tidy patch of lawn is the island's top-ranked shrine, where the *noro* pray for rain and perform rice-planting rites. On L 5/15 is the Inaho rite, when prayers are offered for a good harvest. On L 6/25, there's a harvest festival.
**\*\* Yajiyagama (Cave)** ヤジヤガマ *0:15h by bus to Gushikawa stop, then 0:20h on foot.* This natural cave was used as early as 2,000 years ago for burial, and corpses were left here until recent times. The large cavern near the entrance is blocked off as a sacred space, but an 800-meter-long tunnel, lit by naked bulbs, can be entered; it is said to still contain stray bones.
**Teidā-ishi (Sun Stone)** 太陽石 *0:30h by bus from Nakadomari.* Located near the north shore, in one of the most scenic parts of the island. This large boulder, set in a picturesque grove, bears scratches indicating the directions of neighboring islands. They are supposed to have been used as reference points by which someone observing the sun could tell the time and season.

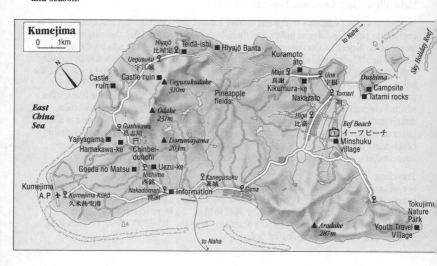

**\* Hiyajō Banta (Cliff)** 比屋定バンタ *0:40h by bus from Nakadomari.* From this vista point one can see to the Kerama islands and also enjoy the dizzying view to the barrier reef 200 meters below.

**\*\*\* Nakazato Village** 仲里村 *0:40h by Nakazato-bound bus from Nakadomari.* The **Kikumura-ke** (house) boasts a 250-year-old cycad palm in its yard. The house is on a street lined with traditional Okinawan houses, though most of their fine stone walls and tall hedgerows of *fukugi* trees were torn up when the road was widened. Back lanes off the main street are better preserved. This neighborhood is well worth walking around to see the women dyeing and weaving Kumejima-tsumugi. Each woman dyes and weaves about 15 bolts per year to help supplement the family income. At the edge of the village is **Kuramoto ato**, a stone-walled enclosure that was once the site of warehouses for the China trade.

**\* Eef Beach** イーフビーチ *0:20h by bus from Nakadomari.* This is a fine, 2-km white sand beach (open 24 hours a day). The Eef Beach Hotel rents windsurfing boards, snorkeling and scuba diving gear, and runs boats out to Sky Holiday Reef and diving destinations.

### Kumejima-tsumugi (Silk Pongee)

Kumejima was the silk-producing center of the Ryūkyū Kingdom, and as silk was reserved for the aristocracy and export trade, the textile woven here was of the finest quality. Today, Kumejima-tsumugi continues to derive its rich, subtle colors from plants and iron-oxide-rich mud; the latter produces a distinctive brown-black color in a process of 70–80 dippings requiring two months. The bright, royal yellow of the *fukugi* tree bark was once a predominant background color. The threads are dyed using the *ikat* technique, with patterns ranging from cross-hatches to stylized swallows, ripples, and flowers. One *tan*, a 12-meter bolt, starts at around Y130,000 (compared to Y300,000 in Tokyo).

**Kumejima Tsumugi Kyōdo Kumiai (Cooperative)** 久米島紬協同組合 (8333). In Nakazato village; a friendly place where one can observe the members at work.

**Kumejima Tsumugi, Inc.** 久米島紬株式会社 (2153). A commercial workshop that adheres strictly to traditional dyeing and hand-weaving methods.

### Kumejima Lodgings (TEL 098)

There is a minshuku village by Eef Beach, and several ryokan at Nakadomari.

☐ **\* Eef Beach Hotel** イーフビーチホテル (985–7111). Fax 985–7117. 548 Janadō, Nakazato-son, Shimajiri-gun, Okinawa-ken. Best on the island; run by ANA. A comfortable small resort hotel right on the beach. Marine sport facilities, rent-a-cycle. Y13,500–18,500. w/meals.

## \* MIYAKO 宮古島

*0:45–1:00h by Nansei flight from Naha, or 10:00–10:30h by boat from Naha-kō to Hirara, the main town.* Miyako is the largest of a cluster of eight pancake-flat islands 330 km south of the *hontō*. The early culture of these islands had affinities to the aboriginal culture of Taiwan. Local dialects and customs are distinct from those of the *hontō*. Miyako and its smaller neighbor, Irabu, are quiet but very pleasant, with some of the friendliest people in Japan. Few of the typical red-tile-roofed houses remain, but one can still buy the famous Miyako-jōfu, with which the islanders paid their taxes to the Ryūkyū Kingdom. Miyako has an interesting nightlife; it is said to have more bars per capita than any other place in Japan.

### Calendar

L 7/15: **\* Kuichā Yuichā.** A local type of Bon dance.

L 8: **\* # Hōnen Matsuri (Hachiguwachi-Odori).** Held on a Sa–M between the 1st and 15th on Taramajima (*3:30h by ferry, 2 per week, south of Miyako*). A colorful harvest festival with a great variety of local performing arts.

L 9: **\* Yūkui.** Ikemajima (*off NW tip of Miyako, served by ferry from Hirara*). On a lucky day at the end of the month. Women aged 51–55, dressed in white and wearing crowns of green leaves, sing sacred songs in a prayer for the island's prosperity. During interludes, the women take off their white outer robes and dance the gay Kuichā Yuichā.

### Getting Around

Motorbikes are recommended. They can be rented in Hirara at **Tomihama Motors** 富浜モーターズ　字西里288 (2-3031) and **Marutama Motors** 丸玉モーターズ　字下里754–1 (2-3393); about Y2000 per day. The legacy of the American Occupation seems to have caused some confusion over the proper side of the road to drive on, especially on Irabu. Miyako also has a bus system that makes a circuit around the island.

### Miyako Sights

**Hirara** 平良 The main town, with most of the hotels, bars, shops. A good place to begin sightseeing. The **Miyako Dentō Kōgeihin Kenkyū Sentā** (*0:03h on foot from the pier*) exhibits the famed Miyako-jōfu, a fine ramie with *kasuri* designs on an indigo ground. The most interesting sight in town is the mausoleum of **Nakasone Toimiyā**, a late 15th-C chieftain lionized for his exploits in conquering the hostile Yaeyama Islands and his diplomacy in saving Miyako from an invasion from the north (*0:02h on foot from the pier, at the northern end of the harbor*). The grave is a mix of the local style and the grand mortuary style of Okinawa island. A little farther north on the same road is **Jintōzeiseki**, a stone 1.4 m in height; from the 17th C, under the domination of Satsuma, anyone taller than the stone had to pay taxes. **Harimizu Utaki** is a small red-tile-roofed shrine in the center of the city. The coastal township of **Hisamatsu** (*0:10h by bus southwest*) boasts several old graves, red-roofed houses, and a monument to the Five Heroes of Hisamatsu, local fishermen who during the Russo-

521

Japanese War (1904–1905) spotted the Baltic fleet steaming north and reported it, giving Admiral Tōgō time to prepare his historic victory in the Tsushima Straits.

**Higashi Henna Misaki** 東平安名岬 *1:00h by bus to Bora, then 1:00h on foot*. On the easternmost end of Miyakojima is this dramatic point graced by a lighthouse. Along the south coast between Hirara and this point are several nice beaches, the Tōkyū Resort Complex, and the Nakazato Tropical Fruit Garden. Sayama Beach, to the north of Hirara, is a pleasant beach with a cave.

**\*\* Irabujima** 伊良部島 *0:15h by hourly ferry from Hirara*. This islet is linked by several bridges to Shimochijima, which has an airstrip, the only blemish on the charmingly rural scenery; you will see horsecarts amid the sugarcane fields. One curiosity worth visiting is **\* Tōri-ike** (west of the airstrip on Shimochijima), which is a big seaside lagoon connected to the ocean by an undersea tunnel. The place has long had religious significance, and local people often refuse to go near it. It is supposed to be a wonderful scuba dive.

### Miyako Diving
**24 Degrees North Miyako** 字下里142 (2-3107 or 2-3784). Y17,500 for boat, tank, gear, and lunch.
**Marine Service Miyako** 下里998-15 (2-9383). Y19,000 for boat, tank, gear, and lunch.

### Miyako Dining and Lodgings (TEL 09807)
**Captain Marian's Restaurant** 西里597-6 (2-7815). Hrs: 11:00–23:00; clsd Tu, NY. Run by one Tony Sipes. For the homesick.
**Isshin-tei** 一心亭　西里113 (2-2113). Hrs: 19:00–24:00; clsd NY. Local cuisine and folk music.
**Hotel New Marukatsu** ホテルニュー丸勝 (2-9936). 303-3 Nishizato, Hirara-shi, Miyako-gun, Okinawa-ken. Probably the best among the rundown "modern" hotels around Hirara harbor. S Y5500, Tw Y10,000.
**Ryokan Yatsushiro** 旅館八城 (2-3020). 1-16 Nishizato, Hirara-shi. Y4000 w/breakfast.
**Minshuku Kawata-sō** 民宿川田荘　下里520 (2-3368). 520 Shimozato, Hirara-shi.
**Minshuku Painagama** 民宿パイナガマ　下里338-5 (2-1555). 338-5 Shimozato, Hirara-shi.
**\* Miyako Tōkyū Resort** 宮古東急リゾート (6-2109). 914 Yonaha, Shimoji-chō. Deluxe. Most of the rooms are twins. S Y10,000+, Tw Y15,000+.
**Irabu Hotel** 伊良部ホテル (8-3421). 57-2 Kuninaka, Irabu-chō. At Kuninaka, by the straits dividing Irabu and Shimochijima. A minshuku, despite its name. Y4000 w/meals.

522

## YAEYAMA ISLANDS
Of all the out-island groups, the Yaeyama Archipelago, consisting of Ishigaki, Taketomi, Iriomote, Kurojima, and Kohama, offers the most variety for the tourist; Ishigaki has the comforts of a town, Iriomote is a national park and has excellent scuba diving, and Taketomi offers its flower-laden Okinawan village.

### \* ISHIGAKI　石垣島　[TEL 09808]
*0:55h by Nansei Airlines from Naha or 0:30h from Miyako; or 13:30h by direct ferry from Naha-kō, or 19:30h via Miyako (departures about once a week)*. Ishigaki airport serves the entire Yaeyama chain, and its harbor is the central hub for boat traffic to the outer islands. Ishigaki, the most developed of the Yaeyama group, has a number of museums, the scenic bay of Kabira, and a few other sights, but they are a pale substitute for the attractions of the outer islands. Except for a quick tour of the main town, better not to linger here.

### Calendar
L 5/4: \*\* **Hārī races.** Ishigaki. See Calendar, p. 508.
L 6: \*\* **Yaeyama Hōnen-sai.** Held for two days, starting on the first "lucky day" of the lunar month. In Ishigaki and various parts of the island. See Calendar, p. 508.
L 7/8: **Shītsui Matsuri.** A harvest thanksgiving festival. Starts on Tsuchi no einu day and lasts for 5 days. Kabira is famous for *mayunganashi* (god's visit).
L 7/14–16: \* **Angamā.** See p. 523 for description.

### Getting Around
The sights in and near Ishigaki harbor are easily seen on foot or taxi; to visit Kabira-wan and the northern tip of the island, use the bus or rent a car at Toyoto Rent-a-Lease (2-4855), Y6500 for 12:00h, or a bicycle at Ishigaki Jitensha Shōkai (2-3255), Y1000/day.

### Getting to the Other Yaeyama Islands
The locations of piers and ferries is a bit chaotic, as there are about five different companies serving the various islands. You have to ask around to find out where the next ferry leaves from. Another annoyance is that there is often no direct service between two out islands, since most service is based from Ishigaki. In such cases, it's often worth chartering a fishing boat.

### Ishigaki Sights
**\*\* Shiritsu Yaeyama Hakubutsukan (Museum)** 市立八重山博物館 Hrs: 9:00–16:30; clsd M, NH, NY. *0:10h on foot from the harbor*. Crafts and folklore objects of the Yaeyama Islands. Of special interest are specimens of the extinct Panari-yaki pottery from tiny Aragusuku Island, Yaeyama-jōfu textiles, and dugout canoes.
**\*\*\* Miyara Donchi** 宮良殿内 (ICP). Open during daylight hours; clsd Tu. *0:15h NE on foot from the harbor*. The Matsushige family, which controlled more than a third of Ishigaki

Island, built this house in 1819. It was modeled on aristocratic dwellings at the royal capital of Shuri. Today, it is the only such house left in all Okinawa. Items of daily use are exhibited here, and there's a fine garden.

**\* Tōrin-ji** 桃林寺 *0:20h on foot from the harbor*. This Okinawa-style Rinzai Zen temple and the adjacent Gongen-dō (1787, ICP), a shrine to the Kumano *gongen*, were founded here in 1614 by order of the Satsuma, after it came to their attention that there were no shrines or temples in the Yaeyama Islands. The Niō statues in the gate date from 1737. Niō are especially revered in Yaeyama, where they are called Nīrumai.

**\*\* Ishigaki-ke Tei-en (Garden)** 石垣家庭園 (ICP). *0:25h on foot from the harbor*. This garden is thought to have been built in 1819. Admission is to the garden only; the house is a youth hostel.

**\* Yaeyama Minzoku-en** 八重山民俗園 Hrs: 9:30–18:00. *0:15h by bus from Ishigaki harbor to Motonagura bus stop*. Exhibits on the history of Yaeyama weaving, and a place to try your hand at the loom and potter's wheel.

**Kabira-wan (Bay)** 川平湾 *0:45h by bus from Ishigaki*. On the north shore of the island. This isle-dotted, sand-fringed cove has a mildly pleasant resort village and is known for cultured black pearls.

**North Ishigaki.** This part of the island tapers into a narrow peninsula, which is said to be scenic. One section in the middle is barely 100 m wide and is called Funakuya, or Boat Crossing, for it is said that fishermen once portaged their boats over this neck of land.

## Ishigaki Shopping

**Dentō Kōgeikan (Traditional Crafts Hall)** 伝統工芸館 (2-5200). Hrs: 9:00–17:00; Sa 9:00–12:00; clsd Su, NH, NY. Between the airport and the harbor. Features Yaeyama fabrics, such as Minsā-ori and Yaeyama-jōfu. There is another sales outlet at Azamiya, near the harbor.

**Minsā Kōgeikan** ミンサー工芸館 (2-3473). Hrs: 8:30–17:30, daily. Textiles.

**Ryūkyū Kuroshinju (Black Pearl) Center** 琉球黒真珠センター (2-5027). Hrs: 9:00–21:30. Near the harbor in Ishigaki (main branch in Kabira-wan).

523

## Ishigaki Dining and Lodgings (TEL 09808)

**Iso** 磯 石垣市大川 9 (2-7721). Hrs: 11:00–22:30 (last order), daily. Near the harbor. Features Yaeyama cooking, based heavily on pork. *Iso teishoku*, Y600.

**Hotel Nikkō Yaeyama** ホテル日航八重山 (3-3311). Fax 3-3201. 559 Ōkawa, Ishigaki-shi, Okinawa-ken. Rather posh resort hotel. S Y12,000, Tw Y20–26,000.

**Hotel Miyahira** ホテルミヤヒラ (2-6111). Fax 3-3236. 4-9 Misaki, Ishigaki-shi. Resort hotel. Tw Y16–20,000.

**Minshuku Yaeyama-sō** 民宿八重山荘 石垣市大川34 (2-3231). 34 Ōkawa, Ishigaki-shi. Y5000 w/meals.

**Ōhama-sō** 大浜荘 川平844 (8-2347). 844 Kabira, Ishigaki-shi. Minshuku at Kabira-wan. Y4000 w/meals.

**YH Yashima Ryokan** YH八洲旅館 (2-3157). 117 Tonoshiro, Ishigaki-shi. Y2800 w/o meals.

## \*\* TAKETOMI 竹富島

*0:15h by ferry from Ishigaki harbor*. This flat island, barely 9 km in circumference, depended entirely on catchment water until a pipeline was connected to Ishigaki. Since then, the island has come alive with bougainvillea, hibiscus, and other tropical flowers, which decorate the typical Okinawan red-roofed houses, many of which are minshuku. Taketomi preserves many crafts and festivals, including the weaving of its own distinctive *minsā* belts. The island is fringed with sandy beaches, but the best recreation is to ramble around, looking at the fine old houses.

### Calendar

**L 7/16: \* Angamā.** In the Yaeyama Islands, Bon is observed by visits to homes by two masked figures of a wrinkled and jolly old man and woman, spirits who've returned from across the sea. They are received in each home, carry on a lively dialogue with the residents, and dance, to the amusement of all.

**L 10: \*\* Tantoi.** From Ki no esaru, continues for 10 days; highlights on days 7 and 8. See Calendar, p. 508.

### Getting Around

Taketomi's sole village is compact and can be seen easily on foot or bicycle. The roads are unpaved, packed white sand, although the locals are threatening to build a paved road around the perimeter, where now there are only quiet beaches. Scooters and bicycles, the principal modes of transportation, can be rented in the center of the village.

### Taketomi Sights

**\* Nishitō Utaki** 西塘御嶽 A shrine dedicated to a 16th-C hero named Nishitō, a Taketomi native who governed the Yaeyama Islands for 25 years.

**\*\* Taketomi Mingeikan** 竹富民芸館 (5-2302). Hrs: 9:00–17:00. Here you can see Taketomi villagers weaving the famous *minsā* belts. Originally, young women wove these to present to their prospective husbands. The belts have a *kasuri* pattern of a white cross and its reverse against an indigo ground.

**\*\* Akayama Oka** 赤山丘 A hillock with an observation tower, Nagomi no Tō, from which there is a fine view over the red-tile roofs of the village and the surrounding area.

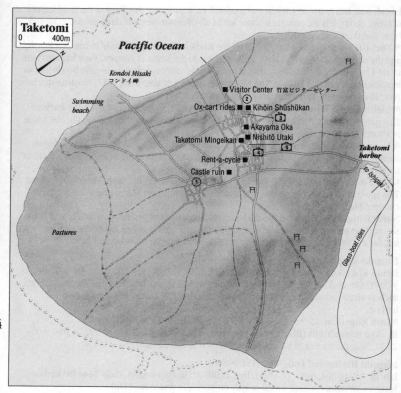

*** **Kihōin Shūshūkan** 喜宝院蒐集館 (5-2202). Hrs: 9:00–17:00. A private collection of more than 3,000 objects from the Yaeyama district, ranging from ancient coins and pottery to examples of local weaving. Local crafts are sold, and there are exhibits on local history as well.

** **Kondoi Misaki** コンドイ岬 *0:40h on foot, on the west shore*. This area has Taketomi's best beach. Walk south along the beach and look for the famous star-shaped sand, actually the skeletons of tiny sea animals. Views of Kohama, Kurojima, and Iriomote.

### Taketomi Dining and Lodgings (TEL 09808)

① **Chirorin-mura** ちろりん村 (5-2145). Hrs: 10:00–2:00 a.m. Coffee and sandwiches.

② **Yarabo** やらぼ (5-2268). Hrs: 11:30–16:00. The place for native cuisine.

③ **Minshuku Izumiya** 民宿泉屋 (5-2250). 377 Taketomi, Taketomi-chō, Yaeyama-gun, Okinawa-ken. Stunningly bedecked with flowers. Runs a diving operation. Y4000 w/meals.

④ **Takana Ryokan** 高那旅館 (5-2151). 499 Taketomi. Also a YH, Y2900 w/meals. Ryokan rate: Y5000 w/meals.

⑤ **Ōyama Ryokan** 大山旅館 (5-2150). 465 Taketomi. Has a modern, air-conditioned annex. Y5000 w/meals.

## KOHAMA 小浜

*0:30h by high-speed boat (7 per day), or 1:20h by a daily ferry, from Ishigaki.* This island boasts very good scuba diving. Rent or borrow a motorcycle and circle around the island, which has cane fields and is pleasantly scenic.

### Kohama Lodgings (TEL 09808)

**Minshuku Omoshiro-sō** 民宿おもしろ荘 (5-3258). 2538 Kohama, Taketomi-chō, Yaeyama-gun, Okinawa-ken. Y4000 w/meals.

**Haimurubushi** はいむるぶし (5-3116). 3000 Higashiomote, Taketomi-chō. A deluxe resort, done in an attractive Okinawan motif; at the time of our visit, none of the highly touted marine sports equipment was operational, which is something to consider at Y25,600 per person.

## ** IRIOMOTE 西表

*0:45h by jetfoil, or 1:30h by ferry from Ishigaki to Ōhara, or 1:00h by jetfoil, 2:40h by ferry to Funaura.* Much fuss is made about the extremely rare Iriomote wildcat, a primitive cousin of the household cat, but the real attraction of this "last wilderness" of Japan is its unspoiled beaches and interior. Most of the island is a national park. Supposedly, one can hike across the park in a long day, but one also has to watch out for the deadly *habu* viper. There are two main towns on Iriomote, Ōhara on the southeast and Funaura on the north. The Funaura area is far more interesting. Some of Japan's best scuba diving can be done from here. Especially famous is **Manta Way**, near the straits between Iriomote and Kohama; it is one of the few places in the world where schools of giant manta rays follow the plankton-rich current.

## Calendar

**L 8–L 9: * Setsu Matsuri.** Sonai. For three days, at the Tsuchi no toi day. One of the last remnants of the ancient thanksgiving rite for the "five grains," which by Okinawan belief were brought to the islands by people from across the sea (see Kudakajima, p. 516). On the first day, homes and tools are purified with a plant called *setsu-kazura*, followed by feasting. On the second day, there's a procession on the beach led by Miroku in the guise of Hotei, followed by offerings of Kyōgen, pole dances, lion dances, and other dances, and a boat race that provokes great excitement among spectators.

## Getting Around

Rent-a-bikes and cycles in Ōhara and Funaura. The two towns are linked by a 0:50h bus ride (2 per day) and high-speed boat (2–3 per day).

## Iriomote Sights

**Funaura** 船浦 This is where the ferry from Ishigaki lands. There are several hotels, min-shuku, and dive shops here and at **Uehara** 上原 , 1 km up the coast road. There is a motorbike rental shop at the top of the hill, to the left. In town, check out **Robinson-goya** (Robinson's hut, 5-6475), which besides being a pleasant coffee shop has caged specimens of the local wildlife.

**Hoshisuna no Hama (Star-sand Beach)** 星砂ノ浜 Out at the tip NW from Funaura is this well-known star-sand beach, but we can't guarantee that you will actually find any of the star-shaped grains.

**** Kampira no Taki (Falls)** カンピラ滝 *0:20h by bus from Funaura to Urauchibashi, then board a boat.* The main tourist attraction on Iriomote is the Urauchigawa; sightseers ride up this diminutive "Amazon of Iriomote" until it becomes unnavigable. Continue on foot 0:30h to Mariudo Falls, the "fall of the god's first bath." Another quarter of an hour brings you to Kampira Falls, less a fall than sculptured flow of whitewater. It is an excellent place to swim, and the butterflies are incredible.

**Iriomote Jūdan (Cross-Island Hike).** From Kampira Falls, continue up into the interior and across the island to Ōhara, a hike that takes about 6:00h. The trails are said to be clearly posted, but people do try to discourage you from going.

**** Sonai** 祖納 This sleepy village has a pleasant beach and a nice minshuku, one of Iriomote's oldest, the Hoshisuna-sō. Be sure to visit the neighboring village of Hoshidate, with its attractive table-coral walls.

***** Shirahama** 白浜 This dock, in a fantastic natural setting, is where Iriomote's only highway ends. From here, sightseeing boats sometimes take tourists around the exquisite bay. The hamlet of **Funauki**, accessible only by boat, is reputed to have a very friendly minshuku.

**Hatomajima** 鳩間島 This tiny islet 4 km north of Iriomote is famous for Hatoma-bushi (ballads) and has a minshuku. There is a highly irregular ferry service from Ishigaki, Funaura, and Shirahama.

525

Iriomote

## Scuba Diving

The best locales are farthest from Funaura—don't let them take you to closer dives. To the east are the famed Manta Way and Barasu-tō (a pinnacle of coral shooting up from the depths). To the west are Sakiyama and Nakanouganjima.

**Unarizaki-sō** うなり崎荘 (5-6406). See Lodgings. Gear rental included in Y5500 per day lodging charge.

**Mistā Sakana** ミスターサカナ (5-6472). 657 Uehara, Taketomi-chō. Expensive (boat, two tanks and lunch run Y12,500 per person), but the man who runs it is well-regarded in diving circles throughout Japan.

## Iriomote Lodgings (TEL 09808)

[1] **Iriomote YH** 西表島YH (5-6255). 870 Uehara, Taketomi-chō, Yaeyama-gun, Okinawa-ken. Right near the Funaura dock. Y3400 w/meals.

[2] **YH Iriomote Midori-sō** YH西表みどり荘 (5-6526). 572-5 Uehara, Taketomi-chō. Y3000 w/meals.

[3] * **Unarizaki-sō** うなり崎荘 (5-6406). 10-172 Uehara, Taketomi-chō. Have you ever wanted to go back to camp? This minshuku offers diving and fairly basic accommodations at reasonable prices, and you get to be "with all the kids." Y5500 w/meals.

[4] ** **Pension Iriomote** ペンションイリオモテ (5-6555). 750 Urauchi, Taketomi-chō. A tasteful pension is a rarity, and this one has a pleasant beachclub nearby that offers windsurfing and good food on a beautiful bay. Y7500 w/meals.

[5] ** **Hoshisuna-sō** 星砂荘 (5-6150). 657 Iriomote, Taketomi-chō. Very friendly, pleasant minshuku in Sonai. Neighbor Yamashita Kenji will take people on hunting and fishing expeditions and cross-country hikes.

## Exploring Yonaguni

*# 0:40h by Nansei Airlines (2 flights per day) or 6:30h by ferry (once every 4 days) from Ishigaki by Fukuyama Kaiun Co. (call 09808-2-4962 in Ishigaki, or 7-2555 in Yonaguni to confirm date and time).* The western extremity of the Okinawan Archipelago is completely off the tourist track. Until very recently, its main villages were purely native style, with thatched roofs and lush hedgerows, but latest reports indicate that the picturesque scenes are vanishing with alarming rapidity.

526

# Readings and Index

527

# RECOMMENDED READING

*Note*: Japanese authors in this list are given with family name last. An asterisk indicates a portable, practical guidebook.

## General

*Appreciations of Japanese Culture*. Donald Keene. Tokyo: Kodansha, 1981. Essays on a broad range of subjects by an eminent Japan scholar.

*The Inland Sea*. Donald Richie. Tokyo: Weatherhill, 1971. Reflections on Japan and the Japanese in a pungent account of the author's Inland Sea journey.

*Mirror, Sword and Jewel*. Karl Singer. Tokyo: Kodansha, 1981. Once you've been to Japan, Singer's acute observations, written in the 1940s, snap into focus.

*Tokyo: Form and Spirit*. Ed. Mildred Friedman. New York: Abrams, 1986. Exhibition catalog. A remarkable group of essays and illustrations by some of the sharpest observers of Japan, its leading architects and designers, ostensibly about the continuity of Japan's esthetic traditions, but illuminating many facets of Japanese life.

## History

*Japan: A Short Cultural History*. George Sansom. Stanford, CA: Stanford University Press, 1952. The best thorough introduction.

*A History of Modern Japan*. Richard Storry. Middlesex: Penguin, 1968. Gripping. The first chapters contain an excellent summary of premodern history.

*The World of the Shining Prince: Court Life in Ancient Japan*. Ivan Morris. Middlesex: Penguin, 1964. A companion to *The Tale of Genji*, this is a richly evocative portrait of the life of Heian courtiers.

*The Nobility of Failure: Tragic Heroes in the History of Japan*. Ivan Morris. Tokyo: Tuttle, 1982. An amusing and captivating study of the Japanese hero, which doubles as a history of Japan through some of its most famous personalities.

*The Western World and Japan: A Study in the Interaction of European and Asiatic Cultures*. George Sansom. Tokyo: Tuttle, 1977.

*Shimoda Story*. Oliver Statler. Tokyo: Tuttle, 1971. An absorbing, novelistic account of Townsend Harris and the opening of Japan.

*From A Ruined Empire*. Ed. Otis Cary. Tokyo: Kodansha, 1984. A collection of vivid letters from the end of the Pacific War by some people who went on to become America's foremost Japan scholars.

*In the Realm of a Dying Emperor: A Portrait of Japan at Century's End*. Norma Field. New York: Pantheon, 1991. A penetrating and disquieting account of three Japanese who refuse to let their society and government evade an honest appraisal of the Pacific War and its aftermath.

## Religion

\* *Buddhist Images*. Taikichi Irie and Shigeru Aoyama. Osaka: Hoikusha Publishing Co., 1982. A simple, generously illustrated pocket guide to Buddhist deities and iconography.

*Zen and Japanese Culture*. Daisetz T. Suzuki. Princeton, NJ: Princeton University Press, 1970. Probably the best book on the subject.

## Merchant Towns, Roads, and Villages

*Traditional Japan*. Charles J. Dunn. Tokyo: Tuttle, 1972. A simple, well-written description of Edo-period society.

*Japanese Inn*. Oliver Statler. Tokyo: Tuttle, 1973. A reconstruction of Japan's history from about 1600 to the present, from the vantage point of a post-town inn.

*Japanese Pilgrimage*. Oliver Statler. New York: Morrow, 1983. While walking Japan's most famous Buddhist pilgrimage, the circuit of eighty-eight temples on Shikoku island, the author muses about past pilgrims and Buddhism.

*Shank's Mare*. Jippensha Ikku. Tokyo: Tuttle, 1960. A comic classic of Edo literature, about two who travel the Tōkaidō.

## Villas and Gardens

*What is Japanese Architecture?* K. Nishi and K. Hozumi. Tokyo: Kodansha, 1985. History and features of traditional Japanese buildings, for the nonspecialist. Well illustrated; would make a good guidebook if it were more portable.

\* *A Guide to the Gardens of Kyoto*. Marc Treib and Ron Herman. Tokyo: Shufunotomo Co. Ltd., 1980. An excellent guide to the history and design of many gardens of Kyoto.

*The World of the Japanese Garden*. Lorraine Kuck. Tokyo: Weatherhill, 1968. Still the definitive work in English on Japanese gardens and their history.

*The Way of Tea*. Rand Castile. Tokyo: Weatherhill, 1979. A handsome, thorough book about the tea ceremony.

## Matsuri

*Festivals of Japan*. Japan Travel Bureau, 1985. A semi-practical, comic-illustrated pocket guide to 271 matsuri.

## Drama

*On the Art of the Nō Drama: The Major Treatises of Zeami*. Trans. J. Thomas Rimer and Yamazaki Masukazu. Princeton: Princeton University Press, 1984. These excellent translations are accompanied by illuminating introductions by the translators.

* *A Guide to Nō*. P. G. O'Neill. Tokyo: Hinoki Shoten, 1953. Play summaries.

* *The Nō plays of Japan*. Trans. Arthur Waley. Tokyo: Tuttle, 1976. These classic translations capture the poetry of the plays. Waley's concise explanations of the theater, and translations of Zeami's essays, are also helpful.

* *20 Plays of the Nō Theater*. Ed. Donald Keene. New York: Columbia University Press, 1970. Complements the Waley translations. A rather hefty volume.

*Five Modern Nō Plays*. Yukio Mishima. Trans. Donald Keene. Tokyo: Tuttle, 1967. Transpositions of several famous plays into modern settings.

* *A Guide to Kyōgen*. Don Kenny. Tokyo: Hinoki Shoten, 1968. Play summaries.

* *The Kabuki Handbook*. Aubrey and Giovanna Halford. New York: Tuttle, 1979. Detailed play summaries and background. Useful for Bunraku as well.

* *Chūshingura*. Chikamatsu Monzaemon. Trans. Donald Keene. Tokyo: Tuttle, 1981.

## Art

*The Arts of Japan*. Seiroku Noma. 2 vols. Tokyo: Kodansha, 1978. By far the best introduction to Japanese art history.

* *Roberts' Guide to Japanese Museums*. Laurance P. Roberts. Tokyo: Kodansha, 1978. A detailed, alphabetized listing of 355 art museums. A useful reference for those who already know where to go.

530

## Crafts

*The Unknown Craftsman*. Yanagi Soetsu. Tokyo: Kodansha, 1972. Essays on the spirit of *mingei*, by the founder of Japan's folk-art movement.

* *Earth 'n' Fire*. Amaury St. Gilles. Tokyo: Shufunotomo, 1980. A guide to kilns.

## Pleasures

*Geisha*. Liza Dalby. Berkeley, University of California Press, 1983. The definitive work on this misunderstood subject, by an American anthropologist who lived as a geisha for a year.

*Furo: The Japanese Bath*. Peter Grilli and Dana Levy. Tokyo: Kodansha, 1985. Reading this lavishly illustrated and entertaining book about the pleasures of the *furo* is the next best thing to being in one.

## Practical Aids

* *JTB Speed Jikokuhyō*. Japan Travel Bureau. Updated monthly. A pocket-sized bilingual timetable. The maps at the beginning of the book serve as an index, with page numbers next to the train lines.

* *Youth Hostel Handbook*. Tokyo: Japan Youth Hostel Association. Updated annually. The single most important book for the budget traveler to have. Basic information in English.

## Language

* *Read Japanese Today*. Len Walsh. Tokyo: Tuttle, 1966. An entertaining book that almost lives up to its title. Basic *kanji* and *kana*, useful for getting around Japan.

*Japanese Kana Workbook*. P. G. O'Neill. Kodansha, 1967. A well-crafted workbook for teaching yourself *kana*.

## Literary Classics

*Japanese Literature: An Introduction for Western Readers*. Donald Keene. Tokyo: Tuttle, 1981. A guide to appreciation.

*The Tale of Genji*. Lady Murasaki. Trans. Edward Seidensticker. Tokyo: Tuttle, 1984. There's also a very different translation by Arthur Waley that is a classic in its own right.

*The Pillow Book of Sei Shonagon*. Trans. Ivan Morris. Middlesex: Penguin, 1981.

*The Ten Foot Square Hut and Tales of the Heike*. Trans. A. L. Sadler. Tokyo: Tuttle, 1981.

*Essays in Idleness: the Tsurezuregusa of Kenko*. Trans. Donald Keene. Tokyo: Tuttle, 1981.

*Oku no Hosomichi*. Bashō. Trans. Dorothy Britton. Tokyo: Kodansha, 1980.

*The Legends of Tōno*. Kunio Yanagita. Trans. Ronald A. Morse. Tokyo: The Japan Foundation, 1975. A record of oral folk tales of old rural Japan.

*The Makioka Sisters*. Junichiro Tanizaki. Trans. Edward Seidensticker. New York: Knopf, 1957. An evocative and moving novel about an Ōsaka family in genteel decline.

## Regional Guidebooks and Histories

* *Exploring Tōhoku*. Jan Brown. Tokyo: Weatherhill, 1982. Enthusiastic and thorough.

* *In and Around Sendai*. Margaret Gardner, James Vardaman, Ruth Vergin. Sendai: Keyaki no Machi Co., Ltd., 1982. Guide to Sendai written by resident Westerners.

*Low City, High City: Tokyo from Edo to the Earthquake*. Edward Seidensticker. New York: Knopf, 1983.

*Tokyo Now and Then: An Explorer's Guide*. Paul Waley. Tokyo: Weatherhill, 1984. The history of the city, site by site, but too hefty to tote around.

\* *Tokyo City Guide*. Judith Connor and Mayumi Yoshida. Tokyo: Ryukotsushin, 1984. An excellent city guide, especially strong on shops and restaurants. Good maps. Distributed in U.S. by Kodansha/Farrar, Straus & Giroux.

\* *Tokyo Access*. Richard Saul Wurman. Los Angeles: Access Press, 1984. The Access guide concept (LA Access, New York Access) applied to Tokyo. The maps are of little practical use, but this book does capture the exciting texture of the city.

\* *Discover Shitamachi*. Sumiko Embutsu. Tokyo: The Shitamachi Times, Ltd., 1984. A charming and detailed walking guide to the old-fashioned quarters of Tokyo.

\* *Exploring Kamakura*. Michael Cooper. Tokyo: Weatherhill, 1981. An interesting, witty guide by a noted scholar. It deserves better maps.

*Kamakura: Its History, Sights and Landmarks*. Tokyo: Japan Times. Lots of background.

\* *Kanazawa: The Other Side of Japan*. Ruth Stevens. Kanazawa: The Society to Introduce Kanazawa to the World, 1979.

\* *Kyoto, A Contemplative Guide*. Gouverneur Mosher. Tokyo: Tuttle, 1982. A classic. A small selection of temples and villas, one from each phase of Kyoto's past, blossoms into a vibrant history of the city.

*Historical Kyoto*; *Historical Nara*; and *Historical Nagasaki*. Herbert Plutschow. Tokyo: Japan Times, 1983. Three fine historical introductions to these cities; not practical guidebooks.

*Okinawa: The History of an Island People*. George H. Kerr. Tokyo: Tuttle, 1960. The melancholy history of these beautiful islands. Well researched and movingly written (for the U.S. military, no less).

531

*JTB Japan in Your Pocket Series*. Japan Travel Bureau. Illustrated with comics. Subjects include daily life, food, festivals, and major sightseeing locales, such as Nikkō and Kyoto.

**Additional Sources**
*National Parks of Japan*. Dorothy Britton and Mary Sutherland. Tokyo: Kodansha, 1981.

*The Anatomy of Dependence*. Takeo Doi. Tokyo: Kodansha, 1973.

*The New Japanese Architecture*. Botond Bognar. New York: Rizzoli, 1990.

*The Elegant Japanese House*. Ed., Teiji Itoh, photography Yukio Futagawa. New York: Weatherhill, 1969. On *sukiya* architecture.

*Traditional Japanese Houses*. Ed., Teiji Itoh, photography Yukio Futagawa. New York: Rizzoli, 1983. Farmhouse architecture.

*A Guide to Japanese Architecture*. Tokyo: Shinkenchiku-sha, Ltd., 1984. Distributed by Japan Architect Co., Ltd. Illustrated listing of major postwar buildings.

*The Japanese Discovery of Europe, 1720-1830*. Donald Keene. Stanford, CA: Stanford University Press, 1969.

*Early Buddhist Japan*. J. Edward Kidder. New York: Praeger, 1972.

*Kodansha Encyclopedia of Japan*. Tokyo: Kodansha, 1983.

*The Maker of Modern Japan: The Life of Shogun Tokugawa Ieyasu*. A. L. Sadler. Tokyo: Tuttle, 1983.

*A History of Japan*. George Sansom. 3 vols. Stanford: Stanford University Press, 1963.

## WHERE TO BUY BOOKS ON JAPAN IN THE UNITED STATES
Kinokuniya
Japan Center, San Francisco, CA 94115  (415-567-7625)

Kinokuniya, New Otani Store
110 S. Los Angeles Street, Los Angeles, CA 90012  (213-687-4480)

Kinokuniya
Yaohan Plaza, 595 River Rd., Edgewater, NJ 07020  (201-941-7580)

Kinokuniya
10 West 49th Street, New York, NY 10020  (212-765-1461)

Paragon Book Gallery (second-hand and out-of-print)
237 West 72nd Street, 2F, New York, NY 10023  (212-496-2378)

Zen Oriental Book Store
521 Fifth Avenue, New York, NY 10017  (212-697-0840)

Books Nippon
115 West 57th Street, New York, NY 10019  (212-582-4622)

# INDEX

新町

540

541